Jewish Languages

PORTA LINGUARUM ORIENTALIUM

Neue Serie

Herausgegeben von Lutz Edzard und Stephan Guth

Band 28

2021

Harrassowitz Verlag · Wiesbaden

Jewish Languages

Text specimens, grammatical, lexical, and cultural sketches

Edited by
Lutz Edzard and Ofra Tirosh-Becker

2021
Harrassowitz Verlag · Wiesbaden

Cover illustration: Rhymed blessing in the vernacular German spoken by Jews (early Yiddish) for anybody who carried this heavy book to the synagogue, Mahzor Worms, fol. 54r; © National Library of Israel. This is the oldest dated Yiddish text known to us.

Bibliografische Information der Deutschen Nationalbibliothek
Die Deutsche Nationalbibliothek verzeichnet diese Publikation in der Deutschen Nationalbibliografie; detaillierte bibliografische Daten sind im Internet über https://dnb.de abrufbar.

Bibliographic information published by the Deutsche Nationalbibliothek
The Deutsche Nationalbibliothek lists this publication in the Deutsche Nationalbibliografie; detailed bibliographic data are available in the internet at https://dnb.de.

For further information about our publishing program consult our website https://www.harrassowitz-verlag.de

Printed on permanent/durable paper.
Printing and binding: Memminger MedienCentrum AG
Printed in Germany

ISSN 0554-7342 eISSN 2748-6850
ISBN 978-3-447-11708-1 eISBN 978-3-447-39194-8

Table of Contents

Preface

Lutz Edzard and Ofra Tirosh-Becker

The study of Jewish languages or language varieties written and spoken by Jewish communities throughout the world has by now been firmly established as a scholarly field encompassing the investigation of linguistic, literary, and cultural-religious aspects. Aharon Maman in his introductory essay to this volume provides a hitherto unsurpassed comprehensive analysis of the various ways to define the term "Jewish language", relieving us as editors of the necessity to discuss the very definition of this term. The maturation of the field of Jewish languages is reflected in flourishing research activities, encompassing conferences, dedicated journals (*Massorot* and *The Journal of Jewish Languages*), multiple publications, and two comprehensive volumes,[1] to which we are honored to add this volume.

The idea for this volume emerged following the 5th International Jewish Languages Conference in Jerusalem, organized by Ofra Tirosh-Becker, recognizing the need for a volume that will not only compile linguistic and cultural reviews but will also make text specimens of Jewish languages available to a broad readership. Hence, this new volume entitled *Jewish Languages: Text specimens, grammatical, lexical, and cultural sketches* accords considerable weight to extensive text specimens with both interlinear and idiomatic translation. The glosses are oriented at the Leipzig Glossing Rules, with language-specific additions and modifications according to the preferences of the individual contributors. Beyond a wealth of linguistic information, all of these texts yield a lot of information on religious, cultural, and historical aspects of Jewish life.

As already stated, a comprehensive comparative essay by Aharon Maman introduces the volume. The main criterion for the inclusion of a language (variety) in this volume was the existence of a sizable amount of religious, literary, scholarly, and other text genres in Hebrew characters produced by Jewish authors. Oral texts recorded with Jewish respondents and available only in transcription play an important role as well. Due to its cultural importance, written Jewish English is likewise included in this volume. The book sections are ordered according to the linguistic affiliation of the treated language varieties, in the following order: Semitic (Neo-Aramaic and Arabic), Germanic (Yiddish and English), Romance (Judezmo/Ladino, Haketia, Italian, French, and Provençal), Greek, Iranian (early Persian and Juhuri/Judeo-Tat(i)), as well as Turkic (Crimean-Turkic, Krymchak, Karaim, and other varieties). While all contributions follow a common structural outline – a "cultural introduction" followed by a "grammatical (and lexical) sketch" and then "text specimens with glosses" – differences nevertheless subsist, depending on the specificity of the Jewish language variety in question. While a

1 Kahn, Lily and Aaron Rubin. 2016. *Handbook of Jewish Languages.* Leiden: Brill; Hary, Benjamin and Sarah Bunin Benor. 2018. *Languages in Jewish Communities, Past and Present.* Boston/Berlin: de Gruyter.

subsection on cultural and orthographic matters may be crucial in one case, a grammatical description of communal specificities may be more relevant in another case. Several indices complete the volume.

Beyond its obvious function as a scholarly reference tool, the authors also hope that the volume will emerge as a pedagogical textbook for courses covering one or several Jewish language varieties, as well as courses in general linguistics and in languages in contact. We are glad that the Harrassowitz series Porta Linguarum Orientalium, after the publication of Stephan Guth's *Die Hauptsprachen der Islamischen Welt: Strukturen, Geschichte, Literaturen* in 2012, which also pursues this very goal, now also features a comparable volume on Jewish language varieties.

We are grateful to all the contributors, who participated in drafting, developing, and proofreading their articles with great stamina. We are also indebted to Stephan Specht of Harrassowitz Verlag and our colleague Stephan Guth from the University of Oslo for taking this volume up in the series Porta Linguarum Orientalium. Thanks are likewise due to Michael Fröhlich of Harrassowitz Verlag for help with a number of technical matters. Additional individual acknowledgments by the authors are found in their respective chapters.

Erlangen and Jerusalem, July 2021 Lutz Edzard and Ofra Tirosh-Becker

Abbreviations

Beyond the global abbreviations listed below, individual chapters may contain specific abbreviations listed there, pertaining, e.g., to encyclopedias, manuscripts, and authors.

Grammatical elements in the glosses

1	first person	ELAT	elative	PASS	passive
2	second person	EXCL	exclamative	PL	plural
3	third person	EZ	*ezafe*	PN	place name
ABL	ablative	F	feminine	POSS	possessive
ACC	accusative	FN	female name	POSTP	postposition
ACT	active	FUT	future	PPP	past passive part.
A(DJ)	adjective	FUTM	future marker	PREP	preposition
ANT	anterior	GEN	genitive	PRES	presentative
AOR	aorist	GER	gerund	PRET	preterite
ASSEV	asseverative	H	head	P(R)F	perfect(ive)
AUX	auxiliary	IMP	imperative	PRN	pronoun
CAUS	causative	IMPF	imperfect	PR(O)G	progressive
CO	casus obliquus	IND	indicative	PROH	prohibitive
COH	cohortative	IND(E)F	indefinite	PROX	proximal
COL(L)	collective	INF	infinitive	PRPN	proper name
COMP	complementizer	INTERJ	interjection	PRS	present
COND	conditional	INTERR	interrogative	PST	past
CONJ	conjunction	IPFV	imperfective	PSTV	presentative
CONT	continuous	IPT	imperative	PTCP	participle
COP	copula	IRR	irrealis	PURP	purposive
CR	casus rectus	ITJ	interjection	QNT	quantifier
CPTV	comparative	IZAF	*izafet*	REFL	reflexive
CS(T)	construct	JUSS	jussive	REL	relative (pronoun)
CVB	converb	L	oblique suffix	REM	remote (distal)
D	direct suffix	LOC	locative	RN	river name
DAT	dative	M	masculine	SBJV	subjunctive
DEF	definite article	M(OD)	modifier	SD	sandhi
DEGR	degree	MN	male name	S(G)	singular
DEICT	deictic/deixis	N(T)	neuter	STAT	stative
DEM	demonstr. (pronoun)	NEG	negative, negation	SUB	subordinating part.
DIM	diminutive	NP	noun phrase	SUBJ	subjunctive
DISJ	disjunctive	NU	nomen unitatis	TOP	topic
DIST	distal	NUM	numeral	VN	verbal noun
DM	discourse marker	OBJ	object	VOC	vocative
DU	dual	OPT	optative	VPT	verbal particle

Languages

A(r)	Arabic	LF	*lingua frankeaḏa*
Aram	Aramaic	Lt.	Latin
BH	Biblical Hebrew	MB	Muslim Baghdadi
BJG	Biblical Jewish Greek	MG	Modern Greek
Blg.	Bulgarian	MHG	Middle High German
Bosn.	Bosnian	MMP	Manichean Middle Persian
CA	Classical Arabic	MSA	Modern Standard Arabic
Cat.	Catalan	MSp.	Middle Spanish
CB	Christian Baghdadi	NENA	North-Eastern Neo-Aramaic
CEA	Colloquial Egyptian Arabic	NP	New Persian
Clt.	Classical Latin	NWJ	Northwest Judezmo
DjK	*djuḏezmo kabá*	OA	Old Arabic
EG	Epirus Greek	OFr.	Old French
EJA	Egyptian Judeo-Arabic	OSp.	Old Spanish
EJP	Early Judaeo-Persian	P	Persian
ENP	Early New Persian	Pol	Polish
Fr.	French	Pt.	Portuguese
Gal.	Galician	SEJ	Southeast Judezmo
Gk.	Greek	SG	Standard Greek
HA	Hebrew-Aramaic	SMG	Standard Modern Greek
H(e/b)	Hebrew	Sp.	Spanish
Hk	Haketía	StG	Standard German
IH	Israeli Hebrew	StY	Standard Yiddish
It.	Italian	SWY	South-Western Yiddish
JB	Jewish Baghdadi	Tk.	Turkish
JG	Judeo-Greek	Vlt.	Vulgar Latin
JLB	Jewish Literary Baghdadi	WY	Western Yiddish
Jud.	Judezmo	Y	Yiddish
L	Ladino	ZMP	Zoroastrian Middle Persian

Other abbreviations

AD	anno domini	LXX	Septuaginta
(B)CE	(before) Christian era	OCP	Obligatory Contour Principle
C	consonant	Od	direct object
DO	direct object (marker)	Oi	indirect object
H	high	SIL	Summer Institute of Linguistics
IPA	International Phonetic Alphabet	V	vowel
L	low	YIVO	Yidisher visnshaftlekher institut

What is a Jewish language?

Aharon Maman, The Hebrew University of Jerusalem

1. Basic definition of *Jewish language*

Jewish language is an attribute given to languages spoken by Jewish communities throughout the world.[1] These Jewish languages were based on vernaculars spoken by the indigenous population of the same geographical space and were basically mere variations of their counterpart base languages out of which they evolved.[2] They are a clear case of languages in contact (Baumgarten 2003: 15), but not in the usual meaning of the term, as the contact occurred internally and unilaterally in the Jewish community, but did hardly have any effect on the entire co-territorial population.[3] Not every language spoken by Jews turned immediately into a Jewish language. This is an essential but insufficient condition. Along the centuries of Jewish wandering outside their Old Country, many Jewish languages emerged out of the languages where Jews were recruited or naturalized in varied locations in the Diaspora. Famous are Judeo-German, the precursor of *Yiddish*,[4] that emerged out of Middle High German (Mittelhochdeutsch),[5] Judeo-Spanish with its versions *Judezmo*, *Ḥaketía*, and *Ladino*,[6] based on old Spanish, and Judeo-Arabic based on Arabic, to name just a few. In some cases, speakers of one Jewish language moved to a different Jewish language, bringing lexical and other lin-

1 This term emerged by the end of the 19th century CE (Baumgarten 2003: 15). A list of Jewish languages is given by Levi 1979, Birnbaum 2011: 8–18, 306–339. See also Baumgarten 2003: 18–19 and n. 14. On definitions of Jewish languages, see below. On the question of '*Jewish* language' vs. '*Judeo*-language' see Nahon 2017: 108, n. 5. It should be stated from the start that due to the endless bibliography in the field, there was no attempt to refer here to every relevant article. This would disproportionally inflate the article and exceed its limits.

2 Cf. Rabin 1979: 41. Aslanov 2011: 391 calls it 'matrix language'. See also Aslanov 2007: 135, where he claims that the French spoken by the Jews of Bordeaux and Bayonne (along the 18th–19th centuries) hardly differed from the French of their non-Jewish neighbors.

3 Some everyday expressions were so common in Judeo-Arabic that even Muslims used them while communicating with their Jewish counterparts. For example, to extend a welcome to a Jew, they would use the Jewish expression *barúx əbbá* (Welcome!) based on Psalm 118: 26. On this phenomenon see Chetrit 2007: 154ff., especially ch. 11, 565–626; and Chetrit 2009, ch. 8, 387–526.

4 On the Yiddish designations see Birnbaum 2011: 47. On the number of Yiddish speakers and its geographical distribution in modern times, see Tapani Salminen, quoted in Moseley 2007: 276.

5 See Moseley 2007: 79–80, 82, 121ff. Although there is no question that Yiddish is structurally a Germanic language and the overwhelming majority of its words are of Germanic stock, it also retains a significant number of Hebrew, Aramaic, Slavic, and even Romance words, as well as various borrowings from other co-territorial languages (Myhill 2004: 127).

6 Sephiha (1986, ch. 2, 51–112) insists on using the term *Judeo-Spanish* for the spoken aspect of the language and reserves the use of *Ladino* for the calque-translation variety, though speakers in some areas use *Ladino* for spoken varieties as well. See also Bentolila, http://www.jewish-languages.org/haketia.html. In this category, Tapani Salminen (in Moseley 2007: 214) counts another three Jewish languages, Italkian, Juhur, and Krimchak.

guistic features from the old pre-language to the new one, such as from Judeo-French[7] to Yiddish, from Judeo-Arabic to Judeo-Spanish and from Yiddish to Jewish English (Spolsky and Benor 2006: 123).

This is not the first attempt to define the nature of *Jewish Languages.*[8] In fact, the notion of Jewish language is quite known and the term is intuitively used by scholars who presented studies on particular Jewish languages or on some of their characteristics. Yet, other scholars tried to define that very notion in terms of linguistics or sociolinguistics. The main aim of this article is to reconsider those definitions and to make a new attempt to provide an elaborate one, though on the way I may have to argue with others' assumptions, or to touch upon the very phenomenon called *Jewish Languages*. Another aim is to show that Jewish languages do not follow a single model, as some scholars tended to assume but at least three different models, according to their nature and development.

One of the most comprehensive definitions was given by the sociolinguist Joshua Fishman.[9] Most scholars who studied one or another Jewish language did not bother to define it, as the identification of any Jewish language is an easy intuitive task, though from the linguistic point of view, their definition and the scientific qualification of their nature are perplexing. A fundamental question is whether Jewish languages are of the nature of a *dialect* vis-à-vis their base language, of an *ethnolect* (Baumgarten 2003: 15, 25), a *religiolect*, a *sociolect*, a *quasilect*,[10] or rather a *jargon* (ibid., n. 40), a *pidgin*, a *creole*,[11] a *slang*, a *lect* (as used, e.g., by Gold 1985: 280ff.), an *idiom*,[12] or something else?[13] On the way to my answer, I will have to sketch the phenomenon called *Jewish language*.

7 On the question whether Judeo-French really existed as a Jewish language or not, see Aslanov 2007: 135 and n. 9.

8 See, e.g., Alvarez-Péreyre 2003a: 398; Myhill 2004: 25ff; Aslanov 2014; Bunin Benor 2016: 131. On the history of the study of Jewish languages see Alvarez-Péreyre 2003.

9 He defined a Jewish language as 'language that is phonologically, morpho-syntactically, lexico-semantically or orthographically different from that of non-Jewish sociocultural networks and that has some demonstrably unique function in the role-repertoire of a Jewish sociocultural network, which function is not normatively present in the role-repertoire of non-Jews and/or is not normatively discharged via varieties identical with those utilized by non-Jews' (Fishman 1985: 4; quoted by Bunin Benor 2008: 1062). Though he added 'determining perspectives... e.g. *the internal Jewish rank and file perspective, the internal Jewish authoritative perspective* (e.g., the halakhic definition of "who is a Jew"), the external (non-Jewish, "general") rank and file perspective and, finally, *the external authoritative* ("specialist") *perspective*,' as there was no unanimity in 'defining Jews per se,' he cast some doubt on the possibility of defining a Jewish language. He, however, listed some essential components of a Jewish language. See Aslanov 2002: 80.

10 See Glinert 1993; Aslanov 2015, §§38–39.

11 On the three latter terms (plus *pidgin-creole*) see Bakker 2008 throughout the chapter, among others the definition he quotes from Holm 2004: 136. On the classification of Jewish languages as such see Baumgarten 2003: 17, n. 13.

12 As Cohen 1985 calls, e.g., Judeo-Arabic along his article.

13 These terms will be discussed further below. Similar questions were, e.g., raised by Baumgarten 2003: 24. See more terms, such as *cryptolect*, *technolect*, in Masson 2003: 153.

2. How did Jewish languages emerge?

2.1 Step 1: The first Jewish component: Hebrew borrowings

Several explanations were suggested as to the emergence of the Jewish languages phenomenon. For instance, the many sources quoted in Baumgarten 1995 (and Baumgarten 1999: 223–224) (including Johann Buxtorf 1603, Andreas Sennert, Wittenberg 1666, Franciscus Haselbauer 1742, and Wilhelm Just Christian Chrysander 1750) refer to Yiddish as a crypto-language ('Geheimsprache') and compare it to the jargons of criminals and the like. Johann Buxtorf explicitly says in his *Synagoga Judaica* (Basel 1603) that the Jews did not want their neighbors to understand their speech.[14] More recently, Max Weinreich (1973; 1980; Alvarez-Péreyre 2003a: 399) claimed that Jewish languages are one of the many mechanisms that Jewish communities have set to maintain the singularity of Jewish society in non-Jewish societies. Wexler (2006: xv, preface, 1[b]) claims that Jewish languages 'were created by Jews who felt a need for a unique linguistic identity to match their unique ethno-religious culture and to replace their two ancestral languages Hebrew and/or Judeo-Aramaic with which they were no longer conversant,' and later (p. xxxi) that 'Judeo-languages were created by converts' – an idea that seems to contradict the former – that 'Yiddish and modern Hebrew are members of the Slavic family of languages' (p. xvii). His *relexification* theory does not seem to be proven.[15] The common implication of these perceptions is that Jewish languages were artificially crafted for one purpose or another. As will be shown later, Jewish languages rather naturally emerged by themselves as an essential necessity. In what follows, I would outline what seems to be the historic reality for any Jewish language.[16]

If one follows the trail of Jewish individuals or families fleeing from the Land of Israel after the destruction of the First Temple (586 BCE) or the Second Temple (70 CE), after the failure of the Bar Kokhva revolt (135 CE), at an earlier or a later period, one may realize that some of the exiles went to Greece or Italy, and others to Babylon, Persia, or anywhere else (cf. e.g., Birnbaum and Aslanov 2007: 302). A certain period of time was required to settle and acclimatize in their new locations.[17] For their communal communications they continued to use their mother tongue, Hebrew, but with their neighbors, the local officials or representatives or the central government, they should have used the vernacular, Greek in Greece,[18] Latin in Latin Europe, Akkadian and later

14 See also Baumgarten 2003: 21–22.

15 According to Romaine (2004, §4.1, 56), *relexification* characterizes pidgins and creoles. See also Myhill (2004: 74). The only domain where *relexification* seems to be fit is where Wexler uses the term in the context of 'the "relexifications" of the Bible in many Jewish speech communities for a population not fluent in Hebrew' (Wexler 2009: 184). *Relexification* here means no more than 'literal translation,' so the use of the term in this context may be misleading.

16 Cf. e.g., Téné 1985: 121 §32.

17 Cf. Alvarez-Péreyre 2007, §§2, 8. Not really 'out of a *desire* for integration into the non-Jewish environment', as Hary (2009: 13) put it, a *wish* ('Wherever Jews have *wished* to distinguish themselves from their neighbors' etc.) according to Hary and Wein (2013: 89) or a *tendency* as may be understood from Bunin Benor (2009: 231: 'Jews have *tended* to speak and write distinctly from their non-Jewish neighbors' [emphasis added to the three quotes]). Her wording on p. 234, 'Wherever Jews have lived, their speech and writing have differed' etc. is objective. It rather was a *necessity*, and the emergence of the Jewish language happened *naturally*.

18 On old literature in Judeo-Greek see Neubauer 1891: 9–10, 14–19. See also Levi 1979: 62.

Aramaic in Babylon, Persian in Persia, and so on, depending on location and language.[19] In the course of time, the mastery of the local language became more and more improved. According to the experience of many immigrants in the various locations during different periods, the younger members of the family or those born in the new location manage a better and easier absorption and control of the vernacular than the first generation of immigrants. It is appropriate to mention here the description of the degree of mastery of Arabic and French by the three consecutive and contemporaneous Jewish generations in Algiers, as was succinctly described by Cohen 1912. This example illustrates the linguistic transformation that took place in Algeria following the French occupation. In three generations of one family, the first spoke Arabic only or with a faintest knowledge of French. The second generation was already bilingual: the children spoke Arabic with their parents and French that they acquired in school with their own children. The third generation only spoke French, thus becoming monolingual again, and hardly knew any Arabic.[20] This example shows what might have happened in different times and places. A parallel can be observed in modern Israel, an immigration state in which the third generation does not master their parents' Jewish languages anymore.

Thus, beginning with a monolingual situation (Hebrew) the first Jewish generation went through a transitional period of kind of bilingualism (Hebrew with a new vernacular) whereas the third generation entered a new monolingual situation and spoke the new Jewish language with a code-switching to the vernacular occurring in their interrelations with the non-Jews.[21] In our initial example, as soon as the exiles began to use the vernacular, they easily noticed that that vernacular was not sufficient to satisfy their cultural needs: the vocabulary of the new language did not have ready-made words and phrases to express the particular needs of Jewish culture and their self-representation,[22] such as the names related to the yearly cycle, as *Šabbat*, *Roš Ḥodeš* (lit., 'head of the month') 'the first day of the Jewish month,' *Ḥanukkah* and *Purim*, *Pesaḥ* 'Passover,' and *Sukkot*, and words pertaining to lifecycle events and objects associated with them as

19 Cf., e.g., Alvarez-Péreyre 2007, §11; Haspelmath and Tadmor 2009: 1 (b); Chetrit 2016: 119. See however Neubauer 1891: 14, who explains why German Jews expelled to Slavic-speaking countries did not bother to immediately switch to the local vernaculars and kept on speaking their former language. The same holds for Judeo-Spanish spoken in Holland and England that was not immediately superseded by the local languages.

20 Cf. Weinreich 1979: 94–95, 107; Cohen, David. 1985: 246; Dean-Olmsted and Skura 2016: 492. The situation described above is parallel to Yaron Tsur's segmentation of colonial Jewish societies into Europeans, Westernized, and natives (Tsur 1996; Tsur 2001: 36–33; Tsur 2016: 23, 212). A slightly different pattern was set by Fishman 1985, esp. for speakers of Yiddish who moved to American English. See also Aslanov 2015, §37.

21 On code-switching see Poplack 2004. It should be emphasized that the very use of Hebrew elements in Jewish languages is not a case of code-Switching, as this only holds when one switches to a different language without changing topic (Poplack 2004: 589), whereas the very insertion of Hebrew terms is necessitated by content (which cannot be expressed by the local language). The case in Jewish languages is one of borrowing, not switching (cf. Poplack 2004: 591).

22 Cf. Weinreich 1979: 57, who says that 'lexical borrowing… can be described as a result of the fact that using ready-made designations is more economical than describing things afresh.' See also, Gold 1985: 280; Aslanov 2011: 392. Cf. also Kazdan's classification of Yiddish 'words of Hebrew origin into… 1) those that have synonyms from other components, 2) those that have no synonyms from other components' (Sasaki 2008: 556).

bərit mila (or in some cases *bərit* only or *mila* only) 'circumcision,' *mohel* 'the person who practices the *bərit mila*,'[23] *təfillin* 'phylacteries' (cf. Aslanov 2002: 84), *Bar-Mitzvah*; words related to the synagogue rites, as *Torah*, *Siddur* 'liturgical Jewish reader,' the names of daily services, *šaḥarit* 'morning service, *minḥa* 'afternoon service,' *ʕarvit* 'evening service' and *musaf* 'additional service in special days; *šəmaʕ* 'a prayer consisting of three Scriptural passages (Deut. 6:4–9, 11:13–21, and Num. 15:37–41) recited in the morning and evening Jewish prayers,' *ʕamida* 'the core of Jewish liturgy recited silently in every prayer, standing;' *ḥazara* 'the aloud repetition of the *ʕamida* by the leader of prayer,' and so on. To fill this vacuum, Hebrew words were *intuitively* borrowed.[24]

Figure 1. A base language before the Hebrew intervention

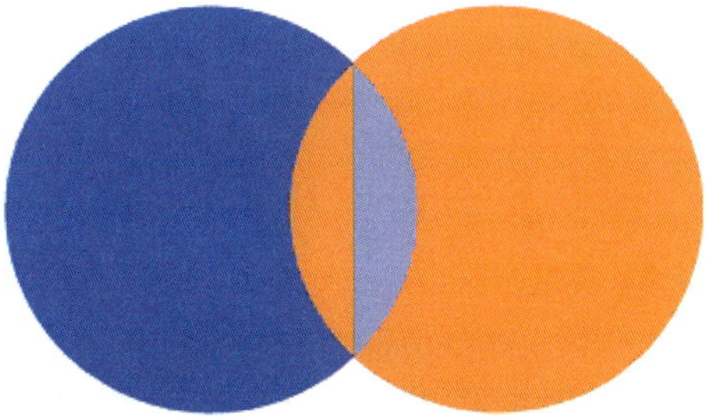

Figure 2. Languages in contact

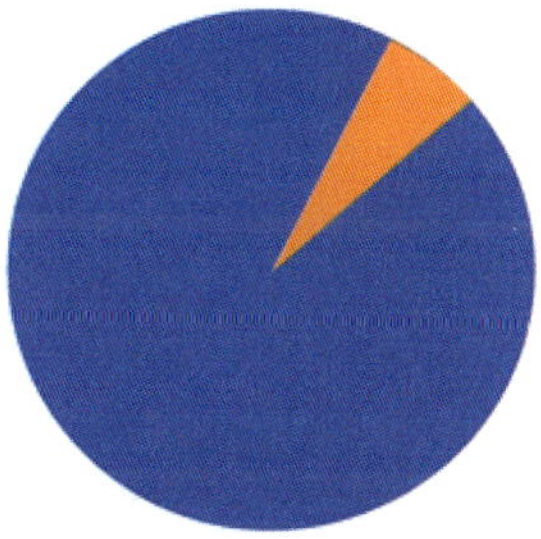

Figure 3. Insertion of the Hebrew component

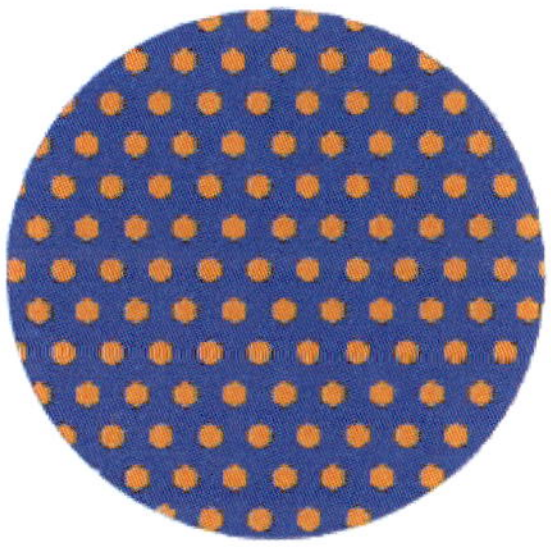

Figure 4. Dispersion of the Hebrew component

23 Amazingly enough, *mohel* does not exist in Judeo-Farsi, but the very fact that such a basic word is not used in a particular community is not evidence of its borrowing in a later period.

24 Cf. Teferra 2016: 13. Notwithstanding the term *borrowing* was criticized by Haugen (1950), who suggested 'importation' instead (Clyne 2004: 801–802), the metaphor is used universally. A good reasoning for it is to be found in Deroy 1956/2013, ch. 1. 'Un emprunt sans restitution,' §§6–16, esp. §6; 16. See also Hickey 2010: 11, 18–20, who justifies this usage, but deals with other used terms as *transfer* ('During language shift, when speakers of language X are switching to language Y, they transfer features of their original native language X to Y. Where these features are already present in Y the transfer is imperceptible but where they are not in Y the transferred features represent an innovation') and *imposition* ('A community contains two groups: a minority with high status and a majority with low status. The minority acquire the language of the majority, eventually relinquishing their original native language. In the process, the majority adopt features of the shift variety of the high-status minority').

Contrarily to natural borrowings which are imported gradually (Deroy 1956/2013, ch. 9. 'Les degrés de la pénétration,' §1), the basic Hebrew nomenclature exemplified above was imported at once. The rate of Hebrew words integrated into the new language spanned between few hundreds and few thousands, depending on the level of personal education and many other factors.[25] The local language, now including the integrated borrowed Hebrew words, took a new shape, was limited to internal communal Jewish use, and was not relevant to communications with non-Jews.[26] The Hebrew words listed above and many more like them were used in any Jewish language, in Yiddish, Judeo-Spanish, Judeo-Arabic, Judeo-Georgian, Judeo-Persian and Judeo-Italian alike, which proves that no equivalents were ready-made in German, Spanish, Arabic, Georgian, Persian, Italian, or any other language. Bar-Asher (2016, §9) states that Hebrew borrowings began around the 2nd cent. CE, as soon as Aramaic supplanted Hebrew.[27] The new reality necessitated[28] the use of the original Hebrew words whenever the need arose for evoking an item of Jewish culture. This is how this type, called a Jewish language, emerged.[29]

Here are two examples of Hebrew words in the context of a base language. It seems convenient to offer examples from Jewish English, a fresh Jewish language that may serve as a laboratory for our case,[30] to which David L. Gold, Bunin Benor and others have been dedicating intensive studies. One example is from *Tora Tidbits* of the 5759/1998 *Vayeshev* weekly portion and one from Weiser 2004's *Frumspeak*:

"It is well known – whether one 'believes' in it or not – that people check their *mezuzot* after something bad happens. There are many stories of defects being found in a *mezuza* – sometimes the particular *p'sul* even relates to the specific tragedy which prompted the *mezuza* check… For two weeks or so, many *shuls* and individuals have been adding the prayer for *atzirat g'shamim* in the weekday *amida*. It is long overdue that we each as individuals and we all as a community do some serious checking of a lot more than our *mezuzot*." (*Tora Tidbits* 23 Kislev 5759, 12-12-98).[31]

The term *Mezuzah* refers to a parchment where the text of the two first sections of the *šəmaʕ* is written in a specific way and attached in a case to the doorpost of a Jewish house as a sign of faith. *p'sul* means 'defect, disqualification.' *Shul* is borrowed from Yiddish, meaning 'synagogue,' originally from German *Schule* 'school.' *ʕaṣirat*

25 See Bar-Asher 1999. On Integration see Clyne 2004: 800.

26 Cf. Gold 1985; Benor 2013, col. 384.

27 See also Aslanov 2011: 390, on the switch from Aramaic to Greek. Cf. Myhill 2009: 172.

28 Clyne 2004: 801. See also Deroy 1956/2013, Introduction, §20 and esp. ch. 6. Nécessité pratique; the notions 'étiquette nécessaire' vs. 'emprunt de luxe' in Deroy 1956/2013, ch. 7. Raisons de cœur, §11.

29 Already Wexler 2006 and Hary 2009: 13ff., later, have argued that Jewish languages emerged out of conversions to Judaism. Even if this were a reality the converts were recruited by an already existing Jewish community, so that conversions might have had a secondary impact only. Bunin Benor (2009: 268) is also opposed to Wexler's view.

30 As Bunin Benor (2009: 231), phrases it: "studying contemporary Jewish languages can contribute to our understanding of historical Jewish languages." Cf., however, Myhill 2004: 29.

31 It does not appear in the archives of the Torah Tidbits website, but it may be found in the very beginning of http://www.seliyahu.org.il/parasha/par5759/epar59011.rtf. Many more examples may be seen in Bunin Benor 2009 and in her website.

gəšamim is the name of a prayer uttered in case of drought. *ʕamida,* lit., 'standing,' is the name of the core of Jewish liturgy recited silently in every prayer, standing.

And here is the one from Weiser's dictionary:[32]

"He never used that *gematria* as a *raya* for his *chidush*; he said it was just a *remez*"; "The *medrash* was a *remez* to the need for *teshuva*" (p. 82; = He never used that *numerology* [= arithmetical value of Hebrew letters of a certain word] as *prove* for his *novel idea*; he said it was just a *hint* [= a way of interpreting a text according to hidden ideas between the lines]"; "The *midrash* was a *hint* to the need for *repentance*").

The Hebrew words incorporated in these examples and in Jewish languages in general are what scholars call *the Hebrew component,* part of which are the *Kulturwörter.* This is a fundamental characteristic of Jewish languages recognized by scholars, and listed by Fishman (1991: 313–315).[33]

The way those imported Hebrew words were integrated into Jewish languages differs from one language to another. In most cases, the mechanism used for the interference of those words and phrases is of the type of 'simple words' (Weinreich 1979: 47). The Hebrew words were simply inserted to the vernacular, i.e. added to its initial lexicon that had no counterparts, in some cases replacing existing words or coexisting with them (Haspelmath and Tadmor 2009: 16, §6.2), a case where *relexification* literally fits. Single words and phrases as well as pragmatic markers and sentence adverbials are borrowed easily. Vocabulary, as an open class with a high degree of awareness by speakers, is the primary source of borrowing from the superstrate (Hickey 2010: 8). The reason is clear: such elements do not require integration into the grammatical system of the borrowing language and can be accommodated without any degree of restructuring (Hickey 2010: 14). In other cases they were adapted into the morpho-syntactic structure of the base language. They are for instance inflected with the local prefixes or suffixes making hybrid compounds,[34] e.g., in Medieval Judeo-Arabic, *al-halaxot* is prefixed with the Arabic definite article *al-* (Blau 1999: 44), in Jewish English, *halakhically* is made out of the Hebrew noun *halakha* and the adverbial suffix *-ically*; *kashered* is inflected the English way as a denominative verb from Hebrew *kasher*. This aspect is well discussed in the study of separate Jewish languages.[35]

The integration of the Hebrew component exhibits a variation in its pronunciation which may reflect different itineraries from its sources to its actual use. For instance,

32 Cf. Baumgarten 2003: 37, n. 89. Aslanov's (2002: 90) opinion is, however, that *yeshivish 'franbreu'* is often a somewhat pedantic and ostentatious mannerism ('maniérisme quelque peu pédant et ostentatoire').

33 See also Mayer-Modena 1999: 104–106, for Judeo-Latin; see, however, Birnbaum and Aslanov 2007: 301. For other Jewish languages see Aslanov 2002: 80; Stillman 2007: *145; and Aslanov 2014: 107. There are complete dictionaries and lists of words for the Hebrew component in one or another Jewish language. A recent one is Bentolila 2015. Cf., however, Gold 1985: 280, who claims that the Hebrew-Aramaic component is 'common, but not essential' to Jewish languages. Though it is undeniable that Jewish languages also borrowed from written texts, there is no way to assume that these were the only source. This is of course obvious but by no means excludes the initial follow-up of the Hebrew spoken just before the exiles discussed above (see the literature quoted in Sasaki 2008: 551).

34 On this phenomenon see Weinreich 1979: 52, Blau 1999:133–149.

35 See, e.g., Sasaki 2008, Bunin Benor 2009: 247; Bunin Benor 2013: 384; Schwarzwald 2015: 57.

šabbāṯ 'Saturday' is pronounce *šávəs* in Judeo-Alsatian as opposed to *šabós* in the local traditional reading of Hebrew (Aslanov 2013: 386), *šábəs* in Yiddish, *səbbát* / *šəbbát* in Judeo-Arabic. The name of the Holiday of Tabernacles is pronounced *sukkót* in Jewish languages of Sephardic communities and in Jewish English drawing from Israeli Hebrew, but *súkkəs* in Yiddish and in Jewish English drawing from it (Bunin Benor 2013: 384).[36]

Parallel to the 1912 Algiers linguistic situation in the example given by Marcel Cohen, regardless of the social dominance of the superimposed new language, Hebrew moved from being a superstratal language for the first generation, who spoke it as a mother tongue before they came in contact with the new vernacular, throughout a transitive period, where it was an adstratal language, towards the status of a substratal language,[37] limited to cultural and religious use and as a source for the Hebrew component in the new Jewish language. Thus, the new complex is not a case of classical bilingualism. Weinreich (1953) saw the true locus of contact-induced change in the bilingual individual, who moves between two linguistic systems. Some scholars go further and consider bilinguals as having a single system (Hickey 2010: 8). In the case of Jewish languages, except for the first generation that generated the complex, i.e. the new Jewish language, the following generations did not speak Hebrew as a mother language, but inherited the Jewish language as is, in many cases without even recognizing the descent and etymology of every word or phrase. As said earlier, Hebrew remained for centuries, until its revival as a naturally spoken language by the end of the 19th century CE, as the language of culture learned for liturgical and national purposes, along with its being transmitted as a Hebrew component in Jewish languages (Maman 2005).

The term 'Hebrew element/component' is used here, bearing in mind that Hebrew culture always had an umbilical link to the Aramaic language (Rabin 1979: n. 2; Stillman 1992: 42; Morag 1999a, n. 3; Bar-Asher 2016, §§14–19; Fassberg 2016: 66). Thus, one should understand it as standing for 'Hebrew-Aramaic,' as Aramaic has always been present in Jewish culture since Biblical times, first in the chapters of the books of Daniel (2:4b–7:28) and Ezra (4:8–6:18 and 7:12–26), and even before, the two words *yəḡar śāhăḏūṯāʔ* in Genesis 31:47 (Fassberg 2016: 66) and the single verse denouncing idolatry in Jeremiah 10:11. Since then, the presence of Aramaic has only intensified. The Aramaic translations of the Bible have always been in use during the last two millennia, both in the Jewish ritual and outside it. The Talmud substrate language is Aramaic, the Zohar is written in Aramaic, and a fairly large number of liturgical songs are in Aramaic. It is therefore not surprising that Aramaic has largely affected Hebrew and is also integrated in Jewish languages. It is only for simplicity that the shortened term 'Hebrew elements' term is used.

36 Cf. also Bunin Benor 2016: 132; for the difference *kašér* / *kóšer* in Jewish English, see Gold 1985: 283. For the purpose of this current study, Weinreich's universally recognized differentiation between the notions of 'whole Hebrew' and 'merged Hebrew' (Weinreich 1980: 351–354) or Morag's differentiation between Classical and integrated Hebrew (Morag 1999a, n. 1; Alvarez-Péreyre 2007, §22) are not necessary.

37 These terms are used universally in the literature dealing with languages in contact. See e.g., Hickey (ed.) 2010: 109, 385, 393, 407, 408, 443, 635.

The fundamental notion of Hebrew being the nucleus of Jewish languages has been recognized universally.[38] To give just one example, Poll (1981) says that 'these languages (whether originally Aramaic, Arabic, Spanish, or German) could not have been transformed into "Jewish" languages if they had not incorporated in them elements of Hebrew as well as specific lexical and syntactic differences which separated them from their languages of origin. Once a language was spoken by Jews in a "Jewish way," Jews considered it a "Jewish language"' (p. 208). 'This language will be known to them and to others as a "Jewish language." This language may be spoken by a relatively small segment of the Jewish population, but because of its Jewish terminology and because of the fact that it will be mainly spoken by Jews in a "Jewish way" about "things Jewish" to Jews, it will be recognized as a "language of Jews" ' (211). Alvarez-Péreyre (2003: 51) adds that this is the only characteristic that is shared by all Jewish languages.[39]

It should be emphasized, however, that the Hebrew component alone is not enough to determine any language as Jewish, as the Hebrew component *per se*, may not turn any language Jewish, unless it represents the nucleus of Jewish culture. For instance, the Arabic spoken by Arabs and Druze in the Galilee and in the Negev in our time includes many Hebrew borrowings such as *maxšev* 'computer,' *šaʕar* 'gate,' *qnás* 'fine,' *teʕuda* 'certificate, document, diploma,' *ramzor* 'traffic light' and many more (Henkin-Roitfarb 201: 156–157; ʕAmmāra 2010: 118–125),[40] but these do not make it Judeo-Arabic, because this Hebrew element does not carry the core of classical Jewish culture. It may be called Israeli-Arabic but not Judeo-Arabic.[41]

2.2 Step 2: The second Jewish component: Hebraisms

The straightforward borrowing of Hebrew terms, as seen in the previous paragraph, was the most convenient process as happens in many other languages in contact (Haspelmath and Tadmor 2009: 47, 55). Yet, another imminent characteristic of Jewish languages consists of Hebraisms, namely the influence of Hebrew on the phraseology and syntax of the base language, of the *calque* type or 'loan translation' (Clyne 2004: 801). In some cases, it is a morpho-semantic phenomenon in which the base language mirrors terms, expressions, or entire Hebrew texts. This feature is dominant in the translations

38 E.g., Weinreich 1931: 198, quoted in Sasaki 2008: 556: 'Yiddish would not have come into being without the Hebrew component.' See also: Fishman 1991:313; Baumgarten 1999: 221, 233, 240; Levy 1999: 418; Aslanov 2002: 80; Alvarez-Péreyre 2003a: 403–406; Baumgarten 2003: 27; Masson 2003: 151, though his notion of *hébréotropisme* does not entirely match the above characteristics; Alvarez-Péreyre 2007, §21; Bar-Asher 2009, §§22–26 ; Kahn and Rubin 2016: 3.

39 See also Alvarez-Péreyre 1999: 16. Yet, Aslanov (2007: 137–138) states that the integration of Hebrew *Kulturwörter* into the Jewish vernacular is not in itself a sufficient criterion to consider this idiom (= used in Bordeaux and Bayonne in the recent centuries) as a Judeo-language.

40 See also Kayyal 2011, esp. ch. 4 and footnotes [5]–[11], and Kayyal 2006; for calques in Judeo-Aramaic see Fassberg 2016: 70.

41 The same holds for the Aramaic culture words borrowed by ancient Muslim Arabic and discussed by Fränkel 1886. This Aramaic nomenclature did not turn that Arabic Jewish or Christian, as it was Islamized regardless of its origins.

of the Bible and other canonical Hebrew texts, beginning in the Septuagint,[42] through Targum Onqelos (Fassberg 2016: 73), medieval Judeo-Latin translations (Blondheim 1925: xi), Saadia's *Tafsīr*, *Taytsh* (old German translation of the Bible), Ladino (or Judeo-Espagnol calque, Sephiha 1984: 745), Judeo-Italian calque (Mayer-Modena 1999: 96), Maghrebi *šurūḥ*,[43] Judeo-Georgean *tabsili* (Enoch 2009), Jewish Malayalam *tamsir* in India (Gamliel 2013; Gamliel 2014: 137, 143ff.), or other literal translations of the Bible and other classic texts, are significant cases of Jewish elements that are not direct Hebrew borrowings but rather their reflection.

This feature may overflow the spoken or practical language. For instance, Nahmany (1953: 19, 39, cf. also Guedj 2016) in his *History of the Jews of Morocco* in Judeo-Maghrebi, used the expression *ʕəmlú fih əs-sráyəʕ* 'they butchered him.' No doubt he borrowed the expression directly from the *šarḥ* to Exodus 12:12 or indirectly from the citation of this verse in the *šarḥ* of the Passover Haggadah, which remains the most popular text in Jewish culture. In both cases, it was referring to *u-ḇə-ḵål ʔĕlōhē miṣrayim ʔeʕĕśe šəfåṭīm*: *uf-ʔilah kəll máṣər naʕməl əs-sráyəʕ* 'and I will make justice to all the gods of Egypt.' The *šarḥ*, by nature, was not a spoken or communicative language at all, but rather a literal translation, a *calque*, of a classical text.

Another example from classical Judeo-Arabic is *yaxruğu mim-mā yulzimu-hu* which is a literal reflection of Hebrew *yeṣeʔ yəḏe ḥoḇaṯo* 'fulfil one's duty'; and *raʔs al-maṯība*, which mirrors *roš yešiḇa* or Aram. *reš meṯiḇta* 'head of a rabbinic academy' (Blau 2006: 76). These processes began hundreds of years ago, but continued up to recent times, such as in the Tunisian satire *Qinat əl-hārəb bə-flus əl-ṭəfla* (p. 5) composed by JB (= Joseph Bijawi), published in the 19th century in Constantinople and Tunis,[44] where a conceited sinner says about himself: *wa-ʔana labs al-geut* 'while I am wearing majesty,' which echoes the Psalmist's expression *haš-Šēm mål̊åḵ gēʔūṯ låḇēš* (Ps 93:1) 'The Lord reigns and is clothed with majesty.' Naturally, there are parallels in other Jewish languages.[45]

42 As indicated by Daniel 1966, precisely on this topic. See e.g., ch. 9. where Heb. *ʕolah* is discussed with regard to its Greek translations ὁλοκαύτωμα and ὁλοκαύτωσις and other coined or adapted terms (p. 239ff.). Cf. also Blondheim 1925: 54–55, 174.

43 *Šurūḥ* (sg. *šarḥ*) are the traditional Judeo-Arabic translations of classical Jewish texts, both biblical and post-biblical, especially of the Maghrebi type, known in the East as *tafsīr*. See Maman 1999, §2.1.1.3. Bar-Asher 1999: 1–129, offers an extensive discussion on the Maghrebi *šarḥ*; see also Bar-Asher 2003, §§12–17; 2009, §§12–17; 2016 §5; Chetrit 2009, references on index, p. 697; Chetrit 2014: 210–121. With regard to the multi-layers of the *šarḥ*, see especially Bar-Asher 1999: 24–27, 30–31, 52–55. See also Baumgarten 2003: 27; Hary 2009: xvi, xxiii.

44 This specific satire is not listed under Bijawi's name in Tobi and Tobi 2014: 283–284.

45 Aslanov (2014: 106) claims that 'Septuagint… the extreme adherence to the syntax of Biblical Hebrew does not make this text a real testimony of Judeo-Greek,' an idea which may be extended to all kinds of literal translations of Jewish texts. Yet, though not spoken, it belongs to this kind of Judaization (see also his formulation in p. 107 re Aquila's Greek translation). A reverse feature is the influence of the local language on a Hebrew word by way of loan-translation, *calibration* in Gold's terminology (Gold 1985: 286–289) such as *khutspe* which absorbed the positive meaning of English 'nerve'.

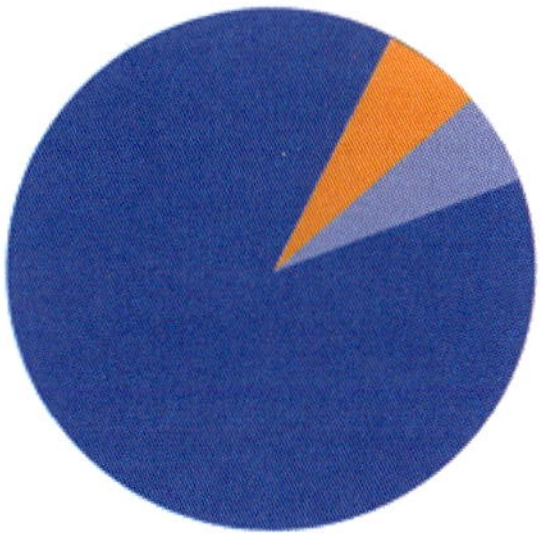

Figure 5. Hebraisms based on interaction

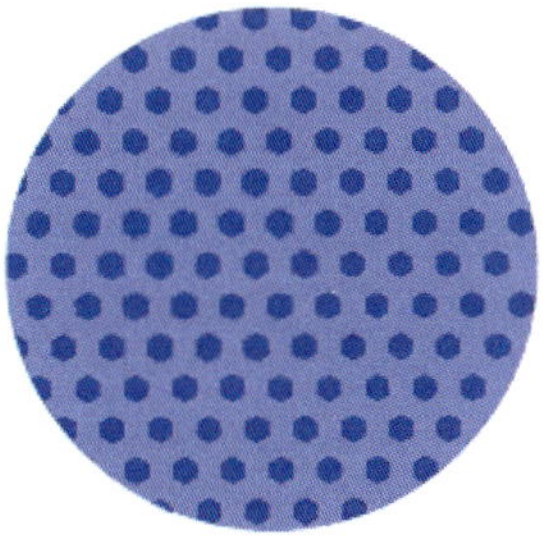

Figure 6. Dispersion of the Jewish component in the base language

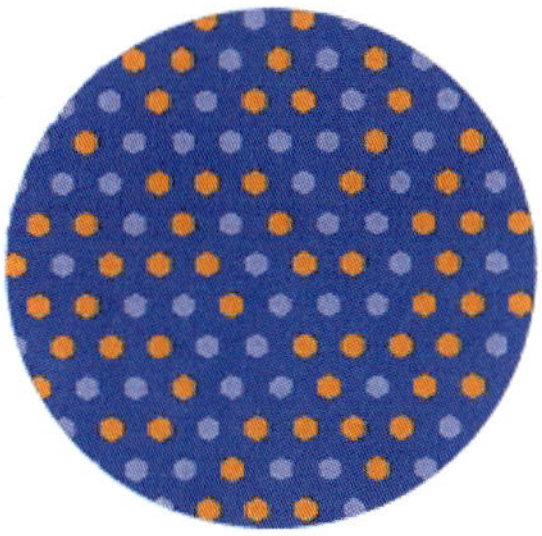

Figure 7. Dispersion of the Hebrew and other Jewish components

2.3 Step 3: The third Jewish component: judaization of local cultural terms

Another salient feature of Jewish languages is the judaization of local cultural terms. A few examples follow. Rav Saadia Gaon (Egypt 882–Iraq 942), David b. Abraham al-Fāsi (Jerusalem, mid-10th cent. CE), and others used the word *Qurʔān* in the context of medieval Judeo-Arabic to refer to the Bible (Blau 2006: 537), and *Rasūl* 'messenger' to refer to Moses (id., p. 248). These words with their new usages are no doubt part of the Jewish component. They are neither Hebrew nor Hebrew calques but rather were created via 'semantic borrowing,' a phenomenon well known from languages in contact. The words *Qurʔān* and *Rasūl* already exist in the base language, i.e., Muslim Arabic, but they are used in Judeo-Arabic in a new meaning, a new referent. This new usage is uniquely Jewish. A Jew would never use *Qurʔān* or *Rasūl* with their internal Jewish meaning (i.e., referring to the Bible and Moses respectively), when talking with a Muslim, as this would immediately arouse a linguistic misunderstanding, if not a theological conflict.[46] Saadia also labels the Torah *šarīʕa*, used in the Islamic context for the 'religious law,' and *Mizraḥ* ('East,' i.e. Jerusalem, towards which one has to turn during his prayers) *qibla* (referring to Mekka in Islamic context).[47] The indigenous speaker may recognize a word or expression, but not understand its Jewish internal meaning. He may understand, for example, the basic meaning of *təsnidá u-təgʕidá* 'bending and back-

46 See however, Tobi 2001:30, who takes a different stand in this regard and claims that words like *Qurʔān* for 'Bible' rather originated in a Jewish milieu in Central Arabia from which they were bequeathed to the Muslims.

47 See Saadia's *Siddur*, Davidzon et al. 1978: 2, 12, 20.

stretching' from the Judeo-Maghrebi adage,[48] but not understand its religious context, 'bending and back stretching in the *ʕamida* prayer.'[49] The implication is that any elements from the overall base language, which undergo internal Jewish dynamics, move from the general substrate to the Jewish component.

An example of this type from nineteenth century German is *Pfingsten* or *Pfingsttag*, discussed by Schwartz (2017: 11–12, n. 49) in his book on Philipp Jaffé (Posen, 1819–1870). These terms appear among others in a letter from Moritz Lazarus (1824–1903) telling that the news about the passing of King Friedrich Wilhelm III on June 7th, 1840, arrived to Posen the next day, when the Jews were in the synagogue close to the end of prayer, 'am zweiten Pfingsttage gegen Abend,' 'on the second day of Pentecost at dusk.' Basically, *Pfingsttag* marks the Christian Pentecost. Hence, German Jews adopted a clear Christian term to indicate the Jewish Holiday, though they also used the term *Wochenfest* which is a pure *calque* of the Hebrew *ḥag Šavuʕot* (lit., "fest of the weeks").[50]

Examples of this type are also noted by Aslanov (2002: 85–86; 2011, p. 393),[51] such as the nickname *coudolo* for the Jewish *matza* 'unleavened bread' in the Venaissin County Provençal, although non-Jews used this word to specify a type of *chametz* 'leavened bread' biscuit. The same holds for *galette* in the language of North African Jews in France whereas the locals used it to indicate a type of widespread round biscuit. Another Christian term presented by Aslanov is the use of *euxaristo* and *euxaristia* in Judeo-Greek for 'blessing' and 'saying a blessing.'[52] The same holds for *torta* meaning 'cake' in Spanish, but 'matza' in Ḥaketia,[53] whereas in Saloniki's Judezmo, it is simply a 'cake' (Nehama 1977, s.v.). These examples show that the Jewish component does not necessarily have to reflect Hebrew. This is another characteristic of Jewish languages recognized by scholars (Fishman 1991: 313–315; Aslanov 2002: 80).

48 In the dictum *təs-ni-dáw / təg-ʕi-dá / mən-ssi-máʕ / lləʕ-mi-dá / uʕ-lí-nu l / sa-bbi-yaḥ / ʕəl-ətt-ríq*, discussed in Maman 2011. A similar – though not identical – linguistic situation parallels what Aslanov (2015, §13) has spotted in the French of the 'pieds noirs' ('black feet').

49 Looking into the nature of the base language is important not only to understand the components of the puzzle called *Jewish language*, but also in order to characterize the nature of the term *Jewish languages*. Bar-Asher 2003 devoted an important chapter to this issue.

50 See also, Gold's example *Laubhüttenfest* 'Feast of Booths' coined in the Enlightenment period (Gold 1985: 293); and 'Jewish Languages Listserv' January 17th, 2017, where Joshua Lebenswerd asked about the 'practice within earlier forms […] of Reform Judaism of replacing Hebrew terminology with translations into the language of the host country.' He gave the following examples from German, English, Swedish, Dutch: *Sukkot* > Laubhüttenfest; Feast of Booths/Tabernacles; Lövhyddofesten; Loofhuttenfeest; *Yom Kippur* > Versöhnungstag; Day of Atonement; Försoningsdagen; Dag van de Vergevingen; *Roš ha-Šana* > Neujahrsfest, Nyårsfesten; *Šəmini ʕaṣeret* > Schlussfest; Slutfesten; *Simḥat Tora* > Torafreude; Torafesten; *Šavuʕot* > Wochenfest; Feast of Weeks; Veckofesten, assuming that many of them were taken from Christian Bible terminology. However, there are other such translations, which are less likely to have occurred in the Christian vocabulary, e.g., *šmone ʕeśre* > Achtzehngebet "the standing prayer;" Tysta bönen 'the silent prayer;' Adertonbönen 'the 18-prayer'; *ḥuppa* > Baldachin; Canopy; Baldakin.'

51 For a few English words that have undergone a similar semantic shift, see Bunin Benor 2009: 260.

52 On the status of old Greek and Latin in Europe see Blondheim 1925: xx ff.

53 Y. Bentolila, personal communication.

3. The Hebrew Script

Let us now examine another outstanding characteristic of Jewish languages, which scholars found noteworthy, the Hebrew script. In most cases, Jewish languages have been written in Hebrew characters, simply to make them easier for the Jewish community to read.[54] Post factum, this of course made them unintelligible to the co-territorial non-Jewish communities. Scholars mentioned this characteristic to be one of the determinants of Jewish languages, in most cases – the first one. So did Birnbaum (2011: 5), Stillman (1992: 44), Hary (2009: 19; repeated in Hary and Wein 2013: 90, §1), Haggai Ben-Shammai in a recent lecture[55] on the characteristics of a Jewish language,[56] and many more. Bunin Benor (2009: 237) did not place it as the first characteristic but as second (§2d). Birnbaum and Aslanov (2007: 302; Birnbaum 2011: 3; 384, n. 2) listed three reasons to prove that Jewish languages are 'creations of the group-forming factor of religion,' two of them related to the *script*: '(2) they are written in the Hebrew alphabet; and (3) the origin of their respective spelling systems is Talmudic orthography.'

According to Bunis (2016:10) 'in the Middle Ages, Spanish Christians do not seem to have perceived the varieties of Ibero-Romance which they heard spoken by Jews as sufficiently distinct from their own varieties to constitute a separate language, warranting a distinctive language name. The Hebrew letters which the Jews used to write their languages, however, were another matter… Jewish writing was therefore perceived by the Christians as distinctively Jewish; and thus medieval Spaniards tended to describe texts *written* by Jews in the Hebrew alphabet, no matter what the actual language, as being in *judiego*, i.e., "Jewish", or, with more specific reference to their alphabet, in *letras judaicas*.'

Of course, anything that arrived to us from Jewish languages of old periods is in writing, from the greatest literary work of Saadia, Juda Halevy, Maimonides and others, to private letters and documents. There are, of course, exceptions, as Ben-Shammai stated in the above-mentioned lecture, biblical translations which used the script of the target language in order to make the Bible available to those who do not know Hebrew.[57]

54 Cf. Deroy 1956/2013, ch. 10. Le sort des immigrés, § 48; Spolsky and Benor 2006: 120. Birnbaum and Aslanov 2007: 302–303, attribute the use of Hebrew script to the Jewish religion.

55 At a conference marking the 90th anniversary of the Institute for Asian and African Studies held at the Hebrew University of Jerusalem on December 14th, 2016, on 'Let the whole country be one language: a dialogue between Jews, Muslims, Christians and others.'

56 The others characteristics discussed by Ben-Shammai are that (2) a Jewish language usually contains a Hebrew component in varying proportions, and (3) quotations from Jewish sources: Bible, rabbinical literature, and other sources relevant to the context, [(4)] the same word has one meaning in Muslim Arabic and another in Jewish Arabic, such as *ʔimām*, which in Muslim Arabic is understood as 'the leader of the congregation in prayer,' whereas in Saadia' Bible translation, *ʔimām* renders 'Cohen'. Ben-Shammai's 2nd and 4th characteristics correspond to my aforementioned 1st and 3rd characteristics, respectively. His 3rd characteristic is not essentially different from his 2nd, which corresponds to my 1st characteristic.

57 Jewish languages sometimes coined expressions based on the square Hebrew script, e.g., in Judeo-Spanish *mem serrada* and in Judeo-Arabic *mīm stuma,* lit., 'closed mem', i.e, reminding the graphic form of a Hebrew final mem, ם, which is closed from all sides, whence 'an inaccessible person.'

Though socio-linguistically the above scholars and many others are extremely right,[58] in my opinion, from a purely linguistic point of view, the script is a technical rather than an essential characteristic, as it is limited to the written aspect of language only. A current proof is that Jewish English does not use Hebrew characters though it is a Jewish language (Gold 1985: 280; Bunin Benor 2009; Bunin Benor 2016: 130). The same holds true for the scripts and transcripts of Ladino (Bentolila 2009) and Bordeaux-Bayonne 18th–19th centuries Judeo-French (Aslanov 2007: 133). Rabin (1979: 43) mentioned Hellenistic Judeo-Greek as an example of a Jewish language that used the original script without transliterating it into Hebrew characters. Other examples were given by Zand 1979 for Judeo-Tajik and by Khan 2016: 31 for Judeo-Arabic. Birnbaum (2011: 5) went as far as to assign a religious value to the script, but the examples he brought do not really prove his point.

As scholars noted with regard to Judeo-Arabic, before the tenth century CE the writers rather used Arabic script and only later they switched to the Hebrew script (Blau 1999: 38–44; Stroumsa 2016: xxii, lii). In fact, the external appearance changed but the content remained the same (cf. Shohat 2015: 52ff.). Had I have transcribed general English or French or any other language as is into Hebrew character, would that make them Jewish? When Turkish switched from Arabic script to Latin transliteration, did this make it less Turkish or less Muslim or more Latin? Take also into consideration what Khan (2016: 31) calls 'the criterion of communicative function in the definition of Judeo-Arabic.' He mentions many Arabic texts written by non-Jewish authors that were transcribed into Hebrew script to make them accessible to the Jewish readership.

In sum, the choice of the Hebrew script is crucial for the cultural-religious aspects of the Jewish languages, sometimes to the point of becoming emblematic.[59]

4. Thorough vs. partial Jewish languages

Thus the Jewish element is that part of Jewish language which did not exist in the base language, before the Jews came into contact and socialized with it, namely the Hebrew component, hebraisms, and judaization of local terms, as well as the intonation in some cases, which may be influenced by the learned texts, as it happened in Ḥaketia.[60] The Jewish element was completely new and was not part of the original language. Even when it superficially sounds exactly like the base language, it does not constitute part of the original substrate. Yet, unlike Rabin (1979: 42) and others who assumed that the language was judaized, it appears that only the Jewish component consisting of the three elements described above underwent judaization. In general, the rest of the base language was kept intact. This of course depends on the degree of distance that a Jewish language kept away from its original base language, a distance which is a crucial factor for its definition, either as an entirely independent language or some kind of variation only of the base language.

58 In this regard see Shaked's (1979) note about the use of Arabic script in the midst of Judeo-Farsi texts in Hebrew characters. See also Baumgarten 2003: 31; Alvarez-Péreyre 2007, §18; Birnbaum and Aslanov 2007: 301; and Myhill 2009: 175.

59 Cf. Lopez-Morillas on Aljamiado, quoted in Hary 2009: 19, n. 31.

60 Bendayán de Bendelac 1990: 16–17, referring to Benoliel.

One aspect relevant to this characterization is that of linguistic competence. Was a speaker of Yiddish able to speak German or Polish with his German or Polish neighbor – simply by removing the Jewish component, in the same way a speaker of Judeo-Arabic was able to speak Arabic with his Arab neighbor or a speaker of Judeo-Georgian with his Georgian neighbor?

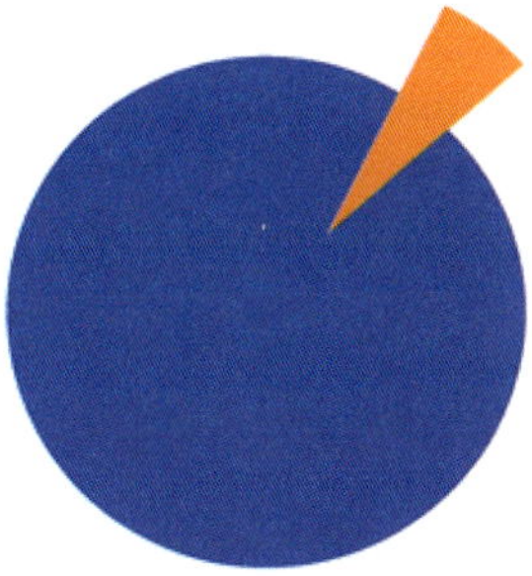

Figure 8. Modularity and mobility of Hebrew component: it may be 'removed.'

In some cases there were only minor differences between the two varieties that Jews and their neighbors spoke, such as in the case of Greek and Latin among Jews and non-Jews in the Roman environment (Blondheim 1925: xxviii, cxxxvi ff.), Old French vs. Rashi's French, Spanish vs. Judeo-Spanish before the expulsion, Georgian vs. Judeo-Georgian (Birnbaum and Aslanov 2007: 301, 302), and Modern Amharic vs. Jewish Amharic (Teferra 2016: 9).[61]

But even in cases where there were substantial differences, Jews were able to use the two varieties. When a Jew in Yemen greeted a neighbor, either Jew or Muslim, using the utterance *kif/kēf ḥālak?* 'How are you', he was using the global substrate, namely the joint language of Jews and Muslims alike. But when he alternatively said *kéṣað kaβoðáx*? lit. 'how is your honor,' that was part of the Jewish component that could only be addressed to another coreligionist. Another example: Jews in the Arabic speaking area expressed the operation of drawing one's attention in various ways, such as: *ra!*, *taṭallaʕ!*, *šuf!*, *xzər/ġzər!*, *ḥəmmər!*, *kəssəʕ!*, and *waggaʕ!*.[62] What does this variation mean? How does the distribution work? Not surprisingly, the Judeo-Arabic distribution exactly corresponds to the one in the local dialects (cf. Shohat 2015: 23, 28, 37, and elsewhere). That is, the basic platform of the Jewish language is identical in this respect to the language of the environment, though not in every detail.[63] Although such a cardinal matter cannot be decided based upon only a few examples, but rather on the basis of

61 According to Teferra (loc. cit.), it appears that there existed almost no specifically Jewish traditional Amharic and it only became essentially different from the general Amharic when Ethiopian Jews immigrated to Israel in the 1980s and 1990s.

62 The latter has been used in Qasbat Tamnuggalt (or Tamluggalt), near the town of Agdəz, halfway between Ouarzazate and Zagora (Morocco), located about 74 kilometers southeast of Marrakesh, on the outskirts of the Sahara. This example is courtesy of the poet Erez Biton, quoting his late father.

63 See, for instance, Blanc's (1979: 49–50; cf. also the examples in Birnbaum 2011: 383) quotes from Brunot and Malka 1939 for the differences between Judeo-Arabic and the Muslim Arabic of Fes, which no doubt emanate from migrations as explained there.

a systematic investigation of the complex modes of expression, the general impression is that the last example represents a linguistic reality.

Blau (1999: ix) says that 'the differences between the various branches of Middle Arabic are not conspicuous' and that 'the Jews everywhere used idioms identical with or closely resembling those of their Gentile neighbors' (Blau 1999: 21, 54–56; cf. Khan 2016: 21). David Cohen (1985: 255; see also 260) voices the opinion that 'a Judeo-Arabic idiom, considering the whole set of its structures, fundamentally remains an Arabic idiom.' Sebag (1991)[64] claims that all the Jews in Tunisia spoke the language of the country, both in their interactions with Muslims and their internal communal interactions.[65] He mentions that what some travelers call 'Jewish speech', which they see as 'corrupt Hebrew', is in fact a 'variant' of the Arabic dialect spoken in the country. He also refers to recent studies which claim that the Jewish speech was not different from that of the Arabs, neither in morphology nor in syntax. It only differed in the pronunciation of the sibilants, such as *š/s* or *ž/z*, and the attenuation of some emphatic consonants as *ṣ*, *ẓ*, and *ṭ*. He adds that against earlier claims, the borrowings from Hebrew were rather rare and limited to a small number of words related to Jewish *halakha* (law code). In this regard, the linguistic situation in Baghdad constitutes a special case. Blanc (1964; Blanc 1979: 50; cf. also Khan 2016: 42–44) has shown that the dialectal differences between Jews, Muslims, and Christians, were due to migrations. This aspect enables us to distinguish between a base language, which is common to co-territorial Jews and non-Jews alike, and a dialect or a substrate, which are different for both populations.

In the same way, it may be assumed that during the initial era of Judeo-German there was a common substrate to both Jewish and non-Jewish German, whereas during the Yiddish era the basic substrate largely drifted away from general German, so much so that Yiddish became an independent Jewish language compared to its base language, not merely because of the Hebrew components. For example, *das ist gestohlen* 'it is stolen' is from the base language. When one converts the main verb to *das ist geganwet*, the syntax is still the same, but the lexicon has changed: *geganwet* substitutes for German *gestohlen*, and though it has a German morphological configuration, it is lexically derived from the Hebrew root √ g-n-b 'steal'. The same holds for *hastu wos geganwet?* 'did you steal something?' which became peculiar to the Jewish speech. Whereas the first sentence is pure German, the second and third are Judeo-German (sometimes referred to as *Taytsh*), to become Yiddish later on. The last sentence is an example quoted by Jean Baumgarten (1995) from Elias Schade's *Mysterium* (Strasbourg 1592). Dr. Oren Roman identified this example as Western Yiddish, preserved especially in Alsace, which is kind of a Nature Reserve for this type of Yiddish.[66] According to Katz (2009: 201), to some Orthodox Jews Yiddish was *yiddish-daytsh* or judaized German. In their case Yiddish was to all intents and purposes German, which became yiddishized through its usage by Jews. Katz (2009: 193) is right in his statement that Jewish langu-

64 Pp. 121–122, par. 6 a, 'langues et écritures'.

65 See also, Sephiha 1984: 744; Shachmon 2007: 21; Morag 1999: 7; Bar-Asher 2009: 27; Aslanov 2014: 104, 118.

66 Personal communication.

ages 'are by no means equal by the empirical measures of number of speakers, geographic extent, duration in history, literary output, or structural and lexical differentiation from the major source language.'

The implication for the case of Yiddish is that the original base language was extensively transformed into an independent Jewish language, because of its unique phonetics, archaisms, and other features.[67] The same is true for Judeo-Spanish when compared to general Spanish. This holds for the processes that occurred prior to the migrations from one original speaking area to other speaking areas. In other words, Yiddish, while still in its natural environment, in the German speaking area, and Judeo-Spanish, while in Spanish speaking area, developed linguistic peculiarities until they became independent languages.[68] When speakers of Yiddish and Judeo-Spanish migrated from their natural environment to the midst of Polish, Greek or Arabic background and became speakers of Eastern Yiddish, Judezmo, and Ḥaketía, respectively, and their languages could be conceived as thorough Jewish languages (to which Bunin Benor (2008: 1070) refers as 'post-co-territorial languages'), they distanced themselves even further from their mother tongues, but kept their linguistic vitality and natural dynamics and created new variations out of new linguistic contacts, e.g., Yiddish with its new Slavic substrate.

This was not the case for other Jewish languages, where the base language remained more or less identical to the co-territorial language (Spolsky and Benor 2006: 120). For instance, Jews who lived in Arab lands did not need more than the base language to hold a conversation with Muslims or local Christians.[69] The nature of the language they used in that conversation did not essentially differ in phonetics, phraseology, or other linguistic characteristics, except for populations that migrated. In some cases, Jews even resorted to Muslim expressions, such as *ṣalli ʕan-nabi!* 'pray for the Prophet!' normally used by Muslims, e.g., when a Jew wanted to finish bargaining with a Muslim the price of a merchandise.[70] The same holds for Judeo-Alsatian (Aslanov 2013: 387) and most of Jewish languages. In this regard, being kind of bilingual speakers, Jews were apt to easily switch from one 'language' to another according to their interlocutor (Weinreich 1979: 73; Myhill 2004: 25–26, 53, 121). This idea may be summed up and formulated as an equation:

BL = Jewish language – JC

i.e., the base language equals the (partial) Jewish language minus the Jewish component

67 Cf., e.g., Bunin Benor 2016: 131. On Yiddish, its past and future, see e.g., Myhill 2004: 126–147 and the cited literature. See also Rabin 1979: 44–45.

68 In Iaacob Hassán's view, Ladino is a dialect of Spanish, whereas other scholars see it as an independent language. See Bentolila 2009: 10–11. See also Myhill 2004: 122–126.

69 This is comparable to the fact the American Jews speak and write in general American English and confine the distinctively Jewish features to in-group speech (Gold 1985: 285; Bunin Benor 2009: 238, 266). Similarly Weinreich (1979: 81) wrote: 'In speaking to a unilingual, the bilingual often tends to limit interference and to eliminate even habitualized borrowings from his speech. He is subject to what has been called interlocutory constraint.'

70 Regularly, however, Jews avoided using Muslim or Christians words (unless judaized as shown earlier). Cf. Gold 1985: 284…285 and Bunin Benor 2009: 239, 262.

Whenever this formula works for a Jewish language it means that it was a 'partial' Jewish language (which is the case for most Jewish languages). If, on the contrary, it does not work in a certain Jewish language, it means that it is a thorough Jewish language, as in the cases of Yiddish and Judeo-Spanish).[71]

This distinction ("partial" vs. "thorough") depends on whether the base language has its own Jewish dynamics to the point that it changes the base language itself, or whether it conforms with its linguistic environment, thereby remaining faithful to the base language. Figuratively, to use a chemical simile, the question is whether a given Jewish language is kind of a mixture or a fusion. If mixture, then once one component is removed, in this case, the Jewish element, all that is left, the base language, is completely identical to the co-territorial language, hence no Jewish characteristic was added to the fundamental substrate. If a fusion, then the Jewish component becomes inseparable. This parallels what Weinreich (1979: 69, 70, 106; Alvarez-Péreyre 2003a: 411) calls 'hybrid languages.' Most Jewish languages are of the blend (mixture) type, whereas only a few reached the level of a fusion ('hybrid languages').[72] The main test is the base language and the linguistic competence for communication between co-territorial Jews and non-Jews.

5. The evolvement of the Jewish element

One remarkable characteristic of Jewish languages is their dynamics in adopting or developing more Hebrew expressions, beyond the basic nomenclature exemplified above. Naturally, with regard to Hebraization (described above in 'step 2' and 'step 3'), Jewish languages differ from one another, as otherwise they are not different from their base languages. In this regard, German *Taytsh* is the equivalent of Medieval Judeo-Arabic *Tafsīr*, Maghrebi *Šarḥ* (n. 43 above), Georgian *Tabsili* (Enoch 2009), Ladino translations, and so on. Yet, even as regards the Hebrew component ('step 1'), many differences evolved in the course of the centuries. The lowest common denominator (of a Hebrew component in all Jewish languages) seems to be inherited from time immemorial, and anything that is particular seems to be institutionalized via a process of selection from early material, or evolved independently in each Jewish language. The internal dynamics operating within this component distanced the Jewish element of one language from that of another to such an extent that apart from a basic Hebrew element common to all Jewish languages, each continued to develop in independent directions.

For instance, *pəloni* ('John Doe') is used in Yiddish, Judezmo and Ḥaketía, literally, but in Iraq it came to be a nickname for the Angel of Death and in Aden a nickname for *Samael*, elsewhere (such as in Yiddish or Judeo-Maghrebi) known by its acronym only,

71 In Weinreich's description (1979: 106), all Jewish languages represent 'unique fusions of various dialects of the stock languages (German, Spanish, Arabic, Persian, etc., as the case may be) with outside admixtures (Hebrew-Aramaic and Slavic, Turkish, etc., again as the case may be)', whereas only in the Yiddish case, 'language loyalty of the Yiddish-speaking community has not been equaled among the speakers of Dzhudezmo ("Judeo-Spanish") or other Jewish languages.' It is common thought today that Judezmo became a full-fledged Jewish language of its own.

72 Cf., however, Goldenberg's stand (Goldenberg 2003b: 427–428) who opposes the idea of 'mixed language', based on Meillet's conception that unless the initial conjugation is changed the language remains the same.

samekh mem 'Satan'. In Yemen, the diphtheria disease was called *bår minnan*, (Aramaic lit. "outside of us, excluding us"), whereas this euphemism was used in Yiddish and elsewhere for 'corpse, 'deceased,' or just literally, 'let this be away from us; Help me God.' In Aden, *Lilith* was nicknamed *falilit* 'criminal' – all these being local developments within the Hebrew component. Local Judeo-Italian examples that developed during World War II are the nicknames *gəvir* 'lord,' *ponel (< poʕel)*, 'worker,' *goy gadol* 'great gentile,' *kelev* 'dog,' *roš* 'head,' all referring to Mussolini (Mayer-Modena, *Dictionary*).[73]

The Hebrew word *haz-zan* (lit., 'he who feeds') was used in Aden as a metonymic nickname for the Challah bread, derived from the beginning of the Grace after meals (*haz-zan ʔet ha-ʕolam* etc. Ben-Zion 2011: 292). The same word appears in Morocco in a sarcastic saying that describes the minimal version of that benediction. The abridged rhymed and rhythmic text says: *barúx šəlḥán* / *barúx ḥəzzán* / *barúx sidná múṣa bən ʕəmrán* (= Blessed is the Table / Blessed is the 'cantor' / Blessed is the Lord and Moses Ben Amram). The leading word, on which the entire adage is based, is *haz-zan*, but it was corrupted and reinterpreted as if it were *ḥəzzan* 'cantor.'[74]

The Hebrew word *zuzim* borrowed from Rabbinic literature (known as well for its Aramaic form *təre zuze* 'two zuzim' from the popular song *Ḥad Gadya* sung at the end of the *Seder* Night) once designated a particular coin or currency, and later became a generic nickname for money. It was incorporated in Judeo-Arabic of some communities such as Aleppo, Syria, Tripoli (Libya). In the same sense *maʕot* 'coins' was used in Georgia and *paḥim* (lit. 'tin') in Tunisia (Henshke 2007: 147; cf. Bentolila 1991: 28).

Variation in the Hebrew component is characterized by a great creativity, normally representing local aspects, e.g., the feminine form of *ʕeved* 'slave' as *ʕavda* (rather than *šifḥa*) in Judeo-Italian *ñavda* 'maidservant' or *vice versa*, the masculinized form *bimḥil* in Yemen (lit. 'with excuse) 'pardon' derived from *bimḥila*, which is current in Yiddish, Judeo-Arabic, Judeo-Georgian, Jewish Neo-Aramaic (Maman 2013: 349, 429), or of a total innovation e.g. *ʕazzifut* (< *ʕazzut panim*) 'chutzpah, sexual misconduct' in Judeo-Spanish (Bentolila 2015: 170).

Creativity is sometimes reflected in graceful and humorous responses or sarcastic reinterpretation to verses from the weekly Torah Portion[75] or to other widely read classical Jewish texts. For example, the biblical instructions for constructing the Menorah brings to mind local innovations. The content of those instructions is: 'One bud shall be under the first pair of branches extending from the lamp stand, a second bud under the second pair, and a third bud under the third pair – six branches in all,' but the biblical Hebrew formulation repeats the first sentence three identical times without abridgments: *wə-ḵap̄tōr taḥaṯ šənē haq-qā̄nīm mim-mɛnn-ā̄h, wə-ḵap̄tōr taḥaṯ šənē haq-qā̄nīm mim-mɛnn-ā̄h, wə-ḵap̄tōr taḥaṯ šənē haq-qā̄nīm mim-mɛnn-ā̄h* (Exod. 25:35), lit. 'and a bud

73 For more examples from Judeo-Italian, see Jochnowitz 2013a.

74 For a detailed discussion see Maman 2011: 134. For a description of this professional role, see Stillman 1988: 82, n. 2. For another expression with *ḥazzan* in Judeo-Egyptian Arabic see Rosenbaum 2013: 390.

75 For a humoristic and sophisticated example of reinterpretation of a biblical passage, see Maman 2011: 35–137.

under two branches of it, and a bud under two branches of it, and a bud under two branches of it.' Regularly one comes across distributive expressions, such as *šana šana* 'year by year,' *yom yom* 'day by day,' but three repetitions in a row stuck out to the ears of listeners, for which reason they sarcastically nicknamed a troublesome person who repeated his words over and over again *kaftor*. This occurred in the Judeo-Arabic of Morocco, Egypt, and Syria, as well as in Ladino, and with slight variations *ve-kaftor* in Italy, *ve-ḵaftor taḥat šenei* in Libya, and *kaftor taḥat* in Tunisia, probably with the connotation of *taḥat* meaning 'bottom' as well.

An example of a humoristic reinterpretation of a Hebrew word from a liturgical text may be seen in the Yemenite expression *maróq baraḥamé-xå hå-rabbím*, borrowed from the High Holiday prayer, 'clear away with Your mercy all of our sins,' then humorously addressed to the person in charge of serving soup, asking for seconds, turning the verb *maroq* from the meaning of 'clearing, cleaning' to a new denominative verb *m-r-q* (*måråq* in the Yemenite pronunciation) meaning 'serving soup' (Ratzhabi 1978: 171). All these examples prove the intensive creativity of Jewish languages, the vitality of their Hebrew component and its particularities in the midst of every single Jewish language.

To give a statistical notion as regards the Hebrew element, I counted the entries under the letter *reš* in the *Synoptic Dictionary* (Maman 2019), randomly selected as a sample. Their thorough examination shows that only a small minority is common to the Jewish languages studied in that dictionary, whereas the majority is peculiar to one or several communities. Altogether, this section (letter *reš*) contains 125 entries with 265 sub-entries. 72 entries (57%) pertain to single communities and 14 entries pertain to two communities (68% altogether). But not all the rest (about 33%) is common to all communities. In fact only 12 entries (10%) are. With a more complete documentation, the rate would get probably higher (up to 20%). The following two entries, e.g., pertain to single communities only: *reviʕit* 'a halachic measure of volume.' Though it is widely used in the realm of *halakha*, the *Synoptic Dictionary* testifies to popular use in Iraq only (*háḏa l-kós kbíġ, bíná kam rebiʕíṯ* 'this cup is large enough to contain a few 'quarters').'[76] *reš gǻluṯ* (lit. 'Head of the Exile,' initially the official Aramaic title of the Exilarch at the time of the Babylonian Geonim) was used in the Yemen as an attribute for a settlement of more than one or two hundred people, i.e., 'a big town.' The sentence *glísna ban-náḏaṛí whí kána reš gǻluṯ* (lit. "we sat in Nadari while it was the head of the exile") means 'we lived in Nadari when it was a big town.'

The entry *roš* 'head' has 27 sub-entries, but only *roš ḥodeš* 'New Moon' and *roš šana* 'New Year' are universal, [77]whereas the remainder is in use in one or another Jewish language only. For instance, in Tunisia and Libya *Roš ḥodeš ḥanuka* is used in the sense of *Rosh Chodesh Ṭevet*, because it always falls in the midst of Hanukkah. In Tunisia alone it is also called *roš ḥodeš lə-bnāt* 'The girls' New Moon,' because of the

76 On a general description of and basic bibliography on Judeo-Arabic in Iraq see Geva-Kleinberger 2013.

77 Including month names, such as *Rosh Chodesh Elul*, *Rosh Chodesh Ṭevet*, and *Rosh Chodesh Nissan*. See e.g., Rosenbaum 2013: 390.

story of Judith. At this New Moon the girls were celebrating with a special meal. In Georgia, *Roš a-šana Tora* was used for 'the New Year's prayer book.'

All other sub-entries are local. For example, *roš* in its basic meaning 'head,' was rare and only used in that sense in Iran, *rošaš hule-hu* (lit. 'his head is sick') 'the patient has a headache.' The expression *ʔavel va-ḥafuy roš* 'mourning and with his head covered,' borrowed from Esther 6:12, is recorded from Morocco and Iraq. *roš keves* 'a sheep's head' is a little more widespread, because of the practice to include it in the first meal of the year among the New Year's symbols. Another phrase was used in the metaphorical and sarcastic sense 'stupid,' *roš trontšo* 'cabbage head,' in Italy (Mayer-Modena; Schwarzwald 2015: 63), where also *roš* and *rošo* were used in the sense of 'leader' with special reference to Mussolini. With other modifiers it also was used in Yemen, Iraq, and Tunisia.[78]

As to the diachronic aspect of the evolution of the Hebrew element in Jewish languages, in some cases it is easy to reconstruct the circumstances, under which a new expression was imported. For instance, *Qabbalat Šabbat* (lit. 'Sabbath's reception') is an old term, but since the spread of Kabbalah in the 16th century, it was used with a new meaning, 'slight dish,' following a Kabbalistic custom of 'slightly tasting the Shabbat dishes' before the prayer of Sabbath's reception. This ceremony was called in Morocco *buyí kallá* 'Come, Bride,' 'bride' being a figurative word for Shabbat. The metonymic expression *buyí kallá* is borrowed from the *piyyuṭ* 'Lekha Dodi' composed by Rabbi Shlomo Halevi Alkabets, a 16th century Safed Kabbalist, and sung since then during the service of the Shabbat's reception. This example makes an explicit and clear connection to the poem.[79]

In sum, the Hebrew vocabulary integrated in Jewish languages is of two types: One part is fundamental and necessary, sometimes collocative, i.e., the speaker or writer has no choice or alternative but to use it; the other part, which constitutes the vast majority of the Hebrew component, was specifically coined or developed for fun, wordplay, flowery language, sarcasm, rhetoric, etc.

6. Modularity and Mobility of the Hebrew Component

Another characteristic of the Hebrew element in most Jewish languages (i.e., those of the blend type) is its modularity and mobility: it is sort of a "building block" that can be easily transferred from one Jewish language to another. This component may pass as is and integrate into a different Jewish language (cf. "step 1"). That was no doubt the case for the North African Jewry, which was speaking Latin prior to the Arab invasion in the seventh century. In comparable scenarios, Greek was superseded in Sicily by Arabic when Arabs conquered the island (Neubauer 1891: 13), when the Jews in the land of Israel moved approximately at the same period from Byzantine Greek; Aramaic was replaced by Arabic (Blau 1999: 22; Myhill 2009: 172; Khan 2016: 23; Fassberg 2016; 65; 85); and Yiddish speakers moved on to American English (Bunin Benor 2009: 246,

78 *rəš* and *råšim* in Yemen, *ros əl-ḥabra* and *ros ha-mišpaḥa* in Tunisia, *roš ha-ḥaxamim*, *roš ha-rabbanim*, and *roš ha-yhudim* in Iraq (Maman 2013: 514).

79 On semantic development in the use of Hebrew words and expressions in Judeo-Maghrebi, see for instance, Tedghi 1996 and Tedghi 2003.

256).[80] In these and similar cases, the Hebrew component, which was in use in Jewish language 1, moved on to Jewish language 2 that was imposed on or became adopted by the same population.[81]

Modularity and mobility do not apply to the second and third Jewish components (cf. 'step 2' and 'step 3' above), i.e. the part of *calques*, semantic borrowing, or independent innovation. These were formally part and parcel of the base language, though only used by Jews. When the Jews moved on from one language to another, as in the earlier examples, this part was lost along with the old basic substrate, because it still belonged to the base language both in lexicon, phraseology and grammar, and though it served as a kind of bridge between the basic substrate and the Hebrew component.

The Hebrew component is evident: it already existed in the vernacular of the Jews before their encounter with any foreign language, consists of every word that is not part and parcel of the new base language, and is not recognized by the indigenous speakers. The other Jewish components sound like the tongue substrate though they did not exist in it prior to the interference of Hebrew and may be recognized but not understood by the indigenous speakers because it was judaized.

It is clear that the Jewish element *per se*, including all of its components, does not constitute a language in itself. It is an additional layer that may integrate and develop within a base language, but it has no independent existence. It only creates a new linguistic texture that justifies the term 'Jewish languages.'

7. Temporariness of Jewish languages

Another feature of Jewish languages that was neither listed above nor in others' works is their temporariness as naturally spoken languages. The fact that Jews moved from one Jewish language to another, under certain circumstances in some places and times, means that Jewish languages were destined to be temporary, not everlasting. There is almost no extant remainder of the Judeo-Latin that was spoken in North Africa[82] prior to the Arab conquests.[83] Jewish languages were an internal Jewish matter that did not affect the speakers of the base languages. It is clear that the Hebrew component, if recorded, as well as any written or recorded literature or documentation in Jewish languages, will be preserved for generations because it is part of the Jewish cultural creativity.[84] The same holds true for the other Jewish components. It is also true that in our generation

80 Weinreich (1979: 113–114) describes a different phenomenon, in which speakers of Yiddish moved from a Slavic environment to an English environment, while they continued to Yiddish. Yet there are also commonalities. Cf. also Gold 1985: 282.

81 Assuming the modular characteristic of the Hebrew element is correct, it is apparent that the model would work for the Chinese, Japanese, or Italian components that were layered onto an English substrate, to take only a few examples of possible combinations of the mixture type. If a Chinese speaker is assimilated into an English-speaking environment, while still observing his or her original culture, and then moves on to a French-speaking area and adopts French as his or her new daily language, the Chinese component embedded in his/her English will inherently move as is to his/her French speech.

82 See Versteegh 2010: 635; Myhill 2004: 118–119.

83 Cf. the case of Judeo-Gascon in Nahon 2017.

84 Cf. Stillman 1988: 3–4.

the Jewish languages are endangered.[85] Even Judeo-Spanish is falling into oblivion. Ḥaketía has already ceased to be spoken (Bentolila 2015: vii), but it seems to be the fate of Judezmo as well. This circumstance may better explain why at the initial stages of Zionism and the revival of the Hebrew speech in Israel there was fierce opposition to Yiddish. In my opinion, this was not because it preserved the Diaspora taste, or because it represented rabbinical culture, as others suggested, but due to a better understanding of the nature of Jewish languages. Most nations or communities speak a single language, and those struggling against Yiddish understood that it was meant to be a temporary language rather than a permanent one; and just as other communities do not hold dual citizenship at the same time, each community tends to speak one language (even in Switzerland each community speaks one language). Therefore, Yiddish should, in their opinion, have disappeared.[86] In a certain sense, the languages of the Jews were a symbol of exilic culture, and when the people of Israel returned to their land, there was no longer any need for Jewish languages. This is also true for other Jewish languages as Ladino, Judeo-Persian, Judeo-Georgian etc. Paradoxically, it is Yiddish that has the best chance to survive, even after losing six million speakers in the Holocaust, because the ultra-Orthodox still use Yiddish in America and Israel. Disappearance of Jewish languages is regrettable from a linguistic point of view, but rather a normal process for the people themselves.

In this context I would like to comment on Ella Shohat's (2015) claim that the concept of "Judeo-Arabic" entails an ethnic-religious "Arab-Jew" identity. Even without attempting a cultural-mental-psychological and historical analysis of the matter, the temporariness of Jewish languages proves that Judeo-Arabic has nothing to do with identity *per se*. Had Judeo-Arabic been part of Jewish identity, it should have on the one hand always been present in its speakers' identity, no matter where they went, and on the other hand it should have been part of any Jew's identity, no matter what other language or Jewish language he or she spoke. Yet in reality, the second and certainly third generations of the immigrants from Arab countries in Israel simply do not speak Judeo-Arabic or any other Jewish language (except Yiddish in certain circles). The first generation just did not care to preserve it and pass it on to their children, which proves that Jewish languages were not an essential part of Jewish culture. The only part that has to do with Jewishness is the prefix *Judeo-* / the adjective *Jewish*, which stand before the hyphen (*Judeo-*), because this is the only part of Jewish languages which persists, stable. Anything that comes after the hyphen (e.g., *-Spanish*) is temporary, so to speak, until conditions necessitate a cardinal change.

85 Out of the Jewish languages listed in Hary 2009: 26–27, many are not spoken any more. Cf also Bunis 2009:167; Myhill 2009:179. In 1985, *The Center for Jewish Languages and Literatures* was founded at the Hebrew University of Jerusalem by Professor Moshe Bar-Asher and since then holds bi-annual international workshops. The rationale behind is the understanding that most of Jewish languages are on the verge of disappearing as naturally spoken languages and that the greatest possible effort should be made to record and analyze as much material as possible, as long as their speakers are still alive. Cf. also Spolsky and Benor 2006: 120; Shohat 2015: 45, regarding Iraqi Judeo-Arabic.

86 See the bibliography in Baumgarten 2003:16, n. 5.

8. Were Jewish languages artificial or cryptic languages?

As implied earlier (see section 2.1), Renaissance Christian Hebraists claimed that the very incorporation of Hebrew words and phrases in "Judeo-languages" such as Rotwelsch was artificial by nature.

Max Weinreich (1973) said that 'the holy tongue influenced Yiddish not orally from mouth to ear but through books and Scripture quotations.'[87] This is certainly not appropriate for the core of the Hebrew component that the exiles took with them from Israel thousands of years ago wherever they went. And it is certainly not appropriate for anything that was developed or created in each community. Creativity of normal expressions does not necessarily mean artificiality, as may be inferred from the earlier examples.

The only case of artificial creativity is that of the cryptic words or expressions.[88] As seen earlier, the Hebrew words *kelev* 'dog,' *goy gadol* 'great gentile' and others (Mayer-Modena) were used in Italy as nicknames for Mussolini during his reign, in order to avoid an explicit mentioning of his name. Indeed, under certain circumstances, such as fear or danger, Jewish languages developed cryptic expressions (cf. Bentolila 1991: 26; Stillman 2007: *146; Shachmon 2013; Chetrit 2014: 208–210). Merchants who feared for their livelihoods instilled Hebrew words in their speech sometimes with changes and apocopations, to make the context obscure for those who were outside of their trade circle, Jews included. In an environment of cognate languages, such as Hebrew and Arabic, words of etymological and typological proximity thwarted sometimes the speakers' intent to use the concealment strategy. To avoid direct use of Hebrew cognate words that sounded like their Arabic equivalents, the interlocutors used alternative words or produced sophisticated forms out of the same words to completely cover up the traces of their etymological provenance. For example, the word *sukkar* 'sugar' is equal in Hebrew and Arabic.[89] Merchant Jews in Morocco who had a monopoly on sugar products for centuries had to find a Hebrew substitute to prevent foreigners from following the conversation. They thus used a metonymic synonym, *l-matoq* 'the sweet' (Bar-Asher 1981: 175), an adjective that has undergone nominalization or substantivization (Maman 2013: 393).[90]

ʔen lanu melex is a cryptic expression in Judeo-Italian, wishing to warn a client that the object is made of tin rather than of a precious metal. The expression is based on a famous liturgical passage, *ʔAvi-nu Malke-nu*, whose source is in the Talmud (Bab. *Taʕanit*, 25v): *ʔen la-nu melex ʔella ʔatta*, 'we have no king but you,' to be understood with reference to the second part of the formula (*ʔella ʔatta*) that sounds like Italian *latta* 'tin' (Mayer-Modena; Maman 2013: 58).

87 Cf. 'Die shprakh von derekh haShas [through the Talmud],' vol. 1, 122; vol. 2, 264.

88 On secret languages, see Bar-Asher's (1999) references in the index, p. 443, especially pp. 160–162; Bar-Asher 2016, §§ 29–32; Chetrit 2009: 241–249, more occurrences referred to in the index, p. 697.

89 For this word's etymology see Deroy 1956/2013, ch. 6. Nécessité pratique, §§ 15–16. On the interplay of Arabic and Hebrew in the Cairo Geniza letters see Cohen 2007.

90 On the circumstances which motivate this phenomenon see Aslanov 2007: 135 and n. 10 and his references.

A trader from Borujerd would say in Judeo-Iranian: *begu hesi* (lit. 'tell him half') 'offer him half the price he demanded.' In Isfahan one would say *ḥaṯi ḥaṯi šutafim* '[let us be] fifty-fifty partners.' In Tripoli, Libya, a broker would demand a profit for mediating in a transaction in the following terms: *miyya l-foq, u-ḥasi ləl-kohin,* 'raise the price by hundred, of which half would go to the priest,' i.e., give me half the profit of the addition. 'Priest' here is not used in its literal meaning and rather refers to the broker who demands an offering as if he were a priest. *Zayin* stands in the cryptic speech of Judeo-Maghrebi for the Hebrew word *zahav* 'gold,' because it begins with *z*.

The cases of cryptic expressions in Jewish languages have been widely discussed in the literature.[91] Does this mean that the entire Hebrew component was meant to turn the language cryptic? This argument was raised by Christian Hebraists especially with regard to the Hebrew component incorporated in Yiddish, and by implication, in any Jewish language.[92] Many of those scholars argued since the 15th century onward, that Yiddish was a crypto-language designed to disguise the intent of the Jews from non-Jews.[93] However, if one looks into the whole range of entries in the *Synoptic Dictionary* (Maman 2019), one may realize that only one percent of the entire Hebrew component, including all Judeo-Arabic dialects, Judeo-Italian, Judeo-Georgian, Judeo-Persian, and Judeo-Aramaic, is somewhat "cryptic".[94] Moreover, one may easily see that not all cryptic expressions were directed against non-Jews. Sometimes this kind of expressions were used because of taboo issues, or when parents wanted to keep a particular issue out of reach of their children; or when traders did not want to disclose a trade secret or wanted to bring a transaction to an end, raise or lower the price, and so on. In conclusion, the total number of these expressions is minor and in no way turned Jewish languages into crypto-languages.

9 The linguistic status of Jewish languages

9.1 What kind of lect are Jewish languages?

Most scholars agree more or less on the characteristics of Jewish languages described above, though some focus primarily on social factors (e.g., Myhill 2004: 25ff.) whereas others emphasize the *structural* characteristics (e.g., Bunis 2016: 6). However, when it comes to their exact nature, which one would expect to be reflected in their names, a certain perplexity is presented. Intuitively, they are just called 'Jewish languages.' Blau (1999: 47 and elsewhere) calls Medieval Judeo-Arabic a 'language,' a 'language in its

91 See, e.g., Levy 1999: 420; Aslanov 2002: 80, 90–92; Henshke 2007: 155–156; Bunin Benor 2009: 262–263, Bar-Asher 2016, §§29–32.

92 Elias Schade, Mysterium, Strasbourg 1592, quoted in Baumgarten 1995 (see the following footnote): 'They have a habit, a way Taytsh, involving several Hebrew words... So the Jews, sometimes they seek to hide their affairs from the Christians used to say: hast du lehem; Der goy: Ikh wil okh das meshalem zeyn; Hastu wos geganwet (das ist gestolen).'

93 The details about this and other arguments may be found in Baumgarten 1995: 113–128.

94 Cf. Bunin Benor 2008: 1072, §7 and her references. On the nomenclature of Jewish Neo-Aramaic and its distribution see Gerrit J. Dimmendaal and F. K. Erhard Voeltz (in Moseley 2007: 620, entries *Lishana Deni* and *Lishanán*) and Fassberg 2016: 101).

own right' (49) and sometimes a 'dialect.'[95] Both Cohen (1912) and Cohen (1964–1975) entitled their books *Le parler arabe des juifs*... Sebag (1991) follows in their footsteps and designates them 'Jewish speech' ('parler judaique') or 'variant' ('variante'),[96] He says that what some travelers call Jewish speech' ('parler judaique'), which they see as 'corrupt Hebrew' ('hébreu corrompu'), is in fact a 'variant' ('variante') of the Arabic dialect spoken in the country. Thus, Sebag does not bother to define the Jewish *lect* beyond the general attributes of *parler* ('speech') and *variante*.[97] Aslanov (2015a: 446) states that Jewish languages are not languages that the Jews spoke where they were, i.e., the common language of the entire population, but linguistic *variants* that they created for themselves in the spaces in which they lived.

9.2 Are Jewish languages dialects of their base languages?

Loewe (1911, quoted in Bunis 2016: 5) referred to these varieties as *Sprachen der Juden* ('languages of the Jews'), whereas Matisiahu/Matthias Mieses in 1915 called them *jüdische Dialekte* ('Jewish dialects'). Fishman (1985) believed that there are no clear linguistic or social criteria that can be used to distinguish between language and dialect (Hary 2009: 10; Hary and Wein 2013: 86–87). Durrell (2004: 201–202) claimed that 'all varieties can be referred to as dialects.' Gamliel (2013: 410) simply calls Judeo-Malayalam a *dialect*. Bar-Asher (2003, e.g., p. 72; Bar-Asher 2009: 27) also designates Jewish languages as *dialects*, as does Goldenberg (2003b: 426).[98] According to Bentolila (2009: 11), the difference between *language* and *dialect* is not based on linguistic terms, but rather on principles such as independence.[99] Whereas a language is autonomous, a dialect is heteronomous,[100] connected to its base language. A regional dialect becomes a language when its speakers achieve political power or cultural strength.[101] Birnbaum (2011: 4, 277ff.) rejected the designation *dialect* for Jewish languages because 'a Jewish structure whose cultural center is Judaism cannot be a dialect of a language which has its focal point in Christian or Islamic culture.' Bunin Benor (2009: 235, §2) wrote that even sociopolitical criteria are not enough for the differentiation between a language and a dialect. Yet, at least intuitively both laymen and scholars use the term *dialect* quite successfully. A typical study may be seen in Dinkin 2009, who discusses the dialect boun-

95 Similarly, Myhill (2004: 28, 29, 109) refers to those varieties as 'languages,' 'versions,' 'varieties,' and even 'debased varieties.' This question is discussed by Bunin Benor 2008: 1066.

96 Pp. 121–122, §6a, 'langues et écritures.'

97 See also Bar-Asher 2003: 71. See, however, Baumgarten 2003: 23.

98 See also Baumgarten 2003: 27 ('*dialectes* juifs des langues majoritaires' – emphasis added). See also Alvarez-Péreyre et Baumgarten 2003: 9, and Myhill 2009: 174. Shohat (2015: 16, 19, and elsewhere) aspires to link Judeo-Arabic to Arabic dialects (and to discard it from Jewish languages altogether).

99 See also Ammon et al. 2004: 269, where definitions of *dialect* from several scholars are presented, most of which are based on the notion of regionality.

100 Not to be confused with *heteroglossic*, a term used by Cohen (1985: 258), to designate the relationship of a language displaced by migration to a different location, where it ceases to be cognate with the new environmental spoken language, such as the case of Yiddish in a Slavic area or Judeo-Spanish in an Arabic or Turkish area.

101 Cf. the criteria for differentiating *language* from *dialect* in a recent article by Maldonado 2016.

daries and phonological change in Upstate New York. It is clear from his definition[102] and discussion that dialects are based on distinctive *phonological* features within the same language spoken in *different areas*. Dialects according to his study are *regional* and the boundaries between them can be traced *geographically*. This is in fact what linguistic *Atlases* are about. Dialectal differences are normally recognized by speakers from both sides of the boundary. Moreover, in the course of time a linguistic feature of one dialect may be diffused to another beyond the boundary that separates the two populations.

An example of dialectal phonetic feature is the split of the phoneme /r/ into several allophones within English, French, Modern Hebrew and other languages with respect to its articulatory and acoustic realization. Such variation marks socio-linguistic, ethnic and regional variations. Another example can be 'words … pronounced with secondary stress on the penultimate syllable, leading to a stress clash between the primary-stressed antepenultimate and the secondary-stressed penultimate, thus: *elementary*' (Dinkin 2009: 18).

Beyond phonological and sound shift differences, dialects develop out of one language by innovations in vocabulary, semantics, phraseology, morphology, grammatical simplification, syntax, either by natural internal development or via external influence from neighboring languages. As the gaps grow, dialects may become independent tongues, as it happened in Latin languages and Arabic dialects, which according to some linguists have reached the level of distinct languages. In the study of the two most prominent Jewish languages, Yiddish and Judeo-Spanish, it is well established that Eastern Yiddish differs from the Western, and Eastern Judeo-Spanish, also known as *Judezmo*, is distinct from Western Judeo-Spanish, *Ḥaketía* (spoken in northern Morocco; Bentolila 2015). In the same way, Eastern Judeo-Arabic is different from its Western counterpart (Myhill 2004: 121; see also Chetrit 2015). The differences are due, in the first place, to the cultural gap between the Mashreq (= East) and Maghreb (= West). Moreover, within these big branches, there are shades and linguistic nuances, dialects and sub-dialects. Roughly speaking, western Judeo-Arabic covers the Maghreb, from Morocco to Libya, and the eastern covers all the territory from Egypt to Iraq (Shinar 1979) without losing sight of the southern Judeo-Arabic as well, of Yemen and Aden. As is well known, within the western dialects there are significant differences, and within each of the Maghreb countries there are differences between Northern and Southern dialects. These dialects differ in their accent and vocabulary, and to a certain extent in morphology and syntax as well.

In the lexicon, some differences are the outcome of borrowings from other languages, others are the outcome of a selection from synonyms in the same language. Whereas, e.g., the words *xubz* 'bread,' *ḥubb* 'love,' *ḥbuba* 'pill,' *waqt*, *zaman* 'time,' *ʕayb* 'shame,' and the nouns designating the body parts, most of the primary colors, and

102 P. 20 and throughout the work. Here is his definition in §1.1: 'A *dialect region* can be roughly defined, in general, as any more or less geographically compact set of communities that share some linguistic feature or set of features that is not generally shared by communities beyond the limits of the region; a *dialect boundary* would then merely be the geographical boundary between two or more such regions.'

animals, such as *baqara* 'cow,' *ṯawr* 'ox,' *ḥimār* 'donkey,' *ğamal* 'camel,' etc., are common to all Arabic dialects; however, if one goes beyond from the basic vocabulary, the differences are increasing, especially with regard to the *realia* terminology. Even within the basic vocabulary of concepts such as the nouns for the primary colors, one may come across differences. Some dialects refer to the 'black' color as *koḥl* and others as *ʔaswad*; and so for *sulṭān* vs. *malik* 'king' and *ḥatta* or *wa-law* vs. *waxxa* 'even though.' Even greeting formulas and trivial questions such as 'How are you?' reveal a variety of phrases according to dialects: in Morocco people would say *aš xbark*?; in Iraq: *aš lónak*?; in Egypt: *iz záyyak*?, and elsewhere in the east and south: *kif ḥálak*? *kef ḥálak?* A parallel distribution holds for the verbs *qabiḍa* vs. *ʔaxaḏa*, 'seize, hold' or *xarağ* vs. *nəğbad* 'went out,' and many more. The variation seems to be the result of an internal stylistic choice between equivalents and it arises from the outset on the basis of a common substrate, that is, these dialects have a strong common core at all levels, and only in their ramifications one finds the East-West and North-South distribution, alongside with the social stratification.[103]

This is similar to British and American pairs such as *nappy / diaper, tap / faucet, petrol / gasoline* or pairs used in Belgian and Swiss French differently than French of France, such as *soixante-dix / septante, quatre-vingts / huitante* (or *octante*), and *quatre-vingt-dix / nonante* (Singleton-Kallen 2004: 532). In some cases, the difference is not in the lexeme but rather in its form. For example, in the Yemen *walif* 'used to' is inflected in the first conjugation (binyan), while in Morocco it is inflected in the second, *mwəlləf*. Sometimes the same word is used in different dialects but with different meanings. For example, *īdăm* is 'a fish stew' in Aden, but 'a cooked fat' in Morocco. *ḥṣəl* means 'achieved' or 'gained' in the East, but 'got into troubles' in the West. This is similar to the American use of *subway* ('underground passenger train') against the British use ('pedestrian underpass' (Singleton-Kallen 2004: l.c.). In some cases one can figure out that the same word was created independently, as in the case of secondary or derivative words. For example, *šahriyya* (derived from *šahr* 'month') indicates 'menstrual cycle' in Aden, but 'monthly salary' in Morocco.

In some cases, the variation stems from the substrate of languages that influenced Arabic in these or other circumstances, such as the English substrate in Aden or the French substrate in North Africa and Lebanon. For example, *inğil* is the word for English 'engine' in Aden (Ben-Zion 2011: 294), but *motor*, borrowed from French *moteur*, in North Africa and elsewhere; and so for *lubya* 'beans' in the West vs. *faṣulya* (from Italian 'fajolia') in the East; *fúrsek* (from Greek 'persika') 'peach' in Aden (Ben-Zion 2011: 185), against *xuxa* in other dialects; 'match' is called *kibrit, zalamit* (< French 'les allumettes'), or *uqida* in different dialects. 'Carrot' is in Eastern Arabic *ğazar*, but in the Maghreb *xizzo*, from Berber. A *knife* is generally referred to as *sakkin*,

103 Maimonides has already noted in his commentary on the Mishnah, order *Ṭeharot*, many dialectical differences between Egypt and the Maghreb (Andalusia and Morocco) with regard to *realia* terms. His dictum *wa-ʕinda-nā fī l-Mağrib* (lit. 'with us in the Maghreb') is well known. Earlier, R. Yona ibn Janāḥ (Spain, mid-11th cent.) mentioned in his Dictionary of Biblical Hebrew *Kitāb al-ʔUṣūl* many parallel *realia* terms designating the same referent in different Arabic dialects, such as כסמת (today identified as 'spelt') for which he gives three alternatives: *kirsinna* in Andalusia, *kinit* in Syria, and *ğalban* (*ğulubban*) in Iraq (Neubauer 1875: 327; Bacher 1896: 226).

but in some Maghrebi dialects it is *aznwi*, also borrowed from Berber. Eventually, there is no fixed criterion, according to which the distance between variations / phases of the same language is enough to consider them as different dialects or even languages. For example, whereas some regard the various Arabic variations as separate languages, others see them as dialects only. It is not sure, how much the speakers' awareness is enough to define the nature of their speech; whether the gap is measurable, or if it is a matter of feeling, of consciousness of the co-territorial speakers.

Against this backdrop, the following observations emerge:

1. the difference between a Jewish language and its base language is *not* geographic, because in many cases (except when Jews lived in separate neighborhoods such as ghettos, which indeed can be considered *dialects*) both coexist in the same space. Furthermore, the fact that the basic Hebrew component is common to all Jewish languages means that it is not a matter of geography or of regional distinction.

2. Dialects develop as an option and not a necessity, whereas supposedly Jewish languages must be created for the cultural needs discussed above.

3. The direction of the development of dialects is not predictable, whereas in a new Jewish language it is entirely predictable. One can expect what vocabulary and Hebrew phrases will enter the new language in its first phase.

4. The specific vocabulary of Jewish languages is external and entirely borrowed from Hebrew and Aramaic.

5. Dialects develop within an existing organic indigenous population, whereas Jewish languages were created among a population of immigrants, notably in the North African case, as a result of the use of a new language.

6. While the differences between dialects develop *gradually* in different areas of the same speakers of an original population, the Hebrew component in every Jewish language was integrated at once. The proof is that when they moved from one language to another, the same Hebrew component moved *en bloc* as one unit from the former language to the new one, for instance, from Latin to Arabic in seventh century's North Africa.

7. A dialectal split may occur in the phonology, sometimes in the vocabulary. In the case of Jewish languages, the phonology is not necessarily different from that of the base language. It is true that it may develop to a point of making a certain variation a dialect or even a language for itself, as in the case of Yiddish. Taytsh was yet ordinary German (Mittelhochdeutsch), but it became unique in phonology, not always because it changed, but because it was conservative compared to the developments undergone by the original language. Yiddish and Judeo-Spanish have reached an independent status because they underwent phonetic changes, etc., and have preserved ancient phenomena as in peripheral languages.[104]

8. Dialects, at least those adjacent in a continuum, are mutually intelligible (Edwards 2009: 63), whereas the Jewish elements of Jewish languages are not intelligible to the adjacent non-Jewish neighbors. It thus follows that Jewish languages are *not* dialects of their base languages, but rather different variations.

104 According to Hary and Wein (2013: 86), Yiddish is in fact a language, not just a dialect.

9.3 Are Jewish languages of the Creole or Pidgin type?

Pidgins and creoles are 'mixed languages with the vocabulary of one language (i.e. the superstrate, also called the lexifier or base language) and the grammar of another (i.e. the substrate).'[105] These 'mixed languages' were created only in certain areas and under certain circumstances. They are full-fledged mixtures of two or more spoken languages, the local one with the colonialists' language. Creolization involves the simplification of grammatical features as gender and distinctions, conjugations and the like (e.g., Myhill 2004: 76).

None of these characteristics or the social ones listed by Bakker (2008: 137–139) for pidgins hold for Jewish languages. While pidgins are 'nobody's mother tongue' (Bakker 2008: 130), which were only used by people who had no common language for communication (Bakker 2008: 136), creoles are extended pidgins that became native languages for certain populations, may only be understood by their speakers, and are the only languages spoken in those areas.

Jews spoke Jewish languages as communal speeches and used the base language with their non-Jewish neighbors (e.g., Weinreich 1979: 104–106). Neither the recipient language nor the donor language in Jewish language were reduced or simplified. Jewish languages were created at once and not in a 'multi-generational scenario' that should be assumed for a creole genesis (Veenstra 2008: 234). To conclude with the words of Birnbaum (2011: 4), "there is much less justification for calling these Jewish tongues 'Creolized' languages than there would be for classifying French or Spanish as 'Creolized Latin'" (cf. Alvarez-Péreyre 2003a: 401–402; Birnbaum and Aslanov 2007: 302).

9.4 Are Jewish languages sociolects?

It appears that scholars felt that the term *dialect* does not fit the nature of most Jewish languages. Alternative terms were thus suggested, such as *ethnolect* and *sociolect*.[106] 'Sociolects are commonly defined as varieties of language determined by social environments or associated with a particular social group' (Durrell 2004: 201b), according to sociological variables such as age, gender, or ethnicity. Any Jewish community was sociologically stratified with prestigious and lower classes, yet they basically spoke the same Jewish language. Naturally, inside each Jewish language, there existed secondary variations depending on gender and scholarship (Bar-Asher 1999: 150–153), but the Jewish language was the same. Thus Jewish languages are *not* sociolects vis-à-vis their base languages.

105 Romaine 2004, §4.1, 55–56. See also Holm 2004, Migge 2004 and Deroy 1956/2013, ch. 14. 'Langues mixtes et langues internationales.' On a Jewish popular poem in *lingua franca* see Mayer-Modena 2012.

106 See, e.g., Aslanov 2002: 81, 93ff.; Aslanov 2011: 389, with regard to Judeo-Greek; Baumgarten 2003: 15. For an introductory study on the notion of 'sociolect' and further bibliography see Durrell 2004. 'Sociolect' is referred to sometimes as 'social dialect' (Durrell 2004: 201a).

9.5 Are Jewish languages religiolects?

Since 1992, Hary has used the term *ethnolect* in the context of Jewish varieties but in the course of time he changed his mind due to the misunderstandings of the term. He turned to using *religiolect* that he found 'a better and more suitable term.'[107] About the same time, O. Schwarzwald used the same term (*apud* Baumgarten 2003: 25, n. 55). Hary and Wein define *religiolect* as 'a language variety with its own history and development, which is used by a religious community… A Jewish *religiolect*, then, is a spoken and/or written variety employed by the Jewish population of a specific area…' (Hary and Wein 2013: 88). In fact, Birnbaum (2011: 3, 307, 385) made a similar claim when he said that "the Jewish languages are creations of the group-forming factor of religion" but did not suggest that term. He himself (Birnbaum 2011: 383) felt that part of the Hebrew component has nothing to do with religion, thus he added a general restriction (cf. also Birnbaum and Aslanov 2007: 302). Bunis (2016: 6) says that '*religiolect* would not seem to be suitable for classifying Jewish languages such as Judezmo and Yiddish.' By implication, one would draw from this statement that *religiolect* would be suitable for other Jewish languages, but it seems more probable that Bunis had in mind other Jewish languages as well, but confined himself to the languages under discussion in that context.

At first sight, *religiolect* sounds a good characterization. Yet, it evokes a few problems. One is that it implies a reduction of Judaism to religion, whereas it is not separable from nationhood, or even more, that it consists of a large scale of diverse beliefs and opinions, theology and philosophy, literature and ethics, *halakha* and *aggada* (legend), *kabbala*, customs, folklore and a way of life, practiced by the Jewish nation since immemorial time. Hary and Wein (2013) support Asad's idea that religion encompasses secularism, so that in their opinion, *religion* covers all parts of the Jewish nation, but this also may cause misunderstandings, as though if religion and secularism may be on the same scale they essentially are exclusive of each other. In this regard, the simple term *Jewish Language* seems to fit better, as it leaves 'Jewish' as is, in its thorough meaning, not as a partial or reduced notion.

Another problem is that *religiolect* literally means a *lect* related to *religion*. This attribute and others of its kind rely, however, upon and are morphologically coined according to the template of *dialect* (dia-lect > religio-lect). But *lect* does not designate in what it differs from *language*, nor does it disclose the nature of Jewish languages.[108] In fact, *dialect* stands in the backdrop of *religiolect* and presumably motivated its use (as it did for the coining of *idiolect*, *ethnolect*, *sociolect*, *castelect*[109]). It seems that *religion* here is only a substitute for *Judeo*- and *lect* only a substitute for *language*, so that *religio-lect* is tautological with *Judeo-language*.

107 On the term see Hary 1992: xiii, n. 1; Hary 2009: xxvi, 12ff.; Hary and Wein 2013: 87 and n. 5. See also Hary 2016: 297, 302, and *passim*.

108 Bunis (2016: 5, n. 18) quotes the definition of *lect* from *American Heritage Dictionary of the English Language, Fifth Edition* (2011) as follows: 'a social or regional variety of speech having a sociolinguistic or functional identity within a speech community.' Hary (2009:12, n. 16) quotes Gold and Prager, who think that *lect* is quite neutral and "does not arrange in any rank of preference," quoted previously by Bunin Benor 2008: 1067.

109 On this term see Hary 2009: 12, n. 20;19, n. 32, and Hary and Wein 2013: 88, n. 11.

Furthermore, the entire Jewish nation represents a religion, so that all Jewish languages at once may be called *religiolect*, but not each Jewish language separately. If we called Yiddish a *religiolect*, a Judeo-Spanish *religiolect*, Judeo-Arabic *religiolect*, and so on, this would imply that they were different *religiolects*, that is, from different religions, not necessarily from one and the same religion.

It is undeniable that part of the basic nomenclature of the Hebrew component in Jewish languages is related to religion (Blau 1999: 153), as Haspelmath and Tadmor (2009: 33, §22; 64–65) prove in their study, and as Hary and Wein (2013: 91) describe in feature 3 of 'the prototype of Jewish varieties.' Another large part of the Hebrew terms, however, is *not* related to religion.[110] Here is a handful of words that have nothing to do with religion: in Yemeni Judeo-Arabic *ʕéġal* (lit. 'calf'), *ʕadullamí* (*nisba* of a place name) and other terms are used as nicknames for the male sexual organ; *safáq waharḥáq* means 'when in doubt, get away from it.' In Borujerd (Iran) *máym dabáš* (lit. 'water and honey') was a children's nickname for tea. In Judeo-Spanish *mem serrada* and in Judeo-Arabic *mīm stuma* (lit. 'closed mem'), as well as in the Yemen and other places, were nicknames for 'a person who is difficult to communicate with, or who does not understand his learning,' because he is 'closed' in all respects like final *mem*. *maʕla maṭṭa* (lit. 'up and down') was used in many communities with the meaning of 'more or less.' *perdizeman* or *perdizemanne* (a combination of Italian *perdere* 'lose' and Hebrew *zeman* 'time'), 'waste of time' and *zarxon* (< Hebrew *seraḥon*) 'stink, bad smell' were used in Judeo-Italien, and *mazal/mazzal* 'luck' in every Jewish language, e.g., in Saqiz, Kurdistan, *maré mazzál* 'lucky man,' *mazzál špirtá awé léh* 'may he have good luck,' and with inflections and combinations such as in Judeo-Spanish *desmazalado* 'unfortunate.' In Yiddish, *klafte* (< Aram. *kalbəṯå*) is well-known for 'bitch.' *škúti makúti* 'quiet [but] blows' was used in Gabes, Tunisia, to refer to someone who looks quiet but would strike blows, i.e., be dangerous. There were also Arabic-Hebrew doublets used for intensification, such as *ʕándhəm flúš u-mamúl* (< Heb. *mamon*) 'they have money and wealth,' 'they are a rich family.' *baʕal basár* was used in the Yemen for 'fat,' and *baʕal gaʔava* in Yiddish and in Georgia for 'arrogant'; *naxašoba*, a word derived from *naḥaš* 'snake,' was used in Judeo-Georgian for 'cunning'; *parnasá* 'livelihood' (pronounced *parnúse* in Yiddish) was used in all Jewish languages.[111]

The implication is that *religiolect* may reflect part of the characteristics of any Jewish language but not all of them. Even if the entire borrowed Hebrew-Aramaic vocabulary were 'religious' this does not make the entire language (including the non-borrowed part) 'religious.' To say that a language is 'religious' just because part of its lexemes and phraseology are related to the religious field is tantamount to saying that a language is 'geographical' because part of its nomenclature is related to geography or 'metaphysical' because part of its lexicon is related to metaphysics, and so on. Since 1912, the Academy of Hebrew language and its forerunner *Vaʕad ha-lašon* ('the com-

110 Cf. Sasaki 2008: 551, regarding earlier studies which 'try to classify the semantic fields of the incorporated Hebrew words, but their attempts are not always successful when confronted with words that are beyond the domains of Judaism.' See also Blondheim 1925: cxxxvii.

111 Cf. also Cohen 1912: 390–408, who classifies the Hebrew component in Algerian Judeo-Arabic into: religion, divine names, formulas, euphemisms, friendship terms, intellectual and affective words, and other words (Tedghi 2003a: 160).

mittee of [Hebrew] Language') have published about 230 professional lexicons such as for land transport (concluded 2003) with 585 terms, diplomacy (1999) with 1038 terms, electronics: radio (1938) including 327 terms, and so on, altogether containing about 100,000 terms.[112] Does this mean that the nature of Hebrew should be reduced according to any of these professional lexicons? All of them are part and parcel of Hebrew. The entire lexicon, the professional included, makes it Hebrew. Any language is a mosaic of several semantic fields made out of professional vocabulary, in the same way a whole country may be a federation of states or regions. Thus, it does not make sense to characterize any language by any of its semantic fields at the expense of the other nume-rous semantic fields. At any rate, it is not the glottonym (or the glottonym category) that counts but rather its content. In this regard the term 'Judeo-language' is good enough (cf. Hary 2009: 5, n.1), provided that 'we recognize that the term is an abstraction' as Bunin Benor (2008: 1069; 2009: 236) puts it.

Glottonyms may reflect the sociolinguistic aspects of the Jewish languages and the attitude of speakers, neighbors and scholars towards them. Bunis (2016) dealt with the Jewishness of Judeo-Spanish in view of both Jews and non-Jews throughout centuries. E.g., Judezmo speakers called the written aspect (in Hebrew characters) of the language *laʕaz*, and the spoken variety *ladino*. Non-Jews in the Ottoman Empire called it Turkish *çıfıt*, *Yahudice*, or *Musevice*. Some scholars called Judezmo a *lĕšon Špánien meʕorav* (Hebrew) 'a mixed language of Spain,' with reference to its place of origin, or *den Levantiren Spanisch*, with reference to the locale, in which this "Spanish" was spoken after the expulsions (Bunis 2016: 2–4).[113]

Having said that, *religiolect* may fit a confined definition as 'languages spoken with-in religious communities, as a vector of sacred texts, liturgical traditions, commentaries on the Scriptures, markers of identity or separation of other minorities' (Baumgarten 2003: 20), that is, related uniquely to religion. In this regard the *yeshivish* (Weiser 2004) may be regarded as a *religiolect*.

9.6 Are Jewish languages ethnolects?

As stated earlier, Hary initially used to call Jewish languages *ethnolects,* but due to misunderstandings of the term, he switched to *religiolects*. Singleton-Kallen (2004: 535–536) saw Jewish languages as ethnolects because of their vocabulary (e.g. *šabbat* 'sabbath'; *miṣva* 'commandment/injunction,' *yom tov* (lit. 'good day') 'holy days;' *košer* 'ritually fit'). Though Judaism is not based on ethnicity, Jewish languages might have at first sight fit into the classification of *ethnolects*. Yet, ethnolects are no more than ethnic *dialects* (Fought 2006: 19, 20, 22, 31, 46) and, as we have seen earlier, Jewish languages do not fall into the category of *dialects*. Indeed, the dialects' main characteristics are in the realms of phonology, grammar, and syntax (Fought 2006: 47–50, 83–84, 128), whereas the main characteristics of spoken Jewish languages are lexical and phraseological. Another difference is that speakers of ethnolects use the grammatical variables intentionally to *index* their ethnicity (Fought 2006: 20–24, 46), whereas speakers of

112 See http://hebrew-terms.huji.ac.il/.

113 See also Sephiha 1984: 746; Bunis 2009: 167; and Aslanov 2011: 396.

Jewish languages were not always aware that a certain lexical item was necessarily Jewish.

9.7 The choice between translational synonyms

In order to catch the nature of Jewish languages, I would take a different route here. As seen earlier, a linguistic problem that the exiles encountered in their new locations was that there were no ready-made counterparts in the host languages for the required Hebrew notions or terms, so that they had no choice but to use the original Hebrew terms that expressed their own culture (Baumgarten 2003: 26). In some cases, however, there may have been equivalent terms that they could have picked up, such as *Pascha* for *Pesaḥ* 'passover' in the Christian countries. In this case the two terms are cognates, the former being the Aramaic form of the latter. Yet, the reason for which Jews were reluctant to use *Pascha* is exactly that it represented the culture of a different or even an opponent religion, the 'Easter.' To express the difference between the two cultures they had to choose the Hebrew word.[114] Similar examples are *šabes* in Yiddish as against German *Sonnabend* or *Samstag*, 'Saturday' (Weinreich 1979: 92 and n. 22), *bəriṯ mila* (or just *bəriṯ* or *mila*) compared to its Arabic counterparts *xtana* or *ṭahāra* (Colin 1993–1994, s.v.) 'circumcision,' *siddur* versus its counterparts *Reader* and *məṣḥaf*, and many more, the former mirroring the Jewish cult whereas the latter the Christian or Muslim cults. The same holds for Hebrew *bəraxa* versus Arabic *baraka*,[115] German *Segnung*, Persian *tabrik*, and so on. Whereas the latter bear a general meaning of 'blessing, benediction,' *bəraxa* refers in most cases to a Hebrew formula to be recited before performing a certain *miṣva*, 'Jewish commandment or ritual,' or in other contexts bearing a mystical connotation. In these cases and many others the choice was not relevant, as the counterparts were not semantically or culturally overlapping.[116] In others, it is the phraseology that may have played an important role in the choice of a Hebrew word out of a potential cluster of parallels. E.g., the word *bəraxa* occurs in some Jewish languages in the phrase *bəraxa lə-ḇaṭṭala*, (lit. 'futile benediction') 'an inappropriate *bəraxa*,' later on used metaphorically to refer to an 'incompetent person' (Maman 2013a). This phrase has no immediate equivalent in any base language, as it is confined to the Jewish culture. As a result of the need to use that word in the framework of a phrase it was also used by itself.

Some eastern Arabic dialects used the word *xanzir* to designate 'pig.' In North Africa, however, Jews considered that word and even its Hebrew cognate *ḥazir* a taboo,

114 Cf. Weinreich 1980 quoted by Bunin Benor 2008: 1072, §6; Mayer-Modena 1999: 99 for a similar phenomenon in Judeo-Italian; Krivoruchko 2013: 408 in Judeo-Greek and Teferra 2016: 9 in Jewish Amharic. Levi (1979: 58) claims that the adoption of new languages by Jews was characterized *by de-Christianization* and *de-Islamization*.

115 In some cases the selection was between a neutral (non-Muslim) Arabic word and a Christian Spanish word. E.g., Judezmo speakers used *alxa* derived from Ar. *al-ḥadd* to designate 'Sunday' and abstained from using Domingo (< *dies dominicus* 'the Lord's Day') which is clearly Christian (See e.g., Stillman 1992: 46; Bunis 2009: 168, and Birnbaum 2011: 316). Interesting enough is also the internal distinction between *broxe* and *bentšən* in Yiddish (Baumgarten 2003: 35).

116 Cf. the American Italian example *giobba* 'job', quoted by Weinreich (1979: 54), that "corresponds to neither *arte, mestiere, professione, impiego,* nor *occupazione,* since it designates a new concept, viz. 'work that is found, and for which one has no attachment and no spiritual interest'."

clearly for religious reasons. Thus the Hebrew word *ḥəlluf* 'substitute' was used as a substitute, as much as Rabbinic Hebrew would nickname it *davar ʔaḥer* 'another thing' for the sake of sublimation or euphemism.[117]

A different type is when a real selection is presented, e.g., the Arabic greeting 'good night,' *təṣbaḥ ʕla xir* (lit. "may you wake up in the morning on good") 'well over the night' versus its Hebrew counterpart *bə-ṭoḇ talin [u-ḇə-raḥamim taqiṣ]* 'May you sleep well [at night] [– and may you mercifully awake].' Whereas the Arabic expression is common and popular, the Hebrew equivalent is limited to well-educated people, those who are well-versed in the classical Hebrew texts. For the latter, it is a clear case of choice, of selection, between one expression and the other, that is between a higher or a lower one, in other words – between one *register* and another, more accurately between a *professional* or *cultural register* and another.[118] The same holds for *bét ha-ḥayyím* (lit. "the house of the living") pronounced in some places *bít aḥayyím* and in Georgia *phet-xaynis*, a famous euphemism for 'cemetery,' along with the more popular *meʕara* (lit. 'cave') in Morocco, itself a Hebrew word recognized even by non-Jews,[119] against its Arabic counterpart *maqbara* ('cemetery'); and so for the euphemisms *bét ha-kiśśé* and *bét ha-kaḇód* (in some places in Yemen *béθ haxsé* and *béθ hak-kå̊βeð*) 'water closet' against their local counterparts everywhere. Speaking with a Muslim, a Jew would use *as-salámu ʕaláy-kum*, but with a coreligionist he would say *šalóm ʕale-xém* 'hello' (lit. 'peace on you').

bli ʕayin ha-raʕ (in Yiddish *k-ayn ará, keynehore*; Bunin Benor 2016: 133; Dean-Olmsted and Skura 2016: 495) or *ben porát yoséf!* (approximately 'a fruitful branch of a tree is Josef'), which is used in the same meaning, 'without evil eye,' (or 'touch wood!'), the latter based on Genesis 49:22, current among Sephardim and considered higher style, are expressions used to defend children, the groom, or wealth, against the evil eye, versus their counterparts in the local languages, such as *mešáḷḷah* in Iran or *xamsa, mašáḷḷah*, or *bla ʕín qbiḥá* in Arab countries. An interesting Hebrew-Aramaic doublet was used in Gabes, Tunisia: *yibáʕʕad ʕalí-na ʕín aráʕ wə-l-ʕín bišá* 'let [God] remove the evil eye from us' (cf. Henshke 2007: 329). Of the same type is *təhé mənuḥatú kaḇód* 'may he be of blessed memory' said when learned people commemorate an important deceased, parallel to the normative expression *zixrono li-braxa* or laymen's Arabic *Alláh yirəḥmú*. In these and similar examples the speaker selects his or her expression out of a few equivalents, i.e., out of different registers in the same language, according to his or her awareness and education. Bunin Benor (2008: 1068; Bunin Benor 2009: 234, 265 and elsewhere), uses a different but quite close terminology, 'distinctly/distinctive [Jewish] linguistic repertoire,' without defining that repertoire as a

117 See, however, Dozy 1927, I, 316a, *ḥəllūf*, where numerous sources are cited. It originally meant a boar, but later was extended to a pig. According to Stillman (1992: 47), 'the word seems to be of Berber origin, *īlaf*. Berber was used in the Western Siwa Oasis, which may explain how the word was transferred to Egyptian Arabic (J.G. Hava. 1951. *Arabic-English Dictionary*. Beirut: Catholic Press, p. 139a, 'wild boar', marks the word with the symbol for Egyptian usage). The word is not in Lane, so it is post-classical, although it is used in literary texts.' See also Stillman 2007: 145.

118 Cf. Deroy 1956/2013, ch. 9. 'Les degrés de la pénétration,' § 25.

119 As attested in Colin 1993–1994, vol. 7, under root √ m-ʕ-r. On the term 'non-Jews' see Hary 2009: 6, n. 2. For more examples see Bar-Asher 2016, §§ 23–24.

cluster of registers. In one place (Bunin Benor 2009: 236) she uses the term 'stylistic repertoire' which is even closer. Earlier, Gold (1985: 286) used the term 'style-shifting' for a similar idea.[120]

9.8 A professional discourse (register)

Thus, a Jewish language is in fact a *professional register* vis-à-vis its base language. *Register* is defined by Durrell (2004, §4, 203) a linguistic 'variation according to use … according to the speech context, characteristically the degree of relative formality which can reflect the relationship between dialogue participants, the communicative situation and the purpose or subject matter.' According to Halliday's table cited in Dittmar 2004: 219, *registers* are characterized by being 'restricted languages, languages for special purposes' used in 'occupational varieties (technical, semitechnical).'[121] 'The register is recognizable as a particular selection of words and structures' (Dittmar 2004: 217). Dittmar (ibid.) also refers to Ferguson's examples of specific registers such as 'baby-register,' 'foreigner talk' or professional as 'sport announcer talk.' He also lists examples of registers ('niveaux de langue') used by French linguists, quoting Ager (1990) and Sanders (1993), e.g., *populaire*, *familier*, *courant*, *soutenu*,[122] and finally a professional one, *académique* / *littéraire* (Dittmar 2004: 218). Later he lists (Dittmar 2004: 221, § 6) other specific subject matter in situational variations e.g., science, *religion*, politics, sports, and law (emphasis added).

An extreme example may be seen in a Maimonides' *responsum*,[123] in which he explains in Judeo-Arabic why the Mishna used a language of *prohibition* where *guilt* is expected, especially where *karète* (spiritual extinction) is involved. Maimonides formulated his *responsum* in Judeo-Arabic, as it was his practice to respond to his correspondents in the language they used in their questions, and routinely used the register that was current in this genre of discourse. The *responsum* is, thus, full of quotes of halakhic Hebrew and Aramaic terminology, as much as required by the topic. Here is the original text with transcription and interlinear glossing ("H" for Hebrew and "A" for Aramaic), followed by Blau's translation (Hebrew and/or Aramaic elements in *italics*):

למא קאלת אלמשנה יום הכפורים אסור באכילה

lammā	*qālati*	*l-mišna*	*yom*	*hak-kippurim*	*ʔasur*	*ba-ʔak̲ila*
when	say.PF.3F.SG	DEF-Mishna^{H}	day^{H}	DEF^{H}-atonement.PL^{H}	forbid.PASS.PTCP.M.SG^{H}	in.DEF^{H}-eat.GER^{H}

After the *Mishna* had stated that on the *Day of Atonement it is forbidden to eat*,

אעתרץ' אלתלמוד כיף יקאל פי ד'לך אסור

iʕtaraḍa	*t-talmud*	*kayfa*	*yuqālu*	*fī*	*d̲ālika*	*ʔasur*
object.PF.3M.SG	DEF-Talmud^{H}	how	say.IPFV.PASS.3M.SG	in	DEM.DIST.M	forbid.PASS.PTCP.M.SG^{H}

the *Talmud* said: "How is it possible to say '*it is forbidden*,'

120 Aslanov (2014:108) raised the question with regard to Judeo-Georgian whether 'those marks of difference are diatopic (pertaining to a geographical-dialectal variation) or diastratic (pertaining to a sociolinguistic contrast between various language *registers*)' (emphasis added).

121 See also Ammon et al. 2004: 235, where the first listed factor that helps to characterize a sublanguage is 'limited subject matter.'

122 See also Ammon et al. 2004: 258.

123 Presented by Blau 199: 145; see also *Peʕamim* 1 (1979): 49.

והוא ענוש כרת פג'אוב אן קולה
wa-huwa ʕanuš karet fa-ğāwaba ʔanna qawla-hū
and-3M.SG punish.PASS.PTCP.M.SG^{H} extinction^{H} CONJ-answer.PF.3M.SG COMP speech.ACC.CS-3M.SG
'whereas it is *punishable with extinction*[124]?" And it answered that, in saying

אסור יריד בה אכילת חצי שיעור אלד'י הוא
ʔasur yurīdu bi-hī ʔakilat ḥaṣi šiʕur allaḏī huwa
forbid.PASS.PTCP.M.SG^{H} want.IPFV.3M.SG in-M.SG.GEN eat.GER.CS^{H} half.CS^{H} measure^{H} REL.M.SG 3M.SG
it is (only) forbidden' it had in view the *eating of half a legal quantity*,[125] which is

אסור ואין חייבין עליו כרת פאעתרץ'
ʔasur we-ʔen ḥayyaḇin ʕal-aw karet fa-ʕtaraḍa
forbid.PASS.PTCP.M.SG^{H} and^{H}-NEG^{H} obliged.PL^{H} upon^{H}-3M.SG^{H} extinction^{H} CONJ-object.PF.3M.SG
forbidden but not punishable with extinction. And it also asked:

איצ'א הא ניחא לר' יוחנן דאמ' חצי שעור
ʔayḍan hā nīḥā le-r[abbi] yoḥanan də-ʔăm[ar] ḥaṣi šiʕur
also DEM.M.SG^{A} appropriate^{A} for^{H}-Rabbi^{H} Yoḥanan^{H} REL^{A}-say.PF.3M.SG^{A} half.CS^{H} measure^{H}
"*This would be right only according to the opinion of Rabbi Yohanan, who said that half the legal quantity*

אסור מן התורה אלא לר' שמעון בן לקיש אלד'י
ʔasur min hat-tora ʔella^{H} le-r[abbi] šimʕon ben laqiš allaḏī
forbid.PASS.PTCP.M.SG^{H} from^{H} DEF^{H}-Tora^{H} if.not for^{H}-Rabbi^{H} Simeon^{H} son.CS^{H} Laqish^{H} REL.M.SG
is forbidden by an enactment founded on the Bible text, but according to the opinion of Rabbi Simeon ben Laqish, who

יקול חצי שעור אינו אסור מאי איכא למימר
yaqūlu ḥaṣi šiʕur ʔen-o ʔasur ma(ʔ)i ʔikkā lə-mēmar
say.IPFV.3M.SG half.CS^{H} measure^{H} NEG.3M.SG^{H} forbid.PASS.PTCP.M.SG^{H} there_is^{A} how^{A} to^{A}-say.INF^{A}
said *that half the legal quantity is not forbidden, how could we explain*

פי קול אלמשנה אסור באכילה וכו'
fī qawli l-mišna ʔasur ba-ʔaḵila we-ḵu[ll-eh]
in speech.GEN.CS DEF-Mishna^{H} forbid.PASS.PTCP.M.SG^{H} in.DEF-eat.GER^{H} and-all.CS-POSS.3M.SG^{A}
the words of the Mishnah '*it is forbidden*,' *etc.* (Blau 1999: 145).[126]

Even without taking account of the content, one may realize what constitutes the larger part. A simple count of the words in the above excerpt shows that about two thirds are in Hebrew and/or Aramaic (45 words) and one third in Arabic (17 words), though Arabic is the base language. This is an extreme case but very instructive, as it proves that these proportions were not only possible but practically existed, especially in the written professional discourse. In other cases of different text types, the percentage of the Hebrew element might have been much narrower, but in any case, its presence made the language completely unintelligible to those who did not know Hebrew, or rather a Judeo-language. To be sure, this kind of terminology was unintelligible to

124 *Karète*, i.e., the soul of the culpable will be cut in this world and the world to come.

125 Thus he did not reach the minimum required for this punishment.

126 For a similar mixed text in Judeo-Spanish see Bentolila 1999, esp. pp. 205ff.

anyone who was not competent in the topic of the discussion, though competent in Judeo-Arabic.[127]

It is true that the Hebrew-Aramaic component, even when it is very small in the discourse,[128] might carry the important nucleus of information, thus making the entire sentence impenetrable to someone who is not familiar with this register. This is no different from a discourse of sportsmen on the subject of sports, physicists on physics, musicians on music, soldiers on military matters ('military language'), or computer professionals on their profession, no matter what base language they speak.

Thus, Maimonides' *responsum* was not only unintelligible to non-Jews, but to Judeo-Arabic speakers as well, because its topic is very professional and only Jewish elites with high levels of Judaic learning who were familiar with that Halakhic matter would understand it precisely.[129] The same holds true for Jewish Babylonian Aramaic.[130] Not anyone mastering that dialect would automatically understand any issue of the Babylonian Talmud, whose base language is that dialect. Only those who are familiar with the subject matter of the Talmud would understand it. André Martinet wrote:[131] 'Who knows all of 'his' language? It will often be easier to understand the foreigner enquiring about the station than to follow the discussion of two local technicians.'[132] This implies that the professional registers are what make a certain discourse opaque to listeners who are not familiar with its terminology. A similar example is the status of most Greek loanwords in English, as Weinreich (1979: 56) states, and borrowed elements in general "all enter the 'learned' stylistic stratum of the recipient language."

This holds true for the text sample analyzed by Bentolila (1999: 217–218), which he characterizes as a 'register'. An opposite example is the 6th century pre-Islamic Arabic poetry of Samawʔal ibn ʕĀdiyā. The fact that it is considered part of the canon of the Arabic literature is because its contents fit in the themes of the *Jāhiliyya* poetry, without any traces of Jewish life. His Jewishness is only known from outside his poetry.[133] In other words, it is the content of culture that makes a language Jewish. This implies not only that Jewish tongues are a clear example of language as a carrier of culture, but that that content, be it short or long, is of the type of *professional registers*.

127 Khan (2016: 30) says that 'the main feature that distinguishes them [= Karaite texts] from Classical Muslim Arabic texts, therefore, is the Jewish subject-matter.'

128 Cf. the statistics supplied by D. Cohen for spoken Tunisian Judeo-Arabic and quoted by Tedghi 2003a: 169. Bar-Asher (1978) presented a differential statistical usage of the Hebrew component among Moroccan speakers from different social layers or learning backgrounds (quoted in Tedghi 2003a: 172).

129 When Blau (1999: 25) speaks about Maimonides' '*Commentary to the Mishna*, a work restricted, owing to its contents, to the Jewish community alone,' we should understand that he means 'Jewish scholars familiar with those contents,' not the entire 'Jewish community.' This is similar to what Bunin Benor (2009: 244–245) writes with regard to the intelligibility of English texts full of halakhic Hebrew-Aramaic terms.

130 On this dialect see Fassberg 2016: 89.

131 In his preface to Weinreich 1979: viii.

132 Cf. also Weinreich 1979: 81.

133 See Goren 1970: 24, Hary 2009: 35.

The fact that there is a common Hebrew component to all Jewish languages that touches precisely upon the areas of Jewish culture testifies to that it is this very component that makes them Jewish. Even that part of Hebrew component which is unique to every Jewish language also attests to similar developments, to their connection to the same sources and the same roots. Thus, when a Jew spoke his Jewish language with a co-religionist in fact they used a *register* of the base language that was only understandable to them, but not to their co-territorial non-Jews, who were not familiar with the Jewish component added to the base language. This holds for most of Jewish languages but not all of them. Naturally, Jewish languages which were spoken outside their outlet, as Yiddish in Slavic environments and Judezmo in Turkey and the Balkans, have no base language as common denominator with the surrounding languages, thus cannot be related to them.

10. Is Hebrew a Jewish language?

Hebrew was the language of speech during the First and Second Temple periods and is the national language in today's Israel (Myhill 2004: 37, 51, and ch. 2). Thus one could conclude that if elements of Hebrew make other languages 'Jewish,' it is only natural to assume that Hebrew as a whole is itself the primary Jewish language.[134]

This seems to be J. Blau's and C. Rabin's standpoint (Rabin 1981) even with regard to Modern Hebrew (Baumgarten 2003: 15, n. 1; cf. Myhill 2009: 179). Yet Rabin claimed that this does not hold for Classical Hebrew, because it was not in diglossia of *High language* and *Low language*, thus it was not a Jewish language (Masson 2003, n. 1 and pp. 144–145). Yet, diglossia is *not* a fundamental feature of Jewish languages. Ornan (1985) opposed the idea of Hebrew being a Jewish language. It seems that the stipulation of a language being characterized as Jewish only when spoken by a bilingual or even trilingual speaker or/and when displaced to a different environment such as Yiddish in a Polish speaking area (Masson, lst ch., 148–149) unnecessarily complicates the matter of things, as Masson 2003 clearly shows. Masson's criticism of that stipulation (p. 150) is justified. Thus, the only relevant tests are the ones listed above.

Furthermore, there is a way to prove that Biblical Hebrew is a Jewish language. Morag 1996 established the theory that biblical Hebrew was the outcome of Judaizing the Canaanite language. He mentioned that Ullendorff had already claimed that monotheism influenced the shaping of biblical Hebrew. That is, whereas Canaanite was a pagan language, Hebrew adapted and translated everything into a language expressing the faith in a single God, including the resulting laws, changing the content of the words of worship and any relevant nomenclature. From this standpoint it is clear that Hebrew is the Jewish language *par excellence* as it bears the Jewish culture from earliest times, and in which the Bible, rabbinic and other literature written throughout the ages, although the platform on which both the Babylonian and Palestinian Talmuds were written is different dialects of Jewish Aramaic. And as Modern Hebrew is based on biblical Hebrew (cf. Masson 2003:154–155), there is no way to discriminate it. The fact that Modern Hebrew features an innovated lexicon fits the fact that every language is com-

134 Levy (1999: 417) puts it simply, 'L'hébreu est une langue juive.'

posed of the nomenclature of many semantic fields, as shown above. Kahn and Rubin (2016: 2) simply assume that "the original Jewish language is, of course, Hebrew."

When Jews returned in our time to Israel, the Jewish part of their former Jewish languages basically remained in the current speech. All the rest was changed by Hebrew, so that the entire language became Jewish. That is why Modern Hebrew should be considered a Jewish language.

11. Epilogue

Though Jewish languages are *Sprachbünde* ('federations of languages'), to use Trubetzkoy's term (Baumgarten 2003: 26, n. 60), as they have some common features, they are not of the same type and do not follow the same model. Those that were dislocated from their natural environment and moved to different areas, such as Eastern Yiddish which moved to a Slavic speaking area and Judeo-Spanish which moved to Turkey, are considered languages *per se*. Yet even this common assumption has been recently seriously challenged by Aslanov (2014: 103ff., and n. 2, esp. 111–119), who holds that they were not really cut off their German and Spanish origins respectively. He would see them as dialects rather than languages of their own. A minority of Jewish languages may belong to a third category set by Aslanov (2014: 104ff.), "Jewish dialects constituting the inlays of a former linguistic continuum, nowadays surrounded by alloglottic coterritorial languages.' Yet the majority of Jewish languages are nothing but variations, as shown earlier – *professional registers*, of their co-territorial languages or dialects.

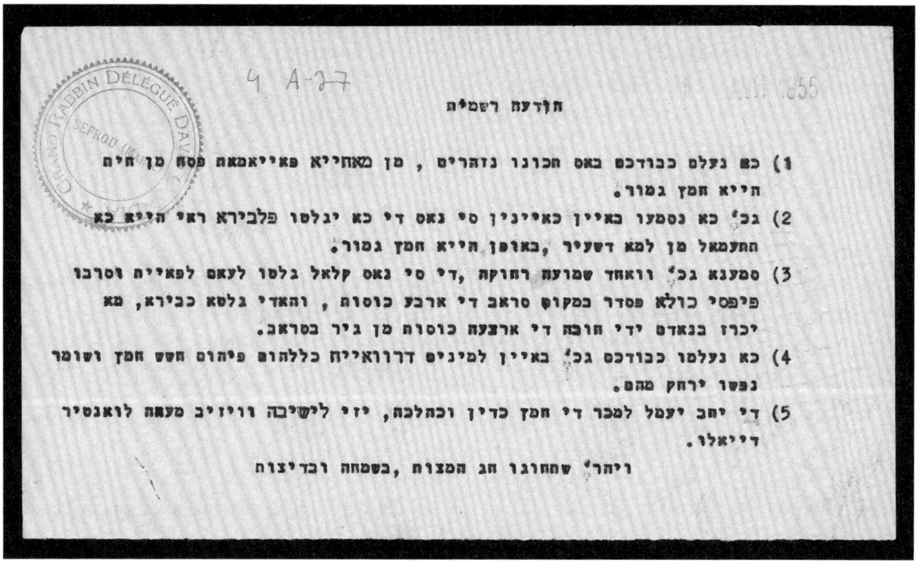
GRAND RABBIN DÉLÉGUÉ DAV…
SEFROU
4 A-27

הודעה רשמית

1) כא נעלם כבודכם באס תכונו נזהרים , מן מאחייא פאייאמאת פסח מן חית הייא חמץ גמור.

2) גכ׳ כא נסמעו באיין כאיינין סי נאס די כא יגלטו פלבירא ראי הייא כא תתעמאל מן למא דשעיר ,באופן הייא חמץ גמור.

3) סמענא גכ׳ וואחד שמועה רחוקה ,די סי נאס קלאל גלטו לעאם לפאיית וסרבו פיפסי כולא פסדר במקום סראב די ארבע כוסות , והאדי גלטא כבירא, מא יכרז בנאדם ידי חובה די ארבעה כוסות מן גיר בסראב.

4) כא נעלמו כבודכם גכ׳ באיין למינים דרוואייח כללהום פיהום חשש חמץ ושומר נפשו ירחק מהם.

5) די יחב יעמל למכר די חמץ כדין וכהלכה, יזי לישיבה וויזיב מעאה לואנסיר דייאלו.

ויהר׳ שתחוגו חג המצות ,בשמחה ובדיצות

Courtesy of the Rabbi David Ovadia Archive, Jerusalem

1. I inform your honor that you should be careful not to use Arak over Passover because it is strictly chametz.

2. We also heard that there are people who were mistaken with bier. It is made out of barley, so that it is completely chametz.

3. We also heard a distant rumor that a few people made a mistake last year and took Pepsi Cola on the Seder night in the capacity of 'the four glasses of wine,' which is a severe mistake, as one does not fulfill his four glasses' duty unless using wine.
4. We also inform your honor that some kinds of perfumes which are not allowed for fear of containing chametz and 'whoever values his life should avoid them'.
5. Whoever wants to make the sale of chametz lawfully and properly should come to the yeshiva and bring with him his own list.
May the Feast of Passover be celebrated with joy and happiness
(signed, R. David Ovadia, Chief Rabbi and delegate of Sefrou, Morocco
Translated from Judeo-Maghrebi by Aharon Maman)

References

Alvarez-Péreyre, Frank. 1999. "Hebrew and the Identity of the Jewish Languages." In Morag et al. 1999, 15–37.

Alvarez-Péreyre, Frank. 2003. "Les langues juives: Construction d'un objet linguistique." In Alvarez-Péreyre and Baumgarten 2003, 43–67.

Alvarez-Péreyre, Frank. 2003a. "Vers une typologie des langues juives?" In Alvarez-Péreyre and Baumgarten 2003, 397–422.

Alvarez-Péreyre, Frank, Georges Drettas, and Gideon Goldenberg. 2003b. "Linguistique des langues juives et linguistique générale: Éléments pour un débat." In Alvarez-Péreyre and Baumgarten 2003, 423–433.

Alvarez-Péreyre, Frank. 2007. "L'hébreu et les langues juives en leur miroir." *Bulletin du Centre de recherche français à Jérusalem*. http://bcrfj.revues.org/233.

Alvarez-Péreyre, Frank and Jean Baumgarten (eds.). 2003. *Linguistique des langues juives et linguistique générale*. Paris: CNRS.

ʕAmmāra, Muḥammad. 2010. *al-luġa al-ʕarabiyya fī ʔIsrāʔīl: siyāqāt wa-tahaddiyāt* (*The Arabic Language in Israel: Contexts and Challenges*). Jordan: Dār al-hudā & Dirāsāt Dār al-fikr http://dirasat-aclp.org/arabic/files/Dirasat_Amara2010_Arabic.pdf.

Ammon, Ulrich, Norbert Dittmar, Klaus J. Mattheier, and Peter Trudgill. 2004. *Sociolinguistics – Handbooks of Linguistics and Communication Science*. 2nd completely revised and extended edition, vol. 1. Berlin/New York: de Gruyter.

Aslanov Cyril. 2002. "Le français des Juifs d'Afrique du Nord est-il un judéo-français?" *Perspectives: Revue de l'Université hébraïque de Jérusalem* 9: 79–101.

Aslanov Cyril. 2007. "Revue de Moshé Bar-Asher, *Les traditions de l'hébreu des communautés juives du Sud-ouest de la France (in Hebrew)*." *Langage et société* 120: 131–138. http://www.cairn.info/revue-langage-et-societe-2007-2-page-131.htm

Aslanov, Cyril. 2011. "Judeo-Greek or Greek Spoken by Jews." *Jews in Byzantium: Dialectics of Minority and Majority Cultures*, ed. R. Bonfil et al., Leiden and Boston 2012, 385–398, Sociolingüística histórica de las lenguas judías, Buenos Aires.

Aslanov, Cyril. 2013. "Judeo-Alsatian, Hebrew Component in." *EHLL*, vol. 2, 386–387.

Aslanov Cyril. 2014. "How Jewish are Jewish Languages?" *Frankfurter Judaistische Beiträge* 39: 103–119.

Aslanov, Cyril. 2015. "Perturbation de la valence des verbes français au contact de l'arabe," *TIPA. Travaux interdisciplinaires sur la parole et le langage*. http://tipa.revues.org/1371; DOI: 10.4000/tipa.1371.

Aslanov, Cyril. 2015a. "Lešonot ha-yehudim ʔo ha-śafot še-be-fi ha-yehudim?" Review of Bernard Spolsky, *The Languages of the Jews: A Sociolinguistic History*, Cambridge: Cambridge University Press, 2014. *Leshonenu* 77: 445–453.

Bacher, Wilhelm. 1896 ed. Yônā Ibn-Ğanāḥ. *Sefer haschoraschim: Wurzelwörterbuch der hebräischen Sprache. Aus dem Arabischen ins Hebräische übersetzt von Yehûdā Ben-Šāʔûl Ibn-Tibbôn*. Berlin: Druck von H. Itzkowski.

Bakker, Peter. 2008. "Pidgins versus Creoles and Pidgincreoles." In: Silvia and John Victor Singler (eds.). *The Handbook of Pidgin and Creole Studies*. Malden, MA, Oxford, Chichester, West Sussex: Wiley-Blackwell, 145–157.

Bar-Asher, Moshe. 1978. "The Hebrew Elements in Moroccan Judeo-Arabic." *Lešonenu* 42: 163–189 (in Hebrew).

Bar-Asher, Moshe. 1999. *Masorot u-lešonot šel Yehude Ṣefon-Afriqa (Traditions linguistiques des juifs d'Afrique du Nord)*. 2nd edition, Jerusalem: ha-Merkaz li-lšonot ha-Yehudim ve-sifruyote-hen, ha-Universiṭa ha-ʕIvrit bi-Yrušalayim; Mosad Byalik; Aškelon: ha-Mixlala ha-ʔezorit, 5759.

Bar-Asher, Moshe. 2003. "Paramètres pour l'étude des judéo-langues et de leur littératures." In Alvarez-Péreyre and Baumgarten 2003, 69–86.

Bar-Asher, Moshe. 2009. "Aspects in the Study of Jewish Languages and Literatures." In David M. Bunis (ed.). *Languages and Literatures of Sephardic and Oriental Jews: Proceedings of the Sixth International Congress for Research on the Sephardi and Oriental Jewish Heritage*. Jerusalem: Bialik Institute, *25–*41.

Bar-Asher, Moshe. 2016. "Jewish Languages and the Hebrew Language." *Journal of Jewish Languages* 4: 125–140.

Bar-Asher, Shalom. 1981. "Jews in North-Africa and Egypt." In Shmuel Ettinger (ed). *History of the Jews in the Islamic Countries*. Jerusalem: Zalman Shazar Center 119–96, 279–326, 329–30.

Baumgarten, Jean. 1995. "L'étude de la composante hébraïque du yiddish: repères historiques et cadres théoriques (Moyen Age – XVIIIe siècle)." In Joseph Tedghi (ed.). *Les interférences de l'hébreu dans les langues juives, Actes de la journée d'étude... mars 1994*, Paris: INALCO, 113–128.

Baumgarten, Jean. 1999. "L'étude de la composante hébraïque du yiddish: repères historiques et outils théoriques." In Morag et al. 1999, 221–241.

Baumgarten, Jean. 2003. "Langues juives ou langues des juifs: Esquisse d'une définition." In Alvarez-Péreyre and Baumgarten 2003, 15–41.

Bendayán de Bendelac, Alegría. 1990. *Voces Jaquetiescas*. Caracas: Centro de Estudios Sefardíes de Caracas: Imprenta Universitaria.

Bentolila, Yaakov. 1991. "ha-ṣaṣa ʔel ha-ʔitalqit ha-yehudit šel Piemonte mi-beʕad le-*Ṭavla maḥzorit* šel Primo Levi.' *Lahon ve-ʕIvrit* 8: 25–30.

Bentolila, Yaakov. 1999. "Alternances d'hébreu et de judéo-espagnol dans un *daroush* marocain." In Morag et al. 1999, 203–219.

Bentolila, Yaakov. 2009. "Iaacob Hassán z"l ke-reformator šel ha-ketiv be-Ladino." *Ladinar* 5: 9–14.

Bentolila, Yaakov. 2015. *Diccionario del elemento hebreo en la ḥaketía*. Cordoba, Spain: UCO Press.

Ben-Zion, Yael. 2011. teʔur lešoni šel ha-lahag ha-ʕaravi be-fi yehude ʕAden (*A linguistic description of the Arabic dialect spoken by the Jews of Aden*). PhD dissertation, Haifa University.

Birnbaum, Salomon A. 2011. *Ein Leben für die Wissenschaft / A Lifetime of Achievement. I: Linguistik/ Linguistics*, ed. Erika Timm. Berlin/Boston: De Gruyter.

Birnbaum, Asher Solomon and Cyril Aslanov. 2007. "Jewish Languages." In Michael Berenbaum and Fred Skolnik (eds.). *Encyclopaedia Judaica*, 2nd ed., vol. 11, 301–303. Detroit: Macmillan Reference USA.

Blanc, Haim. 1964. *Communal Dialects in Baghdad* [*Harvard Middle Eastern monographs* 10]. Cambridge: Harvard University Press.

Blanc, Haim. 1979. "Contemporary Judeo-Arabic." *Peʕamim* 1: 49–52. (in Hebrew).

Blau, Joshua. 1979. "Classical Judeo-Arabic." *Peʕamim* 1: 45–49. (in Hebrew).

Blau, Joshua. 1999. *The Emergence and Linguistic Background of Judeo-Arabic*. Jerusalem: Ben-Zvi Institute.

Blau, Joshua. 2006. *A Dictionary of Mediaeval Judaeo-Arabic Texts*. Jerusalem: The Academy of Hebrew Language.

Blondheim, David S. 1925. *Les parlers judéo-romans et la Vetus latina: Étude sur les rapports entre les traductions bibliques en langue romane des Juifs au moyen âge et les anciennes versions*. Paris: Librairie ancienne Édouard Champion.

Brunot, Louis and Elie Malka. 1939. *Textes judéo-arabes de Fès: textes, transcription, traduction annotée*. Rabat: L'Ecole du Livre.

Bunin Benor, Sarah. 2008. "Towards a New Understanding of Jewish Language in the Twenty-First Century." *Religion Compass* 2/6: 1062–1080.

Bunin Benor, Sarah. 2009. "Do American Jews Speak a "Jewish Language"? A Model of Jewish Linguistic Distinctiveness." *Jewish Quarterly Review* 99/2: 230–269.

Bunin Benor, Sarah. 2013. "Jewish English, Hebrew Component in." *EHLL*, vol. 2, 384–385.

Bunin Benor, Sarah. 2016. "Jewish English." In Kahn and Rubin 2016, 130–137.

Bunis, David M. 2009. "Characteristics of Jewish Languages." In Ehrlich 2009, 167–171.

Bunis, David M. 2016. "Speakers' 'Jewishness' as a Criterion for the Classification of Languages: The Case of the Languages of the Sephardim." *Hispania Judaica* 12: 1–57.

Chetrit, Joseph. 2007. *Diglossie, Hybridation et Diversité intra-linguistique. Études socio-pragmatiques sur les langues juives, le judéo-arabe et le judéo-berbère*. Paris/Louvain: Peeters.

Chetrit, Joseph. 2009. *Lašon u-maʔagare-ha: meḥqarim soṣiyo-pragmaṭiyim ba-ʕArvit ha-Yehudit bi-ṣfon Afriqa u-va-markiv ha-ʕivri še-b-ah: katavot, širim, sipurim u-fitgamim (Trésors et textures d'une langue. Études socio-pragmatiques sur le judéo-arabe en Afrique du Nord et son composant hébraïque: articles, poèmes, récits et proverbs)*. Jerusalem: ha-Merkaz li-lšonot ha-Yehudim ye-sifruyotehen, ha-Universita ha-ʕIvrit bi-Yrušalayim: Mosad Byalik.

Chetrit, Joseph. 2014. "Judeo-Arabic Dialects in North Africa as Communal Languages: Lects, Polylects, and Sociolects." *Journal of Jewish Languages* 2: 202–232.

Chetrit, Joseph. 2015. "Diversity of Judeo-Arabic Dialects in North Africa: *Eqa:l*, *Wqal*, *kjal* and *ʔal* Dialects." *Journal of Jewish Languages* 4: 1–43.

Chetrit, Joseph. 2016. "Jewish Berber." In Kahn and Rubin 2016, 118–129.

Clyne, Michael. 2004. "History of Research on Language Contact." In Ammon et al. 2004, 799–805.

Cohen, Marcel. 1912. *Le parler Arabe des juifs d'Alger*. Paris: Librairie Klincksieck.

Cohen, David. 1964–1975. *Le parler Arabe des juifs de Tunis: vol. 1. Textes et documents linguistiques et ethnographiques*. vol. 2. *Étude linguistique*. Paris: Mouton.

Cohen, David. 1985. "The Arabic Dialects Spoken by North African Jews." In Fishman 1985, 246–260.

Cohen, Mark R., 2007. "On the Interplay of Arabic and Hebrew in the Cairo Geniza Letters.' In Jonathan P. Decter and Michael Rand (eds.). *Studies in Arabic and Hebrew Letters in Honor of Raymond P. Scheindlin*. Piscataway, NJ: Gorgias Press, 17–35.

Colin, Georges. 1993–1994. *Le dictionnaire Colin d'arabe dialectal marocain,* sous la direction de Zakia Iraqui Sinaceur, Institut d'études et de recherches d'arabisation, Rabat, en collaboration avec le C.N.R.S., Paris, Rabat: Éditions al-Manahil, Ministère des affaires culturelles.

Daniel, Suzanne. 1966. *Recherches sur le Vocabulaire du Culte dans la Septante.* Paris: Librairie Klincksieck.

Davidson, Yiśraʔel, Śimḥa Asaf, and Yiśśaxar Yoʕel (eds.). 1978. *Siddur Rav Saʕadja Gaʔon: Kitāb ǧāmiʕ aṣ-ṣalawāt wat-tasābīḥ*. Jerusalem: Ḥevrat meqiṣe nirdamim; Reʔuven Mas.

Evelyn Dean-Olmsted and Susana Skura. 2016. "Jewish Latin American Spanish." In Kahn and Rubin 2016, 489–502.

Deroy, Louis. 1956/2013. *L'emprunt linguistique*. Presses Universitaire de Liège; http://books.openedition.org/pulg/682

Dinkin, Aaron J. 2009. *Dialect Boundaries and Phonological Change in Upstate New York.* Ph.D. Dissertation, University of Pennsylvania, http://repository.upenn.edu/edissertations/79.

Dittmar, Norbert. 2004. "Register." In Ammon et al. 2004, 216–226.

Dozy, Reinhart Pieter Anne. 1927. *Supplément aux dictionnaires arabes.* Paris: Maisonneuve Frères.

Drettas, Georges: See Alvarez-Péreyre 2003b.

Durrell, Martin. 2004. "Sociolect." In Ammon et al. 2004, 200–205.

Edwards, John. 2009. *Language and Identity: An Introduction*. Cambridge: Cambridge University Press.

EHLL = Geoffrey Khan (gen. ed.). *Encyclopedia of Hebrew and Linguistics*, vols. 1–3. Leiden/Boston: Brill, 2013.

Ehrlich, M. Avrum (ed.). 2009. *Encyclopedia of the Jewish Diaspora Origins, Experiences, and Culture*. Santa Barbara: Abc-Clio.

Enoch, Reuven. 2009. *The Study of Tavsili according to the Book of Genesis: Edah Velashon* xxix. Jerusalem: Magnes Press.

Fassberg, Steven E. 2016. "Judeo-Aramaic." In Kahn and Rubin 2016, 64–117.

Fishman, Joshua A. 1985. "The Sociology of Jewish Languages from a General Sociolinguistic Point of View." In Fishman 1985, 3–21.

Fishman, Joshua A. (ed.) 1985. *Readings in the Sociology of Jewish Languages*. Leiden: Brill.

Fishman, Joshua A. 1991. *Yiddish: Turning to Life*. Amsterdam; Phildelphia: J. Benjamins.

Fought, Carmen. 2006. *Language and Ethnicity*. Cambridge: Cambridge University Press.

Fränkel, Siegmund. 1886. *Die aramäischen Fremdwörter im Arabischen*. Leiden: Brill.

Gamliel, Ophira. 2013. "Judeo-Malayalam, Hebrew Component in." *EHLL*, vol. 2, 410–413.

Gamliel, Ophira. 2014. "Sugot targum be-Malayalam yehudit: beḥina lešonit ve-signonit." *Masorot* 16/1: 137–172.

Guedj, David. 2016. "Marbit ha-yehudim, hamon ha-ʕam, kamo-nu, lo yiṣleḥu le-hagiaʕ la-sefer: ha-historya shel yehudei morocco ʻal pi Ḥayim Naḥmani." *Musaf tarbut ve-sifrut, Haaretz*, Dec. 2nd, 2016, p. 4 http://www.haaretz.co.il/literature/study/.premium-1.3140427

Geva-Kleinberger, Aharon. 2013. "Judeo-Arabic, Iraqi, Hebrew Component in." *EHLL*, vol. 2, 391–393.

Glinert, Lewis. 1993. "Language as Quasilect: Hebrew in Contemporary Anglo-Jewry." In Lewis Glinert (ed.). *Hebrew in Ashkenaz: A Language in Exile*. New York: Oxford University Press, 249–264.

Gold, David L. 1985. "Jewish English." In Fishman 1985, 280–298.

Goldenberg, Gideon: See Alvarez-Péreyre 2003b.

Goren. Asher. 1970. *Ancient Arabic Poetry. Selected and translated into Hebrew*, with editorial assistance of H. Ben-Shammai. Jerusalem: The Institute of Asian and African Studies.

Hary, Benjamin. 1992. *Multiglossia in Judeo-Arabic: with an edition, translation and grammatical study of the Cairene Purim scroll*. Leiden/New York: Brill.

Hary, Benjamin H. 2009. *Translating Religion: Linguistic Analysis of Judeo-Arabic Sacred Texts from Egypt*. Leiden and Boston: Brill.

Hary, Benjamin and Martin J. Wein. 2013. "Religiolinguistics: On Jewish-, Christian- and Muslim-Defined Languages.." *International Journal of the Sociology of Language* 220: 85–108.

Hary, Benjamin. 2016. "Il-ʕarabi dyālna (Our Arabic): The History and Politics of Judeo-Arabic." In Joshua Miller and Anita Norich (eds.). *Languages of Modern Jewish Cultures: Comparative Perspectives*. Ann Arbor: University of Michigan Press, ch. 11, 297–320.

Haspelmath, Martin and Uri Tadmor (eds.). 2009. *Loanwords in the World's Languages – A Comparative Handbook*. Berlin: Walter de Gruyter.

Henkin-Roitfarb, Roni. 2013. "Arabic, Hebrew Loanwords in: Modern Period." *EHLL*, vol. 1, 155–161.

Henshke, Yehudit. 2007. *Lašon ʕivri be-dibur ʕarvi: ʔoṣar ha-milim ha-ʕivri ba-ʕAravit ha-mdubberet šel yehude Tunisiya: milon ṿe-diqduq (Hebrew Elements in Daily Spech: A Gramamtical Study and Lexicon of the Hebrew Component of Tunisian Judeo-Arabic)* Jerusalem: Mosad Byalik: ha-Merkaz li-lšonot ha-yehudim ṿe-sifruyote-hem, ha-ʔuniversiṭa ha-ʕivrit bi-Yrušalayim.

Hickey, Raymond (ed.). 2010. *The Handbook of Language Contact*. Chichester, West Sussex; Malden, MA: Wiley-Blackwell.

Hickey, Raymond. 2010. "Language Contact: Reconsideration and Reassessment." In Hickey 2010, 1–28.

Holm, John. 2004. "Pidgin and Creole Studies." In Ammon et al. 2004, 58–67.

Jochnowitz, George. 2013a. "Judeo-Italian, Hebrew Component in." *EHLL*, vol. 2, 409–410.

Kahn, Lily and Aaron D. Rubin. 2016. *Handbook of Jewish Languages*. Leiden and Boston: Brill.

Katz, Dovid. 2009. "Yiddish as a Diaspora Language and Its Future." In: Ehrlich 2009, 193–197.

Kayyal, Mahmoud. 2006. *Targum be-ṣel ha-ʕimmut: normot targum min ha-sifrut ha-ʕivrit ha-ḥadaša la-śafa ha-ʕaravit ba-šanim 1948–1990 (Translation in the Shadow of Confrontation: Norms in the Translations of Modern Hebrew Literature into Arabic between 1948–1990).* Jerusalem: Magnes Press.

Kayyal, Mahmoud. 2011. "at-tadaxxul al-luġawī al-ʕibriy fī al-luġa al-ʕarabiyya al-maktūba fī ʔIsrāʔīl (= The linguistic interference of Hebrew in the written Arabic in Israel)." Website of The Arabic Language Academy in Haifa http://www.arabicac.com/content.asp?id=268

Khan, Geoffrey 2016. "Judeo-Arabic." In Kahn and Rubin 2016, 22–63.

Krivoruchko, Julia G. 2013. "Judeo- Greek, Hebrew Component." *EHLL*, vol. 2, 408–409.

Levi, Avner. 1979. "Lešonot yehudiyot ba-mizraḥ u-va-maʕarav (= Jewish Languages in the East and West)." *Peʕamim: Studies in Oriental Jewry* 1: 58–66.

Levy, Simon. 1999. "Mots et morphèmes hébraïques dans le parler arabe des Juifs de Fès." In Morag et al. 1999, 417–431.

Loewe, Heinrich. 1911. *Die Sprachen der Juden*. Cologne: Jüdischer Verlag.

Maldonado García, María Isabel. 2016. "Saraiki: language or dialect?" *Eurasian Journal of Humanities* 1/2: 40–53 (website: Academia.edu).

Maman, Aharon. 1999. "Linguistic Developments in North Africa 1492–1917." *Sefunot* N.S. 22: 141–190 (= Maman 2014: 3–54).

Maman, Aharon. 2011. "Typology of Creativity in Judeo-Maghrebian."In Steven D. Fraade and Moshe Bar-Asher (eds.). *Studies in the History and Culture of North African Jewry – Proceedings of Symposium at Yale University, April 25, 2010.* New Haven: Yale Program in Judaic Studies; Jerusalem: Hebrew University, Center for Jewish Languages and Literatures, 125–139 (= Maman 2014: 67–76).

Maman, Aharon. 2019. *Synoptic Dictionary of the Hebrew Component in Jewish Languages. Second revised version.* Jerusalem: Magnes Press.

Maman, Aharon. 2013a. "Lešonot *beraxa* ba-ʔaḥadot mi-lešonot ha-yehudim." In Israel Rozenson and Yossi Spanier (eds.). *Minḥat Sapir, Compilation of articles presented to Yiṣḥaq Sapir.* Elkana-Rehovot: Orot Israel College, 277–307 (= Maman 2014: 229–250).

Maman, Aharon. 2005. "he-ʕarutz ha-samuy li-msirat ha-ʕivrit bi-tqufat ha-benayim."*Morešet Israel – Ketav ʕet le-yahadut u-l-ṣiyonut* 1:33–41 (= Maman 2014: 197–203).

Maman, Aharon. 2014. *The Texture of Jewish Languages in North Africa* (in Hebrew). Jerusalem: Mosad Byalik.

Masson, Michel. 2003. "L'hébreu moderne est-il une langue juive?" In Alvarez-Péreyre and Baumgarten 2003, 143–156.

Mayer-Modena, Maria. 1999. "La composante hébraïque dans le judéo-italien de la Renaissance." In Morag et al. 1999, 39–57.

Mayer-Modena, Maria. 2012. "A Lingua-Franca Purim Song." In: Malka Muchnik and Tsvi Sadan (Tsuguya Sasaki) (eds.). *Studies in Modern Hebrew and Jewish Languages, Presented to Ora (Rodrigue) Schwarzwald.* Jerusalem: Carmel, 715–722.

Mayer-Modena, Maria. (forthcoming). *Dictionary of the Hebrew Component in Judeo-Italian.*

Mieses, Matthias/Matisyahu. 1915. *Die Entstehungsursache der jüdischen Dialekte.* Wien: R. Löwit (Hamburg: Helmut Buske, 1979).

Migge, Bettina. 2004. "Pidgin Language and Creole Language." In Ammon et al. 2004, 300–305.

Morag, Shelomo. 1996. "The Beginnings of Hebrew: Some Semantic Considerations." *Studies on Biblical Hebrew*. Jerusalem: Magnes Press, 13–32 (initially published in *Meḥqarim Be-lašon* 1 (1985) 177–196).

Morag, Shelomo. 1999. "The Study of the Language Traditions of the Jewish Communities of the Diaspora." In Morag et al 1999, 3–13.

Morag, Shelomo. 1999a. "The Integrated Corpus of Hebrew Elements in Jewish Languages: Some Aspects of Analysis." In Morag et al 1999, 39–57.

Morag et al. 1999 = Shelomo Morag, Moshe Bar-Asher, and Maria Mayer-Modena (eds.). 1999. *Vena Hebraica in Judaeorum Linguis: Proceedings of the 2nd International Conference on the Hebrew and Aramaic Elements in Jewish Languages*. Milan: Centro Studi Camito-Semitici di Milano.

Moseley, Christopher. 2007. *Encyclopedia of the World's Endangered Languages*. London and New York: Routledge.

Myhill, John. 2004. *Language in Jewish Society: Towards a New Understanding*. Clevedon, UK: Multilingual Matters.

Myhill, John. 2009. "Varieties of Diaspora Languages. In *Encyclopedia of the Jewish Diaspora: Origins, Experiences, and Culture*." In Ehrlich 2009, 171–180.

Nahon, Peter. 2017. "Diglossia among French Sephardim as a Motivation for the Genesis of 'Judeo-Gascon'." *Journal of Jewish Languages* 5: 104–119.

Nahmany, Haim. 1953. *Historya dl-ihud dəl-Maroc bəl-ʕarbiyya (History of the Jews of Morocco, translated from Isaac D. Abou's French book of history)*. Casablanca: Y. Razon.

Nehama, Joseph, avec la collaboration de Jesús Cantera. 1977. *Dictionnaire du judéo-espagnol*. Madrid: Consejo Superior de Investigaciones Cientificas, Instituto Benito Arias Montano.

Neubauer, Adolf Zvi. 1875. *The Book of Hebrew Roots, by Abu'l-Walîd Marwân ibn Janâh, called Rabbî Jônâh. Edited with an appendix, containing extracts from other Hebrew-Arabic dictionaries [by] Adolf Neubauer. With additions and corrections by Wilhelm Bacher.* Oxford: (Amsterdam: Philo Press 1968).

Neubauer, Adolf Zvi. 1891. "On Non-Hebrew Languages Used by Jews." *The Jewish Quarterly Review* 4: 9–19.

Ornan, Uzi. 1985. "ʕIvrit ʔen-ah śafa yehudit (Hebrew is not a Jewish Language)." *Leshonenu* 48–49/2–3: 199–206.

Poll, Solomon. 1981. "The Role of Yiddish in American Ultra-Orthodox and Hassidic Communities." In Yoshua Fishman (ed.). 1981. *Never Say Die! A Thousand Years of Yiddish in Jewish Life and Letters*. The Hague/Paris/New York: Mouton Publishers,197–218.

Poplack, Shana. 2004. "Code-Switching." In Ammon et al. 2004, 589–596.

Rabin, Chaim. 1979. "What Makes the Jewish Languages Special." *Peamim* 1: 40–45 (in Hebrew).

Rabin, Chaim. 1981. "What Constitutes a Jewish Language?" *International Journal of the Sociology of Language* 30: 19–28.

Ratzhabi, Yehuda. 1978. *ʔOṣar lešon ha-qodeš šel-li-vne Teman*. Tel Aviv: Publisher unknown.

Romaine, Suzanne. 2004. "Language-Contact Studies." In Ammon et al. 2004, 49–58.

Rosenbaum, Gabriel M. 2013. "Judeo-Arabic, Egyptian, Hebrew Component in." *EHLL*, vol. 2, 390–391.

Sasaki, Tsuguya. 2008. "The Hebrew Component in Yiddish: Research Possibilities." In Francesco Aspesi et al. (eds.). *Il mio cuore è a Oriente: Studi di linguistica storica, filologia e cultura ebraica dedicati a Maria Luisa Mayer Modena*. Milan: Cisalpino, 547–559.

Schwartz, Daniel R. 2017. *Between Jewish Posen and Scholarly Berlin: the Life and Letters of Philipp Jaffé. Berlin: De Gruyter.*

Schwarzwald, Ora. 2015. "Lešon taštit, magaʕe lašon, ribud ḥevrati u-mištane lašon." *Karmilim* 11: 55–71.

Sebag, Paul.1991. *Histoire des Juifs de Tunisie: des origines à nos jours*. Paris : L'Harmattan.

Sephiha, Vidal Haim. 1984. "Quelques oeuvres judéo-espagnoles éditées à Livourne." *La Rassegna Mensile di Israel*: 743–759.

Sephiha, Vidal Haim. 1986. *Le Judeo Espagnol*. Paris: Editions Entente.

Shachmon, Ori. 2007. *Arabic Dialects of the Jews of North Yemen*. Unpublished Ph.D. dissertation. Jerusalem: The Hebrew University (in Hebrew).

Shachmon, Ori. 2013. "Secret Languages, Hebrew in Yemenite Judeo-Arabic." *EHLL*, vol. 3, 518–520.

Shaked, Shaul. 1979. "Comment." *Peʕamim* 1: 55 (in Hebrew).

Shinar, Pesach. 1979. "Comment." *Peʕamim* 1: 56–57 (in Hebrew).

Shohat, Ella. 2015. "The Question of Judeo-Arabic." *Arab Studies Journal* 23. Washington, DC: Graduate students at the Center for Contemporary Arab Studies, Georgetown University.

Singleton, David and Jeffrey L. Kallen. 2004. "Lexicon." In Ammon et al. 2004, 530–539.

Spolsky, Bernard and Sarah Bunin Benor. 2006. "Jewish Languages." *Encyclopedia of Language and Linguistics*, ed. Keith Brown, 2nd ed., vol. 6, 120–124. Oxford: Elsevier.

Stillman, Norman A. 1988. *The language and Culture of the Jews of Sefrou, Morocco: an ethnolinguistic study* [Journal of Semitic Studies Monograph No. 1]. Manchester: University of Manchester.

Stillman, Norman A. 1992. "Language patterns in Islamic and Judaic societies." In Steven M. Wasserstrom (ed.). *Islam and Judaism: 1400 Years of Shared Values*. Portland, OR: Institute for Judaic Studies in the Pacific Northwest, 41–55.

Stillman, Norman A. 2007. "Verbal Darts: Name-Calling, Cursing, and Gibing in Moroccan Judeo-Arabic." In Aharon Maman, Steve Fassberg, and Yohanan Breuer (eds.), *Shaʕarei Lashon, Studies in Hebrew, Aramaic, and Jewish Languages, Presented to Moshe Bar-Asher, vol. 3: Modern Hebrew and Jewish Languages*, Jerusalem, 141–156.

Stroumsa, Sarah. 2016. *Dāwūd ibn Marwān al-Muqammaṣ. Twenty Chapters, An edition of the Judeo-Arabic text, transliterated into Arabic characters, with a parallel English translation, notes, and introduction*. Provo, Utah: Brigham Young University Press.

Tedghi, Joseph. 1996. "Biṭuyim ʕivriyim šel-lo ki-fšuṭ-am ba-ʕaravit ha-yehudit šel ha-maʕarav." In Bar-Asher Moshe (ed.). *Studies in Hebrew and Jewish Languages, Presented to Shelomo Morag*. Jerusalem: The Hebrew University of. Jerusalem and the Bialik Institute, 539–552.

Tedghi, Joseph. 2003. "De l'évolution sémantique des lexémes hébreux dans le judéo-arabe marocain." In: Jérôme Lentin and Antoine Lonnet (eds.). *Mélanges David Cohen – Études sur le language, les langues, les literatures*. Paris: Maisonneuve & Larose, 689–698.

Tedghi, Joseph. 2003a. "Évolution des recherches sur la composante hébraïque dans les parlers judéo-arabes maghrebins modernes.' In Alvarez-Péreyre and Baumgarten 2003, 157–190.

Teferra, Anbessa. 2016. "Jewish Amharic." In Kahn and Rubin 2016, 8–21.

Téné, David. 1985. "le-ʕinyan ʔaḥdut-ah šel ha-ʕivrit va-ḥaluqat-ah li-tqufot." *Meḥqarim Be-lašon* 1: 101–155.

Tobi, Yosef. 2001. "On the Antiquity of the Judeo-Arabic Biblical Translations and a New Piece of an Ancient Judeo-Arabic Translation to the Pentateuch." In Yosef Tobi and Yitzhak Avishur (eds.). *Ben ʕEver laʕArav* 2. Tel Aviv: Afikim.

Tobi, Yosef and Tsivia Tobi. 2014. *Judeo-Arabic Literature in Tunisia, 1850–1950*. Detroit: Wayne State University Press.

Tsur, Yaron. 1996. "Haskala in a Sectional Colonial Society: Mahdia (Tunisia) 1884." In Harvey E. Goldberg (ed.). *Sephardi and Middle Eastern Jewries – History and Culture in the Modern Era*, New York: Indiana University Press, 146–216.

Tsur, Yaron. 2001. *A Torn Community: The Jews of Morocco and Nationalism, 1943–1954*. Tel Aviv: Am Oved.

Tsur, Yaron. 2016. *Notables and other Jews in the Ottoman Middle-East 1750–1830*. Jerusalem: Mosad Bialik.

Veenstra, Tonjes. 2008. "Creole Genesis: The Impact of the Language Bioprogram Hypothesis." In Silvia Kouwenberg and John Victor Singler (eds.). *The Handbook of Pidgin and Creole Studies*. Malden, MA/Oxford/Chichester/West Sussex: Wiley-Blackwell, 219–241.

Versteegh, Kees. 2010. "Contact and the Development of Arabic." In Hickey (ed.) 2010, 634–651.

Weinreich, Max. 1973. *Die geshikhte von der yidisher shprakh*. New York: YIVO.

Weinreich, Max. 1980. *History of the Yiddish Language,* Chicago/London: University of Chicago Press.

Weinreich, Uriel. 1979. *Languages in Contact: Findings and Problems*. The Hague – Paris/New York: Mouton Publishers.

Weiser, Chaim M. 2004. *Frumspeak – The First Dictionary of Yeshivish*. New York/Oxford.

Wexler, Paul. 2006. *Jewish and non-Jewish Creators of Jewish Languages*. Wiesbaden: Harrassowitz.

Wexler, Paul. 2009. 'Two-Tiered Relexification in Yiddish: Jews, Sorbs, Khazars, and the Kiev-Polessian Dialect.' In: Ehrlich 2009, 184–187.

Zand, Michael. 1979. "Comment." *Peʕamim* 1: 55–56 (in Hebrew).

Jewish Neo-Aramaic

Geoffrey Khan, University of Cambridge

1. Introductory Remarks

Jewish Neo-Aramaic was spoken until the twentieth century in Kurdistan and the adjacent regions of Iran and continues to be spoken today, mainly in Israel, by the older generation of immigrants. It is the vestige of the Aramaic that was spoken more widely by Jews in the Middle East at earlier periods. Distinct Jewish varieties of Aramaic begin to be attested in written sources in the first half of the Common Era. These contrast in particular with specifically Christian varieties of the language which emerge into history at approximately the same period. This communal split between Jewish and Christian dialects has survived in the Neo-Aramaic dialects.

The Jewish Neo-Aramaic dialects belong to the North-Eastern Neo-Aramaic (NENA) subgroup of Neo-Aramaic dialects.[1] This is a highly diverse group of over 150 dialects spoken by Jews and Christians originating form towns and villages east of the Tigris in northern Iraq, south-eastern Turkey and western Iran. The NENA subgroup is distinct from three other subgroups of Neo-Aramaic. These include the western subgroup spoken by Christians and Muslims in the villages of Maʕlula, Baxʕa and Jubbʕadin in the region of Damascus, the Ṭuroyo subgroup, spoken by Christians in the Ṭūr ʕAbdīn region of south-eastern Turkey, and Mandaic, spoken by Mandaeans in the cities of Ahwaz and Kermanshahr in Iran. None of these subgroups is as diverse as NENA. Within NENA itself one may identify a number of subgroups. There is a fundamental split between the dialects spoken by the Jews and those spoken by the Christians. This applies even to cases where Jewish and Christian communities lived in the same town, such as Urmi (north-western Iran), Sanandaj (western Iran), Koy Sanjak and Sulemaniyya (both in north-eastern Iraq). Within Jewish NENA dialects themselves a number of subgroups are identifiable (for details, see below section 3):

(1) *lišana deni* subgroup
(north-west of Iraq in locations to the west of the Great Zab river, east of the river around the Turkish border)

(2) trans-Zab subgroup
(Arbīl and Sulemaniyya provinces of Iraq,
West Azerbaijan province of Iran,
Kurdistan and Kermanshah provinces of Iran)

(3) between (1) and (2) a cluster of dialects in the region of Barzan

1 The term was coined by Hobermann (1988: 557).

Map of the NENA dialect area

At the beginning of the twentieth century the Aramaic-speaking Jews lived in thriving communities in villages and towns throughout the original NENA area. During the upheavals of the First World War the Jews of south-eastern Turkey and the adjacent region of north-western Iran underwent considerable hardship and, like the Aramaic-speaking Christian communities of the region, permanent displacement from their original places of residence. Some Jews, notably those from the region of Salmas (Salamas) in the far north-western tip of Iran, fled into the Caucasus and settled in Tbilisi (Mutzafi 2015). They suffered further under the regime of Stalin, who moved virtually the entire community in 1950 to Almaty in Kazakhstan, where a large proportion of the Jews speaking the Salmas dialect can be found to this day. A few elderly Salmas Jews can still be found in Tbilisi. Other dialects of Jewish communities who were displaced during the First World have become extinct, such as those from the region of Gavar. Since the nineteenth century several Jews of the region emigrated to Palestine through religious motives. This emigration increased after the First World War in the first half the twentieth century due to the activities of the Zionist movement. In the early 1950s, after the foundation of the State of Israel, this migration turned into a mass exodus. As a result, the vast majority of surviving Aramaic-speaking Jews are now resident in Israel. After this exodus virtually no Aramaic-speaking Jews remained in Iraq. The few who did remain were mostly women who converted to Islam.[2] In western Iran, however,

2 Cf. the story of the sister of Yona Sabar narrated by his son Ariel Sabar (2009).

some remained during the time of the Shah but left after the Iranian Revolution in 1979. In Sanandaj, for example, only about 1,000 Jews of a total population of approximately 4,000 migrated to Israel in 1952. Over the subsequent two decades there was a gradual emigration of the Jews from the town either to Tehran or abroad, mostly to Israel. After the Iranian Revolution in 1979 most of the remaining Jews left Sanandaj, the majority settling in Los Angeles in the USA and the remainder in Israel or Europe (Ben-Yaʕqov 1980, 2nd: 149; Khan 2009: 1).

There are some written sources of Jewish Neo-Aramaic, which are datable to the 17th century onwards. These are mainly manuscripts of homilies and Bible translations. Literature of this type was also transmitted orally and after the migration of Jews to Israel a larger corpus was committed to writing.[3] This written material is an important source for the study of the history of Jewish Neo-Aramaic, since it often contains a more archaic form than is found in the surviving spoken dialects. The literature, however, only reflects a limited range of the dialectal diversity. Serious documentation and study of the spoken NENA dialects began only in the second half of the nineteenth century. Much of the early work was carried out by missionaries, whose main concern were the dialects of the Christians, e.g. Stoddard (1860) and Maclean (1895). Some data on the dialects of the Jews were, nevertheless, published by scholars during this period together with material from the Christian dialects, e.g. Socin (1882) on the Jewish dialect of Zakho, Duval (1883) on the Jewish dialect of Salmas, and Maclean (1895, 340–44) on the Jewish dialect of Urmi. Systematic work on the Jewish dialects did not begin, however, until the second half the twentieth century after the Jews had left their original places of residence and migrated to Israel. So far several monograph-length descriptions of dialects have been published, including Garbell (1965a Jewish Urmi and related dialects), Mutzafi (2004a Jewish Koy Sanjak), Mutzafi (2008a Jewish Betanure), Fassberg (2010 Jewish Challa), Greenblatt (2011 Jewish Amedia), Cohen (2012 syntax of Jewish Zakho), Khan (1999 Jewish Arbel), Khan (2004b Jewish Sulemaniyya and Ḥalabja), Khan (2008a Jewish Urmi), Khan (2009 Jewish Sanandaj), in addition to numerous shorter sketches and studies. Several scholars, especially Mutzafi, Hopkins and Khan, have gathered extensive data on most of the other surviving dialects. Much of this material is gradually been made accessible in an online NENA database at the University of Cambridge.

All the Jewish Neo-Aramaic dialects are now on an inexorable trajectory of extinction as living vernaculars within the next couple of decades or so. As remarked, some are known to have already become extinct, in some cases descriptions of these have fortunately been published, e.g. the Jewish dialect of Challa (Fassberg 2010), or at least unpublished data have been collected for future study, e.g. Jewish Nerwa (Mutzafi). The communities who spoke the various dialects in their original location were of varying size. Some dialects were spoken only by a handful of Jewish families and it is these that have now become extinct or are in particular danger of extinction, such as Challa in

3 A large amount of this literature has been edited and studied by Yona Sabar in his numerous publications, e.g. Sabar (1976, 1985, 1991b, 1983, 1988, 1991a, 1994). See also the work of Rees (2008). Sabar was instrumental in having many of the tradents of the oral traditions commit them to writing. Yosef Rivlin also played a role in this respect, see, for example, Rivlin (1959).

south-eastern Turkey (Fassberg 2010), Aradhin (Mutzafi 2002b), Dobe and Hiza (in Iraq). The dialects that were spoken by larger communities in their original locations are in a more healthy state, but every year the number of good speakers dwindles and the opportunities for systematic linguistic documentation vanish with them.

2. Historical Background

There are only scant sources for the history of the Aramaic-speaking Jewish communities. The main written historical sources have been described by Brauer and Patai (1993) and, in greater detail for each community, by Ben Yaʕqov (1980). It is assumed by these authors that the communities have very deep historical roots, but the first clear historical reference to an Aramaic-speaking Jewish population is by the medieval traveller Benjamin of Tudela (12th century), who states that the Jews of the region spoke the Targum language (Brauer and Patai 1993: 58). Mann (1931, 2nd: 16) publishes letters datable to the beginning of the sixteenth century that mention villages in the highlands of Kurdistan that had Jewish communities. Some of these had been abandoned by their Jewish population by the twentieth century or the number of Jewish inhabitants was considerably reduced, reflecting the fact that the Jewish population of the region declined after the sixteenth century. One reason for this reduction is likely to have been the forcible conversion of some Jews to Islam, especially in the nineteenth century in some areas (Soane 1912: 186). After the First World War and the fixing of the border between Iraq and Turkey by the League of Nations in 1925, some Jewish communities that fell within Turkish territory moved down into Iraq. Fieldworkers on the Jewish Neo-Aramaic dialects have gathered a number of oral accounts from older speakers about the recent history of their communities. These frequently talk of migrations around the region, especially from villages into towns. This applies, for example, to the Jews of the towns of Sulemaniyya and Sanandaj, which were founded in the Ottoman period (Khan 2004b: 3, 2009: 1).

The history of the Aramaic-speaking Jewish communities is reflected also in the linguistic history of the Jewish NENA dialects. These are not direct descendants of any of the earlier literary forms of Aramaic (except of course of the written forms of Jewish NENA extant from the 17th century onwards), although they exhibit close affinities to Syriac and Jewish Babylonian Aramaic. The dialects rather have their roots in a vernacular form of Aramaic that existed in antiquity in the region of northern Mesopotamia, which differed from the vernacular underlying the literary languages of Syriac to the west and Jewish Babylonian Aramaic to the south. This is shown by the fact that, although exhibiting numerous innovations, they are more conservative than Syriac and Jewish Babylonian Aramaic in some features (Khan 2007b; Fox 2008). Some of the dialects, moreover, have preserved lexical items of apparently Akkadian origin that do not appear in dictionaries of the earlier forms of literary Aramaic.[4] Structural differences among the NENA dialects are likely to reflect, to some extent, migrations of communities in the northern Mesopotamian region. The clear structural distinction between the Jewish and Christian dialects has been brought about by different migration patterns as

4 For Christian dialects see Krotkoff (1985) and Khan (2002: 515), and for Jewish dialects Y. Sabar (2002: 12).

well as social divisions. Within the Jewish dialects migration history is reflected by concentrations of structural diversity. The greater degree of diversity within the structure of dialects in Iraq compared to those in western Iran, for example, suggests that Iraq was the original heartland of the Aramaic-speaking population and the communities on the eastern periphery in western Iran were the result of migration from this heartland. The Jewish NENA dialects of western Iran also reflect a greater degree of innovation in their structure.

3. Linguistic Structure

3.1 Relationship to Christian Neo-Aramaic

The Jewish NENA dialects are divided into two main subgroups: (1) the so-called *lišana deni* subgroup, which was spoken in the north-west of Iraq in locations to the west of the Great Zab river, such as Zakho, Dohok, Amedia, Betanure, and just to the east of the river around the Turkish border such as Nerwa in Iraq and Challa in south-eastern Turkey. (2) Dialects spoken in locations east of the Great Zab river in the Arbīl and Sulemaniyya provinces of Iraq (e.g. Rustaqa, Ruwanduz, Koy Sanjak, villages of the plain of Arbel,[5] Ḥalabja and Sulemaniyya, also the village of Dobe which is on the western bank of the Great Zab), in the West Azerbaijan province of Iran (e.g. Urmi, Salmas, Shino, Naghada [Solduz], Sablagh [Mahabad]) and further south in the Kurdistan and Kermanshah provinces of Iran (e.g. Saqqiz, Sanandaj, Kerend, and on the Iraqi side of the border in Khanaqin). This subgroup is generally referred to as trans-Zab (following Mutzafi 2008b). In addition, there was a small cluster of dialects in the region of Barzan, located in Iraq between these two areas, which exhibit a linguistic profile that is transitional between the two main subgroups (Mutzafi 2002a, 2004b).

As remarked, the Jewish Neo-Aramaic dialects exhibit numerous differences in their structure from the Christian dialects of the region. The Christian dialects spoken east of the Tigris and the Jewish dialects do, however, clearly exhibit shared innovations and belong to the same Neo-Aramaic subgroup, viz. NENA. One of the most conspicuous innovations of the NENA subgroup is the replacement of the finite verbal forms *yiqṭul* (prefix-conjugation) and *qṭal* (suffix-conjugation) of earlier Aramaic with conjugations based on the active and passive participles respectively. The NENA dialects are distinguished from the adjacently located and closely related Ṭuroyo subgroup by several shared innovations. These include the phonological shift **ġ* > *ʕ* > *ʔ* > *∅*. The voiced velar fricative **ġ* (the erstwhile fricative allophone of the */g/) has been lost in NENA (with the exception of a few lexical items) and has the reflex /ʔ/ or zero, e.g. Jewish Amedia *peʔla*, Jewish Arbel *pela* 'radish' < **paġlā*. The /ʔ/ developed from an early pharyngeal /ʕ/, which is preserved in a few words, e.g. Jewish Amedia *ṛaʕola* 'valley' < **rāġōlā*. A shared innovation of NENA in the verbal system that distinguishes it from Ṭuroyo is the loss of the middle voice so-called T-stems, which have survived, albeit in reduced form, in Ṭuroyo. There are also a variety of shared lexical innovations in the Jewish and Christian NENA dialects, the most conspicuous one being *baxta* 'woman' (of uncertain etymology, but see Mutzafi (2005: 99 n.79)), as opposed to the conservative Ṭuroyo *ʔaṯto*. These innovations of NENA are of a considerable historical

5 The Jews in the town of Arbel itself spoke Arabic (Jastrow 1990).

time-depth. The lexical item *baxta*, for example, appears in an eleventh century source (Khan 2007b: 11).

In general the trans-Zab subgroup of Jewish NENA is more innovative than the *lišana deni* subgroup due to a greater degree of convergence with the non-Semitic languages of the area. The trans-Zab dialects exhibit a greater degree of difference from the neighbouring Christian dialects than is the case with the *lišana deni* subgroup. This is a consequence of the fact that the Christian dialects have in general not undergone a degree of convergence with contact languages that is found in trans-Zab dialects. Conservative features found in Jewish *lišana deni* and the neighbouring Christian dialects include, for example, the preservation of interdental consonants (in some dialects) and the preservation of a predominant SVO word-order, which are not features of Kurdish, the predominant contact language in the region. Trans-Zab dialects, on the other hand, have converged with Kurdish and Azeri Turkish with regard to these features, in that they have lost the interdentals and have a predominantly SOV word order. There is, moreover, a greater proportion of loanwords in their core lexicon than is the case in *lišana deni* dialects. Nevertheless, there are numerous differences between Jewish *lišana deni* dialects and the local Christian dialects. This can be seen in the chart below, which compares the Christian Barwar dialect (Khan 2008b) with the neighbouring Jewish dialect of Betanure (Mutzafi 2008a), together with two other Jewish *lišana deni* dialects, Amedia (Greenblatt 2011) and Nerwa. As can be seen, the Jewish dialects exhibit considerable similarities among themselves, which contrast with the Christian dialect:

	C. Barwar	J. Betanure	J. Amedia	J. Nerwa
loss/preservation of laryngeal	*balota* 'throat'	*baloʔta*	*baloʔta*	*baloʔta*
reflex of **ay*	*lɛša* 'dough'	*leša*	*leša*	*leša*
reflex of **aw*	*tawra* 'ox'	*tora*	*tora*	*tora*
2SG independent pronoun	*ʔati*	*ʔahət* SG.M *ʔahat* SG.F	*ʔahi*	*ʔahət* SG.M *ʔahat* SG.F
3PL pron. suffix	*-ay, -ɛy, -ey*	*-u, -ohun*	*-u, -ohun*	*-u, -ohun*
genitive particle	*diye*	*dide*	*dide*	*dide*
reciprocal pronoun	*ġðaðe*	*ʔəxðe*	*ʔəġde*	*ʔəxde*
deictic copula	*hole*	*wəlle*	*wəlle*	*wəlle*
indicative prefix	*i-*	*k-*	*k-*	*k-*
'tomorrow'	*təmməl*	*bənhe*	*qadöme*	*qadome*
'now'	*diya, hadiya*	*ʔatta*	*ʔatta*	*ʔatta*
'last year'	*šetət wirra*	*šətqel*	*šətqel*	*šətqel*
'quickly'	*jalde*	*hayya*	*hayya*	*hayya*
'big'	*goṛa*	*ʔəṛwa*	*ʔuṛwa*	*ʔuṛwa*
'to descend'	*ṣlaya*	*kwaša*	*kwaša*	*kwaša*
'to stand'	*klaya*	*ḥmala*	*ḥmala*	*ḥmala*
'to sleep'	*ṭlaya*	*ṭwaʔa*	*ṭwaʔa*	*ṭwaʔa*
'to grow up'	*mqărone*	*ṛwaya*	*ṛwaya*	*ṛwaya*
'to speak'	*mṣawoθe*	*mḥakoye*	*mḥakoye*	*mḥakoye*
'he wants'	*băye*	*gbe*	*gbe*	*gbe*
'he knows'	*yăðe*	*kiʔe*	*kiʔe*	*kiye*

3.2 Structural features unique to Jewish Neo-Aramaic

A feature that is unique to all Jewish NENA dialects and contrasts with Christian dialects is the masculine single form and plural form of the adjective 'big', which are *rurwa*/*ruwwa* and *rurwe*/*ruwwe* respectively. This has developed by levelling from the original plural form **rawrḇē* (the original masculine singular form being **rabbā*) (Mutzafi 2014).

The *lišana deni* dialects exhibit a distinctive feature that stands in contrast to the neighbouring Christian dialects and the trans-Zab Jewish dialect in the formation of the independent genitive pronominal form. In most of the *lišana deni* dialects the singular of this is formed by adding pronominal suffixes to the base *did-*, whereas the plural is formed by suffixes to the base *d-*. The singular suffixes are monosyllabic and the plural suffixes are bisyllabic, in some cases lengthened, with the result that the paradigm is bisyllabic in all persons:

	Jewish Betanure	Christian Barwar
3MS	*did-e*	*diy-e*
3FS	*did-a*	*diy-a*
2MS	*did-ox*	*diy-ux*
2FS	*did-ax*	*diy-əx*
1S	*did-i*	*diy-i*
3PL	*d-ohun*	*diy-ey*
2PL	*d-oxun*	*diy-ɛxu*
1PL	*d-eni*	*diy-ən*

Most features that are unique to the Jewish dialects are found in the innovative trans-Zab dialects. As remarked above, most of these have arisen through a greater convergence with contact languages. These features can be divided into those that are general to all trans-Zab dialects and those that are found only in particular dialects of trans-Zab.

Innovative features that are general to trans-Zab include the shift of the interdental consonants /θ/ and /ð/ to the lateral /l/, e.g.

Christian Barwar	Jewish Arbel		
bɛ́θa	*belá*	'house'	< **bayṯā*
ʔéða	*ʔelá*	'festival'	< **ʕēḏā*

Similar sound shifts have been identified in Kurdish (Kapeliuk 1997). As can be seen from the indication of stress position in the table above, the trans-Zab dialects have word-final stress. This contrasts with the general penultimate stress that is found in Jewish *lišana deni* and the Christian dialects and is likely to be induced by contact with the word-final stress position of Kurdish (Khan 2007a: 200).

Another general innovation, under the influence of Kurdish or Azeri Turkish, is the elimination of the distinction between genders in third person singular pronouns, e.g.

Christian Barwar	Jewish Arbel		
ʔaw	*ʔo*	'he'	< **hāhū*
ʔay	*ʔo*	'she'	< **hāhī*

The trans-Zab dialects in or around the Arbīl province of Iraq are in general more diverse in their structure than those in Iran and also are in many cases more conservative. As remarked above, it is likely that Iraq is the original heartland of the subgroup. This Iraq subgroup of trans-Zab includes dialects such as Koy Sanjaq, Qalʕa Dəze, Rwanduz, Rustaqa, Dobe and the Arbel plain. The trans-Zab dialects in Iran may be divided on the basis of shared innovations into (i) the north-western Iran subgroup, which includes the dialects in the West Azerbaijan province of Iran (e.g. Urmi, Salmas, Shino, Naghada [Solduz], Sablagh [Mahabad]) together with the now extinct dialects that were spoken over the border in south-eastern Turkey (e.g. Bashqalan [Başkale] and Gavar [Yüksekova]); and (ii) the west Iran subgroup, which includes dialects of the Kurdistan and Kermanshah provinces of Iran (e.g. Saqqiz, Tikab, Bokan, Sanandaj, Kerend) and adjacent dialects over the border in Iraq (e.g. Sulemaniyya, Ḥalabja, Khanaqin). The dialects of this latter west Iran subgroup are referred to by their speakers as *hulaula*, which is an abstract noun meaning 'Jewishness/Judaism' (< *hūḏāyūṯā*).

In phonology these two Iranian subgroups exhibit unique innovations in the development of the emphatic consonants. These include the developments associated with the original emphatic consonants **ṭ* and **ṣ* and also more recently evolved emphatic phonemes such as the sonorants /ṛ/, /ḷ/ and labials /ṃ/, /ḅ/. Such emphatic consonants involve a coarticulation of pharyngealization. In the Christian dialects of Iraq and also the Jewish *lišana deni* dialects the emphatic consonants maintained their status of pharyngealized consonantal segments, with the phonetic spread of pharyngealization to adjacent vowels and consonants. In the Iraq subgroup of trans-Zab the pharyngealization is weakened, but can still be identified. In the western Iranian subgroup, however, an innovation has taken place whereby the pharyngealization of the emphatic segments has ceased to be a coarticulatory feature but rather surfaces as a pharyngeal segment in the word. This may either be a historical pharyngeal, which has lost its pharyngeal articulation in non-emphatic contexts, e.g. Jewish Sanandaj *tamʕa* 'she tastes' < **ṭāmʕā* vs. *šamya* 'she hears' < **šāmʕā*, or a non-etymological pharyngeal, e.g. *tmaʕni* 'eighty' < *tṃani* (Khan 2013). Such a development seems to have been brought about by convergence with the phonological structure of Kurdish. Some dialects of Kurdish have been shown by Margaret Kahn (1976: 49–52) to have a type of pharyngealization that involves an underlying pharyngeal segment. This pharyngeal, according to Kahn, underlies a word that has a pharyngealized consonant and such words can also be realized with the pharyngeal on the phonetic surface in place of the pharyngealized consonant. One can have variants, therefore, such as *ṭæzi* ~ *tæʕzi* 'fresh'. Kahn was describing Kurdish dialects of the Kurmanji sub-group spoken in the Urmi region. The Jewish trans-Zab dialects where this phenomenon is found were spoken further south in regions where Sorani Kurdish is spoken. Today Sorani Kurdish does not exhibit such a feature. It may be hypothesized that it used to exist in Sorani Kurdish at an earlier period and that the Jewish NENA dialects have preserved the feature whereas the adjacent Kurdish dialects lost it.

In the Jewish Urmi dialect of the north-western Iran subgroup the phonetic spreading of coarticulatory pharyngealization of consonantal segments has been reinterpreted as a suprasegmental phoneme that is a property of an entire word. This has come about under the influence of the vowel harmony of Azeri Turkish, with which the dialect was in contact. The same happened to the Christian dialects of the area, but a unique feature of Jewish Urmi is that the historical emphatic stop **ṭ* became identical with the non-emphatic stop /t/ on the segmental level:

	Iraq	North-western Iran	
	Jewish Arbel	Christian Urmi	Jewish Urmi
**ṭūrā* 'mountain'	*ṭura*	$^{+}$*t̯ura*	$^{+}$*tura*

The original emphatic **ṭ* was distinguished from non-emphatic **t* not only in pharyngealization but also in glottal setting, in that **ṭ* was unaspirated and **t* was aspirated. As remarked, in the Urmi dialects the pharyngealization has become a suprasegmental feature (represented above by a superscribed $^{+}$). In the Christian dialect the glottal setting of **ṭ* is retained and the consonant is pronounced unaspirated (represented above by the symbol /t̯/), which contrasts with aspirated /t/. In the Jewish dialect, however, the glottal setting is not retained and **ṭ* has become totally assimilated to **t* on a segmental level. This can be interpreted as reflecting a greater degree of convergence with the phonology of Azeri, which does not have an unaspirated phoneme equivalent to /t̯/ of Christian Urmi. Furthermore in Jewish Urmi the back vowels /u/ and /o/ are fronted to [y] and [ø] respectively in non-emphatic words, corresponding to the fronting that is found in the Azeri vowel harmony system, whereas this is not systematically found in Christian Urmi (Khan 2013).

In the Jewish Salmas dialect in the north-western Iran subgroup the suprasegmental pharyngealization has been lost in all words that originally used to contain it but the phonetic affect of this feature on vowels has been preserved. This is most conspicuous in the development of long *a* vowels that were originally pharyngealized. These were backed and rounded to the quality /o/, e.g. *xosa* 'back' < **xāṣā*. This has occurred only in morphological stems and not in inflectional vowels:

	Lexical stem	Inflectional ending		
xosa 'back'	*xos-*	*a*	(nominal singular)	< **xāṣā*
tyolana 'player'	*tyol-*	*ana*	(agentive singular)	< **ṭyālānā*

This development in Jewish Salmas has occurred due to contact with various non-Semitic languages, including Russian in the recent history of the dialect.

An example of an innovation in morpho-syntax in the western Iranian subgroup is the loss of the genitive particle *d*. This particle, which combines a head noun with a dependent noun in a genitive construction continues to be used, mainly in the form of a clitic on the head, in the trans-Zab dialects of Iraq and north-western Iran. In the western Iran subgroup, however, it has disappeared. It is possible to explain this as a convergence with Kurdish (Khan 2007a: 202), e.g.

Jewish Arbel/Jewish Urmi	Jewish Sanandaj	
belət Šlomo	*bela Šlomo*	'the house of Šlomo'
		< **baytā d-Šlomo*

In most dialects of the western Iranian subgroup it has survived only as a vestige in genitive pronouns, but in the dialect of Jewish Kerend it is often omitted even in this context (Khan 2009: 11):

Jewish Sanandaj	Jewish Kerend	
bela do	*bela ʔo*	'his house'

This loss of the genitive particle has no doubt come about due to convergence with the local Sorani Kurdish dialects in this area of Iran, known as Ardalānī, which do not mark genitive connection morphologically, e.g. *māl* 'house', *māl pawšaka* 'the house of the king'. Further north in the Urmi region, by contrast, Sorani Kurdish uses a genitive *izafe* particle in such constructions, e.g. Mukri *māl-i pašakay*.

The conservative nature of the Iraq subgroup of trans-Zab vis-à-vis the other trans-Zab subgroups is reflected in some areas of morphology, such as the copula and the patterns of verbs. Compare the form of the present copula across the dialects:

	Iraq	North-western Iran	Western Iran
	Jewish Arbel	Jewish Urmi	Jewish Sanandaj
3MS	*-ile*	*-ile*	*-ye*
2MS	*-wet*	*-ilet*	*-yet*
1S	*-wen*	*-ilen*	*-yena*

In Jewish Arbel the original heterogeneity of the paradigm is preserved, with the /l/ element in the 3rd person and the /w/ element in the 2nd and 1st persons. In Jewish Urmi the /l/ element has been generalized and in Jewish Sanandaj the /l/ has been lost in the 3rd person and replaced by the glide /y/ (*-ye* < *-ile*), then the /y/ element has been generalized.

The north-western Iran and western Iran subgroups exhibit a greater degree of levelling across the vocalism of the verbal patterns. This can be seen, for example, in the forms of the infinitive:

	Iraq	North-western Iran	Western Iran
	Jewish Arbel	Jewish Urmi	Jewish Sanandaj
simplex	*CCaCa*	*CaCoCe*	*CaCoCe*
causative	*maCCoCe*	*CaCoCe*	*CaCoCe*

The Iraq subgroup retains the archaic form of the infinitive of the simplex (historically *peʕal*) form, whereas in the other subgroups this has been levelled with the vocalic pattern of the infinitive of the derived causative form (historically *ʔap̄ʕel*). The Jewish Urmi dialect, in fact, exhibits a complete levelling of vocalic patterns across all conjugations of the simplex and derived forms of the verb (Khan 2008a: 65–67).

Another feature of the Iraq subgroup of trans-Zab that can be regarded as conservative is the occurrence of oblique marking of the subject of past perfective verbs in both transitive and intransitive clauses, e.g.

Jewish Arbel

griš-li	'I pulled' (transitive)
qim-li	'I rose' (intransitive)

The oblique suffix is historically a prepositional phrase consisting of the dative preposition *l-* and a pronominal suffix. These suffixes are glossed as L-suffixes in the glossed texts below (e.g. L.1S = oblique 1st person singular). In the transitive clauses the L-suffix can be interpreted as an ergative marker. In Christian NENA dialects and the Jewish *lišana deni* and Iraqi trans-Zab dialects this ergative suffix is used also as a marker of the subject of intransitive verbs in an alignment profile that may be called 'extended ergative' (Doron and Khan 2012). This profile is likely to have existed in the protoform of the NENA subgroup as a result of partial convergence with Iranian ergative languages of the region. The use of the oblique marker for intransitive subjects is attested in NENA interferences in classical Syriac texts at an early date (Khan 2004a). This is of considerable theoretical interest for studies in language contact and diachrony, in that it involves incomplete pattern matching (Matras and Sakel 2007) and constructional persistence, i.e. the continuing existence of the formal and semantic framework of a particular construction throughout the history of a language (Haig 2004: 55–57).

The innovative trans-Zab dialects of western Iran, however, exhibit a more canonical alignment profile, whereby the subject of transitive verbs are marked by the oblique ergative suffix but unaccusative intransitive verbs are marked by direct nominative suffixes. These direct suffixes are glossed as D-suffixes in the glossed texts below, e.g.

Jewish Sanandaj

grəš-li pull.PST-L.1S	'I pulled' (transitive)
qim-na rise.PST-D.1S	'I rose' (intransitive)

Such ergative alignment, which is unique in NENA to the Jewish dialects of western Iran, is best considered to be the result of innovation rather than archaism, which has arisen, like other innovations in this subgroup, by a greater degree of convergence with Kurdish. Apart from the general innovative character of the subgroup compared to the Iraqi NENA dialects, there is some more specific evidence for this proposal. The past copula, for example, in the western Iranian trans-Zab dialects is conjugated with oblique ergative suffixes, e.g. *ye-le* 'he was', as is the case in extended ergative dialects such as the Iraqi trans-Zab dialect Jewish Arbel: *we-le*. In an ergative alignment system a copula would be expected to have nominative subject suffixes. The presence of ergative suffixes must be a relic from an earlier period in which there was extended ergative marking. The shift to nominative marking of the past copula was blocked by the fact that the resulting form would be identical, or nearly identical, to the present copula. In the north-western Iran subgroup of trans-Zab nominative subject marking is found on the present perfect of intransitive verbs, but the extended ergative system is retained on verbs when they have perfective function, e.g.

Jewish Urmi

qəm-li 'I rose' (perfective)
rise.PST-L.1S

qim-en 'I have risen' (present perfect)
rise.PST-D.1S

The development of such present perfects with nominative subject may also be regarded as an innovation. It is, indeed, probably the first stage of the shift to the nominative marking of the perfective, the development present perfect > perfective being a common pathway of diachronic evolution. There are sporadic examples of perfects with nominative marking in isolated intransitive verbs in some Jewish NENA dialects of Iraq that are otherwise extended ergative. In the Jewish Arbel dialect, for example, it is found in the verb 'to remain', e.g. *piš-i* (remain.PST-D.3PL) 'they have remained' (Khan 1999: 284–285). A few examples are found also in the early written forms of *lišana deni* dialects, e.g. *ʔiṯ-ən* (come.PST-D.1S) 'I have come' (Nerwa texts, 17th century; Y. Sabar 1976: xl). In the Jewish Arbel and *lišana deni* dialects, however, the form was not extended to the general verbal system. It, in fact, has disappeared in the modern forms of the *lišana deni* dialects, and has been completely replaced by perfects expressed by a participle and a copula. The existence of present perfect verbs with nominative subject suffixes is not, however, unique to Jewish NENA, since it is found also in some Christian dialects in the northwestern periphery of NENA in south-eastern Turkey, such as Hertevin (Jastrow 1988: 58–59) and Bohtan (Fox 2009: 56). In Hertevin it is only marginal and has not been fully established in the verbal system, but it is more established in Bohtan, where it has been extended even to transitive verbs.[6]

A general innovation that is unique to the trans-Zab dialects of Jewish Neo-Aramaic is the formation of the perfective stem of the simplex pattern (historical *peʕal*) form on the analogy of that of the causative pattern (historical *ʔap̄ʕel*):

Christian Barwar	Jewish Sanandaj	
simplex	simplex	causative pattern
griš-le pull.PST-L.3MS	*grəš-le* 'he pulled'	cf. *mərxəš-le* 'he caused to walk'
griš-a-le pull.PST-D.3FS-L.3MS	*gərš-a-le* 'he pulled her'	cf. *mərxš-a-le* 'he caused her to walk'

The more conservative trans-Zab dialects of Iraq still retain the *CCiC-a-le* pattern in middle /w/ verbs, e.g.

Jewish Arbel	Jewish Sanandaj
dwiq-a-le hold.PST-D.3FS-L.3MS	*dəwq-a-le* 'he held her'

6 For further details of the development of ergative constructions in NENA see Doron and Khan (2012), Coghill (2016) and Khan (2017). It has generally been assumed by other scholars that the alignment patterns that are found in the western Iranian trans-Zab dialects are more archaic than the majority of dialects with generalized marking of oblique subject suffixes, e.g. Hopkins (1989), Mutzafi (2014), and that the extended ergative profile reflects the decay of the original ergative system (Barotto 2015).

The small cluster of Jewish dialects in the region of Barzan (Mutzafi 2002a, 2004b), which are transitional between the *lišana deni* and trans-Zab subgroups, exhibit features of both of the other subgroups and also some unique features. Among the unique features is the use of the preverbal indicative-marking particles *y-* and *k-*. These are found elsewhere in NENA but not with the distribution that is found in this dialect cluster. In these dialects, for example, they may be combined in the order *y* + *k*, e.g. *y-k-emər* 'he says'. In other NENA dialects such a combination is found only in the reverse order, e.g. Christian Urmi *c-i-patəx* 'he opens'. In some of the dialects of the cluster the *y* is used in positive verbs and the *k* in negated ones, e.g. *y-saxe* 'he swims', *la k-saxe* 'he does not swim'.

3.3 Language contact influences

In numerous places in the foregoing discussion of grammatical structure the point has been made that many of the differences between the *lišana deni* dialects and the trans-Zab dialects have come about by the greater convergence of the latter with contact languages. Here we shall restrict ourselves to some remarks on the lexicon.

As expected, the lexicon of the trans-Zab dialects exhibits a greater influence from contact languages than the *lišana deni* dialects. This is reflected by a greater proportion of loanwords in core areas of the lexicon. The table below shows a series of items in the core lexicon that are of native Aramaic etymology in Jewish Amedia, a *lišana deni* dialect, compared to the corresponding items in the trans-Zab dialects Jewish Urmi and Jewish Sanandaj. In each case at least one of the trans-Zab dialects has a loanword, from Azeri Turkish (T), Kurdish (K) or Persian (P). In some cases both trans-Zab dialects have loanwords.

	Amedia	Urmi	Sanandaj
'eyelash'	*təlpa*	*kəprəg* (T)	*peḷa* (K)
'eyebrow'	*bəgwina*	⁺*qaša* (T)	*gwenya*
'jaw'	*leʔma*	*čanakta* (K/T)	*čanaga* (K)
'spit'	*roqe*	*roqe*	*təf* (K/P)
'arm'	*ʔida*	⁺*qola* (T/K)	*qoḷa* (K)
'mother'	*yəmma*	⁺*daa* (K)	*daăka* (K)
'hail'	*barda*	⁺*dolu* (T)	*tarzăka* (K)
'shade'	*ṭəlla*	*kolga* (T)	*poxa*
'green'	*yaruqa*	⁺*yašəl* (T)	*yăruqa*

Outside of the core vocabulary the extent of influence of contact-languages is greater, especially in nouns. Garbell (1965b) has calculated that in the Jewish Urmi dialect 69% of the total lexicon of nouns are loanwords, and similar proportions can be identified in other trans-Zab dialects (Khan 2004b: 7).

Although nouns are particularly susceptible to being loaned, as is generally the case cross-linguistically, the impact of contact-languages can be seen in all areas of the lexicon in the Jewish NENA dialects. Many verbal roots have been extracted from loanwords. This applies also to Hebrew loanwords, e.g. Jewish Zakho *t-p-l* 'to pray (Muslims)' < Hebrew תְּפִלּ. Some grammatical particles have been borrowed, including discourse connectives and, in the case of some trans-Zab dialects, the Kurdish definite article (Khan 2007a: 201–202).

4. Written and Oral Traditions

4.1 Writing System

When Jewish Neo-Aramaic speakers began to commit their language to writing in the 17th century, they used Hebrew script, as is the norm with other Jewish languages. The orthography was *plene*, corresponding to the contemporary practice of spelling Hebrew (Y. Sabar 1976: xxxi–xxxiv, 2002: 15–21). There are, however, some differences. The most conspicuous one is the use of *ʔaleph* to represent long *ā* in word-medial position, e.g. כמארא *xmāra* 'ass', including in Hebrew loanwords, e.g. נשאמוך *nišāmox* 'your soul' (= נְשָׁמָה), and occasionally also medial short /a/, e.g. כַּאלְוֵוי *kalwe* 'dogs'. In contrast to written Christian Neo-Aramaic, which has incorporated historical elements of Syriac orthography, Jewish Neo-Aramaic orthography is phonetic and not based on that of any early literary form of Jewish Aramaic, e.g. כמשא *xamša* 'five' (= חמשא), שואא *šōʔa* 'seven' (= שבעא). Scribes sometimes write prosthetic vowels that break initial consonantal clusters, e.g. אתרי *ʔətre* 'two', אטלהא *ʔəṭlāha* 'three'. These are generally not pronounced in the surviving spoken language. Spread of emphasis is reflected in spellings with emphatic letters such as צלוצא *ṣloṣa* 'prayer' (= *ṣlōsa* < **slōṯā*), and loss of emphasis by spellings such as שרתי *šarte* < *šarṭe* 'conditions'. Texts written by Jewish Urmi speakers reflect the weakening of pharyngeal consonants in that dialect, e.g. אלחא *ilha* (*ḥet* represents /h/) (Y. Sabar 2013: 481).

Texts written in Israel since the 1950s exhibit some influence from Israeli Hebrew pronunciation, e.g. ח may be used for Neo-Aramaic /x/ and ק for Neo-Aramaic /k/, דוּמַיֵק *dūmāyək* 'eventually', or Hebrew orthography, e.g. the use of ע as in cases such as עֵינַא *ʔena* 'eye' (cf. Hebrew עַיִן), or the use of שׂ in cases such as שְׂעַארֶי *saʕāre* 'barley' (cf. Hebrew שְׂעוֹרִים).

Hebrew vocalization signs came to be used frequently in texts written down in the twentieth century. These reflect Sephardi Hebrew pronunciation, in that the signs *qameṣ* and *pataḥ*, on the one hand, and *ṣere* and *seghol*, on the other, interchange inconsistently. The *shewa* sign is often used to represent /a/, even in closed syllables, e.g. חְכוֹמָא *ḥakōma* 'king'. A noteworthy feature of vocalization is the insertion of epenthetic vowels breaking initial consonantal clusters which are generally not pronounced in the spoken dialects. This is found predominantly in verbal forms in Bible translations, e.g. in the trans-Zab Neo-Aramaic Bible translation studied by Rees (2008: 16) פֵּלִיכְלֶה 'he opened' (spoken dialects: *plixle*).

A distinctive feature of the Bible translations is their close imitation of the syntax of the Hebrew source text. This results in the fact that their syntax deviates radically from the syntax of the spoken dialects (for details see Rees 2008).

4.2 Literature

There is no clear distinction between the written literature and the oral literature of the Neo-Aramaic-speaking Jews, since the majority of their literary heritage originates in oral transmission (Aloni 2014: 22). The many Bible translations published by Sabar, for example, were committed to writing only in the twentieth century at the request of scholars in Israel.

Jewish Neo-Aramaic literature may be divided into the following categories (Y. Sabar 1982: xxxii–xxxvi, 1976: 161–78; Aloni 2014: 22–24):

I. Religious literature, most of which exists today in manuscripts, including:
(i) Homilies on portions of the Pentateuch;
(ii) Expositions on the *Hafṭarot* and *Megillot* in the form of free translations;
(iii) Literal translations of the Bible, mostly written down from oral traditions in the twentieth century;
(iv) Liturgical literature, including dirges (*qinot*), especially for the Ninth of Ab, para-liturgical songs (*pizmonim*) and expositions of the 613 commandments (*ʔazharot*);
(v) Rhymed aggadic narratives (*tafsirim*), loosely based on biblical and midrashic sources. Many of these were published by Rivlin (1959).

II. Oral folk literature. This played a central role in the culture of Neo-Aramaic-speaking Jews. Some of it has been committed to writing by scholars, as part of their documentation of the dialects, and also by native speakers.

In Israel new performance genres have developed among the Neo-Aramaic speaking community. Theatre plays have been produced, notably by the performer and singer Nisan Aviv in the Jewish Urmi dialect (Khan 2008a: xviii, 417). The *lišana deni* community in Jerusalem currently hold monthly cultural gatherings at which they have poetry readings and stand-up comedy entertainment. Speakers of some of the western Iranian trans-Zab dialects have held phone-in radio programmes, organized by speakers of the Sulemaniyya and Sanandaj dialects, including poetry readings and other cultural activities. The participation in these activities dwindles from year to year as the number of competent speakers gradually diminishes.

5. Glossed Texts

The following glossed texts include an extract from an early written form of Jewish Neo-Aramaic of the *lišana deni* variety and samples of two Jewish trans-Zab dialects. The early written Neo-Aramaic is taken from homilies published by Y. Sabar (1976). These are preserved in manuscripts that were written in Nerwa in the 17th century. The tradition of the Neo-Aramaic texts, however, may go back to as early as the 14th century. These texts contain a number of features that are not found in the modern *lišana deni* dialects (Y. Sabar 1976: xxxi–xliii; Goldenberg 2000). As indicated in the discussion above (§3), the trans-Zab dialects exhibit a variety of unique features that are not found in Christian varieties of NENA. The samples are taken from the Jewish dialects of Urmi (north-western Iran) and Sanandaj (western Iran) (Khan 2008a: 2009).

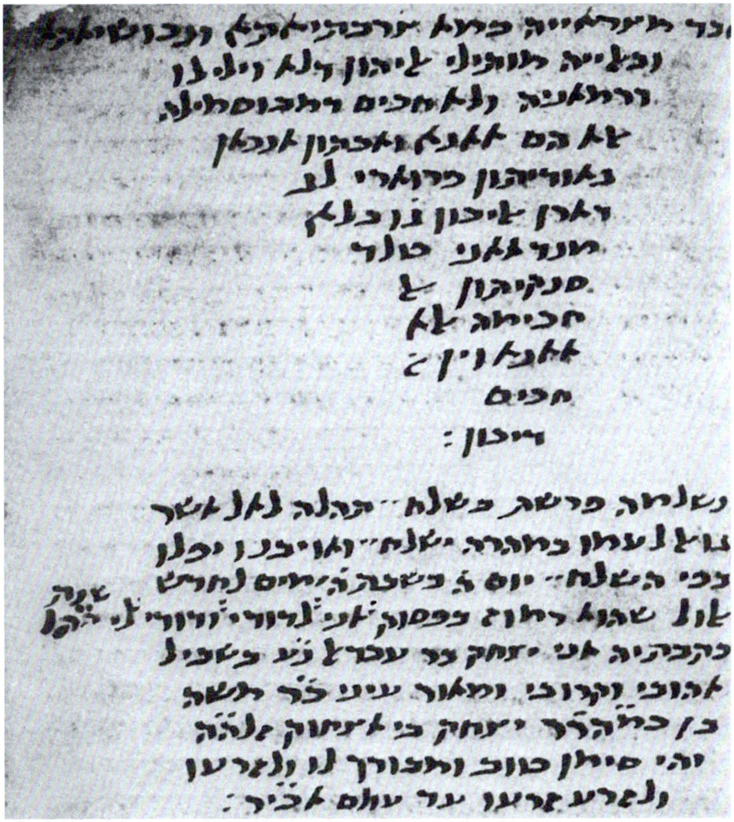

Columbia University Manuscript X893/IPI M58 last page, with colophon

5.1 Nerwa homily (17th century) (Y. Sabar 1976: 5–6, 44–47)

(1) מרו רבותינו ז״ל: אני אנקולוס הגר,

mər-ru rabboṯe-nu z(iḵr-am) l(i-ḇraxa) ʔənni ʔOnqəlos hag-ger,

say.PST-L.3PL master.PL.CS-1PL^{H} memory-3PL.M^{H} for-blessing^{H} that Onqelos DEF-proselyte^{H},

Our masters of blessed memory say that Onqelos the Proselyte,

גר צדק, ע״ה

ger ṣeḏeq, ʕ(ala-w) h(a-šalom)

proselyte^{H} righteous^{H}, upon-3MS^{H} DEF-peace^{H}

the righteous proselyte, may he rest in peace,

(2) אברד כאתד טיטוס הרשע ויוא

ʔəbr-əd xaṯ-əd Ṭiṭos ha-rašaʕ we-wa

son-COMP sister-COMP Titus DEF-wicked^{H} COP.PST.3MS-AUX.PST

was the son of the wicked Titus's sister,

(3) וטיטוס וזירד קיסר ויוא

u-Ṭiṭos wazir-əd Qesar we-wa

and-Titus vizier-COMP Caesar COP.PST.3MS-AUX.PST

and Titus was the vizier of Caesar.

(4) ואו טיטוס רשע אילה דאורה אל בית המקדש

u-ʔo Ṭiṭos rašaʕ=ile d-ʔwər-re ʔəl beṯ hammiqdaš

and-that Titus wicked^{H}=COP.3MS REL-enter.PST-L.3MS to house.CS^{H} sanctuary^{H},

and he is the wicked Titus who entered the Temple

(5) ואודלה פשחתיאתא טומיה

u-ʔwəḏ-le fašḥəty-aṯa ṭumy-e

and-do.PST-L.3MS abomination-PL foul-PL

and committed foul abominations

(6) גו מקדש דה׳ מנד עונות דיני

go miqdaš d-ilaha minn-əd ʕawonoṯ deni

in sanctuary GEN-God from-COMP sins^{H} GEN.1PL

in the sanctuary of the Lord because of our sins

(7) ובאכיר הקב״ה אשקלה אנתקאם מניה

u-b-ʔaxīr h(a)q-(qadoš) b(arux) h(u) ʔšqəl-le ʔəntiqām mənn-e

and-in-end DEF-holy^{H} blessed^{H} 3MS^{H} take.PST-L.3MS vengenace from-POSS.3MS

and in the end the Holy One, blessed be He, took vengeance of him

(8) אל אידד כדא באקא

ʔəlʔiḏ-əd xədda baqa

on hand-COMP one gnat

by means of a gnat

(9) אוורא גו נכירה וזלא גו מוכה

ʔwər-ra go naxir-e u-zəl-la go mox-e

enter.PST-L.3FS in nose-POSS.3MS and-go.PST-L.3FS in brain-POSS.3MS

It entered his nose and went to his brain

(10) ואכלואלה הלד טאלבוא מותה

u-ʔaxl-a-wa-le hall-əd ṭaləb-∅-wa moṯ-e

and-eat.IPFV-D.3FS-AUX.PST-L.3MS until-COMP beg.IPFV-D.3MS-AUX death-POSS.3MS

and it was eating it until he begged for his death

(11) ולא מאיתוא

u-la mayəṯ-∅-wa

and-NEG die.IPFV-D.3MS-AUX

but he did not die

(12) שאקעואלה רישה אל כיפה ואל גודאנה

šaqəʕ-∅-wa-le reš-e ʔəl-kep-e u-ʔəl-gud-ane

strike.IPFV-D.3MS-AUX.PST-L.3MS head-POSS.3MS against-stone-PL and-against-wall-PL

He struck his head against stones and walls

(13) ולא חאג̇מוא

u-la ḥajəm-∅-wa

and-NEG rest.IPFV-D.3MS-AUX.PST

but did not find rest

(14) בד עודאב פשלה ראבה שנה

b-əd ʕüḏāb pəš-le rab-e šənn-e

in-COMP suffering remain.PST-L.3MS many-PL year-PL

in suffering he continued many years

(15) הלד מצולכנו רישה בנראה

hall-əd mṣulxən-nu reš-e b-narʔ-e

until-COMP split.PST-L.3PL head-POSS.3MS with-axe-PL

until they split his head with axes

(16) אלא פרכלא מגו מוכה

ʔəlla prəx-la m-go mox-e

behold fly.PST-L.3FS from-in brain-POSS.3MS

(17) כא באקא אכגן כא זאאד יונה

behold from his brain flew

xa baqa ʔəxjin xa zaʔ-əd yona

one gnat like one young-COMP dove

a gnat the size of a young dove

(18) ומתלה בד עודאב

u-mət-le b-aḏ ʕüḏāb

and-die.PST-L.3MS in-this pain

and he died in this pain.

(19) בתר דאד קצתא אנפליה גו לבד אנקלוס

baṯər d-aḏ qəṣta ʔnpəl-le go ləbb-əd ʔOnqəlos

after GEN-this event fall.PST-L.3MS in heart-COMP Onqelos

After this event the thought came to Onqelos

(20) אברד כאתה טלד פאלט מדינד סוריותא

ʔəbr-əd xaṯ-e ṭla-d paləṭ m-din-əd sorayuṯa

son-COMP sister-POSS.3MS to-COMP leave from-religion-COMP Christianity

the son of his sister, to leave the religion of Christianity

(21) וכומד ויוא אנקלוס גֿו שואלא וגֿו כברא לא אאודוא

u-ku-m-əd we-wa Onqəlos ču šuʔla u-ču xabra la ʔawəḏ-∅-wa

and-all-thing-COMP COP.3MS-AUX.PST Onqelos none matter and-none affair NEG do.IMPV-D.3MS-AUX.PST

and in all cases Onqelos would not do anything at all

(22) דלא בקרתד כלוייה טיטוס

d-la baqart-əd xaloy-e Ṭiṭos

COMP-NEG ask.INF-COMP maternal.uncle-POSS.3MS Titos

without asking his maternal uncle Titus

(23) קמלה זלה ריש קורד טיטוס

qəm-le zəl-le reš qor-əd Ṭiṭos

rise.PST-L.3MS go.PST-L.3MS upon grave-COMP Titus

He set off to the grave of Titus

(24) וקסמלה אליה מעלם דידה נועד כרשיה

u-qsəm-le ʔəll-e m-ʕələm did-e noʕ-əd xərš-e

and-charm.PST-L.3MS on-POSS.3MS from-knowledge GEN-POSS.3MS kind.PL-COMP magic-PL

he performed a spell on him out of his knowledge of all kinds of magic

(25) ומפולטלה מגו קורא ומרילה

u-mpoləṭ-le m-go qora u-mər-re-le

and-bring.out.PST-L.3MS from-in grave and-say.PST-L.3MS-L.3MS

and brought him out of the grave, and said to him

(26) יא כלויי כא בקרתא אתלי אבוך

ya xaloy-i xa baqarta ʔət-li ʔebb-ox

oh maternal.uncle-POSS.1S one question EXIST-L.1S on-POSS.2MS

Oh maternal uncle, I have a question for you

(27) מרי טרוסא דך אודינא

mar-ri ṭrosa dəx ʔoḏ-ena

tell.IMP.SG-L.1S true how do.IRR-D.1MS

tell me honestly what I should do.

(28) אאמר די מרי מריה יא כלויי

ʔamər-∅ də marr-ri mər-re ya xaloy-i

say.IRR-D.3MS please tell.IMP.SG-L.1S say.PST-L.3MS oh maternal.uncle-POSS.1S

He says: Tell me. He said: Oh uncle

(29) בד אאזן אמתגרן ואודן ספארה

bəd ʔaz-ən ʔəmtagr-ən u-ʔoḏ-ən safar-e

FUT go.IRR-D.1MS trade.IRR-D.1MS and-do.IRR-D.1MS journey-PL

I am about to go to trade and travel

(30) די מרי דאימי סלעא זונינא

də mar-ri d-emi səlʕa zon-ena

please say.IMP.SG-L.1S COMP-which merchandise buy.IRR-D.1MS

Tell me what merchandise I should buy.

(31) אמר יא כסי די אכזי אימי סלעא דילא כסאד

ʔamər-∅ ya kass-i, si ʔəxzi ʔemi səlʕa d-ila kasād

say.IRR-D.3MS oh kinsman-POSS.1S go.IMP.SG see.IMP.SG which merchandise COMP-COP.3FS stagnant

Oh my kinsman, go and see what merchandise is in little demand

(32) ונפלתא ונאשא לא גמאינך אבה אאיא זון

u-npəlta u-naša la gə-mʔinəx-∅ ʔəbb-a ʔaya zon!

and-fall.PTCP.FS and-person NEG IND-look.IPFV-D.3MS on-POSS.3MS that buy.IMP.SG

and has gone down (in value), and nobody looks at it – buy that!

(33) דלאבד בד נפלא בקימה

d-labəd bəd napl-a b-qim-e

COMP-without.doubt FUT fall.IRR-D.3FS in-value-POSS.3MS

Certainly it will have gone down in value,

(34) וגרנא ובד מרמא רישא לאזם אי סלעא

u-garn-a u-bəd-marm-a reš-a lazəm ʔay səlʕa

and-become.expensive.IRR-D.3FS and-FUT-raise.IRR-D.3FS head-POSS.3FS must that merchandise

but that merchandise must become valuable and recover

(35) קמלה מתאמא אנקלוס ומפוכרה בגיאנה

qəm-le m-tama ʔOnqəlos u-mfokər-re b-gyan-e

rise.PST-L.3MS from-there Onqelos and-think.PST-L.3MS in-self-POSS.3MS

Onqelos rose from there and thought to himself about it

(36) ומרה אדיו בש סלעא כסאד מנד ישראל ליתן

u-mər-re ʔədyo biš səlʕa kasād mənn-əd Yiśraʔel liṯən

and-say.PST-L.3MS today more merchandise stagnant than-COMP Israel EXIST.NEG

and said: Today there is no merchandise less in demand than Israel

(37) ואמתא בש אתורתא מנה ליתן
u-ʔəmməta biš ʔətwərta mənn-a liṯən
and-nation more break.PTCP.3FS than-POSS.3FS EXIST.NEG
and there is no nation less broken than it

(38) ולאזם בד מארמלא אילאהא אלאיל מכולו אמתיאתא
u-lazəm bəd marəm-∅-la ʔilaha ʔəl-ʔēl m-kull-u ʔəmmət-yaṯa
and must FUT raise.IRR-D.3MS-L.3FS God to-above from-all-POSS.3PL nation-PL
God must surely raise it above all nations.

(39) אדוקלה אורכד ירושלים באידה
ʔədwəq-le ʔurx-əd Yərušalayim b-ʔiḏ-e
seize.PST-L.3MS road-COMP Jerusalem in-hand-POSS.3MS
He took the road to Jerusalem

(40) ואיתילה גו חכמים ומרילו
ʔu-ʔiṯe-le go ḥaḵamim u-mər-re-lu
and-come.PST-L.3MS in sages^{H} and-say.PST-L.3MS-L.3PL
and he came among the sages, and said to them

(41) אמגירולי אאנא פלאן איון איתן אלד דין דישראל
ʔəmgayr-u-li ʔana flan=iwən ʔiṯ-ən ʔəll-əd dīn d-Yiśraʔel
convert.IMP-PL-L.1S I so.and.so=COP.1MS come.PST-D.1MS to-COMP religion COMP-Israel
Convert me! I am so-and-so, I have come to (adopt) the religion of Israel

(42) קמלו חכמים וכולו אנה שרתה
qəm-lu ḥaḵamim u-kull-u ʔanne šart-e
rise.PST-L.3PL sages^{H} and-all-POSS.3PL those demand-PL
Then the sages all those demands

(43) דמריני אד נעמי אוידילא אמד רות
d-mər-reni ʔaḏ Noʕomi ʔəwiḏ-i-la ʔəmm-əd Ruṯ
REL-say.PST-L.1P this Naomi do.PST-D.3PL.-L.3FS with-COMP Ruth
which we said Naomi made of Ruth

(44) כימן דמגוירוואלא הם אאנה מירילו טלאתה אקבלה
kiman d-mgoyər-wa-la hamʔane mir-i-lu ṭlaṯ-e ʔəqbəl-le
when COMP-convert.PST-AUX.PST-L.3FS also they say.PST-D.3PL-L.3PL to-POSS.3MS accept.PST-L.3MS
when she converted, they told the same to him, and he agreed.

(45) וכולו שרתה דמצות וגהוא דתורה בד עולם
u-kull-u šart-e d-məṣwoṯ u-čehwa d-tora b-aḏ ʕolam
and-all-POSS.3PL demand-PL COMP-commandments^{H} and toil COMP-Torah in-this world^{H}
and all the demands of the commandments and the toil of the Torah in this world

(46) ואארא דידה ראבא אבד אי עולם אילה הם אקבלה
u-ʔaʔra did-e raba ʔəbb-əd ʔay ʕolam=ile ham ʔəqbəl-le
and-reward GEN-POSS.3MS great in-COMP that world^{H}=COP.3MS also accept.PST-L.3MS
– and its reward is great in that (other) world – he also accepted

(47) אנגׄר מרוליה יא צדיק לא גמקומא דנאשא אאתה
ʔənjar mər-ru-le ya ṣaddiq la gə-mqom-a d-naša ʔaṯe-∅
then say.PST-L.3PL-L.3MS oh righteous^{H} NEG IND-happen.IPFV-D.3FS COMP-man come.IRR-D.3MS
then they said to him: Oh righteous one, it is not possible for a man to come

(48) ואאור לתכיתד טלניתד שכינה והאוה דלא גזארא
u-ʔawər-∅ l-txeṯ-əd ṭəllaniṯ-əd šəḵina u-hawe-∅ d-la gzara
and-enter.IRR-D.3MS to-under-COMP shade-COMP presence^{H} and-be.IRR-D.3MS COMP-NEG circumcise.INF
and enter under the shade of the Divine Presence while he is uncircumcised

(49) אאמר נעם לרישי קמלה צמלה טלאהא יומאתא
ʔamər-∅ naʕam l-reš-i qəm-le ṣəm-le ṭlaha yom-aṯa
say.IRR-D.3MS indeed on-head-POSS.1S rise.PST-L.3MS fast-L.3MS three day-PL
He says: Indeed, gladly. He thereupon fasted for three days

(50) ואאהון גו ישיבה בקראייא
u-ʔahun go yəšiḇa bə-qraya
and-he in yeshiva^{H} in-read.INF
while he was studying in a yeshiva

(51) יומד טלאהא יומיה זלה אטבילה
yom-əd ṭlaha yom-e zəl-le ʔəṭbəl-le
day-COMP three day-PL go.PST-L.3MS bathe.PST-L.3MS
On the third day he went and had a ritual bath

(52) ויתילה לגו חכמים ואגזרו
u-yṯe-le l-go ḥaḵamim u-gzər-∅-ru
and-come.PST-L.3MS to-in sages^{H} and circumcise.PST-D.3MS-L.3PL
and he came to the sages and they circumcised him.

(53) בתר האדך הקב״ה אנעמלה אליה
baṯər hadax h(a)q(-qadoš) b(arux) h(u) ʔənʕəm-le ʔəll-e
after thus DEF-holy^{H} blessed^{H} 3MS^{H} bestow.PST-L.3MS upon-POSS.3MS
after that, the Holy One, blessed be He, bestowed upon him

(54) מנד רוח הקדש דידה
mənn-əd ruaḥ haq-qodeš did-e
from-COMP spirit^{H} DEF-holy^{H} GEN-POSS.3MS
from His Holy Spirit

(55) ומפצ׳ליה אילה אנואר נבווה עצ׳ים
u-mufẓəl-le ʔəll-e ʔanwār nəbuw-e ʕẓīm
and-confer.PST-L.3MS on-POSS.3MS lights prophecy-PL great
and conferred on him illuminations of the great prophecy,

(56) הלד פשלה תאג׳ אלד כולו חכמי ישראל
hall-əd pəš-le tāj ʔəll-əd kull-u ḥaḵme yiśraʔel
until-COMP become.PST-L.3MS crown to-COMP all-POSS.3PL sage.PL.CS^{H} Israel
until he became the crown of all the sages of Israel.

(57) וכולא אד תורה מנד בראשית ברא
u-kull-a aḏ tora mənn-əd bə-rešiṯ bara
and-all-POSS.3FS this Torah^{H}from-COMP in-beginning create.PRF.3MS^{H}
And all the Torah from ‘God created’ (Gen 1.1)

(58) והל ה׳ אלקיו עמו ויעל אדרילה תרגום אילא
u-hal YHWH ʔeloqaw ʕimm-o wə-yaʕal ʔədre-le targūm ʔəll-a
and until the.Lord[H] God.PL.3MS[H] with-3MS[H] and.go.up.JUSS.3MS[H] put.PST-L.3MS translation on-3FS
until 'The Lord your God be with him and let him go up' (2 Chron 36.23) he put into translation.

(59) כו תניתא אעציתא וכפיתא דאתוא אבד תורה
ku taneṯa ʔəʕṣiṯa u-xpiṯa d-iṯ-wa ʔəbb-əd tora
every word difficult and-covered REL-EXIST-AUX.PST in-COMP Torah[H]
every difficult and obscure word that was in the Torah

(60) אצ׳היראלה ומתופסראלה טלא חכמים
ʔəẓhir-a-le u-mtufsər-a-le ṭla ḥaḵamim
illuminated.PST-D.3FS-L.3MS and-explain.PST-D.3FS-L.3MS to sage.PL[H]
he illuminated and explained to the sages.

(61) ודריאלה שינא גאויהון
u-dəry-a-le šena gaw-ehun
and-put.PST-D.3FS-L.3MS peace in-POSS.3PL
Thus he established peace among them

(62) מנד מאד נאציוא אלד תפסיר דידא
mənn-əd ma-d naṣ-e-wa ʔəll-əd tafsīr did-a
from.COMP what-COMP argue.IMPV-D.3PL-AUX.PST on-COMP interpretation GEN-POSS.3FS
for they used to argue about its interpretation

(63) אילאהא מרזק טלא כולו ישראל האדך
ʔilaha marzəq-∅ ṭla kull-u yiśraʔel hadax
God grant.IRR-D.3MS to all-POSS.3PL Israel[H] thus
May God grant the same to all Israel.

5.2 Jewish Urmi dialect

An acute accent (v́) marks non-nuclear stress. A grave accent (v̀) marks the nuclear stress of an intonation group. A vertical line (ˡ) marks an intonation group boundary.

The Bird who Boasted (Khan 2008a: 404)

(1) *xa-yomá Šlómo ha-mélex ytíw-∅-wa ⁺g-otaġ-èwˡ panjaràˡ*
one-day Solomon DEF-king[H] sit.PRF-D.3MS-AUX.PST in-room-POSS.3MS window
One day King Solomon was sitting in his room and at the window

⁺támaša wadà=we-leˡ batè,ˡ ilanè.ˡ mər-eˡ
watch make.PROG=COP.PST-L.3MS houses trees say.PST-L.3MS
he was watching houses and trees. He said:

xzé-li tre-quš-é gal-⁺dəġde màqul=u.ˡ
see.PST-L.1S two-bird-PL with-each.other speak.PROG=COP.3PL
I saw two birds speaking with each other.

(2) *qúš gorá ba-qúš baxtá mar=è*| *k-y-át-ma baxtà,*|
bird man to-bird woman say.PROG=COP.3MS IND-know.IPFV-D.3FS-what wife
The male bird said to the female bird 'You know what wife,

ya-Šlómo ha-mélex xá-jur jəgr-í madù=le-le.|
this-Solomon DEF-king^{H} one-type anger-POSS.1S bring.PROG=COP.3MS-L.3MS
this King Solomon makes me so angry.

abúl=en ez-én xa-dánka tapúg dah-èn|
want.PROG=COP.1MS go.IRR-D.1MS one-unit kick hit.IRR-D.1SG
I want to go and kick

əl-d-áy $^{+}$*amart-èw,*| *ki-axčà jwằn=ila,*| *maprx-ən-na b-šə́mm-e.*|
OBJ-OBL-DEM palace-POSS.3MS REL-so beautiful=COP.3FS cause.fly.IRR-D.1SG-L.3FS in-sky-PL
his palace, which is so beautiful, and make it fly into the sky'.

(3) *qúš ki-baxtà=ila már=a*| $^{+}$*janəm*| *mà šula-t-tóx mənn-éw?*|
bird who-wife=COP.3FS say.PROG=COP.3FS my.dear^{Turk} what business-EXIST-L.2MS from-POSS.3MS?
The bird who was the wife said 'My dear, what business do you have with him?

Šlómo ha-mélex mà wid=é?| *awùn=ile*| *šúq-le yatə́w-∅*
Solomon the-king^{H} what do.PTCP=COP.3MS sin=COP.3MS leave.IMP.SG-L3MS sit.IRR-D.3MS
What has King Solomon done? It is a shame (to behave in this way), leave him

b-$^{+}$*yān-nòš-ew.*| *mà šula-t-tóx mənn-éw?*|
in-side-self-POSS.3MS what business-EXIST-L.2MS from-POSS.3MS
in peace. What business do you have with him?

bod-má dəmmà mandu=lét?| *bára doq-ì-lox,*| *bára*
for-what blood throw.PROG=COP.2MS afterwards catch.IRR-D.3PL-L.2MS afterwards
Why are you being provocative. They will arrest you afterwards,

$^{+}$*qatl-ì-lox.*|
kill.IRR-D.3PL-L.2MS
then kill you.'

(4) *là,*| *ána b-ez-én àtta šúla od-ə́n-ne.*|
no I FUT-go.IRR-D.1MS now job do.IRR-D.1MS-L.3MS
'No, I shall go and do this job right now.'

Šlómo ha-mélex əl-qűš $^{+}$*sarox=ə̀l-le.*| *mára áġa qùš,*| *mar-xaz-èn.*|
Solomon DEF-king^{H} to-bird shout.PROG=COP.3MS-L.3MS say.PROG Mr bird let-see.IRR-D.1MS
King Solomon shouted to the bird. He said 'Mr bird, let me see.

*āt-kull-óx xa-⁺čangè=let*ˈ *gal-xá* *⁺sbot-í* *⁺məss-én* *əll-ox* *⁺qatl-én.*ˈ
you-all-POSS.2MS one-handful=COP.2MS with-one finger-1S can.PRS-D.1MS OBJ-2MS kill.IRR-D.1MS
You in total are (no more than) a single handful. I can kill you with a single finger of mine.

*ắt mà-jur ⁺məss-éta ⁺əl-amart-í gal-xá-danka tapùk*ˈ
you what-way can.IRR-D.2MS OBJ-palace-POSS.1S with-one-single kick
How could you with a single kick

*mapərx-ə́t-ta b-šə̀mm-e?*ˈ
cause.fly.IRR-D.2MS-L.3FS in-sky-PL
make my palace fly in the air ?'

(5) *mar=è*ˈ *⁺qurbàn-ew xdə́r-ri,*ˈ *ắt mà šulá-t-tox?*ˈ
say.PROG=COP.3MS sacrifice-POSS.3MS become.PST-L.1S you what business-EXIST-L.2MS
He said 'With respect, what has this to do with you?

*ắt bod-má b-šúl-i yarrow=èt?*ˈ
you for-what in-business-POSS.1S enter.PROG=COP.2MS
Why do you interfere with my affairs?

*ắt bod-mà b-šúl-ət góra baxtá yarrow=èt?*ˈ
you for-what in-business-COMP husband wife enter.PROG=COP.2MS
Why are you interfering with the affairs of a husband and wife?

*kúd gorá geb-báxta nóš-ew paqè-∅-la.*ˈ
every husband with-wife self-POSS.3MS inflate.PRS-D.3MS-L.3FS
Every husband boasts to his wife.

*ána geb-báxt-i nóš-i pəqy-à-li.*ˈ *ắt ba-ma-yà maq-ét?*ˈ
I with-wife-POSS.1S self-POSS.1SG inflate.PST-D.3FS-L.1S you for-what-this speak.IRR-D.2MS
I boasted to my wife. Why should you say such a thing?'

(6) *Šlómo ha-mélex ⁺rába xoš-èw idáy=le mən-d-áy măsălà.*ˈ
Solomon DEF-king^{H} much happiness-POSS.3MS come.PROG=COP.3MS from-COMP-this story
King Solomon was very amused with this story.

*már=e sí-lox xà-i,*ˈ *kéf-ox wùd-la!*ˈ
say.PROG=COP.3MS go-L.2MS life-POSS.1SG amusement-POSS.2MS do.IMP-L.3FS
He said 'My dear, enjoy yourself!

*attá fkə́r-ri ắt ma-mar=èt.*ˈ
now understand.PST-L.1S you what-say.PROG=COP.2MS
Now I have understood what you are saying.'

5.3 Jewish Sanandaj dialect

An acute accent (v́) marks non-nuclear stress. A grave accent (v̀) marks the nuclear stress of an intonation group. A vertical line (|) marks an intonation group boundary. Non-standard glosses: EZ = *ezafe* (Iranian attributive complementation marker), PVP = post-verbal particle

Winter (Khan 2009: 430)

(1) *ʔăwăḷán tʷkáne là ʔasr-í-wa.| naš-é g-ez-í-wa wárya*
first shops NEG close.IPFV-D.3PL-AUX.PST people-PL IND-go.IPFV-D.3PL-AUX.PST outside
First of all, they did not close shops. People would go outside

ba-talgà-č.| xor-tʷkan-é là ʔasr-í-wa-lu.| wa-ba-ʕălawà-č|
in-snow-also indeed-shop-PL NEG close.IPFV-D.3PL-AUX.PST-L.PL and-in-addition-also
even in the snow. Indeed they did not close the shops. In addition,

rásm ga-dokà-ye-le| măsălán ga-ʔaxər-e páyiz qárwa sətwà|
custom in-there-COP.PST-L.3MS for.example at-end-EZ autumn close (to) winter
there was a custom there, for example at the end of autumn just before winter

hár xanăwadé ta-nòš-ef,| hár məšpaḥá ta-nòš-ef,| g-ezə̀l-∅-wa|
each family for-self-POSS.3MS each family^{H} for-self-POSS.3MS IND-go.IPFV-D.3MS-AUX.PST
each family, each family went in their turn

xa-dána tórta šăqə̀l-∅-wa-la.|
one-single cow buy.IPFV-D.3MS-AUX.PST-L.3FS
and bought a cow.

k-m-e-wa-l-ó ga-béla nòš-ef.|
IND-bring.IPFV-D.3MS-AUX.PST-L.3FS-PVP in-house self-POSS.3MS
They would bring it back to their home.

(2) *ráb-an k-é-∅-wa dăbəḥ-∅-wa-l-ó baq-èf.|*
rabbi-POSS.1PL IND-come.IPFV-D.3MS-AUX.PST slaughter.IPFV-D.3MS-AUX.PST-L.3FS-PVP for-POSS.3MS
Our rabbi would come and slaughter it for them.
tămíz k-òl-∅-wa-la.| xăé-∅-wa ṭărefà lá-hawy-a,|
clean IND-do.IPFV-D.3MS-AUX.PST-L.3FS see.IPFV-D.3MS-AUX.PST unclean NEG-be.IRR-D.3FS
He cleaned it. He checked lest it be ritually unclean,

xărằb lá-hawy-a.| ʔo-waxtắra qăšàng| ʔo-năqolé-u măqolè-u|
polluted NEG-be.IRR-D.3FS that-time beautiful DEM-unclean-and unclean-and
lest it be polluted. Then he carefully took out what had to be removed,

ʔonyexáe yá gdidìm=yen| xărằb=yen,|
those REL sinews^{H}=COP.3PL polluted=COP.3PL
those parts that were sinews and were polluted,

lá k-əxl-i-lù| *doq-∅-wa-lú-u* *šoḷət-∅-wa-lù.*|
NEG IND-eat.IPFV-D.3PL-L.3PL seize.IPFV-D.3MS-AUX.PST-L.3PL-and throw-D.3MS-AUX.PST-L.3PL
which they did not eat, and threw them away.

(3) *pəsr-ăké k-wə́l-∅-wa-le ba-ʔilá máre bel-ăkè.*|
meat-DEF IND-give.IPFV-D.3MS-AUX.PST-L.3MS in-hand master house-DET
He then gave the meat to the head of the household.

máre bel-ăké mən-d-áy pəsrà| *mătú-∅-wa-le ga-tănurá*
master house-DET from-OBL-that meat put.IPFV-D.3MS-AUX.PST-L.3MS in-oven
The head of the household put out some of this meat and cooked it in an oven.

băšə́l-Ø-wa-le.| *k-əmr-í-wa-le qawurmà.*|
cook.IPFV-D.3MS-AUX.PST-L.3MS IND-say.IPFV-D.3PL-AUX.PST-L.3MS preserved.meat
They called this *qawurma*.

năt-èn-wa-le| *ga-tʷká qărirá măt-ì-wa-le.*|
take.IPFV-D.3PL-AUX.PST-L.3MS in-place cool place.IPFV-D.3PL-AUX.PST-L.3MS
They took it and placed it in a cool place.

yaxčā̆l lìt-wa-lan xor-ʔo-waxtărá.|
fridge NEG.EXIST-AUX.PST-L.1PL still-that-time
We still did not have a fridge at that time.

măt-í-wa-le ga-xá-tʷka qărirà hăwé-∅| *péš-∅ ta-sətwà.*|
place.IPFV-D.3PL-AUX.PST-L.3MS in-one-place cool be.IRR-D.3MS stay.IRR-D.3MS for-winter
They put it in a place that was cool for it to remain until winter.

(4)*ʔáy qawurmá ʔăxà-ye-le*| *galgl-í-wa-le*
this preserved.meat thus-be.PST-L.3MS stir.IPFV-D.3PL-AUX.PST-L.3MS
This *qawurma* was like this, they would stir it round

ga-pliyáw məšxá nòš-ef,| *məšxá tort-ăkè,*| *lá məšxà,*| *denulà.*|
in-middle oil self-POSS.3MS oil cow-DET NEG oil fat
in its own oil, the oil of the cow. Not oil, fat,
ga-denulá nóš-af bašl-í-wa-la qăšàng.| *măt-í-wa-le*
in-fat self-POSS.3FS cook.IPFV-D.3PL-AUX.PST-L.3FS well put.IPFV-D.3PL-AUX.PST-L.3MS
they cooked it well in its own fat. They put it

ga-xá ... ʔó waxtắra qoq-è hit-wa.| *qoq-é xa-zárf,*
in-one that time pot-PL EXIST-AUX.PST pot-PL one-container
in a – at that time there were pots. Pots were a container,

zrúf-ek-yelu mə́n ʔápr-e smoqà.|
containers-INDF-be.PST-L.3PL from clay-EZ red
containers made of red clay

ʔənyexáe măt-í-wa-lu ga-sətwà.|
they place.IPFV-D.3PL-AUX.PST-L.3PL in-winter
They would serve this in winter.

mən-d-óa rába ʔəstəfáda k-ol-ì-wa.|
from-OBL-that much advantage IND-do.IPFV-D.3PL-AUX.PST
They made good use of this.

References

Aloni, Oz. 2014. *The Neo-Aramaic Speaking Jewish Community of Zakho: A Survey of the Oral Culture*. Saarbrücken: Lap Lambert.

Barotto, Alessandra. 2015. "Split Ergativity in the NENA Dialects." In *Neo-Aramaic and Its Linguistic Context*, edited by Geoffrey Khan and Lidia Napiorkowska, 232–249. Piscataway, NJ: Gorgias Press.

Ben-Yaʕqov, Avraham. 1980. *קהילות יהודי כורדסתאן*. Vol. 2. Jerusalem: Kiryat Sepher.

Brauer, Erich, and Raphael Patai. 1993. *The Jews of Kurdistan*. Jewish Folklore and Anthropology Series. Detroit: Wayne State University Press.

Coghill, Eleanor. 2016. *The Rise and Fall of Ergativity in Aramaic: Cycles of Alignment Change*. Oxford Studies in Diachronic and Historical Linguistics 21. Oxford: Oxford University Press.

Cohen, Eran. 2012. *The Syntax of Neo-Aramaic: The Jewish Dialect of Zakho*. Neo-Aramaic Studies. Piscataway: Gorgias Press.

Doron, Edit, and Geoffrey Khan. 2012. "The Typology of Morphological Ergativity in Neo-Aramaic." *Lingua* 122: 225–240.

Duval, Rubens. 1883. *Les dialectes néo-araméens de Salamâs: Textes sur l'état actuel de la Perse et contes populaires publiés avec une traduction française*. Paris: F. Vieweg.

Fassberg, Steven Ellis. 2010. *The Jewish Neo-Aramaic Dialect of Challa*. Studies in Semitic Languages and Linguistics 54. Leiden: Brill.

Fox, Samuel E. 2008. "North-Eastern Neo-Aramaic and the Middle Aramaic Dialects." In *Neo-Aramaic Dialect Studies*, edited by Geoffrey Khan, 1–18. Piscataway, NJ: Gorgias Press.

—. 2009. *The Neo-Aramaic Dialect of Bohtan*. Piscataway: Gorgias.

Garbell, Irene. 1965a. *The Jewish Neo-Aramaic Dialect of Persian Azerbaijan: Linguistic Analysis and Folkloristic Texts*. Janua Linguarum, Series Practica. The Hague: Mouton.

—. 1965b. "The Impact of Kurdish and Turkish on the Jewish Neo-Aramaic Dialect of Persian Azerbaijan and the Adjoining Regions." *Journal of the American Oriental Society* 85 (2): 159–77.

Goldenberg, Gideon. 2000. "Early Neo-Aramaic and Present-Day Dialectal Diversity." *Journal of Semitic Studies* 45 (1): 69–89.

Greenblatt, Jared R. 2011. *The Jewish Neo-Aramaic Dialect of Amadiya*. Studies in Semitic Languages and Linguistics 61. Leiden: Brill.

Haig, Geoffrey. 2004. *Alignment in Kurdish: A Diachronic Perspective. Habilitationsschrift*. Kiel: Christian-Albrechts-Universität zu Kiel.

Hoberman, Robert. 1988. "The History of the Modern Aramaic Pronouns and Pronominal Suffixes." *Journal of the American Oriental Society* 108: 557–75.

Hopkins, Simon. 1989. "Neo-Aramaic Dialects and the Formation of the Preterite." *Journal of Semitic Studies* 37: 74–90.

Jastrow, Otto. 1988. *Der neuaramäische Dialekt von Hertevin (Provinz Siirt)*. Semitica Viva 3. Wiesbaden: O. Harrassowitz.

—. 1990. *Der arabische Dialekt der Juden von ʿAqra und Arbīl*. Semitica Viva 5. Wiesbaden: Harrassowitz.

Kahn, Margaret. 1976. "Borrowing and Variation in a Phonological Description of Kurdish." Ph.D. Thesis, Michigan: University of Michigan.

Kapeliuk, Olga. 1997. "Spirantized *d* and *t* in Neo-Aramaic." *Massorot* 9–10–11: 527–544 (in Hebrew).

Khan, Geoffrey. 1999. *A Grammar of Neo-Aramaic: The Dialect of the Jews of Arbel*. Boston, MA: Brill Academic Publishers.

—. 2002. *The Neo-Aramaic Dialect of Qaraqosh*. Studies in Semitic Languages and Linguistics 36. Boston, MA: Brill.

—. 2004a. "Aramaic and the Impact of Languages in Contact with it through the Ages." In *Lenguas En Contacto: El Testimonio Escrito*, edited by Pedro Bádenas de la Peña, Sofía Torallas Tovar, Eugenio R. Luján, and María Ángeles Gallego, 87–108. Manuales y Anejos de "Emerita" 46. Madrid: Consejo Superior de Investigaciones Científicas.

—. 2004b. *The Jewish Neo-Aramaic Dialect of Sulemaniyya and Ḥalabja*. Studies in Semitic Languages and Linguistics 44. Leiden: Brill.

—. 2007a. "North Eastern Neo-Aramaic." In *Grammatical Borrowing in Cross-Linguistic Perspective*, edited by Yaron Matras and Jeanette Sakel, 197–214. Berlin: Mouton de Gruyter.

—. 2007b. "The North-Eastern Neo-Aramaic Dialects." *Journal of Semitic Studies* 52 (1): 1–20.

—. 2008a. *The Jewish Neo-Aramaic Dialect of Urmi*. Gorgias Neo-Aramaic Studies. Piscataway: Gorgias.

—. 2008b. *The Neo-Aramaic Dialect of Barwar*. Leiden: Brill.

—. 2009. *The Jewish Neo-Aramaic Dialect of Sanandaj*. Piscataway, NJ: Gorgias Press.

—. 2013. "Phonological Emphasis in North-Eastern Neo-Aramaic." In *Base Articulatoire Arrière. Backing and Backness*, edited by Jean Léo Léonard and Samia Naïm, 111–132. Munich: Lincon Europa.

—. 2017. "Ergativity in Neo-Aramaic." In *Oxford Handbook of Ergativity*, edited by Jessica Coon, Diane Massam, and Lisa Travis, 873–99. Oxford: Oxford University Press.

Krotkoff, Georg. 1985. "Studies in Neo-Aramaic Lexicology." In *Biblical and Related Studies Presented to Samuel Iwry*, edited by Ann Kort and Scott Morschauer, 123–134. Winona Lake: Eisenbrauns.

Maclean, Arthur John. 1895. *Grammar of the Dialects of Vernacular Syriac as Spoken by the Eastern Syrians of Kurdistan, North-West Persia, and the Plain of Mosul, with Notices of the Vernacular of the Jews of Azerbaijan and Zakhu Near Mosul*. Cambridge: Cambridge University Press.

Mann, Jacob. 1931. *Texts and Studies in Jewish History and Literature*. The Abraham and Hannah Oppenheim Memorial Publications. Cincinnati: Hebrew Union College Press.

Matras, Yaron, and Jeanette Sakel. 2007. "Investigating the Mechanisms of Pattern Replication in Language Convergence." *Studies in Language* 31 (4): 829–865.

Mutzafi, Hezy. 2002a. "Barzani Jewish Neo-Aramaic and its Dialects." *Mediterranean Language Review* 14: 41–70.

—. 2002b. "On the Jewish Neo-Aramaic Dialect of Aradhin and its Dialectal Affinities." In *Sprich doch mit deinen Knechten Aramäisch, Wir verstehen es!" 60 Beiträge zur Semitistik, Festschrift für Otto Jastrow zum 60. Geburtstag*, edited by Werner Arnold, 479–488. Wiesbaden: Harrassowitz.

—. 2004a. *The Jewish Neo-Aramaic Dialect of Koy Sanjaq (Iraqi Kurdistan)*. Semitica Viva 32. Wiesbaden: Harrassowitz Verlag.

—. 2004b. "Two Texts in Barzani Jewish Neo-Aramaic." *Bulletin of the School of Oriental and African Studies, University of London* 67 (1): 1–13.

—. 2005. "Etymological Notes on North-Eastern Neo-Aramaic." *Aramaic Studies* 3 (1): 83–107.

—. 2008a. *The Jewish Neo-Aramaic Dialect of Betanure (Province of Dihok)*. Semitica Viva 43. Wiesbaden: Harrassowitz.

—. 2008b. "Trans-Zab Jewish Neo-Aramaic." *Bulletin of the School of Oriental and African Studies* 71 (3): 409–431.

—. 2014. "Jewish Neo-Aramaic." *Encyclopedia of the Jews of the Islamic World*. Brill.

—. 2015. “Christian Salamas and Jewish Salmas: Two Separate Types of Neo-Aramaic.” In *Neo-Aramaic and Its Linguistic Context*, edited by Geoffrey Khan and Lidia Napiorkowska, 289–304. Piscataway, NJ: Gorgias Press.

Rees, Margo. 2008. *Lishan Didan, Targum Didan: Translation Language in a Neo-Aramaic Targum Tradition*. Piscataway, NJ: Gorgias Press.

Rivlin, Joseph Joel. 1959. *Shirat Yehude Ha-Targum*. Jerusalem: Bialik Institute.

Sabar, Ariel. 2009. *My Father's Paradise: A Son's Search for His Family's Past*. 1 edition. Algonquin Books.

Sabar, Yona. 1976. *Pəšaṭ Wayəhî BəŠallaḥ. A Neo-Aramaic Midrash on Beshallaḥ (Exodus). Introduction, Phonetic Transcription, Translation, Notes and Glossary*. Wiesbaden: Harrassowitz.

—. 1982. *The Folk Literature of the Kurdistani Jews: An Anthology*. Yale Judaica Series 23. New Haven: Yale University Press.

—. 1983. *Sefer Bereshit ba-ʔAramit Ḥadashah be-Nivam shel Yehude Zakho: we-nosfu ʕalaw Ṭeqsṭim be-Nivim ʔaḥarim shel ʔAramit Ḥadashah u-Millonim*. ʕEdah we-Lashon 9. Jerusalem: Magnes Press, Hebrew University.

—. 1985. *Midrashim ba-ʔAramit Yehude Kurdisṭan le-Parashiyot Wayḥi, Beshallaḥ, Yitro*. Jerusalem: Israel Academy of Science and Humanities.

—. 1988. *Sefer Shemot ba-ʔAramit Ḥadashah be-Nivam shel Yehude Zakho: we-nosfu ʕalaw Ṭeqsṭim be-Nivim ʔaḥerim shel ʔAramit Ḥadashah u-Millon*. ʕEdah we-Lashon 12. Jerusalem: Hebrew University Magnes Press.

—. 1991a. *Sefer Wa-yyiqraʔ be-ʔAramit Ḥadashah be-Nivam shel Yehude Zakho: we-nosfu ʕalaw Ṭeqsṭim be-Nivim ʔaḥerim shel ʔAramit Ḥadashah u-Millon*. ʕEdah we-Lashon 15. Jerusalem: Hebrew University Magnes Press.

—. 1991b. *Targum de-Targum: An Old Neo-Aramaic Version of the Targum on Song of Songs*. Wiesbaden: Harrassowitz.

—. 1994. *Sefer Devarim ba-ʔAramit Ḥadashah be-Nivam shel Yehude Zakho: we-nosfu ʕalaw Ṭeqsṭim be-Nivim ʔaḥerim shel ʔAramit Ḥadashah u-Millon*. ʕEdah we-Lashon 18. Jerusalem: Hebrew Univer-sity Magnes Press.

—. 2002. *Jewish Neo-Aramaic Dictionary*. Semitica Viva 28. Wiesbaden: Harrassowitz.

—. 2013. “Kurdistan, Pronunciation Tradition.” *Encyclopedia of Hebrew Language and Linguistics*. Leiden-Boston: Brill.

Soane, Ely Bannister. 1912. *To Mesopotamia and Kurdistan in Disguise; with Historical Notices of the Kurdish Tribes and the Chaldeans of Kurdistan*. London: J. Murray.

Socin, Albert. 1882. *Die neu-aramäischen Dialekte von Urmia bis Mosul*. Tübingen: H. Laupp.

Stoddard, David Tappan. 1860. *Grammar of the Modern Syriac Language, as Spoken in Oroomiah, Persia, and in Koordistan*. New Haven: Printed for the American Oriental Society by B.L. Hamlen; sold by B. Westermann.

Classical Judeo-Arabic[1]

Lutz Edzard, University of Erlangen-Nürnberg

1. Introduction

Well into the pre-Islamic period, there has been a Jewish presence in the core area of the Arab world, the Arabian peninsula. Bernard Lewis (2014: 67), following Shlomo Dov Goitein, estimates that from the 9th century on, about one percent on average of the population in the Arab lands was Jewish, with a higher percentage in the urban centers. Without romanticizing in any way, Jewish scholarship tends to agree that broadly speaking, the situation of the Jews in the Islamic world was the lesser evil as compared to the situation of the Jews in the Christian world. In his most recommendable book, *A Short History of the Jewish People*, the rabbi and scholar of medieval Arabic and Hebrew poetry, Raymond P. Scheindlin, has pointed out that the relations between Jews and Muslims throughout the ages at times compared favorably to the relations between Jews and Christians. Scheindlin certainly does not block out historical events such as the massacre of the Jewish population of the tribe of the Banū Qurayẓa committed by Muḥammad ibn ʕAbdallāh in the year 627 A.D., the massacre against Jews at the hands of Muslim militants in the oasis Xaybar in the year 628 A.D., or the massacre of Jews in the city of Granada in the year 1066 A.D., where about 1500 Jews lost their life. Rather, he views such events as statistically exceptional in the Jewish-Islamic history, a view shared also by Bernard Lewis. Overall, the situation of the Jews as *ḏimmīs* was safer throughout the centuries as compared to the situation in Christian surroundings, as both authors stress. Many contributions in the volume edited by Abdelwahab Meddeb and Benjamin Stora, *Histoire des relations entre juifs et musulmans des origines à nos jours* (Paris, 2013) follow this line of thought.

In any event, there is no doubt that Jewish-Hebrew and Muslim-Arabic culture fruitfully influenced each other. As already stated by Abraham Geiger in his famous Ph.D. dissertation of 1833, *Was hat Mohammed aus dem Judenthume aufgenommen,* the founder of religion Muḥammad ibn ʕAbdallāh was considerably inspired by Jewish sources during his composition of the Qurʔān. A well-known example is the story of Joseph in Genesis, chapters 37ff., which is partially reflected in sūra 12, *Sūrat Yūsuf*, a sūra with relatively high internal consistency. Conversely, Jewish authors also integrated features of their Arabic surroundings, e.g., the setting of poetry in hemistichs, as was the custom in metrically structured Arabic poetry. The Jewish poet Moses Darʕī, who lived and worked in 11th century Cairo, was among those who applied the formal characteristics of Arabic poetry to Hebrew poetry. Hence, we can witness the metrical and optical division into hemistichs. Here is an example, in which Darʕī states in Judeo-Arabic that he translated two Arabic verses into Hebrew (cf. Yeshaya 2010: 71):

1 This chapter is dedicated to the memory of Professor Joshua Blau (1919–2020), ז"ל.

ממא קלתה איצ׳א פי נקל ביתין

mim-mā *qultu-hū* *ʔayḍan* *fī* *naqli* *baytayni*
from-what.REL say.PF.1SG-3SG.M also in transmission.CS.GEN verse.DU.GEN
What I also said by translating

ערביה אלי אללגה אלעבראניה

ʕarabīyati *ʔilā* *l-luġati* *l-ʕibrīyati*
Arabic.SG.F into DEF-language.GEN DEF-Hebrew.SG.F.GEN
two Arabic verses into the Hebrew language.

רוֹעֶה חֲכָמִים בֶּאֱמֶת יֶחְכָּם וּמִי /

rōʕē *ḥăḵ̊āmīm* *bɛ-ʔĕmɛṯ* *yɛḥk̊ām* *ū-mī*
herd.PTCP.SG.M wise.M.PL in-truth be_wise.IPFV.3SG.M and-who.REL
He who keeps company with wise men will surely be wise (cf. Prov 13:20), but he who

יָגוּר אֱוִילִים לֹא יְחִי מִתְנַשֵּׂא

yā̊gūr *ʔɛ̆wīlīm* *lō(ʔ)* *yĕḥī* *miṯnaśśēm*
dwell.IPFV.3SG.M fool.PL NEG live.JUSS.3SG.M be_elevated.PTCP.SG.M
dwells with fools will not be exalted;

הָעוֹר בְּגוּרוֹ לַסְּפָרִים אַחֲרֵי /

hā̊-ʔōr *bə-gūr-ō* *las-sĕp̄ā̊rīm* *ʔaḥărē*
DEF-leather in-dwell.INF-3SG.M for.DEF-book.PL after
[Like] leather which, when being lodged in books, after

נִבְאַשׁ בְּפֶה נוּשַּׁק וְרָם עַל כִּסֵּא

niḇʔaš *bĕ-p̄ɛ* *nuššaq* *wĕ-rā̊m* *ʕal* *kissē(ʔ)*
stink.PASS.PF.3SG.M with-mouth kiss.PASS.PF.3SG.M and-high on throne
having been odious [due to its stench] will be kissed by a mouth and high on a throne.

Classical Judeo-Arabic can be defined as the literary Arabic language used by Jews in the Arabic diaspora, as opposed to historical and modern Judeo-Arabic vernaculars, the latter of which still have vestiges in present-day Israel. In this context, at least three factors serve as the main arguments for the use of the prefix "Judeo-": Jewish authorship of a text in question, the use of the Hebrew script, and lexical elements specific to the respective Jewish communities. Grammatical features also play a role, but those are not necessarily specific to Jewish communities (at least with respect to the "classical" language register), but may occur in Christian and Muslim "Middle-Arabic" texts as well. The documents subsumed here under the category "classical" testify to all of these criteria, except for a lexicographical entry and a Geniza letter, both written in Arabic script, with only Hebrew words and quotations appearing in Hebrew script. "Literary language" here refers to a register close to Classical/StandardArabic, having in mind that a majority of Judeo-Arabic texts reflect local or communal dialects (see the following chapters). But even in "classical" texts one finds a number of features that have been coined "Middle Arabic" or belonging to the range of the *luġa al-wusṭā*. Still, the term "classical" is understood in this chapter primarily as relating to a relatively high register, rather than to a temporal period. This chapter does not provide a full-fledged grammatical sketch of Classical Arabic. Rather, relevant dialectal or communal features will be presented in contrast to the standard language in the respective chapters on specific Judeo-Arabic varieties.

2. Grammatical features

2.1 Orthography and phonology

Grosso modo, the use of the Hebrew script poses no major problem for the representation of Arabic. The slightly smaller phoneme (or rather: grapheme) inventory of Hebrew necessitates the use of diacritical marks for the rendering of ث *ṯāʔ*, ج *ğīm*, خ *xāʔ*, ذ *ḏāl*, ض *ḍād*, and ظ *ẓāʔ*. What is more, <א> represents both *hamza* (ء) and long *ā* (ا). The spirantized allophones of Hebrew /k/ and /g/, in Judeo-Arabic script <כ'> and <ג>, represent the Arabic phonemes /x/ (/ẖ/) and /ġ/, respectively. There is no way to graphically express *hamza* chairs, so <יוד̈י> and <ביר> represent Classical Arabic يُـــؤَدّي *yuʔaddī* 'leads to' and بِئر *biʔr* 'well', respectively.

Arabic letter		repr. in Hebrew script		phonemic	phonetic
sign	name	sign	name	value (trans.)	value
ا/ء	*ʔalif*	א	*ʔā́lep̄*	/ʔ/	[ʔ]
ب	*bāʔ*	ב	*bēṯ*	/b/	[b]
ت	*tāʔ*	ת	*tāw*	/t/	[t]
ث	*ṯāʔ*	ת'	–	/ṯ/	[θ]
ج	*ğīm*	ג'	*gīmel*	/ğ/	[ʤ, g]
ح	*ḥāʔ*	ח	*ḥēṯ*	/ḥ/	[ħ]
خ	*xāʔ*	כ'	–	/x, ẖ/	[x]
د	*dāl*	ד	*dā́leṯ*	/d/	[d]
ذ	*ḏāl*	ד'	–	/ḏ/	[ð]
ر	*rāʔ*	ר	*rēš*	/r/	[r]
ز	*záyin*	ז	*zāy*	/z/	[z]
س	*sīn*	ס	*sā́meḵ*	/s/	[s]
ش	*šīn*	ש	*šīn*	/š/	[ʃ]
ص	*ṣād*	צ	*ṣāḏē(h)*	/ṣ/	[s]
ض	*ḍād*	צ'	–	/ḍ/	[ɗ]
ط	*ṭāʔ*	ט	*ṭēṯ*	/ṭ/	[ŧ]
ظ	*ẓāʔ*	ט'	–	/ẓ/	[ƶ]
ع	*ʕayn*	ע	*ʕáyin*	/ʕ/	[ʕ]
غ	*ġayn*	ג	–	/ġ/	[ɣ]
ف	*fāʔ*	פ	*pē(h)*	/f/	[f]
ق	*qāf*	ק	*qōp̄*	/q/	[q]
ك	*kāf*	כ	*kap̄*	/k/	[k]
ل	*lām*	ל	*lā́meḏ*	/l/	[l]
م	*mīm*	מ	*mēm*	/m/	[m]
ن	*nūn*	נ	*nūn*	/n/	[n]
ه	*hāʔ*	ה	*hē(ʔ)*	/h/	[h]
و	*wāw*	ו	*wāw*	/w/	[w]
ي	*yāʔ*	י	*yōḏ*	/y/	[j]

While this transcription table represents the dominant status quo in Classical Judeo-Arabic texts, earlier texts dating from the eighth and ninth centuries CE exhibit features as the following: more irregular (presumably phonetic) use of *scriptio plena* and *scriptio defectiva*, lacking representation of pharyngealized consonants (e.g., *dāl* instead of *ḍād*), representation of the assimilation the *lām* of the definite article before the *ḥurūf aš-šamsīya*, and representation of a strong *ʔimāla* by a *yōḏ*, rather than by an *ʔā́lep̄* (cf. Blau and Hopkins 1984; Khan 2007: 527; Khan 2016: 25f.). In contrast, Classical Judeo-Arabic is more oriented at the Classical Arabic orthography. Typical traits include the representation of *ʔalif maqṣūra* by a *yōḏ*, the ubiquitous spelling of the *lām* of the definite article, and the ubiquitous use of the feminine ending *hē(ʔ)*, also in cases, where the Arabic morpho-syntax requires a *tāʔ marbūṭa* (in contrast to the orthography of the Hebrew annexation, where the *hē(ʔ)* changes to a *tāw*) (cf. Khan 2007: 527f.; 2016: 26). Later versions of classicizing Judeo-Arabic again resort to a more unpredictable rendition of short and long vowels, as well as of an erratic representation of the geminated glides *wāw* and *yōḏ*. In later Classical Judeo-Arabic texts, the definite article is often spelled as a separate word (cf. Khan 2007: 528; 2016: 28, 30).

Generally speaking, the unvoweled Hebrew script can, but need not necessarily reveal dialectal features. However, extant manuscripts in the Cairo Geniza exhibit Hebrew voweling marks that reflect the absence of case- and mood-marking final vowels (*šəwā* underneath the final consonant) and a certain degree of vowel harmony.

2.2 Morphology

The morphology of Classical Judeo-Arabic *grosso modo* follows the one of the Standard language. A notable feature is the occurrence of hyper-correct features, e.g., when a longer indicative form *yafʕalūn(a)* 'they do' stands in a context that would require the shortened subjunctive or "apocopate"/jussive form *yafʕalū* 'that they do/let them do'. As the Arabic dialects have regularized the latter form (with alternative means (prefixes) to designate the indicative), the use of the longer form counts as "hypercorrect", as the writer attempts to do "too much" (cf., e.g., Blau 1970; 1999: 28–31). In contrast, an example of a hypocorrect grammatical form would be the example *bāqiyūn(a)* 'remaining, PTCP.PL.M, a blend of dialectal form *bāqiyīn* and the standard form *bāqūn(a)*, where the writer does, grammatically speaking, "too little" to attain the standard register (cf. Blau 1999: 29).

2.3 Syntax

One of the pivotal syntactic features of Middle Arabic, the shift from a "synthetical" syntactic structure to a more "analytical" one, notably in the expression of the Semitic annexation (Hebrew *səmixut*, Arabic *ʔiḍāfa)*, is not yet in place in Classical Judeo-Arabic texts (cf. e.g., Hary 1991). Otherwise, Middle-Arabic syntactic features are limited to a minimum (cf., e.g., Blau 2001 for Saadia Gaon's *Šarḥ*, of which an excerpt is displayed in text one, see below). A Middle-Arabic momentum (alternatively, simply grammatical oversight) may be seen in a non-standard form סבעה עשר סנה *sabʕata ʕašara sana(tan)* found in one manuscript, instead of סבע עשרה סנה *sabʕa ʕašrata sana(tan)* '17 years'. One can observe a tendency to use the Arabic relative marker אלדי'

alladī (later dialectal (י)אל *illi*) across the board, independently of gender and number, reflecting the Hebrew relative marker אֲשֶׁר *ʔăšɛr*.

Medieval Hebrew and Aramaic did, however, have a syntactic impact on Classical Judeo-Arabic. Blau (1999: 82) cites a construction with a cataphoric pronoun *-hu* in front of the preposition *li-*: סמאה לישראל בני בכורי *sammā-hu li-yiśrā̊ʔēl bən-ī ḇəḵōr-ī* 'he called Israel[H] "my[H] first-born[H] son[H]"' (he called it to Israel my son my first-born").

2.4 Lexicon

It comes at no surprise that Judeo-Arabic texts in general are replete with Hebrew words (both proper names and technical terms) testifying to the Biblical and Rabbinical tradition, as in the example just cited (for an overview, cf. Maman 2013). Hebrew vocabulary can also be syntactically embedded, as in גלותנא *gā̊lūṯ-nā* 'our diaspora[H]' or אלצרות אלעצימה *al-ṣā̊rōṯ al-ʕaẓīma* 'the considerable[H] problems[H]' (see below Section 3.3).

Of special interest are Judeo-Arabic calques based on a Hebrew model, e.g., the Arabic verb in binyan V, תאבל *taʔabbala* 'to mourn', based on the Hebrew hiṯpaʕʕēl verb הִתְאַבֵּל *hiṯʔabbēl* with the same meaning (cf. Khan 2007: 531). A comparable example, due to Blau (1999: 134; cf. Hary 2018: 52) is the Judeo-Arabic verb אצדר *ʔaṣdar(a)* 'to arrange [a prayer]' (phonologically reflecting *tafxīm* – suprasegamental assimilation with respect to velarization), based on the Hebrew model [הִסְדִּיר [תְּפִילָּה *hisdīr [təp̄illā̊]*, again with the same meaning. Khan (2007: 531) also cites examples with phonological adaptation, e.g., Judeo-Arabic סופר derived analogically (Hebrew *š* often corresponds to Arabic *s*) from Hebrew שׁוֹפָר *šōp̄ā̊r* 'horn'.

Among the earliest samples of Judeo-Arabic are lists of glosses of rare and/or difficult Biblical Hebrew (and Aramaic words) as well as translated excerpts of Biblical Hebrew texts. Here are a few specimens, mostly representing the phonetic spelling alluded to above, taken from manuscript T-S Ar. 32.10 (cf. Blau and Hopkins 2017: 475): the Hebrew terms אֹחִים *ʔōḥīm* glossed as *numūs* 'ichneuma' (Is 13:21), כְּבִיר הָעִזִּים *kəḇīr hā̊-ʕizzīm* (lit. "net of goat skin") glossed as *mixadda* 'small cushion' (1 Sam 19:13), as well as the Aramaic terms אֲחַשְׁדַּרְפְּנַיָּא *ʔăḥašdarpənayyā* ('the satraps') glossed as *al-baṭāriqa* 'the patricians', סִגְנַיָּא *sig̃nayyā* glossed in a multiple way as *al-muftīyīn* 'the judges', as *al-fuqahāʔ* 'the (religiously) learned ones', and as *al-wuzarāʔ* 'the ministers', and finally גְּדָבְרַיָּא *gəḏaḇrayyā* glossed as *al-xuzzān* 'the treasurers' (all in Daniel 3:2).

place	translation	Arabic	Judeo-Arabic gloss	Hebrew/Aramaic term
Is 13:21	'ichneuma'	نُموس	נ{א}מוס	אֹחִים
1Sam 19:13	'the small cushion'	مخدّة	מכדה	כְּבִיר הָעִזִּים
Daniel 3:2	'(to) the patricians'	البِطارقة	אלבטאריקה	לַאֲחַשְׁדַּרְפְּנַיָּא
Daniel 3:2	'the judges'	المُفتيين	אלמופתין	סִגְנַיָּא
	'the learned ones'	الفُقهاء	אלפוקהא	
	'the leaders'	الأمراء	אלאומרא	
Daniel 3:2	'the ministers'	الوزراء	אלוזרא	אֲדַרְגָּזְרַיָּא
Daniel 3:2	'the treasurers'	الخُزّان	אלכוזאן	גְּדָבְרַיָּא
Daniel 3:3	'the superintendents'	القهارمة	אלקהארמה	דְּתָבְרַיָּא

3. Text samples

3.1 The beginning of the Joseph story (Genesis 37: 1–28) in Hebrew and in Judeo-Arabic

The first example consists of the first twenty-eight verses of Saadia Gaon's (882–942 CE) translation of the Joseph story (Genesis 37), in the edition of Blau (1980b: 20–22). His full name is רבי סעדיה בן יוסף אלפיומי גאון Rabbī Saʕadya ben Yosef al-Fayyūmī Gaʔon in Hebrew and سعيد بن يوسف الفيومي Saʕīd ibn Yūsuf al-Fayyūmī in Arabic. Saadia Gaon's translation of the whole Torah is know by the title *Tafsīr* '(Arabic) interpretation' and represents perfect Classical Arabic. Obviously, one rationale of such translations was that the knowledge of Hebrew of the local Jewish population was not deemed sufficient for the understanding of intricacies of Biblical Hebrew. In contrast with later strictly literal Karaite translations, Saadia Gaon at times strives for elucidation of the specific sense of a Hebrew passage, in a way comparable to the strategy found in the Targum Onqelos. A famous example concerns the semantically unclear passage found in Exodus 23:13 and 34:26, as well as in Deuteronomy 14:21, לֹא-תְבַשֵּׁל גְּדִי, בַּחֲלֵב אִמּוֹ *lō(ʔ)-təḇaššēl gəḏī ba-ḥălēḇ ʔimm-ō* 'you (SG.M) shall not boil a kid (a young goat) in its mother's milk'. While Karaite translations offer a literal rendition, e.g., לא תנצ׳ג׳ אלג׳די בלבן אמה *lā tunḍiği l-ğadya bi-labani ʔummi-hī*, Saadia Gaon translates *ad sensum* (i.e. in the generally understood way) לא תאכל לחמא בלבן *lā taʔkul laḥman bi-labanin* 'you (SG.M) shall not eat meat with milk' (cf., e.g., Freidenreich 2003: 356). The Targum Onqelos likewise offers the interpretation לָא תֵיכְלוּן בְּשַׂר בַּחֲלָב *lā tēḵlūn bəśār ba-ḥălāḇ* 'you (PL.M) shall not eat meat with/in milk' (cf., e.g., Cooper 2012: 117).[2]

In order to gain an impression of Saadia Gaon's style of translation, the Hebrew original of the passage is reproduced here as well (for a characterization of the linguistic and literary style of this translation, cf. Blau 2001; for further linguistic observations on this text cf. Blau 2019).

א וַיֵּשֶׁב יַעֲקֹב, בְּאֶרֶץ מְגוּרֵי אָבִיו
1 וסכן יעקוב פי בלד סכנא אביה

wa-sakana	*yaʕăqōḇ / yaʕqūb*	*fī*	*baladi*	*suknā*	*ʔabī-hi*
and-reside.PF.3SG.M	Jacob	in	land.CS.GEN	residence.CS.GEN	father.CS.GEN-3SG.M

Jacob lived in the land of the residence of his father

בְּאֶרֶץ, כְּנָעַן. ב אֵלֶּה תֹּלְדוֹת יַעֲקֹב,
פי בלד כנעאן 2. והד׳א שרח תאליד יעקוב

fī	*baladi*	*kanʕān*	*wa-hāḏā*	*šarḥu*	*taʔlīdi*	*yaʕăqōḇ*
in	land.CS.GEN	Canaan	and-DEM.M	interpretation.CS.NOM	genealogy.CS.GEN	Jacob

in the land of Canaan. This is the explanation of the genealogy of Jacob.

יוֹסֵף בֶּן-שְׁבַע-עֶשְׂרֵה שָׁנָה הָיָה רֹעֶה
למא כאן יוסף אבן סבע עשרה סנה וכאן ירעי

lammā	*kāna*	*yōsēp̄ / yūsuf*	*sabʕaʕašrata*	*sana(tan)*	*wa-kāna*	*yarʕā*
when	be.PF.3SG.M	Joseph	seventeen	year(.ACC)	and-be.PF.3SG.M	tend.IPFV.3SG.M

When Joseph was 17 years old and was tending

2 I thank my colleague Arik Sadan for having brought my attention to this example.

אֶת-אֶחָיו בַּצֹּאן, וְהוּא נַעַר אֶת-

מע אכ׳ותה אלגנם וכאן נאשיא מע בני בלהה

maʕa ʔixwati-hī l-ġanama wa-kāna nāšiʔan maʕa

with brother.PL.CS.GEN-3SG.M DEF-cattle.ACC and-be.PF.3SG.M grow_up-PTCP.ACC with

with his brothers the small cattle, while he grew up with

בְּנֵי בִלְהָה וְאֶת-בְּנֵי זִלְפָּה, נְשֵׁי אָבִיו;

בני בלהה ומע בני זלפה נסוה̈ אביה

banī bilhā wa-banī zilpā niswati ʔabī-hi

son.PL.CS.GEN Bilha and-son.PL.CS.GEN Zilpa woman.PL.CS.GEN father.CS.GEN-3SG.M

the sons of Bilha and the sons of Zilpa, the wives of his father,

וַיָּבֵא יוֹסֵף אֶת-דִּבָּתָם רָעָה, אֶל-אֲבִיהֶם.

אתי יוסף בשנאעה̈ רדיה̈ ענהם אלי אביהם

ʔatā yōsēp̄ bi-šanāʕatin radī(ʔ)atin ʕan-hum ʔilā ʔabī-him

come.PF.3SG.M Joseph with-ugliness.GEN bad.F.GEN on-3PL.M to father.CS.GEN-3PL.M

Joseph brought/reported bad things from them to their father.[3]

ג וְיִשְׂרָאֵל, אָהַב אֶת-יוֹסֵף מִכָּל-

3. וכאן אסראיל יחבּ יוסף אכת׳ר מן ג׳מיע

wa-kāna ʔisrāʔīl yuḥibbu yōsēp̄ ʔakṯara min ǧamīʕi

and-be.PF.3SG.M Israel love.IPFV.3SG.M Joseph much.ELAT.ACC of totality.CS.GEN

Israel loved Joseph more than all of

בָּנָיו--כִּי-בֶן-זְקֻנִים הוּא, לוֹ; וְעָשָׂה

בניה לאנה אבן שיכ׳וכ׳ה̈ לה פצנע

banī-hi li-ʔanna-hū bnu šayxūxatin la-hū fa-ṣanaʕa

son.CS.PL.GEN-3SG.M for-COMP-3SG.M son.CS.NOM old-age.GEN for-3SG.M CONJ-produce.PF.3SG.M

his sons, because he was the son of his old age. He made

לוֹ, כְּתֹנֶת פַּסִּים. ד וַיִּרְאוּ אֶחָיו, כִּי

לה תוניה̈ דיבאג׳ 4. למא ראו אכ׳ותה אן

la-hū tūnīyata dībāǧin lammā raʔaw ʔixwatu-hū ʔanna

for-3SG.M dress.CS.ACC silk_brocade when see.PF.3PL.M brother.CS.PL-3SG.M COMP

him a dress of silk brocade. When his brothers saw that

-אֹתוֹ אָהַב אֲבִיהֶם מִכָּל-אֶחָיו

אבאהם יחבה אכת׳ר מן ג׳מיעהם

ʔabā-hum yuḥibbu-hū ʔakṯara min ǧamīʕi-him

father.CS.ACC-3PL.M love.IPFV.3SG.M-3SG.M much.ELAT.ACC from totality.CS.GEN-3PL.M

their father loved him more than all of them,

וַיִּשְׂנְאוּ, אֹתוֹ; וְלֹא יָכְלוּ, דַּבְּרוֹ לְשָׁלֹם.

שנוה ולם יטיקו אן יסלּמו עליה

šana(ʔ)ū-hu wa-lam yuṭīqū ʔan yusallimū ʕalay-hi

hate.PF.3PL.M-3SG.M and-NEG be_able.IPFV.APOC.3PL.M COMP greet.IPFV.SUBJ.3PL.M upon-3SG.M

they hated him and were not able to greet him.

3 Here, the Judeo-Arabic text actually disambiguates the Hebrew original, where it is not *a priori* clear whether דִּבָּתָם רָעָה represents a genitivus subjectivus (calumny originating with them) or objectivus (calumny about them).

ה וַיַּחֲלֹם יוֹסֵף חֲלוֹם, וַיַּגֵּד
5. ת׳ם אן יוסף ראי רויא פאכ׳בר

ṯumma ʔinna yōsēp̄ raʔā ruʔyā fa-ʔaxbara
then FOC Joseph see.PF.3SG.M dream.ACC CONJ-inform.PF.3SG.M
Then Joseph had a dream and informed

לְאֶחָיו; וַיּוֹסִפוּ עוֹד, שְׂנֹא אֹתוֹ.
אכ׳ותה בהא פאזדאדו איצ׳א שנאה̈ לה

ʔixwata-hū bi-hā fa-zdādū ʔayḍan šanāʔatan la-hū
brother.PL.CS.ACC-3SG.M in-3SG.F CONJ-increase.PF.3PL.M also hate.ACC for-3SG.M
his brothers about it. Their hatred for him increased even more.

ו וַיֹּאמֶר, אֲלֵיהֶם: שִׁמְעוּ-נָא, הַחֲלוֹם הַזֶּה אֲשֶׁר
6. אד׳ קאל להם אסמעו אלאן הד׳ה אלרויא אלתי

ʔiḏ qāla la-hum ismaʕū l-ʔāna hāḏihī r-ruʔyā llatī
then say.PF.3SG.M for-3SG.M listen.IPT.PL.M DEF-time.ACC DEM.F DEF-dream.ACC REL.F
Then he said to them: listen now to the dream that

חָלָמְתִּי. ז וְהִנֵּה אֲנַחְנוּ מְאַלְּמִים אֲלֻמִּים, בְּתוֹךְ הַשָּׂדֶה, וְהִנֵּה
ראיתהא 7. כאנّא נג׳רז ג׳רזא פי אלצחרא וכאןّ

raʔaytu-hā ka-ʔan-nā nağruzu ğurazan fī ṣ-ṣaḥrāʔi wa-ka-ʔanna
see.PF.1SG-3SG.F as-COMP-1PL bind.IPFV.1PL sheaf.PL.ACC in DEF-desert.GEN and-as-COMP
I dreamt, it was as if we bound sheaves in the desert and it was as if

קָמָה אֲלֻמָּתִי, וְגַם-נִצָּבָה; וְהִנֵּה
ג׳רזתי וקפת ת׳ם אנתצבת וכאןّ

ğurzat-ī waqafat ṯumma ntaṣabat wa-ka-ʔanna
sheaf.CS-1SG rise.PF.3SG.F then stand_upright.PF.3SG.F and-as-COMP
my sheaf rose and (then) stood upright, and it was as if

תְסֻבֶּינָה אֲלֻמֹּתֵיכֶם, וַתִּשְׁתַּחֲוֶיןָ לַאֲלֻמָּתִי.
ג׳רזכם תחיט בהא ותסג׳ד להא

ğuraza-kum tuḥīṭu bi-hā wa-tasğudu la-hā
sheaf.ACC.CS.PL-2PL.M go_round.IPFV.3SG.F in-3SG.F and-bow_down.IPFV.3SG.F for-3SG.F
your sheaves went around it and bowed down to it.

ח וַיֹּאמְרוּ לוֹ, אֶחָיו, הֲמָלֹךְ תִּמְלֹךְ עָלֵינוּ,
8. וקאלו לה אכ׳ותה אמלכא תתמלךְ עלינא

wa-qālū la-hū ʔixwatu-hū ʔa-malikan tatamallaku ʕalay-nā
and-say.PF.3PL.M to-3SG.M brother.CS.PL-3SG.M INT-king.ACC be_king.IPFV.2SG.M over-1PL
His brothers said to him: do you want to be king over us

אִם-מָשׁוֹל תִּמְשֹׁל בָּנוּ; וַיּוֹסִפוּ עוֹד שְׂנֹא
או סלטאנא תתסלט עלינא ואזדאדו איצ׳א שנאה

ʔaw sulṭānan tatasallaṭu ʕalay-nā fa-zdādū ʔayḍan šanāʔatan
or ruler.ACC rule.IPFV.2SG.M over-1PL CONJ-increase.PF.3PL.M also hate.ACC
or be ruler over us. Their hatred for him increased even more.

אֹתוֹ, עַל-חֲלֹמֹתָיו וְעַל-דְּבָרָיו. ט וַיַּחֲלֹם
לה עלי אחלאמה ועלי כלאמה 9. וראי

la-hū ʕalā ʔaḥlāmi-hī wa-ʕalā kalāmi-hī wa-raʔā
for-3SG.M over dream.PL.CS.GEN-3SG.M and-over discourse.CS.GEN-3SG.M and-see.PF.3SG.M
because of his dreams and his words. And he had

עוֹד חֲלוֹם אַחֵר, וַיְסַפֵּר אֹתוֹ לְאֶחָיו;
איצ׳א רויא אכ׳רי פקצ̇הא עלי אכ׳ותה

ʔayḍan ruʔyā ʔuxrā fa-qaṣṣa-hū ʕalā ʔixwati-hī
also dream.ACC other.F.ACC CONJ-tell.PF.3SG.M-3SG.M upon brother.PL.CS.GEN-3SG.M

yet another dream and told it his brothers.

וַיֹּאמֶר, הִנֵּה חָלַמְתִּי חֲלוֹם עוֹד, וְהִנֵּה הַשֶּׁמֶשׁ וְהַיָּרֵחַ
פקאל הוד׳א ראית רויא וכאן̇ אלשמס ואלקמר

fa-qāla huwaḏā raʔaytu ruʔyā wa-ka-ʔanna š-šamsa wa-l-qamara
CONJ-say.PF.3SG.M DEICT see.PF.1SG.M dream.ACC and-as-COMP DEF-sun.ACC and-DEF-moon.ACC

He said: behold, I had a dream, and it was as if the sun and the moon

וְאַחַד עָשָׂר כּוֹכָבִים, מִשְׁתַּחֲוִים לִי. י וַיְסַפֵּר
ואחד עשר כוכב תסג׳ד לי 10. פאד׳ קצ̇הא

wa-ʔaḥada ʕasara kawkab(an) tasǧudu l-ī fa-ʔiḏ qaṣṣa-hū
and eleven star(.ACC) bow_down.IPFV.3SG.F for-1SG CONJ-then tell.PF.3SG.M-3SG.M

and eleven stars bowed down to me. Then he told it

אֶל-אָבִיו, וְאֶל-אֶחָיו, וַיִּגְעַר-בּוֹ
עלי אביה ועלי אכ׳ותה פזג׳ר בה

ʕalā ʔabī-hi wa-ʕalā ʔixwati-hī wa-zaǧara-hū bi-hī
upon father.CS.GEN-3SG.M and-upon brother.PL.CS.GEN-3SG.M and-scold.PF.3SG.M-3SG.M in-3SG.M

his father and his brothers. His father scolded him for it

אָבִיו, וַיֹּאמֶר לוֹ מָה הַחֲלוֹם הַזֶּה אֲשֶׁר חָלָמְתָּ:
אבוה וקאל לה מא הד׳ה אלרויא אלתי ראיתהא

ʔabū-hu wa-qāla la-hū mā hāḏihī r-ruʔyā llatī raʔayta-hā
father.CS-3SG.M and-say.PF.3SG.M to-3SG.M what DEM.F DEF-dream REL.F see.PF.2SG.M-3SG.F

and said to him: what is this dream that you had.

הֲבוֹא נָבוֹא, אֲנִי וְאִמְּךָ וְאַחֶיךָ,
הל נג׳י אנא ואמך ואכ׳ותך

hal naǧī(ʔu) ʔanā wa-ʔummu-ka wa-ʔixwatu-ka
INT come.IPFV.1PL 1SG and-mother.CS-2SG.M and-brother.PL.CS-2SG.M

Do we, myself, your mother and your brothers, come

לְהִשְׁתַּחֲוֺת לְךָ, אָרְצָה. יא וַיְקַנְאוּ-בוֹ,
פנסג׳ד לך עלי אלארץ׳ 11. וחסדה

fa-nasǧudu la-ka ʕalā l-ʔarḍi wa-ḥasada-hū
CONJ-bow_down.IPFV.1PL for-2SG.M upon DEF-earth.GEN and-envy.PF.3SG.M-3SG.M

and bow down to you on the earth? His brothers envied him.

אֶחָיו; וְאָבִיו, שָׁמַר אֶת-הַדָּבָר.
אכ׳ותה ואבוה חפט׳ כלאמה

ʔixwatu-hū wa-ḥafiẓa ʔabū-hu kalāma-hū
brother.PL.CS-3SG.M and-keep.PF.3SG.M father.CS-3SG.M speech.CS.ACC-3SG.M

His father kept his words in mind.

יב וַיֵּלְכוּ, אֶחָיו, לִרְעוֹת אֶת-צֹאן אֲבִיהֶם,
12. ת׳ם מצ׳ו אכ׳ותה לירעו גנם אביהם

ṯumma maḍaw ʔixwatu-hū li-yarʕaw ġanama ʔabī-him
then go_away.PF.3PL brother.PL.CS-3SG.M for-tend.SUBJ.3PL small.cattle.CS father.GEN.CS-3PL.M

Then his brothers went to tend the small cattle of their father

בִּשְׁכֶם. יג וַיֹּאמֶר יִשְׂרָאֵל אֶל-יוֹסֵף, הֲלוֹא אַחֶיךָ רֹעִים
פי נאבלס. 13. פקאל אסראיל ליוסף הוד׳א אכ׳ותך ירעון
fī nābulus. fa-qāla ʔisrāʔīl li-yōsēp̄ huwaḏā ʔixwatu-ka yirʕawna
in Nablus CONJ-say.PF.3SG.M Israel to-Joseph DEICT brother.PL.CS-2SG.M tend.IPFV.3PL.M
in Nablus. Israel said to Joseph: “Your brothers are tending

בִּשְׁכֶם--לְכָה, וְאֶשְׁלָחֲךָ אֲלֵיהֶם; וַיֹּאמֶר לוֹ, הִנֵּנִי.
פי נאבלס תעאל אבעת׳ בך אליהם קאל לה נעם.
fī nābulus taʕāla ʔabʕiṯu bi-ka ʔilay-him qāla la-hū naʕam.
in Nablus come_on.IPT.SG.M send.IPFV.1SG in-2SG.M to-3PL.M say.PF.3SG.M to-3SG.M yes
in Nablus, let me send you to them.” Joseph said [to him] “yes”.

יד וַיֹּאמֶר לוֹ, לֶךְ-נָא רְאֵה אֶת-שְׁלוֹם אַחֶיךָ
14. קאל אמצ׳ אעלם סלאמה̈ אחותך
qāla mḍi ʕlam salāmata ʔixwati-ka
say.PF.3SG.M go_away.IPT.SG.M know.IPT.SG.M well_being.CS.ACC brother.PL.CS.GEN-2SG.M
[His father] said: “Go and find out about the well-being of your brothers

וְאֶת-שְׁלוֹם הַצֹּאן, וַהֲשִׁבֵנִי, דָּבָר;
וסלאמה̈ אלגנם ורד̈ עלי̈ אלג׳ואב
wa-salāmata al-ġanam wa-rudda ʕalay-ya l-ğawāba
and-well_being.CS.ACC DEF-small.cattle and-return.IPT.SG.M on.1SG DEF-answer.ACC
and the well-being of the cattle and report back to me.”

וַיִּשְׁלָחֵהוּ מֵעֵמֶק חֶבְרוֹן, וַיָּבֹא שְׁכֶמָה.
פבעת׳ בה מן עמק חברא פאתי נאבלס.
fa-baʕaṯa bi-hī min ʕamqi ḥabrā fa-ʔatā nābulus.
CONJ-send.PF.3SG.M in-3SG.M from vallyy.CS.GEN Hebron CONJ-come.PF.3SG.M Nablus(.ACC)
So he sent him from the valley of Hebron, and Joseph came to Nablus.

טו וַיִּמְצָאֵהוּ אִישׁ, וְהִנֵּה תֹעֶה בַּשָּׂדֶה; וַיִּשְׁאָלֵהוּ הָאִישׁ לֵאמֹר,
15. פוג׳דה רג׳ל צ׳אלא פי אלצחרא פסאלה
fa-wağada-hū rağulun ḍāllan fī ṣ-ṣaḥrāʔi fa-saʔala-hū
CONJ-find.PF.3SG.M-3SG.M man go_astray.PTCP.ACC in DEF-desert.GEN CONJ-ask.PF.3SG.M-3SG.M
A man found him going astray in the desert and asked him:

מַה-תְּבַקֵּשׁ. טז וַיֹּאמֶר, אֶת-אַחַי אָנֹכִי מְבַקֵּשׁ; הַגִּידָה-נָּא לִי,
מא תטלב. קאל אנא אכ׳ותי אטלב אכ׳ברני
mā taṭlub. qāla ʔanā ʔixwat-ī ʔaṭlubu ʔaxbir-nī
what seek.IPFV.2SG.M SAY.PF.3SG.M 1SG brother.PL.CS-1SG seek.IPFV.1SG inform.IPT.SG.M-1SG.OBJ
“What are you looking for?” Joseph said: “I am looking for my brothers, tell me

אֵיפֹה הֵם רֹעִים. יז וַיֹּאמֶר הָאִישׁ, נָסְעוּ מִזֶּה--
אלאן אין הם ירעון. 17. קאל אלרג׳ל קד רחלו מן הנא
l-ʔāna ʔayna hum yarʕawn. qāla r-rağulu qad raḥalū min hunā
DEF-time.ACC 3PL.M tend.IPFV.3PL.M SAY.PF.3SG.M DEF-man ANT travel.PF.3PL.M from here
now where they are tending.” The man answered: “They traveled from here

כִּי שָׁמַעְתִּי אֹמְרִים, נֵלְכָה דֹּתָיְנָה; וַיֵּלֶךְ יוֹסֵף
וסמעתהם יקולון נמצ׳י אלי דתן פמצ׳י יוסף
wa-samiʕtu-hum yaqūlūna namḍī ʔilā ḏōṯān fa-maḍā yōsēp̄
and-hear.PF.1SG-3PL.M say.IPFV.3PL.M go_away.IPFV.1PL to Dotan CONJ-go_away.PF.3SG.M Joseph
and I heard them saying, “we are going to Dotan”. So Joseph went

אַחַר אֶחָיו, וַיִּמְצָאֵם בְּדֹתָן. יח וַיִּרְאוּ אֹתוֹ,
ורא אכ'ותה פוג'דהם בדתן. 18. פראוה
warāʔa ʔixwati-hī fa-waǧada-hum bi-ḏōṯān fa-raʔaw-hu
after brother.PL.CS.GEN-3SG.M CONJ-find.PF.3SG.M-3PL.M in-Dotan CONJ-see.PF.3PL.M-3SG.M
after his brothers and found them in Dotan. They saw him

מֵרָחֹק; וּבְטֶרֶם יִקְרַב אֲלֵיהֶם, וַיִּתְנַכְּלוּ אֹתוֹ
מן בעיד וקבל אן יקרב אליהם אגתאלוה
min baʕīdin wa-qabla ʔan yaqruba ʔilay-himu ġtālū-hū
from far.GEN and-before COMP approach.SUBJ.3SG.M to-3PL.M conspire_to_kill.PF.3PL.M.3SG.M
from afar and, before he came near to them, conspired

לַהֲמִיתוֹ. יט וַיֹּאמְרוּ, אִישׁ אֶל-אָחִיו: הִנֵּה,
ליקתלוה. 19. פקאלו בעצ'הם לבעץ' הוד'א
li-yaqtulū-hu fa-qālū baʕḍu-hum li-baʕḍin huwaḏā
for-kill.SUBJ.3PL.M-3SG.M CONJ-say-PF.3SG.M some.CS-3PL.M to-some.GEN DEICT
to kill him. One brother said to the other: "Look here

בַּעַל הַחֲלֹמוֹת הַלָּזֶה--בָּא. כ וְעַתָּה לְכוּ
צאחב תלך אלאחלאם קד ג'א. 20. אלאן פתעאלו
ṣāḥibu tilka l-ʔaḥlāmi qad ǧāʔ. al-ʔāna fa-taʕālaw
owner.CS DEM.REM DEF-dream.PL.GEN ANT come.PF.3SG.M DEF-time.ACC CONJ-come_on.IPT.PL.M
the dream guy has arrived. Now, let's

וְנַהַרְגֵהוּ, וְנַשְׁלִכֵהוּ בְּאַחַד הַבֹּרוֹת, וְאָמַרְנוּ,
נקתלה ונטרחה פי אחד אלאבאר ונקול
naqtul-hu wa-natraḥ-hu fī ʔaḥadi l-ʔābāri wa-naqūlu
kill.JUSS.1PL-3SG.M and-throw.JUSS.1PL.3SG.M in one.CS.GEN DEF-WELL.PL.GEN and-say.PFV.1PL
kill him and throw him in one of the wells and we will say,

חַיָּה רָעָה אֲכָלָתְהוּ; וְנִרְאֶה, מַה-יִּהְיוּ
וחש רדי אכלה חתי נריה מא יכון
waḥšun radīyun ʔakala-hū ḥattā nurī-hi[4] *mā yakūnu*
beast wild eat.PF.3SG.M-3SG.M until show.SUBJ.1PL-3SG.M REL be.IPFV.3SG.M
a wild beast has devoured him, so that we will show him what is the result

חֲלֹמֹתָיו. כא וַיִּשְׁמַע רְאוּבֵן,
מן אחלאמה. 21. פסמעהם ראובן וטלב
min l-ʔaḥlāmi fa-samiʕa-hum rəʔūḇēn wa-ṭalaba
from DEF-dream.PL.GEN CONJ-hear.PF.3SG.M-3PLM Reuben and-demand.PF.3SG.M
of the dreams. Reuben heard them and demanded

וַיַּצִּלֵהוּ מִיָּדָם; וַיֹּאמֶר, לֹא נַכֶּנּוּ נָפֶשׁ.
אן יכ'לצה מן אידיהם וקאל לא נקתל נפסא.
ʔan yuxalliṣa-hū min ʔaydī-him wa-qāla lā naqtul nafsan
COMP release.SUBJ.3SG.M-3SG.M from hand.PL.CS.GEN-3PL.M and-say.PF.3SG.M NEG kill.JUSS.1PL soul.ACC
to release him from their hands and said: "Let's not kill a life."

4 So in the edition by Blau (1980b: 21). Another textual variant is ונוריה, pointing to the causative reading in contrast to the Hebrew original.

כב וַיֹּאמֶר אֲלֵהֶם רְאוּבֵן, אַל-תִּשְׁפְּכוּ-דָם--הַשְׁלִיכוּ אֹתוֹ
22. ת׳ם קאל להם ראובן לא תספכו דמא אטרחוה
ṯumma qāla *la-hum* *rəʔūḇēn* *lā* *tasfikū* *daman* *iṭraḥū-hu*
then say.PF.3SG.M to-3PL.M Reuben NEG spill.JUSS.2PL.M blood.ACC throw.IPT.3PL.M-3SG.M
Then Reuben said to the: "Do not spill blood, but throw him

אֶל-הַבּוֹר הַזֶּה אֲשֶׁר בַּמִּדְבָּר, וְיָד אַל-תִּשְׁלְחוּ-בוֹ:
פי הד׳א אלביר אלד׳י פי אלבר ולא תמדו ידכם
fī *hāḏā* *l-biʔri* *llaḏī* *fī* *l-barri* *wa-lā* *tamuddū* *yada-kum*
in DEM.M DEF-well.GEN REL.M in DEF-wilderness and-NEG extend.JUSS.2PL.M hand.CS.ACC-2PL.M
in this pit in the wilderness and do not lay hand

לְמַעַן, הַצִּיל אֹתוֹ מִיָּדָם,
אליה לקבל אן יכ׳לצה מן ידיהם
ʔilay-hi *li-qibali* *ʔan* *yuxalliṣa-hū* *min yaday-him*
to-3SG.M in_order COMP release.SUBJ.3SG.M-3SG.M from hand.DU.CS.GEN-3PL.M
on him." He had made up his mind to release him form their hands

לַהֲשִׁיבוֹ, אֶל-אָבִיו. כג וַיְהִי, כַּאֲשֶׁר-בָּא יוֹסֵף
לירדה אלי אביה. 23. פלמא ג׳א יוסף
li-yarudda-hū *ʔilā* *ʔabī-hi.* *fa-lammā* *ǧāʔa* *yōsēp̄*
for-return.SUBJ.3SG.M-3SG.M to father.CS.GEN-3SG.M CONJ-when come.PF.3SG.M Joseph
in order to return him to his father. When Joseph came

אֶל-אֶחָיו; וַיַּפְשִׁיטוּ אֶת-יוֹסֵף אֶת-כֻּתָּנְתּוֹ, אֶת-כְּתֹנֶת הַפַּסִּים
אלי אכ׳ותה סלכ׳וה תוניתה תוניה̈ אלדיבאג׳
ʔilā *ʔixwati-hī* *salaxū* *tūnīyata-hū* *tūnīyata* *d-dībāǧi*
to brother.PL.CS.GEN-3SG.M strip_off.PF.3PL.M dress.CS.ACC.3SG.M dress.CS.ACC DEF-silk.brocade
to his brothers they stripped of his garment, the silk dress,

אֲשֶׁר עָלָיו. כד וַיִּקָּחֻהוּ--וַיַּשְׁלִכוּ אֹתוֹ, הַבֹּרָה; וְהַבּוֹר
אלד׳ עליה. 24. פאכ׳ד׳וה וטרחוה פי אלג׳ב̇ וכאן אלג׳ב̇
llaḏī *ʕalay-hī.* *fa-ʔaxaḏū-hu* *wa-ṭaraḥū-hu* *fī* *l-ǧubbi* *wa-kāna* *l-ǧubbu*
REL on-3SG.M CONJ-take.PF.3PL.M and-throw.PF.3PL.M in DEF-pit.GEN and-be.PF.3SG.M DEF-pit
which he wore, and they took him and threw him in the pit. The pit was

רֵק, אֵין בּוֹ מָיִם. כה וַיֵּשְׁבוּ, לֶאֱכָל-לֶחֶם,
פארגא ליס פיה מא. 25. ת׳ם ג׳לסו ואכלו טעאמא
fāriġan *laysa* *fī-hi* *māʔ* *ṯumma* *ǧalasū* *wa-ʔakalū* *ṭaʕāman*
empty.ACC NEG.EXIST.3SG.M in-3SG.M water then sit_down.PF.3PL.M and-eat.PF.3PL.M food.ACC
empty, without water. Then they sat down and ate food.

וַיִּשְׂאוּ עֵינֵיהֶם וַיִּרְאוּ, וְהִנֵּה אֹרְחַת יִשְׁמְעֵאלִים
פרפעו עיונהם פנט׳רו פאד׳א בקאפלה אעראב
fa-rafaʕū *ʕuyūna-hum* *fa-naẓarū* *fa-ʔiḏā* *bi-qāfilati* *ʔaʕrābin*
CONJ-lift.PF.3PL.M eye.PL.CS.ACC-3PL.M CONJ-look.PF.3PL.M CONJ-PRES in-caravan.CS.GEN bedouin.PL.GEN
They raised the eyes and looked out, and there was suddenly are caravan of bedouins

בָּאָה מִגִּלְעָד; וּגְמַלֵּיהֶם נֹשְׂאִים, נְכֹאת
ג׳איה̈ מן אלג׳רש וג׳מאלהם מחמלה̈ כ׳רנובא
ǧāyatun *mina l-ǧaraš* *wa-ǧimālu-hum* *muḥammalatun* *xurnūban*
come.PTCP.F from DEF-Jerash and-camel.PL.CS-3PL.M load.PTCP.PASS.F carob.ACC
coming from Jerash, their camels being loaded with Carob,

וּצְרִי וָלֹט--הוֹלְכִים, לְהוֹרִיד מִצְרָיְמָה.
וטריאקא ושאהבלוט מארּין ליחדרו ד'לך אלי מצר.

wa-ṭiryāqan wa-šāhballūṭ[5] *mārrīna li-yaḥdurū ḏālika ʔilā miṣr.*
frankincense.ACC and-chestnut pass_by.PTCP.PL for-bring_down.SUBJ.3PL.M DEM.REM to Egypt

frankincense, and chestnuts, passing by to bring all this to Egypt.

כו וַיֹּאמֶר יְהוּדָה, אֶל-אֶחָיו: מַה-בֶּצַע, כִּי נַהֲרֹג
26. פקאל יהודה לאכ'ותה מא אלטמע אן נקתל

fa-qāla yəhūḏā̊ li-ʔixwati-hī mā ṭ-ṭamaʕu ʔan naqtula
CONJ-say.PF.3SG.M Yehuda to-brother.PL.CS.GEN-3SG.M what DEF-desire COMP kill.SUBJ.1PL

Yehuda said to his brothers: "What is the point in killing

אֶת-אָחִינוּ, וְכִסִּינוּ, אֶת-דָּמוֹ. כז לְכוּ וְנִמְכְּרֶנּוּ
אכ'אנא ונגטי דמה. 27. תעאלו נביעה

ʔaxā-nā wa-nuġaṭṭiya dama-hū. taʕālaw nabīʕ-hu
brother.CS.ACC-1PL and-cover_up.IPFV blood.CS.ACC-3SG.M come_on.IPT.PL.M sell.JUSS.1PL-3SG.M

our brother and covering up his blood. Let's sell him

לַיִּשְׁמְעֵאלִים, וְיָדֵנוּ אַל-תְּהִי-בוֹ, כִּי-אָחִינוּ
ללאעראב וידנא לא תבטש פיה לאנה אכ'ונא

li-l-ʔaʕrābi wa-yadu-nā lā tabṭišu fī-hi li-ʔanna-hū ʔaxū-nā
to-DEF-bedouin.PL.GEN and-hand.CS-1PL NEG attack in-3SG.M for-COMP-3SG.M brother.CS-1PL

to the bedouins so that our hand does not touch him, for he is our brother,

בְשָׂרֵנוּ, הוּא; וַיִּשְׁמְעוּ, אֶחָיו. כח וַיַּעַבְרוּ
כלחמנא פקבלו מנה אכ'ותה. 28. פלמא ג'אזו

ka-laḥmi-nā fa-qabilū min-hu ʔixwatu-hū. fa-lammā ǧāzū
as-flesh.CS.GEN-1PL CONJ-accept.PF.3PL.M from3SG.M brother.PL.CS-3SG.M and-when pass.PF.3PL.M

our flesh [and blood]." His brothers accepted. When

אֲנָשִׁים מִדְיָנִים סֹחֲרִים, וַיִּמְשְׁכוּ וַיַּעֲלוּ אֶת-יוֹסֵף
אלרג'אל אלמדיניון אלתג'אר ג'ד'בו יוסף ואצעדוה

t-riǧālu l-midyanīyūna t-tiǧāru ǧaḏabū yōsēp wa-ʔaṣadū-hu
DEF-man.PL DEF-Midianite.PL DEF-salesman.PL pull.PF.3PL.M Joseph and-lift.PF.3PL.M-3SG.M

the Midianite men, the traders, passed by they pulled and lifted Joseph

מִן-הַבּוֹר, וַיִּמְכְּרוּ אֶת-יוֹסֵף לַיִּשְׁמְעֵאלִים, בְּעֶשְׂרִים כָּסֶף;
מן אלג'בּ ובאעוה להם בעשרין דרהמא

mina l-ǧubbi wa-bāʕū-hu la-hum bi-ʕišrīna dirhaman
from DEF-pit.GEN and-sell.PL.3PL.M-3SG.M for-3PL.M in-twenty dirham.ACC

out of the pit and sold him to the for twenty dirhams.

וַיָּבִיאוּ אֶת-יוֹסֵף, מִצְרָיְמָה.
ואתו בה אלי מצר.

wa-ʔataw bi-hī ʔilā miṣr.
and-come.PF.3PL.M with-3SG.M to Egypt

The Midianites brought him to Egypt.

5 For the rendition of these items in comparison to the Hebrew original see Emmert 2021.

3.2 *First part of Chapter one of Maimonides'* Dalālat al-ḥāʔirīn / more nebokim

The second example consists of the first part of the first chapter of Maimonides' religious-philosophical treatise *Dalālat al-ḥāʔirīn / more nebokim* 'Guide of the Perplexed', which was originally composed in Judeo-Arabic and only later translated into Hebrew by his pupil Ibn Tibbon. The author's full Hebrew name is Rabbī Moše ben Maimon (רבי משה בן מימון) in Hebrew, often abbreviated to the acronym "Rambam" (רמב"ם). His full Arabic name is ʔAbū ʕImrān Mūsā ibn Maimūn ibn ʕUbaydallāh al-Qurtabī (ابـو عـمران مـوسى بـن مـيمون بـن عـبيد الله الـقرطبي). The first section of the *Dalālat al-ḥāʔirīn* represents a close "corpus-linguistic" analysis of Hebrew terms with a view to refute God-related concepts of anthropomorphism. In this context, the first chapter offers a detailed analysis of the Hebrew terms *ṣɛlɛm* and *dəmūṯ*. For the Judeo-Arabic text cf. Munk 1963, vol. 1: יב f. For additional clarity (and unlike in the manuscripts and prints), the Hebrew items and passages are voweled here.

צֶלֶם וּדְמוּת. קד ט'ן אלנאס אן צֶלֶם
ṣɛlɛm ū-ḏəmūṯ qad ẓanna n-nāsu ʔanna ṣɛlɛm
image^{H} and-likeness^{H} ANT think.PF.3SG.M DEF-people.NOM COMP image^{H}
Image and likeness. People have thought that *ṣɛlɛm*[6]

פי אללסאן אלעבראני ידל עלי שכל אלשי
fī l-lisāni l-ʕibrānīyi yadullu ʕalā šakli š-šayʔi
in DEF-language.GEN DEF-Hebrew.GEN point.IPFV.3SG.M upon form.CS.GEN DEF-thing.GEN
in the Hebrew language denotes the shape and the configuration of a thing.

ותכ'טיטה, פודי ד'לך אלי אלתג'סים
wa-taxṭīṭi-hī fa-waddā ḏālika ʔilā t-taǧsīmi
and-design.CS.GEN-3SG.M CONJ-lead.PF.3SG.M DEM.DIST.M to DEF-corporealization.GEN
This [suggestion] led them to the pure doctrine of the corporeality [of God],

אלמחץ' קולה נַעֲשֶׂה אָדָם בְּצַלְמֵנוּ
l-maḥḍi li-qawli-hī naʕăśɛ ʔāḏām bə-ṣalmē-nū
DEF-complete.GEN for-saying.CS.GEN-3SG.M make.IPFV.1PL^{H} man^{H} in-image.CS-1PL^{H}
on account of His saying: "Let us make man in our image,

כִּדְמוּתֵנוּ וט'נוא אן אללה עלי צורה̈ אנסאן
ki-ḏmūṯē-nū wa-ẓannū ʔanna llāha ʕalā ṣūrati ʔinsānin
as-design.CS-1PL^{H} and-think.PF.3PL.M COMP God.ACC upon shape.CS.GEN man.GEN
after our likeness." (Gen 1:26) For they thought that God has a man's form,

אעני שכלה, ותכ'טיטה פלזמהם
ʔaʔnī šakli-hī wa-taxṭīṭi-hī fa-lazima-humu
mean.IPFV.1SG form.CS.GEN-3SG.M and-design.CS.GEN-3SG.M CONJ-be_necessary.PF.3SG.M-3PL.M
I mean his shape and configuration. The pure doctrine of the corporeality

אלתג'סים, אלמחץ' פאעתקדוה, וראוא
t-taǧsīmu l-maḥḍu fa-ʕtaqadū-hu wa-raʔaw
DEF-corporealization.NOM DEF-complete.NOM CONJ-believe.PF.3SG.M-3SG.M and-see-PF.3SG.M
was a necessary consequence [to be accepted by them]. They accordingly believed in it and deemed

6 The to-be-defined term is deliberately not translated here.

אנהם אן פארקוא הד׳א אלאעתקאד כד׳בוא אלנץ,
ʔanna-hum ʔin fāraqū hāḏā l-iʕtiqāda kaḏḏabū n-naṣṣa
COMP.3PL.M if deviate-PF.3PL.M DEM.M DEF-belief.ACC falsify.PF.3PL.M DEF-text.ACC
that if hey abandoned this belief, the would give the lie to the [Biblical] text;

בל יעד̃מון אלאלאה אן לם יכן ג׳סמא
bal yuʕaddimūna l-ʔilāha ʔin lam yakun ğisman
rather annihilate.IPFV-3PL.M DEF-God.ACC if NEG be.APOC.3SG.M body.ACC
that they would even make the deity to be nothing at all unless [they thought that God] he was a body

ד׳א וג׳ה ויד מת׳להם פי אלשכל
ḏā waǧhin wa-yadin miṯla-hum fī š-šakli
possessor.CS.ACC face.GEN and-hand.GEN like-3PL.M in DEF-form.GEN
provided with a face and a hand, like them in shape

ואלתכ׳טיט לכנה אכבר ואבהי בזעמהם
wa-t-taxṭīṭi lākinna-hū ʔakbaru wa-ʔabhā bi-zaʕmi-him
and-DEF-design.GEN however-3SG.M great-ELAT.M and-bright.ELAT.M in-claim.CS.GEN-3PL.M
and configuration. However, He is, in their view, bigger and more resplendent

ומאדתה איצ׳א ליסת בדם ולחם, הד׳א
wa-māddatu-hū ʔayḍan laysat bi-damin wa-laḥmin hāḏā
and-matter.CS.NOM-3SG.M also not_be-IPFV.3SG.F in-blood.GEN and-flesh.GEN DEM.M
[than they themselves], and the matter of which He is composed is not flesh and blood.

גאיה̈ מא ראוה אנה יכון תנזיהא
ġāyatu mā raʔaw-hu ʔanna-hū yakūnu tanzīhan
utmost.CS.NOM REL see.PF.3PL.M-3SG.M COMP-3SG.M be.IPFG.3SG.M not_anthropomorphizing_God.ACC
As they see it, this is as far as one can go in establishing the separateness of God from human attributes.

פי חק אללה אמא מא ינבגי אן יקאל
fīḥaqqi llāhi ʔammā mā yanbaġī ʔan yuqāla
in right.CS.GEN God.GEN as_to REL be_necessary.IPFV.3SG.M COMP say.PASS.SUBJ.3SG.M
Now with respect to which ought to be said in order

פי נפי אלג׳סמאניה̈ ואת׳באת אלוחדאניה̈
fī nafyi l-ğismānīyati wa-ʔiṯbāti l-waḥdānīyati
in negation.CS.GEN DEF-corporeality.GEN and-confirmation.CS.GEN DEF-uniqueness.GEN
to refute [the doctrine of] the corporeality of God and to establish His real unity

אלחקיקיה̈ אלתי לא חקיקה̈ להא אלא בדפע אלג׳סמאניה̈
l-ḥaqīqīyatillatī lā ḥaqīqata la-hā ʔil-lā bi-dafʕi l-ğismānīyati
DEF-true.F.GEN REL.F NEG truth.ACC for-3SG.F if-NEG in-refuting.CS.GEN DEF-corporeality.GEN
– which can have no true reality unless one disproves His corporeality –

פסתערף ברהאן ד׳לך כלה מן הד׳ה אלמקאלה̈
fa-sa-taʕrifu ḏālika kulla-hū min hāḏihī l-maqālati
CONJ-FUT-know.IPFV.2SG.M DEM.DIST.M all.CS.ACC-3SG.M from DEM.F DEF-treatise.GEN
you shall know the demonstration of all this from this Treatise.

ואנמא אלתנביה הנא פי הד׳א אלפצל עלי

wa-ʔinna-mā t-tanbīhu hunā fī hāḏā l-faṣli ʕalā

and-however DEF-alert.NOM here in DEM.M DEF-chapter.GEN upon

However, here in this chapter, an indication is given with a view to

תביין מעני צֶלֶם וּדְמוּת פאקול, אן

tabyīni maʕnā ṣɛlɛm ū-dəmūṯ fa-ʔaqūlu ʔinna

explanation.CS.GEN meaning.CS.GEN image^{H} and-likeness^{H} CONJ-say.IPFV.1SG FOC

elucidating the meaning of *ṣɛlɛm* and *ḏəmūṯ*. Now I say that

אלצורה̈ אלמשהורה̈ ענד אלג׳מהור אלתי הי שכל

ṣ-ṣūrata l-mašhūrata ʕinda l-ǧumhūrati llatī hiya šaklu

DEF-form.ACC DEF-well_known.ACC at DEF-public.GEN REL.F 3SG form.CS.NOM

in the Hebrew the proper term designating the form that is well known among the multitude, namely that form which is the shape

אלשי ותכ׳טיטה אסמהא אלכ׳ציץ בהא פי

š-šayʔi wa-taxṭīṭu-hū smu-hā l-xaṣīṣu bi-hā fī

DEF-thing.GEN and-design-3SG.M name.CS.NOM-3SG.F DEF-specific.NOM in-3SG.F in

and the configuration of a thing, is *tōʔar*.

אללסאן אלעבראני תֹאַר קאל יְפֵה-תֹאַר

l-lisāni l-ʕibrānīyi tōʔar qāla yəpē- tōʔar

DEF-language.GEN DEF-Hebrew.GEN "tōʔar"^{H} say.PF.3SG.M beautiful.CS.M^{H} appearance^{H}

Thus scripture says: "beautiful in form [*tōʔar*]

וִיפֵה מַרְאֶה, מַה-תָּאֳרוֹ, כְּתֹאַר בְּנֵי הַמֶּלֶךְ.

w-īpē marʔɛ ma-ttåʔå̆r-ō kə-ṯōʔar bənē ham-mɛlɛḵ

and-beautiful.CS.M^{H} look^{H} what-appearance.CS-3SG.M^{H} as-appearance.CS^{H} son.CS.PL^{H} DEF-king^{H}

and beautiful in appearance (Gen 39:6)"; "What form [*tåʔå̆r-ō*] is he of? (1 Sam 28:14)"; "As the form [*tōʔar*] of the children of the king (Judg 8:18)"

וקיל פי אלצורה̈ אלצנאעיה̈ יְתָאֳרֵהוּ בַשֶּׂרֶד [...]

wa-qīla fī ṣ-ṣūrati ṣ-ṣināʕīyati yɛṯåʔå̆rē-hū b-aś-śɛrɛḏ

and-say.PASS.3SG.M in DEF-form.GEN DEF-artificial.F.GEN mark.IPFV.3SG.M-3SG.M^{H} with-DEF-line^{H}

This term is also applied to an artificial form: "he marketh [*yɛṯåʔå̆rē-hū*] its form with a line [...]

וּבַמְּחוּגָה יְתָאֳרֵהוּ והד׳ה אסמיה̈ לם תוקע

u-ḇ-am-məḥūḡā yəṯåʔå̆rē-hū wa-hāḏihī smīyatun lam tūqaʕ

and-with-DEF-circle^{H} mark.IPFV.3SG.M-3SG.M^{H} and-DEM.F designation NEG fall.PASS.PF.3SG.F

and he marketh [*yɛṯåʔå̆rē-hū*] its form with a compass (Isa 44:13)." This is a term

עלי אלאלאה תעאלי קט וחאשא וכלא

ʕalā l-ʔilāhi taʕālā qaṭṭu wa-ḥāšā wa-kallā

upon DEF-God.GEN be_lofty.PF.3SG.M ever and-God_forbid and-absolutely_not

that is never applied to the deity, my He be exalted; far and remote may this thought be from us.

אמא צֶלֶם פהו יקע עלי אלצורה̈ אלטביעיה̈

ʔammā ṣɛlɛm fa-huwa yaqaʕu ʕalā ṣ-ṣūrati ṭ-ṭabīʕīyati

FOC "ṣɛlɛm"^{H} CONJ-3G.M fall.IPFV.3SG.M upon DEF-form.GEN DEF-natural.F.GEN

The term image *ṣɛlɛm*, on the other hand, is applied to the natural form,

אעני עלי אלמעני אלד׳י בה תג׳והר אלשי

ʔaʕnī ʕalā l-maʕnā lladī bi-hī taǧawhara š-šayʔu

mean.IPFV.1SG upon DEF-meaning.GEN REL.M in-3SG.M substantiate.PF.3SG.M DEF-thing.NOM

I mean to the notion in virtue of which a thing is constituted as a substance

וצאר מא הו והו חקיקתה מן חית׳ הו ד׳לך

wa-ṣāra mā huwa wa-huwa ḥaqīqatu-hū min ḥaytu huwa dālika

and-become.PF.3SG.M what 3SG.M and-3SG.M truth.CS-3SG.M from where 3SG.M DEM.D.M

and becomes what it is. It is the true reality of the thing in so far as the latter

אלמוג׳וד אלד׳י ד׳לך אלמעני פי אלאנסאן הו אלד׳י ענה

l-mawǧūdu lladī dālika l-maʕnā fī l-ʔinsāni huwa lladī ʕan-hu

DEF-essence REL.M DEM.D.M DEF-meaning.NOM in DEF-man 3SG.M REL.M from-3SG.M

is that particular being. In man that notion is that from which

יכון אלאדראך אלאנסאני ומן אג׳ל הד׳א

yakūnu l-ʔidrāku l-ʔinsānīyu wa-min ʔaǧli hādā

be.IPFV.3SG.M DEF-understanding.NOM DEF-human.NOM and-because.of DEM.M

human apprehension derives. It is on account of this

אלאדראך אלעקלי קיל פיה

l-ʔidrāki l-ʕaqlīyi qīla fī-hi

DEF-understanding.GEN DEF-intellectual.GEN say.PASS.PF.3SG.M in-3SG.M

intellectual apprehension that it is said of man:

בְּצֶלֶם אֱלֹהִים בָּרָא אֹתוֹ ולד׳לך קיל

bə-ṣɛlɛm ʔĕlōhīm bārā(ʔ) ʔōt-ō wa-li-dālika qīla

in-"ṣɛlɛm"[H] God[H] create.PF.3SG.M[H] ACC-3SG.M[H] and-for-DEM.D.M say.PASS.PF.3SG.M

"In the image of God created He him." (Gen 1:27) For this reason also, it is said:

צַלְמָם תִּבְזֶה לאן אלבִזָיוֹן לאחק ללנפס

ṣalm-am tibzɛ li-ʔanna l-bizāyōn lāḥiqun li-n-nafsi

"ṣɛlɛm.CS"-3SG.M[H] despise.IPFV.2SG.M[H] for-COMP DEF-contempt[H] stick.PTCP.SG.M to-DEF-soul.GEN

"Thou contemnest their image." (Ps 73:20) For *contempt* has for its object the soul,

אלתי הי אלצורה֗ אלנועיה֗ לא לאשכאל אלאעצ׳א

llatī hīya ṣ-ṣūratu n-nawʕīyatu lā li-ʔaškāli l-ʔaʕḍāʔi

REL.F 3SG.F DEF-shape.NOM DEF-central.F.NOM NEG to-form.CS.PL.GEN DEF-body_part.PL.GEN

which is the specific form, not the shape and configuration of the parts of the body.

ותכ׳טיטהא וכד׳לך אקול אן אלעלה פי

wa-taxṭīṭi-hā wa-ka-dālika ʔaqūlu ʔinna l-ʕillata fī

and-design.CS.GEN-3SG.F and-as-DEM-D.M say.IPFV.1SG COMP DEF-reason.ACC in

I assert also that the reason why

תסמיה֗ אלאצנאם צְלָמִים כון אלמטלוב מנהא

tasmiyati l-ʔaṣnāmi ṣəlāmīm kawnu l-maṭlūbi min-hā

denomination.CS.GEN DEF-idol.PL.GEN "ṣəlāmīm"[H] being.CS.NOM DEF-seek.PASS.PTCP.GEN from-3SG.F

why idols are called lies in the fact that what was sought in them

מענאהא אלמט׳נון בה לא שכלהא

maʕnā-hā l-maẓnūnu bi-hā lā šaklu-hā

meaning.CS.NOM-3SG.F DEF-think.PASS.PTCP.NOM in-3SG.F NEG form.CS.NOM-3SG.F

was the that what deemed to subsist in them, and no their shape

ותכ׳טיטהא וכד׳לך אקול פי צַלְמֵי טְחֹרֵיהֶם
wa-taxṭīṭu-hā wa-ka-ḏālika ʔaqūlu fī ṣalmē ṭəhōrē-hɛm
and-design.CS.GEN-3SG.F and-as-DEM.DIST.M say.IPFV.1SG in "image".CS.PL^{H} hemorrhoid.CS.PL-3PL.M^{H}
and configuration. I assert similarly with regard to the scriptural expression: "images of your emerods" (1 Sam 6:5)

לאן כאן אלמראד מנהא מעני דפע
li-ʔanna kāna l-murāda min-hā maʕnā dafʕi
for-COMP be.PF.3SG.M DEF-intend.PASS.PTCP.ACC from-SG.F meaning.CS.NOM refuting.CS.GEN
For what was intended by them was the notion of warding off

אד׳יה̈ אלטְחוֹרִים לא שכל אלטְחוֹרִים פאן לם
ʔaḏīyati l-ṭəhōrīm lā šaklu l-ṭəhōrīm fa-ʔin lam
damage.CS.GEN DEF-hemorrhoid.PL^{H} NEG form.CS.NOM DEF-hemorrhoid.PL^{H} CONJ-if NEG
the harm caused by the emerods, and not the shape of the emerods. If, however,

יכן בד מן אן יכון צַלְמֵי טְחֹרֵיהֶם
yakun budda min ʔan yakūna ṣalmē ṭəhōrē-hɛm
be.APOC.3SG.M doubt.ACC from COMP be.SUBJ.3SG.M "image".CS.PL^{H} hemorrhoid.CS.PL-3PL.M^{H}
there should not be no doubt concerning the expression "images of your emerods"

וצְלָמִים מן אג׳ל אלשכל ואלתכ׳טיט פיכון צֶלֶם
wa-ṣəlāmīm min ʔağli š-šakli wa-t-taxṭīṭi fa-yakūnu ṣɛlɛm
and-"ṣəlāmīm"^{H} because.of DEF-form.GEN and-DEF-design.GEN CONJ-be.IPFV.3SG.M "ṣɛlɛm"^{H}
and *ṣəlāmīm* being used in order to denote shape and configuration, it would follow that *ṣɛlɛm*

אסם משתרך או משכך יקאל עלי
ismun muštarakun ʔaw mušakkakun yuqālu ʕalā
noun.NOM share.pass.PTCP.NOM or arouse_doubt.PASS.PTCP.NOM say.PASS.IPFV.3SG.M upon
is an equivocal or amphibolous term applied to

אלצורה̈ אלנועיה̈ ועלי אלצורה̈ אלצנאעיה̈ ומא
ṣ-ṣūrati n-nawʕīyati wa-ʕalā ṣ-ṣūrati ṣ-ṣināʕīyati wa-mā
DEF-form.GEN DEF-central.F.GEN and-upon DEF-form.GEN DEF-artificial.F.GEN and-what
the specific form and also to the artificial form and to what

מאת׳להא מן אשכאל אלאג׳סאם אלטביעיה̈
māṯilu-hā min ʔaškāli l-ʔağsāmi ṭ-ṭabīʕīyati
resemble.CS.PTCP.M-3SG.F from form.CS.PL.GEN DEF-body.PL.GEN DEF-natural.F.GEN
is analogous to the two in the shapes and configurations of the natural bodies.

ותכ׳אטיטהא ויכון אלמראד בה פי קולה
wa-taxāṭīṭi-hā wa-yakūnu l-murādu bi-hī fī qawli-hī
and-design.PL.GEN.3SG.F and-BE.IPFV.3SG.M DEF-intend.PASS.PTCP.NOM in-3SG.M in speech.CS.GEN-3SG.M
That which was meant in the scriptural dictum,

נַעֲשֶׂה אָדָם בְּצַלְמֵנוּ אלצורה̈ אלנועיה̈ אלד׳י הו
naʕăśɛ ʔāḏām bə-ṣalmē-nū ṣ-ṣūratu n-nawʕīyatu llaḏī huwa
make.IPFV.1PL^{H} man^{H} in-ṣɛlɛm.CS-1PL^{H} DEF-form.NOM DEF-central.F.NOM REL.M 3SG.M
"let us make man in our image" was the specific form, which is

אלאדראך אלעקלי לא אלשכל ואלתכ׳טיט

l-ʔidrāku	*l-ʕaqlīyu*	*lā*	*š-šaklu*	*wa-t-taxṭīṭu*
DEF-understanding.NOM	DEF-intellectual.NOM	NEG	DEF-form.NOM	and-DEF-design.NOM

the intellectual apprehension, not the shape and configuration.

פקד בינّא לך אלפרק בין צֶלֶם ותֹאַר

fa-qad	*bayyannā*	*la-ka*	*l-farqa*	*bayna*	*ṣɛlɛm*	*wa-tōʔar*
CONJ-ANT	explain.PF.1PL	for-2SG.M	DEF-difference.ACC	between	"ṣɛlɛm"[H]	and-"tōʔar"[H]

We have explained to you the difference between "ṣɛlɛm" and "tōʔar",

ובינא מעני צֶלֶם

wa-bayyannā	*maʕnā*	*ṣɛlɛm*
and-explain.PF.1PL	meaning.CS.ACC	"ṣɛlɛm"

and have explained the meaning of *ṣɛlɛm*.

3.3 Linguistic and literary intertextuality in Maimonides' ʔIggeret Teman

The third example consists of the first part of the *ʔIggeret Teman*, which was composed in 1173/1174 by Maimonides as a sort of "pep talk" in moral support of the Jewish community in Yemen, which at the time was threatened both by external and internal factors. Maimonides sent the epistle as a response to a message by Yaʕaqov ben Natanaʔel ibn al-Fayyumī (יעקב בן נתנאל אבן אלפיומי), who had expressed his worries about the Yemeni ruler, who threatened to forcibly convert the Jewish community to Islam, as well as his worries about a false Messiah within the Yemeni Jewish community in a letter addressed to Maimonides. For the edition of this text excerpt, together with three contemporary Hebrew translations, cf. Halkin 1952: 4–14.

While this text *grosso modo* sticks to the rules of Classical Arabic, a number of Middle Arabic features can be observed, such as the oblique sound plural ending *-īna* on nouns also in nominative position, the occasional omission of the accusative singular ending *-an*, or the use of the relative marker *allaḏī* irrespective of the gender of the antecedent.

This text witnesses a sizable number of Hebrew cultural and religious terms in Arabic context. First, one can observe direct insertion of Hebrew words or noun phrases in the Arabic context. Among the terms found in predicate or object position are, e.g., חבלי משיח *hɛḇlē mā̊šīaḥ* 'Messianic plagues', גוי *gōy* 'non-Jew', ממזר *mamzēr* 'bastard' (child of a Jewish mother and a non-Jewish father), as well as derogatory משגע *məšuggaʕ* 'madman' (codeword for the founder of religion Muḥammad ibn ʕAbdallāh). The most prominent Hebrew proper nouns in the text are the following: ישראל *yiśrā̊ʔēl* 'Israel', משה *mōšɛ* 'Moses', *dā̄nīʔēl* 'Daniel', *yəšaʕyā̄hū* 'Isaiah', and ישוע הנצרי *yēšūaʕ han-nåṣrī* 'Jesus the Nazarene'.

What is more, Hebrew nouns are often directly preceded by the Arabic definite article *al-* אל, e.g., אלשמד *al-šəmā̊ḏ* 'the forced conversion', אלגלות *al-gālūṯ* 'the diaspora', אלחכמים *al-ḥăkā̊mīm* 'the Sages', אלמשיח *al-māšīaḥ* 'the Messias', and אלתורה *al-tōrā̄* 'the Torah'. Likewise, nouns can be determined by the Arabic pronominal suffix *-nā* נא 'our', e.g., גלותנא *gā̊lūṯ-nā* 'our diaspora'. A mix of Arabic and Hebrew can also occur in noun-adjective phrases, consisting of a Hebrew noun and an Arabic adjective, e.g., אלצרות אלעצימה *al-ṣā̊rōṯ al-ʕaẓīma* 'the considerable problems'.

On the other hand, whole Hebrew noun(-adjective) phrases or even whole verbal phrases can be inserted in the Arabic context, e.g., גזר שמד על ישראל *gāzar šəmād ʕal yiśrāʔēl* 'he imposed forced conversion upon Israel' שמועה רעה *šəmūʕāh rāʕāh* 'bad news', or מזרח ומערב *mizraḥ ū-maʕărāḇ* 'East and West'. The same holds for formulae of respect, notably זכורים לברכה *zəḵūrīm li-ḇrāḵā* 'may their memory be blessed' and cognomina of Moses, notably משה עבדו *mōšɛ ʕaḇd-ō* 'Moses, his servant' and משה רבינו *mōše(h) rabbē-nū* 'Moses, out teacher'. At times, one can detect the allusion to Biblical quotations, e.g., in the example לא זה יצלח ולא זה יצלח *lō(ʔ) zɛ yiṣlaḥ wə-lō(ʔ) zɛ yiṣlaḥ* 'neither one will succeed'. Here an allusion to Jer 22:30 is obvious כִּי לֹא יִצְלַח מִזַּרְעוֹ, אִישׁ יֹשֵׁב עַל-כִּסֵּא דָוִד, וּמֹשֵׁל עוֹד, בִּיהוּדָה 'for no man of his seed shall prosper, sitting upon the throne of David, and ruling any more in Judah'.

In yet other examples, Bible quotations are obvious or explicitly mentioned as such. This can happen by direct insertion without mentioning the speaker, e.g., כָּל-שֹׁמְעוֹ תְּצִלֶּינָה שְׁתֵּי אָזְנָיו 'both the ears of every one that heareth it shall tingle' (1 Sam 3:11), וַיִּהְיוּ לְיִשְׂרָאֵל בַּתָּוֶךְ, אֵלֶּה מִזֶּה וְאֵלֶּה מִזֶּה 'so they were in the midst of Israel, some on this side, and some on that side' (Jos 8:22). In other instances, a prophet is introduced as speaker by קאל אלנבי *qāla n-nabī* 'the prophet said', e.g., before the following Bible quotations: וָאֹמַר, אֲדֹנָי יְהוִה חֲדַל-נָא מִי יָקוּם, יַעֲקֹב: כִּי קָטֹן הוּא 'Then said I: O Lord God, cease, I beseech Thee; how shall Jacob stand? For he is small.' (Amos 7:5) or נְנַתְּקָה אֶת-מוֹסְרוֹתֵימוֹ; וְנַשְׁלִיכָה מִמֶּנּוּ עֲבֹתֵימוֹ. יוֹשֵׁב בַּשָּׁמַיִם יִשְׂחָק: אֲדֹנָי יִלְעַג-לָמוֹ 'Let us break their bands asunder, and cast away their cords from us. He that sitteth in heaven laugheth, the Lord hath them in derision.' (Psalm 2:3–4). In yet other instances, a prophet is explicitly named, e.g., קאל ישעיהו תָּעָה לְבָבִי, פַּלָּצוּת בִּעֲתָתְנִי; אֵת נֶשֶׁף חִשְׁקִי, שָׂם לִי לַחֲרָדָה 'Isaiah said: My heart is bewildered, terror hath overwhelmed me; the twilight that I longed for hath been turned for me into trembling' (Is 21:4) or ובין לנא אלסייד דניאל יִתְבָּרְרוּ וְיִתְלַבְּנוּ וְיִצָּרְפוּ, רַבִּים, וְהִרְשִׁיעוּ רְשָׁעִים, וְלֹא יָבִינוּ כָּל-רְשָׁעִים; וְהַמַּשְׂכִּלִים, יָבִינוּ 'Many shall purify themselves, and make themselves white, and be refined; but the wicked shall do wickedly; and none of the wicked shall understand; but they that are wise shall understand.' (Dan 12:10). At times, God is revealed as speaker through the prophets, e.g., in the following cases: [...] מייזנא אללה לקולה רַק בַּאֲבֹתֶיךָ חָשַׁק יְהוָה, לְאַהֲבָה אוֹתָם; וַיִּבְחַר בְּזַרְעָם אַחֲרֵיהֶם, בָּכֶם מִכָּל-הָעַמִּים כַּיּוֹם הַזֶּה 'God has distinguished us [...]: Only the Lord had a delight in thy fathers to love them, and He chose their seed after them, even you, above all peoples, as it is this day' (Deut 10:15) or והו קולה וּבָעִתִּים הָהֵם, רַבִּים יַעַמְדוּ עַל-מֶלֶךְ הַנֶּגֶב; וּבְנֵי פָּרִיצֵי עַמְּךָ, יִנַּשְּׂאוּ לְהַעֲמִיד חָזוֹן וְנִכְשָׁלוּ 'And [this] is his speech: And in those times there shall many stand up against the king of the south; also the children of the violent among thy people shall lift themselves up to establish the vision; but they shall stumble' (Dan 11: 14).

Last, but not least, one can also observe the use of Islamic formulae in Jewish context (cf. also Cohen 2011), notably cases such as *tabāraka* 'may he be blessed', תעאלי *taʕālā* 'may he be lofty', אלחק *al-ḥaqq*, one of the 99 names of God, and גל אסמה *ǧalla smu-hū* 'may his name be high'.

אמא מא ד׳כרתה מן אמר הד׳א אלקאים

ʔammā mā ḏakarta-hū min ʔamri hāḏā l-qāʔimi

TOP REL mention.PF.2SG.M-3SG.M from matter.CS.GEN DEM.M DEF-stand.PTCP.GEN

You write that the rebel leader[7]

בארץ׳ אלימן אלד׳י גזר שמד על ישראל

bi-ʔarḍi l-yamani llaḏī gāzar šəmāḏ ʕal yiśrå̄ʔēl

in-land.CS.GEN DEF-Yemen.GEN REL.M impose.PF.3SG.M[H] forced_conversion[H] upon[H] Israel[H]

in Yemen decreed compulsory apostasy for the Jews

וג׳בר כל אלמואצ׳ע אלתי קדר עליהא

wa-ǧabara kulla l-mawāḍiʕi llatī qadara ʕalay-hā

and-force.PF.3SG.M all.CS.ACC DEF-place.PL.GEN REL.F have_power.PF.3SG.M upon-3SG.F

by forcing the Jewish inhabitants of all the places he had subdued

מן אלדין כאלד׳י פעל אלכנעני פי בלאד

mina d-dīni ka-llaḏī faʕala l-kanʕanīyu fī bilādi

from DEF-religion.GEN as-REL.M do.PF.3SG.M DEF-Canaanite.NOM in land.CS.PL.GEN

to desert the Jewish religion just as the Berbers had compelled them to do in

אלמגרב פלקד קטע הד׳א אלכ׳בר ט׳הורנא

l-maġribi fa-la-qad qaṭaʕa hāḏā l-xabaru ẓuhūra-nā

DEF-Maghreb.GEN CONJ-ASSEV-ANT cut.PF.3SG.M DEM.M DEF-message.NOM back.CS.PL.ACC-1PL

the Maghreb. Verily, the news has broken our backs

ואבהת ואדהש ג׳מלה̈ ג׳מוענא וחק

wa-ʔabhata wa-ʔadhaša ǧumlata ǧumūʕi-nā wa-ḥaqqun

and-amaze.PF.3SG.M and-astound.PF.3SG.M totality.CS.ACC group.CS.PL.GEN-1PL and-right

and has astounded and dumbfounded the whole of our community. And rightly

לנא והד׳ה שמועה רעה כָּל-שֹׁמְעוֹ--תְּצִלֶּינָה, שְׁתֵּי

la-nā wa-hāḏihī šəmūʕå̄ rå̄ʕå̄ kål-šōməʕ-ō təṣillɛnå̄ štē

for-1PL and-DEM.F rumor[H] bad.F[H] every.CS-hear-PTCP.CS.M-3SG.M[H] ring.IPFV.3PL.F[H] two.CS.F[H]

so. For these are evil tidings, “and whosoever heareth of them, both his ears tingle” (1 Sam 3:11).

אָזְנָיו ולקד צ׳עפת קלובנא ותשושת

ʔåznå̄-w wa-la-qad ḍaʕufat qulūbu-nā wa-tašawwašat

ear.CS.PL-3SG.M[H] and-ASSEV-ANT be_weak.PF.3SG.F heart.CS.PL.NOM-1PL and-be_confused.3SG.F

Indeed our hearts are weakened, our minds are confused,

אפכארנא ונוהנת קואנא להד׳ה אלצרות

ʔafkāru-nā wa-nwahanat quwā-nā li-hāḏihī ṣ-ṣārōṯ

thought.CS.PL.NOM-1PL and-fade.PF.3SG.F force.CS.PL.NOM-1PL for-DEM.F DEF-problem.PL[H]

and the powers of the body wasted because of the dire misfortunes

אלעצ׳ימה אלד׳י בדאנא אלשמד פי טרפי אלעאלם

al-ʕaẓīmati llaḏī badaʔa-nā š-šəmāḏ fī ṭarafayi l-ʕālami

DEF-strong.F.GEN REL.M initiate.PF.3SG.M-1PL DEF-persecution[H] in side.CS.DU DEF-world.GEN

which brought religious persecutions upon us from the two ends of the world,

7 The translation here closely follows the edition by Halkin (1952).

מזרח ומערב וַיִּהְיוּ לְיִשְׂרָאֵל בַּתָּוֶךְ אֵלֶּה מִזֶּה

mizrāḥ ū-maʕărāḇ way-yihyū lə-yiśrāʔēl b-at-tāwɛḵ ʔēllɛ miz-zɛ

east^{H} and-west^{H} and-be.PRET.3PL.M^{H} for-Israel^{H} in-DEF-middle^{H} DEM.PL^{H} from-DEM.M^{H}

the East and the West, “so that the enemies were in the midst of Israel, some on this side,

וְאֵלֶּה מִזֶּה וען מת'ל הד'א אלוקת אלמהול

wə-ʔēllɛ miz-zɛ wa-ʕan miṯli hāḏā l-waqti l-muhawwili

und-DEM.PL^{H} from-DEM.M^{H} and-from like.CS.GEN DEM.M DEF-time.GEN DEF-alarm.PTCP.GEN

and some on that side” (Jos 8:22). The prophet upon learning of such difficult

קאל אלנבי מתשפעא פינא דאעיא לנא

qāla n-nabīyu mutašaffiʕan fī-nā wa-dāʕiyan la-nā

say.PF.3SG.M DEF-prophet.NOM mediate.PTCP.ACC in-1PL and-pray.PRCP.ACC for-1PL

and dreadful time prayed and interceded in our behalf (, as we read),

וָאֹמַר אֲדֹנָי יְהוִה חֲדַל-נָא--מִי יָקוּם

wā-ʔōmar ʔăḏōnā-y YHWH (ʔɛ̆lōhīm) ḥăḏal-nā mī yāqūm

and-say.PF.1SG^{H} Lord.CS.PL-1SG^{H} God^{H} stop.IPT.2SG.M-COH^{H} who^{H} stand.IPFV.3SG.M^{H}

“Then said I, O Lord, cease, I beseech Thee: how shall Jacob stand?

יַעֲקֹב כִּי קָטֹן, הוּא והד'א אמר לא יסתצגרה

yaʕăqōḇ kī qāṭōn hū(ʔ) wa-hāḏā ʔamrun lā yastaṣġiru-hū

Jacob^{H} because^{H} little^{H} 3SG.M^{H} and-DEM.M matter NEG hold_for_little.IPFV.3SG.M-3SG.M

for he is small” (Amos 7:5). Indeed, this is a subject that no religious man dare take lightly,

ד'ו דין ולא יטרחה מן חצל לה

ḏū dīnin wa-lā yaṭraḥu-hū man ḥaṣala la-hū

possessor.CS.NOM religion.GEN and-NEG throw.IPFV.3SG.M-3SG.M REL arrive.PF.3SG.M to-3SG.M

nor any one who believes in Moses put aside.

במשה יקין ולא שך אן הד'ה הי חבלי' משיח

bi-mōšɛ yaqīnun wa-lā šakka ʔanna hāḏihī hiya ḥɛḇlē māšīaḥ

in Moses^{H} faith.NOM and-NEG doubt.ACC COMP DEM.F 3SG.F pain.CS.PL^{H} Messias^{H}

There can be no doubt that these are the Messianic travails

אלתי כאנו אלחכמים ע"ה יסתעיד'ון

allatī kānū l-ḥăḵāmīm ʕ[ālē-hɛm] h[aš-šālōm] yastaʕīḏūna

REL.F be.PF.3PL.M DEF-wise.PL^{H} upon-3PL.M ^{H} DEF-peace^{H} take_refuge.IPFV.3PL.M

concerning which the Sages invoked

באללה מן רויתהא ומבאשרתהא, ואלאנביא

bi-llāhi min ruʔyati-hā wa-mubāšarati-hā wa-l-ʔanbiyāʔu

in-God.GEN from vision.CS.GEN-3SG.F and-direct_contact.CS.GEN-3SG.F and-DEF-prophet.PL.NOM

God that they be spared seeing and experiencing them. Similarly the prophets

ירתעדון מן תכ'יילהא, כמא קאל ישעיהו

yartaʕidūna min taxayyuli-hā ka-mā qāla yəšaʕyāhū

tremble.IPFV.3PL.M from imagination.CS.GEN-3SG.F as-what say.PF.3SG.M Isaiah^{H}

trembled when they envisioned them as we learn from the words of Isaiah

חין וצפהם תָּעָה לְבָבִי, פַּלָּצוּת בִּעֲתַתְנִי;
ḥīna waṣafa-hum tā̊ʕā̊ ləḇā̊ḇ-ī pallā̊ṣūṯ biʕă̊ṯā̊ṯ-nī
when describe.PF.3SG.M-3PL.M err.PF.3SG.M^{H} heart.CS-1SG^{H} terror^{H} afflict.PF.3SG.F-1SG.OBJ^{H}
(when he described them), "My heart panteth, fearfulness affrighteth me,

אֶת נֶשֶׁף חִשְׁקִי, שָׂם לִי לַחֲרָדָה ונאדא אללה
ʔēṯ nɛšɛp̄ ḥišq-ī śā̊m l-ī lə-ḥădā̊rā̊ wa-nādā llāhu
ACC twilight^{H} desire-1SG^{H} put.PF.3SG.M^{H} for-1SG^{H} to-trembling^{H} and-exclaim.PF.3SG.M God.NOM
the twilight I have longed for hath been turned for me into trembling" (Isa 21:4). Note also the divine exclamation in

פי כתאבה באלויל למן שאהדהא וקאל
fī kitābi-hī bi-l-wayli li-man šāhada-hā wa-qāla
in book.CS.GEN in-DEF-woe.GEN for-REL witness.PF.3SG.M-3SG.F and-say.PF.3SG.M
the Torah expressing sympathy for those who will experience them, as we read,

אוֹי, מִי יִחְיֶה מִשֻּׂמוֹ אֵל
ʔōy mī yiḥyɛ miś-śūm-ō ʔēl
alas^{H} who^{H} live.IPFV.3SG.M^{H} from.put.INF.CS-3SG.M^{H} God^{H}
"Alas, who shall live when God doeth this!" (Num 24:23).

ואמא מא ד׳כרתה מן כון בעץ׳ אלקום
wa-ʔamma mā ḏakarta-hū min kawni baʕḍi l-qawmi
and-as_to what mention.PF.2SG.M-3SG.M from existence.CS.GEN some.CS.GEN DEF-people.GEN
You write that the hearts of some people have turned away,

מאלת קלובהם וחדת׳ להם אלשך
mālat qulūbu-hum wa-ḥadaṯa la-humu š-šakku
digress.PF.3SG.F heart.PL.CS.NOM-3PL.M and-occur.PF.3SG.M for-3PL.M DEF-doubt.NOM
uncertainty befalls them

ואכ׳תבטת אעתקאדהם, ובעץ׳ אלנאס מא זאל
wa-xtabaṭati ʕtiqādu-hum, wa-baʕḍu n-nāsi mā zāla
and-go_astray.PF.3SG.F belief.CS.NOM-3PL.M and-some.CS.GEN DEF-people.GEN NEG stop.PF.3SG.M
and their beliefs are weakened, while others have not

יקינהם ולא אצ׳טרבו, פהד׳א אמר
yaqīnu-hum wa-lā ḍṭarabū, fa-hāḏā ʔamrun
conviction.CS.NOM-3PL.M and-NEG be_disturbed.PF.3PL.M CONJ-DEM.SG.M matter.NOM
lost faith nor have they become disquieted.

קד סבק אלאנד׳אר בה וביין לנא אסייד דניאל
qad sabaqa l-ʔinḏāru bi-hī wa-bayyana la-nā s-sayyidu dā̊nīʔēl
ANT precede.PF.3SG.M DEF-warning.NOM in-3SG.M and-explain.PF.3SG.M for-1PL DEF-Sir.NOM Daniel
Concerning this matter we have a divine premonition through Daniel

במא אעלמה אללה אן אד׳א טאל מקאמנא
bi-mā ʔaʕlama-hū llāhu ʔanna ʔiḏā ṭāla maqāmu-nā
in-REL inform.PF.3SG.M-3G.M God-NOM COMP when be_long.PF.3SG.M sojourn.CS.NOM-1PL
who predicted that the prolonged stay of Israel

פי אלגלות ותואלת אלשדאיד עלינא ימרקו כת׳ירון
fī l-gā̊lūṯ wa-tawālati š-šadāʔidu ʕalay-nā yamruqu kaṯīrīna
in DEF-exile^{H} and-continue.PF.3SG.F DEF-difficulty.PL.NOM upon-1PL deviate.IPFV.1SG.M many.PL.M
in the Diaspora, and the continuous persecutions will cause many to drift away

מן אלדין ויתשככו ויצ׳לו. וד׳לך
mina d-dīni *wa-yatašakkakū* *wa-yaḍillū.* *wa-ḏālika*
from DEF-religion.GEN and-be_in_doubt.IPFV.3PL.M and-go_astray.IPFV.3PL.M and-DEM.REM.SG.M
from our faith, to have misgivings, or to go astray, because

למא ישאהדונה מן צ׳עפנא וגלבה̈ מקאומינא
li-mā *yušāhidūna-hū* *min ḍuʕfi-nā* *wa-ġalabati* *muqāwimī-nā*
for-REL witness.IPFV.3PL.M-3SG.M from weakness.CS.GEN-1PL and-victory.CS.GEN opponent.CS.PL.M-1PL
they witnessed our feebleness, and noted the triumph of our adversaries

ואקתדארהם עלינא, ואן אלבעץ׳ לא ישכו
wa-qtidāri-him *ʕalay-nā,* *wa-ʔanna l-baʕḍa* *lā* *yašukkū*
and-domination.CS.GEN-3PL.M upon-1PL and-COMP DEF-few.ACC NEG doubt.IPFV.3PL.M
and their dominion over us, while others would neither oscillate in their belief,

ולא יכ׳תל אעתקאדהם. קאל יִתְבָּרֲרוּ
wa-lā *yaxtallu* *ʕtiqādu-hum.* *qāla* *yiṯbårərū*
and-NEG be_broken.IPFV.3SG.M belief.CS.NOM-3PL.M say.PF.3SG.M be_visible.IPFV.3PL.M[H]
nor be shaken in their convictions. This may be gathered from the verse, "Many shall purify themselves,

וְיִתְלַבְּנוּ וְיִצָּרְפוּ רַבִּים, וְהִרְשִׁיעוּ רְשָׁעִים,
wə-yiṯlabbənū *wə-yiṣṣårəpū* *rabbīm,* *wə-hiršīʕū*
and-be_white.IPFV.3PL.M[H] and-be_redeemed.IPFV.3PL.M[H] many.PL.M[H] and-do_evil.CONSEC.IPFV.3PL.M[H]
make themselves white, and be refined, but the wicked shall do wickedly,

וְלֹא יָבִינוּ כָּל־רְשָׁעִים; וְהַמַּשְׂכִּלִים יָבִינוּ.
rəšåʕīm, wə-lō(?) yåḇīnū *kål-rəšåʕīm;* *wə-ham-maśkīlīm yåḇīnū.*
evil.PL [H] and-NEG[H] understand.IPFV.3PL.M[H]all.CS-evil.PL[H] and-DEF-educated.PL[H] understand.IPFV.3PL.M[H]
and none of the wicked shall understand; but they that are wise shall understand" (Dan 12:10).

ת׳ם ביין אן ולו אלפהמא אלעקלא אלד׳ין
ṯumma bayyana *ʔanna* *wa-lawi* *l-fuhamāʔu* *wa-l-ʕuqalāʔu* *llaḏīna*
then explain.PF.3PL.M COMP and-if DEF-understanding.PL and-DEF-intelligent.PL REL.PL.M
Further on he foretells that even men of understanding and intelligence who

תמר בהם אלשדאיד פית׳בתוא להא, ויבקון
tamurru *bi-himu* *š-šadāʔidu* *fa-yaṯbutū* *la-hā* *wa-yabqawna*
pass.IPFV.3SG.F in-3PL.M DEF-difficulty.PL.M CONJ-be_firm for-3SG.F and-remain.IPFV.3PL.M
would have brooked milder misfortunes and remained

עלי אימאנהם בה׳ ובמשה עבדו,
ʕalā *ʔīmāni-him* *bi-ha[š-šēm]* *ū-ḇə-Mōše* *ʕaḇd-ō*
upon faith.CS.GEN-3PL.M in-DEF[-name][H] and-in-Moses[H] servant.CS-3SG.M[H]
firm in their belief in God and in His servant Moses,

סתמר עליהם אמור אשד ואצעב מן
sa-tamurru *ʕalay-him* *ʔumūrun* *ʔašaddu* *wa-ʔaṣʕabu* *min*
FUT-pass.IPFV.3SG.F upon-3PL.M matter.PL.NOM strong.ELAT.NOM and-difficult.ELAT.NOM from
when they are visited by sterner and harsher afflictions

תלך אלד׳י ת׳בתוא להא. חתי יתוהם
tilka *llaḏī* *ṯabatū* *la-hā.* *ḥattā* *yatawahhama*
DEM.REM.SG.F REL be_firm.PF.3PL.M for-3SG.F until be_under_delusion.SUBJ.3SG.M
than those in the light of which they stood firm, will yield to distrust and will err

בעצ'הם ויצ'ל, ולא יצפו אלא אלקליל.

baʕḍu-hum wa-yaḍillū, wa-lā yaṣfū ʔil-lā l-qalīlu.

some.CS.NOM-3PL.M and-go_astray.SUBJ.3PL.M and-NEG be_pure.IPFV.3PL.M if-NEG DEF-few.NOM

while only a few will remain pure in faith

והו קולה וּמִן-הַמַּשְׂכִּילִים יִכָּשְׁלוּ.

wa-huwa qawlu-hū ū-min-ham-maśkīlīm yikkāšəlū.

and-3SG.M speech.CS.NOM-3SG.M and-from-DEF-educated.PL^{H} stumble.IPFV.3PL.M^{H}

as we read, "And some of them that are wise shall stumble."

ואלאן יא אכ'ותנא ינבגי לכם אג'מעין

wa-l-ʔāna yā ʔixwatu-nā yanbaġī la-kum ʔaǧmaʕīna

and-DEF-time.ACC VOC brother.CS.PL.1PL be_necessary.IPFV.3SG.M for-2PL.M together.PL.ACC

And now, my co-religionists, it is essential for you all

אן תנצתו ותתאמ̈לוא מא אורדה לכם,

ʔan tanṣitū wa-tataʔammalū mā ʔūridu-hū la-kum

COMP listen.SUBJ.2PL.M and-consider.SUBJ.2PL.M REL reveal.IPFV.1SG-3SG.M for-2PL.M

to give attention and consideration to that which I am going to point out to you.

ותלקנוה ללאצאגיר ואלנסא, כי ית'בת

wa-tulaqqinū-hu li-l-ʔaṣāġīri wa-n-nisāʔi kay yaṯbuta

and-suggest.SUBJ.2PL.M-3SG.M for-DEF-little.PL.GEN and-DEF-woman.PL.GEN so_that be_firm.SUBJ.3SG.M

You should impress it upon the minds of your women and children, so that

להם מא צ'עף מן אלאעתקאד ואכתל,

la-hum mā ḍaʕufa mina l-iʕtiqādi wa-xtalla,

for-3PL.M REL weaken.PF.3SG.M from DEF-belief.GEN and-be_damaged.PF.3SG.M

their faith which may be enfeebled and impaired may be strengthened,

ויתמכן פי אנפסהם אליקין אלד'י לא יזול.

wa-yatamakkana fī ʔanfusi-himu l-yaqīnu llaḏī lā yazūlu.

and-consolidate.SUBJ.3SG.M in soul.CS.PL.GEN-3PL.M DEF-faith REL NEG cease.IPFV.3SG.M

and that they be re-established in an unceasing belief.

וד'אך כ'לצנא אללה וכ'לצכם אן הד'א

wa ḏāka xallaṣa-nā llāhu wa-xallaṣa-kum ʔanna hāḏā

and-DEM.DIST.M restitute.STAT.3SG.M-1PL God.NOM and-restitute.STAT.3SG.M-2PL.M COMP DEM.M

May the Lord deliver us and you from religious doubt! Remember, that

הו דין אלחק אלצחיח אלמנזל עלינא

huwa dīnu l-ḥaqqi ṣ-ṣaḥīḥu l-munazzalu ʕalay-nā

3SG.M religion.CS.NOM DEF-truth.GEN DEF-true.NOM DEF-send_down.PTCP.PASS.NOM upon-1PL

ours is the true and authentic Divine religion, revealed to us

עלי יד סייד ג'מיע אלנביין,

ʕalā yadi sayyidi ǧamīʕi n-nabīyīna,

upon hand.CS.GEN master.CS.GEN total.CS.GEN DEF-prophet.PL.GEN

[through Moses], the master of the prophets,

אלמתקדמין ואלמתאחרין, אלד'י מייזנא אללה בה

l-mutaqaddimīna wa-l-mutaʔaxxirīna, llaḏī mayyaza-nā llāhu bi-hī

DEF-precede.PTCP.PL.GEN and-DEF-succeed.PTCP.PL.GEN REL distinguish.PF.3SG.M-1PL God.NOM in-3SG.M

the former as well as the later ones, by means of which God has distinguished us

עלי ג׳מיע אלעאלמין לקולה רַק בַּאֲבֹתֶיךָ
ʕalā ǧamīʕi l-ʕālamīna li-qawli-hī raq ba-ʔăḇōṯɛ-ḵā̊
above total.CS.GEN DEF-world.inhabitant.PL.GEN for-speech.CS.GEN-3SG.M only[H] in-father.CS.PL-2SG.M[H]
from the rest of mankind, as Scripture says, "Only the Lord had a delight in thy fathers

חָשַׁק ה׳ לְאַהֲבָה אוֹתָם; וַיִּבְחַר בְּזַרְעָם
ḥā̊šaq ha[š-šēm] lə-ʔahăḇā̊ ʔōṯ-ā̊m; way-yiḇḥar bə-zarʕ-ā̊m
love.PF.3SG.M[H] DEF[-name][H] for-love[H] ACC-3PL.M[H] and-choose.PRET.3SG.M[H] in-seed.CS-3PL.M[H]
to love them and He chose their seed after them,

אַחֲרֵיהֶם, בָּכֶם מִכָּל-הָעַמִּים, ומא כאן ד׳לך באסתחקאק
ʔaḥărē-hɛm, bā̊-ḵɛm, mik-kål-hā̊-ʕammīm wa-mā kāna ḏālika bi-stiḥqāqin
after-3PL.M[H] in-2PL.M[H] from-all.CS-DEF-people.PL[H] and-NEG be.PF.3SG.M DEM.DIST.M in-merit.GEN
even you above all peoples" (Deut 10:15). This did not happen because of our merits,

לנא בל אנעאמא עלינא במא תקדם לאבאינא
la-nā bal ʔinʕāman ʕalay-nā bi-mā taqaddama li-ʔābāʔi-nā
for-1PL rather show_grace.MAṢDAR.ACC upon-1PL in-REL precede.PL.3SG.M for-father.CS.PL-1PL
but rather as an act of Divine grace, and on account of our forefathers

מן מערפתה וטאעתה כקולה
min maʕrifati-hī wa-ṭāʕati-hī ka-qawli-hī
from knowledge.CS.GEN-3SG.M and-obedience.CS.GEN-3SG.M as-speech.CS.GEN-3SG.M
who were cognizant of God and submitted to Him as we read,

לֹא מֵרֻבְּכֶם מִכָּל-הָעַמִּים חָשַׁק ה׳ בָּכֶם,
lō(ʔ) mē-rubbə-ḵɛm mik-kål-hā̊-ʕammīm ḥā̊šaq ha[š-šēm] bā̊-ḵɛm,
NEG[H] from-multitude.CS-2PL.M[H] from-all.CS-DEF-people.PL[H] love.PF.3SG.M[H] DEF[-name][H] in-2PL.M[H]
"The Lord did not set His love upon you[, nor choose you, because ye were more in number than any people ... but because the Lord loved you, and because He would keep the oath which He swore unto your fathers.]" (Deut 7:7).

ולמא כ׳צ̇צנא בשראיעה ומרסומאתה,
wa-lammā xaṣṣaṣa-nā bi-šarāʔiʕi-hī wa-marsūmāti-hī,
and-when make_special.PF.3SG.M-1PL in-law.CS.PL.GEN-3SG.M and-precept.CS.PL.GEN-3SG.M
God has made us unique by His laws and precepts,

ובאנת פצ׳ילתנא עלי אלגיר
wa-bānat faḍīlatu-nā ʕalā l-ġayri
and-become_obvious.PF.3SG.F precedence.CS.NOM-1PL upon DEF-other.GEN
and our pre-eminence is manifested

בקואנינה ומוצ׳ועאתה, כקולה תע׳
bi-qawānīni-hī wa-mawḍūʕāti-hī ka-qawli-hī taʕ[ālā]
in-law.CS.PL.GEN-3SG.M and-theme.CS.PL.GEN-3SG.M as-speech.CS.GEN-3SG.M be_lofty.STAT.3SG.M
in His rules and statutes, as Scripture says,

ממתנא עלינא וּמִי גּוֹי גָּדוֹל, אֲשֶׁר-לוֹ חֻקִּים
mumattinan ʕalay-nā ū-mī gōy gā̊ḏōl, ʔăšer-l-ō ḥuqqīm
confirm.PTCP.ACC upon-1PL and-who[H] people[H] big[H] REL-for-3SG.M[H] law.PL[H]
in narrating God's mercies to us, "And what great nation is there, that hath statutes

וּמִשְׁפָּטִים צַדִּיקִם, נאצבתנא אלמלל כלהא

ū-mišpåṭīm ṣaddīqīm nāṣabat-nā l-milalu kullu-hā

and-ordinance.PL^{H} just.PL^{H} fight.PF.3SG.F-1PL DEF-religion.PL.NOM all.CS.NOM-3SG.F

and ordinances so righteous [as all this law, which I set before you this day?]" (Deut 4:8). Therefore all the nations rose up against us,

חסדא עלי וטגיאנא ותג׳רדת מלוך אלארץ׳

ḥaṣdan ʕalay-hi wa-ṭuġyānan wa-tağarradat mulūku l-ʔarḍi

envy.ACC upon-3SG.M and-tyranny.ACC and-be-drawn.PF.3SG.F king.CS.PL.NOM DEF-land.GEN

instigated by envy and impiety, and all the kings of the earth applied themselves

לטלבנא מן אג׳לה ט׳למא ועדואנא,

li-ṭalabi-nā min ʔağli-hī ẓulman wa-ʕudwānan

for-persecution.CS.GEN because of-3SG.M sin.ACC and-hostility.ACC

to persecute us, motivated by injustice and enmity.

ירידון מעאנדה אללה ומא יעאנד.

yurīdūna muʕānadata llāhi wa-mā yuʕānad.

want.IPFV.3PL.M opposition.CS.ACC God.GEN and-NEG oppose.IPFV.PASS.3SG.M

They wanted to thwart God, but He cannot be thwarted.

פמא מן זמאן מן חיניד׳ אלי אלאן אלא וכל מלך

fa-mā min zamānin min ḥīnaʔiḏin ʔilā l-ʔāna ʔil-lā wa-kullu malikin

CONJ-NEG from time.GEN from once until DEF-time.ACC if-NEG and-every.CS king.GEN

Ever since the time of Revelation, every despot

גבאר או מתגלב שדיד אוול מא יג׳על גרצ׳ה

ğabbārin ʔaw mutaġallibin šadīdin ʔawwalu mā yağʕalu ġarada-hū

violent.GEN or overpowerer.GEN strong.GEN first.CS REL do.IPFV.3SG.M goal.CS.ACC.3SG.M

or slave that has attained to power, be he violent or ignoble, has made it his first aim

ואוכד אומרה נקץ׳ שריעתנא ופסך׳

wa-ʔawkadu ʔawāmiri-hī naqḍu šarīʕati-nā wa-fasxu

and-strong.ELAT.CS order.PL.CS.GEN-3SG.M destruction.CS law.CS.GEN-1PL and-abolition.CS

and his final purpose to destroy our law, and to vitiate

דיננא באלקהר ואלגלבה באלסיף,

dīni-nā bi-l-qahri wa-l-ġalabatu bi-s-sayfi

religion.CS.GEN-1PL with-DEF-force.GEN and-DEF-overpowering with-DEF-sword.GEN

our religion, by means of the sword, by violence, or by brute force,

מת׳ל עמלק וסיסרא וסנחריב ונבוכדנצר וטיטוס ואדרינוס

miṯla ʕămålēq wa-sīsərå wa-sanḥērīḇ wa-nəḇūḵaḏneṣṣar wa-ṭīṭūs wa-ʔaḏriyanūs

like Amalek and-Sisera and-Sennacherib and-Nebuchadnezzar and-Titus and-Hadrian

such as Amalek, Sisera, Sennacherib, Nebuchadnezzar, Titus, Hadrian,

וגירהם מן אמת׳אלהם. הד׳א הו אלנוע אלואחד

wa-ġayri-him min ʔamṯāli-him. hāḏā huwa n-nawʕu l-wāḥidu

and-other.CS.GEN-3PL.M from example.PL.CS.GEN-3PL.M DEM.M 3SG.M DEF-kind DEF-one

and others like them. This is one

מן אלנועין אלד׳ין ירומון [בהמא] גלבה̈

mina n-nawʕayni llaḏayni yarūmūna [bi-himā] ġalabata

from DEF-kind.DU.GEN REL.DU.GEN wish.IPFV.3PL.M [with-DU.GEN] overpowering.CS.ACC

of the two classes which attempt to foil (or: with which they attempt to foil)

אלארדה אלאלאהיה.
l-ʔirādati l-ʔilāhīya.
DEF-will.GEN DEF-divine.F.GEN
the Divine will.

ואמא אלנוע אלת׳אני פהם חד׳אק אלמלל
wa-ʔammā n-nawʕu t̲-t̲ānī fa-hum hud̲d̲āqu l-milali
CONJ-TOPIC DEF-kind DEF-second CONJ.3PL.M skillful.PL.CS DEF-religious_confession.PL.GEN
The second class consists of the most intelligent

ועלמאיהם מת׳ל אלסריאן ואלפרס ואליונאן. פאן האולי
wa-ʕulamāʔu-hum mit̲la s-suryāni wa-l-farsi wa-l-yūnān. fa-ʔinna hāʔulāʔi
and-learned.PL.CS-3PL.M as DEF-Syrian.COLL and-Persian.COLL and-Greek.COLL CONJ-FOC DEM.PL
and educated among the nations, such as the Syrians, Persians, and Greeks. These

איצ׳א ירומון נקץ׳ אלשריעה ופסכ׳הא בחג׳ג׳
ʔayḍan yarūmūna naqḍa š-šarīʕati wa-fasxa-hā bi-ḥuǧaǧin
also want.IPFV.3PL.M destruction.CS.ACC DEF-law.GEN-1PL and-abolition.CS with-argument.PL.GEN
also endeavor to demolish our law and to vitiate it by means of arguments

יוהמון בהא ומג׳אדלאת יולפונהא, וירומון
yūhimūna bi-hā wa-muǧādalātin yuʔallifūna-hā wa-yarūmūna
deceive.IPFV.3PL.M with-3SG.F and-controversy.PL.GEN compose.IPFV.3PL.M-3SG.F and-wish.IPFV.3PL.M
which they invent, and by means of controversies which they institute. They seek

מן פסך׳ אלשריעה ומחו את׳ארהא בתואליפהם,
min fasxi š-šarīʕati wa-maḥwi ʔāt̲āri-hā bi-taʔālīfi-him
from abolition.GEN DEF-law.GEN and-wiping.CS.GEN trace.PL.CS.GEN-3SG.F in-writing.PL.CS.GEN-3PL.M
to render the Law ineffectual and to wipe out every trace thereof by means of their polemical writings,

מת׳ל מא ירומה אלמתגלבין בסיופהם
mit̲la mā yarūmu-hū l-mutaġallibīna bi-suyūfi-him
like REL wish.IPFV.3SG.M DEF-overpowerer.PL with-sword.PL.CS.GEN-3PL.M
just as the despots plan to do it with the sword.

ולא זה יצלח ולא זה יצלח,
lō(ʔ) zɛ yiṣlaḥ wə-lō(ʔ) zɛ yiṣlaḥ
NEG^H DEM.M^H succeed.IPFV.3SG.M^H and-NEG^H DEM.M^H succeed.IPFV.3SG.M^H
But neither the one nor the other shall succeed.

לאן צ׳מאן אללה תבארך ותע׳ עלי ידי
li-ʔanna ḍamāna llāhi tabāraka wa-taʕ[ālā] ʕalāyaday
for-COMP guarantee.CS.ACC God.GEN be_blessed.STAT.3SG.M and-be_lofty.STAT.3SG.M on hand.CS.DU
We possess the divine assurance given to

ישעיהו קד תקדם לנא באן כל מתגלב
yəšaʕyā̆hū qad taqaddama la-nū bi-ʔanna kulla mutaġallibin
Isaiah ANT precede.PF.3SG.M for-1PL in-COMP every.CS.ACC overpowerer.GEN
Isaiah concerning any tyrant

ירום גלב שריעתנא ואבטאלהא אלמת׳ל
yarūmu ġalaba šarīʕati-nā wa-ʔibṭāla-hā
wish.IPFV.3SG.M overpowering.CS.ACC law.CS.GEN-1PL and-annullation.CS.ACC-3SG.F
that will wish to undermine our Law and to annihilate it

באלתה אלחרביה, יפסד אללה תלך אלאלה
bi-ʔālati-hī l-ḥarbīyati, yufsidu llāhu tilka l-ʔālata
with-tool.PL.CS.GEN-3SG.M DEF-military.F.GEN annihilate.IPFV.3SG.M God DEM.REM.F DEF-tool.ACC
by weapons of war, that the Lord will demolish them

פלא תנג׳ח. והד׳א עלי ג׳הֿה אלמת׳ל
fa-lā tanǧaḥu. wa-hāḏā ʕalā ǧihati l-maṯali
CONJ-NEG succeed.IPFV.3SG.F and-DEM.M on side.CS.GEN DEF-example.GEN
so that they will have no effect. This is only a metaphorical way of saying

אן רומה לא יחצל דאימא. וכד׳לך כל מחאג׳ג׳
ʔanna rawma-hū lā yaḥṣulu dāʔiman. wa-ka-ḏālika kullu muḥāǧiǧin
COMP wish.CS.ACC-3SG.M NEG arrive.IPFV.3SG.M forever and-like-DEM.REM every.CS arguer.GEN
that his efforts will be of no avail, and that he will not accomplish his purpose. In like manner whenever a disputant

ירום אבטאל מא באידינא, יג׳הץ׳ אללה
yarūmu ʔibṭāla mā bi-ʔaydī-nā, yuǧhiḍu llāhu
wish.IPFV.3SG.M abolition.CS.ACC REL in-hand.PL.CS.GEN-1PL abort.IPFV.3SG.M God
shall attempt to demonstrate the falsity of our Law, the Lord will shatter

הג׳תה ויבטלהא וידפעהא ולא
ḥuǧǧata-hū wa-yubṭilu-hā wa-yadfaʕu-hā wa-lā
argument.CS.ACC-3SG.M and-abolish.IPFV.3SG.M-3SG.F and-push.IPFV.3SG.M-3SG.F and-NEG
his arguments and prove them absurd untenable and ineffective so that they will not

תדום. כמא קאל תב׳ ותע׳ ואעדא
tadūm. kamā qāla tab[āraka] wa-taʕ[ālā] wāʕidan
last.IPFV.3SG.M as say.PF.3SG.M be_blessed.STAT.3SG.M and-be_lofty.STAT.3SG.M promise.PTCP.ACC
last. This divine promise is contained in the following verse,

כָּל-כְּלִי יוּצַר עָלַיִךְ, לֹא יִצְלָח, כָּל-לָשׁוֹן
kål-kəlī yūṣar ʕālay-ḵ, lō(ʔ) yiṣlaḥ kål-lāšōn
every.CS-tool^{H} create.IPFV.PASS.3SG.M^{H} against-2SG.F^{H} NEG^{H} succeed.IPFV.3SG.M^{H} every.CS-tongue^{H}
“No weapon that is formed against thee shall prosper; and every tongue

תָּקוּם-אִתָּךְ לַמִּשְׁפָּט, תַּרְשִׁיעִי. וכלאהמא יצ׳נאן
tåqūm ʔitt-åḵ l-am-mišpåṭ, taršīʕī wa-kilā-humā yaẓunnāni
rise.IPFV.3SG.F^{H} with-2SG.F^{H} to-DEF-judgment^{H} condemn.IPFV.2SG.F^{H} and-both-3DU think.IPFV.3DU
that shall rise against thee in judgment thou shalt condemn.” (Is 54:17). Although the exponents of both methods persuade themselves

אן הד׳א בנין ימכן אן יהתדם,
ʔanna hāḏā bunyānun yumkinu ʔan yahtadima,
COMP DEM.M building be_possible.IPFV.3SG.M COMP be_destroyed.SUBJ.3SG.M
that this is a structure which can be demolished,

ויתואמרון קלע קואעדה אלראסכ׳ה אלי אלמא,
wa-yataʔāmarū qalʕa qawāʕidi-hī r-rāsixati ʔilā l-māʔi
and-conspire.IPFV.3PL.M uprooting.CS.ACC fundament.PL.CS.GEN.3SG.M DEF-firm.F.GEN to DEF-water.GEN
and they exert themselves to undermine its firmly established foundations,

פמא יזידון אנפסהם אלא שקאא ותעבא. ואלבניאן עלי מא הו
fa-mā yazīdūna ʔil-lā šaqāʔan wa-taʕaban. wa-l-bunyānu ʕalāmā huwa
CONJ-NEG augment.IPFV.3PL.M if-NEG misery.ACC and-toil.ACC and-DEF-building on REL 3SG.M
they only increase their pain and toil. The structure remains

שדיד יבקי. ואלחק יהזו בהם ויצ׳חך מנהם,
šadīdun yabqā. wa-l-ḥaqqu yahzaʔu bi-him wa-yaḍḥaku min-hum,
firm remain.IPFV.3SG.M and-DEF-true mock.IPFV.3SG.M in-3PL.M and-laugh.IPFV.3SG.M from-3PL.M
remains as firmly planted as ever, while the God of Truth mocks and derides them,

לרומהם בצ׳עף עקלהם מא לא ירום אלאנסאן
li-rawmi-him bi-ḍiʕfi ʕaqli-him mā lā yarūmu l-ʔinsānu.
for-wish.CS.GEN-3PL.M in-weakness.CS.GEN mind.CS.GEN-3PL.M REL NEG wish.IPFV.3SG.M DEF-man
because they endeavor, with their feeble intelligence, to achieve a goal that is beyond the powers of mortal man.

מת׳לה. קאל אלנבי ואצף רומהם והזו
miṯla-hū qāla n-nabīyu wāṣif[an] rawma-hum wa-yahzaʔu
like-3SG.M say.PF.3SG.M DEF-prophet describe.ptcp[acc] wish.CS.ACC-3PL.M and-mock.IPFV.3SG.M
The inspired writer describes their attempt

אלחק בהם: נְנַתְּקָה, אֶת-מוֹסְרוֹתֵימוֹ; וְנַשְׁלִיכָה
l-ḥaqqu bi-him nənattəq-ā̊(h) ʔeṯ mōsərōṯē-mō wə-našlīḵ-ā̊(h)
DEF-true in-3PL.M break.JUSS.1PL-COH^{H} ACC^{H} band.PL.CS-3PL.M^{H} and-cast.JUSS.1PL-COH^{H}
and God's scorn of them in the following verses: "Let us break their bands asunder, and cast away

מִמֶּנּוּ עֲבֹתֵימוֹ. יוֹשֵׁב בַּשָּׁמַיִם יִשְׂחָק: אֲדֹנָי,
mimmɛn-nū ʕăḇōṯē-mō yōšēḇ b-aš-šā̊mayim yiśḥaq ʔăḏōnā̊-y
from-1PL^{H} band.PL.CS-3PL.M^{H} sit.PTCP^{H} in-DEF-heaven^{H} laugh.IPFV.3SG.M^{H} lord.PL.CS-1SG^{H}
their cords from us, He that sitteth in heaven laugheth, the Lord,

יִלְעַג-לָמוֹ.
yilʕaḡ lā̊-mō
derise.IPFV.3SG.M^{H} for-3PL.M^{H}
hath them in derision" (Psalms 2:3-4).

פלם נזל מבליין ממתחנין מן הד׳ין אלפריקין טול איאם
fa-lam nazal mublīyīna min hāḏayni l-farīqayni ṭūla ʔayyāmi
CONJ-NEG stop.APOC.1PL test.PTCP.PASS.PL.ACC from DEM.DU.M.GEN DEF-party.DU.GEN during day.PL.CS.GEN
Both of these parties have harassed and afflicted us incessantly throughout the epoch

דולתנא ובעץ׳ איאם גלותנא.
dawlati-nā wa-baʕḍi ʔayyāmi gā̊lūṯ-nā.
state.CS.GEN and-some.CS.GEN day.PL.CS.GEN exile^{H}-1PL
of our political independence, and partly during the period of our dispersion.

ת׳ם חדת׳ פריק אכ׳ר, רכב חאלה
ṯumma ḥadaṯa farīqun ʔāxaru rakkaba ḥāla-hū
then appear.PF.3SG.M party other construe.PF.3SG.M state.CS.ACC-3SG.M
After that there arose a new sect which combined

מן אלחאלתין ג׳מיעא, אעני אלגלבה ואלמחאג׳ג׳ה
mina l-ḥālatayni ǧamīʕan ʔaʕnī l-ġalabata wa-l-muḥāǧaǧata
from DEF-state.DU.GEN together mean.IPFV.1SG DEF-overpowering.ACC and-DEF-argumentation
the two methods, namely, conquest and controversy, into one,

ואלמנאצ׳רה. וראי אן הד׳א אבלג פי קטע
wa-l-munāẓarata. wa-raʔā ʔanna hāḏā ʔablaġu fī qaṭʕi
and-DEF-dispute.ACC and-see.PF.3SG.M COMP DEM.M appropriate.ELAT in cutting.CS.GEN
because it believed that this procedure would be more effective in wiping out

את׳ר אלמלה, פדבּר אן ידעי אלנבוה,
ʔaṯari l-millati, fa-dabbara ʔan yaddaʕiya n-nubūwata
trace.CS.GEN DEF-religion.GEN CONJ-organize.PF.3SG.M COMP claim.SUBJ.3SG.M DEF-prophethood.ACC
every trace of the Jewish nation and religion. It, therefore, resolved to lay claim to prophecy

ויאתי בשריעה כ׳לאף שריעה̈ אללה ויקול
wa-yaʔtī bi-šarīʕatin xilāfa šarīʕati llāhi wa-yaqūlu
and-come.IPFV.3SG.M with-law.GEN in_contrast_to law.CS.GEN God.GEN and-say.IPFV.3SG.M
and to found a new faith, contrary to our Divine religion, and to contend

אנהא מן אללה איצ׳א כקול אלצאדק, פיחדת׳
ʔanna-hā mina llāhi ʔayḍan ka-qawli ṣ-ṣādiqi fa-yuḥdiṯu
COMP-3SG.F from God.GEN also as-speech.CS.GEN DEF-upright.GEN CONJ-bring.IPFV.3SG.M
that it was equally God-given. Thereby it hoped to raise

אלשך, ויוקע אלחירה, באן הד׳ה תכ׳אלף
š-šakka, wa-yūqiʕu l-ḥayrata, bi-ʔanna hāḏihī tuxālifu
DEF-doubt.ACC and-create.IPFV.3SG.M DEF-confusion.ACC in-COMP DEM.F differ.IPFV.3SG.F
doubts and to create confusion, since one is opposed

מן הד׳ה, והמא ג׳מיעא מנתסבתאן לאלאה ואחד.
min hāḏihī wa-humā ǧamīʕan muntasibatāni li-ʔilāhin wāḥidin.
from DEM.F and-3DU together derive.PTCP.DU.F to-god.GEN one.GEN
to the other and both supposedly emanate from a Divine source,

פיכון ד׳לך מדכ׳ל לתלאף הד׳ה ותלך.
fa-yakūnu ḏālika madxalun li-talafi hāḏihī wa-tilka.
CONJ-be.IPFV.3SG.M DEM.REM entrance to-destruction.CS.GEN DEM.F and-DEM.REM.F
which would lead to the destruction of both religions.

והד׳א מן אלתחייל אלעג׳יב אלד׳י יפעלה אלשכ׳ץ
wa-hāḏā mina t-taḥayyuli l-ʕaǧībi llaḏī yafʕalu-hū
and-DEM.M from DEF-imagination.GEN DEF-miraculous.GEN REL do.IPFV.3SG.M-3SG.M
For such is the remarkable plan contrived

אל׳שדיד אלנכאיה, אנה ירום קתל עדוּוה
š-šaxṣu š-šadīdu n-nikāyati, ʔanna-hū yarūmu qatla ʕadūwi-hī
DEF-person DEF-strong DEF-damage.GEN COMP-3SG.M wish.IPFV.3SG.M killing.CS.ACC enemy.CS.GEN-3SG.M
by a man who is envious and querulous. He will strive to kill his enemy and to save

ובקאה הו. פאד׳א אעיאה ד׳לך דבר
wa-baqāʔa-hū huwa. fa-ʔiḏā ʔaʕayya-hū ḏālika dabbara
and-remaining.CS.ACC-3SG.M 3SG.M CONJ-if be_impossible_to-3SG.M DEM.REM organize.PF.3SG.M
his own life, but when he finds it impossible to attain his objective, he will devise

פי האלה תקתלה ותקתל עדווה.
fī ḥāli-hī taqattula-hū wa-taqattula ʕadūwi-hī.
in state.CS.GEN-3SG.M being_killed.CS.ACC-3SG.M and-being_killed.CS.ACC enemy.CS.GEN-3SG.M
a scheme whereby they both will be slain.

פאול מן עמד עלי הד׳א אלראי ישוע הנצרי שחיק
fa-ʔawwalu man ʕamada ʕalā hāḏā r-raʔyi yēšūaʕ han-nåṣrī šəḥīq
CONJ-first.CS REL rely.PF.3SG.M on DEM.M DEF-opinon Jesus[H] DEF-Christian[H] ground.CS[H/Aram]
The first one to have adopted this plan was Jesus the Nazarene, may his bones be ground to dust.

עצמות והו מו ישראל, ואנה ואן כאן אבוה גוי

ʕăṣā̊mōṯ wa-huwa min yiśrā̊ʔēl, wa-ʔinna-hū wa-ʔin kāna ʔabū-hu gōy

bone.PL^{H} and-3SG.M from Israel^{H} and-FOC-3SG.M and-if be.PF.3SG.M father.CS-3SG.M non-Jew^{H}

He was a Jew because, although his father was a Gentile,

ואמה ישראלית פהו מן ישראל, לאן אלאצל ענדנא

wa-ʔummu-hū yiśrəʔēlīṯ, wa-huwa min yiśrā̊ʔēl, li-ʔanna l-ʔaṣla ʕinda-nā

and-mother.CS-3SG.M Israeli.F^{H} and-3SG.M from Israel^{H} for-COMP DEF-root.ACC at-1PL

his mother was a Jewess. For in accordance with the principles of our law,

גוי ועבד הבא על בת ישראל הולד כשר.

gōy wā̊-ʕɛḇɛḏ hab-bā̊(ʔ) ʕal baṯ yiśrā̊ʔēl haw-wā̊lā̊ḏ kā̊šēr.

non-Jew^{H} and-slave^{H} DEF-come.PTCP^{H} on^{H} daughter.CS^{H} Israel^{H} DEF-newborn^{H} kosher^{H}.

a child born of a Jewess and a Gentile, or of a Jewess and a slave, is legitimate. (Yebamot 45a).

ואנמא נסמיה ממזר עלי ג׳הה̈ אלמבאלגה.

wa-ʔinnamā nusammī-hi mamzēr ʕalā ǧihati l-mubālaġa.

and-however call.IPFV.1PL-3SG.M illegitimate^{H} on DEF-side.CS.GEN DEF-metaphor.GEN

Jesus is only figuratively termed an illegitimate child.

פאוהם אנה מבעות׳ מן אללה ליביין

fa-ʔawhama ʔanna-hū mabʕūṯun mina llāhi li-yubayyina

CONJ-make_believe.PF.3SG.M COMP-3SG.M send.PTCP.PASS from God.GEN for-explain.SUBJ.3SG.M

He impelled people to believe that he was a prophet sent by God to clarify

משכלאת אלתורה, ואנה אלמשיח אלמועוד בה

muškilāti t-tōrā̊, wa-ʔanna-hū l-mā̊šīaḥ al-mawʕūdu bi-hī

problem.CS.ACC DEF-Tora^{H} and-COMP-3SG.M DEF-Messias^{H} DEF-promise.PTCP.PASS in-3SG.M

perplexities in the Torah, and that he was the Messiah that was predicted

עלי ידי כל נבי. פתאוול אלתורה תאוילא

ʕalāyaday kulli nabīyin. fa-taʔawwala t-tōrā̊ taʔwīlan

on hand.DU.CS every.CS.GEN prophet.GEN CONJ-interpret.PF.3SG.M DEF-Tora^{H} interpretation.ACC

by each and every seer. He interpreted the Torah and its precepts in such a fashion

יוד׳י לאבטאל ג׳מלה̈ אלשריעה, ותעטיל ג׳מיע

yuʔaddī li-ʔibṭāli ǧumlati š-šarīʕati, wa-taʕṭīli ǧamīʕi

lead.IPFV.3SG.M to-annullation.CS.GEN totality.CS.GEN DEF-law and-obstruction.CS.GEN total.CS.GEN

as to lead to their total annulment, to the abolition of all

אואמרהא וארתכאב ג׳מיע מנאהיהא עלי מא

ʔawāmiri-hā wa-rtikābi ǧamīʕi manāhī-hā ʕalā mā

precept.PL.CS.GEN-3SG.F and-performance.CS.GEN total.CS.GEN prohibition.CS.GEN-3SG.F on REL

its commandments and to the violation of its prohibitions, according to which

קצד ואגרץ׳. פשער אלחכמים זכורים

qaṣada wa-ʔaġraḍa. fa-šaʕara l-ḥăḵā̊mīm zəḵūrīm

strive.PF.3SG.M and-aim_at.PF.3SG.M CONJ-notice.PF.3SG.M DEF-wise.PL^{H} remember.PTCP.PASS.PL^{H}

he strived for and aimed at. The sages, of blessed memory,

לברכה לגרצ׳ה קבל אן תתמכן שהרתה

li-ḇrā̊ḵā̊ li-ġaraḍi-hī qabla ʔan tatamakkana šuhratu-hū

for-blessing^{H} for-goal.CS.GEN-3SG.M before COMP be_established.SUBJ.3SG.F reputation.CS-3SG.M

having become aware of his plans before his reputation spread

פי אלמלה, פפעלו בה מא כאן אהלא לה.

fī l-millati, fa-faʕalū bi-hī mā kāna ʔahlan la-hū.

in DEF-religion.GEN CONJ-do.PF.3PL.M in-3SG.M REL be.PF.3SG.M welcome.ACC FOR-3SG.M

among our people, meted out fitting punishment to him.

וקד כאן תקדם לנא אלאנד'אר בד'לך עלי יד דניאל,

wa-qad kāna taqaddama la-nū l-ʔinḏāru bi-ḏālika ʕalāyadi dånīʔēl

and-ANT be.PF.3SG.M precede.PF.3SG.M for-1PL DEF-warning in-DEM.REM on hand.CS.GEN Daniel^{H}

Daniel had already alluded to him

וקאל אנה סירום רג'ל מן וקחא ישראל

wa-qāla ʔinna-hū sa-yarūmu rağulun min wuqaḥāʔi yiśråʔēl

and-say.PF.3SG.M FOC-3SG.M FUT-wish.IPFV.3SG.M man from insolent.PL.CS.GEN Israel^{H}

when he presaged the downfall of a wicked one

וכ'וארג'הם אפסאד אלדין באדעאה

wa-xawāriği-him ʔifsāda d-dīni bi-ddiʕāʔi-hī

and-heretic.PL.CS.GEM-3PL.M corruption.CS.ACC DEF-religion.GEN in-claiming.CS.GEN-3SG.M

and a heretic among the Jews who would endeavor to destroy the Law, claim

אלנבוֹוה ותעאטיה אלאמור אלעצ'ימה,

n-nubūwata wa-taʕāṭī-hi l-ʔumūra l-ʕaẓīmata

DEF-prophethood.ACC and-pursuit.CS.GEN-3SG.M DEF-thing.PL.ACC DEF-miraculous.F.ACC

prophecy for himself, make pretenses to miracles,

יעני אנّה משיח, ואן אללה יעת'רה כמא

yaʕnī ʔanna-hū måšīaḥ wa-ʔinna llāha yuʕaṯṯiru-hū kamā

mean.IPFV.3SG.M COMP-3SG.M Messias^{H} and-FOC God.ACC let_stumble.IPFV.3SG.M-3SG.M as

and allege that he is the Messiah – and God lets stumble as

עת'ר. והו קולה וּבְנֵי פָּרִיצֵי עַמְּךָ,

ʕaṯṯara wa-huwa qawlu-hū ū-ḇənē pårīṣē ʕammə-ḵå

let_stumble.PF.3SG.M and-3SG.M speech.CS-3SG.M and-son.PL.CS^{H} insolent.PL.CS^{H} people.CS-2SG.M^{H}

he has let stumble, as it is written, "Also the children of the impudent among thy people

יִנַּשְּׂאוּ לְהַעֲמִיד חָזוֹן--וְנִכְשָׁלוּ. ומן בעדה

yinnaśʔū lə-haʕămīḏ ḥăzōn wə-nikšålū wa-min baʕdi-hī

rise.IPFV.3PL.M^{H} for-pretend.INF^{H} vision^{H} and-stumble.STAT.3PL.M^{H} and-from after.CS.GEN-3SG.M

shall make bold to claim prophecy, but they shall fall." (Dan 11:14).

במדّה טוילה אשתהר דין ינסב אליה מן

bi-muddatin ṭawīlatini štahara dīnun yunsabu ʔilay-hi min

in-while.GEN long.F.GEN be_known.PF.3SG.M religion relate.PASS.IPFV.3SG.M to-3SG.M from

Quite some time after, a religion appeared the origin of which is traced to him by

בני עשו. ומע כאן ד'לך גרצ'ה אלד'י כאן

bənē ʕēśaw. wa-maʕa kāna ḏālika ġaraḍa-hū llaḏī kāna

son.PL.CS^{H} Esau.^{H} and-with be.PF.3SG.M DEM.REM goal.CS.ACC-3SG.M REL be.PF.3SG.M

the descendants of Esau, albeit it was not the intention of this person

יומّל, פמא ד׳לך צ׳ר ישראל, ולא שכו פיה לא ג׳מע
yuʔammilu,[8] *fa-mā ḍarra yiśrå̄ʔēl, wa-lā šakka fī-hi ǧamʕun,*
hope.IPFV.3SG.M CONJ-NEG damage.PF.3SG.M Israel[H] and-NEG doubt.PF.3PL.M in-3SG.M group
to establish a new faith. For he was innocuous to Israel as neither group(s)

ולא פראד, אד׳ באן להם כ׳סרה, וגלבתה
wa-lā furādun, ʔiḏ bāna la-hum xasru-hū wa-ġalabatu-hū
and-NEG single.PL because be_evident.PF.3SG.M for-3PL.M loss.CS.3SG.M and-overpowering.CS-3SG.M
nor individuals were unsettled in their beliefs because of him, since his inconsistencies were so transparent to every one. Finally he was overpowered

ואנקטאעה פי אידינא, אלי אן תםّ עליה מא תםّ.
wa-nqiṭāʕu-hū fī ʔaydī-nā, ʔilā ʔan tamma ʕalay-hi mā tamma
and-being_cut_off.CS-3SG.M in hand.PL.CS.GEN-1PL until COMP end.PF.3SG.M on-3SG.M REL end.PF.3SG.M
and put a stop to by us when he fell into our hands, and his fate is well known.

ת׳ם קאם בעדה משגע יחד׳ו חד׳וה אד׳
ṯumma qāma baʕda-hū məšuggaʕ[9] *yaḥḏū ḥaḏwa-hū ʔiḏ*
then rise.PF.3SG.M after-3SG.M crazy[H] imitate.IPFV.3SG.M imitation.CS.ACC-3SG.M because
After him arose the Madman who emulated his precursor since

פתח לה אלטריק, וזאד מע ד׳לך גרץ׳ אכ׳ר,
fataḥa la-hū ṭ-ṭarīqa, wa-zāda maʕa ḏālika ġarad[an] ʔāxara
open.PF.3SG.M for-3SG.M DEF-way.ACC and-add.PF.3SG.M with DEM.REM goaL[ACC] other.ACC
he paved the way for him. But he added the further objective

והו טלב אלמלך ואלטאעה לה פאחדת׳ מא
wa-huwa ṭalabu l-mulki wa-ṭ-ṭāʕatu la-hū fa-ʔaḥdaṯa mā
and-3SG.M seeking.CS DEF-rule and-DEF-obedience for-3SG.M CONJ-invent.PF.3SG.M REL
of procuring rule and submission, and he invented

שהר. ירידון כלהם אלתשביה בדין אללה
šahara yurīdūna kullu-humu t-tašbīha bi-dīni llāhi
be_known.PF.3SG.M want.IPFV.3PL.M all.CS-3PL.M DEF-equating.ACC with-religion.CS.GEN God.GEN
his well known religion. All of these men purposed to place their teachings on the same level with our divine religion.

סבחאנה, ולא תתשבה אלצנאעה אלאלאהיה באלצנאעה
subḥāna-hū, wa-lā tatašabbahu ṣ-ṣināʕatu l-ʔilāhīyatu bi-ṣ-ṣināʕati
prize.ACC-3SG.M and-NEG be_like.IPFV.3SG.F DEF-craft DEF-divine.F with-DEF-craft.GEN
However, divine institutions do not compare to human practices,

אלבשריה, אלא עלי גר לא מכ׳ברה לה בכלאהמא.
l-bašarīyati ʔil-lā ʕalā ġirrin lā maxbarata la-hū bi-kila-himā
DEF-human.F.GEN if-NEG on inexperienced.GEN NEG experience.ACC for-3SG.M in-both-3DU.GEN
except for a simpleton who lacks knowledge of both.

8 This passage is somewhat unclear. In the light of the three Hebrew translations, a reading ומא כאן appears to be more plausible, unless one were to read: "Even though it was his intention he had hoped for [to damage Israel/to create a new religion], he did not [succeed to] damage Israel." But cf. Halkin 1952: [iv].

9 As mentioned above, a codeword for the founder of religion Muḥammad ibn ʕAbdallāh.

3.4 A lexicographical text: an excerpt from Ibn Janāḥ's Kitāb al ʔUṣūl

The fourth example is an excerpt from the *Kitāb al ʔUṣūl* by Jonah ibn Janāḥ (ca. 990–1055 CE) (in Arabic: ʔAbū l-Walīd Marwān ibn Janāḥ أبـو الـولـيـد مـروان بـن جـنـاح) in the edition of Neubauer (1875). The work, partially building on the sound root theory established by Yehuda Ḥayyūj, counts as the masterpiece of medieval Hebrew lexicography. The original Arabic version was later translated into Hebrew by Yehuda Ibn Tibbon under the title title *Sefer haš-Šorašim* (for the Hebrew version cf. Bacher 1896; cf. also Maman 2004 and Maman 2019: 190f.). The following lemma explains the Hebrew root √ ʔ-b-y (in the original Arabic orthography √ ʔ-b-h, based on the Hebrew orthographical system).

الألف والباء والهاء וְלֹא אָבָה יְהוָה
al-ʔalifu wa-l-bāʔu wa-l-hāʔu wə-lō(ʔ) ʔā̊ḇā̊ YHWH (ʔăḏōn-ā̊y)
DEF-*ʔalif* and-DEF-*bāʔ* and-DEF-*hāʔ* and-NEG^{H} desire.PF.3SG.M^{H} be.IPFV.3SG.M^{H} (master.CS-1PL)^{H}
[The root consisting of] *ʔalif*, *bāʔ*, and *hāʔ*: "Nevertheless the Lord thy God would not harken" (Deut 23:6).

אֱלֹהֶיךָ قد ذكر من تصريف هذا المعنى
ʔɛlōhɛ-ḵā̊ qad ḏukira min taṣrīfi hāḏā l-maʕnā
God.CS-2SG.M^{H} ANT mention.PASS.PF.3SG.M from derivation.CS.GEN DEM.M DEF-meaning.GEN
The derivation of of this meaning was (already) mentioned

في كتاب حروف اللين ما فيه كفاية
fī kitābi ḥurūfi l-līni mā fī-hi kifāyatan
in book.CS.GEN letter.PL.CS.GEN DEF-soft.GEN REL in-3SG.M sufficiency.ACC
sufficiently in the Book of the weak letters ("letters of the weak")

فيلتمس من هناك: ومن هذا المعنى וְתָפֵר
fa-yultamas min hunā wa-min hāḏā l-maʕnā wə-ṯā̊pēr
CONJ-request.PASS.JUSS.3SG.M from here and-from DEM.M DEF-meaning and-fail.IPFV.3SG.F^{H}
and (thus) should be consulted there; to this meaning (belongs also): "and the

הָאֲבִיּוֹנָה ترجمة اللفظ وتبطل الإرادة
hā̊-ʔăḇīyōnā̊ tarǧamatu l-lafẓi wa-tabṭulu l-ʔirādatu
DEF-caperberry^{H} translation.CS.NOM DEF-expression.GEN and-be_void.IPFV.3SG.F DEF-will.NOM
caperberry shall fail (Qoh 12:5)". The translation of this expression is " and the will shall fail",

وذلك كناية عن البضع: وذكر هناك أيضا
wa-ḏālika kināyatun ʕani l-buḍʕi wa-ḏakara hunāka ʔayḍan
and-DEM.DIST.M allusion.NOM from DEF-vulva.GEN and-mention.PF.3SG.M there also
and this is an allusion to sex(ual failure). He also mentioned there

معنى ثانيا وهو לְמִי אוֹי לְמִי אֲבוֹי. כִּי לֹא-
maʕnā ṯāniyan wa-huwa lə-mī ʔōy lə-mī ʔăḇōy kī lō(ʔ)-
meaning.ACC second.ACC and-3SG.M for-who^{H} woe^{H} for-who^{H} desire^{H} because^{H} NEG^{H}
a second meaning: "who crieth: 'Woe'? who 'Alas'?" (Prov 23:29); "for the poor

יֶחְדַּל אֶבְיוֹן ويمكن أن يكون (من) هذ
yɛḥdal ʔɛḇyōn wa-yumkinu ʔan yakūna (min) hāḏā
stop.IPFV.3SG.M^{H} needy^{H} and-be_possible.IPFV.3SG.M COMP be.SUBJ.3SG.M(from) DEM.M
shall never cease" (Deut 15:11). Possibly, "[neither] father nor mother" (Esth 2:7) derives from this

الأصل אָב וְאֵם وهو اسم ناقص اللام
l-ʔaṣli ʔā̊ḇ wə-ʔēm wa-huwa smun nāqiṣu l-lāmi
DEF-root.GEN father^{H}and-mother^{H} and-3SG.M noun.NOM defective.CS.NOM DEF-*lām*.GEN
root, as it [father] is a noun *tertiae infirmae* ("of defective third consonant *lām*"),

كنقصان: אָח وللفظة אָב معان. منها
ka-nuqṣāni ʔā̊ḥ wa-li-l-lafẓati ʔā̊ḇ maʕānin min-hā
as-defectiveness.CS.GEN brother^{H} and-to-DEF-expression.GEN father^{H} meaning.PL from-3SG.F
as the defectiveness of *ʔā̊ḥ*. The term "father" has [several] meanings, among

المعنى المشهور المعروف وهو
l-maʕnā l-mašhūru l-maʕrūfu wa-huwa
DEF-meaning.NOM DEF-make_known.PTCP.PASS.NOM DEF-know.PTCP.PASS.NOM and-3SG.M
them the well-known one, which designates

الأبوّة. ويقال في الله عز وجل
l-ʔubūwa wa-yuqālu fī llāhi ʕazza wa-ǧalla
DEF-fatherhood.NOM and-say.PASS.IPFV.3SG.M in God.GEN be_strong.PF.3SG.M and-be_high.PF.3SG.M
fatherhood, which is used (also) in reference to God – he is lofty and exalted –

(على سبيل الاستعارة للخالق البارئ. مثل
(ʕalā sabīli l-istiʕārati li-l-xāliqi l-bāriʔi miṯla
(upon way.CS.GEN DEF-metaphor.GEN for-DEF-create.PTCP.GEN DEF-create.PTCP.GEN like
in a metaphorical sense for the creator, as in

قوله) הֲלוֹא הוּא אָבִיךָ קָּנֶךָ ومنها
qawli-hī) hă-lō(ʔ) hū(ʔ) ʔā̊ḇī-ḵā̊ qā̊nɛ-ḵā̊ wa-min-hā
speech.CS.GEN-3SG.M INTERR-NEG^{H} 3SG.M^{H} father.CS-2SG.M^{H} create.PTCP.CS-2SG.M^{H} and-from-3SG.F
the biblical quotation "is not He thy father that hath gotten thee?". Also,

الاستاذيّة وهي على ضربين [أيضا] أحدهما استاذيّة
l-ʔustāḏīyatu wa-hiya ʕalā ḍarbayni [ʔayḍan] ʔaḥadu-humā ʔustāḏīyatu
DEF-craft-NOM and-3SG.F over kind.DU.GEN[also] one.CS.NOM-3DU craft.CS.NOM
professional activity derives from it, also in two ways, one of which is professionality

المهن العملية كقولك אֲבִי, כָּל-
l-mihani l-ʕamalīyati ka-qawli-ka ʔā̊ḇī kål-
DEF-profession.PL.CS.GEN DEF-practical.F.GEN as-speech.CS.GEN-2SG.M father.CS^{H} every.CS-^{H}
in practical jobs, as in the biblical quotation "the father of all such as

תֹּפֵשׂ כִּנּוֹר. אֲבִי יֹשֵׁב אֹהֶל والثاني استاذيّة
tōpēś kinnōr ʔā̊ḇī yōšēḇ ʔōhɛl wa-ṯ-ṯānī ʔustāḏīyatu
seize.PTCP.CS^{H} zither^{H} father.CS^{H} sit.PTCP.CS^{H} tent^{H} and-DEF-second.NOM craft.CS.NOM
handle the harp" (Gen 4:21), (or) "the father of such as dwell in tents" (Gen 4:20), and the second of which is professionality in

المهن العلمية كاستاذية الرأي

l-mihani l-ʕilmīyati ka-ʔustāḏīyati r-raʔyi

DEF-profession.PL.CS.GEN DEF-scientific.F.GEN as-craft.CS.GEN DEF-opinion.GEN

scientific jobs, as the professionality in insight (philosophy)

والسنّة والسياسة قالوا וֶהְיֵה לִי לְאָב

wa-s-sunnati wa-s-siyāsati qālū wɛ-hyē(h) l-ī lə-ʔā̊ḇ

and-DEF-law.GEN and-DEF-governing.GEN say.PF.3PL.M and-be.IPT.SG.M[H] for-1SG[H] for-father[H]

and law and governance. One (the Bible) said: "Dwell with me, and be unto me a father

וּלְכֹהֵן וְהָיָה לְאָב לְיוֹשֵׁב יְרוּשָׁלִַם

ū-lə-ḵōhēn wə-hā̊yā̊ lə-ʔā̊ḇ lə-yōšēḇ yərūšā̊la(yi)m

and-to-priest[H] and-be.FUT.CONSEC.3SG.M[H] for-father[H] for-sit.PTCP.CS[H] Jerusalem[H]

and a priest" (Judg 17:10); "and he shall be a father to the inhabitants of Jerusalem" (Is 22:21);

וַיְשִׂימֵנִי לְאָב וְאָבִי רְאֵה--גַּם. אָבִי

wa-yśīmē-nī lə-ʔā̊ḇ wə-ʔā̊ḇ-ī rəʔē(h) gam ʔā̊ḇ-ī

and-put.PRET.3SG.M-1SG.OBJ[H] for-father[H] and-father.CS-1SG[H] see.IPT.SG.M[H] also[H] father.CS-1SG[H]

"and He hath made me a father [to Pharaoh]" (Gen 45:8); "Moreover, my father, see!" (1 Sam 24:11); "My father,

אָבִי רֶכֶב יִשְׂרָאֵל חָלְפוּ עִם אֳנִיּוֹת אֵבֶה

ā̊ḇ-ī rɛḵɛḇ yiśrā̊ʔēl ḥā̊ləpū ʕim ʔŏnīyōṯ ʔēḇɛ

father.CS-1SG[H] chariot.CS[H] Israel[H] pass.PF.3PL.M[H] with[H] ship.PL.CS[H] papyrus[H]

my father, the chariots of Israel" (2K 2:12); "The are passed away as the swift ships" (Job 9:26).

الأقرب فيه عندي أن يكون اسما لواد

al-ʔaqrabu fī-hi ʕind-ī ʔan yakūna sman li-wādin

DEF-near.ELAT.NOM in-3SG.M at-1SG COMP be.SUBJ.3SG.M name.ACC for-valley.GEN

The closest [this term comes to] in my opinion is that it is a name for a valley,

معروف مشهور عندهم وإنما

maʕrūfin mašhūrin ʕinda-hum wa-ʔinna-mā

make_known.PTCP.PASS.GEN know.PTCP.PASS.GEN at-3PL.M and-indeed

which is well-known to them. Indeed,

أقتصر عليه دون غيره من الأودية

ʔaqtaṣiru ʕalay-hi dūna ġayri-hī mina l-ʔawdiyati

confine_oneself.IPFV.1SG upon-3SG.M without other.CS.GEN-3SG.M of DEF-valley.PL.GEN

I confine myself to it [that valley], under exclusion of any other valley

كما أقتصر على רָץ دون غيره من

ka-mā ʔaqtaṣiru ʕalā rā̊ṣ dūna ġayri-hī mina

as-REL confine_oneself.IPFV.1SG upon run.PTCP[H] without other.CS.GEN-3SG.M of

as I confine myself to *rā̊ṣ*, under exclusion of anything other among

الأشياء في قوله וְיָמַי קַלּוּ מִנִּי

l-ʔašyāʔi fī qawli-hī wə-yā̊m-ay qallū minnī

DEF-thing.PL.GEN in speech.CS.GEN-3SG.M and-day.CS.PL-1SG[H] be_light.PF.3PL.M[H] from[H]

the things in the biblical quotation: "Now my days are swifter than

רָץ. ولا معنى للاعتلال عليهم في مثل هذا
rāṣ *wa-lā* *maʕnā* *li-l-iʕtilāli* *ʕalay-him* *fī* *miṯli* *hāḏā*
run.PTCP.SG.M^H and-NEG meaning for-DEF-weakness.GEN upon-3PL.M in like.CS.GEN DEM.M
a runner" (Job 9:25). And the pretext for them has no meaning in contexts like this.

3.5 An excerpt from a Geniza letter (cf. Diem and Edzard 2011)

The fifth example is a short excerpt from a Geniza letter written by an Egyptian Jew in the 11th/12th century CE. In the letter, the author complains about the seemingly unethical behavior of the addressee. While the letter is written in Arabic script, it also contains a few short Hebrew passages. Interestingly, a few Hebrew words are also spelled with Arabic characters. For the edition of the letter cf. Diem and Edzard 2011.

ثم ظننت انك من بنيا إدام
ṯumma ẓanantu *ʔanna-ka* *min* *bənē* *ʔāḏām*[10] *wa-ḥukītu* *mā*
then think.PF.1SG COMP-2SG.M from son.CS.PL^H man^H and-tell.PASS.PF.1SG REL
[…] I then assumed that your are a [decent] human being,

وحكيت ما جرى ممن تعلم وصعب علي
ǧarā *mim-man* *taʕallama* *wa-ṣaʕuba* *ʕalay-ya*
happen.PF.3SG.M from-REL be_informed.PF.3SG.M and-be_difficult.PF.3SG.M upon-1SG
but what had happened was reported to me from a well-informed party. It hit me hard

ما جرى فى حق الشيخ ابو سعيد ذكره
mā *ǧarā* *fī* *ḥaqqi* *š-šayxi* *ʔAbū* *Saʕīd* *ḏakara-hū*
REL happen-PF.3SG.M in right.CS.GEN DEF-sheikh.GEN ʔAbū Saʕīd remember.PF.3SG.M-3SG.M
what had happened with regard to the Sheikh ʔAbū Saʕīd – may God remember him

الله بخير فلم תדין אותי לכף זכות بل
llāhu *bi-xayrin* *fa-lam* *taḏīn*[11] *ʔōṯ-ī* *lə-kap̄* *zəḵūṯ* *bal*
God in-good.GEN CONJ-NEG judge.IPFV-2SG.M^H ACC-1SG^H for-flat_hand^H right^H rather
well […] But have have not acquitted me/given me justice; rather,

حملت عنفك على سو طـ[ـباعـ]ـك
ḥamaltu *ʕunfa-ka* *ʕalā* *sūʔi* *ṭabʕi-ka*
relate.PF.1SG rudeness.CS.ACC-2SG.M upon badness.CS.GEN character.CS.GEN-2SG.M
I explained your rudeness with your bad character

واجريته مجراك وما كفاك حتى
wa-ʔaǧraytu-hū *maǧrā-ka* *wa-mā* *kafā-ka* *ḥattā*
and-relate_back.PF.1SG-3SG.M course.CS.ACC-2SG.M and-NEG suffice-2SG.M until
and have understood it as it befits you. But [all this] was not enough (for you),

حضرت كما قلت واستاذنت على ذلك
ḥaḍarta *ka-mā* *qulta* *wa-staʔḏanta* *ʕalā*
be_present.PF.2SG.M like-REL say.PF.2SG.M and-ask_for_admittance.PF.2SG.M upon
but you (even) appeared, as you said, and asked for admittance, additionally,

10 Interestingly, the two Hebrew words in Arabic characters carry Hebrew vowel marks, a *ṣere* and a *qamaṣ*, respectively.

11 This form vacillates between Arabic (verbal syntax) and Hebrew.

حضرة سيدنا هراب מושה ירום הודו

ḏālika	*haḍrata*	*sayyidi-nā*	*hā̊-rā̊ḇ*[12]	*mōšɛ*	*yā̊rūm*	*hōḏ-ō*
DEM.DIST.M	presence.CS.ACC	master.CS.GEN-1PL	DEF-rabbi[H]	Moshe[H]	be_high-IPFV.3SG.M[H]	glory-3SG.M[H]

his excellence, our master, Rav Moshe – his glory be exalted,

فرسم لك الامتناع

fa-rasama	*la-ka*	*l-imtināʕa*
CONJ-draft.PF.3SG.M	for-2SG.M	DEF-abstinence.ACC

whereupon he instructed you to refrain [from that].

References

Primary sources

Bacher, Wilhelm. 1896. *Wurzelwörterbuch der hebräischen Sprache.* Berlin [= reprint Amsterdam 1969].

Blau, Joshua. 1980b. *Ha-sifrut ha-ʕarvit ha-yehudit: peraqim nivharim.* Jerusalem: The Magnes Press.

Blau, Joshua and Simon Hopkins. 2017. *Early Judaeo-Arabic in Phonetic Spelling. Texts from the end of the first millenium. Part I. General Intorduction and Biblical Texts: Glossaries, Translations, Commentaries and Discussions.* Jerusalem: Ben-Zvi Institute.

Derenbourg, Joseph. 1893. *Version arabe du Pentateuque de r. Saadia ben Iosef al-Fayyoúmi / revue, corrigée et accompagnée de notes hébraïques, avec quelques fragments de traduction française d'après l'arabe par J. Derenbourg.* Paris : E. Leroux.

Diem, Werner and Lutz Edzard. 2011. "Ein unhöflicher Brief und liebliche Verse. Ein Genizadokument des 11.–12. Jahrhunderts n. Chr." *Zeitschrift der Deutschen Morgenländischen Gesellschaft* 161/2: 265–304.

Halkin, Abraham S. (ed.). 1952. Maimonides, Moses. *Epistle to Yemen. The Arab Original and the three Hebrew Versions.* Transl. Boaz Cohen. New York: American Academy for Jewish Research.

Munk, Salomon. 1963. Maimonides, Moses. 1135–1204. *Dalālat al-ḥāʔirīn. Guide des égarés: traité de théologie et de philosophie* / par Moïse Ben Maimoun, dit Maïmonide; traduit ... et accompagné de notes critiques, littéraires et explicatives par S. Munk. – Nouv. éd. Paris: Maisonneuve.

Neubauer, Adolf Zvi. 1875. *The Book of Hebrew Roots by Abū'l Walīd Marwān Ibn Janāḥ, Called Rabbi Jonah.* Oxford: Clarendon Press.

Yeshaya, Joachim J.M.S. 2010. *Medieval Hebrew Poetry in Muslim Egypt. The Secular Poetry of the Karaite Poet Moses ben Abraham Darʕī.* Karaite Texts and Studies, Volume 3. Leiden: Brill.

Secondary sources

Blau, Joshua. 1970. *On Pseudo-Corrections in some Semitic Languages.* Jerusalem: The Israel Academy of Sciences and Humanities.

Blau, Joshua. 1980a. *Diqduq ha-ʕarvit ha-yehudit šel yeme ha-benayim. A Grammar of Mediaeval Judaeo-Arabic.* Second enlarged edition. Jerusalem: The Magnes Press.

Blau, Joshua. 1999. *The Emergence and Linguistic Background of Judaeo-Arabic: A study of the origins of Neo-Arabic and Middle Arabic.* Third edition. Jerusalem: Ben-Zvi Institute.

Blau, Joshua. 2001. "The linguistic character of Saadia Gaon's translation of the Pentateuch." *Oriens* 36: 1–9.

Blau, Joshua. 2006. *A Dictionary of Medieval Judaeo-Arabic Texts.* Jerusalem: The Academy of the Hebrew Language and the Israel Academy of Sciences and Humanities.

Blau, Joshua. 2019. *Notes on Saadya Gaon's Translation of the Torah.* Jerusalem: The Israel Academy of Sciences and Humanities.

Blau, Joshua and Simon Hopkins. 1984. "On Early Judeo-Arabic orthography." *Zeitschrift für Arabische Linguistik* 12: 9–27.

12 Another case of a Hebrew word written in Arabic characters.

Cohen, Mark R. 2007. "On the interplay of Arabic and Hebrew in the Cairo Geniza letters", in: Jonathan P. Decter and Michael Rand (eds.). *Studies in Hebrew and Arabic Letters in Honour of Raymond P. Scheindlin.* Piscataway, NJ: Gorgias Press. 17–35.

Cooper, Alan. 2012. "Once again seething a kid in its mother's milk." *Jewish Studies, an Internet Journal* 10: 109–143.

Emmert, Matthias. 2021. "Zu den lexikalischen Unterschieden in der Josefsgeschichte bei Saadia Gaon im Kontext des hebräischen Urtextes sowie Ms. Sin. Ar. 2 und Ms. Sin. Ar. 4", in: Lutz Edzard (ed.). *Bible Translations – Linguistic and Cultural Issues. Proceedings of the Erlangen Workshop on October 5 and 6, 2018.* Wiesbaden: Harrassowitz. 36–62.

Freidenreich, David M. 2003. "The use of Islamic sources in Saadiah Gaon's 'Tafsīr' of the Torah." *The Jewish Quarterly Review* 93 No. 3/4: 353–395.

Geiger, Abraham. 1833. *Was hat Mohammed aus dem Judenthume aufgenommen.* Ph.D. Dissertation, University of Bonn.

Hary, Benjamin. 1991. "On the use of *ʔilā* and *li* in Judeo-Arabic texts", in: Alan Kaye (ed.). *Semitic Studies in Honor of Wolf Leslau on the Occasion of his Eighty-Fifth Birthday*, 2 vols. Wiesbaden: Harrassowitz. Vol. 1, 595–608.

Hary, Benjamin. 1992. *Multiglossia in Judeo-Arabic. With an edition, translation, and grammatical study of the Cairene Purim Scroll.* Leiden: Brill.

Hary, Benjamin and Howard I. Aronson. 1996. "Adaptations of Hebrew script", in: Peter T. Daniels and William Bright (eds.). *The World's Writing Systems.* New York/Oxford: Oxford University Press. 727–734.

Jastrow, Otto. 1984. "Gibt es einen islamischen Sprachraum? Islamische Idiome in den Sprachen muslimischer Völker", in: Werner Ende and Udo Steinbach (eds.). *Der Islam in der Gegenwart.* Munich: C.H. Beck. 582–589.

Khan, Geoffrey. 2007 "Judaeo-Arabic", in: Kees Versteegh et al. (eds.). *Encyclopedia of Arabic Language and Linguistics.* Volume II: Eg–Lan. Leiden: Brill. 526–536.

Khan, Geoffrey. 2016 "Judeo-Arabic", in: Lily Khan and Aaron D. Rubin (eds). *Handbook of Jewish Languages.* Leiden: Brill. 22–63.

Khan, Geoffrey. 2018. "Judaeo-Arabic", in: Clive Holes (ed.). *Arabic Historical Dialectology.* Oxford: Oxford University Press. 148–169.

Lewis, Bernard. 2014. *The Jews of Islam. With a new introduction by Mark R. Cohen.* Princeton and Oxford: Princeton University Press.

Maman, Aharon. 2004. *Comparative Semitic Philology in the Middle Ages. From Saʕadiah Gaon to Ibn Barūn (10th–12th Century).* Leiden: Brill.

Maman, Aharon. 2013. *Synoptic Dictionary of the Hebrew Component in Jewish Languages.* Jerusalem: Magnes Press.

Maman, Aharon. 2019. "Hebrew to c. 1650", in: John Considine (ed.). *The Cambridge World History of Lexicography.* Cambridge: Cambridge University Press. 182–201.

Meddeb, Abdelwahab and Benjamin Stora. 2013. *Histoire des relations entre juifs et musulmans des origines à nos jours.* Paris: Albin Michel.

Ørum, Olav G. 2018. *Sociohistorical and Linguistic Layers of Arabic in Medieval Cairo: The Case of Judaeo-Arabic.* Oslo: University of Oslo.

Scheindlin, Raymond P. 2000. *A Short History of the Jewish People: From Legendary Times to Modern Statehood.* Oxford: Oxford University Press.

Stillman, Norman A. 1979. *The Jews of the Arab Lands: A History and Source Book.* Philadelphia: The Jewish Publication Society of America.

Wagner. Ester Miriam. 2010. *Linguistic Variety of Judaeo-Arabic in Letters from the Cairo Genizah.* Leiden: Brill.

Iraqi Judeo-Arabic

Lutz Edzard, University of Erlangen-Nürnberg

1. Introduction

The Jewish community in Iraq can be traced back all the way back to the Babylonian exile 586 BC. There were ups and downs in the community's long flourishing history, with the Ottoman period counting as the relatively speaking most prospering time. After the foundation of the State of Israel in 1948, a number of discriminatory laws made the situation of the Iraqi Jewish community unbearable. From the year 1950 to the year 1952, between 120.000 and 123.000 Jews, at the time about 75% of the population, returned to Israel under the auspices of the operation "Ezra and Nehemia". As of today, only a handful of Jews, if any, continue to live in Iraq.[1]

In his seminal study *Communal Dialects in Baghdad*, Haim Blanc established a basic isogloss for Iraqi Arabic dialects in general, terminologically based on the standard Arabic form *qultu* 'I said'. The isogloss has both sociological and geographical implications. In terms of (religious) communal dialects and life style, Jews and Christians speak *qəltu* dialects, while (semi-)nomads and Bedouins speak *gələt* dialects across the board. On the other hand, the sedentary Muslim population (city dwellers) speak *qəltu* dialects north of the Samarra-Falluja line, and *gələt* dialects to the south of this line (cf. Jastrow 2007: 414). According to Blanc (1964a: 168ff.), the *qəltu* dialects are descendents of the spoken Arabic in Abbasid Iraq; in contrast, the *gələt* dialects are due to a re-Bedouinization of central and southern Iraq after the Mongol invasion, a process, which ultimately also affected to urban dialects in the course of the partial sedentarization of the Bedouin population.

At the time of Jewish presence in Iraq, Jewish *qəltu* dialects were represented in Mosul and surroundings (Tigris group) one the one hand, and in ʕĀna, Hīt (cf. Khan 1997), and Kurdistan (cf. Jastrow 2007: 415). In the later area, the socio-linguistic rules of the Jews is noteworthy in two respects. First, they also spoke Aramaic in a few geographical pockets. Second, notably in Arbil, they continued to speak Arabic in an environment, which otherwise had completely shifted to Kurdish and Turkish (cf. Khan 2007: 532).

2. Grammatical features

2.1 Phonology

The consonantal phoneme system of Jewish Baghdadi Arabic (JB) looks as follows (cf. Mansour 2007: 232; traditional Semiticist symbols in angled parentheses).

1 For a precise overview covering the medieval and the modern periods, cf. Rustow 2010 and Simon 2010, respectively.

Table (1) Jewish Baghdadi Arabic consonants

		Labial		Dental		Palato-dental	Palatal	Velar	Uvular	Pharyn-geal	Glottal
		plain	velarized	plain	velarized						
Nasal		m	(mˠ) [ṃ]	n	(nˠ) [ṇ]						
Plos.	-voice	p		t	tˠ [ṭ]			k	q		ʔ [ʔ]
	+voice	b	(bˠ) [ḅ]	d				g			
Affr.	-voice					t͡ʃ [č]					
	+voice					d͡ʒ [ǧ/j]					
Fric.	-voice	f		θ [ṯ]				x [ḫ]		ħ [ḥ]	h
	+voice	(v)		ð [ḏ]	ðˠ [ḏ̣]			ɣ [ġ]		ʕ [ʕ]	
Approximant		w					j [y]				
Lateral				l	(lˠ) [ḷ]						
Trill				r							

At first glance, JB, just as Christian Baghgdadi (CB) and Muslim Baghdadi (MB), matches relatively close the classical Arabic phoneme inventory (for additional phonemes that have entered through loanwords see below). In contrast to JB, Abu Haidar (1991; 2016) does not mention a velarized (bˠ) [ḅ] in MB. Classical Arabic /q/ is retained in JB as an uvular (or post-velar) stop, as in CB, but unlike in MB, where it is pronounced as [g], e.g., JB *qām* vs. MB *gām* 'he got up'. /k/ is retained as [k], as in CB, but unlike in MB, where it is sometimes palatalized to [tʃ], e.g., JB *kam* vs. MB *čam* 'how many'. The classical Arabic interdentals /ð [ḏ], θ [ṯ], ðˠ [ḏ̣]/ are preserved, like in MB (but unlike in CB and the the Jewish dialects of Kurdistan; cf. Jastrow 2007: 415).

/lˠ/ and / bˠ/ are established as phonemes through minimal pairs such as (e.g. *waḷḷa* 'by God!' vs. *walla* 'he went away' and *ḅāḅa* 'father, dad' vs. *bāba* 'her door'. As a suprasegmental phenomenon, velarization harmony obtains to a certain degree.

The pronunciation of /r/ is one of the primary distinguishing features of the *qəltu* dialects of the Tigris group (among them JB) and the southern Kurdistan group. Older Arabic /r/ has shifted to to the velar fricative /ɣ/ [ġ] (as in Christian, but not MB) (cf. Jastrow 2007: 416). However, /r/ has been re-introduced in non-Arabic loans (e.g., *brāxa* 'blessing' < Hebrew בְּרָכָה *bərāḵā*, *qūri* 'teapot' < Persian *qūrī*). In loans from standard Arabic, this sound shift is sometimes blocked, e.g., *ʕaskaġ* 'army' (CA *ʕaskar*) vs. *ḥākəm ʕaskari* 'martial law', the latter expression being more "official". The alternation may also reflect subtle semantic change, e.g., *faġġ* 'he poured, served foot' vs. *farr* 'he threw' (cf. Mansour 2006: 233). In JB, the consonants /p, g, tʃ/ only occur in words of foreign (Hebrew, Persian, Turkish, European) origin, e.g., *plāw* 'cooked rice' (< Persian *palāw*), *zangīn* 'rich, wealthy' (< Turkish *zengin*), *čāy* 'tea' (< Persian *čāy*, Turkish *çay*, as in MB). In a few nouns such as *pēθaḥayyim* 'cemetery', an original *b* is replaced by *p* (cf. Mansour 1991: 33f.).

In stressed position, long *ā*, *ē*, *ī*, *ō*, and *ū* are generally attested in Iraqi dialects, in addition to the diphthongs *aw* and *ay*, the latter only when *w* or *y* is geminated or preceded by the glottal stop. Otherwise, monophthongization obtains, e.g., *biḏ̣ā* 'white' (F) (CA *bayḍāʔ*) and *sudā* 'black' (F) (CA *sawdāʔ*). While the (Jewish) *qəltu* dialects display a system of two short vowels, *ə* and *a*, in unstressed position the *gələt* dialects preserve short *i*, *u*, and *a*. In word-final position, the other short vowels are also attested in

JB. A further feature of JB is a strong *ʔimāla* (*ā* > *ē* > *ī*). While MB reflects CA *ǧāmiʕ* 'mosque' as *jāmiʕ*, CB yields *jēməʕ*, and JB *jīməʕ* (cf. Blanc 1964a: 42).

Total and partial assimilation exceeds the degree of what is found in CA, e.g., *qənna* < *qəlna* 'we said' (CA *qulnā*). Suprasegmental assimilation with respect to voicedness and velarization (*tafxīm*), often resulting in clusters, occurs as well, e.g., *ṭfātəġ* < *ḍfātəġ* (CA *dafātir*) 'notebooks' and *ṣḷā* < *ṣlā* 'prayer, synagogue' (cf. CA *ṣalāh*). Elisions occur as well, e.g., *(l)bōhi* 'yesterday' (cf. CA *al-bāriḥa*) (cf. Mansour 2006: 233).

In the JB *qəltu* dialect, final clusters tend to be opened by an anaptyctic vowel *ə*, but only in the case of high sonority of the syllable coda, e.g., *əbən* 'son', but *məlḥ* 'salt' (cf. Jastrow 2007: 418). Initial clusters are preceded by a prosthetic *ə* in case of high sonority of the onset, e.g., *əġkīk* 'weak' (CA *rakīk*). In the case of the definite article (which would produce a three-consonantal cluster), this also holds before low sonority consonants, e.g., *lə-kbīġ* 'the big one' (CA *al-kabīr*). In medial position, three-consonantal clusters pose no problem, e.g., *pərtqāl* 'orange' (cf. CA *burtuqāl*) (cf. Mansour 2006: 235).

In contrast to the *gələt* dialects, to which MB belongs, the JB *qəltu* dialect does not syncopate CvCvCa(C) sequences (cf. Jastrow 2007: 418).

After a final syllable with a high vowel nucleus (*i*, *ī*, or *ə*) or a coda *y*, the nominal feminine ending *-a* in JB tends to be *-i*, e.g., *jīji* 'hen' (CA *daǧāǧa*) as opposed to regular *-a* as in *kalba* 'female dog'.

Another well-known feature concerns suprasegmental spreading of emphasis (or de-emphatization). The phenomena of *tafxīm* (emphatization) and *tarqīq* (de-emphatization), that are well-documented phonetically, are widely attested in Judeo-Arabic texts, including Jewish Iraqi Arabic varieties. Examples of the former process, i.e. suprasegmental assimilation with respect to velarization, or "A[dvanced] T[ongue] R[oot]" include the following (often, the process originates in an emphatized vowel):

tafxīm in Judeo-Arabic

טמצו *ṭamṣū* reflecting CA طَمَسوا *ṭamasū* 'they effaced'
פרץ *faraṣ* reflecting CA فَرَس *faras* 'horse'
צכ׳ל *ṣaxl* reflecting CA سَخْل *saxl* 'lamb'

In the latter two examples, it is noteworthy that the two liquids (/l/ and /r/) are pronounced with velarization, thus triggering the suprasegmental assimilation of *sīn* to *ṣād*, which in the first instance is conditioned by the velarized /ṭ/. The opposite process (*tarqīq* – de-velarization as a result of partial assimilation) can be observed as well, as in the following examples:

tarqīq in Judeo-Arabic

זגיר *zaġīr* reflecting CA صغير *ṣaġīr* 'little'
אבזאר *ʔabzār* reflecting CA أبصار *ʔabṣār* 'eyes'

2.2 Morphology

The personal independent and dependent (possessive or object) pronouns in MB and JB, as compared with CA, look as follows. Gender distinction in the second and third person plural only survives in rural *gələt* dialects (cf. Jastrow 2007: 418) and is not relevant here.

	Standard (CA)		MB		JB	
	INDEP	DEP	INDEP	DEP	INDEP	DEP
3MS	*huwa*	*-hu*	*huwwa*	*-a*	*huwwi*	*-(n)u*
3FS	*hiya*	*-hā*	*hiyya*	*-ha*	*hiyyi*	*-(h)a*
2MS	*ʔanta*	*-ka*	*inta*	*-(a)k*	*ənta*	*-(a)k*
2FS	*ʔanti*	*-ki*	*inti*	*-(i)č*	*ənti*	*-ək/-ki*
1S	*ʔanā*	*-ī/-nī*	*āni*	*-i/-ni*	*ana*	*-(y)i/-ni*
3PL	*hum*	*-hum*	*humma*	*-hum*	*həmmi*	*-(h)əm*
2PL	*ʔantum*	*-kum*	*intu*	*-kum*	*əntəm*	*-kəm*
1PL	*naḥnu*	*-nā*	*iḥna*	*-na*	*(n)əḥna*	*-na*

The form *-ni* (1S) marks the direct object, otherwise the allomorphs are phonologically conditioned. Indirect object suffixes are prefixed by the dative marker *l-*, i.e. *-l-u* '(to) him', *-l-a* '(to) her', etc. Direct and indirect objects can be combined (in that order), whereby only the latter is morphologically specified, e.g., *jabəlyānu* 'he brought it/him/her/them to him' or *jabəlyāk* 'he brought it/him/her/them to you (MS)' A synchronic interlinear analysis amounts to *jab-əl-yā-nu* bring.PF.3MS-DIR.OBJ-DAT-3MS.OBJ and *jab-əl-yā-k* bring.PF.3MS-DIR.OBJ-DAT-2MS.OBJ, respectively. Diachronically, *l-* is the marker of the indirect object and *yā* (< *ʔiyyā*) the marker of the direct object (cf. Mansour 2006: 236). In Jewish dialects of Mossul and Iraqi Kurdistan, a (sometimes shortened) suffixed personal pronoun functions as copula, e.g., *malīḥ-ūwe* 'he is good' or *malīḥa-ye* 'she is good' (cf. Jastrow 2007: 419).

The demonstrative pronouns in MB and JB are the following.

	NEAR		REMOTE	
	MB	JB	MB	JB
MS	*hāḏa*	*hāḏa* (*hal*)	*hāḏāk(a)*	*hāḏāk*
FS	*hāḏi* (*hāy*)	*hāyi*	*haḏīč*	*haḏīk*
PL	*haḏōla*	*haḏōli* (*hal*)	*haḏōlak*	*haḏōk*

The relative marker (not pronoun) is *əlli*, with the allomorphs *lli* and *l-*, the latter undergoing regressive assimilation as the definite article (see below), e.g., *j-jā* '(he,) who came'. The genitive exponent in use is *māl*.

Interrogative particles in JB include *aškun* 'what' (cf. MB *šənu*), with a shortened prefixed form *aš-* and a suffixed form *-ēš/-eš*, as in *l-eš* 'why', *mani* 'who' (cf. MB *mənu* 'who'), *hayyi* 'which one (of several)' (cf. MB *yāhu*).

The *nomen unitatis* is marked either by the feminine ending *-a* or the affix *-āyi*, e.g., *bəṭṭīxāyi* ‘a single melon’ as opposed to *bəṭṭīx* ‘melon’ (mass noun). Next to the regular sound plural endings *-īn* (M) and *-āt* (F), the Hebrew endings *-īm* (M) and *-ōṯ* (F) apply (mostly) to Hebrew loan words, e.g., *ḥxamīm* ‘rabbis’ and *braxōṯ* ‘blessings’ (cf. Mansour 2007: 237). The Arabic noun *ṣlā* ‘synagogue’ also takes the Hebrew feminine plural marker *-ōṯ*, for obvious semantic reasons, i.e. *ṣlāwōṯ* ‘synagogues’ (cf. Mansour 1991: 41).

The definite article *l-* is regressively assimilated to following alveolar consonants (“sun letters”), e.g., *ṭ-ṭēġ* ‘the bird’ (CA *aṭ-ṭayr*). In front of a CC-onset (triggering an anaptyctic *ə*), this rule is no longer in place, e.g., *lə-ṭyūġ* ‘the birds’ (CA *aṭ-ṭuyūr*). The Iraqi Arabic equivalent to an indefinite article, deriving from CA *fard* ‘individual’, is also found in JB as *faġad* or *fadd*, e.g., *fadd-wēḥəd* ‘a (certain) person’ (cf. Mansour 2007: 239).

The JB cardinal numbers from one to ten in their independent form run as follows (again, in comparison with CA and MB).

	CA	MB	JB
1	*wāḥid, ʔiḥdā* (F)	*wāḥid* (M), *wiḥda* (F)	*wēḥəd* (M), *waḥdi* (M)
2	*iṯnāni* (M), *iṯnatāni* (F)	*ṯnēn* (M), *ṯintēn* (F)	*ṯnēn* (M), *ṯnēn/ṯəntēn* (F)
3	*ṯalāṯa*	*tlāṯa*	*tlāṯi*
4	*ʔarbaʕa*	*arbaʕa*	*aġ(ə)bʕa*
5	*xamsa*	*xamsa*	*xamsi*
6	*sitta*	*sitta*	*sətti*
7	*sabʕa*	*sabʕa*	*sabʕa*
8	*ṯamānya*	*ṯmānya*	*ṯmīni*
9	*tisʕa*	*tisʕa*	*təsʕa*
10	*ʕašra*	*ʕašra*	*ʕašġa*

The numbers eleven and twelve are *daʕaš* and *ṯnaʕaš* in MB, and *idaʕ(ə)š* and *ṯnaʔʕ(ə)š* in JB.

The basic paradigms of the suffix conjugation (perfective) and the prefix conjugation (imperfective) in JB, reflecting the *qəltu* scenario (again as compared with CA and MB) run as follows.

	Standard	MB	JB
1S	*katabtu*	*k(i)tabit*	*ktabtu*
2MS	*katabta*	*k(i)tabit*	*ktabt*
2FS	*katabti*	*k(i)tabti*	*ktabti*
3MS	*kataba*	*kitab*	*katab*
3FS	*katabat*	*kitbat*	*katbit*
1PL	*katabnā*	*k(i)tabna*	*ktabna*
2PL	*katabtum*	*k(i)tabtu*	*ktabtem*
3PL	*katabū*	*kitbaw*	*katbu*

	Standard	MB	JB
1S	*ʔaktubu*	*aktib*	*aktəb*
2MS	*taktubu*	*tiktib*	*təktəb*
2FS	*taktubīna*	*tikitbīn*	*tkətbēn*
3MS	*yaktubu*	*yiktib*	*yəktəb*
3FS	*taktubu*	*tiktib*	*təktəb*
1PL	*naktubu*	*niktib*	*nəktəb*
2PL	*taktubūna*	*tikitbūn*	*tkətbōn*
3PL	*yaktubūna*	*yikitbūn*	*ykətbōn*

The system of binyanim (diatheses) I to X pretty much corresponds to the CA one, with the widespread reduction of form IV in Arabic dialects. The following points pertain to the imperfect paradigm: *qa(d)-* preceding the imperfect marks the present tense, *ġah* the future, while *da-* has an optative quality, comparable to *xalli* with a jussive quality. Mansour (1991: 42) opposes JB *qa(d)* to MB *da* and *gāʕəd.* Stressed *má* expresses the negation of the future and stressed *lá* the prohibitive (negated imperative).

2.3 Syntax

A typical syntactic feature of JB is the Mishnac-Hebrew-style definite noun-adjective phrase, attested already in late Biblical Hebrew, שַׁעַר הָעֶלְיוֹן *šaʕar hā̊-ʕɛlyōn* 'the upper gate' (Ezek 9:2), in which only the adjective is preceded by the definite article and where the distinction between attribution and annexation seems to be blurred (cf. Steiner 1997: 162). Examples are *ʔīd əl-yəmna* 'the right hand' and *ṣlat lə-kbīġi* 'the big synagogue' (cf. Mansour 1991: 44). This construction with the noun in the construct (explicit in the Hebrew script) also occurs on the cover page to the text in section 3.1 below: מטבעת אל וטניה אל יסראליה בגדאד *Maṭbaʕat al-Waṭanīya al-Yisrāʔilīya Baġdād* 'The National Israelite Printing House Baghdad'.

A remarkable feature (not necessarily restricted to JB) is the possessive construction with *māl* + pronominal suffix, e.g., *lə-mʕalləm māl-əm* 'their (M) teacher' (DEF-teacher GEN-3PL) (cf. Mansour 2006: 240). An anticipatory pronoun can be observed in Aramaic-style constructions such as *ʕəqəb ma axḏūw-a lə-flūs* 'after they took [it] the money' (after REL take.PF.3PL-3MS DEF-money) (cf. Jastrow 2007: 422). The same holds for the Aramaic-style doubly-marked genitive, e.g., *ṣdīq-u l-əl-faqīr* (friend.CS-3SG.M for-DEF-friend) 'the poor man's friend' (cf. Mansour 1991: 45).

2.4 Lexicon

JB shares a number of characteristic lexical items with MB (and Christian Arabic), notably the existence marker *aku* 'there is' (negated *māku*) (cf. Jastrow 2018) and a host of loanwords from Persian and Turkish. Blanc (1964a: 134ff.) provides an overview based on the Swadesh-list, which contains 200 lexical items. Sometimes, JB is pinned against MB and CB, e.g., JB *ḏaww* 'fire' against MB *nār* and CB *nāġ*, JB *ənf* 'nose' against MB and CB *xašem*, or JB *ʕāyan* 'to see' against MB and CB *šāf*. In other cases, JB and CB are pinned against MB, e.g., JB and CB *ṭaʕa* 'to give' against MB *niṭa*, JB and CB *zōj* 'husband' against MB *rajel*, or JB *kθīġ* and CB *ktīġ* 'many' against MB *hwāya*. More often, however, dialectal differences are mainly phonological, e.g., JB *(l)bōḥi*, CB *mbēḥa*, and MB *lbārḥa* 'yesterday'.

Specific loanwords from Hebrew and Aramaic are found in both religious and secular matters. An example of the former realm is the term *šəttāxa* 'Passover ceremony' (from the Judeo-Aramaic phrase *haššata haxa* 'this year [we] are here'). Examples of the latter realm include *məzzāl* 'luck' (< Hebrew מַזָּל *mazzå̄l*), *kabōd* 'honor, respect' (< Hebrew כָּבוֹד *kå̄ḇōḏ*), *səkkāna* 'danger' (< Hebrew סַכָּנָה *sakkå̄nå̄*), and *afəllu* 'nevertheless' (< Hebrew אֲפִלּוּ *ʔăpillū* 'even') (cf. Mansour 2006: 240). In addition, a number of Hebrew terms for festivals and ritual context are simply pronounced according to JB phonology, e.g., *mīla* 'circumcision' (< Hebrew מִילָה *mīlå̄*) or *pədyōn* 'redeeming of the first-born son' (< Hebrew פִּדְיוֹן *piḏyōn*) (cf. Mansour 1991: 48f.).

Blanc (1964a: 142ff.) lists a most informative array of Hebrew-based nouns and verbs, either by themselves or embedded in JB idioms. Examples of nouns include *aḇēl* 'terrible, awful' (< Hebrew אָבֵל *ʔå̄ḇēl* 'mourning') in expressions like *meθel aḇēl* 'like a fool', *pēθaḥayyim* 'cemetery' (< Hebrew בֵּית הַחַיִּים *bēṯ ha-ḥayyīm* 'house of the living'), and many more. Examples of verbs include *lāx*, *ylīx* 'to run away' (< Hebrew הָלַךְ *hå̄lak̠* 'to go'), *naggaf* 'to die', in a pejorative sense (< Hebrew נִגַּף *niggap̄* 'to be struck down'), and others. Metaphorically, the name of the fast day *təšʕaḇāḇ* (< Hebrew תִּשְׁעָה בְּאָב *tišʕå̄ bə-ʔå̄ḇ*) may also refer to an unhappy permanently complaining person (cf. Mansour 1991: 49f.)

3. Text samples

3.1 The beginning of the Joseph story (Genesis 37) in a Judeo-Arabic version from Baghdad (1924)

The first text excerpt (for details cf. Edzard 2012) is the beginning of a popularized version of the Joseph story, corresponding to Genesis 37:1–28, with textual additions in the *ḥakawātī* style. Interestingly, the story contains a sizable number of Islamic formulae, starting with the *basmala* (cf. Cohen 2017). Linguistically, the story reflects an intermediate *wusṭā* level (or even a quasi "literary language", cf. Blanc 1964a and Bar Moshe 2019: 7), reflecting, *inter alia*, typical "pseudo-correct" features (cf. Blau 1970) in the verbal system, e.g., *ʔixwat-ak maḍaw li-yarʕawn* 'your brothers went forth to tend'. The negation marker is constantly *lam*. The number syntax clearly deviates from Classical Arabic, e.g., *wa-ʔīdʕašr nuǧūm* 'and eleven stars' (cf. Classical *wa-ʔaḥada ʕasara kawkab(an)* in the version of Saadia Gaon).

No attempt is made here to transcribe the text sample according to the rules of pure JB phonology. The orthography varies between a classicizing and a dialectal level; within the latter, specific JB features, e.g., *r* > *ġ*, are occasionally detectable, though.[2]

קצת יוסף אל צדיק

qiṣṣat yōsēp̄ aṣ ṣiddīq
story.CS Joseph DEF righteous.SG.M
The story of Joseph the righteous

2 According, to Blanc (1964b: 18), a completely voweled version of this story exists, but neither my Israeli colleagues nor myself have so far been able to locate this source.

- בן פורת יוסף -

ב'ה'נ'ו' ב'ס'ט'

קצת יוסף הצדיק עליו השלום

שנת ה'ת'ר'פ'ד'

מנחה שלוחה משאת וארוחה
להתלמיד הנעים האברך

יזכה לתורה ולחופה ולמצות
ולמעשים טובים בחיי אביו ואמו

א'כ'י'ר

מטבעת אל ושנירה ש' ישראייה בנדאד

Title page of *Qiṣṣat Yosef ha-ṣadiq ʕalav ha-šalom*

באסם אללה אל רחמאן אל רחים אייאהו נעבדהו

bi-smi	*llāhi*	*r*	*raḥmāni*	*r*	*raḥīm*	*ʔīya-hū*	*naʕbudu-hū*
in-name.GEN.CS	God	DEF	merciful.GEN	DEF	compassionate	ACC-3SG.M	venerate.IPFV.1PL-3SG.M

In the name of God, the merciful, the compassionate. Him we venerate

וביה נסתעין עלא קום אל צ׳אלמין

wa-bi-hī nastaʕīn ʕalā qawm aẓ ẓālimīn

and-in-3SG.M take_refuge.IPFV.1PL against people.CS.GEN DEF sin.PTCP.PL.M.GEN

and to him we take refuge against the people of the sinners (sinning people)

קאל אסמעו מא ג׳רא עלא יוסף אל צדיק

qāl ismaʕū mā ǧarā ʕālā yōsēp̄ aṣ ṣiddīq

say.PF.3SG.M hear.IPT.PL.M what happen.PF.3SG.M upon Joseph DEF righteous

He said: listen to what happened to Joseph the righteous

למן כאן אבן סבעת עשר סנא וכאן ירעי מע

lamman kān ibn sabʕat ʕašr sana wa-kān yarʕā maʕa

when be.PF.3SG.M son.CS seven ten year and-be.PF.3SG.M tend.IPFV.3SG.M with

when he was 17 years old and was tending with

אכ׳ותו באל גנם וכאן יעקב יחב אלא יוסף

ʔixwat-u bi-l ġanam wa-kān yaʕăqōḇ yuḥibb ʔilā yōsēp̄

brother.PL.CS-3SG.M on-DEF small.cattle and-be.PF.3SG.M Jacob love.IPFV.3SG.M to (ACC) Joseph

his brothers the small cattle. Jacob loved Joseph

אחסן מן אכ׳ותו לאן כאן אבן שיבה להו

ʔaḥsan min ʔixwat-u li-ʔanna kān ibn šayb-uh la-hu

good.ELAT from brother.PL-3SG.M for-COMP be.PF.3SG.M son.CS old_age-3SG.M for-3SG.M

more ("better") than his brothers because he was the son of his old age,

וצנע להו תונייה מן דבאג׳ יעני קמיץ מן בריסם

wa-ṣanaʕ la-hu tūnīya min dibāǧ yaʕnī qamīṣ min brīsam

and-make.PF.3SG.M for-3SG.M dress from silk.brocade mean.IPFV.3SG.M shirt from silk

and he made him a dress of silk brocade, i.e. a shirt of silk.

ושאפו אכ׳ותהו יחבהו אבוהו אחסן מנהום

wa-šāfū ʔixwat-u yuḥibb-hū ʔaḥsan min-hum

and-see.PF.3PL.M brother.PL.CS-3SG.M love.IPFV.3SG.M-3SG.M good.ELAT from-3PL

His brothers saw that he liked him more than them,

פי בקו יבגצ׳והו ולם יחבוהו.

fa baqū yabġuḍū-hu wa-lam yuḥibbū-hū

so continue.PF.3PL.M dislike.IPFV.3SG.M-3SG.M and-not.PF love.IPFV.3PL.M-3SG.M

so they continued to dislike him and did not love him.

יום מן אל אייאם וסאעה מן אל זמאן שאף יוסף חלם

yawm min al ʔayyām wa-sāʕa min az zamān šāf yōsēp̄ ḥulm

day of DEF day.PL and-hour of DEF time see.PF.3SG.M Joseph dream

at a certain time, Joseph had a dream

וקאל יא אכ׳ותי שפת חלם והוד׳א נחנא

wa-qāl yā ʔixwat-ī šuft ḥulm wa-hōḏā niḥnā

and-say.PF.3SG.M VOC brother.PL.CS-1SG see.PF.1SG dream and-DEICT 1PL

and said: oh my brothers, I had a dream, and lo there we were

מחזמין חזאם פי וצט אל ברייה וקאמת חזמתי

muḥazzimīn ḥuzām fī wasṭ[3] *al-barrīya wa-qāmat ḥuzmat-ī*

bind.PTCP.PL bundle.PL in middle.CS DEF-desert and-stand_up.3SG.F bundle.CS-1SG

binding bundles in the middle of the desert, and my bundle stood up

3 Standard Arabic *wasṭ* (*tafxīm* – suprasegmental assimilation with respect to emphasis).

ואנתצבת ואסתדארו חזמאתכום וסג'דו

wa-(ʔi)ntaṣabat wa-(ʔi)stadārū ḥuzāmat-kum wa-sağadū

and-rise_up.PF.3SG.F and-go_round.PF.3PL.M bundle.PL.CS-2PL.M and-bow_down.PF.3PL.M

and stood straight, while your bundles went around and bowed down

לחזמתי. קאלו אכ'ותו והום יתמאהזון

li-ḥuzmat-ī qālū ʔixwat-u wa-hum yatamāhazūn ʕalā

to-bundle.CS-1SG say.PF.3SG.M brother.PL.CS-3SG.M and-3PL be_amazed.IPFV.3PL over

to my bundle. His brothers said, wondering about

עלא אל חלם ותפאסירו הל תריד תציר צלטאן

l ḥulm wa-tafāsīr-u hal turīd taṣīr ṣulṭān

DEF dream and-interpretation.PL.CS-3SG.M INTERR wish.IPFV.2SG.M become.IPFV.2SG.M ruler

the dream and its interpretation(s): do you want to become ruler,

יא יוסף ותחכם עלינא ונסג'ד לך

yā yōsēp̄ wa-taḥkum ʕalay-nā wa-nasğud la-k

VOC Joseph and-rule.IPFV.2SG.M over-1PL and-bow_down.IPFV.1PL for-2SG.M

Joseph, and rule over us, and we bow down to you?

ועאדו יבגצ'והו עלא חלמאתו ועלא

wa-ʕādū yabġuḍū-hu ʕalā ḥalamāt-u wa-ʕalā

and-return.PF.3PL.M dislike.IPFV.3SG.M-3SG.M over dream.PL.CS-3SG.M and-over

and they disliked him even more because of his dreams and its

תפאסירו. וחלם חלם אכ'ר וקאל

tafāsīr-u wa-ḥalam ḥulm ʔāxar wa-qāl

interpretation.PL.CS-3SG.M and-dream.PF.3SG.M dream other and-and-say.PF.3SG.M

interpretation(s). Then he dreamt (yet) another dream and said:

יא אכ'ותי אסמעו חלם אלד'י שפתוהו והוד'א אנא

yā ʔixwat-ī ismaʕū ḥulm allaḏī šuftu-hu wa-hōḏā ʔanā

VOC brother.PL.CS-1SG hear.IPT.PL dream REL see.PF.1SG-3SG.M and-DEICT 1SG

my brothers, listen a(nother) dream that I dreamt. Lo and behold, there I was

בחלמי והוד'א אל שמס ואל קמר ואידעשר נג'ום

bi-ḥulm-ī wa-hōḏā aš šams wa-l qamar wa-ʔīdʕašr nuğūm

in-dream.CS-1SG and-DEICT DEF sun and-DEF moon and-eleven star.PL

in my dream, and the sun and the moon and eleven stars

סאג'דין לי וקאם אבוהו וזברו לחתא

sāğidīn l-ī wa-qām ʔabū-hu wa-zabar-u li-ḥattā

bow_down.PTCP.PL for-1SG and-rise.PF.3SG.M father.CS-3SG.M and-scold.PF.3SG.M-3SG.M for-until

bowed down to me. His father began to/got up and scolded him, lest

אכ'ותהו לא יבגצ'והו. פקאל לו איש

ʔixwatu-hu lā yabġuḍū-hu fa-qāl l-ō ʔēš

brother.PL.CS-3SG.M NEG dislike.IPFV.3SG.M-3SG.M and-say.PF.3SG.M to-3SG.M what

his brothers would hate him (even more). So he said to him: what

האד'א אל חלם אלד'י חלמת וקאמו אכ'ותהו

hāḏā al ḥulm allaḏī ḥalamt wa-qāmū ʔixwat-u

DEM.M DEF dream REL dream.PF.2SG.M and-stand_up.PF.3SG.M brother.PL.CS-3SG.M

is this dream that you dreamt? His brothers got up

וייקולון להו כד׳ב אל חלם אלד׳י חלמת

wa-yaqūlūn	*kiḏb*	*al*	*ḥulm*	*allaḏī*	*ḥalamt*	*wa-lākin*	*yaʕăqōḇ*
and-say.IPFV.3SG.M	lie	DEF	dream	REL	dream.PF.2SG.M	however	Jacob

and said: the dream you dreamt is a lie. Jacob, however,

חפץ׳ האד׳א אל כלאם פי קלבהו.

hafiẓ	*hāḏā*	*al*	*kalām*	*fī*	*qalb-hu.*
keep.PF.3SG.M	DEM.M	DEF	speech	in	heart.CS-3SG.M

kept this speech in his heart.

יום מן אל אייאם מצ׳ו אכ׳ותהו ירעון גנם אבוהום

yōm	*min*	*al*	*ʔayyām*	*maḏaw*	*ʔixwat-hu*	*yirʕawn*	*ġanam*	*ʔabū-hum*
day	from	DEF	day.PL	go_away.PF.3PL	brother.PL.CS-3SG.M	tend.IPFV.3PL	small.cattle.CS	father.CS-3PL

One day, his brothers went forth to tend the small cattle of their father

בשכ׳ם נטר יעקב ולאדהו ומא ג׳ו מן אל גנם

bi-šḵem	*naṭar*	*yaʕăqōḇ*	*wilād-hū*	*wa-mā ğō*	*min*	*al*	*ġanam*
in-Šḵem	watch.PF.3SG.M	Jacob	child.PL.CS-3SG.M	and-NEG come.PF.3PL	from	DEF	small.cattle

in Shkhem (Nablus). Jacob watched out for his sons, but they did not come back from the small cattle.

קאל יעקב ליוסף חביבי יא ולדי קאל אליה נעם

qāl	*yaʕăqōḇ*	*li-yōsēp̄*	*ḥabīb-ī*	*yā*	*walad-ī*	*qāl*	*ʔilay-h*	*naʕam*
say.PF.3SG.M	Jacob	to-Joseph	beloved.CS-1SG	VOC	child.CS-1SG	say.PL.3SG.M	to-3SG.M	yes

Jacob said to to Joseph: "My darling, my son." Joseph said to him: "Yes,

יא אבי. קאל להו הוד׳א אכ׳ותך ראעיין בשכ׳ם

yā	*ʔab-ī*	*qāl*	*la-hū*	*hōḏā*	*ʔixwat-ak*	*rāʕīn*	*bi-šḵem*
VOC	father.CS-1SG	say.PL.3SG.M	to-3SG.M	DEICT	brother.PL.CS-2SG.M	tend.PTCP.PL	in-Šḵem

my father." Jacob said to him: "Look, your brothers are tending in Shkhem (Nablus).

רוח שוף סלאם אכ׳ותך וסלאם אל גנם

rūḥ	*šūf*	*salām*	*ʔixwat-ak*	*wa-salām*	*al*	*ġanam*
go.IPT.SG.M	see.IPT.SG.M	well_being.CS	brother.PL.CS-2SG.M	and-well_being.CS	DEF	small.cattle

Go and see after the well-being of your brothers and the small cattle

ורד לי ג׳וואב וראח יוסף ורא אכ׳ותהו

wa-rudd	*l-ī*	*ğawāb*	*wa-rāḥ*	*yōsēp̄*	*warā(ʔ)*	*ʔixwat-hū*
and-give_back.IPT.SG.M	to-1SG	answer	and-go.PF.3SG.M	Joseph	after	brother.PL.CS.3SG.M

and render me an answer." Joseph went after his brothers,

והווא מתייה בל טריק ומא שאף אחד מנהום

wa-huwa	*mutayyih*	*bi-ṭ*	*ṭarīq*	*wa-mā*	*šāf*	*ʔaḥad*	*min-hum*
and.3SG.M	go_astray.PTCP.SG	in-DEF	way	and-NEG	see.PF.3SG.M	one.M	from-3PL

but went astry on his way and did not see anyone of them.

ואלקאהו מלך גבריאל בל טריק וקאל אלא יוסף

wa-ʔalqā-hū	*mal(ʔ)ak*	*gā̆ḇrīʔēl*	*bi-ṭ*	*ṭarīq*	*wa-qāl*	*ʔilā*	*yōsēp̄*
and-meet.PF.3SG.M-3SG.M	angel	Gabriel	in-DEF	way	and-say.PF.3SG	to	Joseph

The angel Gabriel met him on his way and said to Joseph:

אש תפתש ג׳אובו יוסף וקאל לו

ʔēš	*tufattiš*	*ğāwab-ū*	*yōsēp̄*	*wa-qāl*	*l-ō*
what	seek.IPFV.2SG.M	answer.PF.3SG.M-3SG.M	Joseph	and-say.PF.3SG.M	to-3SG.M

"What are you looking for?"Joseph answered him and said to him:

אלא אכ׳ותי אנא מפתש וין ירעון. קאל לו אל מלך
ʔilā ʔixwat-ī ʔanā mufattiš wēn yarʕawn. qāl l-ō al mal(ʔ)ak
ACC brother.PL.CS-1SG 1SG seek.PTCP.SG where tend.IPFV.3PL say.PF.3SG.M to-3SG.M DEF angel
"I am looking for my brothers, where they are tending." The angel said to him:

אכ׳ותך מצ׳ו לירעון בדותן וראח ווג׳דהום
ʔixwat-ak maḏaw li-yarʕawn bi-ḏōṯā̃n wa-rāḥ wa-wağad-hum
brother.PL.CS-2SG.M go_away.PF.3PL for-tend.IPFV.PL in-Dotan and-go.PF.3SG.M and-find.PF.3SG.M-3PL
Your brothers went forth to tend in Dotan. Joseph went and found them

בדותן ורפעו עייונהום אכ׳ותהו מן בעיד ונצ׳רוהו
bi-ḏōṯā̃n wa-rafaʕū ʕuyūn-hum ʔixwat-hū min baʕīd wa-naẓarū-hu
in-Dotan and-lift.PF.3PL eye.PL.CS-3PL brother.PL.CS-3SG.M from far and-observe.PF.3PL-3SG.M
in Dotan. His brothers lifted their eyes from afar and observed him.

קאל אך אלא אכ׳והו הוד׳א צאחב אל חלאמאת ג׳א
qāl ʔax ʔilā ʔaxū-hu hōḏā ṣāḥib al ḥalāmāt ğā(ʔ)
say.PF.3SG.M brother to brother.CS-3SG.M DEICT possessor.CS DEF dream.PL come.PF.3SG.M
One brother said to the other: "Look, the owner of the dreams has come.

נשוף וין תציר חלאמאתו קאמו אסתדארו עליה
našūf wēn taṣīr ḥalāmāt-ū qāmū (ʔi)stadārū ʕalay-h
see.IPFV.1PL where become.IPFV.3SG.F dream.PL.CS-3SG.M rise.PF.3PL encircle.PF.3PL on-3SG.M
Lets see what has become of his dreams." The rose and encircled him

חתה אן יקתלוהו קאלו בינתהום תעאלו נקתלו
ḥattā ʔan yaqtulū-hu qālū baynat-hum taʕālaw naqtul-ū
until COMP kill.IPFV.SUBJ.3PL-3SG.M say.PF.3PL between-3PL come_on.IPT.PL kill.IPFV.JUSS.1PL-3SG.M
in order to kill him. They said among themselves: "Come on, let's kill him

ונרמיהו בווחד מן אל בייאר ונקול וחשה רדייה
wa-narmī-hu bi-wāḥid min al biʔār wa-naqūl waḥša radīya
and-throw.IPFV.JUSS.1PL-3SG.M in-one from DEF well.PL and-say.IPFV.1PL beast evil.F
in one of the wells. We will say, a wild beast

אכלתו פריסה אנפרס יוסף ונשוף כיף תתתבת
ʔakalat-ū farīsa (ʔi)nfaras yōsēp̄ wa-našūf kayfa tatatabbat
eat.PF.3SG.F-3SG.M prey be_devoured.PF.3SG.M Joseph and-see.IPFV.1PL how be_firm.IPFV.3SG.F
has eaten him, Joseph was devoured as prey, and we will see how will materialize

חלאמאתו. למן ג׳א אליהום קאלו תעאלו
ḥalāmāt-ū lamman ğā(ʔ) ʔilay-hum qālū taʕālaw
dream.PL.CS-3SG.M when come.PF.3SG.M to-3PL say.PF.3PL come_on.IPT.PL
his dreams. When Joseph came up to them they said: "Come on,

נקתלו וקאם ראובן וקאל יא אכ׳ותי
naqtul-ū wa-qām rəʔūḇēn wa-qāl yā ʔixwat-ī
kill.IPFV.JUSS.1PL-3SG.M and-rise.PF.3SG.M Reuben and-say.PF.3SG.M VOC brother.PL.CS-1SG
let's kill him." Reuben rose up and said: "Oh my brothers,

האשא לאללה סובחאן ותעאלה תכ׳טון פי הל ולד
ḥāšā li-llāh subḥān wa-taʕālā taxṭūn fī ha-l walad
beware.STAT.3SG.M for-God praise[CS God] and-be_lofty.STAT.3SG.M sin.IPFV.2PL in DEM-DEF child
God beware – his praise is high and he is lofty – that we sin regarding this child

ותקתלון דם. ארמוהו פי הל ביר אלד׳י פי אל ברייה
wa-taqtulūn dam. irmū-hu fī ha-l bīr allaḏī fī al barrīya
and-kill.IPFV.2PL blood throw.IPT.PL-3SG.M in DEM-DEF well REL in DEF wilderness
and spill (lit.: kill) blood. Throw him in this well in the wilderness

ולא תדמון פיה יד ראד ראובן יכ׳לצהו
wa-lā tamuddūn fī-h yad rād rəʔūḇēn yuxalliṣ-hū
and-NEG extend.IPFV.2PL in-3SG.M hand want.PF.3SG.M Reuben liberate.IPFV.SUBJ.3SG.M-3SG.M
and don't set your hand on him." Reuben wanted to save him

מן ידהום לירג׳עו אלא אבוהום. פי קאמו
min yad-hum li-yurǧiʕ-ū ʔilā ʔabū-hum. fa qāmū
from hand.CS-3PL for-bring_back.IPFV.SUBJ.3SG.M-3SG.M to father.CS-3PL CONJ rise.PF.3PL
from their hand and to return him to their father. The rose,

ושלחו אלא תוניית יוסף ודבחו צכ׳ל מעז
wa-šallaḥū ʔilā tūnīyat yōsēp̄ wa-dabaḥū ṣaxl[4] *maʕz*
and-strip.PF.3PL ACC dress.CS Josep and-slaughter.PF.3PL lamb goat
stripped off the garment of Joseph, slaughtered a small goat,

וטמצו אלא אל תונייה בל דם ושאלו אלא יוסף
wa-ṭamaṣū[5] *ʔilā t tūnīya bi-d dam wa-šālū ʔilā yōsēp̄ wa-ramaw-hu*
and-soak.PF.3PL ACC DEF dress in-DEF blood and-lift.PF.3PL ACC Joseph and-throw.PF.3PL-3SG.M
and soaked his garment in the blood [of the goat]. The lifted Joseph and threw him

ורמוהו בל ביר. ואל ביר נאשף ליס פיה מאיי ולאכן חייאייה
bi-l bīr wa-l bīr nāšif laysa fī-h mayy wa-lākin ḥayʔīya
in-DEF well and-DEF well dry NEG.EXIST.3SG.M in-3SG.M water and-however snake.PL
in the well, which was dry and without water. However, it was full of snakes

ועקארב מתלי. ואסתחמד יוסף לאל בל ביר
wa-ʕaqārib mtilē.[6] *wa-staḥmad yōsēp̄ li-l[lāh] bi-l bīr*
and-scorpion.PL be_filled.PF.3SG.M and-ask_for_grace.PF.3SG.M Joseph to-God in-DEF well
and scorpions. So Joseph asked God for grace in the well

וקאל מן אל צ׳יקא נאדית יא רב ג׳אובני בל נפה
wa-qāl min aḍ ḍāyqā nādayt yā rabb ǧāwib-nī bi-n nafah
and-say.PF.3SG.M from DEF dire_straight call.PF.1SG VOC lord answer.IPT.SG.M-1SG.OBJ in-DEF despair
and said: "From dire straights I am calling to you, oh Lord, answer me in the despair,

יא אללה קאל יוסף יא רבי אשפק עלייא יא רב שפיק
yā llāh qāl yōsēp̄ yā rabb-ī ʔašfiq ʕalay-ya yā rabb šafīq
VOC God say.PF.3SG.M Joseph VOC lord.CS-1SG have_pity.IPT.SG.M on-1SG VOC lord pityful
Oh God." Joseph said: "Oh my Lord, have pity with me, oh Lord, pityful

אנתא חנין ורחים יא רבי ארחם עלייה ועלא שבאבי
ʔanta ḥanīn wa-raḥīm yā rabb-ī irḥam ʕalay-ya wa-ʕalā šabāb-ī
2SG gracious and-merciful VOC lord.CS.-1SG have_mercy.IPT.SG.M on-1SG and-on youth.CS-1SG
you are, gracious and merciful, oh my Lord, have mercy with me and with my youth.

4 Standard Arabic *saxl*.

5 Standard Arabic *ṭamasū* (*tafxīm* – suprasegmental assimilation with respect to emphasis).

6 Standard Arabic *imtalaʔa*.

כון בעוני בהל ביר האד׳א אלד׳י מתלי חייאייה ועקארב

kun *bi-ʕawn-ī* *bi-ha-l* *bīr* *allaḏī* *mtilē* *ḥayʔīya* *wa-ʕaqārib*

be.IPT.SG.M in-help.CS-1SG in-DEM-DEF well REL be_filled.PF.3SG.M snake.PL and-scorpion.PL

Be to my help in this well that is full of snakes and scorpions.

ואנהזמו ורחם אל רחמאן עלא יוסף מן כל צ׳רר

wa-nhazamū *wa-raḥim* *ar raḥmān* *ʕalā* *yōsēp̄* *min kull* *ḍarar*

and-be_repelled.PF.3PL and-have_mercy.PF.3SG.M DEFgracious on Joseph from all.CS damage

So they were repelled, and the Gracious had mercy with Joseph [relieving him] from all damage.

לאכן אכ׳וותו בהל את׳נא וג׳ו גפקת ערב

lākin *ʔixwat-hū* *bi-ha-l* *ʔaṯnā* *wa-ğō* *ġifqat*[7] *ʕarab*

however brother.PL.CS-3SG.M in-DEM-DEF moment and-come.PL.3PL caravan.CS bedouin.COLL

is brothers, however, in this moment – and a caravan of bedouins came,

מחמלין קאל יהודה אש סבב נקתל אלא אכ׳ינא

muḥammalīn *qāl* *yəhūḏā̊* *ʔēš* *sabab* *naqtul* *ʔilā* *ʔaxī-nā*

load.PTCP.PASS.PL say.PF.3SG.M Yehuda what reason kill.IPFV.1PL ACC brother.CS-1PL

heavily loaded – Yehuda said: "What is the reason we kill our brother

נגטי אלא דמו תעאלו נביעהו לל ערב

wa-nuġaṭṭī *dam-ū* *taʕālaw* *nabīʕ-hū* *li-l* *ʕarab*

and-cover_up.IPFV.1PL blood.CS-3SG.M come_on.IPT.PL sell.IPFV.JUSS-3SG.M to-DEF bedouin.COLL

and cover up his blood. Come on, let's sell him to the bedouins,

לאן דמנא ולחמנא הוא קבלו אכ׳וותהו

li-ʔanna dam-nā *wa-laḥm-nā* *hūwa* *qabilū* *ʔixwat-hū*

for-COMP blood.CS-1PL and-flesh.CS-1PL 3SG.M accept.PF.3PL brother.PL.CS.3SG.M

because he is our flesh and blood." His brothers accepted

עלא הל שור וטלעו יוסף מן אל ביר ובעוהו

ʕalā *ha-š* *šūr* *wa-ṭalaʕū* *yōsēp̄* *min al* *bīr* *wa-bāʕū-hu*

on DEM-DEF advice and-lift.PF.3PL Joseph from DEF well and-sell.PF.3PL-3SG.M

that advice and they pulled Joseph up from the well and sold him

לל ערב פי עשרין דרהם פצ׳א

li-l *ʕarab* *fī* *ʕišrīn* *dirham* *fiḍḍa*

to-DEF bedouin.COLL in twenty dirham.CS silver

to the bedouins for twenty silver dirhams.

3.2 A Baghdadi and a Maṣlawi šarḥ *of Psalm 1 (Avishur 2011)*

The following represents a synopsis of Psalm 1 in a Baġdādī and a Maṣlāwī *šarḥ*, compiled by Avishur (2011: 48f.). Here, the transcription is oriented at the colloquial Jewish versions of the city dialects of Baghdad and Mosul.

7 Standard Arabic *rifqat*.

H א אַשְׁרֵי הָאִישׁ-- אֲשֶׁר לֹא הָלַךְ, בַּעֲצַת רְשָׁעִים;
וּבְדֶרֶךְ חַטָּאִים, לֹא עָמָד, וּבְמוֹשַׁב לֵצִים, לֹא יָשָׁב.

B א. יא נייאל אל רג׳ל אלד׳י לם משא בשור אל צ׳אלמין

yā nayyāl əġ ġajəl allaḏī lam mašā bə-šūr əẓ ẓāləmīn
VOC achiever DEF man REL NEG go.PF.3SG.M in-council.CS DEF sin.PTCP.PL.M

ובדרב אל כ׳אטיין לם וקף ובמג׳לס

u-bə-daġb əl xāṭəyīn lam waqaf u-bə-majlis
CONJ-in-way.CS DEF do_wrong.PTCP.PL.M NEG stand.PF.3SG.M CONJ-in-seat.CS

אל פאלתין לם קעד.

əl fālətīn lam qaʕad
DEF do_wrong.PTCP.PL.M NEG sit.PF.3SG.M

M א. הנייל אלרג׳אל אלד׳י לא משי אב משוורת אלצ׳אלמין

ha nayyāl əġ-ġajāl allaḏī lā mašā əb-mišwarat əẓ-ẓāləmīn
VOC achiever DEF-man REL NEG go.PF.3SG.M in-council.CS DEF-sin.PTCP.PL.M

ובדרב אלכ׳טיין לא וקף ובמקעד

u-bə-daġb əl xāṭəyīn lā waqaf u-bə-maqʕad
CONJ-in-way.CS DEF do_wrong.PTCP.PL.M NEG stand.PF.3SG.M CONJ-in-seat.CS

אלג׳האל לא קעד.

əl-jahāl lā qaʕad
DEF-ignorant.PL.M NEG sit.PF.3SG.M

1 Happy is the man that has not walked in the counsel of the wicked,
nor stood in the way of sinners, nor sat in the seat of the scornful.

H ב כִּי אִם בְּתוֹרַת יְהוָה, חֶפְצוֹ; וּבְתוֹרָתוֹ יֶהְגֶּה, יוֹמָם וָלָיְלָה.

B ב. אד׳ אלכאן בשריעת אללה רצ׳אתו

ʔiḏ əl-kān bə-šaġīʕat allāh ġəḏat-o
indeed if-be-PF.3SG.M in-law.CS God wish.CS-3SG.M

ובתוראתו יחכי נהאר וליל.

u-bə-tōrat-o yaḥki nəhaġ wə-lēl
and-in-guidance.CS-3SG.M[H] tell.IPFV.3SG.M day and-night

M ב. כיד׳א אב תורת אללה שג׳לו ובתוראתו יקרא אנהאר וליל.

kiḏa əb-tōrat allāh šəġl-o u-bə-tōrāt-o yəqġaʔ ənhaġ wə-lēl
so in-law.CS[H] God business.CS-3SG.M and-in-guidance.CS-3SG.M read.IPF.-3SG.M day and-night

2 But his delight is in the law of the Lord; and in His law does he meditate day and night.

H ג וְהָיָה-- כְּעֵץ, שָׁתוּל עַל-פַּלְגֵי-מָיִם:
אֲשֶׁר פִּרְיוֹ, יִתֵּן בְּעִתּוֹ--וְעָלֵהוּ לֹא-יִבּוֹל; וְכֹל אֲשֶׁר-יַעֲשֶׂה יַצְלִיחַ.

B ג. ויכון כסוג׳רת אל מג׳רוסא צוב סוואקי אלמאי

w-īkūn kə-sojġət əl majġūsa ṣōb sawaqi l-may
and-be.IPFV.3MS as-tree.CS DEF/REL plant.PTCP.PASS.F at stream.PL.CS DEF-water

אלד׳י ת׳מרתו יעטי בווקתו

əllaḏī ṯamrat-o yuʕṭī bə-waqt-o
REL fruit.CS-3SG.M give.IPFV.3SG.M in-time.CS-3SG.M

ווראקו לם יד׳בל וכל אלד׳י יסווי יעדל.

wə-waraq-o lam yiḏbil wə-kull əllaḏī yəsawwī yaʕdil
and-leaf-3SG.M NEG whither.IPFV.3SG.M and-all.CS REL do.IPFV.3SG.M do_just.IPFV.3SG.M

M ג. ויכון כמא עוד משתול עלא סוואקי אלמייאת

w-īkūn *kamā* *ʕōd* *maštūl* *ʕalā* *sawāqi* *l-mayyāt*
and-be.IPFV.3MS as tree plant.PTCP.PASS upon stream.PL.CS DEF-water.PL

אלד׳י ת׳מרתו יעטי אבוקתו

əlladī *tamrat-o* *yuʕṭī* *əb-waqt-o*
REL fruit.CS-3SG.M give.IPFV.3SG.M in-time.CS-3SG.M

וורקו לא יד׳בל וכל אלד׳י יצנע ינג׳ח.

wə-waġaq-o *lā* *yidbil* *wə-kull* *əlladī* *yəṣnaʕ* *yənjaḥ*
and-leaf-3SG.M NEG whither.IPFV.3SG.M and-all.CS REL do.IPFV.3SG.M succeed.IPFV.3SG.M

3 And he shall be like a tree planted by streams of water,
that brings forth its fruit in its season, and whose leaf does not wither; and in whatsoever he does he shall prosper.

H ד לֹא-כֵן הָרְשָׁעִים: כִּי אִם-כַּמֹּץ, אֲשֶׁר-תִּדְּפֶנּוּ רוּחַ.
B ד. לם היכד׳ אל צ׳אלמין אד׳ אלכאן מת׳ל אל קש

lam *hēkad* *əl* *ẓāləmīn* *ʔid* *əl-kān* *mətl* *əl* *qašš*
NEG like_this DEF sin.PTCP.PL indeed if-be-PF.3SG.M like DEF straw

אלד׳י תדפעהו אל הווא.

əlladī *itdaffaʕ-hu* *əl* *hawwa*
REL push.IPFV.3SG.M-3SG.M DEF airstream

M ד. לא האכד׳ אלצ׳אלמין כיד׳א אם כמא אלקש

lā *hēkad* *əl-ẓāləmīn* *kidā* *əm* *kamā* *əl-qašš*
NEG like_this DEF-sin.PTCP.PL so if like DEF-straw

אד׳ דפעו אלהווא.

əd *daffaʕ-u* *əl-hawwa*
REL push.PF.3SG.M-3SG.M DEF-airstream

4 Not so the wicked; but they are like the chaff which the wind drives away.

H ה עַל-כֵּן, לֹא-יָקֻמוּ רְשָׁעִים--בַּמִּשְׁפָּט; וְחַטָּאִים, בַּעֲדַת צַדִּיקִים.
B ה. עלא היכד׳ לם יקומון אל צ׳אלמין בל שרע

ʕalā *hēkad* *lam* *yaqūmūn* *əẓ* *ẓāləmīn* *b-əš* *šarʕ*
upon like_this NEG stand.IPFV.3PL DEF sin.PTCP.PL.M in-DEF court

ולכ׳אטיין בג׳מאעת אל צאלחין.

wə-l-xāṭəyīn *bə-ğamāʕat* *əṣ* *ṣāləḥīn*
and-DEF-do_wrong.PTCP.PL in-group.CS DEF righteous.PL

M ה. עלא האכ׳ד׳ לא יקומון אלצ׳אלמין בלשרע ולכ׳אטיין אב ג׳מאעת אלצאלחין.

ʕalā *hēkad* *lā* *yaqūmūn* *əẓ-ẓāləmīn* *b-əš-šarʕ*
upon like_this NEG stand.IPFV.3PL DEF-sin.PTCP.PL.M in-DEF court

wə-l-xāṭəyīn *əb-jamāʕat* *əṣ-ṣāləḥīn*
and-DEF-do_wrong.PTCP.PL in-group.CS DEF-righteous.PL

5 Therefore the wicked shall not stand in the judgment, nor sinners in the congregation of the righteous.

H ו כִּי-יוֹדֵעַ יְהוָה, דֶּרֶךְ צַדִּיקִים; וְדֶרֶךְ רְשָׁעִים תֹּאבֵד.
B ו. אד׳ יפתכר אללה דרב אל צאלחין

ʔid *yəftakəġ* *llāh* *dağb* *əṣ* *ṣāləḥīn*
indeed reflect.IPFV.3MS God way.CS DEF righteous.PL

ודרב אל צ׳אלמין תנהפי.

wə-daġb əẓ ẓāləmīn tənhafī
and-way.CS DEF sin.PTCP.PL.M perish.IPFV.3FS

M ו. כיד׳א ופתכר אללה דרב אלצאלחין

kiḏā yəftakər llāh daġb əṣ-ṣāləḥīn
so reflect.IPFV.3MS God way.CS DEF-righteous.PL

ודרב אלצ׳אלמין תנעדם.

wə-daġb əẓ-ẓāləmīn tənʕadəm
and-way.CS DEF-sin.PTCP.PL.M vanish.IPFV.3FS

6 For the Lord regards the way of the righteous; but the way of the wicked shall perish.

3.3 A text in Baghdadi Judeo-Arabic (Mansour 1977: 25–29 and 1991: 184–190)

The following is a purely oral dialectal text, therefore not attested in Hebrew letters, recorded by Jacob Mansour with his mother.[8]

ʔiyyām qabəl kānū yəstḥōn w-ma yəmšōn ʔāčəġ[9] b-əd-daġb
day.PL before be.PF.3PL be_ashamed.IPFV.3PL and-NEG go.IPFV.3PL unveiled[Turk] in-DEF-street
Formerly, they [women] were ashamed (modest) and did not go unveiled in the street,

n-nəswān yləbsōn ʔəzəġ wə-xwīli w-lə-bnāt yləbsōn ʕəbi
DEF-woman.PL wear.IPFV.3PL abaya.PL and-veil.PL DEF-daughter.PL wear.IPFV.3PL abaya.PL
the women wore wrappers and veils, and the young women wore abayas (cloaks)

w-pušyāt[10] walad ʔiδā yġīd yəṭləb bnēti təği
and-veil.PL[Pers] boy when want.IPFV.3SG.M ask_for.IPFV.3SG.M girl come.IPFV.3SG.F
and fine silk veils; when a young man wants to marry a young woman, his mother

ʔəmm-u w-əxt-u yʕanuw-a w-iδa ʕəǧbət-əm
mother-3SG.M and-sister-3SG.M see.IPFV.3PL-3SG.F and-when please.PF.3SG.F-3PL
and his sister come to see her, and when she pleases them

yǧibōn-ū l-walad w-iqədsōn-u w-iδa yʕayən-a
bring.IPFV.3PL-3SG.M DEF-boy and-betrothe.IPFV.3PL-3SG.M and-when see.IPFV.3SG.M-3SG.F
they bring the young man and betroth him, and when her sees her

b-əd-daġb ma yəqdaġ yəʕġəf-a mġaṭṭa wəčč-a
in-DEF-street NEG be_able.IPFV.3SG.M know.IPFV.3SG.M-3SG.F cover.PTCP.PASS.F face-3SG.F
in the street he cannot recognize her, her face being veiled

lēbsi ʕbāyi w-pūšī mən-ṭaraf kānū yxāfōn mn-əl-əmsəlmīn
wear.PTCP.ACT.F abaya and-veil from-side be.PF.3PL fear.IPFV.3PL from-DEF-Muslim.PL
and [she] wearing an abaya and a veil, as they were afraid of the Muslims

8 Following the advice of Otto Jastrow, redundant stress acutes are removed in the transcription.

9 Turkish *açık* 'uncovered, light-colored'.

10 Persian *pošā* 'veil, curtain', Turkish *peçe* 'black veil (worn by women)'.

l-əmsəlmīn yəʔadō[11]*-həm kθīġ məxṣūṣ iδa ylaqōn bnāt*
DEF-Muslim.PL molest.IPFV.3PL-3PL much specialize.PTCP.PASS when meet.IPFV.3PL girl.PL
the Muslims harassed them a lot, especially when they meet young women

yəʔadō-həm kθīġw-ʔakθaġ l-əbnāt yxāfōn yṭəlʕōn b-b-aḥd-əm
molest.IPFV.3PL-3PL much and-many.ELAT DEF-girl.PL fear.IPFV.3PL go_up.IPFV.3PL in-in-one-3PL
they harass them a lot, and most of the young women are afraid to go out alone;

bnēti mā kānət təṭlaʕ b-əl-lēl lə-t-tāli walad lamma
girl NEG be.PF.3SG.F go_up.IPFV.3SG.F in-DEF-night to-DEF-end boy when
a young woman didn't go out at all at night; when a young man

yqaddəs ʕēb yʕayən-a lə-bnēti li-ma yədzawwaǧ
betroth.IPFV.3SG.M shame see.IPFV.3SG.M-3SG.F DEF-girl to-REL marry.IPFV.3SG.M
is engaged it is unusual that he sees the young woman, which he will marry

yaʕni ʔiδa bədlū-ha ma yəqdaġ yḥəss kθīġ
mean.IPFV.3SG.M when exchange.PF.3PL-3SG.F NEG be_able.IPFV.3SG.M feel.IPFV.3SG.M much
i.e. when they exchange her [for another +woman] he cannot feel much;

badlū bnāt w-rahmət ḥkiyyi nōba wēḥəd ġād
exchange.PF.3PL girl.PL and-happen.PF.3SG.F story instance one.M want.PF.3SG.M
the exchanged young women, and there happened a story (case) when a man wanted

yədzawwaǧ w-ʔəmm-u ġāḥət ʕaynət-a lə-bnēti
marry.IPFV.3SG.M and-mother-3SG.M go.PF.3SG.F see.PF.3SG.F-3SG.F DEF-girl
to marry, and his mother went to see the young woman,

w-ʕəǧbət-a w-qədsət-a w-əl-walad ma yaʕġrəf-a
and-please.PF.3SG.F-3SG.F and-betroth.PF.3SG.F-3SG.F and-DEF-boy NEG know.IPFV.3SG.M-3SG.F
and she pleased her and betrothed her, but the young man did not know her

huwwi bə-ġδ̣āt ʔəmm-u lamma sāġ l-ʕəġṣ
3SG.M in-agreement.CS mother-3SG.M when happen.3SG.M DEF-wedding
he – in agreement with his mother; when the wedding happended

dzawwaǧ wə-mn-əṣbaḥ ʕaġaf ʔəllaδi[12] *ḥolā yaʕni*
marry.PF.3SG.M and-from-morning know.PF.3SG.M REL.M/COMP squinting.F mean.IPFV.3SG.M
he married, and from the next morning on he knew that she was squinting, i.e.

ddīġa l-ʕēn-a mən səḥwət-u lə-l-walad ʔəllaδi
turn.IPFV.3SG.F ACC-eye-3SG.F from embarrassment.CS-3SG.M for-DEF-boy REL.M
she turned her eye; from his embarrassment for the young man [himself], who

11 According to Mansour (1991: 185), this verb reflects both CA *ʔāḏā* 'to hurt, harass' (√ ʔ-d-y, IV) and CA *ʔaʕdā* 'to infect' (√ ʕ-d-w, IV).

12 Instead of *ʕaġaf ʔəllaδi* the 1991 edition by Mansour (p. 185) has *qām ḥass biya* 'her woke up and saw that' (rise.PF.3SG.M feel.PF.SG.M in.3SG.F).

samaʕ kəlmət ʔəmm-u ǧann w-šaqqaq
hear.PF.3SG.M word.CS mother.3SG.M become_crazy.PF.3SG.M and-tear.PF.3SG.M
had obeyed the word of his mother he became crazy and tore

ḥwās-u məθəl ma-tṣādfət ʔəllaδi lēʔa w-raḥēl lamma
clothes-3SG.M like REL-happen.PF.3SG.F REL.M/COMP Lea^{H} and-Rahel^{H} when
his clothes; [it was] like that had happened that Lea and Rahel, when

dzawǧu ma bədlu-ha lēʔa ʕawaδ̣ raḥēl bə-l-lēl lamma
marry.PF.3PL NEG exchange.PF.3PL-3SG.F Lea^{H} instead_ofRahel^{H} in-DEF-nightwhen
they married: didn't they exchange Lea for Rahel; in the night when

ṭalaʕ l-ʕəġġīṣ mən-əl-qəbba qāmū ysəwwōn kələlələ
go_up.PF.3SG.M DEF-bridegroom from-DEF-room stand_up.PF.3PL do.IPFV.3PL "*kələlələ*"
the bridegroom when out of the room they began to make [a sound] "*kələlələ*"

yaʕni lēʔa lēʔa w-li-ḥad-ʔəs-saʕa ʕənd-əm hāδa n-nīšān[13] *yqulōn*
mean.IPFV.3SG.M Lea^{H} Lea^{H} and-to-one-DEF-hour with-3PL DEM.M DEF-sign^{Pers} say.IPFV.3PL
i.e. "Lea Lea"; and to this day they have this symbol[ic sound], the say

kələlələ lēli qabl-əl-ʕəġṣ ysəwwōn ḥənni yxəδ̣bō-l-a ḥənni
"*kələlələ*" night before-DEF-wedding do.IPFV.3PL Henna embellish-for-3SG.F Henna
"*kələlələ*". The night before the wedding they put on henna, the embellish her

ʔīd-a w-ġəǧl-a w-ixəllōn ṭəpap ḥənni ʕala ṣabīʕ-a
hand-3SG.F and-foot.3SG.F and-keep.IPFV.3PL ball.PL Henna upon finger.PL-3SG.F
with Henna, her hand, her foot, and they keep rounds of henna on her fingers

w-mən-baʕdēn yǧōn n-nəswān ynətšōn l-ḥənni mən ʔīd-a
and-from-thereafter come.IPFV.3PL DEF-woman.PL beat_off DEF-Henna from hand-3SG.F
and then the women remove the henna from her hand

w-ihələhlōn w-dəqqāqa təqʕəd-ddəqq lēt-əl-ḥənni
and-trill.IPFV.3PL and-drummer.F sit.IPFV.3SG.F-drum.IPFV.3SG.F night.CS-DEF-Henna
and trill, and a female drummer (sits there and) drums during the henna night.

l-ʕəġġīṣ lamma yədzawwaǧ lamma yzəynōn-u
DEF-bridegroom when marry.IPFV.3SG.M when cut_hair.IPFV.3PL-3SG.M
When the bridegroom marries, when they cut his hair

yǧibō-l-u mzayyən lə-l-bēt w-izəynōn-u
bring.IPFV.3PL-for-3SG.M hairdresser to-DEF-house and-cut_hair.IPFV.3PL-3SG.M
they bring a hairdresser to his home and cut his hair

13 Persan *nišān*; Turkish *nişan* 'sign, betrothal'.

w-idəqqō-l-u mazīqa w-iʕəzmōn l-awādəm ʕala zyan
and-drum.IPFV.3PL-for-3SG.M music and-invite.IPFV.3PL DEF-human.PL on hairdressing
and they drum for him music and invite the people to his hairdressing.

māl-u w-lēt-əl-ʕəġṣ yqəʕdōn ʕala bāb-əl-qəbba li-ma
GEN-3SG.M and-night.CS-DEF-wedding sit.IPFV.3PL on door.CS-DEF-room for-REL
And during the wedding night they sit at the door of the until

yəṭlaʕ w-əl-mazīqa qa-ddəqq
go_up.IPFV.3SG.M and-DEF-music CONT-drum.IPFV.3SG.F
he comes out, and the music plays (drums).

l-maġa lamma dğīb bnāt zōğ-a kəll-əš ma
DEF-woman when bring.IPFV.3SG.F daughter.PL husband.3SG.F all-thing NEG
When the (a) woman gives birth to ("brings") daughters her husband cannot

yṭīq yʕayən-əm lə-bnāt həsb-āl-ak ğabət-əm
be_able.IPFV.3SG.M see.IPFV.3SG.M-3PL DEF-daugher.PL according-on-2SG.M bring.PF.3SG.F-3PL
see ("stand") the daughters, as if she had brought them

mən bet-abū-ha w-nōba waḥdi sāġ ʕənd-a
from house.CS-father.CS-3SG.F and-instance one.F travel.PF.3SG.M with-3SG.F
from the house of her father. In one instance, a woman [already] had

xaməs-sətt-əbnāt waqt-əl-waldət zaʕal zōğ-a w-θīni nhāġ
five-six-daughter.PL time.CS-DEF-birth scold.PF.3SG.M husband-3SG.F and-second day
five [or] six daughters. At the time of the birth, her husband scolded her and

nəzzal-a llə-ha w-əl-bənt-a lə-s-səġdāb[14] *ma*
send_down.PF.3SG.M-3SG.F ACC-3SG.F and-ACC-daughter-3SG.F to-DEF-basement NEG
the next day he sent her and her daughter down to the basement, [as] he did not

yġīd-a la llə-ha w-la l-bənt-a zaʕal ʕlī-ha
want.IPFV.3SG.M-3SG.F NEG ACC-3SG.F and-NEG ACC-daughter-3SG.F scold.PF.3SG.M on-3SG.F
want her, neither her and nor her daughter; her scolded her

čənki[15] *ğabət-l-u bnēti yqəllō-l-u l-awādəm*
because[Turk] bring.PF.3SG.F-FOR-3SG.M daughter say.IPFV.3PL-FOR-3SG.M DEF-man.PL
because she had given birth to ("brought him") a daughter. The people say to him

ğabət-əm mən bet-abū-ha w-qat-təʕzal ʕliy-a?
bring.PF.3SG.F-3PL from house.CS-father.CS-3SG.F and-CONT-scold.IPFV.2SG.M on-3SG.F
Has she brought them from her father's house, and you scold her?

14 Persian *sard-ʔāb*; Turkish *serdab* 'basement, underground'.
15 Turkish *çünki/ü* 'because, since'.

lākən lamma dǧīb walad lēt-əs-sətti yqəsmōn šašša[16]
however when bring.IPFV.3SG.F boy night.CS-DEF-sixth distribute.IPFV.3PL *šašša (sweets)*
However, when she gives birth to a son they hand out sweets on the sixth night

w-ikəsġōn təngāyi w-l-ulād yləmmō-həm w-yəṭʕō-həm
and-break.IPFV.3PL pot and-DEF-child.PL gather.IPFV.3PL-3PL and-give.IPFV.3PL.3PL
and break a pot. And the children gather them and they give (them)

l-kəll walad šəqlāyi qəḥəf yaʕni wəṣla mal təngāyi
to-every.CS child fragment.CS bowl mean.IPFV.3SG.M piece GEN pot
to every child a fragment of the bowl, i.e. a piece of the pot.

w-maġa tsawwi zəʕəfġān yaʕni lōn ʔaṣfaġ məθl-əl-kəġkəm
and-woman put.IPFV.3SG.F saffron mean.IPFV.3SG.M color yellow like-DEF-saffron
And a woman prepares saffron, i.e. a yellow color like (the) saffron

wə-ddīġ-l-əm l-kəll walad šwayya b-əl-qəḥəf
and-turn.IPFV.3SG.F for-3PL for-every.CS child thing.DIM in-DEF-bowl
and passes for every child a bit in the [fragment of] the bowl.

w-iǧūḥōn ydəlquw-a b-əd-daġb w-iṣiḥōn šāša šāša
and-go.IPFV.3PL pour_out.IPFV.3PL-3SG.F in-DEF-street and-exclaim.IPFV.3PL "*šašša šašša*"
And they pour it out on the street and shout "*šašša šašša*"

w-iṭəššō-l-əm ḏ̣ūġa w-iləmmū-ha mn-əl-ʔaġḏ̣
and-spread.IPFV.3PL-for-3PL ḍūra and-pick_up.IPFV.3PL-3SG.F from-DEF-floor
And they spread for them ḍūra (roasted maize), and they pick it up from the floor.

w-lēt-ə-θmīni ysəwwōn ʕəqd-əl-yās (əlyās)[17] *yǧibōn*
and-night.CS-DEF-eighth put.IPFV.3PL binding.CS-DEF-privet (or: Elias) bring.IPFV.3PL
and on the eighth night they do the binding of the privet (or: of Elias).

čālġi[18] *kəġsi lyāhu-ṇ-ṇābi w-inəṣbōn-u w-izuġōn-u*
orchestra[Turk] chair.CS Elias-DEF-prophet and-erect.IPFV.3PL-3SG.M and-visit.IPFV.3PL-3SG.M
And they bring an orchestra, [and] the chair of Elias the prophet, and they put him up and pay him a visit.

w-iġəṭṭō-l-u wəčč-u l-walad w-iqəʕdōn-u b-ḥəġġ-əm
and-cover.IPFV.3PL-for-3SG.M face-3SG.M for-son and-place.IPFV.3PL-3SG.M in-lap-3PL
And they cover the face of the boy and place him in their lap.

16 Cf. Hebrew שִׁשָּׁה *šiššā̊* 'six'

17 *ʕəqd-əl-yās* (or: *əlyās*) refers to the ceremony taking place on the night before circumcision. Mansour (1991: 189) explains the name 'binding of the myrtle (privet)' with the similarity of the term *əl-yās* 'the myrtle to *əlyās* 'Elijah': "it was the custom to place a bunch of myrtle on the Prophet Elijah's Chair".

18 Turkish *çalgı* 'musical instrument'.

lamma yfəṭmōn-u l-walad yfərrō-l-u bēḏi b-əš-šaṭṭ
when wean.IPFV.3PL-3SG.M DEF-child swing.IPFV.3PL-for-3SG.M egg in-DEF-river
When they wean the boy they cast (for him) an egg in the river

mən-ṭaraf l-əfṭām māl-u
from-side DEF-weaning GEN-3SG.M
for the sake of his weaning.

ʔiδa ṭalaʕ sənn-u l-fōq ywəznōn-u bə-ṭḥīn
when go_up.PF.3SG.M tooth-3SG.M DEF-up weigh.IPFV.3PL-3SG.M in-flour
When his upper tooth comes out they weigh him in flour

w-isəwwōn-u b-ʕābəʕ w-iqəsmōn-u
and-put.IPFV.3PL-3SG.M in-*ʕābəʕ* and-distribute.IPFV.3PL-3SG.M
and they make it (the flour) to *ʕābəʕ* (a sort of cookie) and distribute it.

ʔiδa ydəqqō-l-u ǧadġi w-iṭib l-ǧadġi
when hit.IPFV.PL-for-3PL smallpox and-heal.IPFV.SG.M DEF-smallpox
When they vaccinate him against smallpox and the smallpox heals

yqəsmō-l-u qēmaġ w-ʕasal
share_with.IPFV.3PL-for-3SG.M cream and-honey
they share for him cream and honey.

3.4 A text in Baghdadi Judeo-Arabic (Bar-Moshe 2019: 133f.)

The following text excerpt entitled *ʕədmō-həm wiya-l-īhūd* 'they executed them with the Jews' was recorded by Bar-Moshe with two speakers. Both the transcription and the translation closely follow the edition by Bar-Moshe.[19]

ʕaqba hadʔət əl-awḏāʕ bas əl-waḏəʕ ətxarḅaṭ
afterwards.ACC calm_down.PF.3SG.F DEF-situation.PL but DEF-situation deteriorate.PF.3SG.M
Afterwards [after the Six-Day War], things calmed down. But the situation got worse,

yaʕni mal-īhūd əwnīki baʕdēn b-əṯ-ṯmīnī wu-səttīn kānu... hā...
mean.IPFV.3SG.M GEN-Jew.COLL there thereafter in-DEF-eight and-sixty be.PF.3PL oh
i.e. [the situation] of the Jews there [in Iraq]. Afterwards, in [19]68 there were … Oh …

b-əl... b-əs-sabʕa wu-səttīn b-aḏāki l-waqt kān wēḥəd wazīr ṣaḥḥa
in-DEF in-DEF-seven and-sixty in-DEM.REM.M DEF-time be.PF.3SG.M one.M minister.CS health
In [19]67, at that time, there was a [public] health minister,

sōni[20] *Israʔel kān-muqtaraḥ ʕal-wizāra ənna-hu l-īhūd*
hate.PTCP.M.CS[H] Israel[H] be.PF.3SG.M-suggest.PTCP.M on.DEF ministry COMP-3SG.M DEF-Jews.COLL
who hated Israel. He suggested to the ministry (government) to take the Jews

19 Thanks to Assaf Bar-Moshe for his kind permission to reproduce this text excerpt.
20 Hebrew שׂוֹנֵא *śōnē(ʔ)* 'hating' (SG.M).

ywəddō-həm əb... əb-kamp ... ʕaqəb Bəġdād əğ-Ğadīda
take.IPFV.3PL-3PL in in-camp following Bəġdād DEF-new.F
to ... to a camp ... out of Baġdād al-Ğadīda

kanu-bēnīn əmkān māl ... mustašfa mal-əmğanīn ā?
be-PF.3PL-build.PTCP.PL place GEN hospital GEN-crazy-PL okay
they were building a place for a psychiatric hospital, okay?

wu-ʕal-asās yaxḏō-həm... yaxəḏ-əm əl-īhūd kəllət-əm
and-on.DEF-basis take.IPFV.3PL-3PL take.IPFV.3SG.M-3PL DEF-Jew.COLL all.CS-3PL
And supposedly they would take them ... all of the Jews,

wu-yəʕtəqəl-əm wnīki b-āḏa l... kamp wnīki yəʕtəqlō-həm i.
and-arrest.IPFV.3SG.M-3PL there in-DEM.SG.M DEF camp there arrest.IPFV.3SG.M-3PL yes
one would imprison them there, in this ... camp, they would imprison them there. Yes.

ma mašət lə-ḥkiyāt kān muʕāraḍa ma muʕāraḍa wu-hāḏa.
NEG walk.PF.3SG.F DEF-story.PL be.PF.3SG.M opposition REL opposition and-DEM.SG.M
[But] it did not happen (lit.: "the stories did not walk"). There was opposition [to that move] and [all] that.

lākən baʕdēn əḥna... mən ğət... mən ṣāġ əl-inqilāb hāḏa
but afterwards 1PL from come.PF.3SG.F from happen.PF.3SG.M DEF-revolution DEM.SG.M
But afterwards we ... when came ... when this revolution happened, [the revolution]

māl... mal-Aḥmad Ḥasan əl-Bakər wu-stawlu l-baʕṯiyīn
GEN GEN-ʔAḥmad Ḥasan al-Bakr and-take_over.PF.3PL DEF-Baathist.PL
of ... of ʔAḥmad Ḥasan al-Bakr, and the Baathists took over

wu-ğā Saddām əHsēn, hāyi b-hayyi sana?
and-come.PF.3PL Ṣaddām Ḥusayn DEM.SG.F in-which year
and Ṣaddām Ḥusayn came – in which year was it?

b-əṯ-ṯmīnī wu-sə... alf wu-təsəʕmīyi wu-ṯmīnī wu-səttīn, b-əl-ōgəst
in-DEF-eight and-s... thousand and-nine-hundred and-eight and-sixty in-DEF-August
In [6]8 ... in 1968, in August

alf wu-təsəʕmīyi wu-ṯmīnī wu-səttīn. wu-badu yətnəklōn[21] b-əl-īhūd
thousand and-nine-hundred and-eight and-sixty and-begin.PF.3PL harass.IPFV.3PL in-DEF-Jew.COLL
1968. And they started to harass the Jews

wu... sawwu hāyi lə-ḥkīyi mal-ğāsūsīyi wu-ğābō-həm əl-īhūd
and do.PF.3PL DEM.SG.F DEF-story GEN-espionage and bring.PF.3PL-3PL DEF-Jew.COLL
and they did this story with espionage (i.e. accused some Jews of spying for Israel) and they brought the Jews

21 Arabic form based on the Hebrew root √ n-k-l in the verb form הִתְנַכֵּל *hiṯnakkēl* 'to harass'.

əmn əl-Baṣġa wu-Bəġdād wu-ʕədmō-həm wu-badət...
from DEF-Baṣra and-Baġdad and-execute.PF.3PL-3Pl and-start.PF.3SG.F
from Basra and Baghdad and executed them. And it started …

kəll saʕa yəġdōn yʕədmōn wēḥəd... wu-aku wuzarā
every year want.IPFV.3PL execute.IPFV.3PL one.M and-EXIST minister.PL
all the time ("every hour") they wanted to execute someone … And there were ministers

kānu mūqufīn hami... yəġdōn yʕədmōn wazīr
be.PF.3PL arrest.PTCP.PASS.PL.M also want.IPFV.3PL execute.IPFV.3PL minister
who were also arrested … When they wanted to execute a minister

yğibōn wēḥəd yhūdī wīya-n-u l... yʕədmōn-u i.
bring.IPFV.3PL one.M Jew.M with-SD-3SG.M t[o] execute.IPFV.3PL-3SG.M yes
they brought a Jew with him … [as an excuse] to execute him. Yes.

ḥətti aškun hāḏa? qa-yəttəhmō... aš yəttəhmōn...
until what DEM.SG.M CONT-accuse.IPFV.3PL what accuse.IPFV.3PL
What was the purpose of that? They accus[e] … what did they accuse of?

yəttəhmōn-u b-əğ-ğāsūsīyi, yaʕni k-ənn-u wiya-l-īhūd.
accuse.IPFV.3PL-3SG.M in-DEF-espionage mean.IPFV.3SG.M as-COMP-3SG with-DEF-Jew-COLL
They accused him [the minister] of spying, i.e. as if he was with the Jews.

lēš hīyi l-baʕṯiyīn ... əl-baʕṯiyīn ... əl... əl-program māl-əm,
for.INT 3SG.F DEF-Baʕṯist.PL DEF-Baʕṯist.PL DEF… DEF-program^{E} GEN-3PL
Was it the Baathists, their program

əl-barnāməğ māl-əm ḏədd-əl-i... əl-gēzaʕ ... ḏədd-l-ihūd? lō! lō!
DEF-program GEN-3PL against-DEF-J… DEF-race^{H} against-DEF-Jew.COLL NEG!^{H} NEG!^{H}
their program against the J…, the race, against the Jews?

hūwi ... l-baʕṯiyīn, taqrīban ən-nəsxa ṭəbq əl-aṣəl mən-əš-šiyuʕīyi.
3SG.M DEF-Baʕṯist.PL approximately DEF-copy according.to DEF-root from-DEF-communism
He … the Baathists [were] more or less a copy of (the origin of the) communism.

wu-hāḏa... hāḏa, Mišēl Aflaq, hūwi lli sūwā-hū ḥəzb əl-baʕṯ
and-DEM.SG DEM.SG.M Michel Aflaq 3SG.M REL make.PF.3SG.M-3SG.M party.CS DEF-resurrection
And this, this Michel Aflaq, he was the one who made the Baath party

b... b-s-Sūrya. wu-kəll-u ʕal-mabādəʔ šiyuʕīyi. yaʕni
in in-DEF-Syria and-all.CS-3SG.M upon-principle.PL communist.SG.F mean.IPFV.3SG.M
in … in Syria. And all of it [was based] on communist principles, meaning

māku tafriqa māku hāḏa. lākən haḏōli qa-yəğdōn yməššōn
NEG.EXIST difference NEG.EXIST DEM.SG.M however DEM.PL PROG.want.IPFV.3PL promote.IPFV.3PL
there was no difference, there was not that. But these [Baathists] wanted to promote

umūr-əm wu-yṯəbtōn wəḏ̣ʕəyət-əm wu-qa-yəğdōn yətxəlṣōn
thing.PL.CS-3PL and-stabilize.IPFV.3PL position.CS.3PL and.PROG-want.IPFV.3PL get_rid_of.IPFV.3PL
their issues and to stabilize their position and they wanted to get rid

mən-kəll əl… haḏōli l-ḏəbbāṭ lə-kbāğ əl… əlli siyāsiyīn əkbāğ,
from-all.CS DEF… DEM.PL DEF-officer.PL DEF-big.PL.M DEF… REL politician.PL big.PL.M
of all… these high-ranking officers that … that (are) high-ranking politicians.

ṭəllʕō-l-əm hāyi ənna-hu yğībō-həm yəttəhmō-həm wiya-ihūdī.
get_out-PF-3PL-for-3PL DEM.SG.F COMP-3SG.M bring.IPFV.3PL-3PL accuse.IPFV.3PL-3PL with-Jew
They got out (invented) for them this [excuse] that they would bring them and accuse them [of cooperation] with a Jew.

wəddēt l-u maktūb ənta. ənta wəddēt l-u hēkəḏ. i. wu-ğabō …
give.PF.2SG.M for-3SG.M letter 2SG.M 2SG.M give.PF.2SG.M for-3SG.M like.this yes and-give.PF.3PL
(For example:) You gave him a letter. You gave [it] to him like this. Yes. And they brought …

yaʕnī l-maṣāləḥ təqtaḏ̣ī? i! i! qa-yəğdōn yətxəlṣōn
mean.IPFV.3SG.M DEF-interest.PL require.IPFV.3SG.F yes! yes! PROG.want.IPFV.3PL get_rid_of.IPFV.3P
That means that the interests [of the Iraqi regime] required [those measures]? Yes! Yes! They wanted to get rid

mənn-əm. b-hal-ṣūra, ttəhmō-həm wiya-ihūd wu-aš-ə… wu-hāḏa
from-3PL in-DEM-form accuse.PF.3PL-3PL with-Jew.COLL and-INT… and-DEM.M
of them. This way, they accused them [of cooperation] with the Jews, and what th...? … and that

wu-ʕədmō-həm wiya-l-ihūd. wu-mən haḏīki hāyi bāʕəd
and-execute.PF.3PL-3PL with-DEF-Jew.COLL and-from then DEM.SG.F after
and they executed them with the Jews. And from that on

əntahət əl… əl-āḏa.
end.PF.3SG.F DE F DEF-DEM.SG.M
ended the … this [the Jewish peaceful existence in Iraq].

3.5 A text in Jewish Maṣlāwī (Jastrow 1989: 291f.)

The following text, as recorded and transcribed by Jastrow (1989: 291f.), equally represents a purely oral dialectal text from Mosul, with linguistic features reminiscent of Anatolian Arabic.[22] Typical features that distinguish Jewish Maṣlāwī (JM) from Muslim Maṣlāwī (MM) are the following (cf. Jastrow 1989: 285–290): a weaker *ʔimāla*, e.g.,

22 Thanks to Otto Jastrow for his kind permission to reproduce this and the following text excerpt.

JM *basētīn* 'gardens', *badle* 'suit', and *hōne* 'here' vs. MM *basītīn*, *badli*, and *hōni*; less anaptyxis in syllable codas in JM as compared with MM, e.g., JM *akalt* 'you (SG.M) ate' vs. MM *akalət*; different plural demonstrative pronouns JM *hōḏe* 'these' vs. MM *haḏōli*; different pronominal suffixes of the third person singular, e.g., JM *nsammī-yu* 'we name him' vs. MM *nsammī-nu* and JM *nsammī-ya* 'we name her' vs. MM *nsammī-ha*; a tendency in JM to shorten the negator *mā* to *ma* in nominal sentences and when preceding a perfect form.

kəbbət əl-bərġəl yaxḏūn əl-bərġəl w yaxḏūn əl-laḥəm
meatball.CS DEF-burġul take.IPFV.3PL DEF-burġul and take.IPFV.3PL DEF-meat
bərġəl meatballs: They take *bərġəl* and they take meat

w əl-laḥəm lāzəm ykūn yaʕni bala səmən
and DEF-meat necessary be.SUBJ.3SG.M mean.IPFV.3SG.M without fat
which must be without any fat, and

w yəṭḥanūn əl-bərġəl maʕ əl-laḥəm yəʕməlūn əl-ʕağīne māl əl-kəbbe
and grind.IPFV.3PL DEF-Burġul with DEF-meat make.IPFV.3PL DEF-dough GEN DEF-Kubbe
and they grind the *bərġəl* together with the meat, the make the dough for the *kəbbe.*

w baʕdēn yaxḏūn əl-laḥəm w yqaṭṭʕūn-u maʕ əl-baṣl
and thereafter take.IPFV.3PL DEF-meat and cut.IPFV.3PL-3SG.M with DEF-onion
Then they take (some other) meat, chop it together with onions,

w yḥəṭṭū-l-u baharāt w yəqlōn-u
and put.IPFV.3PL for-3SG.M spice.PL and fry.IPFV.3PL-3SG.M
add spices and fry it.

b-əl-mōṣəl mā kān margarīna kān yḥəṭṭūn əl-zēt w-əl-baṣl
in-DEF-Mosul NEG be.PF.3SG.M margarine be.PF.3SG.M put.IPFV.3PL DEF-olive_oil and-DEF-onion
In Mosul there was no margarine. They used olive oil and onions

yḥəṭṭūn səmən māl əl-baqaġaw māl əl-ġanam w yəqlōn-u
put.IPFV.3PL fat GEN DEF-cow or GEN DEF-sheep and fry.IPFV.3PL-3SG.M
or butterfat from cows or sheep to fry the meat.

w yḥəṭṭūn əl-baharāt baʕdēn yətrəkūnu yəbġad w mən baʕd mā
and put.IPFV.3PL DEF-spice.PL thereafter leave.IPFV.3PL cool.IPFV.3SG.M and from after REL
They added spices. Then they left it to cool off. When it

yəbġad yaxḏūn əl-kəbbe əl-bərġəl allaḏi ʕəmənnā-ha
cool.IPFV.3SG.M take.IPFV.3PL DEF-meatball DEF-burġul REL.SG.M make.PF.1PL-3SG.F
has cooled off they take the *kəbbe,* that is, the *bərġəl* which we have made

mət̲l əl-ʕağīn w yəftaḥū-wa w yḥəṭṭūn əl-laḥəm ᵊb-baṭna w ...
like DEF-dough and open.IPFV.3PL-3SG.F and put.IPFV.3PL DEF-meat DEF-belly.ACC and ...
into a kind of dough, they open it and put the meat inside.

kān yəʕməlūw-a aw ṭabaqtēn aw ṭabaqa wəḥde yaʕni
be.PF.3SG.M make.IPFV.3PL-3SG.F or layer.DU or layer one.F mean.IPFV.3SG.M
The used to make the *kəbbə* either one layer or two layers.

ṭabaqa wəḥde kān yəʕməlūw-a mət̲l əṭ-ṭappe w baʕdēn
layer one.F be.PF.3SG.M make.IPFV.3PL-3SG.F like DEF-ball and thereafter
The one with one layer they used to make like a ball and

yʕaġġḏ̣ūw-a
broaden.IPFV.3PL-3SG.F
flatten it.

aw id̲a yəʕməlūw-a ṭabaqtēn yəftaḥūn əṭ-ṭabaqa awwal wəḥde
or when make.IPFV.3PL-3SG.F layer.DU open.IPFV.3PL DEF-layer first one.F
When they made it with two layers they would open the layer, the first one,

w yaxd̲ūn ṭabaqa t̲āniya w yaxd̲ūn qəṭʕa māl ᵊqmāš
and take.IPFV.3PL layer second.F and take.IPFV.3PL piece GEN cloth
and then take the second layer, and they would take a piece of cloth.

ydēxlūn əl-laḥəm b-əl-ṭabaqa l-ʔūla w yḥəṭṭūn fōqa ṭ-ṭabaqa
make_enter.IPFV.3PL DEF-meat in-DEF-layer DEF-first.F and put.IPFV.3PL over DEF-layer
They would put the meat into the first layer, put the second layer on top,

t̲-t̲āniya w baʕdēn yḥəṭṭūn ʕalay-a qəṭʕət lə-qmāš w yʕaġġḏ̣ūw-a
DEF-second.F and afterwards put.IPFV.3PL upon-3SG.F piece.CS DEF-cloth and broaden.IPFV.3PL-3SG.F
put a piece of cloth on it and flatten it.

yətrəkūw-a lamman ... faġəd sāʕa ʕal-hawa šwayya yaʕni xāṭər
leave.IPFV.3PL-3SG.F when ... INDEF hour on-air a_bit mean.IPFV.3SG.M so.that
They leave (the ready meatballs) in the open for a while, an hour or so,

təbas ər-rəṭūba mənn-a təṭlaʕ w baʕdēn yəġlōn əl-ṃay
dry.IPFV-3SG.F DEF-moisture from-3SG.F rise.IPFV.3SG.F and thereafter boil.IPFV.3PL DEF-water
so that they dry and the moisture is taken out of them. Then they boil the water.

w əl-ṃay yḥəṭṭū-l-u məlḥ w yḥəṭṭūn əl-kəbbe yḥəṭṭūn
and DEF-water put.IPFV.3PL-for-3SG.M salt and put.IPFV.3PL DEF-meatball put.IPFV.3PL
They add salt to the water and put the meatballs in. They would put

wəḥde w ydīġūw-a b-əd-dəst w baʕdēn yaxd̲ūn aw t̲nēn
one.F and stir.IPFV.3PL-3SG.F in-DEF-pot and afterwards take.IPFV.3PL or two
one (*kəbbe*) and stir it in the pot, and then they would take two

aw ṯāṯe ḥasab əl-kəbəġ māl əd-dəst
or three according DEF-size GEN DEF-pot
or three more, according to the size of the pot.

w lamman tənsələq ᵓṭ-ṭūf ʕal-ṃāy b-ṯat tərbaʕ əs-sāʕa
and when be-cooked.IPFV.3SG.F DEF-surface on.DEF-water in-three.CS quarter.CS.PL DEF-hour
When the *kəbbe* is cooked, it will rise to the surface, after about three quarters of

nəṣṣ sāʕa w yṭallʕūw-a mən əl-ṃāy w yaklūw-a
half.CS hour and take_up.IPFV.3PL-3SG.F from DEF-water and eat.IPFV.3PL-3SG.F
an hour, half an hour. They take it out of the water and eat it.

w hāy kəbbət əl-bərġəl
and DEICT meatball.CS DEF-burġul
So that's *kəbbət əl-bərġəl.*

3.6 A Judeo-Arabic text from Northern Iraq (Shabbat in Arbīl) (Jastrow 1990: 282f.)

Lastly, here is another purely oral dialectal text, as recorded and transcribed by Jastrow (1990: 282f.), in the northern Iraqi city Arbīl. This dialect of Northern Kurdistan exhibits a strong affinity to the dialects of the Mardin group and the more Eastern dialects of Āzəḵ and Siirt (for a list of typical features cf. Jastrow 1990: 6f.).

hadā bə-ʔArbīl kān dāt kall-əm kətīr kānū b-əš-šabbāt
DEICT.M in-Erbil be.PF.3SG.M religion^{H} all.CS-3PL very be.PF.3PL in-DEF-Shabbat^{H}
In Arbīl the people were very religious. They would keep Shabbat

yəmsakū-hu yaʕni qawi əl-šabbāt kəll bēt yəḥaḍḍərūn
maintain.IPFV.3PL-3PL mean.IPFV.3SG.M strong DEF-Shabbat^{H} every.CS house prepare.IPFV.3PL
decisively. All the families ("houses") would prepare

əl-ʔakəl lə-yōm əğ-ğəmʕa w yəmšōn əṣ-ṣala yəḍbəxūn w
DEF-food for-day.CS DEF-assembly and go.IPFV.3PL DEF-synagogue cook.IPFV.3PL and
the food for Friday and go to the synagogue. They would cook and

yəḥaḍḍərūn w yəʕməlūn əl-tabīt əl-tabīt t-īxallaw-a ʕal-ʕūdēn
prepare.IPFV.3PL and make.IPFV.3PL DEF-*tabīt* DEF-*tabīt* FUT-put.IPFV-3SG.F on-wood.PL
prepare beforehand. They would make *tabīt* and put it on (burning) wood

w əl-faḥəm w əl-yəği mən əṣ-ṣala yəqʕadūn əl-ʕāyle
and DEF-charcoal and ?-come.IPFV.3SG.M from DEF-synagogue sit.IPFV.3PL DEF-family
and charcoal. When [the father] came from the synagogue the family sat down,

əl-lūlad w əl-ʔəmm əl-maṛa yāklūn w ... yəqaddəsūn
DEF-child.PL and DEF-mother DEF-woman eat.IPFV.3PL and ... say_blessing.IPFV.3PL
the children and the woman, the mother, and they ate. They pronounced a blessing

w yāklūn w yəpazmənūn[23] *w b-əš-šabbāt yəqūm ... yərūḥ*
and eat.IPFV.3PL and sing.IPFV.3PL[H] and in-Shabbat[H] stand_up.IPFV.3SG.M ... go.IPFV.3SG.M
and ate and sang. On Shabbat [the father] went

əṣ-ṣala yəmšōn əṣ-ṣala w yəği b-əs-sāʕa ʕašra
DEF-synagogue go.IPFV.3PL DEF-synagogue and come.IPFV.3SG in-DEF-hour ten
to the synagogue. They went to the synagogue. At ten o'clock [the father] came

yəqʕad yəsēḥūn kəlla l-lūlād əl-ʔab yəsēḥ-əm w yəftaḥūn
sit.IPFV.3SG.M call.IPFV.3PL all.CS DEF-child.PL DEF-father call.IPFV.3SG.M-3PL and open.IPFV.3PL
and sat down, they called all the children, the father called them, they opened

dəst ət-tabīt yəftaḥū-hu yəqʕadūn yəṣaffəṭ-əm abū-həm ʕaš lūlād
pot.CS DEF-*tabīt* open.IPFV.3PL-3SG.M sit.IPFV.3PL align.IPFV.3SG.M-3PL father.CS-3PL ten child.PL
the pot with the *tabīt*. They sat down, their father placed them in a row; ten children

kānū ʕašra kəll bēt yəqēʕəd-əm w kəll wēḥəd yəṣəbbū-l-u
be.PF.3PL ten every.CS house place.IPFV.3SG.M-3PL and every.CS one.M distribute_food-for-3SG.M
they were, ten [in] each house; he placed them, they distributed

yākəl akal əl-ʔab šərəb ʕaraq w yəġanni w ... w
eat.IPFV.3SG.M eat.PF.3SG.M DEF-father drink.PF.3SG.M Arak and sing.IPFV.3SG.M and ... and
food to everyone, and the father ate, drank Arak, and sang ...

əlli yərūḥ ʕənd rafīq-u w əl-banāt yərūḥūn ʕənd rəfaqāt-əm
DEM.M go.IPFV.3SG.M at friend-3SG.M and DEF-girl.PL go.IPFV.3PL at friend.F.PL-3PL
Then one went to his friend and the girls went to their friends.

w ʕad sāʕa sabʕa bə-l-lēl yəšʕəlūn ḍaw kəlla l-bəyūt
and until hour seven in-DEF-night ignite.IPFV.3PL light all.cs DEF-house.PL
At seven o'clock in the evening they put on light – in all the houses

mā kān ḍaw yəšʕəlūn əḍ-ḍaw w yəğōn ər-rəfaqāt yəqʕadūn
NEG be.PF.3SG.M light ignite.IPFV.3PL DEF-light and come.IPFV.3PL DEF-friend.F.PL sit.IPFV.3PL
there was no light – they put on light. The (girl)friends came and sat down …

w ... w əl-laḥad yəmši kəll wēḥəd ʕaš-šuġl-u wəlla b-əs-sōq
and ... and DEF-one.M go.IPFV.3SG.M every.CS one.M on-work-3SG.M either in-DEF-market
On Sunday everyone went to his work, be it in the suq …

əl-maṛa təšṭġəl b-əl-bēt əl-banāt ... mā yətʕalləmūn ...
DEF-woman be_occupied.IPFV.3SG.F in-DEF-house DEF-girl.PL ... NEG learn.IPFV.3PL
The woman worked at home [and also] the girls, who did not go to school ...

23 Cf. Hebrew פִּזְמוֹן *pizmōn* 'chant'.

References

Primary sources

Anonymous. 1924 (5684). *Qiṣṣat Yosef ha-ṣadiq ʕalav ha-šalom.* Baghdad: Maṭbaʕat al-Waṭanīya al-Yisrāʔilīya.

Avishur, Yitzhak. 2011. *Psalms. Translation into Iraqi Judeo-Arabic from Baghdad and Mosul.* Tel-Aviv/Jaffa: Archeological Center.

Secondary sources

Abu-Haidar, Farida. 1991. *Christian Arabic of Baghdad.* Wiesbaden: Harrassowitz.

Abu-Haidar, Farida. 2006. "Baghdad Arabic", in: Kees Versteegh et al. (eds.). *Encyclopedia of Arabic Language and Linguistics.* Volume I: A–Ed. Leiden: Brill. 222–231.

Arnold, Werner and Assaf Bar-Moshe. 2017. "Linguistic Features Shared by the Jewish Dialects of Baghdad and Aleppo and Their Possible Implications for the History of Both Communities." *Journal of Jewish Languages* 5(1): 22–48.

Avishur, Yitzhak. 1979. "Ha-sifrut ha-ʕamamit šel yehude bavel be-ʕarvit yehudit (הספרות העממית של יהודי בבל בערבית יהודית)." *Peʕamim* 3: 83–90.

Avishur, Yitzhak. 2001. *Ha-ʕivrit še-ba-ʕarvit ha-yehudit* (העברית שבערבית היהודית). Tel-Aviv/Jaffa: Archeological Center.

Bar-Moshe, Assaf. 2019. *The Arabic Dialect of the Jews of Baghdad. Phonology, Morphology, and Texts.* Wiesbaden: Harrassowitz.

Bernstein, Marc S. 2006. *Stories of Joseph. Narrative Migrations between Judaism and Islam.* Detroit: Wayne State University Press.

Blanc, Haim. 1964a. *Communal Dialects in Baghdad.* Cambridge, MA: Harvard University Press.

Blanc, Haim. 1964b. "Notes on the literary idiom of the Baghdadi Jews." In: Lucy S. Dawidowicz (ed..). *Studies in Jewish Languages, Literature and Culture for Max Weinreich on His Seventieth Birthday.* The Hague: Mouton. 18–30.

Blau, Joshua. 1970. *On Pseudo-Corrections in some Semitic Languages.* Jerusalem: The Israel Academy of Sciences and Humanities.

Cohen, Mark R. 2007. "On the interplay of Arabic and Hebrew in the Cairo Geniza letters", in: Jonathan P. Decter and Michael Rand (eds.). *Studies in Hebrew and Arabic Letters in Honour of Raymond P. Scheindlin.* Piscataway, NJ: Gorgias Press. 17–35.

Edzard, Lutz. 2012. "Linguistic features of a Judeo-Arabic text of the *qiṣaṣ al-ʔanbiyāʔ* genre", in: Liesbeth Zack and Arie Schippers (eds.). *Middle Arabic and Mixed Arabic: Diachrony and Synchrony.* Leiden: Brill. 83–94.

Geva-Kleinberger, Aharon. 2013. "Judeo-Arabic, Iraqi, Hebrew Component in", in: Geoffrey Khan et al. (eds.) *Encyclopedia of Hebrew Language and Linguistics.* Vol. 2: G–O. Leiden: Brill. 391–393.

Hary, Benjamin. 1992. *Multiglossia in Judeo-Arabic. With an edition, translation, and grammatical study of the Cairene Purim Scroll.* Leiden: Brill.

Hary, Benjamin and Howard I. Aronson. 1996. "Adaptations of Hebrew script", in: Peter T. Daniels and William Bright (eds.). *The World's Writing Systems.* New York/Oxford: Oxford University Press. 727–734.

Jastrow, Otto. 1984. "Gibt es einen islamischen Sprachraum? Islamische Idiome in den Sprachen muslimischer Völker", in: Werner Ende and Udo Steinbach (eds.). *Der Islam in der Gegenwart.* Munich: C.H. Beck. 582–589.

Jastrow, Otto. 1989. "Notes on Jewish Maṣlāwi." *Jerusalem Studies in Arabic and Islam* 12: 282–293.

Jastrow, Otto. 1990a. *Der arabische Dialekt der Juden von ʕAqra und Arbil.* Wiesbaden: Harrassowitz.

Jastrow, Otto. 1990b. "Die arabischen Dialekte der irakischen Juden", in: Werner Diem and Abdoljavad Falaturi (eds.). *XXIV. Deutscher Orientalistentag vom 26. bis 30. September 1988 in Köln. Ausgewählte Vorträge.* Stuttgart: F. Steiner. 199–206.

Jastrow, Otto. 2001. "Three anecdotes in Jewish Maslawi", in: Judith Rosenhouse and Ami Elad-Bouskila (eds.). *Linguistic and Cultural Studies on Arabic and Hebrew. Essays Presented to Moshe Piamenta for his Eightieth Birthday.* Wiesbaden. Harrassowitz: 61–70.

Jastrow, Otto. 2007. "Iraq", in: Kees Versteegh et al. (eds.). *Encyclopedia of Arabic Language and Linguistics.* Volume II: Eg–Lan. Leiden: Brill. 414–424.

Jastrow, Otto. 2018. "Rescuing Iraqi Arabic *aku* and *māku* from the hands of the Aramaicists." *Zeitschrift für Arabische Linguistik* 67: 90–93.

Khan, Geoffrey, 1997. "The Arabic Dialect of the Karaite Jews of Hit." *Zeitschrift für Arabische Linguistik* 34: 53–10.

Khan, Geoffrey. 2007 "Judaeo-Arabic", in: Kees Versteegh et al. (eds.). *Encyclopedia of Arabic Language and Linguistics.* Volume II: Eg–Lan. Leiden: Brill. 526–536.

Mansour, Jacob. 1974. *The Judaeo-Arabic Dialect of Baghdad. I. Studies in Phonology and Morphology.* Haifa: University of Haifa.

Mansour, Jacob. 1977. *The Judaeo-Arabic Dialect of Baghdad. II. Texts.* Haifa: University of Haifa.

Mansour, Jacob. 1982. *The Judaeo-Arabic Dialect of Baghdad. III. Dictionary. Part one.* Haifa: University of Haifa.

Mansour, Jacob. 1991. *The Jewish Baghdadi Dialect: Studies and Texts in the Judeo-Arabic Dialect of Baghdad.* Or-Yehuda: The Babylonian Jewry Heritage Center, the Institute for Research on Iraqi Jewry.

Mansour, Jacob. 2006. "Baghdad Arabic Jewish", in Kees Versteegh et al. (eds.). *Encyclopedia of Arabic Language and Linguistics.* Volume I: A–Ed. Leiden: Brill. 231–241.

Rustow, Marina. 2010. "Iraq. 1. Medieval Period", in: Norman A. Stillman (ed.). *Encyclopedia of Jews in the Islamic World.* Vol. 2: D–I. Leiden: Brill. 602–609.

Sassoon, Salomon David. 1949. *A History of the Jews in Baghdad.* Letchworth: S.D. Sassoon.

Shohat, Ella. 2015. "The question of Judeo-Arabic." *The Arab Studies Journal* 23/1: 14–65.

Simon, Reeva Spector. 2010. "Iraq. 1. Post-Medieval and Modern Period", in: Norman A. Stillman (ed.). *Encyclopedia of Jews in the Islamic World.* Vol. 2: D–I. Leiden: Brill. 609–617

Steiner, Richard. 1997 "Ancient Hebrew", in: Robert Hetzron (ed.). *The Semitic Languages.* London: Routledge. 145–173.

Wagner, Ewald. 2012. "Vier Abū Nuwās-Anekdoten im literarischen Idiom der Bagdader Juden." *Zeitschrift für Arabische Linguistik* 56: 5–26.

Woodhead, Daniel R. and Wayne Beene. 1967. *A Dictionary of Iraqi Arabic.* Washington, DC: Georgetown University Press.

Yaari, Abraham. 1936–1940. *Ha-dfus ha-ʕivri be-ʔarṣot ha-mizraẋ.* 2 vols. Jerusalem: Hebrew University Press.

The Jewish varieties of Yemeni Arabic

Ori Shachmon, The Hebrew University of Jerusalem

1. Introduction

1.1 The Jewish varieties of Yemeni Arabic

For daily communication Yemeni Jews used Arabic dialects that were typologically similar to the local Muslim vernaculars. The spoken Jewish varieties thus share many characteristics with the Muslim ones, as they are described in Rossi 1939, Diem 1973, Watson 1993, Behnstedt 2016, and others. Nevertheless, in certain cases linguistic differences existed between the speech of Jews and Muslims of the same area. The most evident differentiating factor was the occurrence of Hebrew and Aramaic elements in the Jewish varieties, yet differences in the Arabic dialect itself were also noticeable. When it existed, the distinction ranged from the subtle to the prominent and ear-catching.

As a rule, differences between the speech of Jews and Muslims were less evident in villages than in the big cities, particularly Ṣanʕāʔ. Kara (1986: 123) actually differentiates "Jewish Ṣanʕānī Arabic" from "Muslim Ṣanʕānī Arabic" according to phonological, morphological, and lexical features. In rural areas, however, Jewish-Muslim coexistence was characterized by more integration, cooperation, and brotherhood, and Jews spoke a language very much resembling that of their next-door neighbors. Nonetheless, in certain areas some linguistic features seem to have been more characteristic of Jews than of Muslims.

Section 2 below provides a grammatical sketch of Yemeni Arabic, with special attention to the Jewish varieties and to their distinctive features. Section 3 consists of five text specimens, demonstrating three of the main Jewish varieties, namely the dialect of the Jews of Ṣanʕāʔ, the dialect of the northern Province of Ṣaʕdah, and the dialect of the villages of Lower Yemen. The first two texts exhibit attempts to reduce the spoken dialect to writing, using Hebrew letters, while the three other texts are based on native fluent speech, recorded from the Yemenites in Israel.

1.2 Knowledge and influence of Hebrew and Aramaic

The Jews of Yemen dwelled in more than a thousand different localities (Goitein 1953, 1960), scattered around the vast country from north to south, sometimes as a cohesive community, sometimes only one or two families in an isolated Muslim village. The scope of Hebrew knowledge varied from one locality to another. Moreover, factors such as age, sex, social status and cultural stratification have yielded variation in the practice of Hebrew, even among speakers of the same community.

Jews in the various communities were familiar with several reading traditions. Two of these were Hebrew, namely: the traditional reading of the Bible, based upon the vocalized text, and the traditional reading of post-biblical Rabbinic Hebrew texts, basically transmitted by word of mouth. Two other traditions were Aramaic, namely the Aramaic translation of the Bible or *targūm*, and the reading of the Babylonian Talmud. A fifth reading tradition, practiced mainly in Ṣanʕā, but also in several other communities (Tobi 1991: 133f.), was Saʕadiah Gaon's (born 882) Arabic translation of the Torah and other books of the Bible, or *tafsīr*. The latter was written in medieval Arabic (in Hebrew script), significantly different from the local dialects. These various reading traditions continuously nourished everyday speech and enriched it with many Jewish, Hebrew and Aramaic elements (Tobi 1999). There were also non-Jews, who were familiar with Hebrew and Aramaic elements, which they occasionally interwove into their Arabic speech, especially in situations involving Jews (Shachmon 2014a).

1.3 Writing in Yemeni Judeo-Arabic

In Yemen, Jews have traditionally confined their writing to Hebrew script. The vast majority of Yemeni Jews were unfamiliar with the Arabic script, and those who did have the ability were usually disinclined to read Arabic literature or to write in Arabic characters. Throughout the centuries, learned Yemenites composed a substantial corpus of literary texts and poems in Hebrew only, in Hebrew mixed with Arabic, in Aramaic, or in Judeo-Arabic, on occasion as bilingual or even trilingual texts. Correspondence between the different Jewish communities in Yemen was done in Hebrew, in Judeo-Arabic, or in a mixed form which also reflected the influence of the spoken dialects.

The writing of Yemeni Arabic in Hebrew characters has continued uninterruptedly into the modern era, and after the immigration to Israel as well. In modern times, Yemenite Judeo-Arabic texts often deal with the burning issues of the time. Of such nature is the נשיד עלא שידאד אל-יהוד *našīd ʕala šidād alyihūd* "a poem on the journey of the Jews", which was composed in the 1910s and dealt with the longing of the Jews of Šarʕab for immigration to the Holy Land (Sulami 2001: 16–19). A more recent example is a ballad composed in Israel by a Jewish immigrant from Baraṭ, dealing with the historic arrival of the Egyptian president Anwar al-Sadat to Israel in 1977 (Ben-David 2008: 399–400). Such modern compositions are enriched with new forms, based upon roots and meanings from Modern Hebrew, e.g., אַתְּעָלָה *attʕōlō* "the [Suez] canal" and אלשַׁטָחִים *aššaṭōḥīm* "the [occupied] territories" in the aforementioned ballad. Of a more humorous nature are several compositions by Itamar Pinḥas,[1] offering entertaining Yemeni cover versions of modern Israeli music,[2] or even of classics as the Neapolitan song *Funiculì funiculà*.[3]

1 Itamar Pinḥas is a prolific and talented Israeli Journalist of Yemeni origin, who runs a private institute for the collection and preservation of Yemeni music and has already uploaded to the internet hundreds of short videos, providing insight into various community issues.

2 Pinḥas' cover version of the popular song "Friday", originally performed by the "Benzin" Israeli rock-band, may be watched on www.youtube.com/watch?v=l68G9UfxYjA.

3 A renowned Neapolitan song which was composed in 1880 and has been sung by many famous singers such as Luciano Pavarotti. Pinḥas' Yemeni version is available on www.youtube.com/watch?v=Us2Hmn9Frwo.

While the old generation of immigrants to Israel often continues its former linguistic habits, the younger generations naturally switch to Israeli Hebrew and can no longer speak or comprehend Yemeni Arabic. Against this reality, attempts are made to bridge the growing language gap, with Yemenites preserving their legacy by writing down popular tales, jokes, songs and lullabies in their original Arabic wording. These newly written texts appear in Hebrew letters, either unvocalized or vocalized according to the writer's personal interpretation and preferences. The orthography of such non-scholarly attempts tends to be loose and non-systematic, often revealing the dialectal features of the speaker who put the text down to writing. The internet now offers dozens (if not hundreds) of such popular songs, some performed by prominent Yemeni-Israeli singers, with subtitles in Yemeni-Arabic in Hebrew letters, as well as a Hebrew translation. The subtitles are every now and then projected on large screens during the performance, for the benefit of audience unfamiliar with the Arabic words, and for those who wish to join the singing. Text no. 1 below offers a gloss for one such song entitled *ʕadán ʕadán* "Aden Aden".

A more standardized vocalization is found in the writings of Israeli scholars of Yemeni origin. Dr. Uri Melammed of the Academy of the Hebrew Language has produced a substantial number of texts in vocalized Hebrew script. His book-let ישן בקנקן חדש (lit. "Old [wine] in a new jug") is a collection of Yemeni poems published on the occasion of the seventh anniversary of the death of the founding father of The Association for Society and Culture, Documentation and Research. The texts in this anthology reflect diverse Judeo-Yemeni dialects, and the differences – sometimes only subtle nuances – are reflected in a carefully vocalized transcriptions.

Finally, numerous texts in vocalized Hebrew script appear in a series of works by Rabbi Dr. Aharon Bed-David, born in the Northern province of Yemen and a native speaker of its dialect. Ben-David uses a unique transcription method, yielding an accurate representation of the spoken dialect and a rich and rare source for its study (Shachmon 2017). An extract of Ben-David's work is given in §3.2 below.

1.4 Spoken Jewish Yemeni Arabic today

Nowadays, Jews no longer live in Yemen. A mass of about 50,000 Jews left Yemen to Israel between December 1948 and late 1951 in the famed "Operation On the Wings of Eagles"; others stayed in Yemen until the early 1960s, and several hundreds were brought to Israel in the mid-1990s. The last Jewish families who remained in the northern province into the 21st century were gradually compelled to leave with the outbreak of the violent events in North Yemen since the early 2000s. In Israel the Yemenites have more or less integrated into the general Israeli society, and they all use Israeli Hebrew for daily communication. Similar to other immigrant languages, Jewish Yemeni Arabic is thus gradually dying out.

Nevertheless, Jewish Yemeni Arabic may still be heard in Israel up to the present time. Living among their fellow Yemenites some immigrants maintain their mother-tongue in active use, and are able to produce fluent and coherent speech with only minor interference from Israeli Hebrew. Text no. 3 below was recorded from a Jewish woman, who came to Israel in 1962 from the province of Ṣaʕdah. Text no. 4 was recorded from a Ṣanʕāni who came in 1949, and the narrator of text no. 5 came in the same year from the village of alGades in Lower Yemen. Although the narrators were recorded dozens of years after their immigration, their speech is fluent and lively, providing us with a reliable attestation of their original dialect.

2. Grammatical sketch of the Jewish Yemeni Arabic Varieties

The following linguistic sketch is by no means an exhaustive description of Yemeni Arabic. Rather, it points to certain linguistic features that distinguish the Jewish varieties from their co-territorial Muslim ones.

The core of the description is the dialects of three main areas, namely the capital city of Ṣanʕāʔ and its vicinity, the northern Province of Ṣaʕdah, and the villages of Lower Yemen, around Ibb and Taʕizz. The Muslim dialects of the same areas are well studied and described in the literature (see references to Rossi, Diem, Jastrow, Watson, and Behnstedt), which may serve for comparison between the communal varieties. Information about other Jewish varieties is also provided, based on the available studies (see references to Goitein, Kara, Piamenta, and Ben-David, among others), as well as on many years of my own field-work among the Yemenites in Israel and abroad (see references to Shachmon).[4]

The grammatical description opens with remarks on the phonology of the Jewish varieties (section 2.1), discussing the pronunciation of Arabic and Hebrew consonants (2.1.1–2.1.2), the Arabic and Hebrew vowels (2.1.3–2.1.4) and the syllable structure (2.1.5). I then offer a few insights concerning pausal phenomena (2.1.6) and stress (2.1.7). Section 2.2 deals with morphology, focusing on certain peculiarities of the verbal system (2.2.1), the pronominal system (2.2.2), and the nominal system (2.2.3).

2.1 Phonology

2.1.1 The Arabic Consonants

Despite the considerable diversity of Yemeni dialects, a general classification may be established in accordance with a number of phonological features, most prominent of which are the reflexes of old Arabic *qāf* and *ǧīm*. The current realization of these two sounds allows a rough differentiation between north and central Yemeni on the one hand, and southern Yemeni on the other. A brief discussion of these sounds, as well as of a few others, follows the table.

	North Ṣaʕdah, Ḥaydān, J.Rāziḥ, Baraṭ	Center Ṣanʕāʔ, ʕAmrān, Raydah, Ḏamār	South Ibb, Taʕizz, Ḥugariyyah, Šarʕab, ʕAdan
ج	*ǧ* , *g*[y]	*ǧ*	*g*
ق	*g*	*g*	*q*~ġ

4 My present project, entitled “A systematic survey of the varieties of Yemeni Arabic, as preserved by Jews in Israel and abroad”, is supported by the Israel Science Foundation (grant no. 1009/18).

– OA *jīm*. The reconstructed Semitic velar stop **g* seems to have been preserved in the southwest of the country, while in the central mountains, northern highlands, northern plateau and in the area of Ṣaʕdah it has moved forward and gone through various degrees of affrication and palatalization (Vanhove 2013, Behnstedt 2016). In Ṣanʕāʔ and in Ṣaʕdah it is basically a palato-alveolar affricate, viz. *ğ*, yet in the speech of the Jews who originate in the northern province it is regularly g^y.

– OA *qāf*. In the dialects of the southern mountain range and Aden the reflex of OA *qāf* is a voiceless uvular stop, viz. *q*, which often alternates with the fricative velar *ġ* (Vanhove 2013). In Ṣanʕāʔ and the central mountains, on the other hand, OA *qāf* is realized as a velar stop, which exhibits voiced and unvoiced allophones that often occur side by side even in one utterance, e.g., *gullih~g̥ullih* 'tell him!'.[5] Importantly, the unvoiced allophone of /g/ does not merge with /k/. The distinction between the two is consistently preserved owing to the aspiration of *k*, and therefore *g̥ullih* 'tell him' is clearly distinct from *kullih*, [k^hullih] 'all of it' (cf. Rossi 1937: 461). OA *ṭāʔ* also features two allophones, e.g., *iṭlaʕī~iṭ̮laʕī* 'go up (SG.F)!'; *faṭamt~faṭ̮amt* 'I weaned [the infant]'.[6]

Despite what seems as free alternation of the voiced and unvoiced allophones, each of the two is statistically more likely to occur in certain phonetic environments: the voiced allophone is expected in inter-vocalic positions, as in the example *yigūl* 'he says';[7] the unvoiced allophone is frequent in pre-pause word-final position, e.g., *sáwwag̥* 'he shopped [at the market]', and in gemination, e.g., *ḥag̥g̥him* 'theirs' (not: *ḥakkhim*).[8]

Voice indifference is indeed noticeable in the speech of Yemeni Jews. Moreover, the same applies to the pronunciation of Hebrew /q/ קו"ף and /ṭ/ טי"ת (see 2.1.2 below), so that the voiced and unvoiced allophones alternate in forms of the Hebrew component, and even in newly borrowed Israeli-Hebrew forms, e.g. *ṭaʕīm~ṭ̮aʕīm* 'tasty', or *ṭarí~ṭ̮arí* 'fresh'.

– OA *dāl* and *tāʔ*. The interchange of the two consonants has been reported, mainly for Ṣanʕānī (Rossi 1939: 6; Jastrow 1984: 290). Similarly in Jewish varieties, several scholars pointed to the difficulty to distinguish between דל"ת and תי"ו (Goitein 1934: xiv;

5 Blanc has established the view, that Sībawayhi's distinction of *mahmūsa* vs. *mağhūra* consonants did not have to do with the absence or presence of voice, but rather with the absence or presence of breath. According to Blanc, by classifying OA *qāf* and *ṭāʔ* as *mahğūra*, Sībawayhi meant to indicate their unaspirated pronunciation. It then follows that in Sībawayhi's view *qāf* and *ṭāʔ* were neither voiced nor unvoiced, but rather "voice-indifferent", i.e. exhibited both voiced and unvoiced allophones which alternated freely. The issue of voicing has not been taken into Sībawayhi's consideration, since it was – according to this interpretation – irrelevant (Blanc 1967: 306–307; 1969: 11).The present-day realization of OA *qāf* and *ṭāʔ* in many Yemeni dialects is actually compatible with Blanc's interpretation.

6 *ṭ̮* stands here for voiced *ṭ*, in the literature occasionally (and misleadingly) transcribed as *ḍ*.

7 Other plosives also gain voice in intervocalic position: consider the form *šarikih* 'company', realized as [šarik̬ih] (Watson and Al-ʕAmri 2000: 82 and n. 8; the sound file is available on www.semarch.uni-hd.de. Note that the authors transcribe *šarigih*).

8 Geminate plosives and affricates are generally realized without voice (Jastrow 1984). Note that while the term "geminate devoicing" is often used in this context (cf. Jastrow 1984: 292–293; Watson 1993: 10; Watson 2002: 154), it is not a voiced consonant which is devoiced, but rather a voice-indifferent consonant that surfaces as un-voiced.

Goitein 1960: 363; Morag 1963: 8); Kara 1988: 132). In fact, the voiced realization of the latter has even been marked as a distinctive feature of Jewish-Ṣanʕānī, with forms like [bidgūl] 'you SG.M say' (for *bitgūl*) or [dimsid] 'she massages' (for *timsid*) (Qāfiḥ 1961: 157; Kara 1986: 127).

The principle of voice indifference applies to /d/ and /t/ as well: while the two consonants seem to alternate, with the former gaining voice and the latter becoming unvoiced, the distinction between them is always preserved owing to the aspiration of /t/, which is evident in both its voiced and unvoiced realization (Morag 1963: 39). When asked, informants clearly differentiated between *ǧat* 'she came' and *ǧadd* (the first copy of the geminate invariably delinks, yielding [ǧad̥]) 'grandfather'; or between *šarat* 'she bought' and *šarad* 'he ran away'. Similar to the distribution of /g/, the unvoiced allophone of /d/ is likewise expected in gemination, as in *ǧiddatī* [ǧid̥d̥ati] (not: *ǧittati*);'my grandmother'; and the voiced allophone is frequent in intervocalic position, as in *maratih* [maraṯih] (not: *maradih*) 'his wife'.

– OA *hamza*. The glottal stop as a reflex of OA *hamza* has nearly disappeared, as is the case in most modern Arabic dialects. *hamza* is nevertheless heard in verbs and nouns derived from the OA root √ *sʔl* and in denominative forms as *yitʔaslam* 'he converts to Islam'. In addition, the use of the glottal stop is attested in Yemeni Arabic in two main cases:

• Glottal stop epenthesis, mainly but not exclusively between two identical short vowels, as in *ʕalayyā+asallim* > *ʕalayyā ʔasallim* 'I have to pay', and *yiddī+ibnih* > *yiddī ʔibnih* 'he gives his son'.

• Glottalization of final consonants and final long vowels in pre-pausal position, as in *ḥummēʔ#* 'fever' and *ḥimāʔr#* 'donkey' in text 4 below; *ḥalā~ḥalāʔ#* 'good, agreeable'; *bāṣ~bāʔṣ#* "bus"; *ḥalīb~ḥalīʔb* 'milk' and *fār~fāʔ#* 'mouse' (Watson 2007: 177–182).[9]

A few lexemes exhibit a shift of OA *hamza* to *ʕ*, recalling the old dialectal trait of *ʕanʕana* mentioned by medieval Arab grammarians (Rabin 1951: 194). This shift is rather common in the form OA *alʔān* > *alʕān* 'now', as well as in OA *badaʔa* > *badaʕ* 'start', exemplified in text 4 below. An opposite shift of *ʕ* > *ʔ* is characteristic of the Yemeni coastal plain or Tihāma (Greenman 1979: 54–55; Behnstedt 2016: 8), but I have not encountered this feature in the speech of the Jews.

– OA *h*. The old laryngeal fricative *h* is relatively stable in Yemeni Arabic, and is realized even in intervocalic position, e.g., *nāhī* 'fine, okay'. In the northern dialects, the full realization of *h* in the 3SG.M pronominal suffix is distinctive, as in *yištōh* 'they want it' vs. *yištō* 'they want'. *h* is also heard in the nominal feminine singular suffix, e.g., *madrasih* 'school' in Ṣanʕāʔ / *madrasah* in Ṣaʕdah, although it may be subject to deletion before a vowel-initial word and before the definite article, e.g., *almadrasi lkabīrih* 'the big school' (Watson 2002: 214).

In Ṣanʕānī Arabic, the initial *h* of the independent pronouns *hū, hī, hum*, and *hin* is not realized when the pronoun is suffixed to certain particles, such as *gad* and *ʕād,* as well as to certain question words as *kayf* 'how' or *ayn* 'where' (Watson 2002: 211–212),

9 In the latter, glottalization follows the elision of the final sonorant, see 2.1.6.

and therefore *gad+hum* → *gadum* and *ayn+hī* →*aynī.* In contrast, the dialects around Ṣaʕdah exhibit *gidhū*, *gidhim*, etc. (2.2.2 below).

2.1.2 The Hebrew consonants

Yemeni Jews demonstrate much awareness and sensitivity to linguistic variation, especially the realization of Hebrew ק and ג, which often triggers mutual mimicry, even teasing (Yaakov 2011: 78–80). The pronunciation of these two sounds corresponds with the local reflexes of old Arabic ق and ج: in the Jewish communities of Ṣanʕāʔ and Ṣaʕdah (and in that of Ḥabbān in the east) Hebrew ק is a velar [g] or uvular [G], and ג is a palato-alveolar affricate [ǧ] or [gʸ]. Both sounds exhibit alternating voiced and unvoiced allophones (2.1.1 above). In southern areas, on the other hand, Hebrew ק is an unvoiced uvular stop [q], in Aden and around Ibb occasionally also [ġ], while ג is realized as a voiced velar [g].

In the realization of /bgdkpt/ בגדכפ"ת the Hebrew reading traditions largely preserve the plosive (in Ṣanʕāʔ [b], [ǧ], [d], [k], [p], and [t], respectively) vs. fricative (in Ṣanʕāʔ [ḇ], [ġ], [ḏ], [ḵ], [f], and [ṯ], respectively). Note, that ב=[ḇ] and פּ=[p] or [pʰ] do not have equivalents in the phonemic system of the corresponding local vernacular. However, in daily speech, and particularly in that of women, the usage of the fricative instead of the plosive – and vice versa – is rather frequent. This tendency is exemplified by the form *habdōlō* 'Havdalah', i.e. the Jewish ceremony recited at the termination of Shabbat and holidays, mentioned in text 3 below.

Despite the regular realization of final *h* in the local Arabic dialects (2.1.1 above), Hebrew ה"א in final position is completely silent in Yemeni traditional reading. Morag (1963: 10) indicates certain spoken forms, in which final ה"א is nevertheless realized, as the form אִשָּׁה *iššōh* 'woman', but in the speech of the informants final Hebrew ה"א cannot be heard, e.g., מִלָּה *millō* 'word' in text 2 and הַבְדָּלָה *habdōlō* 'havdalah' in text 3.

2.1.3 The Arabic Vowels

– Short Vowels. A characteristic feature of Ṣanʕāni Arabic is the labialization of short high vowels in words containing emphatic consonants. This labialization, which often yields a shift of OA *i* to *u*, extends beyond the domain of immediate adjacency and applies to other vowels within the phonological word, as in OA *Fāṭimah* > *Fāṭumuh* – p.n. (Watson 1999: 295–296). The emphatic consonants do not exercise such an influence in Lower Yemen, where *yixayyiṭ* 'he embroiders' stands for Ṣanʕānī *yixayyuṭ* (Goitein 1960: 361).

The "coloring" effect of certain consonants is also evident in the dialects of the northern province, yet the circumstances vary. The northern system exhibits two primary vowels, namely *a* and *i*, the latter realized as [u] in the vicinity of velars and labials. For example, the verbal pattern *yifʕal* (e.g., *yismaʕ* 'he hears') yields *yugrab* 'he approaches' with *g* as a 1st radical. Similarly, the pattern *yifʕil* (e.g., *yidfil* 'he spits') yields *yuxriǧ* 'he goes out' and *yidxul* 'he enters', with a back vowel triggered by the occurrence of *x* as 1st or 2nd radical (Shachmon 2007: 41–43, 93–97, 104–112, and 183).[10]

The rural dialects of Lower Yemen tend to lower short high vowels in various positions, e.g., *kuburk* = [kubork] 'I grew up' and *kibirk* = [kiberk] 'you SG.M grew up'. Lowering is especially evident in these dialects in the vicinity of back consonants, and therefore *luʕubk* = [loʕobk] I played' and *liʕibk* = [leʕebk] 'you SG.M played'; and also *aṣaddiqič* = [aṣaddiqeč] 'I believe you SG.F' as opposed to *gaddič* = [gaddič] 'your SG.F grandfather' in text 5 below. Phonologically irrelevant lowering is left unmarked in the transcripts given below.

– Diphthongs. The treatment of the classical diphthongs *ay* and *aw* is a distinctive feature in Yemeni Arabic. The dialects spoken in the central mountains largely preserve the old diphthongs *aw* and *ay*, so that Ṣanʕāni Arabic, for example, exhibits *bayt* 'house', *yawm* 'day', *sawwayt* 'I did', *sawwaw* 'they did', etc. Note, that *ay* and *aw* are occasionally raised and realized as [ey] and [ow] respectively, as heard several times in text 4 below: *bayt sī́dī* = [beyt sīdī] 'my grandfather's house', *śíggayn* = [šig̥g̥eyn] 'two sides', and *šallawnī* = [šallownī] 'they took me'.

On the other hand, diphthongs are regularly subject to monophthongization in many *k*-dialects, with OA *yawm* > *yōm* 'day' and OA *bayʕ* > *bēʕ* 'selling' (Jastrow 1986: 26; Testen 1992: 81). This is also the case in the dialects of the northern province, and the equivalents of the above-mentioned Ṣanʕāni forms would appear in Ṣaʕdah as *bēt*, *yōm*, *sawwēt*, and *sawwō* respectively. Side by side with this general trait of monophthongization, the dialects around Ṣaʕdah exhibit a certain variation of *ē~ey* (Behnstedt 1987: 3–4, 297, 314), as in the examples *xeyrāt* 'much", *eytām* 'orphans', and *Ḥeydān* 'Ḥaydān' (place name). In addition, some northern dialects exhibit pausal alternants of word-final *ē~ay#* and *ō~aw#*, where the diphthongs are either a preservation of their old equivalents or their restoration under specific conditions (see 2.1.6).

Some dialects in Lower Yemen, specifically in the rural area around Ibb, exhibit much fluidity in the treatment of the diphthongs, e.g. *bēt~bayt* (also: *beyt*) 'house', *ṣallēk~ṣallayk* 'you SG.M prayed', or *aštarōk~aštarawk* 'I bought'. This inconsistency tallies with the generally fluid character of the dialects of that area, where many vowels and consonants have a number of phonetic variants (Goitein 1960: 359).

– Long vowels. Final vowels may be effectively long in Yemeni Arabic. In Ṣanʕāʔ, final *ā* – in all but emphatic environments – is subject to *ʔimāla* or raising in pre-pausal position, and is then realized as *ē*, as in *garraynā* > *garraynē#* 'we taught' (Watson 2002: 283). In the Jewish variety of Ṣanʕāni final *ā* is invariably yields *ē*, whether in context or pause. In fact, the raising of *ā* > *ē* is one of the distinctive markers the Jewish variety, against the co-territorial Muslim one; many examples are found in text 4 below: *iḥnḗ* 'we'; *kunnḗ* 'we were'; *ğē* 'he came'; *abūhē* 'her father' *duwḗ* 'medicine'; *hākaḏē* 'thus', etc. Raising in the Jewish variety is plausibly the result of restructuring processes, in which one of two alternating variants in Muslim Ṣanʕāni, namely *ā* and *ē#*, has been generalized to both context and pausal positions in the Jewish variety.

10 That said, there is enough evidence to establish the phonemic value of *u* in the northern dialects as well, e.g. *yidxil* 'let in' in measure IV contrasts with *yidxul* 'enter' of measure I.

2.1.4 The Hebrew vowels

Hebrew vowels are pronounced in a characteristic way, that in some aspects reflects the Babylonian reading tradition:

– *qameṣ*. Hebrew *qameṣ* is realized as a rounded back vowel (usually *ō*), as exemplified by the forms בָּלַם *bōlam* 'he kept his mouth shut' and יִתְבָּרַךְ *yiṯbōrax* 'may He be blessed' in text 2 below.

– *pataḥ* and *seghol*. Tiberian Hebrew *pataḥ* and *seghol* are indistinguishable in Yemenite realization, i.e. both *a*. In open stressed syllables they are pronounced long (Morag 1963: 119, 125), e.g., דֶּרֶךְ *dárax* 'road' in text 2 below.

– *ḥireq* and *šureq*. While the two Hebrew vowels are clearly distinct in the reading traditions, the spoken forms display frequent alternation between *i* and *u*, as in *furṣō* for פִּרְצָה 'loophole' or *mugwō* for מִקְוָה 'ritual bath'. This alternation is plausibly explained by the influence of the local vernaculars, where *i* and *u* often constitute phonetically conditioned variants (2.1.3 above).

– *ḥolem*. The pronunciation of Hebrew *ḥolem* is idiosyncratic in Yemeni pronunciation: in the traditional reading of Ṣanʕāʔ and Ṣaʕdah it is a central rounded vowel, roughly an open *ö*, yet in the communities of southern Yemen *ḥolem* is pronounced as a front non-rounded *ē*, possibly a remnant of its realization in old Hebrew dialects (Morag 1999: 230). Nonetheless, it has been reliably documented that Jewish women in Ṣanʕāʔ and in the northern province frequently pronounce *ē* for Hebrew *ḥolem* (Goitein 1931: 361; Shachmon 2007: 25–26). This may be illustrated in forms like כּוֹס *kēs* 'glass' or תּוֹרָה *tērō* 'Torah' (Kara 1988: 128), as well as the ubiquitous form גּוֹי *ğēy* 'gentile', also in text 3 below.

2.1.5 Syllable structure

Syllable structure is conservative in many parts of Yemen. The long vowels remain long under all circumstances and are not affected by the shift of stress. Changes in syllable structure mainly concern the short vowels that may be subject to quality change, shortening, or elision.

In the dialects of Central and Lower Yemen, the three short vowels are retained in many positions, including open unstressed syllables, e.g., *yibisat* 'it SG.F dried up' and *ṭúluʕat* 'it SG.F went up' in text 2, or *kibire* 'she grew up' in Ibb. Quadrisyllabic words comprising four light syllables are also possible, e.g., *ṭaraḥatih* 'she put it SG.M'' in text 3, or *simiʕato* 'she heard him' (example from Ḥugariyyah). The dialects of the northern province, on the other hand, tend to omit *i* and *u* in unstressed open syllables, e.g., *yibsat* and *ṭulʕat*, and the same holds for the Jewish dialect of Aden, e.g., *xilġat* 'she was born' and *rigʕat* 'she returned'.

Any of the short vowels *a*, *i* or *u* may be subject to syncope that frequently yields initial consonant clusters. Syncope may involve either the elision of a short vowel in the first syllable of a word following a vowel-final previous word, e.g., *anā+daxalt* > *anā́ ‿dxalt* 'I entered'; or the elision of a short vowel in the final syllable of a word preceding a vowel-initial word, e.g. *Yūsif+axūy* > *Yūsf‿axūy* 'Yūsif my brother's.

2.1.6 Pausal phenomena

Yemeni dialects exhibit a number of pausal phenomena (Rossi 1939: 295; Diem 1973: 24; Jastrow 1984: 294; Watson 1993: 10). The modern pausal forms are not necessarily identical to those of Classical Arabic, and in part may reflect the influence of a south-Semitic substratum (Arnold 2010: 231). Following is a brief overview of the main pausal phenomena observed in the speech of Yemeni Jews:

– Vowel raising. In Ṣanʕānī Arabic, final *ā* is subject to raising in pre-pausal position, where it is realized as either *ē* (in neutral environment) or as *ō* (in emphatic environments) (Watson 2002: 283). In Jewish Ṣanʕānī, the pausal allophone *ē* seems to have been generalized, and nearly every final *ā*, whether in context or in pause, is realized as *ē* (see "Long vowels" under 2.1.3 above). Both Muslim and Jewish dialects of the northern province do no seem to raise final *ā*, but certain varieties in that area exhibit an alternation of *ah~eh#* in the nominal feminine ending (Behnstedt 1987: 55).

– Glottalization. Final *ā* in pre-pausal position is frequently glottalized. In Jewish Ṣanʕāni one notices glottalization of final (*ā>) ē,* as in the example *ḥúmmēʔ* 'fever' in text 4 below.

– Silent *lmnr*. Final sonorants are devoiced and often elided in pause, particularly when the sonorant is the last consonant in a final CvCC syllable, e.g. *firn*=[fir] 'oven' (Watson 2007: 177, 181). This feature, however, is more evident in Ṣanʕāʔ and the central mountains than it is in the North. Comparable examples from the Jews of Lower Yemen include *duxn* = [dox] 'pearl millet' and *ʕAmr* = [ʕam] (p.n.). Elision of the sonorant is also typical of final CV̄C syllables, often along with glottalization, e.g., *sanīn* = [sanīʔ] 'years', and *ḥimār* = [ḥimāʔ] 'donkey'. Elision and glottalization are similarly heard in Hebrew forms, e.g., *ghinnōm* = [ghinnōʔ] 'hell' in text 5 below, or the blessing *bōrux haššēm* = [bōrux haššēʔ] 'Thank God', and *w-ʕalēxam šōlöm* = [w-ʕalēxam šōlöʔ] (the response to *šōlöm ʕalēxam* 'peace be upon you').[11]

– Diphthongization. In the northern province the old diphthongs in word-final position are pause-sensitive: they are regularly monophthongized in context (2.1.3), but tend to be retained in pause, e.g. *tištē~ištay#* 'you SG.F want' and *yištō~yištaw#* 'they M want'. Certain northern varieties have generalized the pausal alternant and feature a diphthong in both context and pause, e.g., *yištaw Mōdān* 'heading towards Mōdān' in text 2 below.

Word final *ī* and *ū* are often diphthongized in pre-pausal position. In Ṣanʕāʔ final *ī* may be realized as *ey* and final *ū* as either *aw* or *ow* (Rossi 1939: 35; Watson 1996b: 55). In the northern dialects, final *ī* and *ū* often yield *iy* and *uw* respectively, as in *ismī~ismiy#* 'my name' and *ismaʕū~ismaʕuw#* 'listen! SG.M'.

– Devoicing. The voiced consonants *b*, *d*, and *ğ* are frequently devoiced in utterance-final position, e.g., *ḥaṭab~ḥaṭab̥#* 'wood' or *nōd~nōd̥#* 'wind'. The unvoiced allophones of /g/ and /ṭ/ (see 2.1.1 above) are more likely to appear in pre-pause position, e.g., *sáwwag̥* 'he shopped [at the market]' in text 3 below. Note again, that the pausal devoiced allophone does not overlap with its unvoiced counterpart since the latter is aspirated, and therefor *d̥≠t* ; *g̥≠k* ; etc.

11 The two latter may by heard in Tsur Shezaf's film "The last Jews of Yemen" (www.youtube.com/watch?v=yg7JyMK4QEo, time 05'24).

– Stress shifts. Pre-pausal position is one of the main contextual triggers for stress shifts, as outlined in 2.1.7 below.

2.1.7 Stress patterns

The Yemeni stress patterns differ significantly from those of most eastern Arabic dialects. A prominent feature of Yemeni Arabic is that it stresses the first of two *v̄C*/*vCC* syllables (Watson 2002: 98), e.g., *basā́tīn* 'gardens' and *dáxxalt* 'I brought in', as opposed to *basātī́n* (often *basatī́n*) and *daxxált* in most eastern dialects. In addition, the Yemeni pattern does not necessarily equate long vowels with stress, and may, under certain conditions, yield forms like *fágīr* 'poor' or *Ṣālḥáh* (p.n.), which are unacceptable elsewhere. Yet the most noticeable feature of Yemeni stress is its instability, in the sense that stress may shift and occur in different syllables of the same word in different contexts. As other dialects, Yemeni Arabic features a basic word-stress scheme, which depends upon the syllabic structure of the individual word, and follows a relatively systematic algorithm. But at the same time, stress fluctuates in accordance with prosodic and contextual considerations, predominantly expressive or affective speech, as well as pre- and post-pause position (Naïm-Sanbar 1994; Shachmon 2007: 77–91).

Thus, many forms in Yemeni speech may surface as "irregular". Importantly, from the standpoint of the speakers, the shift of stress from one syllable to another does not alter the lexical meaning of a certain word, yet it may bear additional nuances, and thereby modify the general message of the utterance as a whole. The fluctuation of stress as means of affective speech is illustrated in the following example, in which a Jewish informant from a village north-west of Ṣaʕdah tells with great excitement how he was asked to supply *ʕarag* 'Arak' to a Muslim officer. While, in the first occurrence of the word *ʕarag* the stress is ultimate, in the second occurrence it clearly shifts to the penultimate position: *gāl: anā́ aštī ʕarág. gult lih gult: mā ʕandī ʕárag* 'He said: I want Arak(!). I said to him, I said: I don't have Arak'. The stress shift in this example is an expressive tool, conveying the assertiveness of the officer. Similarly, the speaker in the following example stresses the fact that it was a long time that they had to wait before leaving for Israel, and thus the stress on *sanah* 'year' shifts from the first syllable to the second: *gáʕadū fi-bilād alʔimām sanáh, w-baʕad sánah ʕazamnā alGuds* 'they remained an [entire!] year in theterritory of the Imam, and after a year we left for Israel [lit. Jerusalem]'.[12] Thus, the "irregular" stress patterns are better accounted for individual speech acts, and not as part of the basic grammatical system of the dialect.

The influence of the local stress system is not only evident in the flow of the speech, but also in the reading of Jewish texts, especially those which are unvocalized and without the traditional accent signs, or *ṭəʕāmīm* (Morag 1963: 232, 243, 254). On occasion, the characteristic stress patterns surface even in Hebrew words borrowed from modern Israeli Hebrew after the immigration to Israel, as illustrated by *alḥā́nūt* 'the shop' (Hebrew *ḥanút* 'shop') or *tapū́zīm* 'oranges' (Hebrew *tapuzím* 'oranges'). The following extract, recorded from a Jew from the northern province, demonstrates the shift of stress in modern Hebrew *halxu* 'they went': *naḏaḥū alʕarabī fi-alǧabal. w-hálxū*[IHb],

12 Note that stress shifts are not altogether free and not every syllable may take the stress. For example, the imperfect marker for forms II and V is not likely to become stressed (Watson 2002: 83).

halxū́[IHb] *habayta*[IHb] 'they threw [the corpse of] that Arab in the mountains, and [simply] went! They went home.' Here, the stress-shift delivers the deep shock of the speaker at the act of throwing the corpse into the nearby wadi and simply moving on with life.

2.2 Morphology

2.2.1 Peculiarities of the verbal system

– The perfect. Measure I verbs have the basic pattern *CvCvC* that in Ṣanʕāʔ yields *faʕal*, *fiʕil*, and *fuʕul* as in the examples *katab* 'write', *širib* 'drink', and *kubur* 'grow, become big'. The northern varieties also exhibit the pattern *fuʕil*, as exemplified in text 3 below with *kuṯír* 'increase' and *wuṣíl* 'arrive'. In addition, the conservative pattern *faʕil* was attested in several northern villages, e.g., *samíʕ* 'hear', *labís* 'wear', and *ğalís* 'sit' in text 3 below. In general, the *u*-patterns *fuʕul* and *fuʕil* characterize forms involving velars and/or labials, i.e. sounds which have various degrees of "coloring" or "backing" effects in Yemeni Arabic (see 2.1.3 above).

– *k*-perfect. A group of Yemeni dialects, mainly on the southern high plateau but also in the area of Jabal Rāziḥ in the far northwest, are characterized by a *k*-suffix in the 1SG, 2SG.M, 2SG.F, and 2SG.M/F of the perfect conjugation. For example, OA *katabtu* 'I wrote' may appear as *katabk*, *katubk*, *katbuk*, *katabku*, or *katabk*^{w} in the various *k*-dialects (Diem 1973: 100; Prochazka 1974: 439; Behnstedt, 1987: 133 and Behnstedt 2016: 192–193). Shachmon and Faust (forthcoming) offer a diachronic path through several stages, demonstrating the coloring effect of the labialized *-k*^{w}, and re-constructing the phonological evolution of the various patterns documented in *k*-dialects throughout Yemen.

As far as I know, it was only in the rural area around Ibb that Jews used the *k*-forms. They were first documented in the 1950s from Jews from the village of alGades, with examples like *nazulk* 'I went down' and *suʔulk* 'I asked' (Goitein 1960: 364–365). A short example of a Jewish *k*-dialect from Lower Yemen appears as text no. 5 below.

The Jewish varieties of thc northern province exhibit no *k*-perfect, not even those of Jabal Raziḥ, where *k*-dialects are in use. This is plausibly related to the fact, that the Muslim *k*-speakers lived in the many hamlets scattered over the mountainsides (Watson et al. 2006: 40), while the Jews of that area dwelled mainly in the two larger settlements of alGalʕah and anNaḏ̣īr, closer to the government centre of Qaḏ̣āʔ Rāziḥ (Shachmon 2014a).

– 1SG and 2SG.M perfect. Following the omission of the historical final vowels, old *faʕaltu* and old *faʕalta* both yield *faʕalt,* which is now used for the 1SG and 2SG.M alike. This merger is characteristic of the great majority of modern dialects, both inside and outside the Arabian Peninsula, and in Yemen as well the dialects of Ṣanʕā and Ṣaʕdah exhibit one form for both persons, viz. *faʕalt*. That said, other Yemeni dialects exhibit a range of distinct forms for the 1SG and 2SG.M that avoid the potential ambiguity in the perfect paradigm. This may be done by preserving the final vowel of one of the two persons, e.g. *katabtu* 'I wrote' vs. *katabt* 'you SG.M wrote'; or *katabt* 'I wrote' vs. *katabta* 'you SG.M wrote'; or even of both, viz. *katabtu* vs. *katabta,* as is the case in some dialects of the northern Tihāma (Behnstedt 2016: 194). Aden Arabic is reported to have one form for both persons, yet many Jewish Adanis use a distinct form for the 2SG.M, namely *katabta* (Ahroni 1994: 182, and my own observations).

The various *k*-dialects also maintain the distinction between the 1SG and 2SG.M, with a great variety of forms and patterns: some dialects mark the 1SG with a final vowel, as *qulku* vs. *qulk* ('I said' vs. 'you said') in the dialect of Taʕizz (Prochazka 1974: 439), or with a secondary articulation of the *k* of the 1SG, e.g., *katabkʷ* vs. *katabk*, in some dialects of Lower Yemen (Behnstedt 2016: 193). In others, the differentiation is based upon the inner vowels, with *katubk* vs. *katabk* ('I wrote' vs. 'you wrote') in Jiblih (Diem 1973: 100); or *sarḥuk* vs. *sarḥik* ('I went' vs. 'you went') in Jabal Rāziḥ (Behnstedt 1987: 133). The distinctive inner vowel is the result of back-coloring processes, triggered by a secondary velarization of the *k*, which is still heard in some varieties in Lower Yemen, but has altogether disappeared from others (Shachmon and Faust, forthcoming). Examples from the Jews of alGades and ʕUṯmah include *šurubkʷ* vs. *širibk* 'I/you SG.M drank'; *bakōkʷ* vs. *bakēk* 'I/you SG.M cried'; *qumkʷ* vs. *qimk* 'I/you SG.M stood up', *gassōkʷ* vs. *gassēk* 'I/you SG.M sat', etc. Back-coloring does not occur in varieties which fully preserve the final vowel, as the dialect of Šiʕb asSuḥūl North of Ibb, featuring *širibku, bakēku, qimku, gassēku*, etc.

– Agglutinated 2SG.M forms. The dialects of the Province of Ṣaʕdah exhibit an idiosyncratic 2SG.M perfect of the pattern *faʕaltant,* as exemplified by *naʕaltant* 'you SG.M cursed' and *gultant* 'you SG.M said' in text 2 below. Two similar patterns, viz. *faʕaltint* and *faʕalhant* are characteristic of certain villages of the same province, as well as of Najrān across the Saudi border (Behnstedt 1987: 27; Prochazka 1988: 12, 24, 28, and 77).[13] All three patterns are the outcome of the addition and subsequent agglutination of the 2SG.M independent pronoun *ant* to the basic *faʕalt* form, yet *faʕalhant* reflects a more advanced stage of development, involving the dissimilation of *t* > *h* (Shachmon 2015). The development of agglutinated patterns may be taken to demonstrate another – essentially different – mechanism to avoid ambiguity in the perfect paradigm (see above). While agglutinated forms are reported as marginal in the speech of Muslims around Ṣaʕdah, or to alternate freely with the non-agglutinated form, they are unmistakably predominant in the speech of all Jews originating in that area.

– Prefixes of the verbal measures V, VI, VIII, and X. Rossi (1939: 31) and Watson (1996: 168–169) report *i-/Ø*-prefixes for all four verbal forms in Ṣanʕāʔ, namely *(i)tfaʕʕal, (i)tfāʕal, (i)ftaʕal*, and *(i)staſʕal*, respectively. Jewish Ṣanʕānis indeed use the *i-/Ø*-prefix in these forms. The dialects of Lower Yemen, on the other hand, exhibit an *a*-prefix in these four measures, viz. *atfaʕʕal, atfāʕal, aftaʕal*, and *astafʕal* (Behnstedt 2016: 236, 240), and this is confirmed by Jewish immigrants from the villages around Ibb. However, many dialects in Yemen, including those of the northern province, exhibit two sets of prefixes for the measures discussed, namely: an *i-/Ø*-prefix in measures V–VI, as opposed to an *a*-prefix in measures VIII and X. It is therefore interesting to find that the Jews of Wādi Amlaḥ, to the east of Ṣaʕdah, have generalized the *a*-prefix and use it for all four verbal forms:

13 Comparable forms were also recorded among the Āl Murra, see Ingham 2000: 127, n. 4.

	Ṣanʕāʔ	Ibb	Ṣaʕdah	Amlaḥ
Measure V	*(i)tfaʕʕal*	*atfaʕʕal*	*(i)tfaʕʕal*	*atfaʕʕal*
Measure VI	*(i)tfāʕal*	*atfāʕal*	*(i)tfāʕal*	*atfāʕal*
Measure VIII	*(i)ftaal*	*aftaʕal*	*aftaʕal*	*aftaʕal*
Measure X	*(i)stafʕal*	*astafʕal*	*astafʕal*	*astafʕal*

– Hebrew verbs and Hebrew roots in Arabic patterns. The topic of the Hebrew component in Jewish Yemeni Arabic has been dealt with in Shachmon 2013, including relevant references. In this context, it is sufficient to recall that, as mentioned in 1.2 above, the Hebrew reading traditions continuously nourished the everyday speech of Jews in Yemen. Thus, we find Hebrew verbs incorporated into the various Arabic dialects, either in their original Hebrew form, as בָּלַם *bōlam* 'he kept his mouth shut', demonstrated in text 2 below; or verbs modeled upon Arabic verb formation as תְשַׂטָּא *tšaṭṭā* 'go wild' (from the Hebrew root √ *šṭh* ש.ט.ה 'behave like a fool'), which occurs in text 3 below.

In Israel, the influence of Israeli Hebrew frequently yields hybrid forms such as *yitlaḥem b-ʕaṣmih* 'he was struggling with himself', also in the text 3 below. An intriguing contact phenomenon in the speech of immigrants from Lower Yemen is the use of the 2SG.F *ki*-suffix for Hebrew verbs, e.g. *lēš mā baki almoʕadōn*[H] 'why didn't you SG.F come to the [elderly day-care] club?', for Hebrew בָּאתְ 'you SG.F came', or *antī hifsadkī* 'you missed [all the fun]', for Hebrew הִפְסַדְתְּ 'you SG.F missed'.

– Grammaticalized verbs. Several verbs in Yemeni Arabic exhibit increased morphological fixedness. Most prominent of these are probably *kān* 'to be' and *ʕād* 'still, yet', which – in the same way as a few particles in these dialects – may take the independent pronouns as suffixes in certain parts of the paradigm (see further 2.2.2 below). The following table presents the paradigm of *ʕād*, as it is used with the dependent and/or independent pronouns the dialects of Ṣanʕāʔ and Ṣaʕdah:

<table>
<tr><th></th><th colspan="2">Ṣanʕāʔ</th><th colspan="2">Ṣaʕdah</th></tr>
<tr><th></th><th>+ indep. pron.</th><th>+ dep. pron.</th><th>+ indep. pron.</th><th>+ dep. pron.</th></tr>
<tr><td>1SG</td><td>--------</td><td>ʕādanī</td><td>ʕādanā</td><td>ʕādī, ʕādanī</td></tr>
<tr><td>2SG.M</td><td>ʕādant</td><td>ʕādak</td><td>ʕādant</td><td>ʕādak</td></tr>
<tr><td>2SG.F</td><td>ʕādantī</td><td>ʕādiš</td><td>ʕādantī</td><td>ʕādiš</td></tr>
<tr><td>3SG.M</td><td>ʕād(h)ū</td><td>--------</td><td>--------</td><td>ʕādih</td></tr>
<tr><td>3SG.F</td><td>ʕād(h)ī</td><td>--------</td><td>--------</td><td>ʕādhā</td></tr>
<tr><td>1PL</td><td>ʕādiḥnā</td><td>--------</td><td>ʕādaḥnā</td><td>--------</td></tr>
<tr><td>2SG.M</td><td>--------</td><td>ʕād(a)kum</td><td>--------</td><td rowspan="2">ʕādakum</td></tr>
<tr><td>2SG.F</td><td>--------</td><td>ʕād(a)kin</td><td></td></tr>
<tr><td>3SG.M</td><td colspan="2">ʕād(h)um</td><td colspan="2" rowspan="2">ʕādhim</td></tr>
<tr><td>3SG.F</td><td colspan="2">ʕād(h)in</td></tr>
</table>

Several other verbs seem to have lost their lexical independence:

– *zid*. The fossilized imperative *zid* (lit. 'add!') is used adverbially to denote "again, anymore", as in the example *mā zid šufnā ḥad* 'we could no-longer see anyone', and *mā zid atḥákā* 'he did not speak anymore' in text 2 below. This usage corresponds to Jewish Ṣanʕānī זאד *zād* used by the renown Ḥayyim Ḥibšūš in his memoirs (Leslau 1945/46: 273). In the dialects of the North it is also used as a determiner denoting "another, additional", e.g., *ǧā́bū laná zid lugmah ṣġayyirah* 'they gave us some more bread'.

– *yizʕam*. Several fossilized forms of the root *zʕm* (on occasion also: *sʕm*) are used in the sense of "that is to say" (Piamenta 1990: 200). The form *zaʕm* was recorded in the Jewish dialect of Aden, e.g., *šho zaʕmo* (sic.) 'what do you mean' (Ahroni 1994: 178). In the northern dialects *yizʕam*, lit. 'he states', may also denote "intending to", without necessarily agreeing with its subject: *libsat w-šallat binthā w-nazalat, yizʕam tuxriǧ* 'she got dressed, took her daughter and went down, intending to leave [the house]' (Ben-David 1999: 61).

– *ǧāw*. The idiom *ǧāw*, ubiquitously used by the Jews of Ṣaʕdah, illustrates a case of component merger: the conjunction *w* is combined with the verb *ǧā* 'he came', which is fully fossilized in this construction and is no longer inflectable for gender and number. The merged *ǧā+w* now denotes "it so happened that..." or "it turned out that…", referring to a continuous state in the past.[14] Comparably, the form *jō* was documented in the area of Jabal Rāziḥ, in the west of the northern province, where it denotes "permanent existence or habitude" (Watson et al. 2006: 50 ff.). The complete merger of the two elements allows irregular functioning of the original components, and the form *ǧāw* may take pronominal suffixes, as illustrated in *ǧāwih*, *ǧāwhā*, or *ǧāwhim* 'it so happened that he/she/they …'. *ǧāw* is frequently used as a literary connecting device, often opening a story or an anecdote, bringing a sense of coincidence or chance into the narrative.

2.2.2 Peculiarities of the pronominal system

– Independent pronouns. Many Yemeni dialects, including that of Ṣanʕāʔ, preserve the old distinction between the masculine and feminine in the plural of the second and third persons. The Ṣanʕānī set of pronouns thus consists of five different plural forms (Watson 1996-b: 13). This gender distinction has been lost in the dialects of the northern province that exhibit only one plural form for each of the first, second and third persons (Behnstedt 1987: 64–68).

A distinction between a masculine and a feminine form in the 1SG independent pronoun characterizes several dialects in western and southern Yemen. It is heard in the speech of the Jews of Aden, Ḥugariyyah, and Ibb, who use *anā* for the masculine and *anī* for the feminine (Goitein 1960: 370; Ben-Zion 2011: 74; Ahroni 1994: 182, and my own observations). In Ṣanʕāʔ one form, viz. *anā*, is used for both the masculine and feminine (Watson 1996b: 13). However, due to the structured final *ʔimāla* of *ā* > *ē* in the Jewish variety (2.1.3 above), Jewish *anē* is clearly distinct, as demonstrated in text 4

14 The speakers evidently conceive the two elements as one. Ben-David, himself a native of Wādi Amlaḥ, transcribes the dialect using Hebrew letters, and in the case of *ǧāw* consistently writes גָאו, i.e. as one word. See several examples in Ben David 1999: 59–61.

below. The same applies to the 1PL, which is *iḥnā~iḥnē#* in Muslim Ṣanʕāni, but consistently *iḥnē* in the speech of Jews.[15]

	Ṣanʕāʔ		Ṣaʕdah		Ibb	
	SG	PL	SG	PL	SG	PL
1	Muslim *anā~anē#* Jewish *anē*	Muslim *iḥnā~iḥnē#* Jewish *iḥnē*	*anā*	*aḥnā/iḥnā*	*anā* (M), *anī* (F)	*aḥnā*
2M	*ant*	*antū*	*ant/int*	*antū/intū*	*antā*	*antū*
2F	*antī*	*antayn*	*antī/intī*		*antī*	*antayn~ antēn*
3M	*hū*	*hum*	*hū, huwwa*	*him*	*hū*	*hum*
3F	*hī*	*hin*	*hī, hiyya*		*hī*	*han*

– Suffixed pronouns. As in many Arabian dialects, an epenthetic vowel is regularly inserted whenever a pronoun follows a word ending with a heavy syllable of the type v̄C, ayC, awC or vCC: *ḥagg+nā>ḥagg*[a]*nā* – 'ours' or *bayt+hā* > *bayt*[a]*hā* 'her house'. The inserted vowel is most often *a*, yet in Ṣanʕāʔ it may also be *u* before the 3PL.M pronoun *-hum*, due to vowel harmony, as in *kayf ḥāl*[u]*kum* 'how are you' (Watson 1996a: 9).

	Ṣanʕāʔ		Ṣaʕdah		Ibb	
	SG	PL	SG	PL	SG	PL
1	*-ī* / *-(a)nī*	*(a)nā~(a)nē#* (Muslim) *(a)nē* (Jewish)	*-ī* / *-(a)nī*	*-(a)nā*	*-ī* / *-(a)nī*	*-(a)nā*
2M	*-ak*	*-(a)kum*	*-ak*	*-(a)kum*	*-ak*	*-(a)kum*
2F	*-iš* (Muslim) *-ič* (Jewish)	*-(a)kin*	*-iš*		*-ik, -iš, ič*	*-(a)kin, -(a) kan*
3M	*-ih* (Muslim) *-oh* (Jewish)	*-(a)hum*	*-ih*	*-(a)him~hum*	*-o*	*-(h)om*
3F	*(a)hā~(a)hē#* (Muslim) *(a)hē* (Jewish)	*-(a)hin*	*-(a)hā*		*-e*	*-(h)in ,-(h)an*

Several distinctions between the Jewish and Muslim varieties in Ṣanʕā' may be established, based on the respective paradigms of pronominal suffixes:

The 3SG.M pronominal suffix, which is *-ih* in Muslim Ṣanʕānī, e.g., *baytih* 'his house', is *-oh* in the speech of Ṣanʕānī Jews. The Jewish suffix, which is distinct in Ṣanʕāʔ and its close vicinity, seems common in areas west of Ṣanʕāʔ and in Lower Yemen (Diem 1973: 79, 84, 89, 95). The Jews of the villages around Ibb also use *-uh~ -oh*. The Jews of Aden exhibit either *-ho* or *-o*, which may also surface as *Ø*, e.g.,

15 Note in this context that Rossi (1939: 19) gives only *anēʔ* and *ḥnēʔ* for Ṣanʕāni.

bintoho 'his daughter', *uxto* 'his sister',*ʕalēho* 'on him', but: *abū* 'his father' (Ben-Zion 2011: 75–76).

The 2SG.F pronominal suffix is *-iš* in many Yemeni dialects, as well as in Muslim Ṣanʕānī,[16] yet in Jewish Ṣanʕānī it is regularly *-ič* (Kara 1986: 128), as demonstrated by *aḥǟzīč* 'I tell you SG.F' in text 2 below. The Jewish variant *-ič* differs from its co-territorial Muslim variant *-iš*, yet at the same time it complies with the pronoun used by Muslims in other locations, such as Raydah (Diem 1973: 33). I also hear *-ič/eč* from the Jewish informants from villages in Lower Yemen, alternating with *-iš* and *-ik*.

The 3SG.F and the 1PL pronouns, which historically end in *-ā*, are regularly subject to *ʔimāla* in Jewish Ṣanʕānī, and are *-hē* and *-nē*, respectively. By this, they differ from the Muslim pronouns, which yield *-ā* in all of their context occurrences, but may be raised to *ē* in pre-pausal position (see 2.1.3 and 2.1.6 above).

– The use of independent pronouns as suffixes. As mentioned above (2.2.1), several grammaticalized verbs may take the independent pronouns as suffixes in some parts of the paradigm. In a similar manner, the particles *gad/gid* (< OA *qad*) and *inn* 'that' also take independent pronouns as suffixes. In Ṣanʕānī Arabic there are often two alternative forms, with either the dependent or independent pronoun, e.g., *gadantī kabīrih~gadiš kabīrih* 'you SG.F are old'. The 3PL dependent and independent pronouns are indistinguishable, i.e. both *hum/hin*, and it cannot be determined which of them is suffixed to *gad*. Note, that in Ṣanʕāni Arabic the initial *h* of the pronouns *hū, hī, hum*, and *hin* is silent when suffixed to the particles, e.g. *gad+hū > gadū*.

In the northern dialects, only the independent pronouns may be suffixed to OA *qad > gid*. In Lower Yemen the independent pronouns are suffixed, yet the *d* of old *qad* is elided, e.g., *qad+hū > qāhū* (Jastrow 1986: 28; added to my own observations).

	Ṣanʕāʔ		Ṣaʕdah	alGades
	+ ind. pron.	+ dep. pron.	+ ind. pron.	+ ind. pron.
1SG	*gadanā*	*gadanī*	*g(i)danā*	*qāni*
2SG.M	*gadant*	*gadak*	*gidant*	*qantā*
2SG.F	*gadantī*	*gadiš*	*gidantī*	*qantī*
3.SG.M	*gad(h)ū*	-----	*gidhū*	*qāhū*
3SG.F	*gad(h)ī*	-----	*gidhī*	*qāhī*
1PL	*gadiḥnā*	-----	*gidaḥnā*	*qāḥnā*
2PL.M	*gadantū*	*gad(a)kum*	*gidantū*	*qantum*
2PL.F	*gadantayn*	*gad(a)kin*		*qantayn*
3PL.M	*gad(ah)um*		*gidhim*	*qāhum*
3PL.F	*gad(ah)in*			*qāhan*

16 As convincingly shown by Hopkins, this suffix has nothing to do with the old trait known as *kaš-kaša*. Hopkins states that is more likely "a substrate feature born out of contact with Modern South Arabian" (Hopkins 2004: 27 and the reference given there).

The reflexes of OA *qad* serve in Yemeni Arabic in two main functions: either emphatic, to emphasize certain elements in a nominal phrase, or the action indicated by verb; or temporal, placing the action of the verb further back in time (see Smith 2019 for Jewish Ṣanʕāni, which applies to other varieties as well).

2.2.3 Peculiarities of the nominal system

– The nominal feminine ending. In Ṣanʕāni Arabic the feminine ending corresponding to OA *tāʔ marbūṭah* is regularly subject to raising or *ʔimāla* of the type *ah* > *ih*. This raising is excluded when a guttural consonant occurs immediately to the left of the ending, and therefore: *gahwih* 'coffee' and *sayyārih* 'car', but: *tisʕah* 'nine', *malīḥah* 'good, nice, SG.F', and *karīhah* 'hateful, SG.F' (Watson 2002: 37). That said, the Jewish variety of Ṣanʕāʔ evidently allows raising after gutturals as well, as exemplified in forms like *tisʕih* 'nine' (Kara 1986: 128), *malīḥih* 'good, nice, SG.F' (p.c. with Uri Melammed), and also *šūʕih* 'bad smell' in text 4 below. As in other cases, the peculiarity of the Jewish variety in Ṣanʕāʔ is actually the norm in other localities: forms like *tisʕih* (or: *tisʕeh*) prevail in areas south of Ṣanʕāʔ (Behnstedt 2016: 46).[17]

The raised feminine ending in Ṣanʕāni Arabic is subject to labialization in words containing an emphatic, where the ending *-ih* surfaces as *-uh* (Watson 1996b: 297). Note that his type of labialization occurs even when the high vowel is not immediately adjacent to the emphatic consonant, as is the case in *ṭāguh* 'window' and *ṭālubuh* 'student, SG.F'.

The dialects of Lower Yemen exhibit *ʔimāla* of the type *-ah* > *-ih*, which is prevented when preceded by emphatics, but not by gutturals (Behnstedt 2016: 46). In the texts recorded from the Jewish informants, however, the ending alternates in accordance with the vowel of the previous syllable.[18] This is illustrated in text 5 below, with *kalbah* 'bitch', and *kaḏḏābah* 'liar', SG.F', vs. *xinzīrih* 'sow, female hog' (all used derogatively against a Jewish girl from alGades).

In the dialects of the northern province no *ʔimāla* occurs and the feminine ending is *-ah* without exception, and therefore: *gahwah*, *sayyārah*, *sāʕah*, *tisʕah*, *malīḥah*, *ṭāgah*, and *ṭālibah*.

– Broken plurals of the verbal active participle. The sound plural ending *-īn* is regularly used with the active participle *fāʕil*, and thus *kātib* SG. *kātibīn* 'have written / are [in the state of] writing.PL'. However, broken plurals of the pattern *fuʕūl* are used with several participles denoting motionless state, e.g., *ǧulūs* '[in the state of] sitting.PL' and *rugūd* '[in the state of] sleeping.PL', documented from the Jews of Ṣaʕdah.[19]

17 In most Arabic dialects which exhibit the *ʔimāla* of the feminine ending, raising is hindered by back consonants. However, in some Bedouin dialects of Sinai and the Negev (de Jong 2000: 76; Shawarbah 2012: 88), the pharyngeals *ḥ* and *ʕ* do not prevent the *ʔimāla*, as is the case here.

18 A comparable, though not identical, conditioning, was reported for the dialect of ʕAzāzmih tribe in the Negev (Shawarbah 2012: 88).

19 Comparable forms were documented in Najdi Arabic, e.g., *wugūf* 'are [in the state of] standing' (Ingham 1994: 33). Barth (1894: 464) observed that in Classical Arabic the pattern *fuʕūl* was used with the active participles of verbs denoting durativity.

– Gender-neutral forms. Yemeni dialects, particularly but not exclusively those of the northern province, demonstrate a gradual collapse of gender distinction as the masculine occurs where a feminine form would be expected (Landberg 1909: 723; Behnstedt 2016: map 034), e.g., *mantī sāyir* 'you SG.F don't go'. In many cases the gender-neutralized form is a participle of the pattern *fāʕil*, as *wāgif* 'standing SG.M/F', or the pattern *fāʕī* with third weak roots, as *dāri* 'know'. Such epicene forms are not used with geminate roots, where *fāʕil* yields *fāll*, and therefore *anā ḥāllah fi Sā́gēn* 'I.F live in Sāgēn', and not: **anā ḥāll*. Examples in the derived stems include: *innhā mrayyiʕ-lih* 'she is waiting for him'.

The collapse of gender distinction seems gradual. In certain dialects, it may involve only forms denoting persons, or persons and objects. In other varieties, all participles appear as gender-neutral, and there are dialects where adjectives as a whole have become epicene (Behnstedt 1987: 61–62; Behnstedt 2016: 78–79).

Epicene forms, particularly of the *fāʕil* and *faʕlān* patterns, are also typical of some Levantine Arabic dialects, where they tend to occur in the speech of women describing their own deeds (Dbayyat and Rosenhouse 2006). In Yemen, on the other hand, examples show that the neutral participles may refer to the 3rd person, in the speech of men and women alike (Shachmon 2017b).

– *ī*-ending nouns. Yemeni Arabic regularly marks the *nomen relativum* or *nisba* by the addition of *ī* to nouns, as in *gabīlī* 'a tribesman' or *Ṣaʕdī* 'a native or citizen of Ṣaʕdah'. Yet in addition to this known Semitic function, the termination *ī* may be added to a collective noun to designate an individual of a genus, or *nomen unitatis*, e.g., *gummal* > *gúmmalī* 'a flea' or *ġurrrāb* > *ġurrābī* 'a raven'. This usage is frequent side by side with the more regular Arabic *nomen unitatis* which is based on the addition of the nominal feminine ending *-ah*/*-ih*.[20] In many cases, however, the *ī*-ending singular is not directly derived from the collective or plural, as is the case in *dāyrī* 'a key',[21] *ḏíbbī* 'a fly', or *bugrī* 'a cow'. *-ī* termination is very common in animal names, and especially in the dialects of the province of Ṣaʕdah, which exhibit a series of *ī*-ending animal names (Behnstedt 1987: 96). To this we may also add the form *ġūlī* 'a ghoul, jinni, demon', which, as other *ī*-ending forms, may also appear without the termination, viz. *ġūl*.

Furthermore, though much less common, the termination *ī* also serves to denote the diminutive, as in the examples *buṣlī* 'a little onion' or *šugrī* 'a young cock or chicken'. The form *ṣuġayyirī~zuġayyirī* 'small, young' has a double marking of the diminutive, both by the old Arabic pattern *fuʕayyil* and by the addition of *-ī*. Goitein (1933: 39; 1934: xxiii) offers several examples of *ī*-ending nouns, and suggests that some of them may be viewed as hypochorism.

20 Wagner (1966: 255) remarks that Tigrē also offers these two options to form the *nomen unitatis*, namely either by the termination *-ay* (comparable with Yemeni *-ī*) or by the more prevalent feminine ending *-ä*.

21 This form was documented from Jewish immigrants from Ṣaʕdah, while other dialects use *dāʔir~dāyir* (Rossi 1939: 199; Behnstedt 1992: 394–395; Behnstedt 1993: 77).

3. Text specimens with interlinear glosses

The five texts presented below demonstrate different varieties of Yemeni Arabic, as recorded from Yemenites now living in Israel. The reader may find here many of the distinc-tive features of the Jewish varieties, as discussed in the grammatical sketch above. The first two texts bring to the fore the attempts of Yemeni Israelis to reduce their heritage language to writing, using Hebrew letters (1.3 above). The other three texts are based on my fieldwork among the immigrants, demonstrating the Jewish varieties of the villages around Ṣaʕdah (text no. 3), the capital city of Ṣanʕāʔ (text no. 4), and the rural area around Ibb in Lower Yemen (text no. 5).[22]

3.1 ʕadán ʕadán

The following is a popular song by the renowned Yemeni-Israeli singer Ziyon Golan. The Hebrew transcription (accompanied by Hebrew translation) was prepared in 2011 by Itamar Pinḥas (see 1.3 above) for the "The Association for Society and Culture, Documentation and Research".[23] The phonemic transcript I give here follows the pronunciation of the singer, which is not fully compatible with the Hebrew subtitles. Also noticeable are few instances of inconsistency of pronunciation, such as the alternation of diphthongs and monophthongs (e.g., *ʕalayš* and *mawt* along with *rēt, baḥrēn*). This is plausibly due to the fact that the singer was born in Israel and has been exposed to more than one Yemeni variety.[24]

עדן עדן רית ואן עדן קריבה

ʕadán	*ʕadán*	*ʕádan,*	*rēt*	*w-inn*	*ʕadán*	*garīb-ah*
Aden	Aden	Aden	if.only	and-PSTV	Aden	close-SG.F

Aden, Aden, I wish Aden were close

ואסאפריש מן פגר אלא מג׳יבה

w-asāfir-iš	*min*	*fağr*	*ilā*	*maġībah*
and-travel:IPFV.1SG-you.SG.F	from	dawn	till	sunset

and I will travel to you from dawn till sunset

עדן עדן עדן יא אלי עליש בחרין

ʕadán	*ʕadán*	*ʕádan*	*yā*	*llī*	*ʕalay-š*	^{i}*baḥr-ēn*
Aden	Aden	Aden	ITJ	REL	on-you.SG.F	sea-DU

Aden Aden Aden, with two seas around you

22 I wish to express my thanks and appreciation to Ms. Livnat Barkan for her significant assistance in preparing the interlinear glosses. The following special lexical abbreviations apply: HbC: genuine Hebrew component, i.e. such which was in use by the Jews in Yemen; IHb: Israeli Hebrew component, i.e. born out of the contact with Israeli Hebrew after the immigration; MxC: mixed components, i.e. a blend of Hebrew and Arabic, often formed ad-hoc by the informant.

23 A video including the subtitles is available on www.youtube.com/watch?v=gMiYeyYbwws. My thanks are due to Mr. Adiel Ben-Shalom, the grandson of the founding father of the mentioned association, who drew my attention to this video.

24 Based on personal correspondence with Dr. Uri Melammed of the Academy of the Hebrew Language.

עַיּבְּתי אלמחבוב סנה ושהרין

ʕayyabtī	*al-máḥbūb*	*sanah*	*w-šahr-ēn*
delude:PRF.2SG.F	DEF-love:PTCP.PASS.SG.M	year	and-month-DU

you incited the beloved one [for] one year and two months

חלפת ל-אג׳נִּי, אג׳נִּי ואשִׁל בא-צַוְת

ḥalaft	*^{i}l-aġannī,*	*aġannī*	*w-ašill*	*^{i}b-ṣ-ṣawt*
swear:PRF.1SG	to-sing:IPFV.1SG	sing:IPFV.1SG	and-raise:IPFV.1SG	in-DEF-voice

I swore to sing, sing [I shall] and raise [my] voice

ואסלי עלא קלבי, לַוְמא יִגִּי מַוְת

w-aslī	*ʕalā*	*galb-ī,*	*lōmā*	*yīġī*	*mawt*
and-be_happy:IPFV.1SG	on	heart-1SG	until	come:IPFV.3SG.M	death

and I will let my heart be joyful, until death comes.

עדן, עדן, עדן, רית וין עדן גבותי

ʕAdán	*ʕAdán*	*ʕádan,*	*rēt*	*w-inn*	*ʕadán*	*Ǧábūtī*
Aden	Aden	Aden	if.only	and-COMP	Aden	Djibouti

Aden, Aden, I wish Aden were Djibouti.

וּתְקַנֲּעִי, יא נפס, לא תמותי

w-tgannáʕī	*yā nafs,*	*yā nafs*	*^{i}lā*	*tímūtī*
and-be_contented:IMP.SG.F	ITJ soul	ITJ soul	NEG	die:IPFV.2SG.F

and be contented, O soul, O soul, and you shall not die.

3.2 aṣḥāb assabt

The story of “The companions of Shabbath” was recorded from an immigrant from the village of Rağūzah in the North of Yemen. It depicts a dispute between a Jew and some Muslim officials in Yemen, providing the reader with a meaningful glimpse into a reality, in which Jews were occasionally involved in polemic discussions with their Muslim neighbors (Shachmon 2014a). The text was published by Rabbi Dr. Ahron Ben-David in vocalized Hebrew characters, using a transcription method unique to him (described in detail in Shachmon 2017).[25]

The phonemic transcript offered here basically follows the vocalized Hebrew text, as it was published in *Sefer Ha-Maʕaśim* (“The Book of Tales”), part 1, pp. 90–91. However, I also consulted the original recording, which the author kindly made available to me.[26]

The text contains a considerable number of Hebrew items, yet only a few of them, such as בָּלַם *bōlam* ‘kept his mouth shut’ or יִתְבָּרַךְ *yiṯbōrax* ‘may He be blessed’, belong to the genuine Hebrew component which was part of the dialect back in Yemen. Words of this type are pronounced in accordance with the traditional Yemeni accent, as described in 2.1.2 and 2.1.4 above, and in my transcription below they are all marked with superscript “HbC”. In contrast, Hebrew words and phrases like יָכוֹל לִהְיוֹת *yaxól liyót* ‘could be’ have clearly been adopted after the immigration to Israel. Different from the genuine Hebrew component, these recent borrowings are pronounced as in modern Israeli Hebrew, and I marked them with superscript “IHb”. The interchange of Arabic,

25 The full text in Hebrew letters is re-published here with the kind permission of the author.

26 In the few cases where there were differences between Ben-David’s Hebrew transcript and what I heard on the tape, the transcript here follows the latter.

genuine Hebrew component, and Israeli Hebrew reflects – rather reliably – the linguistic reality of the Yemeni communities in Israel, and the everyday way of speaking in domestic and intra-communal situations.

הָיוּ חֲמִשָּׁה עַסְכַּר מַעְהִם שַׁאוִּשׁ,

hayu ḥamiša ʕáskar maʕ-him šāwiš.

be:PRF.3PL.M[IHb] five[IHb] soldier.PL with-3PL officer.SG.M

There were five soldiers and an officer with them.

וִצְלוּ יְלַא אַלְחַאנוּת חַק דַּאוִּד שׁוּכְּר, פִּ״י מָאדַאן, יִשְׁתַּגִ׳ל.

wiṣilū́ ilā al-ḥā́nūt ḥagg Dā́wid Šukr fī Mōdān, yištaġal.

arrive:PRF.3PL.M to DEF-shop[IHb] of Dāwid Šukr in Mōdān work:IPFV.3SG.M

They arrived at the shop of Dāwid Shukr in Mōdān [while he was] working.

וַאלשֵּׁיךְ גַּאוּ הוּ עִנְדְּהִם. וּוַאחִד מִן אַלנּוּקוּבַּא.

w-aš-šēx ǧā-w hū ʕind-ih, w-wāḥid min an-núgubā

and-DEF-sheikh.SG.M come:PRF.3SG.M-and 3SG at-3SG and-one.SG.M of DEF-nobel.PL

And the sheikh happened to be there, as well as one of the nobles.

הֵם מְדַבְּרִים וּכַּאן יְקוּלוּ

az hem mdabr-im w-bēn-yigūlū́

so[IHb] 3PL[IHb] speak:PTCP.ACT-PL.M[IHb] and-PROG-say:IPFV.3PL.M

So they were speaking and saying

כַּמַא לוּעוּנוּ אַצְחַאבּ אַלסַּבְּת, כַּמַא נוּעוּלוּ.

kamā nuʕulū́ aṣḥāb as-sabt, kamā nuʕulū́

as be_cursed:PRF.3PL.M friend.PL.CS DEF-Sabbath as be_cursed:PRF.3PL.M

"Cursed be the companions of Shabbath, cursed be they".

הַפַּעַם הָרִאשׁוֹנָה וְהַפַּעַם הַשְּׁנִיָּה וְהַפַּעַם הַשְּׁלִישִׁית,

ha-paʕam ha-rišon-a v-ha-paʕam ha-šniy-a v-ha-paʕam ha-šliši-t.

DEF-time[IHb] DEF-first-SG.F[IHb] and-DEF-time[IHb] DEF-second-SG.F[IHb] and-DEF-time[IHb] DEF-third-SG.F[IHb]

[They said this] once, then a second time, then a third time.

אַף אֶחָד לֹא דִּבֵּר. לָמָּה.

af eḥad lo diber. lama?

even[IHb] one[IHb] NEG[IHb] speak:PRF.3SG.M why[IHb]

Nobody spoke. Why?

מַא בִּלַּא אֲנַא וּדַּאוִּד שׁוּכְּר וּמֲרַתִּה, בֵּין אִלַאעִנְדַּךְ כּוּלְּהִם.

mā b-illā̮nā w-Dāwid Šukr w-marat-ih, bēn ilā-ʕind-ak kull-him.

neg exist-except-1SG and-Dāwid Shukr and-wife.CS-3SG among if-at-2SG.M all.CS-3PL

[We were] only me, Dāwid Shukr and his wife, among – you may imagine – all of them.

אָז קִנֵּאתִי מֵהַדָּבָר הַזֶּה.

az ginnēti me-ha-ddavár ha-zza.

Then[IHb] be_distressed:PRF.1SG[HbC] by-DEF-statement[HbC] DEF-DEM.M[HbC]

Then I was distressed by this statement.

קוּלְת יַא שַׁאוִּשׁ אִסְמַע. מַאן הִם אַצְחַאבּ אַלסַּבְּת.

gult yā šāwiš, ismáʕ! man him aṣḥāb as-sabt?

say:PRF.1SG ITJ officer.SG.M listen:IMP.2SG.M who 3PL friend.PL.CS DEF-Sabbath

I said: "O commander, listen! Who are the companions of Shabbath"?

קָאל אַלְיַהוּד. קוּלְתּ לַאאַאאַ.

gāl: al-yihūd. gult: lāāāā!
say:PRF.3SG.M DEF-Jew.PL say:PRF.1SG NEG
He said: "the Jews". I said: "No way!

אַצְחַאבּ אַלסַּבְּת אַלְאַחַד וַאלְגִּמְעַה.

aṣḥāb as-sabt al-aḥád w-al-ğimʕah.
friend.PL.CS DEF-Sabbath DEF-Sunday and-DEF-Friday
The companions of Shabbath are Sunday and Friday".

קָאל הַאהַהַהַה. נְעַלְתַּנְת כּוּל אַלְמִסְלְמִין וְכּוּל אַלְנַּצַארַא.

gāl: hāāā! naʕaltant kull al-mislim-īn w-kull an-naṣārā.
say:PRF.3SG.M ha curse:PRF.2SG.M all.CS DEF-Muslim-PL.M and-all.CS DEF-Christian.PL
He said: "Is that so? You have just cursed all Muslims and all Christians".

לָמַה. עִיד אַלְנַּצַארַא יָאם אַלְאַחַד.

lama? ʕīd an-naṣārā yōm al-áḥad.
Why[IHb] holiday.CS DEF-Christian.PL day DEF-Sunday
Why? The holiday of Christians is Sunday,

וְעִיד אַלְעַרַבּ יָאם אַלְגִּמְעַה.

w-ʕīd al-ʕárab yōm al-ğimʕah.
and-holiday.CS DEF-Arab.PL day DEF-Friday
and the holiday of Muslims is Friday.

קָאל בְּחֵית' מַא תוּכְ'רוּג מִן אַלְחֻכּוּמַה,

gāl: b-ḥēṯ mā tuxriğ min al-ḥukūmah,
say:PRF.3SG.m in-where REL go_out:IPFV.2SG.M from DEF-government
He said: "the moment you go out from the government [court],

יִדְכִ'לְנִי פִּ'לְחַבְּס. לְעַנְת כּוּל אַלְמִסְלְמִין

yixallī-nī fi-l-ḥabs. naʕalt kull al-mislim-īn,
leave:IPFV.3SG.M-1SG.OBJ in-DEF-prison curse:PRF.1SG all.CS DEF-Muslim-PL.M
he will put me in prison". [He claimed that] I cursed all the Muslims,

חַתַּא אַלְאִמַאם. קוּלְתּ מַאנַא ד'י נְעַלְתַּה,

ḥittā‿ l-ʔimām! gult: mānā ḏī naʕalt-ih,
even DEF-Imam say:PRF.1SG NEG.1SG REL curse:PRF.1SG-3SG.M
even the Imam! I said: "It was not me who cursed him,

אַנְתּ ד'י נְעַלְתּ אַצְחַאבּ אַלסַּבְּת.

ant ḏī naʕaltant aṣḥāb as-sabt.
2SG.M REL curse:PRF.2SG.M friend.PL.CS DEF-Sabbath
you were the one who cursed the companions of Shabbath".

סַאלְנִי אַלשֵּׁיךְ אִבְּן נִעְמַה, קָאל

saʔal-nī aš-šēx Bin-Niʕmah, gāl:
ask:PRF.3SG.M-1SG.OBJ DEF-sheikh.SG.M Ibn-Niʕmah say:PRF.3SG.M
Sheikh Ibn-Niʕmah asked me, he said:

מְנֵין אַנְתּ יַא יְהוּדִי.

min-ēn ant yā yihūdī?
from-where 2SG.M ITJ Jew.SG.M
"where are you from, O Jew"?

קוּלְתּ מִן בְּלַאדּ ד׳וּ חְסֵין, מִן בֲּרַט, מִן רֲגּוּזַה.

gult: min bilād Ḏū-Ḥsēn, min Báraṭ, min Rağūzah.

say:PRF.1SG from land.CS Ḏū-Ḥsēn from Báraṭ from Rajūzah

I said: from the land of Ḏū-Ḥsēn, from Baraṭ, from [the village of] Rajūzah.

הַא הוּ יְעְרִף יוּסִף אֲכ׳וּי, הוּ וִיַּאה כְּמוֹ אַחִים.

hā! hū yiʕrif Yūsif, hū wiyyā-h kmo aḥim.

ha 3SG know:IPFV.3SG.M Yusif 3SG with-3SG.M like[IHb] brother.PL[IHb]

Ha! he knows [my brother] Yusif, they are like brothers.

קַאל אִסְמַע יַא שַׁאוִשׁ, אֲנַא וֲכִּיל אַלְיְהוּדִי.

gāl: ismaʕ yā šāwiš, anā wakīl al-yihūdī.

say:PRF.3SG.M listen:IMP.SG.M ITJ officer.SG.M 1SG sponsor.SG.M.CS DEF-Jew.SG.M

He said: "listen, O officer, I shall be the sponsor of the Jew.

אַנְתּ דִ׳י נְעַלְתַּנְתּ אַצְחַאבּ אַלסַבְּתּ.

ant ḏī naʕaltant aṣḥāb as-sabt.

2SG.M REL curse:PRF.2SG.M friend.PL.CS DEF-Shabbath

You are the one who cursed the friends of Shabbath.

והוּ צַאדִק אַלְיְהוּדִי, אַצְחַאבּ אַלסַבְּתּ,

w-hū ṣā́dig al-yihūdī: aṣḥāb as-sabt,

and-3SG be.right:act.PTCP.SG.M DEF-Jew.SG.M friend.PL.CS DEF-Shabbath

and he is right, the Jew: [you said] "the companions of Shabbath",

מַא קוּלְתַּנְתּ אַהְל אַלסַבְּתּ. אַנְתּ קוּלְתַּנְתּ אַצְחַאבּ אַלסַבְּתּ.

mā gultant ahl as-sabt. ant gultant aṣḥāb as-sabt.

NEG say:PRF.2SG.M people.CS DEF-Sabbath 2SG.M say:PRF.2SG.M friend.PL.CS DEF-Sabbath

you did not say: "the people of Shabbath". You said: "the companions of Shabbath".

מַא בִּהּ אַצְחַאבּ אַלסַבְּתּ אִלַּא אַלְאַחַד וַאלְגִּמְעַה.

mā bih aṣḥāb as-sabt illā al-aḥad w-al-ğimʕah.

NEG EXIST friend.PL.CS DEF-Sabbath except DEF-Sunday and-DEF-Friday

There are no "companions of Shabbath" except for Sunday and Friday.

דַ׳לְחִין אֲנַא בַּאסִיר מֲכַּאן אַלְיְהוּדִי.

ḏālḥīn tugʕid al-yihūdī, anā bā́-ˌsīr makān al-yihūdī.

now let_stay:IPFV.2SG.M DEF-Jew.SG.M 1SG FUT-go:IPFV.1SG place.CS DEF-Jew.SG.M

Now let the Jew stay, I will go instead to the place of the Jew.

אֲנַא בַּאקוּל אִנֵּהּ אַנְתּ אַלְדִ׳י לְעַנְתּ אַלְכּוּל.

anā bā-ˌgūl inn-ih ant ḏī naʕaltant al-kull.

1SG FUT-say:IPFV.1SG COMP-3SG 2SG.M REL curse:PRF.2SG.M DEF-all

I will say that you are the one who cursed everybody".

בָּלַם דַ׳אעִנְדַּךְ, מַא זִדּ אַדַּא מִלָּה.

bōlam *ḏā-ʕind-ak*[27], *mā* *zid*[28] *addá̄* *millō*
keep_mouth_shut:PRF.3SG.M[HbC] DEM.SG.M-at-2SG.M no more utter:PRF.3SG.M word[HbC]
He kept his mouth shut, you may imagine, he did not utter another word.

הָעִיקָּר הִם סַארוּ. קַאל בִּן נִעְמַהּ,

ha-ikár *him sārū.* *gāl* *Bin-Niʕmah:*
DEF-main_thing[IHb] 3PL go:PRF.3PL.M say:PRF.3SG.M Ibn-Niʕmah
Anyway they left. Ibn-Niʕmah said:

אִסְמַע. רוּח אַלְבְּלַאד חַקַּךְ.

hā[29]‿ *smaʕ!* *rūḥ* *al-bilād* *ḥagg-ak.*
hey listen:IMP.SG.M go:IMP.SG.M DEF-land of-2SG.M
“Listen! Go to your land,

אִצְ׳וִי בְּלַאדַךְ.

iḏwī! *iḏwī* *gāl* *bilād* *Ḏū-Ḥsēn.*
go_home:IMP.SG.M go_home:IMP.SG.M say:PRF.3SG.M land.CS Ḏū-Ḥsēn
go home, go home”, he said, “to the land of Ḏū-Ḥsēn”.

לַקַטְת נַפְסִי וּצֲ׳וֵית. קְעַדְת שָׁבוּעַ.

lagaṭt *nafs-ī* *w-ḏawēt.* *gaʕadt* *šavuaʕ.*
seize:PRF.1SG self-1SG and-go_home:PRF.1SG stay:PRF.1SG week[IHb]
I took myself and went home. I stayed for a week.

סִרְת אֲנַא מָאדַאן. וּבִּהּ רַהְוַהּ בֵּין מָאדַאן וַאלְמִחְתַּוִיַּהּ.

sirt *anā Mṓdān.* *w-bih* *rahwah bēn* *Mṓdān* *w-alMiḥtáwiyyah.*
go:PRF.1SG 1SG Mōdān and-EXIST hill between Mōdān and-alMiḥtawiyyah
I went to Mōdān. And there was a hill between Mōdān and alMiḥtawiyyah.

טְלִעְת אֲנַא פִ׳לְרַהְוַהּ.

ṭiliʕt *anā* *fi-r-rahwah* *tih-ʕind-ak* *aštī* *alMiḥtawíyyah.*
ascend:PRF.1SG 1SG in-DEF-hill DEM.SG.F-at-2SG.M want:IPFV.1SG alMiḥtawiyyah
I went up the hill, you may imagine, heading alMiḥtawiyyah.

תַאְמִין וִן אַלְכַ׳מְסַה עַסְכַּר וַאלשַׁאוִשׁ

taʔamín *w-inn-ih* *al-xamsah* *al-ʕaskar* *w-aš-šāwiš*
believe:IPFV.2SG.M[IHb] and-PSTV-3SG.M DEF-five DEF-soldier.PL and-DEF-officer.SG.M
Believe [me], and suddenly the five soldiers and the officer

27 The construction of *ḏā*+*ʕind*+suffixed pronoun is a device of narrative lively style, by which the narrator strives to enhance his listeners’ involvement by inviting them to imagine a narrated entity as if it were at (*ʕind-*) their end, indeed right in front of their eyes. It is often accompanied by a gesture of the hand, demonstrating or “pointing” at the item referred to. The whole expression may be taken to denote “as you may imagine”. The demonstrative agrees with the referred item, and may be *ḏā* or *ḏih* for the masculine, and *tih* for the feminine (see *tih-ʕindak* with regard to *rahwah* further below in this text). The suffixed pronoun is in agreement with the addressee, namely *-ak* for the masculine and *-iš* for the feminine.

28 For fossilized *zid* see 2.2.1.

29 The presentational particle *hā*(*ʔ/h*) was documented in various Yemeni dialects (Watson and Al-ʕAmri 2000: 21; Shachmon 2014a: 164). It frequently opens direct speech, often following a speech act verb.

דַ'אעִנְדַךְ קוּבַּאלִי. טַאלְעִין

ḏā-ʕind-ak gubāl-ī. ṭā́lʕ-īn
DEM.SG.M-at-2SG.M in_front_of-1SG ascend:PTCP.ACT-PL.M
just imagine, [appeared] in front of me, going up,

יִשְׁתַו מָאדַאן. קָאל

yištaw Mōdā́n. gāl:
want:IPFV.3PL.M Mōdān say:PRF.3SG.M
heading towards Mōdān. He said:

גַ'רִים סַאק בִּהּ כַּרִים,

"ġarīm sāg bi-h karīm"
opponent.SG.M bring:PRF.3SG.M in-3SG.M generous.SG.M
"An opponent, brought by the generous [one]",

יְקוּל אַלשַּׁאוִּש, כְּלוֹמַר אֲנַא עֲדוּוִּהּ

yigūl aš-šāwiš, zotoméret anā ʕadūww-ih
say:IPFV.3SG.m DEF-officer.SG.M that.is[IHb] 1SG enemy.SG.M-3SG.M
the officer said, that is – I am his enemy

וְהוּ יִתְבָּרַךְ אַדַּאנִי יְלַא יַדִּהּ.

w-hū yiṯbōrax addā-nī ilā́ yad-ih.
and-3SG.M be.blessed:IPFV.3SG.M[HbC] bring:PRF.3SG.M-1SG.OBJ to hand-3SG.M
and He, may He be blessed, brought me into his hands.

קוּלְת אִסְמַע יַא שַׁאוִּש.

gult: ismáʕ yā šāwiš.
say:PRF.1SG listen:IMP.SG.M ITJ officer.SG.M
I said: "listen, O officer,

בֵּין יְקוּלוּ אַנְתוּ בֵּית אַלְעֲפוּ.

bēn-yugūlū́ antū bēt al-ʕafū.
PROG-say:IPFV.3PL.M 2PL.M house.CS DEF-forgiveness
they say that you are people of forgiveness.

יְלַא קִד כֻ'רַגַת מִנִּי כַלְמַה וּמַא אעְגְבַתַךְ,

ilā́ gid xarağat minn-i kálmah mā‿ʕğabat-ak,
if ANT get_out:PRF.3SG.F from-1SG word NEG please:PRF.3SG.F-2SG.M
If a word which did not please you had come out of my [mouth],

לַא תְסַוִּי גַהְדַךְ עֲלַא גַאהִל.

lā tsawwī ğahd-ak ʕalā ğāhil.
NEG make:IPFV.2SG.M ability-2SG.M on boy.SG.M
do not make use of your power against a boy".

קַאל וַאחִד מִן אַלְעַסְכַּר, יָכוֹל לִהְיוֹת

gāl wāḥid min al-ʕaskar, yaxól liyót
say:PRF.3SG.M one.SG.M of DEF-soldier.PL be.able:PTCP.ACT.SG.M[IHb] be:INF[IHb]
One of the officers said – he may have been

אִנִּהּ שֵׁיךְ, קַאל אִסְמַע יַא שַׁאוִּש,

inn-ih šēx, gāl: ismáʕ yā šāwiš,
COMP-3SG.M sheikh.SG.M say:PRF.3SG.M listen:IMP.SG.M ITJ officer.SG.M
a sheikh – he said: "listen, O officer,

לַא תְּסַוִּי גַּהְדַּךּ עֲלַא מַסְכִּין, יִרְחַם אַלַּלָּהּ,

lā tsawwī ǧahd-ak ʕalā maskīn, yirḥam aḷḷā́h,

NEG make:IPFV.2SG.M ability-2SG.M on poor.SG.M have_mercy:IPFV.3SG.M God

do not make use of your force against the poor, may God have mercy [on him],

עֲזוֹב אוֹתָנוּ, כַ׳לָּאנַא נִקְצַד אַלַּלָּה,

ʕázov otanu, xallō-nā nigṣad aḷḷā́h,

leave.IMP:SG.M[IHb] OBJ.1PL[IHb] leave:IMP.PL.M-1PL.OBJ worship:IPFV.1PL God

leave us alone, let us serve God,

כַ׳לִּ מִנַּךּ אַלתְּעִרַּאץ׳. מַא זִד אַתְּחַאכַא.

xállī minn-ak at-tiʕirrāḏ̣. mā zid atḥā́kā

let_go:IMP.SG.M from-2SG.M DEF-interference NEG more speak:PRF.3SG.M

stop interfering". He did not speak anymore.

שַׁלֵּית נַפְסִי וַאלְמִחְתַּוִּיַּה.

šallēt nafs-ī w-alMiḥtawiyyah.

take:PRF.1SG self-1SG and-alMiḥtawiyyah.

I took myself [and headed] towards alMiḥtawiyyah.

אֲבָל קִד דַ׳לֵּית אִנִּהּ פִ׳לדַּרַךּ הַאדִ׳ה, טֲרִיק אַלְמִחְתַּוִּיַּה,

avál gid ḏallēt inn-ih fi-l-dārax[30] hāḏih, ṭarīg al-ḥukūmah,

but[IHb] COP fear:PRF.1SG COMP.3SG.M in-DEF-road[HbC] DEM.SG.F road.CS DEF-government

But I have feared that on this road, the government road,

מַא בִּה מִן יְרַאגִּע עֲלַיַּא

mā bih min yirāǧiʕ ʕalay-yā

NEG EXIST someone stand_up:IPFV.3SG.M on-1SG

there would be no one to stand up for me,

וַלַא מִן יְכַ׳רִּגְנִי.

w-lā min yuxriǧ-nī.

and-NEG someone take_out:IPFV.3SG.M-1SG.OBJ

and no one to release me.

3.3 Garīnah

The speaker in text no. 3 is a Jewish woman, born in the 1930s in the village of Sā́gēn in the province of Ṣaʕdah. She immigrated to Israel in 1962 and I recorded her in March 1997 on the porch of her house in Bnei-Ayish. She lives in a neighborhood with many other immigrants from the same area in north Yemen, and has kept using her mother tongue, so that 35 years after her immigration she was still completely fluent in her native Arabic dialect. As soon as we switched to Arabic she only rarely mixed it with elements from modern Israeli Hebrew.

At the same time, Hebrew components that were part of her dialect already in Yemen are frequently used, reflecting the traditional northern pronunciation of *lašön haggṓḏaš* 'the sacred language'. The pronunciation of the word *ǧēy* (Hebrew גּוֹי 'gentile'), occuring twice in this text, demonstrates the realization of Hebrew *ḥolem* as *ē*, typical of the speech of Jewish women in Ṣanʕā and the north, as opposed to *ö* which is

30 For the pronunciation of Hebrew *seghol* in open stressed syllables see 2.1.4.

the common pronunciation of *ḥolem* in these communities (2.1.4 above).[31] Also noticeable is the use of plosive *b* instead of the fricative *v* in the Hebrew form *habdōlō* 'havdalah', which is also characteristic of the speech of Jewish women (2.1.2).

The narrative deals with Garīnah, an Arabian female demon that somewhat reminds of the Succubus in other mythologies. This demon is said to have exercised a dominating place in popular Islam, but in Yemen the belief in it was apparently widespread among Jews as well. It is believed to assume the shape of various household animals, or to enter a person's body as he sleeps or dreams.

The belief in demons and ghosts prevailed among the Jews of Yemen, particularly those living in rural areas (Ben-David 2005). Many believed that demons lurk them along the mountainous roads, while other demons awaited people inside their houses. As demonstrated in this text, illness was often attributed to a specific demon which entered the ill person's body, and the way to cure him was to "negotiate" the demon's departure and to get its commitment to never come back.[32]

Fieldwork with the author of the story

gaʕátt,	*(i)lā*	*yōm*	*áḥad*	*ab-ī́*	*sáwwag,*
spend-time:PRF.1SG	until	day	one	father-1SG	go_to_the_market:PRF.3SG.M

Time passed [for me], until one day my father went to the market,

yiddī́	*wāḥid*	*yatīm,*	*wald*	*yatīm,*
bring:IPFV.3SG.M	one.SG.M	orphan.SG.M	boy	orphan.SG.M

brought an orphan, an orphan boy,

ḏawwā-h	*al-bēt*	*ʕind-^{a}nā.*
bring.home:PRF.3SG.M-3SG	DEF-house	at-1PL

he brought him to our house.

31 It is however noteworthy, that in this specific word I hear *ē* from northern men as well.

32 The negotiation over the demon's departures echoes Rabbinic traditions in which the soul of Moses negotiates its departure from his body (Lierman 2004: 205). Muslim popular tradition provides a remarkably similar story in which *Nabi Mūsa* refuses to let his soul departure through his mouth, his eyes, his ears, his hands or his legs (Itzchaki 1988,1: 61). Another Yemeni version of this story was documented by Ben-David, with a jinni who possesses a Jewish woman and then negotiates the body part through which it shall leave her body (Ben-David 2005: 105).

wuṣil	*ʕind-^{a}nā*	*f-al-bēt,*
arrive:PRF.3SG.M	at-1PL	in-DEF-house

He came to us, to the house,

gāl:	*bā-yugʕud*	*ind-^{a}nā,*	*níddī-l-ih*	*úkul*
say:PRF.3SG.m	fut-remain:IPFV.3SG.M	at-1PL	give:IPFV.1PL-to-3SG.M	food

he said: he shall stay at our [house], we will give him food

w-yištáġal	*w-yugʕud*	*ʕind-^{a}nā.*
and-work:IPFV.3SG.M	and-remain:IPFV.3SG.M	at-1PL

and he will work and stay with us.

gaʕád	*wagt,*
spend-time:PRF.3SG.M	time

He stayed for some time

w-lā	*darēna,*	*illā*	*w-huwwa*	*bēn-yintafaḏ̣*
and-NEG	know:PRF.1PL	but	and-3SG	PROG-shiver:IPFV.3SG.M

and we have not noticed, but there was he shivering,

bēn-yintafaḏ̣,	*w-bēn-yugʕud*	*galīlah,*
PROG-shiver:IPFV.3SG.M	and-PROG-remain:IPFV.3SG.M	little

he was shivering, and continued [like that] for a while,

w-gām	*tbaxyar*[33].	*w-sār*	*yištaġal,*
and-get.up:PRF.3SG.M	recover:PRF.3SG.M	and-become:PRF.3SG.M	work:IPFV.3SG.M

and he got up and recovered. And he started to work,

w-addā́-l-ih	*áb-ī*	*šaġal,*	*w-yākul*	*maʕ-nā,*
and-give:PRF.3SG.M-to-3SG.M	father-1SG	work	and-eat:IPFV.3SG.M	with-1PL

and my father gave him work [to do], and he would eat with us,

w-nsawwī	*kull*	*aš-šaġal,*	*ḥā́ǧ-āt-nā*	*w-al-kull.*
and-do:IPFV.3SG.M	all.CS	DEF-work	thing.PL.F-1PL	and-DEF-all

and we would do all the work, our things, and everything.

w-gaʕád	*yōm*	*aḥad*
and-remain:PRF.3SG.M	day	one

He remained [like this] for one day,

w-gaʕád	*t̲amān*	*ayyām*	*w-máraḏ̣,*
and-remain:PRF.3SG.M	eight	day.PL	and-become_ill:PRF.3SG.M

and he remained [like this] for eight days, then he became ill,

33 Several verbs derive from the denominative roots *bxr* and *bxyr* (Piamenta 1990: 21). The form בְּכֵ״יְרִין *bxḗrīn* 'well (SG.M)' combines the particle *bi* 'in' and the adjective *xēr* 'good', which have been completely grammaticalized to from the adjective: *bxēr* SG. *bxērīn* (Shachmon 2017b).

w-mā bēn-yugʕud xērāt. ǧális ʕind-^{a}nā xērāt
and-NEG PROG-spend-time:IPFV.3SG.M much stay:PRF.3SG.M at-1PL much
and he did not remain [healthy] for long. He stayed at our [house] for a long time.

kull al-wagt, mā ǧā l-al-wagt kuṯír.
all.CS DEF-time REL come:PRF.3SG.M to-DEF-time intensify:PRF.3SG.M
all the time, as time passed, it became worse.

yōm áḥad hayá xarǧat šabbōṯ
day one be:PRF.3SG.M^{IHb} departure.CS Sabbath^{HbC}
One day, it was Saturday evening,

iḥnā gāʕd-īn yištō yisabbrū habdōlō,
1PL sit:PTCP.ACT-PL.M want:IPFV.3PL.M do:IPFV.3PL.M Havdalah^{HbC}
we were sitting, they intended to make Havdalah,

w-al-wald anǧaḥ yiṣallī w-ragád.
and-DEF-boy finish:PRF.3SG.M pray:IPFV.3SG.M and-sleep:PRF.3SG.M
and the boy finished praying and went to sleep.

nidahhin-ih, ^{i}ndahhin-ih, ^{i}ndahhin-ih,
wake_up:IPFV.1PL-3SG.M wake_up:IPFV.1PL-3SG.M wake_up:IPFV.1PL-3SG.M
We [were trying] to wake him up, trying and trying,

wa-lā ʕa-kalmah wa-lā ḥāǧah. māt bēn yad-ē-nā.
and-NEG on-word and-NEG thing die:PRF.3SG.M between hand-DU.CS-1PL
and he did not [utter] a word, not a thing. He was dying in our hands.

wēš ^{i}nsāwwī? wēš ^{i}nsāwwī? wēš ^{i}nsāwwī?
what do:IPFV.1PL what do:IPFV.1PL what do:IPFV.1PL
What shall we do? what shall we do? what shall we do?

m-iḥnā dārī-n inn mʕi-h Garīnah.
NEG-1PL know:PTCP.ACT-SG.M COMP with-3SG.M Qarina
We did not know that [the she-demon] Qarina is within him.

gāl áb-ī: sīrī yā bint-ī,
say:PRF.3SG.M father-1SG go:IMP.SG.F ITJ daughter-1SG
My father said: "Go, my daughter,

idʕē al-ǧēy. sirt, mā-hū baʕīd.
call:IMP.SG.F DEF-gentile^{HbC} go:PRF.1SG NEG-3SG.M far.away
call the gentile." I went, it was not far away.

dʕēt-l-ih, gult: yā ǧār, taʕāl ʕalē-nā.
call:PRF.1sg-to-3SG.M say:PRF.1SG ITJ neighbor.SG.M come:IMP.SG.M at-1PL
I called him, I said: “O neighbor, come to our house.”

wēš bidd-iš? gult: gāl ab-ī
what want-2SG.F say:PRF.1SG say:PRF.3SG.M father-1SG
“What do you want?” I said: “My father said

inn-ak tiǧī́ w-tiddī́ al-xitmah ḥággat-ak,
COMP-2SG.M come:IPFV.2SG.M and-bring:IPFV.2SG.M DEF-Qurʔān of-2SG.M
that you should come and bring your [copy of the] Qurʔān,

al-xitmah mʕā-k. gāl nā́hī. ǧā wuṣil,
DEF-Qurʔān with-2SG.M say:PRF.3SG.M all.right come:PRF.3SG.M arrive:PRF.3SG.M
[bring] the Qurʔān with you.” He said: “All right.” He came, arrived,

yidahhn-ih yidahhn-ih wa-lā́ šī.
wake.up:IPFV.3SG.M-3SG.M wake.up:IPFV.3SG.M-3SG.M and-NEG thing
he woke him up, woke him up, and nothing.

gāl iddō-l-ī xar klāb,
say:PRF.3SG.M bring:IMP.SG.M-to-1SG feces.CS dog.PL
He said: “Bring me dog feces,

iddō-l-ī mirr iddō-l-ī ṣábir, íʕilgū-l-ī nār.
bring:IMP.PL-to-1SG myrrh bring:IMP.PL-to-1SG aloe light:IMP.PL-to-1SG fire
bring me myrrh, bring me aloe, light me a fire.”

umm-ī gāmat tiʕlig ʕala n-nār
mother-1SG stand up:PRF.3SG.F light:IPFV.3SG.F on DEF-fire
My mother stood up to kindle the fire,

w-áddit-ih. w-illā mānā gid bēn-antafaḍ.
and-bring:PRF.3SG.F-3SG.M and-except NEG.1SG COP PROG-shiver:IPFV.1SG
and she brought it, and there I was shivering,

bēn-abkī́ w-bēn-antafaḍ. gid bēn-aḏill.
PROG-cry:IPFV.1SG and-PROG-shiver:IPFV.1SG COP PROG-fear:IPFV.1SG
I was crying and shivering. I was afraid.

w-huwwa gid huwwa kaḏē, bēn-yintafaḍ bēn-yintafaḍ.
and-3SG.M COP 3SG.M this.way PROG-shiver:IPFV.3SG.M PROG-shiver:IPFV.3SG.M
and he was like that, shivering and shivering.

dʕēnā wāḥid ǧēy w-wāḥid yihūdī,
call:PRF.1PL one.SG.M gentile.SG.M[HbC] and-one.SG.M Jew.SG.M
We called one gentile and one Jew,

w-gʕad wāḥid rāzim ʕalā rās-ih
and-sit:PRF.3SG.M one.SG.M hold:PTCP.ACT.SG.M on head-3SG.M
and one sat holding his head

w-wāḥid rāzim ʕalā riǧl-ih.
and-one.SG.M hold:PTCP.ACT.SG.M on leg-3SG.M
and one holding his leg.

w-al-gēy ṭáraḥ al-xitmah ḥaggat-ih ʕala šigg al-madkah,
and-DEF-gentile.SG.M put:PRF.3SG.M DEF-Qurʔān of.SG.F-3SG.M on side DEF-cushion
And the gentile put his Qurʔān at the end of the cushion,

w-hū mā b-illā bēn-yirā, yištī
and-3SG.M NEG EXIST-except PROG-see:IPFV.3SG.M want:IPFV.3SG.M
and as soon as he saw [the Qurʔān] he wanted

yuṭmur yišill al-xitmah w-ygudd-^{a}hā.
jump:IPFV.3SG.M take:IPFV.3SG.M DEF-Qurʔān and-shred:IPFV.3SG.M-3SG.F
to jump, to take the Qurʔān and shred it.

tēk as-sāʕah hū xállā al-xitmah,
DEM.SG.F DEF-hour 3SG.M leave:PRF.3SG.M DEF-Qurʔān
At that moment he put the Qurʔān down,

fatáḥ-hā al-ğēy gāl
open:PRF.3SG.M-3SG.F DEF-gentile.SG.M^{HbC} say:PRF.3SG.M
the gentile opened it and said:

uxriğ yā malʕū́n
get_out:IMP.SG.M ITJ curse:PTCP.PASS.SG.M
"Get out, damned you!

wēš ant tsawwī fi-hāḏā‿ l-yihūdī
what 2SG.M do:IPFV.2SG.M in-DEM.SG.M DEF-Jew.SG.M
What are you doing inside this Jew?"

gāl: mā́nā xāriğ.
say:PRF.3SG.M NEG.1SG go_out:PTCP.ACT.SG.M
He said: "I am not going out."

gāl: w-aḷḷāh-ī ‿nn tuxriğ.
say:PRF.3SG.M by-God-GEN indeed get_out:IPFV.2SG.M
He said: "By God, get out."

ʕalagat umm-ī an-nār,
light:PRF.3SG.F mother-1SG DEF-fire
My mother lit the fire,

ṭaraḥat-ih w-hū tšaṭṭā kṯīr,
put:PRF.3SG.F-3SG.M and-3SG.M go_wild:PRF.3SG.M^{HbC} much
she put it and he really went wild,

w-bēn-yafriyaʕ w-yitlaḥém b-ʕáṣm-ih,
and-PROG-go_wild:IPFV.3SG.M^{IHb} and-struggle:IPFV.3SG.M^{MxC} in-self-3SG.M^{MxC}
and he went wild and was struggling with himself,

avál hem yígbaḏ̣ū-h. wēš sawwā?
but^{IHb} 3PL.M^{IHb} grasp:IPFV.3PL.M-3SG.M what do:PRF.3SG.M
but they were holding him. What did he do?

šall ar-rawāḥil, ar-rawāḥil hā, w-ṭabx[34] *fi-wağh-ih*
take:PRF.3SG.M DEF-shoe.PL DEF-shoe.PL ha and-hit:PRF.3SG.M in-face-3SG.M
He took the shoes, the shoes, here, and he hit his face

w-hū yiṣīḥ, yiṭbax fi-wağh-ih,
and-3SG.M scream:IPFV.3SG.M beat:IPFV.3SG.M in-face-3SG.M
and he was screaming, beating his face,

yiṭbax yíṭbax yíṭbax yíṭbax
beat:IPFV.3SG.M beat:IPFV.3SG.M beat:IPFV.3SG.M beat:IPFV.3SG.M
beating, beating, beating, beating,

w-hū yiṣīḥ w-hū yiṣīḥ.
and-3SG.M scream:IPFV.3SG.M and-3SG.M scream:IPFV.3SG.M
and he was screaming and screaming.

gāl: uxriğ yā malʕū́n
say:PRF.3SG.M get_out:IMP.SG.M ITJ curse:PTCP.PASS.SG.M
He said: "Get out, damned you,

uxriğ min hāḏā‿ l-yihūdī, mā b-illā yatīm
get.out:IMP.SG.M from DEM.SG.M DEF-Jew.SG.M NEG EXIST-except orphan.SG.M
get out of this Jew, he is just an orphan.

lā mʕ-ih umm w-lā mʕ-ih abb w-lā mʕ-ih axwah.
NEG with-3SG.M mother and-NEG with-3SG.M father and-NEG with-3SG.M brother.PL
He has no mother, he has no father and he has no siblings.

mā b-illā ... yirḥim aḷḷā́h uxriğ minn-ih!
NEG EXIST-except have_mercy:IPFV.3SG.M God get_out:IMP.SG.M from-3SG.M
Just ... may God have mercy [on him], get out of him!"

34 Plausibly a blend of *ṭaxx* and *ṭabaḥ*, which both bear the meaning of hitting and striking.

gāl: inn-ih ḏī daʕā-nī. inn-ih daʕā-nī.
say:PRF.3SG.M indeed-3SG.M REL call:PRF.3SG.M-1SG.OBJ indeed-3SG.M call:PRF.3SG.M-1SG.OBJ
He said: "He is the one who called for me. He called for me."

gāl: wēn daʕā-k?
say:PRF.3SG.M where call:PRF.3SG.M-2SG.M
He said: "Where did he call you from?"

gāl: daʕā-nī min ǧabal Nugúm[35].
say:PRF.3SG.M call:PRF.3SG.M-1SG.OBJ from mountain Nuqm
He said: "He called for me from Mount Nuqm."

gāl: ʕind aḷḷā́h w-ʕind-ak uxriǧ minn-ih!
say:PRF.3SG.M at God and-at-2SG.M get_out:IMP.SG.M from-3SG.M
He said: "By God, get out of him!"

gāl: anā bā-xruǧ minn-ih
say:PRF.3SG.M 1SG FUT-get_out:IPFV.1SG from-3SG.M
He said: "I will get out of him."

gāl: ʕā́hid-nī bi-llāh inn mā tʔūd-ih
say:PRF.3SG.M swear:IMP.SG.M-1SG.OBJ by-God COMP NEG weigh_down:IPFV.2SG.M-3SG.M
He said: "Swear to me by God that you will not weigh him down

wa-lā́ tirǧaʕ fī-h. gāl: miʕāhid l-ak.
and-NEG come_back:IPFV.2SG.M in-3SG.M say:PRF.3SG.M swear:act.PTCP.ACT.SG.M to-2SG.M
and you and [that you] will not come back inside him." He said: "I swear to you."

gāl: minn-ēn bā-tuxriǧ?
say:PRF.3SG.M from-where FUT-get out:IPFV.2SG.M
He said: "Where will you get out from?"

gāl bā-yuxriǧ min ʕēn-ih.
say:PRF.3SG.M FUT-get_out:IPFV.3SG.M from eye-3SG.M
He said he would get out through his eye.

gāl: lā, mā tuxriǧ min ʕēn-ih.
say:PRF.3SG.M NEG NEG get_out:IPFV.2SG.M from eye-3SG.M
He said: "No, do not get out through his eye."

gāl: bā-tuxriǧ min riǧl-ih.
say:PRF.3SG.M FUT-get_out:IPFV.2SG.M from leg-3SG.M
He said: "You will get out through his leg."

35 A mountain east of Ṣanʕāʔ.

gāl:	*lā.*	*gāl*	*bā-yuxriğ*	*mir-rās-ih.*
say:PRF.3SG.M	NEG	say:PRF.3SG.M	FUT-get_out:IPFV.3SG.M	from-head-3SG.M

He said: “No.” He said he would get out through his head.

gāl:	*lā.*	*gāl:*	*bā-yuxriğ*	*min ligf-ih.*
say:PRF.3SG.M	NEG	say:PRF.3SG.M	FUT-get_out:IPFV.3SG.M	from mouth-3SG.M

He said: “No.” He said he would get out through his mouth.

gāl:	*lā.*	*gāl:*	*bā-ṭraḥ-l-ak*	*sī́mān,*
say:PRF.3SG.M	NEG	say:PRF.3SG.M	FUT-put:IPFV.1sg-to-2SG.M	sign[HbC]

He said: “No.” He said: “I will leave a sign for you,

w-amallī-l-ak	*al-kos*	*mayyim*	*fi-l-lahğ,*
and-fill:IPFV.1SG-to-2SG.M	DEF-glass[IHb]	water[IHb]	in-DEF-window

and I will fill the glass with water for you [and put it] at the window,

w-al-ʔamāryah:	*ṣubb*	*al-mā*	*wa-lā́*	*tiksir*	*al-finğā́l.*
and-DEF-sign	pour:IMP.SG.M	DEF-water	and-NEG	break:IPFV.2SG.M	DEF-glass

and the sign [would be]: pour the water without breaking the glass.”

ʕāhad-ih	*bi-llāh*	*avāl*	*gid*	*ṭabaḥ-ih*
swear:PRF.3SG.M-3SG.M	by-God	but[IHb]	COP	beat:PRF.3SG.M-3SG.M

He swore to him by God, but he still beat him,

ṭabaḥ-ih	*w-ḏā.*
beat:PRF.3SG.M-3SG.M	and-DEM.SG.M

he beat him and so.

w-huwwa	*mā*	*rā*	*al-mā*	*la-ḥīn*	*aṣṭabb*
and-3SG.M	as	see:PRF.3SG.M	DEF-water	to-time	be_poured:PRF.3SG.M

And as soon as he saw that the water had been poured

w-aš-šēḏ	*xárağ*	*minn-ih*
and-DEF-demon[HbC]	get_out:PRF.3SG.M	from-3SG.M

the demon got out of him.

hū	*šēḏ*	*ḏī*	*fi-ğōf*	*al-wald,*	*aš-šēḏ*	*fi-ğōf*	*al-wald.*
3SG.M	demon[HbC]	REL	in-interior.CS	DEF-boy	DEF-demon[HbC]	in-interior.CS	DEF-boy

This is a demon inside the boy, the demon is inside the boy.

w-huwwa	*la-ḥīn*	*aṣṭabb*	*al-mā,*	*aṣṭabb*	*al-mā*
and-3SG.M	to-time	be_poured:PRF.3SG.M	DEF-water	be_poured:PRF.3SG.M	DEF-water

And as soon as the water was poured, the water was poured,

hū xarağ. hū xarağ.
3SG.M get_out:PRF.3SG.M 3SG.M get_out:PRF.3SG.M
he got out. He got out.

illā huwwa ḥīn hitḥīl fataḥ ʕiyūn-ih,
PSTV 3SG.M time begin:PRF.3SG.M[IHb] open:PRF.3SG.M eye.PL-3SG.M
And here, as he began to open his eyes,

w-him fállatū-h. kān nugūl-l-ih: Saʕd,
and-3PL let_go:PRF.3PL-3SG.M be:PRF.3SG.M say:IPFV.1PL-to-3SG.M Saʕd
they let go of him. We were calling him: "Saʕd!"

ism-ih Saʕd, ism al-wald Saʕd.
name-3SG.M Saʕd name.CS DEF-boy Saʕd
His name is Saʕd, the boy's name is Saʕd.

kān yigūl-l-ih ab-ī: Saʕd wēš mā-l-ak
be:PRF.3SG.M say:IPFV.3SG.M-TO-3SG.M father-1SG Saʕd what what-to-2SG.M
My father was saying to him: "Saʕd, what is it with you?

wēš mā-l-ak ya-bā? hā-gum ^{i}tgambas
what what-to-2SG.M ITJ-father ITJ-get_up:IMP.SG.M sit:IMP.SG.M
what is it with you, dear? Come on, get up and sit,

wēš mā-l-ak? gāl: wēš mā-l-i? yā ʕamm Sālim
what what-to-2SG.M say:PRF.3SG.M what what-to-1SG ITJ uncle Sālim
what is it with you?" He said: "What is it with me? Uncle Sālim,

wēš sawwēt? gāl: wēš mā-l-ak wēš mā-l-ak?
what do:PRF.1SG say:PRF.3SG.M what what-to-2SG.M what what-to-2SG.M
what did I do?" He said: "What is it with you? what is it with you?

yā walad-ī ant fağaʕt-^{a}nā. wēš mā-l-ak?
ITJ boy-1SG 2SG.M scare:PRF.2SG.M-1PL.OBJ what what-to-2SG.M
My boy, you scared us. What do you have?

wēš bēn-yūğʕa-k? gāl mā l-ī ḥāğah.
what PROG-hurt:IPFV.3SG.M-2SG.M say:PRF.3SG.M NEG to-1SG thing
What hurts you?" He said: "I do not have anything,

mānā dārī šī, anā rāgid, mā sawwēt šī
NEG.1SG know:PTCP.ACT.SG.M thing 1SG sleep:PTCP.ACT.SG.M NEG do:PRF.1SG thing
I do not know anything, I was sleeping, I did not do anything."

3.4 A Crooked Heel

The speaker of text 4 was born in 1942 in Ṣanʕāʔ and immigrated to Israel in 1949.[36] The text recounts his memories as a young boy in Yemen, when – just before a family celebration – he hurt his leg and was given different kinds of popular treatment. By this, the readers (and listeners) get a glimpse into the excitement accompanying the preparations for a Jewish wedding, as experienced from the point of view of a child. One also learns of the fear and uneasiness which characterized life in central Yemen, where – among other restrictions – Jews were only allowed to ride sidesaddle, and not in the ordinary fashion.

Various distinctive traits of Jewish Ṣanʕānī become apparent through this text, most prominent among which are the raising of final *ā* to *ē* in all positions (2.1.3), as well as the characteristic suffixed pronouns *-ič* and *-oh* (2.2.2 above).

tištay aḥā́z-īč mā wugáʕ-l-ī
want:IPFV.2SG.F tell:IPFV.1SG-2SG.F what happen:PRF.3SG.M-to-1SG
Would you like me to tell you what happened to me

ḥīn kunt ğāhil fi-Ṣánʕā, fi-l-yamán?
when be:PRF.1SG boy.SG.M in-Ṣanʕāʔ in-DEF-Yemen
when I was a kid, in Ṣanʕāʔ, in Yemen?

iḥnḗ kunnḗ fi-bayt[37] *sī́d-ī …*
1PL be:PRF.1PL in-house grandfather-1SG
We were in the house of my grandfather …

ánē[38] *kunt ğāhil yumkín ibn xams sitt sinīn.*
1SG be:PRF.1SG boy.SG.M be_possible:IPFV.3SG.M aged.CS five six year.PL
I was a kid, maybe five [or] six years old.

kunt álʕab maʕ al-ʕiyāl nāzil.
be:PRF.1SG play:IPFV.1SG with DEF-child.PL below
I used to play with the kids down [on the street].

w-yawm wāḥid aʕtāsat riğl-ī, w-al-ʕirgūb iʕtáwağ.[39]
and-day one.SG.M be.sprained:PRF.3SG.F leg-1SG and-DEF-heel twist:PRF.3SG.M
And one day my ankle was sprained, and [my] heel became crooked.

36 The text was recorded in Jerusalem in 2011 by the informant's niece Ms. Smadar Gilad, who also prepared a first draft of the transcript. I am grateful to both of them for approving the publication of this text.

37 The diphthong *ay* is maintained, as regular in this dialect, yet in this case it is clearly raised and realized as [ey], see 2.1.3.

38 Despite the resemblance to Israeli Hebrew *aní,* my impression is that *ánē* (on occasion also *ánī*) is a genuine dialectal form.

39 Note that the root *ʕwj* is conjugated here as a sound verb in measure VIII.

kān buh waḥad-íh, kān yugūlū́-l-hē
be:PRF.3SG.M EXIST one-SG.F be:PRF.3SG.M call:IPFV.3PL.M-to-3SG.F
There was one [woman], they used to called her

marat aṭ-ṭāṣī. tiʕrif timsíd ... w-yiddaw-hḗ.
wife.CS aṭ-Ṭāṣī know:IPFV.3SG.F massage:IPFV.3SG.F and-bring:IPFV.3PL.M-3SG.F
aṭ-Ṭāṣī's wife. She knows how to give a massage, they bring her [injuries to treat].

(a)bsarat-nī zġīr sāʕ d̲ayyē yābis ...
see:PRF.3SG.F-1SG little.SG.M like DEICT dry.SG.M
She saw that I was small, like that, dried up ...

másadat másadat másadat
massage:PRF.3SG.F massage:PRF.3SG.F massage:PRF.3SG.F
She massaged, massaged, massaged

w-ṭuluʕat fawg ʕurgūb ríǧl-ī ... yō!
and-get.up:PRF.3SG.F above heel.CS leg-1SG yo
and she went up on the heel of my leg … yo!

baʕd yawm yawm-ayn warramat riǧl-ī.
after day day-DU swell:PRF.3SG.F leg-1SG
After a day [or] two my leg swelled up.

warramat warramat warramat
swell:PRF.3SG.F swell:PRF.3SG.F swell:PRF.3SG.F
It swelled [and] swelled [and] swelled up

(i)lā wugaʕat manfūx-ih. w-ánē kull-ī ḥúmmēʔ, marīḏ!
until happen:PRF.3SG.F swell:PTCP.PASS-SG.F and-1SG all-1SG fever sick.SG.M
until it became swollen. And I was totally feverish, sick!

mā‿start axṭā́ w-lā́ agūm
NEG be_able:PRF.1SG walk:IPFV.1SG and-NEG get_up:IPFV.1SG
I could not walk or get up

w-lā́ ākúl w-lā́ ašráb.
and-NEG eat:IPFV.1SG and-NEG drink:IPFV.1SG
and [I could] not eat and not drink.

fi-hā́d̲āk al-wagt kān ax-ī́ Raḥamī́m
in-DEM.SG.M DEF-time be:PRF.3SG.M brother-1SG Raḥamim
In that time my brother Raḥamim

gad kān a-yitzawwaǧ bint al-ʕizayyrī, Brāxa,
ANT be:PRF.3SG.M FUT-marry:IPFV.3SG.M daughter.CS al-ʕizayyrī Brāxa
was about to get married to alʕizayyrī's daughter, Brāxa,

w-ftağaʕū́	*lā*	*yūgaʕ*	*fī-nī*	*šī*
and-worry:PRF.3PL.M	NEG	happen:IPFV.3SG.M	in-1SG	thing

and they were afraid that something might happen to me

w-al-ʕiris	*yirīḥ-l-oh.*	*az*	*abū-hē,*	*abū*	*Brāxa,*
and-DEF-wedding	go:IPFV.3SG.M-to-3SG.M	then[IHb]	father-3SG.F	father.CS	Brāxa

and the wedding will be gone. Then her father, Brāxa's father,

hū	*kān*	*kabīr,*	*ṭawīl,*	*ḥazág.*
3SG.M	be:PRF.3SG.M	big.SG.M	tall.SG.M	strong.SG.M[IHb]

he was a big, tall, strong [man].

hum	*ğazzā́rīn,*	*ğazzā́rīn,*	*yiʕrifū́*	*kayf*	*yiḏbaḥū́.*
3PL	butcher.PL.M	butcher.PL.M	know:IPFV.3PL.M	how	slaughter:IPFV.3PL.M

They are butchers, butchers, they know how to slaughter.

az ...	*ğē*	*la-ʕind-ī*	*gāl*	*lu-húm*	*yišbaḥū-nī*
then[IHb]	come:PRF.3SG.M	to-at-1SG	say:PRF.3SG.M	to-3.PL	seize:IPFV.3PL.M-1SG

So… he came to me [and] told them to hold me,

w-xazág	*arğil-ī.*	*tubsurī*	*xizgān,*	*haḏáwlē?*
and-make.incision:PRF.3SG.M	leg.PL-1SG	see:IPFV.2SG.F	incision.PL	DEM.PL

and he made an incision in my legs. Do you see incisions, these ones?

gad	*kān*	*kull-oh,*	*riğl-ī,*	*ilā*	*hināyē*	*kān*	*kull-oh*	*middih.*
ANT	be:PRF.3SG.M	all-3SG.M	leg-1SG	until	here	be:PRF.3SG.M	all-3SG.M	pus

All of it, my leg, up until here, was all [full of] pus.

baʕd	*mā*	*xazág*	*ṭaraḥū́*	*šalāyil,*
after	REL	make_incision:PRF.3SG.M	put:PRF.3PL.M	rag.PL

After he made an incision they put rags,

axráğ	*kull*	*al-middih*	*allī*	*kānat*	*fi-riğl-ī.*
take_out:PRF.3SG.M	all.CS	DEF-pus	REL	be:PRF.3SG.F	in-leg-1SG

he took out all of the pus that was in my leg.

rikinū	*gad-(h)ū́*[40]	*malīḥ.*
think:PRF.3PL.M	COP-3SG.M	good.SG.M

They thought that it was OK.

baʕd	*ṯalāṯ*	*arbaʕ*	*ayyām*	*badaʕat*[41]	*riğl-ī*	*tibás.*
after	three	four	day.PL	begin:PRF.3SG.F	leg-1SG	be_dry:IPFV.3SG.F

After three [or] four days my leg began to dry,

40 For the silent *h* see 2.1.1.

41 For the shift of OA *ʔ* to *ʕ* see 2.1.1.

yíbisat,	*hā́kadē.*	*w-ḥúmmē.*	*kull-oh*	*šūʕih*[42]*,*	*mā*	*kān-š*	*ʕīs.*
be_dry:PRF.3SG.F	like.this	and-fever	all-3SG.M	bad_smell	NEG	be:PRF.3SG.M-NEG	good

it became dry, like this. And fever, it all smelled bad, it was not good.

gālū:	*buh*	*gabīlī*	*ʕind*	*al-míslimīn,*
say:PRF.3PL.M	EXIST	tribesman.SG	at	DEF-Muslim.PL.M

They said: there is a tribesman among the Muslims,

nisīr	*la-ʕind-oh*	*w-hū*	*yiʕríf*	*yimsíd*	*malīḥ,*
go:IPFV.1PL	to-at-3SG.M	and-3SG.M	know:IPFV.3SG.M	massage:IPFV.3SG.M	well

let us go to him, he knows how to massage well,

w-kull-oh	*yūgaʕ*	*ʕīs.*
and-all-3SG.M	happen:IPFV.3SG.M	good

and everything will be all right.

šallawnī[43]	*fawg*	*ḥimār,*[44]	*ṭuluʕnā*	*(i)lā*	*Ṣanʕā́.*
take:PRF.3PL.M-1SG	above	donkey	ascend:PRF.1PL	to	Ṣanʕāʔ

They took me on a donkey, we ascended to Ṣanʕāʔ.

fi-ṭ-ṭarīg[45]*,*	*mā*	*dirīt*	*w-gad-(h)ī*	*ḥiǧār*	*fawg*	*ḏahr-ī,*
in-DEF-way	NEG	know:PRF.1SG	and-COP-3SG.F	stone.PL	above	back-1SG

On the way, I did not [even] notice and there were stones [thrown] over my back,

b-yraǧǧimū́	*al-gabāyil.*	*lílmē?*
PROG-stone:IPFV.3PL.M	DEF-tribesman.PL	why

The tribesmen were throwing [stones]. Why?

mā	*yūgáʕ-š*	*inn*	*al-yihūdī*	*yiṭlaʕ*	*fawg*	*al-ḥimār*
NEG	happen:IPFV.3SG.M-NEG	COMP	DEF-Jew.SG.M	ascend:IPFV.3SG.M	above	DEF-donkey

It must not be that a Jew rides a donkey

maʕ	*arǧil-oh*	*ʕala*	*š-šígg-ayn.*[46]
with	leg.PL-3SG.M	on	DEF-side-DU

with his legs on both sides.

w-anē	*ǧāhil,*	*marīḏ.*	*mā*	*ʕād-anē-š*[47]	*ḏākir*
and-1SG	boy.SG.M	sick.SG.M	NEG	still-1SG-NEG	remember:PTCP.ACT.SG.M

And I was [just] a child, sick. I no longer remember

42 For the *ʔimāla* of the feminine ending even when preceded by a guttural see 2.2.3.

43 The diphthong *aw* is realized here as [ow], see 2.1.3.

44 *ḥimār* is pronounced with a glottal closure, viz. [ḥimāʔr], see 2.1.1.

45 *ṭ-ṭarīg* is pronounced with final devoicing and glottalization, viz. [ṭṭarīg̥ʔ], see 2.1.1.

46 The diphthong *ay* is realized here as [ey], see 2.1.3..

47 For *ʕād* taking the independent pronoun as a suffix, see 2.2.2.

mā fiʕíl-l-ī al-mislim hā́ḏē.
what do:PRF.3SG.M-to-1SG DEF-Muslim.SG.M DEM.SG.M
what this Muslim did to me.

raddū-nī ílā l-bayt. ğilist marīḏ
take_back:PRF.3PL.M-1SG.OBJ to DEF-house remain:PRF.1SG sick.SG.M
They took me back to the house. I remained sick

min yawm ilā́ yawm ášwaʕ.
from day to day bad.CPTV
day by day it got worse.

baʕd kam ayyām (a)bsarū́ inn hāḏḗ miš hū malīḥ.
after some day.PL see:PRF.3PL.M COMP DEM.SG.M NEG 3SG.M good.SG.M
Some days later they saw that this was not good.

kān buh fi-lyamán xást-xānih. fi-l-xást-xānih hāḏḗ
be:PRF.3SG.M EXIST in-DEF-Yemen hospital in-DEF-hospital DEM.SG.M
There was in Yemen a hospital. In this hospital

kān ṭabīb, ḥākim ...
be:PRF.3SG.M doctor.SG.M physician.SG.M
there was a doctor, a physician,

yímkin inn-(h)ū[48] italkí. (a)bsár-nī,
be_possible:IPFV.3SG.M COMP-3SG.M Italian.SG.M[IHB] see:PRF.3SG.M-1SG.OBJ
he may have been Italian. He saw me,

(a)bsár riğl-ī, ma-ddā-l-ī šī, duwḗ.
see:PRF.3SG.M leg-1SG NEG-give:PRF.3SG.M-to-1SG thing medicine
he saw my leg, he gave me nothing, [no] medicine.

hā́kaḏā anē ḏākir, kēn? az... nšill-oh…
like.this 1SG remember:PTCP.ACT.SG.M yes[IHb] then[IHb] take:IPFV.1PL-3SG.M
This is what I remember, OK? So … we should take him …

lāzim asīr kull yawm al-ḥammā́m. ḥammām.
necessary go:IPFV.1SG every.CS day DEF-bathhouse bathhouse
I should to go every day to the bathhouse. Bathhouse.

gad kunt ... kān áwwal šī yišillū-nī
ANT be:PRF.1SG be:PRF.3SG.M first thing take:IPFV.3PL.M-1SG
I have been … at first they used to carry me

48 For *inn* taking the independent pronouns as a suffix see 2.2.2. For the silent *h* see 2.1.1.

la-l-ḥammām, w-baʕd kam ayyām
to-DEF-bathhouse and-after some day.PL
to the bathhouse, and some days later

gad kunt axṭā́ bi-l-ʕúṣyā.
ANT be:PRF.1SG walk:IPFV.1SG with-DEF-stick
I was already walking with a stick.

dalḗ dalḗ badaʕat riǧl-ī tiftáḥ min al-ḥámmām,
gently gently begin:PRF.3SG.F leg-1SG open:IPFV.3SG.F from DEF-bathhouse
Very gently, my leg began to open, as a result of [the visits to] the bathhouse,

w-al-xízgān hāḏawlḗ ḥagg arǧil-ī́ tġallagayn.
and-DEF-incision.PL DEM.PL of leg.PL-1SG close:PRF.3PL.F
and these incisions in my legs closed.

badaʕt áʕriǧ, áʕriǧ ʲb-ríǧl-ī b-al-ʕuṣā́.
begin:PRF.1SG limp:IPFV.1SG limp:IPFV.1SG on-leg-1SG with-DEF-stick
I began to limp, limp on my leg with the stick.

mā fiʕíl hā́ḏā‿ l-ḥámmām… al-ḥammā́m hāḏē#,
NEG do:PRF.3SG.M DEM.SG.M DEF-bathhouse DEF-bathhouse DEM.SG.M
This bathhouse did not work… this bathhouse,

yimkin hū … aṣl-oh túrkī.
be_possible:IPFV.3SG.M 3SG.M origin-3SG.M Turkish.SG.M
maybe it was originally Turkish.

3.5 You bitch, you sow![49]

The speaker of text 5 is a Jewish woman born in 1937 in the village of alGades, east of the city of Ibb. Her mother died when she was 11 and she was raised by a step mother, whom her father married shortly after. Similar to what I hear from other Jewish women from Lower Yemen, the informant testifies that she could read Hebrew already as a girl in Yemen, having been taught by her grandfather, Mōri Ḥasan Mūsa. That said, she only practiced writing when she went to school in Israel. She immigrated to Israel in 1949 together with her two older brothers.

I recorded the text in November 2016 in Givat Yeʕarim, the same *moshav* or village described in Goitein 1955 and Goitein 1960. Present in the room at the time of the recording besides me, were the narrator's granddaughter Naama Ben-David and my colleague Tom Fogel. Despite the long years in Israel, the dialect is very much vivid in Givat Yeʕarim, and it was not altogether difficult to get her to tell us a fluent story in her Yemeni mother tongue, although Israeli Hebrew every now and then emerged. It is

49 This text was first published in Shachmon and Fogel 2020 and is re-published here with the permission of the publisher.

worth mentioning that the granddaughter, third generation in Israel, while well acquainted with the dialect, can by no means use it actively.[50]

The text deals with an unpleasant episode that took place while the narrator was herding the family cow, a task which was often carried out by little girls in that rural area (Shachmon and Fogel 2020). It illustrates a number of labialized 1SG perfect *k*-forms (see 2.2.1 above), as well as other peculiar Lower Yemeni features, as the vowel-final (i.e. *t*-less) 3SG.F perfect pattern (Diem 1973: 90; Behnstedt 2016: 203), and the alternation of *-ah*/*-ih* in the nominal feminine ending, in accordance with the vowel of the previous syllable (see 2.2.3).

kāna	*tuhrub*	*ʕan-iyya*	*la-ʕind*	*al-qabīlī.*
be:PRF.3SG.F	escape:IPFV.3SG.F	from-1SG	to-at	DEF-tribesman.

[The cow] used to escape from me to the tribesman['s lot].

al-qabī́lī	*kān,*	*kān*	*gánb-ᵃnā,*	*l-qabī́lī.*
DEF-tribesman	be:PRF.3SG.M	be:PRF.3SG.M	next.to-1PL	DEF-Arab

The tribesman was next to us, the tribesman.

kān	*maʕ-ṓ*	*gam*	*adama.*
be:PRF.3SG.M	with-3SG.M	also^{IHb}	land^{IHb}

He also had land.

al-qabī́lī	*maḥ*	*šim-ó*	*ve-zixr-ó.*
DEF-tribesman	blot_out:PASS.IPFV.3SG.M^{HbC}	name-3SG.M^{HbC}	and-memory-3SG.M^{HbC}

The tribesman, may his name and memory be forgotten,

al-baqar-ah	*daxala*	*la..*	*al-ḥōl*	*ḥaqq*	*al-qabīlī...*
DEF-cow-NU	enter:PRF.3SG.F	to…	DEF-lot	of	DEF-tribesman…

The cow entered … the lot of the Arab …

ma-ze	*tkallam*	*ʕal-iyya!*	*tkallam*	*tkallam:*
what-DEM.SG.M^{IHb}	speak:PRF.3SG.M	on-1SG	speak:PRF.3SG.M	speak:PRF.3SG.M

He cursed me so much! Cursed and cursed:

kalb-ah	*antī*	*xinzīr-ih,*	*antī*	*antī*	*antī*	*antī...*
dog-SG.F	2SG.F	pig-SG.F	2SG.F	SG.F	2SG.F	2SG.F

"(You) bitch! You are a sow! You are, you are, you are, you are…

antī	*yahū́dyy-ih?*	*antī*	*xinźr-ih!*	*amarti*	*l-o*
you:SG.F	Jew-SG.F?	2SG.F	pig-SG.F!	say:PRF.1sg^{IHb}	to-3SG.M^{IHb}

[You claim] you are a Jew? You are a sow!" I said to him:

50 I thank Naama Ben-David for preparing the first draft of the transcription and for patiently checking and verifying the details with her grandmother.

hī háraba háraba háraba ʕal-iyya, háraba.
3SG.F run_away:PRF.3SG.F run_away:PRF.3SG.F run_away:PRF.3SG.F on-1SG escape:PRF.3SG.F
"She escaped, escaped, escaped from me, escaped."

mā ‿ ṣaddiq-ič, mā aṣaddiq-ič, antī káḏḏāb-ah!
NEG believe:IPFV.1SG-2SG.F NEG believe:IPFV.1SG-2SG.F 2SG.F liar-SG.F
"I do not believe you, I do not believe you! You are a liar!

kaḏḏāb-ah! abū-č w-abū-č w-gadd-ik.[51]
liar-SG.F father-2SG.F and-father-2SG.F and-grandfather-2SG.F
Liar! Your father and your father and your grandfather.

anā ša-arūḥ ʕind gadd-ič w-akkallam ʕal-ō.
1SG FUT-go:IPFV.1SG at grandfather-2SG.F and-speak:IPFV.1SG on-3SG.M
I will go to your grandfather and I tell him."

amarti š-yelex yalla l-ghinn-ē ghinnōm.
say:PRF.1SG[IHb] COMP-go:IPFV.3SG.M[IHb] go_ahead.ITJ[IHb] to-hell-PL.M.CS [HbC] hell[HbC]
I said: "let him go, go ahead, to the hell of all hells."

rāḥ la-ʕind ab-ī, la-ʕind gadd-ī, kān ab-ī,
go:PRF.3SG.M to-at father-1SG to-at grandfather-1SG be:PRF.3SG.m father-1SG
He went to my father, to me grandfather. My father was [there],

kān gadd-ī, az hu amar, qal-l-o
be:PRF.3SG.M grandfather-1SG so[IHb] 3SG.M[IHb] say:PRF.3SG.M[IHb] say:PRF.3SG.M-to-3SG.M
my grandfather was [there], then he said, he said to him,

qāl-l-o, wa-lla hāḏī l-kalb-ah daxala l-baqar-ah
say:PRF.3SG.M-to-3SG.M by-God DEM.SG.F DEF-dog-SG.F enter:PRF.3SG.F DEF-cow-NU
he said to him: "By God, this bitch, the cow entered,

akala l-mu-sm-e, akala as-sabū́l. amar
eat:PRF.3SG.F DEF-what-name-3SG.F eat:PRF.3SG.F DEF-crops say:PRF.3SG.M[IHb]
ate the what's-its-name, ate the … crops." He said:

aḷḷah wa-ḷḷah maš b-raḏāʔ-ī, maš b-raḏāʔ-ī yā sī́d-ī, maš b-raḏāʔ-ī.
God by-God NEG in-consent-1SG NEG in-consent-1SG ITJ mister-1SG NEG in-consent-1SG
"God, by God, [this was] not, not with my consent, not with my consent, mister, not with my consent".

51 The common 2SG.F post-consonantal pronominal suffix in the dialect of alGades is *-ič*, yet the informant also uses *-ik*. In fact, I documented three different 2SG.F suffixes in the various village dialects around Ibb, viz. *-ič*, *-ik*, and *-iš* (see 2.2.2 above).

amar l-o hī xinzīr-ih, xinzīr-ih qúlku-l-ak hī xinzīr-ih.
say:PRF.3SG.M[IHb] to-3SG.M[IHb] 3SG.F pig-SG.F pig-SG.F say:PRF.1sg-to-2SG.M 3SG.F pig-SG.F
He said to him: "She is a sow, a sow, I told you she was a sow."

atrawwaḥkʷ al-bēt, bakōkʷ bakōkʷ
go_back:PRF.1SG DEF-house cry:PRF.1SG cry:PRF.1SG
I went home, I cried and cried:

aba aba w-gadd-ī, gadd-ī w-ab-ī, amarti l-ó:
father[IHb] father[IHb] and-grandfather-1SG grandfather-1SG and-father-1SG say:PRF.1SG[IHb] to-3SG.M[IHb]
"Father! Father"! And my grandfather, my grandfather and my father, I said to him:

al-ʕarabī wa-ḷḷah tkallam ʕal-iyya tkallam ʕal-iyya wa-lla
DEF-Arab.SG.M by-God speak:PRF.3SG.M on-1SG speak:PRF.3SG.M on-1SG by-God
"The Arab, by God, cursed me, cursed my, by God

qāl-l-ī xinzīr-ih, qā-l-ī zē qāl-l-ī ...
say:PRF.3SG.M-to-1SG pig-SG.F say:PRF.3SG.M-to-1SG DEM.SG.M[IHb] say:PRF.3SG.M-to-1SG
he called me a sow, he said to me so and so, he said to me" …

amar ab-ū́ ab-ū́. qāl qāl. besēder, qāl.
say:PRF.3SG.M[IHb] father-3SG.M father-3SG.M say:PRF.3SG.M say:PRF.3SG.M Okay[IHb] say:PRF.3SG.M
[My father] said: his father, his father [may he go to hell!]. So he said, so what, he said.

hevī́ zē mu-sm-e, gāb gāb ab-ī,
bring:PRF.3SG.M[IHb] DEM.SG.M[IHb] what-name-3SG.F bring:PRF.3SG.M bring:PRF.3SG.M father-1SG
[The Arab] brought this, what's-its-name, he brought, he brought my father,

gāb gadd-ī, yxāyaʔū al-mu-sm-e,
bring:PRF.3SG.M grandfather-1SG see:IPFV.3PL.M DEF-what-name-3SG.F
he brought my grandfather, so that they would see the what's-its-name,

kān ... al-ḥōl tabaʕ-oh#, aḥsan aḥsan aḥsan m-ʕárabī, mašu
be:PRF.3SG.M DEF-lot of-3SG.M best best best from[IHb]-Arab.SG.M something[IHb]
it was … his lot [was] the best, the best, the best [lot you could see] from an Arab, an [exceptional] thing.

qāl: rūḥ txāyā bint-ak bint-ak
say:PRF.3SG.M go:IMP.SG.M see:IMP.SG.M daughter-2SG.M daughter-2SG.M
[The Arab] said: "Go and see: your daughter, your daughter,

mū sawwa mū sawwa. qāl: hī gāhl-ih aval,
what do:PRF.3SG.F what do:PRF.3SG.F say:PRF.3SG.M 3SG.F child-SG.F but[IHb]
what she did, what she did." [My father] said: "But she is [just] a child,

gāhl-ih gāhl-ih. qāl: lo! hī xinzīr-ih, hī xinzīr-ih mā-(h)ēš
child-SG.F child-SG.F say:PRF.3SG.M NEG[IHb] 3SG.F pig-SG.F 3SG.F pig-SG.F NEG-3SG.F-NEG
a child, a child." He said: "No, she is a sow, she is a sow, she is not,

mā-(h)ēš gāhl-ih, hī xinzīr-ih. tirʕī al-baqar-ah?
NEG-3SG.F-NEG child-SG.F 3SG.F pig-SG.F herd:IPFV.3SG.F DEF-cow-NU
she is not a child, she is a sow. She herds the cow [doesn't she]?"

baqar-ah sōʕ baqar-ah baqar-ah kāna fi maʕ-e ḥálav haláv'.
cow-NU like cow-NU cow-NU be:PRF.3SG.F EXIST with-3SG.F milk[IHb] milk[IHb]
[It was] a cow [as big] as … a great cow, it had great milk.

wa-ḷḷah gadd-ī qál-l-ō xáll-e hī gāhl-ih,
by-God grandfather-1SG say:PRF.3SG.M-to-3SG.M leave:IMP.SG.M-3SG.F 3SG.F child-SG.F
By God, my grandfather said to him: "Let [it] go, she is [just] a child,

hī gāhl-ih hī gāhl-ih, bas maxṭar ṯānī mā-tsawwí-š.
3SG.F child-SG.F 3SG.F child-SG.F just occasion second NEG-do:IPFV.3SG.F-NEG
she is a child, she is a child, but next time she will not do [that again],

mā-tsáwwī-š, qāl wa-ḷḷah hī kalb-ah hī xinzīr-ih.
NEG-do:IPFV.3SG.F-NEG say:PRF.3SG.M by-God 3SG.F dog-SG.F 3SG.F pig-SG.F
she will not do [that]". [The Arab] said: "By God, she is a bitch, she is a sow.

mā tirʕí al-baqar-ah hāḏī hī xinzīr-ih!
as_long_as herd:IPFV.3SG.F DEF-cow-NU DEM.SG.F 3SG.F pig-SG.F
Since she is [capable of] herding this cow, she is [accounted for] a sow!"

ab-ī gāb-l-ō maṣā́rī maḥ-šim-ó
father-1SG bring:PRF.3SG.M-to-3SG.M money blot_out:PASS.IPFV.3SG.M-name-3SG.M[HbC]
My father gave him some money, may his name [and memory] be forgotten,

ve-amar l-ó yaḷḷah xáll-ᵃnā wa-ḷḷah, xall-ᵃnā
and-say:PRF.3SG.M[IHb] to-3SG.M[IHb] go_ahead leave:IMP.SG.M-1PL by-God leave:IMP.SG.M-1PL
and said to him: "Come on, leave us alone, by God, leave us alone,

bas xall-ᵃnā amar l-o aḷḷah yisállim-ak
just leave:IMP.2SG.M-1PL say:PRF.3SG.M[IHb] to-3SG.M[IHb] God preserve:IPFV.3SG.m-2SG.M
just leave us alone." He said to him, "may God protect you (from harm)" –

še-lo iyé-l-o šalom l-ʕōlōm. qāl-l-o wa-ḷḷah
COMP-NEG[IHb] be:IPFV.3SG.M-to-3SG.M[IHb] peace[IHb] to-world[HbC] say:PRF.3SG.M-to-3SG.M by-God
may he never have any protection – [My father] said to him: "By God,

aḷḷāh yisallím-ak *bas xalle* *mu-sm-e*
God preserve:IPFV.3SG.M-2SG.M just leave:IMP.SG.M-3SG.F what-name-3SG.F
may god protect you [from harm)], just leave it alone, the what's-its-name,

hī *gāhl-ih* *mā* *tidrī-š.*
3SG.F child-SG.F NEG know:IPFV.3SG.F-NEG
she is a child, she does not know".

References

Ahroni, Reuben. 1994. *The Jews of the British Crown Colony of Aden.* Leiden: Brill.

Arnold, Werner. 2010. "Pausalformen in den arabischen Dialekten Antiochiens." In: Shabo Talay and Hartmut Bobzin (eds.). *Arabische Welt: Grammatik, Dichtung und Dialekte.* Beiträge einer Tagung im Juli 2008 in Erlangen zu Ehren von Wolfdietrich Fischer, 227–236. Wiesbaden: Reichert Verlag.

Barth, Jakob. 1894. *Die Nominalbildung in den semitischen Sprachen,* 1st ed. Leipzig: J.C. Hinrichs.

Behnstedt, Peter. 1987. *Die Dialekte der Gegend von Ṣaʕdah (Nord-Jemen).* Wiesbaden: Harrassowitz.

—. 1993. *Glossar der jemenitischen Dialektwörter in Eduard Glasers Tagebüchern.* Wien: Österreichische Akademie der Wissenschaften.

—. 2016. *Dialect Atlas of North Yemen and Adjacent Areas.* Leiden: Brill.

Ben-David, Aharon. 1999. הוידה ודאוד מצפון תימן. Israel: Private Publisher.s

—. 2005. "שדים ורוחות במשכנות תימן" In: Shalom Seri and Yisrael Kesar (eds.). *הליכות קדם במשכנות תימן* [English title: "Ancient Customs of the Yemenite Jewish Community."] 91–108. Rehovot: Ahavat Teman.

—. 2008. בית האבן, הליכות יהודי צפון תימן. Israel: Ahavat Teman.

—. 2010, 2015. ספר המעשים. Israel: Ahavat Teman (3 vols.).

Ben-Zion, Yael. 2011. תיאור לשוני של הלהג הערבי שבפי יהודי עדן. Unpublished doctoral dissertation. University of Haifa.

Blanc, Haim. 1967 "The 'sonorous' versus 'muffled' distinction in Old Arabic phonology." In: *To Honor Roman Jakobson: Essays on the Occasion of his Seventieth Birthday*, vol. 1: 295–308. The Hague: Mouton.

—. 1969. "The Fronting of Semitic *g* and the *qāl-gāl* Dialect Split in Arabic." In: *Proceedings of the International Conference on Semitic Studies,* 7–37. Jerusalem: The Israel Academy of Science and Humanities.

Dbayyat, Nisreen and Judith Rosenhouse, J. 2006. "Gender Switch in Female Speech of an Urbanized Arabic Dialect in Israel". *Anthropological Linguistics* 48/2: 169–186.

Diem, Werner. 1973. *Skizzen jemenitischer Dialekte.* Beirut: In Kommission bei F. Steiner, Wiesbaden.

Goitein, Shlomo Dov. 1931. "היסודות העבריים בשפת הדיבור של יהודי תימן" ("Hebrew elements in the spoken language of the Jews of Yemen"), *Leshonenu* 3: 356–380.

—. 1933. "Jemenitische Geschichten." *Zeitschrift für Semitistik* 9: 19–43.

—. 1934. *Jemenica: Sprichwörter und Redensarten aus Zentral-Jemen.* Leipzig: Otto Harrassowitz.

—. 1953. "על החיים הציבוריים של היהודים בארץ תימן" ("The communal organization of the Jews of Yemen"), *Mordecai M. Kaplan Jubilee Volume, on the Occasion of his Seventieth Birthday*, 43–61. New York: Jewish Theological Seminary of America. Reprinted in Goitein 1983, pp. 199–215.

—. 1955. "דיוקנו של כפר אורגים תימני" ("A Portrait of a Yemenite Weavers Village"). *Journal of Jewish Studies* 17: 3–27.

—. 1960. "The Language of Al-Gades, The Main Characteristics of an Arabic Dialect Spoken in Lower Yemen". *Le Muséon* 73: 351–394.

—. 1983. התימנים: הסטוריה, סדרי חברה, חיי הרוח (The Yemenites: History, communal organization, spiritual life). Jerusalem: The Ben Zvi Institute.

Greenman, Joseph. 1979. "A Sketch of the Arabic Dialect of the Central Yamani Tihāmah." *Zeitschrift für Arabische Linguistik* 3: 47–61.

Ingham, Bruce. 1994. *Najdi Arabic, Central Arabian*. Amsterdam/Philadelphia: John Benjamins Publishing Company.

Ingham, Bruce. 2000. "The Dialect of the Miʕdan or 'Marsh arabs'." In: Manwel Mifsud (ed.) *Proceedings of the Third International Conference of AIDA, Malta 1998*, 125–130. Malta: Salesian Press.

Itzchaki, Arie. 1988. אגדה של מקום (*Legends of the Holy-Land*), 2 vols. Tel-Aviv: Modan.

Jastrow, Otto. 1984. "Zur Phonologie und Phonetik des Ṣanʕanischen". In: Horst Kopp and Günther Schweizer (eds.). *Entwicklungsprozesse in der Arabischen Republik Jemen*. Jemen-Studien, Band 1: 289–304. Wiesbaden: Reichert Verlag.

—. 1986. "Alles über Qāt, Ein Text im arabischen Dialekt von Jiblih (Nordjemen)." *Zeitschrift der Deutschen Morgenländischen Gesellschaft* 136: 23–55.

Johnstone, Thomas Muir. 1964. "Further Studies on the Dōsiri dialect of Arabic as spoken in Kuwait." *Bulletin of the School of Oriental and African Studies* 27/1: 77–113.

Jong, Rudolf E. de. 2000. *A Grammar of the Bedouin Dialects of Northern Sinai Littoral*. Leiden: Brill.

Kafih, Joseph. 1961. הליכות תימן: חיי היהודים בצנעא ובנותיה (*Jewish Life in Sanà*). Jerusalem: Ben Zvi Institute for the Study of Jewish Communities in the East.

Kara, Yechiel. 1986. "הערות לחקר הערבית שבפי יהודי תימן" In: *Proceedings of the Ninth Congress of Jewish Studies*, vol. 1: 123–130. Jerusalem: The Magnes Press.

—. 1988. "היסודות העבריים והארמיים בלשון הנשים בתימן: בחינה לשונית". In: Moshe Bar-Asher (ed.) *Studies in Jewish Languages: Bible Translations and Spoken Dialect*, 113–150. Jerusalem: Misgav.

Landberg, Carlo. 1920–1942. *Glossaire Datînois*, Leiden: E.J. Brill.

Leslau, Wolf. 1945–1946 "Linguistic Observations on a Native Yemenite Document." *Jewish Quarterly Review* 36: 261–279.

Lierman, John. 2004. *The New Testament Moses*. Tübingen: Mohr Siebeck.

Morag, Shelomo. 1963. העברית שבפי יהודי תימן (*The Hebrew Language Tradition of the Yemenite Jews*). Jerusalem: Academy of the Hebrew Language.

—. 1999. "The History of the Biblical Text in the Yemenite Community – An Outline." In: Shimon Sharvit (ed.). מחקרים בלשון העברית העתיקה והחדשה, מוגשים למנחם צבי קדרי (*Studies in Ancient and Modern Hebrew in Honour of M.Z. Kaddari*), 219–233. Ramat-Gan: Bar-Ilan University Press.

Naïm-Sanbar, Samia. 1994. "Contribution à l'étude de l'accent yéménite: Le parler des femmes de l'ancienne génération,." *Zeitschrift für Arabische Linguistik* 27: 67–89.

Piamenta, Moshe. 1990, 1991. *Dictionary of Post-Classical Yemeni Arabic*. Leiden: Brill.

Prochazka, Theodore, Jr. 1974. "The Perfect Tense Ending *-k* in the Spoken Arabic of Taʕizz." *Bulletin of the School of Oriental and African Studies* 37/2: 439–442.

—. 1988. *Saudi Arabian Dialects*. London: Kegan Paul International.

Rossi, Ettore. 1937. "Nuove osservazioni sui dialetti del Yemen". *Rivista degli Studi Orientali* 17: 460–472.

—. 1939. *L'arabo parlato a Sanʕâ*. Rome: Istituto per l'Oriente.

Shachmon, Ori. 2007. להגי הערבית המדוברים בפי עולים מצפון תימן (*Arabic Dialects of the Jews of North Yemen*) Unpublished Ph.D. dissertation. Jerusalem: The Hebrew University.

—. 2013. "Judeo-Arabic, Yemen, Hebrew Component." In: Geoffrey Khan (ed.). *Encyclopedia of Hebrew Language and Linguistics*, vol. 2, 402–406. Leiden: Brill

—. 2014a. "*ibn aššarīfah* vs. *ibn aljāriyah*: The Hebrew Component as a Polemic Device," *Jewish Quarterly Review* 104/1: 144–166.

—. 2014b. "Yemenite Judeo-Arabic". *Encyclopedia of Jews in the Islamic World* II. Online Edition.

—. 2015. "Agglutinated Verb Forms in the Northern Province of Yemen". In: Lutz Edzard (ed.) *Arabic and Semitic Linguistics Contextualized. A Festschrift for Jan Retsö*, 260–273. Wiesbaden: Harrassowitz.

—. 2017a. "New sources for the Study of North-Yemenite Arabic: Beit Ha-ʔEven and Sefer Ha-Maʕaśim". *Journal of Semitic Studies* 62/1: 113–135.

—. 2017b. “The Girl and Seven Calves. Observations on the language of a North-Yemenite Fairytale”. *Zeitschrift der Deutschen Morgenländischen Gesellschaft* 167/2: 295–322.

Shachmon, Ori and Tom Fogel. 2020. “On Girls and Cows: Episodes in the Jewish *k*-dialects of Lower Yemen.” *Wiener Zeitschrift für die Kunde des Morgenlandes* 110: 233–256.

Shachmon, Ori and Noam Faust. 2021 forthcoming. “Avoiding of final monopositional vowels: Evidence from the *k*-dialects of Yemen.” *Brill's Journal of Afroasiatic Languages and Linguistics* 12/1.

Shawarbah, Musa. 2012. *A Grammar of Negev Arabic*. Wiesbaden: Harrassowitz.

Smith, Gerald Rex. 2019. “The Particle *qad* in a Nineteenth-Century Yemeni Literary Mixed Arabic Text Ḥabšūš's *Ruʔyā al-Yaman.*” *Zeitschrift für Arabische Linguistik* 69: 39–51.

Sulami, Tuvia. 2011. "שיר על שמואל יבניאלי ובשורתו, שרעב 1914". *Tehuda* 27: 9–20.

Testen, David. 1992. “Extra-Arabic Affiliations of *k*-Yemeni”, in: Ellen Broselow, Mushira Eid, and John J. McCarthy (eds.). *Perspectives on Arabic Linguistics. Papers from the Annual Symposium on Arabic Linguistics IV*, 77–89. Amsterdam: John Benjamins.

Tobi, Yosef. 1991. “Between Tafsir and Sharḥ: Saadia Gaon's Translation of the Bible among the Jews of Yemen.” In: Yitzhak Avishur (ed.). *Studies in the History and Culture of Iraqi Jewry*, vol. 6, 127–138. Or-Yehuda: Babylonian Jewry Heritage Center.

—. 1999. “Aramaic in the Written and Oral Tradition of Yemenite Jews” [Hebrew]. In: מחקרים ביהדות תימן; דברי הקונגרס הבינלאומי השני (*Judaeo-Yemenite Studies, Proceedings of the Second International Congress*), טו-מ. Princeton, New Jersey: Institute of Semitic Studies.

Vanhove, Martine. 2013. “Yemen.” in: *Encyclopedia of Arabic Language and Linguistics*. Online Edition.

Wagner, Ewald. 1966. “Der Jemen als Vermittler äthiopischen Sprachgutes”. *Die Sprache* 12: 252–279.

Watson, Janet. C.E. 1993. *A Syntax of Ṣanʕānī Arabic.* Wiesbaden: Harrassowitz.

—. 1996a. *Ṣbaḥtū! A Course in Sanʕānī Arabic*. Wiesbaden: Harrassowitz.

—. 1996b. “Emphasis in Ṣanʕānī Arabic.” In: James Dickens (ed.). *Three Topics in Arabic Phonology, Occasional Papers of The Centre for Middle Eastern and Islamic Studies* 53: 45–52.

—. 1999 “The Directionality of Emphasis Spread in Arabic.” *Linguistic Inquiry* 30/2: 289–300.

—. 2002. *The Phonology and Morphology of Arabic.* Oxford: Oxford University Press.

—. 2007. “Linguistic leveling in Sanʕani Arabic as reflected in a popular radio serial.” In: Catherine Miller, Enam Al-Wer, Dominique Caubet, and Janet C.E. Watson (eds.). *Arabic in the City: Issues in Dialect Contact and Language Variation,* 166–187. London: Routledge.

Watson, Janet C.E. and ʕAbd al-Salām al-ʕAmri. 2000. *Waṣf Ṣanʕāʔ: Texts in Ṣanʕānī Arabic*. Wiesbaden: Harrassowitz.

Watson, Janet, C.E., Bonnie Glover Stalls, Khalid Al-Razihi, and Shelagh Weir. 2006. “Two Texts from Jabal Rāziḥ, North-west Yemen.” In: Lutz Edzard and Jan Retsö (eds.) *Current Issues in the Analysis of Semitic Grammar and Lexicon*, 40–63. Wiesbaden: Harrassowitz.

Yaakov, Doron. 2011. "לשון ותרבות קהילתית במסורת יהודי תימן". *Tehuda* 27: 75–83.

Modern Spoken Egyptian Judeo-Arabic

Gabriel M. Rosenbaum, The Hebrew University of Jerusalem

1. Introduction

This study reports on some of my main findings from my research on the spoken Arabic of Egyptian Jews (EJA, Egyptian Judeo-Arabic) in the twentieth century.[1] This research, although making some use of printed sources, is mostly based on intensive work with a large number of informants, Egyptian Jews, both Rabbinic and Karaite, who are native speakers of Arabic. Most of the informants are elderly people, living mainly in Israel, Egypt, and France, as well as non-Jewish native speakers of Egyptian Arabic, who live in Egypt. Below are some typical examples of grammatical and lexical characteristics of EJA.

1.1 The linguistic situation in Egypt

The official language of modern Egypt is Arabic. Egyptian society, like other Arabic-speaking societies, is in a state of diglossia, a special case of bilingualism in which two languages, or two linguistic varieties are used, each for different purposes. The two languages (or varieties) used in Arabic-speaking societies are *Fuṣḥā* and *ʕĀmmiyya*. *Fuṣḥā* (standard Arabic, lit.: 'eloquent language, pure language') serves as the language of writing, literature, study, and formal communication, while *ʕĀmmiyya* (colloquial Arabic, lit.: 'the language of the *ʕāmma* – the masses, the common people') is used as the language of spoken everyday communication.

The term *Fuṣḥā* may refer to both classical Arabic and modern standard Arabic; the latter (often referred to as Modern Standard Arabic, MSA) is more or less uniform in various countries and regions in the Arabic-speaking world (except for some vocabulary differences). *ʕĀmmiyya*, whose status has traditionally been regarded as inferior to that of *Fuṣḥā*, differs according to the countries and regions in which it is spoken. Sometimes these differences make communication among speakers from different countries or even regions in one country difficult or almost impossible. In Egypt, however, the differences between the various dialects, in most cases, do not prevent communication and understanding among speakers.

The most prestigious dialect in Egypt is that of Cairo, which is also the main language of Egyptian cinema, theater and songs, and is the most extensively understood dialect in the Arabic-speaking world. It is, therefore, often identified with colloquial Egyptian Arabic in general and often referred to as such (CEA, colloquial Egyptian Arabic).

1 The book based on this research will be published by the Ben-Zvi Institute in Jerusalem (*forthcoming*). Some of its results were published in several articles; see Rosenbaum 2002a; 2002b; 2002c; 2012a; 2012b; 2013a; 2013b; 2016; 2018; 2019.

Arabic-speaking societies do not recognize their mother tongues as respectable languages and refuse to make them national languages. Opposition to using *ʕAmmiyya* as a language of literature has deep roots in Arab culture and also in the modern Arabic-speaking world, Egypt included. It should be noted, however, that today Colloquial Egyptian Arabic has become a second written and literary language in Egypt, in addition to Standard Arabic. So far, Egypt is the only place in the Arabic-speaking world where such a revolutionary change in the linguistic and literary norms has taken place.[2]

1.2 The Arabic-speaking Jews in Egypt

In Egypt, Muslims and Christians (most of whom are Copts) speak what is essentially the same dialect; local variations are geographically rather than religiously or ethnically conditioned. Muslims and Copts in Cairo thus share the Cairene dialect while in Alexandria they share the Alexandrian dialect, except for some lexical peculiarities, for example oath formulas: Jews, Christians, and Muslims each use unique formulas of their own and avoid the use of those of the other groups.[3] The variety spoken by the Jews of Egypt (EJA), however, while being influenced by local dialects, contains many features – in the areas of phonology, morphology, and particularly vocabulary – which are not found in the dialects spoken by their non-Jewish neighbors in various regions in Egypt.

The Jews of Egypt, like many other Jewish communities in other parts of the Arabic-speaking world, spoke, and continue to speak, a distinct Arabic dialect (or variety), differing in a number of respects from the variety spoken by their Muslim and Christian neighbors. While the unique phonological and morphological features of the variety spoken by Jews are constant, irrespective of the circumstances of communication, many distinctive lexical features usually appear only in communication among Jews. In other words, the Jews in Egypt were usually aware of the vocabulary they used, but not of grammar and phonology.

Today there are only a few Jews left in Egypt. EJA, however, is still spoken by Egyptian Jews outside of Egypt, although their number is constantly diminishing, so it seems that this spoken variety will eventually disappear.

1.3 Arabic and Judeo-Arabic written by Jews in Egypt in the twentieth century

Jews in previous centuries wrote Arabic using Hebrew letters, a practice that continued in Egypt up to the twentieth century, when the Arabic script began to be used in books on religious subjects and in Jewish newspapers, such as *al-Šams*, published by Rabbinic Jews and *al-Kalīm*, published by Karaite Jews. Both appeared until the mid-twentieth century. These books and newspapers, which reflect a desire to write in the standard Arabic that is customary in the local culture, sometimes also contain Hebrew words, in Hebrew or in Arabic letters, that are part of the vocabulary either of Hebrew or of EJA, especially in relation to religious and communal life. The writing and publication of

2 On this issue, see, e.g., Rosenbaum 2004; 2011. The first signs of this process started at the end of the nineteenth and the beginning of the twentieth centuries, when the Jews had a flourishing community in Egypt, but the process came to its peak at the end of the twentieth and the beginning of the twenty first centuries, after most of the Jews had left the country.

3 See Rosenbaum 2012b.

such texts in Hebrew letters in Egypt came to an end after almost all the Jews of Egypt had left it towards the end of the 20th century.

1.4 The speakers of modern Egyptian Judeo-Arabic

The Jewish community in Egypt was not homogeneous. Most Egyptian Jews belonged to what today would be called Orthodox Judaism, and in Egypt were called "Rabbinic Jews" (in EJA: SG.M *rabbán*, SG.F *rabbána*, PL *rabbaním*). Rabbinic Jews were divided into many sub-groups according to their geographical origins in the East and West; the majority of Rabbinic Jews were of Sefaradi or Oriental origin, while the Ashkenazi or Western Jews were a minority. A smaller, separate community was that of the Karaite Jews (in EJA: SG.M *ʔarráy* or *ʔárra*, SG.F *ʔarráya*, PL *ʔarrayīn*, with the original consonant ق (*q*), a uvular stop in standard Arabic, realized as a glottal stop; see below, section 2.1).

The great majority of Egyptian Jews lived in the two large cities of Cairo and Alexandria and also in some towns in the Nile Delta.[4]

While there were upper-class Jews who were influential in Egyptian politics, the economy and culture, many Jews were poor or belonged to the lower-middle class. Many of the latter lived in the Jewish quarter in Cairo and in two other mixed Cairene neighborhoods, al-Ẓāhir (in CEA: iḍ-Ḍāhir) and al-Sakakīni, and in several lower-class neighborhoods in Alexandria and in the cities of the Delta. Most lower-class and lower-middle class Jews were native speakers of Arabic, in most cases EJA.

Many Egyptian Jews were bi- or multi-lingual.[5] Often a European language, especially among upper-class Jews and those who lived outside areas with a dense Jewish population, served as the main language of speech. Many Jews spoke European languages as mother tongue, mainly French, Italian, or Judeo-Spanish (Ladino). French, and to a lesser extent English and Italian, were the languages of education of many children.[6] Knowledge of standard Arabic as well as of EJA among Jews who were native speakers of European languages or received their education in those languages was often limited. In families where a foreign language was spoken, many children did not speak Arabic as a mother tongue but rather learned it from their non-Jewish surroundings, and consequently the (occasionally faulty) Arabic they spoke was closer to the variety spoken by non-Jews rather than to EJA.

Thus, the Jews who lived in the poor and low-income neighborhoods were the main preservers of the unique Egyptian Judeo-Arabic variety and its oral cultural heritage.

The largest group of Jews lived in *ḥārt il-yahūd* ('The Jewish Quarter') in Cairo, also called by the Jews in short *il-ḥāra* ('The quarter'). The Karaites had their own separate and much smaller quarter, next to the Rabbinic Jewish Quarter, called *ḥart il-yahūd il-ʔarrayīn* ('The Karaite Jewish Quarter'), or in short *ḥārt il-ʔarrayīn* ('The Karaite Quarter'). Karaite Jews generally assimilated more easily than Rabbinic Jews

4 Krämer 1989: 10–11.

5 See, e.g., Gordon 1977 [1919]: 21.

6 See, e.g., Tignor 1983: 95–97.

into non-Jewish society, and therefore their language variety was closer to the one spoken by non-Jews than the Rabbinic Jews' language variety.

As people's economic situation improved, they tended to leave the Jewish Quarter and move to more prestigious neighborhoods. As a result, the expression *bitūʕ il-ḥāra* ('those from the Quarter') was used disparagingly by upper-class Jews or by Jews who had left the Quarter or had never lived there, to indicate simple, poor, or uneducated, and sometimes uncouth people. The verb *ʔitmaddin*, which in Egyptian Arabic means 'become civilized', was used by Jews, usually mockingly, to refer to someone who had left the Jewish Quarter to live in a better or a more prestigious neighborhood; this term indicated that such a person may have moved out physically, but his essence had not changed.

In the many conversations I had with Cairene Egyptian Jews I encountered two kinds of attitude towards the Jewish Quarter and its residents. According to one, the Quarter was definitely lower-class and so were its inhabitants; others, in contrast, tended to stress the pleasant ambience, the friendly neighborly relations there and its special atmosphere. Many people told me that the years there were the best time of their life. There is no contradiction here: these are just two different points of view regarding one-and-the-same time and place.

1.5 The language of Egyptian Jews: Egyptian Arabic or Egyptian Judeo-Arabic?

Until recently it was believed that the Jews of Egypt did not have a unique vernacular of their own and that the variety they spoke did not differ or differed only minimally from that of their non-Jewish neighbors. As Haim Blanc said in a discussion on Jewish languages:

> One Judeo-Arabic that is quite distinct is, for example, that of the Jews of Baghdad. This dialect is maximally different from the dialects of Muslims and Christians in that city, both from purely linguistic and from socio-cultural aspects. On the other hand, for example, the Arabic spoken by the Jews of Cairo does not possess a typical Jewish uniqueness: it differs from the language of non-Jews only minimally, in both of the above-mentioned aspects.[7]

Blanc referred to this issue also earlier in his preliminary pioneering study of the language of Cairene Jews (Blanc 1974: 207):

> The particular variety of non-standard Cairene discussed here, and the only one alluded to by the abbreviation NSC, was noted among native Cairene Jews, and thus far among them only. I have refrained from labeling it 'Jewish Cairene' or the like because it is not spoken by all Cairene Jews, some of whom speak SC [Standard Cairene]; and because, except for Hebrew words and phrases, there is at present no reason to assume that features of NSC do not occur among non-Jewish Cairenes.

In his study of the Arabic of the Jews of Cairo, Blanc was careful not to label the linguistic variety he was describing as "Jewish Cairene". Notwithstanding his guarded formulation, in the article quoted here and in two other articles describing texts written

7 In Rabin et al. 1979: 50.

in spoken Arabic by Jews in the seventeenth century,[8] Blanc laid the foundations for a description of modern spoken Egyptian Judeo-Arabic.

Beyond Blanc's pioneering articles, however, and a few comments by Tomiche (1968),[9] the spoken dialect of the Jews of Egypt has received scant attention, and extremely little has been written on the basis of data collected from Jewish speakers of Egyptian Arabic. The purpose of my studies on Egyptian Judeo-Arabic is to continue Blanc's work and fill the gap in this area. I am absolutely certain that if Blanc had continued his research on Egyptian Judeo-Arabic he would have reached the same conclusion, that the variety spoken by Egyptian Jews, whose mother tongue is Arabic, is a unique variety, according to the criteria he himself set.

1.6 A note on the transcription

Speakers of Egyptian Arabic, Jews included, usually do not distinguish between the short vowels *e* and *i*, on the one hand, and *o* and *u*, on the other. Standard Egyptian Arabic short vowels *e* and *i* are transcribed *i*, and short vowels *o* and *u* are transcribed *u*, while the vowel *e* originating in Hebrew (*ṣere*, *segol*, and *šwa*) or in another foreign language (and is therefore not performed as *i*) is always marked *e*. The vowel *e* is also written as such in three other words in EJA: the demonstrative pronoun *de*, and the verbs *ge* and *ʔega*.

Vowels in stressed syllables in EJA words that are derived from words originating in Hebrew as well as in European languages, are marked by an acute accent: *á*, *é*, *í*, *ó*, *ú* (as in *tefillá*, *kabéd*, *brindízi*, *kominyón*, and *kippúr* quoted below).

2. Distinctive grammatical characteristics of Spoken Egyptian Judeo-Arabic

2.1 Consonants and vowels

In phonetic articulation, the variety spoken by Jews is nearly identical to that of non-Jews. However, some differences do exist, mostly as a consequence of the introduction of non-Arabic elements into EJA, mainly from Hebrew but also from a number of European languages, including some consonants that are sometimes realized as in the source language and sometimes adapted to the CEA realization.

Most speakers of CEA realize the phoneme /p/ (voiceless *p*) which does not exist in Arabic, as *b* (voiceless *b*: *p* > *b*) when it appears in loan words from European languages, while most speakers of EJA realize it in similar environments as voiceless *p* (*p* = *p*), although some realize it as voiced *b* (*p* > *b*); the former would say *pésaḥ* ('Passover), and the latter *bésaḥ*.

The consonant ق (*q*), realized as a uvular stop in standard Arabic, is realized as a glottal stop (like *hamza*) in Cairo and the cities of Lower Egypt (*q* > *ʔ*), and this is true of the Jews as well, even when uttering words of Hebrew origin, such as *šattaʔ* ('be quiet, don't talk about this now'; see below, section 3.6), from the Hebrew word *šatáq* (שְׁתַק). Occasionally, this consonant may also be realized as a velar stop (*q* > *k*), yield-

8 Blanc 1981; 1985.

9 Preliminary notes on some peculiarities of the dialect spoken by Egyptian Jews were given by Tomiche 1968.

ing, for example, *kaddíš* ('Kaddish' (√ q-d-š), a liturgical prayer also used in commemoration of a death, instead of the more common form *ʔaddíš*).

The phoneme /b/, which in Hebrew is realized as either voiced stop [*b*] or voiced fricative [v], is always realized as voiced stop *b* by Egyptian Jews in words of Hebrew origin, even when in Hebrew it is realized as a fricative, as in *kabéd* (lit: 'heavy'; see also below, section 2.2), versus *kavéd* in Hebrew.

The phoneme /k/, which in Hebrew is realized either as a stop [k] or as a fricative [x/k̲], always retains its original realizations in words of Hebrew origin, as in *kašér* ('kosher') versus *hek̲ál* ('holy ark').

The fricative consonant *v* does not exist in Arabic. In EJA words of Hebrew origin, it is realized as in Hebrew, for example *ʕavón* ('sin').

Gemination of consonants in words borrowed from Hebrew is always retained in EJA, as in *kippúr* ('[Yom] Kippur, the Day of Atonement').

Stress in words borrowed from Hebrew is usually where it would be according to the rules of accentuation in Hebrew; therefore, many such words have ultimate stress, for example *mezuzá, kappará* (quoted below, section 3.4.3), in contrast with CEA, where we would expect the stress to be on the penultima.

Vowels in words of Hebrew origin are usually preserved in EJA. *Shewa mobile* at the beginning of a word or syllable is almost always retained and pronounced *e*, as in *tefillá* ('prayer').

2.2 The definite article, the feminine, and the plural

The CEA definite article *il-* (in MSA: *al-*) is also used before words of non-Arabic origin, for example *lilt il-haggadá* ('The Passover *seder* night'; see below, section 3.9), and in mixed expressions that consist of CEA and non-CEA components, as in *rama l-ʕavonót*, 'cast off his sins' (in the *tašlík̲* ceremony and prayer said on Rosh Hashana, the Jewish New Year, near a body of water). Only in purely Hebrew collocations is the Hebrew definite article *ha-* retained, as in the oath *be-ʔemét ha-torá* ('[I swear] by the truth of the Torah!'). The following is a rare case, in which the prefixed *ha* is perceived as part of the succeeding word, and the Arabic definite article is then attached as well: *il-ha-rambám* ('Maimonides', called in Hebrew by his acronym, *Rambam,* for *Rabbénu Moshé ben Maimón*, and also the synagogue bearing his name in the Jewish quarter in Cairo).[10]

Feminine forms of words of Hebrew origin are usually consistent with Arabic nominal patterns but retain the stress they would have had in Hebrew. For example, *kabedá* is the feminine form of *kabéd* ('pest, disagreeable person'; lit.: 'heavy', influenced by the Hebrew *kavéd* F *kevedá*); *kohená* ('daughter/wife of a *kohén*') is the feminine form of *kohén* ('cohen, priest', versus the Hebrew *kohénet*), and *kašerá* ('kosher woman', a righteous and pious woman). In all of these cases the stress is on the ultima; according to the CEA rules, such words would have the stress on the penultima.

10 This is a common occurrence in Spanish, which contains many words borrowed from Arabic with the Arabic definite article *al-* and also receive the Spanish definite article *el*, as in *el alcázar* ('the fortress, the palace'), from Arabic: القصر (*al-qaṣr*).

In words of Hebrew origin, the Hebrew plural form is usually retained, as in *mamzerím* ('bastards', masculine plural of *mamzér*) and *mitsvót* or *miṣvót* (feminine plural of *mitsvá* or *miṣvá*, 'religious commandments', and also 'reading the Torah and some other honorary roles in the synagogue'), but the Arabic plural suffix *-īn* (*mamzerīn*) is occasionally attested as well.

The masculine form *kinīs* ('synagogue'), as opposed to feminine *kinīsa* ('church'), is used only when it stands alone. When an adjective is added, as in *kinist il-kibīra* ('The Big Synagogue'), it becomes *kinīst*, as the *nomen rectum* of *kinīsa* in the construct state.

2.3 Non-Cairene and non-standard verbal patterns

Verb conjugations in EJA are based on the CEA patterns, but with some significant differences. In some cases, verbs are conjugated in ways that are reminiscent of non-Cairene dialects.

A major characteristic of EJA is the conjugation of verbs in the first person in the imperfect. Whereas Cairene Arabic, as well as Upper Egypt dialects, use the prefixes *a-* and *n-*, respectively, for the imperfect first person singular and plural, Alexandrian Arabic uses the prefix *n-* for the first person singular and the prefix *n-* together with the suffix *-u* for the plural, as is the case in Western Arabic dialects. This pattern, for which Blanc (1974) coined the appellation "nekteb-nektebu", is used by Egyptian Jews who speak Arabic as a mother tongue, regardless of their place of birth or where they used to live. For example, *ʔana ḥa-ninzil* ('I shall go down'), versus *ḥanzil* in CEA; *niktibu bi-raší* ('we write in the Rashi script'), versus *niktib* in CEA. It should be noted that Cairene Jews are the only Cairenes who speak with the "nekteb-nektebu" pattern.

The verbs *ʔaḫad* ('take') and *ʔakal* ('eat') also have shorter forms, *ḫad* and *kal*.[11] Usually CEA speakers stick to one form, either the longer or the shorter. Egyptian Jews, however, tend to prefer the longer forms.[12]

On non-standard verbal patterns in the perfect of the verbs *gih*, derived from the root √ g-y-ʔ, and *ʔarāḥ*, derived from the root √ r-w-ḥ, see below, section 2.5.

2.4 Preference for the vowel u *in verbs and nouns*

A typical feature of EJA is the preferential use of the vowel *u* in some verbs and nouns, as against the use of another vowel in CEA. In Egyptian Arabic, some first form verbs have two possible patterns, *fiʕil* and *fuʕul*, both of which are in use.[13] Today there is a tendency to prefer the *fiʕil* pattern, but Jewish speakers more commonly use the *fuʕul* pattern. For example, Jewish speakers prefer the form *ḫuluṣ* ('come to an end, be finished') to *ḫiliṣ*.

The same is true of nouns with two alternative patterns. Jewish speakers prefer forms with the vowel *u*, while the preferred forms in the standard dialect are usually

11 See Behnstedt and Woidich 1985: maps 262–263.

12 Cf. Blanc 1974: 215.

13 A few verbs may appear in three forms, *faʕal*, *fiʕil*, and *fuʕul*, as in *ṣabar*, *ṣibir*, and *ṣubur* ('to be patient').

those with the vowel *i*. Thus, for example, Jews prefer the form *šubbāk* ('window') to *šibbāk*, which is the more common form used by non-Jews.[14]

A unique feature of EJA is the use of the vowel *u* even in cases where it does not occur at all in CEA, for example *mušṭ* ('comb') in EJA, versus CEA *mišṭ; ṭušt* ('tub' or 'washtub') in EJA, versus CEA *ṭišt;* and *muḫadda* ('pillow') in EJA, versus CEA *miḫadda*. Even some words of Hebrew origin have this pattern as an optional version, substituting *u* for the original vowel: *kutubbá* ('marriage contract'), in addition to Hebrew *ketubbá*; *kuppúr* ('[Yom] Kippur'), in addition to Hebrew *kippúr*, and in the word *ʕurubbá* ('eve of a feast'), of Aramaic origin but not used in Hebrew, in addition to the options *ʕerubbá* and *ʕarubbá*. This feature is also present in older written Judeo-Arabic texts in Hebrew letters and apparently also reflects the tendency to use the vowel *u* in the spoken language.

2.5 Pronouns and typical words

EJA uses several pronouns and some other words that are different from their counterparts in CEA. Some of these existed in the past in Cairene Arabic and have fallen out of use, and others still exist, in various forms, in non-Cairene Egyptian dialects; for many examples see Behnstedt and Woidich 1985; 1994.

Speakers of EJA use the demonstrative pronouns *de* ('this, that; SG.M) and *dōn* ('these, those'; PL.M/F), interchangeably with their CEA parallels *da* ('this, that') and *dōl* ('these, those'), respectively.[15] I also found the form *dōni*, as a variation of *dōn*.[16] Jewish speakers often use the personal pronoun *humman* ('they')[17] instead of CEA *humma,* and *kamāna* ('also, too')[18], instead of CEA *kamān*. Furthermore, in addition to the interrogative pronouns *ʔeh* ('what?'), *lēh* ('why?'), and *ʔizzayy* ('how?'), EJA has retained the interrogative pronouns *ʔēš* ('what?'), *lēš* ('why?'), and *kēf* or *kīf* ('how?'), respectively, which have fallen out of use in the Cairene dialect. In CEA the interrogative pronouns usually appear at the end of the clause, while EJA places them at the beginning, for example *ʔēš ʕāyiz?* ('what do you want?'), as opposed to *ʕāyiz ʔēh?* in CEA.[19] Although fallen out of use, the interrogative pronoun *ʔēš* is still preserved in some CEA collocations, in which it appears at the beginning as in old CEA and in EJA, for example *ʔēš ʕarrafak* ('how do you know?').[20]

14 Since the beginning of the twenty-first century some speakers of CEA have come to prefer the vowel u in some words.

15 See also Blanc 1974: 216.

16 Cf. the form *dōna* in Behnstedt and Woidich 1994: 149.

17 Cf. the forms *humma*, *humman*, and *hummu* in Behnstedt and Woidich 1985: map 147; 1994: 492.

18 Cf. the form *kamāni* and other variations in Behnstedt and Woidich 1994: 421.

19 See also Blanc 1974: 216, and footnote 38 on page 216.

20 Spitta (1880: 80), in his description of Egyptian Arabic grammar at the end of the nineteenth century, mentions both *ʔēš* and *lēš* as existing in CEA. For *ʔēš* cf. Behnstedt and Woidich 1985: map 182, and 1994: 10, and for *lēš* cf. Behnstedt and Woidich 1985: map 182, and 1994: 443.

Jews often realize the number 400 as *ʔurbuʕmiyya,* instead of the CEA *rubʕumiyya*, and a few realize the number 600 as *sittimiyya,* instead of the CEA *suttumiyya*, contrary to the usual tendency in EJA to prefer the vowel *u* to *i*.[21]

In his descriptions of Judeo-Egyptian Arabic of the seventeenth and early twentieth centuries, Blanc demonstrated that some of the morphological features unique to the Jews of Cairo were once used by non-Jewish speakers as well. They fell out of use over time, to be retained only by the Jews.[22] For example, the non-standard form *ʔega* ('he came', versus the standard CEA *gih*), which can be conjugated in all persons in the past tense, appears in non-Cairene and non-Egyptian dialects, but in twentieth-century Cairo it was almost only used by Jews and Christians. In a discussion I had with Manfred Woidich on this issue, he suggested that this verb, as well as some other linguistic peculiarities, might have entered Cairene Arabic through immigrants from greater Syria, and in Cairo are now used mostly by Christians.[23]

In some early descriptions of modern CEA, I found further instances of forms commonly used only by Jewish speakers, such as the verbal form *gu* ('they came'), versus standard CEA *gum*,[24] and the demonstrative pronoun *de* ('this'), used in addition to the CEA form *da*.[25] It should be pointed out that several forms that are no longer used in Cairo are still used in non-Cairene Egyptian dialects.[26]

A very common non-standard EJA form used by many Jewish speakers is the third person feminine singular form *gātit* ('she came'), versus *gat* in CEA.[27] Another non-standard verb form often used in EJA (spoken and written) is the verb *ʔarāḥ* ('went, has gone').[28] In CEA and in MSA it exists in the first form, *rāḥ*, but in EJA the fourth form is more common, also in the figurative meaning 'passed away, died'.

2.6 A note on syntax

The syntax of EJA is almost identical to that of CEA. Blau's comment on (written) medieval Judeo-Arabic syntax can also be applied to contemporary spoken Egyptian Judeo-Arabic:

> Hebrew has almost no influence on grammatical structure [of the Judaeo-Arabic]; even when a sentence contains numerous Hebrew words, in most cases the structure of the sentences remains Arabic. The Hebrew elements are usually adapted to Ara-

21 See also Blanc 1974: 217, and footnote 39 on page 217.

22 Blanc 1974: 207; 1981; 1985.

23 Manfred Woidich, personal communication; on this issue and Syrianisms that crop up in Egyptian Arabic, see Blanc 1974: 215, footnote 37; see also the verb *iga* and other variations in Behnstedt and Woidich 1985: maps 302–304; 1994: 75; see also the form *ega* in Blanc 1974: 215.

24 Cf. Fiske 1904: 84, where *gu* is the only form.

25 Cf. Sacroug 1874: 239.

26 For such forms see Behnstedt and Woidich 1994; for example: 10 (*ʔēš*); 75 (*ʔīǧa*); 421 (*kamāni* [cf. *kamāna* in EJA]); 425 (*kēf* and *kīf*); 443 (*lēš*). See also Blanc 1974: 216.

27 See Blanc 1974: 216; Blau 1995: 68.

28 Cf. Blanc 1974: 215.

bic syntax and there are relatively few (although not completely absent) phenomena which attest to the "foreignness" of the Hebrew words within the Arabic sentence.[29]

Very few EJA syntactic features, however, do exist. In CEA the interrogative pronouns usually appear at the end of the clause, while EJA places them at the beginning (see above, section 2.5).

Another typical EJA syntactic feature that is noticeable among some speakers, mostly women, is a tendency to place some adjectives and adverbs before the modified noun or adjective, respectively, contrary to their regular position in CEA, after the noun or adjective (although a few Egyptians do prepose them in such cases), as in *kitīr kanāyis* ('many synagogues') versus *kanāyis kitīr* in CEA; *hāga ḫāliṣ miš kwayyisa* ('something absolutely not good') *versus hāga miš kwayyisa ḫāliṣ* in CEA.

3. The lexicon of Spoken Egyptian Judeo-Arabic

The description below focuses on the unique vocabulary of Egyptian Judeo-Arabic, that is, words that are used exclusively by Jews, or used by non-Jews as well, but among Jews have a different or an additional meaning.

The main component of this variety consists of words and expressions originating in Hebrew; it also contains words and phrases of Aramaic origin, most of which entered EJA through Hebrew. Another major component is Arabic words that are used by Jews in a different way than by non-Jews. Other components consist of words and phrases that originate in European Romance languages: French, Italian and Judeo-Spanish (Ladino).

As is the case with other Judeo-Arabic dialects, the Hebrew and other components are mixed and combined with components derived from the standard local dialect, resulting in unique combinations. In EJA the non-Arabic components are mixed with the Arabic ones. Borrowed words and phrases often undergo changes in meaning, and sometimes in form as well; some may appear in distorted forms.

As in the vocabularies of other Jewish languages, many uniquely Jewish words and expressions are connected with religious and communal aspects of Jewish life. Several others are used as elements of secret languages for communicating information in the presence of those who are not members of the community.

The vocabulary items described below are typical examples, representing parts of the corpus I collected.

3.1 Words originating in European languages

The EJA lexicon contains words and phrases borrowed from European, mostly Romance languages: French, Italian and Judeo-Spanish (Judeo-Español, also known as Judezmo and nowadays mostly as Ladino). The following are words and phrases derived from these Romance languages,[30] and one word borrowed from Yiddish.

29 Blau 1995: 270; see also Blau 1958, 185–186.

30 For more examples derived from Romance languages see Rosenbaum 2018.

3.1.1 Components derived from French

The word *il-komminuté* (also: *il-komminutá*; see below, section 3.1.2), is derived from French *communauté* ('community'), with the addition of the Egyptian Arabic definite article *il-*, short for *Communauté Israëlite* ('Jewish community'). This term is commonly used to refer to the Chief Rabbinate, which functioned as the governing body of the Jewish community and was responsible for managing its religious and secular affairs.[31]

The word *ser* ('nun'), derived from French *soeur* ('sister; nun'), usually in the sound Arabic plural form *serāt* created by the suffix *-āt* and with the addition of the Arabic definite article *il-* (in this case changed to *is-* because it appears before a "sun letter"):[32] *is-serāt* (lit.: 'the sisters, the nuns'), is used to refer to the nuns who were the teachers at the girls' Catholic school, where many Jewish girls were sent to study. Therefore, the common mixed collocation in EJA *ʕand is-serāt* (lit.: 'at the nuns') actually means 'at the Catholic girls' school'.

The corresponding masculine term *frér*, from French *frère* ('brother; monk'), is also used in EJA to mark the plural (as in French [frères] in which the pronunciation of the plural sounds like that of the singular). Therefore, the mixed collocation *ʕand il-frér* actually means 'at the Catholic boys' school'.

The word *kominyón*; from French *communion*, which in French refers to a Catholic religious ritual (*Eucharist*), in EJA denotes the '*bat mitzvah* celebration' (coming of age ceremony for girls at the age of twelve). In Egypt this term referred to the common ceremony held by the Jewish school for all girls of that age-group.

An example of a distorted term that was very common in EJA is *gudelé*, usually regarded as one word, especially among those who did not speak French. This term is a distorted form of *La goutte de lait* ('Drop of Milk'), the name of a school and orphanage for the poor children of the Jewish community in Cairo. Many speakers pronounced it as a single word, *gudelé*. It is worth mentioning that currently there is an attempt by the diminishing community of Cairene Jews to revive this association, under the title "Drop of Milk". The Jewish community in Egypt today consists of only a few individuals, so that the association's task is to "devote itself to restoring and preserving Jewish institutions throughout Cairo" (Lagnado 2019).

31 Two other terms are synonymous with *il-komminuté* or *il-komminutá*, and are very commonly used in EJA: a. *Il-Ḥak̲ámk̲āna*, a term that consists of the Hebrew word *ḥak̲ám* (lit.: 'wise man'), commonly used to denote 'rabbi' in Oriental Jewish communities and languages, and the suffix *ḫāna*, derived from Persian (through Turkish), meaning a house or a building and used to refer to the location of an institution (on *ḫāna* in Persian see Steingass 1957: 444, and in Turkish see Redhouse 1890: 827. b. *Bēt is-sinyór* (see below, sections 3.1.2 and 3.1.3).

32 "Moon letters" in Arabic are letters that are pronounced when preceded by the definite article, while "sun letters" are letters, to which the consonant *l* of the definite article assimilates, and are thus geminated. The moon letters are *a* (*ʔ*), *b*, *g*/*j*, *ḥ*, *ḫ*, *ʕ*, *ġ*, *f*, *q*, *k*, *m*, *h*, *w*, *y*. The "sun letters" are *t*, *t̲*, *d*, *d̲*, *r*, *z*, *s*, *š*, *ṣ*, *ḍ*, *ṭ*, *ẓ*, *l*, *n*. It should be noted that in Egyptian Arabic the consonants *g* and *k* usually function as sun letters, too.

3.1.2 Components derived from Italian

The word *il-komminutá*, a version of *il-komminuté* (see above, section 3.1.1), is apparently derived from the Italian *comunità*, a cognate of French *communauté* ('Chief Rabbinate'). This second version is as common as the first and is used in the same context.[33]

Another common term, synonymous to *il-komminuté* or *il-komminutá*, is *bēt is-sinyór*. *Is-sinyór* (lit.: 'the lord, the master') denoted the Chief Rabbi in Egypt (mostly among Jews speaking Italian or Judeo-Spanish; in Italian: *signor*; in Judeo-Spanish: *senyór* or *sinyór*),[34] and the term *bēt is-sinyór* (lit.: 'the Chief Rabbi's house') was very common among all Egyptian Rabbinic Jews, denoting 'The Chief Rabbinate'. Some informants believe that the origin of the word *sinyór* is Italian, while others are of the opinion that it is Judeo-Spanish. This term looks as if it is a translation of the mixed EJA term *ḥak̲amk̲āna* (see below, section 3.8.1).

The words *nonno* and *nonna*, borrowed from Italian, are used in EJA to denote 'grandfather' and 'grandmother', respectively, while the words *tsiyo* or *ṣiyo* and *tsiya* or *ṣiya*, from Italian *zio* and *zia* ('uncle' and 'aunt') are used mainly by the Jews of Alexandria, due to the stronger influence of Italian on the language spoken in that city.

A common popular ritual among Jews which derives its name from Italian is the *brindízi*, also *brendézi*: 'Making a toast, having a drink in honor of somebody' (from Italian: *brindisi*). The custom is to raise a glass at family occasions or social gatherings, and to toast someone on that particular occasion. The person who is making the toast holds a glass, and the blessing traditionally opens with the phrase *ʔašrab hāḏa [hāza] l-kās* ('I am going to drink this cup'), followed by the name of a person or referring to an occasion. This opening is then followed by rhyming and comic verse, sometimes prepared beforehand but often improvised. At intimate gatherings this verse can be of a mocking nature.[35]

3.1.3 Components derived from Judeo-Spanish

Some Judeo-Spanish words, used by several groups of Jews in Egypt of *Sefaradí* origin which had immigrated to Egypt from various places around the Mediterranean, entered the Judeo-Arabic spoken by all Jews in Egypt, due to close contact with speakers of Judeo-Spanish.

The word *robbísa*, also *rabbísa* and *ribbísa*, from Judeo-Spanish *rubísa* ('the rabbi's wife'),[36] is the common and only word denoting 'a rabbi's wife' in EJA (in Judeo-

33 For a testimony that refers to this word's pronunciation see Gordon's report on his visit to Cairo, in which he transcribes this term *communita* (1977 [1919]: 21, 23), apparently following the Italian version that he might have heard in Cairo.

34 For the two versions in Judeo-Spanish see section 3.1.3 below.

35 Many *brindīzi* verses in Hebrew, Arabic, Aramaic, and European languages were created by the Choueka family that emigrated from Egypt to Israel and has continued the *brindīzi* tradition at its gatherings in Israel; a collection of these *brindīzi* verses was published in the book *ʔEšté ze hakos* ('I am going to drink this cup'); see Choueka 2001.

36 Bunis 1999: 516 (רוביסה); Nehama and Cantera 1977: 486 (*rubísa*).

Spanish, the three forms *rabi*, *rubi*, and *ribi* are used to denote a 'rabbi',[37] but in EJA only the first version is used). The term *robbísa* (in all three versions) is also used metaphorically as an epithet for a righteous and pious woman, but may also refer to a woman who merely pretends to be such, for example: *ma tiʕmilīš robbīsa!* ('don't pretend to be pious!'). The word *robbísa* also appears in an EJA version of a popular Egyptian lullaby (see below, section 3.9, and text 6).

The word *kurátša* (in Judeo-Spanish: *koráča*)[38] is used to denote 'a fabric bag for carrying the phylacteries, a prayer shawl and a prayer book'. This word is used by rabbinic Jews only, not by Karaites (who do not put on the phylacteries and therefore do not carry them). The corresponding Karaite term is the mixed phrase *kīs ṭalīt* ('a bag for [carrying the] prayer shawl').

The Judeo-Spanish word *mantel*[39] (still used in modern Spanish) is the usual word for 'tablecloth' among Egyptian Jews (*mantél*), versus *mafraš* in standard Egyptian Arabic.

The word *sinyór* mentioned in the previous section, at least in some of its occurences, is probably also of Judeo-Spanish origin (in which there are two versions, *senyór*[40] and *sinyór*)[41]. The plural of this word, *sinyóres* ('Gentlemen'), was used among rabbinic Jews on one specific occasion: the Chief Rabbinate of Cairo employed a person who used to go on Saturdays to visit the synagogues and bring messages from the Chief Rabbinate to the congregation. That person used to enter the synagogue, and when given permission to speak, he would draw the public's attention by loudly calling out *sinyóres!*, in the sense of 'Gentlemen [your attention please – I have a message from the Chief Rabbinate!'].

The Judeo-Spanish expression *Sinyór del mundo!*[42] (lit.: 'Master of the Universe'), an epithet for God,[43] is used in EJA also as an exclamation that conveys a range of feelings from astonishment to discontent.[44] It was sometimes used by speakers of Judeo-Spanish also when speaking Arabic, and thus became familiar to Jews who were not speakers of Judeo-Spanish through their contacts with their Judeo-Spanish-speaking neighbors.

The word *kodyádo* from Judeo-Spanish *kudyado* ('worry, concern, care'),[45] which in EJA means 'it's not important! It does not matter! never mind!', was used mainly by speakers of Judeo-Spanish, but also by those who did not speak it. This word is now known only to a few old informants, and it seems to have gradually fallen out of use by

37 Bunis 1999: 513 (רבי); Nehama and Cantera 1977: 464 (rabi); 480 (ribí); 485 (rubí). See also Bunis 1993: 406 for various variations and derivatives.

38 Nehama and Cantera 1977: 303 (*koráča*).

39 Koén-Sarano and Benchimol 2000: LVI.

40 Nehama and Cantera 1977: 507 (*señór*).

41 Nehama and Cantera 1977: 514 (*siñór*). Cf. above, section 3.1.2: *signor*.

42 Nehama and Cantera 1977: 514 (*Siñór del mundo*).

43 Nehama and Cantera 1977: 514.

44 Cf. Nehama and Cantera 1977: 514.

45 Cf. Bunis 1999: 513 (קוּד׳ייאד׳ו); Koén-Sarano and Benchimol 2000: LII (*kudiado*); Recuero 1977: 86 (*kuđyađo*).

non-speakers of Judeo-Spanish.[46] The mixed expression *ʔēš del kodiādo* ('it doesn't matter, don't worry') mentioned by Tomiche,[47] in the same meaning as *kodyádo* that opens with the EJA interrogative pronoun *ʔēš* ('what'; see above, section 2.5), is today known to only a few informants.[48]

3.1.4 One component derived from Yiddish

The Yiddish word *šlékt* (lit.: 'bad'), also pronounced in EJA *šelékt*, *šlékti*, *šlékten*, and *šléktin* (in Yiddish and German: *schlecht*), was commonly used in Egypt by Jews of Oriental origin as a nickname for Ashkenazi Jews; many of my informants told me that only after they had left Egypt did they discover what this word really meant.[49]

3.2 Wholly or partly Arabic words and expressions

Some of the words and expressions used by Jews are of purely Arabic origin. For example, the word *ʔirāya*, which in CEA means 'reading' as well as 'declaiming verses of the Qurʔān', is used by Rabbinic Jews to denote 'memorial service', and by the Karaites 'reading of a passage from the Torah in the synagogue' (see below, section 3.8.3). *Gabal* means 'mountain', but Cairene Jews use this word, with the prefixed definite article (*il-gabal*), to denote the cemetery, so that *ṭiliʕ il-gabal* (lit.: in CEA: 'he went up the mountain') means in EJA 'he went to visit the cemetery'.

Some Arabic expressions have no meaning outside EJA. For example, it was the custom of the Jews of Egypt to eat goose at the festive meal on the holiday of Shavuót (Pentecost), giving rise to the expression *ʕīd il-wizza* ('feast of the goose'), a popular name for the holiday. According to humorous folk belief, a wife who does not serve her husband goose on Shavuót risks divorce (and according to another version, a husband who does not supply his wife a goose risks the same).

The greeting *gumʕit-ak ḫaḍra* ('may you have a good week'; see below, section 3.5.4), and the responses to it, are said by Jews only and are unknown among non-Jews.

The Jews of Egypt use two words to denote the Shabbat (Saturday), Hebrew *šabbát* and Arabic *sabt*. The Jews invented the neologism *sabbit*, a second-form verb derived from the Arabic term, that means 'spent the Shabbat with', as in *taʕāla sabbit ʕandi-na* ('come and spend the Shabbat with us'). No verb with this meaning exists in CEA (and there is no similar verb in Hebrew). For more Arabic words and expressions connected to the Jewish way of life, see below, section 3.9.

46 This word is mentioned by Tomiche 1968: 1180 (*kodiādo*) as a component that belongs to the EJA vocabulary.

47 Tomiche 1968: 1180.

48 The expression *kodiādo negro* ('it has no importance') mentioned by Tomiche (1968: 1180), was not known to any of my informants.

49 This word appears in Spiro's Dictionary (1973: 321) in the versions *šiliḫt* and *šiliḫtin*, defined as 'Bohemians'; the forms *šilixta* and *šilixtāya* appear in Badawi and Hinds (1986: 476), who define them as 'large ugly woman', marked as possibly derived from Yiddish.

3.3 Hebrew (and Aramaic)

3.3.1 New words and expressions based on Hebrew roots

Some words and expressions in EJA are neologisms created from Hebrew words or roots. For example, the second-form verb *makkit* ('hit, beat') is formed from the root √ m-k-t, otherwise non-existent in Arabic and derived from the Hebrew word *makkót* ('blows', plural of *makká*), whose Hebrew root is √ n-k-y. In EJA this verb is commonly used in the imperative as an element of a secret language: *Makkítu!* ('Hit him! Beat him up!'), especially when a Jew has a fight with a non-Jew.

The EJA verb *ʔitdardim* or *ʔiddardim* ('fell asleep') is also commonly said in the imperative by impatient or angry parents to their children at bedtime: 'Go to sleep! Fall asleep!'[50] Many speakers consider it rude. The verb *dardim* exists in CEA, where, as a secondary form of *radam,* it means 'cover, fill [mainly with earth]', with *ʔitdardim* as its passive form,[51] but neither form is widespread. In EJA, *ʔitdardim* or *ʔiddardim*, from the quadriliteral root √ d-r-d-m, apparently expanded from the Hebrew root √ r-d-m and influenced by the Hebrew verb *nirdám* ('fell asleep'), is used only with the meaning of 'fall asleep', and is very common. This verb looks like the passive form of *dardim* (that does not exist). It also appears in the expressions *ʔitdardim* durdémit *Ḫanóḫ* ('fell asleep like Enoch', or in the imperative 'fall asleep like Enoch'), i.e. 'fell or fall into a deep sleep', usually said in a tone of humorous criticism), and *durdéma taḫdak* ('may you fall into a deep sleep [and not wake up]'), also said in the same tone. The word *durdéma* ('deep sleep') in this expression (in the construct form), and in the phrase *durdéma taḫdak* ('may a deep sleep take you', i.e. 'may you never wake up', said in anger or impatience), is reminiscent of the Hebrew word *tardemá* ('deep sleep') and also has the appearance of being derived from the root √ d-r-d-m. The name of Enoch and the expressions' metaphorical meaning appear to be based on Gen. 5:24: "Enoch walked with God, and he was not; for God took him".

The eighth-form verb *ʔiṭṭabal*, also *ʔiṭṭabal*, meaning 'immersed oneself in a ritual bath' (usually said of a woman: *ʔiṭṭabalit*, *ʔiṭṭabalit*), does not exist in Arabic and is derived from the Hebrew root √ ṭ-b-l, as is the word *ṭabbála* (used in EJA in addition to the CEA word *ballāna*), referring to the (female) supervisor of the ritual bath and formed according to the nominal pattern *faʕʕāl* often used for indicating professions. Egyptian Arabic has an identical word (*ṭabbāla*) meaning 'woman drummer', derived from the Arabic root √ ṭ-b-l and its second-form verbal derivative, *ṭabbil*, which means 'beat a drum', and thus non-Jewish speakers of CEA could not understand the EJA meaning (see also *maṭbal* and *ṭebilá* in section 3.4.3).

3.3.2 Words and expressions whose Hebrew components retain their original form and meaning

The major contributor to distinct EJA vocabulary is Hebrew. Furthermore, some words derived from Aramaic entered EJA through Hebrew, for example: *barminnán* ('God forbid', lit.: in Aramaic: 'except us'; see also *ʕurubbá*, 'eve of a holiday', section 3.4.2

50 See also Khan 1995–1997: 75.

51 See Badawi and Hinds 1986: 284.

below). Many Hebrew words retain their form and meaning in EJA. Some examples are *šeʔer* ('lie'; originally *šeqer*, the uvular stop *q* realized as a glottal stop as is the custom in CEA); *gannáb* ('thief', with the original fricative b (*gannáv*) realized as the stop *b*; *raʕ*, PL *raʕím* ('bad, an evil person'); *nes* ('miracle'); *le-ʕolám va-ʕéd* ('forever'); *yeré šamáyim* ('God-fearing').

3.4 Words and expressions originating in aspects of Jewish life

A considerable portion of the unique vocabulary of EJA refers to aspects of Jewish religious and communal life. The following are typical examples.

3.4.1 The synagogue and prayer: some common terms

Tefillá ('prayer'); *gilyán* ('lifting the Torah scroll in the synagogue'),[52] apparently from Arabic *galla* ('to reveal, to show', but possibly also influenced by the Hebrew verb *gilla* ('to reveal'), or the Hebrew gerund *gelilá* ('rolling up and dressing the Tora scroll'); see below, section 3.5.5.2); *tagliyya* ('carrying the Torah scroll around the synagogue'), apparently from *galla* and *gillá*, too; *šammáš*, PL *šammaším* ('caretaker, beadle of a synagogue'; cf. below, section 3.8, the version *šammás* preferred by the Karaites). This word also means 'the ninth oil-cup from which the Hanukkah menorah, in EJA *ḥanukká*, is lit')[53]; *ḥazzán*, PL *ḥazzaním* ('cantor'); *gabbáy*, pl. *gabbayím* ('administrator of a synagogue'); *tebá* ('prayer rostrum'); *séfer,* PL *sefarím* ('Torah scroll').

3.4.2 Jewish holidays and the Jewish calendar: some common terms

ʕurubbá, ʕerubbá, ʕarubbá (from Aramaic) and also *yóm il-ʕurubbá* ('the eve of a holiday'); *roššaná*, also *roš hašaná* ('Rosh Hashana, the Jewish New Year'). The common version in the spoken language is almost always *roššaná* and is regarded as one word, as is the case with *ṭúbišbáṭ* ('The Fifteenth of Shvat'), which is pronounced and regarded as one word; *sukkót* ('Sukkot, the Feast of Tabernacles'); *purīm* or *burīm* ('Purim'); *pésaḥ* or *bésaḥ* ('Passover'); *ʔéḵa,* the Hebrew title of the Book of *Lamentations*, used to denote 'the Ninth of Av', the fast day on which *Lamentations* is read in the synagogue; this word is used figuratively in a number of expressions (see below, section 3.4.4).

3.4.3 Religious duties and ceremonies

The word *tefilím*, also *tefilín* ('phylacteries'), is also used to refer to the Bar Mitzva ceremony celebrating a boy's coming of age at thirteen. Often prefixed by an Arabic definite article, it is also used in mixed expressions having to do with the Bar Mitzva ceremony: *hayilbis it-tefilím* (lit.: 'he will put on phylacteries', that is, 'he is about to celebrate his Bar-Mitzvah'); *labbisūh it-tefilím* ('they celebrated his Bar Mitzva'). Other examples in this category include *mezuzá* ('mezuzah, a parchment scroll with inscriptions from *Deuteronomy* placed in a case affixed to the doorpost'); *habdalá* ('havdalah, ceremony at termination of Shabbat or holiday'; see below, section 3.5.3); *maṭbal* ('ritual bath'), and *ṭebilá* ('immersion in a ritual bath'; see also *ṭabbála* above, section

52 A homonym in CEA, used by Jews as well, means 'dishwashing' or 'dishes to wash'.

53 In Egypt the custom was to light a menorah (*ṭuštiyya*) consisting of small glass cups with oil and wick.

3.3.1); *ʔiddús* or *ʔaddús* ('*kiddush*', 'the sanctification of the Shabbat or a holiday with a blessing over wine before the meal'). The word originates in the Hebrew word *qidduš*, from the root √ q-d-š, but the EJA version is apparently also influenced by the parallel Arabic root √ q-d-s;[54] *kapparát ʕavonót*, or in the shorter version *kappará*, refers to the ritual of atonement practiced before Yom Kippur or in times of illness or trouble, in which a rooster (for men) or a hen (for women) is slaughtered and its meat is usually given to the poor. The expression is also often used as an exclamation when something breaks or some other bad thing happens: 'let it atone for your sins!', i.e. 'Never mind!'

3.4.4 Words and expressions whose Hebrew components have undergone change in form or meaning

As in other eastern Jewish dialects, the word *ḥaḵám,* which means 'wise, wise man' or 'scholar' in Hebrew, is the usual designation in EJA for a rabbi;[55] from several women I also heard the version *ʕaḵám*. Arabic suffixes of Turkish origin yield *ḥaḵambāša* ('Chief Rabbi') and *ḥaḵamḵāna* ('the Rabbinate, the central institution of the Jewish community"; see above, section 3.1.1, and footnote 31).

The word *ʔéḵa,* designating 'the Ninth of Av' (see above, section 3.4.2), is used figuratively in a number of expressions with negative connotations, as in *yóm ʔéḵa* (lit.: 'day of the Ninth of Av'; 'a bad, unlucky, or disastrous day'); *wišš-i ʔéḵa* (lit: '*ʔéḵa* face', i.e. 'appears grief-striken'); *ʕāmil zayy-i ʕamúd ʔéḵa* (lit.: 'acts like a pillar of the Ninth of Av', i.e. 'stands still, does not move').[56]

The expression *ʔéšet ḥáyil*, also *ʔéšet ḥáyim*, with the consonant *m* replacing the consonant *l* as sometimes occurs in Egyptian Arabic ('woman of valor', *Proverbs* 31:10) is used by Egyptian Jews quite frequently to refer to a righteous, pious woman, loyal to her husband and family. This expression refers more to a woman's moral virtues than to the skills enumerated in *Proverbs* (31:10–31).

The expression *ʔadonáy ʔemét wu-mošé ʔemét* (lit.: 'God is truth and Moses is truth'), as well as the shortened version *ʔadonáy ʔemét* ('God is truth'), is apparently based on the expression *mošé ve-torató ʔemét* ('Moses and his Torah are true/truth")[57]; hence the expression *mošé ʔemét ve-torató ʔemét* ('Moses is true and his Torah is true') that is sometimes quoted in writing in Hebrew on religious matters. The EJA version is an exclamation, made in response to hearing something incredible, meaning: 'Really?! That's amazing! You don't say!'

ʔÓdeš, 'poorhouse' (lit.: 'holiness, sanctity, sacredness'), derived from the Hebrew root √ q-d-š (with the Hebrew uvular stop *q* realized as a glottal stop), refers to free lodging and economic assistance to indigent members of the Jewish community provided by charity funds and wealthy members of the community (although used in secular contexts, this EJA term reminds one of the Arabic-Muslim term *waqf* ('religious endowment'). Thus, the expression *bitūʕ il-ʔōdeš* (lit.: 'those of the *ʔōdeš*') refers to the members of the community who received the free lodging and economic assistance.

54 Cf. the realization of the word קִדּוּשׁ in Western Morocco (Bar-Asher 1998: 156–157).

55 Cf. Maman 2019: 286–288.

56 Cf. Bar-Asher 1998: 157; Maman 2019: 52–54.

57 BT *Baba Batra* 84 b, commenting on *Numbers* 16:32.

3.4.5 Mixed style: expressions consisting of Hebrew and Arabic elements

The linguistic creativity of the speakers of EJA is noticeable in their use of mixed expressions combining Hebrew and non-Hebrew (usually Arabic) elements. The structure and syntax of such expressions are those of CEA, as in *ya way way ya barúḵ ʔadonáy*: this rhyming expression, used in response to extreme fluctuations, for good or ill, in a person's or the world's situation (such as a drought followed by floods, or a very poor person suddenly coming into great wealth), is based on the common Egyptian Arabic pattern *ya... ya...* ('either ... or ...'), into which two contradictory possibilities are inserted. In this case, the initial insertion consists of the onomatopoeic words *way way*, which denote sorrow, while the second is a Hebrew expression meaning 'blessed is God', yielding the meaning 'either things are terrible or they are wonderful; feast or famine'.

Ḥazzán bistanna ʔaddíš ('[like] a cantor waiting for a Kaddish, the liturgical prayer recited for the ascent of the soul of a deceased person [commemoration of a death]'), is said of someone looking for an opportunity to earn something for his livelihood, even at the expense of others. The two nouns are of Hebrew origin, while the verb is in CEA.

In the following expression, the prepositions and the definite article are in Arabic, and the two nouns are in Hebrew. *Min ġēr il-šabatót wil-moʕadím* (lit.: 'without Saturdays and religious festivals'), is a humorous, sometimes sarcastic, response to a person who claims to be younger than he or she is, meaning 'you have not counted Saturdays and religious festivals', i.e. 'you are older than you claim'.

See also the mixed expression *rama l-ʕavonót* ('cast his sins away'), above, section 2.2, in which the verb and definite article are in CEA and the noun is in Hebrew.

3.5 Shabbat (Saturday) vocabulary

3.5.1 A note on the Shabbat and EJA

Šabbát, 'Saturday', is a sacred day for Jews, and also a day of rest, prayer and social activity. Unlike religious feasts which are celebrated once a year, *Šabbát* is celebrated once a week and therefore strongly influences Jewish life and behavior. This is also reflected in many words and expressions related to Saturday activities and usually known to Jews only. Some of this linguistic repertory is shared – in various versions – by other Jewish communities in the East and the West, and others are unique to Egyptian Jews. Some typical examples of this repertory are described below.[58]

3.5.2 The term Shabbat and Shabbat atmosphere

As mentioned above (section 3.2), the Jews of Egypt have two words for 'Saturday', Hebrew *šabbát* and Arabic *sabt*. For Friday and Saturday eve Egyptian Jews use the terms in Egyptian Arabic that mean Saturday and Sunday eve, *lilt is-sabt* and *lilt il-ḥadd*, respectively. Some Rabbinic Jews use the mixed version *lilt iš-šabbát* to refer to Saturday eve.

Activities related to the *Shabbat* begin already on Friday afternoon. Wherever there is a prominent Jewish presence the change in the atmosphere can be felt. This was the

58 For more examples see Rosenbaum 2016.

case in the Jewish quarter and in the predominantly Jewish textile market "al-Ḥamzāwi" in the Al-Azhar neighborhood of Cairo, where shops closed on Friday afternoon and commercial activity stopped until Sunday, and also in the goldsmiths' streets in Egyptian cities and towns, where most of the shops were owned by Jews.[59]

In the Jewish quarter in Cairo it was customary before the commencement of *Shabbat* to announce: *ʔīdu ya girān* (lit.: 'light, oh neighbors'). The beadles of the synagogues in the quarter would make this call to remind the people that the time had come for the traditional oil-lamp (*ṭuštiyya*; see above, footnote 51) lighting for *Shabbat*.

The special preparations for *Shabbat* and the great respect in which this day is held are summed up in the expression *kabód šabbát* ('dignity of *Shabbat*, honor of *Shabbat*'). This expression is also used euphemistically and in a humoristic tone, to denote having sexual intercourse on Saturday.

3.5.3 Shabbat: between Kiddush and Havdalah

Kiddush (lit.: 'sanctification'), the blessing over a cup of wine recited on the eve of *Shabbat* (and holidays), is called in EJA *ʔiddús* or *ʔaddús* (see above, section 3.4.3). The ceremony that contains the blessing over a cup of wine recited on Saturday night (and holidays) that is meant to separate between the Holy Day and the following weekdays is called in EJA *habdalá* (lit.: 'separation', from Hebrew *havdala*), the fricative phoneme /v/ realized as the stop /b/.

A part of the *habdalá* ceremony is the blessing over branches of aromatic plants and smelling them. The custom in Egypt was to smell myrtle leaves (*marsīn*, also *marsīm*; in EJA, some speakers also pronounce this word *barsīm*, which in CEA denotes a species of clover used as animal feed)[60]. Jews who go to the synagogue at the end of the *Shabbat* receive myrtle branches there, rub the fragrant leaves in their hands and recite the blessing *boré atséy besamím* (lit.: '(Blessed art Thou Lord, king of the universe), who created fragrant trees'), which is a part of the *havdala* ceremony. The word *besamím* ('perfumes, fragrances') sometimes also denotes 'myrtle' among Rabbinic Jews, for example: *hāt il-besamím* ('give [me] the myrtle leaves').

3.5.4 Shabbat greetings

Egyptian Jews use common Egyptian Arabic greetings, to which they add some of their own, many of which are related to *Shabbat* and holidays. The most common greeting on Saturday is the Hebrew greeting *šabbát šalóm* ('[may you have] a *Shabbat* of peace').

At the end of the Shabbat, Jews greet each other with *gumʕit-ak ḫaḍra* (or *gumʕit-kum ḫaḍra* in the plural: 'have a good [lit.: green] week'), a greeting used exclusively by Jews. The most common responses are *wu-gumʕit-ak ḫaḍra* (or just *wu-gumʕʕit-ak*: 'May you also have a green week'), or *wu-gumʕit-ak zayy is-salʔ* ('may your week be as green as chard [leaves]'). Other greetings draw upon similes used by Egyptians generally to greet each other in the morning, such as *full* ('jasmine') or *ʔišṭa* ('cream made

59 On the goldsmiths in Egypt and their language see Rosenbaum 2002a, 2013b.

60 Some of my informants told me that they wondered how the same word could refer both to animal feed and to a plant rubbed for its sweet smell at the end of the Shabbat.

from the foam accumulating at the top of the milk'); for example, *wugumʕit-ak zayy il-full* ('may you have a week [white and clean] like jasmine').

Another greeting is derived from Hebrew: *šabúʕa ṭob* ('may you have a good week'); the reply to this greeting is *ʕale-ḵém ve-ʕalé-nu* (lit: 'for you and for us', i.e. 'may you have a good week, too; may we all have a good week').

3.5.5 Saturday rituals: selling readings of the Torah in the synagogue and the process of reading

3.5.5.1 Selling readings of the Torah

On *Shabbat* (and also on holidays) certain rituals called *mitsvót*, also *miṣvót* (lit.: 'commandments' in Hebrew, plural of *mitsvá*, also *miṣvá*) are sold to the highest bidder in the synagogue in a kind of a public auction. This term is used by the Rabbinic Jews only; the Karaite Jews call these activities *ʔirayāt* (lit.: 'readings'; see below, section 3.8.3). These rituals consist of reading passages in the Torah from *parašát ha-šabúʕa* ('weekly section from the Torah read on Saturday'), as well as some other honorary roles which are connected to the process of reading and prayer in the synagogue; these honorary roles are also practiced and sold on the Holidays.

The sums of money that are quoted when selling the commandments often represent Hebrew words in Gematria: 18 (*tamantāšar*) = 'Living' (ח״י, a common abbreviation in Hebrew of the phrase 'Living God', which is one of the names of God), or multiples of this number; 26 (*sitta wi-ʕišrīn*) = "God" (יהוה, the Tetragrammaton); 32 *(ʔitnēn wu-talatīn)* = 'heart' (לב). Sometimes they appeared in other versions to those mentioned above, for example, they could also be multiples of 18 ('Living').

In Egypt the amounts were usually expressed in piasters *(ʔirš*, PL *ʔurūš*, one-hundredth of a *ginēh*, an Egyptian pound) or in *ginēh*. The wealthy people of the congregation would buy 'commandments' for very high prices. The highest sum of money was always paid for the honorary role of *kannidré* (a distorted form of *kol nidré* ['Kol Nidrei', from Aramaic: 'all vows'), taking out the Torah scroll from the holy ark before Kol Nidre, the prayer on Yom Kippur eve asking God to annul one's vows.

The income from the sale of the *mitsvót* or *ʔirayāt* (a practice that still exists in many Jewish congregations) is devoted to the budget of the synagogue, and the sums of money collected are thus regarded as a donation to the synagogue. The person who pays for a *mitsvá* is therefore called *mitnaddéb* ('volunteer'), for example: *mitnaddéb bi-tamatāšar* ('donates eighteen piasters (or Egyptian pounds)'). However, phrases that refer explicitly to selling and buying the *mitsvót* and *ʔirayāt* in the Rabbinic and Karaite synagogues were also commonly used.

3.5.5.2 The Torah reading

The first *mitsvá* sold in a Rabbinic synagogue is *petiḥát ha-heḵál* ('opening the holy ark'); the Hebrew word *heḵál* (lit.: 'palace; a section of the Temple') denotes the ark in which the *sefarím* (SG *séfer*, lit.: 'book'), Torah scrolls written by hand on parchment are kept. The second *mitsvá* is *gilyān* ('lifting the Torah scroll'); this word is derived from the Arab verb *galla* ('to reveal, to show') in the phrase *galla s-séfer* ('showed the Torah, raised the Torah scroll'; see also *galla* and *gillá* above, section 3.4.1). The third *mitsvá* is *rimmoním* (lit.: 'pomegranates'), pomegranate-shaped silverware that adorns the Torah scrolls which are kept in the ark. This *mitsvá* is usually sold during the holidays, and often purchased by parents for their children who receive the honor to remove the *rimmonīm* and return them to the Torah scroll. The word *rimmonim* in EJA is also a nickname for woman's breasts.

Reading portions of the Torah in the synagogue takes place on Mondays, Thursdays, and Saturdays. On Mondays and Thursdays, the portion read is shorter and is divided into three parts, while on Saturdays it is longer and is divided into seven; only on that day the readings are sold. Traditionally, the first portion is read by a *kohén* ('cohen, priest'), the second by a *Leví* ('Levite'), and the rest by any Israelite, a layman (who is neither a *Kohén* nor a *Leví*.

The person who reads the Torah portion is called *ʕolé*, PL *ʕolím* (from Hebrew, lit.: 'one who ascends'). The act of being called up to read the Torah is called *ʕaliyá*, PL *ʕaliyót* (lit.: 'ascent'). This term also appears as the *nomen regens* in possessive phrases while the *nomen rectum* represents one of the readers, for example: *ʕaliyát kohén* ('ascension of the cohen to read the Torah'). The verb 'ascend' in the mixed phrase *ṭiliʕ -s-séfer* ('ascended to read the Torah'), with the first form verb *ṭiliʕ* ('go up, mount'); in this context, a verb in the second form from the same root, *ṭallaʕ*, means 'to call somebody to read the Torah', as in *ṭallaʕū-h -s-séfer* ('they called him up to read the Torah, they let him read the Torah').

After the readings on Saturdays are sold, the readers are called up for reading in the Torah in the following order:

Kohén ('cohen, priest'), the first reader; *Leví* ('Levite'), the second reader; the following readers are all Israelites (in this context, an Israelite is any Jew who is not a cohen or does not belong to the tribe of Levi): *šeliší* (lit.: 'third', 'Israelite'), the third reader; *rebiʕí* (lit.: 'fourth'), the fourth reader; *ḥamišší* (lit.: 'fifth'), the fifth reader; *šišší* (lit.: 'sixth'), the sixth reader; the sixth reader is also called *samúḵ* (lit.: 'adjacent' [to the *mašlīm*]), because he is the last but one reader before the *mašlīm*; *mašlīm* (lit.: 'completing'), the seventh and last reader of *parašát ha-šabúʕa* (see previous section); *mafṭír* (lit.: 'concluding'), an additional reader who rereads the last verses in the weekly Torah portion and then reads the *hafṭará*, a passage from the *Prophets*.

After reading a portion of the Torah, the reader is congratulated by members of the congregation with the words *ḥazzák wu-barúḵ* ('may you be strong and blessed'). The word *ḥazzák* comes from the Hebrew word *ḥazaq* (an imperative form: 'be strong!', derived from the root √ ḥ-z-q), with the uvular stop *q* realized as the velar stop *k*.

When the reading in the Torah is over, it is customary to say blessings for members of the congregation, to wish for the recovery of the sick and to commemorate deceased relatives. These blessings and mentions open with the words *ha-šém ha-ṭób* ('the good name'), an adjective that precedes the person's name mentioned on this occasion.

3.5.6 A typical Jewish dish for Saturday

A typical Jewish dish is *difīna* ('stew', 'cholent'), a dish that contains many ingredients including pulses (in the Egyptian version, mostly chickpeas), commonly put in the oven for a slow cook on Friday eve and eaten on Saturday. This venerable dish exists in many Jewish communities, in various versions and with different names, due to the prohibition on setting fire on the Shabbat. The source of the EJA version of the dish's name is the Arabic root √ d-f-n, that is concerned with burial and hiding (cf. *madfūna* below, section 3.8.4).

3.6 Elements of Jewish secret languages reflecting relations with non-Jews

In many Jewish communities, in the East as well as in the West, unique Jewish vocabulary items serve as a secret language, making it possible to communicate in the presence of non-Jews without the latter understanding what is being said.[61] Merchants and craftsmen often develop secret languages for their own particular professions, enabling them to speak about commercial as well as private matters in the presence of customers, including members of the community who are not of the profession.

The word *goy* is used by Jews in both the East and the West to denote a gentile, a non-Jew. In Egypt and other regions in the East, the Jews make a terminological distinction between Christians, Muslims, and Jews in order to be able to report on a person's affiliation during the process of communication. The Jews of Egypt refer to a Jew as *ben ʕamme-nu*, PL *bené ʕammenu* (lit.: 'a member of our people'); to a Muslim as *goy*, F *goyá*, P. *goyím*; and to a Christian as *ʕarér* (and on a few occasions also *ʕarél*), F *ʕarerá*, PL *ʕarerím*. The latter term, *ʕarér*, is derived from the Hebrew word *ʕarél* ('uncircumcised'), which is used in various Jewish dialects and also appears in written texts.[62]

A common word used as a secret language element is *šattaʔ* (from the Hebrew root √ š-t-q), 'be quiet', i.e., 'don't speak about this now, so that the non-Jew won't hear'.[63] Another word with a similar usage is *be-láḥaš* (lit.: 'in a whisper'), which is how the *il-ʕamidá*, 'the standing prayer', also known in Hebrew as *šemoné ʔesré* ('eighteen [blessings]'), should be said, without the worshipper being heard. In EJA, therefore, *be-láḥaš* became a nickname of this prayer, and in the secret language it is another signal to report on the approach of a stranger and to speak softly in order not to be heard.

The most highly developed Jewish secret language in Egypt is that of the goldsmiths. This was used for centuries by the Jewish (mostly Karaite) goldsmiths in Egypt and was later adopted by their Muslim and Christian colleagues (see below in this section). There are some local variations of this language in different regions of Egypt. For example, 'one' in all versions of the goldsmiths' language is *ʔaḥád*, derived from Hebrew *ʔeḥád* (or the construct form *ʔaḥád*); 'two', on the other hand, is *šanáyin* (derived from Hebrew *šenáyim*, used by the Karaite goldsmiths) in the Cairene version,

61 For some examples see, e.g., Ben-Oren and Moshkowitch 1986; Kendi 1991; Malachi 1985.

62 Cf. the form *ñarelim*, used by the Jews of Piedmont in Italy: Levi 2014: 5. On the use of this term in the masculine and the feminine in Piedmont (and other cities in Italy) and by the Jews of Libya see Bar-Asher 1998: 255, and footnote 57 on page 255.

63 See also Blanc 1974: 217.

while in Alexandria it is *ʔaḥadēn*, a dual form of *ʔaḥád* ('one'), a form that does not exist in Hebrew. In all versions, *yáfet* refers to high quality goods or a good customer; phonetically, this word is similar to Hebrew *yafé* ('beautiful, nice'); it is also the colloquial Arabic form of *yāfiṯ*, standard Arabic for the biblical name Japheth (Yéfet or Yáfet in Hebrew), which, according to rabbinic interpretations, means 'beautiful'.[64] Most of the numbers, such as *šelūša* ('three'), *himišša* ('five'), *šamúnya* ('eight', and in Alexandria also a nickname for a Christian), and *šlušīn* ('thirty'),[65] are of Hebrew origin, but some are not, as *ʕinnitra* ('ten'), *mišṭ* ('twenty', in Cairo), *ʕinnitritēn* ('twenty', in Alexandria), *kwatrīn* ('forty', derived from the word denoting 'four' in the Romance languages (French: *quatre*; Italian: *quattro*; Spanish: *cuatro*), with the Arabic plural suffix *īn*).

The goldsmiths' language has dozens of words for communicating information about customers and goods or giving instructions about how to treat customers. Most are derived either from Hebrew or from the names of goldsmiths' tools, some of which are archaic terms whose original meaning is no longer known to the speakers of the language. For example, a piece of jewelry that was returned by a customer and is then again on display is called *ʔadmón* or *ʔadmūn*, from Hebrew *qadmón* ('ancient'). *Hāt il-gaft* (lit.: 'hand me the tweezers') means 'be quiet, don't talk about this now', similarly to the word *šattaʔ* (see above in this section).[66]

This version of the secret language is still used today by non-Jewish goldsmiths in Cairo, Alexandria and other cities and towns, and also by many merchants in the Khan al-Khalili market in Cairo, especially by those whose shops are located near the goldsmiths' streets. These non-Jewish speakers call this secret language *luġa ʕibriyya* ('Hebrew language'), *luġit il-yahūd* ('the language of the Jews'), and *luġa ʔisraʔīliyya* ('Jewish language').

3.7 Oaths

Egyptian Jews use oath formulas, many of which are not shared by non-Jews.[67] Many of my informants insisted that swearing was a reprehensible habit and that they themselves refrained from pronouncing oaths. However, oaths are very common in the language of Egyptian Jews. Most consist of Hebrew components embedded in Arabic oath formulas. The most commonly used oath formula in CEA is *wi* (also *wu, wa*: 'by ..., I swear by ...'). Other formulas include *wi-ḥyāt* ... ('by the life of ..., I swear by the life of ...'), and *bi-*, similar to *wi-*, also in the Hebrew version *be-*.

The most common and forceful oaths in EJA contain words denoting the Torah. A very frequent one is *be-ʔemét ha-torá* ('[I swear] by the truth of the Torah'). The word *séfer*, which denotes a Torah scroll, appears in a number of oaths, in both the singular form, *wi-s-séfer* ('[I swear] by the Torah scroll') and the plural, *wi-s-sefarím* ('[I swear]

64 BT *Megilla* 9b, commenting on *Genesis* 9:27.

65 The transcriptions here represent the pronunciation of contemporary non-Jewish Goldsmiths in Egypt.

66 For a detailed description of the goldsmiths' secret language see Rosenbaum 2002a; for a concise description see Rosenbaum 2013b.

67 On oath formulas said by the Jews, versus those used by Muslims and Christians, see Rosenbaum 2012b.

by [all] the Torah scrolls'). The strongest and most binding oath is *wi-s-séfer kannidré* ("[I swear] by the Torah scroll of Kol Nidre; see above, section 3.5.5.1). Most of my informants, though not all, knew that the reference was to the Torah scrolls that are taken out of the holy ark for that prayer. All of them agreed that this was a very strong oath, which bound its user to telling the truth. Another common oath is *wi-ḥyāt il-ha-rambám* ('by the life of Maimonides').[68]

A number of oaths mention cult articles or objects in the vicinity of the person making the oath. Examples include *wi-t-tefillím* ('I swear by the phylacteries'); *wi-l-muṣḥāf* ('I swear by the prayer book')[69]; and *wi-ḥyāt iš-šehakól* ('I swear by the drink'). This last oath has its origin in the Hebrew blessing *še-ha-kól nihyá bi-dvar-ó* ('[Blessed art Thou, Lord, king of the universe] by whose word everything was created'), recited before consuming some foods and drinks.

3.8 Distinct vocabulary used by the Karaites

The Karaites, most of whom lived in Cairo, shared some of their vocabulary with the Rabbinic Jews, but also used distinct words and phrases that only they knew and understood. As mentioned above (section 1.2), Karaite Jews generally assimilated more easily than Rabbinic Jews into non-Jewish society; as a result, they sometimes preferred words originating in Arabic over words originating in Hebrew, for example the Arabic version *šammás*, vs. the Hebrew version *šammáš* ('caretaker, beadle of a synagogue') used by the Rabbinic Jews (see above, section 3.4.1; for more examples, see below, section 3.8.3).

A significant part of their vocabulary is related to their unique customs, which rely on traditions which Rabbinic Jews do not share. Thus, for example, the Karaites strictly observe matters of purity and impurity, literally as they are stated in the Bible, giving rise to terms related to practices unknown among Rabbinic Jews; and the prohibition to set fire on Saturday led to the creation of dishes and names of dishes that are unknown to either the Muslim and Christian Egyptians or to Rabbinic Jews. The unique Karaite vocabulary was not understood by non-Jews, and much of it was not known to Rabbinic Jews either. The following are some examples of the unique vocabulary used in the Karaite version of EJA.[70]

3.8.1 The Karaite community

The civil affairs of the Karaite community were managed by a body whose official name was *il-maglis il-milli* (community council').[71] Issues of Karaite religious practice and law were conducted by *dār iš-šarʕ* ('The Rabbinate'; lit.: '[Jewish] law house')[72]; in

68 On the definite article in this word see above, section 22.

69 *Muṣḥāf*, 'prayer book', is a distinct EJA word, as opposed to *muṣḥaf*, 'a volume of the Qurʔān' in CEA and MSA.

70 On the unique EJA vocabulary of the Jewish-Karaite community in Egypt see Rosenbaum 2019.

71 Wehr (1994: 1077) defines this term as: "court of justice of a religious minority (in Egypt abolished since 1956)".

72 In Arabic the term *iš-šarʕ* refers to Islamic law; here it refers to Jewish law.

the spoken language, however, the Karaites also used the term *il-ḥak̠amk̠āna* (see above, section 3.1.2, and footnote 31).

3.8.2 Purity and impurity among the Karaites

The Karaites attach great importance to purity and the avoidance of impurity, such as the impurity of a menstruating woman and the impurity of the dead. Because of this, their vocabulary contains terms on those topics that do not exist in the vocabulary of Rabbinic Jews.

The verb *ṭimyit*, imperfect *tiṭma* (lit.: 'became impure'), from the Hebrew root √ ṭ-m-ʔ,[73] denotes a woman who started menstruating and may therefore not be touched and is forbidden to have sexual intercourse with her husband. This verb also exists in the masculine: *ṭimi*, imperfect *yiṭma*, but its use in the spoken language is rare (a man who adheres to the precautions is not supposed to be in a state of impurity). A woman or a girl during her period is called *ṭaméyya* ('impure').[74] A woman is considered to be impure also after birth as well as in the case of bleeding due to illness. It is also forbidden to touch an object touched by an impure woman.

The term *ṭaharit* (lit.: 'became pure') indicates the opposite situation, that is, a woman who ended her period. This woman is called *ṭahra* ('pure', after bathing – see below).

A woman in a state of impurity when in company should avoid physical contact and sits on a separate chair. Because it is forbidden to touch an impure woman, women are in the habit of reporting on being in this condition, for example: *ʔana ṭaméyya* ('I am impure', that is, 'I am having my period'). This fact is openly communicated and known to all and is not associated with embarrassment or shame.

A man who touches a menstruating woman or her belongings, becomes *ṭami* ('impure'), and it is forbidden to touch him, too.

Bathing in water purifies all conditions of impurity, and according to the Karaite custom is done at home and not in the mikveh. On purification day, the impure woman is assisted by a pure woman, usually the mother, and sometimes a relative or neighbor. The pure woman prepares water in a pure vessel, which the impure woman did not touch (traditionally a metal cup), and pours the water on the impure woman, thus washing her. She then fills water in the vessel, pours the water on the impure woman seven times, and after the seventh time she may call: *ṭahra!* '([You are] pure!'), once or three times.

After the purification process is over, when the woman leaves the bath, she may be greeted with formulas such as *yiṭahhar ʔalbik* ('May God purify your heart [for good deeds and good thoughts]'). Women may bless an unmarried woman with *ʕuʔbāl ma nistaḥamma yōm faraḥik* ('we wish to take a bath on your wedding day', that is, 'we wish that you would get married [soon]'), and a married woman with the blessing

73 Cf. the form טאמי in Bar-Asher 1998: 18; and see the word טמא and its derivatives in the Jewish languages in Maman 2019: 327–329).

74 Following *Leviticus* 15:19–27.

ʕuʔbāl tisaʕ tušhur ('we wish that [this will be the last menstruation cycle and that you give birth] nine months from now').

Men wash themselves, and this is how they become purified. Nowadays, as showers are commonplace, women purify themselves and no longer need the help of pure women, and the use of vessels has ceased.

3.8.3 Shabbat: Karaite vocabulary

Some terms related to prayer and reading the Torah in the synagogue on Saturday are unique to the Karaites. The term *séfer ʔurbān* (lit.: 'book [Torah scroll] of sacrifice') denotes an ancient or old Torah scroll that has gained a higher status than the other Torah scrolls in a particular synagogue. This book is kept separate from the other Torah scrolls in the holy ark, and in Egypt it was common to prepare a showcase inside the synagogue, in which it was on permanent display. The word *ʔurbān* (from Hebrew *qorbán*, derived from the root √ q-r-b), refers to the sacrifices that were made in the Temple, which after the latter's destruction were replaced by the *musáf*, additional prayers that are recited on Shabbat, holidays and the first day of the month. This Torah scroll is taken out of its showcase on holidays and on a Shabbat which is also the first day of the month, and the person who has the honor of carrying it takes it on a round through the congregation.

Towards the end of the prayer the Karaites recite five liturgical poems. The first one is called *piyúṭ parašá* or *biyúṭ barašá* (also: *perašá*, *berašá*; 'liturgical poem of the [weekly Torah] portion'), whose contents are connected to the weekly Torah portion. The other four are called *qedušót* (realized *kedušót*) or *ʔedušót* (PL of *qedušá* or *ʔedušá*, lit.: 'holiness) and deal with the holiness of the Shabbat and keeping the Shabbat. These liturgical texts are included in the Karaites' prayer books.

After reciting the *qedušót* and the *piyúṭ parašá*, the *hazzán* ('cantor') recites blessings over the congregation and over the people of Israel in general. After that the cantor recites *zikronót* (PL of *zékẹr*, lit.: 'memory', which by the Karaites is also used to denote 'memorial service'), blessings to commemorate the memory of the deceased; at first the names of great sages are mentioned, then names of relatives of members of the congregation.

After the recital of the *qedušót* and the *zikronót* there is an intermission, during which the readings of *qedušót* and *piyúṭím* for the following Saturday are sold. Readings in the Torah are then sold in the same kind of auction as in the Rabbinic synagogue. The Torah readings and related activities which are sold in the synagogue and called *mitsvót* by the Rabbinic Jews, are called *ʔirayāt* (lit.: 'readings', PL of *ʔirāya*) by the Karaites.

The first 'reading' sold in the Karaite synagogue is *fatḥ is-sitāra* ('opening the curtain, opening the *paróket*', the ornamented curtain that covers the holy ark). In the two latter cases the Karaites prefer words originating in Arabic over words originating in Hebrew: Arabic *ʔirāya* PL *ʔirayāt* versus Hebrew *mitsvá* PL *mitsvót,* the Arabic gerund *fatḥ* ('opening') versus its Hebrew equivalent *petiḥá* (in the *nomen regens* version *petiḥát*), and the Arabic noun *sitāra* ('curtain') versus the Hebrew noun *hekāl* ('Temple').

In order to encourage the audience to increase the sums offered and to continue the process of selling a certain 'reading', the *gabbáy*, the synagogue administrator, announces: *ḥa-nbārik li-fulān* ('we are about to congratulate so and so [for purchasing the 'reading']'). When the reading is finally sold, the *gabbáy* declares: *bārikna li-fulān* (lit.: 'we have congratulated so and so', i.e. 'congratulation to so and so').

The person who is given the first 'reading' performs two acts: he moves the *paróḵet* aside and opens the ark. The person who opens the ark also takes out the Torah scroll and gives it to the congregant who has been given the second 'reading', called *is-séfer* ('the book', i.e. 'the Torah scroll'). This person holds the Torah scroll, makes a round in the synagogue with it and later puts it back in the ark. As mentioned above in this section, the Karaites, too, use terms of buying and selling in this regard, for example: *yibīʕu s-séfer* ('they are selling the [reading of] the Torah'); *mīn ʔištara s-séfer innahārda?* ('who bought the reading of the book today?').

Then begins the process of selling the readings of the Torah portions and the other honorary roles. The readings of the Torah portions are given names similar to but not identical with those used by Rabbinic Jews. Here, too, the Karaites prefer some Arabic words to the Hebrew ones used by the Rabbinic Jews (the names of the third to the sixth reader):

Kohén ('cohen, priest'), the first reader; *Leví* ('Levite'), the second reader; *it-tālit* (lit.: 'third'), 'Israelite', layman, the third reader; *ir-rābiʕ* (lit.: 'fourth'), the fourth reader; *il-ḫāmis* (lit.: 'fifth'), the fifth reader; *is-sādis* (lit.: 'sixth'), the sixth reader; *mašlīm* (lit: 'completing'), the seventh reader who reads the last portion of *parašát ha-šabúʕa* (see above, section 3.5.5.1); *mafṭír*, the very last reader, who reads the *hafṭará*, passages from the *Prophets*, read after the reading of the Torah (see above, section 3.5.5.2).

It is customary for the *mafṭír* to be also the first reader (i.e. the *kohén*). In this case, the *kohén* reads all of the *hafṭará* by himself, and may also serve as *soméḵ* ('supporter'), a person who helps other readers to read the Torah. But if the *kohén* is not proficient in reading the Torah, the job of the *soméḵ* is performed by someone else who also reads the *hafṭará* instead of the *kohén*. If the *kohén* is only somewhat proficient in reading the Torah, the *soméḵ* starts with reading a few verses, the *kohén* continues with reading the first part of the *hafṭará*, and then the *soméḵ* completes the rest.

The word *ḥazzák* in the greeting *ḥazzák wu-barúḵ* said to those who read the Torah in the synagogue, is realized by some of the Karaites *ḥazzáʔ*, with a glottal stop instead of the original Hebrew uvular stop *q*, that by the Rabbinic Jews is realized in this case as the velar stop *k*.

3.8.4 Karaite foods

The Karaites have many distinctive dishes that do not exist among Egyptian non-Jews or Rabbinic Jews. The names of these foods, most of which are in Arabic or derived from Arab roots, do not exist in CEA and most are not known to Rabbinic Jews or to non-Jews. Many of these foods are meant to be eaten on the Shabbat. Because the Karaites are careful not to use fire (or electric stoves) on the Shabbat, these dishes are prepared beforehand and are eaten cold. The following are just a few examples:

Gamal maḥši (lit.: 'stuffed camel'). A whole chicken breast stuffed with rice and pieces of chicken liver (and sometimes other kinds of meat), seasoned with black pepper. The skin is sewn with a cord that closes the chest. This dish is eaten especially on Saturdays and holidays.

Gilda maḥšiyya (lit.: 'stuffed skin'). Rice and chicken meat or liver stuffed in chicken skin. The skin is sewn, and the stuffed skin is cooked in a soup. This dish is mainly eaten on Saturday morning.

Gōz bi-tōm, also *gōz wi-tōm* (lit.: 'walnuts with garlic'), a thick chicken soup with green chard leaves and garlic, ground and fried. Usually rice, drumsticks or flour are added in order to thicken the soup, and black pepper is added, too. Once the soup is boiling, it is left to cool until it congeals. It is customary to eat it on Saturday.

Ḥāmiḍ (lit.: 'sour'). Thick chicken soup that contains much garlic, turmeric, red pepper, and lemon (which gives the soup its sourish flavor). It is customary to eat it on Saturday noon. This dish also has a version with fish, called *samak bi-lamūn* ('fish with lemon').

Madfūna (lit.: 'buried, hidden'), also realized as *matfūna*. A kind of pie that contains ground chicken meat, eggs, fried onion and baked coriander. It is customary to eat it on Saturday morning. The name of this dish, like the *difīna* of the Rabbinic Jews (see above, section 3.5.6), originates in the Arab root √ d-f-n that is concerned with burial and hiding (but, of course, is not cooked on Saturday like the *difīna*).

3.9 Customs and language

As with any distinct social group, the language of the Jews of Egypt contains expressions and idioms related to the group's way of life.[75] Some of these are connected with special events in the life of the community, religious or secular, and are said only in the context of these events. The following are two typical examples.

Haggadá (lit.: 'telling'), Haggadah, is the traditional text recited at the Passover ceremony, 'Seder', usually preceded with the definite article: *il-haggadá*. In EJA that night is called *lilt il-haggadá* (lit.: 'The night of the Haggadah'). To this day, it is customary among Egyptian Jews (and also in some other communities outside of Egypt) during the Passover ceremony to give each small child in turn a folded napkin with a piece of *ʔafikomán* (also: *ʔafikomén*; 'Afikoman', a piece of unleavened bread eaten at the end of the Passover meal) inside, which they then carry on their shoulders in commemoration of the parcels which the Children of Israel carried as they left Egypt. The leader of the ceremony conducts the following dialogue with each child in turn:

– *Gayy-i mnén?* ('Where are you coming from?).

– *Min miṣráyim* ('From Egypt').

– *Wi-rāyiḥ fēn*? ('And where are you going?').

75 On the religious customs of Egyptian Jews according to written records see, e.g., Ben-Shimon 1908; Israel 1990. On religious as well as everyday life and customs see Hassoun 1981: 107–192 ("Chroniques de la vie quotidienne"); Nini 2000.

–ʕala yerušaláyim ("To Jerusalem).[76]

Several informants reported that in families with many children, when the ceremony became repetitive, the more mischievous children would answer the first question by saying things like *mi-l-madrasa* ('from school'), *min maṣr-i l-gidīda* ('from Heliopolis' [quarter in Cairo]), *min il-maṭbaẖ* ('from the kitchen'), etc.

When Jewish parents want to quiet their tots or put them to sleep, they sing the following lullaby:

ẖud il-bizza wi-skut	'Take the nipple and be quiet'
ẖud il-bizza wi-nām	'Take the nipple and sleep'
ʔumm-ak ir-robbīsa	'Your mother is the Rabbi's wife'
wa-bū-k il-ḥaḵám	'And your father is the Rabbi'

This is a an EJA version of a famous CEA lullaby that has several versions; the following is the most common:

ẖud il-bizza wi-skut	'Take the nipple and be quiet'
ẖud il-bizza wi-nām	'Take the nipple and sleep'
ʔumm-ak is-sayyida	'Your mother is a lady'
wa-bū-k il-ʔimām	'And your father is the Imam (prayer leader at the mosque)'[77]

Some of the verses may be changed in order to adjust them to current political events.[78]

4. Concluding Notes

On the basis of the linguistic usages and vocabulary items described here, representing the repertory of the Arabic variety spoken by the Jews of Egypt (EJA), we may state that they had (and still have) a language variety of their own. The Jews of Egypt (most of whom lived in Cairo and Alexandria and several towns in the Delta, and now reside outside of Egypt), share a common variety which is distinct in quite a number of features from the dialects spoken by their non-Jewish neighbors.

While morphological and phonological features of EJA are constant, its unique vocabulary is more common among Egyptian Jews when they are communicating with each other than when they communicate with non-Jews, who cannot understand most of this unique vocabulary. Thus most of the unique EJA vocabulary was avoided by the Jews when speaking with their non-Jewish neighbors.

The Rabbinic and Karaite Jews in Egypt share many linguistic features, but the theological differences between them also led to linguistic differences. The fact that the Karaites were often socially and linguistically more assimilated into non-Jewish society

76 For a description of this ceremony and a version of the dialogue in French see Hassoun 1981: 174–175. On similar ceremonies among other Jewish communities see Bergman 1960: 72–73; Sperber 1994: 113–114 and footnote 1 on these pages; 1995: 185–187. This tradition still continues among families that emigrated from Egypt and other Middle Eastern countries. In Israel, families whose younger generation no longer speaks Arabic perform the ceremony in Hebrew.

77 Cf. Elder 1927: 113.

78 See, e.g., Elder 1927: 113.

is also reflected in their version of EJA that contained more Arabic and fewer Hebrew elements than that of the Rabbinic Jews.

Hundreds of words and expressions are unique to Jews; many of these are of Hebrew origin, while others consist of a mixture of Hebrew, Arabic, and occasionally Aramaic and some European languages as well. This vocabulary attests to ties with other Jewish dialects in the region, but it also has some distinctive features of its own, amounting, together with the phonological and morphological features described here, to a language variety that may be called "Egyptian Judeo-Arabic dialect" or "spoken Egyptian Judeo-Arabic".

This Judeo-Egyptian variety was occasionally reflected in written texts as well. Certain words and expressions, particularly those having to do with religious and community life, may be found in the Arabic-language Jewish newspapers published in Egypt during the first half of the twentieth century, and in books dealing with the Jewish religion. Many grammatical features and lexical items also appear in earlier written texts, such as those found in the Cairo Genizah, and reflect the existence of a unique EJA dialect.[79] However, many words and expressions used in spoken EJA are not found in written sources, including many of those described here that could be retrieved only through intensive work with informants.

5. Texts

The texts below are excerpts from recordings I made during the 1990s and the 2000s. They appear here for the first time, except for the last text, that was included in my study on the story of Hannah and her seven sons (Rosenbaum 2012a). Long pauses and omitted segments are marked by three dots (…). The full versions, with many other texts, will be included in my study on the spoken Arabic of Egyptian Jews in the twentieth century (see above, footnote 1).

Egyptian Jews who became also speakers of modern Israeli Hebrew, occasionally insert words derived from modern Israeli Hebrew into their speech. Such words are not regarded as EJA lexical items, and are printed here with an uppercase "H" in order to distinguish them from items that belong to the EJA vocabulary.

5.1 Text 1: The language spoken in the Jewish quarter in Cairo

This segment displays the following EJA features: the personal pronoun 3PL *humman* (versus CEA *humma*) and the "*nekteb-nektebu*" pattern 1SG *ma kunti-š nifham-u*.

fīh	*kalām*	*kitīr*	*min bitūʕ*	*ḥart*	*il-yahūd*
EXIST	speech	much	from GEN.EXP	quarter.CS	DEF-Jew.COLL

There are many words [said] by those from the Jewish quarter [in Cairo]

ʔana	*ma*	*ʔaʕrafū-š,*	*yaʕni*	*kalām*	*kānu*	*humman*	*yitkallimū-h.*
1SG	NEG	know.IPFV.1SG-NEG	mean.IPFV.3SG.M	speech	be.PF.3SG.PL	3PL	speak.IPFV.3PL-3SG

that I don't know, that is, words which they used to say.

79 For examples in recent publications see, e.g., Hary 2009 and Ørum 2018.

ʔana ʔamma kānu yitkallimu bitūʕ ḥart il-yahūd ʔuddām-i,
1SG when be.PF.3SG.PL speak.IPFV.3PL-3SG GEN.EXP quarter.CS DEF-Jew.COLL before-1SG
I, when those from the Jewish quarter would speak in my presence,

fīh kalām kitīr ma kunti-š nifham-u,
EXIST speech much NEG be.PF.1SG-NEG understand.IPFV.1SG-3SG.M
there were many words that I did not understand.

kān fīh kalām bināt-hum... bass humman yaʕrafū-h.
be.PF.1SG.M EXIST speech among-3PL only 3PL know.IPFV.3PL-3SG.M
There were words among themselves… that only they knew.

5.2 Text 2: Secret language – be-láḥaš

This segment displays the following EJA features: the interrogative pronoun *ʔēš* (at the beginning of the clause) and the demonstrative pronouns SG.M *de* and PL *dōn*.

be-láḥaš, ʔēš yiʔūlu... taʕraf yaʕni ʔēh be-láḥaš?
in^{H}-whisper^{H} what say.IPFV.3PL know.IPFV.2SG.M mean.IPFV.3SG.M what in^{H}-whisper^{H}
Be-láḥaš, what do they say… so do you know what *be-láḥaš* (lit.: 'in a whisper', a nickname for 'the standing prayer') is?

yaʕni ʕašān ma yifhamū-š ʔilli yikūnu ʔaʕdīn,
mean.IPFV.3SG.M so.that NEG understand.IPFV.3PL-NEG REL be.IPFV.3PL sit.PTCP.PL.M
It means that in order that those [non-Jews] who are present will not understand,

yiʔūlu-l-u be-láḥaš, yaʕni ma titkallim-š, be-láḥaš,
be.IPFV.3PL-to-3SG.M in^{H}-whisper^{H} mean.IPFV.3SG.M NEG speak.IPFV.2SG.M-NEG in^{H}-whisper^{H}
they [the Jewish speakers] tell him [another Jew] *be-láḥaš*, which means 'don't talk', *be-láḥaš*.

wi-de kamān fi t-tigāra... wi-n-nās b-yištiru kida
and-DEM.SG.M also in DEF-commerce and-DEF-people PROG-buy.IPFV.3PL so
And this is also [used] in commerce… while people are buying and so on,

wi-tnēn yahūd bi-yitkallimu fi kalām kida yiʔūlu barḍu be-láḥaš,
and-two Jew.COLL PROG-speak.IPFV.PL in speech so say.IPFV.PL also in^{H}-whisper^{H}
and two Jews are talking and saying something, they also may say *be-láḥaš*,

ḥagāt zayy-i dōn, yaʕni kalām zayy-i sirr-i šwayya.
thing.CS like-SANDHI DEM.PL mean.IPFV.3SG.M speech like-SANDHI secret-SANDHI thing.DIM
things like these, I mean words that are a little bit like a secret.

5.3 Text 3: The disappearing grandfather and his phylactery bag

This segment displays a typical EJA verb pattern *ʔaḫad* (versus *ḫad*), the already mentioned clause-initial interrogative pronoun *ʔēš*, as well as lexical elements from Hebrew, Ladino, and Italian.

ʕandi-na	*b-iʔūlu,*	*ʔiza*	*kān…*	*šuft*	*il-kurátša*	*btāʕ*	*il…*
at-1PL	PROG-say.IPFV.3PL	if	be.PF.3SG.M	see.PF.2SG.M	DEF-phylactery_bag^{L}	GEN.EXP	DEF

We say, if… you see that the phylactery bag of the…

ṣāḥib	*il-bēt*	*muš*	*ʔaʕda,*	*yaʕni*	*ḫalāṣ,*	*rāḥ.*
owner.CS	DEF-house	NEG	sit.PTCP.F	mean.IPFV.SG.M	that's.it ("receipt")	leave.PF.3SG.M

head of the family is missing, that means that that's it, he is gone.

ʔēš	*yaʕni*	*rāḥ?*	*fi*	*waʔtī-ha,*	*ʔana*	*b-āʔūl*	*il-ḥikāya*	*di*
what	mean.IPFV.SG.M	leave.PF.3SG.M	in	time-3SG.F	1SG	PROG-say.IPFV.1SG	DEF-story	DEM.SG.F

What does it mean gone? At that time, I am telling this story

min	*il-famīliya*	*btaʕt-i…*	*nonno,*	*yaʕni*	*ʔabu*	*māma,*
from	DEF-family^{It}	GEN.EXP-1SG	grandfather^{It}	mean.IPFV.3SG.M	father.CS	mom^{It}

about my own family… [my] grandfather ("nonno"), that is my mom's father,

kān	*miggawwiz*	*maʕa*	*waḥda,*	*ʔilli*	*hiyya*	*sitt-i,*	*ʔumm-i*	*māma,*
be.PF.3SG.M	marry.PTCP.M	with	one.F	REL	3SG.F	grandmother-1SG	mother.CS-SANDHI	mom^{It}

was married to someone, who is my grandmother, my mom's mother,

wu-gāb	*minna-ha*	*ḫamas*	*banāt…*	*wi-kānit*	*il-ḥāla*	*ṣaʕba…*
and-bring.PF.3SG.M	from-3SG.F	five	daughter.PL	and-be.PF.3SG.F	DEF-situation	difficult.F

and had with her five daughters… and the situation was difficult,

ma	*ʔidir-š-i*	*gidd-i*	*yaʕni*	*yistaḥmil*	*il-parnasá …*
NEG	can.PF.3SG.M-NEG-SANDHI	grandfather-1SG	mean.IPFV.3SG.M	provide.IPFV.3SG.M	DEF-livelihood^{H}

I mean that my grandfather could not provide for livelihood,

rāḥ	*faṭaš*[80]	*li-amerika.*	*ʔizzayy*	*ʕirfu*	*ʔinn-i*	*ṭafaš?*
leave.PF.3SG.M	flee.PF.SG.M	to-America^{H}	how	know.PF.3SG.PL	COMP-SANDHI	flee.PF.3SG.M

so he fled to America. How did they know that he fled?

dawwaru	*ʕala*	*l-kuratša*	*šel-o –*	*ma-fī-š*	*kurátša!*
search.PF.3PL	upon	DEF-phylactery_bag^{L}	GEN.EXP^{H}-3SG.M^{H}	NEG-EXIST-NEG	phylactery_bag^{L}

They looked for his phylacteries bag – there is no phylacteries bag!

ma-fī-š	*kurátša –*	*yaʕni*	*sāfir.*	*il-yahūdi*	*yisāfir*
NEG-EXIST-NEG	phylactery_bag^{L}	mean.IPFV.3SG.M	travel.PTCP.M	DEF-Jew	travel.IPFV.3SG.M

There is no phylactery bag – it means that he left. A Jew travels

80 Metathesized from *ṭafaš*.

min ġēr kurátša – ʔizzayy ḥa-yilbis tefillím?
from NEG phylactery_bag^{L} how FUT-wear.IPFV.3SG.M phylacteries^{H}
without the phylacteries bag –how will he put on phylacteries?

ʕand-i l-yahūd, ʔiza kān ʔaḫad il-kurátša,
at-SANDHI DEF-Jew.COLL if be.PF.3SG.M take.PF.3SG.M DEF-phylactery_bag^{L}
Among the Jews, if [somebody] took the phylactery bag,

ʔiza il-kurátša muš ʔāʕda, yaʕni ir-rāgil sāfir, ḫalāṣ,
if DEF-phylacter_bag^{L} NEG sit.PTCP.F mean.IPFV.3SG.M DEF-man travel.PTCP.M that's.it
if the phylactery bag does not stay, this means that the man has left, that's it,

wu-muš ḥa-yirgaʕ. ʔiza il-kurátša ʔaʕda ʔahō,
and-NEG FUT-return.IPFV.3SG.M if DEF-phylactery_.bag^{L} sit.PTCP.F PRES
and he will not return. If the phylactery bag stays, "here it is"!

ma gā-š in-nahār-da – yigi bukra. ʕāyiz yiṣalli –
NEG come.PF.3SG.M-NEG today come.IPFV.3SG.M tomorrow want.PTCP.M pray.IPFV.3SG.M
He did not come today – he will come tomorrow. He wants to pray –

ʔizzāy ḥa-yiṣalli min ġēr it-tefillím bitāʕ-u?!
how FUT-pray.IPFV.3SG.M from NEG DEF-phylacteries GEN.EXP-3SG.M
how will he pray without his phylacteries?!

5.4 Text 4: The ritual bath

This segment displays mixed Arabic-Hebrew elements and Hebrew vocabulary.

il-ʕarūsa lli ʕawza titgawwiz bi-trūḥ fi l-maṭbal
DEF-bride REL want.PTCP.F marry.IPFV.3SG.F PROG-go.IPFV.3SG.F in DEF-mikveh$^{A/H}$
The bride who wants to get married goes into the mikveh (ritual bath)

wu-b-titṭibil guwwa ʕašān tibʔa kašerá l-baʕal-á.
and-PROG-immerse.REFL.IPFV.3SG.F$^{A/H}$ inside so.that remain.IPFV.3SG.F kosher.F^{H} for-husband-3SG.F^{H}
and immerses herself in it in order to be permitted to her husband.

5.5 Text 5: Endowment for helping the poor

This segment displays the EJA demonstrative pronoun SG.M *de* and Hebrew vocabulary.

il-ʔódeš de ḥāga tanya. il-ʔódeš de zayy-i biyút min ġēr késef...
DEF-Qódeš^{H} DEM.SG.M thing second.F DEF-Qódeš^{H} DEM.SG.M like-SANDHI house.PL from NEG money^{H}
This *Qódeš* (free lodging and economic assistance; lit: 'holiness, sanctity') is another thing. This "Qódeš" is like homes without [paying] money,

il-biyūt bitūʕ il-fuʔara, huwwa de ʔism-u il-ʔódeš.
DEF-house.PL GEN.EXP DEF-poor.PL 3SG.M DEM.SG.M name-3SG-M DEF-Qódeš^{H}
homes for the poor people, this is what is called "Qódeš".

5.6 Text 6: The virtuous woman

This segments displays both Hebrew and Ladino elements.

ir-robbísa sitt il-ʔéšet ḥáyim[81]*, iṭ-ṭayyiba,*
DEF-robbísa^{L} woman DEF-woman.CS^{H} virtue^{H} DEF.good.F
The *robbísa* (lit.: 'Rabbi's wife') is a virtuous woman, a good person,

bitāʕit il-bēt, ir-robbísa di il-ḥāgga.
GEN.EXP.F.CS DEF-house DEF-robbísa^{L} DEM.SG.F DEF-ḥāgga
one who takes care of her home, [like] the *ḥāgga* (a Muslim woman who has performed the pilgrimage to Mecca).

5.7 Text 7: Reincarnations

This segment also displays Hebrew and Hebrew-Aramaic elements.

wu-fīh barminnán gilgulím baʔa, ʔilli humma ma ʕandu-hum-š-i
and-EXIST except.us^{Aram} reincarnation.PL^{H} remain.PF.3SG.M REL 3PL NEG at-3PL-NEG-SANDHI
And there are, God forbid, reincarnations that have no

tikkūn, wu-b-yitʕabu ktīr ʔawi ʔawi ʔawi. masalan,
rectification^{H} and-PROG-suffer.IPFV.3PL much very very very example.ACC
rectification (of the soul), and they suffer very very very much. For example,

fīh ʔarwāḥ ʔilli hiyya bi-tidḫul gehinnám.
EXIST soul.PL REL 3SG PROG-enter.IPFV.3SG.F hell^{H}
there are souls that go into hell.

5.8: Text 8: Selling the "commandments" at the Rabbinic synagogue

Next to the *nekteb-nektebu* pattern (*niṭallaʕu* 1PL), the demonstrative pronoun SG.M *de*, the clause-initial interrogative pronoun *ʔēš*, and the innovative Arabic component *tallaʕ*, the following segment displays a high degree of Hebrew vocabulary.

Nibīʕ il-miṣvōt... ʔēš il-miṣvōt? ʔabl-i ṣ-ṣala,
sell.IPFV-1PL DEF-commandment.PL^{H} what DEF-commandment.PL^{H} before-SANDHI DEF-prayer
We sell the commandments (*miṣvōt*). What are the commandments? Before the prayer,

ʔabl-i ma niṭallaʕu s-séfer, ʔilli yiftaḥ il-heḵál,
before-SANDHI REL lift.IPFV.1PL DEF-book^{H} REL open.IPFV.3SG.M DEF-ark^{H}
before we take the Torah scroll out of the Holy Ark, the one who opens the Holy Ark...

81 Actually *ʔéšet ḥáyil*, with the consonant *m* replacing the consonant *l*, as sometimes occurs in Egyptian Arabic).

sammū-ha petiḥát ha-hek̲ál, wāḥid yištiri petiḥát ha-hek̲ál
name.PF.3PL-3SG.F opening.CS^{H} DEF^{H}-ark^{H} one.M buy.IPFV.3SG.M opening.CS^{H} DEF^{H}-ark^{H}
they named it the opening of the Holy Ark… someone buys the opening of the Holy Ark

ʕašān yiftaḥ il-hek̲ál bass, wi-yišīl is-séfer torá
so_that open.IPFV.3SG.M DEF-ark^{H} only and-take_out.IPFV.3SG.M DEF-book.CS^{H} Tora^{H}
only to open the Holy Ark, takes out the Torah scroll,

yināwil-hū-l-ak, wu-baʕdēn ʔilli ḥa-yištiri… ʔištara s-séfer,
hand_over.IPFV.3SG.M-3SG.M-FOR-2SG-M and-afterwards REL FUT-buy.IPFV.3SG.M buy.PF.3SG.M DEF-book^{H}
hands it to you. Then whoever buys… bought the [commandment of] the Torah scroll,

yāk̲ud is-séfer minn-u wi-yiwaddī-h li-ġāyit it-tebá.
take.IPFV.3SG.M DEF-book^{H} from-3SG.M and-bring.IPFV.3SG.M-3SG.M to-edge.CS DEF-rostrum^{H}
takes the book from him and brings it to the rostrum.

bardu bi-yidfaʕ filūs… bi-yidfaʕ ʔizzay baʔa?
also PROG-pay.IPFV.3SG.M money PROG-pay.IPFV.3SG.M how remain.PF.3SG.M
He, too, pays money. How does he pay?

ʔana ʔult masal bi-ʕišrīn, gēt ʔinta ʔult-i sitta wi-ʕišrīn,
1SG say.PF.1SG example in-twenty come.PF.2SG.M 2SG.M say.PF.2SG.M-SANDHI six and-twenty
I said, for example, twenty, you came and said twenty-six,

wāḥid ʔāl ʔitnēn wu-k̲amsīn, de li-ġāyit… ʔaḥyānan
one.M say.PF.3SG.M two and-fifty DEM.SG.M to-edge.CS sometimes
[another] one said fifty-two, this [goes on] until… Sometimes

bi-yiwṣal il-petiḥát hek̲ál li-miyya, li-mītēn, tultumiyya…
PROG-reach.3SG.M DEF-opening.CS^{H} ark^{H} to-hundred to-two hundred three hundred
the opening of the Holy Ark reaches one-hundred, two-hundred, three-hundred.

mazād, mazād ʕalani, ma-fī-š ḥadd-i yizʕal min it-tānī.
auction auction public.M NEG-EXIST-NEG one-SANDHI get_angry.IPFV.3SG.M from DEF-second.M
[Like an] auction, a public auction. Nobody gets angry with the other.

ʔinta ʕāwiz? ʔištiri! ʔadd-i ma tidfaʕ – tidfaʕ.
2SG.M want.PTCP.M buy.IMP.SG.M as.much-SANDI REL pay.IPFV.2SG.M pay.IPFV.2SG.M
You want? Buy! As much as you [want to] pay – you pay.

wu-baʕdēn lamma yigi is-séfer ʕala t-tebá
and-afterwards when come.IPFV.3SG.M DEF-book upon DEF-rostrum^{H}
And after that, when the Torah Scroll arrives at the rostrum

*wu- b-italla*ʕ*ū-k,* *tibārik.* *wu-tifḍal*
and-PROG-call_up.IPFV.3PL-2SG.M say_blessing.IPFV.2SG.M and-continue.IPFV.2SG.M
and you are called up [to read the Torah], you say the blessing, and you continue

tiʔrū-l-ak [sic] *il-ḥitta…il-parašá* *bitāʕt-ak,* *bi-taʕmil* *nedabá.*
recite.IPFV.2SG.M-for-2SG.M DEF-part DEF-Tora.section^{H} GEN.EXP.F-2SG.M PROG-do.IPFV.2SG.Mdonation^{H}
reading your part…your Torah-section, and you give a donation.

ma ʔulti-l-ak *ʔana, b-ibīʕu* *il-petiḥá,* *wi-s-séfer* *torá,*
REL say.PF.1SG-to-2SG.M 1SG PROG-sell.IPFV.3PL DEF-opening^{H} and-DEF-book.CS^{H} Tora^{H}
I already told you, they sell the opening [of the Holy Ark], and the [taking out of the] Torah scroll,

wu-gilyān *séfer* *torá,* *wa-ʕaliyá* *la-torá…*
and-lifting.CS^{H} book.CS^{H} Tora^{H} and-calling_up^{H} to.DEF^{H}-Tora^{H}
and the lifting of the Torah scroll, and the calling up to read the Torah…

rimmonīm *kamān b-ibiʕū-ha,* *ʔinnama* *ʔaktar* *wa-ʔaktar* *waʔ-aktar*
ponegranate.PL also PROG-sell.IPFV.3PL-3SG.F but much.ELAT and-much.ELAT and-much.ELAT
The pomegranates are also being sold, but more and more

fi l-ʔaʕyād *yibīʕu* *kull-i* *ḥāga.* *yibīʕu* *yaʕni* *il-petiḥá,*
in DEF- holiday.PL sell.IPFV.3PL all.CS-SANDHI thing sell.IPFV.3PL mean.IPFV.3SG.M DEF-opening^{H}
in the Holidays.They sell everything. That is, they sell the opening [of the Holy Ark],

is-sefarīm, *séfer séfer,* *kam* *séfer b-iṭallaʕu?*
DEF-book.PL^{H} book^{H} book^{H} how.many book^{H} PROG-take_out.IPFV.3PL
the [taking out of the] Torah scrolls, Torah scroll by Torah scroll. How many Torah scrolls are they taking out [of the Holy Ark]?

yibīʕu *kull-i* *s-sefarīm.* *wu-baʕdēn,* *baʕd-i* *de,*
sell.IPFV.3PL all.CS-SANDHI DEF-book.PL^{H} and-afterwards after-SANDHI DEM.SG.M
They sell all of the Torah Scrolls. And afterwards, after that,

yibīʕu *gilyān.* *wu-baʕdēn* *yibīʕu* *kohén,* *yibīʕu* *leví,*
sell.IPFV.3PL-3SG.F lifting^{H} and-afterwards sell.IPFV.3PL kohén^{H} sell.IPFV.3PL leví^{H}
they sell the lifting [of the Torah Scroll]. And afterwards they sell the [reading of the] kohén, the Leví,

šeliší, *rebiʕí,* *ḥamišší,* *mašlím,* *mafṭír…*
third.M^{H} fourth.M^{H} fifth.M^{H} complete.PTCP.M^{H} conclude.PTCP.M^{H}
the third, the fourth, the fifth, the completing [the seventh reader], [and] the last reader [who also reads verses from the *Prophets*]…

wu-kull-i wāḥid ʔilli b-yiṭlaʕ, baʕd-i ma yiʔra
and-every-SANDHI one.M REL PROG-get_up.IPFV.3SG.M after-SANDHI REL recite.IPFV.3SG.M
And everyone who is called to read the Torah, after he reads

wi-yibārik, yiʔūl il-kaddīš bitāʕ-u, yiʔūl
and-bless.IPFV.3SG.M say.IPFV.3SG.M DEF-Kaddish GEN.EXP-3SG.M say.IPFV.3SG.M
and says a blessing, he recites his Kaddish, and says

mitnaddéb kaḥ ve-kaḥ... kohén, leví, šeliší, rebiʕí, ḥamišší, samúḵ,
volunteer.PTCP.M^{H} so^{H} and-so^{H} kohén^{H} leví^{H} third.M^{H} fourth.M^{H} fifth.M^{H} adjacent.M^{H}
"I volunteer [to donate] such and such"... kohén, Leví, the third, the fourth, the fifth, the sixth [lit.: adjacent (to the seventh)],

mašlím, mafṭír.
complete.PTCP.M conclude.PTCP.M
the completing (the seventh), the last one [who also reads verses from the *Prophets*].

5.9 Text 9: Selling the readings at the Karaite synagogue

A specific feature in this segment is the use of the Karaite term *ʔirayāt* (pl. of *ʔirāya*), as opposed to Rabbinical *mitsvót*.

kānu yibīʕu l-ʔirayāt, wi-kull-i wāḥid ʔilli ʕāyiz
be.PF.3PL sell.IPFV.3PL DEF-reading.PL and-every-SANDHI one.M REL want.PTCP.M
They used to sell the 'readings' [of the Torah], and anyone who wants

yiʔra ḥāga yištiri. wu-kānu b-izawwidu kamān bi-l-mazād.
read.IPFV.3SG.M thing buy.IPFV.3SG.M and-be.PF.3PL PROG-raise.IPFV.3PL also in-DEF auction
to read something buys [it]. They also would raise the price through an auction.

dōl talāta, dōl ʔarbaʕa, dōl sabʕa.
DEM.PL three DEM.PL four DEM.PL seven
Those (would offer) three, those four, those seven.

5.10 Text 10: Greetings for Saturday night

The following segment contains the specific terms *gumʕit-ak / gumʕit-kum ḫaḍra* and *gumʕit-ak / gumʕit-kum zayy-i s-salʔ.*

lamma yiʔūlu gumʕit-kum ḫaḍra... yiʔūl lu
when say.IPFV.3PL week.CS-2PL green.F say.IPFV.3SG-M to-3SG.M
When they say "have a good week" (lit.: "have a green week")... [one] says to him

gumʕit-ak zayy-i s-salʔ, yaʕni wāḥid yiʔūl gumʕit-kum ḫaḍra
week.CS-2SG.M like-SANDHI DEF-chard mean.IPFV.3SG.M one.M say.IPFV.3SG.M week.CS-2PL green.F
"have a week [like] chard [leaves]" (i.e. "have a green week too"), that is, when one says "have a green week"

wi-t-tāni yirudd-i ʕalē-h gumʕit-kum zayy-i s-salʔ,
and-DEF.second.M reply.IPFV.3SG.M upon-3SG.M week.CS-2PL like-SANDHI DEF-chard
and the other one replies “have a week like chard”,

yaʕni ʔaẖḍar.
mean.IPFV.3SG.M green.M
it means “green”.

5.11 Text 11: The holiday eve

Next to the demonstrative pronoun SG.M *de* this segment features the Aramaic term *ʕurubbá* and the Hebrew component: *pésaḥ* / *bésaḥ* (with *b* replacing *p*).

il-ʕurubbá yaʕni ʔabl-i l-ʕīd bi-yōm ʕašān yiʕabbu l-ʔakl
DEF-ʕurubbá^{Aram} mean.IPFV.3SG.M before-SD DEF-holiday in-day so.that prepare.IPFV.3PL DEF-food
The ʕurubbá means one day before the holiday,in order to prepare the food

wi-yištiru wi-yiʕmilu... il-ʕurubbá yaʕni l-yōm ʔilli ʔabl-i l-ʕīd...
and-buy.IPFV.3PL and-make.IPFV.3PL DEF-ʕurubbá^{Aram}mean.IPFV.3SG.M DEF-day REL before-SD DEF-holiday
and buy and make [...], the ʕurubbá means the day that comes before the holiday…

kull-i ʕīd fīh il-ʕurubbā, yaʕni dilwaʔti bésaḥ yōm il-gumʕa...
every-SD holiday EXIST DEF ʕurubbá^{Aram} mean.IPFV.3SG.M now Passover^{H} day DEF-assembly
every holiday has a holiday eve, for example now it is Passover, on Friday,

yōm il-ẖamīs lāzim yištiru, yistaḥammu, yiʕabbu kullu
day DEF-five be_necessary.PTCP.M buy.IPFV.3PL bathe.IPFV.3PL prepare.IPFV.3PL everything
so on Thursday they must buy, bathe, and prepare everything,

de ʔism-u il-ʕurubbá, yaʕni ʔabl-i l-ʕīd bi-yōm,
DEM.SG.M name-3SG.M ʕurubbá^{Aram} mean.IPFV.SG.M before-SD DEF-holiday in-day
this is called ʕurubbá (“eve of the holiday”), that is, one day before the holiday,

ʕašān yōm il-ʕīd ma yištaġalū-š.
so.that day.CS DEF-holiday NEG work.IPFV.3PL-NEG
so that on the day of the holiday they will not work.

5.12 Text 12: The feast of the goose

This segment features the Hebrew word *šavuʕót*, once realized as *šabuʕót*, as well as the specifically Judeo-Arabic term *ʕīd il-wizza*.

šabuʕót baʔa ʕīd il-wizza, šavuʕót. yidbaḥu l-wizza
šavuʕót^{H} remain.PF.3SG.M holiday.CS DEF-goose šavuʕót^{H} slaugher.IPFV.3PL DEF-goose
šabuʕót is “the goose feast”, *šavuʕót*. They slaughter the goose

wi-yiʔūlu yaʕni ʔinn-i ʔilli ma yigīb-š-i wizza
and-say.IPFV.3PL mean.IPFV.3SG.M COMP-SD REL NEG bring.IPFV.3SG.M-NEG-SD goose
and say that anyone who does not bring a goose

yiḫāf ʕala mrāt-u yiṭṭallaʔu kida.
fear.IPFV.3SG.M on woman-3SG.M get_divorced.IPFV.3PL so
fears that [he and] his wife will get divorced.

5.13 Text 13: Dreaming of Maimonides in his synagogue

This segment features the demonstrative pronoun SG.M *de* as well as the Hebrew definite article *ha-*, reanalyzed as part of the word (*il-ha-rambām*), and the EJA pronunciation (mostly by women) *ʕak̲ám* (for *ḥak̲ám*).

il-ha-rambām... da... ḥāga kbīra ʔawi da... de ḥāga kbīra ʔawi de,
DEF-DEF^{H}-Rambam^{H} DEM.SG.M thing big.F very DEM.SG.M DEM.SG.M thing big.F very DEM.SG.M
Maimonides, this… a very big thing it is… this is a big thing, it is.

wi-ʔawwil ʕak̲ám fi l-ʕālam kān. ʔism-u mošé ben meymón,
and-first.M wise.M^{H} in DEF-world be.PF.3SG.M name-3SG.M Mošé ben Maymon
The first rabbi in the world he was. His name is Moshe Ben Maimon,

wi-de b-irūḥu yināmu ʕand-u fi l-kinīs wi-yiḥlamu,
and-DEM.SG.M PROG-go.IPFV.3PL sleep.IPFV.3PL at-3SG.M in DEF-synagogue and-dream.IPFV.3PL
and he… they go to sleep at his place in the synagogue, they dream,

yiʕmilu zayy-i ma yiḥlamu wu-b-iṭību.
make.IPFV.3PL like.SD REL dream.IPFV.3PL and-PROG-recover.IPFV.3PL
and they act according to what they dream and recover.

5.14 Text 14: Sleeping at the Maimonides synagogue

This segments features the *nekteb-nektebu* pattern, various EJA phonological phenomena and verbal patterns (notably *ʔaḫad* ('he took') vs. *ḫad* and *gātit* ('she came'), vs. *gat*), as well as Hebrew and French lexical items.

ʔana niḥkī-l-ak ʕala l-ha-rambám. ʔaḫū-ya kān ʕand-u
1SG tell.IPFV.1SG-to-2SG.M on DEF-DEF^{H}-Rambam brother.CS-1SG be.PF.3SG.M at-3SG.M
I'll tell you about Maimonides. My brother was

sana taʔrīban wu-kān yōm... yōm ʔabl-i kippūr.
year approximately and be.PF.3SG.M day day before-SD atonement^{H}
about one year old, and it was the day… one day before Yom Kippur.

māma kānit mitʕawwida trūḥ il-ʔarāfa yōm ʔabl-i kippūr.
Mom be.PF.3SG.F be_accustomed.PTCP.F go.IPFV.3SG.F DEF.cemetary day before-SD atonement^{H}
Mom was accustomed to go to the cemetery one day before Yom Kippur.

ʔarāḥit maʕa papá fi l-ʔarāfa wu-sābit il-walad maʕa l-ẖaddāma,
go.PF.3SG.F with Dad^H in DEF-cemetary and-leave.PF.3SG.F DEF-boy with DEF-servant.F
She went with Dad [Papá] to the cemetery, and left the boy with the maid,

zayy-i l-ʕāda, zayy-i kull-i yōm. il-zāhir ʔinn-i l-ẖaddāma,
like.SD DEF-habitude like-SD every-SD day DEF-appear.PTCP.M COMP-SD servant.F
as usual, like every day. It seems that the maid,

min ġer ma tuqṣud... il-walad ʔitḥaraʔ. bi-ma, ma niʕraf-š.
from NEG REL intend.IPFV.3SG.F DEF-boy be_burned.PF.3SG.M in-what NEG know.IPFV.1SG-NEG
without meaning it… the boy was burned. From what, I don't know.

ṭūl il-lēl ma nām-š, wu-gātit-l-u érysipèle...
length.CS DEF-night NEG sleep.PF.3SG.M-NEG and-come.PF.3SG.F-to-3SG.M erysipelas^Fr
All night he did not sleep, and got erysipelas [said in French: "skin infection"]…

ʔaẖadu ʕarabiyya ḥanṭūr wa-ʔarāḥum il-ha-rambám...
take.PF.3PL horse-drawn.carriage and-go.PF.3PL DEF-DEF^H-Rambam
They took a carriage and went to the Maimonides [synagogue]…

il-walad kubur wi-ʕamalnā-l-u it-tefillím fi l-ha-rambám.
DEF-boy grow_up-PF.3SG.M and-do.PF.1PL-TO-3SG.M DEF-prayer.PL^H in DEF-DEF^H-Rambam
The boy grew up and we celebrated his bar-mitzvah in the Maimonides [synagogue].

5.15 Text 15: Hair-comb and the vowel u *(1)*

Again, this segment features the *nekteb-nektebu* pattern, apart from the EJA preference for *u* over *i* in certain environments (also in the following segment).

ʔiddī-ni l-mušṭ ʕašān nitsarraḥ... mišṭ?
give.IMP.SG.M-1SG.OBJ DEF-comb so.that comb.REFL.IPFV.1SG comb
Give me the comb (*mušṭ*) so that I'll comb my hair… *mišṭ*?

ma kuntiš bi-nʔūl mišṭ, ma naʕraf-š.
NEG be.PF.1SG-NEG PROG-say.IPFV.1SG comb NEG know.IPFV.1SG-NEG
I was not saying *mišṭ*, I don't know [it].

5.16 Text 16: Hair-comb and the vowel u *(2) / (told by a native speaker of Ladino)*

ʔana ʔitʕallimt-i ʕarabi... min gōz-i, min ʕēlit gōz-i,
1SG learn.PF.1SG-SD Arabic from husband-1SG from family.CS husband-1SG
I learned Arabic… from my husband, from my husband's family,

ʕašān fi l-bēt ʕand-i ma kanū-š yaʕrafu ʕarabi ẖāliṣ...
so.that in DEF-house at-1SG NEG be.PF.3PL-NEG know.IPFV.3PL Arabic pure
because in my home they did not know Arabic at all…

min iš-šaġġāla fi l-bēt, wi-kunt-i b-aʔūl mišṭ, wu-ṭišt...
from DEF-employee.F in DEF-house and-be.PF.1SG-SD PROG-say.IPFV.1SG *mišṭ* and-*ṭišt*
[I learned] from the maid in the house, and I was saying *mišṭ* and *ṭišt*…

min iš-šaġġāla.
from DEF-employee.F
[I learned this] from the maid.

5.17 Text 17: A nickname for Ashkenazi Jews

The following segment contains the Yiddish term *šléḵt* 'bad'.

lamma kunna fi maṣr kunna niftikir ʔinn-i l-kilma šléḵt *maʕnā-ha*
when be.PF.1PL in Egypt be.PF.1PL think.IPFV.1PL COMP.SD DEF-word *šléḵt*^{Y} meaning-3SG.F
When we were in Egypt we used to think that the word *šléḵt* meant

ʔinn-i ṣanf il-yahūd ʔilli humma l-ʔaškenáz b-isammū-hum šléḵt.
COMP-SD type.CS DEF-Jew.COLL REL 3PL DEF-Ashkenazi PROG-call.IPFV.3PL-3PL *šléḵt*
that the type of Jews who were Ashkenazi were being called *šléḵt*^{Y}.

hina fhimna ʔinn-i maʕnāt-ha yaʕni kilma muš kwayyisa
here understand.PF.1PL COMP-SD meaning-3SG.F mean.IPFV.3SG.M word NEG good.F
Here [in Israel] we understood that it meant a word that was not good.

yaʕni.
mean.IPFV.3SG.M
[rhetorical element]

5.18: Text 18: Ḥanna and her seven sons

The last segment once more features EJA elements such as *ʔarāḥ* (vs. *rāḥ*), the *nekteb-nektebu* pattern, clause-initial *ʔēš*, the demonstrative pronoun SG.M *de*, as well as a number of Hebrew terms and phrases, notably the term *ʔéḵa*[82].

yōm ʔéḵa, ya sātir[83] *ya rabb, kānit ʔēš ʔisma-ha, ʔēš yiʔulū-l-ha...*
day.CS how^{H} VOC Protector.PTCP.M VOC Lord be.PF.3SG.F what name.SD-SG.F what call.IPFV.3PL to-3SG.F
The day of *ʔéḵa* (Ninth of Av, lit.: 'Day of *Lamentations*'), may God protect us [from such misfortunes], she was… what's her name, how do they call her…

Ḥanna maskīna, di wāḥid, baʕd-i ma gōz-ha māt, ʕanda-ha
Hannah poor.F DEM.SG.F one.M after-SD REL husband-3SG.F die.PF.3SG.M at-3SG.F
poor Hannah. She, somebody – after her husband died, she has

82 The first word in the book of *Lamentations*, which also serves as the Hebrew name of the whole book.

83 An Arabic cognomen of God.

sabaʕ wilād, ʕāwiz yiggawwiz-ha, wi-illi ʕāwiz yiggawwiz-ha
seven boy.PL want.PTCP.M marry.IPFV.3SG.M-3SG.F and-REL want.PTCP.M marry.IPFV.3SG.M-3SG.F
seven sons – he wants to marry her. And he who wants to marry her

de nuṣrāni, wi-hiyya miš ʕayza tiggawwiz-u, yiʔūl la-ha
DEM.SG.M Christian.M and-3SG.F NEG want.PTCP.F marry.IPFV.3SG.F-3SG.M say.IPFV.3SG.M to-3SG.F
is a Christian, and she does not want to marry him. He says to her:

ʔiz-kān miš ḥa-tiggawwizī-ni ḥa-nmawwit-l-ik is-sabaʕ wilād.
if-be.PF.3SG.M NEG FUT-marry.IPFV.2SG.F-1SG.OBJ FUT-kill.IPFV.1SG-to-2SG.F DEF-seven boy.PL
if you don't marry me, I shall kill your seven sons.

wi-hiyya tʔūl-l-u ʔabadan wa-ʔabadan wa-ʔabadan,
nd-3SG.F say-IPFV.3SG.F-to-3SG.M never and-never and-never
And she says to him: never and never and never.

wu-kām tibki wu-tit̩hannén ʔilē-h lo ʕozér šum davár.
and-how.much cry.IPFV.3SG.F and beg.IPFV.3SG.F^{H} to-3SG.M NEG^{H} help.PTCP.M^{H} NEG^{H} thing^{H}
And as much as she cries/is crying and begs/is begging him, nothing helps.

ʔawwil walad ʔatal-hū-l-ha. ʔāl la-ha ḥatggawwizī-ni?
first.M boy kill.PF.3SG.M-3SG.M-to-3SG.F SAY.PF.3SG.M TO-3SG.F FUT-marry.IPFV.2SG.F-1SG.OBJ
Her first son – he killed him. He said to her: will you marry me?

tʔūl-l-u la. tāni walad ʔatal-hū-l-ha.
say.IPFV.3SG.F-to-3SG.M NEG second.M boy kill.PF.3SG.M-3SG.M-to-3SG.F
She says to him: No. Her second son – he killed him.

ḥa-tggawwizī-ni? tʔūl-lu la. tālit walad, rābiʕ walad,
FUT-marry.IPFV.2SG.F-1SG.OBJ say.IPFV.3SG.F-to-3SG.M NEG third.M BOY fourth.M BOY
Will you marry me? She says to him: no. Third son, fourth son,

li-ġāyit ma ʔatal la-ha sabaʕ wilād, wi-tʔūl l-uh:
to-end.CS REL kill.PF.3SG.M to-3SG.F seven boy.PL and.SAY.IPFV.3SG.F to-3SG.M
until he killed her seven sons, while she is saying to him:

ʔana ma nbīʕ-š-i dīn-i wi-niggawwiz nuṣrāni.
1SG NEG sell.IPFV.1SG-NEG-SD religion-1SG and-marry.IPFV.1SG Christian.M
I shall not sell my religion and marry a Christian.

ʔarāḥu l-wilād kullu-hum. ʕamalu ʕalē-hum gumʕit tešaʕ be-ʔav
go.PF.3PL DEF-boy.PL every.CS-3PL make.PF.3PL upon-3PL week.CS nine^{H}-in^{H}-Av^{H}
They died, all the sons. They [the Jews] made in their memory the week of the Ninth of Av

wi-yiṣūmu ṣiyām taʕanít.
and-fast.IPFV.3PL fasting taʕanít[H]
and they fast the *taʕanit* ('fasting').

References

Badawi, El-Said, and Martin Hinds. 1986. *A Dictionary of Egyptian Arabic*. Beirut: Librairie du Liban.

Bar-Asher, Moshé. 1998. *Traditions linguistiques des Juifs d'Afrique du Nord*. Jérusalem: Université hébraïque, Centre des Langues et Littératures Juives and Institut Bialik, and Ashkelon: Institut Universitaire Régional. (in Hebrew)

Behnstedt, Peter, and Manfred Woidich. 1985. *Die ägyptisch-arabischen Dialekte* (vol. 2: *Dialektatlas*. Wiesbaden: Ludwig Reichert.

—. 1994. *Die ägyptisch-arabischen Dialekte* (vol. 4: *Glossar Arabisch-Deutsch*). Wiesbaden: Ludwig Reichert.

Ben-Oren, Guershon, and Wolf Moshkowitch. 1986. "L'argot des commerçants juifs de Géorgie comparé à celui d'autres pays d'Orient". *Massorot* 2: 49–56. (in Hebrew)

Ben-Shimon, Refael. 1908. *Sefer Nehar Mitzrayim* ("The Book of the River of Egypt"). Alexandria: Farag Haim Mizrahi and Sons. 2 Volumes. (in Hebrew)

Bergman, Yehuda. 1960. *Jewish Folklore: Knowledge of the People of Israel, its Beliefs, Characteristics and Popular Customs*. Jerusalem: Reuven Mass. (in Hebrew)

Blanc, Haim. 1974. "The *Nekteb-Nektebu* Imperfect in a Variety of Cairene Arabic." *Israel Oriental Studies* 14: 206–228.

—. 1981. "Egyptian Arabic in the Seventeenth Century: Notes on the Judeo-Arabic Passages of *Darxe No'am* (Venice, 1697)." In Shelomo Morag, Issachar Ben-Ami, and Norman A. Stillman (eds.). *Studies in Judaism and Islam Presented to Shelomo Dov Goitein*. Jerusalem: The Hebrew University, The Magness Press, 185–202.

—. 1985. "Egyptian Judeo-Arabic: More on the Subject of R. Mordekhai b. Yehuda Ha-Levi's *Sefer darxe no'am*." *Sefunot* 18, New Series vol. 3, 299–314. (in Hebrew)

Blau, Joshua. 1958. "On Hebrew Elements in Medieval Judeo-Arabic Texts: Directions and Processes." *Leshonenu* 22: 183–196. (in Hebrew)

—. 1995. *A Grammar of Mediaeval Judaeo-Arabic*. Jerusalem: The Hebrew University, The Magnes Press. (Second enlarged and revised edition 1980; reprinted). (in Hebrew)

Bunis, David M. 1993. *A Lexicon of the Hebrew and Aramaic Elements in Modern Judezmo*. Jerusalem: The Magnes Press, The Hebrew University, and Misgav Yerushalayim. (in Hebrew)

—. 1999. *Judezmo: An Introduction to the Language of the Sepharadic Jews of the Ottoman Empire*. Jerusalem: The Magnes Press, The Hebrew University. (in Hebrew)

Choueka, Aharon, and Sarah Choueka (eds.). 2001. *Eshteh zeh ha-kos: sefer ha-brindizi le-bet Shveka [Choueka]* ["I Shall Drink This Cup: The Brindizi Book of the Choueka Family"]. Jerusalem: Almog Printing. (in Hebrew and other languages)

Elder, Earl E. 1927. *Egyptian Colloquial Arabic Reader*. London: Oxford University Press and Humphry Milford.

[Fiske, Daniel Willard]. 1904. *An Egyptian Alphabet for the Egyptian People*. Florence: The Landi Press.

Gordon, Benjamin L. 1977. *New Judea: Jewish Life in Modern Palestine and Egypt*. New York: Arno Press. (Reprint edition of the 1919 edition, Philadelphia: Julius H. Greenstone)

Hary, Benjamin H. 2009. *Translating Religion: Linguistic Analysis of Judeo-Arabic Sacred Texts from Egypt*. Leiden and Boston: Brill.

Hassoun, Jacques. 1981. "Chroniques de la vie quotidienne". In: *Juifs du Nil*. Paris: Le Sycomore.

Israel, Yom Tov. 1990. *Sefer Minhage Mitzrayim* ("The Book of the Customs of Egypt". Ed. Avraham Yosef. Jerusalem: Makhon Yerushalayim, and Holon: Makhon Or Hamizrah. (1st Edition 1873).

Kendi, Arye. 1991. "Hebrew Words in Hungarian Slang.". *Massorot* 5–6, 185–195. (Hebrew).

Khan, Geoffrey. 1995–1997. "A Note on the Trade Argot of the Karaite Goldsmiths of Cairo." *Mediterranean Language Review* 9: 74–76.

Koén-Sarano, Matilda, and Maymon Benchimol. 2000. *Vokabulario Djudeo-Espanyol (Ladino) – Eebreo, Eebreo – Djudeo-Espanyol (Ladino) Eebreo.* [Beer-Sheva]: Merkaz Eliachar, Universidad Ben-Gurion en el Negev. (Third edition)

Krämer, Gudrun. 1989. *The Jews in Modern Egypt, 1914–1952.* London: I.B. Tauris & Co.

Lagnado, Lucette. 2019. "Preserving the Traces of Egypt's Lost Jews". *The Wall Street Journal.* Feb. 7, 2019. https://www.wsj.com/articles/preserving-the-traces-of-egypts-lost-jews-11549558672.

Levi, Primo. 2014. *Il Sistema Periodico.* Torino: Einaudi.

Malachi, Zvi. 1985. "Hebrew Words in the Secret Language in a Village in Germany." *Leshonenu La'am* 36, booklet 8–10, 216–223. (Hebrew).

Maman, Aharon. 2019. *Synoptic Dictionary of the Hebrew Component in Jewish Languages: Including the Notes of Shelomo Morag.* Jerusalem: The Hebrew University – Jewish Oral Traditions Research Center. (Second revised version)

Nehama, Josheph avec la collaboration de Jesús Cantera. 1977. *Dictionnaire de Judéo-Espagnol.* Madrid: Consejo Superior de Investigaciones Cientificas, Instituto Benito Arias Montano.

Nini, Yehuda. 2000. *From East and West: The Jews of Egypt – Their Everyday Lives and Their Reflection in the Responsa Literature 1882–1914.* Tel-Aviv: Tel-Aviv University. (in Hebrew)

Ørum, Olav G. 2018. *Sociohistorical and Linguistic Layers of Arabic in Medieval Cairo: The Case of Judaeo-Arabic.* Oslo: University of Oslo.

Rabin, Haim et al. 1979. "Jewish Languages: Common, Unique and Problematic Features" (A Scholars' Forum). *Pe'amim* 1: 40–57. (in Hebrew)

Recuero, Pascual. 1977. *Diccionario Básico Ladino-Español.* Barcelona: Ameller Ediciones.

Redhouse, James W. 1890. *A Turkish and English Lexicon.* Constantinople: The American Mission, by A. H. Boyajian.

Rosenbaum, Gabriel M. 2002a. "Hebrew Words and Karaite Goldsmiths' Secret Language Used by Jews and Non-Jews in Modern Egypt." *Pe'amim* 90: 115–153. (in Hebrew)

—. 2002b. "Spoken Jewish Arabic in Modern Egypt: Hebrew and Non-Standard Components." *Massorot* 12: 117–148. (in Hebrew)

—. 2002c. "The Arabic Dialect of Jews in Modern Egypt". *Bulletin of the Israeli Academic Center in Cairo* 25: 35–46.

—. 2004. "Egyptian Arabic as a Written Language." *Jerusalem Studies in Arabic and Islam* [*JSAI*] 29: 281–340.

—. 2011. "The Rise and Expansion of Colloquial Egyptian Arabic as a Literary Language." In Rakefet Sela-Sheffy and Gideon Toury (eds.). *Culture Contacts and the Making of Cultures: Papers in Homage to Itamar Even-Zohar.* Tel-Aviv: Unit of Culture Research, Tel Aviv University. 323–343. (http://www.tau.ac.il/tarbut/Publications/IEZ-Homage/Even-Zohar_Homage_Book.pdf)

—. 2012a. "Hannah and her Seven Sons: Late Egyptian Judeo-Arabic Versions of an Old Hebrew Story." In Johannes den Heijer, Paolo La Spisa, and Laurence Tuerlinckx (eds.). *Publications de l'Institut Orientaliste de Louvain [PIOL]* 61 (*Autour de la langue arabe: Études présentées à Jacques Grand' Henry à l'occasion de son 70e anniversaire*). Louvain-la-Neuve: Institut orientaliste de l'Université catholique de Louvain, Leuven: Peeters.

—. 2012b. "Oaths in Modern Spoken Egyptian Judeo-Arabic with a Comparison to Oaths Taken by Christians and Muslims." *Folia Orientalia* 49: 449–466.

—. 2013a. "Judaeo-Arabic, Egyptian, Hebrew Component in." In Geoffrey Khan (ed.). *Encyclopedia of Hebrew Language and Linguistics* [*EHLL*], vol. 2, 390–391. Leiden and Boston: Brill.

—. 2013b. "Secret Languages, Hebrew in: Egyptian Judeo-Arabic". In Geoffrey Khan (ed.). *Encyclopedia of Hebrew Language and Linguistics* [*EHLL*], vol. 3, 514–515. Leiden and Boston: Brill.

—. 2016. "*Shabbat* (Saturday) in Modern Egypt: Customs and Their Reflection in Spoken Judeo-Arabic." *The Arabist: Budapest Studies in Arabic* 37: 153–165.

—. 2018. "Components of Romance Languages in the Arabic Variety Spoken by Jews in Modern Egypt." In Juliano Mion (ed.). *Mediterranean Contaminations: Middle East, North Africa, and Europe in Con-tact* (Studien zum Modernen Orient 31). Berlin: Klaus Schwarz Verlag.

—. 2019. "The Distinct Vocabulary of the Judeo-Arabic Spoken by the Karaites in Egypt in the Twentieth Century". *Massorot* 19–20, 183–208. (in Hebrew)

—. Forthcoming. *Spoken Egyptian Judeo-Arabic in the Twentieth Century*. Jerusalem: Ben-Zvi Institute. (in Hebrew)

Sacroug, Gabriel. 1874. *The Egyptian Travelling Interpreter or Arabic without a Teacher for English Travellers Visiting Egypt*. Cairo: P. Cumbo.

Sperber, Daniel. 1994. *Customs of Israel: Origins and History.* Jerusalem: Mossad Harav Kook, vol. 3. (in Hebrew)

—. 1995. *Customs of Israel: Origins and History.* Jerusalem: Mossad Harav Kook, vol. 4. (in Hebrew)

Spiro, Socrates. 1973. *An Arabic-English Dictionary of the Colloquial Arabic of Egypt*. Beirut: Librairie du Liban. (New Impression; First Edition 1895)

Spitta, Wilhelm. 1880. *Grammatik des arabischen Vulgärdialectes von Aegypten*. Leipzig: J. C. Hinrichs' sche Buchhandlung.

Steingass, Francis J. 1957. *A Comprehensive Persian-English Dictionary*. London: Routledge & Kegan Paul. (Fourth impression)

Tignor, Robert L. 1983. "The Egyptian Jewish Community and Zionism." *Peʕamim* 16: 89–106. (in Hebrew)

Tomiche, Nada. 1968. "La situation linguistique en Égypte." In André Martinet (ed.). *Le Langage. Encyclopédie de la Pléiade*, vol. 25, 1173–1187. Paris: Gallimard.

Wehr, Hans. 1994. *Arabic-English Dictionary: The Hans Wehr Dictionary of Modern Written Arabic (English and Arabic Edition)*. J. Milton Cowan (ed.). Urbana, Il: Spoken Language Services. (Fourth edition)

North-African Judeo-Arabic

Ofra Tirosh-Becker, The Hebrew University of Jerusalem

1. Introduction

The *Maghreb* is a geographical region encompassing the northern portion of the African continent, from Morocco in the west, Algeria and Tunisia at its center, to Libya in the east. It includes the Mediterranean and Atlantic coastlines as well as the Atlas mountain range that separates the coastlines from the Sahara Desert, stretching for 2,500 km through Morocco, Algeria and Tunisia.

1.1 A brief history of Jews in North Africa

There has been a presence of Jews in the Maghreb for millennia. Jewish settlements in North Africa date back to pre-Roman times, to the Greek colony of Cyrenaica in eastern Libya. In Roman times, Jews were deported also to the Maghreb and many settled in what is now Tunisia. Noteworthy is the Jewish community which settled in Djerba island, off the Tunisian coast, and built the famous *Ghriba* synagogue, which to this day is annually visited by many. Jews thrived in parts of North Africa in the centuries that followed.

The Muslim Arab invasion of the Maghreb took place in the late seventh century. Under Muslim rule Jewish communities developed in important urban centers: in the coastal cities of Tunisia, along the Algerian coast (in Bougie (Béjaïa), Algiers and Tlemcen), and as far as the extreme Maghreb (especially in Fes and in the Atlas Mountains among the Berber populations). The relationships between Muslims and Jews in the Maghreb were relatively good, except for the period in which they were under the rule of the Almohades (12th century), who persecuted non-Muslims.

Already in the seventh century, the Jewish population in North Africa was augmented by Iberian Jewish immigrants, who fled from Christian persecution. A greater wave of immigration of Iberian Jews took place between 1391 and 1492 due to growing persecution of Jews in Spain and Portugal. However, the most significant influx of Jews to the Maghreb followed the 1492 expulsion of Jews by the Spanish Inquisition. On 31 March 1492, the joint Catholic Monarchs of Spain, Isabella and Ferdinand, issued the Alhambra Decree (also known as the Edict of Expulsion) ordering the expulsion of all Jews from Spain by 31 July of that year. Hundreds of thousands of Spanish Jews were driven out of Spain, relocating primarily to the Maghreb, due to its close proximity to Spain, where they quickly prospered. Naturally, some tensions arose between the new immigrants, known as *megorashim* (lit. exiles), and the local inhabitants, known as *toshavim*, over customs and commnal structure.

After the Middle Ages, for three centuries, North Africa was under a loose control of the Ottoman Empire, except for regions in the Moroccan and Algerian Atlas mountain range controlled by local Berber tribes. Ottoman rule was centered in the cities of

Algiers, Tunis, and Tripoli. During the 19th and 20th centuries, North Africa was colonized by France, Spain and Italy. The 1830 French occupation of Algeria marked the beginning of a process by which French culture gradually became dominant among Algerian Jews. This process accelerated after the 1870 Crémieux Decree that granted French citizenship to the majority of the Jewish population in Algeria and deepened their integration. In 1961 French citizenship was also extended to the Jewish communities, who lived in oases towns deep in the Sahara Desert.

Five decades after the occupation of Algeria, in 1881, a French protectorate was established in neighboring Tunisia. Tunisia had begun a process of modern reforms even before the French arrived, and these were accelerated under their rule. French control of Morocco, in the form of a Protectorate that was officially established in 1912, was a colonial regime that preserved the Moroccan monarchy, with its administrative center in Rabat. Unlike to Algerian Jews, French citizenship was not extended to Tunisian or Moroccan Jews. It is noteworthy that from 1912 Morocco's Mediterranean shore in the north as well as its extreme south regions were under a Spanish protectorate. Italian colonization of Libya began in 1911 and lasted until 1943. The country was occupied by Italy after the Italo-Turkish War, which resulted in the establishment of two colonies (Tripolitania and Cyrenaica), later unified in the colony of Italian Libya. The colonization lasted until Libya's occupation by the Allied forces in 1943.

During the 1950s and 1960s all of the North African states gained independence from their colonial European rulers. Libya became independent in 1951, Morocco and Tunisia in 1956, and finally Algeria in 1962. Immediately following their independence and as a result of Israel's independence, most Maghrebi Jews emigrated out of North Africa to Israel, France, Canada. and other countries.

1.2 Multiglossia

The turbulent history of North Africa in general, and of Maghrebi Jews in particular, being subjected to Roman, Spanish, Arab, Turkish, Berber, and European colonial rule over the centuries, had left its mark on their language use. 19th and 20th century North African Jews lived in a multi-lingual environment that included, in addition to their own Judeo-Arabic dialects, also Muslim-Arabic dialects, French/Italian/Spanish as well as Hebrew and Aramaic, their historical cultural languages. Inevitably, this complex reality was reflected in their linguistic behavior. Maghrebi Jews lived in a state of *multiglossia*, a term that refers to a situation where a group of people use multiple languages, or noticeably different varieties of language, on a daily basis to communicate with diverse members of their surrounding societies and for distinct purposes. For example, Algerian Jews used their local Judeo-Arabic dialects for intra-community interactions, French for official discourse with the government, local Muslim Arabic to interact with their Muslim neighbors, and Hebrew to conduct religious rituals and for studying Judaism. Multiglossia, however, is not static as it is affected by changes in the linguistic environment. Thus, with increasing integration of Algerian Jews into French society and culture (especially after receiving citizenship) their multiglossia had gradually shifted as well. While the older generation used Judeo-Arabic as the primary language for intra-community discourse, the younger generations, while still in a stage of multiglossia, preferred using French for intra-community interactions, reserving Judeo-Arabic mainly for interaction with their grandparent generation. Moreover, not all members of the community were proficient to the same level in all languages or varieties.

Linguistic differences among social groups within the Jewish community are often referred to as *sociolects*. For example, proficiency in Hebrew varied significantly among members of the community. The well-educated rabbinic elite held mastery over Hebrew and Aramaic. Educated men in the community, while less proficient in Hebrew, were versed enough in Hebrew to participate in the religious rituals at the synagogue, while uneducated men and the women had only limited knowledge of Hebrew. A notable exception were female family members of local rabbis, who were often well versed in Hebrew.

1.3 North African Judeo-Arabic

Dialects spoken and written by the Jews of the Maghreb are collectively referred to as North African Judeo-Arabic. These should be viewed through two reference frames. The first is the historical prism of Judeo-Arabic, and the second is within the context of Maghrebi Arabic dialects.

Judeo-Arabic had been spoken and written in various forms by Jews throughout the Arabic-speaking world for more than a millennium. Following the spread of Islam in the 7th century, Jewish varieties of Arabic came to exist all around the Arabic-speaking world. Medieval Judeo-Arabic, written in Hebrew script, is the language in which Jewish thinkers and scholars, mainly from the 9th through the 15th centuries, composed their works. These include giants such as Saadia Gaon, Maimonides, and Yehudah Halevi, who composed their seminal cultural contributions in Judeo-Arabic (Blau 1999; Blau 2002).[1] Nonetheless, as demonstrated by the treasure trove found in the Cairo *Genizot,* Judeo-Arabic was far from being only a scholarly language, rather it was a vernacular language serving traders and laymen as much as scholars (Goitein and Friedman 2008). In the late fifteenth century Judeo-Arabic writings began incorporating more local dialectal elements, reflecting a variety of regional Neo Judeo-Arabic dialects that served broader speaker communities. Hence, North-African Judeo-Arabic discussed in this chapter, spoken and written in the 19th and 20th centuries, is an ensemble of Neo Judeo-Arabic dialects, which carry a legacy that can be traced back to Medieval Judeo-Arabic.

The second prism through which North African Judeo-Arabic should be viewed is that of Arabic dialectology. Scholars working on the Judeo-Arabic dialects of the Maghreb classify and describe them either as pre-Hilali or non-Hilali urban dialects, or simply as sedentary dialects (Chetrit 2017). These dialects have characteristic features that distinguish the dialects of the Maghreb from those of the Mashriq (eastern Arabic dialects). There are certain features common to North African Judeo-Arabic dialects that stem from the fact that they are first and foremost Maghrebi dialects (well known are the imperfect 1SG and 1PL forms, see below). Much of the grammatical sketch presented in this chapter is from the perspective of synchronic Arabic dialectology.

1 For a detailed discussion of Medieval Judeo-Arabic see the chapter "Classical Judeo-Arabic" by Lutz Edzard in this book.

1.4 Communal dialects

As articulated by Haim Blanc in his seminal 1964 book on communal dialects in Baghdad, Arabic dialects reflect a wide spectrum of communal varieties. The differences among communal dialects may be manifested not only in the significant Hebrew and Aramaic component characteristic of Judeo-Arabic, but also in a variable range of phonetic, morphological, morphosyntactic and lexical differences.

Communal differences between the Jewish dialects and the Muslim dialects (and Christian dialects, wherever they are present) are well documented throughout the Arabic-speaking world. This concept was first introduced by Blanc in his aforementioned study, where he identified major differences between the Arabic dialects spoken by the Muslims, Jews, and Christians of Baghdad. In that book Blanc also described the *major differentiation* between Muslim and Jewish dialects in some North African cities, notably Oran (Ar. Wahrān, Algeria) and some smaller Algerian towns near the capital Algiers. The Jews of these towns speak sedentary dialects, while the Muslims speak nomad dialects.

Blanc also suggested that in some other North African cities, including Algiers, Fes (Morocco), and Tlemcen (Algeria), there is an *intermediate differentiation* between the two communal dialects, namely a number of dialectal differences that correlate well with communal affiliation (Blanc 1964: 15–16). In Algiers, for example, there are phonological differences between the Jewish and Muslim Arabic dialects: CA /q/ is pronounced by the Jews as [ʔ], but the Muslims pronounce it [q]; CA /t/ is pronounced [t] by the city's Jews, but [tˢ] by its Muslims (M. Cohen 1912: 21, 43–45). The city of Tunis is another example for such *intermediate* communal differentiation (Walters 2011). David Cohen, who studied the Judeo-Arabic of Tunis, documented more than two dozen of such differences in an article he dedicated to this subject. An example is the pronunciation of the CA interdental fricatives *ṯ* (ث), *ḏ* (ذ), *ḏ̣* (ظ) that is preserved in the Muslim dialect, while the city's Jews pronounce them as plosive dental-alveolar *t*, *d*, *ḍ* in line with other urban Maghrebi dialects. Another example is the pronunciation of /h/ by Tunis' Muslims vs. lack of its pronunciation by the city's Jews, leading to different pronunciation of words such as the demonstrative pronoun: *hāḏa* (M) vs. *ada* (J) 'this' (D. Cohen 1970). Additional phenomena that distinguish local Jewish dialects from their Muslim counterparts are discussed in the grammatical sketch below.

1.5 Orthography

Like most other Jewish languages, written Judeo-Arabic consistently uses Hebrew characters.[2] To a large extent, the Hebrew script symbolizes the Jewish identity of the dialect-speaking community. This orthography assigns a Hebrew letter to each Judeo-Arabic character and is based on the similarity between the Hebrew and Arabic consonant system: /ʔ/ = א, /b/ = ב, /d/ = ד, /h/ = ה, and so forth. Diacritic points were added when additional distinctions were necessary: ג or גׄ denotes /ġ/ while ג' or גׂ denotes /ğ/; כ and ך denote /k/ while כׂ and ךׂ denote /x/; צ and ץ denote /ṣ/ while צׂ and ץׂ denote /ḍ/. As the fricative interdental consonants *ṯ*, *ḏ*, and *ḏ̣* were not preserved in North African

2 The Karaites (mainly in the 9th to 11th centuries) were an exception, as they wrote a significant part of their Judeo-Arabic treatises in Arabic script. See Tirosh-Becker 2011, vol. 1: 49–50.

Judeo-Arabic there was no need to use diacritics to distinguish them from their plosive counterparts *t*, *d*, and *ḍ*.[3] The *šadda* is marked by doubling the character. Unlike the classical Judeo-Arabic script that was used in Medieval Judeo-Arabic, the script of North-African Judeo-Arabic is more phonetic in nature, reflecting the spread of emphatic pronunciation, consonant shifts, and vowel quality.

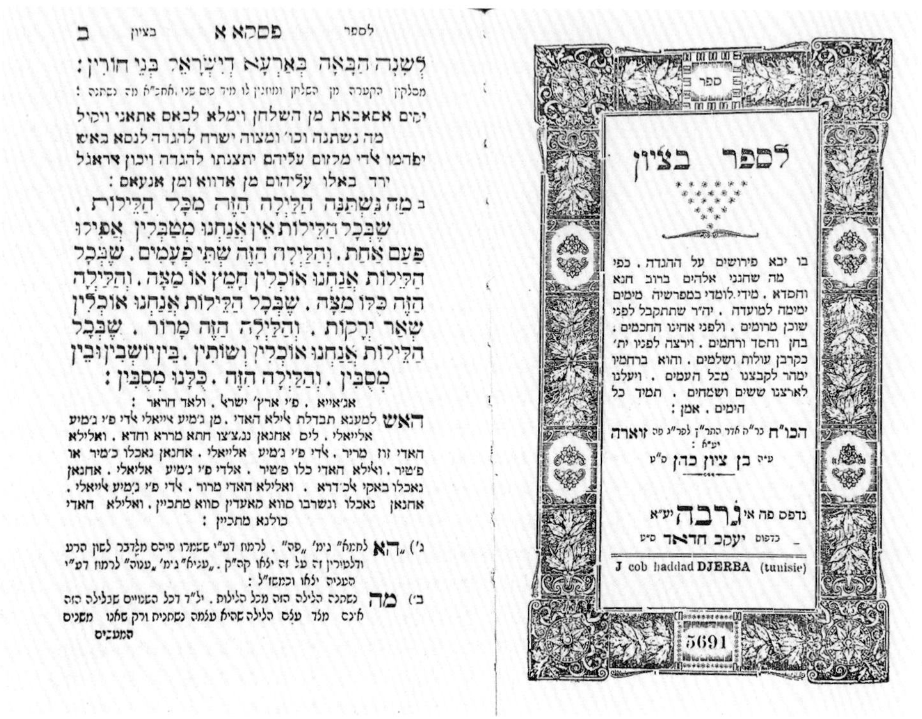
ספר
לספר בציון
בו יבא פירושים על ההגדה . כפי
מה שחנני אלהים ברוב חנא
וחסדא . מידי לומדי במפרשיה מימים
ימימה למועדה . יה״ר שתתקבל לפני
שוכן מרומים . ולפני אחינו החכמים .
בחן וחסד ורחמים . וירצה לפניו ית׳
כקרבן עולות ושלמים . והוא ברחמיו
ימהר לקבצנו מכל העמים . ויעלנו
לארצנו ששים ושמחים . תמיד כל
הימים . אמן :
הכו״ח כר״ה אדר התר״ן לפר״ג פה זוארה יע״א :
ע״ה בן ציון כהן ס״ט
נדפס פה אי גרבה יע״א
בדפוס יעקב חדאד ס״ט
J cob haddad DJERBA (tunisie)
5691

לספר פסקא א בציון ב
לשנה הבאה בארעא דישראל בני חורין :
יקים אסאבאת מן השלחן וימלא לכאס אתאני ויקיל
מה נשתנה וכו׳ ומצוה ישרח להגדה לנסא באש
יפהמו אדי מלזום עליהם יתצנתו להגדה ויכון ארראגל
ירד באלו עליהם מן אדווא ומן אנעאם :
ב מה נשתנה הלילה הזה מכל הלילות .
שבכל הלילות אין אנחנו מטבלין אפילו
פעם אחת . והלילה הזה שתי פעמים . שבכל
הלילות אנחנו אוכלין חמץ או מצה . והלילה
הזה כלו מצה . שבכל הלילות אנחנו אוכלין
שאר ירקות . והלילה הזה מרור . שבכל
הלילות אנחנו אוכלין ושותין . בין יושבין ובין
מסבין . והלילה הזה . כלנו מסבין :
אג׳אייא . פ׳י ארץ׳ ישראל . ולאד חראר :
האש למענא תבדלת לילא האדי . מן ג׳מיע אייאלי אדי פ׳י ג׳מיע
אלייאלי . ליס אחנאן נג׳צ׳צו חתא מררא וחדא . ואלילא
האדי זוז מריר . אדי פ׳י ג׳מיע אלייאלי . אחנאן נאכלו כ׳מיר או
פ׳טיר . ואלילא האדי כלו פ׳טיר . אלדי פ׳י ג׳מיע אליאלי . אחנאן
נאכלו באקי אכ׳דרא . ואלילא האדי מרור . אדי פ׳י ג׳מיע אייאלי .
אחנאן נאכלו ונשרבו סווא קאעדין סווא מתכיין . ואלילא האדי
כולנא מתכיין :

Passover Haggadah, Djerba, Tunisia (Ben Zion Cohen 1931, *le-Sapper be-Zion*, Djerba: Ḥadad imprimerie)

1.6 Literary genres and language registers

A rich literature was written in North African Judeo-Arabic throughout the Maghreb, spanning a variety of literary genres. Judeo-Arabic Bible translation traditions (known as *šarḥ*, pl. *šurūḥ*) were orally transmitted from one generation to the next. Fortunately some of these *šurūḥ* were eventually put down in writing in manuscripts or in print. Judeo-Arabic *šarḥ* traditions exist also for important post-biblical texts such as tractate *ʔAvot* of the Mishnah, the Passover Haggadah, and piyyuṭ *Mi Khamokha* (composed by Rabbi Yehudah Halevi, 1075–1141). A large body of rabbinic literature was composed in Judeo-Arabic by Maghrebi rabbis across the entire region, in large urban centers as well as in small towns. This encompassed commentaries to the Bible and post-biblical literature, translations of rabbinic scholarly works, description of rites and customs, and

3 On early Judeo-Arabic written in phonetic spelling in pre-Saadianic writings see Blau and Hopkins 2017.

more. Secular Judeo-Arabic literature evolved in 19th century North Africa when some of its scholars adhered to the ideology of the European *Jewish Enlightenment* movement. These scholars developed Judeo-Arabic journalism, mainly in Tunisia and Algeria, but also in Morocco and Libya, as well as Judeo-Arabic translations of classical European fiction. Poetry is another literary genre that was popular among Maghrebi Jews, including religious and cultural poems, the *maṭruz* poetry that interweaves Judeo-Arabic and Hebrew, poetry reflecting historical events, and even women's poems (Chetrit 1994).

As discussed above, within the multiglossia state of Maghrebi Jews language proficiency differed between social groups within the community (aka *sociolects*). As literary works targeted different audiences, authors were propelled to select different *registers* for different literary genres. For example, the language used in Bible translations was archaic, elevated and conservative as it was intended for the scholarly elite and due to the revered status of the text. In contrast, a written pamphlet explaining the customs of a certain holiday for the laymen population had to be written in a register that is close to the colloquial dialect in order to be understood (Tirosh-Becker 2014). Some of these register differences will be pointed out in the grammatical sketch below.

2. Grammatical Sketch

The following is a brief grammatical sketch of the most salient properties of North African Judeo-Arabic dialects. As indicated above, there are significant differences between the Jewish dialects within this extended geographical region, which spans from Morocco in the west to Libya in the east, with dialectal variations even within each geographical unit. Therefore, the following grammatical sketch should be viewed as a general introduction to this group of dialects as a whole, rather than a detailed description of each dialectal region. The description below focuses on the characteristics of key dialects in the region's four major countries – Morocco, Algeria, Tunisia and Libya.

For more detailed discussions of the different North African Jewish dialects see the following works and the bibliography therein: Morocco: Heath 2002, Chetrit 2016, Chetrit 2017, Stillman 1988, Heath and Bar-Asher 1982, Bar-Asher 1999; Algeria: M. Cohen 1912, Tirosh-Becker 2012; Tunisia: D. Cohen 1975, Tedghi 2016; Libya: Yoda 2005, D'Anna 2021.

2.1 Phonology

The discussion below focuses on consonants for which there are special pronunciation characteristics in North African Judeo-Arabic dialects.

2.1.1 /q/

The split between the two main realizations of the CA phoneme /q/ is well known. While unvoiced realizations, such as [q], [ʔ], or [k], are characteristic of sedentary Arabic dialects, voiced realizations, mainly [g], are characteristic of nomad and rural Arabic dialects (Fischer and Jastrow 1980: 52). Since the Jewish communities in North Africa were predominantly sedentary city and town dwellers, the /q/ is realized in these communities as an unvoiced consonant.

[q]: The [q] realization is found in numerous Moroccan Judeo-Arabic dialects (Heath 2002: 141–147; Chetrit 2017), as well as in the major cities of Constantine (Algeria), Tunis (Tunisia) and Tripoli (Libya) (Tirosh-Becker 1989:289; D. Cohen 1975: 30–32; Yoda 2010).

[ʔ]: In the main Moroccan urban belt of Rabat-Meknes-Fes and in nearby Ouezzane and Sefrou the Jewish dialects have a glottal stop [ʔ] for /q/. The [ʔ] realization is also pronounced by the Jews of Algiers (Algeria) (Heath 2002: 142; Stillman 1988: 31; M. Cohen 1912: 29).

[k]: In some Moroccan and Algerian Jewish dialects the /q/ had fronted to the velar unvoiced consonant [k] or to the medio-palatal consonant [k^j]. This realization is characteristic to the region of Oujda in northeastern Morocco near the Algerian border, as well as the Judeo-Arabic dialects of Wahrān (Oran) and Tlemcen in western Algeria. It is noteworthy that while the Jews of Tlemcen pronounce /q/ as [k], the Muslims of that city pronounce this phoneme as [q]. The pronunciation [k] is also characteristic of Moroccan Judeo-Arabic dialects spoken east of Moulouya and in the pre-Saharan fringes, an area which extends from Oujda in the northeast to the Draa Valley to the southeast, passing by Tafilalt[4] and the Todgha area (Chetrit 2017; Levy 2009: 341; Tirosh-Becker 2011: 119).

[g]: This realization is characteristic of nomad Muslim dialects. However, in many Jewish dialects there are a few words in which this consonant is realized [g] due to borrowing from nomad or rural Muslim dialects. These borrowed words are often drawn from the semantic fields of agriculture and nomad life, for example, *bəgṛa* (=cow), *gəmṛa* 'moon', *gṛun* 'horns', *nāga* 'female camel', *sāg* 'to lead animals' (Heath 2002: 146; Heath and Bar-Asher; Tirosh-Becker 1989: 289, fn.23; Tirosh-Becker 2011: 119). A [g] realization of /q/ is also found in Moroccan communities, which otherwise pronounce [q], when singing the lyrical romantic poetry of the *ʕrubi* genre, which is of Bedouin origin (Chetrit 2014:217).

2.1.2 Sibilants

An important phonological feature of many Maghrebi dialects is the neutralization of the sibilant pairs /*s/ and /*š/, /*z/ and /*ž/ (Watson 2011: 868). Such sibilant neutralization is prevalent in many Moroccan Judeo-Arabic dialects and in the Judeo-Arabic of Tunis, but not in Algerian and Libyan Judeo-Arabic, which preserve a distinction between the four sibilant phonemes /s/, /š/, /z/, and /ž/.

A phonemic neutralization resulting in the two sibilant phonemes /s/ and /z/ (/*š/ > /s/, /*ž/ > /z/) is a regular feature in most Jewish Moroccan dialects, e.g., *sʕel* (<**saʕala* 'to cough' and < **šaʕala* 'to ignite'), *zbəl* (<**zibl* 'garbage' and <**žabal* 'mountain'). This neutralization is found in the dialects of the main urban belt (Rabat, Meknes, Fes),

4 In Tafilalt the potential phonetic convergence of /q/ > [k] and original *k is avoided by the shift *k > [t] (original *t/*ṯ is pronounced [t^s]), e.g., **qalb* > *klb* 'heart', **kalb* > *tlb* 'dog' (Heath and Bar-Asher 1982: 39). In free speech of women from Oujda there are vestiges of the affricated realization [t^s], [$t^š$] for *k, particularly in the suffixes *-k*, *-lk*, used as a declension mark of the second-person singular, or in the verb *kan* (Chetrit 2017).

the Atlantic strip, Marrakesh, Tafilalt and in most of the small southern towns (Heath 2002: 132). The sibilant phonemes /s/ and /z/ vary in their realization from one community to another, ranging from pronunciations close to [s] and [z] to realizations close to [š] and [ž] (Chetrit 2017: §2.1). However, even in such dialects a few words may exhibit sibilant differentiation due to dialect-switching or borrowing from local Muslim dialects or by influence of Hebrew (e.g., the root √ *qdš*).

In the Judeo-Arabic of Tunis the phonemic neutralization of the sibilants resulted in the two phonemes /š/ and /ž/ (/*s/ > /š/, /*z/ > /ž/), e.g., *tbəššəm* (<**tabassama* 'he smiled'), *žmān* (<**zamān* 'time'). Nonetheless, when occurring next to emphatic consonants, the neutralized phonemes are pronounced [ṣ] and [ẓ], e.g., *ṣṭaḥ* 'terrace', *əẓṛaq* 'blue'. The [s] and [z] realizations are found only when adjacent to non-emphatic [r], e.g., *yāser* 'much' (D. Cohen 1975: 20–26).

While sibilant neutralization is prevalent in Moroccan and Tunisian Judeo-Arabic, the distinction between the four sibilant phonemes /s/, /š/, /z/, and /ž/ is maintained in Algerian Judeo-Arabic (the cities of Algiers and Constantine) and Libyan Judeo-Arabic (the city of Tripoli), e.g., *nsa* 'women', *šra* 'to buy', *zbəl* 'garbage', and *žbəl* 'mountain' (M. Cohen 1912: 23–24; Tirosh-Becker 1989: 290–291; Yoda 2005: 17–20). Specific realizations of these phonemes vary throughout these regions. Speakers of the Jewish community of Constantine (Algeria) realize the phoneme /ž/ as either [ž] or [ğ] (= [d͡ž]) (Tirosh-Becker 1989: 296–297). The distinction between the four sibilant phonemes is also maintained in the northeastern Moroccan Jewish dialects of Debdou and Oujda, which are near the Algerian border (Heath 2002: 132), and by bilingual Judeo-Arabic/Berber (Judeo-Berber) speaking small rural Jewish communities in Morocco (in Berber there is a distinctive differentiation between the realizations of these consonants) (Chetrit 2017: §2.1).

When two sibilant phonemes appear within the same word, assimilation or dissimilation may occur in dialects that maintain the difference between the four sibilant phonemes. Such assimilation/dissimilation is observed in various Maghrebi Muslim dialects as well (Fischer and Jastrow 1980: 252–253). For example, CA *šams* 'sun' undergoes assimilation to *šəmš* in the Judeo-Arabic of Algiers and a different assimilation to *səms* in the Judeo-Arabic of Tripoli. Additional examples are CA *zawǧ* 'two, pair' > *zuz* by the Jews of Tripoli, CA *ǧayš* > *ǧays* by the Jews of Constantine (M. Cohen 1912: 85; Tirosh-Becker 1989: 291; Yoda 2005: 74).

2.1.3 Interdentals

The shift of the interdental fricatives to their plosive dental-alveolar counterparts *ṯ* > *t* (ت < ث), *ḏ* > *d* (د < ذ), *ḏ̣* > *ḍ* (ض < ظ) is characteristic of urban North African dialects (Watson 2011: 872; Ph. Marçais 1977: 8–9). This shift is prevalent in North African Judeo-Arabic dialects as well, as the majority of Jews in this region were city and town dwellers (sedentary dialects). Examples are **ṯāni* > *tāni* 'second', **ḏirāʕ* > *drāʕ* 'arm', *ḏ̣alām* > *ḍlam* 'darkness'. The only known Jewish community that preserved the interdental fricatives is in the desert community of Tozeur, Tunisia (Saada 1981: 125). In Tunis the pronunciation of the historical interdental fricatives is one of the conspicuous differences between the Arabic dialects of Jews and Muslims in this city. While Tunis'

Muslims preserve the fricative pronunciation of these consonants *ṯ, ḏ, ḏ̣*, the city's Jews pronounced them as plosive *t, d, ḍ* in line with other sedentary Maghrebi dialects (D. Cohen 1970).

2.1.4 /t/

The realizations of the synchronic phoneme /t/ vary from one dialect to another, regardless of its origin (**t* or **ṯ*). They range from a dental [t] to a slightly affricated [ţ], the clearly affricated [t^{s}] or [t$^{\check{s}}$], to clear-cut affrication in the form of a double consonant [t͡s] or [t͡š]. A palatalized realization [t^{y}] and an aspirated realization [t^{h}] are also documented in Maghrebi Judeo-Arabic dialects, although these are less common.

[t]: This realization is found in the Judeo-Arabic of Tunis and Algiers (M. Cohen 1912: 21; D. Cohen 1970: 19). It is also heard in Constantine, although the prevalent pronunciation in the Judeo-Arabic of that city is [t$^{\check{s}}$] (Tirosh-Becker 1989: 298). It is also found in the Moroccan Judeo-Arabic of the towns along the Atlantic coast (e.g., Marrakesh), where the realization varies from [t] to [ţ], although it is always pronounced [t] before the liquid consonants [l], [n], and [r] (Chetrit 2017: §2.1).

[t^{s}]: In the old urban Maghrebi Judeo-Arabic of Meknes, Fes and Sefrou the /t/ is either moderately [t^{s}] or strongly [t͡s] affricated, except before [l], [r], and [n], e.g., *tlat^{s}a/tlat͡sa* 'three', *t^{s}aḥt l-frās/t͡saḥt l-frās* 'under the bed' (Stillman 1988: 31–32; Chetrit 2017: §2.1). The realization [t^{s}] (with variation to slight affrication [ţ]) is found in the Moroccan Judeo-Arabic of communities east of the Atlas range, from Oujda in the north, through Tafilalt in the center, to Zagora in the south (Chetrit 2017: §2.1). In Constantinian Judeo-Arabic the affrication [t^{s}] is frequent in final position, e.g., *imūt^{s}* 'he dies/he will die' (Tirosh-Becker 1989: 298).

[t$^{\check{s}}$]: This realization is characteristic of the Judeo-Arabic of Constantine regardless of position in the word, e.g., *yət$^{\check{s}}$kəlləm* 'he talks/he will talk', *t$^{\check{s}}$kəlt$^{\check{s}}$* 'I trust'. Both [t^{s}] and [t$^{\check{s}}$] are found throughout the entire borough of Constantine (Tirosh-Becker 1989: 298).

[č] (=[t͡š]):[5] The affricate alternant [č] is characteristic of the Judeo-Arabic of Tripoli (Libya), in contrast to the pronunciation [t] by that city's Muslims, e.g., *čmənya* 'eight', *kəčbəč* 'she wrote'. This affrication does not take place when /t/ stands before *l, n, s, š, ṣ*, e.g., *tlāča* 'three', *tsəkkər* 'you shut' (Yoda 2010: 53–54).

2.1.5 Glottal consonants

/ʔ/

The glottal stop /ʔ/ weakened in North African Judeo-Arabic dialects, regardless of its position in the word, whether initial, medial or final. In many dialects the glottal stop was lost in an initial position, e.g., *ʔiyyām* > *iyyām* 'days', *ʔana* > *ana* 'I', *ʔinsān* > *insān* 'man'. The glottal stop sometimes disappears together with its vowel: *ʔawlād* > *ulād* 'children'. In Tunisia hyper-restoration of the silenced /ʔ/ sometimes leads to forms such as *halaf* (< *alaf*) 'thousands', *hummo* (< *ʔummo*) 'his mother' (Saada 1964: 16).

5 As the examples with this realization are from Tripoli, Libya, we adopt here the notation [č] used by S. Yoda (2005).

At times the silencing of the /ʔ/ causes a morphological change, such as the disappearance of the fourth verbal stem *ʔafʕala* from many Maghrebi dialects, such as the dialects of Algiers, Constantine (Algeria), Tunis, Sefrou (Morocco), and Tripoli (Libya). For example, *ʔaʕṭa* > *ʕṭa* 'gave', which conjugates as the first verbal stem (M. Cohen 2012: 211–212; D. Cohen 1975: 37; Tirosh-Becker 2012: 417; Yoda 2005: 142; Stillman 1988: 47). The weakening of initial glottal stop also affects the morphology of the pattern *ʔafʕalu* that is used to denote colors, disabilities, and the elative (e.g., CA *ʔaḥmar* 'red', *ʔaʕwar* 'blind', and *ʔakbar* 'greater'). In Algiers and Constantine, but not in Tunis, these terms are constructed using the pattern *fʕəl*, e.g., *ḥməṛ* 'red', *kbər* 'greater' (M. Cohen 2012: 314–315; D. Cohen 1975: 203).

In a medial position, when the glottal stop appears in CA with a *sukūn*, it drops in these dialects, and the preceding vowel is lengthened, for example, *biʔr* > *bīr* 'a well', *kaʔs* > *kās* 'a glass'. When the medial glottal stop is vocalized with a *kasra* it weakens and is realized as [y], for example, *dāʔim* > *dāyəm* 'always', *xāʔif* > *xāyəf* 'afraid'.

Silencing of the glottal stop in final position is also common, e.g., *nisāʔ* > *nisa* 'women', *xibāʔ* > *xba* 'tent', *šaqāʔ* > *šqa* 'hard work'. Similar examples are found already in medieval Judeo-Arabic manuscripts, e.g., *samāʔ* > *sama* (סמא) 'sky'.

The silencing of the glottal stop may lead to changes in conjugation of verbs whose roots contain a glottal stop, as will be detailed in the discussion on verb morphology below.

Preservation of the glottal stop is rare in North African Judeo-Arabic. In Constantinian Judeo-Arabic the glottal stop is sometimes preserved between two vowels, either within a single word or between two consecutive words. Examples are verbal forms of roots whose first radical is a glottal stop, such as *ʔaddbuni* 'they tormented me'. The glottal stop is preserved in Constantine also in monosyllabic words such as *əl-ʔax* 'the brother', and in some retained CA words. In Morocco the glottal stop exists only as a demarcation in loanwords, as in *iṣṛaʔil* 'Israel, the modern state', vs. *iṣṛayl* 'the Jewish people' (Chetrit 2017), or is reintroduced in literary borrowings (Heath 2002: 179).

/h/

In many Moroccan Judeo-Arabic dialects and in the Judeo-Arabic of Constantine (east Algeria), as well as in most Muslim dialects throughout North Africa, the glottal fricative /h/ is preserved. An exception is the enclitic 3SGM pronoun *-hu* > *-u* postconsonantally, e.g., in Morocco *bn-u* 'his son', but *bən-ha* 'her son' (Chetrit 2017; Heath 2002: 180–181, 240–241), and in Constantine *fūmm-u* 'his mouth', but *waqqəṛū-h* 'respect him!'.

In contrast, in the Judeo-Arabic of Algiers and Tunis the glottal fricative /h/ has dropped, leaving only the accompanying vowel, e.g., *den* (< *dhen*) 'he painted', *alál* (< *hilāl*) 'crescent moon'. In some cases, the missing *h* is echoed by compensatory lengthening of the adjacent vowel or doubling of the adjacent consonant, e.g., *qāwa* (< *qahwa*) 'coffee', *ddab* or *dabb* (< *ḏahab*) 'gold'. In Algiers, the /h/ was silenced in the speech of most of the city's Jews, and could be heard mainly in eloquent speech, where the /h/ was reconstructed imitating dialects which preserved this consonant. In Tunis, the pronunciation of /h/ (by Muslims) or lack of its pronunciation (by Jews) is a known communal distinction, leading to different pronunciation of words such as the demonstrative pronoun: *hāḏa* (M) vs. *āda* (J) 'this' (D. Cohen 1970). The loss of the *h* affects the conjugation of verbs with an original third-radical *h*, which subsequently conjugate as weak verbs, e.g., *šba* (< *šbah*) 'resembled'. In the Tunisian towns of Tozeur and Djerba the *h* is retained, at least in certain cases (M. Cohen 1912: 32–33; D. Cohen 1975: 34–35; Tedghi 2016).

Loss of the glottal fricative /h/ is also characteristic of the Judeo-Arabic of Tripoli (Libya), where it is one of the most conspicuous differences between the city's Muslim and Jewish dialects. When the original *h* appears before a vowel it tends to be silenced, e.g., *ādā* (< *hāḏa*) 'this (M)', but following a consonant it tends to be pronounced as a voiced *h*, [ɦ], e.g., *ḍɦəṛ* (< *ḏahṛ*) 'back', *šɦəṛ* (< *šahṛ*) 'month'. When a word with an original *h* is followed by a suffix pronoun beginning with a vowel, the *h* drops and the adjacent vowel is lengthened in compensation, e.g., *ḍāṛ-i* (< *ḍɦəṛ* + *-i*) 'my back'. Lengthening of the adjacent vowel may occur in other cases as well, e.g., *kṛā* (< *kariha*) 'he hated' (Yoda 2010; Yoda 2005: 75–79).

2.1.6 Pharyngeal Consonants

In North African Judeo-Arabic the voiced and unvoiced fricative pharyngeal consonants /ʕ/ and /ḥ/ are preserved. However, as is found in many eastern and western Arabic dialects, they undergo assimilation when they are adjacent to each other or adjacent to the glottal fricative /h/: *ʕh* > *ḥḥ*, *ʕḥ* > *ḥḥ*, *ḥh* > *ḥḥ*, and *hḥ* > *ḥḥ*. For example, *itebbaḥ-ḥum* (< *itebbaʕ-hum*) 'he will chase them', *ḅṛuḥḥa* (<*bi-rūḥihā*) 'by herself' (M. Cohen 1912: 75; Yoda 2005: 79–80).[6]

The voiced pharyngeal fricative /ʕ/ is occasionally lost in the X-teen numerals of many Moroccan dialects, e.g., *ḥḍaš* 'eleven', *ṭnaš* 'twelve' (Heath 2002: 179). The same forms appear in the Judeo-Arabic of Algiers and Tunis, with a long *ā* (M. Cohen 1912: 356–357; D. Cohen 1975: 231–232).

2.1.7 Spread of emphasis

Emphatic pronunciation of consonants via pharyngealization (or velarization) is fundamental to Arabic and is known as *tafxīm* (تفخيم). The emphatic consonants in CA[7] are /ṭ/ (ط), /ḍ/ (ض), /ḏ̣/ (ظ), and /ṣ/ (ص). In most modern Arabic dialects, the presence of an emphatic phoneme in the word causes adjacent consonants to be pronounced emphatically and adjacent vowels to be lowered or backed. This assimilation is often denoted as 'spread of emphasis' or 'harmonization'. In some dialects it is only the consonant or vowel immediately adjacent to the emphatic consonant that is affected, whereas in other dialects emphasis may spread to the entire word (and even beyond the word boundary), namely as a suprasegmental phenomenon. This phenomenon is prevalent in all North African Judeo-Arabic dialects (Fischer and Jastrow 1980: 56–57; Heath 2002: 149–159).

6 This phenomenon is already mentioned by the famous 8th century Arab grammarian Sībawayhi in his treatise *al-Kitāb* (Levin 1994: 220–221).

7 The Arab grammarian Sībawayhi (8th century) adds several additional emphatic consonants (as allophones), whose emphasis is not reflected in the Arabic script.

The emphatic pronunciation of consonants that were not emphatic in CA is usually not phonematic, except for the *r,* as in many Maghrebi dialects there is a phonematic distinction between /r/ and /ṛ/, e.g., *žrā* 'he ran' vs. *žṛā* 'it happened' (Fischer and Jastrow, 1980: 253). Consonants that tend to accept secondary emphasis are first and foremost the non-emphatic counterparts /t/, /d/, and /s/ of the emphatic CA consonants /ṭ/ (ط), /ḍ/ (ض), /ḏ̣/ (ظ), and /ṣ/ (ص). Other phonemes that may accept an emphatic realization are *ḅ, f̣, ḷ, ṇ, ṃ, ỵ, ẉ, ẓ*. Examples, *ṭḷəḅt* (< *ṭalabtu*) 'I asked', *əṣ-ṣəḷṭāṇ* (< *əs-sulṭān*) 'the sultan', *ḍāḷəṃ* (< *ḏ̣ālim*) 'unjust', *tṣeḷḷi* (< *tuṣallī*) 'you (SG) will pray', *f̣i ḍ-ḍayqa* (< *fi ḍ-ḍayqa*) 'in distress'. While in the Judeo-Arabic of Algiers emphasis may spread in both directions, affecting phonemes that precede or follow the emphatic CA consonants, in the Judeo-Arabic dialects of Fes and Meknes (in Morocco) and Tunis (in Tunisia) emphasis tends to spread mainly to phonemes that precede the original emphatic consonant (M. Cohen 1912: 90; Heath 1987: 321; Heath 2002: 149ff.; D. Cohen 1975: 14, 32).

Fieldwork interview with Haim Twito, hailed from Constantine, Algeria

2.1.8 Vowels

The CA vowel system includes three long vowels (*ā, ū, ī*), three short vowels (*a, u, i*) and the *sukūn* (سُكُون ;ـْ), which marks the absence of a vowel after a consonant. The three long vowels *ā, ū, ī* were preserved in most North African Judeo-Arabic dialects, although in many Moroccan dialects they are no longer pronounced as long rather as full vowels (Heath 2002: 187). In many of the North African Judeo-Arabic dialects two additional long vowels were added to the vowel system as a result of monophthongization:

ay > *ē* and *aw* > *ō*. Short vowels are often omitted in open syllables in most Maghrebi dialects. These dialects typically have only two short vowels in their vowel system, a centralized short vowel *ə* and one of the 'original' short vowels, e.g., in the Judeo-Arabic dialect of Tunis the short vowels are /ə/ and /u/. In the Judeo-Arabic of Algiers and Constantine there is only a single short vowel phoneme /ə/, which may be colored as [a] adjacent to emphatic and back consonants, as [i] near the consonant *y* and as [u] when adjacent to labial consonants (M. Cohen 1912: 104).

2.1.9 Diphthongs

In the Judeo-Arabic of Algiers the CA short diphthongs *ay* and *aw* are frequently monophthongized as *ay* > *ī* and *aw* > *ū* (M. Cohen 1912: 111). The same is frequent in Moroccan Judeo-Arabic dialects although the vowel is realized as full and not long. In contrast, in the Judeo-Arabic dialects of Constantine (Algeria) and of Tunis these diphthongs are typically preserved, although they are monophthongized in certain contexts e.g., *kayfa* > *kīf* 'how' (Constantine), *yawm* > *yūm* 'day' (Tunis). In Constantine the monophthongization is sometimes *ay* > *ē* and *aw* > *ō*, e.g., *lawz* > *lōz* 'nut', *rāʔiḥa* > *rayḥa* > *rēḥ* 'smell' (D. Cohen 1975: 67–70; Tirosh-Becker 1988: 123–133). In many North African Judeo-Arabic dialects new diphthongs were formed as a result of various processes, such as the disappearance of the original *hamza*, e.g., *min ʔayna?* > *mnayn?* 'from where?' (many Moroccan dialects), or the addition of the plural morpheme *-u* to a singular form ending with a vowel, e.g., *ktəbti* + *-u* > *ktəbtīw* (Constantine), *bakā* + *-u* > *bkāw* (Algiers).

2.1.10 Consonant Clusters and Syllable Structure

One of the outstanding features of the Maghrebi dialects is the omission of short vowels in open syllables, which results in consonant clusters even at the beginning of words. For example, *ǧabal* 'mountain' or *zibl* 'garbage' > *zbəl* (Sefrou), *nahār* > *nhāṛ* 'day', *buḥūr* > *bḥūṛ* 'seas', *kataba* > *ktəb* 'he wrote' (Constantine), *ḥanaš* > *ḥnəš* 'snake' (Tunis), *qafaṣ* > *qfọṣ* 'cage', *tələbsu* > *tləbsu* 'you will wear' (Algiers). This is especially marked in the Judeo-Arabic dialects of Morocco, where consonantal clusters of three, four, five, and even more elements are frequent, in particular when morphemes are added to triliteral or quadriliteral verbs, e.g., *kṭəbt-lha* (CCəCC-CCV) 'I/you wrote her' (Stillman 1988: 36–37; Chetrit 2016: 22).

As a result of phonological processes or morphological concatenation a consonantal cluster of three (or more) consonants may be formed. In such cases, an epenthetic auxiliary vowel (either ultrashort or short) may be inserted to break up the cluster. Dialects have one of three choices with regards to the auxiliary vowel: insert the vowel after the second consonant CC_2VC, insert the vowel before the second consonant CVC_2C, or leave the consonantal cluster CC_2C without epenthesis. The addition of an auxiliary vowel often leads to the phenomenon of syllabic alternations, either CCVC > CVCC that is known as *Aufsprengen* or *ressaut,* or CVCC > CCVC that is known as *Umspringen* or *sursaut.*

The process of the *Aufsprengen* (or *ressaut*) syllable alternation, CCVC > CVCC, can be described as follows: Starting from *taktubu* (CVC_1-$\mathbf{C_2V}$-C_3V) the short vowel in the open syllable C_2V is omitted, forming a consonantal cluster > **taktbu* (CV$\mathbf{C_1C_2}$-$\mathbf{C_3}$V). Then an auxiliary vowel is inserted after C_1 to break up the cluster, initially as an ultrashort vowel which then becomes a short vowel > **tәkәtbu* (CV-$\mathbf{C_1{}^VC_2}$-$\mathbf{C_3}$V) > **tәkәtbu* (**CV**-C_1VC_2-C_3V). Finally, the short vowel that precedes the cluster, which is now in an open syllable, is omitted > *tkәtbu* (**CCVC**-CV) 'you will write/you are writing' (Constantine, Algeria). The word *msәlmin* 'Muslims' (Tripoli, Libya) is another example for the CCVC > CVCC *Aufsprengen* syllable alternation: *mә**slәm*** + *in* > **mәslmin* > **mә**sәlm**in* > *msә**lm**in*. The second process of syllable alternation CVCC > CCVC, known as *Umspringen* or *sursaut,* is the following: *qaṣr* ($C_1VC_2C_3$) > **qaṣәṛ* ($C_1VC_2{}^VC_3$) > **qaṣәṛ* (C_1V-C_2VC_3) > *qṣәṛ* ($C_1C_2VC_3$) 'palace' (Constantine, Algeria). These processes were first described by Stumme (1896: 5–6) and are realized in various North African Judeo-Arabic dialects (Fischer and Jastrow 1980: 254–256; D. Cohen 1975: 76–79; M. Cohen 1912: 147–148; Tirosh-Becker 1988: 136–142).

In CA long vowels can only exceptionally occur in closed syllables (participles of verbs *mediae geminatae*), while in North-African Judeo-Arabic dialects this is possible in general. For example, *zdād* 'born', *nqūm* 'I will rise', *xōf* 'fear' (Constantine, Algeria). Of special note is the imperative SG form of hollow verbs – *xāf* (خَف) 'fear!', *fīq* (فِق) 'wake up!', *qūm* (قُم) 'rise!' – which is common to many Maghrebi dialects, including the Jewish dialects of Algiers, Tunis, and Constantine.

2.2 Morphology

2.2.1 Verb

Conjugation

The most conspicuous morphological phenomenon that characterizes Maghrebi Arabic dialects, both sedentary and nomad, and distinguishes them from other Arabic dialects is the conjugation of the imperfect 1SG and 1PL forms. In Maghrebi dialects the 1SG form has the prefix *n-* (and not *ʔa-* as in CA and in eastern dialects) and the 1PL form received the transparent plural morpheme *-u*. Thus, in the 1st verbal stem (Grundstamm) these forms are *nәfʕәl* (1SG) / *nәfʕlu* or *nfәʕlu* (1PL), while in CA the forms are *ʔafʕalu* (1SG) / *nafʕalu* (1PL) (Fischer and Jastrow 1980: 261–262). Examples: *nsәrb* / *nsәrbu* 'I/we (will) drink' (Verbal Stem I; Sefrou, Morocco), *nәktәb* / *nәktbu* 'I/we (will) write' (Verbal Stem I; Tunis), *nkәddeb* / *nkәddbu* 'I/we (will) lie' (Verbal Stem II; Algiers), *nәčʕәllәm* / *nәčʕәllmu* 'I/we (will) learn' (Verbal Stem V; Tripoli, Libya).

In many Maghrebi sedentary dialects, the distinction between the 2SG.M and 2SG.F perfect forms was lost, and the common 2SG.C form that is used is either *ktәbt* (e.g., Judeo-Arabic of Algiers, Tunis and many Moroccan towns) or *ktәbti* (e.g., Judeo-Arabic of the Moroccan northwest from Rabat to Marakesh). In many Moroccan Judeo-Arabic dialects the converged form *ktәbt* is used not only for 2SG.C but also for 1SG (Heath 2002: 220–221). In the Judeo-Arabic of Constantine (Algeria) there is a free alternation between the two 2SG.C perfect forms, *ktәbt* and *ktәbti*. This phenomenon reflects the location of the city of Constantine on a regional dialectal junction, where the form *ktәbt* is used to its northwest (e.g., Algiers' Jews and Jijel's Muslims) and the form *ktәbti* is used to its northeast (e.g., by Skikda and Edough Muslims). When a pronominal object suffix is added to a 2SG.C perfect form in Constantin's Judeo-Arabic the alternant *ktәbti* is always selected, e.g., *trəktīh* 'you left him' (Tirosh-Becker 2012: 424). In contrast to the above, the Judeo-Arabic of Tripoli (Libya) maintains the distinction between the 2SG.M and 2SG.F perfect forms: *kčəbč* (2SG.M) 'you (M) wrote' / *kčəbči* (2SG.F) 'you (F) wrote' (Yoda 2005: 146).

The distinction between 2PL.M and 2PL.F forms in the perfect conjugation has ceased to exist in many sedentary Arabic dialects (Fischer and Jastrow 1980: 61–64). The common form in North African dialects ends with the suffix *-tu*, for example *ktəbtu* ('you [PL] wrote'). However, in the Judeo-Arabic dialects of Constantine (Algeria) and of the Moroccan Atlantic strip the 2PL.C perfect suffix is *-tīw* (e.g., *ktəbtīw* 'you (PL) wrote', *qultīw* 'you (PL) said'). In this form the plural morpheme *-u* is realized as a semi-vowel *w* when added to the 2SG.C morpheme *-ti* that ends with a vowel: *ktəbti* + *-u* > *ktəbtīw* (Tirosh-Becker 2012: 424–425; Heath 2002: 221).

Verbal stems

The Simple Stem (Stem I)

In CA, Stem I verbs are classified according to the C_2 vowel in their perfect form – *CaCaCa*, *CaCiCa* or *CaCuCa*. While a distinction according to stem vowels is preserved in most modern Arabic dialects, it is not preserved in North African Judeo-Arabic dialects due to the phonetic processes that converged all three forms to a mono-syllabic form *CCəC*, with the short central vowel *ə*. Namely, the short final vowel of *CaCaCa* drops > *CaCaC,* then the short vowel in the open syllable drops > *CCaC*, and finally the remaining short vowel is centralized > *CCəC* (the same occurs for *CaCiCa* and *CaCuCa*). Examples: *kataba* > *ktəb* 'wrote', *šariba* > *šrəb* 'drank', *kaṯura* > *ktər* 'increased (in number)'.

Verbal Stem IV

The CA verbal Stem IV (*ʔafʕala*) has ceased to function as a productive category in Maghrebi dialects, including North African Judeo-Arabic dialects (Fischer and Jastrow 1980: 46). A few participle forms of this verbal stem are found in the conservative language of the Bible translations (*šurūḥ*) from Constantine (Algeria), Meknes, and Fes (Morocco). Such forms were also documented in the Judeo-Arabic dialect of Algiers where they are used as adjectives or nouns. Examples are the adjective *muxīf* 'awe-inspiring, revered', *muġīt* 'savior', *muʕīn* 'assistant' (Tirosh-Becker 2012: 417; Bar-Asher 2001, 2: 54, 399, 518; Tedghi 2006: 305; M. Cohen 1912: 212).

Passive Voice Verbal Stems

In CA the passive voice of the simple verbal stem (Stem I) is denoted by the 'internal passive' form (*fuʕila*) or by verbal Stem VII (*ʔinfaʕala*).[8] In modern Arabic dialects there are two verbal stem options to denote the passive voice of a simple verb: a verbal stem with an initial *n-* that originates from CA verbal Stem VII (*ʔinfaʕala* > *nəfʕəl*) and a verbal stem with an initial *t*/*tt-* (*ttəfʕəl*, *tfəʕəl*). While in some Maghrebi dialects both verbal stems are used side by side, in other dialects the *t*/*tt-* stem is dominant and the *n*-stem is disappearing (Retsö 1983; Ph. Marçais 1977: 62–67; Fischer and Jastrow 1980:

8 We will not discuss the 'internal passive' forms as they are not used in these dialects.

264). The *n-* stem is in common use, often alongside the *t/tt-* stem, in the western and central Maghreb, including the Judeo-Arabic dialect of Algiers and Constantine in Algeria, and of Fes, Tetouan, Sefrou, and Tafilalt in Morocco. It is also in common use in the Judeo-Arabic of Tripoli in Libya (M. Cohen 1912: 218; Tirosh-Becker 1989: 305–309; Tirosh-Becker 2012: 417; Stillman 1988: 244; Heath and Bar-Asher 1982: 68; Yoda 2005: 177). In the eastern Maghreb there is preference for the *t/tt-* stem over the *n-* stem, including in the Judeo-Arabic dialect of Tunis and in Tunisian Muslim dialects (D. Cohen 1975: 123, 125). Examples for *n-* stem forms: *ntəmm* 'was finished', *yinġāt* 'will be saved' (Constantine), *nəǧla* 'he was exiled' (Algiers), *nəkšəf* 'her was found (Tripoli); examples for *t/tt-* stem forms: *tfəžʕu* 'they were scared' (Tunis), *ttənsīt* 'I was forgotten', *yittaṛma* 'he will be thrown' (Constantine).

Verbal Stem VIII

The use of Verbal Stem VIII with the infix *t* (*ʔiftaʕala*) has diminished in Maghrebi dialects, including Judeo-Arabic dialects throughout this region. This verbal stem, *ftəʕl* (< *ʔiftaʕala*), is documented mainly in Judeo-Arabic Bible translations (*šarḥ*, pl. *šurūḥ*) from Constantine (Algeria) and from Morocco, a literary genre that is known to preserve many archaic language features. Examples from Maghrebi *šurūḥ* are: *ʕətməl* / *ʕətmal* (עתמל/עתמאל) 'was done' (Morocco), *irtaʕdu* (ירתעדו) 'they will tremble' (Constantine, Algeria). Limited use of verbal Stem VIII is found in the Judeo-Arabic dialects of Algiers, Tunis, Sefrou, Tafilalt (Morocco), and Tripoli (Libya). Example, *ḥṭaz* 'was needed' (Sefrou), *xṭaṛ* 'he selected' (Algiers), *ždād* 'he was born' (Tunis), *ščaq* 'he longed' (Tripoli) (M. Cohen 1912: 222–227; D. Cohen 1975: 126; Ph. Marçais 1977: 63–64; Yoda 2005: 179–181; Tirosh-Becker 2012: 416; Stillman 1988: 47; Bar-Asher 2010: 184).

Verbal Stem X

The modern Arabic verbal stem *stəfʕəl*, which reflects CA Verbal Stem X (*ʔistafʕala*) without the prosthetic *alif*, is common in Maghrebi Judeo-Arabic dialects, although its use lessens in some dialects (e.g., the Judeo-Arabic dialect of Tafilalt in southeast Morocco and in some Maghrebi Muslim dialects). The initial *st-* is often pronounced emphatically *ṣṭ-* when the adjacent consonant is emphatic. Examples, *stənǧəm* 'he consulted the stars' (Algiers), *stəʕrəf* 'he acknowledged' (Tripoli), *ṣṭaṛǧīt* 'I hoped' (Constantine). Assimilations of the prefixes *st* > *ss* and *ṣṭ* > *ṣṣ* are frequent and freely alternate with the unassimilated form. Examples, *ssənna* (< *stənna*) 'he expected' (Algiers), *əṣṣəṛǧa* (< *əṣṭəṛǧa*) 'hope!' (Constantine). Assimilation is apparent also in the verb *ṣqṣi* (< *staqṣii*) 'he asked',[9] which is very common in Moroccan Judeo-Arabic dialects (M. Cohen 1912: 235; Heath 2002: 393–394; Tirosh-Becker 2011b; Yoda 2005: 181). In the Jewish dialect of Tunis, where *s* > *š*, the prefix of this Verbal Stem is *št-*, e.g., *štaʕžəb* 'he was surprised', *štaġla* 'he found it expensive', *štənna* 'he expected'. Near emphatic consonants the prefix becomes *ṣṭ-* in agreement with the emphatic realization of **s* in this context, e.g., *ṣṭḥaqq* 'it lacked', *ṣṭaṛwaḥ* 'he has a cold' (D. Cohen 1975: 130–131).

9 The word *ṣqṣi* has local variants according to the local realization of the /q/ (see section on phonology above).

The Verbal Stem fʕāl / fʕal

A well-known North African dialectal phenomenon is the use of the verbal stem *fʕāl* / *fʕal* to indicate a process of change in the properties of an object or a person, e.g., *smān* 'he gained weight', *ḍyāq* 'he became narrow'. The verbal stem *fʕāl* with a long vowel is used in the Judeo-Arabic of Algeria and Tunis, while the verbal stem *fʕal* is used in the Judeo-Arabic dialects or Morocco and Tripoli (Libya), e.g., *sman* 'he gained weight', *zyan* 'he became beautiful'. It was suggested that this verbal stem originates either from CA verbal Stem XI (*ʔifʕālla*) or CA verbal stem IX (*ʔifʕalla*) (Fischer and Jastrow 1980: 264). However, while CA verbal stems IX and XI were limited to colors and defects, in Maghrebi Arabic dialects the *fʕāl* / *fʕal* stem has a much broader use, also indicating a process of change in material properties and human psychological aspects, e.g., *čqal* 'he became heavy', *qbaḥ* 'he became impudent' (Tripoli) (M. Cohen 1912: 236–237; D. Cohen 1975: 121; Heath 2002: 2019; Tirosh-Becker 2012: 423; Yoda 2005: 183).

Verb types

Following are a few comments on the conjugation of some verb types. The silencing of the glottal stop may lead to changes in conjugation of verbs whose roots first radical is a glottal stop. Of special note are the CA verbs *ʔakala* (أَكَلَ 'ate') and *ʔaxaḏa* (أَخَذَ 'took'), which have undergone a variety of changes in Arabic dialects once the initial glottal stop was lost (Fischer and Jastrow 1980: 67). Among the Jewish dialects of the Maghreb there are three distinct paths of change in these verbs (Heath 2002: 379–386, 571).[10] In most Moroccan Judeo-Arabic dialects the perfect forms of these verbs are *kəl* and *xəd*, reflecting a strong bilateral stem. In Tafilalt (southeastern Morocco), the forms *kal* and *xad*, that reflect a hollow triliteral stem, are used.[11] In the Judeo-Arabic dialects of eastern Morocco, Algiers, Constantine, Tunis, and Tripoli (Libya), the perfect forms of these verbs reflect a weak triliteral stem, *kla* and *xda*. In these dialects the imperative forms of these verbs are *kūl* and *xūd*, reflecting a hollow triliteral stem, and not a weak triliteral stem as in the perfect forms (on the long vowel in the imperative form of hollow triliteral stems in Maghrebi dialects see in the phonology section above). Finally, the imperfect forms *nākul*, *tākul* (CA *taʔkulu*) exhibit a long vowel compensating for the loss of the original glottal stop (M. Cohen 1912: 198–199; D. Cohen 1975: 108–110; Tirosh-Becker 2012: 423–424; Yoda 2005: 189).

Another example for a paradigmatic stem-shape alternation is in the passive participle forms of hollow triliteral roots, which follow the pattern of roots with a weak first radical. Examples from Constantinian Judeo-Arabic are the participle forms *mawxūf* 'is feared' of the hollow triliteral root √ *xwf*, *mawǧūb* 'is brought' of the hollow triliteral root √ *ǧyb*, and *mawqūl* 'is told' of the hollow triliteral root √ *qwl*. While their perfect forms are *xāf*, *ǧāb*, and *qāl*, as expected of hollow triliteral roots, their dialectal passive participle forms *mawxūf*, *mawǧūb*, and *mawqūl* follow the pattern of roots with a weak first radical, such as *mawǧūd* 'exists' whose root is √ *wǧd*. In CA we would have ex-

10 A fourth possibility, *kəll*, with a geminate triliteral stem, occurs in a few Muslim Moroccan dialects, but is not documented in Jewish Moroccan dialects, see Heath 2002: 381.

11 The Jews of Tafilalt pronounce it *tal*, due to the **k* > *t* shift in their dialect, see Heath and Bar-Asher 1982:67.

pected the passive participle *maxūf* (مَخُوف) for the root √ *xwf* (Tirosh-Becker 2012: 422). Similar examples, without the diphthongs *aw*, are found in other North African Judeo-Arabic dialects: *mūṣūb* 'is found' from the root √ *ṣwb* (Algiers), *muqul* 'is told' (Tripoli, Libya) (M. Cohen 1912: 191; Yoda 2005: 162).

Preverbs

In Arabic dialects a variety of preverbs (or their contracted forms) precede the imperfect form of the verb to denote temporal aspects (Fischer and Jastrow 1980: 75). In North African Judeo-Arabic dialects a durative aspect of an action that is taking place right now is denoted by preceding the imperfect form with the preverbs *kāyən* 'lit. existing' or *qāʕəd* 'lit. sitting', or their phonetically contracted forms *ka-, ta-*, or *qa-*. The marker *ka-* is dominant in Moroccan Judeo-Arabic dialects of the urban belt (Rabat-Meknes-Fes) with scattered attestations further south, while the marker *ta-* is the dominant form in southern Moroccan Jewish dialects, e.g., *ka ymsi w-izi* 'he is coming and going'. In the Judeo-Arabic of Tunis and Tripoli (Libya) the preverb is *qāʕəd* 'lit. sitting' or its shorter version *qa-*, e.g., *qāʕəd iṣāwəb ḥwālu* 'he is improving', *qa yākəl* 'he is eating' (Tunis), *ša qa čəʕməl* 'what are you doing?' (Tripoli) (D. Cohen 1975: 136–137; Chetrit 2017; Yoda 2005: 193).

Future actions are denoted by preceding the imperfect form with the future preverb *maši* 'lit. going', or its contracted forms *maš* or *ma-*. The preverb *maši* is dominant in Moroccan Jewish dialects (especially in the urban belt from Rabat to Fes-Sefrou and in the Marrakesh area) and in the Judeo-Arabic dialects of Algiers and Tunis, e.g., *mas tʔtelni* 'it will kill me' (Fes), *māši nəxrəǧ* 'I am about to exit' (Algiers) (Heath 2002: 216; M. Cohen 1912: 258).

In the Judeo-Arabic of Tunis and of Tripoli (Libya) a desire for a future action, i.e., 'I would like to do something', or an intent, is expressed by preceding the imperfect verb with the preverb *ḥebb* 'to love', e.g., *nḥebb nakəl ksəsu* 'I want to eat couscous' (Tripoli) (D. Cohen 1975: 137; Yoda 2005: 194).

In the Judeo-Arabic of Sefrou (Morocco) the future is indicated by prefixing the marker *a-* to the imperfect form, e.g., *a-nsmaʕ* 'I will listen', *a-ihezzu* 'they would lift'. The future marker *a-* seems to be unique to the Jewish dialect of Sefrou. The imperfect verb with the prefix *a-* is also used to express the subjunctive mood of CA (Stillman 1988: 40–41).

2.2.2 Demonstrative pronouns

Demonstrative pronouns for near deixis

North African Judeo-Arabic dialects have the following system of demonstrative pronouns for near deixis, with appropriate phonetic adaptations in each dialect. In the Judeo-Arabic of Constantine (Algeria) these pronouns are:

SG.M	*hāda*	
SG.F	*hādi*	} *hād*
PL.C	*hādu*	

These pronouns reflect the phonetic shift of the fricative interdentals to their plosive counterparts (*ḏ* > *d*) that is characteristic of urban North African Judeo-Arabic (see above): CA *hāḏā* (هٰذا) > *hāda*, CA *hāḏihi* (هٰذِهِ) > *hādi*. Before a definite noun, a single short form *hād* is used regardless of gender or number, e.g., *səddūr hāda* but *hād əs-səddūr* 'this book', *hād əl-bnāt* 'these girls.' The short form *hād* is common throughout the Maghreb (Ph. Marçais 1977: 197). In Moroccan dialects the first vowel in these pronouns is *a*: *hada* (SG.M), *hadi* (SG.F), *hadu* (PL.C). The *h* is often omitted in the dialect of Algiers. In the Judeo-Arabic dialects of Tunis, where *h* is not pronounced, the demonstrative pronouns for near deixis are *āda* (SG.M), *ādi* (SG.F), *ādu* (PL.C). Before a definite noun these pronouns are shortened to *ād*. The same is true for the Judeo-Arabic of Tripoli (Libya) with slight variations: *ada* (SG.M), *adi* (SG.F), *aḍun* ~ *aḍuni* (PL.C); before a definite noun these pronouns are shortened to *ad* (Heath 2002: 271; M. Cohen 1912: 346; D. Cohen 1975: 225; Yoda 2005:127).

In the conservative language of some North African Bible translations (*šurūḥ*) the plural demonstrative pronoun for near deixis is *hāwlay* (האולאי), which reflects the CA form *hāʔulāʔi* (هٰـؤُلاءِ) and differs from the local dialectal form *hādu*. The pronoun *hāwlay* is found in the *šarḥ* traditions from Constantine (Algeria) and from Meknes and Fes (Morocco), e.g., *hāwlay əḍ-ḍālṃīṇ* (האולאי אלצ'אלמין) 'these evil people' (Constantine). Although there are other Maghrebi *šarḥ* traditions in which the colloquial form *hādu* is employed (Bar-Asher 2001, 3:94; Bar-Asher 2010: 184; Tirosh-Becker 2012: 412–413).

Demonstrative pronouns for distal deixis

The following system of demonstrative pronouns is used for distal deixis in the Judeo-Arabic dialect of Constantine (Algeria):

SG.M *hādāk*
SG.F *hādīk*
PL.C *hādūk*

The corresponding CA pronouns are *ḏālika* (ذٰلِكَ), *tilka* (تِلْكَ), *ʔūlāʔika* (أُولٰئِكَ). In Moroccan dialects these pronouns are: *hadak* (SG.M), *hadik* (SG.F), *haduk* (PL.C), and the *ha* is dropped before a definite noun, e.g., *dak l-wəld* 'that boy', *dik l-bənt* 'that girl'. The *h* is often omitted in the dialect of Algiers. In the Judeo-Arabic dialects of Tunis, where *h* is not pronounced, the demonstrative pronouns for distal deixis are *adāk* (SG.M), *adīk* (SG.F), *adūk* (PL.C). The same is true for the Judeo-Arabic of Tripoli (Libya) with slight variations: *adak* ~ *dak* (SG.M), *adik* ~ *dik* (SG.F), *aḍuk* ~ *ḍuk* (PL.C) (Heath 2002: 272; D. Cohen 1975: 225; Yoda 2005:127).

2.2.3 Relative marker

In North African Arabic dialects, the relative marker has evolved in one of two ways, each preserving a different element of the CA relative marker *ʔallaḏī* (اَلَّذِي). The first is the relative marker *əlli* ~ *lli* that preserves the alveolar liquid element *ll* of the CA marker, and the second is *əddi* ~ *ddi* ~ *di* that reflects the original interdental element *ḏi* (Fischer and Jastrow 1980: 84–85).

In the Judeo-Arabic dialects of the central and eastern Maghreb – i.e., the Jewish dialects of Algiers, Constantine (Algeria), Tunis and Tripoli (Libya) – the relative marker is *əlli* ~ *lli* ~ *li*. Of interest is that while the Jews of Constantine used both *əlli* and *lli*, the Muslims of that city use only the marker *lli* (Tirosh-Becker 2012: 415–416; M. Cohen 1912: 349; D. Cohen 1975: 221; Yoda 2005: 131; Laraba 1981: 109).

Unlike the rest of the Maghreb, Moroccan Judeo-Arabic dialects use *di* as the relative marker, and it is attested in all regions of Morocco (Meknes, Sefrou, Casablanca, Marrakesh, Tafilalt, and more). In contrast, the ubiquitous relative marker used by Muslims throughout Morocco is *lli*. The marker *lli* is sporadically used by Moroccan Jews as well, suggesting an influence of the local Muslim dialects (Heath 2002: 474).

It is noteworthy that the main relative marker that is used in the conservative language of Bible translations (*šurūḥ*) from Constantine is *əldi* (אלדי), which reflects the CA form *ʔallaḏī* (ٱلَّذِي). However, in contrast to the inflection of *ʔallaḏī* in CA, the marker *əldi* was mostly invariable already in Medieval Judeo-Arabic (Blau 2002: 55) and is completely invariable in the Constantinian *šarḥ*. Example, *əldi tnəbba ʕla Yehuda wi-Yerušalayim* '(a person) who prophecized on Judea and Jerusalem' (Isaiah 1:1). The relative marker *əldi* is also characteristic of the literary language of the Jews of Tunis (Tirosh-Becker 2012: 416; D. Cohen 1975: 221).

2.2.4 Genitive exponents

The genitive (possessive) exponents that are common to many Maghrebi dialects are *ntāʕ* ~ *mtāʕ* ~ *tāʕ*, *dyāl*, and *di* ~ *d-*. All, except for *di*/*d-*, may accept a pronominal suffix, e.g., *mtāʕ-u* 'his', *dyāl-hum* 'theirs' (Ph. Marçais 1977: 168–170, 223). These forms are used interchangeably in Judeo-Arabic dialects throughout the Maghreb, although *dyāl*, and its shorter versions *di* ~ *d-*, are the dominant forms in Moroccan Judeo-Arabic dialects. While *dyāl* is frequently used in Constantinian Judeo-Arabic alongside *ntāʕ* ~ *tāʕ*, the short form *di* is not attested in this dialect. As described in the phonology section above, sometimes the assimilation *ntāʕ-hum* > *ntāḥ-ḥum* may occur (Tirosh-Becker 2019: 206 207; M. Cohen 1912: 74–75, 363–364; D. Cohen 1975: 252; Stillman 1988: 52; Heath 2002: 461). Examples:

ntāʕ ~ *mtāʕ*: *l-mḥəbba ntāʕ-kum* 'your love' (Gahrdaia, Algeria), *məsyāsa mtāʕ addāb* 'a gold bracelet' (Algiers)

tāʕ: *l-kəlb tāʕ-kum* 'your (PL) dog' (Constantine, Algeria), *ṣḥāb tāʕ-u* 'his friends' (Tunis)

dyāl: *l-braxa dyāl ṇṭiḷat yadayim* 'the blessing of washing hands' (Constantine, Algeria), *ət-tšuva dyāl-u* 'his repentance' (Algiers), *ḍ-ḍaṛ dyali* 'my house' (Sefrou, Morocco), *lə-qbūṛ dyal-u* 'his tomb' (Tunis)

di / *ddi*: *ḍ-ḍaṛ ddi-l-i* 'my house' (Rabat, Morocco), *l-ʕamr di bənadam* 'the life of a human being' (Algiers)

d-: *r-rabban d-l-blad* 'the Rabbi of the town' (Sefrou, Morocco)

2.3 Lexicon

The Jews of North Africa lived in a thriving multi-lingual environment that included local Arabic and Berber dialects, French, Spanish (mainly Morocco) or Italian (Libya), alongside Hebrew (and Aramaic) which is central to Jewish culture and heritage. Many of the speakers were in as state of *multiglossia* (see detailed discussion in the introduction above). All aforementioned languages have left footprints in the lexicon of Judeo-Arabic speaking Jews in North Africa.

2.3.1 Hebrew (Aramaic) component

North African Judeo-Arabic, like all other Jewish languages, has a significant Hebrew and Aramaic component embedded within it. These mainly include terms and phrases that reflect Jewish religion, culture and heritage, Jewish life cycle events, communal functions and roles, and the like. For the sake of simplicity, this component can be referred to as 'Hebrew' as the Aramaic element in itself is limited and there is no distinction in usage between the two. However, only the rabbinic elite possessed broader knowledge of Aramaic, and thus their *sociolect* includes more Aramaic lexemes. These Hebrew and Aramaic loanwords undergo phonetic, morphological and semantic adaptations upon embedding into Judeo-Arabic (M. Cohen 1912: 388–408; Stillman 1988: 53–58; Yoda 2005: 361).

Among the considerable Hebrew component, we find many Jewish religious and communal concepts, such as *t-tōra* 'the Torah' (< תורה), *skka* 'Sukka' (< סכה), *ṭəbila* 'ritual immersion' (< טבילה), *l-gifen* 'Qiddush wine or Qiddush blessing' (< הגפן) (Sefrou, Morocco); *qa^h^al* 'congregation' (< קהל), *šəmmāš* 'beadle' (< שמש), *məṣva* 'a commandment to be performed as a religious duty' (< מצווה) (Algiers), *məggid* 'a person who assists the reader of the Torah in the synagogue' (< מגיד) (Constantine, Algeria); *ḥačan* 'bridegroom' (< חתן), *ẓḍaqa* 'charity' (< צדקה), *ṃuil* 'circumciser' (< מוהל) (Tripoli, Libya). Nonetheless, Hebrew secular concepts are also in wide use, e.g., *ṣāṛa* 'trouble' (< צרה), *ṣaʕar* 'sorrow' (< צער), *gibboṛ* 'a strong person' (< גיבור) (Sefrou, Morocco); *mamon* 'money' (< ממון), *maggefa* 'plague' (< מגיפה) (Algiers); *šəggi-noṛ* 'blind' (Aramaic *saggi nəhor* סגי נהור), *šəkkana* 'danger' (< סכנה) (Tunisia). "Function" words of Jewish Aramaic origin were also used, e.g., *(ə)ḍṛabba* 'all the more' (< Aramaic אדרבא) (Tunisia).

Hebrew elements are prominent in blessings, greetings and similar expressions exchanges between community members, such are *sabbaṭ salom* 'a peaceful Sabbath' (< שבת שלום), *sabuʕa ṭob* 'have a good week' (< שבוע טוב), *barux hab-ba* 'welcome!' also 'you are free to do what you like' (< ברוך הבא), *hassim iṭbarax* 'the blessed Lord' (< השם יתברך), *bs-simman ṭob* 'congratulations! (< בסימן טוב; lit. with a good sign)' (Sefrou), *rəbbono šēl ʕolam* 'Good Lord! (< ריבונו של עולם; lit. master of the universe!)' (Algiers), *šibaḥ la-(y)il* 'praise the Lord' (< שבח לאל) (Tunisia).

Many Hebrew personal names undergo local adaptations in Judeo-Arabic so that they seem closer to Arabic forms. In Sefrou (Morocco) we find *Bṛaham* 'Abraham', *Ṣḥaʔ* 'Isaac (Heb. *Itzḥaq*)', *Müsi* 'Moses (Heb. *Moše*)', and *Dabi* 'David', while in Tripoli (Libya) these are pronounced *Muši* 'Moses' and *Dawid* 'David'.

Some Hebrew roots were weaved into Arabic verbal stems making them an integral part of Judeo-Arabic. Examples from Algiers – *tməlšən* 'he informed on (someone)' (< Heb. *malšin* מלשין 'informer'), *tšəbbəš* 'he was confused, bewildered, perplexed' (< Heb. root √ *šbš* 'to disrupt'), *itmūmar* 'he converted' (< Heb. *mumar* מומר 'a convert'); from Morocco (Sefrou) – *piyyəṭ* 'he sang a religious poem' (< Heb. *piyyuṭ* פיוט 'religious poem'); from Libya (Tripoli) – *čfənnəq* 'he was spoiled' (< Heb. *hitpanneq* התפנק 'he was spoiled'), *xnəb* 'he stole' (< Heb. *ganav* גנב 'he stole').

While many Hebrew loanwords are shared by Jews across many communities (with local adaptations), some vary from area to area. An example is the Hebrew loanword used to denote a Jewish cemetery that differs between eastern and western Maghreb. Jews of the western Maghreb communities (Morocco and western Algeria) use the Hebrew word *meʕara* (מערה 'cave') to denote a cemetery, while Jews who live in central and eastern Maghreb communities (Algiers, eastern Algeria, Tunisia, and Libya) use the Hebrew phrase *betaḥayim* (בית החיים 'house of the living') for the same purpose. Another example, the Jews of Algiers and Constantine use the original Hebrew term *miqve* (מקווה) to denote the 'ritual bath' used for ritual immersion, while in western Algeria and in Morocco it is referred to as *ṭəbila* (Sefrou) (טבילה 'immersion'), probably referring to the term בית טבילה 'house of immersion' that is used in the Mishnah. A variety of Hebrew terms were used in different communities to denote the anniversary of the day of death of a loved one, also known by the Yiddish term *yahrzeit*: in Constantine (east Algeria) the term for *yahrzeit* was the Hebrew word *həzkir* / *həzker* (< הֶזְכֵּר; from the root √ *zkr* that denotes 'memory'); in the towns of Tlemcen and Aïn Témouchent (western Algeria) the term was *həsgir* (< הֶסְגֵּר, from the root √ *sgr* that denotes 'closure'); in Tétouan and other northern Moroccan towns, as well as some speakers in eastern Algeria (Tlemcen and Aïn Témouchent) the Hebrew term was *naḥala* (< נחלה, 'heritage'); in Tafilalt (southeastern Morocco) as well as in Libya, the easternmost part of the Maghreb, the term used was *pəqida* (< פְּקִידָה; from the root √ *pqd* that denotes 'to remember' [biblical]); finally, many Moroccan Jews adopted the Yiddish term *yahrzeit* itself in their Judeo-Arabic speech, which was sometimes pronounced *yaʔərṣyaṭ* based on "spelling pronunciation" of the written word יארצייט (Bar-Asher 1999: 154, 300, 312).

Some Hebrew words preserve archaic traditions of Hebrew terms or expressions. For example, while the pronunciation *ha-qadoš barux hu* 'God (lit. the Holy One Blessed be He)' (< הקדוש ברוך הוא) is common across North Africa, the Jews of Algiers pronounce this phrase *a-qodeš baruxu*. The pronunciation *qodeš* (and not *qadoš*) preserved an archaic version of this expression which is documented in ancient manuscripts of rabbinic literature (הקודש ברוך הוא).

In some communities the Hebrew component also served as a *concealed language* understood only by community members, enabling merchants and traders to communicate without being understood by others. Thus, Hebrew words, e.g., for items such as gold, silver or money, replaced their Arabic counterparts within the Judeo-Arabic conversation, and Hebrew numbers or Hebrew letters were used for counting (the simple and widespread alphanumeric code of assigning a numerical value to each Hebrew letter, known as *gematria,* is used throughout the Jewish world). When Algiers' Jews wanted to silence each other in the presence of strangers they said *bla dabar* (< *bəlo dibbur* בלא דיבור 'without speech') avoiding the more common Hebrew word *šeket!* (< *šeqeṭ!* !שקט) due to its similarity to the Arabic word *uskut!* (أسكت).

2.3.2 French component

As French was the *lingua franca* in North Africa during much of the nineteenth and twentieth centuries, numerous French words were integrated into North African Judeo-Arabic, first and foremost into Algerian Judeo-Arabic as Algerian Jews received citizenship from France in 1870. Many French words also entered Moroccan and Tunisian Judeo-Arabic when these became French Protectorates. This French component was used to refer to modern (typically secular) concepts, administration and government organizations, modern technology and more.

Among the many French words used by North African Jews are *journal*, *commander*, *franc*, *bureau*, *monsieur*, *prezidan* (Fr. *le president*), *l-kumitē* (Fr. *le comité*), *timbr* 'stamp' (Fr. *timbre*), *əl-gato* 'cake' (Fr. *gâteau*). Modern technical vocabulary is also French, e.g., *lavyon* 'airplane' (Fr. *l'avion*), *l-fṛen* 'car brakes' (Fr. *freins*), etc. French loanwords were sometimes embedded in Arabic noun patterns, such as the use of the Arabic broken plural form, e.g., *konsul* 'consul' – *kanāsil* 'consuls' (Constantine, Algeria),[12] or the use of the Arabic plural morpheme *-at*.

2.3.3 Spanish component

There is an extensive vocabulary of Spanish loanwords in Moroccan Judeo-Arabic dialects. A considerable number of these loanwords are shared among the urban Arabic dialects of northern and central Morocco, both Jewish and non-Jewish. These words have been penetrating into Moroccan Arabic from the Middle Ages to modern times due to the close interactions with the Iberian Peninsula (Stillman 1988: 59–60). Included are words such as *busta* 'post office' (Sp. *posta*), *familiya* 'family' (Sp. *familia*), *sala* 'living room' (Sp. *sala*), *suppa* 'soup' (Sp. *sopa*), *swerṭi* 'luck' (Sp. *suerte*).

As Jews arrived in Morocco from Spain in several waves during the fourteenth and fifteenth centuries, bringing with them speakers of Castilian Judezmo, there are Spanish loanwords that are unique to Moroccan Judeo-Arabic. The Judeo-Arabic of Meknes, for example, contains a fairly large number of lexical elements of Judeo-Spanish or Spanish origin. These lexemes belong to different categories of material culture and to social attributes and roles. For example, *banyo* 'wash basin' (Sp. *baño*), *küna* 'cradle' (Sp. *cuna*), *rodiyya* 'table napkin' (Sp. *rodilla*), *saya* 'skirt' (Sp. *sayo*), *kutsärä*, pl. *kwätsär*, 'spoon' (Sp. *cuchara*), and even abstract nouns such as *əl-mizirja* 'misery' (Sp. *miseria*) (Stillman 1988; Chetrit 2017).

A smaller number of Spanish loanwords are found also in Algerian Judeo-Arabic, as Algeria also received Jewish immigrants from Spain in the fourteenth and fifteenth centuries. Among the Spanish loanwords in the Judeo-Arabic of Algiers are *šītā* 'brush', *šnūġa* 'synagogue', and *šlāda* 'salad'. Spanish words that were borrowed at a later period are *kānṭaṛa* 'small chest' and *botəlya* 'bottle' (Sp. *botella*). Spanish words are more

12 The same phenomenon can be seen in the Hebrew component as well, e.g., *fasuq* '[biblical] verse' (< פסוק) pl. *fawāsiq* 'verses'.

common in the Judeo-Arabic of Oran (Ar. Wahrān) due to its long history under Spanish rule and its status as a bustling port city.

Finally, as Castilian speaking Jews who fled the Iberian persecutions and expulsion of the 14th and 15th centuries also reached Tunisia, a few Spanish loanwords were embedded in Tunisian Judeo-Arabic as well. Examples are *garfu* 'fork' (Sp. *garfio* 'fork, hook'), *villu* 'veil of the bride' (Sp. *velo*).

2.3.4 Italian component

Libya was under Italian rule from 1911 until its independence in 1951. Hence, many Italian loanwords have been introduced into Libyan Judeo-Arabic and are an integral part of daily speech. Recent Italian loanwords have not been completely phonologically arabicized and maintain consonants and vowels that are not part of the local phonetic system (e.g., the consonants *v*, *p*, and the vowels *e*, *o*). Examples from the Judeo-Arabic of Tripoli, *žornāle* 'newspaper' (It. *giornale*), *bandyēra* 'flag' (It. *bandiera*). Some Italian words take Arabic plural endings (CA *-āt*), such as *žornāliyač* 'newspapers', *banndyērač* 'flags.' Other loanwords, such as *baninu* 'sandwich' (It. *panino*) retain their original plural form in Judeo-Arabic, *banini* 'sandwiches' (It. *panini*). Other examples are činma 'cinema', *familya* 'family' (It. *famiglia*), *filəm* (pl. *filmač*) 'film', *firma* 'signature', *fṛuṭṭa* 'fruit' (Yoda 2005: 6, 313ff.).

Tunisian Judeo-Arabic also includes loanwords from Italian introduced by the Jews from Livorno, who originated from Spain and Portugal, and settled in Tunis and other coastal towns in the eighteenth and nineteenth centuries. The Italian vocabulary integrated in Tunisian Judeo-Arabic encompasses a variety of semantic fields and most particularly those connected with everyday life. Examples, *(a)bukāṭu* 'lawyer' (It. *avvocato*), *šušīta* 'society' (It. *società*), *brīma* 'excellent, unparalleled' (It. *prima*), *rigālo* 'present' (It. *regalo*) (Tedghi 2016).

A limited number of Italian words are present also in the Judeo-Arabic of Algiers, due to immigration of Jewish traders from Livorno to Algeria. Among the Italian loanwords in Algiers' Judeo-Arabic are words such as *sōldi* 'a silver coin', *mərkāṭi* 'trader' (It. *mercante*) also used to denote 'a rich person', and *pyano* 'floor' (It. *piano*).

2.3.5 Berber component

The Berber population is widespread throughout North Africa. However, because the Jews were a sedentary (mainly urban) population, while Berbers are predominantly nomads, the interaction between the two was fairly limited. Hence, Berber loanwords are extremely few in North African Judeo-Arabic, and these are also shared with the Muslim Arabic dialects in the region. Berber loanwords are typically from the semantic fields of agriculture and botany. A few of the Berber words in North African Judeo-Arabic are *šlāġəm* 'mustaches' and *fəkrūn* 'torture, suffering' (Algiers), *aznun* 'a ceiling window', *taʕṛabat* 'explicitly' (Tafilalt, Morocco). The Berber feminine form is adopted in some words in the Judeo-Arabic of Sefrou, e.g., *ṭaxerrazṭ* 'shoemaking'. Only a few Berber words were documented as being used by Jews, but not by their Muslim neighbors, e.g., *zāwəš* 'sparrow' (Algiers).

3 Text specimens with inter-linear glosses

The texts below were chosen to represent a variety of North African Judeo-Arabic dialects, and different genres. Texts 1 is a *šarḥ* (translation) tradition of Psalms Chapter 33 from Constantine, Algeria. Text 2 is an article published in the Judeo-Arabic journal *əl-Ḥikma* from Constantine, Algeria. Text 3 is a folk tale told in Tunisian Judeo-Arabic. Text 4 is a description of the celebration on the eve of *Shavuʕot* (Tabernacles) from Sefrou, Morocco. Text 5 is a fairy tale from Tripoli, Libya, Texts 1 and 2 were printed in Hebrew characters, while texts 3, 4, and 5 are oral texts.

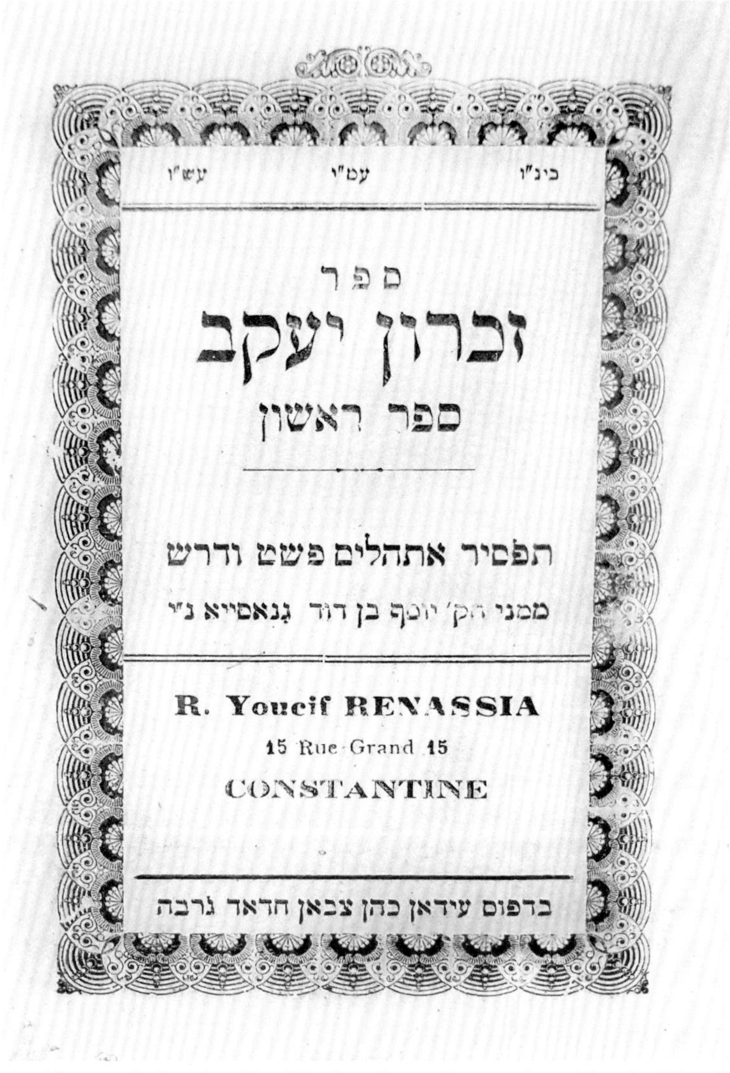
כינ"ו עמ"ו עש"ו

ספר

זכרון יעקב

ספר ראשון

תפסיר אתהלים פשט ודרש

ממני הק' יוסף בן דוד גנאסייא נ"י

R. Youcif RENASSIA

15 Rue Grand 15

CONSTANTINE

בדפוס עידאן כהן צבאן חדאד גרבה

A Judeo-Arabic translation (*šarḥ*) of Psalms from Constantine, Algeria (Yosef Renassia 1954(?), *Zikhron Yaʕakov*, Djerba: Ḥadad imprimerie)

Text 1: A šarḥ *of Psalm 33 from Constantine, Algeria*

The *šarḥ* (translation) of Psalms according to the tradition of the Jewish community of Constantine (Eastern Algeria) was put down in writing and published by Rabbi Yosef Renassia (1879–1962), a prominent leader of this community. Rabbi Renassia published more than 100 volumes written in Judeo-Arabic, encompassing Bible translations (*šurūḥ*) and commentaries, translations and exegeses of post-biblical texts, liturgical texts, translations of historiographic and halakhic books, dictionaries, grammar books, and more (Tirosh-Becker 2012). The translation of Psalms was published in the book *Zikhron Yaʕaqov*, 5 vols, Ḥadad imprimerie, Djerba 1954(?). The transcription below is based on my recording of Rabbi Daniel Renassia reciting from the book *Zikhron Yaʕaqov* (recorded in 1987; Dimona, Israel). Rabbi Daniel Renassia was the son of Rabbi Yosef Renassia, and studied the *šarḥ* tradition from his father. I indicated in footnotes wherever the version recited by Rabbi Daniel Renassia differed from the printed text (denoting it as DR).

1 רַנְּנוּ צַדִּיקִים, בַּיהוָה; לַיְשָׁרִים, נָאוָה תְהִלָּה.
רננו יא עאדלין באללאה ללמסגמין[13] תואתי אשוכראן

rannənu	*yā*	*ʕādlīn*[14]	*b-aḷḷāh*	*l-ᵊl-msəggmīn*	*twāti*	*əš-šukrān*
sing:IMP.PL	VOC	virtuous:PL.M	in-God,	DEF-righteous:PL.M	deserve:IPFV.3SG.F[15]	DEF-thanks:SG.M

Sing of God o virtuous! The righteous deserve thanks.

2 הוֹדוּ לַיהוָה בְּכִנּוֹר; בְּנֵבֶל עָשׂוֹר, זַמְּרוּ-לוֹ.
אשכרו לאללאה באלעוד ברבאב למעשר מגדו ליה

əšəkru	*l-aḷḷāh*	*b-əl-ʕūd*	*bə-rbāb*[16]	*l-mʕaššər*[17]	*məğğdu*[18]	*lī-h*
thank:IMP.PL	to-God	with-DEF-*ʕūd*	with-*rbāb*	DEF-be_ten.PTCP.SG.M[19]	praise:IMP.PL	to-3SG.M

Thank the Lord with an *ʕūd* (= a type of local string instrument, similar to the lute), praise Him with a ten-string *rbāb* (= a type of local bowed string instrument).

3 שִׁירוּ-לוֹ, שִׁיר חָדָשׁ; הֵיטִיבוּ נַגֵּן, בִּתְרוּעָה.
סבחו ליה תסביח גדיד חסנו אנג׳מא בתבויק

səbbḥu	*lī-h*	*təsbīḥ*	*ğdīd,*	*ḥassnu*[20]	*ən-nəġma*	*b-taḅẉīq*
praise:IMP.PL	to-3SG.M	praise	new	well_perform:IMP.PL	DEF-tune	in-horn_playing

Praise Him with a new praise-song, improve the tune playing the horn.

13 In Algerian Judeo-Arabic the *šadda* is indicated by doubling of letters in Hebrew-script texts, e.g., קדדם (*qəddəm*). However, the doubling is not always reflected in this printed Hebrew-script text, although it is pronounced (e.g., ללמסגמין = *msəggmīn*; סבחו = *səbbḥu*).

14 The version recited by Rabbi Daniel Renassia (henceforth DR): *l-ʕādlīn*.

15 *šukrān* is a SG.M form. The 3SG.F form *twāti* may be an attraction to the Hebrew SG.F form נָאוָה.

16 DR: *u-rbāb*.

17 DR pronounced it as *l-mʕassər* influenced by the Hebrew word *ʕaśor* (עָשׂוֹר).

18 Speakers of this dialect realize the phoneme /ž/ (ج) either as [ž] or [ğ] (=[d̲ž]) (Tirosh-Becker 1989: 296–297).

19 This participle form translates a noun denoting a musical instrument.

20 Lowering of the vowel *ə* > *a* due to the pharyngeal *ḥ*. DR adds an alternative translation to this word: *ġannīw* (= sing:IMP.PL).

4 כִּי-יָשָׁר דְּבַר-יְהוָה; וְכָל-מַעֲשֵׂהוּ, בֶּאֱמוּנָה.

אין מסגם כלאם אללאה וגמיע פ׳ועלו בלאמאן

ʔin[21] *msəggəm klām aḷḷāh u-ğmīʕ fuʕl-u bə-l-ʔamān*

because righteous:SG.M speech.CS God and-all.CS action-3SG.M with-DEF-faith

Because of all the Lord's words are righteous, and all His actions are with faith.

5 אֹהֵב, צְדָקָה וּמִשְׁפָּט; חֶסֶד יְהוָה, מָלְאָה הָאָרֶץ.

יחב עדלא וחכם פ׳צ׳ל אללאה תעמרת אלארץ׳

yəḥəbb ʕadla u-ḥukm,[22] *fḍəḷ*[23] *aḷḷāh tʕammrət əl-ʔaṛḍ*

love:IPFV.3SG.M justice and-law grace.CS God fill:PF.3SG.F DEF-earth

Loves justice and law, the Lord's grace fills the earth.

6 בִּדְבַר יְהוָה, שָׁמַיִם נַעֲשׂוּ; וּבְרוּחַ פִּיו, כָּל-צְבָאָם.

בכלאם אללאה סמאואת נכ׳לקו ובריח פ׳ומו גמיע גיסהום[24]

b-klām aḷḷāh smāwāt nxəlqu, u-b-rīḥ fūmm-u ğmīʕ ğayš-hum

by-speech.CS God sky:PL create:PASS.PF.3PL and-by-breath.CS mouth-3SG.M all.CS army-3PL

By God's speech the skies were created, and with the breath of his mouth all their armies [were created].

7 כֹּנֵס כַּנֵּד, מֵי הַיָּם; נֹתֵן בְּאוֹצָרוֹת תְּהוֹמוֹת.

יגממע כיף אצור מייא לבחאר[25] יגעל פ׳למכ׳אזן אתהום

yiğəmmaʕ[26] *kīf əṣ-ṣūṛ miya l-bḥaṛ, yiğʕal f-l-mxāzən ət-təhom*

collect:IPFV.3SG.M as DEF-wall water:PL.CS DEF-sea place:IPFV.3SG.M in-DEF-storehouse:PL DEF-deep[H]

Collects the waters of the seas as a wall, places the deep in storehouses.

8 יִירְאוּ מֵיְהוָה, כָּל-הָאָרֶץ; מִמֶּנּוּ יָגוּרוּ, כָּל-יֹשְׁבֵי תֵבֵל.

יכ׳אפ׳ו מן אללאה גמיע אלארץ׳ מנו יכ׳אפ׳ו גמיע סוכאן אדנייא

ʸixāfu mən aḷḷāh ğmīʕ əl-aṛḍ, mən-u yixāfu ğmīʕ sukkān əd-dənya

fear:IPFV.3PL of God all.CS DEF-earth of-3SG.M fear:IPFV.3PL all.CS dweller:PL.CS DEF-world

The entire earth will fear the Lord, all the dwellers of the world will fear Him.

9 כִּי הוּא אָמַר וַיֶּהִי; הוּא-צִוָּה, וַיַּעֲמֹד.

אין הווא קאל וכאן הווא וצצא ווקף

ʔin huwa[27] *qāl u-kān, huwa wuṣṣa*[28] *u-wqaf*

because 3SG.M speak:PF.3SG.M and-be:PF.3SG.M 3SG.M order:PF.3SG.M and-stand:PF.3SG.M

Because He spoke it became so, He ordered and it stood [still].

21 The glottal stop is often omitted in this dialect, although it is realized in certain circumstances.

22 DR: *əl-ʕadla u-l-ḥukm* (= DEF-justice and-DEF-law).

23 The entire word is pronounced emphatically.

24 The Hebrew transcription גיסהום reflects a *š* > *s* shift (ש < ס), but DR pronounced it with a *š* (*ğayš-hum*).

25 The mater lectionis א in the word בחאר reflects vowel quality (*a*) and not length. The short vowel is pronounced *a* due to the adjacent pharyngal consonant *ḥ*.

26 The short vowel *ə* of the imperfect prefix *yə-* is frequently pronounced *i* due to assimilation to the adjacent *y*. See additional examples in verse 16.

27 The 3SG.M personal pronoun is pronounced either *huwa* or *huwwa.*

28 Since this verbal form וצצא comes after a word that ends with a vowel, the initial *waw* is pronounced as a consonantal *w* (hiatus).

10 יְהוָה, הֵפִיר עֲצַת-גּוֹיִם; הֵנִיא, מַחְשְׁבוֹת עַמִּים.
אללאה בטטל צ׳בארת אלאומום בטטל תכ׳מימאת אלאומום

ʔaḷḷāh bəṭṭal ḍbāṛət əl-umūm, bəṭṭal təxmīmāt əl-umūm
God annul:PF.3SG.M counsel.CS DEF-nation:PL annul:PF.3SG.M thought:PL.CS DEF-nation:PL

The Lord annulled the counsel of the nations, annulled the thoughts of the nations.

11 עֲצַת יְהוָה, לְעוֹלָם תַּעֲמֹד; מַחְשְׁבוֹת לִבּוֹ, לְדֹר וָדֹר.
צ׳בארת אללאה לדואם תוקף תכ׳מימאת קלבו לגיל וגיל

ḍbāṛət aḷḷāh l-dwām tūqəf,[29] *təxmīmāt qəlb-u l-ǧīl u-ǧīl.*
counsel.CS God for-ever stand:IPFV.3SG.F thought:PL.CS heart-3SG.M for-generation and-generation.

The counsel of the Lord will stand for ever, the thoughts of His heart [will stand] for generations.

12 אַשְׁרֵי הַגּוֹי, אֲשֶׁר-יְהוָה אֱלֹהָיו; הָעָם, בָּחַר לְנַחֲלָה לוֹ.
אסקל אלקום אלדי אללאה אילאהו אלקום כ׳תאר ללוראתא ליה

ʔaṣqəl əl-qawm əldi aḷḷāh ilāh-u, əl-qawm xtāṛ l-l-urāta lī-h
blessed:ELAT[30] DEF-people REL God god-3SG.M DEF-people choose:PF.3SG.M for-DEF-heritage to-3SG.M

Blessed are the people that the Lord is their god, the people He has chosen as His heritage.

13 מִשָּׁמַיִם, הִבִּיט יְהוָה; רָאָה, אֶת-כָּל-בְּנֵי הָאָדָם.
מן אסמא מקקן אללאה נצ׳ר אילא גמיע ולאד בן אדם

mən əs-smā maqqan aḷḷāh, ṇḍəṛ ila ǧmīʕ ulād bənadəm
from DEF-sky observe:PF.3SG.M God watch:PF.3SG.M ACC all.CS son:PL.CS son-of-man

From the sky the Lord observed, watched all the sons of man.

14 מִמְּכוֹן-שִׁבְתּוֹ הִשְׁגִּיחַ-- אֶל כָּל-יֹשְׁבֵי הָאָרֶץ.
מן צואב סוכנאנו מקקן עלא גמיע סוכאן אלארץ׳

mən ṣwāb suknān-u maqqan ʕla ǧmīʕ sukkān əl-aṛḍ
from place.CS dwelling-3SG.M observe:PF.3SG.M on all.cs dweller:PL.CS DEF-earth

From his dwelling-place he observed all the dwellers of the earth.

15 הַיֹּצֵר יַחַד לִבָּם; הַמֵּבִין, אֶל-כָּל-מַעֲשֵׂיהֶם.
אלכ׳אלק גמיע קלבהום אלפ׳אהם אילא גמיע פ׳עאיילהום

əl-xāləq[31] *ǧmīʕ qəlb-hum, əl-fāhəm ila ǧmīʕ fʕāyəl-hum*
DEF-creator:PTCP.CS all.CS heart-3PL DEF-understand:PTCP ACC all.CS action:PL-3PL

The creator of all their hearts, [He] who understands all their actions.

16 אֵין-הַמֶּלֶךְ, נוֹשָׁע בְּרָב-חָיִל; גִּבּוֹר, לֹא-יִנָּצֵל בְּרָב-כֹּחַ.
ליש אצולטאן ינג׳את בכתרת גיס

layš əṣ-ṣulṭān yinġāt b-kutrət ǧays,[32]
NEG DEF-king be_saved:IPFV.3SG.M by-lots.CS army

קוי (גבבאר) ליש ינפ׳ך בכתרת גהד

qwi (ǧəbbār) layš yinfəkk b-kutrət ǧəhd
mighty_man (hero) NEG be_rescued:IPFV.3SG.M by-lots.cs strength.

The king is not saved by multitude of armies, a hero is not rescued by lots of strength.

29 In this dialect, imperfect singular forms of verbs with a first radical *waw* have two alternating realizations: *tūqəf* or *twukaf.*

30 Elative form, see Fischer 2001: 76–77.

31 DR: *əldi yəxlaq* (REL create:IMPF.3SG.M; = 'that who creates').

32 DR recited alternative renderings: *əl-ǧays, əl-qwi, əl-ǧəhd.*

17 שֶׁקֶר הַסּוּס, לִתְשׁוּעָה; וּבְרֹב חֵילוֹ, לֹא יְמַלֵּט.
כדב אלכ'יל ללמג'יתא ובכתרת גייסו[33] ליש ימננע (רוחו)

kdəb	*əl-xēl*	*l-l-məğīta*	*u-b-kutrət*	*ğays-u*	*layš*	*yimənnaʕ*	*(rūḥ-u)*
lie	DEF-horse:COLL	for-DEF-rescue	and-by-lots.CS	army:3SG.M	NEG	be_strengthened:IPFV.3SG.M	(soul-3SG.M)

The horse is a lie for rescue, and by the multitude of his army he will not be able to escape.

18 הִנֵּה עֵין יְהוָה, אֶל-יְרֵאָיו; לַמְיַחֲלִים לְחַסְדּוֹ.
הודא עין אללאה אילא כ'איפ'ינו ללמצרגין לפ'צ'לו

hawda	*ʕayn*	*aḷḷāh*	*ila*	*xāyfīn-u*	*l-l-mṣṣərğīn*[34]	*l-fəḍl-u*
PRES	eye.CS	God	to	afraid:PTCP.PL-3SG.M	to-DEF-hope:PTCP.PL	to-grace-3SG.M

Behold the Lord's eye [turns] to those who fear him, those who hope for His grace.

19 לְהַצִּיל מִמָּוֶת נַפְשָׁם; וּלְחַיּוֹתָם, בָּרָעָב.
ליפ'ך מן אלמות רוחהום וליעיישהום פ'לגוע

li-yfəkk	*mən*	*əl-mowt*	*rūḥ-hum*	*u-l-yʕayyəš-hum*	*f-l-ğūʕ*
for-save:SUBJ.3SG.M	from	DEF-death	soul-3PL	and-for-resuscitate:SUBJ.3SG.M-3PL	in-DEF-hunger

To save their souls from death, and to resuscitate them from hunger.

20 נַפְשֵׁנוּ, חִכְּתָה לַיהוָה; עֶזְרֵנוּ וּמָגִנֵּנוּ הוּא.
רוחנא צתרגאת לאללאה מעוונתנא ומצ'רקתנא הווא

rūḥ-na	*ṣtərğāt*	*l-aḷḷāh*	*mʕawwənt-na*	*u-mḍərqət-na*	*huwa*
soul-1PL	hope:PF.3SG.F	to-God	aid-1PL	and shield-1PL	3SG.M

Our soul hopes for the Lord, He is our aid and our shield.

21 כִּי-בוֹ, יִשְׂמַח לִבֵּנוּ: כִּי בְשֵׁם קָדְשׁוֹ בָטָחְנוּ.
אין ביה יפ'רח קלבנא אין ביסם קודשו[35] תכלנא

ʔin	*bī-h*	*yifraḥ*	*qəlb-na,*	*ʔin*	*b-ism*	*qudš-u*	*tkəl-na*
because	in-3SG.M	rejoice:IPFV.3SG.M	heart-1PL	because	in-name.CS	holiness-3SG.M	trust:PF.1PL

Because in Him our heart will rejoice, because in the name of His holiness we trusted.

22 יְהִי-חַסְדְּךָ יְהוָה עָלֵינוּ: כַּאֲשֶׁר, יִחַלְנוּ לָךְ.
יכון פ'צ'לך אללאה עלינא כיף אלדי צתרגינא ליך

ʸikūn	*fəḍl-ək*[36]	*aḷḷāh*[37]	*ʕlē-na*	*kīf*	*əldi*	*ṣtərğīna*	*l-ək*
be:IPFV.3SG.M	grace-2SG.M	God	on-1PL	as	REL	hope:PF.1PL	for-2SG.M

Your grace Lord shall be upon us, as we hoped for You.

Text 2: The journal əl-Ḥikma from Algeria

Following are two newspaper articles published in the Judeo-Arabic journal *əl-Ḥikma* from Constantine, Algeria. The journal *əl-Ḥikma* (*La Philosophie*) was the only Judeo-Arabic journal published in Algeria in the twentieth century, printed in Hebrew characters in Constantine (eastern Algeria) in 1912–1913 and 1922–1923. The journal's editor Rabbi Avraham Zerbib (1870–1942), though a religious leader, was also an avid sup-

33 The spelling the Arabic word جَيْش as גייס with a ס (= /s/) and not גייש with a ש (= /š/) reflects a dissimilation caused by the proximity of the two sibilants.

34 This is a plural participle form of the tenth verbal stem of the root √ r-ğ-w, with *st* > *ṣṣ*.

35 The spelling with ש (*š*) instead of ס (*s*) reflects the influence of the Hebrew word קָדְשׁוֹ (*qodšo*).

36 The entire word is pronounced emphatically.

37 DR: *yā aḷḷāh* (added *yāʔ al-nidāʔ*).

porter of the Jewish enlightenment movement (*haskala*). Hence, the journal is a mosaic of articles on religious themes, discussions of secular and philosophical topics, news from around the Jewish world, serialized stories as well as greetings, obituaries, advertisments and more. The first of these two texts, about the passing of Eliezer Ben-Yehudah, the 'reviver' of the Hebrew language, was written by the editor Avraham Zerbib and published in issue 21 of year 2 on January 12, 1923 (for a detailed discussion see Tirosh-Becker 2015). The second text, a news article about the Jewish community in America, published in issue 6 of year 1 on July 21, 1922.

Text 2.1

פנומרו אסאבק עלמנה[38] בלפטירה מתע החכם המפורסם
f-ən-numero əs-sābəq ʕlləmna b-l-fṭiṛa mtāʕ he-ḥaxam ha-məfursam
in-DEF-issue^{FR} DEF-previous inform:PF.1PL in-DEF-death^{H} GEN DEF-scholar^{H} DEF-famous^{H}
In the previous issue we informed [our readership] of the passing of the famous scholar

ה׳ר אליעזר בנ[39] יהודה נ׳ע.
ha-rav Eliʕezer ben Yehuda n[uḥ-o] ʕ[eden].
DEF-rabbi^{H} Eliʕezer^{H} ben^{H} Yehuda^{H} rest-3SG.M heaven.
rabbi Eliʕezer ben Yehuda, may he rest in peace.

פלג׳ורנל דאר היום סמאה אב אלסאנ אלעברי
f-əl-jurnal doʔar ha-yom səmmā-h ʔab əl-lsān əl-ʕibri,
in-DEF-journal^{FR} Doʔar^{H} ha-Yom^{H} entitle:PF.3SG.M-3G.M father-CS DEF-language DEF-Hebrew^{H}
In the journal *Doʔar Ha-Yom*[40] he was entitled 'father of the Hebrew language',

פלחיכמה סמאה מוחיי לסאנ לעברי.
f-əl-ḥikma səmma-h muḥyī[41] *lsān əl-ʕibri.*
in-DEF-Ḥikma entitle:PF.3SG.M-3SG.M reviver.CS [DEF-]language DEF-Hebrew^{H}.
in *əl-Ḥikma*[42] he was entitled 'the reviver of the Hebrew language'.

האד לכייס יסאהל האד אלחוג׳ה ואלו לסאנ העברי קדים.
hād əl-kiyyəs issahəl[43] *hād əl-ḥuğğa*[44] *wa-law lsān ha-ʕibri qdīm.*
DEM DEF-wise_man merit:IPFV.3SG.M DEM DEF-title and-if language DEF-Hebrew^{H} ancient.
This wise man merits this title even if the Hebrew language is ancient.

38 The 1PL suffix *-na* in *ʕlləmna* is written here with a *he* instead of an *aleph*. In Algerian Judeo-Arabic texts *aleph* and *he* often interchange in the orthography of when denoting the final vowel *a*.

39 In this journal the printer does not use the character ן for final *nun*, and uses the initial/medial *nun* sign נ instead.

40 *Doʔar Ha-Yom* was a Hebrew language journal published in Jerusalem (1919–1936) by Itamar ben Avi, Eliʕezer ben Yehuda's son.

41 In the Judeo-Arabic of Constantine the fourth verbal form had significantly weakened, although some participle forms are still in use, such as *muḥyī* 'reviver'.

42 The Algerian journal in which this article was published (see above).

43 The form *issahəl* is an imperfect of Form X (استأهل > استهّل), with an *st* > *ss* assimilation; see Ben Sedira 1995: 262. The *aleph* in יסאהל indicates vowel quality and not quantity.

44 Speakers of the Jewish community of Constantine (Algeria) realize the phoneme /ž/ either as [ž] or [ğ] (=[d͜ž]), see Tirosh-Becker 1989: 296–297.

הווא יתסמא אב לשונ העברי מנ סבב אתנך
huwa yətsəmma ʔab lašon ha-ʕibri mən sabab ət-tanax
3SG.M be_entitled:IPFV.3SG.M father.CS language^{H} DEF-Hebrew^{H} from cause DEF-Bible^{H}
He is entitled father of the Hebrew language because the Bible

לי פיידינה מה פיהש לכלאם אלכול אלמלזום
ᵊlli f-yiddī-na mā fī-hə-š l-kalām əl-kūl əl-malzūm
REL in-hand:PL-1PL NEG in-it-NEG DEF-word:PL DEF-all DEF-be_necessary.PTCP.PASS
that is in our hands does not have all the necessary words,

והחכם אליעזר בנ יהודה ראה יבדאע לכלאם
wa-he-ḥaxam Eliʕezer ben Yehuda rā-h yibdaʕ əl-kalām
and-DEF-scholar^{H} Eliʕezer^{H} ben^{H} Yehuda^{H} PRES-3SG.M invent:IPFV.3SG.M DEF-word:PL
and the scholar Eliʕezer ben Yehuda invented the words

לי יכוץ מנ לסאנ ביהא לי יתסמא אב הלשונ
lli yixuṣṣ mən lsān bī-ha lli yətsəmma ʔab hal-lašon
REL lack:IPFV.3SG.M from language in-3SG.F REL be_entitled:IPFV.3SG.M father.CS^{H} DEF-language^{H}
that lacked in the language. [He] was entitled the father of the language,

ראה יולד לכלאם ללסאנ לעברי. אוחנה סמינאה
rā-h yūləd[45] *əl-klām əl-lsān əl-ʕbri. uḥna sammīna-h*
PRES-3SG.M father:IPFV.3SG.M DEF-word:PL DEF-language DEF-Hebrew^{H} 1PL entitle:PF.1PL-3SG.M
because he fathered the words of the Hebrew Language. We entitled him

מוחיי אלסאנ לעברי מנ סבת ליהוד פלגלות
muḥyī əl-lsān əl-ʕibri mən səbbət əl-yahūd f-əl-galut
reviver.CS DEF-language DEF-Hebrew^{H} from cause.CS DEF-Jew:COLL in-DEF-diaspora^{H}
reviver of the Hebrew language because the Jews in the diaspora

צארו יתכלמו בלסאנ לווטנ פאיינ ראהום
ṣāṛu yitkəllmu bi-lsān əl-uṭan fayn rā-hum
became:PF.3PL.M speak:IPFV.3PL.M in-language.CS DEF-country where PRES-3PL
became speakers of the language of the country where they were [living]

ולסאנ לעברי תנסא מנהום
u-l-lsān əl-ʕibri ttənsa mən-hum
and-DEF-language DEF-Hebrew^{H} be_forgotten:PF.3SG.M from-3PL
and they forgot the Hebrew language (lit. the Hebrew language was forgotten by them),

והאד אלכייס ואקף ילזזם[46] ליהוד יתכלמו
u-hād əl-kiyyəs wāqəf ilazzəm əl-yahūd yətkəllmu
and-DEM DEF-wise_man stand:PTCP demand:IPFV.3SG.M DEF-Jew:COLL speak:IPFV.3PL.M
and this wise man demanded that the Jews speak

בלסאנ לעברי פי כל מסאלה. אלמות דייאלו חאיירת ארץ ישראל
b-l-lsān əl-ʕibri fī kəll msāla. əl-mawt dyāl-u ḥayyrət ʔereṣ yisraʔel
in-DEF-language DEF-Hebrew^{H} in all.CS matter DEF-death of-3SG.M shake:PF.3SG.F land.CS^{H} Israel^{H}
Hebrew for all matters. His death shook the entire Land of Israel

45 Judeo-Arabic speakers from Constantine use two alternative forms *yūləd* and *yuwləd*, the second form is with the diphthong *uw*.

46 Printing mistake in the journal: יללזם.

בכמאלהא ועמלולו להספדים למלזומין.

bi-kmāl-ha wa-ʕamlu-lu ǝl-hespedim ǝl-malzūmīn.

in-full-3SG.M and-do:PF-3PL-for-3SG.M DEF-eulogy:PL^{H} DEF-require:PTCP.PASS.PL

and they composed the required eulogies.

ראנה נכתבו לכבודו להספדים לי תעמלו לכבודו

rā-na nkǝtbu li-xvod-o ǝl-hespedim lli ttʕamlu li-xvod-o

PRES-1PL write:IPFV.1PL for-honor-3SG.M^{H} DEF-eulogy:PL^{H} REL be_done:PF.3PL.M for-honor-3SG.M^{H}

We will publish in his honor the eulogies that were composed in his honor

באש נביינו לאבידה מתע בן אדם כביר. מאוושי דאע[47]

bāš nbayynu ǝl-ʔaveda mtāʕ bǝnadǝm kbīr. māwšī ḍāʕ

in_order_to elucidate:IPFV.1PL DEF-loss^{H} GEN person^{H} distinguished he.NEG be_lost:PF.3SG.M

in order to elucidate the loss of [this] distinguished person. He was not only lost

לאהלו פקט אלא דאע לליהוד מתע[48] אלמונדו

l-ahl-u faqaṭ ǝlla ḍāʕ l-ǝl-yahūd mtāʕ ǝl-mundo

to-family-3SG.M only rather be_lost:PF.3SG.M to-DEF-Jew:COLL GEN DEF-world^{SP}

to his family rather he was lost to the world's Jews

בחאל מה קאל לפסוק "וכל בית ישראל

bḥāl ma qāl ǝl-pasuq: "wǝ-xol bet yisraʔel

like REL say:PF.3SG.M DEF-verse^{H} "and-entire.CS^{H} house.cs^{H} Isreal^{H}

as the verse says: "and the entire house of Israel

יבכו את השריפה אשר שרף ה'".[49]

yivku ʔet has-sǝrefa ʔašer saraf ʔadonay".

weep:IPFV.3PL.M^{H} ACC^{H} DEF-burning^{H} REL^{H} kindle:PF.3SG.M^{H} t[he-name]^{H} (Lord^{H})".

shall weep the burning that the Lord has kindled".

Text 2.2

לאמיריך מן קבל כאנת תחת חכומת אנגליז וחין נאס לאמיריך

l-amǝrik mǝnqbǝl kānǝt taḥt ḥkūmǝt ingliz u-ḥīn nās ǝl-amǝrik

DEF-America^{FR} from before be:PRF.3SG.F under rule.CS English and-when people.CS DEF-America^{FR}

America was once under England's rule, and when the American people

חאבו יכונו מחאררינ מנ חכומת אנגליז, ויחכמו עלה רוחהום.

ḥabbu ʸikūnu mḥarrǝrīn mǝn ḥkūmǝt ingliz, u-yaḥkǝmu ʕla rūḥ-hum

want:PF.3PL be:IPFV.3PL free:PTCP.PL from rule.CS English and-rule:IPFV.3PL.M on soul-3PL

wanted to be free from England's rule, and rule themselves.

47 The orthography in which Hebrew ד is used to transcribe Arabic *ḍ* is not common in Algerian Judeo-Arabic texts. The common transcription for Judeo-Arabic *ḍ* is צ'. In Moroccan Judeo-Arabic one finds ד or צ' to transcribe *ḍ*. See Bar-Asher 1999: 82. For the uses of ד vs. צ' in a variety of earlier Judeo-Arabic texts see Blau and Hopkins 2017: 26.

48 The origin of the possession particle *mtāʕ* is the Arabic noun متاع 'belongings'. The particle *mtāʕ* (and its variants *ntāʕ* and *tāʕ*) are in frequent use in Algerian Judeo-Arabic. The orthography of this word is either מתאע or מתע (despite the long vowel *ā* that is typically transcribed with an *aleph*).

49 Lev 10:6.

תמא יהודי איסמו חיים סולימוו[50] עטא סת מייה וסתין אלף דולאר
təmma yahūdi ism-u Ḥayim Solomon ʕṭa sətt miya wa-səttin alf
there Jew name-3SG.M Ḥayim[H] Solomon give:PF.3SG.M six hundred and-sixty thousand
There was a Jew named Ḥayim Solomon who gave six hundred and sixty thousand

לי הומאן תלאתה מליון ותלת מייאת אלף פרנך
dollar lli hummān tlāta millyon u-tlāt myāt alf frank
dollar[EN] REL 3PL three million and-three hundred.PL thousand franc[FR]
dollars, which are three million and three hundred thousand francs

לדמת מצרוף ריפוליסיון מתע לאמיריך. וחין נפטר,
l-dəmmət maṣṛūf revolusyon mtāʕ l-amərik. u-ḥīn nəfṭaṛ
in-order expenses.CS revolution[FR] GEN DEF-America[FR] and-when die:PF.3SG.M[H]
in order [to pay for] the expenses of the American revolution. And when he died,

אדאוולה ואפקת באיין האד לפלוס ירג'עו לוולדו
əd-dawla wāfqət bayn hād əl-flūs yirəǧʕu li-wuld-u
DEF-government approve:PF.3SG.F COMP DEM DEF-money:PL return:IPFV.3PL to-offspring-3SG.M
the government approved that this money will return to his offspring.

אנהאר לי בעתו אלחוכאם לכווארט באש יכתם פיהום
ən-nhār lli baʕtu əl-ḥukkām əl-kwārət[51] bāš yixtəm fi-hum
DEF-day REL send:PF.3PL DEF-authority:PL DEF-document:pl[FR] in-order sign:IPFV:3SG.M in-3PL
The day on which the authorities sent the documents for him to sign

ויקבד לפלוס כאן יום[52] שבת.
u-yiqbəḍ əl-flūs kān yom šabbat.
and-receive:IPFV.3SG.M DEF-money:PL be:PF.3SG.M day[H] Sabbath[H]
and receive the money was Saturday.

מה האבש יכתם האד לוולד פשבת קאלהום:
mā ḥabb-š yixtəm hād əl-wuld f-šabbat, qāl-l-hum:
NEG want:PF.3SG.M-NEG sign:IPFV:3SG.M DEM DEF-offspring on-Sabbath[H] say:PF.3SG.M-to-3PL
[However] that offspring did not want to sign on the Sabbath, and told them

"האתה יום לתנין". יום לחאד נפטר לוולד עלה גפלה.
"ḥatta yawm ət-tnēn". yawm əl-ḥadd nəfṭaṛ əl-wuld ʕla ġafla
"until day DEF-second" day DEF-first die:PF.3SG.M[H] DEF-offspring on suddenly
"[wait] until Monday". On Sunday the offspring died suddenly.

ומן האדאך אזמן לפלוס בקאו פלכיס מתע טריזור.
u-mən hādāk əz-zmān əl-flūs bqāw f-l-kīs mtāʕ ət-trezor
and-from DEM.REM DEF-time DEF-money:PL remain:PF.3PL in-DEF-pocket GEN DEF-treasury[FR]
And from that time the money remained in the pocket of the treasury.

50 The name *Solomon* was incorrectly spelled as סולימוו (and not סולומון). Ḥayim Solomon (1740–1785) was a Jewish American businessman who aided the Continental Army and was possibly their prime financier during the American Revolutionary War against Great Britain. See Jane Frances Amler (2004), *Haym Salomon: Patriot Banker of the American Revolution*, New York: Rosen-PowerPlus Books, p. 6.

51 An Arabic broken plural of the French word *carte*.

52 It is not clear whether יום stands for the Arabic word *yawm* 'day' or the Hebrew word *yom*. See also Aharon Maman (1989), "On Identifying the Hebrew Element in Judeo-Maghrebian", *Massorot* 3–4: 171–201 (in Hebrew).

חין כאן פריזידאן מתע לאמיריך, מסיו טאפט[53]

ḥīn kān presidañ mtāʕ əl-amərik məsyu Taft

when be:PF.3SG.M president^{FR} GEN DEF-America^{FR} mister^{FR} Taft^{EN}

When Taft was the president of America

חאב בלינתיריס מתע האד לפלוס יטלעו סכולה

ḥabb b-l-intiris mtāʕ hād əl-flūs iṭəllʕu skola[54]

want:PF.3SG.M in-DEF-interest^{IT} GEN DEF-money:PL build:IPFV.3PL school^{IT}

he wanted to use the interest on this money to build a school

עלה איסם חיים סולומון, אדאוולה מה ואפקתש להאד אשי.

ʕla ʔism Ḥayim Solomon əd-dawla mā wāfqət-š l-hād əš-ši

on name Ḥayim^{H} Solomon DEF-government NEG approve:PRF.3SG.F-NEG to-DEM DEF-thing

named after Ḥayim Solomon, [however] the government did not approve it.

אליום חופדאן חופדאנו טלבו האד לוראתה, וקאלו

əl-yawm ḥufdān ḥufdān-u ṭalbu hād l-urāta wa-qālu

DEF-day grandson:PL.CS grandson:PL-3SG.M request:PF.3PL DEM DEF-inheritance and-say:PF.3PL

Today his great grandsons request this inheritance, and they said

נחבו נדיוו ראץ אלמאל בלא אנתיריס.

nḥabbu nddīw rāṣ əl-māl b-lā intiris

want:IPFV.1PL restore:IPFV.1PL head.CS DEF-money with-NEG interest^{IT}.

we want to restore the principal sum without the interest.

Text 3: A story on the 'evil eye' from Tunis, Tunisia

The following text is a folk story about the 'evil eye' in Tunisian Judeo-Arabic, told by an informant from the capital Tunis. This oral text was recorded and transcribed by David Cohen, who studied and documented the Judeo-Arabic dialect of Tunisian Jews during many years. This short story is included in his book *Le Parler Arabe des Juifs de Tunis: Textes et documents linguistiques et ethnographiques* (The Hague – Paris, 1964). It appears in phonetic transcription accompanied by a French translation on pages 103–104, and is brought here based on this transcription.[55] The text exhibits many of the characteristic llinguistic traits of the Tunisian Judeo-Arabic dialect. Key linguistic features of this dialect are discussed in more detail in the grammatical sketch above and are indicated in footnotes. For a more detailed account of the Judeo-Arabic dialect of Tunis see Cohen, David, 1975. *Le parler arabe des Juifs de Tunis. Vol. II: Étude linguistique*. The Hague – Paris: Mouton.

53 William Howard Taft (1857–1930) was the 27th President of the United States (1909–1913).

54 Italian *scuola*.

55 Minimal changes to the transcription include transcribing خ as *x* (not *ḫ*).

əl-ʕäyn mūš ădṛå[56] *ntāʕ nšă*[57] *bə-l-köll.*
DEF-eye NEG conversation GEN woman:PL.F in-DEF-all
The [evil] eye is not at all women's talk.

u-kān təqra mnīḥ f-əṭ-ṭūṛa təlqa bå̆ršä klām u-măʕšiyūt
and-be:COND[58] read:IPFV.2SG.M well[59] in-DEF-Torah[H] find:IPFV.2SG.M many saying:PL and-tale:PL[H]
And if you read the Torah well, you will find many sayings and tales

ʕäl "ʕăyn ā-ṛăʕ" ṣīmọṣṣilinu.[60] *ānä ṣāṛət qbält-i u-qbālət*
on[H] eye[H] DEF-evil[H] God_save_us[H] 1SG happen:PF.3SG.F in_front_of-1SG and-in_front_of
about the "evil eye", God save us. It happened in front of me and in front of

bå̆ṛšä nāš... ẓṛāt ʕlä wāḥəd ṣnåyʕi məškīn f-əṣ-ṣūq
many people ... happen:PF.3SG.F on one craftsman unfortunate in-DEF-market
many people ... It happened to an unfortunate craftsman in the market

ʕănd-u uləd ẓġīr, ṣwīnăʕ, bāš yəbäʕt-u yăqdi băʕd əl-qădyāt
at-3SG.M boy young employee:DIM for send:IPFV.3SG.M-3SG.M run:IPFV.3SG.M some.CS DEF-errand:PL
who had a young boy, a junior employee, [that he would] send to run some of the errands for him.

ūwä kān wăkkāl tbå̆ṛkoḷḷå mənāk əl-wăkkālīn lə-ġwāl.
3SG.M be:PF.3SG.M eater be_praised.STAT.3SG.M.God from DEM.PL DEF-eater:PL DEF-monstrous:PL
He [the craftsman] was an eater of those monstrous eaters, God bless him.

ṣbāḥ tʕăddä ʕlä ḥänūt-u wāḥəd ṣăyyād mālti yăʕṛf-u
morning pass:PF.3SG.M on store[H]-3SG.M one fisherman Maltese know:IPFV.3SG.M-3SG.M
One morning a Maltese fisherman passed his store, known to him

mäġrūm, ʕăṛṛa ʕlä qọfft-u wå̆ṛṛå buṛīya dkå̆ṛ
enthusiast remove_the_cover:PF.3SG.M on basket-3SG.M show:PF.3SG mullet male
as an enthusiast, removed the cover of his basket, showed a male mullet

tăʕməl myät ălf kăyf. xdā-ä, bʕăt-tä
do:IPFV.3SG.M hundred.CS thousand pleasure:PL take:PF.3SG.M-3SG.F send:pf.3SG.M-3SG.F
that makes your mouth water (lit. "a hundred thousand pleasures"). He [the craftsman] took it, sent it

56 In the Tunisian Judeo-Arabic dialect the unvoiced glottal fricative *h* almost disappeared, e.g., *adṛå* (هذرة), *ūwä* (هو).

57 In the Tunisian Judeo-Arabic dialect *s* > *š*, except before an emphatic consonant. The pronunciation [s] only occurs before non-emphatic *r*. On the special sibilant shifts in Tunisian Judeo-Arabic see the grammatical description above.

58 Frozen in the be:PF.3SG.M form.

59 An adjective that serves here as an adverb.

60 *ṣīmọṣṣilinu* = Hebrew השם יצילנו (*haš-šem yaṣṣīle-nū* 'God save us').

l-əl-qăllăy mʕä l-ulīyed. qăl-l-u nḥä'bb-ək tqăṛqəš-ša
to-DEF-fryer with DEF-boy:DIM tell:PF.3SG.M-to-3SG.M want:IPFV.1SG-2SG.M scale-3SG.F
to the fryer with the young boy. He told him [the fryer]: I want you to scale it,

tfərrăġ-ġä u-tməllăḥ-ḥä u-tăqlīy-ä äkkăk mən-ġīr ma tqoṣ-ṣa.
empty-3SG.F and salt-3SG.F and-fry-3SG.F like.DEM from-other RELcut_to_pieces:IPFV.2SG.M-3SG.F
and empty it, and salt it, and fry it like this keeping it whole (lit. "without cutting it to pieces").

ʕănd lūwel l-ulīyəd mšä l-əl-qăllăy u-žăb ḥaš-ăk[61]
at mid-day DEF-boy:DIM go:PF.3SG.M to-DEF-fryer and-bring:PF.3SG.M with_all_due_respect
At mid-day the young boy went to the fryer and brought [back], with all due respect,

ăk əl-ḥūtä moqlīyä. xdă-ä əṛ-ṛăžəl wə-qʕăd åy åy, åy åy,
DEM DEF-fish fry:PTCP take:pf.3SG.M-3SG.F DEF-man and-sit:PF.3SG.M EXC
that fried fish. The man took it and sat, ay ay, ay ay

bdä b-əṛ-ṛåṣ kəmməl b-əd-dənbä mä xăllä kăn əš-šäwk.
start:PF.3SG.M with-DEF-head finish:PF.3SG.M with-DEF-tail NEG leave:PF.3SG.M but DEF-fishbone:PL
started with the head, finished with the tail, leaving nothing but fishbones.

w-ăk l-ūləd wăqəf qbălt-u šăkət yəqšăʕ fī.
and-DEM DEF-boy stand:PTCP before-3SG.M silent:PTCP look:IPFV:3SG.M at.3SG.M
And that boy stands before him silent, looking at him.

wăqt əlli blăʕ l-äxxər loqmä, ṛma ʕăyn-u ʕăṣ-ṣḥan l-ūləd,
when REL swallow:PF.3SG.M DEF-last bite throw:PF.3SG.M eye-3SG.M on-DEF-plate DEF-boy
When he swallowed the last bite, the boy eyed the plate,

ūwä zərbi, u-kīf li l-kəlmä xăržət mənqălb-u, qāl: klä,
3SG.M Djerbi and-as_if REL DEF-word come_out:PF.3SG.F from heart-3SG.M say:PF.3SG.M eat:PF.3SG.M
he is from Djerba, and, as if the word came out of his heart, he said: [he] ate,

l-köll. ăyy, ṣīmoṣṣilīnu. lă-ʕšīyä əṛ-ṛăžəl ṛăwwăḥ əl-dăṛ-u,
DEF-all EXC God_save_us[H] DEF-evening DEF-man go:PF.3SG.M to-home-3SG.M
everything. Ayy, God save us. In the evening the man went to his home,

ḥăšš nəfš-u šwīyä mxălwoḍ, žūf-u tūžʕ-u,
feel:PF.3SG.M self-3SG.M thing:DIM be_shaken:PTCP stomach-3SG.M hurt:IPFV:3SG.F-3SG.M
felt himself a little shaken, his stomach hurt him,

61 Literally *ḥāšā* (حاشا) means 'except' (Beaussier 1958: 207). *ḥaš-ăk* literally means 'except you', but it is used here to express the phrase 'with all due respect'. Tunisian Jews warded off the 'evil eye' by saying the words *xämšä* (= five, i.e., the form of the palm) or the word *ḥūtä* (= fish), hence the informant added the phrase 'with all due respect' before saying 'fish' (D. Cohen 1964: 99).

mädäbī[62] *yitqăyyä,* *ā̆t* *tṛonžīyä,* *əž-žūf* *təzri,*
would_like_to throw_up:IPFV.3SG.M bring:SG.M verbena [tea] DEF-stomach run:IPFV.3SG.F
[and he] wanted to throw up. He was given melissa tea , he had diarrhea (lit. “the stomach ran”),

əṛ-ṛāžəl mərxi *ră̌xwä* *qwīyä,* *ʕăyyṭu* *ṭbīb,* *ṣīmọṣṣilīnu,* *ṣīmọṣṣilīnu,*
DEF-man weak:PTCP weakness strong:F call:PF.3 PL.M physician God_save_us[H] God_save_us[H]
the man was very weak, [they] called a physician, God save us, God save us,

əṭ-ṭbīb *uṣăl* *lqā* *mīyət.*
DEF-physician arrive:PF.3SG.M find:PF.3SG.M.3SG.M dead.
the physician arrived and found him dead.

Text 4: A text on the eve of Shavuʕot from Sefrou, Morocco

This is an oral text in which an informant from Sefrou, Morocco describes the Jewish celebration customs of this community on the eve of the Jewish holiday of *Shavuʕot* (Tabernacles). The text was recorded, transcribed, and translated by Norman A. Stillman, who recorded Sefriwi Jews during the 1970’s, and published it among other recorded texts in his book *The Language and Culture of the Jews of Sefrou, Morocco: An Ethnolinguistic Study*, (Journal of Semitic Studies, Monograph no. 11), Louvain: University of Manchester 1988 (p. 121).[63] The text exhibits many of the characteristic linguistic traits of this Moroccan Judeo-Arabic dialect, which although classified among the ‘old urban Maghrebi Arabic’ dialects also reflects other features, including some unique ones. In the footnotes I refer to key linguistic phenomena discussed in more detail in the grammatical description above. For a more detailed account of the Judeo-Arabic dialect of Sefrou see Stillman 1988.

lilt *Sabüʕotˤ* *tḥak*[64] *u-tˤ-tˤora* *l-ʕaziza.*
eve.CS Shavuʕot[H] laughter and-DEF-Torah[H] DEF-beloved.F
On the eve of Shavuʕot there is laughter and the beloved Torah.

bəzzaf *ḍ-ḍyaṛ* *kanu* *yʕamid* *l-ʔəraya*[65] *f-ḍ-ḍyaṛ.*
many DEF-home:PL be:PF.3PL.M hold:IPFV.3SG.M DEF-reading in-DEF-home:PL
In many households they would hold reading sessions at home.

62 One of the ways to express a wish in Tunisian Judeo-Arabic is *mädäbīya* (= je voudrais bien que), see D. Cohen 1975: 263. See also Beaussier 1958: 917 (ما ذا بي = je voudrais bien que, lit. “what is in me”).

63 I thank Prof. Stillman for granting me permission to cite this sample text. The responsibility for the glosses is mine.

64 *ḍ* > *t* (√ ضحك).

65 The pronunciation of /q/ as [ʔ] is characteristic of many key urban Judeo-Arabic dialects in Morocco.

u-baba	*ʕaziz-i*	*kan*	*izib*[66]	*l-ʕaniyyin*	*f-ṣ-ṣbaḥ*
and-father	dear-1SG	be:PF.3SG.M	bring:IPFV.3SG.M	DEF-poor:PL^{H}	in-DEF-morning

My dear father would bring in the poor folk in the morning

yiferraʔ-l-hom	*l-flüs*	*b-s-st^{s}ẹṛa –*	*ya*	*ḥasani,*	*ya*	*frank.*
distribute:IPFV.3SG.M-to-3PL	DEF-money:PL	in-DEF-secret –	DISJ	ḥasani	DISJ	franc

and distribute money among them in secret – a Ḥasani[67] there, a franc there.

yiʔraw	*w-igüzü*	*t^{s}-t^{s}ḥameḍ*	*u-maḥya.*
read:IPFV.3PL	and-eat:IPFV:3PL	DEF-salad:PL	and-maḥya

They would read and eat salads and drink *maḥya.*

f-ṣ-ṣbaḥ	*yimsiw*	*yṣeḷḷiw*	*wi-yirzʕu*	*l-s-sʕüda.*
in-DEF-morning	go:IPFV.3PL	pray:IPFV.3PL	and-return:IPFV.3PL	to-DEF-feast^{H}

In the morning they would go to pray and return for a festive meal.

kunna	*nʕamlu*	*ṭ-ṭenbor*	*d-l-beḍ*	*l-məsluʔin*	*u-tlat^{s}in*	*kilu*	*d-kaʕak*[68]
be:PF.1PL	do:IPFV.1PL	DEF-kettle	GEN-DEF-egg:PL	DEF-boil:PTCP.PL	and-thirty	kilo	GEN-kaʕak

We would fill a large kettle with boiled eggs and thirty kilos of *kaʕak*

b-nāfiʕ	*u-zinzlan*	*u-skakṛ.*
with-anise	and-sesame_seed:PL	and-sugar:PL.DIM

with anise and sesame seed and lots of sugar (lit. a little sugar).[69]

a-imsiw	*r-rzal,*	*iziw*	*n-nsa*	*yedůʔů*	*s-sʕüda*	*t^{s}a*	*huma.*
FUTM-go:IPFV.3PL	DEF-man:PL	come:IPFV.3PL	DEF-woman:PL	taste:IPFV.3PL	DEF-feast^{H}	also	3PL.F

When the men went, the women would come to taste from the festive food as well.

fi Pisaḥ	*di*	*ʕand-ů*	*bnit^{s}a*[70]	*aw*	*weld*	*d-xems*	*snin*
on Passover^{H}	REL	at-3SG.M	daughter:DIM	DISJ	son	GEN-five	year:PL

On Passover, whoever had a young daughter or a son five years old

a-iṣefṭů	*xiṭba*	*a-iʕamlu*	*mlak*	*Pisaḥ.*
FUTM-send:IPFV.3PL	proposal	FUTM-do:IPFV.3PL	engagement.CS	Passover^{H}

would send a proposal that they make a Passover engagement.

bü-l-weld	*izib*	*l-xiṭba*	*l-ḍar*	*l-bint^{s}.*	*u-f-Sabüʕot^{s}*
father.CS-DEF-boy	bring:IPFV.3SG.M	DEF-proposal	to-home.CS	DEF-girl	and-on-Shavuʕot^{H}

The boy's father would bring the proposal to the girl's house. On Shavuʕot

66 *ğ > z.*

67 The ḥasani was a dirham equal to one-half of a franc, see Stillman 1988: 122 fn. 3.

68 A type of a round biscuit.

69 The diminutive form may carry an emphatic meaning expanding the base concept, see Stillman 1988: 122 fn.4. For Classical Arabic, cf. Wright 1955:166D.

70 *bnit^{s}a* is a diminutive form of *bint^{s}* 'daughter'. On diminutive forms in southeast Moroccan Judeo-Arabic see Bar-Asher 1986.

huwa ṭlaʔ. a-izi s-sammas d-ṣ-ṣla
3SG.M divorce:PF.3SG.M FUTM-come:IPFV.3SG.M beadle[H] GEN-DEF-synagogue
he would make a divorce. The beadle of the synagogue would come

bas yaʕṭi l-giṭ.
in_order_to give:IPFV.3SG.M DEF-bill_of_divorce[H]
to give the bill of divorce.

a-ya-ṛḇḇ-i, ṣdaʔ-ha hada l-xibza b-l-gṛůn.
EXCL-VOC-Lord-1SG marriage_settlement-3SG.F DEM DEF-bread with-DEF-horn:PL
"O Lord, her marriage settlement is this braided roll!"

kan l-weld di ma yḥebb-s iṭellaʔ u-yebki.
be:PF.3SG.M DEF-boy REL NEG want:IPFV.3SG.M-NEG divorce:IPFV.3SG.M and-cry:IPFV.3SG.M
A child who did not want to be divorced would cry.

u-kanu zğaṛt^{s} [71] *u-d-denya tḥek ü-tlʕeb.*
and-be:PF.3PL ululation and-DEF-everyone laugh:PF.3SG.M and-enjoy_oneself:PF.3SG.M
There would be ululation and everyone would laugh and enjoy themselves.

daʔ[72] *n-nhar l-weld kan ilbis z-zellaba, bedʕiya, u-belġa*
DEM.REM DEF-day DEF-boy be:PF.3SG.M wear:IPFV.3SG.M DEF-jellaba badʕiyya and-belġa
On that day the boy would wear a jellaba,[73] a badʕiyya,[74] pointed slippers,

u-ṭ-ṭarḇůs l-kḥel. zman kan silṭan ʔebiḥ
and-DEF-tarboosh DEF-black time be:PF.3SG.M sultan wicked
and a black tarboosh. Once there was a wicked sultan,

di ʔal l-ihüd ilbesu ġir ṭ-ṭarḇůs l-kḥel.
REL say:PF.3SG.M DEF-Jew:COLL wear:IPFV.3PL only DEF-tarboosh DEF-black
who said that the Jews could only wear a black tarboosh.

di yilbis ṭarḇůs l-ḥmer d-l-msilmin u-xerz bi-h
REL wear:IPFV.3SG.M tarboosh DEF-red GEN-DEF-Muslim:PL and-go_outside:PF.3SG with-3SG.M
Anyone who wore the red tarboosh of the Muslims and went outside with it

71 The form *zğaṛt*^{s} reflects a *d* > *t*^{s} shift in the word زَغَارِيد (sg. زَغْرُودَة).

72 The distal demonstrative *daʔ* (< *hadak*) is unique to Sefriwi Judeo-Arabic. The shift of final *k* to *ʔ* occurs in a few words in this dialect (Stillman 1988: 33).

73 A long-sleeved, hooded outer robe which was originally a Muslim garment.

74 In its masculine version, this garment was a sleeveless vest.

yigezru-h[75].	*l-bint^{s}*	*l-ʕazmi*	*u-iʕakkṛů-l-ha.*
tear:IPFV.3PL.M^{H}-3SG.M	DEF-girl	DEF-ʕazmi	and-put_make_up:IPFV.3PL-to-3SG.F

would be torn to pieces. The girl [would wear] the ʕazmi[76] and would have make-up put on her.

f-ḍ-ḍhọr	*m-s-sṭiḥan*	*u-s-srazm*	*di*	*ygüz*
in-DEF-noon	from-DEF-rooftop:PL	and-window:PL	REL	pass:IPFV.3SG.M

At noon water would be poured from the rooftops and the windows upon any passer-by.

yexwiw	*ʕali-h*	*l-ma.*	*a-it^{s}rassu*[77]	*d-denya.*
pour:IPFV.3PL.M	on-3SG.M	DEF-water	FUTM-be_splashed:IPFV.3PL	DEF-everyone

Everyone would be splashed with water.

yallah,	*kanü*	*l-bat^{s}üt^{s}*	*d-l-ʔezdir*	*bas*	*yʕamru*	*bi-l-ma.*
indeed	be:PF.3PL	DEF-water_gun:PL	GEN-DEF-tin	in_order_to	fill:IPFV.3Pl	with-DEF-water

Indeed, there were tin water guns that people would fill with water.

Text 5: "The Sultan and [the] three sisters" from Tripoli, Libya

This text excerpt consists of the first paragraph of a fairy tale "The Sultan and [the] three sisters", narrated by Mĕrĕ Ḥəžžaž Liluf, a Jew born in 1925 in Tripoli, Libya. The tale was recoded and transcribed by Sumikazu Yoda, who published this text in his book *The Arabic Dialect of the Jews of Tripoli (Libya)*, Wiesbaden: Harrassowitz 2005 (pp. 298f.).[78] The text exhibits linguistic features of the Tripolitan Judeo-Arabic dialect. In the footnotes I refer to key linguistic phenomena. For a detailed account of this dialect see Yoda 2005.

kan	*u*	*ma*	*kan*	*ʕala*	*waḥəṭ*[79]	*ṣəlṭaṇ.*	*adak*	*əṣ-ṣəlṭaṇ*	*ma*	*ʕənd-u-š*
be.PF.3SF.M	and	REL	be.PF.3SF.M	on	one.M	sultan	DEM.REM	DEF-sultan	NEG	at-3SG.M-NEG

Once upon a time there was a Sultan. That Sultan had no

əzġaṛ.	*lila*	*məl-lyali*	*ṭaṛ*	*əʕl-i*	*n-nʕas.*	*ṭəḅḅəḥ*	*ḥəl-l-uzir*[80]
little.PL	night	from.DEF-night.PL	fly.PF.3SG.M	on-3SG.M	DEF-sleepiness	call.PF.3SG.M	on-DEF-minister

children. One night sleep evaded him. He called his minister

75 The Hebrew root √ *gzr* is interwoven into an Arabic stem.

76 A female garment, which was very similar to the Muslim caftan, and was worn only on festive occasions.

77 *š* > *s* (√ رشش).

78 I thank Prof. Yoda for granting me permission to cite this sample text. The responsibility for the glosses and the translation is mine.

79 *d* > *ṭ* because of the emphatic consonant *ṣ* in the following word and the spread of emphatic pronunciation.

80 In the hiatus *ḥʕ* > *ḥḥ*.

ənčaʕ-u[81] *w qal-l-u čəʕla,*[82] *aná ma ʕənd-i-š ənʕas, nḥəbb*
GEN-3SG.M and say.PF.3SG.M-to-3SG.M come_on.IMP 1SG NEG at-1SG.NEG sleepiness want.IPFV.1SG
and said to him: Come on, I cannot sleep, I want

ənṭəlʕu. nləbsu bŏrgēzĕ,[83] *u ənṭəlʕu naraw l-blad.*
go_out.IPFV.1PL dress.JUSS.1PL bourgeois[It] and go_out.IPFV.1PL see.IPFV.1PL DEF-country
that we go out. Let's wear civilian clothes and let's go out to see the country.

lbəs bŏrgēzĕ ṣ-ṣəlṭan u l-uzir, w xadu lə-ḥṣənna nčaʕ-əm
dress.PF.3SG.M bourgeois[It] DEF-sultan and DEF-minister and take.PF.3PL DEF-horse.PL GEN-3PL
The Sultan and the minister put on civilian clothes, took their horses,

u ṭəlʕu. bdaw yəmšiw f-əl-blad yḍəwwṛu na na na na,
and go_out.PF.3PL begin.PF.3PL go.IPFV.3PL in-DEF-country look-for.IPFV.3Pl IDEOPHONE (X 4)
and went out. They began to go around in the country, looking around,

wəṣlu l-l-xla. ṣabu ḍəww zġəyyər məm-bʕid, mšəʕul.[84]
arrive.PF.3PL to-DEF-desert find.PF.3PL light little.DIM from-far light.PTCP.PASS
and reached the desert. They perceived a little light from afar, lit.

qal-l-u əyya nčəbbʕu ṭ-ṭriq w naraw əḍ-ḍəww ada šawa uwa.
say.PF.3SG.M-to-3SG.M INTERJ follow.IPFV.1PL DEF-way and see.IPFV.1PL DEF-light DEM what 3SG.M
He said to him: Let's follow the way and see what the light is.

mšaw mšaw mšaw, ṣabu zriba zġəyyra. qal-l-u əsməḥ
go.PF.PL go.PF.PL go.PF.PL find.PF.3PL hut small.DIM say.PF.3SG.M-to-3SG.M hear.IPT
The went and went, and found a small hut. He said to him: Listen

ḥəss əd-duwa. sməʕ əd-duwa, wəqfu, qəʕdu, yəṭṣənnču ysəmʕu
sound.CS DEF-speech hear.PF.3SG.M DEF-speech stand.PF.3PL stay.3PF.PL listen.IPFV.3PL hear.IPFV.3PL
to the sound of the speech. He listened to the speech. They stood still, paying attention and listening

d-duwa ša čəmma ša iya d-duwa. kanu fia tlač əbnač, adik əz-zriba.
DEF-speech what there what 3SG.F DEF-speech be.PF.3PL in.3SG.F three girl.PL DEM.F DEF-hut
to the speech. What is there? What is the speech? In it were three girls, (in) that hut.

əl-bənt lə-kbira qalč, qa čədwi l-əxč-a, qalt-l-a,
DEF-girl DEF-big.F say.PF.3SG.F CONT speak.IPFV.3SG.F to.sister-3SG.F say.PF.3SG.F-to-3SG.F
The elder girl said, while speaking to her sister, she said to her:

81 *mtāʕ* > *ntāʕ* > *nčaʕ*. The origin of the possessive exponent *mtāʕ* is the Arabic noun متاع (= belongings).

82 Classical Arabic *taʕāla* (imperative of form VI). [č] (= ṯš) is the common realization of the phoneme /t/ in this dialect. There are more examples for this pronunciation in the text. See Yoda 2005: 71–74.

83 Italian *borghese*.

84 *mšəʕul* < **məšʕul*, see Yoda 2005:110.

ḥnan žiʕanin, u ma da bi-ya yaxəd-ni s-sənfaz[85] *čə-ṣ-ṣəḷṭaṇ,*
1PL hungry.PL and REL DEM in-1SG take.IPFV.3SG.M-1SG DEF-doughnut_maker GEN-DEF-sultan
We are hungry, and I would like the doughnut maker of the Sultan to marry me,

nəšbəʕ aná nakəl aná qbəl ma yakəl əṣ-ṣəḷṭaṇ.
be_satiated.IPFV.1SG 1SG eat.IPFV.1SG 1SG before REL eat.IPFV.3SG.M DEF-sultan
I will be satiated, I will eat before the Sultan eats.

ža əṣ-ṣəḷṭaṇ qal l-uzir, qal-lu əkčəb, li
come.PF.3SG.M DEF-sultan say.PF.3SG.M to.DEF-minister say.PF.3SG.M-to-3SG.M write.IMP REL
Thereupon the Sultan said to the minister, he said to him: Write (it)!

tsəmʕ-u-kəčb-u. ət-čanya qalt-l-a, aná ma da bi-ya
hear.IPFV.2SG.M-3SG.M-write.IMP.3SG.M DEF-second.F say.PF.3SG.F-to.3SG.F 1SG REL DEM in-1SG
Write what you hear! The second (girl) said to her: I would like

yaxəd-ni ṭ-ṭəḅḅax, li-yəʕməl makla l-əṣ-ṣəḷṭaṇ, nəšbəʕ aná
take.IPFV.3SG.M-1SG DEF.cook REL-make.IPFV.3SG.M food for-DEF-sultanbe_satiated.IPFV.1SG 1SG
the cook to marry me, he who makes food for the Sultan, I will be satiated

qbəl ma yəšbəʕ əṣ-ṣəḷṭaṇ. qal-l-u qəyyəd ya wzir!
before REL be_satiated.IPFV.3SG.M DEF-sultan say.PF.3SG.M-to-3SG.M register.IMP VOC minister
before the Sultan is satiated. He said to him: Register (that), oh minister!

əz-zġira qalt-l-əm, aná ka yaxəd-ni əṣ-ṣəḷṭaṇ l-ʕam l-əwwəl
DEF-small say.PF.3SG.F-to.3PL 1SG if take.IPFV.3SG.M-1SG DEF-sultan DEF-year DEF-first
The youngest (girl) said to them: If the Sultan marries me, in the first year

nžib-l-u wəld, əl-ʕam ət-čani nžib-l-u wəld,
give.IPFV.1SG-to-3SG.M boy DEF-year DEF-second give.IPFV.1SG-to-3SG.M boy
I will give birth to a boy for him, in the second year I will give birth to a boy for him,

u l-ʕam l-čaləč nžib-l-u bənč. qal-l-u, qəyyəd
and DEF-year DEF-third give.IPFV.1SG-to-3SG.M girl say.PF.3SG.M-to-3SG.M register.IPT
and in the third year I will give birth to a girl for him. He said to him: Register

ya wzir. qəyyd-u w mšaw, ṛəwwḥu.
VOC minister register.PF.3SG.M-3SG.M and go.PF.3PL return.PF.3PL
oh minister! He registered it, and they went away, and returned.

85 Note the *n* preceding the *f* in the word *sənfaz* (= doughnut maker), see Yoda 2005: 338. Compare سفنج (*sfinğ*), Beaussier 1958: 477.

References

Bar-Asher, Moshe. 1986. "Le diminutif dans les dialectes judéo-arabes du Tafilalet (Maroc)." *Massorot* 2: 1–14.

Bar-Asher, Moshe. 1999. *Traditions Linguistiques des Juifs d'Afrique du Nord.* 2nd extended edition. Jerusalem: The Bialik Institute and the Hebrew University.

Bar-Asher, Moshe and Jeffrey Heath. 1982. "A Judeo-Arabic Dialect of Tafilalt (southeastern Morocco)." *Zeitschrift für Arabische Linguistik* 9: 32–78.

Beaussier, Marcelin. 1958. *Dictionnaire pratique arabe-français.* Algiers: La Maison des Livres.

Blanc, Haim. 1964. *Communal Dialects in Baghdad.* Cambridge: Harvard University Press.

Blau, Joshua. 1999. *The Emergence and Linguistic Background of Judaeo-Arabic: A Study of the Origins of Middle Arabic.* 3rd revised edition. Jerusalem: Ben-Zvi Institute.

Blau, Joshua. 2002. *A Handbook of Early Middle Arabic.* Jerusalem: The Max Schloessinger Memorial Foundation.

Blau, Joshua and Simon Hopkins. 2017. *Early Judaeo-Arabic in Phonetic Spelling*, Part 1. Jerusalem: The Ben-Zevi Institute.

Brunot, Louis and Elie Malka. 1939. *Textes judéo-arabes de Fès: textes, transcription, traduction annotée.* Rabat: L'Ecole du Livre.

Brunot, Louis. 1950. "Sur le thème verbal FʕaI en dialectal marocain." *Mélanges offerts à William Marçais par l'Institut d'études islamiques de l'Université de Paris.* Paris: G.-P. Maisonneuve, 55–62.

Chetrit, Joseph. 1994. *Written Judeo-Arabic Poetry in North Africa.* Jerusalem: Misgav Yerushalayim.

Chetrit, Joseph. 2007. *Diglossie, hybridation et diversité intra-linguistique: études socio-pragmatiques sur les langues juives, le judéo-arabe et le judéo-berbère.* Paris: Peeters.

Chetrit, Joseph. 2013. "Formation and Diversity of Jewish Languages and of Judeo-Arabic in North Africa, I: Middle Judeo-Arabic and its Forms of Hybridization." *Journal of Jewish Languages* 1(2): 177–206.

Chetrit, Joseph. 2014. "Judeo-Arabic Dialects in North Africa as Communal Languages: Lects, Polylects and Sociolects." *Journal of Jewish Languages* 2(2): 204–234.

Chetrit, Joseph. 2016. "Diversity of Judeo-Arabic Dialects in North Africa: Eqa:l, Wqal, Kʲal, and ʔal Dialects." *Journal of Jewish Languages* 4(1): 1–43.

Chetrit, Joseph. 2017. "Moroccan Judeo-Arabic." *Encyclopedia of Jews in the Islamic World*, exec. ed. Norman A. Stillman. First published online: 2017.

Cohen, David. 1964. *Le Parler arabe des Juifs de Tunis: Textes et documents linguistiques et ethnographiques.* The Hague – Paris: Mouton.

Cohen, David. 1970. "Les deux parlers arabes de Tunis – Notes de phonologie compare.", *Études de linguistique sémitique et arabe*, ed. David Cohen. Paris – the Hague: Mouton, 150–171.

Cohen, David. 1975. *Le parler arabe des Juifs de Tunis. Vol. II: Étude linguistique.* The Hague – Paris: Mouton.

Cohen, Marcel. 1912. *Le parler arabe des Juifs d'Alger.* Paris: H. Champion.

D'Anna, Luca. 2021. "The Judeo-Arabic Dialect of Yefren (Libya): Phonological and Morphological Notes." *Journal of Jewish Languages* 9(1): 1–31.

Fischer, Wolfdietrich and Otto Jastrow. 1980. *Handbuch der arabischen Dialekte.* Wiesbaden: Harrassowitz.

Fischer, Wolfdietrich. 2001. *A Grammar of Classical Arabic*, 3rd revised edition. New Haven – London: Yale University Press.

Goitein, Shelomo Dov and Mordechai Akiva Friedman. 2008. *India Traders of the Middle Ages: Documents from the Cairo Geniza: India Book.* Leiden: Brill.

Grand'Henry, Jacques. 1972. *Le parler arabe de Cherchell, Algérie.* Louvain-la-Neuve: Université catholique de Louvain.

Heath, Jeffrey. 1987. *Ablaut and Ambiguity: Phonology of a Moroccan Arabic Dialect.* Albany: State University of New York Press.

Heath, Jeffrey. 2002. *Jewish and Muslim Dialects of Moroccan Arabic.* London: Routledge Curzon.

Heath, Jeffrey and Moshe Bar-Asher. 1982. "A Judeo-Arabic Dialect of Tafilalt (Southeastern Morocco)." *Zeitschrift für Arabische Linguistik* 9: 32–78.

Henshke, Yehudit. 2007. *Hebrew Elements in Daily Speech: A Grammatical Study and Lexicon of the Hebrew Component of Tunisian Judeo-Arabic*. Jerusalem: Bialik Institute (in Hebrew).

Laraba, Ahmed. 1981. *A Linguistic Description of the Algerian Arabic Dialect of Constantine*. Ph.D. thesis. University of Manchester.

Levin, Arye. 1994. "Sībawayhi's Attitude to the Spoken Language." *Jerusalem Studies in Arabic and Islam* 17: 205–244.

Levy, Simon. 2009. *Parlers arabes des Juifs du Maroc: Histoire, sociolinguistique et geographie dialectale*. Zaragoza: Instituto de Estudios Islamicos y del Oriente Proximo.

Maman, Aharon. 1989. "On Identifying the Hebrew Element in Judeo-Maghrebian." *Massorot* 3–4: 171–201 (in Hebrew).

Marçais, Philippe. 1956. *Le Parler arabe de Djidjelli: Nord constantois Algerie*. Paris: Adrien-Maisonneuve.

Marçais, Philippe. 1977. *Esquisse grammaticale de l'arabe maghrebin*. Paris: Adrien-Maisonneuve.

Marçais, William. 1902. *Le dialecte arabe parlé à Tlemcen*. Paris: Ernest Leroux.

Retsö, Jan. 1983. *The Finite Passive Voice in Modern Arabic Dialects*. Göteborg: Acta Universitatis Gothoburgensis.

Saada, Lucienne. 1956. "Introduction à l'étude du parler arabe des Juifs de Sousse." *Les Cahiers de Tunisie* 6: 518–532.

Saada, Lucienne. 1964. "Caractéristiques du parler arabe de l'ile de Djerba (Tunisie)." *Comptes rendus du GLECS (Groupe Linguistique d'Etudes Chamito-Sémitiques)* 10: 15–21.

Saada, Lucienne. 1981. *Études sur le parler arabe de Tozeur (Tunisie)*. Paris: Geuthner.

Stillman, Norman A. 1988. *The Language and Culture of the Jews of Sefrou, Morocco: An Ethnolinguistic Study* (Journal of Semitic Studies, Monograph no. 11). Louvain: University of Manchester.

Stumme, Hans. 1896. *Grammatik des tunisischen Arabisch: nebst Glossar*. Leipzig: J.C. Hinrichs.

Taine-Cheikh, Catherine. 2000. "Deux macro-discriminants de la dialectologie arabe (la réalisation du qâf et des interdentales)." *Matériaux arabes et sudarabiques (GELLAS)*, Nouvelle série no. 9 (1998–99): 11–51.

Talmoudi, Fathi. 1980. *The Arabic Dialect of Sūsa (Tunisia)*. Göteborg: Acta Universitatis Gothoburgensis.

Tedghi, Joseph. 2006. "Translation of Hebrew Prayers into Judeo-Arabic by Shmuel Malka." *Massorot* 13–14: 279–314 (in Hebrew).

Tedghi, Joseph. 2016. "Tunisian Judeo-Arabic.", *Encyclopedia of Jews in the Islamic World*, exec. ed. Norman A. Stillman. First published online: 2016.

Tirosh-Becker, Ofra. 1988. *Phonology and Topics in Morphology of the Judeo-Arabic Translation of Psalms from Constantine (Algeria)*. Masters thesis. The Hebrew University of Jerusalem (in Hebrew).

Tirosh-Becker, Ofra. 1989. "A Characterization of the Judeo-Arabic Language of Constantine." *Massorot* 3–4: 285–312 (in Hebrew).

Tirosh-Becker, Ofra. 2011. *Rabbinic Excerpts in Medieval Karaite Literature*, 2 vols. Jerusalem: The Bialik Institute and the Hebrew University (in Hebrew).

Tirosh-Becker, Ofra. 2011a. "Languages of Algerian Jewry." *Algeria: Jewish Communities in the East in the Nineteenth and Twentieth Centuries*, ed. Haim Saadoun. Jerusalem: Ben-Zvi Institute, 117–132 (in Hebrew).

Tirosh-Becker, Ofra. 2011b. "On Dialectal Roots in Judeo-Arabic Texts from Constantine (East Algeria)." *Revue des Études Juives* 170 (1–2): 227–253.

Tirosh-Becker, Ofra. 2012. "Mixed Linguistic Features in a Judeo-Arabic Text from Algeria: The *Šarḥ* to the *Hafṭarot* from Constantine." *Language and Nature: Papers presented to John Huehnergard on the Occasion of his 60th Birthday*, eds. Rebecca Hasselbach and Naʿama Pat-El. Chicago: The Oriental Institute, 391–406.

Tirosh-Becker, Ofra. 2014. "A Reflection of a Linguistic Reality: An Algerian Judeo-Arabic Book for the New Year." *Studies in the Culture of North African Jewry,* vol. 3, eds. Moshe Bar-Asher and Steven D. Fraade. New Haven – Jerusalem: Yale University and the The Hebrew University of Jerusalem, 193–216.

Tirosh-Becker, Ofra. 2015. "Eliʕezer Ben-Yehuda and Algerian Jews: Relationship and Language." *Arabic and Semitic Linguistics Contextualized. A Festschrift for Jan Retsö,* ed. Lutz Edzard. Wiesbaden: Harrassowitz, 430–447.

Tirosh-Becker, Ofra. 2019. "Linguistic Analysis of an Algerian Judeo-Arabic text from the 19th century." *La Linguistique* 55(1): 192–211.

Walters, Keith. 2011. "Communal Dialects." *Encyclopedia of Arabic Language and Linguistics*, eds. Lutz Edzard and Rudolf de Jong. First published online: 2011.

Watson, Janet C.E. 2011. "Arabic Dialects (general article)." *The Semitic Languages: An International Handbook*, eds. Stefan Weninger, Geoffrey Khan, Michael P. Streck, and Janet C.E. Watson. Berlin – Boston: De Gruyter Mouton, 851–896.

Wright, William. 1955. *A Grammar of the Arabic Language*, 3rd edition. Cambridge: Cambridge University Press.

Yoda, Sumikazu. 2005. *The Arabic Dialect of the Jews of Tripoli (Libya)*. Wiesbaden: Harrassowitz.

Yoda, Sumikazu. 2010. "Libyan Judeo-Arabic." *Encyclopedia of Jews in the Islamic World*, exec. ed. Norman A. Stillman. First published online: 2010.

Yiddish

Lutz Edzard, University of Erlangen-Nürnberg

1. Introduction

1.1 Overview

Yiddish (etymologically simply "Jewish") is an umbrella term for a diachronically and geographically broad spectrum of varieties of German with a significant Hebrew adstratum, spoken and written by Jews. As a *linguistic* term for the language varieties, Yiddish was first used in English in 1886 in the novella Children of Gibeon by Walter Besant. Later, Salomon Birnbaum and Max Weinreich, among others, were pivotal figures in the establishment of *Yiddish* (in the anglicized version with a geminated *d*) as a linguistic term. Opinions differ as to whether the varieties of German spoken by Jews grammatically differed right away from the varieties spoken by their Christian neighbors or whether such differences only emerged in the course of time (see below section 1.3). Lexically speaking, of course, there is no question as to the the early-on specificity of Romance and Hebrew adstratum and the later specificity of Slavic adstratum.

In the upper Rhine area, Jewish presence can be deducted from documents as early as in the third century AD (cf., e.g., Battenberg 1990: 25). Two decrees from 321 and 331AD, attested in the Codex Theodosianus, a collection of late Roman imperial law finished in 438, testify to a Jewish community in Cologne in the fourth century. Contemporary Jewish communities are also assumed to have existed in Mainz, Speyer, Worms, Trier, Augsburg, Regensburg, and Vienna, i.e. cities lying at the rivers Rhine, Maas, and Danube. In the following centuries, after the Romans were driven out of the Germanic provinces, there is a marked lack of documentary evidence regarding the Jewish communities in these areas, in contrast to the regions of Aquitania, Gallia Narbonensis, and Gallia Lugdunensis. Later, from the ninth century on, archeological documentary evidence exists regarding Jewish communities in the cities of Cologne, Mainz, Speyer, and Worms. Remnants of the earliest Rhenish synagogue dating back to the ninth century were found in Cologne. Two prominent figures in 10th/11th century Mainz were the rabbis Yehuda ben Meir and Gershom ben Yehuda, who founded a widely known Yeshiva in this city. The Yeshivot in Speyer and Worms likewise gained transregional fame. Salomo ben Isaac, known as Rashi, born in Troyes in 1040, studied for a period in Worms. Due to pogroms and massive persecution from the 11th century on, which exacerbated during the time of the pest in the middle of the 14th century, eastward migration occurred, which resulted in a basic dichotomy of Eastern vs. Western Yiddish. Eastern Yiddish successively extended from Poland and Lithuania over Ukraine, Belarus to the Eastern Russian province Birobidjan.

While Western Yiddish is generally assumed to have died out in the late 18th century, remnants survived in Alsace and parts of Switzerland, where the last attestations date to the 1970s. While Western Yiddish *grosso modo* had adapted to its linguistic environment, Eastern Yiddish conserved historical (medieval) features, with morphological and especially lexical Slavic impact. What is more, Eastern Yiddish assumed the role of a linguistic standard. From the late 19th century on, Yiddish speakers emigrated to England and North America, the result of which was both an English impact on Yiddish and Yiddish loanwords in colloquial English. From 1917 to 1920, Yiddish was one of the official languages in Ukraine. Thereafter, it also had official status in the 1920s and 1930s in Belarus, next to Russian, White-Russian, and Polish. In spite of blatantly anti-Semitic politics, Yiddish was tolerated in the Stalinist Sowjet Union. Prominent Yiddish newspapers were *Der Emes* ('the truth'), from 1920 to 1939 in Moscow, *Der Shtern* ('the star') from 1925 to 1941 in Ukraine, and *Oktjabr* ('October), from 1925 to 1941 in Belarus. A milestone was the establishment of the YIVO (*Yidisher visnshaftlekher institut* (ייִדישער וויסנשאַפֿטלעכער אינסטיטוט) by Max Weinreich 1925 in Vilna. Since 1940, the Institute resides in New York. In 1928, the Jewish autonomous *oblast* with its capital Birobidjan was founded in Eastern Russia. Yiddish was supposed to become the official language, but never gained the majority of speakers.

The number of eleven to thirteen million speakers of Yiddish prior to World War II was reduced by approximately 5.800.000 (85% of 6.000.000 – percentage according to Birnbaum) in the course of the Nazi genocide.

In the early 21st century, speakers of Yiddish, significantly within the ultra-orthodox Haredi community, are found in parts of New York (mostly Brooklyn), Montreal, London, and Jerusalem (notably Meʔa Šeʕarim).

1.2 Theories of origin

The traditional theory regarding the origin of Yiddish and the history of Ashkenazic Jewry, which is in line with standard Jewish historiography, may be called the "Rhine hypothesis". This theory, mainly associated with Max Weinreich, Salomon Birnbaum, and Jechiel Bin-Nun (cf. Beider 2015: 1ff.) points to the Rhine-Moselle valley (iconically referred to as "Lot(h)er", etymologically related to the (today's) French region Lorraine/Lothringen) as the cradle of Ashkenazy Jewry, with influx mainly from Northern France and (possibly) Italy, from where further Jewish settlement proceeded. Jews, who later moved eastward, merged there with pre-existing Slavic-speaking Jewish communities. The German element of Yiddish is described as a blend of elements from various High German dialects ("high" in this context always to be understood geographically, i.e. as opposed to "low(er) Northern German, not in the Fergusonian sense). Yiddish turned out to be the sole language of Jews both in northern areas (Cologne) and in Southern areas (Mainz, Worms, Speyer). Weinreich's periodicization approximately looks as follows: Early Yiddish from the 9th century in two stages up to ca. 1250; Old Yiddish up to ca. 1500; Middle Yiddish with a gradual split into Western and Eastern Yiddish up to ca. 1750; New Yiddish thereafter. Within the first stage of Old Yiddish, Romance, German, and Hebrew-Aramaic elements converge; in the second stage of Old Yiddish, in the course of southward and eastward migration, dialects such as Alemannic, East Franconian, and Bavarian also contribute to the make-up of Yiddish. However, as early as in the 10th century, a Jewish community existed in the Bavarian town of Regensburg, an argument for a polygenetic origin of Yiddish (see below). While this theory does not explicitly suppose any "Proto-Yiddish", but rather develops the idea of a fusion language (*shmeltsshprakh*) or a "non-genetic" language in terms of Thomason and Kaufman (1988: 11), it still can be labeled essentially "monogenetic" (cf. Beider 2015: 4).

From the 1980s on, the so-called Danube hypothesis gained weight. Propagated in a number of publications by Dovid Katz, and ultimately going back to Mieses 1924, an Austro-Bavarian origin of Yiddish was postulated (cf. Beider 2015: 5ff.) as well as an independent origin of the Jewish communities in the Rhineland and in Southern Germany/Austria. The hypothesis underlines the fact that, while Rhenish German dialects and Yiddish virtually share no similarities, the contrary holds for Bavarian (as a linguistic term also encompassing most of Austria's dialects) and Yiddish. Here is a list of relevant features (cf. Jacobs 2005: 16, based on a list established by Faber and King (1984), juxtaposing Middle High German (MHG), Standard Yiddish (StY), and (Modern) Standard German (StG) forms; cf. also Beider 2015: 89f.):

1. apocope of final vowels, e.g., MHG *bluome* 'flower' (Blume) and *tage* 'days' (StG *Tage*) vs. Standard Yiddish (StY) *blum* and *teg*;
2. non-application of syllable-final devoicing, e.g., MHG *rat* 'wheel' (StG *Rad*) vs. StY *rod*;
3. a direct causal relationship between the last two rules;
4. early and complete unrounding of front rounded vowels, e.g., MHG (and StG) *über* 'over' vs. StY *iber*;
5. retention of the archaic Bavarian independent pronouns *ets* (PL.NOM) and *enk* (PL.OBL) 'you' in certain dialects of Central Yiddish;
6. lack of umlaut in the present indicative of the second and third person singular of strong verbs, e.g., StY *ikh trog* 'I carry', *du trogst* 'you carry', and *er trogt* 'he carries' vs. StG *ich trage*, *du trägst*, *er trägt*;
7. loss of [phonologically] distinctive vowel length, as found in most German dialects;
8. diminutive formation with an *l*-based diminutive rather than the *k*-based diminutive in StG; what is more, Bavarian and Yiddish share a, intense diminutive ("iminutive"), e.g., StY *shtot* 'city', *shtetl* 'market town', *shtetələ* 'little market town' (in Austrian Bavarian, a comparable situation obtains, e.g., *shtuob* 'room', 1st diminutive *shtiabl*, 2nd diminutive *shtiabarl*)

Eggers (1998) presents additional evidence, notably he merger of the *ich*-laut and the *ach*-laut in Yiddish and Bavarian. An additional Bavarian feature is the appearance of a prosthetic *daleth* in verbal forms that begin with *er*- in standard German, e.g., both Yiddish and Bavarian *dertseyln* 'to narrate' (cf. Standard German *erzählen*) (cf. Baumgarten 2005: 14).

On the syntactic and stylistic levels, the Bavarian scenario is plausible as well. For instance a kind of "smikhut kfula" construction (doubly marked genitive) is found in both Yiddish and Bavarian, *dem man-s bukh* 'the book of the man' as compared with Bavarian *dem Mo sei Buach* (cf. Standard German *das Buch des Mannes*). The same holds for appositional structures such as *a froy a sheyne* 'a beautiful woman', which would be equally idiomatic in Bavarian, *a Frau a schene* (cf. Standard German *eine schöne Frau*). In predication, similar parallels obtain, e.g., Yiddish *er iz an ungeduldiker* 'he is [an] impatient one' as compared with Bavarian *er is a ungeduldiger* (cf. Standard German *er ist ungeduldig*) (cf. Kiefer 2000: 1406). While these features originally are associated more with the Western regions, they also were taken to the Eastern regions by migration and continued cultural contact.

Eggers (1998) and Jacobs (2005) further elaborate the Danube hypothesis. For the former, Bohemia also forms part of the cradle of Yiddish in the 12th/13th century. For the latter, the Danube hypothesis constitutes more of a further elaboration of the Rhine hypothesis than of an antithesis.

Like the Rhineland hypothesis, the Danube hypothesis is basically monogenetic. Of two groups of Ashkenazi Jews, in the 15th century referred to (in the orthography of Katz) as the "Bney Hes" (influenced by Rhenish German and "Loez", i.e. Romance elements) and the "Bney Khes" (influenced by Danubian German and Hebrew-Aramaic), the language of the Bney Khes was identified with "Proto-Yiddish", which later split into West Yiddish and East Yiddish.

In contrast, Beider (2015: 7ff.) develops a polygenetic model, with three major contributing communities: (i) Jews from Western Germany, "West Canaanites" from the Czech lands; and (iii) East Canaanites from Ukrainian and Belarusian territories. The ancestral role of Middle High German is explicitly mentioned and in the period around 1500 both a "Proto West Yiddish" and a "Proto East Yiddish" is assumed. While he integrates elements of the proposals by Weinreich, Bin-Nun, and Katz into his model, East Franconian is identified as the most important donor to the West Yiddish variety. Old Czech influence on the Eastern branch takes place early on, later supplemented by East Slavic elements. The Bohemian German dialect, which shares features with Bavarian, has an important impact on Eastern Yiddish. Beider also assumes continued mutual influences between the Western and Eastern branches (for a graphic elaboration, cf. Beider 2015: 69).

The most important cross-references between Yiddish and German dialects according to Beider (2018: 291, extrapolated from Beider 2015: 214f.) are (the transcription is slightly adjusted):

1. merger of MHG *â* and *ô*: in South Western Yiddish and East Franconian;
2. raising of lengthened MHG *a*: Eastern Yiddish, Czech Yiddish, Bohemian; and Silesian;
3. diminutive plural suffix *-lekh*: all Yiddish varieties, parts of East Franconian, and the older period of Bohemian;

4a. reflexes of Old West Germanic **p* in initial position: *pf* in South Western Yiddish and East Franconian; *f* in Eastern Yiddish and Czech Yiddish, *f* in Silesian and *pf* in Bohemian;

4b. reflexes of Old West Germanic **p* in gemination: *pf* in South Western Yiddish, *p* in Eastern Yiddish and Czech Yiddish, *p* in Silesian and Bohemian;

5. German neutralization of consonants: South Western Yiddish and East Franconian;
6. /št/-reflexes of internal MHG *st*: South Western Yiddish and East Franconian;
7. /a:/ for MHG *ei* and *ou*: South Western Yiddish, East Franconian and Bohemian;
8. main diminutive singular suffix: *-(e)l* in Czech Yiddish, Eastern Yiddish, Bohemian and Silesian;
9. Unrounding of front rounded vowels: all Yiddish dialects, Bohemian, and Silesian;
10. Voiced and/or *lenes* reflexes of intervocalic MHG *v*: Czech Yiddish, Eastern Yiddish, Bohemian, and Silesian;
11. Apocope of unstressed vowels: all Yiddish dialects, East Franconian (except for the final *-e* in feminine nouns), and Bohemian.

As mentioned above, feature 9 equally applies to Bavarian, but not Alemannic and Franconian dialects, e.g., *Glück* > *glik* 'luck' or *böse* > *bese* 'evil' [modern Eastern Yiddish *beyz*] (Timm 1986: 16). According to Timm (1986: 14), feature 11 can be traced back to Bavaria in the early 13th century.

Paul Wexler's theory can be summarized as follows: Out of a Judeo-Romance variety (Weinreich's Loez) and Ashkenazic Judeo-German, Western Yiddish developed through a process of German re-lexification. Independently, out of a Sorbian (Slavic), proper Yiddish (Eastern Yiddish) developed, equally through a process of German relexification (cf., e.g., Wexler 1993; cf. also Fleischer 2014a: 109). This theory has not gotten real ground in the scholarly discussion and will not be pursued here any further (for a balanced assessment, cf. Kahn 2016: 646f.). Even though this theory also constitutes a polygenetic model, Beider (2015) markedly distances himself from this approach.

Independently of which of the preceding models one follows, it is *a priori* plausible that Jewish communities in some way related to the linguistic features of their Gentile neighbors. Thus, it is hardly surprising (and not confusing) that Yiddish partially adopted Central German, Southern German, and Eastern dialect features in the course of time and migrations. From a personal point of view, let it be stated that this writer (who had no personal exposure to Yiddish as a child, but native exposure to Bavarian, and grew up in a diglossic environment of Bavarian and StG) has no problem at all to follow, e.g., Yiddish recordings by Chava Turniansky on Youtube. Later, as a high school student in Munich, I also heard artists like Leonard Bernstein and Menachem Pressler (Beaux Arts Trio) communicating with German orchestra musicians and the audience in Yiddish without any problems. Conversely, speakers of Yiddish usually face no problems in figuring out written or spoken German (Norman A. Stillman, personal communication). In other words, there is a high degree of mutual intelligibility between speakers of Southern German dialects and speakers of Yiddish.

Erika Timm (1986: 13) has summarized the situation as follows:

"Doch auch wenn man das genetische Band bewußt locker hält, bilden hier in der Sache die deutsche Schriftsprache, die deutschen Mundarten und – von Südwesten nach Osten – die jiddischen Mundarten praktisch ein Kontinuum zunehmender Vereinfachungen."

("Even when one keeps the genetic juncture deliberately loose, the German written language, colloquial German varieties, and – from the Southwest to the East –factually represent a continuum of gradually increasing leveling.")

In the following, she plausibly characterizes features in Yiddish and German dialects as "analytical", as opposed to the more synthetical structure of written German. Parallels to the linguistic scenario in the Arab(ic) and Semitic world (diglossia/polyglossia) in general are obvious (notably as regards the expression of the genitive).

1.3 Definition of Yiddish

The common denominator of what constitutes Yiddish is threefold (cf. Beider 2015: 10): it can be defined as the vernacular Jewish language in which (i) the German component is quantitatively and structurally dominant; (ii) that represents an ancestor of (at least) some modern Yiddish varieties; that is distinct from local German dialects and Standard German as well.

Again, it is important to consider the native intra-communal terms for the language. Besides the term *yidiš* 'Jewish' (until the late 19th century not used for the language variety itself), the self-referential denominations *lošn aškenaz* 'language of Ashkenaz', *tayts̆* '[Midde High] German' ("deutsch"), *mame-lošn* 'mother tongue', and *lošn-qoydeš* 'holy tongue' also play a role, each with different ethnic, linguistic, familiar-emotional, and religious implications, respectively. Here is a tabular overview:

לשון־אַשכּנז	*lošn aškenaz*	'language of Ashkenaz'
טײַטש	*taytš*	'[Midde High] German' ("deutsch")
מאַמע־לשון	*mame-lošn*	'mother tongue'
אידיש/יידיש	*yidiš*	'Jewish'

As initially stated, the latter term was only used from the later 19th century on as a *linguistic* term. According to Kiefer (2000: 1400) the terminus post quem is 1913 (Birnbaum), an opinion outdated by now (see above). Hebrew as the language of Jewish liturgy was traditionally referred to as לשון־ קודש *lošn-qoydeš* 'holy tongue'.

One can discern two basic approaches to the determination of the origin of Yiddish: a "Germanistic" approach and a "Jewish-oriented" approach. The "Germanistic" approach derives Yiddish from the linguistic spectrum of Middle High German and does not assume a specifically Jewish linguistic variety spoken by Jews prior to the 15th century AD. Aharon Maman (this volume: 39) states that "Taytsh was yet ordinary German (Mittelhochdeutsch), but it became unique in phonology, not always because it changed, but because it was conservative compared to the developments undergone by the original language". In contrast, the "Jewish" approach (or varieties thereof) assumes a much older Jewish origin of Yiddish by way of German re-lexification of a Romance substrate in the course of eastward migration, or even a Slavic substrate in the course of westward migration, in contact with the pre-existing Jewish communities. The names of the approaches, as suggested by Beider (2015: 10), appear in quotation marks, as they are not *a priori* linked to non-Jewish or Jewish researchers, respectively. Beider (2015: 28ff.) convincingly points out that each of these lines of research has its merits and that these two basic approaches should not be played out against each other. Rather, they both yield important contributions to the understanding of the development of Yiddish. Historically, the "Germanistic approach unfortunately was marred by normative and prejudiced statements about words "misspelt" by Jews, e.g., *un* instead of *und* 'and' or *mir* for *wir* 'we'. The majority of scholars of Yiddish (notably Weinreich, Katz, and Jacobs) represent the "Jewish-oriented" approach. Alexander Beider himself seeks to innovate and enrich the "Germanistic" approach within historical linguistics with elements of the "Jewish-oriented" approach. Jürg Fleischer as one of the leading scholars on Western Yiddish can also be said to subscribe to that evolutionary "Germanistic" approach.

The characterization of Yiddish as a "fusion language" (*shmelstsshprakh*), as opposed to a full-fledged pidgin or creole language, is a major contribution by the "Jewish oriented" approach (cf. Jacobs 2005: 17ff. and Beider 2015: 19ff).

In any event, both the historical and modern status of Yiddish as a *language* of its own (as opposed to an ethnolect, religiolect or the like) is nowadays uncontroversial, given its grammatical (phonological and morphological), and not only lexical, features. Still, one should keep in mind the famous adage attributed to an auditor of one of Max Weinreich's lectures:

אַ שפּראַך איז אַ דיאַלעקט מיט אַן אַרמיי און פֿלאָט.

A	*shprakh*	*iz*	*a*	*dialekt*	*mit*	*an*	*armey*	*un*	*flot.*
INDEF	language	be.3SG.PRS	INDEF	dialect	with	INDEF	army	and	navy

"A language is a dialect with an army and navy."

This well-known quotation captures the circumstance that linguistic specificity in practice cannot be considered independently of political considerations. Obviously, political and cultural considerations also can play a role in an entirely non-religious context, e.g., in the well-known case of the mutually intelligible Scandinavian languages Norwegian, Swedish, and Danish.

The fact that (especially Eastern) Yiddish incorporates substantial Semitic (Hebrew and Aramaic), Romance, and Slavic lexical stocks is beyond question. An often cited "anecdotal" citation is the following, in which the lexical origin of each word is indexically marked:

דער זיידע האָט געבענטשט חנוכּה ליכט.

der	*zeyde*	*hot*	*gebentsht*	*khanike*	*likht.*
DEF.SG.M^{Germanic}	grandfather^{Slavic}	have.3SG.PRS^{Germanic}	bless.PPP^{Romance}	Hanukka^{Hebrew}	light^{Germanic}

"The grandfather blessed the Hanukka candles."

Another comparable cause célèbre is the sentence provide by Weinreich (1:33)

נאָכן בענטשן האָט דער זיידע געקויפֿט אַ ספֿר.

nokhn	*bentshn*	*hot*	*der*	*zeyde*	*gekoyft*	*a*	*seyfer*
after.DEF.DAT.NT^{G}	bless^{R}.INF	have.3SG.PRS^{G}	DEF.SG.M^{G}	grandfather^{Sl}	buy.PPP^{G}	INDEF^{G}	book^{H}

"After the blessing (grace after meals), the grandfather bought a religious book."

Still, the lexicon in itself is not a sufficient criterion for classifying a linguistic variety as a language of its own. Beider (2015: 22) argues accordingly regarding one of the oldest attested Yiddish documents, a Hebrew prayer book (*maḥăzor*) from Worms, dated 1272 AD:

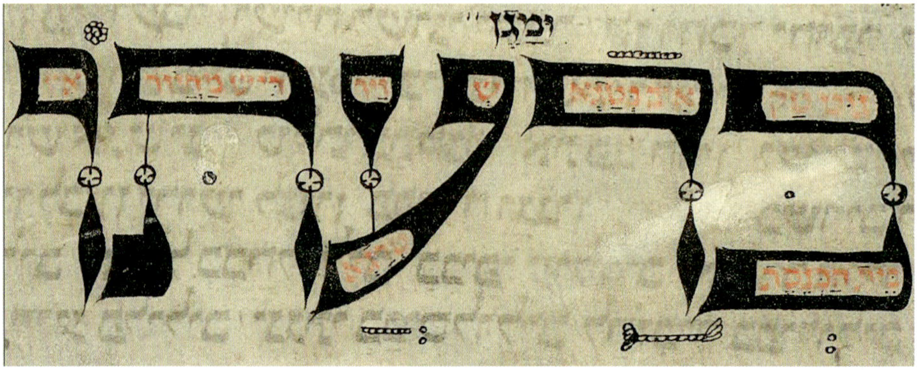

גוּט טַק אִים בְּטַגְּא שְׁ וַיר דִּיש מַחֲזוֹר אִין בֵּיתַ הַכְּנֶסֶתַ טְרַגְּא

gut	*tak*	*im*	*betage*	*s'waer*	*dis*	*maḥăzor*	*in*	*beyṯ*	*ha-kneseṯ*
good	day	3SG.M.DAT	shine.3SG.PRS.CONJ	REL	DEM.NT	prayer.book^H	in	house.CS^H	DEF-assembly^H
trage									
carry.3SG.PRS									

"May a good day come to him who carries this prayer book into the synagogue."

While this fragment contains two Hebrew noun phrases, *maḥăzor* 'Hebrew prayer book' and *beyṯ ha-kneseṯ* 'the synagogue', the remaining lexicon and grammatical structure does not differ in any marked way from Middle High German. Interestingly, the phrase *tak betage* emulates the Semitic figura etymologica.

A proper description of the diachronic and synchronic wealth of Yiddish dialects is a task much beyond this article. Beider 2015 constitutes an analysis of hitherto unsurpassed sophistication, far too complex to be summed up here (but cf. Beider 2018). Section 2 will therefore be restricted to Standard Yiddish (as deriving from Eastern Yiddish). Specific comments on varieties, when applicable, will precede the text samples in section 3.

The following sample taken from a Wikipedia entry on Bavarian (https://en.wikipedia.org/wiki/Bavarian_language) clearly illustrates the Sitz im Leben of Yiddish within the spectrum of High German dialects. (Again, "H(igh)" vs. "L(ow)" always refers to German geography, i.e. the "higher" German South against the "lower" German North, and not to registers "H" vs. "L" in a Fergusonian sense.)

Austrian	*s Bóarische is a Grubbm fő Dialektt im Siin fåm dœtschn Shbroochråm.*
Bavarian	*'s Bóarische is a Grubbm fő Dialektt im Siin fóm daitschn Shproochraum.*
Yiddish (Southeastern)	בײַריש איז אַ גרופּע פֿון דיאַלעקטן אין דרום פֿון דײַטשיש שפּראַך־קאָנטינוום *Bayrish iz a grupe fun dialektn in dorem fun daytshish shprakh-kontinuum.*
Standard German	*Das Bairische ist eine Gruppe von Dialekten im Süden des deutschen Sprachraumes.*
English	*Bavarian is a group of dialects in the South of the German Sprachraum.*

Besides the Yiddish term for "South", דרום *dorem* (< Hebrew דָּרוֹם *dā̊rōm*), the example sentence also contains an "internationalism", קאָנטינוום *kontinuum* (cf. Kahn 2016: 700f.).

Following a suggestion by Jürg Fleischer, the term "Judeo-German" may be meaningful in a context, where standard German is transcribed in Hebrew letters, e.g. in the title of the Purim play by Joseph Herz from 1828 (see below section 3.9) אסתר אדער דיא בעלאָנטע טוגנד – איינע פּאָזזע אין פיער אַבשניטטען אין יידיש־דייתשער מונדארט פאָן יוסף הערץ *Esther oder die belohnte Tugend. Eine Posse in vier Abschnitten in jüdisch-deutscher Mundart* ('Esther or the rewarded virtue: a farce in four sections in Jewish-German vernacular'). The play itself then is set entirely in a Franconian variety of Western Yiddish.

1.4 Attestation and literature

This is only an extremely short overview, for details cf. Baumgarten 2005 and Frakes 2004 for the older period of Yiddish and Shmeruk and Prager 2007 for a comprehensive overview of the whole period of Yiddish. Roughly, one can discern three periods: Old Yiddish literature, Hasidic and Haskala literature, and Modern Yiddish literature. The authenticity of a number of Yiddish glosses in Rashi's Bible and Talmud commentaries (cf. the editio princeps by Darmesteter and Blondheim 1929) is controversial. Timm (1985) considers a few examples as authentic (i.e. not as later additions), notably the term װינדלשטיין *wendelstein* rendering Hebrew לוּלִים *lūllīm* 'wound stairs' in 1 K 6:8, corresponding to Old French *viz* 'screw, wound stairs' (cf. Timm 1985: 75f.). The already mentioned Hebrew prayer book from Worms, dated 1272 AD, counts as the oldest extant Yiddish document. As in other Jewish language varieties, translation of religious core texts emerged soon. In addition, chivalric romances and epic poems, comparable to standard German literature of the time emerged (cf. Sample 3.6., the beginning of the epos *Dukus Horant*, below), e.g., the *Shmuel Bukh*, a midrashic epic from the second half of the 15th century. A towering figure of Old Yiddish literature in the 16th century is Elijah Levita (cf. also Sample 3.7 below), who became famous with the *Bovo Bukh* (בָּבָא-בוּך, בּוֹבוֹ-בוּך), another chivalric romance, first printed in 1541. A further milestone in Old Yiddish literature is the *Mayse Bukh* ('book of tales', < Hebrew מַעֲשֶׂה *maʕăśɛ*), comprising both religious material and folktales. An important Yiddish prose work of 1590, structurally similar to the weekly Torah portions of the Pentateuch is the *Tsenerene* (cf. Song 3:11: צְאֶנָה וּרְאֶינָה בְּנוֹת צִיּוֹן, *ṣəʔɛnā̊ u-rəʔɛnā̊* 'Go forth and see, Oh daughters of Zion').

Hasidic mysticism constitutes a further hallmark in Yiddish literature. Rabbi Israel ben Eliezer (ca. 1698 – 1760), known as the Baal Shem Tov, counts as the crucial figure in this connection. Nachman of Breslov (נחמן מברסלב), also known as Reb Nachman of Bratslav, Reb Nachman Breslover (רבי נחמן ברעסלאָווער), or Nachman from Uman (1772 – 1810) is another towering personality associated with that period. Representatives of a more secular maskilic counter-movement were mainly Israel Aksenfeld (1787 – 1886, Solomon (or Shloyme) Ettinger (1802 – 1856), and Isaac Mayer Dick (1807 – 1893).

1864 is often cited as a *terminus post quem* for Modern Yiddish literature, meaning that the name *yidish* – perhaps first appearing in 1865 – began to appear at the modern Yiddish literature period. In that year, Mendele Mocher Sforim (1836 – 1917) (Yiddish:

מענדעלע מוכר ספרים, Hebrew: מנדלי מוכר ספרים, lit. “Mendele the book peddler”, born Sholem Yankev Abramovich) published his novel *Dos kleyne mentshele* (“The little person”). Together with Sholem Rabinovitsh (1859 – 1916), better known under his pen name as Sholem Aleichem (שלום עליכם), and Isaac Leib Peretz (1852 – 1915) (יצחק־לייבוש פרץ), he forms the “classical” trio of modern Yiddish writers, who greatly enhanced the literary impact of this language variety. Yiddish literature has flourished ever since, in the first half of the twentieth century also among women writers, e.g., Celia Dropkin (1887 – 1956), Anna Margolin (1887 – 1952), Kadia Molodowsky (1894 – 1975), and others. Not only Yiddish prose witnessed prolific writers, but also poetry, e.g., Mordechai Gebirtig (1877 – 1942) (Yiddish: מרדכי געבירטיג), cf. Sample 3.3 below. The awarding of the Literature Nobel Prize in 1978 to Isaac Bashevis Singer (1902 – 1991) (Yiddish: יצחק באַשעוויס זינגער) was a major boost to modern Yiddish literature. Yiddish literature flourishes to this day, including in popular genres such as spy novels (cf. Kahn 2016: 712f.). Classical newspapers were already mentioned above, *The Forward* (פֿאָרווערטס *forverts*) in New York still publishes today in Yiddish.

2. Grammatical sketch

2.1 Phonology and orthography

The consonantal phoneme inventory of Yiddish, enriched by phonemes found in Hebrew-Aramaic and Slavic terms, can be represented as follows:

		Labial	Alveolar		Postalveolar		Dorsal	Glottal
			soft	hard	soft	hard		
Nasal		m	nʲ	n			(ŋ)	
Plosive	voiceless	p		t			k	(ʔ)
	voiced	b		d			g	
Affricate	voiceless		tsʲ	ts	tʃʲ	tʃ		
	voiced		dzʲ	dz	dʒʲ	dʒ		
Fricative	voiceless	f	sʲ	s		ʃ	χ	h
	voiced	v	zʲ	z		ʒ	ɣ	
Rhotic					r			
Approximant	central						j	
	lateral			l			ʎ	

Thereby, in spite of general stability, the realization of individual consonants may vary, notably of /r/, as in German dialects, between an alveolar trill, a uvular trill, or a voiced uvular fricative (Kahn 2016: 664). Nasal assimilation of /m/ and /n/ obtains, again, as in spoken German, in cases such as /lign/ [ligŋ] ‘lie (untruth)‘ and /lebn/ [lebm] ’live’ (Jacobs 2015: 113).

The vowel system (monophthongs), subject to regional variation, can be represented as follows:

	Front	Central	Back
Close	ɪ		ʊ
Open-mid	ɛ	ɜ	ɔ
Open	a		

In addition, the following diphthongs are part and parcel of Yiddish:

Front nucleus	Central nucleus	Back nucleus
ɛɪ	aɪ	ɔɪ

As advocated by adherents of Standard Yiddish, the Hebrew characters are used in the following way to represent Yiddish consonants. Thereby, certain graphemes are restricted to words of Hebrew origin:

sign	name	phonemic transcription	phonetic value	comment
א	*shtumer alef*	/ʔ/	[Ø]	
אַ	*pasekh alef*	/ʔ/	[ɑ]	
אָ	*komets alef*	/ʔ/	[ɔ]	
ב	*beys*	/b/	[b]	also בּ
בֿ	*veys*	/v, b̲/	[v]	ב /b̲/ in Semitic words
ג	*giml*	/g/	[g]	
ד	*daled*	/d/	[d]	
ה	*hey*	/h/	[h]	
ו	*vov*	/u (w)/	[ʊ]	
וּ	*melupm vov*	/u/	[ʊ]	also ו
וו	*tsvey vovn*	/v/	[v]	
וי	*vov-yud*	/oy/	[ɔj]	
ז	*zayen*	/z/	[z]	
זש	*zayen-shin*	/zh/		
ח	*khes*	/kh, ḥ/	[x]	/ḥ/ in Semitic words ([x])
ט	*tes*	/t, ṭ/	[t]	
טש	*tes-shin*	/tsh/	[tʃ]	
י	*yud*	/i, y/	[ɪ, j, ◌ʲ]	◌ʲ after coronals and before vowel palatalization of Slavic words
יִ	*khirek yud*	/i/	[ɪ]	also י
יי	*tsvey yudn*	/ey/	[ɛj]	
ײַ	*pasekh tsvey yudn*	/ay/	[ɑj]	

sign	name	phonemic transcription	phonetic value	comment
כּ	*kof*	/k/	[k]	כּ in Semitic words
כ/ך	*khof, lange khof*	/kh, k̲/	[x]	
ל	*lamed*	/l/	[l, ł, ʎ]	
מ/ם	*mem, shlos mem*	/m/	[m]	
נ/ן	*nun, lange nun*	/n/	[n]	
ס	*samekh*	/s/	[s]	
ע	*ayin*	/e, ʕ/	[ɛ̆]	[ɛ̆]/[ĭ], when unstressed
פּ	*pey*	/p/	[p]	
פֿ/ף	*fey, lange fey*	/f, p/	[f]	also פ
צ/ץ	*tsadek, lange tsadek*	/ts, ṣ/	[ts]	
ק	*kuf*	/k, q/	[k]	
ר	*reysh*	/r/	[ʀ]	[r]
ש	*shin*	/sh, š/	[ʃ]	[ʃ]
שׂ	*sin*	/s, ś/	[s]	ש in Semitic words
תּ	*tof*	/t/	[t]	תּ in Semitic words
ת	*sof*	/s, t̲/	[s]	in Semitic words, never word-initialדן

Prior to the 19th century, no standard existed and quite a bit of orthographic variation is found (e.g., word-final *-e* can be represented by both ע and י), in addition to "Germanizing" spelling, for instance, employing vowel-lengthening ה *h*, e.g., שטוהל *shtul* 'chair' (cf. Standard German *Stuhl*). The YIVO standard orthography established in 1936 is largely phonetic (see below), and widely employed, also in the Romanization of Yiddish lemmata and text samples. The Soviet orthography (after 1917) also resorted to a phonetic spelling of Hebrew terms, e.g., קאַלע *kale* instead of כלה 'bride' (cf. Kahn 2016: 668). Modern Haredi orthography partially returns to a Germanizing spelling. Notably, Hebrew vowel marks precede the various *matres lectionis* in Yiddish (just as in Masoretic Hebrew spelling, e.g., וָואס *vos* in contrast to וואָס 'what' (for details, cf. the summary in Kahn 2016: 669).

In the YIVO system, words of Hebrew-Aramaic origin are spelled according to the Hebrew norm (in marked contrast to the Soviet spelling system of Yiddish), even though they are pronounced differently in Yiddish context. The German stock, however is essentially spelled phonetically. Thus MHG *ich* 'I' graphically always surfaces as איך, not *יכה. Syllable-final devoicing is represented in examples such as הונט *hunt* [hunt] 'dog'. In contrast, voicing is orthographically rendered in examples such as זײַן *zayn* (cf. German *sein*) or זיסער *ziser* 'sweeter' (cf. German *süßer*). Syllable onsets /st/ and /sp/, which are pronounced [sht] and [shp] also in most standard German varieties, are regularly spelled phonetically שט and שפ, e.g., שטאָט *shtot* 'city' (cf. German *Stadt*) or שפּיל

shpil (cf. German *Spiel*). In comparison with German orthography, homorganic consonants are freely inserted to reflect actual pronunciation, e.g., אונדזער *undzer* 'our' (cf. Standard German *unser*) (cf., e.g., Jacobs 2005: 112, 127 and Edzard 2018). The same phenomenon occurs, e.g., in Spanish *Alhambra* (cf. Arabic *al-ḥamrāʔ* 'the red one (F)'). Yiddish orthography also regularly reflects the absence of vowels in non-hypercorrect speech, e.g., in verbal forms such as ווינטשן *vuntshn* 'to wish' (cf. German *wünschen*).

Graphic minimal pairs between homonyms of Hebrew-Aramaic stock and Slavic stock include examples such as Hebrew-based term סוֹד [sod] 'secret' vs. סאָד [sod] 'orchard' (cf. Jacobs 2005: 48f.). In more recent varieties of Western Yiddish, as in older periods of Yiddish in general, the orthography is often more oriented at German spelling (also of dialects), including gemination of consonants, e.g., נעממע *nemme* 'to take' (border regions of East Franconian; cf. Standard German *nehmen*).

In the following, a phonemic transcription is used throughout.

Consonants

Yiddish almost entirely reflects the High-German consonantal shift. As in Standard High German, Germanic /p/ shifts to /f/ in words like *schlafen, laufen, helfen, hoffen*: *shlofn* 'to sleep', *loyfn* 'to run', *helfn* 'to help', *hofn* 'to hope'. As in East Middle German syllable-/word-final /p/ remains unshifted. e.g., Standard High German *Kopf, Zopf, Topf* wind up as *kop* 'head', *tsop* 'braid', *top* 'pot'. The attachment of diminutive suffixes does not alter this situation *kepl, tepl* ('little head', 'little pot'). Regarding word-initial /pf/ in Standard German, as, e.g., in *Pfanne*, *Pfeffer*, *pfeifen*, *Pfeil*, *Pferd*, *Pflanze*, Yiddish simplifies the affricate to /f/, as does East Middle German *fan* 'pan', *fefer* 'pepper', *fayfn* 'to whistle', *fayl* 'arrow', *ferd* 'horse', *flanzn* 'plant'. In contrast, Western Middle German keeps the /p/ in this position, and High German "Oberdeutsch") shifts to /pf/, as in Stand German. West Germanic /p/ at the beginning of the syllable coda remains /p/, as in *epl* 'apple', *shepn* 'to scoop, bucket' (cf. Standard German *Apfel*, *schöpfen*).

Proto-Germanic	Standard German	Yiddish
*slēpaną	*schlafen*	שלאָפן *shlofn* 'sleep'
*pannōn	*Pfanne*	פֿאַן *fan* 'pan'
*aplaz	*Apfel*	עפּל *epl* 'apple'

As in many Bavarian and Alemannic dialects, ח/כ/ך (*ch*) is pronounced as [x] also after ײ (*i*), ײ (*ey*), (*ay*), as well as after ר (*r*), e.g., ליכט *likht* ([lɪxt]) 'light'.

Vowels

Germanic linguistics owes a very sophisticated system of indexing of proto-vowels to Max Weinreich (for an overview, cf. notably Katz 1983: 1023f.; cf. also Kiefer 2000: 1402); for dialectal details cf. Jacobs 2005: 90–108 and Beider 2015: 116–156). The following description is somewhat simplified and oriented at Standard Yiddish, with only occasional references to dialectal differences.

Yiddish shares a number of sound shifts with Southern ("Ober" – Higher) and Central ("Mittel") German dialects: de-rounding of the high vowels *ö* > *e*, *ü* > *i* (e.g., MHG *jüde* > Yiddish *jid* 'Jew'), the diphthongization of MHG viz. regional early NHG long *ê* > *ey*, *ô* > *ou*, in East Yiddish further > /oi/, *œ* (> *ê*) > *ey* (e.g., MHG. *gên* > Yiddish *geyn* 'to go', MHG *brôt* > Yiddish *broyt* 'bread', MHG *schœne* > Yiddish *sheyn* 'beautiful'), the lowering of the long central vowel MHG *â* > *ô*/*û* (e.g., MHG *schlâfen* > NE Yiddish *shlofn,* S Yiddish *shlufn* 'to sleep').

Old High German	German	Yiddish	Example
a / ā	a [a:]	אָ *(o)*	שאָף (*shof*) 'sheep'
a	a [a]	אַ *(a)*	זאַלץ (*salts*) 'salt'
ō	o [o:]	וי *(oy)*	ברויט (*broyt*) 'bread'
ō [ø:]	ö [ø:]	יי *(ey)*	בייז (*beyz*) 'evil'
e	e [e:]		אייזל (*eyzl*) 'donkey'
o [ø]	ö [œ]	ע *(e)*	קעפּ (*kep*) 'heads'
e	e [ɛ]		ענג (*eng*) 'tight'
u [y:], [ʏ]	ü [y:], [ʏ]	י *(i)*	איבער (*iber*) 'over'
ou	au [ao]	וי *(oy)*	אויג (*oyg*) 'eye'
ū	au [ao]		הויז (*hoyz*) 'house'
ei	ei [ae]	יי *(ey)*	שטיין (*shteyn*) 'stone'
ī	ei [ae]	ײַ *(ay)*	ווײַן (*vayn*) 'wine'
iu	eu [oe]		נײַ (*nay*) 'new'

The development of /ei/, /ø:/, and /iu/ towards the corresponding Yiddish sounds passed via the intermediate stages /ei/ > /e:/ > /ey/, e.g., *bein* > *bēn* > *beyn*); /ø:/ > /e:/ > /ey/ (*schoni* > *schœne* > *schēn* > *sheyn* 'beautiful'); /iu/ > /y:/ > /i:/ > /ay/, e.g., *niuwi* > *nü(we)* > *nī* > *nay* 'new').

2.2 Morphology

Yiddish morphology is by and large Germanic-based, with both specific retentions and innovations, as well as Slavic and Hebrew influences. In the nominal realm, nouns denoting quality are often derived by mere umlaut, e.g., *hoykh* 'high' > *heykh* 'hight' or *groys* 'big' > *greys* '(large) size)' (as in colloquial German the final *-e* of the corresponding terms *Höhe* and *Größe* is absent) (cf. Jacobs 2005: 155f.). Prefixes and suffixes in nominal derivation likewise do not necessarily match the situation in standard German, e.g., *bashefenish* 'creature', *kleynkayt* 'smallness', or *klugshaft* 'prudence' (cf. Standard German *Schöpfung*, *Kleinheit*, *Klugheit*) (cf. Jacobs 2005: 156f.). The often pejorative agent suffix *-nik* (fem. *nitse*) is of Slavic origin (see below). There is a broad range of feminine extensions in addition to standard *-in*, including *-ke* (e.g., *shnayderke* 'female tailor') and *-she* (e.g., *doktershe* 'female doctor'). Except for the diminutive and iminutive, all emotive (endearing or pejorative) suffixes, usually attached to proper names and kinship terms, are of Slavic origin, e.g., *moysh-inke* and *avrem-tshik.*

Pronoun

The Yiddish pronominal system looks as follows:

	NOM		DAT		ACC	
1SG	איך	*ikh*	מיר	*mir*	מיך	*mikh*
2SG	דו	*du*	דיר	*dir*	דיך	*dikh*
3SG.M	ער	*er*	אים	*im*	אים	*im*
3SG.F	זי	*zi*	איר	*ir*	זי	*zi*
3SG.NT	עס	*es*	אים	*im*	עס	*es*
1PL	מיר	*mir*	אונדז	*undz*	אונדז	*undz*
2PL/POL	איר	*ir*	אײַך	*aykh*	אײַך	*aykh*
3PL	זיי	*zey*	זיי	*zey*	זיי	*zey*

While the system, all the way from Old High German, is rather stable, the morphological syncretism in the third person singular (dative and accusative) is noteworthy. The Modern Standard German polite form *Sie* (3PL), attested since the late 18th century, is not in use in Yiddish; rather, one resorts to the from *ir* (2PL).

Third person pronouns agree in gender with the noun they refer to. Thus even inanimate objects are sometimes referred to as *er* or *zi* if they are masculine or feminine, respectively. Neuter nouns are referred to by *es*.

Nouns

Gender

As in both Standard German and German dialects, Yiddish nouns can be classified into three genders: masculine (זכר *zokher*), feminine (נקבה *nekeyve*) and neuter (נייטראַל *neytral*). To a large extent, the gender of a noun is unpredictable, even though there are some regular patterns. The following generalizations apply:

– Nouns denoting specifically male humans and animals are usually masculine, and nouns denoting specifically female humans and animals are usually feminine.

– Nouns ending in an unstressed *schwa* (*-e*, phonetically [ə]) are usually feminine, except for iminutives that are neuter, irrespective of the original gender of the noun.

– Nouns built on most of the common suffixes of abstract-nouns, such as -ונג *-ung* and -הײַט *-hayt*, are feminine.

– Diminutive nouns with the suffix *-l* or *-le* are neuter in the standard language, also when referring to humans, including diminutives on personal names.

– Loanwords are generally assigned masculine gender by default, unless they end in a *schwa* (*-e*), in which case they are usually feminine.

An interesting feature of Hebrew-stock compound nouns is the rule that the head noun determinines the gender of the compound in accordance with the rules for German, e.g., *der/dos seyfer* 'the religious book' + *di toyre* 'the Torah' yields, *di seyfer-toyre* 'the Torah scroll' (in Hebrew, agreement in this case would be with *seyfer*).

Case

There are three cases in Yiddish: nominative, accusative and dative. The nominative case generally refers to the subject, the accusative to the direct object and the dative to an indirect object. Nouns themselves are normally not inflected for case, and case is indicated by the inflection of a related definite article or adjective. In a few situations, case inflection of the noun is optional or obligatory, including certain kinship terms (טאַטע *tate* 'father', מאַמע *mame* 'mother') and the words ייִד *yid* 'Jew' and האַרץ *harts* 'heart'. In those cases, masculine nouns take the ending ן- *-n* in the accusative and dative singular, and feminine and neuter nouns take ן- *-n* only in the dative singular.

Yiddish does not have a genitive case. However, when the possessor is a human or occasionally other living beings, possession may be indicated with a suffixed ס- *-s* (like the English possessive *-'s*). Otherwise, possession is normally indicated in an analytical way by the preposition פֿון *fun* 'of'.

Another genitive-like construction, quasi-appositional, the quantitative, is used to describe quantities of objects: אַ פֿול גלאָז הייסע טיי *a ful gloz heyse tey* 'a full cup of hot tea'; אַ גרופּע יונגע מענטשן *a grupe yunge mentshn* 'a group of young people'. The quantity is simply followed by the object described. This construction may not be used if the object has a definite article: אַ פֿול גלאָז פֿון דער הייסער טיי *a ful gloz fun der heyser tey* (a full cup of the hot tea).

Number

The following morphological features apply as regards plural marking in Yiddish:
– umlaut and *-n* endings (as in High German dialects);
– no *-e* ending (as in High German dialects);
– *-(e)s* ending (German; also with Hebrew and Slavic nouns);
– *-im* ending (mostly with Hebrew nouns);
– the Hebrew dual ending *-ayim* is only found exceptionally in Yiddish, e.g., *yodayem* 'hands' (pejorative) (cf. Jacobs 2005: 163).

There is a very large number of nouns with irregular plural forms, including *-es* (these are usually nouns of Slavic origin), and *-er* with umlaut (e.g., מאַן *man* 'man' vs. מענער *mener* 'men'; קינד *kind* 'child' vs. קינדער *kinder* 'children'), or umlaut alone (e.g., האַנט *hant* 'hand', cf. הענט *hent* 'hands'). The *-(e)s* plural ending is far more widespread than in both standard German and German dialects, e.g., לעבנס *lebns* 'lives' (cf. StG *Leben*), זינגערס *zingers* 'singers' (cf. StG *Sänger*), or פֿראַגעס *frages* 'questions' (cf. StG *Fragen*). Polysyllabic words with final stress usually take an *-n* ending, e.g., קאָנטאַקטן *kontaktn* 'constacts' (cf. StG *Kontakte*) (for details, cf. Jacobs 164f.). Some words do not change in the plural (e.g., פֿיש *fish* 'fish'), as in the well-known dish געפֿילטע פֿיש *gefilte fish*, lit. "filled fish". Many words of Hebrew origin form the plural with *-im*, and plural words of Hebrew origin, which end in וֹת-, are pronounced *-es*, e.g., זכרונות *zikhroynes* 'memories' (this also holds for the abstract ending וּת-, e.g., in רחמנות *raḥmones* 'pity'). Many plural forms of words are characterized by a stem vowel mutation (umlaut).

Here is an overview of Yiddish plural formation:

	singular		plural	gloss
שוועסטער	*shvester* (Schwester)	שוועסטער	*shvester*	'sister'
טיש	*tish* (Tisch)	טישן	*tishn*	'table'
ים	*yam* (Meer)	ימען	*yamen*	'sea' (Hebrew)
קויש	*koysh* (Korb)	קוישן	*koyshn*	'basket' (Slavic)
טאָג	*tog* (Tag)	טעג	*teg*	'day'
גאָרטן	*gortn* (Garten)	גערטנער	*gertner*	'garden'
קול	*kol* (Stimme)	קולער	*keler*	'voice' (Hebrew)
סאָד	*sod* (Obstgarten)	סעדער	*seder*	'orchard' (Slavic)
שטעקן	*shtekn* (Stecken)	שטעקנס	*shtekns*	'staff (baton)'
מומע	*mume* (Tante, Muhme)	מומעס	*mumes*	'aunt'
חיה	*khaye* (Tier)	חיות	*khayes*	'animal' (Hebrew)
נודניק	*nudnik* (Langweiler)	נודניקעס	*nudnikes*	'boring person' (Slavic)
פויער	*poyer* (Bauer)	פויערים	*poyerim*	'peasant'
נס	*nes* (Wunder)	נסים	*nisim*	'wonder' (Hebrew)
שטח	*shetekh* (Gegend)	שטחים	*shtokhim*	'area' (Hebrew)
מלבוש	*malbesh* (Kleidungstück)	מלבושים	*malbúshim*	'piece of clothing' (Hebrew)

Article

The definite article in Yiddish functions as follows, with a syncretism comparable to the syncretism in the system of personal pronouns:

	NOM		DAT		ACC	
SG.M	דער	*der*	דעם	*dem*	דעם	*dem*
SG.F	די	*di*	דער	*der*	די	*di*
SG.NT	דאָס	*dos*	דעם	*dem*	דאָס	*dos*
PL	די	*di*	די	*di*	די	*di*

Comparable to the strategy in Bavarian (*dem Mo sei* 'the man's …'), the genitive is expressed by a combination of the dative definite article and a residue of the genitive *-s*.

masculine	NOM	*der man* (*der Mann*) 'the man'
	GEN	*dem mans* ... (... *des Mannes* / *des Mannes* ...) 'the man's …'
	DAT	*dem man* (*dem Mann*) '(to) the man'
	ACC	*dem man* (*den Mann*) 'the man'
feminine	NOM	*di froy* (*die Frau*) 'the woman'
	GEN	*der froys* ... (... *der Frau*), 'the woman's …'
	DAT	*der froy* (*der Frau*) '(to) the woman'
	ACC	*di froy* (*die Frau*) 'the woman'
neuter (not in north-eastern Yiddish)		
	NOM	*dos kind* (*das Kind*) 'the child'
	GEN	*dem kinds* … (... *des Kindes* / *des Kindes* ...) 'the child's …'
	DAT	*dem kind* (*dem Kind*) '(to) the child'
	ACC	*dos kind* (*das Kind*) 'the child'

In the plural, *di* is used in all genders and numbers, e.g., *di mener/froyen/kinder zingen* / cf. StG *die Männer/Frauen/Kinder singen* 'the men/women/children sing', *ikh gib dos buch di mener/froyen/kinder* / cf. StG *ich gebe das Buch den Männern/Frauen/Kindern* 'I give the book to the men/women/children'.

Residues of case inflection of the nouns include a clitic *-s* (see above), independently of gender, in possessive constructions, e.g., *dem man-s bukh* 'the book of the man' – cf. the analytical construction in dialectal German *dem Mann sein Buch, der froy-s bukh* 'the book of the woman', *dem kind-s bukh* 'the book of the child'– cf. StG *das Buch des Mannes*, *der Frau*, *des Kindes*.

What is more, adjectives used as nouns, personal names, and a few words denoting persons, *yid* 'Jew', *mentsh* 'human being, person', and *rebe* 'rabbi' can take the suffix *-n* in oblique cases (cf. Jacobs 2005: 161f.), e.g.,
– *der tate* 'father', genitive *dem tatn-s*, dative/accusative *dem tatn* (likewise: *zeyde* 'grandfather', *rebe* 'Chasidic rabbi, schoolteacher');
– *der mentsh* 'man(kind)', genitive *dem mentshn-s,* dative/accusative *dem mentsh* or *dem mentshn* (likewise: *jid* 'Jew(ish man)');
– *di mame* 'mother' – genitive *der mame's,* dative *der mame* or *der mamen*, accusative *di mame* (likewise: *bobe* 'grandmother', *mume* (Tante) 'aunt').

The accusative *-(e)n* appears after proper names, in conjunction of a first and a last name only with the last name, e.g., *ikh ze Dovidn* 'I see David', but *ikh ken Arn Barnboymen* 'I know Aaron Birnbaum' (the ending can be omitted for stylistic reasons).

A frozen ending *-n* is found in the following examples, *tsum hartsn* ('to the heart'), *in der emesn* ('in truth'), *in der luftn* ('in the air'), *in der vokhn* ('in the week' (during week days), *far akht togn* ('eight days ago') (cf. the regular Yiddish plural *teg* 'days'), *ba laytn* ('among decent people').

The indefinite article is אַ *a*, which becomes אַן *an* before a noun or an adjective beginning with a vowel. Yiddish, like English or Standard German and German dialects, does not have a plural indefinite article. No inflection applies, i.e., *a man, a froy, a kind* 'a man, a woman, a child' (all three Yiddish cases) (*ein/einem/einen Mann*, *eine/einer Frau*, *ein/einem Kind*). According to Timm (1986: 11) this reflects a MHG tendency to level inflection, in contrast to tendencies in the formal written language.

Adjectives

Attributives are inflected to agree with the gender, number, and case of the noun they modify, while predicate adjectives remain uninflected (but see below for non-limited conditions). For example, one says דער גוטער מאַן *der guter man* 'the good man', but דער מאַן איז גוט *der man iz gut* 'the man is good'. In other words, there is no difference, as in Standard German, between a strong and a weak inflection (except occasionally for neuter), e.g., regarding the noun-adjective phrases 'a/the old man', 'to an/the old woman', and 'a/the little child' (Standard German in parentheses):

	INDEF		DEF	
NOM M	*an alter man*	(*ein alter Mann*)	*der alter man*	(*der alte Mann*)
DAT F	*an alter froy*	(*einer alten Frau*)	*der alter froy*	(*der alten Frau*)
NOM N	*a kleyn kind*	(*ein kleines Kind*)	*dos kleyne kind*	(*das kleine Kind*)

Timm (1986: 13) reports a similar syncretism for Ripuarian (Northern Middle Franconian).

When an adjective is used in predicative position, its ending changes as if it were followed by another noun: דער מאַן איז אַ גוטער *der man iz a guter* 'the man is a good [one].' Neuter singular attributive adjectives have no case ending unless the whole noun phrase is introduced by the definite article.

Summing up, definite attributive adjectives function as follows:

	NOM		DAT		ACC	
SG.M	גוטער	*guter*	גוטן	*gutn*	גוטן	*gutn*
SG.F	גוטע	*gute*	גוטער	*guter*	גוטע	*gute*
SG.NT	גוטע	*gute*	גוטן	*gutn*	גוטע	*gute*
PL	גוטע	*gute*	גוטע	*gute*	גוטע	*gute*

A separate absolutive from is attested in the singular neuter, *guts*. Otherwise, and unlike in Standard German, no differences surface between the definite and the absolutive forms.

For phonotactic reasons, the ending *-n* becomes *-en* after a stressed vowel, as well as after *m*, *ng*, or *nk*; and it becomes *-em* after *n*, an example of the Obligatory Contour Principle. Again, Yiddish is slightly simpler than German in that German *-m* and *-n* both correspond to *-n* in Yiddish (or, in the case of the definite article, *dem*), and Yiddish does not have a genitive case. The "definite" and "absolutive" versions of the neuter gender are a relic of the strong vs. weak adjective endings of German (*das gute Bier* vs. *gutes Bier* '(the) good beer').

A class of quantifiers and pronominal adjectives, including איין *eyn* 'one', קיין *keyn* 'none', and possessive pronouns such as מײַן *mayn* 'my, mine' and זײַן *zayn* 'his', display behavior opposite to that of ordinary adjectives: they are inflected for gender, number and case when used predicatively but not when used attributively (absolutively, they behave as normal adjectives) (cf. Timm 1986: 10f.).

Adjectives normally precedes the noun, but they may follow the nouns by way of apposition for stylistic purposes: אַ שיינע פֿרוי *a sheyne froy* or אַ פֿרוי אַ שיינע *a froy a sheyne* ('a beautiful woman'). Depending on the semantics of the adjective, temporarily limited vs. non-limited conditions can be distinguished in this way, e.g., *er iz gliklikh* 'he is happy (right now)' vs. *er iz a gliklikher* 'he is happy (by nature)' (cf. Jacobs 2005: 173). As mentioned above, Bavarian features similar noun adjective phrases.

As already mentioned above, there are two kinds, or, if one so pleases, stages of diminutives in Yiddish, a diminutive I designating the smaller unit and a diminutive II ("iminutive"):

Diminutive I (smaller unit)

singular: *-l* – plural *-lekh*: *bet* (Bett) – dim. I *betl,* pl. *betlekh* 'little bed'; accompanied by umlaut: *hant* (*Hand*) – dim. I *hentl* 'little hand'.

Diminutive II (imminutive: affective nuance)

singular *-ele* – plural *-elekh*: *bet* (Bett) – dim. II *betele,* pl. *betelekh* 'dear little bed'; accompanied by umlaut: *hant* (Hand) – dim. II *hentele* 'dear little hand'.

Adverbs

Yiddish features a number of adverbial affixes that are are not found as such in Standard German (cf. Jacobs 2005: 195ff.). Those include the prefixes *a-*, e.g., *a-ponem* 'apparently' (Hebrew) and *a-heym* 'homewards', as well as several Hebrew prepositions such as *be-*, e.g., *be-sod* 'secretly' and *bi-ksav* 'in writing' and *le-*, e.g., *le-sof* 'finally', also with Germanic elements, e.g., *le-vayter* 'until further'. A specifically Yiddish and productive suffix is *-erhayt*, e.g., *gezunt-erhayt* 'in good health'. Other "optional" adverbial suffixes such as *-ert* (e.g., *its-ert* 'now' are also found in southern German dialects, notably Bavarian and Franconian (*jetz-ert* 'now').

Prepositions

Simple Yiddish prepositions of Germanic stock include the following items:

אַדאנק	*adank*	'thanks to'
אויסער	*oyser*	'besides'
אונטער	*unter*	'under'
איבער	*iber*	'over'
אַרום	*arum*	'around, about'

Simple Yiddish prepositions of Hebrew stock include the following items:

במקום	*bimkem*	'instead of'	(< Hebrew בִּמְקוֹם *bi-məqōm*)
לגבי	*legabe*	'in relation to'	(< Hebrew לְגַבֵּי *lə-ḡabbē*)
לכבד	*lekoved*	'in honor of'	(< Hebrew לִכְבוֹד *li-ḵbōḏ*)
לשם	*leshem*	'for the sake of'	(< Hebrew לְשֵׁם *lə-šēm*)
מצד	*mitsad*	'on the part of'	(< Hebrew מִצַּד *miṣ-ṣaḏ*)

In this context, one has to beware of lexical *faux-amis* between StG and Yiddish, e.g., Yiddish *vegn* 'about' vs. StG *wegen* 'because of' (see below).

Verbs

Yiddish verbs are conjugated for person and number (singular and plural). The infinitive of a verb ends in ן- *-n* or, in some phonotactically conditioned cases (see above), ען- *-en*.

Present tense

The present tense of regular verbs is conjugated for person and number, as follows (examples קויפֿן *koyfn* 'buy', פֿאַרלירן *farlirn* 'lose', as well as "irregular" האָבן *hobn* 'to have' and זײַן *zayn* 'to be'):

				'buy'		'lose'		'be'		'have'
INF			קויפֿן	*koyfn*	פֿאַרלירן	*farlirn*	זײַן	*zayn*	האָבן	*hobn*
1SG	איך	*ikh*	קויף	*koyf*	פֿאַרליר	*farlir*	בין	*bin*	האָב	*hob*
2SG	דו	*du*	קויפֿסט	*koyfst*	פֿאַרלירסט	*farlirst*	ביסט	*bist*	האָסט	*host*
3SG	ער	*er /*								
	זי	*zi /*								
	עס	*es*	קויפֿט	*koyft*	פֿאַרלירט	*farlirt*	איז	*iz*	האָט	*hot*
1PL	מיר	*mir*	קויפֿן	*koyfn*	פֿאַרלירן	*farlirn*	זענען	*zenen/zaynen*	האָבן	*hobn*
2PL/POL	איר	*ir*	קויפֿט	*koyft*	פֿאַרלירט	*farlirt*	זענט/זײַט	*zent/zayt*	האָט	*hot*
3PL	זיי	*zey*	קויפֿן	*koyfn*	פֿאַרלירן	*farlirn*	זענען/זײַנען	*zenen/zaynen*	האָבן	*hobn*

Certain simplifications (as compared with StG) obtain. In the present paradigm, neither *e-i* change nor umlaut occurs, e.g., regarding *helf(e)n* 'to help' and *fal(le)n* 'to fall:

	Yiddish	StG	gloss
INF	*helfn / faln*	helfen / fallen	'to help'
3SG.PRS	*er helft / er falt*	*er hilft /er fällt*	'he helps' / 'he falls'

According to Timm (1986: 13), exactly the same syncretisms can be observed in Southern West-Middle German.

As in StG and German dialects in general, the imperative singular consists of the stem of the present tense or the infinitive, the imperative plural is identical with the second person plural (without the pronoun), e.g.,

For a historical perspective, useful for Yiddish modal forms (see below), here are also the present tense paradigms of the (auxiliary) verbs "to be", "to have", "to want", and "to do" in Middle High German.

	pronoun	'be'	'have'	'want'	'do'
1SG	*ich*	*bin*	*hān*	*wil(e)*	*tuon*
2SG	*dû*	*bist*	*hâst*	*wil(e)/wilt*	*tuost*
3SG	*er*	*ist*	*hât*	*wil(e)*	*tuot*
1PL	*wir*	*sîn/sint/birn*	*hân*	*wel(le)n*	*tuon*
2PL	*ir*	*sît/sint/birt/bint*	*hât*	*wel(le)t*	*tuot*
3PL	*sie*	*sint*	*hânt*	*wel(le)nt/wellen*	*tuon*

Past participle

The past participle is used extensively in Yiddish. The majority of verbs (so-called weak verbs) form the past participle by adding -גע *ge-* and ט- *-t* to the stem, e.g., געקויפֿט *ge-koyft* 'bought'. However, strong verbs form the past participle with -גע and ן- *-n*, accompanied by a vowel change, e. g. געהאָלפֿן *geholfn* 'helped' from the stem -העלפֿ *helf-* 'help'. The vowel change is unpredictable, and there is no way to tell from the infinitive whether a verb is weak or strong.

The prefix -גע is omitted in past participles of verbs whose first syllable does not bear primary stress. There are two classes of verbs for which this happens: verbs with one of several unstressed stem prefixes, such as -פֿאַר *far-* or -באַ *ba-*; and verbs built on the stressed suffix -יר *-ir*, usually used for loanwords. Thus the past participles of פֿאַרקויפֿן *farkoyfn* 'to sell' and אַבאָנירן *abonirn* 'to subscribe' are, respectively, merely פֿאַרקויפֿט *farkoyft* and אַבאָנירט *abonirt*.

Past tense

Like other varieties of High German and unlike literary German, Yiddish does not make use of the inflected past tense (preterite). Instead, the auxiliary verbs האָבן *hobn* 'to have' or זײַן *zayn* 'to be' are used with the past participle of the verb. Most verbs take האָבן *hobn*, while about 30 verbs of motion or status and some of their derivatives take זײַן *zayn*. Transitive derivatives of these exceptional verbs usually take האָבן *hobn*: איך בין געגאַנגען *ikh bin gegangen* ('I went') vs. איך האָב איבערגעגאַנגען דעם טײַך *ikh hob ibergegangen dem taykh* (I walked across the river).

For illustration, the past tense of איך קויף *ikh koyf* 'I buy' is איך האָב געקויפֿט *ikh hob gekoyft*, and the past tense of איך קום *ikh kum* 'I come' is איך בין געקומען *ikh bin gekumen* 'I came'. The distribution of the auxiliaries האָבן *hobn* and זײַן *zayn* cannot be automatically deduced from StG. While there is overlap in some cases, differences obtain in other cases: ער איז געשטאַנען *er iz geshtanen* 'he stood' (StG *er ist/hat gestanden*), but זי איז געשלאָפֿן *si iz geshlofn* 'she slept' (StG *sie hat geschlafen*). Regional differences exist(ed) as well: North-eastern Yiddish (Lithuania, Belarus) only featured *hobn* as an auxiliary verb.

Here are some additional forms of both strong and weak verbs in Yiddish, as well as a small number of irregular verbs.

– strong verb			
infinitive	3SG.PRS	past participle perfect (PPP)	gloss
shraybn (*schreiben*)	*shraybt*	*geshribn*	'to write'
zingen (*singen*)	*zingt*	*gezungen*	'to sing'
shlofn (*schlafen*)	*shloft*	*geshlofn*	'to sleep'
– weak verb			
makhn (*machen*)	*makht*	*gemakht*	'to do, make'
redn (*reden*)	*redt*	*geredt*	'to talk'
strashen (*drohen*)	*strashet*	*gestrashet*	'to threaten'
irregular			
hobn (*haben*)	*hot*	*gehat*	'to have'
veln (*wollen*)	*vil* (full verb) /		
	vel (auxiliary)	*gevolt*	'to want, will'
– periphrastic			
moyde zayn (*zugeben*)	*iz moyde*	*moyde geven*	'to admit'

As there is no preterite in Yiddish, the plu(squam)perfect is formed by a combination of the perfect of האָבן *hobn* and the passive participle of the relevant verb, e.g., איך האָב געהאַט געקויפֿט *ikh hob gehat gekoyft* 'I had bought'.

The future tense is expressed by the conjugated forms of the auxiliary וועלן *veln* 'to want, will' (StG *wollen*; comparable to English future formation with *will*), e.g., איך וועל קויפֿן *ikh vel koyfn* 'I will/shall buy'.

As in Standard German (including dialects), the passive is expressed by the auxiliary ווערן *vern* (StG *werden*) in combination with the passive participle, e.g., דאָס בוך ווערט געקויפֿט *dos bukh vert gekoyft* 'the book is (being) bought'.

The conditional is expressed with וואָלט *volt* 'would' (historically a subjunctive belonging to וועלן *veln* (*wollen*) 'to want') plus participle perfect, e.g., ער וואָלט געהאָלפֿן *er volt geholfn* 'he would help' (StG *er würde helfen / er hülfe*).

What is more, Yiddish features a system of *aktionsarten*, inspired by the verbal system in Slavic, especially in Yiddish in a Slavic environment, less so in Western Yiddish.

– *shraybn* (*schreiben*, as a state: imperfective) vs. *onshraybn* (*schreiben* in the sense of to finish writing: perfective: *ikh shrayb a bukh* = (*ich bin dabei, ein Buch zu schreiben*, "ich bin am Schreiben", 'I am in the course of writing' vs. *ikh hob ongeshribn a bu^h* = *ich habe das Buch fertig geschrieben* 'I finished writing the book'. The imperfective aktionsart is also attested in the construction known as "Rheinische Verlaufsform", e.g., *ich bin am Schreiben* 'I am writing (lit. "at the writing") right now'.

– *interesirn zikh* (*sich interessieren* 'to be interested', as a state: imperfective) vs. *farinteresirn zikh* (*Interesse an etwas gewinnen* 'to take an interest in': perfective/resultative).

Compound verbs

Yiddish features a number of phrasal verbs containing Semitic elements. Masculine singular present tense forms of active Semitic verbs are followed by the auxiliary זײַן (*zayn* 'to be'), while present tenses of passive Semitic verbs are followed by the auxiliary ווערן (*vern* 'to become'). The reflexive particle זיך (*zikh*) is added, when reflexive Hebrew verbs are used. Several other auxiliary verbs are occasionally used in some cases:

מסכּים זײַן	*maskim zeyn*	'to agree' ("to be agreeing")
מודה זײַן	*moyde zeyn*	'to admit' ("to be admitting")
זוכה זײַן	*zoykhe zeyn*	'to deserve, live to' ("to be deserving")
קונה־שם זײַן	*koyne shem zeyn*	'to gain popularity' ("to be buying name")
נעלם ווערן	*nelam vern*	'to disappear' ("to become disappear")
זיך נתגלגל ווערן	*zikh nisgalgel vern*	'to reincarnate' ("to become overturning")
תּשובֿה טאָן	*tshuve ton*	'to repent' ("to do regret")
נקמה נעמען	*nekome nemen*	'to take revenge' ("to take revenge")

Similar constructions (conflated complements) exist with the auxiliary *hobn* 'to have', e.g., הנאה האָבן *hanoe hobn* 'to enjoy' ("to have joy").

Numerals

The Latin transcription of Yiddish numbers looks as follows:

0 *nul*	10 *tsen*		100 *hundert* 1.000 *toyznt* 1000.000 *milyon*
1 *eyns*	11 *elf*		
2 *tsvey*	12 *tsvelf*	20 *tsvantsik*	
3 *dray*	13 *draytsn*	30 *draysik*	
4 *fir*	14 *fertsn*	40 *fertsik*	
5 *finf*	15 *fuftsn*	50 *fuftsik*	
6 *seks*	...		
7 *zibn*			
8 *akht*			
9 *nayn*			

Conjunctions

Yiddish features a number of coordinating and subordinating conjunctions, some of which are of Slavic or Hebrew origin. Generally, conjunctions have no impact on mode and position of the verb, the latter in marked contrast to modern Standard German. Here is a small selection.

Paratactic

און / אונ'	*un*	'and'
אָדער	*oder*	'or'
אָבער	*ober*	'but'
ווײַל	*vayl*	'because'

Hypotactic

הגם	*hagam*	'although' (< Hebrew הֲגַם *hă-ḡam*)
כאָטש	*khotsh* (Sl.)	'although'
אַז	*az*	'that'
אויב	*oyb*	'if/whether'
בכדי	*bikhdey*	'so that' (< Hebrew בִּכְדֵי *bi-ḵdē*)
הן ... הן	*hen ... hen*	'both … and' (< Hebrew הֵן הֵן *hēn hēn*)
אָדער ... אָדער	*oder ... oder*	'either … or'

2.3 Syntax

Word order

As Timm (1986: 6ff.) convincingly states (cf. the statement by Aharon Maman above), Yiddish has not undergone syntactic developments typical of the German in the 16th and 17th centuries. In general, Yiddish from that period on exhibits far less hypotaxis in comparison to contemporary standard German documents. This also holds for broadened attribute constructions.What is more, Yiddish refrains from using bracketing constructions and avoids final verb position in hypotactic clauses, e.g. (Timm 1986: 9):

	Yiddish	StG
present	*er sucht oys a bukh*	*er sucht ein Buch aus*
perfect	*er hot oysgesukht a bukh*	*er hat ein Buch ausgesucht*
hypotactic	*ven er hot oysgesukht a bukh*	*als er ein Buch ausgesucht hat*

('he chooses a book, he chose a book, when he chose a book')

(Cf. also below *mir hobn arayngeleygt dos feygele* vs. StG *wir haben das Vögelein hineingelegt* 'we put in the little bird' in text sample 3.5 below.)

On the other hand, Yiddish conserves verb-initial constructions à la *sah ein Knab ein Röslein stehen* ('a boy saw a little rose (standing)'), which vanished in StG; these are found regularly in Yiddish, e.g., *iz der yid tsurik geshprungen* 'the Jew jumped back' (an example from 1614, cf. Timm 1986: 9).

Taube (2014) demonstrates another conservative feature of Yiddish, namely conservative *az*-clauses. Whereas the conjunction *az* (cf. StG *als* 'when, as') usually introduces subordinate clauses, it can also serve "superordination" in marking salient linguistic events in independent clauses, e.g. (apud Taube 2014: 235)

די בריליאַנטענע שטערן האָבן אָנגעהויבן איינציקוויז אויסלעשן זיך

di	*brilyantene*	*shtern*	*hobn*	*ongehoybn*	*eyntsikvayz*	*oysleshn*	*zikh*
DEF.PL	shining.PL	star(.PL)	have.PRS.3PL	begin.PPP	sole.ADV	extinguish.INF	REF

'The diamond stars began to go out one by one

אזוי ווי די בענטשליכט אז עס האָט זיך פּלוצעם

azoy	*vi*	*di*	*bentshlikht,*	*az*	*es*	*hot*	*zikh*	*plutsem*
so	like	DEF.PL	blessing^{F}.light(.PL)	when	PRON.3SG.NT	have.PRS.3SG	REF	suddenly

like Shabbath candles, when suddenly

געלאָזט הערן אַ קנאַק.

gelozt	*hern*	*a*	*knak*
let.PPP	hear.INF	INDEF	bang

a bang was heard.'

This type of syntactic construction is well attested in older German narrative (e.g., fairy tales).

Accusative existentials

In connection with the modern Hebrew existential *yeš ʔet* (EXIST ACC) construction (cf., e.g., Glinert 1989: 149), Taube (2016) has discussed co-occurring constructions in Slavic and Germanic that may be seen as a trigger behind the unusual occurrence of a *nota accusativi* after an existential marker. At any rate, this construction (*es gibt* 'there is' + accusative) is wide-spread in Standard German, German dialects, and Yiddish.

Relative clauses

A remarkable feature of Eastern Yiddish is relative clauses introduced by וואָס *vos* 'what', independently of the gender and the number of the antecedent, e.g. (cf. Fleischer 2014b: 137ff.).

דער בחור וואָס איך זע

der bokher vos ikh ze
DEF.SG.M boy REL 1SG see.PRS.1SG
'the boy that I see'

אַ ייִדענע וואָס זי האָט געהייסן יענטע

a yidene vos zi hot geheysn Yente'
INDEF Jewess REL 3SG.F have.PRS.3SG be_named.PPP Yente
'a Jewish woman, whose name was Yente'

די קינדער וואָס דו האָסט געהאָלפֿן

di kinder vos du host geholfn
DEF.PL child.PL REL 2SG have.PRS.2SG help.PPP
'the children whom you helped'

Taube (2012) and Fleischer (2014b) consider Slavic (mostly Polish) adstratum most likely in this case. The fact remains that – as also acknowledged by these authors – the overlap between interrogative and relative elements is a commonality between Semitic, Southern German dialects, and Slavic. In this author's view, Bavarian examples such as

dea hund dea / dea vos / vos doa lafft
DEF.SG.M dog DEF.SG.M / DEF.SG.M REL / REL there run.PRS.3SG
'the dog that is running over there' (adapted from Fleischer 2014b: 144)

perfectly illustrate the inner-Germanic transition from the "classical" relative pronouns/markers (overlapping with the German definite articles) to relative marking with interrogative elements such as "what" and "where" (the latter being attested in Semitic, Bavarian, and modern Greek).

Tautological infinitive

Another syntactic construction specific to Yiddish (as opposed to its German environment) is the "tautological infinitive" (Yudl Mark), inner object, or *figura etymologica*, a construction which stresses the activity in question. The Biblical Hebrew locus classicus for this construction, (infinitive absolute + finite verb) is the following (Gen 37:8):

הֲמָלֹךְ תִּמְלֹךְ עָלֵינוּ אִם-מָשׁוֹל תִּמְשֹׁל בָּנוּ

hă-mā̊lōḵ timlōḵ ʕā̊lē-nū ʔim mā̊šōl timšōl bā̊-nū
INT-reign.INF.ABS reign.IPFV.2SG.M upon-1PL if rule.INF.ABS rule.IPFV.2SG.M on-1PL
'Do you want to be king over us or rule over us?

Yiddish frequently features this construction, e.g., קומען קומט ער ניט *kumen kumt er nit* 'he does not come' (cf. Fleischer 2014b: 155), טראָגן טראָג איך מיין אַלטן מאַנטל *trogn trog ikh mayn altn mantl* 'I wear my old coat a lot', or אויפֿהערן האָט די גבירה שוין ניט אויפֿגעהערט צו לאַכן *oyfhern hot di gvire shoyn nit oyfgehert tsu lakhn* 'the lady just wouldn't stop laughing' (cf. Mark 1978). Still, Fleischer (2014b: 155) argues for a Slavic origin of the construction in Yiddish. In contrast, Goldenberg (1971) points to the occurrence of this construction in *both* German and Yiddish. The construction is also found in Judezmo, e.g., *vinir no vino* 'he didn't come' (David Bunis, written communication).

Pseudo-coordination

Yiddish provides insight in a large spectrum of linguistic matters. Yuasa and Sadock (2002) illustrate that point with the phenomenon of pseudo-coordination, i.e. a sort of *ad sensum* construction, in Yiddish.

דער טאַטע מיט דער מאַמע זינגען אינײנעם

der	*tate*	*mit*	*der*	*mamen*	*zingen*	*ineynem*
DEF.SG.M	father	with	DEF.F.DAT	mother.DAT	sing.PRS.3PL	together

'Father and mother are singing together.'

Even though the mother is syntactically subordinated to the father in this construction, plural agreement obtains, thus placing the mother semantically on the subject level.

Negation

Sentential negation is expressed by ניט *nit* or נישט *nisht* 'not' after the verb. Negated indefinite noun phrases, singular or plural, are preceded by the negative article קיין *keyn* instead of the indefinite article אַ *a* or אַן *an*. Negated definite noun phrases use the definite article as usual.

Yiddish allows and often requires double negation, e.g., קיינער איז דאָרטן נישט געווען *keyner iz dortn nisht geven* (lit. "no one was not there") or איך האָב קיינעם נישט געזען *ikh hob keynem nisht gezen* (lit. "I didn't see no one"). In colloquial speech even triple and multiple negations may occasionally be used: איך האָב נישט געוווּסט קיין גאָרנישט נישט *ikh hob nisht gevust keyn gornisht nisht* (literally: "I did not know no nothing not").

Typologically, such examples are reminiscent of multiple negation in Southern German dialects, e.g., Bavarian *I hob koa Lust net* 'I do not want' (lit. "I have no desire not") or Black American English ("Ebonics") *dey ain't got no right to drive no buses* 'they are not allowed to drive (any) buses' (lit. "they are not got no right ..."; quotation from a council woman in Oakland, CA, speaking out against bus drivers under influence).

2.4 Lexicon

Lexical archaisms

Yiddish features a number of lexical archaisms, from the perspective of both StG and German dialects. An example is the verb אָנהייבן *onheybn* 'to begin'. In StG, three relevant verbs with the same meaning exist: *anfangen* (mainly colloquial language), *beginnen* (mainly written language), and *anheben* (poetic, archaizing) (cf. Timm 2005: 434f.). According to Timm (2005: 435), אָנהייבן *onheybn* gained weight in Yiddish between 1400 and 1600, to the expense of b*egin(n)en*, still frequent in Middle High German. In the nominal realm, one likewise encounters archaic אין אָנהייב *in onheyb* 'in [the] beginning', as compared to StG *am Anfang*. Idiomatically, *Anhieb* survives in the StG term *auf Anhieb* 'right away'.

Hebrew-Aramaic loanwords

Following the terminology of Max Weinreich, two layers can be distinguished in this context: "whole Hebrew" affecting intertextually interwoven Hebrew passages, and "merged Hebrew" affecting single Hebrew words and phrases. Importantly, Hebrew-Aramaic elements not only pertain to the cultural religious realm, but permeate the whole vocabulary, thus accounting for the character of Yiddish of the "fusion language". The main changes from the Tiberian standard to standard Yiddish pronunciation are the following: The Biblical Hebrew phoneme /ḥ/ (itself reflecting both historical /ḥ/ and /x/) generally winds up as [x], the sibilants /s/, /ś/, /š/ as [s] and [š], and the emphatic sibilant /ṣ/ as [ts], with regional variants. /t/ winds up as [s], e.g., פתיכה *psike* 'ritual opening of the ark in the synagogue'. *qā̊māṣ gā̊ḏōl* in non-stressed position is reflected by [o] (as in Ashkenazi pronunciation of Hebrew in general), with few exceptions such as *khaver* 'friend' < Hebrew חָבֵר *ḥā̊ḇēr*, in final position it is reflected by [e/ə], as is *pattā̊ḥ* (*páṯaḥ*). Stressed *ḥōlā̊m (ḥōlem)* and *ṣērē (ṣēre)* are usually diphthongized to [oy] and [ey], respectively. Unstressed *qibbūṣ*/*šūrūq* can also surface as [i] or [e], e.g., מלבוש *malbesh* 'piece of clothing' < Hebrew מַלְבּוּשׁ *malbūš* 'clothing'. *ḥōlā̊m* (*ḥōlem*) in the final syllable coda turns out [e]. Ultimate stress in Hebrew falls back on the penultimate or even antepenultimate. Here are some relevant examples (cf. also Beider 2015: 276ff.)

	Hebrew term	Standard Yiddish form	gloss
מִשְׁפָּחָה	*mišpā̊ḥā̊*	*mishpókhe*	'family'
עֲבוֹדָה	*ʕăḇōḏā̊*	*avóyde*	'worship, work'
חֲתֻנָּה	*ḥăṯunnā̊*	*khásene*	'wedding'
חֲנֻכָּה	*ḥănukkā̊*	*khánike*	'Hanukkah'
עוֹלָמוֹת	*ʕōlā̊mōṯ*	*óylemes*	'worlds'
נְקֵבָה	*nəqēḇā̊*	*nekéyve*	'female'
נַחַת	*naḥaṯ*	*nákhes*	'pleasure'
תַּחַת	*taḥaṯ*	*tókhes*	'buttocks'

As Bunis (2005) has demonstrated, the fusion character of Jewish languages such as Judezmo and Yiddish is very prominent in the realm on all kinds of agent nouns. Hebrew stems can take Germanic suffixes, e.g., *khaver-l* '(dear) little friend' (cf. Hebrew חָבֵר *ḥā̊ḇēr* 'friend') and *bokher-l* '(dear) young man' (cf. Hebrew בָּחוּר *bā̊ḥūr* 'young man'); conversely, Germanic stems can take Semitic suffixes, e.g., *poyer-im* 'peasants' (cf. German *Bauer* 'peasant') or *tayvlon-im* 'devils' (cf. German *Teufel* or Bavarian *Deivl* ~ *Deivi* 'devil') (cf. Bunis 2005: 105f.).

By the same token, Hebrew verb stems can be integrated into Germanic patterns, e.g., *akhlen* 'to eat' (< Hebrew לֶאֱכוֹל *le-ʔĕḵōl* 'to eat'), *dabern* / *dibern* 'to speak (informally)' (< Hebrew לְדַבֵּר *lə-dabbēr*), or *nablen* 'to make obscene remarks, to slaughter an animal in a non-kosher way' (< Hebrew לִנְבּוֹל *li-nbōl* 'to be vile' and נְבֵלָה *nəḇēlā̊* 'carcass of an animal not killed in accordance with Jewish law'). While the previous examples are based on the Hebrew root, other examples are based specifically on certain nouns, adjectives, or participles, e.g., *geshemen* 'to rain' (< Hebrew גֶּשֶׁם *gešem* 'rain'), *mishpetn* 'to judge' (< Hebrew מִשְׁפָּט *mišpåṭ* 'judgment'), or *meymesn* 'to beat, kill' (< Hebrew מֵמִית *mēmīṯ* 'killing' (PTCP.SG.M)). In yet other examples, Germanic prefixes are added, e.g., *farkhideshn* 'to amaze' (< Hebrew חִדּוּשׁ *ḥiddūš* 'remarkable thing'), *baganv(en)en* 'to steal' (< Hebrew גַּנָּב *gannåḇ* 'thief'), or *aynshmuesn* 'to persuade' (< Hebrew שְׁמוּעוֹת *šəmūʕōṯ* 'talk') (cf. Beider 2015: 333ff.)

In some cases, Hebrew-based compounds in Yiddish are oriented at the Germanic order of constituents, e.g., *akhbrosh* 'impudent fellow' (< עַכְבָּר *ʕaḵbår* 'mouse' + ראֹשׁ *rō()š* 'head' (cf. Kutscher 1982: 218) or *shabes-goy* 'Gentile to perform domestic chores forbidden to Jews on Shabbath' (< שַׁבָּת *šabbåṯ* + גּוֹי *gōy* 'non-Jew'). Yiddish also features a number of compounds (pseudo-attributions or pseudo-annexations) that take an external plural ending, e.g., *yontoyvim* 'holidays' (< יוֹם טוֹב *yōm ṭōḇ* 'good day' (SG)) or *ameratsim* 'ignoramuses' (< עַם הָאָרֶץ *ʕam hå-ʔåreṣ* 'people of the land'); the latter term is also prominent in Judezmo (cf. Bunis 1993; this volume).

Often, doublets of Hebrew-Aramaic based and Germanic based words exist. According to Kahn (2016: 694f.), the difference may lie in a contrast between (1) a religious and a non-religious meaning, (2) a pejorative vs. a neutral meaning, or (3) a more general vs. a specific meaning; alternatively, true synonymy may obtain (4):

(1)	ספֿר	*seyfer*	'Jewish religious book	בוך	*bukh*	'[secular] book'
(2)	אכלען	*akhlen*	'to eat gluttonously'	עסן	*esn*	'to eat' (neutral)
(3)	חלומען	*kholemen*	'to dream'	טרויען	*troymen*	'to dream (of an ideal)'
(4)	חבֿר	*khaver*	'friend'	פֿרײַנט	*fraynt*	'friend'

An even more differentiated case is שאלה *shayle* 'Jewish legal question' (Hebrew) vs. קשיא *kashe* 'philosophical question//problem' (Aramaic) vs. פֿראַגע *frage* 'question (general request for information)' (Germanic) (cf. Kahn 2016: 695).

Romance loanwords

Disregarding given names and toponyms, prominent Romance loanwords in Yiddish include the following:

בענטשן *bentshn* 'recite the grace after meals' (Jewish) < Latin *benedicere* 'to pray, bless'
דאַוונען *davnen* 'to pray' (Jewish) < Latin *divinus* 'divine'
ליינען *leynen* 'to read' < Old French *leyer* < Latin *legere* 'to read'
ניטל *nitl* 'Christmas' < Latin *natalis* 'born'

Further items include the following (cf. Beider 2015: 390ff.):

בראָטערן *brote(r)n/brete(r)n* 'embroider' < French *broder*
טאָלמע *tolm(e)* 'bridal canopy' < Latin/Greek *thalamus* 'inner room' (also in Judeo-French and Judezmo)
שאַרמען *shormen* 'to bewitch' < French *charmer*
ווירען *viren* 'to make lines' < French *virer*
WY פּילצל *piltsl* 'house maiden' < French *pucelle* 'maiden'

WY פּראַיען *prāyen* ‘to invite’ < French *prayer* ‘to ask’
SWY באַפען *bāfen* ‘to drink’ < Old French *beivre*

In the realm of onomastics, a prominent Romance Yiddish name is, e.g., Cohn-Bendit (containing the elements “priest” and “pray, bless”), the last name of a German-French politician and publicist.

On the morphological level, one has suggested that the plural morpheme *-(e)s* in Yiddish is of Romance origin.

Slavic loanwords

Among the most prominent Slavic loanwords are those designating family relations:
טאַטע *tate* ‘father, dad’, Protoslavic *tata*
מאַמע *mame* ‘mother’
זיידע *zeyde* ‘grandfather’, cf. Russian *дед* (*ded*) and Polish *dziadek*
באָבע (*bobe*) ‘grandmother’, Protoslavic *baba*

Max Weinreich has identified, *inter alia*, the following items as Polish loanwords in Yiddish:
בלאָנדזשען *blondzhen, blonken* (Polish *błądzić, błąkać się*) ‘to stray’
גאָמבע *gombe*/*gembe* (*gęba*) ‘chin’
גלאָמב *glomb* (*głąb*) ‘stalk’
דעמב *demb* (*dąb*) ‘oak’
דראָנג *drong* (*drąg*) ‘pole’
וואָנצע *vontse* (*wąsy*) ‘moustache’
ווענטקע *vent*(*k*)*e* (*wędka*) ‘fishing rod’
טעמפּ *temp* (*tępy*) ‘dull’
כראָמסקע *khromske* (< *chrząstka*) ‘cartilage’
לאָנקע *lonke* (*łąka*) ‘meadow’
פּאַראָנטקעס *parondkes* (*porządki*) ‘cleaning’
פּאַרענטש *parentsh* (*poręcz*) ‘railing’
פּלאָנטע(ר)ן *plonte*(*r*)*n* (*plątać*) ‘to confuse’
פּענטען *penten* (*pętać*) ‘to fetter’
פּענכער *penkher* (*pęcherz*) ‘bladder’
פּרענט *prent* (*pręt*) ‘rod’
קורטשענטע *kurtshente* (*kurczę*, plural: *kurczęta*) [dialect] ‘hen’
ראָנד *rond* (*rząd*) ‘row’

The typically Polish feature here is the retention of the nasalized vowel *ą* and *ę*, represented by an additional *n* in the Yiddish items.

Further terms are
אינדיק *indik* ‘turkey’, cognate to Polish *indyk*
בוריק *burik* ‘beet’, cf. Polish *burak* and Ukrainian *буряк* (*burják*)
גאָמלקע *gomlke* ‘cottage cheese’, cf. regional Polish *gomółka*
נעבעך *nebekh* ‘sadly, unfortunately’, cf. Old Polish *niebog*, from Proto-Slavic **nebogъ*

סאָד *sod* 'orchard', cf. Polish *sad*, Russian *сад* (*sad*)
פּלייצע *pleytse* 'upper body, shoulder', cf. Polish *plecy*, Proto-Slavic **pleťe* ('shoulder')
קישקע *kishke* 'intestines, bowel', cf. Polish *kiszka*, Russian *кишка́* (kišká), and Ukrainian *ки́шка* (*kýška*), ultimately from Proto-Slavic **kyša*, **kyšьka* ('intestine, stomach').

Beider (2015: 430f.) adduces the following lexical items, for which an Old Czech origin is plausible:
טרייבערן *treybern* 'to remove forbidden parts from meat to make it kosher' < Old Czech *třiebiti* 'to clean, uproot'
ביילִיק *beylik* 'white meat' < Old Czech *biel-* 'white'
זאָדיק *zodik* '(butchery) hindquarters' < Old Czech *zadek* 'behind, backside'
פּלייצע *pleytse* 'shoulder' < Old Czech *plecě*
פּאַרעווע *parev(e)* 'neither dairy, nor meat (food)' < Old Czech *párový* 'paired, two-fold'
פּיסק *pisk* 'mouth' < Old Czech *pysk* 'lip'

Function terms include
כאָטש *khotsh* 'at least, although', cf. Polish *choć* and Russian *хоть (xot')*

As already mentioned, Slavic suffixes such as *-nik* and *-ke* are also prominent in Yiddish.

Interesting, especially in the light of Yiddish being a "fusion language", are blends between Slavic and Germanic elements (and, of course, between Hebrew-Aramaic and Germanic elements, see below). Just as with Hebrew-Aramaic and French stems, Slavic stems can be followed by a German(ic) infinitive ending *-(e)n*, as in *blondzhen*, *blonken* (Polish: *błądzić*, *błąkać się*) 'to stray' above. The Yiddish term *pamelekh* 'slow', for example, represents a contamination of Germanic **gemēlekh* (StG *gemächlich*) and Polish *pomału* (cf. U. Weinreich 1955: 604). Idioms can likewise be composed of different elements, e.g., *bobe-mayse* 'old wives' tales', according to U. Weinreich (1955: 606) a calque of Slavic *babska historia*.

Faux amis / doublets as compared with standard German

When analyzing Yiddish texts, one has to be careful not to deduct the meaning of a given verb or noun automatically from Standard German (or a German dialect for that matter). Notable faux amis include:
shmekn: 'to smell' (Yiddish) vs. *schmecken* 'to taste' (StG)
farzukhn: 'to taste' (Yiddish) vs. *versuchen* 'to try' (StG)
yortsayt: 'anniversary of a death' (Yiddish) vs. *Jahreszeit* 'season' (StG)
makher: 'a fixer, an important person, a "hot shot"' (Yiddish) vs. *Macher* 'someone who does' (StG), e.g., *Uhrmacher* 'watchmaker' (as a loan in StG, the meaning "a person who gets things done" can also be understood in German)
shvitser: ' a person who boasts' (Yiddish) vs. *Schwitzer* 'a person who sweats' (StG)
vegn: 'on the topic of' (Yiddish) vs. *wegen* 'because of' (StG)

Faux amis / doublets as compared with modern Hebrew

Similar doublets also exist in Hebrew itself, marked by a (slightly) different pronunciation or different stress:

mašqé 'something to drink' (Hebrew) vs. *mášqe* 'a(n alcoholic) drink' (Kutscher 1982: 229f.)
moser 'a person who transmits' vs. *moyser* 'a traitor (within the Jewish community)'
taxlit 'goal, purpose' (Hebrew) vs. *tax(e)les* 'final negotiation process'

Lexical impact on modern standard German and dialects

Just as Yiddish has had a lexical impact on German dialects and jargons (notably *Rotwelsch*), it has also left its traces in the standard language. This goes beyond the observation that a considerable cultural stock of Biblical Hebrew nouns have entered standard German in religious or other cultural context, as evidenced by terms such as אָמֵן *ʔā̊mēn* ('verily') 'Amen', מַצָּה *maṣṣā̊* 'Matze', 'unleavened bread', שִׁבֹּלֶת *šibbōlɛṯ* '(corn) ear', 'Schibbolet', 'decisive factor, not just in linguistics'. A number of terms, however, are part and parcel of standard German precisely in their Yiddish form, e.g., *Chuzpe* 'insolence' < חֻצְפָּה *ḥuṣpā̊*, *Dalles* 'dire straits' < דַּלּוּת *dallūṯ* ('poverty'), *Ische* 'young woman, girl' < אִשָּׁה *ʔiššā̊*, *Maloche* 'work' < מְלָאכָה *məlā̊ḵā̊*, *meschugge* 'crazy' < מְשֻׁגָּע *məšuggā̊ʕ*, *Mischpoke* 'family, group' < מִשְׁפָּחָה *mišpā̊ḥā̊*, *Schabbes* 'Saturday' < שַׁבָּת *šabbā̊ṯ*, *Schickse* 'Christian young woman' < שֶׁקֶץ *šɛqɛṣ* ('s.th. revolting'), *Tacheles* 'final details in a negotiating process' < תַּכְלִית *taḵlīṯ* ('goal, purpose'). In other cases, Hebrew stems have been integrated into the German morphological system, e.g., *(be-) dibbern* 'to talk (about)' < דִּבֵּר *dibbēr* ('he said').

Other Hebrew terms and expressions have been adapted in a way that they phonologically overlap with preexisting and etymologically totally unrelated German terms and expressions. Examples of single terms include *Moos*, *Mäuse*, or *Most* 'money' < מָעוֹת *mā̊ʕōṯ* ('small mints'), in a popular association with *Moos* 'moss', *Mäuse* 'mice', and *Most* 'must' ('new wine'), or *Kluft* 'clothes' קְלִפָּה *qəlippā̊* ('shell'), in a popular association with *Kluft* 'cleavage'. The classical examples of whole expressions borrowed in this way are *Hals- und Beinbruch* (a positive wish), properly "success and blessing" < הַצְלָחָה וּבְרָכָה *haṣlā̊ḥā̊ u-ḇrā̊ḵā̊*, in popular etymological association with "breaking neck and leg(s)", *es zieht wie Hechtsuppe* 'it is draughty' < הֵיךְ סוּפָה *hēḵ sūpā̊* ('like a hurricane'), in popular etymological association with "pike soup" (cf. Althaus 2006: 157f.), and *einen guten Rutsch* (ACC) 'a New Year's wish' < רֹאשׁ *rō(ʔ)š* ('head, beginning [of the year]'), in popular etymological association with "good slipping".

Lexical impact on English

A study by Schultz (2019), based on the Oxford English Dictionary, analyzes about 290 Yiddish loanwords in (mainly American) English. The following categories are suggested by the author: (1) language and linguistics, (2) criminality (3) entertainment and leisure activities, (4) gastronomy, (5) faith and religion, and (6) people and everyday life. Derogatory terms could be added to this list. In the following, only a few terms, not previously mentioned, are given (cf. also the contribution by Sarah Bunin Benor in this volume):

bagel: a ring-shaped bread roll made by boiling or steaming, and then baking, the dough (בייגל *beygl*)
bris: the circumcision of a male child (ברית *bris* < Hebrew בְּרִית *bərīṯ* 'covenant')
klezmer: a musical tradition of the Ashkenazi Jews in Eastern Europe (כליזמר or קלעזמער, < Hebrew כְּלִי *kəlī* 'tool, vessel' + זֶמֶר *zemer* 'singing')
latke: potato pancake, especially during Hanukkah (לאַטקע < Russian латка *latka* 'pastry/patch' or Ukrainian оладка *oladka* 'pancake/fritter'
nudnik: a pest, "pain in the neck", a bore (נודניק *nudnik*, from נודיען *nudyen* 'to bore'; cf. Polish: *nudny* 'boring, annoying'
shmuck: a contemptible or foolish person; a jerk (שמאָק *shmok* 'penis, fool')
shtick: a comic theme; a defining habit or distinguishing feature or business (שטיק *shtik* 'piece'; cf. German *Stück* 'piece')
tumler: 'entertainer, master of ceremonies' from טומלען, *tumlen* 'make a racket'; cf. German *(sich) tummeln* 'go among people'
yarmulke: skullcap worn by observant Jews (יאַרמלקע *yarmlke*, from Polish *jarmułka* and Ukrainian ярмулка (< Turkish *yağmurluk* 'raincoat, oilskin')
zaftig 'full-figured' (זאַפֿטיק *zaftik* 'juicy'; cf. German *saftig* 'juicy')

Lexical and stylistic impact on modern Hebrew

Just as Yiddish had always coexisted with Hebrew in the religious and traditional study sphere, it coexisted culturally with revived Hebrew in the Haskala period, as authors such as Mendele and Bialik published in both languages. A phonological feature is the penultimate stress on many Hebrew proper names, e.g., חנה *x̱ána* 'Hannah'. On the morphological level, modern oppositions in the binyan system may be explained by recourse to Yiddish aspectual prefixes such as e.g., -פֿאַר *far-*, -צע *tse-*, -אָנ *on-*, -דער *der-*) (cf. Farstey 2013: 1027). Yiddish suffixes are used to express the diminutive and endearment, e.g., קטנצ'יק *qaṭančiq* 'little thing/person' and אבאלֶה *ʔabale* 'dad (endearment)'. Yiddish terms in colloquial registers of modern Hebrew include *bis* 'bite (of food)' (alternating with native נגיסה *negisa*) and שלוק *šluq* 'sip'(alternating with native לגימה *legima*). געוואַלד *gevald* 'help!' (lit. "violence") and נעבעך *nebex* 'poor, unfortunate' are examples of Yiddish terms occurring also in modern literary Hebrew (cf. again Farstey 2013: 1028).

In the realm of slang, especially sexually loaded vocabulary and slurs, Yiddish also plays a prominent role (cf. notably Ben Israel 2011). The term נודניק *nudniq*, for instance, refers to a boring and/or obnoxious person. The iminuitve form פייגעלע *feygele* ('little bird') may be used as a derogatory term for homosexuals. The term שמוק *šmoq* 'prick', whose etymology is debated, either from Old Polish *smok* 'dragon' (cf. Bulgarian *smok* 'grass snake') or German *Schmuck* 'embellishment', refers to a contemptible person. The Yiddish-based term שטרונגול *šṭrungul* '(large) prick' constitutes the base of the verb לשטרנגל *le-šṭrangel* 'to screw someone to the bone' (not necessarily in a sexual sense) (Ben Israel 2011: 44).

The Yiddish hypocoristic *šm-* echo pattern (cf., e.g., Southern 2005) is also found in Israeli Hebrew. Former Prime Minister Menachem Begin, for instance, once referred to the United Nations (in Hebrew אומות מאוחדות *ʔumot meʔux̱adot*) as *ʔum šmum*.

Excursus on Western Yiddish

Western Yiddish is quite diversified, and often its analysis is complicated by ambiguities in the Hebrew script. What is of help are manuals in transcription (e.g., Callenberg 1736), which in spite of *mala fide* intentions (ridiculing) or anti-Semitic undertone, provide information regarding the pronunciation. Also one has noted the somewhat artificial style (oriented at standard German models) of some older Western Yiddish texts. Western Yiddish texts exhibit more similarities with (groups of) particular local varieties (cf. the Franconian and Swiss examples below), without, however, overlapping with a specific dialect alone. What remains is the strong fusion language character of these documents.

In any event, there are clear differences between Western and Eastern Yiddish, in spite of "the (original) unity of Western and Eastern Yiddish" (cf. Fleischer 2014a) or as a result of an ultimately polygenetic scenario, depending on the view one takes. More recent lexical isoglosses between Western Yiddish and Eastern Yiddish include the following (cf. Katz 1983: 1025):

Western Yiddish	Eastern Yiddish	gloss
bárkhes/bérkhes	*khále*	'Shabbath bread'
méme	*máme*	'mother'
éte	*táte*	'father'
fråle	*bóbe*	'grandmother'
hárle	*zéyde*	'grandfather'
óumern	*tseyln sfire*	'to count the 49 days between Pesach and Shavuot'
orn	*dav(e)nen*	'to pray'
shnodern	*menader zeyn*	'to commit oneself to contribute'
tetshn	*blozn shoyfer*	'to play ("blow") the Shofar'
tfile	*sider*	'prayer book'
trendl	*dreydl*	'teetotum'

The pronunciation of the letter ח *ḥet* is a major phonological *shibbolet* between Western and Eastern Yiddish. In the West (the Rhineland, Alsace, Swabia, Switzerland, Franconia, and a large part of Bavaria), it was pronounced [h], thus similar to or in fact identical with the pronunciation of ה *he*. In the East (Austria, the town of Regensburg, Bohemia-Moravia, Eastern Germany, Hungary, and Poland), is was pronounced as a velar [x], like a postvocalic fricative or unpointed כ *kaf*. This gave rise to the distinction in the literature between *Bne Hes* and *Bne Ḵes*, in reference to the Biblical Hebrew expression בְּנֵי חֵת *bənē ḥēṯ* 'children of Heth, Hittites' in Gen 23.3–20 (cf. Beider 2013: 373). The differences between the two groups also affect a number of other names of letters.

Interestingly, Western Yiddish has also had an impact on the speech of non-Jewish speakers. A *cause célèbre* is the (by now extinct) language of cattle traders in and around the Franconian village of Schopfloch, known as "Lachoudisch" (cf., e.g., Matras 1996 and Hofmann 1998). The term "Lachoudisch" is coined after לשון־קודש *loshn-*

qoydesh 'holy tongue', referring to the wealth of Hebrew terms and idioms in the jargon. Here is an illustration (example due to Alfred Klepsch):

Ich	*hob*	*bei*	*dene*	*Kaffriechem*	*hej*	*Bores*	*und*	*schnej*	*Ejgele*	*kannicht.*
1SG	have.PRS.1SG	at	DEM.PL	peasant.PL.DAT^H	five^H	cow.PL^H	and	two^H	little_calf.PL^H	buy.PPP^H

I bought five cows and two little calfs from these peasants.

This short sentence in condensed form contains six Hebrew-Yiddish elements, *Kaffriechem* 'peasants' (based on כְּפָר *kəp̄år* 'village'), *hej* 'five' (the letter ה *hē,* "5"), *Bores* 'cows' (< פָּרוֹת *pårōṯ*), *schnej* 'two' (< שְׁנֵי *šənē*), *Ejgele* 'little calf' (עֵגֶל *ʕēḡel*), with the impression of an iminutive, and *kannicht* 'bought', properly 'I bought' (קָנִיתִי *qånīṯī*). It is especially intriguing that the Hebrew final verb *qånīṯī* is integrated into a fictitious Germanic past participle passive.

In modern Franconian (just as in other parts of Germany), terms such as *Ische*, in the sense of "girlfriend" *and Schiggsn*, used in a derogatory way for women in general, are not unusual.

3. Sample texts

The following text samples are ordered and structured as follows. The first five text samples, from Biblical, literary (including one example of poetry), scholarly, and pedagogical sources illustrate Eastern Yiddish (Yiddish par excellence). The subsequent five text samples illustrate the history of Yiddish from its earliest sources in the times of Middle High German, which could still be labeled "Judeo-German", over two classical texts all the way to two texts from the nineteenth and twentieth century, respectively. While the transcription of the older texts, just as of the more recent Western Yiddish texts, follows the transcription in the scholarly editions, all other texts are transcribed (or "normalized" in Aronson's (1996) terminology) in a YIVO-like manner.

3.1 The first five verses of Genesis 1 (Blumgarten 1928: 1)

The first sample represents a relatively late Yiddish text, the beginning of Solomon Blumgarten's (known by the pen name "Yehoash") Yiddish rendition of the beginning of Genesis 1 (cf. also Kahn 2016: 709f.).

בְּרֵאשִׁית בָּרָא אֱלֹהִים אֵת הַשָּׁמַיִם וְאֵת הָאָרֶץ׃ 1
אין אָנהייב האָט גאָט באַשאַפֿן דעם הימל און די ערד 1

In	*onheyb*	*hot*	*got*	*bashafn*	*dem*	*himl*	*un*	*di*	*erd*
in	beginning	have.3SG.PRS	God	create.PPP	DEF.M.ACC	heaven	and	DEF.F	earth

1 In the beginning God created the heaven and the earth

וְהָאָרֶץ הָיְתָה תֹהוּ וָבֹהוּ וְחֹשֶׁךְ עַל־פְּנֵי תְהוֹם
און די ערד איז געווען וויסט און ליידיק,

Un	*di*	*erd*	*iz*	*geven*	*vist*	*un*	*leydik*
and	DEF.F	earth	be.3SG.PRS	be.PPP	desert	and	empty

2 Now the earth was unformed and void,

און פֿינצטערניש איז געווען אויפֿן געזיכט פֿון תּהום
un fintsternish iz geven oyfn gezikht fun thom[1]
and darkness be.3SG.PRS be.PPP on.DAT face of deep_ocean[H]
and darknes was upon the face of the deep;

וְר֣וּחַ אֱלֹהִ֔ים מְרַחֶ֖פֶת עַל־פְּנֵ֥י הַמָּֽיִם׃ 2
, און דער גײַסט פֿון גאָט האָט געשוועבט אויפֿן געזיכט פֿון די וואַסערן 2
un der gayst fun got hot geshvebt oyfn gezikht fun di vasern
and DEF.M spirit of God have.3SG.PRS hover.PPP on.DAT face of DEF.PL water.PL
and the spirit of God hovered over the face of the waters.

וַיֹּ֥אמֶר אֱלֹהִ֖ים יְהִ֣י א֑וֹר
האָט גאָט געזאָגט: זאָל ווערן ליכט.

Hot got gezogt: zol vern likht
have.3SG.PRS God say.PPP shall.3SG.PRS become.INF light
3 And God said: "Let there be light."

וַֽיְהִי־אֽוֹר׃ 3
און עס איז געוואָרן ליכט 3

Un es iz gevorn likht
and 3SG.NT be.3SG.PRS become.PPP light
And there was light.

וַיַּ֧רְא אֱלֹהִ֛ים אֶת־הָא֖וֹר כִּי־ט֑וֹב
און גאָט האָט געזען דאָס ליכט אַז עס איז גוט;
Un got hot gezen dos likht az es iz gut
and God have.3SG.PRS see.PPP DEF.NT light COMP 3SG.NT be.3SG.PRS good
4 And God saw the light, that it was good;

וַיַּבְדֵּ֣ל אֱלֹהִ֔ים בֵּ֥ין הָא֖וֹר
און גאָט האָט פֿאַנאַנדערגעשיידט צווישן דעם ליכט
un got hot fanandergesheydt tsvishn dem likht
and God have.3SG.PRS divide.PPP between DEF.NT.DAT light
and God divided the light

וּבֵ֥ין הַחֹֽשֶׁךְ׃ 4
און צווישן דער פֿינצטערניש 4
un tsvishn der fintsternish
and between DEF.F.DAT darkness
from the darkness.

וַיִּקְרָ֨א אֱלֹהִ֤ים ׀ לָאוֹר֙ י֔וֹם
און גאָט האָט גערופֿן דאָס ליכט טאָג,
Un got hot gerufn dos likht tog
and God have.3SG.PRS call.PPP DEF.NT light day
5 And God called the light Day,

וְלַחֹ֖שֶׁךְ קָ֣רָא לָ֑יְלָה
און די פֿינצטערניש האָט ער גערופֿן נאַכט.
un di fintsternish hot er gerufn nakht
and DEF.F.ACC darkness have.3SG.PRS 3SG.M call.PPP night
and the darkness He called Night.

1 Hebrew תְּהוֹם *təhōm* 'ocean, chaos'.

וַֽיְהִי־עֶ֥רֶב

און עס איז געווען אָוונט

Un es iz geven ovnt

and 3SG.NT be.3SG.PRS be.PPP evening

And there was evening

וַֽיְהִי־בֹ֖קֶר י֥וֹם אֶחָֽד׃ 5

און עס איז געווען פֿרימאָרגן, איין טאָג 5

un es iz geven frimorgn eyn tog

and 3SG.NT be.3SG.PRS be.PPP early_morning one.M day

and there was morning, one day.

3.2 A literary prose excerpt (cf. Erlikh 1977: 49; Aronson 1996: 740f.)

The second sample is taken from the exemplary overview of Yiddish orthography by Aronson (1996). The excerpt is found in *Khelemer dertseylungen* 'Stories from Khelem' by Borekh Mortkhe Erlikh.

נאָך דער חתנה פֿון גרשמען מיט נחמהען

Nokh der khasene[2] *fun Gershemen mit Nekhomen*

after DEF.F.DAT wedding^{H} of Gershom.DAT with Nekhome.DAT

After the marriage of Gershom and Nekhome,

האָט זיך דאָס פּאָרפֿאָלק געלעבט שטיל און באַשיידן.

hot zikh dos porfolk gelebt shtil un basheydn.

have.3SG.PRS REFL DEF.NT couple live.PPP quiet and modest

the married couple lived quietly and modestly.

צו דער ריכטיקער צײַט איז נחמה געלעגן געוואָרן,

tsu der rikhtiker tsayt iz Nekhome gelegn gevorn,

at DEF.F.DAT right.F.DAT time be.3SG.PRS Nekhome lie.PPP become.PPP

After the proper time Nekhome gave birth,

געהאַט אַ ייִנגעלע און דער ברית איז פֿאָרגעקומען

gehat a yingele un der bris[3] *iz forgekumen*

have.PPP INDEF boy.IM and DEF.M circumcision^{H} be.3SG.PRS occur.PPP

had a boy, and the ritual circumcision occurred

כדת משה וישׂראל. די שטיל געבענטשטע ליבע האָט זיך

ke-das[4] *Moyshe ve-Yisroel. di shtil gebenshte libe hot zikh*

as^{H}-religion.CS^{H} Moses and^{H}-Israel DEF.F quiet bless.PPP love have.3SG.PRS REFL

according to the law of Moses and Israel. A quietly blessed love

2 Hebrew חֲתֻנָּה *ḥătunnā̊* 'wedding'.

3 Hebrew בְּרִית מִילָה *bərīṯ mīlā̊* '(ritual) circumcision'.

4 Hebrew דַּת *daṯ* 'religion'.

אאַרויסגעריסן פֿון דער פֿרום־צניעטדדיקער געצוימטקייט

aroysgerisn fun der frum-tsniesdiker[5] *getsoymtkeyt*
tear_out.PPP from DEF.F.DAT pious-virtuous[H].F.DAT decency
arose from their pious and virtuous restraint

און האָט געאַנקערט אן דער פֿרייד פֿון זייער בשותפותדקן

un hot geankert in der freyd fun zeyer beshutfesdikn[6]
and have.3SG.PRS anchor.PPP in DEF.F.DAT joy of POSS.3PL common[H].M.DAT
and became anchored in the joy of their common

ייִנגלע מענדעלע -- אַזוי האָבן זיי אים א נאָמען געגעבן.

yingele Mendele azoy hobn zey im a nomen gegebn.
boy.IM Mendele thus have.3PL.PRS 3PL 3SG.DAT INDEF name give.PPP
boy Mendele – so they had named him.

די עלטרן פֿוןביידע צדדים, סײַ פון קאָצק אונג סײַ פֿון כעלעם,

di eltern fun beyde tsodim,[7] *say fun kotsk un say fun khelem,*
DEF.PL parents of both side.PL[H] be.it of Kotsk and be.it of Khelem
Their parents from both sides, both from Kotsk and from Khelem (two Polish towns),

האָבן גהאַט פֿון זיי נחת.

hobn gehat fun zey nakhes.[8]
have.3PL.PRS have.PPP from 3PL pleasure[H]
had pleasure from them.

3.3 A Yiddish poem by Mordechai Gebirtig (cf. Jaldati and Rebling 1985: 176–179)

The third sample is a famous poem by Mordechai Gebirtig (1877–1942), who was murdered in the Cracow ghetto in 1942. He composed this song (both lyrics and music) in 1938, in reaction to a pogrom in the Polish town of Przytyk. The song is found in various anthologies.

ס'ברענט! ברידערלעך, ס'ברענט!

s'brent! briderlekh, s'brent!
3SG.NT'burn.3SG.PRS brother.IM.PL 3SG.NT'burn.3SG.PRS
It is burning, dear brothers, it is burning.

אוי, אונדזער אָרעם שטעטל נעבעך ברענט!

oy, undzer orem shtetl nebekh brent!
EXCL POSS.1PL poor city.DIM unfortunately[Pol] burn.3SG.PRS
Our poor little town, a pity, burns!

בייזע ווינטן מיט ירגזון

beyze vintn mit yirgozn[9]
evil.PL wind.PL with rage[H]
Evil winds blow with rage,

5 Hebrew צָנוּעַ *ṣā̊nūaʕ* 'modest'.
6 Hebrew שֻׁתַּף *šuttap̄* 'he/it was shares'.
7 Hebrew צְדָדִים *ṣəḏā̊ḏīm* 'sides'.
8 Hebrew נַחַת *naḥaṯ* 'pleasure'.
9 Hebrew רֹגֶז *rōḡɛz* 'rage'.

רײַסן, ברעכן און צעבלאָזן

raysn, brekhn un tseblozn
tear.3PL.PRS break.3PL.PRS and blow_away.3PL.PRS
Tear, break, and blow away.

שטאַרקער נאָך די ווילדע פֿלאַמען,

shtarker nokh di vilde flamen,
strong.COMPAR even DEF.PL wild.PL flame.PL
The wild flames are even stronger,

אַלץ אַרום שוין ברענט!

alts arum shoyn brent!
everything around already burn.3SG.PRS
Everything around already burns.

[פּזמון]
און איר שטייט און קוקט אַזוי זיך

[chorus]
un ir shteyt un kukt azoy zikh
and 2PL stand.2PL.PRS and look.2PL.PRS like_that REFL/self
And you stand and look like this

מיט פֿאַרלייגטע הענט,

mit farleygte hent,
with fold.PPP.PL hand.PL
With folded hands

און איר שטייט און קוקט אַזוי זיך –

un ir shteyt un kukt azoy zikh
and 2PL stand.2PL.PRS and look.2PL.PRS like_that REFL/self
And you stand and look like this

אונדזער שטעטל ברענט ...

undzer shtetl brent ...
POSS.1PL city.DIM burn.3SG.PRS
(While) our little town burns.

ס'ברענט! ברידערלעך, ס'ברענט!

s'brent! briderlekh, s'brent!
3SG.NT'burn.3SG.PRS brother.IM.PL 3SG.NT'burn.3SG.PRS
It is burning, dear brothers, it is burning.

אוי, אונדזער אָרעם שטעטל נעבעך ברענט!

oy, undzer orem shtetl nebekh brent!
EXCL POSS.1PL poor city.DIM unfortunately[Pol] burn.3SG.PRS
Our poor little town, a pity, burns!

ס'האָבן שוין די פֿײַערצונגען

s'hobn shoyn di fayertsungen
3SG.NT'have.3PL.PRS already DEF.PL firetongue.PL
The tongues of the fire have already

דאָס גאַנצע שטעטל אײַנגעשלונגען –

dos gantse shtetl ayngeshlungen –
DEF.NT whole city.DIM devour.PPP
Swallowed the entire little town.

און די בייזע ווינטן הוזשען,

un di beyze vintn huzshen,
and DEF.PL evil.PL wind.PL blow.3PL.PRS
And the evil winds are blowing,

ס׳גאַנצע שטעטל ברענט!

s'gantse shtetl brent!
DEF.NT'whole city.DIM burn.3SG.IPF
The entire little town is burning!

[פזמון]
און איר שטייט און קוקט אַזוי זיך...

[chorus]
un ir shteyt un kukt azoy zikh
and 2PL stand.2PL.PRS and look.2PL.PRS like_that REFL/self
And you stand and look like this

ס׳ברענט! ברידערלעך, ס׳ברענט!

s'brent! briderlekh, s'brent!
3SG.NT'burn.3SG.PRS brother.IM.PL 3SG.NT'burn.3SG.PRS
It is burning, dear brothers, it is burning.

אוי, עס קען חלילה קומען דער מאָמענט

oy, es ken kholile[10] *kumen der moment*
EXCL 3SG.NT can.3SG.PRS beware^H come.INF DEF.M moment
O, beware, the moment can come,

אונדזער שטאָט מיט אונדז צוזאַמען

undzer shtot mit undz tsuzamen
POSS.1PL city with 1PL.DAT together
Where our city together with us

זאָל אויף אַש אַוועק אין פֿלאַמען,

zol oyf ash avek in flamen,
shall.3SG.IPF on ash away in flame.PL
Shall be [on] ash, gone away in flames,

בלײַבן זאָל – ווי נאָך אַ שלאַכט –

blaybn zol– vi nokh a shlakht –
remain.INF shall.3SG.PRS as after INDEF battle
As after a battle shall remain

נאָר פוסטע, שוואַרצע ווענט.

nor puste, shvartse vent.
only empty.PL black.PL wall.PL
Just empty black walls.

[פזמון]
און איר שטייט און קוקט אַזוי זיך...

[chorus]
un ir shteyt un kukt azoy zikh
and 2PL stand.2PL.PRS and look.2PL.PRS like_that REFL/self
And you stand and look like this

10 Hebrew חָלִילָה *ḥålīlå* 'God beware'.

ס׳ברענט! ברידערלעך, ס׳ברענט!

s'brent! briderlekh, s'brent!
3SG.NT'burn.3SG.PRS brother.IM.PL 3SG.NT'burn.3SG.PRS
It is burning, dear brothers, it is burning.

די הילף איז נאָר אין אײַך אליין געווענדט.

di hilf iz nor in aykh aleyn gevendt.
DEF.F help be.3SG.PRS only in 2PL.DAT alone turn.PPP
You are the only source of help.

אויב דאָס שטעטל איז אײַך טײַער,

oyb dos shtetl iz aykh tayer,
if DEF.NT city.DIM be.3SG.PRS 2PL.DAT precious
If you value your little town,

נעמט די כּלים – לעשט דאָס פֿײַער,

nemt di keylim[11] – lesht dos fayer,
take.PL.IPT DEF.PL tool/vessel.PL^H extinguish.PL.IPT DEF.NT fire
Take up the tools to put out the fire,

לעשט מיט אײַער אייגן בלוט,

lesht mit ayer eygn blut,
extinguish.PL.IPT with POSS.2PL own blood
Put out the fire with your own blood.

באַווײַזט, אַז איר דאָס קענט!

bavayzt, az ir dos kent!
prove.PL.IPT COMP 2PL DEF.NT can.2PL.PRS
Prove that you are able to do that!

[פזמון אחרון]
שטייט ניט, ברידער, אָט אַזוי זיך

[final chorus]
shteyt nit, brider, ot azoy zikh
stand.PL.IPT NEG brother.PL there like_this REFL/self
Don't stand there like this

מיט פֿאַרלייגטע הענט,

mit farleygte hent,
with fold.PPP.PL hand.PL
With folded hands,

שטייט ניט, ברידער, לעשט דאָס פֿײַער –

shteyt nit, brider, lesht dos fayer –
stand.PL.IPT NEG brother.PL extinguish.PL.IPT DEF.NT fire
Don't stand (around), brothers, put out the fire –

אונדזער שטעטל ברענט!

undzer shtetl brent ...
POSS.1PL city.DIM burn.3SG.PRS
Our little town is burning ...

11 Hebrew כֵּלִים *kēlīm* 'vessels, tools'.

3.4 A modern scholarly text excerpt by Max Weinreich (cf. Frakes 2004: xliv f.)

The following sample is due to the doyen of Yiddish studies, Max Weinreich, and shows Yiddish in its role as a scholarly metalanguage.

ווען מיר שוין זוכה זײַן צו אַן 'אַלט-ייִדישער טעקסט-ביבליאָטעק',
ven vir shoyn zoykhe[12] *zayn tsu an alt-yidisher tekst-bibliotek*
if 1PL already be_worthy.PTCP.SG.M^H be.1SG.PRS to INDEF old-Yiddish.F.DAT text-library
If we live to see [the publication of] an Old Yiddish Text library

וואָס זאָל געבן איטליכן לעזער א השגה וועגן אונזר האָב-און-גוטס,
vos zol gebn etlikhen lezer a hasoge[13] *vegen unzer hob-un-guts,*
REL shall.3SG.PRS give.INF every.DAT reader INDEF idea^H about POSS.1PL have-and-good
that can give every reader an idea of our possession (heritage),

דאַן וועט זיך ארויסווײַזן, אז דאָס איז גאָרניט
dan vet zikh aroysvayzn, az dos iz gornit
then AUX.3SG.PRS REFL.3 become_clear.INF COMP PRON.NT be.3SG.PRS not.at.all
then it will become clear that this is not at all

'דאָס ביסל אָרעמקייט', ווי מען האָט זיך אײַנגעוויינט צו טראַכטן,
dos bisl oremkeyt vi men hot zikh ayngeveynt tsu trakhtn,
DEF.NT little ("bite.DIM") poverty as one.INDEF have.3SG.PRS REFL.3 get_used_to.PPP to think.INF
that little poverty (stricken pittance) that one has got used to think,

נאָר אַז ייִדן האָבן באַוויזן צו באַשאַפן אין 15טן, 16טן, 17טן,
nor az yidn hobn bavayzn tsu bashafn in 15tn 16tn 17tn
only COMP Jew.PL have.3PL.PRS prove.PPP to create.INF in 15.ORD.DAT 16.ORD.DAT 17.ORD.DAT
rather that Jews have documented that they created in the 15th, 16th, 17th,

18טן י״ה אַ ליטעראַטור אַ ברייטע, א ווײַט-פֿאַרצווײַגטע,
18th yorhundert a literature a breyte a vayt-fartsvaygte,
18.ORD.DAT century INDEF literature INDEF broad.F INDEF wide-branch.PPP
and 18th century a broad multi-faceted literature

וואָס האָט באַפֿרידיגט זייערע גייַסטיגע באַדערפֿנישן.
vos hot bafridigt zeyere gaystige baderfnishn.
REL have.3SG.PRS satisfy.PPP POSS.3PL intellectual.PL need.PL
that satisfied their intellectual needs.

און ס'איז א גרויסער טעות, אז פֿאר ייִדישע גײַסטיגע באַדערפֿנישן
un s'iz a groyser toes[14] *az far yidishe gaystige baderfnishn*
and 3SG.NT'be.3SG.PRS INDEF big error^H COMP for Jewish.PL intellectual.PL need.PL
And it is a great error [to think] that for Jewish intellectual needs

12 Hebrew זוֹכֶה *zōk̲ɛ* 'deserving' (SG.M).

13 Hebrew הַשָּׂגָה *haśśā̊gā̊* 'reaching' (verbal noun), 'impression.'

14 Hebrew טָעוּת *ṭā̊ʕūṯ* 'error'.

זײַנען יעמאָלט גענוג געווען טײַטש-חומש און מוסר-ספֿרים.

zaynen jemolt genug geven taytsh-chumesh[15] *un muser-seforim.*[16]
be.3PL.PRS any.time enough be.PPP Yiddish-Pentateuch[H] and moral-religious.book.PL[H]
a Yiddish Pentateuch and ethical books would have ever sufficed.

ס'איז א ווילדע אײַנריידעניש, אַז ביז דער עמאַנסיפּאַציע

s'iz vilde aynreydnish az biz der emantsipatsiye
3SG.NT'be.3SG.PRS wild.F misconception ("in-talk") COMP until DEF.F.DAT emancipation
It is a wild misconception (to think) that until the (time of) the Emancipation

איז דער ייִד געווען כולו רוחניות און האָט נאָר געקלערט

iz der yid geven kull-o[17] *rukhnies*[18] *un hot nor geklert*
be.3SG.PRS DEF.M Jew be.PPP all-3SG.M[H] spirituality[H] and have.3SG.PRS only contemplate.PPP
the Jew consisted totally of spirituality and has only contemplated

וועגן תורה און מצוות. גאָט צו דאַנקען, די וועלט-פֿרעמדקײַט פֿון ייִד

vegen toyre[19] *un mitsves.*[20] *got tsu danken, di velt-fremdkayt fun yidn*
about Torah[H] and commandment.PL[H] God to thank.INF DEF.F world-remoteness of Jew.PL
the Torah and the commandments. Thank God, the unworldliness of Jews

איז אַלעמאָל געווען א סך קלענער, ווי מען פּרובֿט אונז

iz alemal geven a sakh[21] *klener, vi men provt*
be.3SG.PRS always be.PPP INDEF lot[H] little.COMPAR than one.INDEF try.3SG.PRS
has always been much smaller than one has tried

אײַנשמועסן, און דווקא די ייִדישע ליטעראַטור, וואו ס'האָט

unz aynshmuesn,[22] *un davke*[23] *di yidishe literatur, vo s'hot*
1PL.DAT make.hear[H].INF and precisely[H] DEF.F Yiddish.F literature where.REL 3SG.NT'have.3SG.PRS
to make us think, and precisely Yiddish literature, where

זיך אָפּגעשפּילט דאָס טאָג-טעגליכע לעבן פֿון ייִדישן פֿאָלק,

zikh opgeshpilt dos tag-teglikhe leben fun yidishn folk,
REFL.3 play.PPP DEF.NT day-daily life of Jewish.DAT people
the daily life of the Jewish people plays,

גיט אונז די בעסטע ראיות, אַז אין געטאָ האָט מען אויך געוואוסט,

git unz di beste rayes[24] *az in geto hot men oykh gevoust,*
give.3SG.PRS 1PL.DAT DEF.PL best.PL proof.PL COMP in ghetto have.3SG.PRS one.INDEF also know.PPP
provides us with the best proof that in the ghetto people also knew

15 Hebrew חָמֵשׁ *ḥåmēš* 'five'.
16 Hebrew מוּסָר *mūsår* 'ethics'; סְפָרִים *səp̄årīm* '(religious) books'.
17 Hebrew כֻּלּוֹ *kull-ō* 'all of him/it'.
18 Hebrew רוּחָנִיּוּת *rūḥånīyūṯ* 'spirituality'.
19 Hebrew תּוֹרָה *tōrå* 'education' (the Pentateuch).
20 Hebrew מִצְוֹות *miṣwōṯ* 'commandments'
21 Hebrew סָךְ *såḵ* 'a lot'.
22 Hebrew לְהַשְׁמִיעַ *lə-hašmīʕ* 'to make hear' or Hebrew שְׁמוּעוֹת *šəmūʕōṯ* 'talk'.
23 Hebrew-Aramaic דַּוְקָא *dawqå* 'of all things, precisely, (in) spite'.
24 Hebrew רְאָיוֹת *rəʔåyōṯ* 'proofs'.

וואָס הייסט ליבע אונ׳ לעבן און לעבנסלוסט. געוויס, די שרײַבער
vos heist libe un leben un lebenslust. gevis, di shrayber
what.REL mean.3SG.PRS love and life and lust_of_life surely DEF.PL writer.PL
what love and life and lust of life mean. Sure enough, the majority of authors

פֿון די ספֿרים זײַנען געווען דאָס רוב אַסקעטיש געשטימט —
fun di seforim zaynen geven dos rov[25] *asketish geshtimt* –
of DEF.PL religious.book.PL^{H} be.3PL.PRS be.PPP DEF.NT majority^{H} ascetic.(ADV) tune.PPP
of religious books were ascetically tuned –

אָבער דער ייִד פֿון אַ גאַנץ יאָר האָט געהאַט א געזונטן חוש
ober der yid fun a gants yor hot gehat a gezunt chush[26]
but DEF.M Jew of INDEF whole year have.3SG.PRS have.PPP INDEF healthy sense^{H}
but the secular Jew had a healthy sense

צום לעבן. און דאָס יונגוואַרג האָט זיך אַפֿילו
tsum leben. un dos yungvarg hot zikh afilu[27]
to.DEF.M.DAT life and DEF.NT young-people have.3SG.PRS REFL.3 even^{H}
of life. And the young people even

הינטער די געטאָ-מויערן געקווייקט מיטן ביסל זון,
hinter di geto-moyern gekvikt mitn bisl zun,
back DEF.PL ghetto-wall.PL rejoice.PPP with.INDEF little ("bite.DIM") sun
had a good time behind the ghetto walls with a little sun,

וואָס פֿלעגט אַהין אַרײַנדרינגן.
vos flegt ahin arayndringn.
REL use.3SG.PRS there intrude.INF
which used to enter there.

3.5 A modern pedagogical text (Yefroikin and Mark 1964: 5f.)

The following sample represents a pedagogical text of an intermediate level (3 = ג in a series) for young readers. In this case, a standard German translation is added as well for contrast, with an attempt to imitate Yiddish expressions that, however, are idiomatically much closer to Southern German dialects than to Standard German.

אַ פֿייגעלע
a feygele
INDEF bird.IM
A little bird (Ein Vögelein)

עס איז געווען פֿרײַטיק. מיר זײַנען געגאַנגען אַהיים,
es iz geven fraytik mir zaynen gegangen aheym,
3SG.NT be.1SG.PRS be.PPP Friday 1PL be.1PL.PRS go.PPP home
It was Friday (Es ist Freitag gewesen). We went home, (Wir sind heimgegangen,)

25 Hebrew רוֹב *rōḇ* 'majority'
26 Hebrew חוּשׁ *ḥūš* 'sense, feeling'.
27 Hebrew אֲפִלּוּ *ʔăp̄illū* 'even'.

עטלעכע ייִנגלער צוזאַמן. געגאַנגן זײַנען מיר גיך,

etlekhe yingler tsuzamen gegangen zaynen mir gikh
all.PL boy.DIM.PL together go.PPP be.1PL.PRS 1PL quickly
all boys together. (etliche Jünglein zusammen.)
We went quickly, (Gegangen sind wir schnell (“quick”/“keck”)),

ווײַל מיר זײַנען געווען הונגריק.

wayl mir zaynen geven hungrik
because 1PL be.1PL.PRS be.PPP hungry
because we were hungry. (weil wir hungrig gewesen sind.)

פלוצלינג האָט איינער פֿון אונדז אויסגעשריען: "אוי, אַ פֿייגעלע",

plutsling hot eyner fon undz oysgeshriyen oy a feygele
suddenly have.3SG.PRS one of 1PL.DAT exclaim.PPP oh INDEF bird.IM
Suddenly, one of us shouted (Plötzlich hat einer von uns ausgeschrien): “oh, a little bird”, (“oh, ein Vögelein”)

האָבן מיר זיך אַלע אָפּגעשטעלט. אַ קליין יונג פֿייגעלע

hobn mir zikh ale opgeshtelt a kleyn yung feygele
have.PL.PRS 1PL REFL all stop.PPP INDEF little young bird.IM
[and] we all stopped. (wir haben uns alle abgestellt.)

איז געזעסן אויף דער ערד. דאָס פֿייגעלע האָט געציטערט.

iz gezesn oyf der erd dos feygele hot getsitert
be.3SG.IPF sit.PPP on DEF.F.DAT earth DEF.NT bird.DIM have.3SG.PRS tremble.PPP
A little young bird sat on the ground. The little bird trembled.
(Ein kleines junges Vögelein ist auf der Erde gesessen. Das Vögelein hat gezittert.)

עס האָט געמאַכט מיט די פֿליגעלעך, אַבער ניט געקענט פליען.

es hot gemakht mit di fligelekh aber nit gekent fliyen
3SG.NT have.3SG.PRS do.PPP with DEF.PL wing.IM.PL but NEG be_able.PPP fly.INF
It has moved with the [its] little wings, (Es hat [Bewegungen] gemacht mit den Flügelein,) but it could not fly. (aber es hat nicht fliegen gekonnt.)

עס האָט געעפֿנט דאָס געלע שנעבעלע ווי אַ קליין קינד

es hot geefnet dos gele shnebele wi a kleyn kind
3SG.NT have.3SG.PRS open.PPP DEF.NT yellow beak.IM like INDEF little child
It opened the [its] yellow beak (Es hat das gelbe Schnäbelein geöffnet) like a little child (wie ein kleines Kind).

וואָס וויל עסן. מיר האָבן שטאַרק רחמנות געהאַט

vos vil esn mir hobn shtark raḥmones[28] *gehat*
REL want.3SG.PRS eat.INF 1PL have.PL.PRS strong pity[H] have.PPP
that wants to eat. (wie ein kleines Kind, das essen will.) We had strong pity
(Wir haben starkes Mitleid gehabt)

אויפֿן פֿייגעלע. מיר האָבן אָנגעהויבן טראַכטן:

oyf-n feygele mir hobn angehoybn trakhten
over-DEF.NT.DAT bird.IM 1PL have.PL.PRS begin.PPP (“lifted”) consider.INF
with the little bird. (mit dem Vögelein.) We started to consider:
(Wir haben angehoben zu trachten:)

28 Hebrew רַחְמָנוּת *raḥmā̊nūṯ* ‘pity’.

וואָס טוט מען מיטן פֿייגעלע? יאָסל האָט געזאָגט:

wos tut men mit-n feygele Yosl hot gezogt
what do.3SG.IPF one with-DEF.NT.DAT bird.IM Yosl have.3SG.PRS say.PPP
what does one with the little bird? (was tut man mit dem Vögelein?) Yosl said: (Yosl hat gesagt:)

"מע דאַרף עס לאָזן זיצן אויף דער ערד

me darf es lozn zitsn oyf der erd
one may.3SG.PRS 3SG.NT let.INF sit.INF on DEF.F.DAT earth
"one may let it sit on the ground" ("man darf es auf der Erde sitzen lassen")

ביז דעם פֿייגעלעס מאַמע וועט קומען".

bis dem feygele-s mame vet komen
until DEF.NT.DAT bird.DIM-GEN mom will.3SG.PRS come.INF
"until the mom of the little bird will come."
("bis dem Vögelein seine Mama kommen wird.")

דוד האָט געגעבן אַן עצה:

David hot gegebn an eytse[29]
David have.3SG.IPF give.PPP INDEF advice[H]
David advised: (David hat einen Rat gegeben:)

"זאָל מען עס געבן אַ וואָרף אין דער הייך,

zol men es gebn a vorf in der heykh
shall.3SG.PRS one 3SG.NT give.INF INDEF thrust in DEF.F.DAT height
"should one give it a thrust in the air" ("height"),
("soll man ihm einen Wurf in die Höhe geben")

וועט עס אַליין אַוועקפֿליִען". און הערשל האָט געזאָגט:

vet es aleyn avekfliyen un Hershl hot gezogt
will.3SG.PRS 3SG.NT alone fly_away.INF and Hershl have.3SG.PRS say.PPP
"it will fly away by itself" ("alone"). ("wird es alleine wegfliegen.") And Hershl said: (Und Hershl hat gesagt:)

"דאָס פֿייגעלע קען ניט פֿליִען. לאָמיר עס נעמען אַהיים".

dos feygele ken nit fliyen lo-mir es nemen aheym
DEF.NT bird.IM can.3SG.PRS NEG fly.INF let.JUSS-1PL 3SG.NT take.INF home
"the little bird cannot fly." ("das Vögelein kann nicht fliegen.") "Let us take it home".
("Laß es uns heimnehmen.")

מיר האָבן דאָס פֿייגעלע געבראַכט אַהיים.

mir hobn dos feygele gebrakht aheym
1PL have.3SG.PRS DEF.NT bird.IM bring.PPP home
We brought the little bird home. (Wir haben das Vögelein heimgebracht.)

מיר האָבן אַלע פֿאַרגעסן אַז מיר זײַנען הונגעריק.

mir hobn ale fargesn az mir zaynen hungerik
1PL have.3SG.PRS all forget.PPP COMP 1PL be.1PL.PRS hungry
We all forgot that we were hungry.
(Wir haben alle vergessen, daß wir hungrig sind (waren).)

29 Hebrew עֵצָה *ʕēṣå̄* 'advice'.

מיר האָבן געגעבן דעם פֿייגעלע וואַסער.

mir hobn gegebn dem feygele vaser
1PL have.3SG.PRS give.PPP DEF.NT.DAT bird.IM water
We gave the little bird water. (Wir haben dem Vögelein Wasser gegeben.)

אַבער דאָס פֿייגעלע האָט נאָר געציטערט בײַ אונדז אין די הענט.

aber dos feygele hot nor getsitert bey undz in di hent
but DEF.NT bird.IM have.3SG.PRS only tremble.PPP at 1PL.DAT in DEF.PL hand.PL
But the little bird only trembled in our hands.
(Aber das Vögelein hat nur gezittert bei uns in den Händen.)

דאָס פֿייגעלע האָט פֿאַרוואָרפֿן דאָס קעפּעלע

dos feygele hot farworfn dos kepele
DEF.NT bird.IM have.3SG.PRS misplace.PPP DEF.NT head.IM
The little bird misplaced the [its] little head (Das Vögelein hat das Köpflein verworfen)

אויף אַ זײַט, פֿאַרמאַכט די אייגעלעך. עס איז געווען טויט.

oyf a zayt, farmakht di eygelekh es iz gewen toyt
on INDEF side make.PPP DEF.PL eye.IM.PL 3SG.NT be.3SG.PRS be.PPP dead
to the side, [and] closed the [its] little eyes. It was dead.
(auf eine Seite, hat die Äugelein [zu] gemacht. Es ist tot gewesen.)

מיר האָבן אויסגעגראָבן אין הויף אַ טיף גריבעלע.

mir hobn oysgegrobn in hoyf a tif gribele
1PL have.3SG.PRS dig_out.PPP in courtyard INDEF deep pit.IM
We dug out a deep little pit in the courtyard.
(Wir haben im Hof ein tiefes Grübelein ausgegraben.)

מיר האָבן ארײַנגעלייגט דאָס פֿייגעלע אין גריבעלע און פֿאַרשאָטן מיט זאמד.

mir hobn arayngeleygt dos feygele in gribele un farshotn mit zamd
1PL have.3SG.PRS lay_in.PPP DEF.NT bird.IM in pit.IM and pour.PPP with sand
We placed the bird in the little pit and covered [it] with sand.
(Wir haben das Vögelein hineingelegt in [das] Grübelein und mit Sand verschüttet.)

איבער דעם האָבן מיר געשטעלט אַ ברעטעלע

iber dem hobn mir geshtelt a bretele
over DEF.NT.DAT have.3SG.PRS 1PL placed.PPP INDEF board.IM
Un top of it we placed a little board
(Über dem [Grübelein] haben wir ein Brettlein gestellt)

מיט אַן איפֿשריפֿט: "דאָ ליגט דאָס קליינע פֿייגעלע"

mit an oyfshrift do ligt dos kleyne feygele
with INDEF.F.DAT inscription there lie.3SG.PRS DEF.NT little bird.IM
with an inscription: (mit einer Aufschrift:) "there lies the little bird"
("da liegt das kleine Vögelein")

און אָנגעשריבן אַלע נעמען פֿון די קינדער וואָס זײַנען דערבײַ געווען:

un angeshribn ale nemen fun di kinder wos zaynen derbay gewen
and write_on.PPP all name.PL of DEF.PL child.PL REL be.3PL.PRS present be.PPP
and wrote all the names of the children that were present:
(und [wir haben] angeschrieben alle Namen von den Kindern, die dabei gewesen sind:)

בערל, יאָסל, דוד, הערשל.

Berl	*Yosl*	*Dovid*	*Hershl*
Berl	Yosl	David	Hershl

Berl, Yosl, David, Hershl.

3.6 An Old-Yiddish text: Dukus Horant (cf. Fuks 1957: 41; Ganz et al. 1964: 132f.; Dunphy 2007: 76)

This Old-Yiddish text dating back to the 14th century, based on the manuscript C.Y. revolving around the Hildesaga shows how Yiddish emerged from Middle High German dialects. According to Fuks (1957: xxxiv ff.), its linguistic features point to an Upper-German location. A rounding *a* > *o* can already be observed. On the other hand, *î* and *û* are not diphthongized, as in the Alemannic region. The following picture represents the beginning of the text (fol. 21r. of Codex C.Y., T.–S.10.K22).

עש ווש אין טוצן ריכן איין קוינק וויט ארקנט

ʕs	*uus*	*ʔin*	*tuš̯n*	*rikn*	*ʔiin*	*quniq*	*uuit*	*ʔrqnt*
Ez	*waz*	*in*	*tiutschen*	*rîchen*	*ein*	*kunic*	*wît*	*erkant,*
3SG.NT	be.3SG.PRET	in	German.PL.DAT	empire.PL.DAT	INDEF.M	king	wide(.ADV)	know.PPP

There was in German lands a famous king,

איין דעגן אלזא קונא איטנא ווש ער גננט

ʔiin	*dʕgn*	*ʔlsʔ*	*qunʔ*	*ʔitnʔ*	*uus*	*ʕr*	*gnnt*
ein	*degen*	*alsô*	*kuone*	*Etene*	*waz*	*er*	*genant.*
INDEF.M	epée/warrior	so	potent	PN	be.3SG.PRET	3SG.M	call.PPP

a most valiant hero Etene was his name

ער וויש מילדא און שונא

ʕr uus mildʔ ʔun šunʔ
Er waz milde unde schône,
3SG.M be.3SG.PRET mild and beautiful
He was generous and fair

ער טרוק דער אירן קרונא

ʕr truq dʕr ʔirn qrunʔ
er truog der êren krône.
3SG.M bear.3SG.PRET DEF.F.GEN honor.GEN crown
and bore the crown of honor.

3.7 Medieval West-Yiddish: Paris un Wiene (Verona 1594: fol. ב - ג; Timm 1996: 3–5, 7; Shmeruk 1996: 47f. and 51)

The next sample, equally an epos, was, according to Timm (1996: cxxxvii), probably composed between 1532 and 1553. Formally, it represents a poem in stanzas, a sort of love story between the protagonists in a chivalric setting. Timm uses a number of additional diacritical signs (in order to be able to reconstruct the original Hebrew orthography not featured in her book) and orients her transcription at German orthography. An unmarked <s> marks voiced /z/ (ז), while <ṡ> and <ś> mark s (ס) and ś (שׁ), respectively. The diphthong/digraph <וי> is rendered as *ö*, *ou*, or *ü*, depending on Middle High German correspondences. Letters not in italics reflect textual emendations by Timm. Here is the title page of the Verona manuscript (1594) (cf. Timm 1996: cli).

קיין מענש קונט שטין נאך גין פֿון שטט

1 *Kain mensch kunt šten noch gen fun štat*
no human.being can.3SG.PRET stand.INF nor go.INF from city
No human being could stand or go away

נוך אדליר נוך אקשׂ נאך ליבן

noch adeler noch okś noch leben,
nor eagle nor ox nor lion
nor eagle, ox or lion,

נוך קונט זיך רירן קיין בלט

noch kunt sich riren kain blat,
nor can.3SG.PRET REFL.3 move.INF no leaf
nor could a leaf move,

קיין די[נ]ג העט ענד נאך קענט זיך אן היבן

kain ding het end noch kent sich an-heben –
no thing have.3SG.PRS end nor can.3SG.CONJ2 REFL.3 begin.INF ("lift")
nor could could anything come to an end or begin –

אז זייא דען גוֹט דטר עז גישטט

es sei? den got, der es geštat,
3SG.NT be.3SG.CONJ1 because god REL.SG.M 3SG.NT allow.3SG.PRS
except for God, who would allow it,

אונ׳ איז זיין הייליקליכֿן נאמן עבן

un' is sein hailiklichen namen eben.
and be.3SG.PRS POSS.3SG(.DAT) holy.DAT name.DAT equal
and it is alright for his holy name.

ער בישאף דיא וועלט אויז נישט אזו קליגלך

er beschaf di? welt ous nischt aso klüglich;
3SG.M create.3SG.PRET DEF.F world out.of nothing so wise.ADV
He created the world from nothing in such a wise way;

דרום איז אך נישט ווידר זיין נאמן מויגליך

drum is ach nischt wider sein namen müglich.
therefore be.3SG.PRS also nothing against POSS.3SG.M name.ACC possible
therefore, nothing is possible against his will.

דרום ביט איך אינ׳ רויף אין אן

2 *Drum bit ich in un' rüf in an,*
Therefore beg.1SG.PRS 1SG 3SG.ACC and call.1SG.PRS 3SG.ACC to
Therefore I beg him an call upon him,

דאז ער מיט מיר אך לושׂ זיין ווילן

das er mit mir ach loś sein wilen,
COMP 3SG with 1SG.DAT also let.3SG.PRS POSS.3SG will.ACC
that he leaves his will also with me,

דאז איך דאז בוך אויז מאכֿן קאן

das ich das buch ous-machen kan,
COMP 1SG DEF.NT book finish.INF("out make") can.3SG.PRS
so that I can finish this book,

אז איך עז אין זין האב טון דער ווילן

as ich es in sin hab tun der-welen,
like 1SG 3SG.NT in sense have.1SG.PRS do.INF will.INF
as I like to do it,

און׳ הילף מיר אז ער הולף דען מאן

un' hilf mir, as er hulf den man,
and help.3SG.CONJ 1SG.DAT like 3SG help.1SG.PRET DEF.M.ACC man
and my he help me, like he helped the man,

דאז דיא גנץ וועלט איז נאך אים הילן

das di? ganz welt is noch im hilen,
COMP DEF.F whole world be.3SG.PRS yet in.DEF.NT.DAT ring.INF
that the whole world still rings,

דאז איך אז ער מיין ביכֿלן קיין ריימן

das ich as er mein bichlein kan reimen
COMP 1SG like 3SG POSS.1SG.M book.DIM can.1SG.PRS rhyme.INF
so that I can rhyme my book (endearing) like he (did)

און׳ אל דיא ריד אזו שמיטן און׳ ליימן

un' al di? red aso schmiten un leimen.
and all DEF.F speech so forge.INF and glue.INF
and forge and glue together all the speech.

אום דיזן מאן איז מיר וואל אנד

3 *Um disen man is mir wol and,*
because.of DEM.M.DAT man be.3SG.PRS 1SG.DAT well painful
This man worries me quite a bit,

אז ווער ער מיין פאטר אדר שוויעהר

as wer er mein fater oder schweher,
as.if be.3SG.CONJ.2 3SG POSS.1SG.M father or father_in_law
as if he were my father or father-in-law,

און דא ער זוך אוס דיזם לנד

un do er zoch ous disem land,
and when 3SG draw.3SG.PRET out.of DEM.NT.DAT land
and when he drew out of this land,

דו ליש איך אום אים מענכֿי טרעהר

do liś ich um im menche treher.
then let.1SG.PRET 1SG because.of 3SG.DAT some.PL tear.PL
I shed quite many tears because of him.

זיין נאמן טוט אים ניט אויף שנד

sein namen tut im nit ouf schand:
POSS.3SG.M name do.3SG.PRS 3SG.DAT NEG on shame
His name is no shame onto him:

איך מאן דען אלטן רבי אליה בעהר

ich man den alten rabi Elje Beher.
1SG think.1SG.PRS DEF.M.ACC old.M.ACC rabbi Eliya Baḥur (= Elia Levita)
I am talking about old Rabbi Eliya Baḥur.

זיין נמן לעבט אל צייט אונ׳ טוט ניט שטערבן

sein namen lebt al zeit un' tut nit šterben;
POSS.3SG.M name live.3SG.PRS all time and do.3SG.PRS NEG die.INF
His name lives forever and will not die;

דאז זיין דיא בויכֿר די ער האט טון דרוורבן

das sein diʔ bücher die er hot tun derwerben.
PRON.SG.NT be.3PL.PRS DEF.PL book.PL REL.PL 3SG have.3SG.PRS do.INF do.well.and.finish.INF
these are the books that he has finished.

ער האט אין דער הייליגי שפרוך

4 *Er hot in der hailige sprach*
3SG have.3SG.PRS in DEF.F.DAT holy.F language
In the holy language

זעקס אדר עכֿט שון לושׂן דרויקן

seks oder echt schon losen druken;
six or eight already let.INF print.INF
he has already made print six or eight [books];

דאז גוטשׂ איז גרושׂ דיא ער איז הוך

das gutś is groś, diʔ er is hoch,
DEF.NT good.NT be.3SG.PRS big DEF.F honor be.3SG.PRS high
the good is great, the honor is high,

אונ׳ נימנט קאן אים זיא צוקן

un' nimant kan im siʔ zuken.
and nobody can.3SG.PRS 3SG.DAT 3SG.F.ACC take_away.INF
and nobody can take them away from him.

זינט דער ווערדר מאן אוישׂ דעם לנד צוך

sint der werder man ouś dem land zoch,
since DEF.SG.M worthy man out.of DEF.SG.M.DAT land draw.3SG.PRET
since the worthy man drew from the land,

דו זיין מיר הוינליך און דיא קלוקן

do sein mir hünlich on diʔ kluken –
there be.1PL.PRS 1PL chicken.DIM at DEF.PL.F chick.PL
we are chicken upon the little chicks –

וויא וואל פֿיל לויט האלטן זיין ספֿרים ערליך

wiʔ-wol fil löut halten sein seforim erlich
although much people hold.3PL.PRS POSS.3PL religious.book.PL[H] honest(.ADV)
even though many people keep his religious books honestly

גלייך אז דיא זויא דיא קעטן אדר פערליך

gleich as diʔ söu diʔ keten oder perlich.
equal as DEF.PL.F sow.PL DEF.PL.F necklace.PL or pearl.DIM.PL
as the sows keep the necklaces and (little) pearls.

איך פֿוירכֿט מיך איך ריד צוא פֿיל

5 *Ich fürcht mich, ich red zuʔ fil;*
1SG fear.1SG.PRS REFL.1SG 1SG talk.1SG.PRS too much
I am afraid I am talking too much;

דרום וויל איך זיין ספֿרים ליגן נידר

drum wil ich sein seforim legen nider,
therefore will.1SG.PRS 1SG POSS.3PL religious.book.PL[H] lay.INF down
therefore I will put down his religious books,

אונ׳ פֿון טויש דינג איך רידן וויל

un' fun töusch ding ich reden wil.
and of German (= Yiddish) thing 1SG talk.INF will.1SG.PRS
and talk about Yiddish things.

דוך מושׂ איך קומן אויף אין ווידר

doch muś ich kumen ouf in wider:
however must.1SG.PRS 1SG come.INF on 3SG.ACC again
But I must return to him:

ווער ווערט איץ מאכֿן פורים שפיל

wer wert iz machen purim[30]-špil,
who AUX.3SG.PRS now make.INF Purim[H] play
who will now prepare a Purim play

ווער שפרוך ווער כלה לידר

wer špruch, wer cale[31]-lider?
who poem(.PL) ("speech") who bride[H] song.PL
who (will prepare) poems and bride songs?

ווער ווער גנצי בויכֿר ריימן אונ׳ שרייבן

wer wert ganze bücher reimen un' schreiben,
who AUX.3SG.PRS whole.PL book.PL rhyme.INF and write.INF
Who will rhyme and write complete books,

דז איר מיט לכֿן ווערט דיא צייט ור טרייבן

das ir mit lachen wert di? zeit ver-treiben?
COMP 2PL with laugh.INF AUX.2PL.PRS DEF.F time spend_time.INF ("drive away")
so that you will spend the time laughing?
[…]

דא טוט דיא הקדמה פֿאלענדן

Do tut di? hakdome[32] folenden.
there do.3SG.PRS DEF.F introduction[H] end.INF
Here, the introduction ends.

גאט זאל אונז משיח באלד זענדן

got sol uns Mošiaḥ[33] bald senden!
god shall.3SG.PRS 1PL.DAT Messias[H] soon send.INF
God shall send us the Messiah soon!

30 Hebrew פּוּרִים *pūrīm* 'lots, Purim festival'

31 Hebrew כַּלָּה *kālā̊* 'bride'

32 Hebrew הַקְדָּמָה *haqdāmā̊* 'introduction'.

33 Hebrew מָשִׁיחַ *māšīaḥ* 'anointed'.

דאז זאל גישעהן אין אונזרן טאגן

das sol geschehen in unseren tagen.
PRON.NT shall.3SG.PRS happen.INF in POSS.1PL.DAT day.PL.DAT
That shall happen in our days.

דרוף וועלן מיר אל אמו זאגן

druf welen mir al omen[34] *sagen.*
thereon will.1PL.PRS 1PL all Amen[H] say.INF
Upon this we all want to say "Amen".

3.8 Memoirs of Glikl (cf. Kaufmann 1896: 1f; Turniansky 2006: 6, 8)

The Memoirs of Glikl (1645 Hamburg – 1724 Metz) were composed between the years 1691 and 1719. The author's full name is Glikl bas Judah Leib (גליקל בת יהודה לייב) and her memoirs count as the first autobiography of a woman in Germany. The orthography reflects Middle Yiddish. <ש> can represent both /s/ and /š/. The texts contains a considerable amount of "whole Hebrew", transcribed here according to the *EHLL* standard for medieval Hebrew, as well as merged Hebrew, transcribed according to Yiddish conventions. As is typical of Western Yiddish texts, Slavic lexical adstrate is completely absent.

שנת תתנ"א אתכיל לכתוב זה מרוב דאגות וצרות

šnat tn"ʔ ʔatḥīl li-ḵtoḇ ze me-roḇ degaʔot we-ṣarot
year.CS[H] [5]451 (=1691) begin.1SG.IPFV[H] to-write.INF[H] DEM.M[H] from-much.CS[H] worry.PL[H] and-sorrow.PL[H]
I am starting to write this in the year 1691, driven by many worries, sorrows,

ומכאובי לב וויא ווייטר פולגין ווערט, וה' (השם) ישמחנו

u-mik-keʔuḇe leḇ vi vayter folgen vert, we-haš-šem yiśammeḥe-nu
and-from-pain.PL.CS[H] heart[H] as furtheron follow.INF AUX.3SG.PRS and-the-name[H] gladden.3SG.PRS-1PL[H]
and heart pains, as will follow. And may God make us glad (as long)

כימות ענותינו וישלח משיחינו וגואלינו ממהרה

k-imot ʕanwate-nu[35] *we-yišlaḥ mašīḥe-nu we-goʔele-nu mim-mohora*
as-day.PL.CS[H] humiliation.CS-1PL[H] and-send.3SG.M.IPFV[H] Messias.CS-1PL[H] and-redeemer.CS-1PL[H] from-tomorrow[H]
as in the days of our humiliation, and may he send our Messiah and Redeemer soon.

אמן. כל מה שברא הקב"ה (הקדוש ברוך הוא) לא ברא

ʔamen. kol ma še-bara(ʔ) haq-qadoš baruḵ hu(ʔ) lo(ʔ)bara(ʔ)
Amen[H] all[H] what[H] REL-create.3SG.M.PF[H] DEF-holy.M[H] bless.PTCP.PASS.M[H] 3SG.M[H] NEG[H] create.3SG.M.PF[H]
Amen. Everything that God created – may he be blessed – he createds

אלא לכבודו, והעולם בחסד יבנה מיר ווישין

ʔella li-ḵḇod-o we-ha-ʕolam be-ḥesed yibbane mir visen
except_for[H] for-honor.CS-3SG.M[H] and-DEF-world[H] in-grace[H] build.PASS.3SG.M.PRS[H] 1PL know.1PL.PRS
only for his honor, and the world will be built with grace. We know

34 Hebrew אָמֵן ʔā̊mēn 'secure'.

35 Allusion to Psalm 90:15.

דאז המקום ב״ה (ברוך השם) וב״ש (ברוך שמו)

daz ham-maqom baruḵ haš-šem we-baruḵ šm-o

COMP DEF-place^{H} bless.PTCP.PASS.M^{H} DEF-name^{H} and-bless.PTCP.PASS.M^{H} name.CS-3SG^{H}

that God – may he and his name be blessed –

אליש בישאפין אונ׳ גיטאן מיט אייטיל חסד ורחמים כי המקום

ales beshafen un getan mit aytel ḥesed we-raḥamim ki ham-maqom

everything create.PPP and do.PPP with proper grace^{H} and-pity^{H} because^{H} DEF-place^{H}

has created everything with proper grace and compassion, because God

ב״ה (ברוך השם) האט ניט ניטיג אייניש פון זיין בישעפנים,

baruḵ haš-šem hat nit netig aynes fun zayn beshafenis[36]

bless.PTCP.PASS.M^{H} DEF-name^{H} have.3SG.PRS NEG necessary one.NT of POSS.3SG creation

– may he be blessed – does not need any one of his creatures.

אביר דאש הש״י (השם יתברך) זוא פיל ארלייא האט בישאפין איזט

aber daz haš-šem yitbareḵ zo fil erlei hat beshafhen izt

but COMP DEF-name^{H} bless.PASS.3SG.M.PRS^{H} so many.a.thing have.3SG.PRS create.PPP be.3SG.PRS

But the circumstance that God – may he be blessed – has created so many a thing is

אליש צו זייניר גרושי ער אונ׳ האט אליש מיט חסד ורחמים

ales tsu zayner grose er un hat ales mit ḥesed we-raḥamim

all.NT to POSS.3SG.F.DAT big.F honor and have.3SG.PRS all.NT with grace^{H} and-pity.PL^{H}

all to his great honor, and he has created everything with grace and pity

בישאפין דאז עש אונש זינדיגע מענשין אליש צו נוטץ קומט,

beshafen daz es uns zindige menshen ales tsu nutts komt,

create.PPP COMP 3SG.NT 1PL.OBJ sinful.PL human.being.PL all.NT to benefit come.3SG.PRS

so that it comes to benefit us sinful human beings.

דאן אליש וואז בישאפין איזט קומט אונש מענשין אליש צו נוטצין,

den ales waz beshafen izt komt uns menshen ales zu nuttsen,

because all.NT REL create.PPP be.3SG.PRS come.3SG.PRS 1PL.OBJ human.being.PL all.NT to benefit

Because everything that was created comes to benefit us human beings

דאז מיר מענשין שונט ניט ביגרייפין אודיר ביטראכטין קענין,

daz mir menshen shont nit begrayfen oder betrakhten kenen,

PRON.NT 1PL human.being.PL already NEG comprehend.INF or look.at.INF can.1PL.PRS

(also) that which we human beings cannot comprehend and contemplate.

אליש וויא דוד המלך ע״ה (עליו השלום) גיפראגט האט

al(e)s vi dawid ham-meleḵ ʕal-aw haš-šalom gefragt hat

as like David DEF-king^{H} upon.3SG.M^{H} DEF-peace^{H} ask.PPP have.3SG.PRS

It is like when King David – peace be upon him – asked

וואור צו איין נאר אונ׳ איין וועשפא אונ׳ איין שפין איזט בישאפין ווארדן,

vor tsu ayn nar un ayn vespe un ayn shpin izt beshafen vorden,

where to INDEF diot and INDEF wasp and INDEF spider be.3SG.PRS create.PPP AUX.PPP

why an idiot, and a wasp, and a spider were created,

36 The *-im* ending as possible basis of Pappenheim's translation ("creatures") could also be explained as being dissimilated from an *-(en)* ending because of the preceding *n* (a kind of OCP effect).

דען איהם האט גידאכט וואז קומין דיא דרייארלייא צו נוטץ אין דער וועלט,
den im hat gedakht waz komen di drayerlay tsu nutts
because 3SG.M.DAT have.3SG.PRS think.PPP what come.3PL.PRS DEF.PL three_kind to benefit
because he wondered what benefit could come from these three

אביר ער איזט ענטליך גיוואר וואררין דאז איהם זעלבירט
in der velt, aber er izt entlikh gevar vorden daz im zelbert
in DEF.F.DAT world but 3SG.M be.3SG.PRS finally aware AUX.PPP COMP 3SG.M.DAT self
in the world, but he finally became aware of the fact that he himself

אלי דרייארלי זענין צו נוטץ קומין אונ׳ איהם זיין חיות
ale drayerlay zenen tsu nutts komen un im zayn khayes[37]
all.PL three_kind be.3PL.PRS to benefit come.3PL.PRS and 3SG.M.DAT POSS.3SG life^{H}
had benefitted from the three and that they saved his life,

גאט צו פאר ערהאלטין אלש וויא אין ספר מלכים בישריבן איזט,
got tsu par erhalten als vi in seyfer melakim beshribn izt,
God to pair maintain.3PL.PRS like as in book.CS^{H} king.PL^{H} describe.PPP be.3SG.PRS
together with God, as is described in the Book of Kings.[38]

ווער ווישין וויל קאן אין עשרים וארבע לייאין,
ver visen vil kan in ʕeśrim we-ʔarbaʕ leien
who.REL know.INF want.3SG.PRS can.3SG.PRS in twenty and-four read.INF
Whoever wants to know can read in [the] twenty-four [books] (the Hebrew Bible).

נון איזט אויך ווישיקליך וויא פיל טריפזאל אילנדווידרווילין דאז מיר
nun izt oukh visiklikh vi fil tribzal elend vidervilen
now 3SG.PRS also known how much sadness misery adversity
Now, one also knows how much sadness, misery, and adversities

זינדיגי מענשין אין דיזיר פרגענקליכי וועלט האבין צו דעם
daz mir zindige menshen in dizer fergenklikhe velt haben
COMP 1PL sinful.PL human.being.PL in DEM.F.DAT transitory.F world have.1PL.PRS
we sinful human beings have in this transitory world.

פינדין מיר וויא פיל פרוימי לייט זיינין אין דער וועלט
tsu dem finden mir vi fil froume layt zaynen in der velt
to PRON.NT.DAT find.1PL.PRS 1PL how many pious.PL people be.3PL.PRS in DEF.F.DAT world
Moreover, we find how many pious people there are in the world,

דיא עש גאר איבל גיט אונ׳ בעולם הזה גאר אילינדליך לעבן,
di es gar ibel get un ba-ʕolam haz-ze gar elendikh lebn,
REL.PL 3SG.NT DEGR evil go.3SG.PRS and in.DEF-world^{H} DEF-DEM.M^{H} DEGR miserable live.3PL.PRS
who are doing badly and live in this world in a miserable way;

קיגן דעסין פינדיט מאן ווידערום כמה רשעים דיא אין גרויש וואול
kegn desen findet man viderum kama rešaʕim di in grous vol
against PRON.NT.GEN find.3SG.PRS ONE.INDEF again some^{H} evil.PL^{H} REL.PL in big wealth
in contrast, one finds a lot of evildoers, who spend their days in great wealth

37 Hebrew חַיּוּת *ḥayyūṯ* 'life'.

38 The story is not found as such in the Book of Kings; rather, it is reminiscent of the Book of Samuel (cf. Turniansky 2006: 7, n. 99).

טעגין אונ׳ עשירות לעבן אונ׳ עש גיט אינין

tegen un ashires[39] *lebn un es get inen*

spend_the_day.3PL.PRS and rich.ADV^{H} live.3PL.PRS and 3SG.NT go.3SG.PRS PRON.PL.DAT

and live in rich circumstances, and their children

איר קינדר גאר וואול, דאר עש נעביך דען גירעכטין גאטישפערכטיג גאר איביל

ir kinder gar vol dar es den gerekhten gotesferkhtig gar ibel

POSS.PL child.PL DEGR well while 3SG.NT DEF.PL.DAT just.PL.DAT god-fearing DEGR evil.ADV

are well off, whereas the just and god-fearing is doing badly,

אים אונ׳ זייני קינדיר גיאט נון וועלטין מיר אונז גידאנקין מאכין

im und zayne kinder get nun velten mir unz gedanken makhen

3SG.M.DAT and POSS.PL child.PL go.3SG.PRS now want.1PL.PRET 1PL 1PL.DAT thought.PL make.INF

he and his children. Now, we wanted to consider,

וויא קאן דאז זיין גאט דער אלמעכטיגי איזט יוא איין גירעכטיר ריכטיר,

vi kan daz zayn got der almekhtige izt yo ayn gerekhter rikhter,

how can.3SG.PRS PRON.NT be.INF god DEF.M almighty be.3SG.PRS DM INDEF just.M judge

how can that be, God Almighty being a just judge.

איך האב מיר אביר גידאכט גם זה הבל דען דיא מעשים

ikh hab mir aber gedakht gam ze hebel den di maʕaśim

1SG have.1SG.PRS 1SG.DAT however think.PPP also^{H} DEM.M^{H} wind^{H} because DEF.PL deed.PL^{H}

But I considered that also this (thought) is futile, because as concerns God's deeds

פון הש״י ב״ה זענין און מיגליך

fun haš-šem yitbarek̲ baruk̲ hu(?) zenen un meglikh

of DEF-name^{H} bless.PASS.3SG.M.PRS^{H} bless.PTCP.PASS.M^{H} 3SG.M^{H} be.3PL.PRS im possible

– may he be blessed – it is impossible

אויז צו טראכטין אודיר אויז צו גרינדין, משה רבינו ע״ה

ouz tsu trakhten oder tsu grinden, moše rabbe-nu ʕal-aw haš-šalom

out to figure_out.INF or to get_to_bottom.INF Moše master.CS-1PL^{H} upon-3SG^{H} DEF-peace^{H}

to figure them out and to get to the bottom of them. Moshe, our master – peace be upon

האט עש גערין וואלין אונ׳ גיזאגט הודיענו נא את דרכיך,

hat es geren velen un gezagt hodiʕe-nu na(?) derak̲e-k̲a[40]

have.3SG.PRS 3SG.NT.OBJ gladly want.INF and say.PPP inform.IPT.SG.M^{H} COH^{H} way.PL.CS-2SG.M^{H}

them – wanted (to know) it eagerly and said "inform us concerning your ways",

אביר דאך ניט דאר צוקומין, דארום זאלין מיר דאז ניט טראכטין

aber dokh nit dar tsu-komen darum zolen mir daz nit trakhten

but DM NEG there to-come.INF therefore shall.1PL.PRS 1PL PRON.NT NEG figure_out.INF

but did not arrive at that. Therefore, we should not (try to) figure out that.

דיזיש איזט עכ״פ (על כל פנים) גוויש דאז דיזיר עולם איזט פון ניקש אנדרשט

dizes izt ʕal kol panim gevis daz dizer ʕolam izt niks anderst

DEM.NT be.3SG.PRS on^{H} all.CS^{H} face^{H} sure COMP DEM.M world^{H} be.3SG.PRS nothing different

What is for sure, anyhow, is that this world was created for nothing other

39 Hebrew עֲשִׁירוּת *ʕăšīrūt̲* 'wealth'.

40 Cf. Exodus 33:13.

וועגין ווארין בישאפֿין אליש פון עולם הבא וועגין, און
vegen voren beshafhen al(e)s) fun ʕolam hab-ba(?) vegen
because.of AUX.PPP create.PPP than of world^{H} DEF-come.PTCP.M^{H} because.of
than the coming world.

דארום האט אונש המקום ב״ה אך
darum hat uns ham-maqom baruḵ hu(?) akh
therefore have.3SG.PRS 1PL.ACC DEF-place^{H} bless.PTCP.PASS.M^{H} 3SG.M^{H} certainly
Therefore, God – may he be blessed – created us certainly

ברוב חסדיו אין דיזין עולם בישאפֿין דער ניקש און פֿאר גענקליך
be-roḇ ḥasd-aw in dizen ʕolam beshafen der niks un ver genklikh
in much.CS^{H} grace.PL.CS-3SG^{H} in DEM.M.DAT world^{H} create.PPP REL.M nothing and trans itory
with all his grace in this world, which is nil and transitory.

איזט, זוא מיר נון וואול טון אונ׳ אונזרין גראישן הערין וואל דינין ברענגט
izt, zo mir nun vol tun un unzren grousen heren vol dinen brengt
be.3SG.PRS if 1PL now well do.INF and 1PL.DAT big.M.DAT lord.DAT well serve.INF bring.3SG.PRS
If we do well and serve our great lord, he will bring

ער אונש און ערגענקליך איניז איביגי אויז דער בישוועהרליכי מיא זעליגי
er unz un ergenklikh iniz evige ous der beshverlikhe mi zelige
3SG 1PL.ACC un conditioned into.NT.ACC eternal.NT out.of DEF.M.DAT hard.F trouble some
us unconditioned in the eternal (world) out of the hard and troublesome

וועלט אין אייטיל רויאונג אונ׳ זעניפֿטקייט
velt in eitel rouung un zeneftkayt
world in proper quietness and mellowness
world, in proper quietness and mellowness.

3.9 Modern West-Yiddish: A text from Franconia, the Fürth Megille (cf. Herz 1854; 1871: 11f.; Klepsch 2008)[41]

The following sample is an excerpt modern Western Yiddish sample, the so-called *Fürth Megille*, a Purim play by the 19th century Jewish author Josef Herz entitled אסתר אדער דיא בעלאָנטע טוגנד (*Esther oder die belohnte Tugend*) 'Esther or the rewarded virtue'. This subtitle refers to an English novel, *Pamela or virtue rewarded*, by Samuel Richardson, published 1740 in London (cf. Klepsch 2008: 4). While the title represents Standard German (see above), the style in the play itself is close to the local Franconian dialect, mixed with Suebian and Hessian features, with a lot of Hebrew lexical adstratum. The Hebrew orthography is oriented at the German orthography, representing, *inter alia*, vowel-lengthening *h* by ה (e.g., איהן *ihn* 'him'), and even imitating German gemination (e.g., נעממע *nemme* 'to take'). The Latin transcription ("normalization") follows the 19th century source of the play (cf. also Klepsch 2008). On the following page, the cover of the print of 1854 is reproduced.

41 For a number of valuable hints in this context I am indebted to Alfred Klepsch and Mechthild Habermann.

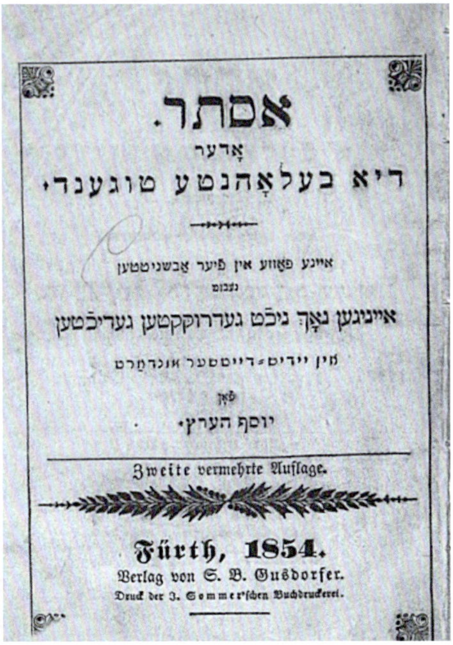

אסתר.
אָדער
דיא בעלאָהנטע טוגענד.

איינע פאָסע אין פיער אבשניטטען

איינינען נאָך ניכט געדרוקקטען געדיכטען

אין יידיש=דייטשער אונדהאַרט

פאָן

יוסף הערץ.

Zweite vermehrte Auflage.

Fürth, 1854.

Verlag von S. B. Gusdorfer.

Druck der J. Sommer'schen Buchdruckerei.

Charbonah: חרבונה:

דער מלך ווילל נעממע אַ פֿראַה.

Der Melech will nemme a Frah.
DEF.M king[H] want.3SG.PRS take.INF INDEF woman/wife
The king wants to marry.

דוי האָב איך איהן דיא עצה גיהבען,

Do hob ich ihn die Eze gib'n,
there have.1SG.PRS 1SG 3SG.OBJ DEF.F advice[H] give.PPP
I gave him the advice

Recka: רעקאַ:

ער זאָלל נעממע אונזר צעטולפע ליהבען!

Er soll nemme unser Zetulpe lib'n.
3SG.M shall.3SG.PRS take.INF POSS.1PL.OBJ PN dear.OBJ
Let him marry our dear Zetulpe.

Charbonah: חרבונה:

אַ מיין גיה מיר מיט דער טאָכֿטער נעהר,

A mei geh' mir mit der Tochter nehr,
INTERJ go.IPT.SG 1SG.DAT with DEF.F.DAT daughter only
Oh, just leave me alone with the daughter,

מיט דער איז אַאַך ניט פֿיל / שאָן עבבעס דער מעהר!

Mit der is aach nit viel dermehr!
with PRON.SG.F.DAT be.3SG.PRS also NEG much more
Not much is going on with her!

דיא איז, וויא זיא אַללעוויל בעוונות אַללע זעננע –

Die is, wie sie alleweil Beavones[42] *alle senne –*
PRON.SG.F be.3SG.PRS as 3PL always unfortunately[H] all.PL see.3PL.PRS
She is, as everyone unfortunately can see –

זיכֿט זיא דען מעהר ניין אין צאינה וראינה?

Sicht sie denn mer 'nein in Zennerenne[43]
see.3SG.PRS 3SG.F DM more into in womens's_religious_literature
Does she look more into women's religious literature,

אין תהלים אָדער מעמדות,

In Tillim oder Ma'amodes,[44]
in psalm.PL[H] or collection_of_religious_writings[H]
the Psalms or (other) religious writings,

וויל דאַז אומשטאַנזגזאַגט, אויז דער מודע איז!

Weil das umschtahnsgsagt,[45] *aus der Mude is!*
because PRON.NT unfortunately out.of DEF.F.GEN fashion be.3SG.PRS
as this is unfortunately out of fashion.

איך דאַרף מיך דאָך דוי גלייך אוויפֿשליצצען

Ich derf mich doch do gleich aufschlitz'n,
1SG may.1SG.PRS 1SG.ACC DM there at.once cut_up.INF
I may just cut me up,

טוט זיא שבת ניקז, וויא איבער ביכֿער זיצען.

Tut sie Schabbes nix, wie über Bücher sitzen.
do.3SG.PRS 3SG.F Shabbat[H] nothing than over book.PL sit.INF
doesn't she do on Shabbat anything else than to study books.

דע שטן איז אָרענטליך אין זיא דריננע

Der Suden[46] *is ornlich in sie drinne,*
DEF.M Satan[H] be.3SG.PRS pretty.much in 3SG.F inside
The devil is pretty much in her,

איך מעכֿט נאָר וויססען, וואַאז זִיא שיהנעס דראַן גפֿיננע?

Ich mecht nor wissen, waas sie Schehns dran g'finne?
1SG wish.1SG.PRS only know.INF what.REL 3PL beautiful.NMLZ.NT at.that find.3PL.PRS
if I only knew what they like about that.

42 Hebrew בְּעֲווֹנוֹתֵינוּ הָרַבִּים *bə-ʕăwōnōṯē-nū hā̊-rabbīm* 'because of our many sins' (cf. Klepsch 2004: 335).

43 *Tsene-rene*, a Yiddish prose work of the 1590ies, structurally similar to the weekly Torah portions of the Pentateuch. Cf. Song 3:11: צְאֶנָה וּרְאֶינָה בְּנוֹת צִיּוֹן, *ṣəʔɛnā̊ u-rəʔɛnā̊* 'Go forth and see[, O ye daughters of Zion.]'

44 Hebrew תְּהִלִּים *təhillīm* 'psalms'; מַעֲמָדוֹת *maʕămā̊ḏōṯ* 'stands, post' (cf. Klepsch 2004: 946).

45 Franconian expression of complaint, dismay (cf. Klepsch 2004: 1457, following Copeland and Süsskind 1976: 154).

46 Hebrew שָׂטָן *śā̊ṭā̊n* 'devil'.

וואַז טוט דוי אַלז פֿאָר שטות דרינגע שטיהן?

Was tut do alles for Schtuß[47] *drinne stehn?*
what do.3SG.PRS there all.NT for nonsense[H] therein stand.INF
What kind of nonsense is therein?

וויא דער האַנזעל טוט צו דער גריהטעל גיהן?

Wie der Hansel tut zu die/der Greth'l gehn,
as DEF.M PN do.3SG.PRS to DEF.F.DAT PN go.INF
As Hänsel goes to Gretel.

לבסוף דעננע זיא זיך נעממע;

Li'bsuff[48] *denne sie sich nemme,*
Finally[H] do.3PL.PRS 3PL REFL take.INF
Finally they marry

וואַטט ער אַ טאַאַטע, און זיא אַ מעממע!

Wart er a Taate (un) sie *<wart>* *a Memme!*
become.3SG.PRET 3SG.M INDEF father[Slav] (and) 3SG.F become.3SG.PRET INDEF mother
He becomes a father and she a mother!

דוי האָסטו דאַז מעשה, פֿון א ביז ת.

Dau hoß'tu das Ma'aseh[49] *vun Oleph bis Tuhf.*
there have.2SG.PR'2SG DEF.NT business[H] from *ʔalep̄*[H] to *taw*[H]
There you have the business from A to Z.

שטיהט יוי כלומר אַ מויל עבעס דרינגע פֿון אַ גרוהף,

Steht jau Klomer[50] *a mul ebbes drinne von a Gruhf,*
stand.3SG.PRS DM as.one.says[H] INDEF time something inside of INDEF count
There is something in it about a count,

פֿון אַ פֿאַשט אָדער אַ גרויזען האַרר

Vun a Farscht oder a graußen Harr;
of INDEF duke or INDEF big.SG.M.DAT master
a duke, or a great lord;

Recka: רעקאַ:

גיה דוא זימפעל! דו שבשן! דו נַרר!

Geh' du Simpel! Du Schabschen![51] *Du Narr!*
go.SG.IPT 2SG simpleton 2SG idiot[H] 2SG jester
Come on, you simpleton, you idiot, you jester!

וואַז איז דיר דראַהן קשה? פֿון דיינעתוויהגען

Was is Dir drahn koscheh?[52] *vun Deinetwihg'n*
what be.3SG.PRS 2SF.DAT at.that problematic[H] from because.of.POSS.2SG.GEN
What is your problem? As far as you are concerned,

47 Hebrew שְׁטוּת *šəṭūṯ* 'nonsense'.
48 Hebrew לְבַסּוֹף *lə-ḇas-sōp̄* 'finally' ("to-in.the-end").
49 Hebrew מַעֲשֶׂה *maʕăśɛ* 'deed'.
50 Hebrew כְּלוֹמַר *kə-l-ōmar* 'so to say'.
51 Hebrew שַׁבְּשָׁן *šabbəšā̊n* 'idiot' ("who errs").
52 Hebrew קָשֶׁה *qā̊šɛ* 'difficult'.

קעננעט זיא חטשה גרויע צעפף אַאַך קריהגען!

Kennet sie chodsche graue Zöpf' aach krihg'n!
can.3SG.SUBJ1 3SG.F even^{Slav} grey.PL braid.PL also get.INF
she could even get grey braids!

התך האָט איהר גערעט זוי אַ גוטען שידיך

Hodach hott ihr gered't sau a guten Schiddich,[53]
PN have.3SG.PRS 3SG.F.DAT talk.PPP SOW INDEF good.M.ACC (arranged) marriage)
Hodach has talked to her about a damned good marriage

וואָרים האָסטו דיהן ניט גטוין? זאַג אַ מויל? איך בנטטיך!

Worem hoß'tu dihn nit getaun? sag e mol? ich bitt' Dich!
why have.2SG.PRS'2SG PRON.M.ACC NEG do.PPP say.SG.IPT one time 1SG beg.1SG.PRS 2SG.ACC
Why didn't you do that? Come on, I beg your pardon!

3.10 Modern West-Yiddish: Purim in Endingen (cf. Fleischer 2005: 73–76)

The last sample, for which no version in Hebrew script is available, is based on a recording with Isaak Guggenheim-Bloch in 1957, in Endingen, part of the Surbtal region in Switzerland. The text style is by no means identical with co-territorial High-Alemannic. As evidence for that circumstance, Fleischer (2005: 6) mentions diphthongization and monophthongization that happened in Early High German, most High German dialects, and also in Western Yiddish, but not in Alemannic. The text is presented here in Fleischer's phonetic transcription, which strictly follows the oral recording (in contrast to a slightly deviating pre-existing written German version in the Florence Guggenheim Archive, Cb §b 4c). The footnotes also draw on the notes by Fleischer (2005: 77–79) to this text. Thanks to Jürg Fleischer for his kind permission to reproduce this text.

ə pu:rəm ts en(d)iŋə da:z is epəs gəvẽ:
INDEF Purim^{H} to Endingen 3SG.NT be.3SG.PRS something be.PPP
Purim in Endingen, this was something:

ə ʃenər feʃt hot s ga:r nid ge:.
INDEF beautiful.COMPAR party have.3SG.PRS 3SG.NT at_all NEG give.PPP
A more beautiful feast has not existed at all.

əm ta:nəs estər[54] *"esst er"*[55]*, das hot mər nid gek^{h}ent,*
at.DAT fasting.CS^{H} Esther^{H} eat.3SG.PRS 3SG.M DEF.NT have.3SG.PRS one.INDEF NEG know.PPP
On Esther fasting "he eats", one did not know this,

mə hot siɛ fon je:hɛ:r ans faʃtə gəvent.
one.INDEF have.3SG.PRS REFL from time_immemorial at.DEF.NT.ACC fasting become_used_to.PPP
one has gotten used to fasting from time immemorial.

53 Hebrew שִׁדּוּךְ *šiddūḵ* '[arranged] marriage'.

54 Hebrew תַּעֲנִית אֶסְתֵּר *taʕănīṯ ʔɛstēr* 'Esther's fasting [on the eve of Purim]'.

55 Dialectal wordplay *esst er* 'he eats' (Standard German *ißt er* "eats he").

und ts na:xt i dər sinago:g tsu də məgilə[56]
and to night in DEF.F.DAT synagogue to DEF.F scroll[H]
And at night in the synagogue on the occasion of the book Esther

ist baiənand gəve: di gants kʰilə[57]*.*
be.3SG.PRS together be.PPP DEF.F whole congregation[H]
the whole congregation was together.

un ts mɔrgəds nɔ:x ʃu:l, dau sin ɛ:rʃt di simxəs[58] *a:gaŋə,*
and to in.the.morning after divine.service there be.3PL.PRS first DEF.PL joy.PL[H] begin.PPP
An in the morning after the divine service, the joys only started,

den mit kʰafi und ausgənetsti[59] *kʰiɕliɕ is siɕ jedər məhanə*[60]*.*
because with coffee and "net_out".PPP kake.IM.PL be.3SG.PRS REFL everyone.M enjoy.PTCP[H]
because with coffee and "outnetted" cakes everyone enjoyed themselves.

am bu:rəm hen ali midənand raxmo:nəs[61]*,*
at.DAT Purim have.3PL.PRS all with_each_other pity[H]
On Purim, everyone has pity with each other,

a:m ʃikt əm andərə ʃlaxmo:nəs[62]*.*
one.M send.3SG.PRS one.M.DAT other Purim.gifts[H]
one sends Purim gifts to the/each other.

lugəd, jets seit mə ʃou maski:rti kʰindər uf də ʃtraus!
look.2PL.IPT now see.3SG.PRS one.INDEF already mask.PPP.PL child.PL on DEF.F street
Look, now one already sees masked children on the street!

si hen li:dliɕ un gədiɕtliɕ gəlɛnt un ge fun hauz tsu hauz.
3PL have.3PL.PRS song.IM.PL and poem.IM.PL learn.PPP and go.3PL.PRS from house to house
They have memorized songs and poems and go from house to house.

un əm nɔməta:g ɛ:rʃt, da la:fəd ibəral maskən umənan
and at.M.DAT afternoon first there run.3PL.PRS everywhere mask.PL around
And in the afternoon even more so, masks run around everywhere

56 Hebrew מְגִלָּה *məḡillā̊* 'scroll [here: of the book Esther]'.

57 Hebrew קְהִלָּה *qəhillā̊* 'congregation'.

58 Hebrew שְׂמָחוֹת *śəmā̊ḥōṯ* (CS: *śimḥōṯ*) 'joys, family feasts'.

59 The meaning of this verb, possibly referring to a netlike pattern on the cakes, is not entirely clear (cf. Fleischer 2005: 77).

60 Hebrew מְהַנֶּה *məhannɛ* 'giving pleasure', here part of a phrasal verb.

61 Hebrew רַחְמָנוּת *raḥmā̊nūṯ* 'pity'.

62 Cf. Hebrew וּמִשְׁלוֹחַ מָנוֹת *ū-mi-šlōaḥ mā̊nōṯ* 'and from the sending of meals' (Esther 9:19).

aləs is luftig, aləs frait siɛ, und is aus rand und band.
all.NT be.3SG.PRS funny all.NT rejoice.3SG.PRS REFL and be.3SG.PRS out.of rim and ribbon
Everyone is merry, everyone rejoices and is out of control (utterly happy).

un je:dər ə bislə bedu:x[63] *jəhu:de*
and every.M INDEF a.little wealthy[H] Jew[H]
And every somewhat wealthy Jew

maxt pu:rəm ts na:xt ə bu:rəmsu:də[64].
make.3SG.PRS Purim[H] to night INDEF Purim.meal[H]
prepares a Purim meal on Purim night.

di maskə gen bai im ãĩ un auz
DEF.F mask.PL go.3PL.PRS at 3SG.M.DAT in and out
The masks come to him and go from him

un maxəd undərobsiɛ faft s gants hauz
and make.3PL.PRS upside_down almost DEF.NT whole house
and turn the whole house almost upside down.

un meŋgə bəkʰumt epəs fun saini nəfɛ:rəs[65] *ts hɛ:rə*
and many_a_one get.3SG.PRS something of POSS.3SG.PL sin.PL[H] to hear.INF
And many a one gets to hear something of their sins

inərə maskə kʰa mə jo niks fərvɛ:rə
INDEF.F.DAT mask can.3SG.PRS one.INDEF after_all nothing withhold.INF
one cannot say no to a mask, after all.

hait is də pu:rəmbal əm fitsə,
today be.3SG.PRS DEF.M Purim.ball in.DEF.M.DAT shooter
Today, the Purim ball is on at the "Schütze" (name of a locality)

fərusən is ə gri:rə, abər baim dantsə kʰumt mə ts fvitsə.
outside be.3SG.PRS INDEF cold[H] but at.DEF.DAT dance.INF come.3SG.PRS one.INDEF to sweat.INF
outside it is cold, but in the course of dancing one gets to sweat.

əs vərd gəjo:lt, gəlɛrmt un gəlaxt,
3SG.NT AUX.3SG.PRS cheer.PPP make_noise.PPP and laugh.PPP
One cheers, makes noise, and laughs,

63 Hebrew בָּטוּחַ *bå̄ṭūaḥ* 'safe', in the German(ized) form *betucht* 'wealthy' associated with 'Tuch' = '[precious] cloth', an attribute of wealthy people.

64 Hebrew סְעוּדָה *səʕūḏå̄* 'meal'.

65 Hebrew עֲבֵרוֹת *ʕăḇērōṯ* 'transgressions, sins', the initial *n* in *nəfɛ:rəs* being a reflex of Hebrew /ʕ/.

un meĩ as a:nər vɔrt halbə gəlo:nə gəmaxt,
and more than one.M AUX.3SG.PRS half crazy make.PPP
and more than one gets half crazy,

den am bu:rəm
because at.DEF.DAT Purim[H]
because on Purim

hen di en(d)iŋər fərgesə iri jəsu:rəm[66]
have.3PL.PRS DEF.PL people_from_Endingen forget.PPP POSS.3PL sorrow.PL[H]
the people of Endingen forget their sorrows.

ts na:xt ten siɕ soga:r eltəri vaibər fərʃtelə
to night do.3PL.PRS REFL even older.PL woman.PL dissimulate.INF
At night, even older women disguise themselves

s ʃeinələ, di beil, di edəl, di gelə.
DEF.NT Scheinele DEF.F Beil DEF.F Edel DEF.F Gelle
Scheinele, Beil, Edel, and Gelle.

si gen uf də tantssa:l tsum intrigi:rə
3PL go.3PL.PRS on DEF.DAT dancehall to conspire.INF
The go up to the dancehall to conspire

und iri manə ausʃpioni:rə.
and POSS.3PL man.PL spy_on.INF
and to spy on their husbands.

un meŋsmol is ax pasi:rt
and sometimes be.3SG.PRS also happen.PPP
And sometimes it also happens

as a:nə hot tsvai ʃe:[67] *kʰarizi:rt*[68]
COMP one.M have.3SG.PRS two hour[H] flirt/pet.INF
that a certain person has flirted for two hours

un hot gəma:nt, vas ər dau kʰen fiʃe
and have.3SG.PRS think.PPP REL 3SG there can.3SG.PRS fish.INF
and thought he could "fish" [another woman]

66 Hebrew יִסּוּרִים *yissūrīm* 'pains'.

67 Hebrew שָׁעָה *šåʕå* 'hour'.

68 French *caresser* 'to pet'.

un vu siɕ hot demaski:rt, vɛr is əs? sai aigəni iʃe[69]
and when REFL have.3SG.PRS unmask.PPP who be.3SG.PRS 3SG.NT POSS.3SG own.ADJ woman^H
and when [she] unmasked herself, who is it? – his own wife.

am pu:rəm is aləs oni sɔrgə,
at.DEF.M.DAT Purim^H be.3SG.PRS everything without sorrow
On Purim, everything is without sorrow,

(ə)s vɔrd gətantst bis fri: am mɔrgə.
3SG.NT AUX.3SP.PRS dance.PPP until early.ADV at.DEF.M.DAT morning
one dances until the early morning hours.

s is ən abər ax bald tsait,
3SG.NT be.3SG.PRS then but also soon time
But it is then also [high] time,

das də juŋ sai ma:dlə ha:m bəglait.
COMP DEF.M boy POSS.3SG girl.IM home escort.3SG.PRS
that the boy escorts his girl home.

uf əm vɛ:g ten si siɕ nɔx gu:t undərhaltə,
on DEF.M.DAT way do.3PL.PRS 3PL REFL further well converse.INF
On the way they still have a good conversation,

und hi: und da: ax ə kʰus ãĩʃaltə.
and here and there also INDEF kiss intersperse/switch_on.INF
and exchange a kiss here and there.

un meŋsmol hot s əsiɕ ax ge:bə
and sometimes have.3SG.PRS 3SG.NT REFL also give.PPP
And sometimes it also happened

das tsvai ənundər gfundə hen tsum ʃidiɕ[70] *fɔr s gants le:bə.*
COMP two each-other find.PPP have.3SG.PRS to.DEF.M.DAT marriage^H for DEF.NT whole life
the two [people] found each other for marriage for the[ir] whole life.

das is pu:rəm aus alt en(d)iŋər tsait,
PRON.SG.NT be.3SG.PRS Purim^H from/out_of old Endingen.ADJ time
That is Purim from the old time of Endingen,

uns abər hait nɔr nɔx di ərinərig blaibt.
1PL.DAT but today only still DEF.F recollection rest.3SG.PRS
but we only have the recollection [thereof] today.

69 Hebrew אִשָּׁה *ʔiššā̊* 'woman'.

70 Hebrew שִׁדּוּךְ *šiddūḵ* '[arranged] marriage'.

References

Primary sources

Blumgarten, Solomon ("Yehoash"). 1926. תורה נביאים וכתובים. reprint, 3 vols. New York: Forward.

Darmesteter, Arsène and David S. Blondheim. 1929. *Les gloses françaises dans les commentaires talmudiques de Raschi. Tome premier. Texte des gloses.* Paris: Librairie ancienne Honoré Champion.

Dunphy, Graeme. 2007. "Literary Transitions: From 1300–1500." *Early Modern German Literature* (= The Camden House History of German Literature, vol. 4), ed. Max Reinhart, 43–87. Rochester, New York/Woodbridge: Camden House.

Erlikh, Borekh Mortkhe. 1977. *Khelemer dertseylungen.* Tel Aviv: Farlag Mikhoel.

Fleischer, Jürg. 2005. *Westjiddisch in der Schweiz und Südwestdeutschland. Tonaufnahmen und Texte zum Surbtaler und Hegauer Jiddisch.* Tübingen: Niemeyer.

Frakes, Jerold C. 2004. *Early Yiddish Texts 1100–1750. With Introduction and Commentary.* Oxford: Oxford University Press.

Friedman, Sara. 2019. *Glikl. Memoires 1691–1719.* Edited and Annotated with an Introduction by Chava Turniansky Translated by Sara Friedman. Waltham, MA: Brandeis University Press.

Fuks, Lajb. 1957. *The Oldest Known Literary Documents of Yiddish Literature (c. 1382).* Leiden: Brill.

Ganz, Peter F., Frederick Norman, and Werner Schwarz (eds.). 1964. *Dukus Horant* (Altdeutsche Textbibliothek, Ergänzungsreihe 2). Tübingen: Niemeyer.

Herz, Joseph. 1828. אסתר אדער דיא בעלאָנטע טוגנד – איינע פּאָזזע אין פיער אַבשניטטען אין יידיש־דייתשער מונדארט פאָן יוסף הערץ *Esther oder die belohnte Tugend. Eine Posse in vier Abschnitten in jüdisch-deutscher Mundart.* Fürth: Gusdorfer.

Herz, Joseph. 1871. *Esther oder die belohnte Tugend. Eine Posse in vier Abschnitten. Nebst einigen Gedichten vermischten Inhalts in jüdischem Dialekt.* Vom Hebräischen ins Deutsche übertragen von J. Suhler. Fürth: Gusdorfer.

Jaldati, Lin and Eberhard Rebling. 1985. *Es brennt, Brüder, es brennt. Jiddische Lieder.* Berlin: Rütten & Loening.

Kaufmann, David. 1896. *Die Memoiren der Glückel von Hameln.* Frankfurt a.M.: J. Kauffmann.

Meyer, Thomas. 2012. *Wolkenbruchs wunderliche Reise in die Arme einer Schickse.* Zürich: Salis Verlag.

Shmeruk, Chone. 1996. *Paris un' Viena. Edited with Introduction, Notes and Appendices by Chone Shmeruk in Collaboration with Erika Timm.* Jerusalem: The Israel Academy of Sciences and Humanities 1996. (in Hebrew)

Süss, Hermann. 1984. "Die Fürther Megille." *Nachrichten für den jüdischen Bürger Fürths*, September 1984: 13–17.

Timm, Erika and Gustav A. Beckmann. 1996. *Paris un Wiene. Ein jiddischer Stanzenroman des 16. Jahrhunderts von (oder aus dem Umkreis von) Elia Levita.* Tübingen: Niemeyer.

Timm, Erika. 2003. "Ein neu entdeckter literarischer Text in hebräischen Lettern aus der Zeit vor 1349." *Zeitschrift für deutsches Altertum und deutsche Literatur* 142: 417–443.

Turniansky, Chava. 2006. *Glikl. Zikronot (Zikhroynes) 1691–1719 (Glikl. Memoires 1691–1719).* Edited and translated from the Yiddish by Chava Turniansky. Jerusalem: The Zalman Shazar Center for Jewish History and The Ben-Zion Dinur Center for Research in Jewish History, The Hebrew University. (in Hebrew).

Yefroikin, Zalman and Yudel Mark. 1964. *Yiddishe kinder (Jewish children).* Part III. New York: Education Department of the Workmen's Circle.

Secondary sources

Althaus, Hans-Peter. 2003 (2nd ed.). *Kleines Lexikon deutscher Wörter jiddischer Herkunft.* Munich: C.H. Beck.

Althaus, Hans-Peter. 2006 (2nd ed.). *Chuzpe, Schmus & Tacheles. Jiddische Wortgeschichten.* Munich: C.H. Beck.

Aptroot, Marion and Björn Hansen (eds.). 2014. *Yiddish Language Structures.* Berlin: de Gruyter.

Aronson. Howard I. 1996. "Yiddish." *The World's Writing Systems*, eds. Peter T. Daniels and William Bright, 727–734. New York/Oxford: Oxford University Press.

Aslanov, Cyril. 2013. "The Romance component in Yiddish: a reassessment." *Journal of Jewish Languages* 1: 261–273.

Battenberg, Friedrich. 1990. *Das europäische Zeitalter der Juden.* Darmstadt: Wissenschaftliche Buchgesellschaft.

Baumgarten, Jean. 2005. *Introduction to Old Yiddish Literature.* Edited and translated by Jerold C. Frakes. Oxford: Oxford Univesity Press.

Beider, Alexander. 2013, "*Bne Hes* and *Bne Ḵes*." *Encyclopedia of Hebrew Language and Linguistics*, ed. Geoffrey Khan, vol. 1: 373–375. Leiden: Brill.

Beider, Alexander. 2015. *Origins of Yiddish Dialects.* Oxford: Oxford University Press.

Beider, Alexander. 2018. "Yiddish in Eastern Europe." *Languages in Jewish Communities, Past and Present*, eds. Benjamin Hary and Sarah Bunin Benor, 276–312. Berlin: de Gruyter.

Ben Israel, Danny. 2011. *Zubi! The REAL Hebrew you were never taught in school.* New York: Penguin Group.

Bin-Nun (Fischer), Jechiel. 1936. *Das Jiddische und sein Verhältnis zu den deutschen Mundarten, unter besonderer Berücksichtigung der ostgalizischen Mundart. Erster Teil – Lautlehre (einschließlich Phonetik der ostgalizischen Mundart. Erste Hälfte: Allgemeiner Teil.* Leipzig: Buchdruckerei Oswald Schmidt.

Birnbaum, Solomon A. 1979. *Yiddish. A Survey and Grammar.* Toronto: University of Toronto Press.

Bunis, David M. 1993. *A Lexicon of the Hebrew and Aramaic Elements in Modern Judezmo.* Jerusalem: The Magnes Press.

Bunis, David M. 2005. "A Theory of Hebrew-Based Fusion Lexemes in Jewish Languages as Illustrated by Morphologically Derived Animate Nouns in Judezmo and Yiddish." *Mediterranean Language Review* 16: 1–115.

Bunis, David M. 2013. "Writing more or less 'Jewishly' in Judezmo and Yiddish." *Journal of Jewish Languages* 1: 9–75.

Callenberg, Johann Heinrich. 1736. *Jüdischteutsches Wörterbüchlein.* Halle: Institutum Judaicum et Muhammedaicum.

Copeland, Robert M. and Nathan Süsskind. 1976. *The Language of Herz's Esther: A Study in Judeo-German Dialectology*. University of Alabama.

Edzard, Lutz. 2014. "Hebrew and Hebrew–Yiddish terms and expressions in contemporary German: some (socio-)linguistic observations." *Proceedings of the Oslo–Austin Workshop in Semitic Linguistics. Oslo, May 23 and 24, 2013*, eds. Lutz Edzard and John Huehnergard, 127–143. Wiesbaden: Harrassowitz.

Edzard, Lutz. 2018. "Script as a Medium of Linguistic and Cultural Features: The Case of Jewish Languages." *Reading Slowly. A Festschrift for Jens E. Braarvig*, eds. Lutz Edzard, Jens W. Borgland, and Ute Hüsken, 159–172. Wiesbaden: Harrassowitz.

Eggers, Eckhard. 1988. *Sprachwandel und Sprachmischung im Jiddischen.* Frankfurt/New York: Peter Lang.

Faber, Alice and Robert King. 1984. "Yiddish and the settlement history of Ashkenazic Jewry." *Mankind Quarterly* 24: 393–425.

Farstey, Hava. 2013. "Yiddish influence on Hebrew." *Encyclopedia of Hebrew Language and Linguistics*, ed. Geoffrey Khan, vol. 3: 1024–1032. Leiden: Brill.

Fleischer, Jürg and Lea Schäfer. 2012. "Der Kasus nach Präposition in westjiddischen Quellen des (langen) 19. Jahrhunderts." *לקט. ייִדישע שטודיעס הייַנט Jiddistik heute*, eds. Marion Aptroot, Efrat Gal-Ed, Roland Gruschka, and Sion Neuberg , 415–436. Düsseldorf: Düsseldorf University Press.

Fleischer, Jürg. 2014a. "The (original) unity of Western and Eastern Yiddish: an assessment based on morphosyntactic phenomena." *Yiddish Language Structures*, eds. Marion Aptroot and Björn Hansen, 107–123. Berlin: de Gruyter Mouton.

Fleischer, Jürg. 2014b. "Slavic influence in Eastern Yiddish syntax: the case of *vos* relative clauses." In: Ghil'ad Zuckermann (ed.). *Jewish Language Contact* (Special Issue, *International Journal of the Sociology of Language* 226): 137–161.

Fleischer, Jürg. 2018. "Western Yiddish and Judeo-German." *Languages in Jewish Communities, Past and Present*, eds. Benjamin Hary and Sarah Bunin Benor, 239–275. Berlin: de Gruyter.

Glinert, Lewis. 1989. *The Grammar of Modern Hebrew*. Cambridge: Cambridge University Press.

Goldenberg, Gideon. 1971. "Tautological Infinitive." *Israel Oriental Studies* 1: 36–85.

Guggenheim-Grünberg, Florence. 1973. *Jiddisch auf alemannischem Sprachgebiet*. Zürich: Joris.

Hofmann, Hans-Rainer. 1998. *Lachoudisch sprechen. Mit Wörterverzeichnis*. Dinkelsbühl: Brunnen Verlag.

Jacobs, Neil G. 1990. *Economy in Yiddish Vocalism. A study in the interplay of Hebrew and non-Hebrew components*. Wiesbaden: Harrassowitz.

Jacobs, Neil G. 2005. *Yiddish: A Linguistic Introduction*. Cambridge: Cambridge University Press.

Kahn, Lily. 2016. "Yiddish." *Handbook of Jewish Languages*, eds. Lily Kahn and Aaron D. Rubin, 297–364. Leiden: Brill.

Katz, Dovid. 1983. "Zur Dialektologie des Jiddischen." *Dialektologie: Ein Handbuch zur deutschen und allgemeinen Dialektforschung*, eds. Werner Besch, Ulrich Knoop, Wolfgang Putschke, and Herbert Ernst Wiegant, 1018–1041. Berlin/New York: de Gruyter.

Katz, Dovid. 1987. *Grammar of the Yiddish Language*. London: Duckworth.

Kiefer, Ulrike. 2000. "Das Jiddische in Beziehung zum Mittelhochdeutschen." *Sprachgeschichte. Ein Handbuch zur Geschichte der deutschen Sprache und ihrer Erforschung. 2., vollständig neu bearbeitete und werweiterte Auflage*, eds. Werner Besch, Anne Betten, Oskar Reichmann, and Stefan Sonderegger, 1399–1408. Berlin: de Gruyter.

Kleine, Ane. 2003. "Standard Yiddish." *Journal of the International Phonetic Association* 33 (2): 261–265.

Klepsch, Alfred.2004. *Westjiddisches Wörterbuch. Auf der Basis dialektologischer Erhebungen in Mittelfranken*. Berlin: de Gruyter.

Klepsch, Alfred. 2008. "Aussterben und Fortleben des Jiddischen in Franken." In: Horst Haider Munske (ed.): *Sterben die Dialekte aus? Vorträge am Interdisziplinären Zentrum für Dialektforschung an der Friedrich-Alexander-Universität Erlangen-Nürnberg, 22.10.-10.12.2007*. <<http://www.dialektforschung.phil.uni-erlangen.de/sterbendialekte>>

Kluge, Friedrich. 2011 (25th ed.). *Etymologisches Wörterbuch der deutschen Sprache*. Bearbeitet von Elmar Seebold, 25. durchgesehene und erweiterte Auflage. Berlin/New York: Walter de Gruyter.

Krogh, Steffen. 2001. *Das Ostjiddische im Sprachkontakt. Deutsch im Spannungsfeld zwischen Semitisch und Slavisch*. Tübingen: Niemeyer.

Kutscher, Eduard Yechezkel and Raphael Kutscher 1982. *A History of the Hebrew Language*. Jerusalem: Magnes Press.

Maman, Aharon. 2019. *Synoptic Dictionary of the Hebrew Component in Jewish Languages. Second revised version*. Jerusalem: Magnes Press.

Manaster Ramer, Alexis and Meyer Wolf. 1996. "Yiddish origins: the Austro-Bavarian problem." *Folia Linguistica Historica* 17: 193–209.

Mark, Yudel. 1978. *Grammatik fun der Yiddisher Klal-shprakh* גראַמאַטיק פֿון דער ייִדישער כּלל־שפּראַך. New York: Congress for Jewish Culture.

Matras, Yaron. 1991. "Zur Rekonstruktion des jüdischdeutschen Wortschatzes in den Mundarten ehemaliger 'Judendörfer' in Südwestdeutschland." *Zeitschrift für Dialektologie und Linguistik* 58: 267–293.

Matras, Yaron. 1996. "Sondersprachliche Hebraismen." *Rotwelsch-Dialekte. Symposium Münster 10. bis 12. März 1995*, ed. Klaus Siewert, 97–106. Wiesbaden: Harrassowitz.

Merkle Ludwig. 1975. *Bairische Grammatik*. Munich: Heimeran Verlag.

Mieses, Matthias. 1915. *Die Entstehungsursache der jüdischen Dialekte*. Vienna: R. Löwit; reprint: 1979 Hamburg: Helmut Buske.

Mieses, Matthias. 1924. *Die Jiddische Sprache: eine historische Grammatik des Idioms der integralen Juden Ost- und Mitteleuropas.* Berlin/Vienna: B. Harz.

Nachama, Andreas. 2005. *Jiddisch im Berliner Jargon.* Berlin: Jaron Verlag.

Paul, Herrmann. 2007. *Mittelhochdeutsche Grammatik.* Neu bearbeitet von Thomas Klein, Hans-Joachim Solm und Klaus-Peter Wegera. Mit einer Syntax von Ingeborg Schöbler, neubearbeitet und erweitert von Heinz-Peter Prell. 27th ed. Tübingen: Niemeyer.

Röll, Walter. 1966. "Das älteste jüdisch-deutsche Sprachdenkmal: ein Verspaar im Wormser Machsor von 1272/1273." *Zeitschrift für Mundartforschung* 33: 127–138.

Rowley, Anthony R. 2011 "Bavarian: Successful dialect or failed language?" *Handbook of Language and Ethnic Identity.* Volume 2: *The Success-Failure Continuum in Language and Ethnic Identity Efforts*, eds. Joshua A. Fishman and Ofelia Garía, 209–309. Oxford /New York: Oxford University Press.

Rubin, Aaron. 2005. *Studies in Semitic Grammaticalization.* Winona Lake, Indiana: Eisenbrauns.

Sadan, Tsvi. 2013. "Yiddish, Hebrew component in." *Encyclopedia of Hebrew Language and Linguistics*, ed. Geoffrey Khan, vol. 3: 1034–1038. Leiden: Brill.

Schäfer, Lea. 2014. *Imitationen des Jiddischen in der deutschsprachigen Literatur. Studien zur Struktur fiktionaler Sprache.* Dissertation, University of Marburg.

Schultz, Julia. 2019. "The impact of Yiddish on the English language: An overview of lexical borrowing in the variety of subject areas and spheres of life influenced by Yiddish over time." *English Today* 35/3: 2–7.

Shmeruk, Chone and Leonard Prager. 2007. "Yiddish literature." *Encyclopaedia Judaica*, 2nd edition, eds. Michael Berenbaum and Fred Skolnok, vol. 21: 338–372. Detroit: Macmillan Reference USA.

Southern, Mark R.V. 2005. *Contagious Couplings: transmission of expressives in Yiddish echo phrases.* Westport, CT: Praeger Publishers.

Stern, Heidi. 2000. *Wörterbuch zum jiddischen Lehnwortschatz in den deutschen Dialekten.* Tübingen: Niemeyer.

Taube, Moshe. 1987. "The development of aspectual auxiliaries in Yiddish." *Word* 38: 13–25.

Taube, Moshe. 2012. "On the relative marker *vos* and Yiddish post-modifiers." *Leket: Yidddish Studies Today*, eds. Marion Aptroot et al., 467–481. Düsseldorf: Düsseldorf University Press.

Taube, Moshe. 2014. "On superordinate *az*-clauses in Yiddish narrative." *Yiddish Language Structures*, eds. Marion Aptroot and Björn Hansen, 231–251. Berlin: de Gruyter Mouton.

Taube, Moshe. 2016. "The usual suspects: Slavic, Yiddish, and the accusative existentials and possessives in Modern Hebrew." *Language Contact and the Development of Modern Hebrew*, ed. Edit Doron, 25–35. Leiden: Brill.

Thomason, Sarah Grey and Terrence Kaufman (1988), *Language Contact, Creolization, and Genetic Linguistics.* Berkeley, The University of California Press.

Timm, Erika. 1985. "Zur Frage der Echtheit von Raschis jiddischen Glossen." *Beiträge zur Geschichte der deutschen Sprache und Literatur* 107: 45–81.

Timm, Erika. 1986. "Das Jiddische as Kontrastsprache bei der Erforschung des Frühneuhochdeutschen." *Zeitschrift für Germanistische Linguistik* 14: 1–22.

Timm, Erika 1987. *Graphische und phonische Struktur des Westjiddischen unter besonderer Berücksichtigung der Zeit um 1600* (Hermaea 52). Tübingen: Niemeyer.

Timm, Erika. 2001. "Glikls Sprache vor ihrem sozialhistorischen und geographischen Hintergrund." Die Hamburger Kauffrau Glikl. Jüdische Existenz in der frühen Neuzeit, ed. Monika Richarz. Hamburg: Christians, 49–67.

Timm, Erika. 2005, unter Mitarbeit von Gustav Adolf Beckmann. *Historische jiddische Semantik. Die Bibelübersetzungssprache als Faktor der Auseinanderentwicklung des jiddischen und des deutschen Wortschatzes.* Tübingen: Niemeyer.

Trudgill, Peter. 1986. *Dialects in Contact.* Oxford: Blackwell.

Vennemann, Theo. 2012. *Germania Semitica*, edited by Patrizia Noel Aziz Hanna. Berlin/New York: Mouton de Gruyter.

Wagner, Esther-Miriam. 2013. "Germanic languages, Hebrew loanwords in." *Encyclopedia of Hebrew Language and Linguistics*, ed. Geoffrey Khan, vol. 2: 57–60. Leiden: Brill.

Weinreich, Max. 2008. *History of the Yiddish Language*. Translated by Shlomo Noble. New Haven: Yale University Press. [Translation of Weinreich's four-volume *Geshikhte fun der yidisher shprakh* געשיכטע פֿון דער ייִדישער שפּראַך]

Weinreich, Uriel. 1955. "Yiddish blend with a Slavic element." *Word* 11/4: 603–610.

Weinreich, Uriel. 1969 (5th ed.). *College Yiddish. An Introduction to the Yiddish Language and to Jewish Life and Culture.* New York: YIVO Institute for Jewish Research.

Weinreich, Uriel. 1977. *Modern English–Yiddish, Yiddish–English Dictionary.* New York: Schocken Books.

Wexler, Paul. 1993. *The Ashkenazic Jews: A Slavo-Turkic People in Search of a Jewish Identity*. Columbus, OH: Slavica.

Wolf, Siegmund A. 1962. *Jiddisches Wörterbuch. Wortschatz des deutschen Grundbestandes der jiddischen (jüdischdeutschen) Sprache.* Mannheim: Bibliographisches Institut. [1986. Hamburg: Buske]

Wolf, Siegmund A. 1985. *Wörterbuch des Rotwelschen. Deutsche Gaunersprache.* Hamburg: Buske.

Yuasa, Etsuyo and Jerry M. Sadock. 2002. "Pseudo-subordination: a mismatch between syntax and semantics." *Journal of Linguistics* 38: 87–111.

Written Jewish English

Sarah Bunin Benor, Hebrew Union College

1. Introduction

In 1981, pioneering sociologist of language Joshua Fishman wrote, "The ultimate Jewish sociolinguistic reality today is the fact that English or some Jewish variant thereof is probably the most widespread JL [Jewish Language] of our time" (Fishman 1981: 15). If we exclude Modern Hebrew from the list of "Jewish languages," this remains true in 2021. Due to the concentration of Jews in Israel and the United States, as well as smaller communities in the United Kingdom, Canada, South Africa, Australia, and New Zealand, the vast majority of Jews in the world today speak either Modern Hebrew or some variety of English.

Much scholarship about Jewish languages excludes Jewish English, Jewish Latin American Spanish, Jewish Hungarian, Jewish Russian, and other varieties that came into existence only in the post-Emancipation era (e.g., Weinreich 2008 [1973], Birnbaum 1979, Rabin et al. 1979, Bunis 1981, Wexler 1981, Alvarez-Péreyre 2003). There are several reasons for this omission, including the orientation toward antiquity and the Middle Ages in Jewish studies and the sense that the Emancipation and Enlightenment periods represented a radical break with the past (Benor 2009: 266).

Another reason contemporary Jewish languages are often considered to be in a different analytic category from Jewish languages of the past is that the former are not generally written in the traditional Hebrew (Aramaic) script and instead follow orthographic norms of their local non-Jewish correlates with the insertion of Hebrew words in Hebrew letters or transcription. This transition is primarily due to increased literacy rates throughout the developed world and the fact that Latin (or Cyrillic, etc.) letters are now accessible to anyone with an elementary education (Benor 2009: 249). Another factor in the lack of Hebrew letters in contemporary Jewish languages is Jews' increased integration into society (Gold 1985: 294) and, at least in the case of American Jews, their comparatively low levels of knowledge of Hebrew. Although the orthographic difference is significant, I believe it should not lead to the exclusion of contemporary communities from comparative Jewish linguistic analysis. As Rabin writes, "the use of Hebrew characters would be a secondary, but not necessary, mark of a Jewish language" (Rabin 1981: 21).

Despite the general trend to see Jewish languages as a phenomenon of the past, several scholars have included Jewish English – and sometimes additional post-Emancipation Jewish language varieties – in their comparative Jewish linguistic analyses (Rabin 1981, Gold 1981a, Fishman 1981, Steinmetz 1981, Gold and Prager 1981–1987, Gold 1985, Gold 1986, Prager 1986, Weiser 1995, Spolsky and Benor 2006, Benor 2008, Hary 2009, Benor 2009, Tirosh-Becker and Benor (eds.) 2013–, Kahn and Rubin 2016, Hary and Benor 2018). These comparative studies and collections of research on multiple Jewish languages get around the sticky issue of distinguishing between languages and dialects by defining the term "Jewish language" as referring to what others might call languages and dialects (Fishman 1981, Bar-Asher 2002, Tirosh-Becker and Benor (eds.) 2013–) or by replacing the terms "Jewish language" and "Jewish dialect" with "Jewish lect" (Gold 1981a; Gold and Prager 1981–1987) or "Jewish religiolect" (Hary 2009). See also Maman, this volume.

Although I include any Jewish community in comparative Jewish linguistic analysis, I also feel it is important to distinguish between different types of Jewish languages. In previous work (Benor 2008), I pointed out the difference between "coterritorial languages" like Judeo-Arabic and Jewish English (situations where Jews live in an area where the non-Jewish correlate/base language is spoken) and "post-coterritorial languages" like Judezmo/Ladino and Yiddish (situations where Jews' non-Jewish neighbors mostly speak unrelated languages, like Slavic languages in the case of Yiddish and Balkan languages in the case of Judezmo). Even so, I still include both types under the umbrella category "Jewish languages" to facilitate comparative analysis.

I also call for changing the central question of Jewish linguistics from "Does [a given Jewish community] speak a Jewish language?" to "To what extent does a given excerpt of speech or writing by a Jew make use of a distinctively Jewish linguistic repertoire?" (Benor 2008: 1068). A Jewish community's distinctive linguistic repertoire (based on the broader construct "ethnolinguistic repertoire" – Benor 2010) is defined as the collection of differences between their language and that of their non-Jewish neighbors. This repertoire can include Hebrew and Aramaic loanwords, loanwords and grammatical influences from more recently spoken ancestral languages, systematic phonological and syntactic features, prosodic and discourse features, and more. In this article I describe the distinctive Jewish linguistic repertoire of Jews in the United States of America and discuss the variation among different types of Jews there. Then I analyze eight excerpts of Jewish English writing in order to answer the question, "To what extent, and how, does a given excerpt of writing by American Jews make use of a distinctively Jewish linguistic repertoire?"

2. Distinctive features of Jewish English

Previous research on Jewish English has pointed to a repertoire of distinctive features used in Jewish English that distinguish the language from its non-Jewish correlate, English. The most common and most salient feature is the use of several hundred loanwords from Hebrew, Aramaic, Yiddish, Ladino, Judeo-Arabic, and other languages (see analysis in Steinmetz 1981, Gold 1985, 1986, Benor 2000, 2012, and several dictionaries: Rosten 1968, Steinmetz 1987, Bluestein 1989, Glinert 1992, Weiser 1995, Eisenberg and Scolnic 2001, Steinmetz 2005, Benor 2012). In addition to the lexicon, Jewish English has distinctive features at all levels of language, including the following (Jewish variants appear first, and general American English versions are presented as contrasts):

- Phonology
  - hyperarticulation of word-final /t/ (right => [rayt^h] vs. [rayʔ]) (Benor 2001, Levon 2008)

- final devoicing ([goingk][J] vs. [going], [liars] vs. [liarz]) (Benor 2012: 102)
- non-raising of pre-nasal /æ/ (the vowel in "candle" and "lamb" sounds like the vowel in "glad") (Benor 2012: 103)
- New York State regional features outside of New York City (e.g., [harrible] vs. [horrible]) (Knack 1991, Benor 2011)

• Syntax (Benor 2012: 91, 96–102)
- periphrastic Hebrew loan verbs ("Don't be[Y] *mevatel*[H] my *zman*[H]" ['Don't waste my time']; "May you be[Y] *zocheh*[H] to build a *bayis*[H/Y] *ne?eman*[H] *b'yisroel*[H/Y]!" ['May you merit creating a faithful home in the Jewish community'])
- preposition deletion ("Her bus gets in 10:15," vs. "Her bus gets in at 10:15")
- present for present perfect tense, sometimes with "already": ("I live here already eight years," vs. "I've lived here for eight years")
- "so" insertion: "If you like him, so tell him" vs. "If you like him, then tell him"
- "should": "I want that you should take her number"[J] vs. "I want you to take her number"
- "to": "coming to us for dinner" vs. "coming to our house for dinner"
- phrasal verbs: "What do we learn out from this?" vs. "What do we learn from this?"

• Prosody (Weinreich 1956: 640, Benor 2012: 103–104, Burdin 2017)
- chanting and quasi-chanting contours
- high-falling pitch boundaries: used at the end of introductory phrases and embedded clauses to indicate a "dramatized transition"

• Discourse
- highly engaged speech style (Tannen 1981, Schiffrin 1984, Benor 2011)
- fast speech rate (Benor 2012: 104–105)
- hesitation click (Benor 2012: 105)
- verb-initial sentences in continuing narrative (e.g., "Said the rabbi…")

• Lexical semantics: distinctive meanings of English words (Benor 2012)
- e.g., "continuity" for 'generational transmission of Judaism' in Jewish communal organizations
- e.g., "egalitarian" for 'non-Orthodox Jewish [prayer group or service] in which men and women can participate equally and a *mechitzah* (boundary separating women from men) is not used'

These features are influenced by several sources, including Yiddish (an ancestral language of a large percentage of English-speaking Jews), Modern Hebrew (which many Jews learn in school and when they spend time with Israelis in Israel or locally), traditional text study, and the concentration of Jews in the New York area historically and today. Although some of these features stem from other languages, they are only included in this list if they are used by native English speakers several generations removed from immigration.

Even though a linguist can describe such a pool of features, no one Jew will use all of them. Some will use none, some a few, and some many. The diversity is not just in degree, but in the choice of which features each person uses. As I found in my survey-based research (Benor 2011), linguistic variation correlates with several factors, including community affiliation (Reform, Conservative, Modern Orthodox, Hasidic, etc.), generational distance from immigration, ancestral languages, the percentage of one's friends who are Jewish, time spent in Israel, and Shabbat observance. The phonological and syntactic features are found primarily in Orthodox communities, and the use of certain Yiddish loanwords is limited primarily to older Ashkenazi Jews and those involved in Yiddish cultural activities. There is also variation in the pronunciation of Hebrew loanwords: Haredi Orthodox Jews tend to use Ashkenazi norms like penultimate stress, the Hebrew *qamaṣ* vowel as [o] or [ʌ], and the Hebrew grapheme <ת> as [s], while Modern Orthodox and non-Orthodox Jews are more likely to use Israeli Hebrew norms, like ultimate stress, *qamaṣ* as [a], and ת as [t]. Another area of diversity is location in the English-speaking world (Canada, UK, Australia, etc.), about which further research is needed.

Some of the features listed above, especially in phonology, prosody, and discourse, are not discernible in written Jewish English. Even the syntactic features are rare in written language. Some can be found in relatively informal writing, such as on Internet forums like hashkafa.com, theyeshivaworld.com, and imamother.com, but most appear only in spoken Jewish English, especially in Haredi Orthodox communities (Yeshivish and Hasidic). Therefore, the excerpts analyzed below focus primarily on lexicon, especially loanwords from Hebrew and Yiddish.

3. Texts

The excerpts below offer a glimpse into the diversity of American Jews. Most come from e-mails sent to the distribution lists of Jewish organizations, one comes from a blog post, and one comes from a text book. All excerpts that are not publicly available are reprinted here with permission of the authors or institutions that distributed them. Names have been changed unless the individuals gave permission for their names to be used.

In contrast to other articles in this volume, most of these excerpts are not immediately glossed, because the glosses would be mostly the same as the originals. Instead, loanwords and other distinctive features are marked with a superscript "H" (Hebrew), "Y" (Yiddish), "Aram" (Aramaic), or "L" (Ladino), depending on the origin, and then glossed and discussed in the analysis that follows each excerpt. The authors' original orthographic conventions are preserved, including whether they set apart loanwords using italics, capitalization, or quotation marks, and whether they present them in English or Hebrew characters.

3.1 Excerpt #1: Email from coordinator to independent minyan *e-mail list:*

From: [Allison Berger]
Date: Tue, Apr 28, 2015 at 10:30 PM
Subject: Shabbat^{H} Together
To: [Independent minyan^{H} e-mail list]

Shalom[H],

Just a friendly reminder that we will be meeting this Shabbat[H] May 2nd, Acherei[H] Mot[H]-Kedoshim[H]. This is your chance: to make the minyan[H], to sign up to leyn[Y] [or] to be part of the kahal[H].

We will be meeting the first and third Shabbatot[H] starting this Shabbat[H]. The third Shabbat[H] will continue with meditation and with the kids' programming.

kol[H] tuv[H],

[Allison]

This excerpt exhibits a common feature of Jewish English written communication, Hebrew loanwords for greetings/openings and closings, in this case *Shalom* ('hello, peace') and *kol tuv* ('all goodness'). In addition, several loanwords are used to describe Jewish ritual observance: one Yiddish word, *leyn* ('chant Torah'), and four Hebrew words and phrases, *Shabbat* ('Sabbath'), *Acherei Mot-Kedoshim* (lit. 'after death-holy – the name of a double Torah portion read in the spring'), *minyan* ('quorum of 10 adult Jews [male or female in this egalitarian prayer group]', and *kahal* ('community, congregation'). The word *minyan* in the name of the group refers to a volunteer-led prayer group (in contrast to a synagogue, which generally has a rabbi and other professional staff), and the phrase "make the *minyan*" in this case refers to arriving early to make sure ten people are present in order to recite certain prayers. The word *Shabbat* is pluralized according to the Modern Hebrew norm, *Shabbatot*, as opposed to the Ashkenazi/Yiddish *Shabosim*, or the English-inflected *Shabbat*s or *Shabbos*es.

Readers who are not familiar with this type of Jewish English might understand the gist of this e-mail but not the details. They would likely feel that the message was not directed to them, as the author does not translate the Hebrew and Yiddish loanwords. Some synagogues and other Jewish communal organizations avoid using so many loanwords or use them with parenthetical translations. An independent minyan e-mail list can include the loanwords without translation because they expect members to have a shared cultural and religious background and knowledge of Jewish English (although they might call it "Jewish language" or "English with Hebrew words," rather than "Jewish English").

3.2 Excerpt #2: Humorous "halachic" *question*

Subject: Xmas Halakhah redux

Date: Thu, 24 Dec 2009 17:37:31 -0600

From: Saul Kelner שאול קלנר

To: [Jewish professional email list]

Chaverim[H],

In 2006 I inquired as to the halachah[H] on whether Chinese food should be eaten Erev[H] Chag[H] or Yom[H] Chag[H]. (There was a makhloket[H], of course, but we decided to follow Beis[H/Y] Fendrick whose teshuva[H] is reproduced below).

I need another psak[H] on a perhaps even more difficult matter:

Q: Nashville has no good Chinese food. For proper observance of Christmas, is it permissible to eat other Asian cuisines instead? If permissible, then are any particular cuisines preferred (Japanese, Korean, Indian, Thai etc.)?
I checked Hilchos[H/Y] Xmas, which [David Leibowitz] had pointed me in his 2006 tshuvah[H], but I found no guidance on this particular matter…
Thank you. Gut[Y] nitlnacht[Y].
Shaul Kelner
…

Sue Fendrick's Psak[H] on when Chinese Food Should be Eaten, Erev[H] or Yom[H]
Shaul, The halakhah[H] for Ashkenazim[H] is that you go out for Chinese food and to a movie on Christmas Day. If you only go out to the movies on Christmas day, b'diavad[Aram] you are yotzei[H] even if you didn't get Chinese food. If you eat Chinese food on Christmas Eve rather than Christmas Day, you do [so] without the bracha[H] ("… v'tzivanu[H] le'echol[H] ochel[H] sini[H]"). Reform and some Reconstructionist Jews get takeout on Christmas Eve.

This e-mail was sent to an e-mail list of Jewish communal professionals – rabbis, educators, nonprofit leaders, etc. In contrast to Excerpt #1, which was intended to convey information, this excerpt was intended primarily for entertainment. The authors of the query and of the *psak* ('rabbinic ruling') are aware that there are not actually serious *halachic* ('Jewish legal') rulings on when Jews should eat Chinese food and go to the movies on Christmas (two activities common among American Jews, because many other restaurants and entertainment venues are closed on that holiday). They use an exaggerated version of *halachic* Jewish English, with which they are familiar from other contexts, to heighten the humorous, parodic nature of the exchange.

Again, the e-mail uses loanwords for the opening and the closing. *Chaverim* is Hebrew for 'friends', and *Gut nitlnacht* is Yiddish for 'good Christmas Eve'. The author presents his name in both English and Hebrew letters in the "from" field of the email (Saul Kelner שאול קלנר) but only in English letters (the Hebrew version, Shaul) in the signature. The subject of the email uses the humorous phrase "Xmas *halakhah*" ('the laws of Christmas'). "Xmas," which includes the Greek letter X, chi, from the Greek *Christos* ('Christ'), is a common way of abbreviating "Christmas" in English, not a specifically Jewish convention. But many Jews use "Xmas" (or *nitlnacht* or the more tongue-in-cheek *kratsmach*, Yiddish 'scratch me') to avoid writing the name "Christ." The phrase "Xmas *halakhah*" has English syntax and uses *halakhah* ('law') as a mass noun (in contrast to a count noun, like "a *halakhah*," perhaps on the model of "law"), while a Hebrew version might be *Hilxot ḥag ha-molad*. This use of Hebrew words with English syntax is common in Jewish English, as it is in other Jewish languages. Note that later the author uses "*Hilchos* Xmas," based on the title of the document he cites, which uses a more Hebraic syntax with an Ashkenazi rendering of the ת at the end of *Hilchos*.

The excerpt includes several other loanwords: *Erev/Erev Chag* ('eve/eve of holiday') *Yom/Yom Chag* ('day/day of holiday'), *makhloket* ('dispute'), *Beis* ('house [of] / school of thought'), *teshuva/tshuvah* ('responsum'), *psak* ('ruling'), *Ashkenazim* ('Jews of Central/Eastern European descent'), *b'di-avad* (Aramaic 'after the fact'), *yotzei* ('released from obligation via fulfillment'), *bracha* ('blessing'), as well as a code switch to Whole Hebrew (Weinreich 2008) for part of a faux blessing: "*v'tzivanu le'echol ochel sini*" ('and commanded us to eat Chinese food').

All of the Hebrew loanwords are common in *halachic* dialogue, and their use here indexes the exchange as being part of that body of literature and discourse. Most of the words are rendered with Modern Hebrew phonological norms – *b'di-avad* rather than Ashkenazi *b'dieved*, *makhloket* rather than *makhlokes* or *makhloykes*, and *bracha* rather than *broche*. Exceptions are *Beis* (rather than Modern Hebrew *Beit*) and *yotzei* (rather than Modern Hebrew *yotze*), as Jewish English often preserves the diphthong-monophtong distinction between *ṣere* and *segol*. Given the norms of Jewish English, it is likely that the writers pronounced some of the words with penultimate stress, especially *Ashkenazim*, *tshuvah*, and *bracha*, while Modern Hebrew would use ultimate stress. This is due to a combination of Yiddish/Ashkenazi influence and English stress patterns, which are primarily penultimate.

Another hallmark of this excerpt is orthographic variation. Kelner writes *halakhah* in the subject line and *halachah* in the body of the email, and Fendrick writes *halakhah*. Kelner uses both *teshuva* and *tshuvah*, reflecting both variability in the realization of the word-initial consonant-*šəwā-nāʕ*-consonant sequence (Benor 2012: 149–150) and variability in transcription (<h> reflects the silent Hebrew word-final *he* and is optional in Jewish English transcription). Such variability is common in Jewish English. Some words have a very common spelling, like *chutzpah* ('nerve, gall') and *aliyah* ('moving to Israel, blessings for Torah reading'), but most loanwords in Jewish English have multiple common spellings, such as *Chanukah/Hannukah/Chanukkah*, etc. (see Benor, Krasner, and Avni 2020, chapter 6). Given the lack of standards in this relatively young language, it is not surprising that even in one e-mail the same word is spelled in multiple ways.

Like Excerpt #1, this excerpt does not offer parenthetical glosses of loanwords. The authors assume that recipients of their e-mails will be familiar with the type of Jewish English that characterizes *halachic* discourse and will understand the humor.

3.3 Excerpt #3: "A Simple Jew" blog post, 2009: "All You Need To Do Is Ask!"

Early Sunday morning, I asked the Sudilkover[Y] Rebbe[H/Y] what we should be doing about the situation in Eretz[H] Yisroel[H/Y].

The Rebbe[H/Y] answered with the following parable:

A person is travelling through a desert and has run out of water. All of a suden [sic!] an angel appears to him and tells him that if [he] asks for just one thing, Hashem[H] will answer him.

What do you think that this thirsty person should ask for?

The Rebbe[H/Y] said that most people answer this question by saying that the man dying of thirst should ask for a glass of water. However, the truly intelligent person answers this question by saying that he should ask to be saved and returned to the comfort of his home.

In this time of sakana[H] (danger), we can certainly say more kapitlach[Y] of Tehillim[H], however we need not focus our tefillos[H/Y] on interim goals of the IDF's success in Gaza or the safety of civilians during rocket attacks, we need only to focus our tefillos[H/Y] on the ultimate goal; Moshiach[H/Y].
The Rebbe[H/Y] said that people are spending too much time listening to the news and not enough time internalizing the hints that are being sent to us. Each day, Hashem[H] is telling us "My precious children, I will send you Moshiach[H/Y] and release you from golus[H/Y], all you need to do is ask!"

Comments:
…
But haven't Yidden[Y] been asking that for thousands of years already? I'm not saying not to ask, but to make it sound like one just has to ask and it will be granted presto? We have to do work on ourselves, do teshuvoh[H/Y], etc., so the requests will have a better chance of being granted.

I went to daaven[Y] to Hashem[H] by the Lubavetcher[Y] Rebbe's[H/Y] Ohel[H] a couple [of] days ago.
Before I opened my mouth, I stood there for a while wondering if praying to find my zivug[H], or praying for parnasa[H], or praying for health of ill family, or the chayalim[H] and Jews in S. Israel was really paramount to using the time to pray for Geulah[H]...

– There is no contradiction.
Truly and sincerely praying for the latter (Geulah[H]) will include all of the former.
Moshiach[H/Y] Now!

BH[H/Y]
There is some sort of confusion. I do not know if this was a misprint, but to not pray for Jews in IDF, CHAS[H] VESHALOM![H] Chazal,[H] our sages have rulled [sic] that in matters of Pikuah[H] Nefesh[H] (Protection of lives), even the concern of bringing Moshiach[H/Y] must be put asside [sic] for the moment. Kol[H] Vahomor[H] (how much more so) Rambam[H] has rulled [sic] that "one should know, that any Mitzvah[H] can be the one to tip the scales of the world to good and usher in the complete Redemption". How much more so then [sic] the Mitzvah[H] [of] protecting Jewish lives!...

A linguistic analysis of this blog post and its responses leads us to believe that the authors are Orthodox Jews toward the Black Hat / Haredi end of the Modern Orthodox to Haredi continuum (see Benor 2012). The Hebrew words are rendered with Ashkenazi phonological norms, such as *Moshiach* ('Messiah') vs. Israeli *Mashiach*, *Eretz Yisroel* ('Land of Israel') vs. Israeli *Eretz Yisrael*, *tefillos* ('prayers') vs. Israeli *tfilot*, *golus* ('exile, Diaspora') vs. Israeli *galut*, *teshuvoh* ('repentance') vs. Israeli *tshuva*. We can assume the writers pronounce these words with penultimate stress, in contrast to Israeli ultimate stress. We can assume the same for several Hebrew loanwords that do not have [o] for *qamaṣ* or [s] for ת: *Tehillim* ('Psalms'), *zivug* ('match'), *parnasa* ('livelihood, income'), *Geulah* ('redemption'), *chas veshalom* ('God forbid'), *mitzvah* ('commandment'), and *Rambam* ('Maimonides'). One word is pronounced with penultimate stress in both Ashkenazi and Israeli Hebrew: *ohel* ('grave structure'). Two words are pronounced with ultimate stress in both Ashkenazi and Israeli Hebrew: *Hashem* ('God') and *Chazal* (an acronym of *ḥaḵamenu ziḵronam li-ḇraḵa* 'Our Sages, may their memory be blessed'). The Israeli Hebrew loanword *chayalim* 'soldiers' is likely pronounced with ultimate stress and [a] rather than [o] or [ʌ] for *qamaṣ*, because it is seen as an Israeli Hebrew loanword rather than one from the Rabbinic tradition.

In addition to Ashkenazi Hebrew, the excerpt also features a few Yiddish loanwords: *kapitlach* ('chapters'), *Yidden* ('Jews'), and *daaven* ('pray'). Two of the names of rabbis use Yiddish morphology – the masculine adjectival suffix *-er*: the *Sudilkover Rebbe* and the *Lubavetcher Rebbe*. This use of Ashkenazi and Yiddish lexical, phonological, and morphological features helps readers (both linguists and the general Orthodox public) to identify the authors as locating themselves toward the Haredi end of the Modern Orthodox to Haredi continuum, because Modern Orthodox and non-Orthodox Jews would likely use more Modern Hebrew features.

The authors assume that readers will understand most of their loanwords and phrases, but they offer glosses of four: "*sakana* (danger)," "*Chazal*, our sages," "*Pikuah Nefesh* (Protection of lives)," and "*Kol Vahomor* (how much more so)." These translations are surprising, because all four of the phrases are common in American Orthodox communities. It seems that the blogger feels that *sakana* is a less common loanword, and the author of the comment starting with "BH" may be directing his comment at a broader audience, as he translates three of his eight loanwords.

The spelling *Kol* is also surprising, as *kal vachomer* is much more common. This and several other instances of variation in the spelling of Hebrew and Yiddish loanwords, as in Excerpt #2, indicate that orthographic norms in Jewish English have not yet fully crystalized.

This excerpt also includes incorrect spellings of English words, such as "suden" (sudden), "rulled" (ruled), and "asside" (aside). Certainly many Haredi Orthodox writers have perfect English spelling. But some do not, and this can be attributed to the greater emphasis the Haredi education system places on Judaic studies compared to secular studies. It is also possible that the authors who used these non-standard spellings spoke Yiddish or Hebrew as their first language (especially the author of the comment starting with "BH") and/or did not attend school in an English-speaking country (reflecting the transnational orientation of Jewish English-speaking Orthodox communities).

Aside from the few spelling irregularities, most of the English is standard. The few exceptions reflect calque influence from Textual Hebrew, Israeli Hebrew, and Yiddish. The author who wrote "complete Redemption" may have been thinking of the Hebrew phrase *geula shlema*. The word "situation" may be inspired by Israeli Hebrew *matzav* ('situation'), which is generally understood by Israel-oriented English-speaking Jews to refer to the political and military situation in Israel and the surrounding region. One of the commenters uses "by" in its Yiddish-influenced usage: "I went to *daaven* to *Hashem* *by* the *Lubavetcher Rebbe*'s *Ohel*." Standard English would render this sentence: 'I went to pray to God at the Lubavitcher Rabbi's grave'. The Yiddish preposition *bay* has several meanings, including 'at [a location]', and Orthodox Jewish English has incorporated this usage in the cognate (and homophonic) English word "by." This is a frequently used feature of Orthodox Jewish English (Benor 2012), and it is becoming more and more common in younger generations (Benor 2011: 150).

A final feature of this excerpt is acronyms, IDF and *BH*. IDF is a common way that Israel-oriented Jews refer to the Israeli Defense Forces. Many Orthodox Jews use "BH" (*Be'ezras Hashem* – 'with God's help' or *Baruch Hashem* – 'bless[ed be] God'), "BS"D" (*b-siyata di-šmaya* – Aramaic 'with the help of heaven'), or variants like "B"H," "BSD," or "בס״ד," at the top of written correspondence (handwritten or electronic).

3.4 Excerpt #4: Bnei Akiva Camp Moshava parent update (8/15):

Dvar[H] Torah[H] By Rabbi [Dov Greenberg]
Rosh[H] Moreh[H] Camp Moshava[H]

In פרשת עקב, the Torah[H] commands us to "bentsch"[Y] after we eat. The source for the mitzvah[H] to recite Birkat[H] Hamazon[H] is the passuk[H]: (Devarim[H] 8:10) וְאָכַלְתָּ וְשָׂבָעְתָּ וּבֵרַכְתָּ אֶת יְקֹוָק אֱלֹהֶיךָ עַל הָאָרֶץ הַטֹּבָה אֲשֶׁר נָתַן לָךְ: – "And you will eat and be sated, and you shall bless the Lord, your God, for the good land He has given you."

The very next passuk[H] warns "not to forget Hashem[H], your G-d, by not keeping His commandments, His ordinances, and His statutes, which I command you this day": הִשָּׁמֶר לְךָ פֶּן תִּשְׁכַּח אֶת יְקֹוָק אֱלֹהֶיךָ לְבִלְתִּי שְׁמֹר מִצְוֹתָיו וּמִשְׁפָּטָיו וְחֻקֹּתָיו אֲשֶׁר אָנֹכִי מְצַוְּךָ הַיּוֹם

Similiarly [sic], in the second blessing of Birkat[H] Hamazon[H], we thank G-d for the food, and Land, and for the Torah: ... נוֹדֶה לְּךָ, ה' אֱלֹקינוּ, עַל שֶׁהִנְחַלְתָּ לַאֲבוֹתֵינוּ אֶרֶץ חֶמְדָּה טוֹבָה וּרְחָבָה, וְעַל תּוֹרָתְךָ שֶׁלִּמַּדְתָּנוּ, וְעַל חֻקֶּיךָ שֶׁהוֹדַעְתָּנוּ

This needs explanation. Why is the mitzvah[H] to bless G-d for the food we ate and for the Land which provided us the food, followed the idea of the importance to keep the Torah[H] and mitzvot[H]?

The Chatam[H] Sofer[H] (in Torat[H] Moshe[H]) explains that the role of eating in our lives can easily be misunderstood. The act of eating is materialistic, and we share this behavior with animals, as they, too, eat in order to survive. A Jew's task is to elevate his eating to be an essential aid to provide himself with the physical needs in order to better serve Hashem[H] and to grow spiritually.

In our code of law – the Shulchan[H] Aruch[H] (O.C. 231) – there is an entire chapter, named "בכל דרכיך דעהו" – "Know Him in all your ways". The Halacha[H] gives a detailed description of how the Jew is to channel his materialistic actions to help him better serve G-d. Eat, drink, sleep, and rest... all in order to serve Hashem[H].

For this reason the pesukim[H] in the Torah[H] and the beracha[H] in bentsching[Y] connect eating food and the Torah[H] and mitzvot[H], to ensure that we maintain the proper perspective to food and materialism.

As an added point, it can be said that our connection to the Land of Israel can also be easily misunderstood. Some could see it as any other land, meant for a geographic location for our nation, and for growing produce, providing materialistic needs. However, the pesukim[H] and the bracha[H] place the Land in context of Torah[H] and Mitzvot[H]. We now understand that the Land of Israel too is part of our connection to our service of Hashem[H]. Eretz[H] Yisrael[H] is the place where our spiritual growth should reach the greatest heights - as individuals and as a People. The Land is holy, and we have mitzvot[H] that can only be performed there (like Shmitta[H] which is being observed this year in Israel). I look forward to returning home to Israel at the end of the summer, to complete the year of Shmitta[H], and to continue eating the holy fruits of the Land.

This excerpt, written by an American-born rabbi who lives in Israel during the year and teaches at a Modern Orthodox Zionist camp in Pennsylvania in the summers, is filled with Hebrew loanwords and phrases and a few code switches into biblical and liturgical Hebrew. Loanwords include *Dvar Torah* ('brief teaching from Jewish sources'), *Moshava* ('name of the camp, lit. colony'), *Torah* ('Pentateuch'), *mitzvah* ('commandment'), *Birkat Hamazon* ('blessing after meals'), *passuk* ('verse'), *Hashem* ('God'), *Halacha* ('Jewish law'), and *Shmitta* ('agricultural sabbatical year'). Most refer to religious observance and the rabbinic tradition. Some have simple, common English equivalents, and others do not. The author assumes that the campers' parents who read this excerpt are familiar with Orthodox Jewish English and does not translate most of the loanwords he uses. He does explain that the *Shulchan Aruch* is "our code of law," and he does translate two of the three Hebrew liturgical quotes, indicating that he sees his audience as not necessarily completely proficient in the Hebrew rabbinic tradition.

More than other excerpts presented in this paper, this excerpt uses Hebrew letters for the Whole Hebrew code switches and a few of the loan phrases in the titles of chapters: פרשת עקב (*Parašat ʕeqeḇ* – a Torah portion) and בכל דרכיך דעהו (*bə-ḵol darḵē-ḵā dāʕē-hū* 'Know Him in all your ways' – a chapter from *Shulchan Aruch*, named after a quote from Proverbs 3:6). Other Hebrew names of books and authors are transcribed: *Devarim*, *Chatam Sofer*, *Torat Moshe*, and *Shulchan Aruch*.

The quotes in Hebrew orthography replace the Hebrew later *hey* with *qof* in God's names – אֱלֹקֵינוּ and יְקֹוָק – as writing with God's name is supposed to be kept in a *genizah* (storeroom of a synagogue) rather than discarded (although the author misses one: אֱלֹהֶיךָ). The author does the same with the English word "God," rendering it as "G-d," a common convention in English writing by religious Jews.

The only Yiddish word used, "*bentsch*," is presented in quotation marks on first appearance. That may indicate that the author feels that Yiddish loanwords are not as legitimate in Jewish English as Hebrew loanwords. *Bentsch* comes from the Romance component of Yiddish, likely Judeo-Italian *benedice* ('he blesses'), and it was used in Yiddish for 'bless' so speakers in the Germanic milieu could avoid the German word *segnen*, which meant not only 'bless' but also 'make the sign [of the cross]' (Weinreich 2008). In Jewish English, *bentsch* means not only 'bless' but also and more commonly 'say the blessings after meals'.

Later in the excerpt, the word *bentsch* is combined with English morphology: *bentsch*ing, a common practice in Jewish English. Most Yiddish verbs that are not periphrastic in Yiddish (*bentshn* 'to bless', *davenen* 'to pray', *kashern* 'to render kosher', *paskenen* 'to make a legal ruling') are used as direct verbs in English: they *daven*ed, we need to *kasher* our kitchen, he *pasken*s). In contrast, Hebrew-origin verbs that are periphrastic in Yiddish, like *zoyche zayn* ('merit') and *mekayem zayn* ('fulfill, realize'), are also periphrastic in Orthodox Jewish English, e.g., "we should be *zoche* to witness the coming of the *Moshiach*" ('we should merit witnessing the coming of the Messiah') and "The *Avos* were *mekayem* the *mitzvos* based on their understanding of how to serve *hashem*"[1] ('the patriarchs fulfilled the commandments based on their understanding of how to serve God').

Despite the presence of this Yiddish word, most of the loanwords in this excerpt are rendered with Israeli Hebrew norms, rather than Ashkenazi or Yiddish norms: *birkat* rather than *birkas*, *mitzvot* rather than *mitzvos*, and *passuk* rather than *posuk*. Based on my visit to the camp, which includes many Israeli and American staff members, I can share that there is great variation – *mítzvʌh* is more common than *mitzváh*, and *Tórah* is more common than *Toráh*, although both Ashkenazi and Israeli forms are used, sometimes by the same person within the same sentence.

In this excerpt, *mitzvah* is pluralized with Modern Hebrew morphology: *mitzvot*, rather than English morphology: *mitzvah*s or Ashkenazi Hebrew *mitzvos*. *Passuk* is pluralized as *pesukim*, which honors the *šəwā nāʕ* (Hebrew [ə] vowel) after the first consonant. It is possible that the author pronounces it as schwa to be strict about Hebrew grammar, or perhaps he has Sephardi heritage and pronounces it as [ɛ]. It is also possible that he pronounces it more like the Israeli Hebrew [psukím] but writes it with an <e> to more accurately reflect Biblical/Rabbinic Hebrew grammar (a common Jewish English writing convention). We see the same with *beracha*, which the author may pronounce as American Sephardi [bɛɹaxá], Israeli [bʁaxá], or, more likely, American Israeli [bɹaxá] or American Ashkenazi [bɹʌ́xʌ].

Aside from the use of loanwords and code switching, the English in this excerpt is mostly identical to non-Jewish English. Even the one spelling mistake is the kind of typo one would expect from any American: "Similiarly" rather than "Similarly." However, there are a few semantic influences or calques of Hebrew words and phrases with English lexical material. One example is the words "materialism" and "materialistic," as in "The act of eating is materialistic." Within contemporary American English, "materialistic" generally refers to being overly concerned with money and material possessions. The use in this excerpt seems to be a calque of *gašmiyut*[H] ('materialism, indulgence in earthly pleasures'), in contrast to *ruḥaniyut*[H] ('spirituality'). Similarly, "our service of Hashem" may be a calque of *ʕab̲odat Ha-šem.*[H] According to a Google search of English websites, "our service to God" is more common than "our service of God," although both are common. In observant Jewish circles, which use the word *Hashem*, the reverse is true: "Our service of Hashem" is more common than "our service to Hashem," which may reflect calque influence of *ʕab̲odat Ha-šem.*[H] The final calque phrase is "the Land of Israel" and its shortened version, "the Land." This phrase is commonly used in English-speaking Jewish communities to refer to *ʔEreṣ Yiśraʔel*[H] (which is used later in this excerpt), sometimes in contrast to the State of Israel and

1 http://jewishworker.blogspot.com/2010/11/did-avos-kepp-all-613-mitzvos.html

sometimes to refer to the geographic area in historical periods when Jews did not have sovereignty there.

Another interesting feature is the phrase "*Rosh Moreh*," which is the title given to Rabbi Greenberg in the introductory material (likely written by someone in the camp office). This is surprising, as the more common descriptor of Rabbi Greenberg's position at Camp Moshava is *Rosh Morim* (head of teachers). *Rosh* means 'head', and *Moreh* means 'teacher'. *Rosh Moreh* has a different sense in Hebrew ('head of teacher'). It is possible that the person compiling this email knew that Rabbi Greenberg was the head teacher and simply translated those words into Hebrew. Such calques of English phrases into Hebrew sometimes occur in Jewish English, and they are often the topic of intense ideological discussion, as many English speakers with strong Hebrew knowledge consider them to be mistakes.

3.5 Excerpt #5: Yiddish culture group email

From: **Living Traditions**
Date: Sat, Nov 27, 2010 at 8:01 AM
Subject: KlezKamp 2010 Updates

Dear friends,
New York Times Arts reporter [Jim Baskin] spent a delightful few days with us at last year's Klez[Y]Kamp and has just written about it in today's edition of the paper of record. If you've been on the fence about joining us, now–shvartse[Y] fraytik[Y]–is the time to register for Klez[Y]Kamp. There are still limited bus seats available between NYC and the hotel, either one-way or round-trip…

Two other announcements:
* For family reasons, teaching staff accordionist/musicologist [Benjy Shapiro] will not be joining us. We wish him and his mishpokhe[Y] good health and full recovery.
* An error in the Klez[Y]Kamp brochure made it appear that the all-in-Yiddish classes taught by Forverts columnist [Sura Melamed] are the same. Please note: her AM1 class, Laytish[Y] Mame[Y] Loshn[Y], is about her late father, the eminent linguist Dr. [Moyshe Melamed]. Her AM2 class, Vos[Y] Heyst[Y] Haynt[Y] a[Y] Yiddishe[Y] Tsaytung[Y] in[Y] Amerika[Y], explores Yiddish journalism in the US today. Our apologies for any mixups.
See you at Klez[Y]Kamp!

So far, all of the excerpts analyzed in this chapter have been written by and for religiously oriented Jews. Excerpt #5 comes from the email distribution list of a secular Yiddish-oriented organization, "Living Traditions." For 30 years, this group held an annual conference for people – Jewish and not – who were interested in *klezmer* music and Yiddish language and culture. While other excerpts infuse their English with many Hebrew words and a few Yiddish words, this one uses several Yiddish words, some of which come from the Hebrew component of Yiddish.

There are two code switches into Yiddish in the discussion of Sura Melamed's classes: *laytish mame loshn* ('authentic mother-tongue/Yiddish'), and *vos heyst haynt a yiddishe tsaytung in amerika* ('what it means to be a Yiddish newspaper in America today'). Because these classes were to be taught in Yiddish, their titles are given in Yiddish – with enough explanation that even people who would not understand the classes can discern what they are about.

In contrast, the rest of the excerpt is written in English with a few Yiddish loanwords: *Yiddish* ('Jewish Eastern European language, lit. Jewish'), *Forverts* ('Forward'), *Klez*Kamp ('Jewish Eastern European music camp'), *mishpokhe* ('family'), and *shvartse fraytik* ('black Friday'). Of these words, *Yiddish*, *Klez(mer)*, and *mishpokhe* are part of the Hebrew component of Yiddish, and the other words are from its Germanic component.

Forverts ('forward') is the name of the American Yiddish newspaper, published daily from 1897 and weekly more recently, which spawned an English version, the *Forward*. *Klez*Kamp combines the first half of the Yiddish word *klezmer* (Jewish Eastern European music – from Hebrew *kley zemer* – 'vessels of melody') with a non-standard alliterative spelling of the English word "camp." *Mishpokhe* is the Yiddish/Hebrew word for family. While *Yiddish*, *Forverts*, and *klezmer* refer to referents specific to Yiddish culture and could not have been written in English, the author could have written "family" instead of *mishpokhe*. This word seems to be used for identity purposes, to highlight the Yiddish orientation of this organization.

The same can be said for *shvartse fraytik*, a direct translation of the American English phrase "Black Friday" (the day after Thanksgiving when many stores are flooded with discount seekers buying gifts for Christmas, which comes a month later). While the other loanwords, including *mishpokhe*, are commonly known in Yiddish culture circles, *shvartse fraytik* is not. This nonce translation of an English phrase into Yiddish might be interpreted as humorous, as it highlights the incongruity of American materialism and the cultural orientation of Yiddishist and klezmer circles.

The only other potentially distinctive feature in this excerpt is the phrase "we wish him … full recovery," which might be influenced by the Hebrew/Yiddish *refuʔa šlema / refue shleyme*. This phrase might be used in non-Jewish circles, but it would more likely be "we wish him a full recovery."

This email is distinguished from the other excerpts in its spelling of Yiddish/Hebrew words. For the most part, it follows the YIVO standard transcription system (with the exception of *yiddishe*, which would be *yidishe*). While most American Jews would write *mishpacha* even if they pronounce it [mispʌ́xʌ], the YIVO system calls for the use of <kh> for the [x] sound and <o> for the stressed *komets* (*qamaṣ*) vowel. Yiddish culture organizations often follow the YIVO system, using uncommon spellings like *khanike* and *bar mitsve*, while most Americans would write *Chanukah/Hannukah* and *Bar Mitzvah*. This allows these organizations to emphasize the centrality of the Yiddish language in their activities and worldview, even when they are using words that also come from Hebrew.

3.6 Excerpt #6: Habonim Dror Camp Galil parent update (6/15)

This morning, the Bogrim[H] (post-ninth graders) were up and at it as soon as the rest of camp (*machaneh*[H]) woke up. Can you guess what for? If you said, packing for *tiyul*[H], a hiking trip, then you'd be correct! The rest of *machaneh*[H], however, took their time mak-ing their way to the flag pole (*toren*[H]) this morning.

By 8:30 though, everyone was there and we raised the flags. Today during *ivrit*[H] *shimushit*[H], the skit to teach the useful Hebrew word of the day. The word of the day was *chizar*[H], which means "alien," which is also the persona of one of the counselors (*madrichim*[H]) who preforms [sic] the skit each day. After *ivrit*[H] *shimushit*[H] ended, we all walked down to the dining hall (*chadar*[H] *ochel*[H]) for breakfast. This morning, we had scrambled eggs with cheese on top, as well as cereal and yogurt options. Then, everyone split off into the groups for their chores (*avodot*[H])! After about half an hour of *avoda*[H], the *chanichim*[H] had time to clean up their cabin (*tzrif*[H]) before it was time for their age group discussions (*peulot*[H]). Today, each age group (*shichva*[H]) was in a different place than they were yesterday. The Amelim[H] (post-third and fourth graders) were in the *Moadon*[H], or the "clubhouse," writing messages to each other and drawing pictures. The Chotrim[H] (post-fifth graders) were in the Mini-Mo[H] (which is somewhat of a mini-*moadon*[H]), talking about Judaism and eating fruit. The Sayarim[H] (post-sixth graders) were at the pool today for instructional swim. When I arrived, they were using kick boards to swim across the pool. The Tzophim[H] (post-seventh graders) were in the *refet*[H], or "barn" (it's not really a barn though-we don't have animals living there or hay on the ground!). The Bonim[H] were in the *chadar*[H] *ochel*[H], playing games before beginning a more serious conversation about their *kvutsa*[H] (small, united community).

The Bogrim[H], of course, were not here today, but I'm sure that they are having a blast hiking and camping somewhere in the Poconos. I can only hope that it won't rain on them, because outside my window the outlook is not promising. Earlier today, however, the weather was perfect, especially for sports, which happened right after the *peulot*[H] came to an end. It was so warm during sports, in fact, that a (delightfully) overwhelming amount of *chanichim*[H] participated in free swim today. Free swim has always been a particularly fun part of *machaneh*[H], in my opinion, so it was great seeing the surge of kids who were interested in it today. When free swim came to an end, everyone had a chance to wash up before lunch, which was, drumroll please, latkes[Y]!

How can one attend a Jewish summer camp and not like latkes[Y], am I right? Truth be told, actually, I never would have eaten them my first summer at *machaneh*[H] (picky eater, what can you do). Along with the latkes[Y], we had green beans, applesauce, and a salad bar. When lunch concluded, everyone spread out around *machaneh*[H] to enjoy some rest time (*menucha*[H]). I walked around and saw many different things going on at once. First of all, *menucha*[H] is usually when the *chanichim*[H] get their mail, so those who received letters, emails or packages were very excited to see what they said. Other things happening at that time included basketball games, a soccer game, the use of musical instruments, and a few frisbee catches too. *Menucha*[H] transitioned into electives (*chugim*[H]) after a little while.

Today, some of the *chanichim*[H] visited the art room (*beit*[H] *omanut*[H]), while others played in the new sand on the volleyball court. The second set of *peulot*[H] for the day came after *chugim*[H], and many of the age groups (*schavot*[H] [sic]) continued with the same conversations that they had begun earlier in the day, except of course the Sayarim[H] did not go back down to the pool, but started a new *peula*[H] instead. *Kibud*[H] (snack time) came next. Apples can usually be expected during *kibud*[H], which isn't a bad thing because they are always crisp and cold when we get them. In a little while, everyone will come together again to sing and lower the flags for the evening. Then, we'll head down to dinner. Last night, we had lasagna, so I wonder what tonight will be! After dinner, there will be some free time (*chofesh*[H]) before the evening activity, *tochnit*[H] *erev*[H]! I was invited to hang out with the Tzophim[H] tonight during their *tochnit*[H] *erev*[H], which will include get-ting into pijamas [sic] and playing board games all together, so that's what I'll be doing!

Excerpt #6 is also from a relatively secular institution, a progressive Zionist summer camp. The many Hebrew loanwords in this parent update refer not to religious life, as in most of the excerpts above, but rather to several camp-related referents:

- activities: *tiyul* 'hiking trip', *tochnit erev* 'evening activity', *kibud* 'snack', *peulot* 'discussions', *chugim* 'electives', *menucha* 'rest time', *chofesh* 'free time', *ivrit shimushit* '[the skit to teach the] useful Hebrew [word of the day]'
- locations: *toren* 'flag pole', *tzrif* 'cabin', *refet* 'barn', *beit omanut* 'art room', *chadar ochel* 'dining hall', *moadon* 'clubhouse'
- roles: *madrichim* 'counselors', *tzevet* 'staff', *chanichim* 'campers'
- groupings: *kvutsa* 'small, united community', *shichva/shchavot* 'age group(s)'
- age divisions: *Chotrim* 'rowers', *Bogrim* 'graduates', *Amelim* 'workers', *Tzophim* 'scouts', *Sayarim* 'patrols/scouts', and *Bonim* 'builders'.

Camp is referred to with a Hebrew loanword, *machaneh*, and the name of the camp includes three Hebrew words: *Habonim* ('the builders'), *Dror* ('freedom') (these two words together reflect a historical merger of two youth movements), and *Galil* ('Galilee region in Israel').

By using so many Hebrew words in the everyday life of camp, this Zionist institution highlights the importance of Hebrew and makes camp feel like a distinct environment from campers' homes, schools, and synagogues. This phenomenon is quite common: a large percentage of the many Jewish sleep-away camps across North America and else-where in the English-speaking world use some Hebrew loanwords within their local variety of English, and some use hundreds of Hebrew words, creating a special register of "Camp Hebraized English."[2] Note that all of the Hebrew words used in this excerpt are nouns or noun phrases, whereas in the excerpts above there are also a few adjectives, adverbs, verbs, interjections, and greetings. This is common in Camp Hebraized English.

2 See Benor, Krasner, and Avni 2020.

One Yiddish word is used, *latkes* ('potato pancakes'), a food term that most Ashkenazi American Jews are familiar with. A Modern Hebrew word that is not generally found in Camp Hebraized English is used in the context of teaching selected words (*ivrit shimushit*): *chizar*, an unusual transcription of *chayzar* 'alien creature'. The "usefulness" of this word is debatable, but the fact that the camp teaches Hebrew words on a regular basis is an additional indication of the value of Hebrew at this camp.

In contrast to the other excerpts above, the Hebrew loanwords use only Israeli phonological norms (e.g., *beit*, rather than Ashkenazi *beis*). I know from observation at this camp that Hebrew loanwords are generally pronounced with ultimate stress and that they are otherwise rendered with American rather than Israeli phonology (an especially notable difference is American retroflex approximant [ɹ] rather than Israeli uvular trill [ʁ]), with the addition of the [x] phoneme.

The Hebrew words in this excerpt are pluralized according to Hebrew morphological norms. For example, the masculine noun *chug* receives the masculine plural suffix *-im* (*chugim*), and the feminine noun *avoda* receives the feminine plural suffix *-ot* (*avodot*). Even irregular nouns receive the appropriate Hebrew plural morphology: *shichva* becomes *shchavot* (although here there is a typo and it is spelled *schavot*). These morphological norms are generally followed at camp, although sometimes one hears exceptions, like *tzrif*s instead of *tzrifim* and *tiyul*s instead of *tiyulim*. Although not evident in the update, the camp also tends to use the Hebrew morphological system of distinguishing between males and females, e.g., *madricha* for a female counselor and *Amelim* (masc.) and *Amelot* (fem.) to refer to boys and girls of that age group.[3]

Despite this general trend of following Israeli Hebrew linguistic norms, some of the Hebrew words have distinctive usages and meanings in this excerpt (as they do at camp), such as *peula* 'discussion', which is 'action/activity' in Modern Hebrew, *refet* 'barn without animals', which is 'cowshed, dairy section of a farm' in Modern Hebrew, and *moadon* which is shortened to *mo*. These are common trends in Jewish English: many loanwords undergo semantic shift and are sometimes clipped and otherwise altered phonologically. For example, *tish* means 'table' in Yiddish but in Jewish English means 'celebration, such as for a groom before his wedding or led by a rebbe with his Hasidim'. Another example is *shmooze*, from Yiddish *shmuesn* ('chat'), which has spread beyond Jewish communities and has acquired a more specialized meaning, 'kiss up, chat up', and transitive use (e.g., "she spent the whole party *shmoozing* up the district manager").

The author of this parent update made the decision to represent language as used at camp. But because she is aware that these Hebrew words are not widely known in American Jewish communities, she not only highlights most of them by using italics but also translates most of them on first use. She varies the order of her translation, sometimes using the English word first, sometimes the Hebrew. Only four of the words are not translated: the common Ashkenazi Jewish food term *latkes* 'potato pancakes', *tzevet*

3 See Benor, Krasner, and Avni 2020, chapter 8, regarding the adoption of innovative gender suffixes in Habonim Dror camps, such as *Amelimot* (gender-inclusive double plural of this age group) and *chanichol* (gender-neutral 'camper').

('staff'), *chanichim* ('campers'), and one of the division names, *Bonim* (lit. 'builders'). The other divisions are described according to age group but are not translated literally.

The English has two spelling errors – preforms (performs) and pijamas (pajamas) – and a few grammatical "errors" according to standard norms of written English (a sentence fragment in the second sentence of the second paragraph and "amount" vs. "number"). These are the types of errors that Americans of diverse backgrounds make in their writing. Aside from loanwords, this excerpt does not include any other elements of the distinctive Jewish linguistic repertoire. The vast majority of loanwords used here are unique to the environment of Hebrew-rich camps (Benor, Krasner, and Avni 2020) and are not generally found in other Jewish communal settings.

3.7 Excerpt #7: Sephardic Adventure Camp parent update (6/15)

Queridos[L] Madres[L] y[L] Padres[L],

Today was our first full Sunday up at Camp, and it means that we've officially been here for a full week! Although it's a little quieter than usual because the CIT's left for their overnight this morning, we kicked off the week by dressing up in our beloved Hawks gear and had a fun-filled, green and blue Seahawks day sponsored by the [Rosenberg] family!! Aside from our jerseys and t-shirts, we also had Seahawks colored tablecloths, and a gorgeously decorated cake baked by our very own [Batsheva].

We were blessed with a number of wonderful visitors today as well! Board President, [Barbara Franco], and her husband [Daniel] spent the day with us baking borekas[L], running for touchdowns, and testing out the Lost Lake waters via kayak. Rabbi [Evans] joined us at breakfast, and taught shiurim[H] for B-1 and G-2, where they learned about the mitzvah[H] to keep one's body healthy. [Joe] and [Judy Franco] also came down from Seattle with plans to sleep over tonight! [Judy] spent the day in the Mess Hall teaching all of our campers how to shape and bake borekas[L]!

Campers gathered in the field for a mid-morning all-camp football game, where a number of highlight reel worthy plays took place! G-3 counselor [Sara Rosenberg] had three interceptions, B-2 member [Leon Franco] caught the ball after it went through the hands of his father [Daniel] who was trying to make an interception, and [Joseph Soriano] broke B-1 counselor [Avi Hassan]'s ankles as he juked him on a run towards the end zone!! Fun was had by all, and we celebrated with a baked potato lunch. The slightly rainy afternoon was a great change of pace, and made for a relaxed and activity-filled evening leading up to our University of Washington improvisation crew who put on a show for us for the night activity!

Please remember to check all the food for nuts that you send to camp!

Al vuermos[L],

[Lauren Evans]

Like Galil's update (#6), this excerpt from Sephardic Adventure Camp was intended to update parents about their children's activities and was written by a staff member. While Galil's update is filled with Hebrew loan-words, this one has only a few. It uses "Camp" rather than "*machaneh*," "Mess Hall," rather than "*chadar ochel*," and "night activity" rather than "*tochnit erev.*" The Hebrew words that do appear here – *shiurim* ('classes') and *miitzvah* ('commandment') – refer to Jewish religious practices and concepts and are used in similar ways in other religiously observant Jewish communities in the United States. Although it is not evident from this written document, these words may have been pronounced differently from the penultimate-stressed *shiúrɪm* and *mítzvʌh* heard in many Ashkenazi-dominated American settings. At Sephardic Adventure Camp, the rabbis likely pronounced them with ultimate stress (*shiurím* and *mitzváh*), as in Israel and Sephardi communities, and the latter could have been pronounced with [s] instead of [ts]: *misváh*. However, even in Sephardi communities like this one, Ashkenazi norms have become common (not just Hebrew pronunciation but also Yiddish loanwords like *shul* 'synagogue' and *daven* 'pray'), and I did hear both Sephardi and Ashkenazi variants when I visited this camp.

In addition to Hebrew, this text has another source of lexical enrichment: Ladino (the term used in American Sephardic communities for Judezmo or Judeo-Spanish). Sephardic Adventure Camp is geared toward the descendants of Ladino-speaking Sephardi Jewish immigrants from Rhodes and Turkey, most of whom came to Seattle (a city in the Pacific Northwest region of the United States) in the early 20th century. One of the camp's goals is to foster Sephardi identity, and they do so by preparing Sephardi foods, using Sephardi prayer traditions and melodies, teaching Sephardi Hebrew *zemirot* ('songs') for Shabbat, and incorporating Ladino words and songs into the camp experience. Bunks are given Ladino nicknames, teams get extra points in Color War for using Ladino on their banners, and campers are taught vocabulary during "Ladino word of the day."

In this excerpt, Ladino is used for one food term, the opening, and the closing. *Borekas*, savory pastries stuffed with potatoes, cheese, and other foods, are a common feature of Sephardic cultural events. There is some debate about whether to pronounce this word *borekas* (like in Turkey) or *burekas* (like in Rhodes), as the Seattle Sephardic community includes members from both dialect regions. At least in this parent update, the Turkish version won out.

The opening and closing point not only to the importance of Ladino but also to its attrition. The opening, "*Queridos Madres y Padres*" ('Dear Mothers and Fathers'), is identical in Ladino and Spanish, and the author could have learned it from her family or from a high school Spanish class (see Kirschen 2015 on contact between Ladino and Spanish in the United States). The orthography is standard Spanish, compared to Ladino *keridos madres i padres*, an ideologically fraught distinction within Ladino maintenance circles (see Brink-Danan 2011). The closing, "*Al vuermos*" seems to have a mistake, as it is generally "*al vermos*" ('until we see each other'). In an e-mail exchange with me, Lauren Evans reported that she learned that closing from an advisor with some Ladino knowledge, but that advisor reports not being familiar with that phrase. It is likely that at some point, someone looked up Ladino conversational closings and found "*al vermos*," and over time, as in the game Telephone/Operator, that morphed into "*al vuermos*." The vast majority of people who read this update have little Ladino knowledge and would likely assume (based on the source) that *al vuermos* is Ladino and is intended to highlight the camp's Sephardi identity.

Like the Hebrew and Yiddish openings and closings in Excerpts #1 and #2, the Ladino opening and closing in this excerpt mark the primarily English message as Sephardi and Ladino-oriented (see Ahlers 2006 and Avineri 2012 on similar language framing in Native American ceremonies and Yiddish culture groups). And the use of Spanish orthography in the greeting and the mistake in the closing may point to the predominance of Spanish and the attrition of Ladino four generations after this community's immigration to the United States.

3.8 Excerpt #8: "Rocket to Mars" Hebrew decoding curriculum

Audrey returned to her earlier suggestion. "Shall we speak in Mars language from now on?" "All right," Mark agreed. "לֶתְּ בְּגִנ." ("Let's begin.")

> From now on Audrey and Mark will be speaking Mars language which, as you know, is English words written in Hebrew. Read it as you do Hebrew, from right to left. You will have no trouble understanding the words if you read them aloud to yourself.

אָדְרִי שְׁפּוֹק — "This רַקִת שְׁפּ אִז בְּגִנִינְג תּוּ מֵק רִיל שְׁפִּיד."

[Audrey spoke — "This rocket ship is beginning to make real speed."]

"יֶת אִנְדִיד," מַרְק תֶד.

["Yes indeed," Mark said.]

"שׁוּן אִת will בִּי קַמִינְג אִנְתּוּ the רַקִת תְּתֵישְׁנ אַנ מוּנ נָמְבְּר תּוּ."

["Soon it will be coming into the rocket station on moon number two."]

מַרְק שֶׁד נוֹ מָר פָּר אֵי מוֹמֶנת. אִנְתֶּד he גֵזְד at אֵי פּתְתְּר אַנ the רַקִת דָר. אִת שֶׁד —

[Mark said no more for a moment. Instead he gazed at a poster on the rocket door. It said –]

לֵק through the בִּג תֶּלְתְקוֹפּ אַנ מוּנ נָמְבְּר תּוּ

[Look through the big telescope on moon number two.]

This excerpt is a rare example of English written in Hebrew letters. It comes from a 1950s curriculum used to teach American Reform Jews how to decode and recite Hebrew. The author, Rabbi Dr. Sylvan Schwartzman, felt that children would have an easier time learning the Hebrew writing system if they could sound out words in their native language before reading prayers and Torah in Hebrew. This pedagogical technique has not been the norm in American Hebrew education (see Benor, Avineri, and Greninger 2020), but even in the 2020s some teachers use similar techniques informally to supplement their Hebrew decoding curricula. For example, educator Stacey Lasky had her students read this quote, along with names of Star Wars characters (not knowing about the similar-themed Rocket-to-Mars curriculum):

לֶטס רִיד נֵיימס אֶנד פלֵייסֶס אִן הִיבּרוּ

[Let's read names and places in Hebrew.]

Both of these excerpts represent English sounds using Hebrew letters with *niqud* (the system of points that represents vowels and modifies some consonants), emulating the Hebrew writing that students are learning to decode. "Rocket to Mars" uses letters in positions that would be ungrammatical in Hebrew – ת at the beginning of a word and

ת at the end – and uses no *sofiyot* (final letters). The curriculum uses English letters for select words, especially those with [ð], [θ], [w], and [æ] – sounds that do not appear in Ashkenazi Hebrew. It follows Ashkenazi Hebrew pronunciation norms, including ת pronounced as [s] and *qamaṣ* as [o]. In 1953, when the curriculum was written, these pronunciations were the norm in the American Reform movement. Over the following 12 to 20 years, most Reform congregations and schools transitioned to pronunciation norms that emulated Israeli Hebrew, rendering ת as [t] and *qamaṣ* as [a] (Benor 2013). Today, pedagogical instances of English written in Hebrew letters, such as Lasky's excerpt above, follow Israeli norms for these sounds. However, they still tend – as both of these excerpts do – to distinguish be-tween *tsere* as the diphthong [ey] and *segol* as the monophthong [ɛ] – a feature of Ashkenazi vocalization that is often maintained in American Hebrew recitation but not in Israeli Hebrew.

In addition to pedagogical examples like these, American Jews have created hundreds of instances of material culture featuring English words in Hebrew letters, especially representing locations, universities, sports teams, and political candidates (e.g., "ווייק פורסט הלל" – "Wake Forest Hillel" printed on a T-shirt). Such products sometimes include additional English words, as in "טראמפ פנס קיפ אמריקה גרייט!" ("Trump, Pence: Keep America great!" printed on a kipah). These products serve to highlight their owners' Jewish identities, in addition to their various American affiliations (see details in Benor 2020).

4 Conclusion

As the excerpts above demonstrate, written Jewish English is mostly intelligible to non-Jewish English speakers (except in the rare excerpts that are written in Hebrew characters). It is distinct primarily at the lexical level, as it incorporates hundreds of loanwords from Hebrew, Aramaic, Yiddish, and Ladino, as well as calque translations of Hebrew phrases and Yiddish grammatical structures. Jewish English differs orthographically from many Jewish languages of the past, as it is written in Latin/English letters, except for select instances with pedagogical or performative intent. Loanwords are generally rendered with English transcription, but sometimes they are inserted in Hebrew letters, especially in long quotes from the Biblical and Rabbinic tradition. Textual Hebrew/Aramaic, Israeli Hebrew, and Yiddish all play important roles in how Hebrew words are used within Jewish English (Benor 2000), and non-Hebrew loanwords from Ladino and Yiddish play smaller roles in specific subgroups of American Jews (as do Judeo-Arabic, Russian, Farsi, Spanish, and other languages).

The analysis leads to three questions. First, how distinct is the English of Jews from that of their non-Jewish neighbors? It depends on the writer, the audience, the topic, and the venue/medium of communication. Some excerpts of writing by and for Jews are nearly identical to "Standard English," and others have so many Hebrew and Yiddish words that they are unintelligible to most English-proficient readers. In rare cases, Jewish English is written in Hebrew letters, making it even less accessible to most English readers.

Should Jewish English (as an umbrella term encompassing this variation) be considered a separate language from English? Again, it depends. Depending on the excerpt, we might consider it a language, a dialect, or just English with a series of specialized vocabulary. And depending on the criteria for considering an entity to be a language or a dialect – mutual intelligibility, speakers' recognition, etc. – a given excerpt could be classified in multiple ways. Therefore, I believe this question is unproductive.

Should Jewish English be considered a Jewish language? It depends how "Jewish languages" are delineated. If a Hebrew writing system is a required criterion for inclusion, then Jewish English would be excluded, as would Jewish Malayalam, Judeo-Georgian, Jewish Latin American Spanish, 20th-century Ladino/Judezmo, and other language varieties. If we move beyond required linguistic or orthographic criteria for membership in the analytic category of Jewish languages, then we can allow for more productive comparative analysis of Jewish languages past and present.

A conclusion we can draw from this analysis about Jewish languages is that we cannot assume that writing accurately reflects the spoken language of the time. The excerpts presented here differ from general English primarily in lexicon and do not reflect the many other distinctive linguistic features in the Jewish English ethnolinguistic repertoire. Archaeology and historical linguistics will look much different in the future and may involve analysis of audio and video recordings. But assuming only written records were available, a linguist in the year 2700 might assume that 21st-century Jewish English differed from English only in the use of Hebrew, Yiddish, and Ladino loanwords. Similarly, the written remnants we have of language in some ancient and medieval Jewish communities suggest that their language was mostly identical to the non-Jewish language of the time, except for being written in Hebrew letters and incorporating a few Hebrew loanwords (e.g., Judeo-Persian, Judeo-Greek, Judeo-French, Judeo-Catalan; see Gold 1981b, Fudeman 2010, Edzard 2014, and Baum 2016). In line with Gold 1981b and Benor 2009, the current analysis suggests that those and other Jewish communities of the past may have had a much more elaborate distinctive linguistic repertoire beyond what we are able to discern in the few written documents they left behind.

References

Dictionaries

Benor, Sarah Bunin. 2012–present. *Jewish English Lexicon.* https://jel.jewish-languages.org/. Shared with a Crea-tive Commons Attribution 4.0 International License.

Bluestein, Gene. 1989. *Anglish/Yinglish: Yiddish in American Life and Literature.* Athens: University of Georgia Press.

Eisenberg, Joyce, and Ellen Scolnic. 2001. *The JPS Dictionary of Jewish Words.* Philadelphia: Jewish Publication Society.

Glinert, Lewis. 1992. *The Joys of Hebrew.* Oxford: Oxford University Press.

Rosten, Leo. 1968. *The Joys of Yiddish.* New York: McGraw-Hill.

Steinmetz, Sol. 1986. *Yiddish and English: A Century of Yiddish in America* Tuscaloosa: University of Alabama Press.

Steinmetz, Sol. 2005. *Dictionary of Jewish Usage: A Guide to the Use of Jewish Terms.* Lanham: Rowman and Littlefield.

Weiser, Chaim. 1995. *Frumspeak: The First Dictionary of Yeshivish.* Northvale: Jason Aronson.

Other references

Ahlers, Jocelyn C. 2006. "Framing Discourse: Creating Community through Native Language Use." *Journal of Linguistic Anthropology* 16/1: 58–75.

Avineri, Netta Rose. 2012. Heritage Language Socialization Practices in Secular Yiddish Educational Contexts: The Creation of a Metalinguistic Community. PhD Dissertation, UCLA. http://www.bjpa.org/publications/details.cfm?PublicationID=14333.

Alvarez-Péreyre, Frank. 2003. "Vers une typologie des langues juives?" In *Linguistique des langues juives et linguistique générale*, ed. F. Alvarez-Péreyre and J. Baumgarten. Paris: CNRS. 397–421.

Bar-Asher, Moshe. 2002. "Beḥinot be-ḥeqer lešonot ha-yehudim ve-sifruyotehem." *Peʕamim* 93: 77–89.

Baum, Ilil. 2016. "Hebrew-Catalan Medieval Wedding Songs: Satirical Functions of the Hebrew Component and Other Linguistic Aspects." *Journal of Jewish Languages* 4/2: 166–202.

Benor, Sarah. 2000. "Loan Words in the English of Modern Orthodox Jews: Yiddish or Hebrew?" *Proceedings of the Berkeley Linguistic Society's 25th Annual Meeting, 1999*. Steve S. Chang, Lily Liaw, and Josef Ruppenhofer, eds. Berkeley: Berkeley Linguistic Society. 287–298.

Benor, Sarah Bunin. 2001. "The Learned /t/: Phonological Variation in Orthodox Jewish English." *Penn Working Papers in Linguistics: Selected Papers from NWAV 29*. Tara Sanchez and Daniel Ezra Johnson, eds. Philadelphia: Univ. of Penn. Linguistics. 1–16.

Benor, Sarah Bunin. 2008. "Towards a New Understanding of Jewish Language in the 21st Century." *Religion Compass* 2/6: 1062–1080.

Benor, Sarah Bunin. 2009. "Do American Jews Speak a 'Jewish Language'? A Model of Jewish Linguistic Distinctiveness." *Jewish Quarterly Review* 99/2: 230–269.

Benor, Sarah Bunin. 2010. "Ethnolinguistic Repertoire: Shifting the Analytic Focus in Language and Ethnicity." *Journal of Sociolinguistics* 14/2: 159–183.

Benor, Sarah Bunin. 2011. "*Mensch*, *Bentsh*, and *Balagan*: Variation in the American Jewish Linguistic Repertoire." *Language and Communication* 31/2: 141–154.

Benor, Sarah Bunin. 2012. *Becoming Frum: How Newcomers Learn the Language and Culture of Orthodox Judaism*. New Brunswick, NJ: Rutgers University Press.

Benor, Sarah Bunin. 2013. "From Sabbath to Shabbat: Changing Language of Reform Sisterhood Leaders, 1913–2012." In *Sisterhood: A Centennial History of Women of Reform Judaism*, ed. Carole B. Balin, Dana Herman, Jonathan D. Sarna, and Gary P. Zola. Cincinnati: American Jewish Archives. 314–337.

Benor, Sarah Bunin. 2020. "Bivalent Writing: Hebrew and English Alphabets in Jewish English." *Journal of Jewish Languages* 8/1–2: 108–157.

Benor, Sarah Bunin, Jonathan Krasner, and Sharon Avni. 2020. *Hebrew Infusion: Language and Community at American Jewish Summer Camps*. New Brunswick, NJ: Rutgers University Press.

Benor, Sarah Bunin, Netta Avineri, and Nicki Greninger. 2020. "Let's Stop Calling It 'Hebrew School': Rationales, Goals, and Practices of Hebrew Education in Part-Time Jewish Schools." Washington, DC: Consortium for Studies in Applied Jewish Education. https://www.casje.org/HebrewEdPartTime.

Birnbaum, Salomo A. 1979. *Yiddish: A Survey and a Grammar*. Manchester: Manchester University Press.

Brink-Danan, Marcy. 2011. "The Meaning of Ladino: The Semiotics of an Online Speech Community." *Language and Communication* 31: 107–118.

Bunis, David M. 1981. "A Comparative Linguistic Analysis of Judezmo and Yiddish." *International Journal of the Sociology of Language* 30: 49–70.

Burdin, Rachel Steindel. 2017. "New Notes on the Rise-Fall Contour." *Journal of Jewish Languages* 5/2: 145–173.

Edzard, Alexandra. 2014. "A Judeo-French Wedding Song from the Mid-13th Century: Literary Contacts between Jews and Christians." *Journal of Jewish Languages* 2/1: 78–98.

Fishman, Joshua A. 1981. "The Sociology of Jewish Languages from the Perspective of the General Sociology of Language: A Preliminary Formulation." *International Journal of the Sociology of Language* 30: 5–16.

Fudeman, Kirsten. 2010. *Vernacular Voices: Language and Identity in Medieval French Jewish Communities*. Philadelphia, PA: University of Pennsylvania Press.

Gold, David. 1981a. "Jewish Intralinguistics as a Field of Study." *International Journal of the Sociology of Language* 30: 31–46.

Gold, David. 1981b. "Recent American Studies in Jewish Languages (Review-Essay)." *Jewish Language Review* 1: 11–88.

Gold, David. 1985. "Jewish English." In *Readings in the Sociology of Jewish Languages*, ed. Joshua Fishman. Leiden: Brill. 280–298.

Gold, David. 1986. "On Jewish English in the United States." *Jewish Language Review* 6: 121–35.

Gold, David, and Leonard Prager. 1981–1987. *Jewish Language Review*. Haifa: Association for the Study of Jewish Languages.

Hary, Benjamin. 2009. *Translating Religion: Linguistic Analysis of Judeo-Arabic Sacred Texts from Egypt*. Leiden: Brill.

Hary, Benjamin, and Sarah Bunin Benor (eds.). 2018. *Languages in Jewish Communities, Past and Present*. Berlin: De Gruyter Mouton.

Kahn, Lily, and Aaron Rubin (eds). 2016. *Handbook of Jewish Languages*. Leiden: Brill.

Kirschen, Bryan. 2015. *Judeo-Spanish Encounters Modern Spanish: Language Contact and Diglossia among the Sephardim of Los Angeles and New York City*. PhD Dissertation, University of California Los Angeles.

Knack, Rebecca. 1991. Ethnic Boundaries in Linguistic Variation. In *New Ways of Analyzing Sound Change*. Penelope Eckert, ed. San Diego: Academic Press. 251–272.

Levon, Erez. 2006. "Mosaic Identity and Style: Phonological Variation among Reform American Jews." *Journal of Sociolinguistics* 10: 185–205.

Maman, Aharon. This volume.

Prager, Leonard. 1986. "A Preliminary Checklist of English Names of Jewish Lects." *Jewish Language Review* 6: 225–236.

Rabin, Chaim et al. 1979. "The Jewish Languages: Commonalities, Differences and Problems" (in Hebrew). *Peʕamim* 1: 40–57.

Rabin, Chaim. 1981. "What Constitutes a Jewish Language?" *International Journal of the Sociology of Language* 30: 19–28.

Schiffrin, Deborah. 1984. "Jewish Argument as Sociability." *Language in Society* 13: 311–335.

Spolsky, Bernard, and Sarah Bunin Benor. 2006. "Jewish Languages." In *Encyclopedia of Language and Linguistics*. Keith Brown, ed. 2nd edition. Vol. 6. Oxford: Elsevier. 120–124.

Steinmetz, Sol. 1981. "Jewish English in the United States." *American Speech* 56/1: 3–16.

Tannen, Deborah. 1981. "New York Jewish Conversational Style." *International Journal of the Sociology of Language* 30: 133–49.

Tirosh-Becker, Ofra, and Sarah Bunin Benor (eds.). 2013–. *Journal of Jewish Languages*. Leiden: Brill.

Weinreich, Max. 2008 [1973]. *History of the Yiddish Language*. New Haven: Yale University Press.

Wexler, Paul. 1981. "Jewish Interlinguistics: Facts and Conceptual Framework." *Language* 57/1: 99–145.

Judezmo/Ladino/Judeo-Spanish

David M. Bunis, The Hebrew University of Jerusalem

1. Introductory remarks

In medieval Christian ספרד/*Sĕfarad* or Iberia, Jews primarily used Hebrew when writing for Jews literate in that language, and their local everyday variety of Ibero-Romance when writing for other Jews.[1] In their Hebrew writings the Iberian Jews referred to their everyday vernacular as לעז/*laʕaz* 'Laʕaz (i.e., Romance)' or לעז ספרד/ספרדי / *laʕaz Sĕfarad/sĕfaradi* 'Laʕaz of Sĕfarad/Spain / Sephardic/Spanish Laʕaz';[2] in the vernacular itself, as we shall see, the language came to be known by diverse names. The medieval Jews' Ibero-Romance diverged somewhat from the varieties of Ibero-Romance used by their Christian neighbors – first and foremost on account of the distinctive elements it incorporated from Hebrew and Aramaic, Old Jewish Greek (through Old Jewish Latin), and (Jewish) Ibero-Arabic, as well as certain elements of Romance origin used by Jews which differed in form or meaning from the cognates used by non-Jews.[3] Furthermore, unlike the Christians of Iberia, who wrote their Romance in the Latin alphabet taught by representatives of the Catholic Church, the Jews usually wrote their Romance in the Hebrew letters taught by Jewish instructors of religion.[4]

In 1492 the Jews of Castile and Aragon were expelled from their dwelling-place of many centuries together with most of the Muslims still remaining in Spain when the Christian Reconquista brought an end to the Muslim conquest begun in 711. Like most of the Muslims, some of the Jewish exiles crossed the Mediterranean to North Africa, settling primarily in what was to become Spanish Morocco;[5] small numbers migrated to

1 The present article was prepared with the support of grants from the Israel Science Foundation, nos. 41105/11 and 1930/17. For a taxonomy of names for Judezmo and other Jewish languages, see Bunis 2008a. For a structural introduction to Judezmo, see Bunis 2016; for more sociolinguistic approaches, see Bunis 2018; Schwarzwald 2018.

2 לעז/*laʕaz* originally denoted 'foreign, non-Jewish language': in the biblical context (e.g., Psalms 114:1) it referred to Ancient Egyptian; in the Mishnah, usually Greek; and from the Middle Ages, '(esp. Jewish) Romance' – and among the Sephardim, speakers both of Jewish Arabic (as illustrated in the writings of Maimonides, Abraham Ibn Ezra) and of Jewish varieties of Ibero-Romance (e.g., Nahmanides and others), specifically '(Jewish) Ibero-Romance', and eventually what was to become 'Judezmo/Ladino/Judeo-Spanish'.

3 For a comparison of the Ibero-Romance used by Muslims, Jews and Christians in Medieval Spain, see Bunis 2015.

4 A historical overview of Judezmo spelling in the traditional Judezmo (i.e., Hebrew-letter) alphabet is offered in Bunis 2005a.

5 For a selection of representative texts in Ḥaketía, the primarily Ibero-Romance language used into modern times by the descendants of Jewish exiles from Christian Iberia in North Africa, see the chapter by Yaakov Bentolila in the present volume.

Italy and other parts of Western Europe;[6] but the great majority immigrated to the Ottoman Empire, at the invitation of Sultan Bayezid II (1447–1512). At first, most of these "Ottoman Sephardim" settled in the two major points of their arrival in the empire, the port cities of Constantinople and Salonika. In time, some made their way to other parts of the empire, establishing Sephardic communities in all the major, and many minor, cities then under Ottoman rule. From those regions, especially from the eighteenth century, some migrated to the Austro-Hungarian Empire, with a preference for Vienna.

In whichever parts of the Ottoman and Austro-Hungarian empires they settled, these descendants of medieval Iberian Jewry tended to maintain their own language. In the sixteenth century the diverse varieties of Jewish Ibero-Romance which they had brought to the Ottoman Empire in the late fifteenth century began to coalesce into a single language, bearing the closest resemblance to the popular medieval Jewish Castilian faintly echoed in texts surviving from Iberia,[7] but having some variant forms reminiscent of the normative Spanish beginning to emerge in the fifteenth century. In many instances, the latter variants would become obsolete among the Jews, causing their language to diverge increasingly from normative Spanish even in its Ibero-Romance component. In the major population centers – Istanbul, Salonika, Izmir, Edirne – the Jews tended to preserve the phonological system which had been used in medieval Spain. For example, into the modern era, Judezmo speakers universally preserved the sounds [ʤ] in גֿינטי/*djente* 'people', [ʒ] in מוזֿיר/*mujer* 'woman', and [ʃ] in לישוס/*leshos* 'far', whereas all three sounds came to be pronounced [χ] or [h] in Modern Spanish.[8] All of the Jews of the former Ottoman regions also continued to distinguish phonemically (e.g., intervocalically) between *b* and *v* (e.g., אבאשאר/*abashar* 'to descend', אבֿאגאר/*avag̱ar* 'softly'), and *s* and *z* (e.g., קאסאר/*kasar* 'to hunt' vs. קאזאר/*kazar* 'to marry'), as in Old Spanish. (In later Spanish these pairs merged: between vowels, the first pair became the bilabial fricative [β], and in Andalusian the second pair merged as voiceless [s]). But at the other structural levels, the language of the Ottoman Sephardim evolved ever further over the centuries from its original medieval sources, especially through the speakers' strong tendencies toward analogical leveling and simplification; the evanescence of forms characteristic of a small socioeconomic elite and the normatization of popular variants and innovative forms; the expansion of the Hebrew-Aramaic component, reflecting the overall pre-dominance of Judaism, its texts and institutions, in the everyday lives of the

6 On published reflections of Sephardic Ibero-Romance in Italy, see Bunis 1994, 1997a, 2008b; Minervini 1994; Arnold 2006.

7 For a selection of Jewish Ibero-Romance texts from medieval Spain see Minervini 1992.

8 Except when using I.P.A. transcription symbols enclosed within square brackets [ ], the Judezmo citations reproduced in the present article are transcribed from sources originally in the traditional Hebrew-letter Judezmo alphabet, using a variant of the romanized orthography devised by Moshe Shaul and advocated by the Israel National Authority for Ladino Culture (for a summary see *Aki Yerushalayim* 35:96 [2014], 2). Note the values of the following special symbols: *ch* = [ʧ]; *d* = [d]; *ḏ* = [ð]; *dj* = [ʤ]; *g̱* = [ɣ]; *h* = [χ]; *i* =[i]; *j* = [ʒ]; *ny* = [ɲ]; *r* = flapped [ɾ] or trilled [r] (depending on the particular word and the regional Judezmo dialect being cited); *rr* = trilled [r]; *s* = [z] before a word-initial voiced phone, otherwise = [s]; *sh* = [ʒ] before a word-initial voiced phone, otherwise = [ʃ]; *u* = [u] or, preceding a vowel, [w]; *v* = [v]; *y* = [j]; *z* = [z]. The stress in words ending in a vowel or *-n* or *-s* is generally penultimate, and that in words ending in other consonants is ordinarily ultimate; exceptional stress is indicated by an acute accent mark over the stressed vowel.

speakers;[9] the selective adoption of elements from local contact languages such as Turkish and Greek, reflecting intensive, daily interaction with their non-Jewish neighbors, as well as of elements from languages of European imperialism such as Italian, French, and German, learned in formal educational settings as well as in commerce – and the synthesis of all of these features into a unique new structural entity.

1.1 Historical phases

The structure of the language as a whole would undergo significant modifications over time, permitting the division of the language into distinct historical phases and subphases. For example, in *Old Sephardic Laʕaz* – or in retrospect, *Old Judezmo* (earliest origins through 1492) – the morphemes denoting the first- and second-person plural in ־אר/*-ar* verbs in the preterite indicative tense were apparently ־אמוש/*-amos* and ־אשטי(י)ש/*-aste(y)s*, respectively, as in Spanish of this period; in *Middle Judezmo* (approximately 1493–c.1796), these were supplemented by ־ימוס/*-emos* and (by at least 1739) ־ימוס/*-imos* and ־אסטיש/*-ástesh* variants; and in *Modern Judezmo* (approximately c. 1797–present) the earlier variants were supplanted by the normatized morphemes ־ימוס/*-imos* and (from at at least 1797) ־אטיש/*-átesh*.

1.2 Regional dialectology

In the Old Judezmo phase the Hispanic component of the Jews' everyday language probably bore a closer resemblance to that used by non-Jews of the same region than to the Hispanic component used by non-Jews in other regions. From the beginnings of the Middle Judezmo phase, an incipient locally based regional dialectology may be discerned, as the language underwent increasing subdivision by major and minor isoglosses dividing the extensive extra-Iberian territory in which it was spoken. By the Modern Judezmo phase, the language was divided into two major geographic dialect regions. In the Northwest dialect region (NWJ) – former Yugoslavia, Northwestern Greece, Western Bulgaria, Romania, and also Vienna, all falling mostly under the linguistic and cultural sway of the Austro-Hungarian Empire – speakers traditionally preserved medieval *f-* (e.g., פֿאזיר/*fazer* 'to do'), and medieval final nonstressed *-e* and *-o* became *-i* and *-u* (e.g., דיינטי/*dyenti* 'tooth', אוזו/*oju* 'eye'); in the Southeast dialect region (SEJ) – essentially Turkey and Eastern Bulgaria – *f-* was lost (thus, אזיר/*azer* 'to do'), and *-e* and *-o* were preserved (*dyente*, *ojo*). Salonika constituted a transition area, traditionally having *f(azer)* but *(dyent)e* and *(oj)o*. Additionally, the metathesis of historical [-rð-] as [-ðr-] is characteristic of the Southeast (including Salonika), whereas the original sequence is preserved as [-rd-] in parts of the Northwest, e.g., SEJ טאדֿראר/*tadrar* vs. Bosnian Judezmo טארדאר/*tardar* 'to delay'. At the syntactic level, Salonika and the Northwest dialects posit object and reflexive pronouns before verbal infinitives when following prepositions, e.g., פארה מי דאר / *para me dar* 'in order to give me' (a variant known in Old Spanish), while the Southeast dialects prefer post-positing them after the infinitive, e.g., synonymous פארה דארמי *para darme* (as in modern normative Spanish).

9 Bunis 1993a is an attempt at a comprehensive inventory of elements of Hebrew-Aramaic origin in Modern Judezmo. Contributions toward a structural analysis of those elements include Crews 1962, Bunis 1981, 1993a, 1997b, 2005b, 2006–2007, 2007, 2009, 2013a, 2013b, 2020.

Lexically, the Southeast (including Salonika) dialects generally express ‘what?’ and ‘one must’, respectively, as קואלו?/*kualo?* and קאלי/*kale*; while the Northwest dialects prefer לוקי?/*luké?* and פרימי/*premi*. There is also some subdivision within the two major dialect regions. For example, in Salonika and its environs (e.g., Bitola), the gerund doubles as the second-person-plural imperative, e.g., ב̄יניינדו!/*vinyendo*/*-u!* ‘come!’, while most of the Southeast dialects instead use the historical imperative ending in -V́*ð* (the -*ð* may become voiceless -*θ* or drop), e.g., ב̄יני[ד̄]!/*vení(ð)*/*(θ)!* ‘come!’ (cf. Sp[anish]. *¡venid!*).[10] Within the Northwest, Bitola and some nearby dialects show the raising of historical nonstressed word-final -*a* to -*e*, e.g., Bitola קאזי/*kaze* vs. Salonika קאזה/*kaza* ‘house’ (cf. Sp. *casa*); and Sarajevo shows the lowering of stressed *e* to *a* when preceding *r* + consonant or, historically, a trilled *rr*, e.g., Sarajevo פוארטה/*puarta* vs. Salonika פואירטה/*puerta* ‘door’. The numerals 12–15 differ significantly from city to city, e.g., Salonika טריג̄י/*tredje*, Istanbul טריג̄י/טריזי/*tredje*/*treze*, Izmir טרילזי/*trelze*, Sarajevo טרידזי/*tredzi* ‘13’. Influence from the divergent local contact languages also resulted in some additional phonological isoglosses distinguishing Southeast from Northwest Judezmo (e.g., SEJ, spoken alongside Greek, distinguishes word-medial /d/ vs. /ð/ and /g/ vs. /ɣ/ phonemes, as in modern Greek, while in NWJ, spoken alongside South Slavic, which lack *ð* and *ɣ*, the former pair collapsed as /d/, and the latter, as /g/).[11] For example, SEJ /nidá/ ‘menstruating woman’ < Hebrew נדה/*nidda*, /níðo/ ‘nest’ (Spanish *nido*), /pigúl/ ‘hooligan’ < Hebrew פגול/*piggul* ‘abomination’, /paɣar/ ‘to pay’ (Spanish *pagar*) versus NWJ /nidá/, /nídu/, /pigúl/, /pagár/.

1.3 Social-level and literary variation

From the sixteenth century one may also distinguish several spoken and literary stylistic and social-level registers; the distinctions separating the registers would increase over time. Social-level registers reflected societal variables such as age, gender, level of religiosity, type of education received, type of occupation practiced, and so on. For example, in the early sixteenth century a small socioeconomic elite, apparently retaining a sensitivity to the Castilian-dominated language esthetics of the Christian socioeconomic counterparts they had left in Iberia, employed language varieties rather close to theirs, and avoided non-Hispanic elements such as words of Hebrew origin as well as incorporations from the local contact languages. The language varieties used by the more numerous, socioeconomically more modest sectors had more in common, in their Hispanic component, with the language varieties used by the more popular sectors of fifteenth-century Christian Iberia, and they also included a significant Hebrew-origin component and a growing Turkish and Balkan component. Within a century, as the younger generations of the families who had constituted the socioeconomic elite assimilated in language to the more popular sectors, their primarily popular and constantly evolving Castilian-dominated Hispanic component, with some additions from other popular Ibero-Romance varieties, and important contributions of Hebrew-Aramaic and Turkish-Balkan origin, became the predominant language of the majority of the Ottoman

10 Unless otherwise noted, ‘Sp.’ denotes normative modern Spanish.

11 Quintana 2006 provides extensive diachronic and synchronic coverage of Judezmo regional dialectology.

Sephardim, and came to be referred to by their non-Jewish neighbors as the 'Jewish language'. In the Modern Judezmo phase, younger speakers who acquired French and Italian through commercial contacts or formal schooling tended to relexify their Judezmo, replacing traditional elements of Hebrew-Aramaic and Turkish-Balkan with Gallicisms and Italianisms,[12] leaving those speakers who were unfamiliar with the European prestige languages baffled by the younger generation's נואיבֿו לינגואזֿי / *nuevo linguaje* 'new language'.[13] As the speech of westernized/Europeanized/secularized males became enriched through borrowings from French and Italian and depleted of 'eastern' elements of Hebrew and Turkish origin, the language of traditional females lacking a western education began to seem more old-fashioned and conservative, with greater preservation of 'eastern' elements and even more traditional, popular forms of Hispanisms than used by males, who now, especially in their written language, tended to alter the forms of their Hispanisms under French and Italian influence (e.g., גֿודֿייו/*djuḏió* > זֿודֿייו/*juḏió* 'Jew', under the influence of French *juif*). Individuals, especially males, with a more religious orientation tended to employ more elements of Hebrew-Aramaic origin than their more secular, religiously less-educated counterparts; while males whose professions or trades brought them into close contact with the local non-Jewish population tended to incorporate into their speech more local borrowings than those less in touch with non-Jewish neighbors. In general it may be said that, in the late nineteenth and twentieth centuries, the Jewish encounter with diverse new language attitudes – those gaining popularity among the local non-Jews, as well as those introduced by local representatives of European Jewish language-related social movements such as the Haskalah and political Zionism – caused Judezmo speakers of all orientations to introspect about their language and effect changes in it. Stylistic divergence related to context and text type, on the other hand, reflected variables such as everyday spoken contexts versus special educational settings (e.g., Bible-translation lessons), and literary frameworks such as traditional religious texts versus westernized journalistic reportage.

1.4 Language names

One aspect of the language in which historical, regional and social factors have jointly played a role is the name used by speakers to denote their tongue. During the sixteenth century, writers in the language used diverse names for it, including names which had also been used by Spanish Christians, such as לאדֿינו/*laḏino* – an allusion to the popular *Latin* antecedents of all varieties of Ibero-Romance (cf. Lat. LATINUS); רומאנסי/*romanse* – an acknowledgment of its primarily *Romance-origin* lexicon and structure (cf. Lat. ROMANICE); and איספאנייול/*espanyol* – connecting the language with its original homeland, *Hispania* or Spain (cf. Lat. HISPANIA). The linguanym *laḏino* remained in use among the Jews into the twenty-first century, especially to denote the Jews' everyday vernacular, or more specifically the special calque-translation language used to render sacred Hebrew and Aramaic texts into the vernacular, especially in opposition to לשון הקודש/*lashón (akóḏesh)* 'the (Holy) Tongue', or 'Hebrew' proper. Among the Jews, *laḏino* never acquired meanings such as 'shrewd' or 'mestizo', which are the primary

12 On French elements in Modern Judezmo see Sephiha; on Italianisms, see Minervini 2014.

13 On 'new language' and related concepts among Judezmo speakers, see Bunis 2014.

senses in which the corresponding Spanish word is used today in Spain and Latin America; it instead carried distinctive secondary senses such as 'translation', 'meaning', and, as an adjective, 'refined'. Unlike the case among Spanish Christians, the name *romanse* did not survive among the Ottoman Jews beyond the sixteenth century; in the seventeenth and eighteenth centuries the use of *espanyol*, too, became rare; probably neither term had had deep roots in the speech tradition of the Jews.

Distinctively, among the Ottoman Jews several unique linguanyms arose which were apparently unknown among Spanish Christians. Two of them had a geographic dimension: from the sixteenth century, some Jews referred to their vernacular as פֿראנקו/*franko*, perhaps an adaptation of Turkish *Frenkçe*, a generic term for a language used by the *Frenkler* '(Christian) Western Europeans' of *Frengistan* 'Western Europe', from whence the Sephardim had immigrated to the empire. In the eighteenth and nineteenth centuries, some Jews called their language ליבֿאנטינו/*levantino* 'language of the Levant', demonstrating the Jews' identification of their language with the Levant in which they resided. But perhaps most characteristically, from at least the first half of the eighteenth century, Ottoman Sephardim used the term גֿודיזמו/*djuḏezmo* (cf. Spanish *judaísmo* 'Judaism') to denote the concept 'Jewish (or Judean) language' (as well as 'Judaism') (e.g., *djuḏezmo* is the translation of *yĕhudit* 'Judean/Jewish language (meaning Hebrew)', appearing in Avraham Asa's Constantinople 1743 translation of II Kings 18:26); and by the early nineteenth century they were clearly using it to denote the group language of the Ottoman Jews (e.g., *djuḏezmo* appears in that sense in responsum no. 67 of Mənašše 1836: 74a, from 1824: *Me disho ke no le avlara en djuḏezmo* 'He told me not to speak to him in Judezmo), just as their non-Jewish neighbors referred to the Jews' language as 'Jewish' (e.g., *Yahudice* and derogatory *çıfıt* in Turkish). *Djuḏezmo*, and semantically analogous גֿו־/גֿידֿייו//*dju-/djiḏyó* 'Jewish', seem to have been the most popular native names for the language until the second half of the nineteenth century, when the Haskalah scholars of Central and Eastern Europe began to acquaint the speakers with the argument that their language was a kind of 'Jewish Spanish' – and a corrupt Spanish at that – which philologists began to call 'Judeo-Spanish'; Ottoman Jewish intellectuals then adopted that term in its French form, זֿודיאו־איספאנייול/*judeo-espanyol* (< Fr[ench]. *judéo-espagnol*). Today, popular speakers often simply call their language איספאנייול/*(e)spanyol* (mostly in the SEJ region) or אישפאנייול/*(i)shpanyol* (in the NWJ region); the term seems to have reentered the Jews' language in the nineteenth century, under Haskalah influence (cf. Fr. *espagnol*, It[alian]. *spagnolo*, T[ur]k[ish]. *İspanyol*, Serbo-Cr[oatian]. *Španjolski*, Ger[man]. *Spanisch*), resulting in the lack of a clear-cut terminological distinction in the language of some contemporary speakers between Judezmo and Castilian – leading some speakers to use מואיסטרו איס־/אישפאנייול / (SEJ/NWJ) *muestro/-u (e)s-/(i)shpanyol* 'our Spanyol/Spanish' to specify Judezmo in opposition to Castilian.

2. Grammatical sketch

Everyday Modern Judezmo of the Ottoman regions and successor states diverges from its normative non-Jewish correlate, Modern Spanish, in many respects. Only a brief summary of the most salient divergences not discussed in the preceding section will be offered here.

2.1 Nouns

Nouns carry masculine or feminine gender; those incorporated from Turkish, which does not distinguish grammatical gender, are usually assigned masculine or feminine gender based on their final sequences: e.g., those with a final consonant are masculine (m. חאמאל/*hamal* 'porter', Tk. *hamal* < Ar. *ḥamal*), those with final *-a* are feminine (f. טאבאקה/*tabaká* 'storey', cf. Tk. *tabaka* < Ar. *ṭabaqa*); exceptions derive from the natural gender of an animate referent (e.g., m. פאשה/*pashá* 'pasha' < Tk. *paşa*, f. האנום/*hanum* 'lady' < Tk. *hanım*). Substantives of non-Hispanic origin generally femininize with Hispanic-origin *-a* (m. בעל הבית/*balabáy* 'householder' (< Heb. בעל הבית / *baʕal ha-bayit*) > f. באלאבאייה/*balabay+a* 'housewife', m. סילאניקלי/*selaniklí* 'Salonikan' (Tk. *Selânikli*) > f. סילאניקליאה/*selaniklí+a*); there are also other femininizing suffixes (e.g., רבי/*rubí* 'religious teacher, leader'(Hb. רבי/*rabbi* > *rub+isa* 'rabbi's wife'). Nouns with initial stressed *a-* generally accept the feminine definite and indefinite article, לה/*la* and אונה/*una*, e.g., לה/אונה אלמה / *la*/*una alma* 'the/a soul' (Sp. *el*/*un alma*); nouns in *-or* are also generally feminine, e.g., לה קאלור / *la kalor* (Sp. *el calor*).

Some native nominal suffixes diverge in meaning and productivity from their Spanish analogues, e.g., ־אדֿה/*-ada* denoting duration of time, etc., as in נוגֿאדֿה/*nochada* '(entire) evening' (Sp. *noche*); and there are innovative uses of suffixes, e.g., ־דֿירו/*-dero* denoting a 'strong compulsion', e.g., גומיטאדֿירו/*gomitadero* 'persistant wretching' (Old Sp. *v-/gomitar*, Sp. *vomitar* 'to vomit'). Nominal coinages, as well as other lexemes, are created using affixes of diverse etymological origins, such as Hispanic and Ibero-Arabic, e.g., חאזינו/*hazino* 'ill' [cf. Ar[abic]. *ḥazīn* 'sad'] > חאזינורה/־דאדֿ/*hazinura*/*-dad* 'illness' (cf. Sp. *-ura*, *-dad*); Hebrew and Hispanic, e.g., *sedaká* 'charity' [Heb. צדקה/*ṣĕdaqa*] > סידֿאקירו/*sedak+ero* 'charity collector' (cf. Sp. *-ero*), *garón* 'throat' [Heb. גרון/*garon*] > גארונידֿאדֿ/*garon+edad* 'gluttony' (cf. Sp. *-edad*), *haragán* 'lazy' [Sp. *haragán*] > חאראגאנודֿ/־ות/*haragan+ud* 'laziness' (cf. Heb. ־ות/*-ut*); Hebrew and Turkish, e.g., פזמון/*pizmón* 'hymn' [Heb.] > פיזמונגֿי/*pizmon+djí* 'singer of hymns' (cf. Tk. *-ci*), פורים/*purim* 'Purim' [Heb.] > פורימליק/*purim+lik* 'Purim present' (cf. Tk. *-lik*), *haham* 'rabbi' [Heb. חכם/*ḥakam*] < האחאמבאשי/*hahambashí* 'chief rabbi' (cf. Tk. *başı*). Contact with French and Italian led to the rise of allomorphemic variants of native nominal markers and other affixes, e.g., native abstract nominal-marking ־דאדֿ/*-dad* > טה־/*-tá* (< It. *-tà*) / ־טאדֿ/*-tád* (It. *-tà* + Sp. *-dad*), e.g., גֿינירוזיטאדֿ/־טה/*djenerozitá(d)* 'generosity' (cf. It. *generosità*, Sp. *generosidad*), and also to the incorporation of new affixes, e.g., ־יסטו/־יסטה / *-isto*/*-ista* '-ist' (< Fr. *-iste* / It./Sp. *-ista*), e.g., איבֿאנזֿיליסטו/־ה / *evanjelisto*/*-a* 'evangelist'.

Nouns of Hebrew-Aramaic origin often pluralize with the Hebrew morphemes ־ים/*-im* (חזנים/*hazan+im* 'cantor+s'), ־ות/*-od* (השכבה/*eshkavá* > השכבות/*eshkav+-od* 'eulogy/-ies'); so do some others (פאפאס/*papás* > פאפאזים/*papaz+im* 'priest+s', קאסאבה/*kasabá* > קאסאבודֿ/־ת/*kasab+od* 'small town+s', Tk. *papaz*, *kasaba*). Most other nouns pluralize with Hispanic-origin *-(e)s* (איסקולאס/*eskola+s* 'school+s' (< It. *scuola*), מילדאריס/*meldar+es* 'religious school+s' (< Gk. *meletáō*), סילאניקליס/*selaniklí+s* 'Salonikans'), including some Hebraisms (e.g., גארוניס/*garon+es* 'throat+s' < גרון/*garon*); while some nouns, mostly Hebrew-Aramaisms, show tautological *-im/-in+es* (מלאך/*malah* > מאלאחינים/ *malah+in+es* 'angel+s' < מלאך/*mal?ak*) or *-od̲+es* (ברכה/*berahá* > ביראחודֿים/*berah+od̲ +es* 'blessings' < ברכה/*bĕrak̲a*).[14]

2.2 Pronouns and pronominal adjectives

Pronouns and pronominal adjectives in the modern language are distinctive in that they include preservations of Old Spanish variants later rejected in normative Spanish, and innovative forms: e.g., 1pl. subject pronoun מוזוטרוס/־אס//*mozotros*/*-as* (and innovative מוזוס/*mozós*) 'we' (Sp. *nosotros*); 2pl. subject pronoun בֿוזוטרוס/־אס//*vozotros*/*-as* (and innovative בֿוזוס/*vozós*) 'you' (Jud. variant, OSp. *vosotros*/*-as*); 2pl. object/reflexive pronoun בֿוס/*vos* 'you' (Sp. *os*); enclitic reflexive 3sg. ־סי/*-se* vs. 3pl. ־סין/*-sen* (Sp. *-se* only). The three levels of direct address are: intimate (2sg.) טו/*tu*; respectful (3) m. sg. איל/*el*, pl. אילייוס/*eyos* / f. sg. איליה/*eya*, pl. אילייאס/*eyas*; highly respectful (2pl.) m. בֿוזוטרוס/ *vozotros* / בֿוזוס/*vozós*, f. בֿוזוטראס /*vozotras* (Sp. *tu*, *Usted*/*-es*) 'you'. The order of a first or second person object pronoun and a reflexive is מי סי / *me se*, טי סי / *te se* (Sp. *se me*). The pronouns מוס/*mos* 'us' and בֿוס/*vos* '(2pl.) you' reduce to מו/*mo* and בֿו/*vo* before another pronoun with initial *l-*, e.g., מו לו דישירון / *mo lo disheron* 'they told us it' (Sp. *nos lo*, etc.). Under French and Italian influence, the pronominal adjective denoting a third-person-plural possessor is always formally plural סוס/*sus*, e.g., סוס קאזה / *sus kaza* 'their house' (Sp. *su casa* 'their house' vs. *sus casas* 'their houses'). מי/*mi* and טי/*ti* are used after (אה) קומו / *komo (a)*, e.g., קומו מי / *komo mi* 'like me' (Sp. *como yo*), and after קון/ *kon* 'with', e.g., קון מי / *kon mi* 'with me' (Sp. *conmigo*). Pleonastic use of object and reflexive pronouns is common, e.g., ייה טי לה טרושי לה פרינדה / *ya te* la *trushe* la *prenda* 'I brought (it) to you the pledge'. There are diverse sorts of final metatheses when enclitic pronouns occur with infinitives, gerunds, and imperatives, e.g., דאלדי/*dalde* 'to give him; give him!' (Sp. *darle*, *¡dadle!*), דאנדובֿולדו/*dándovoldó* 'giving it (m.sg.) to you (2pl.)', דאמידֿ/*damed̲* '(2pl.) give me!' (Sp. *¡dadme!*), דאמילדו/*dameldo* 'give it (2pl.) to me' (Sp. *dármelo*).

2.3 Verbs

Verb conjugations and participles diverge from normative Modern Spanish in numerous respects. Some forms correspond to obsolete and/or popular variants absent in the modern norm: e.g., classes of conjugations represented by forms such as present indicative דו/*do* 'I give' (norm.Sp. *doy*), סיירבֿו/*syervo* 'I serve' (Sp. *sirvo*), סוס/*sos* '(2sg.) you are' (Sp. *eres*), preterite indicative טרושו/*trusho* 's/he brought' (Sp. *trajo*), imperfect איאה/*ía* 'I was going' (Sp. *iba*) and טראאיבֿה/*traíva* 'I was carrying' (Sp. *traía*), future טירני/*terné* 'I shall have' (Sp. *tendré*), pluperfect forms with auxiliary אבֿיר/*aver* / טיניר/ *tener* (+ בושקאדֿו/*bushkad̲o*) 'to have (looked for)' (Sp. [only] *haber [buscado]*), past participle טובֿידֿו/*tuvid̲o* 'had' (Sp. *tenido*), present participle טובֿיינדו/*tuvyendo* 'having' (Sp. *teniendo*). Some verb forms resemble analogues in non-Castilian varieties of Ibero-Romance (although they may be internal innovations in Judezmo); e.g., אינדו/*indo* 'going' (cf. Sp. *yendo*, Pt. *indo*). Other forms reflect internal phonological tendencies,

14 On plural formation in Judezmo see Bunis 1985. For a graded introduction to Modern Judezmo see Bunis 1993c.

e.g., -V*ys* > -V*sh*: ש(טומא)/*(tomá)sh* 'you (2pl. indic.) take' (Sp. *tomáis*); while still others reflect analogical leveling: e.g., 1sg. preterite indicative *-í* as in טומי/*tomí* 'I took' (cf. Sp. *tomé* but *comí* 'I ate', *salí* 'I went out'), 1sg. present indicative אימפיסו/*empeso* 'I begin' (infinitive *empesar* 'to begin'; Sp. *empiezo* (inf. *empezar*)), 2sg./pl. preterite indicative חואיטיס/-ש *huítes*/*-sh* '(2sg./pl) you were' (Sp. *fuiste*/*-eis*), 2sg. imperative !אימפיסה/*empesa!* 'begin!' (Sp. *¡empieza!*). There are some distinctive reductions, e.g., 1sg. pres. indic. near-future בֿו אה / *vo a* > בֿה/*va* 'I am going to' (Sp. *voy a*).

Verbal neologisms were created through novel concatenations of bases and affixes of diverse etymological origins: e.g., בואינו/*bueno* 'good' + *-iguar* > אבוניגואר/*aboniguar* 'to do good', חאזינו/*hazino* 'ill' + *en- -ear+se* > אינחאזיניארסי/*enhazinearse* 'to become ill', Heb. ד-ר-ש/*d-r-š* + *-ar* > דארסאר/*darsar* 'to sermonize', Hebrew-origin חמץ/*hamés* 'leavened food' (Heb. חמץ/*ḥameṣ*) + *des- -ear* > דיסחאמיסיאר/*des·hamesear* 'to get rid of leavened food before Passover', Tk. *konuş-* > קונושיאר/*konushear* 'to speak', Tk. *boya-* (3sg. past def. *boyadı*) > בוייאדיאר/*boyadear* 'to paint', Jud. *kushak* [Tk. *kuşak*] 'belt' + *a- -ar+se* > אקושאקארסי/*akushakarse* 'to put on one's belt'.

At the syntactic level, too, there are numerous divergences between Judezmo and modern normative Spanish worth noting. For example, the 'then' clause of 'if-then' verbal constructions may be expressed by the imperfect indicative instead of the conditional: e.g., סי סינטייראש סו אבֿלה ... דאבֿאש קרידיטו / *si sintyérash su avla [...] dávash krédito* 'If you heard his talk [...] you would have given him credit' (Sp. *si hubierais oído [...] habrías dado*). The imperfect indicative may also be used in the 'if' clause, instead of the subjunctive: e.g., סי לו סאבֿיאמוס, לוס מאטאבֿאמוס / *si lo savíamos, los matávamos* 'If we knew it, we would have killed them' (Sp. *si lo hubiéramos sabido, los habríamos matado*). The past participle often appears after finite verbs of 'necessity' or 'want' such as קאליר/*kaler* 'to be necessary' and קיריר/*kerer* 'to want': e.g., נו קאלי דיג̃ו / *no kale dicho* 'it is unnecessary to say' (Sp. *no hay que decir*, Cat. *no cal dir*); with respect to *kale*, this use was added in the Late Middle Judezmo phase to the earlier use of *kale* + subjunctive, e.g., לה סוכה קאלי קי סיאה די טיירה / *la suká kale ke sea de tyera* 'the booth has to be of earth', and *kale* + infinitive, e.g., קאלי סאליר דילה סוכה / *kale salir de·la suká* 'one has to leave the booth'. Unlike normative Spanish, which requires third-person *singular* forms of existential *haber* when used to denote 'there is/are', regardless of the number of the subject, analogous Judezmo אבֿיר/*aver* shows number agreement: e.g., אבֿיאן דוס פרוכיות / *avían dos parohiyod̲* 'there were two Torah-ark curtains' (Sp. *había dos cortinas*). Perhaps under Turkish influence, the predicate (nouns, adjectives, past participles) generally precedes קי/*ke* + the subjunctive form of verbs in oaths and blessings, סאנו קי איסטיס / *sano ke estés* 'be well'; פאסאדֿו קי סיאה / *pasad̲o ke sea* 'may it [this unpleasantness, etc.] be behind you' (cf. Tk. *sağol*; *geçmiş olsun*).

2.4 Adjectives

Adjectives in Judezmo do not diverge greatly in their structure or function from Spanish; but some structures are distinctive, e.g., איל דיזמאזאלאדֿו די מאיר / *el dezmazalad̲o de Mair* 'unlucky Mair'. Under French influence, from the Modern Judezmo phase there is overt gender concord between a substantive and its non-Turkish-origin qualifier, even if the qualifier ends in a liquid: e.g., m.sg. קומירסייאל/*komersyal* vs. f.sg. קומירסייאלה/

komersyala 'commercial' (Sp. m./f.sg. *comercial*; Fr. m. *commercial*, f.sg. *commerciale*). טאל/*tal* 'such' and קואל/*kual* 'which' are distinguished in gender and number as טאל/*tal*, טאלה/*tala*, טאלוס/*talos*, טאלאס/*talas* and קואל/*kual*, קואלה/*kuala*, קואלוס/*kualos*, קואלאס/*kualas*, respectively (Sp. *tal*, *tales; cual, cuales*). Some adjectives of Turkish origin only appear in the masculine singular form, e.g., קאדיר/*kadir* 'capable' (Tk. *kadir* < Ar. *qādir*): אילייאס סון קאדיר די איסטו / *eyas son kadir de esto* '(f.pl.) They are capable of this'. Generally speaking, there are only two sets of demonstratives, proximals (m.sg. איסטי/*este* 'this', etc.) and distals (m.sg. אקיל/*akel*, etc.) (Sp. *este* vs. *ese* vs. *aquel*). Under Turkish influence, some nouns may be used collectively and receive a singular adjective, e.g., מונגֿה פארה / *muncha pará* 'a lot of money' (cf. Tk. *çok para*, Sp. pl. *muchos ducados*). Judezmo uses comparative constructions rejected in normative Spanish, e.g., מאס מיזֿור / *mas mijor* 'better' (Sp. *mejor*). The superlative may be expressed distinctively through reduplication, e.g., מונגֿו מונגֿו / *muncho muncho* 'very much', or with ביין/*bien*, e.g., *bien grande* 'very large'. The absolute superlative may show a repetition of the article, e.g., לה קאזה לה מאס גראנדי / *la kaza la mas grande* 'the biggest house' (Sp. *la casa más grande*). The Spanish superlative suffix *-ísimo* has no productive Judezmo analogue.

2.5 Numerals

Numerals diverge from Spanish in some cardinal forms, e.g., סיש/*sesh* 'six', מואיבֿי/*mueve* 'nine', בינטי/*vente* '20', טרינטה/*trenta* '30', שישינטה/*sheshenta* '60', סיין/*syen* '100' (Sp. *seis*, *nueve*, *veinte*, *treinta*, *sesenta*, *ciento*), as well as in some ordinal forms, e.g., פרימו/פרימיר(ו)/*primo/primer(o)* 'first', קואטרינ(ו)/*kuatren(o)* 'fourth' (Sp. *primer[o]*, *cuarto*); an alternate ordinal form is exemplified by איל די קואטרו / *el de kuatro* 'the fourth'. Each digit of a complex numeral is separated by אי/*i* 'and', e.g., סיין אי סינקואינטה אי מואיבֿי / *sien i sinkuenta i mueve* '159' (Sp. *ciento cincuenta y nueve*). When a noun is qualified by a complex numeral ending in 'one', the noun appears in the singular, e.g., סיין אי אונה נוגֿי / *syen i una noche* '101 nights'.

2.6 Adverbs

Adverbs in Judezmo tend to resemble their Spanish counterparts in form and function. However, *-mente* '-ly' is rarely used; and adjectives often have adverbial function, e.g., בואינו/*bueno* 'good; well'. Intensification may be expressed through reduplication, e.g., אבֿאגאר אבֿאגאר / *avagar avagar* 'slowly; softly'. Perhaps under Italian influence, טאנטו/*tanto* is often used instead of טאן/*tan* 'so', e.g., איל בֿה טאנטו אבֿאגאר / *el va tanto avagar* 'he goes so slowly' (Sp. *Va tan despacio*). There are some distinctive constructions, e.g., אין לוקי / *en lo ke* + (+ finite verb) 'while (+ gerund)' (Sp. *al* + infinitive). Adverbial clauses with אין/*en* + gerund (vs. Sp. *al* + infinitive) are common: אין קיטאנדולו / *en kitándolo* 'upon removing it' (Sp. *al quitarlo*).

2.7 Prepositions

The forms and functions of Judezmo and Spanish prepositions differ in many respects. For example, the functions of pairs such as פור/*por* and פארה/*para*, די/*de* and דיזדי/*dizde* and others do not exactly match those of their Spanish cognates, *por*, *para*, *de*, *desde*, and so on. In representations of language from at least the early seventeenth century, the ‘personal *a*’ which in normative Spanish obligatorily precedes a human direct object is frequently absent in Judezmo: e.g., נו הארבֿין לוס תלמידים / *No harven los talmidim* ‘They should not beat the pupils’ (Sp. *No golpeen a los alumnos*). There is frequent omission of אה/*a* ‘to’ between איר/ייר//*(y)ir* ‘to go’ and the infinitive in analytic, near-future constructions, especially when there is a vowel at the end of the finite form of *(y)ir* and/or the beginning of the following infinitive; אה/*a* is also omitted in various other positions in which it is obligatory in Spanish: e.g., בֿה אזיר זיארה / *Va azer ziara* ‘He is going to make a pilgrimage [to the graves of Jewish saints]’ (Sp. *Va a hacer una peregrinación*). There are various other uses of prepositions in divergence from normative Modern Spanish: e.g., דין / די אין ... אין / *den* / *de en* ... *en* ‘from ... to’: דין בֿאנדה אין בֿאנדה / *den vanda en vanda* ‘from one side to another’ (Sp. *de lado a lado*); אניל/*anel* ‘to him’ (Sp. *a el*).

2.8 Time and age expressions

Past time may be expressed by constructions such as: אגורה/*agora* + time expression (e.g., אגורה און אנייו דארסו איל חכם / *agora un anyo darsó el haham* ‘a year ago the rabbi lectured’); *atrás* + time expression (e.g., דוס אוראס אטראס סאליירון / *dos oras atrás salyeron* ‘they went out two hours ago); time expression + *antes* (e.g., אונה אוריקה אנטיס / *una orika antes* ‘just about an hour ago’); *ay* + time expression (e.g., איי סיש אנייוס קי איסטו אקי / *ay sesh anyos ke estó akí* ‘I have been here six years’; these constructions correspond to Spanish *hacer* + time expression. As in Old Spanish, age is expressed by *ser* + *de edad de*, e.g., אירה די אידֿאדֿ די דוס אנייוס / *era de edad de dos anyos* ‘he was two years old’ (Sp. *tenía dos años [de edad]*); under French influence, an alternate construction is *ser* + *aedado de*, e.g., איס אאידֿאדֿו די דוס אנייוס / *es aedado de dos anyos* ‘he is two years old’ (Sp. *tiene dos años*, Fr. *il est âgé de deux ans*).

2.9 Negation

Negation expressing limitation (‘only’) takes the form negative expression + קי/*ke*: e.g., נו (איסקאפארון) קי (סייטי פריסונאס) / *no (eskaparon) ke (syete presonas)* ‘only (seven people escaped)’ (cf. Sp. *no ... más de*, Fr. *ne ... que*). Unlike normative Spanish, from the Late Middle Judezmo phase, and especially during the Modern Judezmo period, the negative particle נו(ן)/*no(n)* was often used pleonastically after a negative element: e.g., דינגונו נו סי קישו / *dinguno* no *se keshó* ‘no one complained’ (Sp. *nadie se quejó*).

In all spheres of morphology and lexicon, Ottoman and post-Ottoman Judezmo were enriched by incorporations from Hebrew as well as contact languages,[15] resulting in further grammatical divergence from Spanish.[16]

15 On the influence of Turkish in Judezmo see Varol-Bornes 1996, Bunis 2008, 2009, 2013. For South Slavic influence see Bunis 2017.

16 For extensive notes on structural innovation in contemporary Judezmo, especially that of Istanbul, see Varol-Bornes 2008.

3. Sample texts

3.1 A note on the sample texts

The texts constituting most of the remainder of the present article are intended to illustrate the major historical, stylistic and social varieties or registers of Judezmo used among its speakers from the sixteenth century into the modern phase of the language. The major distinctive features of each of the represented varieties and historical phases will be noted in the remarks introducing each text, including details on language name, orthography, phonology, morphology, lexicon, syntax and semantics. Note that where authors used ד for both /d/ and /ð/, I respected their orthography in the Hebrew-letter transcriptions appearing in the texts; in the romanizations, however, I have distinguished /d/ from /ð/ by means of *d* vs. *d̲*, in accordance with SEJ phonology.

3.2 The Hebrew-letter graphemes of Modern Judezmo

The following chart outlines the principal Hebrew-letter graphemes used to denote the phonemes of Judezmo in the modern phase of the language as exemplified in the sample texts offered in the present article. Following World War II, most Judezmo speakers made the transition to the Roman alphabet. The chart below also introduces the predominant contemporary Latin-letter Judezmo orthography; it was proposed by Moshe Shaul and is advocated by the Autoridad Nasionala del Ladino i Su Kultura he helped found in Jerusalem, 1997, as well as by Ladinokomunita and other internet and online social media sites.[17] It is presently used in the Judezmo periodicals *Aki Yerushalayim* (Jerusalem) and *El Amaneser* (Istanbul). IPA symbols are used below to indicate the phonological values of the orthographic symbols:

Vowels

IPA	Israel Ladino Authority	*Rashí* Letters	*Merubá* Letters
[a]	a	(־)א־, ־ה	(־)א־, ־ה
[e]	e	י	י
[i]	i	י	י
[o]	o	ו	ו
[u]	u	ו	ו

Semi-consonants

IPA	Israel Ladino Authority	*Rashí* Letters	*Merubá* Letters
[u]	u	ו	ו
[j]	i, y	י, יי, לייי	י, יי, לייי

17 The Romanization system was first elaborated in Shaul 1979. For further discussion of Judezmo in Romanization see section 3.13 below.

Consonants

	Modern Judezmo Graphemes			Pre-Modern Judezmo Allographs
IPA	Israel Ladino Authority	*Rashí* Letters	*Merubá* Letters	
[b]	b	ב	ב	
[d]	d	ד	ד	
[ð]	d	ד̆	ד̄	ד/ד
[ʣ]	dz	דז	דז	
[ʤ]	dj	ג̆	ג̄	
[f]	f	פ̆	פ̄	
[g]	g	ג	ג	
[h]				ה/ה
[γ]	g	ג	ג	
[k]	k	ק	ק	
[k´]	k, ky	ק̆	ק̄	
[l]	l	ל	ל	
[ʎ]				לי(י)/לי(י)
[m]	m	מ, ־ם	מ, ־ם	
[n]	n	נ, ־ן	נ, ־ן	
[nj/ɲ]	ny	ניי	ניי	
[p]	p	פ	פ	
[r]	r	ר	ר	
[rr]	rr	ר, רר	ר, רר	ר/ר
[s]	s	ס	ס	ש/ס, ס/ס
[ʃ]	sh	ש, ש̆	ש, ש̄	ג̄/ג̆, ש/ש, ש̄/ש̆
[t]	t	ט	ט	
[θ]	t, th	־ד̆, ־ת	־ד̄/־ד, ־ת	-ד/־ד, ־ת/־ת
[ʦ]	ts	צ , ־ץ / טס	צ, ־ץ/ טס	
[ʧ]	ch	ג̆	ג̄	
[v]	v	ב̆	ב̄	ב̄/ב̆, ו/ו
[χ]	h	ח	ח	
[z]	z	ז	ז	ז/ז, ־ש־/־ש־
[ʒ]	j	ז̆	ז̄	ג̄/ג̆

3.3 Sacred Hebrew-Aramaic texts and their literal Judezmo renditions: Ottoman Judezmo speakers' Ideal Whole Hebrew reading pronunciation and Judezmo calque-translation tradition[18]

In many ways constituting a parallel to the calque-translation varieties used among speakers of other Jewish languages to render sacred Hebrew and Aramaic texts into an archaizing, literal version of the vernacular, the Judezmo sacred-text calque-translation variety is sometimes known among native speakers as *laḏino*. As this name suggests, the Judezmo calque-translation variety harks back to the early varieties of *Latin*-derived Hispano-Romance used by the Jews of Iberia in the early Late Middle Ages. Probably as in medieval times, in the Ottoman Empire this variety was used in the elementary religious schools as part of the *lashón i laḏino* (i.e., Hebrew and vernacular calque translation) study technique traditionally used to impart a basic understanding of the original Hebrew or Aramaic text of the holy writ through a literal translation in a variety of the student's vernacular. In this technique, Hebrew words, phrases, and ultimately entire verses were recited or chanted alternately in the original language, using the Whole Hebrew-Aramaic reading pronunciation unique to Judezmo speakers in the local Sephardic community,[19] and in the literal translation;[20] teachers generally complemented the translations of the biblical verses under study with impromptu *perushim* (explications) based on the classical Bible commentaries as well as on local interpretation traditions.

Since the primary focus of such studies was always the Hebrew (or in the case of some texts, the Aramaic) classical text, the calque translation attempted to provide a mirror image of the original, rendering as literally as possible the morphology and syntax of the original, with even some occasional attempts at phonological matching, grounded in the conservative preservation of translation patterns undoubtedly established during the earliest period in which the Iberian Jews began to use varieties of Ibero-Romance, with additional influence – especially lexical – from the Jewish Hispano-Arabic calque-translation tradition which had earlier been used among the Jews of Muslim Spain.[21] As a result, in the Ottoman regions, this register included morphological, syntactical, and lexical elements long archaic or obsolete not only in Spanish, but in

18 Note the following notational conventions, not ordinarily used in the accepted Leipzig glosses format, which are incorporated in this section in the glosses, both in the Hebrew text and in the parallel Judezmo calque translation: An underline (_) is used in the Judezmo translation to denote the boundary between morphemes in the Hebrew text which in the Judezmo translation constitutes a word boundary. The double underline (‗) is used in the Hebrew-letter Judezmo translation of the Hebrew text, as well as in the Romanization of the Hebrew text and its Romanized Judezmo translation, to denote a מקף/*maqaf* or Biblical hyphen (i.e., < ־ >). In the Romanization of the Judezmo texts, the middle dot (<·>) is used to indicate a boundary between two words in Modern Judezmo in Romanization which are spelled in the present Hebrew-letter Judezmo texts as one word. In preparing the Leipzig glosses, I was helped by Ms. Adi Bukshpan of the Hebrew University of Jerusalem; for some Spanish parallels see Gonzálvez García 2010. Note the additional gloss abbreviations used here: PRON.PREP = post-prepositional pronoun, PROX = proximal demonstrative, DIS = distal demonstrative, HYP = hypocoristic.

19 On the concept Whole (as opposed to Merged) Hebrew as elaborated by the Yiddish linguist Max Weinreich, with specific reference to Judezmo speakers, see Bunis 2013a.

20 On Judezmo speakers' oral and written calque-translation techniques see Bunis 1996.

21 Judeo-Arabisms preserved in the Judezmo Bible translation tradition are discussed in Bunis 2017b.

everyday Judezmo as well. Since the variety was intended as a *translation* of Hebrew and Aramaic, elements from the latter languages which in fact came to constitute an integral part of the everyday Judezmo of the Ottoman Sephardim were usually avoided in the calque translations of sacred texts; so, too, were elements incorporated over the centuries from local Ottoman contact languages such as Turkish, Greek and South Slavic. Thus, into the modern era, the lexicon of the traditional sacred-text translations was essentially limited to elements of medieval Hispanic and Hispano-Arabic origin.

The sample text offered below, recounting the binding of Isaac (Genesis 22:1–18), well illustrates the features of the calque-translation variety used by Modern Judezmo speakers. This version was published in the Bible translation edited by Yisraʔel Bĕḵar Ḥayyim of Belgrade in Vienna, 1813–16, which constitutes an adaptation of that published by Avraham ben Yiṣḥaq Asa of Constantinople, 1739–44, which in turn is apparently an amalgam of written translations first published in Constantinople in the mid-sixteenth century and local oral translations known to Asa. The maximal vernacular-language mirror-imaging of the original syntactic constructions and semantic senses of the lexemes in the Hebrew text is brought to the fore in the sample text, which includes many structures that are of a type which appear only in traditional Jewish Ibero-Romance sacred-text translations. The sharp contrast between such translations and the corresponding non-calque Spanish translations ordinarily used by contemporary Spanish speakers may be demonstrated through the citations below of the equivalent phrases found in the Modern Spanish Bible translation available online from La Iglesia de Jesucristo de los Santos de los Últimos Días.[22]

The general feature of literalism in the translations is illustrated by Judezmo constructions which calque the precise word-for-word structure and literal meaning of the Hebrew but which, when examined in the light of ordinary, everyday Judezmo, are often found to lack the semantic sense carried by the Hebrew source constructions. The Judezmo calque-translations sometimes lack elements ordinarily required by the primarily Hispanic-origin syntax of Judezmo but which do not have overt representatives in the Hebrew text. For example, biblical consecutive *waw* is consistently reflected overtly as literal *i* 'and' rather than receiving zero reflection (as for example in the corresponding Spanish and English equivalents of the second phrase below); after *i*, however, the verb is translated in Judezmo as the temporally converse tense implied by the Hebrew syntax rather than as that expressed literally by the Hebrew verb form, thus illustrating the fact that the literality of the calque-translation language does in fact have certain limits. Examples of phenomena of this type appearing in the sample text include:[23]

22 https://www.lds.org/scriptures/bible?lang=spa

23 In the analytic portion of this section the Biblical Hebrew receives its standard romanization; in the sample text the Biblical Hebrew is instead transcribed according to the Whole Hebrew reading tradition of Southeast Judezmo speakers.

Hebrew	Calque Judezmo	Modern Literary Spanish	English equivalent
wa-yhi	*I_fue* [not **I_será* or *I_akonteserá*]	Y aconteció	And it came to pass
wa-yiśśa Aḇraham	*i_als-ó Avraam*	alzó Abraham	Abraham lifted up
šenit	*segunda vez*	por segunda vez	a second time

The principle of literality is further actualized through the absence in the translation of the copula (סיר/*ser*) or the verb of location/state (איסטאר/*estar*), ordinarily obligatory in Judezmo (as in Hispanic) syntax, if corresponding elements are absent in the Hebrew text; for example:

Hebrew	Calque Judezmo	Modern Literary Spanish	English equivalent
wĕ-ʔayye ha-śe lĕ-ʕola	*i_adó el_karnero por_alsasyón*	pero, ¿dónde *está* el cordero para el holocausto?	but where *is* the lamb for a burnt-offering?

In translations of Hebrew expressions composed of verbs and nouns employing the same root, the calque Judezmo analogue also uses verbs and nouns displaying the same base; not all of the members of such calques actually have analogues in Spanish; for example, Judezmo אלסאסייון/*alsasyón* in the following expression does not have a correspondent (**alzación*) in ordinary Spanish:

Hebrew	Calque Judezmo	Modern Literary Spanish	English equivalent
wĕ-haʕale-hu … lĕ-ʕola	*I_áls-a-lo … a_alsasyón*	y ofrécelo … en holocausto	And offer him … for a burnt offering

As part of the attempt toward systematic one-to-one correspondences between Hebrew constructions and their calque Judezmo analogues, specific Hebrew verb tenses and other verbal constructions are usually rendered automatically and systematically by particular Judezmo analogues. Thus, the singular present participle is regularly translated by the archaic apocopated present participle; for example, *yare* is rendered by apocopated *temyén* (cf. full present participle *temyente*) in:

Hebrew	Calque Judezmo	Modern Literary Spanish	English equivalent
ki_yĕre ʔElohim ʔatta	*ke_temyén_de el_Dyo tu*	que temes a Dios	that thou art a God-fearing man

Similarly, the Hebrew simple past is universally translated by the Judezmo preterite tense, rather than the present, or a compound past tense, as the context might require in ordinary language; for example:

Hebrew	Calque Judezmo	Modern Literary Spanish	English equivalent
ʕak̲šaw yadaʕti	*agora supe* ['I knew']	ahora sé ['I know']	now I know
ʔamar_lo	*disho_a_el* ['told to him']	le había dicho ['had told him']	had told him

The *nifʕal* is customarily translated by the passive construction *ser* + past participle, as for example in the following instance, in which the Hebrew future-tense verb form is translated literally by a future passive:

Hebrew	Calque Judezmo	Modern Literary Spanish	English equivalent
yeʔamer	*será dicho* ['it will be said']	se dice ['it is said']	it is said

The infinitive absolute is reflected as the infinitive + finite form of the same verb; for example:

Hebrew	Calque Judezmo	Modern Literary Spanish	English equivalent
Ki_b̲arek̲ a-b̲arek̲ĕk̲a wĕ-harba ʔarbe ʔet̲_zarʕak̲a	*Ke_bendezir te_bendeziré i_muchiguar muchiguaré a_tu_semen* ['to bless I will bless you…']	de cierto te bendeciré grandemente y multiplicaré en gran manera tu descendencia	that in blessing I will bless thee, and in multiplying I will multiply thy seed

With the result of writing the verb and pronoun together as a single word, as in the Hebrew source constructions, object and reflexive pronouns are posited enclitically after verbs in the present, preterite and imperfect tenses, as in archaic (but not Modern) Judezmo; and, as in medieval Judezmo and Spanish, they are infixed between the infinitive and future inflections in future forms; for example:[24]

Hebrew	Calque Judezmo	Modern Literary Spanish	English equivalent
wa_yaqom	*i_alevantóse*	y se levantó	and rose up
wĕ-ništaḥawwe	*i_enkorvarmosemos*	[adoraremos]	and we will worship

Similarly, post-positioning the indirect object pronoun after an overt preposition brings the Judezmo translation structurally closer to the Hebrew than positing it before the verb, as in the first analogue in Spanish below, or post-positing it after the verb but without an overt preposition, as in the second Spanish instance:

Hebrew	Calque Judezmo	Modern Literary Spanish	English equivalent
ʔašer ʔomar ʔele-k̲a	*ke diré a_ti*	que yo te diré	which I will tell thee of
wĕ-lek̲_lĕ-k̲a	*i_anda_a_ti*	y vete	and get thee

24 Note that the verb used in the Spanish translation, *adorar*, is not a pronominal, as opposed to Judezmo pronominal *enkorvarse*, reflecting the *hitpaʕel* in the Hebrew text.

In the third person, Hebrew *ʔet* + pronominal suffix in the sense of 'with' is more closely mirrored in calque Judezmo through the use of post-prepositional *(kon) el* than of reflexive Spanish *consigo*:

Hebrew	Calque Judezmo	Modern Literary Spanish	English equivalent
ʔittó	*kon_el*	consigo	with him

The Hebrew object marker *ʔet* is systematically translated as *a* in the Judezmo calque text, although in ordinary Judezmo this element is only used, as in Spanish, before an object which is human (and optionally, animate) and definite; for example:

Hebrew	Calque Judezmo	Modern Literary Spanish	English equivalent
Wa-yaḥaḇoš ʔet_ḥamoro	*i_sinchó **a**_su_azno*	y ensilló su asno	and [he] saddled his ass

On the other hand, since the definite article is absent in the possessor element in Hebrew construct forms, it is also absent in the Judezmo equivalent, although this runs counter to ordinary Judezmo syntax; but when the definite determiner (*ha-*) does appear in the Hebrew text, it is translated literally rather than, say, a demonstrative; for example:

Hebrew	Calque Judezmo	Modern Literary Spanish	English equivalent
šem ha-maqom	*nombre_de_**el**_lugar*	**el** nombre de **aquel** lugar	the name of that place

Where the article is repeated in the Hebrew text, as in demonstrative or other attributive constructions, the repetition is reflected in the calque translation, although this too is contrary to ordinary Judezmo syntax; for example:

Hebrew	Calque Judezmo	Modern Literary Spanish	English equivalent
ha-dĕḇarim ha-ʔelle	*las_palavras las_estas*	estas cosas	these things

The Hebrew article is also reflected in the translation in other instances, such as references to the name of the Divinity and to toponyms; for example:

Hebrew	Calque Judezmo	Modern Literary Spanish	English equivalent
wĕ-ha-ʔelohim	*i_el_Dio*	Dios	God
ʔel_ʔereṣ Ha-moriyya	*a_tiera_de la_Moriá*	a tierra de Moriah	to the land of Moriah

Hebrew elements tend to be automatically and systematically translated by particular Judezmo elements, often regardless of whether the translations are suitable semantically in the context of Judezmo or not; for example, in the verbal system one finds:

Systematic correspondences	Hebrew	Calque Judezmo	Modern Literary Spanish	English equivalent
yašaḇ = estar	*Šĕḇú la-ḵem po*	*Estad_a vos akí*	Esperad aquí	Abide ye here
halaḵ = andar	*wa-yeleḵ*	*i_anduvo*	y fue	and went

The choice of the Judezmo analogue of a given Hebrew word may be determined by the number and/or gender of the Hebrew source lexeme; for example, the plural number and masculine gender of the equivalent of 'wood' correspond in the Judezmo rendition, but diverge in the Spanish equivalent:

Hebrew	Calque Judezmo	Modern Literary Spanish	English equivalent
ʕaṣe ʕola	*lenyos_de alsasyón*	leña para el holocausto	wood for the burnt offering

Distinctive translations meant to syntactically approximate Hebrew numerical use include constructions such as:

Hebrew	Calque Judezmo	Modern Literary Spanish	English equivalent
šĕne-hem	*ambos eyos*	los dos	both of them
yaḥdaw	*a·una*	juntos	together
ʔeṯ_šĕne nĕʕaraw	*a_dos sus mosos*	a dos criados suyos	two of his young men

Various other archaic or otherwise distinctive forms occur throughout such texts; in the sample text below these include:

Hebrew	Calque Judezmo	Modern Literary Spanish	English equivalent
hinneni	*Ek me*	Heme aquí	Here I am
wĕ-ʔayye	*i adó?*	¿donde?	where
ha-mizbeaḥ	*la ara*	un altar	the altar
wĕ-hinne-ʔayil	*i ek_barvéz*	y he aquí un carnero	and behold … a ram
wa-yišlaḥ Aḇraham ʔeṯ-yaḏo	*I_tendió Avraam a_su mano*	Y extendió Abraham su mano	And Abraham stretched forth his hand
mĕʔuma	*ninguna koza*	nada	[not] anything

In order to effect as close a correspondence between the Hebrew and Judezmo elements as possible, some Hebrew elements are translated by the Judezmo elements bearing the closest phonological proximity to the target elements; for example:

Hebrew	Calque Judezmo	Modern Literary Spanish	English equivalent
ʕaḏ_ko	*asta akí*	hasta allá	yonder
ki ʕaḵšaw	*ke agora*	porque ya	for now

Despite the tendency toward linguistic conservatism characteristic of the Judezmo calque translation language, it does occasionally reflect innovations in the contemporary language spoken at the time a particular written translation was prepared. For example, in Judezmo translation texts from the sixteenth century, the second person singular preterite indicative morpheme is *-ste* (e.g., היזישטי/*hiziste* in the 1547 Constantinople Pentateuch, Genesis 22:16), as in normative Spanish of the period; but from the eighteenth through early nineteenth centuries one instead finds innovative *-stes* (under the influence of *-s* as the 2sg. marker in other tenses), cf. *ʕasita* = *izistes* in our sample text (as opposed to *hiciste* in the Spanish translation). Furthermore, where the original text uses a particular lexical or syntactic element, the translation offers an overt corresponding element; but the translation also occasionally adds an element not corresponding to an overt element in the original, generally in adherence to requirements of Hispanic syntax. For example, the three components *mi_*, *maʕal*, and *la* of the adverbial construction *mi_maʕal la(-ʕeṣim)* 'upon the (wood)' are reflected literally as three components of Hispanic origin, דיארִיבֿה אה (לוס ליניייוס) / *de ariva a (los lenyos)*, as opposed to simple *sobre* in the Spanish translation; but the single adverbial element *taḥat* 'under' is also translated by means of three components, אין לוגאר די / *en lugar de*, in conformance with Hispanic syntax (and as in the Spanish translation) and, in this instance, diverging from the predominant, one-to-one component-to-component, calque-translation technique.

In instances of semantic ambiguity in the original text, the calque translation often reflects the interpretation incorporated in earlier traditional translations, such as Onqelos, or in later rabbinical commentaries. For instance, *šaʕar (ʔoyĕḇaw)* is translated as קונסיז׳ו די (סוס אינימיגוס) / *konsejo_de (sus_enemigos)*; since biblical *šaʕar*, literally meaning 'gate' (including 'city gate'), also came to denote the 'counsel' offered by the elders who gathered at the city gate; in this instance the Spanish translation uses the more literal, less interpretative "puertas de sus enemigos" 'gates of his enemies', similar to 'gate of his enemies' in the English. Rabbinical commentators interpreted the phrase *ʕeqeḇ ʔašer* in some biblical verses as a conjunctive phrase denoting causality; but in Psalms 19:12 and Proverbs 22:4 *ʕeqeḇ* was understood as something akin to English 'reward', and this would seem to explain the glossing of the word as פריסייו / *presyo* 'price' in the Judezmo rendition.

In order to highlight the techniques used in the calque-Judezmo text to mirror-image the original Hebrew, the Hebrew text itself has been added to the translation text below. The Romanization of the Hebrew represents the Ideal Whole Hebrew of Judezmo speakers in Salonika,[25] a major Ottoman Judezmo speech community and one in which the largest number of distinct grapheme-to-phoneme correspondences was maintained, probably in most respects closely resembling the realization of Ideal Whole Hebrew in medieval Castile.

The Ideal Whole Hebrew of Modern Judezmo speakers in Salonika featured a five-vowel system, corresponding to the five vowels of Judezmo (and Spanish): ִ חיריק/*ḥiriq* = [i]; ֵ צירה/*ṣere* / ֶ סגול/*segol* / ֱ חטף סגול / *ḥaṭaf segol* / ְ שווא נעה / *šĕwa naʕa* 'vocalic *šĕwa*' = [e]; ָ קמץ גדול / *qameṣ gadol* / ַ פַּתח/*pataḥ* / ֲ חטף פַּתח / *ḥaṭaf pataḥ* = [a]; ֹ חולם/

25 The concept 'Ideal Whole Hebrew' of Judezmo speakers, denoting the idealized form of Hebrew proper (e.g., its phonology, morphology, and so on) advocated for use in formal contexts by the Judezmo-speaking Ottoman rabbis, and its converse, Judezmo speakers' 'Real Whole Hebrew', denoting the Hebrew actually realized by Judezmo speakers, for example, in informal contexts or by speakers lacking complete competence in Ideal Whole Hebrew, were first elaborated in Bunis 1981.

ḥolam / ָ קמץ קטן / *qameṣ qaṭan* / ֳ חטף קמץ / ֳ *ḥaṭaf qameṣ* = [o]; וּ שורוק/*šuruq* / ֻ קבוץ *qubbuṣ* = [u]. A vocalic *šĕwa* (שווא נעה / *šĕwa naʕa*) was realized [e] when under conditions similar to its traditional classification in 'Sephardic Hebrew', e.g., שְׁמַע/*šĕmaʕ* = *shemá(h)* 'listen!', הַמְבורך/*ha-mĕḇorak̲* = *amevorah* 'the blessed', מצַוְּךָ/*mĕsawwĕka* = *mesavehá* 'order you', לְבָבְךָ/*lĕḇaḇĕk̲a* = *levavehá* 'your heart', נַפְשְׁךָ/*nafšĕk̲a* = *nafshehá* 'your soul', לְהַרְרֵי/*lĕharĕre* = *learere* 'to the mountains of'. In other instances the *šĕwa* was considered silent (שווא נחה / *šĕwa naḥa*), receiving zero realization, e.g., וַיְכֻלּוּ/*wa-yk̲ullu* = *vayhulú* 'and they finished', וּבְכָל/*u-ḇ-k̲ol* = *uvhol* 'and with all'. A *qameṣ* preceding a *ḥaṭaf qameṣ* was realized *a*, e.g., נָעֳמִי/*Naomí*. Furthermore, Judezmo speakers' Whole Hebrew shows some distinctive vocalisms; for example, medieval Iberian transcriptions of Hebrew in Romanization show that the personal name מאיר was pronounced *Mair*, as in Judezmo today (cf. Ashkenazic-derived Israeli Hebrew *Méir*).

With the exceptions of ח/*ḥet* and כ/*k̲af*, both realized locally among Judezmo speakers as a fricative somewhere on the continuum between [χ] and [h], the realization of the consonants basically corresponded to that of phones existing in the Hispanic component of the Jews' everyday language and lacked characteristically Semitic phones: א/*ʔalef* = phonological zero, בּ/*bet* = [b], ב/*ḇet* = [v], גּ/*gimel* = [g], ג/*g̱imel* = [γ], דּ/*dalet* = [d], ד/*ḏalet* = [ð], ה/*he* = phonological zero, ו/*waw* = [v], ז/*zayin* = [z], ח/*ḥet* = [χ], ט/*ṭet* = [t], י/*yod* = [y] (with a tendency toward zero when adjacent to a front vowel), כּ/*kaf* = [k], כ/־ך / *k̲af* = [χ], ל/*lamed* = [l], מ/־ם / *mem* = [m], נ/־ן / *nun* = [n], ס/*samek̲* = [s], ע/*ʕayin* = phonological zero (or [χ] at the end of a syllable), פּ/*pe* = [p], פ/־ף / *fe* = [f], צ/־ץ / *ṣade* = (SEJ) [s] or (NWJ) [ʦ], ק/*qof* = [k], ר/*reš* = flapped or trilled apical [r], שׁ/*šin* = [ʃ] or [s], שׂ/*śin* = [s], תּ/*taw* = [t], ת / (unpointed) *taw* = [t] in syllable-initial position, and (SEJ) [θ] or [ð] / (NWJ) [t] or [d] in syllable-final position. The stress is as indicated by the טעמים/*ṭĕʕamim* of the biblical text.

3.4 Sample text: The Binding of Isaac (Genesis 22:1–18)

(1) וַיְהִי אַחַר הַדְּבָרִים הָאֵלֶּה וְהָאֱלֹהִים

אי_פ̄ואי דיספואיס_די לאס_פאלאב̄ראס לאס_איסטאס אי_איל_דייו

Va_yí	*aharé*	*a_devar-im*	*a_ele*	*ve_A_eloim*
I_fue	*después_de*	*las_palavra-s*	*las_est-as*	*i_el_Dyo*
and_be.PRET.3SG[26]	after-ADV	DEF.F.PL_word-PL	DEF.F.PL_PROX.F.PL	and_DEF.M.SG_God

And it was after these things that God

נִסָּה אֶת־אַבְרָהָם וַיֹּאמֶר אֵלָיו אַבְרָהָם

פריב̄ו אה_אברהם אי_דישו אה_איל אברהם

nisá	*eḏ_Avraam*	*va_yó-mer*	*el_av*	*"Avraam"*[27]
prev-ó	*a_Avraam*	*i_dish-o*	*a_el*	*"Avraam"*
prove-PRET.3SG	OBJ_Avraam	and_say-PRET.3SG	to_PRON.PREP.3SG.M	Abraham

did prove Abraham, and said unto him: "Abraham";

26 Unless otherwise noted, verb forms (e.g., present, preterite, imperfect, future) are in the indicative mode; other modes (subjunctive, conditional) will be explicitly noted.

27 I have added quotation marks and various punctuation marks in the romanizations in conformance with Modern Judezmo use; they do not appear in the Hebrew-letter texts.

וַיֹּאמֶר הִנֵּנִי׃

אי_דישו איק_מי :

va_yó-mer	*"Ine_ni":*
i_dish-o	*"Ek_me" :*
and_say-PRET.3SG	behold.ADV_PRON.ACC.1SG

and he said: "Here am I".

(2) וַיֹּאמֶר קַח־נָא אֶת־בִּנְךָ אֶת־יְחִידְךָ

אי_דישו טומה_אגורה אה_טו_איזו אה_טו_אוניקו

Va_yó-mer	*"Kah_na*	*ed_bin-há*	*ed_yehide-há*
I_dish-o	*"Tom-a_agora*	*a_tu_ijo*	*a_tu_únik-o*
and_say-PRET.3SG	take-IMP.2SG_now-JUS	OBJ_POSS.2SG_son	OBJ_POSS.2SG_only-M.SG

And He said: "Take now thy son, thine only,

אֲשֶׁר־אָהַבְתָּ אֶת־יִצְחָק וְלֶךְ־לְךָ אֶל־אֶרֶץ הַמֹּרִיָּה

קי_אמאסטיס אה_יצחק אי_אנדה_אה_טי אה_טיירה_די לה_מוריה

asher_aav-ta	*ed_Yis·hak*	*ve_leh_le-há*	*el_eres*	*A_moriá*
ke_am-astes	*a_Yis·hak*	*i_and-a_a_ti*	*a_tyera_de*	*la_Moriá*
REL_love-PRET.2SG	OBJ_Isaac	and_go-IMP.2SG_to_PRON.PREP.2SG	to_land_of	DEF.F.SG_Moriah

whom thou lovest, Isaac, and get thee into the land of Moriah;

וְהַעֲלֵהוּ שָׁם לְעֹלָה עַל אַחַד

אי_אלסאלו אאי אה_אלסאסייון סובֿרי אונו_די

Ve_aale-u	*sham*	*le_olá*	*al*	*ahad*
I_áls-a-lo	*aí*	*a_alsasyón*	*sovre*	*un-o_de*
And_raise-IMP.2SG.M-PRON.ACC.3SG.M	there.ADV	to_offering	on.ADV	one.NUM.M.SG_of

and offer him there for a burnt-offering upon one of

הֶהָרִים אֲשֶׁר אֹמַר אֵלֶיךָ׃

לוס_מונטיס קי דירי א_טי :

e_ar-im	*asher*	*o-mar*	*ele_ha" :*
los_monte-s	*ke*	*dir-é*	*a_ti :*
DEF.M.PL_mountain-PL	REL	say-FUT.1SG	to_PRON.PREP.2SG

the mountains which I will tell thee of".

(3) וַיַּשְׁכֵּם אַבְרָהָם בַּבֹּקֶר וַיַּחֲבֹשׁ אֶת־חֲמֹרוֹ

אי_מאדרוגו אברהם פור_לה_מאנייאנה אי_סינגֿו אה_סו_אזנו

Va_ya-shkem	*Avraam*	*b_a_bóker*	*va_ya-havósh*	*ed_hamor-ó*
I_madrug-ó[28]	*Avraam*	*por_la_manyana*	*i_sinch-ó*	*a_su_azno*
and_rise=early-PRET.3SG	Abraham	in_DEF.F.SG_morning	and_saddle-PRET.3SG	OBJ_POSS.3SG_ass

And Abraham rose early in the morning, and saddled his ass,

28 Since the volume containing the Judezmo translation was prepared by a speaker from Belgrade, in the Northwest Judezmo dialect region in which the phonemes /ð/ and /ɣ/ are absent, and the text was also published in Vienna, also a part of that region, the grapheme ד̄, denoting /ð/, does not appear in the original work. Nevertheless, the transcription has here been 'normalized' in conformance with the Southeastern Judezmo pronunciation used by the great majority of Modern Judezmo speakers; and thus the Romanization incorporates *d̲* and *g̲*, denoting /ð/ and /ɣ/, respectively, and the vowels are also transcribed in accordance with the phonology of that region.

וַיִּקַּח אֶת־שְׁנֵי נְעָרָיו אִתּוֹ וְאֵת יִצְחָק
אי_טומו אה_דוס סוס_מוסוס קונ_יל אי_אה יצחק

va_yi-kah	*ed̲_shené*	*near_av*	*it_ó*	*ve_ed̲*	*Yis·hak*
i_tom-ó	*a_dos*	*su-s_moso-s*	*kon_el*	*i_a*	*Yis·hak*
and_take-PRET.3SG	OBJ_two.NUM	POSS.3-PL-servant-PL	with_PRON.PREP.3SG.M	and_OBJ	Isaac

and took two of his young men with him, and Isaac

בְּנוֹ וַיְבַקַּע עֲצֵי עֹלָה וַיָּקָם
סו_איזֿו אי_פארטייו ליניוס_די אלסאסייון אי_אליבֿאנטוסי

ben-ó	*va_y-vaká*	*asé*	*olá*	*va_yá-kom*
su_ijo	*i_part-yó*	*lenyo-s_de*	*alsasyón*	*i_alevant-ó-se*
POSS.3SG_son	and_cleave-PRET.3SG	wood-PL_of	offering	and_rise-PRET.3SG-REFL.3SG

his son; and he cleaved wood for the burnt-offering, and rose up,

וַיֵּלֶךְ אֶל־הַמָּקוֹם אֲשֶׁר־אָמַר־לוֹ הָאֱלֹהִים.
אי_אנדובֿו א_איל_לוגאר קי_דישו_א_איל איל_דייו :

va_yé-leh	*el_a_makom*	*asher_amar_l_o*	*A_eloim :*
i_anduv-o	*a_el_lugar*	*ke_dish-o_a_el*	*el_Dyo :*
and_go-PRET.3SG	to_DEF.M.SG_place	REL_say-PRET.3SG_to_PRON.PREP.3SG.M	DEF.M.SG_God

and went unto the place of which God had told him.

(4) בַּיּוֹם הַשְּׁלִישִׁי וַיִּשָּׂא אַבְרָהָם אֶת־עֵינָיו
אינ_יל_דיאה איל_טריסירו אי_אלסו אברהם אה_סוס_אוזֿוס

B_a_yom	*a_shelishí*	*va_yi-sá*	*Avraam*	*ed̲_en_av*
En_el_día	*el_treser-o*	*i_als-ó*	*Avraam*	*a_su-s_ojo-s*
on_DEF.M.SG_day	DEF.M.SG_third.M.SG	and_raise-PRET.3SG	Abraham	OBJ_POSS.3-PL_eye-PL

On the third day Abraham lifted up his eyes,

וַיַּרְא אֶת־הַמָּקוֹם מֵרָחֹק.
אי_בֿידו אה_איל_לוגאר_די_לישוס :

va_y-ar	*ed̲_a_makom*	*me_rahok :*
i_vid̲-o	*a_el_lugar*	*de_leshos :*
and_see-PRET.3SG	OBJ_DEF.M.SG_place	from_afar

and saw the place afar off.

(5) וַיֹּאמֶר אַבְרָהָם אֶל־נְעָרָיו שְׁבוּ־לָכֶם פֹּה
אי_דישו אברהם א_סוס_מוסוס איסטאד_א_בֿוס אקי

Va_yó-mer	*Avraam*	*el_near_av*	*"Shev-ú_la_hem*	*po*
I_dish-o	*Avraam*	*a_su-s_moso-s*	*"Esta-d̲_a_vos*	*akí*
And_say-PRET.3SG	Abraham	to_POSS.3SG-PL_servant-PL	be-IMP.2PL_to_PRON.PREP.2PL	here.ADV

And Abraham said unto his young men: "Abide ye here

עִם־הַחֲמוֹר וַאֲנִי וְהַנַּעַר נֵלְכָה עַד־כֹּה
קון_איל_אזנו אי_ייו אי_איל_מוסו אנדארימוס אסטה_אקי

im a_hamor	*va_aní*	*ve_a_náar*	*ne-lehá*	*ad̲_ko*
kon el_azno	*i_yo*	*i_el_moso*	*and-aremos*	*asta_akí*
with DEF.M.SG_ass	and_1SG	and_DEF.M.SG_servant	go-FUT.1PL	until_here-ADV

with the ass, and I and the lad will go yonder;

וְנִשְׁתַּחֲוֶה וְנָשׁוּבָה אֲלֵיכֶם.
אי_אינקורבֿארמוסימוס אי_טורנארימוס אבֿוס :

ve_ni-shtahav-é   *ve_na-shuva*   *ale_hem" :*
i_enkorv-ar-mos-emos[29]   *i_torn-aremos*   *a_vos" :*
and_bow down-INF-REFL.1PL-FUT.1PL   and_return.FUT.1PL   to_PRON.PREP.2PL

and we will worship, and come back to you".

(6) וַיִּקַּח אַבְרָהָם אֶת־עֲצֵי הָעֹלָה וַיָּשֶׂם עַל־יִצְחָק
אי_טומו אברהם אה_ליניוס_די·לה_אלסאסיון אי_פוזו סובֿרי_יצחק

Va_yi-kah   *Avraam*   *ed_asé*   *a_olá*   *va_yá-sem*   *al_Yis·hak*
I_tom-ó   *Avraam*   *a_lenyo-s_de*   *la_alsasyón*   *i_puz-o*   *sovre_Yis·hak*
And_take.PRET.3SG   Abraham   OBJ_wood-PL_of   DEF.F.SG_offering   and_lay-PRET.3SG   on_Isaac

And Abraham took the wood of the burnt-offering, and laid it upon Isaac

בְּנוֹ וַיִּקַּח בְּיָדוֹ   אֶת־הָאֵשׁ וְאֶת־הַמַּאֲכֶלֶת
סו_איזֿו אי_טומו אינ·סו_מאנו א_איל_פֿואיגו אי_אה_איל_קוגֿילייו

ben_ó   *va_yi-kah*   *be_yad_ó*   *ed_a_ésh*   *ve_ed_a_maahéled*
su_ijo   *i_tom-ó*   *en_su_mano*   *a_el_fuego*   *i_a_el_kuchiyo*
POSS.3SG_son   and_take-PRET.3SG   in_POSS.3SG_hand   OBJ_DEF.M.SG_fire   and_OBJ_DEF.M.SG_knife

his son; and he took in his hand the fire and the knife;

וַיֵּלְכוּ שְׁנֵיהֶם יַחְדָּו.
אי_אנדובֿיירון אנבוס_אילייוס אאונה :

va_ye-leh-ú   *shene_em*   *yahd-av :*
i_anduv-yeron   *anb-os_eyos*   *a-úna :*
and_go-PRET.3PL   both-M.PL_3PL.M   together-ADV

and they went both of them together.

(7) וַיֹּאמֶר יִצְחָק אֶל־אַבְרָהָם אָבִיו וַיֹּאמֶר אָבִי
אי_דישו יצחק אה_אברהם סו_פאדרי אי_דישו מי_פאדרי

Va_yó-mer   *Yis·hak*   *el_Avraam*   *av_iv*   *va_yó-mer*   *"Av_í"*
I_dish-o   *Yis·hak*   *a_Avraam*   *su_padre*   *i_dish-o*   *"Mi_padre"*
And_say-PRET.3SG   Isaac   to_Abraham   POSS.3SG_father   and_say-PRET.3SG   POSS.1SG_father

And Isaac spoke unto Abraham his father, and said: "My father".

וַיֹּאמֶר הִנֶּנִּי בְנִי וַיֹּאמֶר הִנֵּה הָאֵשׁ
אי_דישו איק_מי מי_איזֿו אי_דישו איק איל_פֿואיגו

va_yó-mer   *"Ine_ni*   *ven_í"*   *va_yó-mer*   *"Iné*   *a_ésh*
i_dish-o   *"Ek_me*   *mi_ijo"*   *i_dish-o*   *Ek*   *el_fuego*
and_say-PRET.3SG   behold_PRON.ACC.1SG   POSS.1SG_son   and_say-PRET.3SG   behold   DEF.M.SG_fire

And he said: "Here am I, my son". And he said:"Behold the fire

וְהָעֵצִים וְאַיֵּה הַשֶּׂה לְעֹלָה.
אי_לוס_ליניוס אי_אדו איל_קארנירו פור_אלסאסיון :

ve_a_es-im   *ve_ayé*   *a_sé*   *le_olá" :*
i_los_lenyo-s   *i_adó*   *el_karnero*   *por_alsasyón" :*
and_DEF.M.PL_wood-PL   and_where?   DEF.M.SG_lamb   for_offering

and the wood; but where is the lamb for a burnt-offering?"

29 In most Southeast Judezmo dialects this is realized *enkorvármozémos*.

(8) וַיֹּאמֶר אַבְרָהָם אֱלֹהִים יִרְאֶה־לּוֹ
אי_דישו אברהם איל_דייו אמוסטראראה_א_איל
Va_yó-mer Avraam "Eloim yi-re_l_ó
I_dish-o Avraam "El_Dyo amostr-ará_a_el
And_say-PRET.3SG Abraham DEF.M.SG_God show-FUT.3SG_to_PRON.PREP.2SG.M
And Abraham said: "God will provide Himself

הַשֶּׂה לְעֹלָה בְּנִי וַיֵּלְכוּ שְׁנֵיהֶם יַחְדָּו.
איל_קארנירו פור_אלסאסייון מי_איזֿו אי_אנדובֿיירון אנבוס_איליוס א_אונה :
a_sé le_olá ben_í" va_ye-leh-ú shene_em yahd_av :
el_karnero por_alsasyón mi_ijo" i_anduv-yeron anb-os_eyos a_úna :
DEF.M.SG_lamb for_offering POSS.1SG_son and_go-PRET.3PL both-M.PL_3PL together.ADV
the lamb for a burnt-offering, my son". So they went both of them together.

(9) וַיָּבֹאוּ אֶל־הַמָּקוֹם אֲשֶׁר אָמַר־לוֹ הָאֱלֹהִים
אי_בֿיניירון אאיל_לוגאר קי דישו_אאיל איל_דייו
Va_ya-vo-u el_a_makom asher amar_l_o A_eloim
I_vin-yeron a_el_lugar ke dish-o_a_el el_Dyo
and_come-PRET.3PL to_DEF.M.SG_place REL say-PRET.3SG_to_PRON.PREP.3SG.M DEF.M.SG_God
And they came to the place which God had told him of;

וַיִּבֶן שָׁם אַבְרָהָם אֶת־הַמִּזְבֵּחַ וַיַּעֲרֹךְ
אי_פֿראגואו אאי אברהם א_לה_ארה אי_אורדינו
va_yi-ven sham Avraam ed_a_mizbéah va_ya-aroh
i_fragu-ó aí Avraam a_la_ara i_orden-ó
and_build-PRET.3SG there-ADV Abraham OBJ_DEF.F.SG_altar and_arrange-PRET.3SG
and there Abraham built the altar, and laid

אֶת־הָעֵצִים וַיַּעֲקֹד אֶת־יִצְחָק בְּנוֹ וַיָּשֶׂם
א_לוס_ליניוס אי_אטו אה_יצחק סו_איזֿו אי_פוזו
ed_a_es-im va_y-akod ed_Yis·hak ben_ó va_yá-sem
a_los_lenyo-s i_at-ó a_Yis·hak su_ijo i_puz-o
OBJ_DEF.M.PL_wood-PL and_tie-PRET.3SG OBJ_Isaac POSS.3.SG_son and_place-PRET.3SG
the wood, and bound Isaac his son, and laid

אֹתוֹ עַל־הַמִּזְבֵּחַ מִמַּעַל לָעֵצִים.
א_איל סובֿרי_לה_ארה די_אריבֿה א_לוס_ליניוס :
ot_ó al_a_mizbéah mi_máal l_a_es-im :
a_el sovre_la_ara de_ariva a_los_lenyo-s :
OBJ_PRON.ACC.3SG.M upon_DEF.F.SG_altar from_on.top to_DEF.M.PL_wood-PL
him on the altar, upon the wood.

(10) וַיִּשְׁלַח אַבְרָהָם אֶת־יָדוֹ וַיִּקַּח אֶת־הַמַּאֲכֶלֶת
אי_טינדייו אברהם אה_סו_מאנו אי_טומו א_איל_קוג̃יליו
Va_yi-shlah Avraam ed_yad_ó va_yi-kah ed_a_maahéled
I_tend-yó Avraam a_su_mano i_tom-ó a_el_kuchiyo
and_extend-PRET.3SG Abraham OBJ_POSS.3SG_hand and_take-PRET.3SG OBJ_DEF.M.SG_knife
And Abraham stretched forth his hand, and took the knife

לִשְׁחֹט אֶת־בְּנוֹ.
פור_דיגוייאר א_סו_איזו :

li_sh·hot	*eḏ_ben_ó :*
por_degoy-ar	*a_su_ijo :*
for_behead-INF	OBJ_POSS.3SG_son

to slay his son.

(11) וַיִּקְרָא אֵלָיו מַלְאַךְ יְהוָה מִן־הַשָּׁמַיִם
אי_ייאמו אה_איל אנג׳יל_די ה[שם]' די_לוס_סיילוס

Va_yi-krá	*el_av*	*malah*	*Aḏonay*	*min_a_shamáy-im*
I_yam-ó	*a_el*	*ándjel_de*	*A[_shem]*	*de_los_syelo-s*
and_call-PRET.3SG	to_PRON.PREP.3SG.M	angel_of	the[_Name]	of_DEF.M.PL_heaven-PL

And the angel of the Lord called unto him out of heaven,

וַיֹּאמֶר אַבְרָהָם אַבְרָהָם וַיֹּאמֶר הִנֵּנִי.
אי_דישו אברהם אברהם אי_דישו איק_מי :

va_yó-mer	*"Avraam*	*Avraam"*	*va_yó-mer*	*"Ine_ni" :*
i_dish-o	*"Avraam*	*Avraam"*	*i_dish-o*	*"Ek_me" :*
and_say-PRET.3SG	Abraham	Abraham	and_say-PRET.3SG	behold_PRON.ACC.1SG.M

and said: "Abraham, Abraham". And he said: "Here am I".

(12) וַיֹּאמֶר אַל־תִּשְׁלַח יָדְךָ אֶל־הַנַּעַר
אי_דישו נון_טיינדאס טו_מאנו אה_איל_מוסו

Va_yó-mer	*"Al_ti-shlah*	*yaḏ_ehá*	*el_a_náar*
I_dish-o	*"Non_tyenda-s*	*tu_mano*	*a_el_moso*
and_say-PRET.3SG	NEG_extend-SUBJ.PRS.2SG	POSS.2SG_hand	to_DEF.M.SG_lad

And he said: "Lay not thy hand upon the lad,

וְאַל־תַּעַשׂ לוֹ מְאוּמָה: כִּי עַתָּה
אי_נון_אגאס א_איל נינגונה_קוזה קי אגורה

ve_al_ta-as	*l_o*	*meuma*	*ki*	*atá*
i_non_aga-s	*a_el*	*ningun-a_koza*	*ke*	*ag̱ora*
and_NEG_do.SUBJ.PRS-2SG	to_PRON.PREP.3SG.M	no-F.SG_thing	CONJ	now.ADV

neither do thou any thing unto him; for now

יָדַעְתִּי כִּי־יְרֵא אֱלֹהִים אַתָּה וְלֹא חָשַׂכְתָּ
סופי קי_טימיין_די איל_דייו טו אי_נון ב̃ידאסטי[ס]

yaḏa-ti	*ki_yer-é*	*Eloim*	*atá*	*ve_ló*	*hasah-ta*
sup-e	*ke_tem-yén_de*	*el_Dyo*	*tu*	*i_non*	*veḏ-aste[s]*[30]
know.PRET-1SG	COMP_PRS.PTCP.APOC[31]_of	DEF.M.SG_God	2SG	and_NEG	withhold-PRET.2SG

I know that thou art a God-fearing man, seeing thou hast not withheld

אֶת־בִּנְךָ אֶת־יְחִידְךָ מִמֶּנִּי.
א_טו_איזו א_טו_אוניקו די_מי :

eḏ_bin_há	*eḏ_yehiḏ_ehá*	*mi_meni":*
a_tu_ijo	*a_tu_únik-o*	*de_mi" :*
OBJ_POSS.2SG_son	OBJ_POSS.2SG_only-M.SG	from_PRON.PREP.1SG

thy son, thine only son, from Me".

30 The editor of the translation evidently copied the archaic form ב̃ידאסטי/*veḏaste* from a pre-modern translation. By his period the corresponding form used in calque translations was generally ב̃ידאסטיס/*veḏastes*, and in actual speech, ב̃ידאטיס/*veḏates*.

31 PRS.PTCP.APOC = apocopated present participle.

(13) וַיִּשָּׂא אַבְרָהָם אֶת־עֵינָיו וַיַּרְא וְהִנֵּה־אַיִל

אי_אלסו אברהם א_סוס_אוזוס אי_בֿידו אי_איק_בארבֿיז

Va_yi-sá	*Avraam*	*ed_en_av*	*va_y-ar*	*ve_iné_áyil*
I_als-ó	*Avraam*	*a_su-s_ojo-s*	*i_vid-o*	*i_ek_barvéz*
and_raise-PRET.3SG	Abraham	OBJ_POSS.3-PL_eye-PL	and_see-PRET.3SG	and_behold_ram

And Abraham lifted up his eyes, and looked, and behold behind him a ram

אַחַר נֶאֱחַז בַּסְּבַךְ בְּקַרְנָיו

דיספואיס_קי פֿואי_טראבֿאדו אין_לה_ראמה פור_סוס_קואירנוס

ahar	*ne_eház*	*b_a_sevah*	*be_karn_av*
después_ke	*fue_travad-o*	*en_la_rama*	*por_su-s_kuerno-s*
after_REL	PASS.AUX.PRET.3SG_catch.PTCP-M.SG	in_DEF.F.SG_thicket	by_POSS.3PL_horn-PL

caught in the thicket by his horns.

וַיֵּלֶךְ אַבְרָהָם וַיִּקַּח אֶת־הָאַיִל

אי_אנדובֿו אברהם אי_טומו אה_איל_בארבֿיז

va_yé-leh	*Avraam*	*va_yi-kah*	*ed_a_áyil*
i_anduv-o	*Avraam*	*i_tom-ó*	*a_el_barvéz*
and_go.PRET-3SG	Abraham	and_take-PRET.3SG	OBJ_DEF.M.SG_ram

And Abraham went and took the ram,

וַיַּעֲלֵהוּ לְעֹלָה תַּחַת בְּנוֹ.

אי_אלסולו פור_אלסאסייון אין_לוגאר_די סו_איזו :

va_ya-ale-u	*le_olá*	*táhad*	*ben_ó :*
i_als-ó-lo	*por_alsasyón*	*en_lugar_de*	*su_ijo :*
and_raise-PRET.3SG-PRON.ACC.3SG.M	for_offering	in_place_of	POSS.3SG_son

and offered him up for a burnt-offering instead of his son.

(14) וַיִּקְרָא אַבְרָהָם שֵׁם־הַמָּקוֹם הַהוּא יְהוָה יִרְאֶה,

אי_ייאמו אברהם נומברי_די_איל_לוגאר איל_איסטי ה[שם]' בֿירה

Va_yi-krá	*Avraam*	*shem_a_makom*	*a_ú*	*Adonay*	*yi-ré*
I_yam-ó	*Avraam*	*nombre_de_el_lugar*	*el_este*	*A[_shem]'*	*ver-á*
And_call-PRET.3SG	Abraham	name_of_DEF.M.SG_place	DEF.M.SG_PROX.M.SG	the[_Name]	see-FUT.3SG

And Abraham called the name of that place Adonai-yireh [will see];

אֲשֶׁר יֵאָמֵר הַיּוֹם בְּהַר יְהוָה

קי סירה_דיגֿו אויי אין_מונטי_די ה[שם]'

asher	*ye_amer*	*ayom*	*be_ar*	*A[donay]*
ke	*ser-á_dich-o*	*oy*	*en_monte_de*	*A[shem]'*
REL	PASS.AUX-FUT.3SG_say.PTCP-M.SG	today	in_mountain_of	the[_Name]

as it is said to this day: "In the mount where the Lord

יֵרָאֶה.

סירה_אפאריסידו :

ye_raé :
ser-á_aparesid-o :
PASS.AUX-FUT.3SG_appear.PTCP-M.SG

is seen".

(15) וַיִּקְרָא מַלְאַךְ יְהוָה אֶל־אַבְרָהָם שֵׁנִית
אי_ייאמו אנגֿיל_די ה[שם]' אה_אברהם סיגונדה_בֿיז
Va_yi-krá malah A[ḏonay] el_Avraam sheni_ḏ
I_yam-ó ándjel_de A[shem]' a_Avraam seg̱und-a_vez
And_call-PRET.3SG angel_of the[_Name] to_Abraham second.NUM-F.SG_time
And the angel of the Lord called unto Abraham a second time

מִן־הַשָּׁמָיִם.
די_לוס_סיילוס :
min_a_shamáy-im :
de_los_syelo-s :
from_DEF.M.PL_heaven-PL
out of heaven,

(16) וַיֹּאמֶר בִּי נִשְׁבַּעְתִּי נְאֻם־יְהוָה: כִּי יַעַן אֲשֶׁר
אי_דישו אין_מי גֿורי דיגֿו_די_ה[שם]' קי פורקי
Va_yó-mer "B_i nishba-ti neum_A[ḏonay] ki yaan asher
I_dish-o "En_mi djur-í dicho_de_A[_shem] ke porke
And_say.PRET-3SG in_PRON.PREP.1SG swear-PRET.1SG saying_of_the[_Name] CONJ because
and said: "By Myself have I sworn, saith the Lord, because

עָשִׂיתָ אֶת־הַדָּבָר הַזֶּה וְלֹא חָשַׂכְתָּ
איזיסטיס א_לה_קוזה לה_איסטה אי_נון בֿידאסטי[ס]
asi-ta eḏ_a_davar a_zé ve_ló hasah-ta
iz-istes a_la_koza la_esta i_non veḏ-aste[s]
do.PRET-2SG OBJ_DEF.F.SG_thing DEF.F.SG_PROX.F.SG and_NEG withhold-PRET.2SG
thou hast done this thing, and hast not withheld

אֶת־בִּנְךָ אֶת־יְחִידֶךָ.
א_טו_איז̃ו א_טו_אוניקו :
eḏ_bin_há eḏ_yehiḏe_ha :
a_tu_ijo a_tu_único-o :
OBJ_POSS.2SG_son OBJ_POSS.2SG_only-M.SG
thy son, thine only son,

(17) כִּי־בָרֵךְ אֲבָרֶכְךָ וְהַרְבָּה אַרְבֶּה אֶת־זַרְעֲךָ
קי_בינדיזיר טי_בינדיזירי אי_מוגֿיגוארי מוגֿיגוארי א_טו_סימין
Ki_vareh a-varehe_há ve_arbá arb-é eḏ_zara_há
Ke_bendez-ir te_bendezir-é i_muchigu-ar muchig̱uar-é a_tu_semen
COMP_bless-INF PRON.ACC.2SG_bless-FUT.1SG and_multiply-INF multiply-FUT.1SG OBJ_POSS.2SG_seed
that in blessing I will bless thee, and in multiplying I will multiply thy seed

כְּכוֹכְבֵי הַשָּׁמַיִם וְכַחוֹל אֲשֶׁר עַל־שְׂפַת הַיָּם
קומו_איסטריללייאס_די לוס_סיילוס אי_קומו_ארינה קי סובֿרי_אורילייה_די·_לה_מאר
ke_hohev-é a_shamáy-im ve_ha_hol asher al_sefa_ḏ a_yam
komo_estreya-s_de los_syelo-s i_komo_arena ke sovre_oriya_de la_mar
as.ADV_star-PL_of DEF.M.PL_heaven-PL and_as.ADV_sand REL upon_shore_of DEF.F.SG_sea
as the stars of the heaven, and as the sand which is upon the seashore;

וְיִרַשׁ זַרְעֲךָ אֵת שַׁעַר אֹיְבָיו.
אי_אירידארה טו_סימין אה קונסיזֿו_די סוס_אינימיגוס :

ve_y-irásh	*zara_há*	*eḏ*	*sháar*	*oyev_av :*
i_ereḏar-á	*tu_semen*	*a*	*konsejo_de*	*su-s_enemigo-s :*
and_inherit-FUT.3SG	POSS.2SG_seed	OBJ	gate/advice_of	POSS.3-PL_enemy-PL

and thy seed shall possess the gate of his enemies;

(18) וְהִתְבָּרְכוּ בְזַרְעֲךָ כֹּל גּוֹיֵי הָאָרֶץ
אי_בינדיזירסיאן קון_טו_סימין טודאס ג̃ינטיס_די לה_טיירה

Ve_iḏ-barah-ú	*ve_zara_há*	*kol*	*goy-é*	*a_ares*
I_bendez-ir-se-án	*kon_tu_semen*	*toḏ-as*	*djente-s_de*	*la_tyera*
and_bless-INF-PASS.3-FUT.3PL	with_POSS.2SG_seed	all-F.PL	people-PL_of	DEF.F.SG_earth

and in thy seed shall be blessed all the nations of the earth;

עֵקֶב אֲשֶׁר שָׁמַעְתָּ בְּקֹלִי.
פריסייו קי אולייסטיס אין_מי_בוז :

ékev	*asher*	*shama-ta*	*be_kol_í :*
presyo	*ke*	*oy-istes*	*en_mi_boz:*
price	REL	hear-PRET.2SG	in_POSS.1SG_voice

because thou hast hearkened to My voice".

3.5 Representation of Conversational Judezmo from 17th-century Gaza, Eretz Yisrael (Ottoman Gaza Sanjak), c. 1677

Representations of spoken Judezmo from various regions and during diverse historical phases of the language are dispersed throughout the extensive responsa literature produced by the major rabbinical authorities of the Ottoman Empire from the sixteenth century on.[32] Most such passages, which for the early period of Ottoman Judezmo constitute the only texts purporting to be verbatim transcriptions of actual speech, consist of eye-witness or second-hand testimony concerning problems between family members, friends or associates such as family legacies, business controversies, and especially the *ʕaguna* or 'straw widow', whose husband had left home and never returned; without having a halakhically-reliable witness testify to her husband's death, the widow could not remarry and thus remained the victim of social and economic insecurity.[33]

The sample passage, from the responsa of Rabbi Moše Ben Ḥabib (b. Salonika 1654, d. Jerusalem 1696),[34] is evidently a typical representation of the kind of Judezmo used in the Land of Israel in the seventeenth century, when Judezmo-speaking Jews resided in many parts of the region, in contact with speakers of Arabic, Judeo-Arabic, Turkish, and other non-Jewish and Jewish languages. Our passage concerns a struggle between a Jewish man and a local Arab who wished to take possession of the former's wife and children. As reported to the rabbinical court by the Jew's widow, based on eye-

32 For a rich selection from the sixteenth century see Benaim 2011.

33 According to Jewish law, the עגונה/*ʕaguna* or 'straw widow' (literally, 'anchored woman') is a woman whose husband is not with her for reasons such as his presumed death (but his body has not been identified by reliable witnesses), or because he has abandoned her but refuses to divorce her (see Hacohen c.2004).

34 Moše Ben Ḥabib, *Š[ĕʔelot] u-t[šuvot] m[orenu] ha-ra[v] M[oše] Ben Ḥabib*, no. 6, at the end of the Jerusalem 1989 edition of his *ʕEzrat našim*. For further discussion see Bunis 2021.

witness testimony recounted to her by sympathetic Arabs, the corpse of the widow's husband was found by the Arabs near a body of water. As is generally the case with such passages, it is introduced by the rabbinical author in Hebrew – the principal or framing language of the responsa collection itself. After identifying for the readers the woman who testified before the judges, the author reproduces her ostensibly verbatim first-person testimony, following which the place and date of the hearing are noted. The section of Judezmo testimony is followed by the rabbi's Hebrew evaluation of the case and his decision concerning the reliability of the testimony and, ultimately, the woman's marital status.

The Judezmo passage offers several features characteristic of speech – if somewhat formal speech – of the period.[35] As typical during the long traditional phase of Judezmo preceding World War I, and in accommodation to the context of the interaction represented – testimony offered orally to respected rabbinical scholars – the speaker addresses her interlocutors indirectly, in the third person implying polite speech, with the expression *"Savrán sus mersedes"* 'Know [literally, you will know], your mercies'; the verb phrase is perhaps a calque of rabbinical Hebrew phrases formulated in the third-person future such as *yedaʕ adoni* / ידע אדוני 'he will know, sir'.[36] Her testimony is then related in the first person. As often occurring in natural speech, but of course also crucial in this particular case of witness testimony, the speaker refers to a particular local place (*Azá* 'Gaza'); and a specific person (her husband, *Shemuel Eshkenazí*). But no less typically, she uses generalizations, customary among people of the period in question, when referring to the times of the occurrences related (*un anyo antes de la landre* 'a year before the plague'); to the people with whom she interacted (*un djuḏyó sal[o]niklí i un franko,*[37] *ke·no konesía p[o]r·djuḏyó o por kristyano* 'a Salonikan Jew and a European, whom I didn't know to be a Jew or a Christian'); generalizations are also expressed through the use of deictic phrases such as *por esta plátika* 'because of *this* argument', *akel djuḏyó ke harvó a·los alarves* 'that Jew who beat the Arabs'. Furthermore, there are also vague references to non-specific subjects of verb phrases (e.g., *disho el saloniklí a mi mariḏo ke·lo keriyan matar a el* 'the Salonikan told my husband that *they* wanted to kill him'; *akel djuḏyó ... lo akavaron de matar* '*that Jew* ... *they* ended up killing him'); and non-specific places (e.g., *Estuve ayí disde noche de lunes* 'I was *there* from Sunday night'). The speaker uses the nebulous connective *En esto* 'In this' to express the time between events.

Complex sentences are avoided; phrase upon phrase and sentence upon sentence are conjoined by *i* 'and': e.g., *salí de Azá ... i kuatro días después ke salimos ... i por esta plátika ... i día de martes me kontó el alarve* 'I departed Gaza ... and four days after we departed ... and because of this conversation ... and Tuesday the Arab told me'). Complex verbs are particularly avoided; all verbs appear either in the preterite or imperfect tense (*salí* 'I departed', *me espertí* 'I awoke', *bushkí* 'I looked for'; *konesía* 'I

35 On some characteristics of Judezmo speech as represented in writing, see Bunis and Bunis 2011.

36 For example, cf. Eliyyahu Mizraḥi (Constantinople, c. 1450–1526) 1559–61, no. 74. The similar phrase of address *Sabrán, señores* 'Know, gentlemen' is found only once in the online CORDE historical corpus of the Real Academia Española.

37 *Franko* 'western European'.

knew', *keriyan* 'they wanted'). The phrasing sometimes borders on the colloquial: e.g., *le dyo en la kavesa koza de sekaná* 'he gave him a serious/dangerous hit on the head', *se·alevantó el saloniklí i harvó a·los alarves* 'the Salonikan got up and beat the Arabs', *noche de lunes me durmí, i·mi marido kon mi* 'Sunday night I fell asleep, and my husband with me'; *por esta plátika se ensendyó pleyto entre eyos* 'because of this conversation a fight flared up between them'. There are references to speech acts (e.g., *disho* 'said'), to the experience of emotion (e.g., *tuvo miedo de venir* 'he was afraid to come'), and to the will of the individuals described (e.g., *lo keriyan matar a el* 'they wanted to kill him').

The speaker's language well illustrates features of the morphology of popular Judezmo at the time: e.g., the first-person plural possessive adjective *muestro* (cf. *muestras manos* 'our hands'; vs. Sp. *nuestro*); the finite verb form *(no) konesía* 'did (not) know' (Sp. *no conocía*); the first-person singular and plural preterite markers in *-ar* verbs, *-í* and *-imos*, respectively, e.g., *bushkí* 'I looked for', *apanyimos* 'we seized' (Sp. *busqué, apañamos*). The passage also illustrates the etymological makeup of the lexicon used by Ottoman Judezmo speakers at the time: most elements are of Iberian origin, typically as used in popular and regional speech, e.g., *se·alevantó* 'he rose up' (cf. normative Sp. *se levantó*), and include some lexemes generally avoided in the more conservative sacred-text translation language (e.g., *aharvar* 'to beat' < Ibero-Arabic *ḥarb* + *-ar*, rather than the Hispanic-origin near-synonym *batir*). Elements of Hebrew origin used popularly also appear, e.g., post-biblical *(koza de) sekaná* 'dangerous' < Judezmo speakers' Whole Hebrew סְכָּנָה/*sekaná* [Israeli Hebrew סַכָּנָה/*sakaná*]); the city of Gaza is referred to by its biblical Hebrew-origin name (e.g., Genesis 10:19), *Azá* (Heb. עזה/*ʕAzza*), and typically, the personal names and a family name cited by the speaker are also of Hebrew origin: feminine *Rahel* < רחל/*Raḥel*, masculine *Shemuel* < שמואל/*Šĕmuʔel*, the surname *Eshkenazí* < אשכנזי/*Aškĕnazi*. As typical of rabbinical texts, but perhaps less so of actual popular speech, the speaker refers to the day of the event described by means of the Hebrew expression יום ד' / *yom dáled* (literally, 'day four [according to the Jewish calendar]) 'Wednesday', instead of more expected Hispanic-origin *myérkoles*. The speaker also uses a few local borrowings, illustrating the many which had begun to enter Judezmo early on in the sixteenth century; for example, a 'Salonikan Jew' is referred to as a *djudyó saloniklí* (cf. G[reek] *[Thes]saloniki* 'Salonika' | Tk. *Selânikli* 'Salonikan').

3.6 Sample text: Seventeenth-Century Conversational Judezmo

עדות [...] העגונה מ[רת]' רחל בת בתו

Edud [...]	*a-aguná,*	*ma[r-a-d]'*	*Rahel,*	*bad*	*bit-ó*
testimony^H	DEF-woman.unable.to.remarry^H	Mrs.^H	Rachel	daughter.CS^H	daughter-POSS.M.3SG^H

Testimony [...] of the straw widow, Mrs. Rachel, daughter of the daughter

של החכם י' פרימו נ[שמתו]"ע[דן] ואמרה [...] שאבראן
shel e-haham Y. Primo, n[ishmat-ó] e[d̲en], ve-amer-á[38] *[...] "Savr-án*
of[H] DEF-scholar[H] Y. Primo soul-POSS.M.3SG[H] paradise[H] and-say-PAST.F.3SG[H] know-FUT.3PL
of the scholar Y. Primo, [may] his soul [dwell in] Paradise, and she said [...] "Know,

שוש מירשידיש קומו, און אנייו אנטיש די·לה לאנדרי, שאלי
su-s mersed̲-es, komo, un anyo antes de·la landre, sal-í
POSS-3PL mercy-PL how.ADV INDEF.M.SG year before of·DEF.F.SG plague depart-PRET.1SG
your mercies, that, a year before the plague, I departed

די עזה יום ד[לת]' קון מי מארידו, שמואל אשכנזי, אי·און
de Azá yom dá[led̲][39]*kon mi marid̲o, Shemuel Eshkenazí, i·un*
from Gaza day[h] four[h] with POSS.1SG husband Shemuel Eshkenazi and·INDEF.M.SG
Gaza on Wednesday with my husband, Šĕmuʔel Aškĕnazi, and a

ג̃ודייו שאל[ו]ניקלי אי·און פ̄ראנקו, קינו קונישיאה פ[ו]ר·ג̃ודייו
djud̲yó sal[o]nik-lí i·un franko, ke·no kones-ía p[o]r·djud̲yó
Jew Salonika-ADJ.M.SG and·INDEF.M.SG European REL·NEG know-IMPF.1SG for·Jew
Salonikan Jew and a Western European, whom I didn't know to be a Jew

או פור קרישטייאנו; אי קואטרו דיאש דישפואיש קי שאלימוש, נוג̃י די אלחד,
o por kristyano; i kuatro día-s después ke sal-imos, noche de alh[a]d̲,
or for Christian and four.NUM day-PL after CONJ depart-PRET.1PL night of Sunday
or a Christian; and four days after we departed, Saturday night,

דישו איל שאלוניקלי אה מי מארידו קי·לו קירילייאן מאטאר
dish-o el saloniklí a mi marid̲o ke·lo ker-iyan mat-ar
say-PRET.3SG DEF.M.SG Salonikan to my husband COMP·PRON.ACC.3SG.M want-IMPF.3PL kill-INF
the Salonikan told my husband that they wanted to kill (him)

אה איל פארה טומארלי לה מוג̃יר אי·לוש איג̃וש,
a[40] *el para tom-ar-le la mujer i·los ijo-s,*
OBJ PRON.PREP.3SG.M for take-INF-PRON.DAT.3SG DEF.F.SG wife and·DEF.M.PL child-PL
him in order to take his wife and children,

אי·פור אישטה פלאטיקה שי אינשינדייו פלייטו אינטרי אילייוש
i·por est-a plátika se ensend-yó pleyto entre eyos
and·for PROX-F.SG conversation PASS ignite-PRET.3SG fight among PRON.PREP.3PL.M
and because of this conversation a fight flared up between them

אי שי·אליב̄אנטו איל שאלוניקלי אי הארב̄ו א·לוש אלארב̄יש,
i se·alevant-ó el saloniklí i harv-ó a·los alarve-s,
and REF·raise-PRET.3SG DEF.M.SG Salonikan and beat-PRET.3SG OBJ·DEF.M.PL Arab-PL
the Salonikan got up and beat the Arabs,

38 H[ebrew]. *ʕEdut ... ha-ʕaguna ma[rat]' Raḥel bat bitto šel he-ḥa[xam]' Y. Primo n[išmato]' ʕe[den] wĕ-ʔamĕra'*.

39 Here and in the following, a small "h" marks a word of Hebrew origin, which I consider to be an integral part of Judezmo, as opposed to words marked with an uppercase "H", which represent parts of Whole Hebrew phrases.

40 In language other than calque translations of Hebrew and Aramaic, in which *a* corresponds to Hebrew *ʔet* and precedes any direct object, *a* precedes direct objects which are definite and human (and sometimes animate in general).

אי אה אונו די אילייוש לי דייו אין לה קאבֿישה

i a un-o de eyos le dyo en la kavesa

and to INDEF-M.SG of PRON.PREP.3PL.M PRON.DAT.3SG give.PRET.3SG in DEF.F.SG head

and to one of them he gave a dangerous blow to the head.

קוזה די סכנה. אין אישטו, נוגֿי די לוניש מי דורמי,

koza de sekaná. En esto, noche de lunes me durm-í,

thing of danger[h] in this night of Monday REF.1SG sleep-PRET.1SG

With this, Sunday night I fell asleep,

אי מי מארידו קון מי. קואנדו מי דיספירטי, בושֿקי

i·mi marido kon mi. Kuando me despert-í,[41] *bushk-í*

and·POSS.1SG husband with PRON-PREP.1SG when REF.1SG awake-PRET.1SG search-PRET.1SG

and my husband with me. When I awoke, I looked

אה מי מארידו אי נו לו אליי, אי דיאה די מארטיש

a mi marido i·no lo ay-í, i día de martes

OBJ POSS.1SG husband and·NEG PRON.ACC.3SG.M find-PRET.1SG and day of Tuesday

for my husband and didn't find him, and Tuesday

מי קונטו איל אלארבֿי קי אקיל גֿודייו קי חארבֿו

me kont-ó el alarve ke akel djudyó ke harv-ó

PRON.DAT.1SG tell-PRET.3SG DEF.M.SG Arab REL DIST.M.SG Jew REL beat-PRET.3SG

the Arab told me that that Jew who beat

א·לוש אלארבֿיש, לו אקאבֿארון די מאטאר. אישטובֿי אליי

a·los alarve-s, lo akav-aron de mat-ar. Estuv-e ayí

OBJ·DEF.M.PL Arab-PL PRON.ACC.3SG.M finish-PRET.3PL of kill-INF be-PRET.1SG there.ADV

the Arabs, they ended up killing him. I was there

דישדי נוגֿי די לוניש פֿאשטה איל אוטרו מארטיש קי ויני אה עזה

disde noche de lunes asta el otr-o martes, ke vin-e a Azá

since night of Monday until DEF.M.SG other-M.SG Tuesday CONJ come-PRET.1SG to Gaza

from Sunday night until the next Tuesday, when I came to Gaza

קון אונה אלארבֿה. דישפואיש די אוגֿו דיאש אין עזה וינו

kon una alarva. Después de ocho día-s en Azá vin-o

with INDEF.F.SG Arab_woman afterwards.ADV of eight day-PL in Gaza come-PRET.3SG

with an Arab woman. After eight days in Gaza there came

אונה אלארבֿה אי מי דישֿו, שאבֿריש קומו

una alarva i me dish-o, "Savr-[é]s komo,

INDEF.F.SG Arab_woman and PRON.DAT.1SG say-PRET.3SG know-FUT.2SG how.ADV

an Arab woman and told me "Know that

41 Lack of vocalization in the text makes it impossible to know whether Hebrew-letter first-person preterite *-ar* conjugation verb forms such as דישפירטי <dyšpyrṭy> 'I awoke' were meant to be read with final *-é*: *desperté*, as in Spanish, or *-í*: *despertí*, as is documented in some Judezmo texts from at least the 18th century (e.g., Asa 1739 Gen. 28:15). Spellings such as אפאניימוש <ʔpʔnyymwš> 'we grabbed' and טופימוש <ṭwpymwš> in the present text demonstrate that the plural inflection had a front vowel, but it is unclear whether it denoted *-e(mos)*, as already documented in some vocalized texts in the 16th century (e.g., Paquda c1568: 16b), or *-i(mos)*, a form known from at least the 18th century (Asa 1739: Ex. 14:12). In the present article, the first-person preterite forms are systematically transcribed as singular *-í* and *-imos*, respectively.

טו מארידו לו אפאניימוס פארה טראאירלו אקי,
tu marido̱, lo apany-imos para tra-er-lo akí,
POSS.2SG husband PRON.ACC.3SG.M grab-PRET.1PL for bring-INF-PRON.ACC.3SG.M here.ADV
we grabbed your husband to bring him here,

אי טובֿו מיידו די ויניר אי שי פֿוייו די מואישטראש מאנוש.
i tuv-o myeḏo de ven-ir, i se fuy-ó de·muestr-as mano-s.
and have-PRET.3SG fear of come-INF and REF flee-PRET.3SG from·our-F.PL hand-PL
and he was afraid to come, and he fled from our hands.

אה קאבֿו די דוש טריש דיאש פֿואימוש, לו טופימוש מוארטו
A kavo de dos tres día-s fu-imos, lo top-imos muert-o
at end of two three day-PL go-PRET.1PL PRON.ACC.3SG.M find-PRET.1PL dead-M.SG
At the end of two or three days we went, [and] found him dead

אל לאדו די אונה אגואה. והיה זה פה ירושלים
al laḏo de una agua". Ve-ayá ze po Yerushaláyim,
at.DEF.M.SG side of INDEF.F.SG water and-be.PST.3SG.M[H] this[H] here[H] Jerusalem[H]
near a [body of] water". And this [testimony] was [taken down] in Jerusalem,

ת[יבנה]"ו[תיכונן] בחודש שבט
ti[-bané] ve[-tikonén], be-hóḏesh shevat
build[-FUT.PASS.3SG.F][H] and[-establish.FUT.PASS.3SG.F][H] in-month[H] Shevat[H]
may it be rebuilt and securely established, in the month of Shevat

שנת התל"ז ליצירה [...]
shena-ḏ e.ta[v].lá[meḏ].za[yin] la-yesirá [...][42]
year-CS[H] 5437[H] to.DEF-creation[H]
of the year 5437 [= c. January 1677] of the Creation [of the world ...]

3.7 Rabbinical Judezmo

From the earliest Judezmo literary writings documented in the Ottoman Empire through those created into the middle of the nineteenth century, the predominant literary register used in original compositions was the rabbinical Judezmo register. All of the features which were to characterize that register are already present in documents produced in medieval Iberia, such as the *taqqanot* (or community regulations) of Valladolid, formulated by the rabbis of Castile in 1432. The general impression made by texts in this register is that their authors, like some of the testifiers in the Ottoman rabbinical courts, would have preferred to express themselves entirely in Hebrew – the language believed by the rabbis to have been spoken by all of mankind before the separation of nations and languages after the Tower of Babel, the oldest and most sacred language of all Jewry, the language whose continued use by the Jews of Ancient Egypt earned them the merit of the Exodus and the establishment of the Jewish people with Hebrew as their national language, the favorite and most customary language of rabbinical composition, and the language which, according to rabbinical argument, will be spoken by all Jews with the coming of the Messiah. But since, as was also true of most Jews in other communities using other Jewish languages, the great majority of the Judezmo speakers of the Ottoman Empire could not comprehend a text written entirely in Hebrew, rabbinical

42 Heb. *Wĕ-haya ze po Yĕrušalayim ti[bbane] wĕ-[tikkonen] bĕ-ḥodeš šĕvaṭ šĕnat htl"z la-yĕṣira.*

authors reached a compromise by which they sought *lĕ-zakkot ʔet ha-rabbim* 'to earn merit for the masses', as they often referred to it, by constructing a rabbinical Judezmo literary framework which in many ways resembled a rabbinical text in Hebrew, but in fact, expressed most of the content or message of the text in a variety of the vernacular. As was noted, in rabbinical texts in the language of the Ottoman Sephardim, the vernacular itself was generally referred to as *ladino*, using phrases such as *avlar el ladino* 'to speak Ladino/Judezmo', as illustrated in the sample text below. It goes without saying that the authors expected most of the male members of their community to be able to comprehend their texts without great difficulty, although problems concerning language were sometimes addressed, directly or indirectly, by the authors, as in the sample text.

As illustrated in the Modern Rabbinical Judezmo passage below – constituting most of the preface to *Sefer Wĕ-hokiaḥ Avraham* [And Abraham Reproved], by Rabbi Avraham Palachi (1809–1899), a son of the prolific scholar and Izmir chief rabbi Ḥayyim Palachi (1788–1868) and himself a chief rabbi of Izmir[43] – the techniques used by the authors of Rabbinical Judezmo writings to create a Hebrew framework or skeleton for their works included:

(a) Hebrew rather than Judezmo book titles, generally composed of a phrase from the sacred sources often incorporating the author's own name, e.g., *Sefer Wĕ-hokiaḥ Avraham* – a citation from Genesis 21:25, including the author's first name;

(b) Hebrew chapter and section titles, e.g., *Idnaselud amehaber* 'Author's apology';[44]

(c) code-switching between wholly Hebrew and wholly Judezmo portions of the text, often in mid-sentence, e.g., *syendo lo ragal al leshonó a eskrivir en ladino* 'because *he is not accustomed* to writing in Ladino', in which the Judezmo conjunction *syendo* is followed by a Hebrew phrase with a finite verb, *lo ragal al leshonó*, with the return to Judezmo introduced by the Judezmo preposition *a*. Other transitional elements utilized for code-switching include: Hebrew prepositional elements in non-lexicalized expressions such as *le-* 'in order to' in *no ize aataká segunda leipakéah rasón ashoel* 'I did not proofread the work a second time *in order to accede to the* wishes of the one requesting it [i.e., the appearance of the book]', *la-* 'to the' in *se enbyó ladefús* 'it was sent *to the press*'), *be-* 'in' in (*toparás ...*) *bekamá devarim* 'you will find *in a few things*', or the conjunction *ve-* 'and', e.g., *velifamim* '*and* sometimes';

(d) plentiful citation of passages from sacred and rabbinical sources in Hebrew and Aramaic, e.g., (Heb.) *Veehad amarbé veehad amamit uvilvad sheyidkavén libó lashamáyim* 'One may do much or one may do little, it is all one (and the same), provided that he direct his heart to Heaven',[45] or (Aram[aic].) *Nekot mia palgá* 'Be satisfied with

43 Palachi's original introduction appeared in the edition of volume one published in Salonika, 1853, ff. 7a–8b; an abridged version appeared in the edition published in Izmir, 1877, ff. [i]b–[ii]b. Divergences between the two versions are pointed out here in the footnotes.

44 Here and throughout the present article, the Romanization of Whole Hebrew-Aramaic (or possibly Whole Hebrew) passages in the Judezmo texts is an attempt to reconstruct the oral pronunciation of such elements as traditionally used by the Judezmo-speaking rabbis of the Ottoman Empire, based on linguistic descriptions and observation of the traditions of the living bearers of this tradition today. It should be kept in mind, however, that such reconstructions are in fact hypothetical.

45 Cf. Talmud Bavli, Berakot 17a.

half'.[46] There are also innovative adaptations of traditional expressions, e.g., *azen limud leshón aloazim ikar velimud atorá araí* 'They make the study of the language of the foreigners *the main thing and the study of the Torah transitory*', based on Hebrew expressions containing oppositions such as *ʕiqqar* 'root, main thing' vs. *ṭafel* 'grafted part, adjunct', and *qevaʕ* 'permanent' vs. *ʔaraʕi* 'temporary'. The following popular saying, originating in Judezmo itself, also alludes to Jewish study practices: *El Shemyidbarah* [Heb. שם יתברך / *šem yitbarak*] *no konta ojas sinó oras* '"The Name [i.e., God] Blessed Be He" does not count [the number of] pages [studied] but [the number of] hours [devoted to study]' (note the near homonyms *ojas/oras*).

The quantitatively predominant component in this as in most varieties of Judezmo, and that giving the register its fundamental morphological, syntactic and lexical structure, is the Hispanic component. Palachi suggested that the Jews' spoken language (presumably he meant its Iberian component) had its roots in Portugal (*el shóresh es de Portugal*).[47] In the sample text, as in Judezmo rabbinical works generally, the Hispanic component may be subdivided into two major subcategories. The first subcategory consists of archaic, literary lexemes and somewhat artificial calque-translation constructions used in rendering citations from sacred sources literally into the vernacular, as well as in creating original phrases which nevertheless incorporate features of Hebrew, as opposed to ordinary Judezmo, syntax. Typical of this subcategory in the sample passage are lexemes such as דיפרינדיר/*deprender* instead of אמ־/אימביזארסי / *a-/embezarse* 'to learn', and noun-phrase constructions such as קאדָה אונו אי אונו / *kada uno i uno* 'each (and every) one' (cf. Heb. *kol ʔeḥad wĕ-ʔeḥad*) and *(El ladino ke avlamos por muestra parte no es aunado kon otros lugares) en kuantos byervos* '(The Ladino which we speak in our area is not identical with that in other areas) in a few/certain words' (cf. Heb. *bĕ-kama dĕvarim*, in which there is no explicit indefinite article, since Hebrew lacks one; as in Spanish, ordinary Judezmo syntax would require the indefinite article אונוס/*unos* before קואנטוס/*kuantos*, cf. synonymous Spanish *en* unas *cuantas palabras*). The second, and predominant subcategory of the Hispanic component in Rabbinical Judezmo approximates popular, everyday spoken Judezmo, occasionally including features specific to the author's own regional variety (in the case of our sample text, forms such as

46 Aramaic נקוט מיהא פלגא = be satisfied with half [at least you escaped half of the punishment of *karet*] (cf. Talmud Bavli, Moʕed Qaṭan, 28a).

47 Several factors might have led Palachi to conclude that Judezmo had its roots in Portuguese. Contemporary Judezmo and Portuguese words both contain some common features which are absent from the cognate words in contemporary Spanish (although they had existed in medieval Spanish): e.g., voiced /z/ in Judezmo קאזה/*kaza* (as in Old Spanish *casa*) and Portuguese *casa* 'house', and *g/g* in Judezmo אגורה/*agora* and Portuguese (and Old Spanish) *agora* 'now', versus Modern Spanish *casa* [ˈkasa] and *ahora* [aˈora]. Furthermore, some Sephardic families in Izmir were aware that certain of their ancestors had lived in medieval Portugal and were forced to convert to Catholicism there, from whence they eventually emigrated to Italy in order to return to the open practice of Judaism, eventually immigrating to Izmir where they congregated around the 'Qahal Portugal' or Portuguese Synagogue. Palachi evidentally had also read an article on the language of the Sephardim published in the opening issue of the Judezmo periodical *Šaʕare Mizraḥ* (1845–46), published in Izmir by Rafaʔel ʕUzziʔel, which could have prompted Palachi to conclude that the language of the Izmir Sephardim had its roots in Portugal – although in his paper ʕUzziʔel generally stressed the *Spanish* origins of the Ottoman Sephardim. For a romanization and analysis of ʕUzziʔel's article touching on language, see Bunis 1993b.

טאמיין/*tamyén* 'also', קאלי/*kale* 'one must') rather than other regional varieties (e.g., synonymous טאמביין/*tambyén*, פרימי/*premi*); frequent use of hypocoristic forms, used to create a sense of group-identity and intimacy between author and reader (e.g., ליבֿריקו גֿיקו / *livriko chiko* 'little book'); forms characteristic of popular Judezmo universally (e.g., איסטונסים/*estonses* 'then', מונגֿו/*muncho* 'a lot', בֿאמוס אבֿלאר *vamos avlar* 'we will speak', נו סי טירנה דימיניסטיר / *no se terná demenester* 'will not be necessary' [vs. Mod. Sp. *entonces*, *mucho*, *vamos a hablar*, *no habrá necesidad de*], and idiomatic expressions, some of them based on adaptations of idioms in contact languages, such as *Si es todo en lashón akódesh ... no entra ni sale en nada* 'If the whole [book] is in Hebrew ... he can make no sense of it at all').

As in all varieties of Judezmo documented before the mid-nineteenth century, the rabbinical register includes elements, primarily lexical, of Hebrew and Aramaic origin – referred to in the sample text not as 'Hebrew words' per se but as 'words from the Language of Holiness' (i.e., *byervos de lashón akódesh*) which were fully incorporated into Judezmo. The author noted that most of the Hebraisms he used were 'words usual in the speech of all' (*son byervos murgalim befí akol*); the meaning of those words unknown to a given reader could be learned by consulting a more learned friend (*demanda a otro ke save i se enbeza*), thus enriching his acquaintance with the holy tongue (*se enbeza algunos byervos en lashón akódesh*).

Particularly distinctive of the elements of Hebrew-Aramaic origin in this register is their relatively high percentage, and their representation not only in the form of substantives directly connected with Jewish religion and civilization, but also lexemes not necessarily bearing an immediate connection to Judaism. As typical of Rabbinical Judezmo texts, the Hebrew-Aramaisms appearing in the present sample include numerous lexemes – some perhaps limited to the language of those learned in Jewish texts and traditions, but many others belonging to the language of all Judezmo speakers before the modern era – having a direct relation to the topic of the piece, rabbinic writing in Judezmo: e.g., כתיבה/*ketivá* 'writing', לשון/*lashón* [pl. *leshonod*] 'language' and the names of languages customary in rabbinic writing, such as לשון הקודש / *lashón akódesh* 'Holy Tongue', ארמי/*aramí* 'Aramaic', (לשון) לעז / *(lashón) laaz* 'Judezmo (language)', לשון אשכנז / *lashón Eshkenáz* 'Yiddish', מצרי/*misrí* 'Egyptian' (cf. also מצרים/*Misráyim* 'Egypt'), אשורי/*ashurí* 'Assyrian', ערבי/*araví* 'Arabic', יוני/*yevaní* 'Greek', איטלקי/*italkí* 'Italian', צרפתי/*sarfatí* 'French' (there are also names not of Hebrew-Aramaic origin, e.g., Romance-origin לאדינו/איספאנייול / *ladino/espanyol* 'Judezmo', לאטינו/*latino* 'Latin', and Ottoman-origin פֿארסי/*farsí* [< Ar. *fārsī*] 'Persian'), book-related terms such as קונטרס/*kuntrés* 'tract', אגרת שלומים / *igéred shelomim* 'letter of greeting', העתקה/*aataká* 'copying, proofreading', דפוס/*defús* 'press', and the subdivision of works into parts such as the חלק/*hélek* 'part, section', פרק/*pérek* (pl. פרקים/*perakim*) 'chapter(s)', דף/*daf* 'folio', עמוד/*amud* 'page/column', אות/*od* '(paragraph) letter'; related concepts such as מוסר השכל / *musar askel* 'moral', (ליבֿרו די) מוסר / *(livro de) musar* 'ethical (work)', טעויות הדפוס / *tauyod adefús* 'typographical errors', לוח הטעויות / *lúah atauyod* 'errata list', אמרי אינשי / *ameré enashé* 'popular saying'; and the titles of works cited, which are invariably rabbinic works in Hebrew or Aramaic (e.g., איל זוהר / *el Zóar* 'the Zohar') or Judezmo (e.g., ס[פר]' מעם לועז / *Sé[fer] Meam Loéz* 'Book of *Me-ʕam loʕez'*; the first volume, by

Yaʕaqov K̲ulí, appeared in Constantinople, 1730). Other characteristic substantives in the sample text include terms denoting sectors of the Jewish population, such as the חכמים/*hahamim* 'rabbinical scholars', רבנים/*rabanim* 'rabbis', למדן/*lamdán* 'man devoted to and learned in Jewish sources', בחור/*bahur* 'young, unmarried student/scholar', עם הארץ/*amares* 'ignoramus (in Jewish matters)', and the individual בן אדם / *ben ad̲am* 'son of Adam, i.e., human being'; concepts recalling incidents recounted in the Bible, e.g., דור הפלגה / *dor apalagá* 'generation of secession (after the Tower of Babel)'; Jewish legal terms, e.g., איסור גדול / *isur g̲adol* 'major prohibition'. Some substantives carry a more abstract sense, e.g., terms relating to causality, origins, sensations and behavior such as סיבה / *sibá* 'reason, cause', שורש/*shóresh* 'root (e.g., of a language)', חשק/*héshek* 'desire, urge', טעם/*táam* 'savory taste', הרגל/*ergel* 'habit'. A formal characteristic of the Hebrew-Aramaic-origin substantives occurring in rabbinical texts is the almost universal indication of plural forms by using morphemes of Hebrew-Aramaic origin, e.g., חכם/ *haham* 'rabbinical scholar' > pl. חכמים/*hahamim*, לשון/*lashón* 'language' > pl. לשונות/ *leshonod̲*, עם הארץ/*amares* 'ignoramus' > pl. עמי הארצות / *amé aarasod̲*). In more popular texts, on the other hand, the Hispanic-origin plural marker *-(e)s* is often used instead, e.g., חאחאמים/*hahames*, אמאריסים/*amáreses*.

Rabbinical Judezmo texts also exhibit a higher percentage of lexemes belonging to parts of speech other than the substantive than texts in other registers. For example, the sample text includes periphrastic or analytic verbs constructed of an auxiliary verb of Hispanic origin and an invariant complement of Hebrew or Aramaic origin such as: אזיר העתקה / *azer aataká* 'to copy, proofread', סיר מסדר (איל לשון) / *ser mesader* (*el lashón*) 'to put (the language) in good order', טיניר הצלחה / *tener aslahá* 'to succeed', סיר משבח / *ser meshabéah* 'to praise', and pronominal verbs with סי/*se* such as סירסי סומך / *serse someh* 'to count on', סירסי מונע די / *serse monea de* 'to refrain from', as well as idiomatic constructions incorporating other Hispanic-origin verbs such as קונטאר לכף זכות / *kontar lehaf zahud̲* 'to give the benefit of the doubt', קאלייר טעות / *kayer taud̲* 'to be erroneous'. In texts in other registers, the relatively fewer verbs of Hebrew-Aramaic origin tend to be synthetic, with the stem originating in Hebrew-Aramaic and the inflections of Hispanic origin, e.g., דארסאר/*darsar* 'to lecture', cf. Heb. ד־ר־ש/*d-r-š* + Sp. *-ar*, אינחירימאר/ *enheremar* 'to excommunicate', cf. חרם/*hérem* 'excommunication' < Heb. חרם/*ḥerem* + Sp. *en- -ar* (such verbs also appear in the body of Palachi's text, although they are absent from the brief sample below). Palachi's sample also exemplifies the use in texts in this genre of adjectives of Hebrew-Aramaic origin such as מסודר/*mesudar* 'ordered'; of conjunctions such as יען/*yaan* 'because'; and of adverbs and adverbial expressions such as אפילו/*afilú* 'even', בכלל/*bihlal* 'among (others)', לפעמים/*lifamim* 'occasionally', מכל וכל / *mikol vahol* 'completely', דרך אגב / *déreh agav* 'incidentally', לכף זכות / *lehaf zahud̲* '(judge) favorably'.

The sample is typically rich in free-standing introductory or connective phrases which perhaps lie in the gray area between the Merged Hebrew component of Judezmo and Judezmo speakers' Whole Hebrew, e.g., זאת ועוד (קי איל לאדינו קי אב̄לאמוס...) / *Zod̲ vaod̲ (ke el lad̲ino ke avlamos...)* 'Furthermore [literally, 'this and more'] (that the Ladino which we speak…)'; וזוהי סיבה (קי...) / *vezoi sibá (ke...)* 'and this is the reason (that…)', רוב ה(פרקים) / *rov a(perakim)* 'most of (the chapters)'; ואף גם זאת / *veaf gam zod̲* 'and also in this;' ועל הרוב / *Veal arov* 'And mostly'; (די דיזיר) וחלילה לי / *Vehalila li (de dezir)* 'Heaven forbid me (from saying)'; רצוני לומר / *Resoní lomar* 'My intention is to say'; וכדומה / *vehadomé* 'et cetera'. Some of the Hebraisms appear in Hispanic guise: that is, they are calques of Hebrew idioms, expressed through Hispanisms, e.g., *(ke sea) una ora antes* '(that it be) as soon as possible' (cf. Heb. שעה אחת קודם / *šaʕa ʔaḥat qodem*). To save space, rabbinical authors in Judezmo, as in Hebrew, make extensive use of abbreviations, usually of words of Hebrew-Aramaic origin, e.g., ש״ית = *Shem-yid̲barah* (שם יתברך) 'The Name Blessed be He (i.e., God)', הי״ו = *Ashem yishmereu vihayeu* (השם ישמרהו ויחיהו) 'May God protect and grant him life' (added after the name of a living Jew cited in the text). Hebrew letters and their names are also used with their numerical value to indicate numbers, for example, of pages or folios, as in עמוד אלף / *amud̲ álef* 'column one'. As the text illustrates, characteristic of the Hebrew-letter spelling of rabbinic Judezmo is the use of word-final ייא- for *-ya*, probably to avoid the word-final ייה- more usual in non-rabbinic texts, since יה/*Ya* is a name of God in Hebrew. As customary in rabbinic Judezmo texts whenever possible, Palachi even used a phrase from the sources as an abbreviation of his name: אפ״י זוטרי / *Ape zutré* (cf. Aram. *ʔappe zuṭre* 'little faces'), i.e., the first three letters represent **א**[ברהם] **פ**[אלאג׳]**י** / ***A**[vraham]* ***P**[alach]**i***. The author noted that in his work he expressed some ideas entirely in Hebrew rather than Judezmo, since in the latter the phraseology seemed to him more 'heavy' (*en su lad̲ino vyene la avla pezgad̲a*).

As is also typical of Judezmo rabbinic works, Palachi's language includes local borrowings, mostly of Turkish (i.e., etymologically Turkish, Arabic and Persian) origin, many of which began to be incorporated in the language of the first generations of Sephardim born in the Ottoman Empire. In the sample text, 'foundation' is denoted by טימיל/*temel* (cf. Tk. *temel* < G[reek]. *themélio*); the adverb מאחסוס/*mahsús* (cf. Tk. *mahsus* < Ar. *maxṣūs*) denotes 'intentionally'; and one finds the synthetic verbs (with Turkish-origin stems and Hispanic-origin inflections) ייאקישיאר/*yakishear* 'to fit, be suitable' (cf. Tk. *yakış-*), ביגינאר/*beg̲enear* 'to like' (cf. Tk. *beğen-*), אקסאדיאר/*aksadear* 'to limp, be halting' (cf. Tk. 3sg. past def. *aksadı* [infin. *aksa-*]).[48] The verb אטאקאנאר/*atakanar* 'to order, compose, correct', occurring in our text as the past participle (with adjectival function) *atakanad̲o (en lad̲ino)* 'composed, arranged (in Judezmo)', appears to constitute a semantic merger reflecting both Turkish *tak-* 'to set', *takın-* 'to put on' and nearly homophonous Hebrew תיקן/*tiqqen* 'to correct, put in order'.

Especially worthy of note in this selection is the general attitude expressed by the author to Judezmo and its component structure, and to Hebrew. Palachi apologizes for any of his Judezmo formulations which the reader may find uncharacteristic or incorrect – thus implying that, to his way of thinking and that of his potential readers, there *are* 'correct' Judezmo formulations (*asigún es su regla del lad̲ino*), as opposed to faulty ones. Apparently influenced by an apologetic article on the contemporary state of Judezmo in the mid-nineteenth century which Rafaʔel ʕUzziʔel published in 1845 in the earli-

48 When a Turkish verbal stem ends in a consonant, the Judezmo derivative is created by adding the Hispanic-origin verbalizer *-ear*; when it ends in a vowel, *-ear* is added to the third-person singular past definite form in *-dı*, thus supplying a kind of consonantal bridge enabling the attachment of the inflectional endings to the stem.

est Judezmo newspaper, *Šaʕare Mizraḥ* [Gates of the East], Palachi echoes ʕUzziʔel's Haskalah-style critique of the lexicon of the everyday language of the Sephardim of Izmir, noting that:

(1) it diverged lexically from that of varieties used elsewhere (*no es aunad̲o kon otros lugares en kuantos byervos ke son demud̲ad̲os {i se risferensy[a]n}*[49] *de sivdad̲ a sivdad̲*);

(2) it consisted of lexemes drawn from diverse etymological sources (*lo·tenemos mesklad̲o de otros leshonod̲ · {komo italkí, aramí, sarfatí, yevaní, latino, sefarad̲í, araví, farsí, ashurí, misrí, vehadomé})*;[50]

Palachi also explained that what the reader might consider flaws in his work were the result of his not re-reading the material before submitting it to the printer (*no ize aataká sigunda*). In some instances Palachi was perhaps referring to calques of Hebrew syntax, e.g., *aataká sigunda* 'a second proofreading' (cf. Heb. העתקה שניה / *haʕataqa šĕniyya*), instead of more natural Judezmo *sigunda aataká*, corresponding to Hispanic syntax. He might also have been thinking of noun-adjective concord based on the gender of the more frequent Hispanic-origin synonym of a Hebrew-origin word used in the text: e.g., his use in the phrase *bekamá devarim ke están eskritas* 'in a few things/ words that are written' of the feminine plural adjective איסקריטאס/*eskritas* 'written' to qualify the word דברים/*devarim*, the etymon of which is masculine plural in Hebrew (and generally also in Judezmo), can be explained by its being a partial synonym of the more frequent Hispanic-origin feminine plural *kozas* 'things'. Note, however, that Hebrew *dĕḇarim* means both 'words' and 'things', which could have caused Palachi to think of feminine plural קוזאס/*kozas* as a synonym for *devarim*; but in Judezmo itself, *kozas* does not have the additional sense of 'words', which is instead ordinarily conveyed by ביירב̄וס/*byervos*, as used by Palachi in the text.

3.8 Sample text: Nineteenth-Century Rabbinical Judezmo

התנצלות המחבר

Id̲naselud̲ a-mehaber,
Apology.CS[h] DEF-author[h]
Apology of the author,

ה[שם] י[שמרהו]"ו[יחיו]

A[-shem]	*yi[-shmere-u]"*	*vi[-hae-u]*
DEF-name[h] [=God]	FUT.3SG.M-save-PRON.ACC.3SG.M[h]	and.FUT.3SG.M-keep.alive-PRON.ACC.3SG.M[h]

may God protect him and grant him life

49 The text enclosed within angular brackets was omitted in the second edition.

50 Palachi's list of languages contributing to Judezmo derives essentially from Abraham Mi-Šaʕar-Arye/Portaleone's *Sefer Šilṭe Ha-gibborim* [Shields of the Heroes] (Mantua, 1612), as Palachi himself notes; most of the languages listed did in fact contribute to Judezmo, directly or indirectly, but others – e.g., Latin, Assyrian, Egyptian – while having contributed to Hebrew, made no direct impact on Judezmo.

מודעת זאת בכל האר״ש קי טודו מודו די אומברי
Mud̲á-ad̲ zod̲ be-hol a-ares[51] *ke tod̲-o mod̲o de ombre*
inform.ADJ-F.SG^{H} PROX.F.SG^{H} in-all.CS^{H} DEF-land^{H} COMP all-M.SG manner of man
It is known everywhere that everyone

קי איס למדן אפילו איל מאס ג̃יקו קומו איסקריב̃י
ke es lamdán, afilú el mas chik-o, komo eskriv-e
REL be.PRS.3SG learned_man^{h} even.ADV^{h} DEF.M.SG most.ADV little-M.SG as.ADV write-PRS.3SG
who is learned,[52] even minimally, when he writes

חידושי תו[רה]׳ איל הרגל די לה כתי[בה]׳ לי אזי פינה
hidush-é to'[rá], el ergel de la keti'[vá] le az-e pena
novella-CS.PL^{h53} Torah^{h} DEF.M.SG habit^{h} of DEF.F.SG writing^{h} PRON.DAT.3SG make-PRS.3SG effort
Torah novellae, the habit of writing makes it difficult for him

אה איסקריב̃יר בל׳[שון]׳ לעז אין בואינה ריגלה סיינדו
a eskriv-ir be-la'[shón] laaz en buen-a regla syendo
to write-INF in-language.CS^{h} Judezmo^{h} in good-F.SG order be.GER
to write in Judezmo properly because

לא רגל על לשונו אה איסקריב̃יר אין לאדינו אפי[לו]׳
lo ragal al leshon-ó a eskriv-ir en lad̲ino afi'[lú]
NEG^{H} be.accustomed.PAST.3SG.M^{H} on.PREP^{H} tongue-POSS.3SG.M^{H} to write-INF in Ladino even.ADV^{h}
he is not accustomed to writing in Ladino even

אגרת שלומים. אי קון איסטו, נו מי אפ̄יאי איל
igéred̲ shelomim. I kon est-o, no me afe-e el
letter.CS^{h} well-being.PL^{h} and with PROX-M.SG NEG PRON.DAT.1SG blame-SUBJ.PRS.3SG 3SG.M
a letter of greeting. Therefore, let not the one

קי מילדה אין איסטי ליב̃ריקו ג̃יקו קואנדו ב̃י
ke meld-a en est-e livr-iko chik-o kuando ve
REL read-PRES.3SG in PROX-M.SG book-DIM.M.SG little-M.SG when see.PRS.3SG
who reads [in] this meager little book find fault with me when he sees

קי לה אב̃לה נו לי קורי בואינה או קי אלגונוס ביירב̃וס
ke la avla no le kor-e buen-a o ke algun-os byervo-s
COMP DEF.F.SG speech NEG PRON.DAT.3SG run-PRS.3SG well-F.SG or COMP some-M.PL word-PL
that the language does not flow well or that some words

נו איסטאן איסקריטוס אסיגון איס סו ריגלה דיל לאדינו ·
no est-án eskrit-os asigún es su regla del lad̲ino ·
NEG be-PRS.3PL written-M.PL as be.PRS.3SG POSS.3SG rule of.DEF.M.SG Ladino ·
are not written as is the rule in Ladino ·

51 מודעת זאת בכל האר״ש; cf. Isaiah 12:5 ... הארץ The last word is here spelled האר״ש, evidently meant by the author to have a secondary meaning as an abbreviation; the precise meaning of that abbreviation is unclear. Superscript "H" is used here to indicate Whole Hebrew words, which are not ordinarily a part of Judezmo, as opposed to the other words of Hebrew origin in the text, which are part of the Merged Hebrew component of Judezmo and marked with superscript "h".

52 That is, learned in Hebrew religious texts.

53 The abbreviation CS is used here to denote a construct form of a Hebrew-origin noun.

זאת ועוד קי איל לאדינו קי אבֿלאמוס פור מואיסטרה פארטי
Zod̲ va-od̲ ke el lad̲ino ke avl-amos por muestr-a[54] *parte*
this.F.SG^{H} and-more^{H} COMP DEF.M.SG Ladino REL speak-PRS.1PL for POSS.1PL-F.SG area
And furthermore, because the Ladino which we speak in our area

נו איס אאונאדו קון אוטרוס לוגאריס אין קואנטוס בײרבֿוס
no es aunad̲-o kon otr-os lugar-es en kuant-os byervo-s
NEG be.PRS.3SG identical-M.SG with other-M.PL place-PL in some-M.PL word-PL
is not identical with that in other areas in certain words

קי סון דימודאדוס {אי סי ריספֿירינסיאן} די סיבֿדאד אה סיבֿדאד
ke son demud̲ad̲-os {i se risferensy-[a]n}[55] *de sivdad̲ a sivdad̲*
REL be.PRS.3PL different-M.PL and REF diverge-PRS.3PL from city to city
which are different {and diverge} from city to city,

אי איל איספאנײול קי אבֿלאמוס קי איל שורש איס
i el espanyol ke avl-amos, ke el shóresh es
and DEF.M.SG Spanish REL speak-PRS.1PL REL DEF.M.SG root^{h} be.PRS.3SG
and the Spanish/Espanyol that we speak, the root of which is

די פורטוגאל לו טינימוס מיסקלאדו די אוטרוס לשונות ·
de Portugal, lo·ten-emos meskl-ad̲o de otr-os leshon-od̲ ·
from Portugal PRON.ACC.M.SG·AUX-PRS.1PL mix-PTCP.M.SG of other-M.PL language-PL^{h}
in Portugal, we have mixed with other languages ·

{קומו איטאלקי ארמי צרפתי יוני לאטינו ספרדי ערבי פֿארסי
{komo italkí, aramí, sarfatí, yevaní, latino, sefarad̲í, araví, farsí,
such as Italian^{h} Aramaic^{h} French^{h} Greek^{h} Latin Spanish^{h} Arabic^{h} Persian^{h}
{such as Italian, Aramaic, French, Greek, Latin, Spanish, Arabic, Persian,

אשורי מצרי וכדומה להן עי[ין]' בס[פר]' שלטי הגבו[רים]' ד[ף]"ד[לד]
ashurí, misrí, vehad̲omé, ayén be-Séfer Shilt-é A-gibor-im, da[f] dá[led̲]
Assyrian^{h} Egyptian^{h} etc.^{h} vid.^{H} in-book.CS^{H} sign-CS.PL^{H} DEF-hero-M.PL^{H} folio^{h} 4.NUM^{H}
Assyrian, Egyptian, etc., see *Sefer Šilṭe Ha-gibborim* [Shields of the Heroes], f. 4a}[56] ·

ע[מוד]"א[לף]} · אי נו סי טופה קין סיפה אבֿלאר
amud̲ álef} i no se top-a ken sep-a avl-ar
page/column^{h} 1.NUM^{h} and NEG IMPRS find.PRS.3SG REL know-SUBJ.PRS.3SG speak-INF
and no one is found who can speak

איל לאדינו אין און לשון טודה סו אבֿלה.
el lad̲ino en un lashón tod̲-a su avla.
DEF.M.SG Ladino in one.NUM language^{h} all-F.SG POSS.3SG speech
Ladino using [only] one language in all of his speech.

סי טאמיין סי טופה אוטרה סיבה קי איל לשון
Si tamyén[57] *se top-a otr-a sibá ke el lashón*
but also IMPRS find-PRS.3SG other-F.SG reason^{h} COMP DEF.M.SG language^{h}
And there is also another reason why the language

54 1st ed.: *nuestra*/נואיסטרה

55 The text enclosed within curly brackets was omitted in the second edition.

56 Cf. Mi-Šaʕar-Arye/Portaleone1612, f. 4a.

57 1st ed.: *tambyén*/טאמביין

דיל דיטו קונטרס נו איסטה מסודר בואינו
del dit-o kuntrés no est-á mesudar bueno
of.DEF.M.SG aforementioned-M.SG tract NEG be-PRS.3SG organized^{h} well.ADV
of this tract is not well ordered

יען רוב הפרקים נו איזי העתקה סיגונדה
yaan rov a-perak-im no ize aataká seg̱und-a
because^{h} most.CS^{h} DEF-chapter-M.PL^{h} NEG do.PRET.1SG proofreading^{h} second-F.SG
because [for] most of the chapters I did not do a second proofreading,

להפקח רצון השואל ה[שם] י[שמרהו]"
le-ipakéah resón a-shoel A[-shem] yi[-shmere-u]"
to-be_attentive.INF^{H} will.CS^{H} DEF-ask.PTCP.SG.M^{H} DEF-God^{h} FUT.3SG.M-save-PRON.ACC.3SG.M^{h}
in order to be attentive to the will of the seeker, May God protect him

ו[חייהו] קי סיאה אונה אורה אנטיס
vi[-haye-u][58] *ke sea un-a ora antes,*
and.FUT.3SG.M-keep alive-PRON.ACC.3SG.M^{h} COMP be.SUBJ.PRS.3SG one.NUM-F.SG hour before
and grant him life, as quickly as possible,

אי לוקי מי סאליו די לה בוקה אלה פינדולה
i lo·ke me sal-yó de la boka a·la péndola
and DEF.N.SG·REL REF.1SG leave-PRET.3SG from DEF.F.SG mouth to·DEF.F.SG pen
and what left my mouth [and went] to the pen,

דיטה כתיבה פרופייה סי אינביאו לדפוס וזוהי סיבה
dit-a ketivá propy-a se enb-yó la-defús, ve-zo-i sibá
aforementioned-F.SG writing^{h} same-F.SG PASS send-PRET.3SG to.DEF-press^{H} and-this-F.SG^{H} reason^{H}
this same writing was sent to the press and this is the reason

קינו סי פודו סיר מסדר איל לשון בנועם שיח
ke·no se puḏ-o ser mesader el lashón be-nóam síah
COMP·NEG PASS be_able-PRET.3SG be.INF organize.PTCP.M.SG^{h} DEF.M.SG language^{h} in-pleasant^{H} conversation^{H}
that the language could not be well ordered in a pleasant conversational style

להיות דורשה ומגיה ולקיים הכינה וגם חקרה
li-yoḏ doresh-á u-magía u-l-kayem ahiná ve-gam hakirá
to-be^{H} teach^{H}-PRS.3SG.M and-proofread^{H} and-to-perform.INF^{H} preparation^{H} and-also^{H} investigation^{H}
in order both to write and proofread and prepare and investigate

אי מי פֿואי סומך אל קי מילדה אין איל
i me fuí someh al ke meld-a en el
and REF.1SG be-PRET.1SG.M rely.PTCP.M.SG^{h} on.DEF.M.SG COMP read-PRS.3SG in PRON.PREP.3SG.M
and I counted on the one reading it

קי ייה מי קונטה לכף זכות. אי טופאראס טאמיין
ke ya[59] *me kont-a le-haf̱ zahuḏ. I topar-ás tamyén*[60]
COMP already PRON.ACC.1SG count-PRS.3SG to-palm.CS^{h} right^{h} and find-FUT.2SG also
to surely give me the benefit of the doubt. And you will also find

58 להפקח רצון השואל ה[שם] י[שמרהו]"ו[יחיהו]

59 *Ya*/ייה was omitted in the second edition.

60 Here the 1st ed. has *tamién*/טאמיין, evidently adhering to the author's native Izmir Judezmo variant; the Salonika dialect prefers *tambyén*/טאמביין. See Quintana 2006: 222.

בכמה דברים קי איסטאן איסקריטאס בלשון הקדש

be-kamá devar-im ke est-án eskrit-as be-la[shón] a-kó[d̲esh]

in-several^{H} thing-M.PL^{H} REL be-PRS.3PL written-PTCP.F.PL in-language.CS^{H}DEF-sanctity^{H}

in a few things that *they* are written in the Holy Tongue

פור סיבה קי אין סו לאדינו בֿייני לה אבֿלה פיזגאדה

por sibá ke en su lad̲ino vyen-e la avla pezgad̲-a,

for reason^{h} COMP in POSS.3SG Ladino_translation come-PRS.3SG DEF.F.SG speech heavy-F.SG

because in its Ladino translation the language comes out heavy,

ולפעמים קאיי טעות בדפוס אי נו סי אינטיינדי

ve-lifamim kay-e taud̲ b-a-defús i no se entyend-e

and-sometimes^{h} fall-PRS.3SG error^{h} in-DEF-printing^{h} and NEG PASS understand-PRS.3SG

and sometimes there is an error in printing and the word is not understood

איל ביירבֿו דיל טודו ואף גם זאת סי גאנה

el byervo del[61] *tod̲o, ve-af gam zod̲ se g̲an-a,*

DEF.M.SG word of.M.SG all.M.SG and-even^{h} also^{h} DEM.F.SG^{h} REF benefit-PRS.3SG

at all, and also in this one benefits,

קי איל ע[ם]"ה[ארץ] אי איל בחור קי מילדה סי אינביזה

ke el amares i el bahur ke meld-a se enbez-a

CONJ DEF.M.SG unlearned_person^{h} and DEF.M.SG young_man^{h} REL read-PRS.3SG REF learn-PRS.3SG

because the unlearned person and the young man[62] who reads [it] learns

אלגונוס ביירבֿוס אין לשון הקדש קי קואנדו איל ליבֿרו איסטה

algun-os byervo-s en lashón a-kód̲esh, ke kuando el livro est-á

some-M.PL word-PL in language.CS^{h} DEF-sanctity^{h} CONJ when DEF.M.SG book be-PRS.3SG

a few words in the Holy Tongue, because when the book is

אטאקאנאדו אין לאדינו לי אינטרה איל חשק די מילדאר

atakanad̲-o en lad̲ino le entr-a el héshek de meld-ar

arranged-M.SG in Ladino PRON.DAT.3SG enter-PRS.3SG DEF.M.SG urge^{h} of read-INF

arranged in Ladino he feels a desire to read

אין איל פור סיר ליבֿרו קי אינטיינדי לוקי מילדה ·

en el por ser livro ke entyend-e lo·ke meld-a;

in PRON.PREP.3SG because be.INF book REL understand-PRS.3SG DEF.N·REL read-PRS.3SG

[in] it, being a book in which he understands what he reads;

לי קידה אלגונוס קואנטוס ביירבֿוס די לשון הקדש

le ked̲-a algun-os[63] *kuant-os byervo-s de lashón a-kód̲esh*

PRON.DAT.3SG remain-PRS.3SG some-M.PL few-M.PL word-PL of language.CS^{h} DEF-sanctity^{h}

there remain a few words from the Holy Tongue

קינו לוס סאבֿי איסטונסיס דימאנדה אה אוטרו

ke·no los sav-e, estonses demand-a a otr-o

REL·NEG PRON.ACC.3PL.M know-PRS.3SG then ask-PRS.3SG OBJ another-M.SG

which he does not know, then he asks someone else

61 1st ed.: *de el* / די איל

62 *Or*: 'yeshiva student'.

63 1st ed.: *unos*/אונוס

קי סאבֿי אי סי אינביזה אי לי קידה אין טינו

ke sav-e i se enbez-a i le ked̲-a en tino

REL know-PRS.3SG and REF learn-PRS.3SG and PRON.DAT.3SG remain-PRS.3SG in mind

who knows and he learns and it remains in his mind

אה דיפרינדיר לוקי פואידי קי סי איס טודו אין לשון הקדש

a deprend-er lo·ke pued̲-e, ke si es tod̲-o en lashón a-kód̲esh

to learn-INF DEF.N·REL be able-PRS.3SG CONJ if be.PRS.3SG all-M.SG in language.CS^h DEF-sanctity^h

to learn what he can, because if everything is in the Holy Tongue

נו טומה אה מילדארלו פורקי סאבֿי אין סי

no tom-a a meld-ar-lo, porke sav-e en si

NEG take-PRS.3SG to read-INF-PRON.ACC.3SG.M because know-PRS.3SG in 3SG.REF

he won't take it to read, because he knows himself

קי נו אינטרה ני סאלי אין נאדה · ועל הרוב

ke no entr-a ni sal-e en nad̲a · Ve-al a-rov

COMP NEG enter-PRS.3SG nor go out-PRS.3SG in nothing and-on^H DEF-most^H

that he will make no sense of it at all. And mostly

ייא סון ביירבֿוס מורגלים בפי הכל אי אפי[לו]'

ya son byervo-s murgal-im be-fí a-kol, i afi[lú]

already.ADV be.PRS.3PL word-PL usual-M.PL^h in-mouth.CS^h DEF-all^h and even.ADV^h

they are words usual in the speech of all, and even

קי נו טופארה אקיאה אורה קין לי אינביזי איל ביירבֿו

ke·no topar-á ake-a ora ken le enbez-e el byervo

REL·NEG find-FUT.3SG DIST.F.SG hour who PRON.DAT.3SG learn-SUBJ.PRS.3SG DEF.M.SG word

if he should not find at that moment someone to teach him the word

קי נו אינטינדייו נקוט מיהא פלגא אין קיטאנדו

ke no·entend-yó, nekot mia palgá,[64] *en kit-ando*

REL NEG·understand-PRET.3SG take-IMP.2SG.M^AM from-PRON.PREP.3SG.M^AM half^AM on exclude-GER

he did not understand, he will be rewarded for what he does study, [for] on excluding

מיס טעיות קינו איסטה לה אבֿלה בואינה אי אין קיטאנדו

mi-s tau-yod̲, ke·no est-á la avla buen-a, i en kit-ando

POSS.1SG-PL error-F.PL^h REL-NEG be-PRS.3SG DEF.F.SG speech good-F.SG and on exclude-GER

my errors, where the language is not good, and excluding

טעיות הדפוס אי ביירבֿוס די לשון הקדש קי נו סי

tau-yod̲ a-defús i byervo-s de lashón a-kód̲esh ke·no se

error-CS.F.PL^h DEF-printing^h and word-PL from language.CS^h DEF-sanctity^h REL·NEG PASS

the typographical errors and the words from the Holy Tongue which are not

אינטיינדין אינריבֿה די איסטו לו מאס מונג̃ו דיל פרק ייא

entyend-en, enriva de esto lo mas muncho del pérek ya

understand-PRS.3PL above of PROX.N DEF.N more many of.DEF.M.SG chapter^h already

understood, beyond this the majority of the chapter

64 Aramaic נקוט מיהא פלגא *nĕqoṭ miha palga* 'be satisfied with half [at least you escaped half of the punishment of *karet*]' (cf. Talmud Bavli, Moʕed Qaṭan, 28a).

לֿי קידה פארה אינטינדירלו בואינו,
le keḏ-a para entend-er-lo bueno,
PRON.DAT.3SG remain-PRS.3SG for understand-INF-PRON.ACC.3SG.M well
is left for him to understand well,

ואחד המרבה ואחד הממעיט ובלֿבד
ve-ehaḏ a-marbé ve-ehaḏ a-mamit, u-vi-lvaḏ
and-one.NUM.M^{H} DEF-increase.PRS.3SG.M^{H} and-one.NUM.M^{H} DEF-decrease.PRS.3SG.M^{H} and-in-only^{H}
and “One may do much or one may do little, it is all one, provided

שיתכוין לֿבו לֿשמים והיינו דאמרי אינשי
she-yiḏ-kavén lib-ó la-shamáy-im, ve-aynú de-ameré enash-é,
COMP-FUT.3SG.M-direct^{H} heart-POSS.3SG.M^{H} to.DEF-heaven-PL^{H} and-this^{H} REL-say-PRS.PL^{AM} person-PL^{AM}
that he direct his heart to Heaven”,[65] and this is as the popular proverb says,

איל ש[ם]"ית[ברך] נו קונטה אוזֿאס סינו אוראס ·
“El She[m]” Yiḏ[-barah] no kont-a oja-s sinó ora-s”.
DEF.M.SG name^{h} FUT.PASS.3SG.M-bless^{h} NEG count-PRS.3SG page-PL but hour-PL
“The Name [i.e., God] Blessed Be He” does not count [the number of] pages [studied] but [the number of] hours [devoted to study]”.

איל טימֿיל איס החזק במוסר אל תרף
El temel es “Ahazek ba-musar al téref”,
DEF.M.SG main_principle be.PRS.3SG hold.IMP.2SG.M^{H} in.DEF-moral^{H} NEG^{H} let_go.JUSS.2SG.M^{H}
The main principle is “Take fast hold of instruction, let her not go”,[66]

רצוני לומר נו טי אפֿלושיס דינו טומאר איל ליבֿרו
reson-í lo-mar, no te aflosh-es de·no tom-ar el livro
wish.CS-POSS.1SG^{H} to-say.INF^{H} NEG REF.2SG weaken-SUBJ.PRS.2SG of·NEG take-INF DEF.M.SG book
by which I mean to say, do not be weak so as not to take the book

די מוסר אמֿילדאר פור בֿיר קי לה אבֿלה טי אפריטה
de musar a-meld-ar, por ver ke la avla te apret-a
of morals^{h} to-read-INF for see.INF COMP DEF.F.SG speech PRON.ACC.2SG oppress-IND.PRS.3SG
of ethics to read, after seeing that the language oppresses you

אי טי קאנסה אה איל מֿילדאר או קי איל דפוס
i te kans-a a el meld-ar, o ke el defús
and PRON.ACC.2SG tire-PRS.3SG to DEF.M.SG read-INF or COMP DEF.M.SG print^{h}
and tires you upon reading, or that the printed text

נו איסטה בואינו אי בֿאס אפינאר, סינו לֿאזרה אה אינטינדיר
no est-á buen-o i vas apen-ar, sinó lazr-a a entend-er,
NEG be-PRS.3SG good-M.SG and go.2SG suffer-INF but strive-IMP.2SG to understand-INF
is not good and you will struggle, but rather strive to understand,

אי לֿוקי פואידיס אינטינדיר קי טי אבאסטי
i lo·ke pueḏ-es entend-er ke te abast-e,
and DEF.N·REL be_able-PRS.2SG understand-INF COMP PRON.DAT.2SG suffice-SUBJ.PRS.3SG
and what you can understand let be enough for you,

65 Cf. Talmud Bavli, Beraḵot 17a.

66 Cf. Proverbs 4:13.

בודק עד המקום שידו מגעת וכל אדם
"Boḏek aḏ a-makom she-yaḏ-ó magá-aḏ",[67] *ve-"Kol aḏam*
examine.PRS.3SG.M^{H} until^{H} DEF-place^{H} REL-hand-POSS.3SG.M^{H} reach-3SG.F^{H} and-every^{H} man^{H}
"He examines up until the place where his hand reaches", "and everyone

אינו חייב אלא כשיעורו [...] אי אאון קי ב̄יריש
en-ó hayav elá ke-shiur-ó"[68] *[...] i aún ke ver-ésh*
not-3SG.M^{H} culpable^{H} only^{H} as-measure-POSS.3SG.M^{H} and even COMP see-FUT.2PL
is culpable only in accordance with its standard" [...] And even though you will see,

קי סי טופה בכלל קי איי מוסר ללמדנים
ke se top-a, bihlal, ke ay musar la-lamdan-im
COMP IMPRS find-PRS.3SG among_others^{h} REL exist.PRS moral^{H} to.DEF-scholar-M.PL^{H}
among others, that there are morality lessons for Torah scholars

אי נו ייאקישיאה אין לאדינו לתופסי התורה חלילה לי
i no yakishe-a en laḏino le-tofes-é a-torá, halila li
and NEG fit-PRS.3SG in Ladino to-grasp.PTCP-CS.M.PL^{H} DEF-Torah^{H} heaven.forbid^{H} PRON.DAT.1SG^{H}
and it is not fitting in Ladino for graspers of the Torah, Heaven forbid that I

די דיזיר מוסר אה ת[למידי]"ח[כמים] אפילו אה איל מאס ג̄יקו
de dez-ir musar a ta[lmiḏ-é]"ha[ham-im], afilú a·el mas chik-o,
to say-INF morality^{h} to pupil-CS.M.PL^{h}scholar-M.PL^{h} even^{h} to·DEF.M.SG most small-M.SG
should preach morality to Torah scholars, even the most minor of them,

סינו איס קי ב̄ינו דרך אגב אי נו איס מאחסוס
sinó es ke vin-o déreh agav i no es mahsús,
but be.PRS.3SG COMP come-PRET.3SG way.CS^{h} incidentally^{h} and NEG be.PRS.3SG purposely
but rather it came out incidentally and is not on purpose,

אי סי טאמיין קי לפעמים איס להוכיח את עצמי
i si tamyén[69] *ke lifamim es le-ohíah eḏ asm-í*
and if also COMP sometimes^{h} be.PRS.3SG to-prove.INF^{H} OBJ^{H} self-POSS.1SG^{H}
and also sometimes it is to reprove myself,

אי פארה קי לו טינגה לזכרון בין עיני [...]
i para ke lo teng-a le-zikarón ben en-áy [...]
and for COMP PRON.ACC.3SG.M have-SUBJ.PRS.1SG to-memory^{H} between^{H} eye-DUAL.POSS.1SG^{H}
so that I keep it as a reminder in front of my own eyes[70] [...]

איל קי ביגיניארה אמילדאר בקונטרס קטן הלזה קי טינגה
El ke beḡenear-á a-meld-ar be-kuntrés[71] *katán a-lazé ke teng-a*
3M.SG¸REL deign-FUT.3SG to-read-INF in-booklet^{H} little^{H} DEF-DEM^{H} COMP have-SUBJ.PRS.3SG
He who will deign to read in this little tract should have

67 Cf. Talmud Bavli, Bava Mĕṣiʕa, 7a; Maimonides, *Mišne Tora*, *Sefer Zĕmanim*, *Hilḵot ḥameṣ u-maṣa*, chap. 2, sec. 5.

68 Cf. Talmud Bavli, Šabbat, chap. 10, 90b.

69 1st ed.: *tambyén*/טאמביין

70 Cf. Ex 13:9.

71 From Latin *commentarius*.

לנגד עיניו לוח הטעיות אנדי לי אקסאדיאה איל לשון
le-neged en-av lúah a-tau-yod ande le aksade-a el lashón,
to-against^{H} eye-POSS.3SG.M^{H} list.CS^{H} DEF-mistake-PL^{H} where PRON.DAT.3SG halt-PRS.3SG DEF.M.SG language^{H}
before his eyes the errata list for where the language is halting,

פארה קי קורה אין סו מילדאר אי קי טופי טעם
para ke kor-a en su meld-ar i ke top-e táam
for COMP run-SUBJ.PRS.3SG in POSS.3SG read-INF and COMP find-SUBJ.PRS.3SG savor^{h}
so that he can run quickly in his reading and find savor

אין לו קי מילדה [...] סהדי במרומים כי לא היה
en lo ke meld-a [...] Saad-í ba-merom-im[72] *ki lo ayá*
in DEF.N REL read-PRS.3SG Witness-POSS.1SG^{AM} in.DEF-height-M.PL^{H} COMP^{H} NEG^{H} be-PAST.3SG.M^{H}
in what he reads […] My witness is in the heavens that it would not have been

רצוני לסדר תוכחות מוסר בלשון לעז אילולא
reson-í le-sader tohah-od musar be-lashón laaz ilu-lé
will-POSS.1SG^{H} to-compose.INF^{H} rebuke-CS.F.PL^{H} morality^{H} in-language.CS^{H} LaʕAz^{H} if-not^{AM}
my will to compose moral rebukes in the Laʕaz language if they had not

דהכריחוני · אי איס קי ביֿדי בס[פר]'
de-ihrih-u-ni · i es ke vid-e be-Sé[fer]'
COMP-force.PAST.3PL-PRON.ACC.1SG^{AM} and be.PRS.3SG COMP see-PRET.1SG in-Book.CS^{H}
forced me ·And the fact is, that I saw in *Sefer*

תורת האשם, אות ד[לת] ר[יש] וז[ה]"ל[שונו]
Tora-d A-asham, od dá[led] re[sh], ve-zé" le[shon-ó]:
Torah-CS^{H} DEF-guilt^{H} letter^{H} 4.NUM^{H} 200.NUM^{H} and-PROX.M.SG"^{H} language-POSS.3SG.M^{H}
Torat Ha-Ašam [Law of Guilt], section 204,[73] and this is its language:

טוב להזהר אה אוזארסי אבֿלאר בלשון הקדש
"Tov le-izaer a uz-ar-se avl-ar be-lashón a-kódesh,
good^{H} to-be careful.INF^{H} to accustom-INF-REF speak-INF in-language.CS^{H} DEF-sanctity^{H}
"It is good to accustom oneself to speak in the Holy Tongue,

כי אז יצליח בכל מעשיו אסיגון דיזי איל זהר
ki az ya-slíah be-hol maas-av, asigún diz-e el Zóar,
CONJ^{H} then.ADV^{H} FUT-succeed.3SG.M^{H} in-all.CS^{H} deed-PL.POSS.3SG.M^{H} as say-PRS.3SG DEF.M.SG Zohar^{H}
because then one will succeed in all his deeds, as the Zohar [Book of Splendor] says,

פ[רשת]' נח קי דור הפלגה לוקי טובֿיירון הצלחה
pe[rasha-d] Nóah, ke dor apalagá lo·ke tuv-yeron aslahá
chapter-CS^{h} Noah^{h} COMP generation.CS^{h} division^{h} DEF.N·REL have-PRET.3PL success^{h}
in the chapter Noah, that the Generation of Division[74] was successful

72 Cf. Job 16:19.

73 The reference is to Yĕhuda Altshuler, *Sefer Torat Ha-Ašam*, in his *Sefer Wa-yḥal Moše* [And Moses Besought], Prague 1613, f. 41a, sec. 204.

74 During the period of the Tower of Babel (Gen. 11:1–9).

נו פֿואי סינו פורקי אבֿלאבֿאן בלשון הקדש

no fue sinó porke avl-avan be-lashón a-kódesh,

NEG be.PRET.3SG but.only because speak-IMPF.3PL in-language.CS^H DEF-sanctity^H

for no other reason than because they spoke in the Holy Tongue,

ע[ד]"כ[אן] ובספר קב הישר פ[רשת]' פ[א]"ב[ית] טופאראס

ad kan, Ve-be-Sé[fer] Kav A-yashar, pe[rasha-d] pe" be[d], topar-ás

until^H here^H and-in-book.CS^H *Qav^H Ha-yašar^H* chapter-CS^H 80.NUM^H 2.NUM^H find-FUT.2SG

until here [is the citation], And in *Sefer Qav Ha-yašar* [The Just Measure],[75] chapter 82, you will find

מוסר השכל אה לוס קי מיטין אלוס איזוס גֿיקוס אין לה איסקולה

musar_askel a los ke met-en a·los ijo-s chik-os en la eskola

moral_lesson^h to DEF.M.PL REL put-PRS.3PL OBJ·DEF.M.PL son-PL young-M.PL in DEF.F.SG school

a moral lesson for those who put their young children in the Western European-style school

אה אינביזארסין לשונות הגוים אי נו טיינין

a enbez-ar-sen leshon-od a-goyim i no tyen-en

to learn-INF-REF.3PL language-CS.PL^h DEF-Gentiles^h and NEG have-PRS.3PL

to learn languages of the Gentiles and do not have in

איל טינו אין לשון הקדש דיל טודו ני אין ייבֿארלוס

el tino en lashón a-kódesh del todo ni en yev-ar-los

DEF.M.SG thought in language.CS^h DEF-sanctity^h of.DEF.M.SG all nor in bring-INF-PRON.ACC.3PL.M

mind the Holy Tongue at all nor in bringing them

לבית המדרש סינו אזין לימוד לשון הלועזים

le-ved a-midrash sinó az-en limud lashón a-loaz-im

to-house.CS^H DEF-study^H but make-PRS.3PL study.CS^H language.CS^H DEF-foreigner-M.PL^H

to the traditional Jewish study hall but rather they make the study of the language of the foreigners

עיקר ולימוד התורה עראי אי איס איסור גדול

ikar ve-limud a-torá araí i es isur gadol

main_thing^H and-study.CS^H DEF-Torah^H temporary^H and be.PRS.3SG prohibition^h great^h

the main thing and the study of the Torah transitory and it is a great prohibition

לוקי אזין אי נו סאבֿין קי לוקי סאלימוס די מצרים

lo·ke az-en, i no sav-en ke lo·ke sal-imos de Misráyim

DEF.N·REL do-PRS.3PL and NEG know-PRS.3PL COMP DEF.N·REL leave-PRET.1PL from Egypt^h

what they do, and they do not know that the reason we left [the bondage] of Egypt

פֿואי בזכות שלא שינו את לשונם [...] קאלי דיזיר

fue bi-zhud she-ló shin-ú ed leshon-am [...] Kal-e dez-ir

be.PRET.3SG in-merit^H COMP-NEG^H change-PAST.3PL^H OBJ^H language-POSS.3PL.M^H must-PRS.3SG say-INF

was in merit of the fact that they did not change their language […] It must be said

פור ספרים שנדפסו בל[שון]' לעז קי איס לצורך

por sefar-im she-ni-dpes-ú be-la[shón] laaz ke es le-sóreh

for book-M.PL^H REL-PASS-print-PAST.3PL^H in-language.CS^H LaSaz^H COMP be.PRS.3SG for-need.CS^H

concerning books that were published in the Laʕaz language that it is for the need

75 See Ṣĕvi Hirsch Kaidanover, *Sefer Qav Ha-yašar*, Frankfurt am Main 1705, ff. 171a–171b; Kaidanover was referring particularly to French.

עמי הארצות לזכות את הרבים אי אסיגון איזיירון

am-é a-aras-od̲, le-zakod̲ ed̲ a-rab-im, i asigún iz-yeron

people-CS.M.PL[H] DEF-land-F.PL[H] to-earn_merit[H] OBJ[H] DEF-many-M.PL[H] and as do-PRET.3PL

of the unlearned,[76] to earn merit for the masses, and as several rabbis did,

כמה רבנים קומו ס[פר]' מעם לועז המאיר לעולם

kamá raban-im komo Sé[fer] Meam Loéz, a-mair[H] *la-olam,*

a_few[H] rabbi-M.PL[H] like book[H] *Me-ʕAm*[H] *Loʕez*[H] DEF-illuminate.PRS.3SG.M to.DEF-world[H]

as in the *Sefer Me-ʕAm Loʕez* [From a People of Strange Language],[77] which illuminates the world,

ובספר יערות דבש ח"א בכמה מקומות אזי

ve-be-Séfer Yearod̲ Devásh, hé[lek]" á[lef], be-kamá mekom-od̲, az-e

and-in-book[H] *Yĕʕarot*[H] *Dĕvaš*[H] part"[H] one.NUM[H] in-a_few[H] place-F.PL[H] do.PRS.3SG

and in *Sefer Yĕʕarot Dĕvaš* [Forests of Honey],[78] part one, in several places, it gives

תוכחות אה קי מילדין לוס עמי הארצות

tohah-od̲ musar a ke meld-en los am-é a-aras-od̲

rebuke-CS.F.PL[h] moral[h] to REL read-SUBJ.PRS.3PL DEF.M.PL people-CS.M.PL[h] DEF-land-F.PL[h]

moral instructions that the unlearned should read

בספרי מוסר קי איי בלשון אשכנז אי לוס

be-sifr-é musar ke ay be-lashón Eshkenáz i los

in-book-CS.M.PL[H] moral[H] REL exist.PRS in-language.CS[H] Ashkĕnaz[H] and PRON.ACC.3PL.M

ethical works that there are in the language of Ashkĕnaz[79] and he praises them,

איס משבח קי ייא טופאן אמילדאר אין איל לשון

es meshabéah, ke ya top-an a-meld-ar en el lashón

be.PRS.3SG praise.PTCP.M.SG[h] CONJ already.ADV find-PRS.3PL to-read-INF in DEF.M.SG language[h]

because they find material to read in the language

קי אינטיינדין קאדה אונו אי אונו [...] בביאת משיחנו נו סי

ke entyend-en kad̲a uno i uno [...] Be-via-d̲ meshih-enu no se

REL understand-PRS.3PL each one and one [...] in-coming-CS[H] messiah-POSS.1PL[H] NEG IMPRS

which each one understands [...]With the coming of our messiah there will be no

טירנה דימיניסטיר ליבֿרוס בלשון לעז מכל וכל סיינדו קי

tern-á de-menester livro-s be-lashón laaz mi-kol va-hol, syendo ke

have-FUT.3SG of-need book-PL in-language.CS[H] Laʕaz[H] from-all[H] and-all[H] be.GERUND COMP

need for books in Laʕaz at all, since

טודוס בֿאמוס אבֿלאר בל[שון]"הק[דש] [...] אי נו פור איסטו

tod̲-os va-mos avl-ar be-la[shón]" a-kó[d̲esh] [...] i no por esto

all-M.PL go-PRS.1PL speak-INF in-language.CS"[H] DEF-sanctity[H] [...] and NEG for PROX.N

all of us will speak in the Holy Tongue [...] But not for this reason

76 That is, those ignorant of Hebrew and Jewish studies.

77 The reference is to Yaʕaqov K̲ulí (כ'ולי), *Sefer Me-ʕAm Loʕez*, Constantinople, 1730 and subsequent volumes of biblical exegesis by K̲uli and his successors, the earliest volumes enjoying several editions (see Romero 1992).

78 Cf. Jonathan Eybeschütz, *Sefer Yĕʕarot Dĕvaš*, 3d ed., Karlsruhe 1779, chapter 1, passim.

79 That is, Yiddish; the name אשכנז/Aškĕnaz appears in the Bible (Genesis 10:3) with reference to a descendant of Noah, as well as to a kingdom (Jeremiah 51:27). In the Middle Ages the word came to denote the German-speaking lands.

סי סיאה מונע איל בן אדם דינו איסקריבֿיר ספר

se sea monea el ben adam de·no eskriv-ir séfer

REF be.SUBJ.PRS.3SG refrain.PRS.3SG.M^{h} DEF.M.SG son.CS^{h} man^{h} of·NEG write-INF book^{H}

should a person refrain from writing a book

בלשון לעז קי אפי[לו]׳ בלשון הקדש אין אתה יודע

be-lashón laaz, ke afi[lú] be-lashón a-kódesh "en atá yodea

in-language.CS^{H}LaʕazH CONJ even.ADV^{h} in-language.CS^{H}DEF-sanctity^{H} NEG^{H} 2SG.M^{H} know.PRS.M.SG^{H}

in the La'az language, because even in the Holy Tongue you do not know

אזה יכשר קי איסטונסיס בֿה סיר ולא ילמדו עוד

ezé yi-hshar",[80] ke estonses va ser "Ve-ló ye-lamed-ú od

which^{H} FUT-succeed.3SG.M^{H} CONJ then.ADV go.PRS.3SG be.INF and-NEG^{H} FUT-teach-3PL.M^{H} further^{H}

which one will succeed, for then it will be "And they shall teach no more

איש את רעהו ומלאה הארץ דעה את ה׳ [...]

ish ed ree-u", u-"Mle-á a-ares deá ed Adonay" [...]

man^{H} OBJ^{H} friend-POSS.3SG.M^{H} and-full-F.SG^{H}DEF-land^{H} knowledge^{H}OBJ^{H} Lord^{H}

every man his neighbor",[81] and "The earth shall be full of the knowledge of the Lord"[82] [...]

ממני יצאו הדברים בשליש ראשון לח[ודש]׳ תשרי מש[נת]׳

Mi-meni yase-ú a-devar-im[83] ba-shelísh rishón le-hódesh tishrí mi-shena-d

from-1SG^{H} depart-PAST.3PL^{H} DEF-word-M.PL^{H}in.DEF-third^{H} first^{H} to-month.CS^{H} Tishre^{H} from-year-CS^{H}

From me these words departed during the first third of the month of Tishre of the year

בחסד ואמת יכופר עון וביראת ה[שם]׳ סור

"Be-hésed ve-emed ye-hupar avón u-v-yira-d A-shem sur

in-mercy^{H} and-truth^{H} FUT-expiate.PASS.3SG.M^{H} iniquity^{H} and-in-fear-CS^{H} DEF-Name^{H} depart.IMP^{H}

"By mercy and truth is iniquity expiated, and by the fear of the Lord depart

מרע לפר[ט]"ק[טן] לחיים טובים ולשלום,

me-rá",[84] li-f[rat]" ka[tán], le-hayim tov-im u-l-shalom,

from-evil^{H} to-specification"^{H} small^{H} to-life^{H} good-M.PL^{H} and-to-peace^{H}

from evil", according to the abbreviated date,[85] and for a good life and peace,

א[ברהם]פ[אלאג]"י זוטרי ס[ופו]"ט[וב]

A[vraam] P[alach]"i zutarí, s[of-ó]" t[ov]

A[vraham] P[alach]i minor^{AM} end-POSS.3SG.M"^{H} good^{H}

A[vraham] P[alach]i the minor [scholar], may his end be good.

80 Cf. Ecclesiastes 11:6.

81 Jeremiah 31:3.

82 Isaiah 11:9.

83 2nd ed.: *beyom za[yin]"ha[f] lehódesh rahamim*/ ביום ז"ך לחודש רחמים, i.e., on the 27th day of the month of Raḥamim (i.e., Elul, called *Raḥamim* 'Mercy' because of the hopes for divine compassion during the month preceding Rosh Hashanah, the Jewish New Year).

84 Cf. Proverbs 16:6.

85 That is, the indication of the Hebrew year alluded to in the verse, without specifying the fifth millennium, resulting from the calculation of the numerical value of the Hebrew letters spelling the word *u-v-yirʔat*/10+200+1+400+[2+]6 = וביראת: i.e., 617 rather than 5617 (i.e., 1856 CE).

3.9 Europeanized Judezmo (as compared with its popular equivalent)

From their earliest days in the Ottoman Empire, Judezmo speakers engaged in trade with Jews and non-Jews from the port cities of Italy, including residents in or visitors to the empire and residents of Italy. One result was a certain Italian linguistic influence on Ottoman Judezmo from as early as the sixteenth century on, especially in lexical spheres related to commerce. From the eighteenth century, the immigration to the empire of *francos* or Christians and Jews from Italy in response to the Ottoman 'capitulations' meant to attract Western Europeans to the empire led to more direct and intensive interaction between speakers of Judezmo and Italian locally. Once in the empire, Italian-speaking Jews and their descendants attained leadership roles, became local commercial entrepreneurs, and served as physicians, educators and supporters of 'progressive' undertakings such as the establishment of a Jewish press in Ottoman Jewish communities, thus further encouraging Judezmo speakers to acquire a knowledge of Italian and incorporate borrowings from it into their spoken and especially literary language.

The colonialist interests of the French, too, resulted in the dissemination of French "civilisation" in the empire and caused the French language to enjoy considerable prestige and commercial use there. The establishment in Paris, 1860, of the Alliance Israélite Universelle, and its subsequent attempts to propogate French language and culture among Jews girls and boys of the empire as a means of westernizing and modernizing them and facilitating their interaction with Western Europeans also led to significant French linguistic influence on Judezmo, especially from the second half of the nineteenth century.

In the regions of the Judezmo-speaking world which fell under Austro-Hungarian influence – in the South Slavic lands, Romania, Hungary, and of course Austria (i.e., Vienna) – Judezmo speakers acquired varying degrees of fluency in German from the late eighteenth century, and their Judezmo began to exhibit clear German influence.

On the whole, the Spaniards demonstrated little or no colonialist interests in the Ottoman regions, and made no attempt to propagate their language there. But individual Spanish men of letters, and particularly the Spanish senator Angel Pulido y Fernández, became aware of the presence in the Ottoman regions, North Africa and elsewhere, of descendants of the Jews who had been expelled from their country in the late fifteenth century. They came to view these Jews, whom Pulido called 'Spaniards without a country', as a potential local Spanish interest group with whose assistance they could promote Spanish interests in the empire. From the second half of the nineteenth century, Pulido and a few other Spaniards urged the Sephardim to replace Judezmo with Spanish. A few Sephardic intellectuals in Vienna and Sarajevo made the attempt, but hardly any Ottoman Sephardim took up the call with any vigor. Nevertheless, a handful of Judezmo writers throughout the region began replacing a few Judezmo elements with their Spanish counterparts (e.g., ב̄ידרה/*veḏrá* > ב̄ירדאד̄/*verdaḏ* 'true', Sp. *verdad*), and incorporated a few words from the Spanish dictionary, interpreted as if Spanish graphemics and phonology were identical with those of French (e.g., ז̄יריגונזה/*jerigonza* [ʒeriˈgonza] 'jargon', vs. Sp. *jerigonza* [χeriˈγonθa/-sa]) – but the words were rejected by most Judezmo speakers.[86] In the final analysis, Spanish may be said to have made only a trivial impact on popular, spoken Judezmo, if one considers only those borrowings in Modern Judezmo which are distinctly Spanish, as opposed to borrowings the origin of which could be attributed to Western Romance in general: e.g., אינטירבֿאלו/*entervalo* 'interval' in the sample text could reflect French *intervalle*, Italian *intervallo*, or Spanish *intervalo*.

Especially from the middle of the nineteenth century, many Ottoman Jews grew dissatisfied with the low social status from which the Jews of the Ottoman regions suffered, and also with the traditional communal Jewish language traditionally associated with them. There was a growing belief that greater social status and economic opportunities could be attained if Judezmo were replaced by a more prestigious Western European language such as French, Italian, and, in regions under Austro-Hungarian influence, German. The result was an increasing tendency among members of the community who had received a western-style rather than traditional Jewish education, to prefer to use a western language – particularly French in the Southeast Judezmo speech region, German in the Northwest – over Judezmo for writing and even for speech.

From the second half of the nineteenth century, writers who continued to create literature in Judezmo grew highly sensitive to the 'language question' and issues concerning the linguistic future of their community. The topic was widely discussed in sober articles and letters published in the Judezmo press, and also in satirical works directly or indirectly touching on the changes the language was undergoing under French and Italian influence, and on the occasional clashes and even misunderstandings arising between those community members who continued to maintain the more traditional, popular varieties of Judezmo, and those whose language evidenced increasing transformation under western influence. The mid-nineteenth century saw the rise of what came to be referred to in the Judezmo press as the נואיבֿו לינגואזֿי / *nuevo linguaje* 'new language' or גֿודֿיזמו פֿראנקיאדֿו / *djudezmo frankeado* 'Europeanized Judezmo', a literary variety bearing the unmistakable imprint of Italian, French, and in areas under Austro-Hungarian influence, German. The first Judezmo periodical to exemplify the incipient use of this variety was Rafaʔel ʕUzziʔel's periodical, *Šaʕare Mizraḥ*, or *Puertas de Oriente* 'Gates of the East' (Izmir, 1845–46). Variants of the variety were quickly adopted by many subsequent Judezmo journalists with a positive orientation toward Western Europe and a critical attitude toward the language and culture which had developed naturally among the Jews of the Ottoman Empire over the four centuries and more since their arrival from Iberia. But some writers, especially those of the second and third generations of Judezmo journalists, rejected the 'new language' in favor of a literary language based on traditional speech – at least for use in fictional depictions of Ottoman Sephardic folk life.

The following satirical sample text from the Southeast region illustrates the coexistence of and growing competition between popular and Europeanized Judezmo for literary and even oral use from the late nineteenth century. In the text, Alexandre Benghiat, a Judezmo journalist in Izmir, poked fun at writers using either style by re-

86 For numerous examples see Bunis 2011a, esp. 377–390.

counting a short tale of frustrated romance in two parallel versions, one אין פֿראנקיאדו/*en frankeaḏo*, i.e., in Westernized Judezmo exhibiting influences from French, Italian and perhaps Castilian, the second אין פארה מינודה / *en pará menuḏa*, 'in smaller change', this ironic designation of the linguistic style itself alluding to the extensive use in popular Judezmo of borrowings drawn from local contact languages, especially Turkish (cf. Tk. *para* 'money'). The rubric of the piece, פֿאנטאזיאה/*Fantazía*, known among Europeanized Judezmo speakers to denote a whimsical piece of make-believe, also reflects the influence on the *lingua frankeaḏa* or 'Europeanized Judezmo' of terms such as French *fantaisie*, Italian *fantasia* and German *Phantasie*.

The Europeanized version of the piece incorporates lexemes which must have struck popular readers of the time as neologistic, high-flown, and not entirely comprehensible, as compared with their older, more familiar and much less pretentious analogues in the 'cheaper' version of the text; the latter analogues were undoubtedly perceived as old-fashioned, somewhat vulgar, and worn-out by those readers who were by then well on the way to Europeanization. The two texts exemplify numerous types of divergences separating the two language styles at all linguistic levels:

Phonologically, the text in Europeanized language (henceforth, LF = *lingua frankeaḏa* 'Europeanized language') illustrates correspondences in borrowings from French and Italian versus their cognates or analogues in more veteran, Hispanic-origin material in popular Judezmo (henceforth, DjK = *djuḏezmo kabá* 'common Judezmo') such as *b* in LF פוסיבלי/*posible* 'possible' (Fr. *possible*), *v* in DjK אמאבֿה/*amava* 'loved'; *an* in borrowings from French in LF such as אנטוסייאסמאדו/*antusyasmaḏo* 'excited' (Fr. *enthousiasmé*) versus *en* in native Hispanisms such as אינשארופאדו/*ensharopaḏo* 'smitten' (cf. OSp. *xaropado* < Ar. *šarab*); *-el* in adjectives from French in LF such as *eternel* 'eternal' vs. corresponding adjectives – all of them of recent Italian, French or Spanish origin in the language – with *-al* such as נאטוראל/*natural* 'natural' (cf. It. *naturale*, Sp. *natural*, but Fr. *naturel*); *-uizir* in verbs borrowed from or influenced by French in LF such as רידואיזיר/*reduizir* 'to reduce' (cf. Fr. *réduire*) versus *-uzir* in older, Hispanic-origin verbs (e.g., רילוזיר/*reluzir* 'to shine', OSp.); the diphthong *ua* in Gallicisms in LF such as טואליטה/*tualeta* 'toilet' vs. *e* in old Judezmo lexemes such as טילה/*tela* 'cloth'; the sequence *-ly-* in Italianisms in LF such as אורגולייוזו/*orgoliozo* (It. *orgoglioso*), corresponding to *-y-* in Hispanisms such as קאייארסי/*kayarse* 'to be quiet' (Sp. *callarse*); and the replacement of French (and sometimes Italian) final *-e* in masculine nouns by Judezmo *-o*, e.g., m. קאלמו/*kalmo* 'calm' (cf. Fr. m. *calme* vs. It., Sp. f. *calma*). In LF adaptations from the Castilian dictionary, the Spanish grapheme *j* was identified with French *j* [ʒ], and thus was transcribed by ז̄ in Judezmo rather than by ח, which would have reflected its actual Spanish realization as [χ], e.g., טארז̄יטה/*tarjeta* 'calling card' in the present text.[87] Morphologically, the incorporation of a borrowing from French or Italian into Judezmo involved the identification of the Gallo-Italic morpheme in the donor form with its Hispanic-origin analogue in the recipient language, and the replacement of the one with the other: e.g., French verbal infinitive-marking *-er* > Judezmo

87 In fact, the Spanish word *tarjeta* simply means 'card' of any kind, but Judezmo speakers perhaps had direct contact with the word only in the context of Spanish calling cards, *tarjetas de visita*. The corresponding term in the DjK version is in fact *karta de vijita*.

-ar, as in *affectionner* > אפיקסייונאר/*afeksyonar* ‘to love’, French *-ement* > Judezmo *-amyento*, as in *dévouement* > דיבֿואמיינטו/*devuamyento* ‘devotion’.

The DjK:LF lexical correspondences occurring in the text illustrate the extensive relexification of popular Judezmo, primarily under the influence of French and Italian, which produced Europeanized Judezmo. The result was an increasingly palpable distinction between what western-educated speakers began to perceive as the ‘ordinary’ or even ‘low’ prestige variety of the language (DjK), composed primarily of popular Hispanisms, Turkish-Balkanisms and Hebraisms, and what they came to consider the ‘high’ prestige variety (LF), rich in Gallo-Italianisms. The disparity between the two varieties is illustrated by the following correspondences in the two versions of the text:

	‘Ordinary’ or ‘low’ variety (*“en pará menuḏa”* = Dj[uḏezmo]K[abá])	‘High’ variety (*“en frankeaḏo”* = L[ingua]F[rankeaḏa])
Nouns and noun phrases	*ombre* (cf. Sp. *hombre*)	*individuo* (cf. It., Sp. *individuo*)
	manyas dulses (cf. Sp. *mañas dulces*)	*karákter naívo* (cf. Fr. *caractère*; *naïf*, *-ve*)
	repozo (cf. OSp. *reposo*)	*kalmo* (Fr. *calme*)
	kamareta onde eya se atakanava i se vestía (OSp. *camareta, donde, se vestía*; Tk. *takın-*)	*kabineto de tualeta* (It. *gabinetto*; Fr. *cabinet de toilette*)
	terbiyetsizlik (cf. Tk. *terbiyesizlik*)	*deskortéz* (cf. Sp. *descortés*)
Verbs and verbal expressions	*amar* (cf. Sp.)	*afeksyonar* (cf. Fr. *affectionner*)
	dezir (cf. OSp. *dezir*)	*komunikar* (cf. Fr. *communiquer*, It. *comunicare*, Sp. *comunicar*)
	irse para (Sp.)	*dirijirse verso* (cf. Fr. *se diriger vers*, It. *dirigersi verso*, Sp. *dirigirse hacia*)
	entrar (Sp.)	*entrodu(i)zirse* (cf. Fr. *s’introduire*)
	entender (Sp.)	*aperseverse de* (cf. Fr. *s’apercevoir de*)
	boltarse atrás (cf. Pt. *voltar atrás*)	*retornarse sovre sus pasos* (cf. Fr. *se retourner*)
	azerse triaki (OSp. *hazerse*, Tk. *tıryakı*)	*(deshar) molestar su amor propyo* (cf. It. *molestare il suo amor proprio*, etc.)
Adjectival expressions	*muy de muy feḏorento* (OSp. *muy*, *de*, *fedor* + *-ento*)	*sin límito* (cf. It. *senza limiti*)
Adverbs and adverbial expressions	*para* Adverbs... | *para* | *verso*	*verso* ‘toward’ (cf. Fr. *vers*, It. *verso*)
	para syempre (Sp.)	*eternel* (cf. Fr. *eternel*)
	para esto (Sp.)	*a este efeto* (cf. Fr. *à cet effet*, It. *effetto*)
Conjunctions	*para*	*afín de* (cf. Fr. *afin de*, Sp. *a fin de*, It. *al fine di*,)

Some of the correspondences in the two versions of the text seem to shed light on the author’s perception of the historical origins of the pairs of lexemes he used. For example, Benghiat used רימיטיר/*remeter* ‘to deliver’ in the DjK version, corresponding to פריזינטאר/*prezentar* in the LF version (cf. Fr. *présenter*), although its sense more closely corresponds to French *remettre* ‘offer, present’ than to Spanish *remeter* (‘to re-enter, ‘to tuck in’) and thus it would appear to be a Gallicism. Benghiat identified the terms מאנסיבֿו/*mansevo* ‘young man’ and מוג̃אג̃ה/*muchacha* ‘lass’ (in the Izmir dialect), which are widely used in popular Judezmo, as part of the older, native (i.e., Hispanic-origin) lexicon, while synonymous גֿובֿין/*djoven* and גֿובֿינה/*djóvena* were apparently perceived as borrowings, perhaps under the influence of It. m./f. *giovane*, Fr. m./f. *jeune* – although Judezmo גֿובֿין/*djoven* is in fact probably as old as the language itself, cf. Sp. *joven* 'young man/woman'. (On the other hand, the *-n* vs. *-na* gender distinction in this pair of modern Judezmo words perhaps points to the influence of French pairs such as *chien* 'male dog' vs. *chienne* 'female dog', having an overtly-marked gender distinction, since Judezmo speakers perceive French feminine *-e* as corresponding to Judezmo feminine *-a*). Similarly, the indefinite article appears in the phrase אנסי אונה מוזֿיר / *ansí una mujer* 'such a woman' in both the DjK and LF versions, although this construction would seem to be rooted in a fusion of foreign constructions such as French *une telle femme* and Italian *una tale donna* / *una donna così* (vs. Sp. *tal mujer* [rare *una tal mujer*]).

Some usages involving borrowings from French and Italian seem to reflect influence from the Hispanic origins of the language and diverge from actual French or Italian usage. For example, אפֿיקסייונאדה/*afeksyona<u>d</u>a* is used in the text as a free-standing feminine noun denoting the 'loved one' – as opposed to the more restricted use of *affectionnée* as an attributive adjective in French – on analogy with Hispanic-origin pairs in Judezmo such as *kerer* 'to love', *keri<u>d</u>a* the 'loved one' (cf. Sp. *querer*, *querida*). In some instances, Benghiat uses recent European borrowings in both the LF and DjK text versions, e.g., LF דיסידירסי פור / *desidirse por* = DjK דיטירמינארסי פור / *determinarse por* 'to make up one's mind to' (cf. Sp. *decidirse*, *determinarse*), thus suggesting that he does not recognize the latter as imports from French or Spanish.

Interestingly, Benghiat incorporates in the LF version several words belonging to the lexicon of the calque-translation language traditionally used in rendering traditional Hebrew or Aramaic texts in the vernacular; these correspond to more everyday lexemes in the DjK version. Judezmo speakers tend to sense that some such words are archaic, stylized and not part of everyday speech (as some are, in fact, in Spanish as well); perhaps Benghiat identified them as being part of Castilian and thus suitable for use in the somewhat artificial LF version of his story: e.g., LF דואינייו/*duenyo* (cf. Sp. *dueño*) vs. DjK פאטרון/*patrón* 'owner'; LF אלדיאה/*aldea* (Sp.) vs. DjK קאזאל/*kazal* 'village'; LF אלבֿוראדה/*alvora<u>d</u>a* (OSp. *alb-/alvorada*, MSp. *alborada*) vs. DjK דימאדרוגאדה/*demadruga<u>d</u>a* 'dawn'; LF ארריינדה/*aryenda* vs. DjK גֿיפֿליק/*chiflik* 'plantation' and ארריינדירו/*aryendero* 'plantation owner' (vs. DjK איל/*el* 'he'); LF מוסה/*mosa* 'lass' (cf. Sp. *moza*) vs. DjK מוגֿאגֿה/*muchacha* 'lass'. Nevertheless, Benghiat's use of קאמפו/*kampo* in the sense of 'farm' would suggest influence from French *champ*, although the word appears in biblical calque translations in the Spanish sense of 'field' (*campo*).

Perhaps most characteristic for Benghiat of the popular as opposed to Europeanized register was the rich Turkish-Balkan component which popular Judezmo included. Examples of lexemes belonging to this component which Benghiat used in the DjK version include nouns and adjectives referring to behavior: טירביליייטסיזליק/*terbiyetsizlik* 'discourtesy' (cf. Tk. *terbiyesizlik* < Ar. *tarbiye* + *tā marbūṭa* [cf. Per. *terbiye(t)*] + Tk. *-siz* + *-lik*), טריאקי/*triakí* 'depressed' (cf. Tk. *tıryakı* < Ar. *tiryāqī* < Gk. *thēriakē*); to agriculture: גֿיפֿליק/*chiflik* 'plantation' (cf. Tk. *çiftlik*); and to grooming: אטאקאנארסי/*atakanarse* 'to make one's toilette' (cf. Tk. *takın-*, with possible influence from Hebrew ת־ק־ן/*t-q-n* 'to repair, put in order').

3.10 Sample Text: Twentieth-Century Europeanized Judezmo (and its Popular Analogue)

[Alexandre Benghiat], *El Meseret*/איל מֿיסירֿיט 25:36 (Izmir, 1921), p. 3:

פֿאנטאזיאה

Fantazía

Fantasy

אין פרֿאנקיאדו:

En frankeaḏo:

In Europeanized_language

In Europeanized language:

און אינדיבֿידואו, דואינייו די אונה אריינדה, אפֿיקסייונאבֿה אה אונה מוסה

Un individuo, duenyo de un-a aryenda, afeksiyon-ava a un-a mosa

INDF.M.SG individual squire of INDF-F.SG estate love-IMPF.3SG OBJ INDF-F.SG maiden

A certain individual, the squire of an estate, adored a maiden

די לה אלדיאה בֿיזינה. אנטוסייאסמאדו סובֿרי טודו פור איל קאראקטיר נאאיבֿו

de la aldea vezin-a. Antusyasmaḏ-o sovre toḏo por el karákter naív-o

in DEF.F.SG hamlet adjacent-F.SG excited-M.SG over all by DEF.M.SG character naïve-M.SG

the adjacent hamlet. Excited in particular by the naïve character

די לה ניניה, אי קונסיבֿיינדו פור אילייה און איטירניל דיבֿואמיינטו,

de la ninya, i konsiv-yendo por eya un eternel devuamyento,

of DEF.F.SG girl and feel-GERUND for PRON.PREP.3SG.F INDF.M.SG eternal devotion

of the young lady, and overcome by a sense of eternal devotion for her,

איל אריינדירו סי דיסידייו פור קומוניקארסילו.

el aryendero se desid-yó por komunik-ár-se-lo.

DEF.M.SG squire REF.3 resolve-PRET.3SG to communicate-INF-DAT.3-N.SG

the squire resolved to communicate this to her.

אה איסטי איפֿיטו, אה לה אלבֿוראדה די און דיאה די קאלמו, איל סי

A est-e efeto, a la alvoraḏa de un día de kalmo, el se

to PROX-M.SG end at DEF.F.SG dawn of INDF.M.SG day of serenity 3SG REF.3

Toward this end, at the dawn of a calm day, he

דיריזֿו בֿירסו איל קאמפו די סו אפֿיקסייונאדה אי, פריזינטאנדולי

dirij-ó verso el kampo de su afeksyonaḏa i, prezent-ándo-le

direct-PRET.3SG towards DEF.M.SG farm of 3SG.POSS beloved_woman and present-GER-DAT.3SG

directed himself toward the farm of his beloved and, presenting to her

סו טארזֿיטה, סי אינטרודושֿו אין סו קאבֿיניטו די טואליטה.

su tarjeta,se entrod-usho en su kabineto de tualeta.

his card REF.3 introduce-PRET.3SG in POSS.3 room of toilette

his card, he was introduced into her toilette room.

אורגולייוזה סין לימיטו, לה גֿובֿינה רידואיזייו לה בֿיזֿיטה

Orgolyoz-a sin límito, la djóvena reduiz-yó la vijita

conceited-F.SG without.ADV limit DEF.F.SG young_woman reduce-PRET.3SG DEF.F.SG visit

Conceited beyond measure, the young woman reduced his visit

אל מאס קורטו אינטירבֿאלו די טיימפו פוסיבלי, אי איל גֿובֿין, קי
al mas kort-o entervalo de tyempo posible, i el djoven, ke
to.DEF.M.SG moreshort-M.SG interval of time possible and DEF.M.SG young_man REL
to the shortest interval possible, and the young man, who

סי אפירסיבֿייו די איסטה טינידה דיסקורטיז, ריטורנו סובֿרי
se apersev-yó de esta tenida deskortéz, retorn-ó sovre
REF.3 notice-PRET.3SG of PROX.F.SG meeting discourteous return-PRET.3SG on.ADV
noticed this discourteous meeting, retraced

סוס פאסוס פארה מאס נו דישאר מוליסטאר סו אמור פרופייו פור אנסי
su-s paso-s para mas no desh-ar molest-ar su amor propy-o por ansí
POSS.3PL step-PL for more no allow-INF disturb-INF POSS.3 dignity self-M.SG by such-ADV
his steps, never again to allow his pride to be wounded by such

אונה סינייורה.
una sinyora.
INDF.F.SG lady
a lady.

אין פארה מינודה:
En pará menud-a:
In money small-F.SG
In cheap currency [i.e., the same narrative, in more popular language]:

און אומברי, פאטרון די און גֿיפֿליק, אמאבֿה אה אונה מוגֿאגֿה
Un ombre, patrón de un chiflik, am-ava a un-a muchacha
INDF.M.SG man owner of INDF.M.SG farm love-IMPF.3SG OBJ INDF-F.SG girl
A man, the owner of a farm, loved a girl

דיל קאזאל בֿיזינו. אינשֿארופאדו סובֿרי טודו פור לאס
del kazal vezin-o. Ensharopad-o sovre todo por las
from.DEF.M.SG village neighboring-M.SG sweetened-M.SG above all by DEF.F.PL
in the nearby village. Smitten especially by the

מאנייאס דולסיס די לה מוגֿאגה, אי קיזֿינדו סאקרֿיפֿיקארסי אה אילייה
manya-s dulse-s de la muchacha, i kij-endo sakrifik-ar-se a eya
habit-PL sweet-PL of DEF.F.SG girl and want-GER dedicate-INF-REF.3 to PRON.PREP.3SG.F
sweet habits of the girl, and wanting to dedicate himself to her

פארה סיימפרי, איל סי דיטירמינו פור דיזירסילו.
para syempre, el se determin-ó por dez-ír-se-lo.
for always 3SG.M REF.3 resolve-PRET.3SG for say-INF-REF.3-PRON.ACC.3SG.M
forever, he resolved to tell her so.

פארה איסטו, אין לה דימאדרוגאדה די און דיאה די ריפוזו, איל סי פֿואי
Para esto, en la demadrugada de un día de repozo, el se fue
for this in DEF.F.SG dawn of INDF.M.SG day of quiet 3SG REF.3 go-PRET.3SG
For this, at the break of one quiet day, he went

פארה איל קאזאל די סו קירידה אי, רימיטיינדולי סו קארטה די בֿיזֿיטה,
para el kazal de su keriḏa i, remet-yéndo-le su karta de vijita,
to DEF.M.SG village of his beloved and hand_over-GER-PRON.DAT.3SG 3SG.POSS card of visit
to his beloved's village and, handing over his visitor's card,

אינטרו אין לה קאמאריטה אונדי איליה סי אטאקאנאבֿה אי
entr-ó en la kamareta onde eya se atakan-ava i
enter-PRET.3SG in DEF.F.SG room where-ADV 3SG.F REF.3 beautify-IMPF.3SG and
he entered the room where she applied her makeup and

סי בֿיסטיאה.
se vest-ía.
REF dress-IMPF.3.SG
dressed.

סי קומו איליה אירה מויי די מויי פֿידורינטה, לה מוגֿאגֿה
Si komo eya era muy de muy feḏorent-a, la muchacha
Since she be-IMPF.3SG very INT very conceited-F.SG DEF.F.SG girl
Since she was really stuck-up, the girl

אקורטו מונגֿו לה בֿיזֿיטה, אי איל מאנסיבֿו, קי אינטינדייו
akort-ó muncho la vijita, i el mansevo, ke entend-yó
cut-PRET.3SG much.ADV DEF.F.SG visit and DEF.M.SG young man REL understand-PRET.3SG
cut his visit very short, and the young fellow, who understood

איל טירביאיטסיזליק, סי בולטו אטראס, אפֿין די נו אזירסי טריאקי
el terbietsizlik, se bolt-ó atrás, afín de no az-er-se triakí
DEF.M.SG rudeness REF.3 turn-PRET.3SG back-ADV in_order_to.CONJ NEG do-INF-REF.3 depressed
the rudeness, turned back home, so as not to get depressed

פור אנסי אונה מוזֿיר.
por ansí un-a mujer.
for such.ADV DEF-F.SG woman
over such a woman.

3.11 Modern literary Judezmo based on popular language

For factual journalistic reportage aimed at the more westernized sectors of the speech community, most Judezmo writers preferred to use *djuḏezmo frankeaḏo* 'Europeanized Judezmo'. But among those who intentionally wrote for the popular sectors, and especially those imbued with a sense that, over the centuries, the Ottoman Sephardim had created a rich, unique Jewish group language from the diverse linguistic raw materials at their disposal – a language the future of which was increasingly endangered due to competition from the *nuevo linguaje* 'new language' and, ultimately, from local state and international prestige languages to which increasing numbers of Judezmo speakers were transferring – the *djuḏezmo kabá* 'popular variety' was the more favored register.[88] In it, such writers consciously sought to create "authentic" ethnic literature, pictures of everyday life, as it were, documenting for posterity the Ottoman Sephardic folk community, its life style, typical characters, institutions, and habits and customs which the

88 On the 'Judezmist' ideology of such writers, see Bunis 2011b; 2012.

writers – themselves already highly westernized – recognized as on the very brink of disappearance as a result of the rapid westernization and secularization their community was undergoing. The sample text below is an exemplary representative of Judezmo creative writing based on the Jewish folk idiom of Salonika. Its author's nostalgic reminiscences of the custom of summoning the community's men to early-morning prayers before *el Fuego* – the catastrophic Great Salonika Fire of August 1917[89] – brought to his mind the people of the past generation who had maintained the custom, their patterns of behavior and turns of speech; his mental recreation naturally lent itself to expression using the language of the individuals recalled.

In the piece, the reader will not find the plethora of Gallo-Italianisms which constitute the *sine quibus non* of the 'new language'; nevertheless, by the time the piece was written, many such elements had already been incorporated in popular speech and especially writing, and several of them appear here. With the exception of the common noun *depó* 'depot' (Fr. *dépôt*, also Tk. reflex *depo*) and the indefinite adjective *kualunke* 'any' (cf. It. *cualunque*), these are literary terms, used in the piece as transitional or contradictory elements in relating the story: *malgra̱do* 'despite' (cf. It. *malgrado*, also Fr. *malgré*), *vizaví de* 'in relation to' (Fr. *vis-à-vis*), *portanto* 'nevertheless' (Fr. *pourtant*), *enfin* (Fr. *enfin*, It. *infine*, vs. Sp. *por fin*). In the middle of this for the most part popular-styled piece, the author reminded the editor of the periodical, to whom the piece was ostensibly addressed, that both the writer and the editor were themselves members of the Europeanized sector of Jewish Salonika who rejoiced in the use of such expressions, by switching to French in mid-piece and addressing him with the words: *Or, mon sher Chaketón* (Fr. *Or, mon cher Chaketón*).

Nevertheless, as in everyday popular Judezmo of the period, the lion's share of the Romance component employed in the piece reflects the popular Hispanisms used among rank-and-file Judezmo speakers for generations. These lexemes diverge from their normative Spanish analogues; some are unique to Judezmo. Exemplifying large categories of such elements in Judezmo, those appearing in the text include:

• forms characteristic of the author's local regional dialect, e.g., *fazerse* 'to become' (cf. Istanbul Jud. *azerse*, OSp. *fazerse*, MSp. *hacerse*);

• forms corresponding to analogues in popular Spanish, e.g., *myentres* 'during', *delantre de* 'before' (normative Spanish *mientras*, *delante de*), and lexemes with *m* rather than *n* before the [w] glide (e.g., *muevo* 'new', Sp. *nuevo*);[90]

• forms corresponding to variants which had existed in medieval Spanish but were rejected in the later normative language, such as the verbs *kombidar* 'to invite' (cf. premodern Sp. *combidar*, MSp. *invitar*), *despareser* 'to disappear' (cf. OSp. *desparecer*, MSp. *desaparecer*, perhaps with influence from Fr. *disparaître*), and finite verb forms such as *estó* 'I am' (< *estar* 'to be'), *ía* 'I was going', *vía* 'I was seeing' (Sp. *estoy*, *iba*, *veía*);

• forms resembling correspondents in non-Castilian varieties of Ibero-Romance, e.g., *inda* 'still' (cf. Pt. *ainda*, Gal. *aínda*), *a poko a poko* 'little by little' (cf. Cat. *a poc a poc*), and the modal expression *kale ke* 'one must' (cf. Cat. *cal*);

89 See Papastathis and Hekimoglou 2010.

90 In this and the subsequent uses of "Sp.", the reference is to contemporary normative Spanish.

• distinctive Judezmo phonological forms such as *akodrarse* 'to recall' (with metathesis of historical *rð* > *ðr*; Sp. *acordarse*), *luvia* 'rain' (with depalatalization of historical initial [ʎ] to [l] when a later syllable contains a [j] glide; Sp. *lluvia*), and (f.pl.) *akeas* 'those' (with the loss of a reflection of historical [ʎ] (Sp. <ll>) in forms in which it was historically preceded by a front vowel and followed by another vowel; Sp. *aquellas*);
• distinctive lexical forms such as the substantives *nochada* 'evening' (Sp. *noche*), *empajada* 'pitcher' (Sp. *jarra*, *cántaro*), the adjective *aperkantado* 'under a spell' (cf. Lat. *praecantatio*), and the adverb *ande* 'where' (Sp. *donde*);
• numerical formulations rejected in normative Spanish, e.g., *syen i sinkuenta (anyos)* '150 (years)' (Sp. *ciento cincuenta*);
• interjections meant to grant blessing, such as *Sus ijos ... ke bivan* 'His children ... may they live!' and to override the evil eye, such as *De muerte non!* 'May such a difficult state not be the result of death!';
• morpho-syntactic characteristics such as first-person plural pronouns with *m-* rather than *n-* before *o* or the *u* glide (e.g., *mos* 'us', *muevo* 'new'; Sp. *nos*), the pronoun *mi* rather than *yo* being used after *komo [a]* (Sp. *como yo* 'like me'), and *debasho* + noun 'under' (Sp. *debajo de*).
• idiomatic constructions such as *ande ay de dar dyente i de travar algún mekam* 'where there's something to sink your teeth into and some tune to sing out';
• elements carrying primary senses distinct from their Spanish counterparts, e.g., *sentir* Judezmo 'to hear' (cf. Sp. *lo siento* 'I'm sorry').

There is also a significant popular Hebrew-Aramaic component, including lexemes denoting practices and concepts standing at the epicenter of traditional Sephardic Jewish life – *sabá* 'the Sabbath' (Heb. שבת/*šabbat*), *pizmonim* 'religious hymns' (Heb. פזמונים/*pizmonim*), the *zemirod* (Heb. זמירות/*zĕmirot*) prayers, or *primera tefillá* 'first (i.e., morning) prayer' (Heb. תפלה/*tĕfilla*/),[91] and *selihod* 'penitential prayers' (Heb. סליחות/*sĕliḥot*) to which the men recalled in the piece are called to recite; the *hazán* (Heb. חזן/*ḥazzan*) 'cantor' who leads the prayers, the *minyán* (Heb. מנין/*minyan*/) or 'prayer quorum' required for public prayers, and the *azer la agbaá* (Heb. הגבהה/*hagbaha*) or 'elevation of the Torah scroll' during the prayer service.

But not all lexemes of Hebrew-Aramaic origin have a direct relation to the practice of Judaism; some references, such as abstract concepts, body parts (represented in the text by *garón* 'throat', Heb. גרון/*garon*), and parts of speech other than substantives are also denoted by Hebrew-Aramaisms. The text includes characteristic fusion formations combining morphemes of Hebrew and other origins, such as *henozo* 'graceful' (cf. Heb. חן/*ḥen*+ OSp. *-oso*), the hypocoristic common noun form *midraziko* 'little study hall', occurring in the text together with its primitive form, *midrash* (Heb. מדרש/*midraš*), and the hypocoristic forms of the masculine personal names, *Daviko* (< *David*, cf. Heb. דוד / *David*+ Jud. *-iko* [Sp. *-ico*]), *Moshón* (< *Moshé*, cf. Heb. משה/*Moše*+ Jud. *-ón* [Sp.]), *Avramaki* (< *Avram*, cf. Heb. אברהם/*ʔAvraham*+ Jud. *-aki* < Gk. *-áki*]). The text also in-

91 The word is realized by some speakers with geminated *l*:. Although there is historical justification for this (cf. Heb. *tĕfilla*), perhaps it is actually the result of influence by Turkish words of Arabic origin such as *Allah*, *bismillah*. Such gemination in Judezmo seems only to occur with the resonants *l*, *n*, *m*, and *r*.

cludes the rhetorical question expression *Aitahén baolam?* 'Is such a thing possible?" (Heb. ?הייתכן בעולם / *ha-yittaḵen ba-ʕolam?*); and innovative usages such as "*beshem* x", literally 'in the name of x', but meaning 'whenever x is concerned' (and thus, *beshem ziafet* 'whenever there is a feast'). The personal names of local heros appear in their distinctive Judezmo forms: e.g., *Shemuel, Yakó* (שמואל/*Šĕmu'el*, יעקב/*Yaʕaqov*).[92] The traditional honorific title *Han* (< *haham* 'rabbinical scholar' < Heb. חכם/*ḥaḵam*) precedes the textual reference to *Moshón*, and *Harbí* (< *haham ribí* < Heb. חכם רבי / *ḥaḵam ribbi*) precedes *Saul* (Heb. שאול/*Šaʔul*); while the memorial expression *alav ashalom* 'peace upon him' (Heb. עליו השלום / *ʕalaw ha-šalom*) is added after the name of a deceased person, *Liau Koén* (Heb. אליהו כהן / *ʔEliyyahu Kohen*). As characteristic of popular Judezmo, some elements of Jewish realia are denoted both by their Hebrew-origin names and their Hispanic-origin equivalents: *séfer torá / livro de la ley* 'book of the Law (i.e., Torah scroll)'. The text even provides a fragment illustrating the popular realization of a Whole Hebrew-Aramaic blessing used after mentioning the Name of God: *Baruhú barúshemó, amén* (Heb. ברוך הוא וברוך שמו, אמן / *baruḵ hu u-varuḵ šĕmo, ʔamen*).[93]

The elements of Turkish-Balkan origin in the text represent the culmination of the process begun at the beginning of the sixteenth century whereby Judezmo speakers incorporated elements from local languages, especially popular urban Turkish, reflecting their acclimatization to the everyday milieu, animate and inanimate, which became familiar to and relished by Ottoman Judezmo speakers. Over the centuries, the speech group selectively assimilated elements from their surroundings, making them a part of the Ottoman Jewish identity, particularly with respect to cuisine and costume, music and folklore, and at the linguistic level, intimate colloquial language as well as more abstract expression. The text offers numerous examples of the wide range of semantic fields containing representatives from the Ottoman-Balkan lexicon; it also demonstrates the unique Judezmo adaptation of such elements at the phonological, morphological, and stylistic levels.

The endearing title of address, *kuzum* 'my dear' (Tk. *kuzum*), for example, is one of many such terms and phrases of endearment borrowed from Turkish; while *papú* 'grandpa' (Gk. *pappoús*) exemplifies local terms incorporated into the kinship lexicon.

The fields of entertainment, leisure-time diversions, music and art as practiced in the Ottoman regions are represented by the name for a typical Ottoman Sephardic-style feast, *ziafet* (Tk. *ziyafet* < Ar. *ḍiyāfa* + *tāʔ marbūṭa*), by a term for festive enjoyment, *djimbush* (Tk. *cümbüş*), and by the name given to an Ottoman-style melody or musical mode, *mekam* (Tk. *makam* < Ar. *maqām*). The traditional Ottoman-fashioned articles of clothing worn by Judezmo speakers before westernization in the modern era are exemplified textually by *kirín* 'men's fur-lined overcoat' (Tk. *kırım*), *kushak* 'sash' (Tk. *kuşak*), *rizá* 'handkerchief' (cf. Tk. *rida* < Ar. *ridāʔ*, Blg. *rizá* 'shirt'), *fezezika* 'small fez hat' (Tk. *fes* + Jud. [< Sp.] hypocoristic *-ezika*), *konduryas de papuchi* (cf. Tk. *kundura* + Jud. [< Sp.] *-ia*, *pabuç*; Gk. *papoútsia*). The lexical component relating to agriculture,

92 On the popular phonological realization of Hebraisms in Judezmo see Crews 1962.

93 For an analysis of the popular realization of Hebrew among the Jews of Spain, which is reflected in Modern Judezmo, see Bunis 2013b.

a vocation practiced by, and associated by the Jews with, the Turks, is represented by *(lana) yerlía* 'locally-derived (wool)' (cf. Tk. *yerli* + Jud. [< Sp.] femininizing *-a*). A Turkism representing denotations of the physical surroundings, one of the many other semantic fields put into words by Judezmo speakers using borrowings from Turkish, is *kyushé* 'corner' (Tk. *köşe*). Many local regions, cities, and neighborhoods and quarters inhabited by or known to the Jews carried Judezmo names of local origin, as illustrated in the text by *Chamekchí* (evidently deriving from the name of a local mosque),[94] *el Kalvasará* (cf. Tk. *Kervansaray* 'caravansary, or inn with a central courtyard for travellers'),[95] and *el Medán* (cf. Tk. *meydan* 'square, large open space'). By World War II many such names – especially those of Turkish origin in the newly-established Balkan states – had been replaced by others, of Balkan origin, just as many of the Ottoman architectural structures distinguishing them were replaced by new buildings.

The local contributions to the Judezmo lexicon were not limited to nouns; the wide range of semantic spheres represented by non-substantive borrowings, as well as the morphological devices used to incorporate free and bound morphemes of local origins into the Judezmo grammatical system, are represented by verbs and derivational forms in the text expressing emotion and psychological state, such as *embrenear (el alma)* 'to cheer up (the soul)' (Tk. *imren-* + Sp. *-ear*), *churudear* 'to wear out' (Tk. *çürü-*, 3sg. past def. *çürüdü*), *dignidear* 'to recover one's senses' (Tk. *dikil-*), *soreado* 'used up', p.part. of *sorear* 'to use up' (Tk. *sür-*).

The rich inventory of Turkish-origin Judezmo interjections, exclamations, blessings and oaths is represented by the exclamation *ayde!* (Tk. *haydi*), used to draw someone's attention. Judezmo speakers also borrowed from their neighbors techniques of wordplay and linguistic irony, some based on the semantic distinctiveness of near homophones belonging to the diverse etymological components of Judezmo, as exemplified by the writer's ironic warning to the reader not to misread בוז, here meant to denote *boz* 'voice' (OSp.), as *buz* 'ice' (Tk.), both lexemes traditionally spelled identically in the traditional alphabet. Illustrating the tendency of Judezmo writers to avoid lexical monotony through the use in a single text of nearly synonymous terms and expressions deriving from different etymological components of the language, the writer expressed the rhetorical question 'Is such a thing possible?' both by means of Hebrew-origin *Ayitahén baolam?* (discussed above) and Turkish-origin *Uchulurme?* (Tk. *güç olur mu* 'Would it be difficult?'). The text is an exemplary illustration of the use of popular Judezmo, complemented here and there by elements from other registers of the modern language, as the basis for distinctively culturally-embedded creative writing. Orthographically, too, the piece exemplifies the ultimate popularization of the Hebrew-letter orthography. Hebrew-origin words are often spelled phonemically, e.g., *tefillá*/טיפֿיללה instead of תפלה for 'prayer', and the occasional use of double *reš* (רר) to represent trilled [r], e.g., *tarrasika*/טאררסיקה 'little terrace', alternating with *tarasika*/טאראסיקה.

94 The reference is unclear: perhaps it refers to the Akça/Akçe Mescid/-t (> Jud. *Chamekchí*?) Mahallesi, a neighborhood in Salonika centered around the mosque by that name (Sarısakal, [3]); or possibly to the name of a Jewish dispensary once maintained in the city's Aghias Triados neighborhood. Warm thanks to Dr. E.A. Hekimoglou and Mr. Jacky Benmayor of Thessaloniki for the second suggestion.

95 Perhaps Hamza Bey Kervansarayı (Sarısakal, [11]).

3.12 Sample text: Twentieth-Century Literary Judezmo Based on Popular Language
"Charlemagne", *El Chaketón* / 3:27 איל גֿאקיטון (Salonika 1922), p. 2

ייה אימפיסארון לאס זמירות!

Ya empes-aron las zemir-od!
already.ADV start-PRET.3PL DEF.F.PL prayer-F.PL[h]
They've already started the first morning prayers!

קוזום גֿאקיטון,

Kuzum Chaketón,
Dear.INTERJ Chaketón (lit: a hit, blow)
My dear Chaketón,

אונה נוגֿי די לה סימאנה פאסאדה, לה בורינה די לה לובֿייה קי

Un-a noche de la semana pasad-a, la borina de la luvya ke
One.NUM-F.SG night of DEF.F.SG week last-F.SG DEF.F.SG torrent of DEF.F.SG rain REL
One night last week, the torrential rain that

מוס גֿורודיאו – די מואירטי נון – אינטירוס,

mos churude-ó – de muerte non!– enter-os,
PRON.ACC.1PL wear out-PRET.3SG of death NEG complete-M.PL
wore us out – but not to the point of death! – through and through,

מי אובֿליגו אה קידארמי אין לה קאזה די

me ovlig-ó a ked-ar-me en la kaza de
PRON.ACC.1SG obligate-PRET.3SG to remain-INF-REFL.1SG in DEF.F.SG house of
forced me to stay in the home of

אונו די מיס נומירוזוס אמיגוס פור איל גֿאמיקגֿי,

un-o de mi-s numeroz-os amigo-s por el Chamekchí,
one.NUM-M.SG of 1SG.POSS-PL numerous-M.PL friend.M-PL by DEF.M.SG Chamekchí
one of my numerous friends in Chamekchí [or Akça/Akçe Mescid/-t Mahallesi],

אנדי אובֿו און זיאפֿיט. איסטו ייה סי קי נון

ande uv-o un ziafet. Est-o ya se ke non
where there is-PRET.3SG INDF.M.SG feast PROX-N.SG already.ADV know.PRS.1SG REL NEG
where there was a feast. This, I know, will not

טי בֿה בֿיניר די מֿואיבו, סיינדו טו, קומו טודו איל מונדו,

te va ven-ir de muevo, syendo tu, komo todo el mundo,
2SG.DAT go.PRS.3SG arrive-INF of new be.GER 2SG like.ADV all.M.SG DEF.M.SG world
be new for you, since you, like everyone else,

ייה סאבֿיס קי, בישים זיאפֿיט או קואלונקי גֿימבוש אנדי

ya save-s ke, beshem ziafet o kualunke djimbush ande
already.ADV know-PRS.2SG REL every.[96]ADJ[H] feast or any.SG entertainment where.ADV
already know that, whenever there's a feast or any festive gathering where

איי די דאר דיינטי אי די טראבֿאר אלגון מיקאם חינוזו, אה מי

ay de dar dyente i de trav-ar algún mekam henoz-o, a mi
there_is.PRS of give.INF tooth and of pull-INF some.M.SG tune lovely-M.SG to PRON.PREP.1SG
there's something to sink your teeth into and some lovely tune to sing out, I'm the one

96 Literally, 'in the name of'.

קאלי קי קומבידין אימפרימירו. אור, מון שיר גֿאקיטון, גֿוסטו
kal-e ke kombid̲-en emprimero. Or, mon sher Chaketón, djusto
need.to-PRS.3SG REL invite-SUBJ.PRS-3PL firstly.ADV now[Fr] my[Fr] dear[Fr] Chaketón precisely.ADV
they have to invite first. Now, my dear Chaketón, precisely

אין איל מומינטו אנדי, דיספואיס די אבֿיר בֿאזייאדו לה אולטימה אימפאזֿאדה
en el momento ande, después de av-er vazy-ad̲o la últim-a empajad̲a
in DEF.M.SG moment where after of have.PFV-INF pour-PTCP DEF.F.SG last-F.SG pitcher
at the moment when, after having drained the last pitcher

די בֿינו, אי סוריאדו לו פוקו די בוס (מילדאד בוֹז אי נו בוּז),
de vino, i sore-ad̲o lo poko de bos (meldad̲ <boz> i no <buz>),
of wine and use.up-PTCP DEF.N.SG little of voice read.IMP.2PL voice and NEG ice
of wine and used up what little voice (read *voice*, not *ice*) was left,

אין איל פונטו, דיגו, אנדי מוס איסטאבֿאמוס אפארייזֿאנדו אה
en el punto, dig-o, ande mos est-ávamos aparej-ando a
in DEF.M.SG moment say-PRS.1.SG where REF.1PL AUX-IMPF.1PL ready-GER to
at that moment, I say, when we were getting ready to

אינקאשארמוס דיבאשו לה קולגֿה, קומו און גריטו מי
enkash-ar-mos debasho la kolcha, komo un grito me
insert-INF-REF.1PL under DEF.F.SG blanket like INDF.M.SG scream PRON.DAT.1SG
climb under the blanket, like a scream I

פאריסייו סינטיר:
pares-yó sent-ir:
seem-PRET.3SG hear-INF
seemed to hear:

– איידי, אירמאנוס! איידי, קי ייה אימפיסארון לאס
– Ayde, ermano-s! Ayde, ke ya empes-aron las
get_going.INTERJ brother-M.PL get_going.INTERJ REL already.ADV start-PRET.3PL DEF.F.PL
– Come on, brothers! Come on, 'cause they've already started the

זמירות!
zemir-od̲!
prayer-F.PL[h]
first morning prayers!

מאראבֿיאדו, אפירקאנטאדו, ייו אקוסטי אוריזֿה. ייו נו מי
Maraviad̲-o, aperkantad̲-o, yo akost-í oreja. Yo no me
amazed-M.SG enchanted-M.SG 1SG harken-PRET.1SG ear 1SG NEG REFL.1SG
Amazed, bewitched, I sharpened my ears. I couldn't

לו איסטאבֿה פֿיאנדו. אוגֿולורמי? אאיטאחין באאולאם?
lo est-ava fi-ando. Uchulurme? Aitahén baolam?
DEF.M.SG AUX.IMPF.3SG trust-GER is_it_possible.INTERJ (Tk. phrase) could it happen? (Hb. phrase)
believe it. Could it be? Was it possible?

אינדה איי סליחות? אינדה איי פרימירה טיפֿילה?
Inda ay selih-od̲? inda ay primer-a tefillá?
still.ADV EXIST.PRS penitential_prayer-f.PL[h] still.ADV EXIST.PRS first-F.SG prayer[h]
Is there still such a thing as "penitential prayers"? Is there still such a thing as "the first prayer"?

מי פאריסייו קי מי איסטאבֿה סונייאנדו אנטיס מיזמו קי

Me pares-yó ke me est-ava sony-ando antes mezmo ke

1SG.DAT seem-PRET.3SG REL REFL.1SG AUX-IMPF.3SG dream-GER before even.ADV REL

It seemed to me as if I were dreaming before I even

אלקאנסארה אה סיראר לוס אוזֿוס. פורטאנטו, דיגנידיאנדו בואינו,

alkans-ara a ser-ar los ojo-s. Portanto, dignide-ando bueno,

achieve-SUBJ.IMPF.1SG to close-INF DEF.M.PL eye-PL nevertheless regain_awareness-GER well.ADV

managed to close my eyes. Nevertheless, forcing myself well awake,

ייו מי קונבֿינסי קי ייו איסטאבֿה ביין סינטיינדו. אונה בוס

yo me konvens-í ke yo est-ava byen sint-yendo. Una bos

1SG REFL.1SG convince-PRET.1SG REL 1SG AUX.IMPF.3SG well.ADV hear-GER INDF.F.SG voice

I convinced myself that I was hearing right. A powerful voice,

פֿואירטי, מאלגראדו קי טימבלאבֿה, גריטאבֿה:

fuerte, malgrado ke tembl-ava, grit-ava:

strong although COMP shake-IMPF.3SG shout-IMPF.3SG

I convinced myself that I was hearing right. A powerful voice, although it shook, was shouting:

איידי, שמואל אקוניס, אברהם [ב]ן׳ דוד, חאן מושון!

–Ayde, Shemuel Akunes, Avram [Be]"n David, Han Moshón!

get_going.INTERJ Shemuel Akunes Avram [Be]"n David Han.HON Moshon

– Come on, Shemuel Akunes, Avram [Be]"n David, Han Moshón!

איידי, קי ייה אימפיסארון זמירות!

Ayde, ke ya empes-aron zemir-od!

get going.INTERJ CONJ already.ADV start-PRET.3PL prayer-F.PL[h]

Come on, 'cause they've already started the first morning prayers!

קואנטו אבֿיאה, קוזום גֿאקיטון, קי נו סינטיאה

Kuanto av-ía, kuzum Chaketón, ke no sent-ía

How_long.ADV EXIST-IMPF.3SG dear.INTERJ Chaketon, COMP NEG hear.IMPF.1SG

How long it had been, Chaketón my pet, that I hadn't heard

ייאמאר אה סליחות! דיל פֿואיגו אקי, איסטי פואיגו קי

yam-ar a selih-od! Del Fuego akí, est-e fuego ke

call-INF to penitential prayer-F.PL[H] from.DEF.M.SG fire here PROX-M.SG fire REL

the call to penitential prayers! Since the time of the Fire, that fire that

מוס ארוזֿו קומו לה פילוטה דילה פלאסה אל דיפו,

mos arroj-ó komo la pelota de-la Plasa al Depó,

PRON.ACC.1PL hurl-PRET.3SG like DEF.F.SG ball of-DEF.F.SG Market to.DEF.M.SG Depot

hurled us like a football from the Market to the Depot,

קריאיאה – אי קומו מי, קואנטוס! – קי איסטי בֿייזֿו אוזו

kre-ía – i komo mi, kuant-os! – ke est-e vyej-o uzo

believe-IMPF.1SG and like PRON.PREP.1SG many-M.PL COMP PROX-M.SG old-M.SG custom

I thought – and like me, so many others – that this old custom

ייה אבֿיאה דיספאריסידו. אי קואנדו סינטי אקיאה בוס

ya av-ía despares-ido. I kuando sent-í ake-a bos

already.ADV PFV.AUX-IMPF.3SG disappear-PTCP and when hear-PRET.1SG DEM-F.SG voice

had completely disappeared. And when I heard that voice

אין לה סולידאד דילה נוגֿאדה, ייו מי אקודרי די אקיל

en la soledad̲ de-la nochad̲a, yo me akod̲r-í de akel

in DEF.F.SG solitude of-DEF.F.SG night 1SG PRON.REFL.1SG remember-PRET.1SG of DIST.M.SG

voice in the solitude of the night, I was reminded of that

בואין טיאו ליאאו כהן, עליו השלום, איל פאפו די אברהם

buen Tío Liau Koén, alav ashalom, el papú de Avram,

good uncle.HON Liau Koen on.PRON.3SG.M[h] DEF.peace[h] DEF.M.SG grandfather of Avram

good Uncle Liau Koén, may he rest in peace, the grandfather of Avram,

איל די קאטוגֿה, קי אליבֿאנטאבֿה איל קאלבֿאסארה, לה קארניסיריאה אי

el de Katucha, ke alevant-ava el Kalvasará, la Karnesería i

DEF.M.SG of Katucha REL raise-IMPF.3SG DEF.M.SG Kalvasara DEF.F.SG meat market and

Katucha's husband, who used to wake up the whole Kalvasará, Meat Market and

איל מידאן אינטירוס קון סוס ייאמאדאס אה סליחות. אי

el Medán enter-os kon su-s yamad̲a-s a selih-od̲. I

DEF.M.SG open_square whole-M.PL with 3SG.POSS-PL call-PL to penitential_prayer-F.PL[H] and

the Open Square neighborhoods with his calls to penitential prayers. And

מיינטריס קי לה לובֿייה גוטיאבֿה אפֿואירה, אלה קאמה ייו פאריסיאה

myentres ke la luvya g̲ote-ava afuera, a·la kama yo pares-ía

while COMP DEF.F.SG rain drip-IMPF.3SG outside.ADV in·DEF.F.SG bed 1SG seem-IMPF.1SG

while the rain dripped outside, in bed I seemed

ביבֿיר די מואיבֿו אקיאס נוגֿאדאס די אינבֿיירנו. אי ייו לו בֿיאה

biv-ir de muevo ake-as nochad̲a-s de envierno. I yo lo v-ía

live-INF of new DIST-F.PL night-PL of winter and 1SG PRON.ACC.3SG.M see-IMPF.1SG

to relive those winter nights. And I saw

אה טיאו ליאאו קון לה נייבֿי, קון לה לובֿייה, קון איל איירי אי קון

a Tío Liau kon la nyeve, kon la luvya, kon el ayre i kon

OBJ uncle.HON Liau with DEF.F.SG snow with DEF.F.SG rain with DEF.M.SG air and with

Uncle Liau in the snow, in the rain, in the gusts and in

לה טראמונטאנה, קי סי מיטיאה לאס קונדורייאס די פאפוגֿי

la tramontana, ke se met-ía las kondurya-s de papuchi

DEF.F.SG northwind REL REFL.3SG put-IMPF.3.SG DEF.F.PL shoe-PL of house_slippers

the north wind, when he used to put on his slippers

דיספואיס די אבֿירסי ביין אטאדו לוס פיאליס די לאנה יירליאה גודרה,

después de av-er-se byen at-ad̲o los peal-es de lana yerlí-a g̲od̲r-a,

after of PV.AUX-INF-REFL.3SG well.ADV tie-PTCP DEF.M.PL socks-PL of wool local-F.SG thick-F.SG

after having carefully tied his socks of thick, coarse local wool,

פור אנדי נון פאסאבֿה ני טירוס די 42, סי איגֿאבֿה אקיל

por ande non pas-ava ni tiro-s de 42, se ech-ava akel

for where NEG pass.IMPF.3SG neither bullet-M.PL of 42 REFL.3SG throw.IMPF.3SG DIST.M.SG

which not even 42 mm bullets could not penetrate, put that

קירין אלוס אומברוס, סי אימברוזֿאבֿה איל גארון אין און קושאק די

kirín a·los ombro-s, se embruj-ava el garón en un kushak de

fur_coat to·DEF.M.PL shoulder-PL REF.3SG wrap-IMPF.3SG DEF.M.SG neck in INDF.M.SG scarf of

fur-lined coat over his shoulders, wrapped his neck in a scarf

דוס מיטרוס די לונגורה, סי אינקאלקאבֿה ביין ביין לה

dos metro-s de longura, se enkalk-ava byen byen la

two.NUM meter-PL of length REF.3SG push-IMPF.3SG well.ADV well.ADV DEF.F.SG

two meters long, pushed way down his

פֿיזיזיקה ארודיאדה די אונה גראנדי ריזה די קאשוניס קי לי טאפאבֿה

fez-ezika arroḏeaḏ-a de una grande rizá de kashon-es ke le tap-ava

fez-F.DIM wrapped-F.SG of INDF.F.SG big-SG kerchief of drawer-PL REL 3SG.DAT cover-IMPF.3SG

little fez wrapped around with a big, clumsy kerchief that covered his head

אסטה לאס אוריזֿאס, אי סאליאה אה ייאמאר מינייאן פארה לה פרימירה טיפֿילה.

asta las oreja-s, i sal-ía a yam-ar minyán para la primer-a tefilá.

up_to DEF.F.PL ear-PL and exit-IMPF.3SG to call-INF quorum[h] for DEF.F.SG first-F.SG prayer[h]

up to the ears, and went out to call together a quorum for the first morning prayers.

אי טיאו ליאאו איאה קאמינאנדו אי קאנטאנדו אקיאוס פיזמונים קי

I Tío Liau ía kamin-ando i kant-ando akeo-s pizmon-im ke

and uncle.HON Liau go.IMPF.3SG walk-GER and sing-GER DIST.M-PL hymn-M.PL[h] REL

And Uncle Liau walked along and sang those hymns that

אימבריניאבֿאן איל אלמה אי ארראנקאבֿאן סייטי אנסייאס....

embrene-avan el alma i arrank-avan syete ansya-s....

cheer-IMPF.3PL DEF.M.SG soul and tear-IMPF.3PL seven.NUM sorrow.F-PL

cheered your spirits and tore all your sorrow out....

מי אקודרי טאמביין, גֿאקיטון, די טיאו בינייאמין אבֿראם –

Me akoḏr-í tambyén, Chaketón, de Tío Binyamín Avram –

REFL.1SG remember-PRET.1SG also Chaketon of Uncle.HON Benyamin Avram

I remembered too, Chaketón, Uncle Binyamín Avram –

קי ביבֿה סיין אי סינקואינטה אנייוס – איל פאדרי

ke biv-a syen i sinkuenta anyo-s – el paḏre

COMP live-SUBJ.PRS.3SG hundred.NUM and fifty.NUM year-M.PL DEF.M.SG father

may he live 150 years – the father

די אבֿראמאקי איל מיאו, קי סי מיטיאה דילה טאראסיקה

de Avram-aki el mí-o, ke se met-ía de·la taras-ika

of Avram-HYP.M DEF.M.SG 1SG.POSS-M.SG REL REF.3SG put-IMPF.3SG of·DEF.F.SG terrace-DIM.F

of my Avramaki, who used to station himself on the terrace

די סו קאזה, די אנדי סי אפֿירראבֿה קון איל אוזֿו איל

de su kaza, de ande se aferr-ava kon el ojo el Medán

of 3SG.POSS house from where REL grasp-IMPF.3SG with DEF.M.SG eye DEF.M.SG open_square

of his house, from where his eyes could take in the

מידאן אינטירו, אה דיספירטאר אה ביניקו סאלטיאיל, אה ייאקו כהן, אה דאבֿיקו

enter-o, a despert-ar a Ben-iko Saltiel, a Yakó Koén, a Dav-iko

whole-M.SG to wake-INF OBJ Ben-HYP.M.SG Saltiel, OBJ Yako Koen OBJ Dav-HYP.M.SG

whole Open Square, to wake up Beniko Saltiel, Yakó Koén, Daviko,

אלמאליח, אי אה חארבי סאאול אמארילייו קון טודוס סוס איזֿוס,

Almaleh, i a Harbí Saul Amariyo kon toḏ-os su-s ijo-s,

Almaleh and OBJ Harbi-HON Saul Amariyo with all-M.PL 3PL.POSS.-PL son-PL

Almaleh, and Harbí Saul Amariyo with all his sons,

קי ייה פֿורמאן – קי ביבֿאן – אה אילייוס סולוס מידייו
ke ya form-an – ke biv-an – a eyos sol-os medy-o
REL already.ADV constitute-PRS.3PL REL live-SUBJ.PRS.3PL to PRON.PREP.3.M.PL alone-M.PL half-M.SG
who – may they live long – constitute unto themselves half a

מינייאן. מי אקודרי, אינפֿין, קואנדו טיאו בינייאמין
minyán. Me akodr-í, enfin, kuando Tío Binyamín
quorum[H] REF.1SG remember-PRET.1SG finally when Uncle.HON Binyamin
prayer quorum. I remembered, in the end, how Uncle Binyamín

סי מיטיאה דיאה די סאבה אלה טאראסיקה סוייה, קי אירה
se met-ía día de sabá a·la taras-ika suy-a, ke era
REF.3SG put-IMPF.3.SG day of Saturday to·DEF.F.SG terrace-DIM.F.SG 3SG.POSS-F.SG REL be.IMPF.3.SG
used to go out on the day of the Sabbath onto his terrace, that was

ג̃וסטו בֿיזאבֿי דיל מידראזיקו די לה קייושי די לה פלאסה,
djusto vizaví del midraz-iko de la kyushé de la plasa,
precisely.ADV opposite.ADV from.DEF.M.SG study_hall[h]-DIM.M.SG of DEF.F.SG corner of DEF.F.SG market
just opposite the little study hall at the corner of the market,

אה דיזיר די אינפֿרינטי לה טיפֿיללה ג̃ונטו קון טודוס. אי אירה בֿיראמינטי
a dez-ir de enfrente la tefillá djunto kon tod-os. I era veramente
to say-INF of in_front_of.ADV DEF.F.SG prayer[h] together with all.M-PL and be.IMPF.3SG truly.ADV
to say the morning prayers together with those in it. And it was truly

סאבֿרוזו קואנדו טיאו בינייאמין ריספונדיאה, דילה טאררסיקה,
savroz-o kuando Tío Binyamín respond-ía, de·la tarras-ika,
sweet-M.SG when Uncle.HON Binyamin reply-IMPF.3SG from·DEF.F.SG terrace-DIM.F.SG
sweet when Uncle Binyamín used to respond, from his terrace,

אל חאזאן דיל מידראש: ״בארוחו בארושימו, אמין״.
al hazán del midrash: "Baruhú barúshemó, amén".
to.DEF.M.SG cantor[h] of.DEF.M.SG study hall[h] blessed.3SG[h] blessed.name.POSS.3SG.M[h] certain[h]
to the cantor of the study hall: "Blessed Be He, Blessed be His Name, amen".

קואנדו קיטאבֿאן איל סיפֿיר טורה אי קי אזיאן לה אגבאאה,
Kuando kit-avan el séfer torá i ke az-ían la agbaá,
when take_out-IMPF.3PL DEF.M.SG scroll.CS[h] Torah[h] and CONJ do-IMPF.3PL DEF.F.SG raising[h]
When they took out the Torah scroll and raised it up high,

אבולטאנדו איל ליבֿרו דילה לייי די טודאס לאס פארטיס פארה קי
abolt-ando el livro de·la ley de tod-as las parte-s para ke
turn-GER DEF.M.SG book of·DEF.F.SG law of all.F-PL DEF.F.PL side-PL for COMP
turning the Book of the Law to all directions so that

ביזין טודוס, טיאו בינייאמין גריטאבֿה די לה טאראסה קי
bez-en tod-os, Tío Binyamín grit-ava de la tarasa ke
kiss-SUBJ.PRS.3PL all.M-PL Uncle Binyamin shout-IMPF.3SG from DEF.F.SG terrace COMP
all should kiss toward it, Uncle Binyamín used to shout from his terrace that

נון סי אולבֿידאראן די אבולטאר אי פור אנדי איל...
non se ulvid-aran de abolt-ar i por ande el...
NEG REF.3 forget-SUBJ.IMPF.3PL to turn-INF also for where PRON.PREP.3M.SG
they shouldn't forget to turn also toward him…

אח! קומו מוס איסטאמוס פֿאזיינדו בֿייזֿוס אה פוקו אה פוקו, קוזום
Ah! Komo mos est-amos faz-yendo vyejo-s a poko a poko, kuzum
INTERJ how PRON.REFL.1PL AUX-PRS.1PL do-GER old.M-PL by little by little dear.INTERJ
Ah! How old we're growing little by little, dear

גֿאקיטון. פאריסי קי ייה בֿה אזיר סינקו מאלאנייוס די איסטו
Chaketón. Pares-e ke ya va az-er sinko malanyo-s de est-o
Chaketon seem-PRS.3SG COMP already.ADV go.PRS.3SG do-INF five.NUM bad_year-PL of PROX-N.SG
Chaketón. Does it seem like it's already going to be five miserable years since all of this

קי טי איסטו קונטאנדו? אי פאריסי קי איס אויי קי
ke te est-ó kont-ando? I pares-e ke es oy ke
COMP PRON.DAT.2SG AUX-1SG tell-GER and seem-PRS.3SG COMP be-PRS.3SG today COMP
that I'm telling you [ceased]? And it seems like today that

איסטו בֿיינדו דילאנטרי די מיס אוזֿוס טודאס איסטאס שינאס מימוראבֿליס...
est-ó vyendo delantre de mi-s ojo-s tod-as est-as shena-s memoravle-s…
AUX-1SG see-GER in_front of 1SG.POSS-PL eye-PL all.F-PL PROX-F.PL scene-PL memorable-PL
I'm still seeing before my eyes all of these memorable scenes…
Charlemagne[97]
Charlemagne

3.13 Twenty-first century Judezmo in Romanization

From the Middle Ages until the middle of the nineteenth century, Judezmo texts meant for openly-practicing Jewish readers were almost always written in Hebrew letters, often referred to by Judezmo speakers over the centuries by terms expressing group identification such as ליטרה גֿודֿיקה / *letra djuḏeka* 'Judaic letters,'[98] ליטראס גֿודֿיזמאס / *letras djuḏezmas* 'Jewish letters,'[99] ליטראס זֿודֿיאס / *letras judías* 'Jewish letters',[100] אין גֿודֿיזמו קון ליטראס די רש״י / *en djuḏezmo kon letras de Rashí* 'in Judezmo (/Jewish) in Rashi letters',[101] לאס ליטראס סאנטאס / *las letras santas* 'the holy letters,'[102] or simply נואיסטרה ליטרה / *nuestra letra* 'our letters.'[103] The Latin alphabet, on the other hand, was denoted by terms of distancing such as ליטרה די גויים / *letra de goyim* 'Gentile letters',[104] or איסקריטורה די גויים / *eskritura de goyim* 'Gentile writing'.[105]

A few texts from medieval Iberia written in the Latin alphabet by Jews for Jews have survived; but these were meant for crypto-Jews who no longer had knowledge of the Hebrew alphabet.[106] The same is true of the Jewish Hispanic texts in Romanization produced in the 'Spanish-Portuguese' communities in parts of Western Europe such as Ferrara, Venice, Amsterdam and London, which were founded mainly by Iberian-origin

97 The author's name appeared in the original text in Roman rather than Hebrew letters.
98 Ḵuli 1730: 54b.
99 *Guerta de Estorya* 2 (2nd. ed., Salonika, 1891], p. 147 (from Vienna, 1865).
100 Elia R. Karmona (ed.), *El Djugetón* 4:1 (Constantinople, 1912), p. 4.
101 Alexandre Benghiat (ed.), *El Meseret* 25:51 (Izmir, 1921), p. 6.
102 Ḵuli 1730: 197a.
103 Ḵuli 1730: 66b.
104 [Maʔir Benveniste], *Sefer šulḥan ha-panim*, Salonika, 1568, f. 3b.
105 Eliʕezer ben Šem Ṭov Papo, *Sefer Dammeśeq Eliʕezer*, Belgrade, 1861, f. 61a.
106 On such texts see Bunis 2013b: 21.

crypto-Jews who left Iberia to return to the open practice of their ancestral faith. However, the Sephardim of the Ottoman Empire and North Africa, mostly descendants of fully practicing Jews who had left Iberia with the expulsions, continued the Iberian Jewish tradition of writing and printing their everyday language in the Hebrew alphabet well into the modern era– those in New York, until 1948, when the city's last Hebrew-letter Judezmo periodical לה בֿארה / *La Vara* closed.

However, from the late eighteenth century political, economic and social developments brought Judezmo speakers into increasingly close contact with Western European civilization, especially as represented linguistically by Italian and French and culminating in the informal and formal study of those languages by children from Judezmo-speaking homes. Those who began to study in Western-European-style schools such as those established by the Alliance Israélite Universelle and Società Dante Alighieri became accustomed to writing French or Italian in the Roman alphabet, and more and more of them began to adapt the one or the other of those writing systems, or eclectic combinations of the two, to the writing of their traditional group language, rather than employing the Hebrew letters they might have learned to use previously in the elementary Jewish religious schools they had attended when younger. In a Judezmo educational manual entitled לה גואירטה די אורו / *La guerta de oro* 'The golden garden' meant for Sephardim in the east considering emigration to Western Europe (Livorno, 1778, p. 1), Sarajevo-born author David Behar Mošé ʕAtías introduced readers to the Romanization used for Italian:

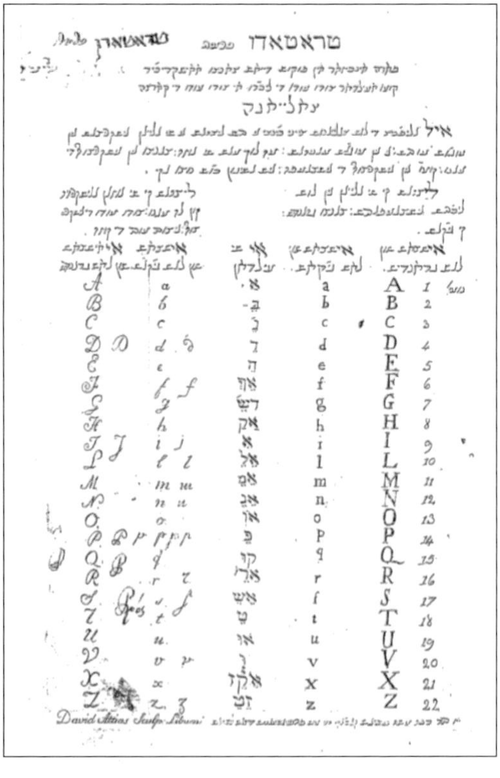

In 1866 a transition from the Hebrew alphabet to a Castilian-based Romanization was proposed for Judezmo in the Viennese Judezmo periodical איל נאסייונאל / *El Nasyonal*, edited by Josef Kalwo; but there is no evidence that such a transition in that periodical ever took place.[107] Saadí Aleví Eshkenazí, founding editor of the Salonika Hebrew-letter Judezmo periodical לה איפוקה / *La Epoka*, also proposed such a shift, and from issue 5:204 (dated 17 November 1879) of the paper he occasionally published illustrative passages in Romanized Judezmo, such as the following text printed in the paper in both Hebrew letters and in a highly eclectic Romanization based primarily on Italian and French:

A nuestros meldadores.

Los carateres que empleamos los judios de Turquia por escrévir nuestro espaniol no son basticientes y munchas vezes se azen yeros grandes por no saver si la yod se deve meldar por hirék ò por cerè, y la vav por holem ò por schurek, y cetera

Seria un gran progreso si nos uzavamos à escrévir esta lingua con caracteres latinos segun se escrive el verdadero espaniol. La dificultad es tan chica y los vantajes tan grandes que mos maraviamos como no se izo asta oy esta reforma tan importante y tan facile.

No entendemos seguir por oras la ortografia del vero espaniol, ma solamente un semplice troco de caracteres ebraicos en caracteres latinos.

Quièn no conose oy las 20 ò 25 letras menesterozas para escrivir nuestro linguaje? De nuestra parte, por mostrar al publico la posiblidad y la facilidad de esta escritura, nos proponemos de publicar cada semana un chico facto con caracteres latinos.

סאלוניקי 61 נוב׳ימברי 1879

אנואיסטרוס מילדאדורים.

לוס קאראקטיריס קי אימפליאמוס לוס ג׳ודיוס די טורקיאה פור איסקריב׳יר נואיסטרו איספאנייול נון סון באסטיסייינטיס אי מונג׳אס ב׳יזיס סי אזין ייירוס גראנדיס פור נון סאב׳יר סי לה יוד סי דיב׳י מילדאר פור חיריק או פור צירי, אי לה ואו פור חולים או פור שוריק, אי קיטירה.

סיריאה און גראן פרוגריסו סי מוס אוזאב׳אמוס אה איסקריב׳יר איסטה ליגואה קון קאראקטירים לאטינוס סיגון סי איסקריב׳י איל ב׳ירדאדירו איספאנייול. לה די־פ׳יקולטאד איס טאן ג׳יקה אי לוס ב׳אנטאז׳יס טאן גראנדיס, קי מוס מאראב׳יאמוס קומו נון סי איזו אסטה אויי איסטה רי־פ׳ורמה טאן אינפורטאנטי אי טאן פ׳אסיל.

נון אינטינדימוס סיגיר פור אורה לה אורטוגראפ׳יאה דיל ב׳ירו איספאנייול מה סולאמינטי און סינפליג׳י טרוקו די קאראקטירים איבראאיקוס אין קאראקטירים לאטינוס.

קיין נון קונוסי אוי לאס 20 או ב׳ינטי אי סינקו ליטראס מיניסטירוזאס פארה איסקריב׳יר מואיסטרו ליגואז׳י? די מואיסטרה פארטי, פור מוסטראר אל פוב׳ליקו לה פוסיב׳ילידאד אי לה פ׳אסילידאד די איסטה איסקריטורה, מוס פרופונימוס די פוב׳ליקאר קאדה סימאנה און ג׳יקו פ׳אטו קון קאראקטירים לאטינוס.

But the readers of *La Epoka* apparently expressed no enthusiasm over the idea and the paper continued to appear in the Hebrew alphabet for another 33 years until it closed in 1912. The founder's son, Šĕmuʔel/Sam Levy, who was one of the editors of the paper, went so far as to write that "איל דיאה אנדי אונו די לוס איסקריב̄ידורים ג̄ודיאו-איספאנייוליס אימפליארה און סולו ביירב̄ו אין קאראקטירים לאטינוס, אקיל דיאה איל ג̄ודיאו-איספאנייול איס מואירטו אי

107 The original Hebrew-letter proposal is reproduced in Romanization in Bunis 2011c: 69–72.

אינטיראדו" / *"El dia ande uno de los eskrividores djudeo-espanyoles empleará un solo byervo en karakteres latinos, akel día el djudeo-espanyol es muerto i enterado".*[108]

Nonetheless, like the Judezmo-speaking children who studied in the French and Italian schools, those who received their education in the state schools established from the first half of the nineteenth century with the dismemberment of the Ottoman Empire began to write Judezmo in romanizations such as that based on Serbo-Croatian, Romanian and Modern Turkish, and in Bulgaria, in the Cyrillic alphabet. In some places, such as Salonika, Jerusalem and New York, Judezmo publications continued to appear in the Hebrew alphabet into the 1930s and 40s. But increasingly from that time, and especially after World War II, the Judezmo speakers as a community shifted from the use of the Hebrew-based Judezmo alphabet to the Roman alphabet, using various foreign-language models and diverse adaptations or combinations of those models.

In 1979 Izmir-born Judezmo journalist Moshe Shaul, who had immigrated to Israel in 1949, proposed the use of a highly intuitive, phonemic-based Romanization, incorporating graphemes, including some digraphs, already familiar to many Judezmo speakers from English, French, Turkish and Serbo-Croatian.[109] A slightly revised version of Shaul's Romanization, sometimes known as the *Aki Yerushalayim* (Here is Jerusalem) orthography (after the name of the Latin-letter Judezmo periodical Shaul established in Jerusalem in 1979), is the system advocated today by the Israel National Authority for Ladino Language and Its Culture (and thus henceforth to be called here the Israel Ladino Authority orthography). The system is also used in contemporary Latin-letter Judezmo periodicals such as *El Amaneser* of Istanbul, in popular social network venues such as Ladinokomunita (founded by Izmir-born Rachel Amado Bortnick, who since 1958 has resided in the United States), and by most Judezmo writers and rank-and-file native speakers today.

The principal Romanizations which have been used for writing Judezmo since the mid-nineteenth century,[110] including that advocated by the Israel National Authority for Ladino Language and Culture,[111] are summarized in the following table:

Major Romanizations of Judezmo (19th-21 Centuries)						
	Italian	French	Serbo-Croatian	Turkish (expanded)	Israel Ladino Authority	
VOWELS						
[i]	i				i	*tino* 'attention'
[e]	e				e	*meldar* 'to read'
[a]	a				a	*kaza* 'house'
[o]	o	o, eau	o		o	*topar* 'to find'
[u]	u	u, ou	u		u	*buz* 'ice'

108 *La Epoka* 28: 1377 (1902), p. 9.

109 Shaul 1979.

110 For a more detailed diachronic look at the use of the Latin alphabet for the writing of Judezmo see Bunis 2019.

111 The illustrative words are here transcribed as pronounced in the major cities of the Southeastern Judezmo dialect region, e.g., Salonika, Istanbul, Izmir, where the majority of Judezmo speakers traditionally resided (for phonological details see Quintana Rodríguez 2006).

GLIDES						
[j]	i		j	i, y	y-/-i-/-y	*yamar* 'to call'; *nasion* 'nation'; *boy* 'size'
[w]	u				u	*muezes* 'walnuts'
CONSONANTS						
[p]	p				p	*papu* 'grandfather'
[b]	b				b	*bavajadas* 'nonsense'
[f]	f				f	*haftona* 'beating'
[v]	v				v	*kovdo* 'elbow'
[t]	t				t	*tavan* 'roof'
[θ]	d/t			t', d', t, d	t	*zahut* [za'χuð/-uθ] 'merit'
[d]	d				d	*lazdrar* 'to make an effort'
[ð]	d			d', d	d	*tadrar* 'to delay'
[k]	c[a/o/u]/ ch[i/e]/q[u]	c/q[u]	k		k	*kapak* 'lid'
[χ]	h				h	*herem* 'excommunication'
[g]	g[a/o/u]/ gh[e/i]	g[a/o/u] /gu[e/i]	g	g	g	*sangre* 'blood'
[ɣ]	g			ğ, g	g	*agora* 'now'
[h]	h				'h	*'Herzl* 'Herzl'
[ks]	x			ks	ks	*aksion* 'action'
[gz]	x		gz	gz	gz	*examen* 'exam'
[ʧ]	ci	tch	č, ć	ç	ch	*chiko* 'small'
[ʤ]	gi	dj	dž, đ	c	dj	*adjustar* 'to add'
[ʦ]	z(z)	ts/tz	c	ts/tz	ts, tz	*ts-/tzadikim* 'Jewish righteous men'; *pitsa* 'pizza'
[ʃ]	sci	ch	š	ş	sh	*shavon* 'soap'
[ʒ]	j/g(e/i)		ž	j	j	*mujer* 'woman, wife'
[s]	s-/-ss-/-s		s		s	*engrandeserse* 'to grow up'
[z]	s		z		z	*kezo* 'cheese'
[l]	l				l	*lonso* 'bear'
[ɾ]	r				r	*karo* 'dear'
[r]	rr		r(r)	rr	rr	*karro* 'cart'
[n]	n				n	*Na!* 'Behold!'
[ɲ]	gn		nj	ny	ny	*inyeta* 'granddaughter'
[m]	m				m	*tamam* 'okay, that's it'

Notes on the Israel Ladino Authority Romanization

The following are some notes on the Romanization endorsed by the Israel Ladino Authority as compared with earlier romanizations, and vacillation among contemporary users of the system as first proposed by Moshe Shaul in 1979.

d, ð. The sound [d], and the variant sounds [ð] (the latter, occurring before a voiced sound) and allophonic [θ] (occurring before a voiceless sound and at the end of a breath group) are distinct phonemes, /d/ versus /ð/, in the Southeastern dialects of Judezmo (i.e., those of present-day Turkey, Greece and Western Bulgaria). Starting in the 1820s, two distinct graphemes were used systematically to represent /d/ versus /ð/ in many Judezmo publications from the Southeast: ד was used for /d/ versus ד̄/ד׳ for /ð/ (e.g., לאד̄ינו/*laðino* in De Kastro 1823: 1a). This may be illustrated in the minimal pair (female personal name) *Ida* [ˈida], denoted by אידה in the periodical *La Epoka* of Salonika (23 April 1877, p. 1) versus (common noun) *iḏa* [ˈiða] 'departure, going away', denoted by איד̄ה in *La Epoka* (6 May 1878, p. 3). The early Turkish-based variants of the Romanization used by the Jews of Turkey (e.g., in Meşulam c1932) distinguished these phonemes graphemically as *d* for occlusive /d/ [d] versus the allographs *d'* for voiced fricative [ð] (especially in words of Hispanic origin and as the reflection of unpointed ד/*dalet* in words of Hebrew-Aramaic origin, e.g., הגדה/*agad'a* 'Passover Haggadah') and *t'* for voiceless [θ] (especially reflecting word-final unpointed ת/*taw* in words of Hebrew-Aramaic origin, e.g., זכות/*za-/zehut'* 'merit'). However, the Israel Ladino Authority-endorsed orthography does not distinguish graphemically between these phonemes, using *d* for [d] and [ð] (e.g., *agada*), and usually *t* for the reflection of Hebrew-Aramaic origin word-final *taw* (e.g., *za-/zehut*). Nonetheless, some contemporary writers use the grapheme *d* for [d] versus *ḏ* (e.g., *naḏa* 'nothing' in Perahya 1997: 164) or *d'* (e.g., *nád'a* 'nothing' in Perahya 2012: 347) for [ð] and [θ].

g, γ. Nor does the Ladino Authority-endorsed system distinguish graphemically between occlusive [g] and fricative [γ], which are also distinct phonemes in the Southeastern Judezmo dialects; rather, it uses *g* for both phonemes. These two phonemes were usually not distinguished in the Hebrew-letter Judezmo orthography used in publications from the Southeastern region. For example, the same grapheme, ג, was used to denote both the /g/ phoneme of *(Viktor) Ugó* / אוגו '(Victor) Hugo' [uˈgo] in *La Epoka* (17 February 1879, p. 2) and the /γ/ phoneme of nearly homophonous [ˈjuγo]/ייוגו 'yoke' in *La Epoka* (22 October 1877, p. 2). Nevertheless, the two phonemes came to be distinguished sporadically in some variants of the Turkish-based Romanization as *g* for /g/ (e.g., *lungo* 'long') versus *ğ* for /γ/ (e.g., *luğar* 'place'). Some contemporary writers use *g* for [g] versus *g̱* for [γ].

k, s, sh, z, h, s.h, 'h. Regardless of the corresponding graphemes in cognate words in Spanish, French or Italian – which causes some consternation to advocates of a system that would bring Judezmo closer to contemporary Romance languages – the grapheme *k* is used universally for the sound [k]; *s* and *sh* are used to denote [s] and [ʃ], respectively, in word-initial, word-medial, and word-final position before a voiceless sound and at the end of a breath-group; and *z* is used to denote [z] in word-initial, word-medial, and sometimes word-final position (e.g., *boz*/*bos* 'voice'). Reflecting a feature of the phonemic system of Judezmo, the graphemes *s* and *sh* in word-final position when preceding a voiced sound denote the voiced phones [z] and [ʒ], respectively, e.g., *dos ombres* [doz ˈombres] 'two men', *sesh oras* [seʒ ˈoras] 'six hours'. The grapheme *h* is used for the voiceless velar fricative [χ], rather than for breathed [h] as in English; the latter sound does not exist in Judezmo except in borrowings from languages such as English, German and, among some writers, Israeli Hebrew, and for it the grapheme *'h* is used. The potential ambiguity of the consonant sequence *sh*, which might have been interpreted as both the phoneme /ʃ/ (i.e., *sh*) and the cluster *s* + χ – e.g., *deshar* [deˈʃar] 'to leave', *deshamesar* [desχameˈsar] 'to get rid of leavened food before Passover' – was resolved by the use of a period to separate the sequence *s* + χ; thus, the latter word is spelled *des.hamesar*.

ny, *y*. Moshe Shaul had originally suggested that the phoneme [ɲ] be represented by *ni* (e.g., *banio* 'bath', cf. Sp. *baño*), but he later shifted to *ny*, which is the grapheme universally accepted today. The original system advocated the use of *y* for the [j] glide at the beginning and end of words, and word-medially in between vowels. Elsewhere, perhaps under the influence of Romance languages, *i* was to be used (e.g., *nasion* 'nation'); but today many contemporary speakers seem to prefer *y* in all positions (e.g., *nasyon*); the latter use would seem to stress the actual glide-like character of this phoneme, in opposition to the use of *i* for the monophthong [i] only; perhaps the preference for *y* is also influenced by the traditional use of double *yod* (יי) for the [j] glide in the Hebrew-letter system when it occurs before the phonemes *a* (א, ה), and *o* and *u* (ו) (e.g., נאסייון/*nasyón*). Additionally, some contemporary writers use *y* to separate a front vowel and an adjacent vowel, e.g., *diya* 'day' (versus Sp. *día*).

r, *rr*. In the traditional Hebrew-letter orthography the opposition between flapped [ɾ] and trilled [r], which is phonemic in dialects of the Southeastern region, did not begin to be distinguished graphemically until the second half of the nineteenth century, e.g., קארו/*karo* '(m.sg.) dear' in *La Epoka* (14 February 1876, p. 3) versus קאררו/*karro* 'cart' in *La Epoka* (24 January 1876, p. 3). From that time on the רר grapheme for trilled *rr* was used by some writers, albeit only sporadically. In early variants of Judezmo in Romanization, too, the flapped /r/ versus trilled /rr/ opposition was sometimes marked by the graphemes *r* versus *rr*. In the system accepted by the Israel Ladino Authority this opposition is meant to be upheld systematically.

ts/*tz*. The letter צ/*tsadi* in words of Hebrew origin was traditionally reflected as [s] in Judezmo of the Southeast region, although in the Northwest, especially among educated people, it was sometimes reflected as [c] (i.e., *ts*). However, under the apparent influence of the Hebrew reading traditions of Ashkenazi and Italian Jews, and, especially from the early twentieth century, of that of Hebrew educators from Eretz Israel/Palestine in the Ottoman Jewish communities, some Southeast Judezmo speakers began to reflect *tsadi* as [c] as well. Apparently under Israeli Hebrew influence the letter *tsadi* is today sometimes reflected as *ts* or *tz* in Hebrew borrowings, although some writers use more traditional *s* (e.g., צדקה/*sedaka*/*tsedaka*/*tzedaka* 'charity'). Writers also use *ts* or variant *tz* for the sound [c] in borrowings from languages such as Italian (e.g., *pitsa* 'pizza').

Spelling variation. The spelling of personal names reflects the use of the persons referred to, e.g., *Koen*, *Kohen*, *Coen*, *Cohen*. Where Judezmo has its own names for countries and cities, those are accepted, with tolerance for individual and regional variants, e.g., *(la) Grecha/Gresya* for 'Greece', *Salonik/Saloniko/Selanik*, etc. for 'Salonika', *Estambol* for 'Istanbul', *Ezmir* for 'Izmir'. In other instances the contemporary official local names are used, e.g., *Mo-/Manastir* or *Bitola*. Some freedom is also allowed in the transcription of words the pronunciation of which diverges regionally, stylistically and so on. For example, depending on their pronunciation of the word for 'Sunday', some writers spell it *alhad* (denoting [alˈχað] or [alˈχad]), and others *alhat* (denoting [alˈχaθ] or [alˈχat]), or *alha* (representing [alˈχa]). The Ladino Authority does not necessarily attempt to adjudicate in such matters.

Lexical stress is phonemic in Judezmo, e.g., *pára* 'in order to' versus *pará* 'Turkish *para*, a unit of Turkish currency', but the Ladino Authority-endorsed system does not advocate the indication of irregular stress. Nevertheless, some contemporary writers who use the system (e.g., Matilda Koen-Sarano) mark irregular stress by means of an acute accent. This is beneficial for students of the language who are not necessarily familiar with the irregular stress of some words. In certain instances it can even clarify readings for native speakers, for example, the difference between *rio* 'river' and *rió* '(third-person singular preterite tense) laughed', or *riza* 'laughter' and *rizá* 'handkerchief', or *aria* 'aria' and *aría* '(3sg.) would do', which pairs would be written identically as *rio*, *riza* and *aria* in the orthographic system endorsed by the Ladino Authority.

Although it could perhaps benefit from some further fine tuning, the Latin-letter orthographic system endorsed by the Israel Ladino Authority is relatively simple and rather intuitive. It offers contemporary Judezmo writers an easy-to-use orthography requiring little special training and no familiarity with the spelling systems of the correlate languages (Spanish, Hebrew, Turkish, French, etc.) from which Judezmo has derived much of its lexicon and grammar, but from which it must be seen today as entirely independent.

3.14 Sample text: A reminiscence about Jewish life in mid-twentieth-century Istanbul

Roz Kohen, "Los Sedakeros del Kal Apollon", from her *Estambol Djudyo: Una Koleksyon de Rekuerdos i Ilustrasyones / Jewish Istanbul: A Collection of Memoirs and Illustrations* (Istanbul: Libra Publishing, 2012, pages 189–196).[112]

Heirs to what may be called the popular 'Judezmist' writers of the early modern era of Judezmo literature which began in the 1770s,[113] a group of contemporary Judezmo writers are now using the Roman alphabet instead of the traditional Hebrew letters in an attempt to document the last living remains of the language. At the same time they are recording what they remember of the distinct character of Sephardic life during their childhood, when many members of the community were still using Judezmo as their

112 The Judezmo text, as retrieved from http://judeo-spanishmemoires.blogspot.com/) is reprinted here with the permission of Roz Kohen and Libra Publishing. It was originally published in Judezmo in the Istanbul Judezmo periodical *El Amaneser* (year 5, number 62, April 2010) and in the Izmir Jewish community newsletter *Diyalog, Izmir Musevileri e-Haber Bülteni 010,* Temmuz – Ağustos 2010). Ms. Kohen's original English version was a free adaptation of her Judezmo text; in consideration of the particular needs of the present anthology it was retranslated here, more closely following the original Judezmo, by the author of the present article. I take this opportunity to express warm thanks to Roz Kohen for her important and useful comments on this section.

113 On popular 'Judezmism' and its principles see Bunis 2011b.

primary in-group language. One of the most gifted of the contemporary Judezmist writers is undoubtedly Roz Kohen, who was born in Istanbul in 1949 to a family of Romaniote or Byzantine Jewish descent, grew up in the city's once highly Jewish Galata neighborhood with Judezmo as her family language, and in 1981 emigrated to the United States.

From the introductory notes to one of her collections of short pieces on Jewish life in Istanbul in the 1950s, from which the present text is taken, it is clear that Kohen writes with a consciousness of the rich cultural sources – Jewish, medieval Iberian, and Ottoman – which contributed to the unique variant of modern Sephardic language and culture she experienced first-hand in her youth. She is aware of the myriad lexical resources of which the language she heard as a child was comprised ("*[La verzyon de] El Djudeo-Espanyol kon la kuala me engrandesi teniya biervos en Turko, Grego, Fransez i Ebreo*"), and unlike those writers today who advocate a more *frankeado* or Western Europeanizing style, she unhesitatingly interweaves representatives of all those linguistic components into her writing. By doing so she manages to capture the spirit of the popular language of the Sephardim of mid-twentieth-century Istanbul, in which, as Kohen has noted, "*uzavan a eksprimir sus sentimyentos los mas personales. De mizmo ke proverbos, dichas, bendisiones i maldisiones. Esto todo se armonizava de una manera otentika kon la intonasion espesiala de la lingua*" 'they expressed their most personal feelings. Including the use of proverbs, sayings, blessings and curses. All of it harmonized in an authentic way with the special intonation of the language'. (In her English rendition of the comment Kohen expressed this as 'The tone of their voices and the nature of the topics discussed were shaped by the sentimentality embedded in the language. Blessing, cursing, name branding, clichés and proverbs were part of the everyday Judeo-Spanish they spoke'). Engaged in a kind of artistic 'language and culture salvage' (*"Esto todo ke desparesio en muestro tiempo aze parte de mi pasado"* 'All of this, which has disappeared during our lifetime, forms a part of my past'), Kohen noted that in her writings 'I used as many of the expressions as I could remember in an effort to capture the values, culture and humor ... of the language our ancestors communicated with for centuries'. Fully aware of the fact that much of the Judezmo lexicon and grammar derive historically from Ibero-Romance, and that scientists interested in the language often refer to it as 'Judeo-Spanish', nonetheless in her own creative writing Kohen prefers to use the popular communal language name *Djudyo* (Jewish),[114] by means of which contemporary community members identify their group language with their primarily Jewish identity.

As illustrated by the sample selection, like the first generations of popular Judezmist writers, Roz Kohen – whether consciously or unconsciously – tends to use those

114 *Djuḏyó*/גֿודֿייו as a language name seems first to appear, in the sense of 'Hebrew/Jewish language', in De Kastro 1823:120a "אילייוס נו סאבֿיאן קי אינטינדיאה יוסף קי דישירון, נו סאבֿי אבֿלאר אין גֿודֿייו"/*Eyos no savían ke entendía Yosef ke disheron, 'No save avlar en djuðyó*"Joseph's brothers did not know that he understood what they said; "He doesn't know how to speak in Jewish"' (cf. Genesis 42:23). That language name has essentially replaced *djuḏezmo* amongst those contemporary speakers in and from Turkey who continue to refer to their language as 'Jewish'.

variants of elements of Ibero-Romance origin which diverge in form or meaning from modern Castilian: e.g., *leshor* for 'distance' (OSp. *lexanía*), *kaleja* 'narrow street' (Sp. *calleja*), *ande* for 'where' (Sp. *donde*), *merkar* 'to purchase' (Sp. *comprar*), *dainda* 'still' (Sp. *todavía*), *fraguar* 'to build' (Sp. *construir*, etc.), *los proves* 'the poor' (Sp. *los pobres*), *emportantes* 'important' (S. *importantes*) and many others. Even the word for 'truth; true', which today tends to be used by speakers in a form closer to Spanish than its traditional Judezmo form, *veḏrá*, occurs in the text in a reduced form diverging from normative Spanish *verdad*: *verda*. In her Romanization variant, too, the author shows graphemes distancing it from Spanish, such as predominant *y* instead of *i* for the [j] glide (e.g., *syempre* 'always', *dezeyos* 'desires', cf. Sp. *siempre*, *deseos*), and a few instances of word-final *z* before a following voiced consonant (e.g., *moz dizian* 'they told us', *doz butikas* 'two shops', cf. Sp. *nos*, *dos*). As usual in the current prevailing Romanization, the phonemes /d/ vs. /ð/ and /g/ vs. /ɣ/ are not distinguished, and /r/ vs. /rr/ are distinguished only sporadically (e.g., *borrachones*, *serrada* but *deredor*, *baryendo*). Exemplifying the cosmopolitan and polyglot character of the speech community, Kohen also incorporates a few foreign graphemes into her text: *ğ* and *ş* from Turkish in *uğradeyar* and the alternate spelling of the synagogue name, *Neve Şalom*; *é* and *tch* from French in *rez-de-chaussée* and *etchos* (the latter, in her footnote 1); and, as in French and Italian, but unlike Spanish, the apostrophe occasionally used between words (*el kal d'Apollon*) and in abbreviated spoken forms (e.g., *la punta'l* [< *punta del*] *pino*).

Nowadays even in the writings of the popular Judezmists the Hebrew-Aramaic component is generally smaller than that used by their predecessors. Kohen's piece illustrates this as well. Although some of the elements of Hebew-Aramaic origin she uses refer to the institutions and practice of traditional Judaism, e.g., *(karne) kasher* 'kosher (meat)' (illustrating the use of a masculine adjective, כשר, with a feminine noun), (*echar azete al*) *kal* '(donating oil to the) synagogue' (exemplifying the Judezmo speakers' zero realization of the Hebrew letter ה"א/*he* < קהל), *shamash* (שמש) 'synagogue beadle', some others have a broader reference, e.g., *mazal* (< מזל) 'fortune', *balabayes* 'hosts' (the pluralization of the Hebrew base, reduced from בעל הבית/*báal abáyiḏ*, reflecting Hispanic-origin *-es*), *sedakeros i sedakeras* 'male and female beggars' (a fusion of צדקה/*seḏaká* 'charity' + Hispanic-origin actor-marking *-ero*).

While the more *frankeaḏo* writers refrain in particular from using elements of Turkish and Balkan-language origin, thus in a sense negating the centuries of co-existence between the Sephardim and their Ottoman and post-Ottoman neighbors, Kohen unhesitatingly makes use of such elements as they suit the scene and context she recreates. Although she herself is a native Turkish speaker and is fully aware of the corresponding forms in Turkish proper, the forms she uses in her Judezmo writings are characteristically those of local Judezmo speakers. For example, *la male* (vs. Tk. *mahalle* < Ar. *maḥalla*) denotes the local 'neighborhood' in which the scene she describes takes place, and the prominent 'tower' symbolizing Istanbul's Galata neighborhood is called *la Kula* (vs. Tk. *kule*). Local practitioners of vocations are referred to by such names as *kunduradji* 'shoemaker' (Tk. *kunduracı*) and plural *elektrikchis* 'electricians' (Tk. *elektrikçiler*); the term *eskirubadjis* 'old clothes dealers' would seem to derive from Turkish *eski* 'old' + *ruba* (cf. Jud. *ropa* 'clothes', Bosn. *ruba* 'goods') + profession-marking

-dji (Tk. *-cı*). Items sold by neighborhood merchants include *fostanes* (*de novya)* '(bridal) gowns' (Gk. *foustáni*), *defteres* (*para la eskola*) 'school notebooks' (Tk. *defter* < Ar. *daftar*), and *penches* (Tk. *pençe*) taps put on shoes for reinforcement; they are paid for in *groshes* "pennies" (literally, Turkish currency of little value', cf. Mod. Tk. *kuruş*). Demonstrating that the Turkish-Balkan borrowings in Judezmo are not limited to nouns, the verb *uğradeyar* 'to stop by' (cf. Tk. *uğradı*, the 3sg. past-tense form of the verb *uğra-* + Jud. verbalizing *-e(y)ar*) also appears within the context of the family visit depicted.

Although the Jews in and from Turkey continue to maintain a strong Jewish identity, the acquisition by recent generations of Western European languages and to a considerable extent the cultural orientation of the peoples who speak those languages has caused the contemporary Turkish Jews to maintain a sense of *kozmopolitizmo i el sentimyento de una apartenensia kultura ancha i de umanizmo* ('cosmopolitanism and a feeling of broad cultural belonging and of humanism'). Kohen's piece contains clear signs of the Western Europeanization of the recent generations. The profound impact of French and Italian, disseminated in the community both formally, through instruction in foreign-language educational institutions, and through direct interaction with French and Italian speakers and writers in commercial and social relations, is reflected in borrowings such as *rez de chaussée* 'ground floor' (Fr. *rez-de-chaussée*), *kestyones* 'questions', *kontrasto* (It. *contrasto*, Fr. *contraste*, which according to the principles of borrowing of Gallicisms into Judezmo would naturally yield *kontrasto*, vs. Sp. *contraste*), the m.pl. adjective *orozos* 'happy' (cf. Fr. *heureux* + Jud. *-ozo* [< OSp. *-oso*]), the pronominal use of *pasarse* 'to occur' (cf. Fr. *se passer* vs. Sp. *pasar*), the formally plural possessive adjective *sus* qualifying a formally singular noun in *en sus mano* 'in their hand' in reflection of the distinctive third-person plural *leur* of French, and internationalisms such as *entuziasmo* (cf. It., Sp. *entusiasmo*; borrowing from French would instead have yielded *antuziasmo*) and *personajes* 'personages' (cf. Fr. *personnages*, perhaps Sp. *personajes* – but only if pronounced according to the rules of French, versus actual Spanish [persoˈnaχes]), titles of respect and kinship such as *Musyu* 'sir' (as distinct from the Turkish reflex *mösyö*) and *tant* 'aunt' (Fr. *tante*), and even *Sarina* and *Dora*,[115] representatives of the female personal names of Italian and French origin which during the past several generations have tended to replace the names of Hebrew, Spanish, Turkish, and Greek origin used in the preceding generations.

The passage recreates a recurrent neighborhood stroll which the author used to take with her mother in the Galata neighborhood of the Pera or Beyoğlu district of Istanbul (Tk. İstanbul). At the trip's epicenter was the Knesset Israel Synagogue on Büyükhendek Street, which opened to the Galata Tower square. Known popularly as the Apollon Synagogue after the Apollon Building which provided entrance to it, the synagogue was opened on March 18, 1923; it closed in 1982 and an office building was built in its place.

115 As Roz Kohen pointed out in a personal communication from 3 December 2020, *Dora* can reflect Greek *Dóra* 'Gift', or perhaps more likely in the present instance, it may be a shortened form of Dorothea (Dorothy) and Theodora 'God's Gift', from *dõron* 'gift' + *theós* 'god', a short form of Isadora, Isidora, or other such compounds, versions of which are also used in French and Italian.

LOS SEDAKERO-S DEL KAL APOLLON
DEF.M.SG beggar.M-PL of.M.SG synagogue Apollon
The Beggars of the Apollon Synagogue[116]

En los anyo-s 50 del siglo pasad-o uz-avamos a
In DEF.M.PL year-PL 50 of.M.SG century past.PTCP-M.SG use-IMPF.1PL to
In the 50s of the past century, we used to

vijit-ar kon mi Madre el entorno de la Kula
visit-INF with POSS.1SG mother DEF.M.SG environs of DEF.F.SG Kula
visit with my mother the area of the Galata Tower.

La Kula era leshor de sinko punto-s de kamino del
DEF.F.SG Kula be.IMPF.3SG distance of five minute-PL of road of.M.SG
The Galata Tower was a distance of five minutes from the road of the

apartamento Melek, ande mor-avamos. Mi Madre me tom-ava
apartment Melek where reside-IMPF.1PL POSS.1SG mother PRON.ACC.1SG take-IMPF.3SG
the Melek Apartment Building where we resided. My mother took me

de la mano i mos met-iamos en kamino kon grande entuziazmo.
from DEF.F.SG hand and REF.1PL put-IMPF.1PL on way with great enthusiasm.
by the hand and we set out on our way with great enthusiasm.

Syempre era mas o menos lo mizm-o:
Always be.IMPF.3SG more or less DEF.N same-M.SG
It was always more or less the same:

vijit-ar la prim-a de mi padre Djentil, ke mor-ava
visit-INF DEF.F.SG cousin-F.SG of POSS.1SG father Djentil REL reside-IMPF.3SG
to visit my father's cousin Djentil, who lived

un-os kuant-os apartamento-s despues del kal Apollon;
INDEF-M.PL several-M.PL apartment-PL after of.M.PL synagogue Apollon
a few apartment buildings after the Apollon Synagogue;

merk-ar karne kasher ande Musyu Dalva; uğradey-ar ande la tant Sarina
buy-INF meat.F.SG kosher.M.SG at Monsieur Dalva; stop.by-INF at DEF.F.SG aunt Sarina
to buy kosher meat at Monsieur Dalva's; to stop by at Aunt Sarina,

ke biv-ia enfrente del Bit Pazar; ech-ar un-a boz
REL live-IMPF.3SG opposite of.DEF.M.SG Flea Market; throw-INF INDF-F.SG voice
who lived opposite the Flea Market; to call out

116 https://www.nevesalom.org/apollonEng.html

al rez de chaussée de Dora Adato; i, de·vez-es en kuando
to.DEF.M.SG floor of ground of Dora Adato; and, from·time-PL in when
at the ground floor [apartment] of Dora Adato; and, from time to time,

ech-ar azete al kal.
throw-INF oil to.DEF.M.SG synagogue
to donate oil to the Synagogue.

En akeyo-s tyempo-s el kal de Neve Şalom (Neve Shalom)
In DIST.M-PL time-PL DEF.M.SG synagogue of *Neve Şalom*
In those days the Neve Şalom Synagogue

dainda no era fraguad-o, i el kal d'-Apollon,
still NEG AUX.IMPF.3SG build.PTCP-M.SG and DEF.M.SG Synagogue of-Apollon
still was not built, and the Apollon Synagogue,

ke mi Madre lo yam-ava el kal de los prove-s,
REL POSS.1SG mother PRON.ACC.3SG.M call-IMPF.3SG DEF.M.SG synagogue of DEF.M.PL poor-PL
which my mother called the synagogue of the poor,

era el kal lo mas frekuentad-o.
be.IMPF.3SG DEF.M.SG synagogue DEF.N more patronize.PTCP-M.SG
was the synagogue that was the most patronized.

La Kula, en akeyo-s anyos era serrad-a.
DEF.F.SG Galata·Tower in DIST.M-PL year-PL AUX.IMPF.3SG close.PTCP-F.SG
The Galata Tower, in those years was closed.

Apares-iya muy eskayid-a i pas-avamos al·deredor·de eya
appear-IMPF.3SG very be_rundown.PTCP-F.SG and pass-IMPF.1PL to.DEF.M.SG·around·of PRON.3SG.F
It appeared very rundown and we used to pass around it

komo si no egzist-iya. Me akodr-o tambien del kunduradji,
as if NEG exist-IMPF.3SG REF.1SG remember-PRS.1SG also of.DEF.M.SG shoemaker
as if it did not exist. I also remember the shoemaker,

Musyu Navon, ke ten-iya un-a butik-ita chik-it-ika i brusk-a,
Monsieur Navon, REL have-IMPF.3SG INDF-F.SG shop-DIM.F.SG small-DIM-DIM.F.SG and rough-F.SG
Monsieur Navon, who had a very small and rough little shop,

ande moz ech-ava penche-s muev-as a los kalsado-s vyej-os
where PRON.DAT.1PL throw-IMPF.3SG shoe_tap-PL new-F.PL onto DEF.M.PL shoe-PL old-M.PL
where he used to put new taps on old shoes

por un-os kuant-os grosh-es. Un-a otr-a butika ke konos-iyamos
for INDF-M.PL few-M.PL kuruş-PL INDF-F.SG other-F.SG shop REL be_familiar_with-IMPF.1PL
for a few pennies. Another shop we knew

bueno en la Kula era la butika de Pardo,
well.ADV in DEF.F.SG Galata Tower area be.IMPF.3SG DEF.F.SG shop of Pardo
well in the Galata Tower area was the shop of Pardo,

kon su-s fostan-es de novya ke alkil-ava. Un-os kuant-os elektrikchi-s
with POSS.3-PL dress-PL of bride REL rent-IMPF.3SG INDF-M.PL few-M.PL electrician-PL
with his bridal gowns that he rented. A few electricians,

ke adov-avan lampa-s vyej-as, i mas abasho un-as doz butika-s
REL repair-IMPF.3PL lamp-PL old-F.PL and more down some-F.PL two shop-PL
who repaired old lamps, and further down some two shops,

ke vend-ian livro-s i defteres para la eskola. Mas i mas
REL sell-IMPF.3PL book-PL and notebook.PL for DEF.F.SG school more and more
that sold books and notebooks for school. Most of all

me akodr-o de los eskirubadji-s kon el sako en la espalda;
REF.1SG remember-PRS.1SG of DEF.M.PLold-clothes_man-PL with DEF.M.PLsack on DEF.F.SG back;
I remember the old-clothes men with the sack on their back;

los vendedor-es de fruta-s i de pishkado-s.
DEF.M.PLseller-PL of fruit-PL and of fish-PL
the sellers of fruit and of fish.

El deredor de la Kula en akeyo-s anyo-s ten-iya
DEF.M.SG environs of DEF.F.SG Galata Tower in DIST-M.PL year-PL have-IMPF.3SG
The area surrounding the Galata Tower in those years had

un ayre muy eskayid-a kon su-s apartamento-s vyej-os,
INDF.M.SG atmosphere very rundown.PTCP-F.SG with POSS.3-PL apartment-PL old-M.PL
a rundown atmosphere with its old,

deskolorad-os i su-s entrada-s kon golor de mofo i areskur-as,
discolored-M.PL and POSS.3-PL entrance-PL with smell of mold and dark-F.PL
discolored apartment buildings and its entrances having a smell of mold and dark,

kon un-os kuant-osborrachon-es kon las bocha-s de ispirto en su-s mano,
with INDF-M.PL few-M.PL drunk-PL with DEF.F.PL bottle-PL of liquor in POSS.3-PL hand
with a few drunks with the liquor bottles in their hands,

i los butikaryo-s bary-endo las entradas i ech-ando agua-s a
and DEF.M.PLshopkeeper-PL sweep-GER DEF.F.PL entrance-PL and throw-GER water-PL onto
and the shopkeepers sweeping the entrances and pouring water onto

las kaye-s para espant-ar a los gato-s ke era-n numeroz-os
DEF.F.PL street-PL in order to frighten-INF to DEF.M.PLcat-PL REL be.IMPF-3PL numerous-M.PL
the streets to frighten away the cats which were numerous.

La entrada del Kal Apollon no era diferente del resto
DEF.F.SG entrance of.M.SG Synagogue Apollon NEG be.IMPF.3SG different from.DEF.M.SG rest
The entrance of the Apollon Synagogue was no different from the rest

de la kaleja. I mas i mas, komo "al tinyozo
of DEF.F.SG street and more and more like to.DEF.M.SG scalp-ringworm sufferer
of the street. And still more, as in [the proverb] "[Add] to the bald man's pate

un gran-iko mas", era-n los sedakero-s i sedakera-s
INDF.M.SG scab-DIM.M.SG more be.IMPF-3PL DEF.M.PL male beggar.M-PL and female beggar-F.PL
yet another pimple,"[117] there were the male and female beggars

asent-ados en la puerta del kal.
sit-PTCP.M.PL in DEF.F.SG door of.M.SG synagogue
seated at the door of the synagogue.

Asentad-os en las eskalona-s de laja en la entrada del kal
sit.PTCP-M.PL in DEF.M.PL step-PL of marble in DEF.F.SG entrance of.DEF.M.SG synagogue
Seated on the marble steps at the entrance of the synagogue

de los prove-s, avl-ando syempre en Djudyo,
of DEF.M.PL poor-PL speak-GER always in Jewish
of the poor, speaking always in Jewish [Judezmo]

era-n yen-os de bendisyon-es i alavasyon-es:
be-IMPF.3PL full-M.PL of blessing-PL and praise-PL
they were full of blessings and praise:

"Presyad-a, asi ke te veyga de tod-o bueno,
Precious-F.SG thus COMP PRON.ACC.2SG see.SUBJ.PRS.3SG of all-M.SG good
"Precious woman, so may I see you with all that's good,

Ke veyga-s novya a tu ija, ke tenga-s el mazal
COMP see.SUBJ.PRS-2SG bride OBJ POSS.2SG daughter COMP have.SUBJ.PRS-2SG DEF.M.SG luck[h]
may you see your daughter a bride, may you have luck

en la punta-l pino, tod-o bueno ke tenga-s
in DEF.F.SG top-[of.]DEF.M.SG pine tree all-M.SG good REL have.SUBJ.PRS-2SG
as high as the top of a pine tree, all good may you have

i ke los dezeyo-s de tu alma ke se agan verda".
and COMP DEF.M.PL desire-PL of POSS.2.SG soul COMP IMPRS.3SG make.SUBJ.PRS-3PL true
and may the desires of your soul come true."

117 Here the translation reflects Istanbul usage as explained to me by Roz Kohen. The literal meaning is '[Add] to the scalp-ringworm sufferer['s scalp] yet another crusty scab'.

En	*mizm-o*	*tyempo*	*sav-iyan*	*todo*	*lo*	*ke*	*se*	*pas-ava*
In	same-M.SG	time	know-IMPF.3PL	everything	DEF.N	REL	REF.3SG	happen-IMPF.3SG

At the same time they knew everything that happened

en	*la*	*male*	*i*	*era-n*	*komo*	*los*	*balabay-es*	*del*	*kal,*
in	DEF.F.SG	neighborhood	and	be.IMPF-3PL	like	DEF.M.PL	host-PL	of.DEF.M.SG	synagogue

in the neighborhood and they were like the hosts of the synagogue,

dando	*avizo-s*	*i*	*prunt-ando*	*kestyones:*
give.GER	announcement-PL	and	ask-GER	question-PL

making announcements and asking questions:

"El	*Shamash*[i]	*ya*	*vin-o,*	*va-s*	*a*	*ech-ar*
DEF.M.SG	synagogue beadle	already	arrive.PRET-3SG	go.PRS-2SG	to	throw-INF

"The synagogue beadle has already arrived, are you going to donate

azete	*al*	*kal?"*
oil	to.DEF.M.SG	synagogue

oil to the synagogue?"

Me	*akodr-o*	*tambien*	*ke*	*kant-avan*	*en*	*Djudyo*	*kant-ika-s*	*alegre-s,*
REF.1SG	remember-PRS.1SG	also	COMP	sing-IMPF.3PL	in	Jewish	song-DIM.F-PL	happy-PL

I remember too that they used to sing in Jewish little happy songs,

en	*kontrasto*	*kon*	*su-s*	*vistido-s*	*eskayid-os,*
in	contrast	with	POSS.3-PL	garment-PL	be.rundown.PTCP-M.PL

in contrast with their rundown clothes,

su-s	*kara-s*	*flak-as*	*i*	*su-s*	*boka-s*	*sin*	*dyente-s.*
POSS.3-PL	face-PL	thin-F.PL	and	POSS.3-PL	mouth-PL	without	tooth-PL

their thin faces and their toothless mouths.

Pares-iyan	*oroz-os*	*kon*	*su-s*	*karas*	*de*	*riza.*
seem-IMPF.3PL	happy-M.PL	with	POSS.3-PL	face-PL	of	laughter

They seemed fortunate with their laughing faces.

Me	*akodr-o*	*tambien*	*ke*	*los*	*grande-s*	*mos*	*espant-avan*
REF.1SG	remember-PRS.1SG	also	COMP	DEF.M.PL	adult-PL	PRON.ACC.1PL	scare-IMPF.3PL

I remember too that the adults used to scared us

kon	*avla-s*	*sovre*	*zingano-s,*	*sedaker-os*	*i*	*Sanpavlo.*[ii]
with	talk-PL	about	Romany-PL	beggar-M.PL	and	Sanpavlo

with talk about Romany, beggars and 'Sanpavlo'.

I	*moz*	*diz-ian*	*ke*	*si*	*no*	*mos*	*komport-aramos*	*bien,*
and	PRON.DAT.1PL	tell-IMPF.3PL	COMP	if	NEG	REF.1PL	behave-SUBJ.1PL	well.ADV

And they used to tell us that if we did not behave well,

un-a zingan-a o un sedaker-o i mizmo Sanpavlo el mizm-o,
INDF-F.SG Romany-F.SG or INDF.M.SG beggar-M.SG and even.ADV Sanpavlo 3SG.M oneself-M.SG
a Romany woman or a beggar or even 'Sanpavlo' himself

moz pued-ia arevat-ar-mos.
PRON.ACC.1PL be.able-IMPF.3SG snatch-INF-PRON.ACC.1PL
might snatch us away.

No sav-iya kualo "Sanpavlo" ker-ia dizir, ma este byervo,
NEG know-IMPF.3SG what 'Sanpavlo' want-IMPF.3SG say-INF but PROX.M.SG word
I didn't know what 'Sanpavlo' meant, but this word,

dich-o kon boz alt-a ya me arevent-ava la fiel.
say.PTCP-M.SG with voice high-F.SG already PRON.DAT.1SG burst-IMPF.3SG DEF.F.SG gall.
said in a loud voice, was enough to burst my gall bladder.

Kon estos prospekto-s en mi-s penseryo-s, la entrada al kal
With PROX.M.PL prospect-PL in POSS.1-PL thought-PL DEF.F.SG entrance to.DEF.M.SG synagogue
With these prospects in my mind, the entrance

de Apollon me dava un sentimyento de espanto
of Apollon PRON.DAT.1SG give.IMPF.3SG INDF.M.SG feeling of fear
to the Apollon Synagogue gave me a feeling of fear

meskIad-o de un-a kuryozita.
mixed-M.SG of INDF-F.SG curiosity
mixed with curiosity.

Las vijita-s a los miembro-s de famiya ke mor-aron
DEF.F.PL visit-PL to DEF.M.PL member-PL of family REL reside-PRET.3PL
The visits to the members of the family who resided

en el deredor de la Kula, el uzo de ech-ar azete
in DEF.M.SG environs of DEF.F.SG Galata Tower DEF.M.SG custom of throw-INF oil
in the area of the Galata Tower, the custom of donating oil

al kal, su-s personaje-s estrany-os kon los sedakero-s
to.DEF.M.SG synagogue POSS.3-PL personage-PL strange-M.PL with DEF.M.SG beggar.M-PL
to the synagogue, its strange personages with the beggars

en la puerta del Kal Apollon, no egzist-en mas.
in DEF.F.SG door of.DEF.M.SG Synagogue Apollon NEG exist-PRS.3PL more
at the door of the Apollon Synagogue, no longer exist.

Esto todo ke despares-io en muestr-o tiempo aze parte
PROX.N.SG all REL disappear-PRET.3SG in POSS.1PL-M.SG time make-PRS.3SG part
All of this, which disappeared in our time, forms a part

de mi pasado. Kada ves ke vijit-o a Estambol, en el fondo
of POSS.1SG past each time REL visit-PRS.1SG OBJ Istanbul in DEF.M.SG bottom
of my past. Each time I visit Istanbul, deep inside

de un-a Kula i de su entorno, modernizad-o i restorad-o,
of INDF-F.SG tower and of POSS.3SG surrounding area modernized-M.SG and restored-M.SG
a tower and its surrounding area, modernized and restored,

su-s rekuedro-s se arebiv-en i me pares-e oy-ir
POSS.3-PL memory-PL REF.3SG revive-PRS.3PL and PRON.DAT.1SG seem-PRS.3SG hear-INF
their memories are revived and I seem to hear

las boz-es de los sedakero-s de Apollon.
DEF.F.PL voice-PL of DEF.M.PL beggar.M-PL of Apollon
the voices of the beggars of Apollon.

Roz Kohen's footnotes:
[i]Shamash *(Ebreo) – Alguno kargad-o kon los etcho-s sekretari-os*
Beadle (Hebrew) – someone encharged-M.SG with DEF.M.PL matter-PL secretarial-M.PL
Shamash (Hebrew) – Someone in charge of secretarial matters

del kal.
DEF.M.SG synagogue
of the synagogue.

[ii]Sanpavlo – *Pavlo, el Apostol ke biv-yo entre el anyo 5 i 67,*
Sanpavlo – Paul DEF.M.SG Apostle REL live-PRET.3SG between DEF.M.SG year 5 and 67
Sanpavlo – Paul, the Apostle who lived between the year 5 and 67 [CE],

tambien konosid-o komo San Pavlo o Saulo de Tarso. El se deskriv-e
also known-M.SG as Saint Paul or Saul of Tarsus 3SG.M REF.3SG describe-PRS.3SG
also known as Saint Paul or Saul of Tarsus. He is described

komo uno de los mas emportante-s misyonariyo-s Kristyan-os.
as one.M.SG of DEF.M.PL most important-PL missionary-PL Christian-M.PL
as one of the most important Christian Missionaries.

References

Arnold, Rafael. 2006. *Spracharkaden. Die Sprache der sephardischen Juden in Italien im 16. und 17. Jahrhundert*. Heidelberg: Winter.

Asa, Avraham. 1739. *Ḥeleq rišon me-ha-ʔarbaʕ wĕ-ʕeśrim wĕ-hu ḥamišša ḥumĕšše tora ʕim laʕaz*. Constantinople.

—. 1743. *Sefer neḇiʔim rišonim ... ʕim laʕaz.* Constantinople

Benaim, Annette. 2011. *16th-Century Judeo-Spanish Testimonies*. Leiden: Brill.

Ben Ḥabib, Moše. 1731. *Š[ĕ'elot] u-t[šuvot] m[orenu] ha-ra[v] M[oše] Ben Ḥabib*. At the end of his *ʕEzrat našim*, Constantinople (Jerusalem 1989).

Bunis, David M. 1981. *A Phonological and Morphological Analysis of the Hebrew and Aramaic Component of Judezmo*. Unpub. PhD. diss., Columbia University.

—. 1985. "Plural Formation in Modern East Judezmo." In *Jerusalem Studies in Judeo-Romance Languages*, edited by Joseph Sermoneta and Isaac Benabu. Jerusalem: Magnes Press, 41–67.

—. 1993a. *A Lexicon of the Hebrew and Aramaic Elements in Modern Judezmo*. Jerusalem: Magnes Press.

—. 1993b. "The Earliest Judezmo Newspapers: Sociolinguistic Reflections." *Mediterranean Language Review* 6–7, 5–66.

—. 1993c. *The Judezmo Language: An Introduction*. Jerusalem: Magnes. (In Hebrew)

—. 1994. "Tres formas de ladinar la Biblia en Italia en los siglos XVI–XVII." In *Introducción a la Biblia de Ferrara*, edited by Iacob M. Hassán. Madrid: Consejo Superior de Investigaciones Científicas, 315–345.

—. 1996. "Translating from the Head and from the Heart: The Essentially Oral Nature of the Ladino Bible-Translation Tradition." In *Hommage à Haïm Vidal Sephiha*, edited by Winfried Busse, Heinrich Kohring, and Moshe Shaul. Bern: Peter Lang, 337–357.

—. 1997a. "Phonological Characteristics of Ibero-Romance Elements in the First Printed Ladino Bible Glossary (*Sefer Hešeq Šelomo*, Venice, 1587/88)." In *Hispano-Jewish Civilization After 1492*, edited by Michel Abitbol, Galit Hasan-Rokem and Tom-Tov Assis. Jerusalem: Misgav Yerushalayim, 203–252.

—. 1997b. "The Use of Hebrew and Aramaic Elements in the Creation of Satire by Speakers of Judezmo." *Massorot* 9–10–11: 319–333. (In Hebrew).

—. 2003. "Ottoman Judezmo Diminutives and Other Hypocoristics." In *Linguistique des langues juives et linguistique générale*, edited by Frank Alvarez-Pereyre and Jean Baumgarten. Paris: CNRS, 193–246.

—. 2005a. "Writing as a Symbol of Religio-National Identity: On the Historical Development of Judezmo Spelling." *Peʕamim* 101–102, 111–171. (In Hebrew)

—. 2005b. "A Theory of Hebrew-Based Fusion Lexemes in Jewish Languages as Illustrated by Animate Nouns in Judezmo and Yiddish." *Mediterranean Language Review* 16: 1–115.

—. 2006–2007. "Judezmo Inanimate Fusion Nouns with Non-Romance Affixes." *Yod* 11–12: 359–410.

—. 2007. "Judezmo and Haketia Inanimate Nouns with Hebrew-Origin Bases and Romance-Origin Affixes." In *Shaʕarei Lashon: Studies in Hebrew, Aramaic and Jewish Languages Presented to Moshe Bar-Asher*, edited by Aharon Maman, Steven E. Fassberg, and Yochanan Breuer, vol. 3, Jerusalem: The Bialik Institute, *40–63.

—. 2008a. "The Names of Jewish Languages: A Taxonomy." In *Il mio cuore è a Oriente. Studi di linguistica storica, filologia e cultura ebraica dedicati a Maria Luisa Mayer Modena*, edited by Francesco Aspesi, Vermondo Brugnatelli, Anna Linda Callow and Claudia Rosenzweig. Milan: Cisalpino, 415–433.

—. 2008b. "Jewish Ibero-Romance in Livorno." *Italia* 18: 7–64.

—. 2008c. "The Differential Impact of Arabic on Ḥaketía and Turkish on Judezmo." *El Presente* (Beer Sheva) 2: 177–207.

—. 2009. "Judezmo Analytic Verbs with a Hebrew-Origin Participle: Evidence of Ottoman Influence." In *Languages and Literatures of Sephardic and Oriental Jewry*, edited by David M. Bunis. Jerusalem: Misgav Yerushalayim and Bialik Institute, 94–166.

—. 2011a. "Judezmo Glossaries and Dictionaries by Native Speakers and the Language Ideologies behind Them." In *Lexicología y lexicografía judeoespañolas*, edited by Winfried Busse and Michael Studemund-Halevy. Berne: Peter Lang, 353–446.

—. 2011b. "A Doctrine of Popular Judezmism as Extrapolated from the Judezmo Press, c. 1845–1948." *Satirical Texts in Judeo-Spanish By and About the Jews of Thessaloniki*, edited by Rena Molho, Hilary Pomeroy and Elena Romero. Thessaloniki: Ets Ahaim Foundation, 244–268.

—. 2011c. "The Changing Faces of Sephardic Identity as Reflected in Judezmo Sources." *Judenspanisch* 13: 43–71.

—. 2012. "The Anti-Castilianist Credo of Judezmo Journalist Hizkia M. Franco (1875–1953)." In *Homenaje a Elena Romero*, edited by Aitor García Moreno, *ehumanista* 20 (http://www.ehumanista.ucsb.edu/volumes/volume_20/pdfs/articles/monographic%20issue/5%20Bunis.v20.pdf), 63–97.

—. 2013a. " 'Whole Hebrew': A Revised Definition." In *A Touch of Grace: Presented to Chava Turniansky*, vol. 2, edited by Yisrael Bartal, Galit Hasan-Rokem, Ada Rapaport-Albert, Claudia Rosenzweig, Vicki Schifriss and Erika Timm. Jerusalem: Zalman Shazar Center & Center for Research on Polish Jewry, *37–68.

—. 2013b. "The Whole Hebrew Reading Tradition of Ottoman Judezmo Speakers: The Medieval Iberian Roots." *Hispania Judaica Bulletin* (Hebrew University of Jerusalem. Jerusalem) 9, 15–67.

—. 2013c. "From Early Middle to Late Middle Judezmo: The Ottoman Component as a Demarcating Factor." *El Prezente* (Beer Sheva) 7 / *Menorah* (Belgrade) 3: 115–163.

—. 2014. "Linguistic Conservatism versus Linguistic Pragmatism: Judezmo Speakers on 'Old' and 'New' Language." In *Around the Point: The Literatures of Jews in Jewish and Non-Jewish Languages*, edited by Hillel Weiss, Roman Katsman and Dov-Ber Kotlerman. Cambridge: Cambridge Scholars Publishing, 135–182.

—. 2015. "Jewish and Arab Medieval Ibero-Romance: Toward a Comparative Study." In *In the Iberian Peninsula and Beyond*, vol. 2, edited by José Alberto R. S. Tavim, Maria Filomena Lopes de Barro, Lúcia Liba Mucznik. Cambridge: Cambridge Scholars, 64–148.

—. 2016. "Judezmo (Ladino)." In *Handbook of Jewish Languages*, edited by Lily Kahn and Aaron D. Rubin. Leiden: Brill, 365–450.

— . 2017a. "Lexical Elements of Slavic Origin in Judezmo on South Slavic Territory, 16–19th Centuries: Uriel Weinreich and the History of Contact Linguistics." *Journal of Jewish Languages* 5: 217–252.

—. 2018. "Judezmo (Ladino/Judeo-Spanish): A Historical and Sociolinguistic Portrait." In *Languages in Jewish Communities, Past and Present*, edited by Benjamin Hary and Sarah Bunin Benor. Berlin–Boston: De Gruyter, 185–238.

—. 2018–2019. "The Language and Personal Names of Judezmo Speakers in Ereṣ Israel during the Time of Nathan of Gaza: Clues from Seventeenth-Century Ottoman Rabbis." *El Prezente* 12–13: 31–72.

—. 2019. "La ortografia de Aki Yerushalayim: Un pinakulo de la estoria de la romanizasion del djudezmo (djudeo-espanyol)." *Aki Yerushalayim* 101: 8–24 (http://www.akiyerushalayim.com/ay/101/101_03_ortografia.htm).

—. 2020. "Adjectives of Hebrew and Aramaic Origin in Judezmo and Yiddish." *Journal of Jewish Languages* 8: 189–268.

Bunis, David M., and Mattat Adar-Bunis. 2011. "Spoken Judezmo in Written Judezmo: Dialogues in *Sefer Me-ʕam Loʕez* on Leviticus and Numbers (Istanbul 1753–64) by Rabbi Yiṣḥaq Magriso." *Peʕamim* 125–127, 412–505. (In Hebrew).

Crews, Cynthia M. 1962. "The Vulgar Pronunciation of Hebrew in the Judeo-Spanish of Salonica." *The Journal of Jewish Studies* 13, 83–95.

De Kastro, Avraham. (tr.). 1823. *Toledot adam en ladino.* Constantinople.

Gonzálvez García, Francisco. 2010. "Contrasting Constructions in English and Spanish: The Influence of Semantic, Pragmatic, and Discourse Factors." In *Contrastive Studies in Construction Grammar*, edited by Hans C. Boas. Amsterdam: John Benjamins Publishing Company, 43–86.

Hacohen, Aviad. c.2004. *Tears of the Oppressed: An Examination of the Agunah Problem.* Jersey City, NJ: Ktav.

Ḳulí, Yaʕaqov. 1730. *Sefer Me-ʕAm Loʕez ... Berešit.* Constantinople.

Měnašše, Yaʕaqov Rěfa'el. 1836. *Běʔer ha-mayim, ʔEven Ha-ʕezer.* Salonika.

Meşulam, David. c1932. *La agad'a de pesah.* Istanbul.

Minervini, Laura. 1992. *Testi giudeospagnoli medievali (Castiglia e Aragona).* 2 vols. Naples: Liguori.

—. 1994. " 'Llevaron de acá nuestra lengua'. Gli usi linguistici degli ebrei spagnoli in Italia." *Medioevo Romanzo*, 19, 133–192.

—. 2014. El léxico de origen italiano en el judeoespañol de Oriente. In *La lengua de los sefardíes: tres contribuciones a su historia*, edited by Winfried Busse. Tübingen: Stauffenburg, 65–104.

Mi-Šaʕar-Arye/Portaleone, Abraham. 1612. *Sefer Šilṭe Ha-gibborim.* Mantua.

Mizraḥi, Eliyyahu. 1559–61. *Responsa*. Constantinople.

Papastathis, Ch. K., and Hekimoglou, E. A. 2010. *The Great Fire of Thessaloniki (1917)*. Thessaloniki: E. N. Manos. Retrieved from file:///G:/Local%20Disk/Seattle%202013/Salonika%20postcards/The_Great_Fire_of_Thessaloniki_1917.pdf.

Paquda, Baḥye Ibn. c1568. *Sefer ḥobat ha-lěbabot bě-laʕaz*, translated by Ṣaddiq Formón. Salonika.

Perahya, Klara et al. 1997. *Diksyonaryo Judeo Espanyol – Türkçe / Sözlük Türkçe – Judeo Espanyol*. Istanbul: Gözlem.

Perahya, Klara. 2012. *Diksyonaryo Judeo-Espanyol–Turko / Ladino–Türkçe Sözlük*. 2nd edition, enlarged, edited by Karen Gerson Şarhon. Istanbul: Gözlem and Sefarad Kültürü Merkezi.

Quintana Rodríguez, Aldina. 2006. *Geografía lingüística del judeoespañol: Estudio sincrónico y diacrónico*. Bern: Peter Lang.

Romero, Elena. 1992. *La creación literaria en lengua sefardí*. Madrid: Mapfre.

Sarısakal, Bari. *Selanik Mahalleleri 1913*. Retrieved from http://www.bakisarisakal.com/SELAN%C4%B0K%20MAHALLELER%C4%B0.pdf.

Schwarzwald, Ora (Rodrigue). 2018. "Judeo-Spanish throughout the Sephardic Diaspora." In *Languages in Jewish Communities, Past and Present*, edited by Benjamin Hary and Sarah Bunin Benor. Berlin–Boston: De Gruyter, 145–184.

Sephiha, Haim Vidal. 1973. "Le judéo-fragnol." *Ethno-psychologie* 2–3: 239–249.

Shaul, Moshe. 1979. "Es ke ay menester de una nueva ortografia para el djudeo-espaniol?" *Aki Yerushalayim* 1, 3–4.

Varol-Bornes. Marie-Christine. 1996. "Influencia del turco en el judeoespañol de Turquía." In *Hommage à Haim Vidal Sephiha*, edited by Winfried Busse and Marie-Christine Varol-Bornes. Bern: Peter Lang, 213–238.

Varol-Bornes, Marie-Christine. 2008. *Le judéo-espagnol vernaculaire d'Istanbul*. Bern: Peter Lang.

Haketia – the Judeo-Spanish of North-Africa

Yaakov Bentolila, The Ben-Gurion University of the Negev

1. The Origin of Haketia

Jews were expelled from Spain starting in 1391, followed by greater numbers in 1492. These exiles (*megorašim* in Hebrew) included an important contingent that settled in North Africa, in Morocco and Algeria, where they continued using the Spanish they brought with them. However, after two or three centuries, those living in the main cities of the Maghreb assimilated into the indigenous Jewish communities (the *tošabim*), and adopted their Judeo-Arabic dialect.

The communities established in the north, in parts of Algeria and later in Gibraltar (Benabu 2008) continued using Spanish. However, the influence of local (Muslim or Jewish) Arab dialects, together with the traditional Hebrew superstratum, resulted in the evolution of a Judeo-Spanish variant known as Haketia. The name Haketia probably comes from the Arabic root حكي (√ ḥ-k-y) meaning speech or chitchat, as it is an oral variant that borrows many words from the local Maghrebian dialects.

The dialect also presents a higher written register, sharing in the general Judeo-Spanish (*koiné*) language common to the whole Sephardíc diaspora (Bentolila 2008). In Morocco the name "Ladino" was reserved for this variety. The register avoids using typical vernacular words (Bentolila 1999). It was used for translation of religious texts, such as the Passover Haggadá, sermons and rabbinical treatises, texts that understandably borrow a high proportion of words from Hebrew. We will use the name Haketia for both the oral and written varieties.

2. Overview of the language

2.1 State of the research

The first researcher of Haketia was José Benoliel, who wrote a detailed description of the dialect. His essay, which offers the first Glossary of Haketia, was serialized in the prestigious *Boletín de la Real Academia Española* (Benoliel 1926–1952). Benoliel's work provides the most important knowledge base for Haketia. He saved from oblivion many details in the fields of cultural heritage (oral texts, proverbs, etc.), grammar (phonology and morphology) and vocabulary. However, some of the features he listed had limited usage, due to the process of *re-hispanización* of Haketia already begun, as evidenced later with the discovery of the Protocols of the Community Council of Tangier dating from the second half of the 19th century (Pimienta and Pimienta 2010). Modern Spanish influence is evident not only in documents of formal register like these protocols, but also in manuscripts of narrative and popular character dating from the early nineteenth century (Bentolila 2007b).

The work of Benoliel certainly contributed to a nascent scientific interest in the dialect shared by illustrious figures of philological work in Spain,[1] encouraging scholars to further study the linguistic aspects of Haketia, including Alegria [Bendayán de] Bendelac (1987, 1990, 1995), Isaac Benharroch (2004), Paul Benichou (1945, 1960), Yaakov Bentolila (1985, 1992, 1999, 2003, 2007b, 2007c, 2008, 2010, 2011, 2012, 2015b), Iacob Hassan (1968, 1977a, 1977b, 1998), Jacobo Israel Garzón (2013), Juan Martínez Ruiz (1957, 1960, 1966, 1982a, 1982b) and Haim Vidal Sephiha (1968, 1976, 1980, 1981a, 1981b). Nina Pinto-Abecasis was[2] a promising representative of the younger generation of researchers; she contributed with a folklorist approach, valuable studies of language and culture of Haketia speakers (Pinto-Abecasis 2008, 2014, forthcoming).

Many of the linguistic features of present day Haketia have evolved under the influence of modern Spanish. Due to the re-Hispanization of Haketia in recent generations, many archaic features, evidenced in ancient texts,[3] have disappeared from current use. Some however are preserved in sayings and proverbs. Many have been brought to life again, sometimes in an exaggerated way, in humorous texts of contemporary authorship. In the following paragraphs we will describe some of the principal features of the language,[4] with special focus on those presented in the five texts at the end of this article.

2.2 Conventions of transcription

Ladino and Haketia texts were traditionally written in Hebrew characters (see *infra*, Texts 1 through 3), but in modern times, since the beginning of the 20th century, the Latin alphabet has been used increasingly. For transcription of the former and for the rendering of recent texts, we will use the following conventions of transcription.

ĝ Denotes the voiced post-alveolar sibilant [IPA ʒ] in words of Spanish origin spelled with <g>; e.g., *reĝo* ('set of rules') and *ĝente* ('people, SP *gente*).

h/ɦ In Spanish words, according to current orthography, the initial <h> is silent: *hablar* ('to speak') is pronounced [ablar]. Sometimes, this letter is actualized as a glottal voiced approximant in Haketia; to represent these cases, we use the sign <ɦ>: *ɦablar*, *ɦazer* ('to do'). In words of Hebrew or Arabic origin, we use <h> or <ɦ>: *kehiłlá* ('community'), *meɦrez* ('mortar'), according to the spelling and pronunciation in these languages.

Ḥ ḥ Denotes the voiceless pharyngeal fricative [IPA ħ] current in Arabic and in Hebrew.

1 Many studies are mainly focused on the description of oral literature, namely stories, romances, ballads and songs. Among those studied traditions of Morocco is worth mentioning the works of Manuel Alvar (1969), Oro Anahory-Librowicz (1998), Samuel Armistead (1973, 1976), Samuel Armistead and Joseph Silverman (1974, 1976), Paul Benichou (1946), Kelly Benoudis Basilio (2007), Paloma Diaz-Mas (1994), Arcadio de Larrea Palacín (1943, 1952, 1954), Juan Martínez Ruiz (1962, 1963a, 1963b, 1968, 1977), Zarita Nahón (1977), Manuel Ortega (1919) and Susana Weich-Shahak (1997, 2008).

2 Sorrowfully, Nina passed away prematurely in the summer of 2019; she was only 48.

3 E.g., the word *presona* (Text N° 1), today *persona.*

4 For a more comprehensive description, see: Benoliel 1977, Israel Garzon 2013.

J j This letter denotes the voiceless palatal fricative [IPA χ], as in modern Spanish spelling.

Ĵ ĵ Denotes the voiced post-alveolar sibilant [ʒ] in words of Spanish origin spelled with <j>; e.g., *hiĵa* ('daughter'; SP *hija*) and *ĵudezmo* ('religiosity'; SP *judaismo*).

K k This letter denotes the voiceless velar stop in words of Hebrew origin, regardless of whether the etymons are spelled with <כ> *kaf* or <ק> *qof*: *Ḥanuká*, *kehil·lá*, *madrakes* 'mattresses',[5] etc.

l·l We use this digraph to denote the gemination of [l] in Hebrew or Arabic words, in order to avoid the script <ll> pronounced in Spanish as palatal approximant [IPA λ or j]: HK *kehil·lá* ←≠→ SP *silla* ('chair').

Q q Mostly in words of Arabic origin, it represents [q], the voiceless uvular stop, as in *se qadeó* ('it was finished'), *qemmear* ('to stand [somebody or something]').

Š š This letter designates the voiceless post-alveolar sibilant [IPA ʃ]; for example: *šabbat šalom* ('formula for shabbat greetings'). It is also used to transcribe Spanish archaisms originally written with <x>, such as *šabon* ('soap'), *dišéramos* ('we would say'), *quešarse* ('to complain'), *bašo* ('low'), etc.

Y y Represents the palatal approximant [IPA j], transcribing the sound of the Hebrew *yod* <י> pronounced as in the word *yes*.

Z z Represents the voiced alveolar sibilant [z], in words of Hebrew origin written with <ז> *zayin*, and in Spanish words where an /s/ assimilates to an adjacent vowel: *zejut* (← HB *zəḵūṯ* 'merit'), *caza* or *cazza* (SP *casa* 'house'), *meza* or *mezza* (SP mesa 'table').

ʕ Represents the voiced pharyngeal fricative [IPA ʕ] in words of Semitic origin.

2.3 Phonetics and phonology

The following are characteristics of the phonetics and phonology of Haketia.

a) The pharyngeal fricatives /ḥ/ and /ʕ/, in words of Arabic or Hebrew origin. For example: (Text Nº 4) *yaḥasrá* (AR 'what a pity'), *yʕatik* (AR 'will give you'), *ḥanukía*; (Text Nº 3) *Maʕarab* (HB 'Morocco').

b) The glottal fricative /h/ (frequently voiced [ɦ]) in Hebrew words, like in *kehil·lá* (Text Nº 3, 'community'), or Arabic words, like in *ɦaraĵ* (Text Nº 5, 'uproar'). An etymological <h> written but no longer pronounced in Spanish words may be retained in Haketia, as seen in Text Nº 3 האזין [*hazen*] and האביינדו [*habiendo*] (SP *hacen* 'they do' and *habiendo* '[since] they have done', respectively); but אורורוסו [*orroroso*] (SP *horroroso* 'dreadful') and אירמאנוס [*ermanos*] (SP *hermanos* 'brothers') are examples with the current Spanish silent <h>.

c) Texts written in Hebrew letters show occurrences of a trilled /r/, as in אורורוסו [*orroroso*]. In this respect Spanish influence is widespread in the actual Haketic speech, as evidenced in *Marruecos* ('Morocco'; *infra* Text Nº 4). Older texts show occurrences of a simple alveolar tap (IPA [ɾ]): טיירה [*tiera*] (Text Nº 2, SP *tierra*).

5 From Arabic? The etymology of this word is uncertain.

d) The voiceless uvular stop /q/, in words of Arabic origin: *qadear* ('to finish, to terminate').

e) The voiced sibilant [z], not only in Hebrew or Arabic words but also in the actualization of an original /s/ as a result of assimilation between vowels: *laz alegríaz* (Text Nº 5); this [z] can evolve in a second phase from sibilant to an interdental fricative [IPA ð]: *mosotros* ('we') → [mozotros] → [*moðotros*].

f) The postalveolar sibilants, the voiced [ĵ] (IPA ʒ) as in *hiĵas* (Text Nº 1, 'daughters', SP *hijas* [iχas]) and *muĵer* ('wife, woman', SP *mujer*) and the unvoiced [š] as in *šabon*, *enšawar* (SP *jabón* 'soap' and *enjuagar* 'to rinse'); in actual spoken Haketia, influenced by modern Spanish <j>, most of these cases are pronounced as the voiceless velar fricative [χ].

g) The sibilant [š] is a phoneme in Haketia in words of Arabic or Hebrew origin; often it was pronounced [s], principally by women: *šabbat šalom* → *sabbat salom*; *kidduš* ('blessing of the wine') → *kiddús*, etc.; next to a voiced consonant, this [s] can be pronounced as [z]: *ḥešván* → [ḥesván] → *ḥezván* ('name of a Hebrew month'). On the other hand, [š] may be the actualization of an /s/ before a /k/ as in *mošca* [moška] ('fly', SP *mosca*), and *bušcar* [buškar] (Text Nº 1, 'to look at', SP *buscar*).

h) The profusion of gemination, especially in loanwords from Arabic or Hebrew, even when absent in the original form, as in *berajjá* (← HB *bərāḵā*); also, by consonantal assimilation, at word boundaries, like in *salimos de Pésaḥ* → *salímod-de Pésaḥ* (Text Nº 5).

i) Assimilation to velar sounds; for example: *bueno* ('good') → [wueno] → *güeno*, *puerta* ('door, gate') → *cuerta* [kuerta]; the same phenomenon is evident when a vowel /a/ diphthongizes after a velar consonant; for example: *Ḥanukká* (= HB *Ḥănukkā*) → *Ḥanukkwá*.

j) Consolidation of the consonant [n] with the vowel [i] in the palatal nasal [ñ] (IPA ɲ): *quinientos* (=SP 'five hundred') → *quiñentos* [kiɲentos] (Text Nº 5).

k) Reduction of [y] after an accented [i]: *maravilla* [maravíya] (= SP 'wonder') → *maravía*.

l) In some communities, particularly in Tetuan, consonant elision: *poned* (= 'put [2PL. IMP]') → *poné* (Text Nº 1), → *comites* ('you ate') → *comite*.

2.4 Morphology

Stress

Spanish words stressed in the antepenultimate syllable are reproduced as acute in Haketia: *música* → *muzicá* ('music'), *última* → *ultimá* ('last' F.).

Verb

The verb presents three conjugations in line with Spanish, identifiable by the suffixes: {-ar} (e.g., *mirar* 'look, see'), {-er} (e.g., *comer* 'eat') and {-ir} (e.g., *abrir* 'open'); although some verbs that are conjugated in Spanish in {-ir}, would articulate in Haketia according to the second conjugation; for example: *durmer* ('sleep', SP *dormir*), *dizer* ('tell', SP *decir*), *cubrer* ('cover', SP *cubrir*).

Haketic verbal forms coincide in the majority of cases with the Spanish. The following table shows the principal cases where Haketia differs from Spanish:

Spanish	Haketia	Forms
tengo *tomo*	*tengo/tengoy* *tomo/tomoy*	1SG.PRS.IND
somos	*somos/semos*	1PL.PRS.IND
tenéis *coméis* *habéis*	*tenís* *comís* *habís*	2PL.PRS.IND
fregué, *enseñé* *tuve* *hube* *fui* *estuve*	*freguí,* *enseñí* *tuvi* *hubi* *fui/fi* *estuvi*	1SG.PST.IND
tomaste *tuviste* *fuiste* *estuviste*	*tomates* *tuvites* *fuites/fites* *estuvites*	2SG.PRS.IND
fue	*fue/fe*	3SG.PST.IND
empezamos *fuimos*	*empecimos* *fimos*	1PL.PST.IND
tomasteis *tuvisteis* *hubisteis* *fuisteis* *estuvisteis*	*tomatis* *tuvitis* *hubitis* *fitis* *estuvitis*	2PL.PST.IND
fueron	*feron*	3PL.PST.IND
veréis *tendréis*	*verís* *tendrís*	2PL.FUT.IND
entrad	*entrái*	2PL.IMP
toméis	*tomís*	2PL.PRS.SBJV
tuviereis	*tuvieris*	2PL.IMPF.SBJV

2.5 Lexicon

In addition to an important number of Spanish words, the Haketia lexicon contains words of both dialectal Arabic and Hebrew origin. A survey of the entries recorded in Benoliel's glossary (Benoliel 1977) shows 34.5% of Arabic terms against 18.5% of Hebrew terms.

Words of Arabic origin

Words of Arabic origin[6] serve to designate objects and concepts from everyday life; e.g., *zinzelá* 'earthquake' (< Arabic *zalzala*), *estormía* 'cushion' (< Moroccan Arabic *ṣṭeṛmiya*), *rabuz* 'bellow' (< Moroccan Arabic *ṛabuz*), *mehrez* 'mortar' (< Moroccan Arabic *mahrez*). In higher registers, religious writings and other formal records of the language, there is a clear tendency to exclude them. For example, sermons given at ceremonies like *bar mizvas* and memorials use a language that members of those com-

6 See: Bunis 2008; El-Madkouri Maataoui 2004; Israel Garzón 2013: 63–68.

munities would call Ladino, based on Spanish and Hebrew only, clearly avoiding the use of Arabic words (Bentolila 1999). The communities differed regarding the proportion of Arabic words in the currently spoken Haketia, with more in Tangier and Chauen for example and less in Tetuan.

Words of Hebrew origin

The Hebrew component[7] assumes the expression of religious and cultural concepts, e.g., *šabbat* ('shabbat'), *Pésaḥ* ('Passover'), *šabuot* ('Pentecost'); legal concepts, e.g., *neeman* ('trustee'), *get* ('bill of divorce'); historical and sociological concepts, e.g., *galut* ('exile'), *kehiŀlá* ('community'), *goyim* ('gentiles').

Hebrew nouns and adjectives have been incorporated with notable frequency, but verbs are scarce e.g., *niftar* ('died'), *nizkar* ('mentioned'), used mainly in set phrases like *min haššamáyim tenuḥamu* ('be comforted from heaven'), or lexicalized, like *misabberaj* ('blessing') or *vaydabber* ('topic'). To express actions using Hebrew words, Haketia resorts to verbs such as *hazer* ('to do'), *dezir* or *dizer* ('to say'), etc.: *hazer ḥanifut* ('to do flattery = to flatter'), *hazer una kusiá* ('to do a difficulty = to raise an objection'), *dezir berajjá* ('to say a blessing'), *dezir tefillá* ('to say a prayer').

Whole Hebrew and Merged Hebrew

Components of Hebrew or Aramaic origin constitute one of the most important characteristics of any Jewish language. The transfer of a word from one language to another can take place with or without linguistic adjustment. Without adjustment, the word is used in the receiving language as it is understood and articulated in the donor language; with adjustment, the word adapts itself to the system of the receiving language – to its phonetics, its morphology or even to a change of meaning. Regarding Hebrew words in Jewish languages, acquisition of a word without linguistic adjustment is generally referred to as "whole Hebrew", whereas with adjustment it is referred to as "merged Hebrew".[8]

Whole Hebrew

Any word or expression belonging to the category of "whole Hebrew" may be inserted into both oral and written texts in Haketia. There are however cases of "whole Hebrew" in which Haketia offers its own version of a word that does not appear in the Bible and, therefore, lacks canonical configuration; for example: *kemeʕá* ('amulet') and *taŀlet* ('liturgical shawl'), other traditions exhibit *kaméaʕ* and *taŀlit* respectively, etc. There is another interesting case when a word is created in Haketia from a Hebrew root, as in *hamayot* ('making a fuss') or in *doḥaká* ('trouble').

Merged Hebrew

Hebrew words integrated into Haketia may exhibit changes in phonetics, morphology or meaning, as illustrated by the following examples:

7 See Bentolila 2015b.

8 See Weinreich 1954; Bar-Asher 2012: 23–35.

Phonetic change – /š/ → [s], for example: *šammáš* ('caretaker') → *sammás*; *kušiá* ('difficulty, question') → *kusiá*.

Morphological change – the use of Spanish prefixes and suffixes, e.g., *enkaˤasarse* ('to get angry') from Hebrew *kaˤas* ('anger'), *desḥamezar* ('to clean for Passover') from Hebrew *ḥāmēṣ* ('bread and the like').

Modification of meaning – *šajén* (HB 'neighbor') → *sajén* (HK 'Christian, Spanish'). The change of meaning of a word is in itself a phenomenon of merging, even without any alteration of phonetics or morphology: *ḥarboná* (HB Biblical proper name → HK 'beating, reprimanding'), *ḥalḥalá* (HB 'fear, quake' → HK 'hurry, trouble, urgency').

Loan translations

Another category of merging is found in translations in which Hebrew words taken from canonical texts are replaced with the corresponding Spanish expression, generally known from Ladino versions: *el amo del ˤolám* ← *ribbōnō šel ˤōlām* (HB 'master of [the] world'), *hiĵas de Israel* (Text Nº 1) ← *bənōṯ yiśrāʔēl* (HB 'daughters of Israel'). A special case of what may be called "morphological translation" is found in *se tenbló la tiera* (Text Nº 2, 'the ground shook itself'); this abnormal reflexive is a calque from a Hebrew *hitpaˤel*: *hizdaˤzəˤā*.

On the other hand some Hebrew expressions may show loan translations from Spanish. For example: *ʔōr ləyōm šel ʔarbāˤā yāmim ləḥ[odeš] nisān miš[šənaṯ] tqṣd* (Text Nº 2, 'On the eve of the 4th of Nissan 5594') – both *šel* and *mi-* translate the Spanish preposition *de* 'of'.

2.6 Decline of Haketia

As soon as 1860, with the short two year Spanish occupation of Tetuan, speakers of Haketia were increasingly exposed to modern Spanish, and with the establishment of the Spanish protectorate in 1912 it did not take long for the young people to favor the use of modern Spanish, a prestigious European language. Haketia was thus relegated to use mainly in domestic contexts. In the diglossia that evolved, Haketia became the Low Variant, especially among the youngsters of the community. Indeed, the Spanish regime was offering not only seductive distractions, but also cultural emancipation and higher education. Modern Spanish, with all its linguistic richness, became their first language.

Benoliel's description of Haketia (Benoliel 1926–1952) had already, during the second quarter of the XXth century, conferred on the language some status worthy of respect. A new appreciation of Haketia evolved after the achievement of the longed for western-oriented emancipation and was aided by the distancing of communities immigrating to other countries. From afar, when Haketia could be seen not as defective Spanish, but as an idiosyncratic dialect worthy of interest, evoking its memory brought an increasing nostalgia with the resumption of some of its uses – particularly encouraging and consolidating community identity. The renewed interest in Haketia was shared both by learned persons and laymen, some very talented and creative, producing literary writings and theatrical works, often humorous in nature.[9]

9 See Levy 1992, 2008, 2014.

In communities living in the diaspora, outside the State of Israel, Haketia often fills the role normally played by Hebrew in naming religious and traditional concepts. For example, what is called in Israel a *bar-mitsvá*, is called in the haketic diaspora *tefel·limes*; *berit milá* ('circumcision') is called *sercusión*; *kal·lá* ('fiancée') *novia*; *roš haššaná* ('new year') *rosaná*; *šabbat* ('shabbath') *Sabbá* or *Sabbad*; *taref* ('unclean') *terefá*; etc.

3. Text specimens with inter-linear glosses

3.1 Text N° 1: The preface to Dat Yehudit

This text is a short citation from the Preface to *Dat Yehudit* (Laredo and Levy 1835), a Ladino treatise, written in North-Africa, on the religious duties of women.

סיניוראס היגאס די ישראל אביריד לוס אוֹכוס
Señora-s hiĵa-s de Israel ab<e>rid los ojo-s
Lady-PL daughter-PL of Israel open.IMP.PL DEF.M.PL eye-PL
Ladies, daughters of Israel, open your eyes

דיל אינטינדימינטו אי פוני מיינטיס
d-el entendimiento y poné miente-s
of-DEF.M judgment and put.IMP.PL mind-PL
and look

אין איסטי מונדו אי סו ריגו אי סו וידה אי סו מואירטי
en este mundo y su regô y su vida y su muerte
in DEM.M.SG world and POSS.3SG.M set_of_rules and POSS.3SG.M life and POSS.3SG.M death
at this ongoing world – see in it both life and death

אי ויריס ביין קלאראמינטי קי נו בינימוס אאיסטי מונדו
y ver-ís bien claramente que no venimos a-este mundo
and see-2PL.FUT well clearly COMP NEG come.1PL.PRS to-DEM.M.SG world
and understand that we are not here only

פארה קומיר אי ביביר אי פאסאר טיימפו קי סי
para comer y beber y pasar tiempo que si
to.PURP eat.INF and drink.INF and cross.INF time CONJ if
to eat, drink and pass the time away. If

פואירה פור איסו איסטין סיגוראס קי נו סי קריארה
fuera por eso esten seguras que no se creara
be_1[10].3SG.SBJV.IMPF for.PURP that.N be_2[11].2PL.IMP confident.F.PL COMP NEG PRN.PASS create.3SG.SBJV
this was so, {the world} would never have been created.

מונדו סי נו סיירטאמינטי קי לוקי בינימוס אאיסטי
mundo, si<>no ciertamente que lo-que venimos a-este
world, if.not certainly CONJ DEF.N-CONJ come.1PL.PRS to-DEM.M.SG
Indeed, we only came to this

10 be_1 = *ser*.

11 be_2 = *estar*.

מונדו איס פארה האזיר גוסטו דיל שי״ת אי אאיסטו
mundo es para hazer gusto d-el šy"t y a-esto
world be$_{1}$.3SG.PRS to.PURP make.INF pleasure of-DEM.M.SG šy"t^{H}[12] and for-DEM.N
world to please the Blessed Name and so

דיבי לה פריסונה בושקאר אי פריגונטאר פור לוקי לי
debe la presona bušcar y preguntar por lo-que le
must.3SG.PRS DEF.F.SG person seek.INF and ask.INF for DEF.N-CONJ 3SG.DAT
each person should ask himself what he

פאלטה דיל גודיזמו פארה האזירלו סיינדו קי פארה
falta d-el ĵudezmo para hazer-lo siendo que para
lack.3SG.PRS of-DEF.M.SG Judaism to.PURP make.INF-3SG.M be$_{1}$.GER CONJ for.PURP
is missing [in his observance] of Judaism, this being

איסו סי קריאו
eso se creó
DEM.N PRN.PASS create.3SG.PST
the purpose for which he was created.

3.2 Text N° 2: Earthquake in Tetuan

This text is a short citation, from an 1835 chronicle about an earthquake that occurred in Tetuan, recorded in the Sassoon Manuscript 672 (microfilm 8959) held in the Institute of Microfilmed Hebrew Manuscripts (The National Library of Israel).[13]

אור ליום של ארבעה ימים לח ניסן מש תקצד
ʾōr lə-yōm šel ʾarbāʿā yāmīm lə-ḥ[ōdeš] nisān mi-š[šənaṯ] tqṣd
light^{H} for^{H}-day^{H} of^{H} four^{H} day.PL^{H} for^{H}-month.CS^{H} nisan^{H} of^{H}-year.CS tqṣd^{H}
On the eve of the 4th of Nissan 5594

לפק אה לאס אוגו די לה נוגי סי
li-p̄[rāṭ] q[āṭān] a la-s ocho de la noche se
for^{H}-computation^{H} small^{H} at the.F-PL eight of DEF.F.SG night PRN.PASS
at eight o'clock in the evening,

טינבלו לה טיירה דיג?א/ו/ן? זינזלה פואירטי אי דיספואיס די
tenbló la tiera de-un zinzelá fuerte y después de
shake.3SG.PST DEF.F.SG earth of.CAUS-INDEF earthquake^{A} strong and after PREP
the ground shook with a strong earthquake and since

איסטאר סיראדאס לאס קוואירטאס די לה סיבדאד –
estar cerada-s la-s cuerta-s de la ciḇdad –
be$_{2}$.INF close.F-PL DEF.F-PL door-PL of DEF.F.SG city
the city gates were closed,

אורדינארון לוס קונסוליס קי סי אבייראן לאס קוואירטאס
ordenaron los consul-es que se ab<r>ieran la-s cuerta-s
order.3PL.PST DEF.M.PL consul-PL COMP PRN.PASS open.3PL.SUBJ.IMPF DEF.F-PL door-PL
the consuls ordered them to be opened

12 Acronym: *Šy"t* (*šem yiṯbārak̠* = 'the Name (God), may He be blessed').

13 See Bentolila 2007b.

אי דורמיירון באסטאנטי גינטי אה פוואירה די

y durmieron bastante ĝente a fuera de

and sleep.3PL.PST enough people PREP outside of

and many people slept outside

לה סיבדאד אה לה נוגי סיגיינטי דורמיירון באסטנטי

la cibdad. A la noche siguiente durmieron bastante

DEF.F.SG city. PREP DEF.F.SG night following sleep.3PL.PST enough

the walls. The next night, many people [again] slept

גינטי אה פוואירה דיל איספאנטו קי דיזיאן קי אלה

ĝente a fuera, d-el espanto que dezian que a-la

people PREP outside of.CAUS-DEF.M.SG fright COMP say.3PL.IMPF COMP PREP-DEF.F.SG

outside the city walls, frightened by a rumour,

אוטרה נוגי אלאס אונאס אברה זינזלה עד

otra noche a-la-s una-s [h]abrá zinzelá ʕ[ad]" k[ān]

other.F.SG night PREP-DEF.F-PL one.F-PL[14] be.3SG.FUT earthquake^{A} until^{H} here^{H}

of another earthquake to take place at one o'clock. End [of the chronicle]

3.3 Text N° 3: Sir Moses Montefiore

This text is a short citation from Protocol 96 dealing with the expected visit of Sir Moses Montefiore in Morocco (Pimienta and Pimienta 2010).

איל סי פריסידינטי פריזינטו אין כונטה אונאס קארטאס

El Se[ñor] Presidente prezentó en junta un-a-s carta-s

DEF.M.SG mister president show.3SG.PST in committee INDF-F-PL letter-PL

The president presented to the Board some letters

קי ריסיבייו פור איספריסו די לוס דיינים די פיס,

que recibió por espreso de los dayyan-im de Fes,

REL get.3SG.PST by express from DEF.M.PL rabbi^{H}-PL^{H} from Fez

that he received by express mail from the Rabbis of Fez,

קוייו קונטינידו סי אינסיררה,

cuyo contenido se encierra,

PRN.POSS.M.SG contents PRN.PASS enclose.3SG.PRS

the contents of which are enclosed.

קי האביינדו לייגאדו אה סו קונוסימיינטו

que habiendo llegado a su conocimiento

COMP have.GER get.PTCP.M.SG to POSS.3SG.M knowledge

[The Fez Rabbis say] that their attention has been drawn to

לה לייגאדה אה איסטה דיל ויניראבלי קאבליירו שר משה מונטיפיורי

la llegada a ésta d-el venerable caballero Sar^{H} Mošé Montefiore

DEF.F.SG arrival to DEM.F.SG of-DEF.M.SG venerable gentleman sir Mošé Montefiore

the [expected] arrival of the venerable gentleman Sir Moses Montefiore.

14 Plural, as in *a las ocho* (line 2, 'at eight o'clock'), but singular in Spanish: *a la una* ('at one o'clock').

האזין פריזינטי אין קורטוס טירמינוס

hazen prezente en corto-s término-s
make.3PL.PRS present in short.M-PL term-PL
[They want to use this opportunity to] describe briefly

איל לאמינטאבלי איסטאדו די איסה קהלה

el lamentable estado de esa kehil·lá
DEF.M.SG sad situation of DEM.DIST.F.SG community^{H}
the lamentable situation of their community

אי איל אוררורוסו גלות קי סופרין נואיסטרוס אירמאנוס

y el [h]orroroso galut que sufren nuestro-s [h]ermano-s
and DEF.M.SG dreadful exile^{H} REL endure.3PL.PRS POSS.1-PL brother-PL
and the dreadful harassment undergone by our brothers

אין איל אינטירייור דיל מערב

en el interior d-el Maˤarab
in DEF.M.SG interior of-DEF.M.SG Morocco^{H}
in the Moroccan inland.

3.4 Text N° 4: A Moroccan Home

Below is a short citation from a text representing spoken Haketia, and written by Mrs. Sonia Benelbaz de Binisti, living in Caracas, about the Moroccan-style decor of his home, especially during the Hanuka festivities.

Con bien vos entre Ḥanuká!
with good 2PL.DAT enter.3SG.SBJV.PRS Hanuka^{H}
Happy Hanuka!

Ewa entrái a mi palacito encender-emos la-s mecha-s de Ḥanuká!
INTJ^{A} enter.IMP.PL PREP POSS.1SG living_room.DIM light-1PL.FUT DEF.F-PL wick-PL of Hanuka^{H}
Welcome to my living room and let's light the Chanukah candles!

Ama que ħiba
INTJ^{A} EXCL magnificence^{A}
How magnificent!

La ḥanukía sta šaˤaleteando,
DEF.F.SG Hanuka-menorah^{H} be$_{2}$.3SG.PRS shine^{A}.GER
The menorah shines,

la freguí con alma y corassón. Da-ca que
PRN.F.SG.ACC rub.1SG.PST with soul and heart give.IMP.SG-here COMP
I have polished it with all my heart and soul.

la mirara la descansada de mi abuela,
PRN.F.SG.ACC see.3SG.SBJV.IMPF DEF.F.SG rested.F.SG of POSS.1SG grandmother
I wish my grandmother, may she rest in peace, could see it,

Mamá Raquel, que su alma sté en gan ʕéden
Mama^{A} Raquel, COMP POSS.3SG soul be$_{2}$.3SG.SBJV.PRS in garden.CS^{H} Eden^{H}
Mama Raquel, may her soul rest in the garden of Eden.

Ella la gustaba todo cómo y cómo.
she REFL.F.SG like.3SG.IMPF everything how.EXCL and how.EXCL
She used to like everything to be just perfect.

Me dišera: La y-ʕati-k saḥḥa,
1SG.DAT say.3SG.SBJV.IMPF God^{A} 3SG-give.SBJV.FUT^{A}-2SG.ACC^{A} health^{A}
She would say to me: “may God give you health.

a immá, ansí t'-enseñí.
INTJ^{A} mother^{A} thus 2SG.ACC-teach.1SG.PST
Oh my child, this is [exactly] how I taught you.”

En mi palacito, dirás que stas en Marruecos,
In POSS.1SG living_room.DIM say.2SG.FUT COMP be$_{2}$.2SG.PRS in Morocco,
In my living room you would say that you are back in Morocco,

en los año-s de ya-ḥasrá
in DEF.M.PL year-PL of INTJ^{A}-pity^{A}
all those nostalgic years ago.

Alai los madrak-es faršado-s, la-s zarbiya-s
DEM DEF.PL.M mattress-PL tidy-PL the.F-PL carpet^{A}-PL
Look at the tidy mattresses, the carpets,

La-s senía-s con su-s tippad-es, la-s lampa-s de assófar,
the.F-PL tray^{A}-PL with POSS-PL teapot^{E}-PL DEF.F-PL lamp-PL of brass^{A}
the trays with their teapots, the lamps of brass,

La-s estormia-s, el rabúz, el meħrez,
DEF.F-PL cushion^{A}-PL DEF.M.SG bellows^{A} DEF.M.SG mortar^{A}
the cushions, the bellows, the mortar,

el tas para enšawar-se la-s manos
DEF.M.SG jug^{A} for.PURP rinse.INF-REFL DEF.F-PL hand-PL
the jug for hand washing,

y hazer la netila-t yad-aim.
and do.INF DEF.F.SG ablution-CS^{H} hand-DU^{H}
and doing the ritual ablutions.

Cada cozza pertenecía a un-a abuela, gran tía, bizabuela,
each thing belong.3SG.IMPF to INDF-F.SG grandmother grand aunt great_grandmother
Each thing belonged to a grandmother, a great aunt, a great grandmother,

ḥatta de Maine, la abuela de mi abuela.
even[A] of Maine.PRPN DEF.F.SG grandmother of POSS.1SG grandmother
even to Maine, my grandmother's grandmother.

Toda-s la-s generacion-es están cabe mi.
all.FM-PL the.F-PL generation-PL be$_{2}$.PRS.3PL near DAT.1SG
All the generations are [still] with me,

Bendicho ste el amod-el ʕolám
blessed be$_{2}$.3SG.SBJV.PRS DEF.M.SG master of-DEF.M.SG world[H]
blessed be God

uno se mete en el foyo pero se mos quedan su-s atuendo-s
one REFL put.3SG.PRS in DEF.M.SG hole but REFL DAT.1PL remain.3PL.PRS POSS-PL thing-PL
After death and burial, [only] their possessions remain

Y cada vez que mi-s ojo-s miran un-a ḥaĵa
and each time CONJ POSS.1SG-PL eye-PL see.3PL.PRS INDF-F.SG object[A]
and each time I look at one of these things

es como si miraran la persona.
be$_{1}$.3SG.PRS how if see.3PL.SBJV.IMPF DEF.F.SG person
it is as if I can [actually] see the [loved] one {to whom it belonged}.

3.5 Text N° 5: Leaving Tangier

This text is a short citation from Levy 2008 (p. 270); it deals with the author's emotional remembering of his departure from Tangier to immigrate to Canada.

Como salímod de Pésaḥ, empecímoz a preparar la cercusión.
How leave.1PL.PST PREP Pesah, start.1PL.PST to prepare.INF DEF.F.SG circumcision
Immediately after Passover, we started to prepare for the circumcision

En medio de la-z alegría-z y d-el ħaraĵ,
In middle of DEF.F-PL joy-PL and of-DEF.M.SG uproar[A]
In the middle of all the joy and excitement

yo me la-z apañaba pa[ra e]scapar-me de vez en cuando
1SG REFL.1SG OBJ.F-PL manage.1SG.IMPF to escape.INF-REFL.1SG from time in when
I managed to slip away from time to time.

Un-a horita a-la nochecer y me iba,
one-F hour.DIM at-DEF.M.SG nightfall and REFL.1SG go.IMPF.1SG
after nightfall, for a short stroll

sólo uaḥdí a pasear por la playa. Y miéntraz
alone alone[A] to stroll.INF by DEF.F.SG beach And meanwhile
alone on the beach. And while

andaba metiendo bien los pie-z descálso-z en la arena,
walk.IMPF.1SG put.GER well DEF.M.PL foot-PL barefoot-PL in DEF.F.SG sand
walking barefoot in the sand,

me ponía a jammear en muestro destino, en esa
REFL.1SG put.IMPF.1SG to meditate[A].INF on POSS.1M.SG destiny PREP DEM.DIST.F.SG
I started pondering our destiny at this

hoja d-el libro de muestra vida que se estaba volteando.
page of-DEF.M.SG book of POSS.1F.SG life COMP REFL be$_2$.IMPF.3SG turn.GER
turning point in our life.

Esta cercusión – me lo dizía y me lo repitía,
DEF.F.SG circumcision - REFL.1SG DEF.N.ACC say.1SG.IMPF and REFL.1SG DEF.N.ACC repeat.1SG.IMPF
This circumcision – I told myself again and again,

como pa[ra] convencer-me yo mizmo –
as to.PURP convince.INF-REFL.1SG 1SG 1SG.REFL –
as if to convince myself –

iba a ser la ultimá que ibamoz a festejar
go.3SG.IMPF to be$_1$.INF DEF.F.SG last.F.SG REL go.1PL.IMPF to celebrate.INF
[that this one] will be the last we were to celebrate

en la tierra de muéstro-z antepasado-s,
in DEF.F.SG land of POSS.1PL ancestor-PL
in the land of our ancestors;

¿la ultimá de cuánta-s?
¿DEF.F.SG last.F.SG of QNT.F-PL?
the last of how many?

¿Cuánto-z varon-es se cercusieron en muestra familia
¿QNT.M-PL boy-PL PRN.PASS circumcise.3PL.PST in POSS.1F.SG family
How many boys were circumcised in our family

dezde que el primero de los primero-s
since PREP DEF.M.SG first.M.SG of DEF.M.PL first.M-PL
since the first of [our ancestors]

puzzo el pie en Maruécoz
put.3SG.PST DEF.M.SG foot in Morocco
made his first step on [the soil of] Morocco?

haría de eso mil áño-z o maz, o quiñentos,
do.3SG.COND of DEM.DIST.N thousand year-PL or more, or five_hundred,
maybe a thousand or more years ago, or five hundred,

sigún sómoz descendiénte-z de los Tošab-im
PREP be$_{1}$.1PL.PRS descendant-PL from DEF.M.PL resident^{H}-PL^{H}
depending on whether we are descendants of the [original] residents

o de loz Megoraš-im?
or from the.M.PL exile^{H}-PL^{H}
or of the exiles [from Spain in 1492]?

References

Alexander, Tamar, and Yaakov Bentolila. 1998. "Elementos hispánicos y jaquéticos en los refranes judeo-españoles de Marruecos". *Jewish Studies in the Turn of the 20th Century*, edited by Angel Sáenz-Badillos and Judit Targarona-Borrás. Leiden: Brill, 421–429.

—. 2008. *La palabra en su hora es oro – El refrán judeo-español en el Norte de Marruecos*. Jerusalem: Ben-Zvi Institute.

—. 2010a. "On the Meaning of Personal Names in Haketic Proverbs and Idioms." *Image and Identity: Studies in Jewish Folklore*, edited by D. Ben-Amos, D., Tamar Alexander and P. Tokofsky. Wayne: Wayne State University Press, 263–293.

—. 2010b "A Soft Tongue Breaks the Bone: Canonic Hebrew Sources as Reflected in Judeo-Spanish Proverbs from Morocco." *Or Le-Mayer. Studies in Bible Semitic Languages Rabbinic Litterature, and Ancient Civilizations. Presented to Mayer Gruber on the Occasion of His Sixty-Fifth Birthday*, edited by Shamir Yona. Beer-Sheva: Ben-Gurion University of the Negev Press, *9–*37.

—. 2010c. "Personal Names in Judeo-Spanish Proverbs from Northern Morocco." *Pleasant Are Their Names*, edited by Aaron Demsky. Bethesda, Maryland: University Press of Maryland, 263–293.

—. 2015. "Judeo-Spanish Haketic Proverbs from Northern Morocco: Sources and Studies." *Bis Dat, Qui Cito Dat – Gegengabe in Paremiology, Folklore, Language, and Literature, Honoring Wolfgang Mieder on His Seventieth Birthday*, edited by Christian Grandl and Kevin J. McKenna. Frankfurt: Peter Lang, 17–28.

Alvar, Manuel. 1959. "El romance de Gerineldo entre los sefarditas marroquíes." *Boletín de la Universidad de Granada* 31: 9.

Anahory-Librowicz, Oro. 1998. "Romances judeoespañoles de Gibraltar." *Sefarad* 58.1: 5–29.

Armistead, Samuel G. 1973. "El cancionero judeo-español de Marruecos en el siglo XVIII (Incipits de los Ben-Ṣûr) ". *Nueva Revista de Filología Hispánica* 22: 280–290.

—. 1976. "El romancero judeo-español de Marruecos: Breve historia de las encuestas de campo." *Poesía: Reunión de Málaga de 1974*, edited by M. Alvar. Málaga: Cátedra-Seminarío Menéndez Pidal, 245–256.

Armistead, Samuel G., and Joseph H. Silverman. 1974. "Four Moroccan Judeo-Spanish Folksongs, Incipit (1824–1825)." *Hispanic Review* 42.1: 83–87.

—. 1976. "La colección Nahón de romances judeo-españoles de Tánger." *La Coronica* 5.1: 7–16.

Aslanov, Cyril. 2008. "La haquetía entre hispanidad y aloglotismo: divergencia y convergencia." *El Presente – Estudios sobre la cultura sefardí: La cultura Judeo-Española del Norte de Marruecos*, edited by Tamar Alexánder and Yaakov Bentolila Beer Sheva: Sentro Moshe David Gaon de Kultura Djudeo-Espanyola y la Universidad Ben-Gurion del Neguev, vol. 2, 209–222.

Bar-Asher, Moshe. 2012. *Studies in Modern Hebrew.* Jerusalem: The Academy for the Hebrew Language.

Benabu, Isaac. 2008. "Jewish Languages and Life after Death: Traces of Ḥaketía among the Jews of Gibraltar." *El Presente – Estudios sobre la cultura sefardí: La cultura Judeo-Española del Norte de Marruecos*, edited by Tamar Alexánder and Yaakov Bentolila Beer Sheva: Sentro Moshe David Gaon de Kultura Djudeo-Espanyola y la Universidad Ben-Gurion del Neguev, vol. 2, 243–252.

Benaim Bunan, Gladys. 2007. *Tu boca en los cielos – La haketía de Menashé y Alfonso*. Beverly Hills, CA: Laredo Publishing Co.

Benarroch, Carlos. 1970. "Ojeada sobre el judeo-español de Marruecos." *Actas del primer simposio de Estudios Sefardíes:* 263–275.

Benarrosch, Amram. 2004. *Palabras de allá, un sabor de haketía – en memoria de Rachel Benarrosch.* Rehovot: Yail.

Benazeraf, Raphael. 1978. *Refranero: Recueil de "Refranes" (proverbes) judéo-espagnols du Maroc (Hakitía).* Paris: Imprimerie Continentale..

Bendelac, Alegria. 1985. "L'héritage espagnol dans les communautés sépharades du Nord du Maroc." *Judaica España*: 43–50.

—. 1986. "Différents modes d'expression de l'intensité affective utilisés en Jaquetia." *Contrastes* 12: 43–52.

—. 1987. *Los Nuestros: Sejiná, Letuarios, Jaquetía y Fraja. Un retrato de los sefardíes del norte de Marruecos a través de sus recuerdos y de su lengua (1860–1984).* New York: Peter Lang.

—. 1998. "En busca de la jaquetía y de sus hablantes. Génesis de un diccionario." *La lengua y la literatura españolas en África*, edited by Celia Casado-Fresnillo. Melilla: V Centenario de Melilla, S.A., 43–68.

—. 1990. *Voces Jaquetiescas*. Caracas: Centro de estudios sefardíes de Caracas

—. 1995. *Diccionario del Judeoespañol de los Safardíes del Norte de Marruecos*. Caracas: Centro de estudios sefardíes de Caracas.

Benharroch, Isaac. 2004. *Diccionario de Haquetía*. Caracas: Asociación Israelita de Venezuela y Centro de Estudios Sefardíes.

Bénichou, Paul. 1944. "Romances judeo-españoles de Marruecos." *Revista de Filología Hispánica* 6.

—. 1945. "Observaciones sobre el judeo-español de Marruecos." *Revista de Filología Hispánica* Año 7.3: 209–258.

—. 1946. *Romances Judeo-españoles de Marruecos*. Buenos Aires: Universidad de Buenos Aires – Instituto de Filología.

—. 1960. "Notas sobre el judeo-español de Marruecos." *Nueva Revista de Filología Hispánica* 14: 307–312.

—. 1968. *Romancero judeo-español de Marruecos, 2nd ed.* Madrid: Castalia.

Benoliel, José. "Dialecto judeo-hispano-marroquí o hakitia", Boletín de la Real Academia de la Lengua Española, vol. XIII, fasc. 62 (1926): 209–233; fasc. 63 (1926): 342–363; 64 (1926): 507–538; vol. XIV, fasc. 66 (1927): 137–168; fasc. 67 (1927): 196–234; fasc. 68 (1927): 357–373; fasc. 69 (1927): 566–580; vol. XV, fasc. 71 (1928): 47–61; fasc. 72 (1928): 188–223, y vol. XXXII fasc. 136 (1952): 255–289. Reedited in Benoliel 1977 and Benoliel 2009.

—. 1977. *Dialecto judeo-hispano-marroquí o hakitia*. Madrid: R. Benazeraf.

—. 2009. *Diccionario básico jaquetía-español - Edición, introducción y notas: Jacobo Israel Garzón.* Madrid: Hebraica Ediciones.

Benoudis Basilio, Kelly (ed.) 2007. *Romances de Alcácer Quibir*. Lisbon: Colibri.

Bentolila, Yaakov. 1985. "Le composant hébraïque dans le judéo-espagnol marocain." *Judeo-Romance Languages*, edited by Isaac Benabu and Joseph Sermoneta. Jerusalem: The Hebrew University of Jerusalem, Misgav Yerushalayim, 27–40.

—. 1992. "The Hebrew Elements in Hakitia", *Miqqedem Umiyyam* 5: 59–66. (in Hebrew)

—. 1999. "Alternances d'hébreu et de judéo-espagnol dans un Daroush marocain." *Vena Hebraica in Judaeorum Linguis*, edited by Shelomo Morag, Moshe Bar-Asher, and Maria Mayer Modena. Le livre ed. Milan: Università degli Studi di Milano and The Hebrew University of Jerusalem, 203–219.

—. 2003. "Le processus d'hispanisation de la hakétia à la lumière de quelques sources littéraires." *Linguistique des langues juives et linguistique générale*, edited by Frank Alvarez-Péreyre and Jean Baumgarten. Paris: CNRS éditions. 2003: 247–265.

—. 2004. "Hébreu et judéo-espagnol dans des fiches didactiques trouvées à Tétouan." *Présence juive au Maghreb: Hommage à Haïm Zafrani*, edited by N. Serfaty and Joseph Tedghi. Paris: Editions Bouchene, 259–273.

—. 2007a. "Haketia: el djudeo-espanyol de la Afrika del Nord." *Judeo-Spanish (Ladino) – Proceedings of the Conference 6–7 November 2005*. Collana di Studi Ebraici. Livorno: Salomone Belforte, 85–89.

—. 2007b. "The Flood that Befell the City of Tetuan and Other Stories: Chronicles written in North African Judeo-Spanish." *Sha'arei Lashon, Studies in Hebrew, Aramaic and Jewish Languages presented to Moshe Bar-Asher*, edited by Aharon Maman, Steven E. Fassberg and Yonathan Breuer. Jerusalem: The Bialik Institute:, vol. 3: 259–277. (in Hebrew)

—. 2007c. "The Study of Moroccan Judeo-Spanish (Hakitia)." *Mikan* 8. Studies in Sephardic Culture, El Prezente 1: 159–164. (in Hebrew).

—. 2008. "La lengua común (coiné) judeo-española entre el Este y el Oeste." *El Presente – Estudios sobre la cultura sefardí: La cultura Judeo-Española del Norte de Marruecos*, edited by Tamar Alexánder and Yaakov Bentolila Beer Sheva: Sentro Moshe David Gaon de Kultura Djudeo-Espanyola y la Universidad Ben-Gurion del Neguev, vol. 2, 159–176.

—. 2010. "Haketia." *Encyclopedia of Jews in the Islamic World*, edited by Norman Stillman. Leiden: Brill online.

—. 2011. "The Hispanic *jota* in the Nord African Judeo-Spanish." *Hikrei Ma'arav u-Mizraḥ – Studies in Language, Literature and History, presented to Joseph Chetrit*, edited by Yosef Tobi and Dennis Kurzon. Jerusalem: Carmel ,vol. A, 43–58.

—. 2012. "Un cantar de castigo en el judeo-español de Marruecos." *Studies in Modern Hebrew and Jewish Languages Presented to Ora (Rodrigue) Schwarzwald*, edited by Malka Muchnik and Tsvi Sadan. Jerusalem: Karmel, 580–598. (in Hebrew)

—. 2015a. "Cómo se trokan los proverbios." *Dameta Letamar – Studies in Honor of Tamar Alexander*, edited by Eliezer Papo et al. Vol. 3. El Prezente 8–9; Mikan 15. Beer Sheva: Moshe David Gaon Center for Ladino Culture, the Ben-Gurion University, 1–9.

—. 2015b. *Diccionario del elemento hebreo en la ḥaketía*, Córdoba: UCO Press – CNERU (Córdoba Near Eastern Research Unit) – CSIC (Consejo Superior de Investigaciones científicas).

—. 2015c. "The Nineteenth-Century Book of Records fron the Jewish Community of Tangier and its Contribution to a Dictionary of Hebrew Elements in Haketía." *Studies in the History and Culture of North African Jewry*, edited by Moshe Bar-Asher and Steven D. Fraade. Jerusalem and New Haven: The Center for Jewish Languages and Literatures, Hebrew University, Jerusalem. The Program of Judaic Studies, Yale University, New Haven, 49–62.

Botbol Hachuel, Abraham. 1982. "El judeo-español, el ladino y la haketía." *Magen* 44, jul.-sept., 58–62.

Bunis, David M. 2008. "The Differential Impact of Arabic on Ḥaketía and Turkish on Judezmo." *El Presente – Estudios sobre la cultura sefardí: La cultura Judeo-Española del Norte de Marruecos*, edited by Tamar Alexánder and Yaakov Bentolila Beer Sheva: Sentro Moshe David Gaon de Kultura Djudeo-Espanyola y la Universidad Ben-Gurion del Neguev, vol. 2, 177–208.

Castro, Américo. 1922. "Entre los hebreos marroquíes, la lengua española en Marruecos." *Revista Hispano-Africana* 1.5: 145–146.

Chetrit, Joseph. 1985. "Judeo-Arabic and Judeo-Spanish in Morocco and their Sociolinguistic Interaction." *Readings in the Sociology of Jewish Languages*, edited by Joshua Fishman. Leiden: Brill, 261–279.

Cohen Aflalo, Esther. 2000. *Lo que yo sé – Manual de Haketía*. Madrid: Cyan, Proyectos y Producciones editoriales.

Díaz-Mas, Paloma. 1994. "Los romances tetuaníes del manuscrito de Luna Bennaim." *De balada y lírica II. Tercer coloquio internacional del romancero.* Madrid: Fundación Menéndez Pidal, Universidad Complutense de Madrid.

El-Madkouri Maataoui, Mohamed. "Los arabismos en el judeo-hispano-marroquí (Hakitía)." *Revista electrónica de estudios filológicos* 8.

Hassán, Iacob. 1968. "De los restos dejados por el judeo-español en el español de los judíos del norte de Africa." *Actas del XI Congreso Internacional de Lingüistica y Filología Románica*: 2127–2140.

—. 1977a. "Más hebraísmos en la poesía sefardí de Marruecos: Realidad y ficción léxicas." *Sefarad* 37: 373–428.

—. 1977b. "Un cantar ¿sefardí? sobre el ¿naufragio? de 1638." *El siglo XVII hispanomarroquí*, edited by Mohammed Salhi. Rabat: Facultad de letras, 311–331.

—. 1998. "Tetsimonios antiguos de la jaquetía." *La lengua y la literatura españolas en Africa*, edited by Casado-Fresnillo, Celia. Melilla: V Centenario de Melilla, S.A., 147–169.

IPA *The International Phonetic Alphabet and the IPA Chart* https://www.internationalphoneticassociation.org/content/ipa-chart

Israel Garzón, Jacobo. 2013. *Jaquetía – Dialecto judeo-español del Norte de Marruecos. Gramática elemental.* Madrid: Hebraica.

Jalfón de Bentolila, Estrella. 2008. *El Tetuán de los sefarditas.* Beverly Hills: Laredo Publishing Co. Inc.

Laredo, Abraham e Isaac Levy. 1835. *Dat Yehudit* ['La religión de la judía']. Liorna. (in Ladino)

Larrea Palacín, Arcadio de. 1943. *Cuentos populares de los judíos del norte de Marruecos.* Tetuán.

—. 1952. *Cancionero del Norte de Marruecos: Romances de Tetuán.* Vol. I-II. Madrid: Instituto de Estudios Africanos.

—. 1954. *Cancionero judío del norte de Marruecos: Canciones rituales hispano-judías.* Vol. III. Madrid.

Levy, Simon. 1991. "Judéo-espagnol et judéo-arabe marocains le sort des morphèmes de pluriel et d'emprunts au terme de quatre siècles de plurilinguisme." *Yod* 33–34: 141–155.

Levy, Solly. 1992. *YAHASRA – Escenas haquetiescas.* Montréal: Institut de la culture sépharade de la Communauté sépharade du Québec.

—. 2006. "Defensa e ilustracion de la Haquetia." *Sefardica* 16: 165–184.

—. 2008. *El libro de Selomó.* Madrid: Hebraica Ediciones.

– 2014. *El segundo libro de Selomó.* Barcelona: Tirocinio.

Martínez Ruiz, Juan. 1952. "Lengua y literatura de los sefarditas de Alcazarquivir." *Revista de la Universidad de Madrid* 1: 567–569.

—. 1957. "H aspirada y h muda en el judeo-español de Alcazarquivir." *Tamuda* 5: 150–161.

—. 1960. "Morfólogía del judeo-español de Alcazarquivir." *Miscelanea Filológica dedicada a Mons. A. Griera* ,103–128.

—. 1962. "La poesía tradicional sefardita de Alcazarquivír." *Archivum* 12: 79–215.

—. 1963a. "Poesía sefardí de carácter tradicional (Alcazarquivir)." *Archivum* 13: 79–215.

—. 1963b. "Textos judeo-españoles de Alcazarquivir." *Revista de Dialectología y Tradiciones populares* 19: 78–115.

—. 1966. "Arabismos en el judeo-español de Alcazarquivir (Marruecos) 1948–51." *Revista de Filología Española* 49: 39–71.

—. 1968. "Un cantar de boda paralelístico bilingüe en la tradición sefardí de Alcazarquivir (Marruecos)." *Revista de Filología Española* 51: 169–181.

—. 1977. "Ficción y realidad judeo-española en el Aita Tettauen, de Benito Pérez Galdós." *Revista de Filología Española* 54,: 145–177.

—. 1982a. "Aragonismos en el judeo-español de Alcazarquivir." *Miscelánea de Estudios Arabes y Hebraicos, Universidad de Granada* 31.2: 119–133.

—. 1982b. *Lenguas en contacto: judeo-español y árabe marroquí: interferencias léxicas, fonéticas y sintácticas.* Actas del Cuarto Congreso Internacional de Hispanistas.

Nahon, Zarita. 1977. *Romances judeo-españoles de Tánger. Recogidos por Zarita Nahon*. Madrid: Cátedra – Seminario Menéndez Pidal.

Ortega, Manuel. 1919. *Los hebreos en Marruecos*. Madrid: Hispano-Africana.

Pimienta, Gladys. 1991. "Espagnol et Haketia à travers les chansons judéo-espagnoles du Maroc." *Yod* 33–34: 133–139.

—. 1994. "Un inventario en Haketia." *Aki Yerushalayim* 50: 30–33.

—. 2004. "Djoha en haketia." *Aki Yerushalayim* 76: 34–37.

Pimienta, Gladys and Sidney Pimienta (transcription by). 2010. *Libro de Actas de la Junta Selecta de la Comunidad hebrea de Tánger (1860–1883) – Nacimiento y desarrollo de una comunidad organizada*. Paris and Jerusalem: Jem y Erez editors.

Pimienta, Jimmy. 1991. "Une chronique en Haketia." *Yod* 33–34: 99–114.

Pimienta, Sydney. 1991. "Actas de la communauté juive de Tanger (1860–1875)." *Yod* 33–34: 115–131.

—. 1992. *Libro de Actas de la Junta Selecta de la Comunidad Hebrea de Tanger, desde 6 Heshvan 5621 hasta 21 Iyyar 5635 – Indice transcrito del aljamiado al espanol por Sidney Salomon Pimienta*. Paris.

Pinto-Abecasis, Nina. 2008. "El entramado de las relaciones entre las comunidades judías del Marruecos español en el espejo del chiste y del mote." *El Presente – Estudios sobre la cultura sefardí: La cultura Judeo-Española del Norte de Marruecos*, edited by Tamar Alexánder and Yaakov Bentolila Beer Sheva: Sentro Moshe David Gaon de Kultura Djudeo-Espanyola y la Universidad Ben-Gurion del Neguev, vol. 2, 283–290.

—. 2014. *The Peacock, the Ironed Man and the Half-Woman – Nicknames, humor and foolklore in the day-to-day speech of Tetuan's Haketia-speaking Jews*. Jerusalem: Ben-Zvi Institute and the Hebrew University of Jerusalem. 2014. [in Hebrew].

—. forthcoming. *Tetuan – Site of Contacts between Cultures*. (in Hebrew)

Rechnitz, Florette M. 1978. "Tres romances de Tánger." *Estudios sefardíes* 1: 121–128.

Sephiha, Haim Vidal. 1968. "Vestiges du judéo-espagnol vernaculaire du Maroc (Hakitia) parmi les Juifs de l'Oranie." *Judaïsme d'Afrique du Nord aux XIXe-XXe siècles*, edited by M. Abitbol, Jerusalem: Institut Ben-Zvi, 160–166.

—. 1976. "Extinction du judéo-espagnol vernaculaire du Maroc ou Hakitía." *Yod* 2,1: 83–88.

—. 1980. "Le Judéo-espagnol au Maroc." *Juifs du Maroc, Identité et Dialógue*. Grenoble: La Pensée sauvage, 85–97.

—. 1981a. "Le judéo-espagnol du Maroc ou Haketiya." *Combat pour la Diaspora* 6: 77–80.

—. 1981b. "Archaïcité et sacré en judéo-espagnol oranais." *Ethnolingüistique. – Contributions théoriques et méthodologiques*. Paris: Selaf, 151–155.

Weich-Shahak, Susana. 1977. *Romancero sefardí de Marruecos: antología de tradición oral*. Le livre ed. Madrid: Editorial Alpuerto, S. A.

—. 2008. "*Me vaya kapará* – La haketía en el repertorio musical sefardí." *El Presente – Estudios sobre la cultura sefardí: La cultura Judeo-Española del Norte de Marruecos*, edited by Tamar Alexánder and Yaakov Bentolila Beer Sheva: Sentro Moshe David Gaon de Kultura Djudeo-Espanyola y la Universidad Ben-Gurion del Neguev, vol. 2, 291–300.

Weinreich, Max. 1954. "Prehistory and Early History of Yiddish: Facts and Conceptual Frameworks." *The Field of Yiddish*, edited by Uriel Weinreich. New York: Linguistic Circle of New York, 73–101.

Judeo-Italian

Michael Ryzhik, Bar-Ilan University

1. Introduction: Overview of Judeo-Italian

This article is divided in three parts: 1. an introduction dedicated to general problems concerning Judeo-Italian and to a brief description of its written sources; 2. a grammatical sketch;[1] and 3. an anthology, representing three sources discussed in the first part: a 13th century *Elegy for the 9th of Av*, translations of the Siddur from the 15th–17th centuries, and an excerpt of a 16th century sermon, accompanied by morpheme-by-morpheme glossing.

1.1 General remarks

Judeo-Italian is the common name for different modes of speech and writing (dialects, k*oinè*) that were used by Italian Jews. The history of Jews on the Appenine peninsula is very long and concerns almost all parts of it,[2] and so also the history of Judeo-Italian. Generally speaking, the whole complex of Judeo-Italian modes of speech may be divided into two major groups: medieval and modern. They differ from each other in many aspects, both linguistic and methodological, and not only diachronically. Medieval Judeo-Italian dialects are conserved in written sources. These written sources represent mostly translations of classical Hebrew texts, such as the Hebrew Bible and some excerpts from the post-biblical literature, and several translations of the Siddur, but also the *Elegy for the 9th of Av*, an original poetic composition of the 13th century, and some 16th century sermons (see below). All of these represent the high level of the language. On the other side, modern Judeo-Italian is represented by spoken ghetto dialects. These dialects were formed after the establishing of ghettos in the second half of the 16th century and functioned up to the Second World War when two different factors caused their disappearance: the Catastrophe of the European Jewry and the final victory of the Italian language over the dialects also in the everyday life. In this period, Hebrew and Italian were used for writing, and Judeo-Italian only served for everyday talk, representing the low level of the language. As a consequence, also the type of documentation is very different: instead of translations of sacred texts there are lists of words and expressions[3] made mostly by amateurs without special preparation, who were interested first of all in strange and unusual (if not simply comic) features, and not in a systematic description of ghetto speech.[4]

1 Words and short fragments that are used in this part as examples of discussed linguistic or cultural features are not accompanied by morpheme-by-morpheme glossing.

2 For general ideas (and many details) see, e.g., Milano 1963.

3 For a comprehensive bibliography see now Aprile 2012.

4 Of course there are exceptions, as extensive scientific descriptions, see Giacomelli and Terracini (Terracini 1937, 1951, 1962), Mayer-Modena and Massariello 1973, and Massariello 1980.

This article is dedicated to the earlier, medieval-renaissance period of Judeo-Italian (13th-17th centuries). The main reason is practical: relatively long text-specimens can be found in this period. For later periods we have only few texts that represent not so much a live usage, as a "reflected dialectal literature", as similar compositions in Christian Italian dialects were called by Benedetto Croce.[5] Such are, e.g., the sonetto collections by Crescenzo Del Monte, written in Judeo-Romanesco;[6] they are particularly rich in Hebrew-Aramaic elements, but the Romance component is of great importance as well. The well-known scholar David (Umberto) Cassuto wrote a play with his children in Judeo-Fiorentino, "Gnora Luna",[7] which may serve as an important source of this dialect in the first half of the 20th century. The Second World War and the Holocaust with subsequent post-war changes in the style of life led to a drastic fall in the active use of Judeo-Italian. In the last decades of the 20th century, some representatives of "reflected dialectal literature" appeared that represent the last phases of Judeo-Italian, as for example "Chiacchere alla giudia" by Mirella Calò,[8] a collection of short dialogues in the Judeo-Romanesco of the 1980s that successfully strive to be realistic and modern, but are also extremely nostalgic. However, as stated, these texts are not authentic representatives of Judeo-Italian.

The second reason (which is of course closely related to the first) to discuss mostly the earlier texts is that they are much richer in Judeo-Italian elements and so can give a fuller understanding of the nature of Judeo-Italian dialects in their written form.

Some important facts characterized the general lines of development of Judeo-Italian from its very beginning. Generally speaking, Judeo-Italian underwent a homo-glossic development: it developed in the Italian milieu, while Yiddish and Ladino were spoken and written in a hetero-glossic situation, Yiddish mostly in Eastern Europe, and Ladino mostly in Turkey and in North Africa. But this general factor must be complemented by another one: the main direction of migration of Jews in Italy was from South to North,[9] so the Jewish variants of the local dialects are generally more Southern (i.e. have more Southern traits) than their Christian counterparts.[10] Yet another phenomenon is that, as other Jewish languages did as well, Judeo-Italian dialects conserved numerous archaic traits.[11]

5 Croce 1952.

6 Del Monte 1927, 1932, and1955.

7 Bene Kedem 1932 (Bene Kedem is an acronym of of *Bene [= children of] Kassuto David Moshe*).

8 Calò 1990.

9 See, e.g., Milano 1963, *passim*.

10 See Colorni 1970 on Judeo-Mantuan. E.g., in the field of phonology, Judeo-Mantuan lacks the vowels *ü* and *ö*, typical of the Lombardic dialects (as a result of Gallic substrate) and usual in the Mantuan non-Jewish dialect; so *cor* 'heart' and not *cör* (as in the Mantuan non-Jewish dialect) *fiol* 'son' and not *fiöl*, *mur* 'wall' and not *mür*, *du* 'two' and not *dü*.

11 So Mancini (1992) has demonstrated that the language of the Roman ghetto in the Renaissance and Baroque period was based on the Roman dialect of the "first stage", e.g. on the medieval Roman dialect, and not on the Roman dialect of the "second stage", which was formed in the 16th century, mostly under the massive influence of the Florentine traits. Del Monte (1935) has shown that also the ghetto dialect of the first half of the 20th century had great affinity with the old Roman dialect.

As a consequence of mutual work of these factors, i.e. the conservation of Southern and archaic traits and constant movement from place to place in a homo-glossic environment, Judeo-Italian dialects are mostly formed as a result of koineization. According to Cuomo[12] and Sermoneta, [13] this is the case in the central-southern Judeo-Italian dialects, in which medieval texts are written . On the base of 16th–17th centuries compositions, written in more northern parts of Italy, one can speak of a central-northern koine.[14] Let us consider one example of such a dialect mixture. In a Jewish (Hebrew) calendar for 1573 printed in the Venetian Ghetto, we find the Julian names of months and names of Christian festivals and saints.[15] These names are written in Hebrew characters and are those used by the Venetian Jews in their vernacular. There are clear Southern traits in their phonology:

– assimilation *mb* > *mm* characteristic of the South,[16] e.g., סיטימר / סיטימרו (*settemer* / *settemro*), נובימר / נובימרו (*novemer* / *novemro*), דיצימר / דיצימרו (*dicemer* / *dicemro*);

– shift *st* > *št*: שטיפן (*Štefano*), בשטיאן (*Baštian*), קרישטופן (*Crištofan*), אגושטין (*Agoštin*). This shift is characteristic of some southern regions, first of all Abruzzo.[17] It is found also in some northern regions (Romagna), but there it is accompanied by the shift *sk* > *šk*, while in the language of our calendar this latter shift does not take place: פרנציסקו (*Francesco*), פסקווה (*Pasqua*), precisely as in Abruzzo.

But there are also some Northern phonological traits:

– omission of the last vowel: דיצימר (*Dicemer*), נובימר (*Novemer*), סיטימר (*Settemer*), יואן (Ioan), קרניוואל (*carneval*), קרישטופן (*Crištofan*), אגושטין (*Agoštin*). This phenomenon is typically northern.[18]

– Sonorization of intervocalic *t* (only in two cases; in other occurrences the *t* is conserved): וידו (*Vido* < *Vito*) and לנונציאדה (*l'Annunziada* < *l'Annunziata*). This is also a typical northern trait.[19] Finally, there are traits of dubious origin, e.g., names of the third declination that normally have the suffix *-e*, have an ending in *-o*: סיטימרו (< *settembre*), אוטוברו (< *ottobre*), נטאלו (< *Natale*) 'Christmas', מיקילו (< *Michele*). It may be a northern trait, i.e. erroneous reconstruction of the dropped last vowel,[20] but it may be also typical central-southern trait, i.e. a metaplasm of declination.[21]

12 Cuomo 1976.

13 Sermoneta 1976.

14 Mayer-Modena 1997: 953.

15 Bonfil 2012. For the analysis of the language see Michael Ryzhik, "La lingua dei calendari ebraici veneziani cinquecenteschi", *Rassegna Mensile di Israel*, in press.

16 Rohlfs 1966–69, 254. It is interesting that in the names of months this assimilation is documented only in Sicilian (Giorgio Piccitto, Giovanni Tropea, and Salvatore C. Trovato, *Vocabolario siciliano*, 5 vol., Centro di studi filologici e linguistici siciliani, 1977–2002, s.v), in other dialects the normative influence of the official (ecclesiastical) language has changed them to forms with *mbr* (*dicembre*). But in Judeo-Italian this corrective influence did not exist.

17 Rohlfs 1966–69:156, 158; Cuomo 1988a: 40.

18 Rohlfs 1966–69: 143, 146.

19 Rohlfs 1966–69: 201.

20 Rohlfs 1966–69: 353.

21 Cuomo 1988: 42–43; Ryzhik 2007: 10.

Another (metalinguistic) factor that was important for the development of medieval and Renaissance Judeo-Italian (and decisive in its disappearance in the 16th century) is the great influence of the Italian cultural trends on the culture of the Italian Jewry,[22] more precisely on their general attitude to language. Italy had always been divided in many dialects zones; from the 13th century on there were different attempts to create a literary language based on different dialects or their mixture. The successful attempt was the one based on the Florentine / Tuscany dialect of 14th century, sanctified by the writings of the "three crowns", Dante, Petrarch, and Bocaccio and proclaimed as a literary language of the Appennine peninsula by the Pope secretary and great humanist writer Pietro Bembo in 1525. This was not the end of the story; until the late 19th century there were vivid discussions about different aspects of the literary Italian language, under the name of *Questione della lingua*,[23] but the second half of the 16th century marked the end of writing in dialects or dialect-colored language and the transition to the literary language based on the Florentine dialect. In this process, two different factors played a role: the unifying effect of printing on the one hand, and normativizing legislation of the Tridentine Council (1545–1563) in the questions of the ecclesiastic language on the other. As a result, the dialects disappeared from printed books and from written texts. This also affected the Jewish Italian world: written ("illustrious") Judeo-Italian disappeared and was replaced by Hebrew and quasi-Italian (in the beginning, a quite Toscanized Judeo-Italian that quickly gave place to common Italian). This late Judeo-Italian was still written in Hebrew characters and it contains some phonological, morphological, and lexical traits of the medieval Judeo-Italian, but these traits also disappeared during the 17th century, as did the writing in Hebrew characters.

1.2 Medieval Judeo-Italian: phases and sources

The writing of the Romance dialects in Hebrew characters in the territory of Italy began almost simultaneously with the writing in Latin characters, and sometimes preceded it. In Salento, for example, one of the earliest cases of writing in the local dialect is the case of the Romance glosses to the *Mishna*. As Cuomo has demonstrated,[24] these glosses, founded on the margins of the Mishnah manuscript Ms Parma 138, were written in the 11th century in the Otranto dialect (or in some dialect very close to it). These are the earliest witnesses of the Judeo-Italian.

– The earliest sources of Judeo-Italian: the *Elegy for the 9th of Av*
(for the full text see below, section 3.1)

One of the earliest poetical texts in the central-southern dialects is also written in Hebrew characters. It is the *Elegy for the 9th of Av*, written in the 13th or 14th century,[25]

22 See, e.g., the classic study by Bonfil 1994.

23 See, e.g., Migliorini 1987, *passim*; Marazzini 1993 and the bibliography. Many other articles in the same volume are useful, especially L. Serianni, "La prosa", pp. 451–580.

24 Cuomo 1977.

25 For its dating see Contini 1960, vol. 1: 35f: "the archaic jester style and its similarity to the *Sant' Alessio* have suggested to Cassuto, not followed by all scientists, to date it in the earlier 13th century or even in the preceding century; but it is not possible to date it earlier than the 13th century".

published by Cassuto, Contini, and Natale 2018.[26] This beginning of the Judeo-Italian literature may be easily called splendid. Here is the beginning of the *Elegy* in the transliteration of Contini (*loc.cit.*):

La ienti de Sïòn plange e lutta;
dice: "taupina, male so' condutta
em manu de lo nemicu ke m'ao strutta".
La notte e la die sta plorando,
li soi grandezi remembrando,
e mo pe lo mundu vao gattivandu.

The people of Zion cry and mourn / say: "miserable, I am badly led / in the hand of the enemy that has destroyed me" / night and day they are crying / remembering its greatness / and now around the world wanders in captivity

The full text of the *Elegy* according to the Ms Ferrara[27] is reproduced and analyzed in section 3. The complete *Elegy* contains several stories that are found in the tractate *Niddah* (ff. 57a-58b) of the Babylonian Talmud, and in the parallel text in the Midrash *Eka Rabbah*, between other stories about the destruction of the Second Temple and the successive expulsion and captivity. This text is very typical of the Italianized Jewish culture. On the one hand, not only the theme of the elegy, but also the rhythm, four stressed words in each line,[28] and the rhyme structure, e.g,. the monorhyme terzets, are typical traits of the Hebrew elegies. On the other hand, there are multiple similarities with the contemporary Marchigian poetry, as the Ritmo di Sant'Alessio or the Ritmo Laurenziano.[29] Even more importantly, the language has many traits of the central-southern dialects, first of all of the ancient Marchigiano and ancient Romanesco, e.g., assimilation of the cluster *-nv-* (*'mmediati* 'invidiati' 'envied', v. 15), but with hypercorrections (*afflambato* 'affiammato' 'burnt', v. 30); the change of the sibilant to the affricate in the cluster *-ns-* (*pinzaru* 'thought'); the conservation of the clusters labial + *l* (*plange* 'cries', *plorando* 'crying', and *templo* 'temple', but also *pianto* 'cry'); *ge-* turns to /y/ (*ienti* 'people'); the 1SG.PRES form of the verb 'avere' *aju* 'I have' (v. 64), the future form *faraio* 'I will do' (v. 84), the 3SG.PRES forms *ao* 'has', *vao* 'goes', *fao* 'does' (*passim*); the interchangeability of the final *i* and *e*: *porti* 'doors', *donni* 'women', *flambi* 'fires' / M *figlie* 'sons', *isse* 'these'.[30] But there are signs of the learned scripture/elevated style, so the assimilation of the cluster *-nd-* is found in the elegy (*bennerelli* 'venderli' 'to sell them', v. 72), but it is rare (examples include *grandi* 'big', *plorando* 'crying', *remembrando* 'remembering', etc.); see also the above-mentioned hypercorrection *mm* > *mb*. Maybe the conservation of the cluster *-nd-* (which does not show signs of hypercorrection) is not due to learned scripture/elevated style, but a remnant of the Salento basis of Judeo-Italian.[31]

26 Cassuto 1929, Contini 1960: 37–42, Natale 2018.
27 For characteristic of manuscripts see Cassuto 1929.
28 One of the stresses may be secondary, in the polysyllabic word, or may fall on the proclitic.
29 See Contini 1960 for both these texts.
30 See Contini 1960: 37–42.
31 For a Salentian conservation of this cluster see Rohlfs 1966–69: 253.

This was the illustrious beginning of the Judeo-Italian, the Salentinian glosses of the Mishnah and the Marchegiano-Romanesco (but as we have seen also somewhat Abruzzese-Salentine) elegy. As already mentioned, the first stage of Judeo-Italian, which can be called 'classical' or 'medieval' Judeo-Italian, is represented mostly by the vulgarizations (translations) of the classical Hebrew texts, such as the Bible and the Talmudic and liturgical literature. The language of these texts is generally homogenous, it is central-southern according to its characteristic traits (as we have seen in the case of the *Elegy for the 9th of Av*), and it may be characterized as 'high' or 'written', which is not surprising taking in consideration the content of these texts. In contrast, the late Judeo-Italian represents different ghetto dialects, heterogeneous as belonging to different zones, almost all northern (as spoken in the northern communities),[32] and 'low', as functioning as the spoken general language;[33] this 'lowness' is expressed even in the self-nomination of the Livorno Jewish dialect, *bagitto* ('low' in Judeo-Iberic).

1.3 The time limits of medieval Judeo-Italian

The first important question that must be asked concens what may be called the *terminus ante quem* of medieval (classic) Judeo-Italian When does medieval Judeo-Italian of texts end, and does modern Judeo-Italian of the spoken ghetto dialects begin? The situation is different from the scenario in the two great Indo-European Jewish languages, Yiddish and Ladino. First, in the case of these languages the great change occurs with the change of the linguistic milieu: the latter two became heteroglossic after the eastward migration in the case of the Yiddish and with the expulsion from the Spain in the case of the Ladino, respectively, while Judeo-Italian remained in the same homoglossic Italian surrounding. Second, both Yiddish and Ladino remained the main written languages for the Ashkenazic and Sephardic Jews, respectively, while written Judeo-Italian ceased to exist in the modern period.

In the case of Judeo-Italian, the reasons for the changes and their characters must be searched not in the transfer of the Jews to another country, but in the changes that occurred in the same country, in Italy. The main factors of this change were of two different types: the establishment of the ghetto one the one hand and the Toscanization of the written Italian on the other hand. The spoken ghetto dialects emerged with the establishment of the ghettoes in the middle of the 16th century (the first one, in Rome, was established in the 1555). This is also the time of the expulsion of Jews from Southern Italy, which began in 1493, almost simultaneously with the expulsion from Spain (Southern Italy was governed by Spanish royal families and was practically under Spanish rule). This is one of the reasons of the great difference between the central-southern character of medieval Judeo-Italian and the (light-)northern one of late Judeo-Italian. But the real reason of the death of medieval Judeo-Italian used in the translation of the sacred texts seems to be the same one that caused the Toscanization of the all written forms of the language in Italy in the 16th century – the debates around the *questione della lingua*, which led to the unification and Toscanization of the written Italian. In the

32 With the evident exceptions of some communities such as of Rome, Florence, and Pitigliano.

33 Sometimes used consciously as the 'secret language', also of the (half)-criminal population. See, e.g., Mayer-Modena 1997; and see now Aprile 2012 and the bibliography there.

case of the Jewish communities, Judeo-Italian yielded not only to literary Italian, but also to Hebrew, whose cultivation had always been very strong in the Italian Jewry. As Bonfil has demonstrated, this switch to the two literary languages occurred in the middle of the 16th century.[34] It can be demonstrated that the texts belonging to the same genres, or the translations of the same texts, lose their Judeo-Italian character in the course of the 16th century. We will present three examples: (1) one Judeo-Italian text in the Haggada of Pesah, which was changed to the Hebrew version, (2) the change in the language of sermons, and (3) the change in the language of the Bible translations.

(1) The Jews of Corfu in the late medieval and earlier modern period were of South-Italian origin, mostly from Puglia, expelled from the Kingdom of Naples at the beginning of the 16th century. Their dialect is called *pugghisu* (i.e. *pugliese*, 'Apulian'), and it is indeed an Apulian dialect. Some additions or directives to the Seder and to the Passover Haggada in earlier manuscripts from Corfu are written in this language.[35] The most original is the directive how to split *matza* for *afikoman* and what to say during this action. The text in *pugghisu* is found in several manuscripts, it is more or less standard, cited here according to Ms. Brit.Or. 5978, c. 41r:

פִּיָאמוּ לָה מַצָּה דֵי מֶנְזוּ קוּן לִי דוֹאִי שֶׁינְיָאלִי אֵי לָא שְׁפַּרְטִימוּ אַמֶנְצוּ אֵי דִיצִימוּ קוּשִׁי קוֹמוּ
שְׁפַּרְטִימוּ קִשְׁטָא *מַצָּה* קוּשִׁי שְׁפַּרְטִיאוּ ה׳ק׳ב׳ה׳ לוּ מַארִי רוּבִּיוּ אֵי פַּשַּׁארוּן לִי פַּאדְרִי נוֹשְׁטְרִי אִין
מֶנְזוּ דִי אִישׁוּ. אִין דוֹדִיצִי וֵיאִי. אֵי פִּיצִי קוֹן אִישִׁי *נִסִּים וְנִפְלָאוֹת* קוּשִׁי קוּ פַּצָּה קוּנוֹאִי קִשְׁטוּ אַנוּ
אַקַה. לוּ אַנוּ קֵיוֵינִי אָה לָה טֵירָה דִי יִשְׂרָאֵל אוֹמִינִי לִיבֵּרִי. לָה מֶנְזָה לַמֶנְטִימוּ שׁוֹטָא לָה טוֹבַיָּה פֵּיר
אַפִּיקוֹמִין. אֵי דִיצִימוּ *זֵכֶר* לְמִשְׁאֲרוֹתֵיהֶם צרורות בְּשִׂמְלוֹתָם. אֵיל אַלְטְרָא מֶנְזָא אוּפְרָא לִי דוֹאִי *מַצּוֹת*
פִּיר הַמּוֹצִיא

Piggiamu la *matsa* de menzu cun li doi segnali e la spartimu a menzu e dicimu cusi comu spartimu kista *matsa* cusi spartiu HQBH lu Mari Rubbiu e passarun li padri nostri in menzu di isso in dodici vei. E fici con issi *nissim ve niflaʔot* cusi cu faccia cunnoi. Kistu annu acca. Lu annu che veni alla Terra di Israel omini liberi. La menza la mentimu sotta la tovajja per *afiqomin*. E dicimu זֵכֶר לְמִשְׁאֲרוֹתֵיהֶם צרורות בְּשִׂמְלוֹתָם. E l'altra menza ufra li doi *matsot* pir *ha motsi*.

Translation: We take the middle *maṣa* with two signs and split it in the middle and say: "As we have split this *maṣa* so HQBH had split the Red Sea and our fathers passed in the middle of it in twelve ways. And he made with them *nissim ve niflaʔot* so will he make with us. This year here. Next year free men in the Land of Israel. We put the one half under the tablecloth for the *afikomin*. And we say זֵכֶר לְמִשְׁאֲרוֹתֵיהֶם צרורות בְּשִׂמְלוֹתָם.[36] And the other half between the two *maṣot* for *hamoṣi*.

But in later manuscripts this text was translated into Hebrew.[37] While the original texts is almost the same and unchangeable in all manuscripts, Hebrew translations differ from each other (they are also made with multiple errors and written in very 'popular' Hebrew orthography). Here are three versions:

34 Bonfil 1994.

35 Sermoneta 1990; Ryzhik 2013b.

36 Exodus 12:34.

37 Ryzhik 2013b.

Ms. JTS 5439, c. 3v:

לוקיחים מצה האצעית עם שני שימנים ומפרידין אותה ואומרים כשם שאנו מפרידין זה המצה כך הפריד הב"ה את ים סוף ועברו [אבותינו] בתוכו בשנים עשר דרכים ועשה עמהם ניסים ונפלאות כך יעשה עמנו השתא הכא לשנה הבא בהרעא דישראל בני חורין חציה משים אותה בין שתי המצות להמוציא וחציה תחת המפה להפקומין ואומר זכר למשארותם צרורות בסמלותם

Translation: They take the middle *maṣa* with two signs and split it and say as we split this *maṣa* so HBH had split the Dead Sea and [our fathers] have passed in twelve ways and he had made with them wonders and miracles [ניסים ונפלאות] so he will do with us, this year here, the next year in the land of Israel free men. He puts a half of it between the two *maṣot* for *hamoṣi* and a half under the tablecloth for *afikomin* and says in memory of משארותם צרורות בסמלותם.

JTS 4181:

לוקח המצה האמצעית מהשני סימנין ויבצעיה לשנים ויתן חציה תחת המפה לשומרה לשם אפיקומין וחציה משים בין שתי השלמות ונוהגים לומר חולקים אנו מצה זו כשם שחלק ייי ים סוף להעביר בתוכו את אבותינו והוציאם ממצרים כך יוציא אותנו מזה הגלות

He takes the middle maṣa of the two signs and will split it in two and will give half of it under the tablecloth to keep it for *afikomin*, and a half of it he puts between the two intact <*maṣot*> and there is custom to say: we divide this *maṣa* as God has divided Red Sea to make our fathers pass it and has taken them out from Egypt so he will take us out from this expulsion

JTS 4821:

ונוהגים לומר כשחולקין אותה חולקין אנו זאת האפיקומין כשם שבקע הקב"ה את ים סוף והעביר בתוכו את אבותינו כן יוציא אותנו מגלות זה

There is custom to say dividing it: we divide this *afikomin* as HQBH has split the Dead Sea and took our fathers across it, so he will take us out from this expulsion

We see that the three cited Hebrew translations, while undoubtedly translated from the same Judeo-Italian original, differ in the lexicon (e.g., *spartimu* 'we divide' is translated by three different Hebrew verbs: הפריד, חלק, בצע) and in syntax (e.g., singular vs. plural: לוקיחין/לוקח; participle vs. future: משים/יתן). It means that translations were many and made *ad hoc*, as a part of a general trend of substitution of Judeo-Italian by Hebrew.

In this case we can say that the substitution and disappearance of Judeo-Italian happened in the course of the 16th-17th centuries. In some other cases we can be more precise. Such is the case of three short prayers in the Maḥzor that are written after the Passover liturgy: *Seder hattarat qelalot* (Order of the annulation of the curses), *Mi še-berak̠* ('He that is blessed'), *Hazkarat nešamot* ('Commemoration of the souls [of the passed away']). In all medieval manuscripts of the Maḥzorim these prayers are composed in a mixture of Judeo-Italian and Hebrew. The fixed liturgical formulas common to all rites are written in Hebrew, while expressions that are found only in the Italian rite are written in Judeo-Italian. The texts of these prayers are (almost) identical in all manuscripts.[38]

38 Scazzocchio 1988. Scazzocchio described these prayers in the Ms Casatenense 71(2881), but they are found in all medieval manuscripts of the Maḥzor.

In order to follow the withdrawal of the Judeo-Italian and a change to the Hebrew it is important to study what happened in the printed editions in the 16th century.[39] In the first printed editions of the Siddur according to the Italian rite, Soncino 1486 and Fano 1506, these texts are written in Judeo-Italian, as in the medieval manuscripts. But in the Rimini edition of 1521 a Hebrew translation is printed aside the usual Judeo-Italian text, just as in the famous Bologna Maḥzor of 1540. The following editions of the Siddur, Mantua 1560, Venice 1587, 1606, 1626, up to our days are all printed in Hebrew.

We see that at least in this case the developments are exactly parallel to the processes in the Christian Italian world, conditioned by the grammarians of the beginning of the 16th century and by the decisions of the Council of Trent. It must be noted that the period from 1540 to 1560 is the period in which decisive changes occurred in the post-biblical Hebrew tradition as it is represented in the printed editions of the Siddur (the same editions that are quoted above); for example, the medieval way to vocalize the degree Rabbi, רַבִּי *rebbi*, is replaced by the modern Italian form, רִבִּי *ribbi*, which most probably arrived with the expelled Spanish Jews.[40] It seems that this is not just accidental.

(2) The next example of the changes that occurred in medieval Judeo-Italian in the 16th century and led to its Toscanization and subsequent disappearance is the case of the sermons. The rabbinical sermons in Italy were printed in Hebrew. But it is clear that they were pronounced from the pulpit in Italian, and up to the second half of the 16th century in Judeo-Italian. Some of these sermons are conserved in manuscripts. The comparison of the sermons that were written in the first half of the century with the sermons written in the second half reveals a clear difference in their language that became much more Toscanized, according to the general trend in Italy in this epoch.[41] First, here are some short fragments of a sermon of Rabbi Samuel ben Rafael Modena, from the year 1535:[42]

> Eccelentissimi signori *mevoʔar nigle* che intutti le cose che loomo fao intenne che lo faccia di ben considerare e penzare che lo *takhlit* di quella *peʕulla* sia allonore e allareverenzia de lo *Eloqim yitbarach* quanno questo sia se bene inquella *peʕulla* nesuggerissa alcuna *ʕavera* o vero alcuna cosa che nelcospetto dellovolghe paresse inconveniente essenno che inquella *ʕavera* o inquello incoveniente ne risulta larevenzia e lonore d'*Eloqim yit<barakh> ʔen safeq <without doubt>* che simila *peʕulla* è molto grata e molto accetto inanzi *H<a>B<arukh H<u>*. E questo si vede per quello che daršeno *haḵamim be-m<aseḵet> Beraḵot* [...] (196b)
>
> Translation: Reverend Gentlemen, it is absolutely clear that in all things that he does a man must consider and think that the final aim of this action must be to honor and to respect God Almighty in any case. Even if there is in this action

39 For details see Ryzhik 2010.

40 Ryzhik 2012.

41 Ryzhik 2008b.

42 Ms. Moscow Russian State Library, Ms. Guenzburg 1317. A longer example of his sermon is cited and analyzed in section 3. In this section I cite sermons, written in Hebrew characters, in Latin transcription. In section 3, the sermon is cited in Hebrew characters.

> something that is similar to sin or to inconvenience in the eyes of the people, it is welcome and accepted before God, because from this sin and from this inconvenience come out honor and reverence of Him. And it is proved by the comments of our Sages in the tractate *Berak̲ot* [...]

There are clear traits of the medieval Judeo-Italian that we have already seen in the *Elegy for the 9th of Av*: the assimilation *nd* > *nn* (*intenne* 'means', *quanno* 'when', *essenno* 'being'), the change of the sibilant to the affricate in the cluster *-ns-* (*penzare* 'to think'; also *ls* > *lts*: *volze* 'wants', 188b), the verb 3SG present form *fao* 'does' (in other parts of the sermons also *ao* 'has', *vao* and the masculine article *lo* (in other parts of the sermon also plural *li*). Other traits are found in other parts of Samuel Modena's sermons, as the conservation of the clusters of labial + *l* (*plu*, 184b), the anaptyctic vowel in the word *patere* 'father' (185b), and *onne* 'each' instead of *ogni* (184b and *passim*).

A significant part of the lexicon is consists of untranslated Hebrew words, mostly fixed and well-known formulas, which later entered the Judeo-Italian dialects of the ghetto (and are mostly common to Jewish languages). In the quoted fragment we see also the synthetic Hebrew-Italian verb *daršeno* 'they comment', with a Hebrew root (√ d-r-š) and an Italian suffix (*-eno*). This type of word-formation is relatively rare in medieval Judeo-Italian, but this impression may be only due to the documentation, based largely on the translations of the Bible and of the Siddur; these translations prefer to use Romance equivalents of Hebrew words and not the Hebrew component itself. In Samuel Modena's sermons there also very specific words proper of Medieval Judeo-Italian, as the verb *nescere*, *ennescere* 'to teach':[43] che la *Torah* ennesce a lo *ben ʔadam* a ingegnarsi (190b).

If we compare this language to the sermons of R. Yaʕaqov ben Mordecai Pogetto, written in 1579 we see that their language is quite different:[44]

> Due consolazioni grandissime debbano avere e sui onoratissimi madre fratelli e sorella nella morte di questi due *qedoši<m>* a i quali vi hanno davere riguardo, una particolare e laltra universale, la particolare lessere morti ambedue giovani di tenera età percioche morendo a tenpo immaturato non si po dire se non che siano eletti di Dio senza peccare, dicano *RZL p<ereq> q<ama> deḤagiga* <...> ma la consolazione universale è la *texiyyat ha-metim* la quale ha d'essere a tutti li eletti de la *umma ha-Israelit alibba di-xule ʕalma* che tutti ciabbiamo a rivedere insieme, oltra al felicissimo bene che hanno quelle anime benedette di stare per in sino a quel tempo in compagna di beati spirti kemo *še-amar ha-malax li-Ihošuaʕ* <...> dove possano <...> contemplare e vedere linfinita sua bellezza e di quella infinitamente godere <...> (45a).

> Translation: There are two great consolations that must take in consideration the mother, the brothers and the sister of these two dead saint, one particular and one universal. The particular one is that they are dead in their childhood, so that were chosen by God when they were yet without sin, as say our Sages in the

43 About this verb see Cuomo 1976, p. 49. And see below in this article.

44 Ms. JTS 1588.

first chapter of Ḥagiga <...> while the universal consolation is the Resurrection from the Death, which must happen to all the chosen of Israel according to all opinions, when we will meet and see each other together. Up to that time these blessed souls also have the happiest well-being in the company of beatified spirits as have said angel to Yehošuaʕ <...> where they can <...> contemplate and see His infinite beauty and enjoy it infinitely <...>

All the southern and ancient traits which we have seen in the sermon of Samuel Modena are eliminated (*grandissime* 'very big', *morendo* 'dying', *essendo* 'being' without assimilation; in other parts of the sermon also *conserva* and not *conzerva*, p. 42b; *fa* 'does', and not *fao*, p. 43a ; *il* and not *lo*, *passim*). In addition, the period be-came much more complex, "baroque", and not simple and medieval; for the sake of illustration, here is an example from another (anonymous) preacher of the second half of the 16th century:[45]

E tanto più in noi si accresce l'obbligo di ringraziarLo quanto che li beneficii che abbiamo ricevuto da Lui avanzano e eccedene ogni altre maggior favore e singular grazia che pò mai sperare alcun *nivra* di ottenere o particolarmente per averci eletti per *ʕam ha-nivḥar* e per soi *banim ḥavivim* onde per questo solo con solennità celebrare il suo *yom ha-toleda* ben dovemo noi celebrare questo santissimo giorno nel quale non solo i nostri antecessori ma anco li nostri proprii *nešamot* si troverono presenti a quel degnissimo spettacolo di *mattan Torah* nel quale ottenero tutte le *nešamot* una nova e degna riforma come dice il *pasuq* [...]

And so much more increases the duty to thank Him, as the benefits that we have received from Him advance and exceed any other major favor and singular grace that may hope any creature, especially that He has obtained and chosen us as His chosen people and as his beloved children. Therefore only for this reason we must celebrate solemnly His birthday, we must celebrate this most sacred day in which our ancestors, but also our own souls, were present at this most respectable play of Giving of the Torah, during which all our souls have received new and honorable reform, as it is said [...]

Here the normal 16th century Italian is used, but not exclusively: the Giving of the Torah is described as a *spettacolo*, 'play, show, performance', a very Italian trait, and the change that happens with the soul in this context is called *riforma*, in the spirit of the century. Nevertheless, one trait remains, i.e. the vast use of the Hebrew component; this use of Hebrew disappears only when the written Judeo-Italian finally turns out to be Italian. But it remains very strong in the "modern" Judeo-Italian, in the spoken ghetto dialects.

(3) The third example of the changes that Judeo-Italian underwent during the 15th-17th centuries concerns the translations of the Siddur.[46] The Siddur contains texts of different origin, Bible verses, excerpts of Mishnaic literature, as well as prayers written in different periods of the Jewish history. These translations, made explicitly for women

45 Ms. London British Library Or. 10109 (Gaster 434), f. 81a.

46 See about them Cassuto 1930b; Ryzhik 2007; and now Ryzhik 2013a. The translations of *Šemaʕ Israel* and *Šemona ʕEśre* in three manuscripts are given in section 3.

but used also by men, were based on the common tradition, but were not canonized, and their language changes from one manuscript to another. Three manuscripts of the 15th century are known,[47] three identical printed editions from the 16th century,[48] and one manuscript from the 17th century.[49] This last one is quite different from the earlier ones, which are written in "classic Medieval Judeo-Italian", i.e. are rich in central and southern dialectal traits, as demonstrated by the quotations from the *Elegy for the 9th of Av* or Samuel Modena's sermons cited above. In contrast, the Siddur has clear northern traits, notably phonological ones:

– absence of gemination;

– intervocalic sonorization (סְטִיפִּדִי = *stipidi* 'doorposts' instead of *stipiti*);[50]

– dropping of the final vowel, e.g., רַאייוֹנַאר קְוֶוילִי [...] סֵידֵיר טוּאוֹ = *rajjonar queli [...] seder tuo* 'thinking them [...] your sitting' נֵיל קַאמִינַאר טוּאוֹ [...] נֵיל יַיאצֵיר טוּאוֹ אֶי נֵיל רִיצַאר טוּאוֹ = *nel caminar tuo [...] nel jacer tuo e nel rizar tuo* 'in your going [...] in your going to bed and in your coming up';[51]

– absence of the assimilation *nd* > *nn*[52] (which is obligatory in F and 15th century manuscripts), e.g., in the *Ba-me madliqin*: *demandato* 'asked', *quando* 'when', *dimanda* 'asks', *condanato 'sentenced'.*

To illustrate the difference, here are two parallel segments. The first is the fragment from the Mishnah Shabbat 2:2–4 (*Ba-me madliqin*) from the print edition Fano 1506 (F), and the second is the parallel fragment from the manuscript translation of the 17th century (S):

> ב. אֵי נוֹן אַצֵּינֵינוֹ נֶילוֹ אוֹלְיוֹ קֶי אֵי אַרְצַה נֶילוֹ יוֹם טוֹב: רְבִּי יִשְׁמָעֵאל דִיצֵי נוֹן אַצֵּינְנוֹ נֶילוֹ אוֹלְיוֹ פֵּיטְרוֹלְיוֹ פֵּיר קַשׁוֹנֵי דֵי לוֹ אוֹנוֹרֵי דֵי לוֹ סַבְּיטוֹ: אֵי חֲכָמִים דַנוֹ הֵתֵּר אֶין טוּטִי לִי אוֹלְיוֹרַה: נֶילוֹ אוֹלְיוֹ דֵי לִינוֹרַה נֶילוֹ אוֹלְיוֹ די לִי נוֹצִי: נֶילוֹ אוֹלְיוֹ דֵי לִי רַדִיצִי נֶילוֹ אוֹלְיוֹ דֵי פֵּישֵׁי נֶילוֹ אוֹלְיוֹ דֵי צוּקִי סַאלְוָוטִיקִי נֶילוֹ אוֹלְיוֹ פֵּטְרוֹלְיוֹ אֵי נֵילַה פְּיצֵי: רְבִּי טַרְפוֹן דִיצֵי נוֹן אַצֵּינְנוֹ סְינוֹ נֶילוֹ אוֹלְיוֹ דֵי לַה אוּלִיוַה סוֹלַה מֵינְטִי: ג. אוֹנֵי קֶי יֵיסְי דֵי לוֹ לִינוֹ נוֹן אַצֵּינֵינוֹ אֶין אֵיסוֹ סְינוֹ נֶילוֹ לִינוֹ אוֹנֵי קֶי יֵיסְי דֵי לוֹ לִינוֹ נוֹן אֶין פֵּילוּטַה לוֹ אֶין פֵּילוּטַמֵינְטוֹ דֵי לִי פַּוֵוילְיוֹנִי סְינוֹ נֶילוֹ לִינוֹ: לוֹ לוּצִינְיוֹ דֵי לוֹ פַּאנוֹ קֶי טוֹרְצֵיסִי אֵיסוֹ אֵי נוֹן אַבְּרוּשַׁוו אֵיסוֹ רְבִּי אֱלִיעֶזֶר דִיצֵי אֶין פְּילוּטַה אֵי אֵיסַה אֵי נוֹן אַצֵּינְנוֹ אֶין אֵיסה: רְבִּי עֲקִיבָא דִיצֵי מוּנַה אֵי אֵיסַה אֵי אַצְּינֵימוֹ אֶין אֵיסַה: ד. נוֹן דֵיאוֹ פוֹרַרֵי לוֹ אוּמוֹ לַה קוֹצַה דֵי לוֹ אוֹבוֹ אֵי אֵינְפְּיָה אֵיסַה דֵי אוֹלְיוֹ אֵי דַיֵיה אֵיסַה סוֹפְּרֵי בוֹקַה דֵי לַה קַנֵילַה פֵּיר קַשׁוֹנֵי קֶי אֵיסַה גוֹצַה אֵי אַבֵּירְסִי קֶי אֵיסַה אֵי דֵיפִיטִילְיוֹ אֵי רְבִּי יְהוּדַה לוֹ אֵי מַתִּיר: מַה סְי אַפִּיצַאסְי אֵיסַה לוֹ

47 Ms. Parma de' Rossi ital. 7, written in the 1484 (according to the colophone) in Florence or in its nearest neighborhood. Its sigla in this article is Q1; Ms. London 625 [Or. 2443], written in the 1483 in Montalboddo [Ostra] (according to the colophone), its sigla in this article is Q2; Ms. JTS Mic. 4076, written in the 15th century in the same zone (Tuscany-Umbria), there is no colophone. Its sigla in this article is Q3.

48 We will use the *editio princeps* Fano 1506, its sigla is F. In the scientific literature it is called *Rite of Fano* (*rito di Fano*).

49 Ms. London Or. 10517 written in the Northern Italy. Its sigla in this article is S.

50 Rohlfs 1966–69: 201.

51 The language of S is very Toscanized and normalized. So the dialectal northern traits are very attenuated, e.g., the dropping of the final vowel happens almost only after the /r/. But as can be seen, in all cited cases the dropping occurs before the consonant, the position that usually defends the final vowel. Significantly, this dropping is almost obligatory in S.

52 Rohlfs 1966–69: 253.

פִּיטִילְיֵירוֹ דַּה פְּרִימַה אֵי מוּתַּר פֵּיר קַשׁוֹנֵי קֵי אֶיסוֹ אֵי וַשֵׁילוֹ אוּנוֹ: נוֹן דֵּיאוֹ אֵינְפְּיִרֵי לוֹ אוֹמוֹ לַה סְקוּדֵּילַה דִּי אוֹלְיוֹ אֵי דְּיַה אֵיסַה אַפְּרֵיסוֹ אַלַה קַנֵּילַה פֵּיר קַשׁוֹנֵי קֵי אֵיסַה גוֹצַה אֵי רְבִּי יְהוּדָה לֵי מַתִּיר:

F : (2) E non accenneno nello olio che è arsa nello *yom tov*: Rebbi Yishmael dice non accenneno nello olio petrolio per cascione de lo onore de lo sabbeto: E *hakhamim* danno *hetter* en tutti li oliora: Nello olio de linora nello olio de li noci: Nello olio de li radici nello olio de pesce nello olio de zucchi salvatichi nello olio petrolio e nella pece: Rebbi Tarfon dice non accenneno senno nello olio de la uliva sola mente: (3) Onne che iesse de lo lino non accenneno en esso se-nno nello lino. Onne che iesse de lo lino non en pelluta lo en en pellutamento de lo paviglioni se-nno nello lino: Lo lucigno de lo panno che torcessi esso e non abbrusciavo esso Rebbi Eliezer dice en pelluta è essa e non accenneno en essa: Rebbi Aqiva dice munna è essa e accenneno en essa: (4) Non deo forare lo omo la cozza de lo ovo e enpia essa de olio e dia essa sopre bocca de la cannella per cascione che essa goccia e abersi che essa è de-fitiglio e Rebbi Yehuda lo è *mattir*: Ma se appicciase essa lo fitigliaro da prima è *muttar* per cascione che esso è vascello uno: Non deo inpiire lo omo la scudella de olio e dia essa appresso alla cannella per cascione che essa goccia e Rebbi Yehuda le *mattir*:

ב. נוֹן סִי דֵיוֵוי אִינְפִּיצַאר קוֹן אוֹלְייוֹ דִי תְרוּמַה קֵי דֶיוֵוי אֶיסֶיר בְּרוּיַיאטוֹ נִיאַנְקוֹ דִי יוֹם טוֹב, רַבִּי יִשְׁמַעְאֵל דִיצֵי נוֹן ס׳ אִינְפִּיצָה קוֹן אוּלְייוֹ דִי פֶּיצֵי פֶּיר אוֹנוֹר דֶיל שַׁבָּת, אֶי לִי חֲכָמִים קוֹנְצֵידוֹנוֹ קוֹן אוֹנְיִי סוֹרְטֶי דִי אוֹלְייוֹ, קוֹן אוֹלְייוֹ דִי פַּאפַּאבְרוֹ, קוֹן אוֹלְייוֹ דִי נוֹצֶי, קוֹן אוֹלְייוֹ דֵי רַאוִיצוֹן קוֹן גְרַאסַה דִי פֶּישֶׁי, קוֹן אוֹלְייוֹ דִי פוֹנְגִי, אֶי קוֹן פֶּיצֶי אֶי טֶירְמֶינְטִינַה, רַבִּי טַרְפוֹן דִיצֶי נוֹן ס״אִינְפִּיצַה סַאלְווֹ קוֹן אוֹלְייוֹ ד״אוֹלִיוַה, סוֹלַאמֶינְטֶי, **ג**. דִי אוֹנְיִי קוֹסַה קֵי אֶישֶׁי דַה לֶינְיוֹ נוֹן סִי נֶי פַה סְטוּפִּינִי, פֶּיר אִינְפִּיצַאר סוֹלוֹ דִי לִינוֹ, אֶיט אוֹנְיִי קוֹסַה קֵי אֶישֶׁי דִי לֶינְייוֹ אֶי קֵי סֵי נֶי פַה פַּאדִילְייוֹנֵי נוֹן אִינְמוֹנְדַאנוֹ אִינְמוֹנְדַאצִייוֹנִי קְוַואנְדוֹ וִי אֶי אוֹן מוֹרְטוֹ אִין קְוֵוילוֹ פַּאדִילְייוֹנֵי סוֹלוֹ דִי לִינוֹ, אוּן סְטוֹפִּינוֹ דִי פַּאנוֹ קֵי לוֹ אַוֵויסֶי סְטוֹרְטוֹ אֶי נוֹן ל״אַוֵויסֵי סְטְרִינַאטוֹ רַבִּי אֱלִיעֶזֶר דִיצֶי אִינְמוֹנְדַה אֶי קְוֵוילָה אֶי נוֹן ס״אִינְפִּיצָה קוֹן קְוֵוילָה, רַבִּי עֲקִיבַה דִיצֶי פּוּרַה אֶיקְוֵוילה אֶיט אֶי לֶיצִיטוֹ אִינְפִּיצַאר קוֹן קְוֵוילַה, **ד**. נוֹן דֵיוֵוי פוֹרַאר ל״אוֹמוֹ אוּנַה קַאנַה קֵי נַאשֶׁי נֵיל פַּאנְטַאנוֹ אֶיט אִימְפִּירְלַה דִי אוֹלְייוֹ אֶי פּוֹנֵירְלָה סוֹפְּרַה ל״אוֹרְלוֹ ד״אוּנַה לוּמֶי אִיצִייוֹ קֵי גוֹצִייאַסֶי אַנְקוֹר בֶין קִי אֶיסַה קַאנַה פּוֹסֵר דִי טֶירַה, אֶי רַבִּי יְהוּדַה קוֹנְצֵידֶי, מַה סֶי ל״אַוֵויסֶי אַטַאקַאטוֹ אִיל בּוֹקַאלֶירוֹ דַה פְּרִינְצִיפִּייוֹ אֶי לֵיצִיטוֹ, פוֹאִי קֵי סִי דִימַאנְדַה טוּטוֹ אוּן וַואסוֹ, נוֹן דֵיוֵוי ל״אוֹמוֹ אֶימְפִּירֵי אוּנַה סְקוּדֶילַה דִי אוֹלְייוֹ אֶי פּוֹנֶירְלַה אַל לַאטוֹ דִי אוּנַה לוּמֶי אֶי פּוֹנֶיר אִיל קַאפּוֹ דֵיל סְטוֹפִּינוֹ אִין קְוֵוילַה סְקוּדֶילָה אַצִייוֹ קֵי סְפּוֹצָה אֶי טִירִי ל״אוֹלְייוֹ אֶיט רַבִּי יְהוּדַה לוֹ קוֹנְצֵידֶי,.

S: (2) Non si deve inpicciar con olio di *terumah* che deve esser bruggiato nianco di *yom tov*, Rabbi Yishmael dice non si inpiccia con ulio di pece per onor del shabbat, e li *hakhamim* concedono con ogni sorte di olio, con olio di papavero. con olio di noce, con olio di ravizon con grassa di pesce, con olio di fonghi, e con pece e termintina. Rabbi Tarfon dice non s'inpiccia salvo con olio d'oliva, solamente. (3) Di ogni cosa che esce da legno non si ne fa stupini, per inpicciar solo di lino, et ogni cosa che esce di legno e che se ne fa padiglione non inmondano inmondazione quando vi è on morto in quello padiglione solo di lino, un stopino di panno che lo avesse storto e non l'avesse strinato. Rabbi Eliezer dice inmonda è quella e non s'inpiccia con quella, Rabbi Aqiva dice pura è quella et è lecito inpicciar con quella. (4) Non deve forar l'omo una canna che nasce nel pantano et inpirla di olio e ponerla sopra l'orlo d'una lume acciò che gocciasse ancor ben che essa canna fosser di terra, e Rabbi dimanda tutto un vaso, non deve l'omo empire una scudella di olio e ponerla al lato di una lume e poner il capo del stopino in quella scudella acciò che spozza e tiri l'olio et Rabbi Yehuda lo concede.

Translation:[53] (2) We may not light on Yom Tov with oil that must be destroyed by burning. Rabbi Yishmael says: We must not light with tar, out of respect for the honour due the Sabbath. But the Sages permit [lighting] with all [these] oils: with sesame oil, nut oil, radish oil, tar, or petrolium. Rabbi Tarfon says: We must light only with olive oil. (3) We must not light with any product of a tree, with the exception of linen. And no tree-product can contract contamination from sheltering [a contaminated object], with the exception of linen. If a wick was made from a cloth that was twisted but not singed, Rabbi Eliezer says: It accepts contamination and we may not light with it. Rabbi Akiva says: It does not accept contamination and we may light with it. (4) One may not pierce an egg-shell, fill it with oil, and put it over the mouth of a lamp so that [the oil] will drip down, even if [the container is] of earthenware. Rabbi Yehudah permits this. But i the potter originally attached it, it is permitted, because it is a single vessel. One may not fill a bowl with oil, put it next to lamp, and put the end of the wick into [the bowl] so that it will draw [oil]. Rabbi Yehudah permits this.

It can be seen that the late 15th century translation (documented in the print edition from 1506) is rich in medieval Judeo-Italian (southern-central) traits mentioned above: *nd* > *nn* (*accenneno* '(they) fire'), *mn* > *nn* (*onne* 'each' instead of *ogni*), *rs* > *rz* (*arza* 'burns'), analogical 3SG present verb form *deo* 'must', verbal form *iesse* (instead of *esce*), perfect form *abbrusciavo* 'I singed', plural noun form on *-ora* (*oliora* 'oils'). While the 17th century translation is Toscanized with some northern traits, e.g., sonorization of the intervocalic consonants, as *bruggiato* 'singed' (in the 1506 edition *abbrusciavo*). The Hebrew component is richer in the 15th century translation (in the 17th century translation only *yom tov* and *ḥak̲amim* occur), and not directly dependent on the Hebrew text (וחכמים מתירים *ve-hak̲amim mattirim* 'and Sages permit' is translated not *e hak̲amim sono mattirim*, but *e hak̲amim danno hetter*). But also the 17th century translation is not written in Golden Tuscany Italian, e.g., as concerns the above-cited form *fonghi* 'fungus' (instead of *funghi*) we see the absence of the anaphony, which may be a northern trait.[54]

So we see that in the course of the 16th century happen decisive changes in the Judeo-Italian, that are parallel to the corresponding changes in the common Italian. It must be underlined that all the discussed texts, comprising those from the 17th century, are written in Hebrew characters. Very soon, in the 17th and especially in the 18th century, also characters will be changed to Latin, and the medieval written Judeo-Italian will cease to exist.

53 Translation according to R. Nosson Scherman, R. Meir Zlotowitz (eds.), *The Complete ArtScroll Siddur*, Menorah Publications Ltd., Brooklyn NY, 1993.

54 Rohlfs 1966–69: 70.

2. The main linguistic traits of Judeo-Italian

The sources of Medieval Judeo-Italian are not rich. There are mostly translations, of the Bible and of the Siddur[55] (both listed by Cassuto).[56] From a linguistic point of view, some other important sources exist, such as glossaries, and of special importance is the three-language Bible dictionary *Maqre Dardeqe*.[57] This dictionary comprises all the lexicon of the Bible. In contrast, there are no medieval translations of the Torah and of the Hagiographies (the full Bible translation is conserved in the 16th century manuscripts, and it seems that is was written in the same period). For the same reason, the translations of the ritual are important, which comprise many citations from these parts of the Bible (especially from the Psalms). There are also collections of excerpts from the Midrash,[58] from the grammatical treatises,[59] philosophical glossaries,[60] and some other translations and some original texts.[61]

The most complex description of the phonology and the morphology of medieval Judeo-Italian is due to Cuomo in her book dedicated to the 15th century translation of the Book of Jonah.[62] The language is more or less the same, at least in the general lines, in all sources of medieval Judeo-Italian (dialectal differences will be described below).

2.1 Orthography

The Hebrew characters correspond to the Italian sounds as follows. The list is made on the basis of the Siddur translations,[63] but it is equally valid for other sources.

– Consonants

א = Ø; בּ = *b*; ב with the sign of *rafeh* = *v*; ב without *dagesh* or *rafeh* it may be *b* or *v*, e.g., בֵּינֵידִיצִייוֹנֵי = *benedizione* ‘benediction’, אבֵירֵי = *avere* ‘to have’; ג = (affricated) *g* before *a*, *o*, *u*, *ua*, = *gh* before *e*, *i*, e.g., לֵיגַארַאִי = *legarai* ‘(I) tied’, גוֹבֵירְנַה = *governa* ‘governs’, לַרְגוּרַה = *largura* ‘vast space, convenience’, גְוַאַרְדֵיטִי = *guardeti* ‘(you) see’, אַלְבֵירְגֵירַאִי = *albergherai* ‘(I) shall dwell’, לֵיגִי = *leghi* ‘(you) tie’; ד = *d*; ה is used in Italian words only as *mater lectionis* for /a/ at the end of the word, e.g., טֶירַה = *terra* ‘earth’; ו is used as *mater lectionis* for /o/ and /u/, but also as a consonant /v/ or as a part of the diphthong /ua/; ז is almost absolutely out of use in Italian words;[64] ח is not in use in the Italian words; ט = *t*; י is used as *mater lectionis* for /i/ or /e/, and also as a palatal consonant /j/ and for the affricate /dʒ/ (the distinction between the latter two usages is very difficult), e.g., סֵינְייוֹ = *segno* ‘sign’, פִּילְיוֹלִי = *figloli* ‘sons’, אוֹיִי = *ojji* ‘today’; רַאיוֹנַאר = *rajonar* ‘to discuss’, לֵיֵי = *lejje* ‘law’; כ is very rare in use in Italian words. In

55 About these translations see note 45 above.

56 For the Siddur, see the precedent note. For the Bible translations, see Cassuto 1930a; Cassuto 1930c; Cassuto 1934.

57 Perez Trebot, *Sefer Maqre Dardeqe*, Napoli [without the name of the editing house], 1488 (= *Maqre Dardeqe* below). See Fiorentino 1937; Fiorentino 1951; Cuomo 1988b; Tirosh-Becker 1990.

58 See Cuomo 1985; Cuomo 1986.

59 Sermoneta 1967.

60 Debenedetti Stow 1990.

61 Modena 2001; but it is somewhat late in its language.

62 Cuomo 1988a.

63 Ryzhik 2013a.

64 About its use in the Jewish-Italian see Cuomo 1976: 30–33.

the Siddur translations it is found only in Q2 and almost only for the Italian word *che*[65] (כְּי in its graphics), which is the automatic translation of Hebrew כִּי in Judeo-Italian; its transliteration is /k/; ל = *l*; מ = *m*; נ = *n*; ס = *s*; ע is not used in Italian words; פּ = *p*, פ with the sign of *rafeh* = *f*, פ without *dagesh* or *rafeh* is *p* or *f*, according to the etymological context, e.g., פַּטְרִי = *patri* 'fathers', פְֿרַה = *fra* 'between', אֵינְפֵּירְיאוֹ = *enperio* 'power', פַֿאקוּלְטַה = *faculta* 'property'; צ can signify either the affricate /ts/ or the affricate /tš/. The choice between the two must be made according to etymology, e.g., רִיצַאר = *rizar* 'to come up', לַנְצוֹלִי = *lanzoli* 'flaps', צִיֵילִי = *cieli* 'skies', יַיאצֵיר = *jacer* 'to lay down'; ק = *c* before *a*, *o*, *u*, = *q* before *ua*, *ue*, *ui*, = *ch* before *e* or *i*, e.g., קָאסָה = *casa* 'house', אוּנִיקוֹ = *unico* 'unique', סְקוּדִיאַטוֹרֵי = *scudiatore* 'defender', קְוַואלֵי = *quale* 'which', קְוֵויסְטוֹ = *questo* 'this', אַקְוִויסְטַאטוֹר = *aquistator* 'purchaser', קֵי = *che* 'that', אַנְטִיקִי = *antichi* 'ancient (PL)'; ר = *r*; שׁ = *š*; in transcriptions I use *sci* before other vowels than *e* (*a*, *o*, *u*, *i*), *sc* before *e*, and *š* before consonants,[66] e.g., שׁוֹלְיִי = *sciolji* '(you) untie', גְוַרִישִׁי = *guarisci* '(you) cure', דִישֶׁינְדֵיר = *discender* 'to come down', נוֹשְׁטְרוֹ = *noštro* 'our'; ת is rare in Italian words. It is found in the written Judeo-Italian name of God,[67] דוֹמֵדֶת דֵית. Besides this name the ת is found very rarely, only in Q2, in the words נוֹשְׁתְרָא, תּוֹרְנָא, תְּינְפוֹ, אסְינְיֶיאתְי, מורתורְי, and לַסָא[ס]תִי.

– Vowels

Qamaṣ and *pataḥ* = a; *ṣere* and *segol* = e; *ḥiriq* = i; *ḥolam* = o; *shuruq* and *qubbuts* = u. The *shwa* has a twofold character. In the Judeo-Italian translation of the *Siddur* all letters are vocalized, e.g., each one has a vocal sign, meaning that also the consonant which precedes another consonant without a intercession by the vowel is marked by *shwa*. This *shwa quiesciens* has no correspondence in the transcription, e.g., נוֹשְׁטְרוֹ = *noštro*. But *shwa* may be also the sign of vowel (/*e*/), frequently even with a *mater lectionis jod* after it, e.g., קוֹרְי (*core* 'heart'), פוֹרְטְי (*porte* 'gates'), וְוִירֵיטֵיווֹלֵי (*veretevole* 'deserving confidence'), רָבֵּיפְֿיקְי (*rabbefechi* 'revive'), מְיאְי (*mee* 'mine'); without *mater lectionis*: אֵיסְרְי (*essere*'to be'). So also in the *Elegy for the 9th of Av*. This type of *shwa* is especially frequent in Q2 (there it is used more than *ṣere* or *segol*), but it is frequent also in F, Q1 and Q3 (but absent in S).

– Consonant gemination

Gemination is phonemic in the central-southern Italian dialects, so it must find expression in the transliteration of F and the 15th century manuscripts of translations, made and written in this zone and belonging to the central-southern tradition (*coiné*, in the terminology of Cuomo and Sermonetta).[68] The gemination in these sources is often marked by *dagesh forte*, e.g., טוּטּוֹ = *tutto*, קוֹמַנּוֹ = *comanno* (*comando* with the southern characteristic assimilation *nd* > *nn*). But in most cases, the *dagesh* is ommitted. Almost always it is clear that the omission is casual and the consonant must be duplicated according to

65 Besides כי there is only one time כּוֹמְי = *kome*, also in Q2.

66 שׁ before consonant is found (and widely spread in the 15th century manuscripts Q1, Q2, Q3) only before *t*, see below.

67 *Domedet Det* is the common name for God in medieval Judeo-Italian (see Sermoneta 1969: 393–394). It seems that *Domedet* derives from *Dominus*, and *Det* from *Deus*. The fact that the last letters in both names are *taw rafa* may be explained by the ancient pronunciation of the *taw rafa* as /s/ (and not as /d/ as commonly in the Italian Hebrew in the late Middle Ages and up to the 20th century).

68 Cuomo 1976, Sermoneta 1976.

the grammar of these dialects, e.g., טוּטוֹ = *tutto* ‘all’, אֶנְטֵינֵי = *entenne* (*intendi* ‘hear’), פָוֵילַארֵי = *fauellare* ‘to speak’.

In S, *dagesh* is totally absent. This manuscript was written in Northern Italy and presents many linguistic features of this zone. One of the main phonological traits of the northern Italian dialects is the complete loss of gemination, so the omission of *dagesh* is not just graphical, e.g., טוּטוֹ = *tuto* (for *tutto* ‘all’), אַנִי = *ani* (for *anni* ‘years’).

– Word division

The words are often written joined, and not only in the sense of the closely written letters of the consonantal text, but also joined by the vocalization on the word frontier, e.g., קוֹנְטוּטוֹ לַנִימוֹ (*con tutto l’animo* ‘with the whole soul’). Most frequently, this joining happens with the article, e.g., לַמָלָאטִי (*l’ammalati* ‘the sick (persons)’), but also other types of joining are found, e.g., אֵינֵיסִי (*en essi* ‘in these’). Only the late S uses the apostrophe to divide between the /l/ of the article and the word beginning with a vowel. This apostrophe is then doubled, e.g., לְ״אַנִימַה = *l’anima* ‘the soul’, לְ״אוֹלְיוֹ = *l’oljo* ‘the oil’. S also uses the single apostrophe, usually after the preposition ‘a’ (to), e.g., אַ' ווֹאִי = *a’uoi* ‘to you’.

2.2 Phonology

As already stated, the phonological traits are mostly the general central-southern ones.

– Consonants

This part is best described by Cuomo.[69] The traits are central-southern ones:

- *-nd-* > *nn*: *granna* ‘big (F)’, *munna* ‘pure (F)’, *segunna* ‘second (F)’. So also always in the *Rite of Fano*. And so mostly in the sermons of Rabbi Samuel ben Rafael Modena (1535, see above), but already with some exceptions in scholarly Latinized forms, as *onorandissimo* ‘very reverend’, *indotto* ‘learned’ (p. 184b). About the conservation of the cluster *nd* in the *Elegy for the 9th of Av* see above.
- An important phenomenon is the conservation of preconsonantal *l*: *alzaro* ‘(they) rose up’, *vultato* ‘turned’, *multo* ‘much’, etc., as the velarization or palatalization of such an *l* is a general trait in all dialectal zones relevant for Judeo-Italian.[70] This holds for Judeo-Italian texts, beginning with the *laʕazim* in the *ʕArukh* studied by Cuomo.[71]
- *l* is maintained in the classic Judeo-Italian texts also in postconsonantal position, e.g., in the Book of Jona: *clama* ‘cries’, *flumo* ‘stream’, *tenpelo* ‘Temple’, *schelarire* ‘to clear’, *plu* ‘more’. According to Cuomo, it is one of the characteristic traits of the central-southern Judeo-Italian texts, with the exception of the *Maqre Dardeqe*. In the 15th century manuscripts of the Siddur translations, the *l* is maintained: *locli* ‘the eyes’ (also with an epenthetic vowel: *occheli* [Q3]), *loflore* ‘the flower’, *florire* ‘to flower’. In the *Rite of Fano*, *l* in such a position is mostly palatalized, e.g., *piacimento* ‘pleasure’ (6b, 7a), *chiamaj* ‘(you) call’ (5a), *chiameti* (5b), *chiama* (71b), *injenocchiameroci* (5a), *locchiu* (5b), *fiore*, *fiorire* (27a), but also *injenoclare* ‘to bow’ (‘inginnocchiare’, 57b).

69 Cuomo 1988a: 37–42.

70 Cuomo 1988a: 37; Ernst 1970: 75–80 (but there is also some evidence of the conservation of the *l* in this position in some local non-Jewish texts, not always explained as a scholar correction).

71 Cuomo 1974: 137.

This testifies to the Toscanization of medieval Judeo-Italian mentioned above. But even as late as 1535 in the sermons by Samuel Modena the *l* is mostly conserved: *plu*, *declarato* 'declared', *declarare* 'to declare' (184b), *declareremo* 'we will declare' (185a), with metathesis: *replubbeca* 'republic' (184b). But also *chiara* 'clear' (184b).

• Partial assimilation occurs in *-ns-*, *-rs-*, *-ls-* > *nz*, *rz*, *lz*, in all Judeo-Italian texts, except the *ʕArukh*.[72] So also in the *Rite of Fano*: *laperzone* 'the person' (6b), *reverzeno* (*reverseno*) '(they) reverse'(169a), *reconzola* 'comforts' (5b), *reconzolarajo* '(I) will comfort' (7a), *penzava* 'thought' (169a), *non volze* 'didn't want' (7a), *falzitade* 'falsification' (32b), *ravvolze* 'turns around' (48a), but there are also several cases indicative of Toscanization: *consigliamo* 'we) advise' (32b), *consiglio* 'advice' (33b).

• All consonantal clusters that yield an affricate /dʒ/ in the Tuscany dialects yield the palatal fricative /j/ in medieval Judeo-Italian.[73] So always in the medieval and 15th century texts. This fricative is signified by *jod* or *jod* (״י/י). But in the 17th century translation of the Siddur this sign already signifies a voiced palatal affricate, as is clear from such orthography as *abruyyava* = *abbrucciava* 'burned', where *yy* must signify /dʒ/. In the very late Italian translation of the *Pirqe Avot* written in Hebrew characters[74] this sound is signified by the digraph *gimel jod* (גי׳), under the influence of the common Italian orthography, e.g., רַאגְיוֹנֵי *ragjone* 'reason' (but also in this late printed edition the ancient orthography remains, e.g., רַאיוֹנוֹרֵנוֹ = *rajonorono* '(they) reasoned').

As an example of the general phonological phenomena that characterize medieval Judeo-Italian may serve the epenthetic vowel, *-e-* which appears in the consonantal clusters consonant + *r*, *l*. This trait is generalized and becomes a rule in the translation of the Book of Jona studied by Cuomo,[75] where she calls it "sbalordativo" for its regularity. It appears always in posttonic position (*libero* 'free', *supera* 'above', *ventera* 'belly', *senpere* 'always'), while in pretonic position it appears when the cluster consonant + *r*, *l* is preceded by a third consonant (*ingheluttire* 'to swallow', *schelarire* 'to clear', but *clama* 'calls', *sacrifizio* 'sacrifice'). This trait is present in some other medieval Judeo-Italian texts, although not with such a consistency. It is well documented in the Judeo-Italian texts in the Hebrew Siddur, discussed above: *lu-pateri* 'the father', *alteri* 'others' (see above), but it is almost absent in the 15th century translations of the Siddur. In the *Ritual of Fano* we find almost only *patre* 'father', *nostri* 'ours', *nostra* 'our (F)', *nostro* 'our (M)', (passim); only once *colpi nosteri* 'our sins' (33a), but on the same page several times *nostri*. According to Cuomo, this trait is somewhat peculiar when compared with other central-southern dialects, especially those of Lazio, where the epenthetic *-e-* is present in the symmetric clusters *l*+consonant.[76]

There is another trait which is very important for searching for the origins of Judeo-Italian. It is the sort of consonant clusters *st*, *sk*, *sp*. In the *Ritual of Fano* these clusters are conserved (i.e., written סט, ספ, סק), and so in the 17th century S. While in the three 15th century manuscript translations (Q1, Q2, Q3) the distribution is *št* / *sk*, *sp* (שט / סק,

72 Cuomo 1988a: 26, 39; Cuomo 1974: 137.

73 Cuomo 1988a: 24–25, 39.

74 Venezia 1710. It can be hardly named "Judeo-Italian", as the language is very normative.

75 Cuomo 1988a, p. 41; Cuomo 1976: 30–53, at 36.

76 See the discussion in Cuomo 1988a: 42.

ספ; e.g., נוֹשְׁטְרָה / סְקוֹמְפֶּירַה, סְפְּרַאנְצָה). The distribution in such a strict form is characteristic of the Abruzzese dialects.[77] The same trait can also be observed in the ancient *Elegy for the 9th of Av*, as Natale has recently remarked.[78] Such a consistency may point to Abruzzo as the cradle of Judeo-Italian. This consistency remains also in later times, i.e. this trait is conserved also in some northern Judeo-Italian dialects, e.g., in the Judeo-Venetian of the late 16th century.[79]

– Vowels

Cuomo provides an elaborate analysis of the accented vowels in translation of the Book of Jona:[80] /ū/ > always *u* (e.g., *annunzia* 'declares', *fiumi* 'streams', *dejuno* 'fast'); /ī/ > generally *i* (*figlio* 'son', *dissero* '(they) said', *ira* 'wrath'); /ŭ, ō/ > always *u*, independently of the final vowel (*supera* 'above', *majjuro* 'great', *cumo* 'as', *respuse* 'answered', *dudeci* 'twelve', *multo* 'much'); /ŏ/ > *o* when final *-a* (*opera 'deed', misericordia* 'mercy'), *-e* (*sorta* 'lot', *morta* 'death', *coro* 'heart'),[81] *-o*; *u* when final *-i* (*furza* 'forse' 'maybe', *umeni* 'men'), *-u* (*pupelo* 'people', *turto* 'twisted'); /ĭ, ē/ > always *e*, independently of the final vowel (*secca* 'dry', *furtezza* 'strength', *pescio* 'fish', *cenera* 'ashes', *temo* 'I am afraid', *celi* 'skies', *scese* 'came down', *quvesto* 'this', *temero* '(they) were afraid'); /ĕ/ > always *e*, independently of the final vowel (*tenpesta* 'tempest', *essere* 'to be', *vascelli* 'vessels', *prezzo* 'price', *vento* 'wind'). This vocal system is evidently asymmetric (/ŭ, ō/ > always *u*, while /ĭ, ē/ > always *e*; /ŏ/ > *o* or *u* as a result of metaphony, while /ĕ/ > always *e*, independently of the final vowel). Cuomo suggests several possible explanations of this phenomenon. First, it may be explained by the tendency of the manuscript Parma[82] to regularity of paradigm. Second, maybe the closed *o* was very closed, and more similar to *u*, than to the open *o*. The third proposed explanation is very interesting from the socio-linguistic point of view, as it underlines the common destiny of Judeo-Italian with non-Jewish Italian: in the discussed period the diphthong was considered as a plebeian trait in Rome and in the zones culturally dependent of it, and the described Judeo-Italian system is the consequence of the conscious elimination of diphthongs (*iɛ* > *e*; *uɔ, uɛ* > *u*). Thus, monophthongization is important as a witness to the aspiration to the "high language". In accented syllables, *u* is dominant as well, but not in the final position.[83]

In other vocalized sources, as the Siddur translations, the picture is much more similar to the general Tuscany scheme. So in the *Rite of Fano*: *popoli* 'peoples', *comenza* 'begins' [5a] *profonno* 'profound' [17a]), but with clear remnants of the paradigma described by Cuomo, e.g., *rispuse* 'answered' [5a], *locchiu* 'the eye' [5b]. The existence of different vocal schemes, some of which are closer to the Ms Parma system and some of which are more Toscanized, can be seen if we compare the above-men-

77 Rohlfs 1966–69: 156, 158.

78 Natale 2018: 5, n. 26

79 Ryzhik 2017.

80 Cuomo, 1988a: 28–34.

81 About the general metaplasm of the class *-e* to the classes *-o* and *-a* see below.

82 Ms Palatina di Parma 3068, the translation of the books of Prophets, containing also the Book of Jona.

83 Cuomo 1988a: 34–37.

tioned short prayers *Seder hattarat qelalot* ('Order of the annulation of the curses'), *Mi še-beraḵ* ('He that blessed'), *Hazkarat nešamot* ('Commemoration of the souls [the deceased]') in different manuscripts. So in the Ms Leeds, Brothertorn Library, MS Roth 58: *fusseru* 'were', *muljere* 'wife', *neputi* 'grandchildren', *lu nefeš* (also in the function of objective suffix: *lu salva* 'save him'), but also in final position: *avesseru* 'have had', *essu* 'this', *sianu* 'will be'; and probably with metaphony: *jodea* / *judio* 'Jew'. Also in this manuscript, which is relatively consistent, there is at least one case of alternative forms: *posti* / *pusti* 'posted'. The form *sorori* 'sisters' is also found. The picture is different in the Ms Parma Bibl. Pal. Cod. Parm. 3134 (Parma De Rossi 260): *fussero*, *avessero*, *siano* (but *essu*), *sorori*, *nepoti*, *lo nefeš*. Yet another scheme, with even more *u*, we find in the Ms Parma Biblioteca Palatina Cod. Parm. 2573 (Parma de Rossi 63): *judeu*, *fusseru*, *neputi*, *sururi*. It must be underlined that in all these manuscripts the scheme remains asymmetric, as in the Book of Jona, and there is no corresponding shift *e* > *i*. These multiple differences in the vocalization evidently reflect different dialects; maybe for this reason, and under the influence of the general Italian trend to unify the language, in some later manuscripts of the Siddur, as in the Ms. Paris Bibliotheque Nationale Heb. 1130, the discussed prayers are not vocalized, although the rest of the texts of the Siddur (which are Hebrew) are vocalized. But in the last source in which these segments appear, the Mahzor Bologna 1540, they are vocalized, and the vocalization (as other dialectal traits) is very similar (if not identical) to the medieval one: *fusseru posti*, *judio* / *judea*.

2.3 Morphology

– Noun

Several traits are characteristic of the medieval Judeo-Italian texts.

• The metaplasm, e.g., the redistribution of the nouns of the 3rd declination (with the ending *-e*) to the 1st and 2nd declinations (feminine nouns receive the ending *-a*, e.g., *cittada* 'city', *salvaziuna* 'salvation') and the masculine nouns with the ending *-o*, e.g., *pescio* 'fish', *granno* 'great'). As in the case of the epenthetic *e* discussed above, this trait can be deduced from the Book of Jona studied by Cuomo (from which these examples are taken),[84] with the only exception of the monosyllables *dì* (*dė*) 'of' and *re* 'king'. The metaplasm is well documented in another Judeo-Italian texts, too, e.g., in the *Rite of Fano*: *lo nome tuo granno* 'your great name' (22a), but generally the nouns and the adjectives of the 3rd declination don't change there.

Here is a place to mention the inner distinction in the *Rite of Fano*: the *Hošanot*, the ancient *piyyuṭim* (religious poetry) for the Festival of Sukkot, are translated in a somewhat more ancient and southern language.[85] And here we find more cases of the metaplasm than in the other parts of the Siddur translation, e.g., *fina* (= *fine* 'end', 175b) in *Hošanot* / *fine* (18b, 70a) elsewhere; *jenta* (= *gente* 'people', 176a) in *Hošanot* / *jente* (77a) elsewhere.

84 See the discussion in Cuomo 1988a: 42–44.

85 Ryzhik 2014.

• The plural ending of the 1st declination is *-i* instead of *-e* (*operi* 'deeds'). This trait was considered the "most constant characteristic of Judeo-Italian",[86] but it can be differently explained in different sources, partly as phonological phenomenon, partly as a consequence of analogical morphological processes.[87] It seems to be evidently non-phonological in the *Rite of Fano*, as such forms (e.g., *li stradi* 'the ways', 18b) exist in parallel with generally conserved nouns of the 3rd declination (on the same page: *pastore* 'shepherd', *nome* 'name'), and even to those that are similar to plural form but in reality are the remnants of the 4th Latin declination (see immediately below): *la grannezze* 'the greatness' on the same page.

• As has just been stated, Judeo-Italian conserves many abstract nouns with the ending *-ezze* in the singular, e.g., in the *Rite of Fano*: *fortezze mea* 'my strength'(5a), *allegrezze* 'merriness' (5b, singular שמחה in the Hebrew original), *la tristezze* 'the grief' (7a), *la altezze* 'the height' (17a) etc. These remnants of the Latin declination with the ending *-ities* are wide-spread in the southern dialects.[88]

– The noun forms with the suffix *-isc-* are wide-spread in Judeo-Italian, e.g., in different 15th century translations of the Siddur: *fioriscimento* 'flowering', *guariscitore* 'healer', *libertiscemento* 'liberation', *entaljetiscemento* 'intelletto' 'intellect'.[89] Such forms are characteristic of southern Italian dialects as well.[90]

• The plural forms with the ancient and dialectal ending *-ora*.[91] It is particularly wide-spread in the already mentioned translation of the *Hošanot* in the *Rite of Fano*: *trivora* ('tribes', 161b, שבטים), *albergora* ('camps', 167b, מחנים). Its ending is found also with *-e* instead of *-a*: *li albergore toi* ('your camps' 176b); a shift *-ora* > *-orae* is documented well in the Salentine dialects;[92] it is not the only trait that underlines the affinity between the extreme Southern dialects and Judeo-Italian.

– Possessive adjectives

The system of the possessive adjectives is described by Cuomo for the Book of Jona:[93]

PS	SG (M/F)	PL
1	*mio*/*mea*	–
2	*tuo*/*toa*	*tui*
3	*suo*/*soa*	*sui*

This paradigm, as Cuomo concludes, is most similar to that described by Ernst[94] for the high forms of the ancient Roman dialect.

Other Medieval Judeo-Italian texts have slightly different paradigms, e.g. in the *Rite of Fano*: *mio* (5a), *tuo* (18b), *suo* (5b), *mea* (5a), *toa* (5a), *toi* (masc. 5b, fem. 28b), *soi* (masc. 17a, fem. 5a). This is the paradigm also in other (manuscript) 15th century trans-

86 Terracini 1956: 243–258, at 254.
87 See the discussion in Cuomo 1988a: 46–47.
88 Rohlfs 1966–69: 355.
89 Ryzhik 2013a: 229–260, 250–251.
90 Rohlfs 1966–69: 524.
91 Mostly southern, see Rohlfs 1966–69: 370.
92 Rohlfs 1966–69: *ibid.*
93 Cuomo 1988a: 48–50.
94 Ernst 1970: 128.

lations of the Siddur, with only one exception, an additional example of dialect differences inside Judeo-Italian. In Q3 we find the 2SG possessive adjective *tuu* (instead of *tuo*), typical of the Marchigian dialect.[95] According to Rohlfs, this form is found in Ancona, a city rich in Jewish traditions. But the language in Q3 is not purely "Anconian": *tuu* and *suu* are systematically used, the standard form *mio* for 1SG occurs as well, while the Anconian dialect has *miu* (Rohlfs, ibid.).

– Verb

The verbal morphology of Judeo-Italian is well described and analyzed by Sermoneta,[96] and especially by Cuomo.[97] Not surprisingly, it is Central-Southern in its general traits. Here are some of the most salient features.

The ancient Roman dialect has 3SG present indicative forms *ao* 'has', *fao* 'does', *dao* 'gives', *stao* 'stays', *vao* 'goes'.[98] These forms are well represented in the Judeo-Italian texts: [99] *ao*, *vao*, *fao* in the *Elegy for the 9th of Av* (but also *sta*), *vao*, *stao* in the Book of Jonah, *veo* in the translation of Song of Songs (but *fa* and *sta*),[100] *fao* in the translation of Psalms.[101] We see that the distribution is lexical (*fao* / *sta* in the *Elegy*, *veo* / *fa*, *sta* in the translation of Psalms), so that isoglosses are found between different sources of Judeo-Italian. These isoglosses exist also between the different 15th century translations of the Siddur. The form *fao* is the only one used in F, as in the following examples: *fao fiatare lo uento e fao scennjere la-pjojja* 'he makes blow the wind and makes fall the rain' (Heb. משיב הרוח ומוריד הגשם), *fao fiorire a-noi saluezione en appresso* 'he makes blossom for us salvation soon' (Heb. מצמיח לנו ישועה בקרוב). The form *fao* is also found in Q3; e.g., *e fao uenire sconperatore* 'and he makes the redeemer come' (Heb. ומביא גואל), but it is otherwise very rare in Q3; in other occurrences, *fa* is used). In Q1 and Q2, this form is absent (only *fa*).[102]

According to Ernst, these forms begin to cede in the 14th century, yielding to short forms (*fa*, *de*, *vo*) and finally disappear in the 16th century,[103] the last cited source being *Anedotti* edited by Vatasso, written between 1476 and 1478.[104] But in Judeo-Italian as late as 1535 we find such forms in the sermons of Samuel Modena, e.g., *fao* (196b), *vao* (188b); they disappear only in the second half of the 16th century.[105]

95 Rohlfs 1966–69: 427.
96 Sermoneta 1967.
97 Cuomo 1988a: 56–71.
98 Ernst 1970: 144.
99 Cuomo 1988a: 58.
100 Sermoneta 1974: 84.
101 Sermoneta 1978: 196–239, at 215.
102 Ryzhik 2013a: 251.
103 Ernst 1970: 144.
104 Cuomo 1988a: 58.
105 Ryzhik 2012.

The 1SG present indicative of *sapere* 'to know' is *saccio*.[106] So in the *Rite of Fano* (6b, 127a) and in all other 15th century translations of the Siddur. The form is southern, and it remains in Judeo-Romanesco up to the 20th century.[107]

The ending of the 1SG future indicative is the southern *-rajo*.[108] So also in the *Rite of Fano*: *e darajo erva nel canpo tuo* 'and I will give grass in your camp'(23*r*); *e da linemici mei serajo salvato* 'and I will be saved from my enemies'(70*r*); *e darajo essi e farajo moltepecare essi e darajo lo santovario mio en fraessi asenpre* 'and I will give these and will multiply these and will give my sanctuary between them forever' (76*v*).

The ending of the 3SG past perfect (*passato remoto*) is the Central-Southern *-ao* / *-avo*. These forms also serve as the present in the translations of the Siddur, as in the *Ritual of Fano*: *scanpao* 'escaped' (5a), *amao* 'loved'(7a).

2.4 Syntax

Generally the syntax of the Judeo-Italian translations strictly follows the Hebrew original. But it is not mechanical, at least there are some interesting phenomena as translators search to find compromises between Hebrew and Italian (Semitic and Indo-European) syntactic structures.[109] Here three different traits related to the verb.

• The use of the verbal copula (different forms of the verb *essere* 'to be') does not exist in Hebrew, so it may be introduced or not in the translations to a language such as Italian, in which its use is almost obligatory.[110] It is particularly evident in the translation of the concluding formula of the benedictions, ברוך אתה ה', 'Blessed are you, You God', which is usually followed by the participle that describe some quality of God (who creates, who loves, who heals). There are two problematic questions in the translation of this formula into Italian:[111] (a) How should the nominal phrase ברוך אתה 'Blessed are You' be translated (with or without the verbal copula)? (b) In which person should the verb that translates the Hebrew participle (second – because it is subordinated to אתה, 'tu' – or third) occur? It appears that all these possibilities are realized in the different translations. The copula is present in F and Q2 (*benedetto sii tu* 'blessed be you') and is absent from Q1 and Q3 (*benedetto tu* 'blessed you'). The verb that translates the participle is in the second person in F (e.g., *che fai fiorire* 'who makes flower') and appears in the third person in Q1, Q2, and Q3 (*fa* / *fao*).

• The Hebrew preterite may be translated by *passato remoto* or by *passato prossimo*. *Passato prossimo* is characteristic for the northern, *passato remoto* for the southern dialects.[112] Accordingly to this distinction, the use of the tense *passato remoto* is documented in the *Rite of Fano* and 15th century manuscripts, which represent the classic Medi-

106 Cuomo 1988a, p. 67.

107 Del Monte 1955: 10, 45; Calò 1990: 36.

108 Cuomo 1988a: 59.

109 Cuomo 1988a: 73–98.

110 Cuomo 1988a:85–86.

111 Ryzhik 2009.

112 See Rohlfs 1966–69: 672, 673.

eval Judeo-Italian, while *passato prossimo* is found in the 17th century S, e.g., in Num 15:41 (in the *Šemaʕ Israel*):

The Hebrew original: אֲנִי יְהוָה אֱלֹהֵיכֶם אֲשֶׁר הוֹצֵאתִי אֶתְכֶם מֵאֶרֶץ מִצְרַיִם
I am God your Lord that have taken you from the Land of Egypt

Q1: אִיאוֹ דוֹמֵדֶת לוֹ דֵית בוֹשְׁטְרוֹ קֵי טְרַאסִי בוֹאִי דְלַטֵירַה דֵי מִצְרַיִם
io Domedet lo Det voštro che trassi voi della-terra de Misraim

Q2: אִיאוֹ דוֹמְדֵיד דֵיד בוֹשְׁטְרוֹ קְי טַרַאסְי בוֹאְי דַלַטֵירָה דְמִצְרָיִם
io Domeded Ded voštro che trasse voe dalla-terra de-Misraim

Q3: אִיאוֹ סוֹ דוֹמֵדֵת דֵית ווֹשְׁטְרוֹ קֵיטְרַאסֵי ווֹאִי דַלַטֵירָה דְמִצְרַיִם
io so Domeded Det uoštro che-trasse uoi dalla-terra de-Misraim

S: אִיאוֹ אִיל סִינְיוֹר אִידִיאוֹ ווֹסְטְרוֹ קְוַואל אוֹ קַאוַואטוֹ ווֹאִי דַה לַה טֶירָה דֵי מִצְרָיִם
io il Sinjor Idio uostro qual o cauato[113] *uoi da la tera de Misraim*

So we see that there is clear line of development that can be called historic-geographic, from the medieval Judeo-Italian rich in the ancient (and /or) southern traits to the post-medieval Judeo-Italian, Toscanized and rich in the northern traits.

• The past conjunctive *(congiuntivo passato)* is not used in the Judeo-Italian translations, as it has no Hebrew counterpart. But in the original Judeo-Italian texts, as in the short Judeo-Italian prayers in the Hebrew Siddur (see above) this form is found: *fusseru posti* 'were posted', *avesseru posti* 'have posted'.

2.5 Lexicon

Generally the Judeo-Italian Romance component is not very different from the lexicon of the medieval central-southern dialects, but there are some lexemes which are used (almost) exclusively in Judeo-Italian, and some of them are important key-words.[114] Here are several words which are particular for Judeo-Italian.

• The verb *nescere* 'to teach'. This is one of the most characteristic verbs for medieval Judeo-Italian.[115] e.g., in the *Rite of Fano*: *e per la lejje toa che nescesti noi* 'and for Your law that you have taught us' (179b); *tu cordolji allomo sapere e nesce allomo intelletto* 'You give to the man knowledge and teach the man intellect' (78a); or in the 16th century sermons: la *Tora ennesce a lo ben adam.*[116] In the non-Jewish sources this verb is extremely rare and is documented only in 13th century texts written in the ancient Roman dialects (also here it is very rare), e.g., in the *Storie de Troia e de Roma*, 1252/1258: *Et a li cavaleri novilemente nescea cavallaria*; *De Adriano imperatore. [...] Questo fece granne spesa ad nescere lectera greca* 'and he taught chivalry to the knights in the noble way; about emperor Adrian [...] this has made great expenses to teach the Greek language'.[117]

113 In this case the used lexemes (*trarre* / *cavare*) are also different.

114 See Cuomo 1988a, pp. 99–103; Ryzhik 2008b.

115 Cuomo 1976: 49.

116 Ryzhik 2008b: 539.

117 Ryzhik 2008a: 168.

• *Semonire* 'seduce, tempt'. The verb form יִפְתֶּה *yifte* 'will seduce' in Dt 11:16 from the *Šemaʕ Israel* is translated by the verb *semonire* in the all translations, including the 17th century's S:

The Hebrew original: הִשָּׁמְרוּ לָכֶם, פֶּן יִפְתֶּה לְבַבְכֶם וְסַרְתֶּם

F: גְוַארְדֵיטִי אַווֹאִי אֶין קְוָונוֹ סְימוּנִיסְקַה לוֹ קוֹרֵי ווֹסְטְרוֹ אֵי צֵיסָרִיטְיֵוִי

guardeti a-uoi en quanno semonisca lo core uostro e cessarete-ue

Q1: [גְוַארְדֵּיטִי אַבוֹאִי אֵינְקְוַאנוֹ סֵיסֵימוֹנִיסְקַה לוֹקוֹרֵי בוֹשְׁטְרוֹ אצֵיסַרֵי

guardeti a-voi enquanno se-semonisca lo-core voštro a-cessare

Q2: גְוָורַדְּטְי אָבוֹיְי נוֹן קְוָואנוֹ סְיסִימוֹנִיסְקָא לוֹקוֹרְי בוֹשְׁטְרוֹ אֵיצְסְרִיטְיְוִי

guardete a-voje non quanno se-simonisca lo-core voštro e-cesserite-ue

Q3: גְוַורְדֵיטִיבֵּי אַווֹאִי קֵינוֹן סֵי סֵימוֹנִיסְקָה לוֹקוֹרֵי ווֹשְׁטְרוֹ אֵי צֵיסַרֵיטִיבֵּי

guardeti-ve a-uoi che-non se semonisca lo-core uoštro e cessareti-ve

S: גְוַארְדַאטֶיוִוי אַ׳ ווֹאִי קֵי נוֹן [וְוִי] סִימוֹנִיסְקַה אִיל קוֹר ווֹסְטְרוֹ אֶי וְוִי לֵיוַוארֵיטֶי

guardate-ui a' uoi che non [ui] simonisca il cor uostro e ui leuarete

In the Christian translations other words are used in this verse: [118]

Vulgata: *cavete ne forte decipiatur cor vestrum*

Bibbia Volgare: *Guardatevi ne per ventura il vostro cuore sie ingannato*

Diodati: *guardatevi che talora il vostro cuore non sia sedotto*

Brucioli: *Guardateui dunque, che perauentura il vostro cuore non sia disuiato*

The verb 'semonire' is found only in the Judeo-Italian sources, such as Judah Romano's glosses published by Debenedetti Stow and in the *Maqre Dardeqe*.[119] In both works, the root פתה is translated by the word סימונימנטו = *simonimento*, and as a Biblical example is cited properly in our verse (Dt 11:16).

In spite of its evident Christian origin (from *simonia*, the trade by the sacred objects, from the name of Simon the Magus from the Acts of Apostles), the verb *semonire* in the general sense of seduction is completely absent from the Christian sources and present only in the Jewish ones. Maybe this complete absence from the Christian sources is the reason of the conservation in Judeo-Italian of this verb with such a clear Christian etymology.

Anyway, on the example of this verb we see the existence of the common tradition which underlays the Judeo-Italian translations, from the ancient to the more recent ones.

• Sometimes a specifically Judeo-Italian word is found exceptionally in a Christian source, too. This is the case with the word גואל *goʔel* 'redeemer', whose traditional translation is *sconperatore* or similar, e.g., in the first benediction of the prayer *Šemona ʕeśre*:

118 As a Christian translation for the comparison with Jewish-Italian ones I use the Vulgata Clementina, the Bibbia Volgare, originally published by Nicolas Jenson in Venice, 1471, and the translations of Brucioli [Bruccioli, Antonio,1562. Bibbia (trad.), Ginevra, F. Durone] and Diodati [Diodati, Giovanni, 1607. *La Bibbia, cioè, I libri del Vecchio e del Nuouo Testamento nuouamente traslatati in lingua Italiana da Giovanni Diodati, di nation Lucchese*, Ginevra, Jean de Tournes].

119 Debenedetti Stow 1990: 246; *Maqre Dardeqe*, s.v.

The Hebrew original: ומביא גואל לבני בניהם למען שמו באהבה

F: אֵי פַּאִי וֵוינִירֵי לוֹ סְקוֹנְפֵּירַטוֹרֵי אַלְי פִּילְיוֹלְי דִּי לִי פִּילְיוֹלְי לוֹרוֹ פֵּיר לוֹ נוֹמֵי סוּאוֹ אֵין אָמוֹרֵי

e fai uenire lo sconperatore alle filjoli de li filjoli loro per lo nome suo en amore

Q1: אֵיפָא וֵינִירֵי אֵיסְקוֹנְפֵּירַאטוֹרִי אַלִי פִּילְיוֹלִי דְלִי פִּילְיוֹלִי לוֹרוֹ פֵּיר לוֹנוֹמֵי סוּאוֹ קוֹן אַמוֹרֵי

e-fa uenire esconperatore alli filjoli delli filjoli loro per lo-nome suo con amore

Q2: אֵי פַּא וְוִינִירִי] אֶיסְקוֹנְפָּרָאטוֹרִי אַלִּיפִילְיוֹלִי דְלִיפִלְיוֹלִי לוֹרוֹ פִּיר לוֹנוֹמֶי סוּאוֹ קוֹן אַמוֹרִי]

[e fa uenire] esconparatore alli-filjoli delli-filjoli loro per lo-nome suo con amore

Q3: אֵי פָּאוֹ וֵינִירֵי סְקוֹנְפֵּירָטוֹרֵי אַלִּי פִּילְיוֹלִי דֵילִי פִּילְיוֹלִי לוֹרוֹ פֵּיר לוֹ נוֹמֵי סוּאוּ קוֹן אָמוֹרֵי

e fao uenire sconperatore alli filjoli delli filjoli loro per lo nome suu con amore

S: אֵי קוֹנְדוּצֵי סְקוֹמְפֶּירַאטוֹר אַ׳ לִי פִּילְיוֹלִי דֵי לִי פִּילְיוֹלִי לוֹרוֹ פֶּיר אִיל נוֹמֵי סוּאוֹ קוֹן אַמוֹרֵי

e conduce scomperator a' li filjoli de li filjoli loro per il nome suo con amore

The verb *scomparare* 'to redeem' is very common in Jewish Italian, and the form סקונפיראו = *sconperao* is found also in the *Maqre Dardeqe* as a translation of the root √ g-ʔ-l.[120] The word is documented at the end of the 16th century in the elegy in Judeo-Italian published by Roth.[121] In the Christian sources, however, this word is found only in one Venetian document written in 1371.[122] So in this case the tradition is established very well in Judeo-Italian, as opposed to the Christian world.

• The Hebrew and Aramaic component is rich in medieval Judeo-Italian,[123] but not in the Bible translations, where every word is translated into Italian, with very rare exceptions (such as תפילין *tefillin*, for the Hebrew טוטפת = *filatteri* 'phylacteries', the translation of which is based on the ancient tradition, at least from Onkelos). There are more Hebrew-based words in the translations of the Siddur, mostly synthetic verbs, such as אינכוונרסי *inqawwanarsi* 'to think intensively' from the Hebrew reflexive verv התכוון *hitkawwen*, or מחלארי *mahlare* 'to forgive', from Hebrew מחל *maḥal*. Orthography may be some-times 'Italianized': the verb קעסארי *kaʕasare* 'be angry' from the Hebrew כעס is written with ק instead of כ, as כ is not used in the Judeo-Italian Romance component (see above). Interesting are the cases in which one Hebrew word translates another, e.g., the Hebrew word תימן *teman* 'South' is translated by another Hebrew word with the same significance דרום *darom* (*Rite of Fano*, 18b); i.e., this word seems to be used in the everyday vernacular of the Jews of Italy.

There are many Hebrew words in Judeo-Italian sermons. Sometimes Judeo-Italian is prevalent in the beginning and in the final part of sermon, i.e. in the introduction and in the conclusion, while the central part, dedicated to halachic or similar themes, is

120 Cuomo 1985:69–126, at 111.

121 Roth 1950: 155.

122 "Nui, Johann de Bona, rector di Ragusa, iudesi, consilieri et comun dela dita terra, a vui, misser lo consolo deli Viniciani in Salonich, et ser Lucha Pençin dela dita çitade de Vinesia, over a çaschuno altro de qualchuncha stado over condicion si sia che vorra' scomparar Çugno de Sorgo, nostro çintil homo de Ragusa, da carçere", in Lettera "autentica" del rettore di Ragusa Johann de Bona a dei giudici e consiglieri della città, al console dei Veneziani a Salonicco, a Lucha Pençin veneziano (*Monumenta Ragusina. Libri Reformationum*, t. IV, a cura di Josip Gelcic, Monumenta spectantia historiam slavorum meridionalium, XXVIII, 1896, pp. 129–130).

123 See Modena 1999.

almost exclusively Hebrew. But also the introductory and concluding parts are rich in Hebrew, as can be seen in text that is cited below in the section 3. But it is not real Hebrew component; it is more testimony to the common knowledge of Hebrew of the public that heard sermons, the 16th century Jews of Italy.

3. Sample texts

3.1 Elegy for the 9th of Av
(according to Ms Ferrara; P in parentheses refers to Ms Parma, see Cassuto 1929)

1. לַאיֵנְטִי דְּצִיוֹן פַלְנְיִי אֵילוּטָא

la=ienti de=Ṣiyon palnj-i {corr.to planj-i} e=lutt-a
DEF.SG.F=people of=Ṣiyon cry-PRS.3SG and=mourn-PRS.3SG
The people of Zion cry and mourn

2. דִיצֵי טָאוּפִינָא מָלֵי סוֹ קוֹנְדוּטָא

dic-e taupin-a male so condu-tt-a
say-PRS.3SG miserable-SG.F bad.ADV be:PRS.1SG lead-PTCP-SG.F
say: "miserable, I am badly led

3. אַמָאנוּ דְלוֹנֵימִיקוּ קֵי מָאוֹשְׁטְרוּטָא

a{P: em}=manu de-llo=nemicu ke m=ao=štru-tt-a
to{P: in}=hand of-DEF.SG.M=enemy REL 1SG.OBJ=have:PRS.3SG=destroy-PTCP-SG.F
in the hand of the enemy that has destroyed me"

4. לָא נוֹטִי אֵלָא דִיאֵי שְׁטַא פְלוֹרַנְדוֹ

la notti e=la die šta plor-ando
DEF.SG.F night and=DEF.SG.F day stay.PRS.3SG cry-GER
night and day they are crying

5. לִי סוֹאִי גְרַנְדֵיצִי רְמֵימְרַאנְדוֹ

li so-i grandezz-i remembr-ando
DEF.PL.M 3SG.POSS-PL greatness-F.PL remember-GER
remembering its greatness

6. אֵימוֹ פְילוֹמוּנְדוּ בָאוֹ גַאטִיבַאנְדוֹ

e=mo pello=mundu va-o gattiv-ando
and=now for.DEF.SG.M=world go-PRS.3SG capture-GER
and now around the world wanders in captivity

7. סוֹפְרֵי אוֹנִי יֵינְטִי פוֹאִי נַאלְצָטָא

sopre onni jenti foi nalz-at-a
above every people be:PRF.3SG elevate-PTCP-SG.F
Above all people it was elevated

8. אֵידוֹנִי אֶינְפֵרִיאוֹ אֲדוֹרְנָטָא

e=d=onni enperio adorn-at-a
and=of=every empire adorn-PTCP-SG.F
and adorned of every empire

9. דַאדֵיאוֹ סַנְטוֹ קֵירָא אֲמָאטָא

da=Dio santo k=era am-at-a
by=God holy as=be:IMPF.3SG love-PTCP-SG.F
when it was loved by holy God

10. אֵילִי סִינְיוֹרִי דָאוֹנִּי קַנְטוֹ

e=li sinjor-i da=onni canto
and=DEF.PL.M nobleman-M.PL from=every side
and the noblemen from everywhere

11. יִיאֲנוּ אֲדוֹפְרִירִי אַלוֹטֶימְפְלוֹ סַנְטוֹ

ji-anu ad=offr-ire a=llo=templo santo
come:PST-3PL to=offer-INF to=DEF.SG.M=temple holy
went to offer <sacrifices> at the holy temple

12. דְלוֹגַרַנְטִי אוֹנוֹרִי קָא בְיאָה טַנְטוֹ

de=llo=granti onori k=av-ea tanto
of=DEF.SG.M=great honor when=have-PST.3SG much
when it had a lot of great honor

13. לִיפִילְיֵי דְיִשְׂרָאֵל אֵירָנוֹ אֲדוֹרְנָטִי

li=filj-e de=Israel er-ano adorn-at-i
DEF.PL.M=son-M.PL of=Israel be:PST-3PL adorn-PTCP-M.PL
The sons of Israel were adorned

14. דְסִיצִירְדוֹטִי אֵילִיוִיטִי אַוַונְטָטִי

de=sicerdot-i e=liviti avant-at-i
by=priest-M.PL and=Levite-M.PL praise-PTCP-M.PL
Praised by priests and Levites

15. אֵידוֹנִי יֵינְטִי פוֹרוֹמְדִיאָטִי

e=d=onni jenti foro=mmedi-at-i
and=by=every people be:PRF.3PL.envy-PTCP-M.PL
and were envied by every people

16. לִינוֹשְׁטְרִי פַטְרִי מָלֵי פִינְצָארוּ

li=noštr-i patr-i male pinz-aru
DEF.PL.M=1PL.POSS-M.PL father-M.PL bad.ADV think-PRF.3PL
Our fathers wrongly thought

17. קְיקוֹנְטְרָא דֵיאוֹ רְיבִילַרוּ

ke=contra Deo revill-aru
COMP=against God rebel-PRF.3PL
when against God rebelled

18. לוּבֵינִי קְילִיפִיצִי נוֹ רְמֶמְרָארוֹ

lu=beni ke=li=fic-i no rememmr-aro
DEF.SG.M=good REL=DEF.PL.M.DAT=do:PRF-3SG NEG remember-PRF.3PL
the good that he done to them, did not remember

19. פִי קְוִישְׁטוֹ דֵיאוּ לִיפוֹאִי אֲדִירָאטוֹ

pi quišto Deu li=foi adir-at-o
for DEM.M God DEF.PL.M.DAT=be:PRF.3SG angry-PTCP-SG.M
For this God became angry with them

20. אֶידְנְפֵרְיוּ לוֹרוֹ פוֹאִי קַצָאטוֹ

e=d=enperiu loro foi cacci-at-o
and=from=empire 3PL.POSS be:PRF.3SG expell-PTCP-SG.M
and he <Jewish people> was expelled from their empire

21. קָאלוֹ סוֹאִי נוֹמִי אַבִּירוֹ סְקוֹרְדָאטוּ

ka=lo *soi {P: soo}* *nome* *abb-ero* *scord-at-u*
because=DEF.SG.M 3SG.M.POSS name have:PRF-3PL forget-PTCP-SG.M
because they had forgotten his name

22. סוֹפְּרֵי אִיסֵי מַנְדָאוֹ סִיגַרְנְדִי אוֹשְׁטִי

sopre *iss-e* *mand-ao* *si=grand-i* *ošt-i*
over DEM-PL send-PRF.3SG so=great-SG.F army-SG.F
Over these He sent such a great army

23. קִי פוֹאִי סִי דוּרָא אֵיסִי פוֹרְטִי

chi *foi* *sì* *dur-a* *e=ssì* *fort-i*
REL be:PRF.3SG so hard-SG.F and=so strong-3SG
that was so hard and so strong

24. קֵירוֹפְּי מוּרָא אֵינְפְרַנְצִי פוֹרְטִי

ke=ropp-e *mur-a* *e=nfranz-i* *port-i*
COMP=break:PRF-3SG wall-PL and=crush:PRF-3SG gate-F.PL
that it broke the walls and crushed the gates

25. גְוואִי קַוְונְטָא יֵינְטִי פוֹאִי מְצִיאָטָא

guai *quant-a* *jenti* *foi* *meci-at-a*
woe how.many-SG.F people be:PRF.3SG assassinate-PTCP-SG.F
Woe, how many people were killed

26. קִיטוּטָא לָטֵירָא יִיאָה אֶנְסַנְגְוִוינֵטָטָא

ke=tutt-a *la=terra* *ji-a* *ensangvinata-t-a*
COMP=all-SG.F DEF.SG.F=soil go:PST-3SG soak.with.blood-PTCP-SG.F
that all the soil was soaked with blood

27. אוֹיְ צִיוֹן קֵיסִי דֵיסְפִילְיָיטָא

oi *Ṣion* *ke=si* *desfilj-at-a*
oj Zion COMP=be:PRS.2SG lose.child-PTSP-SG.F
Oh, Zion, that you lost your children.

28. לוֹטֶימְפְּלוֹ סַנְטוֹ אַבִּירוֹ דְסִירְטָטוֹ

lo=templo *sant-o* *abb-ero* *desirta-t-o*
DEF.SG.M=temple holy-SG.M have:PRF-3PL desolate-PTCP-SG.M
They have desolated the holy temple

29. קֵינְגַרנְטִי אוֹנוֹרֵי פוֹאִי דְפִיקָאטוֹ

ke=n=garnti {corr. to: granti} *onore* *foi* *defic-at-o*
that=in=great honor be:PRF.3SG build-PTCP-SG.M
that was built in great honor

30. אֵיפוֹקוֹ דַצֵילוֹ לַאבִּי אַפַלְמַאטוֹ

e=foco da=celo l=abb-e afalma-t-o {corr. to: aflamma-t-o}
and=fire from=heaven it=have:PRF-3SG burn-PTCP-SG.M
and fire from heaven had burnt it

31. סְפְּרִיקָארוֹ טוֹרִי אֵיגְרַנְדִי פָּלַאצָא

sprec-aro *torri* *e=grand-i* *palazz-a*
waste-PRF.3PL tower-M.PL and=big-M.PL palace-N.PL
The towers and grand palaces were wasted

32. אֵילוֹ בַנְדוֹ יִיאָה פֵאוֹנִי פְלָאצָא

e=lo bando ji-a pe=onni plazza
and=DEF.SG.M ban go-PRF.3SG for=every square
and a ban went in every square:

33. פִי אַפוֹנַמְינטוֹ סִי דְיסְפַאצָא

fi a=fonnamento si desfazz-a
down to-foundation REFL undo:SBJV-3SG
“Let it be undone, down to its foundations!”

34. בְידִיסִי דוֹנִי לָא דְיסְפָרֵי

vedi-si donn-i là disf-are
see:PRF3SG-REFL woman-F.PL destroy-INF
Women were seen destroyed

35. אֵיֵינְטִילִי אוֹמֶנִי דְגַרנדִי אַפָרִי

e=ientil-i omeni de=garnd-i {corr. to: grand-i} affar-i
and=gentile-M.PL man-M.PL of=great-M.PL deed-M.PL
and refined people of great deeds

36. קֶינוּלָא גְוִיסָא סִינוֹ פוֹאִי רְיצִיטָרֵי

ch=en=nulla guisa si=no po-i recit-are
COMP=in=NEG.F way REFL=NEG can:PRS-2SG narrate-INF
that in no way it can be narrated.

37. אֵיטְרִי נָאבִי מִיסְרוֹ פִימָארֵי

e=ttri nav-i mis-ero pi mare
and=three boat-F.PL put:PRF-3PL at sea
And three boats were sent in the sea

38. צֵינְצָא רִימוֹ אֵינְטֵינדָא קִיסָא יוּטָרֵי

zenza rimo (entend-a ki=s=a iut-are)
without row (hear:SBJV-3SG who=know:PRS.3SG help-INF)
without a row (hear who can help!)

39. אֵיטוּטִי אַמָארֵי סֵיפְרִיסְרוֹ יֵיטָרֵי

e=tutt-i a=mare se=pris-ero iett-are
and=all-M.PL in=sea REFL=start:PRF-3PL throw-INF
and all of them started to jump in the sea

40. אֶלָטְרִי נְיבִינֵרוֹ דוֹנֵי קַנְטוֹ טוּטִי

elatr-i {corr. to: e=altr-i} ne=vinn-ero d=onni canto tutt-i
and=other-M.PL they:GEN=sell:PRF-3PL from=every corner all-M.PL
Others were sold everywhere

41. צֵינְצָא אֲבִירִי נוֹנְדִירְי פֶּרְקַוונְטוֹ

zenza av-eri non=de-re per=quanto
without have-INF NEG=say-INF for=how.much
Without saying for how much

42. אוֹי קֵי פָרָאִי פוֹפלוֹ סַנְטוֹ

Oi, ke fa-r-ai popolo santo?
Woe, what do-FUT-2SG people holy?
Woe, what will you do, holy people?

43. אֵילִילְוִיטִי אֵילִיסַצִירְדוֹטִי

e=li=levit-i *e=li=sacerdot-i*
and=DEF.PL.M=levite-M.PL and=DEF.PL.M=priest-M.PL
and the Levites and the priests

44. קוֹמוֹ בְּישְׁטִי אַלְיָיא פוֹרוֹ בְּינדוּטִי

como beštiali-a f-oro vend-ut-i
as beast-M.PL be:PRF-3PL sell-PTCP-M.PL
were sold like beasts

45. אֵינְפַריי לַאלְטְרָא יֵינטֵי פוֹאִי סְפֶּרְדוּטִי

e=nfra l=altr-a iente poi sperd-ut-i
and=between DEF.SG.F=other-SG.F people then disperse-PTCP-M.PL
and were dispersed then between the other people

46. טַנְטוֹ אֵירָא דוּרָא לוֹרוֹ סִינְיוֹרִיאָה

tanto er-a dur-a loro sinioria
so be:PAST-3SG hard-SG.F 3PL.POSS government
So hard was their rule

47. לַנוֹטֵי פְּרֵיגָא דִּיאוֹ קֵי פוֹרְסִי דִּיאָה

La=notte preg-a Dio ke fors-i dia
DEF.SG.F=night pray:PST-3PL God COMP be:SBJV-3SG day
that at night they prayed God that it would be day

48. לָדִיאָה לָנוֹטִי טַנְטוֹ סְקוּרִיאָה

la=dia la=notti tanto scur-ia
DEF.SG.F=day DEF.SG.F=night so become_dark:PAST-3SG
at day that it would be night, so it was dark

49. קִיבּוֹלֵי אָאוֹדִירֵי קְרוּדֵלְיטָטִי

ki=bol-e aod-ire crudeltate
who=want:PRS-3SG hear-INF cruelty
Who wants to hear about the cruelty

50. קֵי אַדִּיבְינִי דְסוֹרֵי אֵיפַרטִי

ke addevenn-i de=sore e=farte {corr. to: frate}
REL happen:PRF-3SG of=sister and=brother
that happened to a brother and a sister

51. קִינְקְוִילָא אוֹרָא פוֹרוֹ גַאטִיבָאטִי

ki=n=quill-a ora f-oro gattiv-at-i
COMP=in=DEM.DIST-SG.F moment be:PRF-3PL enslave-PTCP-M.PL
that at that moment were caught

52. נֵילָא פְּרִיסָא פוֹרוֹ דְבִיסָאטִי

ne-lla prisa f-oro devis-at-i
in-DEF.SG.F captivity be:PRF-3PL divide-PTCP-M.PL
in captivity they were divided

53. קִי אַבִּי לָסוֹרוֹ אֵיקִי לוֹפְרַטִי

ki abb-e la=soro e=kki lo=frate
who have:PRF-3SG DEF.SG.F=sister and=who DEF.SG.M=brother
somebody had the sister and somebody had the brother

54. אֶינְגַא טִיבַנְצָא פוֹרוֹ מְינָאטִי

en=gattivanza f-oro men-at-i
in=captivity be:PRF-3PL lead-PTCP-M.PL
they were led in captivity

55. לוֹ סִינְיוֹרְי דְלָסוֹרוֹ מְיצִיאָרוֹ

lo signore de-lla=soro meciaro
DEF.SG.M lord of-DEF.SG.F=sister assassin
The owner of the sister, the assassin

56. לַאבְּי וֶונדוּטָא אֲדוּנוֹ טַבֵירְנַארוֹ

l=abb-e vend-ut-a ad=uno tabernaro
PRON.3F.SG.OBJ=have:PRF-3SG sell-PTCP-SG.F to=one inn_keeper
sold her to an inn keeper

57. קְי דְלוֹבִינוֹ לַאלְמְרִיאָרוֹ

ke de-llo=vino là=l=embri-aro
REL from-DEF.SG.M=wine there=PRON.3SG.M.OBJ-make.drunk:PRF-3PL
that made him there drunk from the wine

58. אֵילוֹ פְּרָטְי פוּאְי טְרָדָטוֹ

e=lo frate fu-e trad-at-o
and=DEF.SG.M brother be:PRF-3SG trade-PTCP-SG.M
and the brother was traded

59. אֲדוּנָה פוּטָנָא פִּיפְּיקָאטוֹ

ad=una puttana pi peccato
to=one.F whore for sin
to one whore for sin

60. אוֹי פוֹפוֹלוֹ סַנְטוֹ מָלְי סִי גְוִידָטוֹ

oy popolo santo male si guid-at-o
oh people holy bad.ADV be:PRS.3SG lead-PTCP-SG.M
Oh, holy people, you were lead wrongly!

61. בֵינִּי אוּנָא אוֹרָא קֵי סַאדוּנָארוֹ

venn-i una ore che s=adun-aro
arrive:PRF-3SG one hour REL REFL=meet:PRF-3PL
Arrived an hour in which they met,

62. קְוִילָא פוּטָאנָא אֵילוֹ טָאבֵירְנָארוֹ

quilla puttana e=lo tavernaro
DEM.DIST.F whore and=DEF.SG.M inn_keeper
this whore and inn keeper

63. אִילוּנָא אֵילַלְטרוֹ לוֹרְיצִיטָרוֹ

e=l=una e=l=altro lo=recit-aro
and=DEF.SG.F=one and=DEF.SG.M=other PRON.3SG.M.OBj=tell:PRF-3PL
and narrated each other:

64. אוּנָא דוֹנָא אַייוּ בֵּילָא קַוונְטוֹ רוֹסָא

una donna ai-u bella quanto rosa
one woman have:PRS-1SG beautiful.F as rose
A woman I have, beautiful like a rose

65. בֵּינֵי קְירִידוֹ קְי יֵינְטִי קוֹסָא

Bene	*crid-o*	*k-è*	*ienti*	*cosa*
well	believe:PRS-1SG	COMP-be:PRS:3SG	gentle	thing

Really I believe she is a gentle creature

66. דְלַיֵינְטִי טְרִישְׁטָא אֵידוֹלוֹרוֹסָא

de-lla=ienti	*trišta*	*e=dolorosa*
of-DEF.SG.F=people	sad	and=pained

from the people sad and painful

67. קְווִילָה רְיסְפּוּנְדִי קִיאוֹ אַיְיוֹ אוּנוֹ נְנְפַנְטִי

quilla	*respund-i*	*k=io*	*ai-o*	*uno*	*nnfanti*
DEM.DIST.F	answer:PRF-3SG	COMP=1SG	have:PRS-1SG	one	boy

She responded that "I have a youth

68. קְיֵרִי סִי יֵינְטִי אֶידְּבִינַנְטִי

ked=è	*sì*	*ienti*	*ed=evinanti*
that=be:PRS:3SG	so	gentle	and=pretty

that is so gentle and pretty

69. פְּלוֹ קִילָא שְׁטִילָא דַאלִיבַנְטִי

plo	*ki=la*	*štilla*	*da=livanti*
more	than=DEF.SG.F	star	of=morning

more than the morning star"

70. אִינְקוִישׁטוֹ פִינְצָרוֹ פָּרֵינְטִיצִי אַפָּרִי

in=quišto	*pinz-aro*	*parentezze*	*a=f-ari*
in=DEM.M	think:PRF-3PL	marriage	to=do-INF

So they thought to make a marriage

71. אִילִילוֹרוֹ פִילְיֵי אַסִירְבִינְטָארִי

e=li=loro	*figli*	*asservent-ari*
and=DEF.PL.M=3PL.POSS	children	enslave-INF

and to enslave their children

72. אֵיבְּינְרִילִי פְּי גָוַדַאנְיָרִי

e=benn-ere-lli	*pe*	*guadagn-are*
and=sell-INF-3PL.OBJ	for	profit INF

and to sell them to earn from it.

73. פוֹרוֹ קוֹנְיֵינְטִי אֲדוּנָא קָמִינָאטָא

f-oro	*coniun-t-i*	*ad=una caminata*
be:PRF-3PL	gather-PTCP-3PL	to=one room

They were gathered in a small room

74. לָדוֹנָא דָקַנְטוֹ אֵי זְבִיאָטָא

la=donna	*da=canto*	*è*	*svi-at-a*
DEF.SG.F=woman	from=aside	be:PRS:3SG	go.aside-PTCP-SG.F

the woman turned to a corner

75. דִיצִי טְרִישְׁטָא מַלֵא פוֹאִי נָאטָא

dec-e	*trišta*	*male*	*fo-i*	*n-at-a*
say:PRF-3SG	sad	bad.ADV	be:PRF-1SG	bear-PTCP-SG.F

said: "I was born unlucky!"

76. דִּיסְאצְירְדּוֹטִי אִיאוֹ פוֹאִי פִּילְיוֹלָא

de=secerdot-i io fo-i figliola
of=priest-PL 1SG be:PRF-1SG daughter
I was a daughter of a priest

77. סִינְיוּרִי דְלִיְי אֵידְסְקוֹלָא

signur-i de=lije e=de=scola
nobleman-PL of=law and=of=synagogue
reverend persons of law and the synagogue

78. אִימּוֹ קוּאוּנוֹ סֵירְבוֹ שְׁטָאוֹ סוֹלָא

e=mmo cu=uno servo šta-o sol-a
and=now with=one slave stay:PRS-1SG alone.sg.f
and now I am alone with a slave"

79. קוֹסִי לוֹנְפַנְטִי שְׁטָוָוא דָקַנְטוֹ

così lo=nfanti šta-va da=canto
so DEF.SG.M=boy stay-PST.3SG from=aside
In the same way the youth stayed in a corner

80. פָּצִיאָה לָמֵינְטוֹ אֶיגְרָנְדִי פָּלַנְטוֹ

fac-ia lamento e=grandi palanto {corr. to: planto}
do-PST.3SG lament and=great cry
and made a lament and great cry

81. קָא פוֹאִי פִּילְייוֹ דוּנוֹ אוֹמוֹ סַנְטוֹ

ca fo-i figlio d=uno omo santo
COMP be:PRF-1SG son of=one man holy
that "I was son of a holy man"

82. מוֹסוֹ אֲדוּנָאטוֹ קוּנָא סֶירְיֵינְטְי

mo=so adun-at-o c=un-a seriente
now=be:PRS.1SG gather-PTCP-SG.M with=one-F slave
Now, I am put together with a slave

83. נְידְּמִיאָה לִיְי נְידְּמִיאָה יֵינְטֵי

né=de=mi-a lije né=de=mi-a iente
NEG=of=POSS.1SG-F law NEG=of=POSS.1SG-F people
not of my law, nor of my people:

84. קוֹמוֹ פַרָאייוֹ טְרִישְׁטוֹ דוֹלֵינְטֵי

como fa-r-aio trišto dol-ente?
how do-FUT-1SG sad ache-PTCP.PRS
what shall I do, sad and painful?

85. אֵינְקְוִילוֹ פְּלַנְטוֹ סַאבְּירוֹ אָאוֹדוּטִי

en=quillo planto s=abb-ero aod-ut-i
in=DEM.DIST.M cry REFL=have:PRF-3PL hear-PTCP-PL
In this cry they heard each other

86. אֵילוּנוֹ אֵילַלְטרוֹ קוֹנוֹשׁוּטִי

e=l=uno e=l=altro conoš-ut-i
and=DEF.SG=one and=DEF.SG=other recognize-PTCP-PL
and one the other recognized

87. סורו אֵיפְרָטֵי אוֹבִי סִימוֹ בִינוּטִי

soro e=frate ovi s-imo ven-ut-i
sister and=brother where be:PRS-1PL come-PTCP-PL
"Brother and sister, where have we come?"

88. אֵילוּנוֹ אֵללַטְרוֹ סְיאַבְּרָאצָרוֹ

e=l=uno e=l=altro se=abbrazz-aro
and=DEF.SG=one and=DEF.SG=other REFL=embrace-PRF.3PL
and embraced one another

89. אֵיקוֹנְגְרֶנְדִי פַּלְנְטוֹ לָמֵינְטָרוֹ

e=con=grandi palnto {corr. to: planto} lament-aro
and=with=great cry lament-PRF.3PL
and with great cry lamented

90. פִי קֵמוֹרִירוֹ אֵיפַּזְמָארוֹ

fi ke=mor-iro e=pasm-aro
until COMP=die-PRF:3PL and=faint-PRF.3PL
until they died and fainted

91. קְוִישְׁטָא קְרוּדֵילִי קִי אָאוֹדִיסִי

quišt-a crudeli chi aodiss-e
DEM-F cruel REL hear-PST.SBJV.3SG
The one that would hear this cruel story

92. קִי גְרַנְדִי קוֹרְדוֹלְייוֹ נוֹלִי פְּרִינְדִיסִי

ki grandi cordoglio no=li prind-isse
REL great condolence NEG=OBJ.3SG.M take-PST.SBJV.3SG
who would not be taken by great compassion

93. אֵיגַרְנְדִי לָמֵינְטוֹ נוֹנֵי פָצִיסִי

e=garnde {corr. to: grande} lamento no=ne fac-isse
and=great lament NEG=GEN do-PST.SBJV.3SG
and would not make a great lament

94. קִיפּוֹאִי קוֹנְרֵטַי לַאלְטְרִי טוֹרְמֵינְטִי

ki=pò-i conretai {corr. to: cont-are} l=altr-i torment-i
who=can-PRS.3SG narrate-INF DEF.PL=other-PL torment-PL
Who can narrate the other torments

95. קֵי סְפִיסוֹ סְפִיסוֹ סוֹ קוֹמְבֵינְנְטִי

ke spisso spisso so comven-ent-i
REL often often be:PRS.3PL happen-PRS.PTCP-PL
that happen very often

96. פְּלוֹ דוֹרִי קֶפְלָמְבִי אַרְדֵינְטִי

plo dor-i ke=flamb-i ard-ent-i
more hard-PL than=flame-PL burn-PRS.PTCP-PL
harder, than burning flames

97. סַנְטוֹ דִיאוֹ נוֹשְׁטְרוֹ סִינְיוֹרִי

santo Dio noštro Signore
holy God POSS.1PL Lord
Holy God, our Lord

98. רִיטוֹרְנָא רֵיטוֹ לוֹטוֹאוֹ פוֹרוֹרִי

retorn=a reto lo=too forore
return:IMP.2SG=to back DEF.SG.M=POSS.2SG.M fury
turn back your anger

99. אֶינוֹ גְוַורְדָרִי אַנוֹאִי פִּיקָדוֹרִי

e=no guard-ari a=noi piccador-i
and=NEG see-INF to=1PL sinner-PL
and do not pay attention to us sinners

100. פְּלוֹטוֹאוֹ נוֹמְו סַנְטוֹ אֶבִינְדִיטוֹ

pe=lo=too nome santo e=bindi-tt-o
for=DEF.SG.M=POSS.2SG.M name holy and=bless-PTCP-SG.M
for your holy and blessed name

101. לְנוֹשְׁטְרוֹ קוֹרְו אַיוּשְׁטָא אַדְרִיטוֹ

le=noštro core aiušt-a a=dderitto
to=POSS.1PL heart straighten-IMP.2SG to=right
straighten our heart

102. קְיטְי סִירְבָאמוֹ אִינְפַטוֹ אֵינְדִיטוֹ

ke=te sirv-amo in=fatto e=n=ditto
COMP=2SG.DAT serve-PRS.1PL in=act and=in=speech
so that we will serve You in act and word

103. אֵירְמֶימְרָא לַפְּרִימָא אֲמָנְצָא

e=rememmr-a la=prim-a amanza
and=remember-IMP.2SG DEF.SG.F=first-SG.F love
and remember the first love

104. אֵיטְרָאִי נוֹאִי דְקְוִישְׁטָא גַאטִיבַנְצָא

e=tra-i noi de=quišt-a gattivanza
and=draw_out-IMP.2SG OBJ.1PL from=DEM-F slavery
and draw us out from this slavery

105. דְקְוִישְׁטָא טֵינְיבְרִי אֵיסְקוּרַנְצָא

de=quišt-a tenebri e=scuranza
from=DEM-F darkness and=darkness
from this darkness and gloom

106. אֵילוֹ נְמִיקוֹ קֵיטַנְטוֹ אֲוַונְטָטוֹ

e=lo nemico k=è=tanto avant-at-o
and=DEF.SG.M enemy REL=be:PRS.3SG=so favor-PTCP-SG.M
and the enemy that you so favoured

107. נֶילוֹטוֹאוֹ פוּרוֹרִי סִיאָה דְיֵיטָטוֹ

ne=llo=too furori si-a deiett-at-o
in=DEF.SG.M=POSS.2SG.M fury be:PRS.SBJV-3SG throw_down-PTCP-SG.M
in your fury let be thrown down

108. דַאקַנְטוֹ אֶנְקַנְטוֹ דְסִירְדאטוֹ

da=canto a=canto desered-at-o {P: desert-at-o}
from=side to=side disinherit-PTCP-SG.M {P: desert-PTCP-SG.M}
let him be deserted from the one end to another

109. אֵיצְיטוֹ פַּצָּא קוֹמוֹ אָאוֹפַּטוֹ

e=cetto fazz-a como ao=fa-tt-o
and=soon do:PRS.SBJV-3SG as have:PRS.3SG=do-PTCP-SG.M
and do to him quickly like he has done to us

110. אֵיסִיאָה שְׁטְרוּטוֹ אֵידְיסְפַּטוֹ

e=si-a štrut-t-o e=desfa-tt-o
and=be:PRS.SBJV-3SG destroy-PTCP-SG.M and=undo-PTCP-SG.M
and let him be destroyed and undone

111. קָא פַּאוֹ רוּמְפֵּירְי לַאלִיְי אֵילוֹפַּטוֹ

ka fa-o rump-ere la=lije e=lo=patto
CONJ do:PRS-3SG break-INF DEF.SG.F=law and=DEF.SG.M=pact
because he made us break the law and the pact

112. אֵידְרִיצָּא שְׁטָרְדִי נְאוֹנִי קַנְטוֹ

e=derizz-a štrad-i n=onni canto
and=straighten-IMP.2SG way-PL in=every side
And straighten ways everywhere

113. אֲדָרוּנָאֵרֵי אֶינְקְוִילוֹ סַנְטוֹ

ad=arunare {corr. to: adun-are, so in P} en=quillo santo
to=assemble-INF in=DEM.DIST.M holy
to assemble us in that holy (temple)

114. קְוִילוֹ פּוֹפּוֹלוֹ קָא מַשְׁטִי טַנְטוֹ

quillo popolo k=am-ašti tanto
DEM.DIST.M people REL=love-PRF.2SG so
this people that you loved so much

115. אֵילוֹ סַנְטוֹ טֵימְפּלוֹ קְי דְגַוְושְׁטָטוֹ

e=lo santo templo k=è deguašt-at-o
and=DEF.SG.M holy temple REL=be:PRS.3SG destroy-PTCP-SG.M
and your holy temple that is destroyed

116. דְלָטוֹאָה מָנוֹ סִיאָה דְפִיקָאטוֹ

de=la=toa mano si-a defec-at-o
from=DEF.SG.F=POSS.2F.SG hand be:PRS.SBJV-3SG rebuild-PTCP-SG.M
let it be built by your hand

117. לוֹטוֹאוֹ פְּרוּפֵיטָא קוֹמוֹ אָאוֹ פְּרוֹפְטִיאָטוֹ

lo=too prufeta como ao profeti-at-o
DEF.SG.M=POSS.2SG.M prophet as have:PRS.3SG prophesize-PTCP-SG.M
like your prophet had prophesized

118. לְוִיטִי אֵיסְצֵירְדוֹטִי אֶטוּטָא יֵינְטִי

levit-i e=secerdot-i e=tutt-a ienti
levite-PL and=priest-PL and=all-F people
Levites and priests and all the people

119. אֶינְטְרוֹ צִיוֹן שְׁטַרְי גָאוֹ יֵינְטֵי

entro Sion št-are gaoi-ent-e
inside Zion stay-INF be_happy-PRS.PTCP-PL
in Zion to stay happy

120. לוֹסַנְטוֹ טוֹאִי נוֹמֵי בֵּינֵדִיצֵינְטִי

lo=santo toe nome benedic-ent-i
DEF.SG.M=holy POSS.2SG.M name bless-PRS.PTCP-PL
blessing you holy name

3.2 Šemaʕ Israel *and first benedictions of* Šemona ʕEśre *in the* Rite of Fano*,*
a 15th century manuscript and a 17th century manuscript

F = Siddur stampato, Fano 1506
Q3 =Ms. JTS Mic. 4076, sec. 15
S = London Or. 10517, sec. 17

The translation is accompanied by the Hebrew text, which is naturally the same in the case of *Šemaʕ Israel*, but also (almost) absolutely standard in the case of *Šemona ʕEśre* according to the Italian rite.[124]

Šemaʕ Israel

שמע ישראל ה׳ אלהינו ה׳ אחד:
F: אֶין טֵינִי יִשְׂרָאֵל דוֹמְידֵית דֵית נוֹסְטְרוֹ דוֹמְידֵית אוּנוֹ:
F: *entenn-i Israʔel Domedet Det nostro Domedet uno:*
hear-IMP.2SG Israel Domedet Det POSS.1PL Domedet one
Hear, Israel, Domedet Det our Domedet one

Q3: אִינְטֵינִּי יִשְׂרָאֵל דוֹמֵדֵת דֵית נוֹשְׁטְרוֹ דוֹמֵדֵת אוּנוֹ
Q3: *intenni Israʔel Domedet Det noštro Domedet uno*
Hear, Israel, Domedet Det our Domedet one

S: אַבְדִי יִשְׂרַאֵל אִיל סִינְיְיוֹר אִידִיאוֹ נוֹסְטְרוֹ אֶי סִינְיְיוֹר אוּנִיקוֹ
S: *avdi Israʔel il SinjorIdio nostro è Sinjor unico*
Hear, Israel, the Lord our God is the unique Lord

ברוך שם כבוד מלכותו לעולם ועד:
F: בְּינֵדִיטוֹ סִיאָה לוֹ נוֹמֵי דְי לוֹ אוֹנוֹרֵי דְּי לוֹ אֵינְפֵּירִיאוֹ
F: *Benede-tt-o si-a lo nome de lo onore de lo enperio*
bless-PTCP-SG.M be:SBJV-3SG DEF.SG.M name of DEF.SG.M honor of DEF.SG.M empire
סוּאוֹ אַסֵיקוֹלוֹ אֵי אַסֵינְפְּרֵי:
suo a=secolo e a=senpre:
POSS.3SG.M to=eternity and to=forever
blessed be the name of the honor of his empire in eternity and forever

Q3: בֵּנֵדִיטוֹ לוֹנוֹמֵי דֵילוֹנוֹרֵי דֵילוֹנְפֵּירִיאוֹ סוּאוּ אַסֵיקוֹלוֹ אֵי אַסֵינְפְּרֵי
Q3: *Benedetto lo-nome de-ll=onore dello=nperio suu a=secolo e a=senpre*
blessed be the name of the honor of his empire in eternity and forever

S: לוֹדַאטוֹ אֶי אִיל נוֹמֵי דֵיל אוֹנוֹר סוּאוֹ אֶימְפֶּירִיאַלֵי אַ׳ סֶימְפֶּיר אִין אֵיטֶירְנוֹ:
S: *lodato è il nome de-l onor suo emperia-le a' semper in eterno:*
praised be the name of his imperial honor forever in eternity

124 Only version F is accompanied by an interlinear translation.

ואהבת את ה׳ אלהיך בכל לבבך ובכל נפשך ובכל מאדך:

F: אֵי אַמָרַאִי אַדוֹמְידֵית דֵית טוּאוֹ אְין טוּטוֹ לוֹ קוֹרֵי טוּאוֹ

F: *e am-ar-ai a=Domedet Det uo en tutto lo core tuo*

and love-FUT-2SG to-Domedet Det POSS.2SG.M in all DEF.SG.M heart POSS.2SG.M

אְין טוּטוֹ לָאנִימוֹ טוּאוֹ אֵי אְין טוּטוֹ לוֹ אַוִירְי טוּאוֹ:

en tutto l=animo tuo e en tutto lo av-ire tuo:

in all DEF.SG.M=soul POSS.2SG.M and in all DEF.SG.M have-INF POSS.2SG.M

Q3: אֵי אָמָרָאִי דוֹמֵדֵת דֵית טוּאוּ קוֹן טוּטוֹ לוֹקוֹרֵי טוּאוּ אֵי קוֹן טוּטוֹ לַנֵימוֹ טוּאוּ אֵי קוֹן טוּטוֹ לוֹ אָוֵירֵי טוּאוֹ

Q3: *e amarai Domedet Det tuu con tutto lo=core tuu e con tutto l=anemo tuu e con tutto lo avere tuo*

F, Q3: and you shall love your Domedet Det with all you heart and with all your soul and with all your possession

S: אֶי אַמֵירָאִי אִיל סִינְיִיוֹר אִידִיאוֹ טוּאוֹ קוֹן טוּטוֹ אִיל קוֹר טוּאוֹ אֶי קוֹן טוּטָה לְ״אַנִימַה טוּאַה אֶי קוֹן טוּטַה לַה פַאקוּלְטַה טוּאַה

S: *e amerai il Sinjor Idio tuo con tuto il cor tuo e con tuta l'=anima tua e con tuta la faculta tua*

S: and you shall love your Lord God with all your heart and with all your soul and with all your ability

והיו הדברים האלה אשר אנכי מצוך היום על לבבך:

F: אֵי סִיאֵינוֹ לִי פָּרַוולִי קְוֵויסְטִי קִי אִיאוֹ קוֹמָנוֹ אַטִי אוֹייו

F: *e si-eno li parauol-i quest-i che io comann-o a=ti ojjo*

and be:SBJV.3PL DEF.PL.F word-F.PL DEM-F.PL REL 1SG command-PRS.1SG to=2SG.DAT today

סוֹפְּרֵי לוֹ קוֹרֵי טוּאוֹ

sopre lo core tuo

above DEF.SG.M heart POSS.2SG.M

Q3: אֵי סִיאָנוֹ לִי פָּרָבוֹלִי קְוֵישְׁטִי קֵי אֵיאוֹ קוֹמַנוֹ טִי אוֹיֵי סוֹפְּרֵי לוֹקוֹרֵי טוּאוּ

Q3: *e siano li paravoli quešti che io comanno ti ojje sopre lo=core tuu*

S: אֶי סַארַאנוֹ לִי פַּארוֹלֵי מֶיאִי קְוֶויסְטֶי קְוַואלֵי אִיאוֹ קוֹמַאנְדוֹ אָ׳ טֶי אוֹיִי סוֹפְּרַה אִיל קוֹר טוּאוֹ

S: *e sarano li parole mei queste quale io comando a' te ojji sopra il cor tuo*

F, Q3, S: and will be these my words that I command to you today on your heart

ושננתם לבניך ודברת בם בשבתך בביתך

F: אֵי מָאלְטָרַאִי אֵיסִי אָלִי פִּילְיוֹלִי טוֹאִי אֵי פַּוִילַרָאִי אְינֵיסִי

F: *e malt-ar-ai ess-i a-lli filjol-i to-i e fauell-ar-ai en=ess-i*

and teach-FUT-2SG DEM-PL to-DEF.PL.M son-M.PL POSS.2SG-M.PL and speak-FUT-2SG in=DEM-PL

נְי לוֹ סְידֵירֵי טוּאוֹ נְי לַקָאסָה טוֹאָה:

ne lo sed-ere tuo ne la=casa to-a:

in DEF.PL.M sit-INF POSS.2SG.M in DEF.SG.F=house POSS.2F.SG

Q3: אֵי מֵילְטָרָאִי אֵיסִי אַלִיפִּילְיוֹלִי טוֹאִי אֵי פַּוֵילָרָאִי אֵינֵיסִי נֵילוֹ סֵידֵירֵי טוּאוֹ נֵילָקָסָה טוֹאָה

Q3: *e meltarai essi alli=filjoli toi e fauellarai enn=essi nello sedere tuo nella=casa toa*

F, Q3: and teach these to the your children and speak about them in your sitting in your house

S: אֶי פַּארַאִי רַאיוֹנַאר קְוֶוילִי אַלִי פִּילְיִיוֹלִי טוֹאִי אֶי פַּארְלַארַאִי אִין קְוֶוילִי נֵיל סֵידֵיר טוּאוֹ נֵי לֵי קַאסֵי טוּאֶי

S: *e farai rajonar queli ali filjoli toi e parlarai in queli nel seder tuo ne le case toe*

S: and do your children to talk over them and speak about them in your sitting in the your houses

ובלכתך בדרך ובשכבך ובקומך:

F: אֵינֶילוֹ יִירְי טוּאוֹ פֵּיר לַה וִויאָה אֵי נֶילוֹ קוֹלְקָאְרֵי טוּאוֹ

F: *e=ne-llo ji-re tuo per la via e ne-llo colic-are tuo*
and=in-DEF.SG.M go-INF POSS.2SG.M by DEF.SG.F way and in=DEF.SG.M lie.down-INF POSS.2SG.M

אֵי נֶילוֹ לֶיוָורֵי טוּאוֹ

e ne-llo lev-are tuo
and in-DEF.SG.M come.up-INF POSS.2SG.M

Q3: אֵי נֵילוֹ יִירֵי טוּאוּ פֵּיר לָוִיאָה אֵינֵּי לוֹקוֹלְקָארֵי טוּאוּ אֵינֵילוֹ לֵיבָֿארֵי טוּאוּ

Q3: *e nello jire tuu per la=via e=nne lo=colcare tuu e=nello levare tuu*

S: אֶי נֵיל קַאמִינַאר טוּאוֹ פֵּיר לַה וִויאַה אֶי נֵיל יַיאצֵיר טוּאוֹ אֶי נֵיל רִיצַאר טוּאוֹ

S: *e nel caminar tuo per la via e nel jacer tuo e nel rizar tuo*

F, Q3, S: and in your going by your way and in your lying down and in your coming up

וקשרתם לאות על ידך והיו לטטפת בין עיניך:

F: אֵי לֵיגִי אֵיסִי אָסֵינוֹ סוֹפְרֵי לִי מָאנִי טוֹאִי אֵי סִיאֵינוֹ

F: *e legh-i ess-i a=senno sopre li man-i to-i e si-eno*
and bind-IMP.2SG DEM-PL to=sign above DEF.PL.F hand-F.PL POSS.2-F.PL and be:SBJV-3PL

אָתְפִּילִין אֶין פְּרַה לִי אוֹקְיֵי טוֹאִי

a=tefillin en fra li occhj-i to-i
to=tefillin in between DEF.PL.M eye-M.PL POSS.2-F.PL

And bind them as a sign on your hands and let them be tefillin between your eyes

Q3: אֵי לֵיגָארָאִי אֵיסִי אַסֵינוֹ סוֹפְרֵי לַמָאנוֹ טוֹאָה אֵיסֵירָאנוֹ אַתְפִּלִין אִינְפְּרָה לוֹקְלִי טוֹאִי

Q3: *e legarai essi a=senno sopre la=mano toae=seranno a=tefillin infra l=ocli toi*
and you shall bind them as a sign on the your hand and they will be tefillin between your eyes

S: אֵי לִיגַארַאִי קְוֵוילִי פֶּיר סֵינְייוֹ סוֹפְרַה לַה מַאנוֹ טוּאַה אֶי סַארַאנוֹ פֶּיר פְּרוֹנְטַאלִי אֶינְפְּרָה לִי אוֹקְיֵי טוֹאִי

S: *e legarai queli per senjo sopra la mano tua e sarano per frontali enfra li ochji toi*

F, Q3, S: and you shall bind them on the your hand and they will be frontals between your eyes

וכתבתם על מזזות ביתך ובשעריך:

F: אֵי סְקְרִיוִוי אֵיסִי סוֹפְרֵי לִי בָּאלִיסְטְרָטִי דְי לַה קַסַה טוֹאַה

F: *e scriu-i ess-i sopre li balistrat-i de la casa to-a*
and write-IMP.2SG DEM-PL above DEF.PL.M doorpost-PL of DEF.SG.F house POSS.2-SG.F

אֵי נְי לִי פוֹרְטִי טוֹאִי:

e ne li port-i to-i:
and in DEF.PL.F door-PL POSS.2-PL

Q3: אֵי סְקְרִיוֵירָאִי אֵיסִי סוֹפְרֵי לִיבַלֵישְׁטְרַאטִיקִי דֵי לָקָסָה טוֹאָה אֵי דֵילִי פוֹרְטִי טוֹאִי

Q3: *e scriuerai essi sopre li-baleštratichi de la-casa toa e delli porti toi*

S: אֶי סְקְרִיוֵירָאִי קְוֵוילֵי סוֹפְרה לִי סְטִיפִּידִי דֵי לַה קַאסַה טוּאַה אֶי נֵי לֵי פוֹרְטֵי טוּאֵי

S: *e scriuerai quele sopra li stipidi de la casa tua e ne le porte tue*

F, Q3, S: and write them above the doorposts of the your house and in [Q3: of] the your doors (gates)

והיה אם שמע תשמעו אל מצותי אשר אנכי מצוה אתכם היום לאהבה את ה׳ אלהיכם ולעבדו בכל לבבכם ובכל נפשכם:

F: אֵי סַרַה סֵי אֶין טֵינֵינוֹ אֶין טֵינֵירֵיטִי אַלִי קוֹמָנַמֵינְטִי מֵיאִי

F: *e sara se entenne-nno en tenn-er-eti a-lli comannament-i me-i*

and be.FUT.3SG if hear-GER hear-FUT-2PL to-DEF.PL.M command-PL POSS.1SG-PL

קֵי אִיאוֹ קוֹמַנוֹ אַווֹאִי אוֹייוֹ אַאָמָארֵי דוֹמְדֵית דֵית ווֹסְטְרוֹ אֵי אַה סֵירְוִוירֵי אֵיסוֹ

che io comann-o a-uoi ojjo a=am-are Domedet Det uostr-o e aseru-ire

that 1SG command-1SG to=2PL today to=love-INF Domedet Det POSS.2PL and to serve-INF

אֶין טוּטוֹ לוֹ קוֹרֵי ווֹסְטְרוֹ אֵי אֶין טוּטוֹ לוֹ אָנֵימוֹ ווֹסְטְרוֹ

esso en tutt-o lo core uostr-o e en tutt-o lo anemo uostr-o

3SG.M in all-SG.M DEF.SG.M heart POSS.2PL-SG.M and in all-SG.M DEF.SG.M soul POSS.2PL-SG.M

Q3: אֵיסֵירָה סֵי אֵינְטֵינֵּנוֹ אֵינְטֵינֵּירֵיטִי אַלִּי קוֹמָנָּמֵינְטִי מֵיאִי קֵי אִיאוֹ קוֹמַאנּוֹ אַווֹאִי אוֹיֵי אַה אָמָארֵי דוֹמֵדֵת דֵית ווֹשְׁטְרוֹ אֵי אַסֵירְוִירֵי אֵיסוֹ קוֹן טוּטוֹ לוֹקוֹרֵי ווֹשְׁטְרוֹ אֵי קוֹן טוּטוֹ לַנֵימוֹ ווֹשְׁטְרוֹ

Q3: *e=sera se entennanno entennereti alli comannamenti mei che io comanno a-uoi ojje a amare Domeder Det uoštro e a=seruire esso con tutto lo=core uoštro e con tutto l=animo uoštro*

S: אֶי סַארַה סֶי אַבְדֵינְדוֹ אַבְדִירֵיטֵי אַלִי פְּרֵיצֶיפְּטִי מֶיאִי קְוַואלִי אִיאוֹ קוֹמַאנְדוֹ אַ׳ ווֹאִי אוֹיִי אַד״אַמַאר אִיל סִינְיוֹר אִידִיאוֹ ווֹסְטְרוֹ אֶיט אַ׳ סֶירְוִויר קְוֵוילוֹ קוֹן טוּטוֹ אִיל קוֹר ווֹסְטְרוֹ אֶי קוֹן טוּטַה ל״אַנִימַה ווֹסְטְרַה

S: *e sara se avdendo avdirete a-li precepti mei quali io comando a' uoi ojji ad'amar il Sinjor Idio uostro et a' seruir quelo con tuto il cor uostro e con tuta l'anima uostra*

F, Q3, S: And it will be if you shall really hear my commandments that I command you today and love your Domedet Det and serve him with [F: in] all your heart and with [F: in] your soul

ונתתי מטר ארצכם בעתו יורה ומלקוש ואספת דגנך ותירשך ויצהרך:

F: אֵי דַרָאייוֹ פְּיוֹיַיה נֶילַה טֵירַה ווֹסְטַרַה נֶילוֹ טֵינְפּוֹ סוּאוֹ

F: *e d-ar-ajjo pjojja ne-lla terra uostr-a ne-llo tenpo su-o*

and give-FUT-1SG rain in-DEF.SG.F land POSS.2PL-SG.F in-DEF.SG.M time POSS.3-SG.M

פְּרִימוֹנִייקוֹ אֵי טַרְדִיאוֹ אֵי אַרֵיקוֹלְיֵירַאִי לוֹ לָווֹרֵי טוּאוֹ

primonjico e tardio e arreccolj-er-ai lo lauore tu-o

first_rain and late_rain and collect-FUT-2SG DEF.SG.M grain POSS.2SG-SG.M

אֵי לוֹ מוֹסְטוֹ טוּאוֹ אֵי לוֹ אוֹלְיוֹ טוּאוֹ:

e lo most-o tu-o e lo oljo tu-o:

and DEF.SG.M young_wine POSS.2SG-SG.M and DEF.SG.M olive_oil POSS.2SG-SG.M

Q3: אֵי דָרָאיוֹ לַפְּלוֹיָה דֵילָטֵירָה ווֹשְׁטְרָה נֵילוֹ טֵינְפּוֹ סוּאוּ פְּרִימוֹטֵיקוֹ אֵי טַרְדִיאוֹ אֵי רֵיקוֹלְיֵירָאִי לוֹלָבֿוֹרֵי טוּאוּ אֵי לוֹ מוֹשְׁטוֹ טוּאוּ אֵי לוֹלְיוֹ טוּאוּ

Q3: *e darajo la-ploja della-terra uoštra nello tenpo suu primoteco e tardio e reccoljerai lo-lavore tuu e lo mošto tuu e l-oljo tuu*

S: אֵי אִיאוֹ דַארוֹ לַה פִּייוֹיֵיה דֵי לַה טֶירַה ווֹסְטְרַה נֵיל טֶימְפּוֹ סוּאוֹ טֶימְפּוֹרִיטָה אֶי טַארְדִיוַוה אֶי רֵידוּנִיראִי אִיל פוֹרְמֵינְטוֹ טוּאוֹ אֶיט אִיל מוֹסְטוֹ טוּאוֹ אֶי ל״אוֹלְיוֹ טוּאוֹ

S: *e io daro la pijoiie de la tera uostra ne-l tempo suo temporita e tardiua e redunerai il formento tuo et il mosto tuo e l'oljo tuo*

F, Q3, S: And I shall give the rain of the your land in its time, earlier and late, and you shall collect your grain, your young wine and your olive oil

ונתתי עשב בשדך לבהמתך ואכלת ושבעת:

F: אֵי דַרָאיוֹ אֵירְוַוה נֵילוֹ קַנְפּוֹ טוּאוֹ פֵּיר לַבֵּיסְטִיאַה טוֹאַה

F: *e d-ar-ajo erua ne-llo canpo tu-o per la-bestia to-a*
and give-FUT-1SG grass in-DEF.SG.M field POSS.2SG-SG.M for DEF.SG.F-animal POSS2SG-SG.F

אֵי מָנֵיקָרַאִי אֵי סטוֹלֵּרַאִי:

e manec-ar-ai e satoll-er-ai:
and eat-FUT-2SG and be.sated-FUT-2SG

Q3: אֵי דָרָאיוֹ אֵירְבָה נֵילוֹקַנְפּוֹ טוּאוּ פֵּיר לַבֵּישְׁטִיאָה טוֹאָה אֵי מַנֵיקָרָאִי אֵי סַטוֹלָּרָאִי

Q3: *e da-ajo erba nello-canpo tuu per la-beštia toa e manecarai e satollarai*

S: אֵי אִיאוֹ דַארוֹ ל״אֶירְבַה נֶיל קַאמְפּוֹ טוּאוֹ פֶּיר לַה ייוּמֶינְטֶי טוּאַה אֶי מַאנְיֵירַאִי אֶי טִי סַאצִיאַרַאִי

S: *e io daro l'erba nel campo tuo per la jumente tua e manjerai e ti saziarai*

F, Q3, S: And I shall give grass in the your field for the your animals and you shall eat and you will be sated

השמרו לכם פן יפתה לבבכם וסרתם ועבדתם אלהים אחרים והשתחויתם להם:

F: גְוַוארְדֵיטִי אַוּוֹאִי אֶין קְוָונוֹ סֵימוּנִיסְקַה לוֹ קוֹרֵי ווֹסְטְרוֹ אֵי

F: *guard-eti a-uoi en quanno semon-isca lo core uostr-o e*
guard-IMP.2PL to-2PL.DAT in when seduce-SBJV.3SG DEF.SG.M heart POSS.2PL-SG.M and

צֵיסָרִיטֶיוֵוי אֵי סֵירְוֵוירֵיטִי דֵיאִי אַלְטְרִי אֵי סַאלוּטַרֵיטִי אַה אֵיסִי

cess-ar-ete-ue e seru-er-eti de-i altr-i e salut-ar-eti a essi
cease-FUT-2PL-REFL.2PL and serve-FUT-2PL god-PL other-PL and salute-FUT-2PL to DEM.PL

Q3: גְוורְדֵיטִיבֵּי אַווֹאִי קֵינוֹן סֵי סֵימוֹנִיסְקָה לוֹקוֹרֵי ווֹשְׁטְרוֹ אֵי צֵיסַרֵיטִיבֵּי אֵי סֵירְוֵירֵיטִי דֵיאִי אַלְטְרִי אֵי סַלוּטָרֵיטִי אַה אֵיסִי

Q3: *guardetive a-uoi che-non se semonisca lo-core uoštro e cessaretive e seruereti dei altri e salutareti a essi*

S: גְוַוארְדַאטֶיוִוי אַ׳ ווֹאִי קֵי נוֹן [וִוי] סִימוֹנִיסְקַה אִיל קוֹר ווֹסְטְרוֹ אֶי וִוי לֵיוַוארֵיטֶי אֶי סֶירְוִוירֶיטֵי אִידוֹלִי אַלְטְרִי אֶי סַאלוּטַארֵיטֵי אַ׳ קְוֵוילִי

S: *guardateui a' uoi che non [ui] simonisca il cor uostro e ui leuarete e seruirete idoli altri e salutarete a' queli*

F, Q3, S: beware you lest your heart be seduced and you turn astray and serve other gods and bow to them

וחרה אף ה׳ בכם ועצר את השמים ולא יהיה מטר והאדמה לא תתן את יבולה ואבדתם מהרה מעל הארץ הטבה אשר ה׳ נתן לכם:

F: אֵי אַדִירַרָאסִי לוֹ פּוֹרוֹרֵי דֵי דוֹמְדֵית אֶין ווֹאִי אֵי

F: *e adir-ar-a-si lo forore de Domedet en uoi e*
and get.angry-FUT-3SG-REFL.3SG DEF.SG.M wrath of Domedet in 2PL and

סְטְרֵינְיֵירָאסֵי לִיצֵילִי אֵי נוֹן סַרַה פְּיוֹיַה אֵי לַאטֵירַה נוֹן

strenj-er-a-se li- cel-i e non sara pjojja e la-terra non
tighten-FUT-3SG-REFL.3SG DEF.PL.M sky-PL and NEG be.FUT.3SG rain and DEF.SG.F-earth NEG

דַרָה לוֹ לַוורֵי סוּאוֹ אֵי דְיפֵירְדֵירְיטֵיוֵוי אֶין אַיינוֹ דַה סוֹפְּרֵי

dara lo lauore suo e deperd-ere-te-ue en ajino da sopre
give.FUT.3SG DEF.SG.M grain POSS.3SG.M and lose-FUT-2PL-REFL.2PL in swift of above

לַטֵירַה בּוֹנַה קֵי דוֹמְדֵית דֵיאוֹ אָווֹאִי

la-terra bon-a che Domedet deo a-uoi
DEF.SG.F-earth good-SG.F REL Domedet give.PRS.3SG to-DAT.2PL

Q3: אֵי אַדִירָרַסֵי לוֹפוּרוֹרֵי דֵי דוֹמֵדִית אִין וואִי אֵי שְׁטְרֵינְיֵירָאסֵי לִי צֵילִי אֵינוֹן סֵירָה פְלוֹיָה אֵילָּה טֵירָה נוֹן דָרָה לוֹלָבוֹרֵי סוּאוּ אֵי דֵיפֵּירְדֵירֵיטִיבֵי אֵינָאיִינוֹ דַסוֹפְרֵי לַטֵירָה בּוֹנָה קֵי דוֹמֵדֶת דָאוֹ אַוואִי

Q3: *e adirarase lo-furore de Domedet in uoi e štrenjerase li celi e-non sera ploja ella terra non dara lo-lavore suu e deperderetive enajino da-sopre la-terra bona che Domedet dao a-uoi*

S: אֶי סִי אַדִירֵירָה אִיל פוּרוֹר דֵיל סִינְיִיוֹר אִין וואִי אֶי סְטְרִנְיֵרָה לִי צִיֵילִי אֶי נוֹן סַארַה פִּיוֹיַיה אֶי לַה טֶירַה נוֹן דַארַה אִיל פְרוּטוֹ סוּאוֹ, אֶי וִוי דִיפֶּירְדִירֵיטֵי טוֹסְטוֹ דַה סוֹפְרַה לַה טֶירַה בוֹנַה קְוַאלֵי אִיל סִינְיִיוֹר דַה אַ׳ וואִי

S: *e si adirera il furor del Sinjor in uoi e strinjera li cieli e non sara pijoja e la tera non dara il fruto suo, e ui diperdirete tosto da sopra la tera bona quale il Sinjor da a' uoi*

F, Q3, S: and the wrath of God will blaze against you and he will restrain the heaven and there will be no rain and the earth will not yield its produce, and you will swiftly be expelled from the good land which God gives you

ושמתם את דברי אלה על לבבכם ועל נפשכם

F: אֵי פוֹנְרֵיטִי לִי פַּרָאוולִי מֵיאִי קְוֵויסְטִי סוֹפְרֵי לוֹ קוֹרֵי ווֹסְטְרוֹ

F: *e*	*pon-er-eti*	*li*	*parauol-i*	*me-i*	*questi*	*sopre*	*lo*	*core*	*uostr-o*
and	put-FUT-2PL	DEF.PL.F	word-PL	POSS.1SG-PL	DEM.PL.M	above	DEF.SG.M	heart	POSS.2PL-SG.M

אֵי סוֹפְרֵי לוֹ אָנֵימוֹ ווֹסְטְרוֹ:

e	*sopre*	*lo*	*anemo*	*uostr-o:*
and	above	DEF.SG.M	soul	POSS.2PL-SG.M

Q3: אֵי פוֹנֵירֵיטִי לִי פָּרַבּוֹלִי מֵיאִי קְוֵישְׁטִי סוֹפְרֵי לוֹקוֹרֵי ווֹשְׁטְרוֹ אֵי סוֹפְרֵי לַנֵימוֹ ווֹשְׁטְרוֹ

Q3: *e ponereti li paravolli mei quešti sopre lo-core uoštro e sopre l-anemo uoštro*

S: אֶי פוֹנֵירֵיטֵי לֵי פַּארוֹלֵי מִיאֵי קְוֵויסְטִי סוֹפְרָה אִיל קוֹר ווֹסְטְרוֹ אֶי סוֹפְרָה ל״אַנִימָה ווֹסְטְרָה

S: *e ponerete le parole mie questi sopra il cor uostro e sopra l'anima uostra*

F, Q3, S: and you shall place these my words upon your heart and upon your soul

וקשרתם אתם לאות על ידכם והיו לטוטפת בין עיניכם:

F: אֵי לְיגַרֵיטִי אֵיסִי אַסֵינוֹ סוֹפְרֵי לִי מַאנִי ווֹסְטְרִי אֵי סַרָאנוֹ אַתְּפִּילִין אִין פְּרַה לוֹקְיֵי ווֹסְטְרִי

F: *e*	*leg-ar-eti*	*essi*	*a-senno*	*sopre*	*li*	*man-i*	*uostr-i*	*e*	*sar-anno*
and	bind-FUT-2PL	DEM.PL	to-sign	above	DEF.PL.F	hand-PL	POSS.2PL-PL	and	be.FUT-3PL

a-tefillin	*in fra*	*l-occhj-i*	*uostr-i*
to-tefillin	in between	DEF.PL.M-eye-PL	POSS.PL-PL

Q3: אֵי לֵיגָארֵיטִי אֵיסִי אָסֵינוֹ סוֹפְרֵי לִימָאנוֹ ווֹשְׁטְרִי אֵי סֵירַאנוֹ אַתְּפִּלִין סוֹפְרֵי לוֹקְלִי ווֹשְׁטְרִי

Q3: *e llegareti essi a-ssenno sopre li-mano uoštri e seranno a-tefillin sopre l-ocli uoštri*

S: אֶי לִיגַארֵיטֵי קְוֵוילֵי פֶּיר סֶינְיִיוֹ סוֹפְרַה לִי מַאנִי ווֹסְטְרִי אֶי סַארַאנוֹ אַ׳ פְרוֹנְטַאלִי אֶינְפְרַה לִי אוֹקְיֵי ווֹסְטְרִי

S: *e ligarete quele per senjo sopra li man-i uostri e sarano a' frontali enfra li occhji uostri*

F, Q3, S: and you will bind them for a sign upon your arms and they will be tefillin between your eyes

ולמדתם אתם את בניכם לדבר בם בשבתך בביתך ובלכתך בדרך ובשכבך ובקומך:

F: אֵי נֵישְׁרֵיטִי אֵיסִי אַלִי פִּילְיוֹלִי ווֹסְטְרִי אַפַּוֵוילַאֵרִי אֶינֵיסִי נֶילוֹ

F: *e nesc-er-eti essi a-lli filjol-i uostr-i a-fauell-are en=essi ne-llo*

and teach-FUT-2PL DEM.PL to-DEF.PL.M son-PL POSS.2PL-PL to-speak-INF in=DEM.PL in-DEF.SG.M

סֵידֵירֵי טוּאוֹ נֵילַה קַסַה טוֹאַה אֵי נֶילוֹ יִירֵי טוּאוֹ

sed-ere tu-o ne-lla casa to-a e ne-llo j-ire tu-o

seat-INF POSS.2SG-SG.M in-DEF.SG.F house POSS.2SG-SG.F and in-DEF.SG.M go-INF POSS.2SG-SG.M

פֵּיר לַה וִויאַה נֶילוֹ קוֹלְקַאֵרִי טוּאוֹ אֵי נֶילוֹ לֵיוַואֵרִי טוּאוֹ

per la uia ne-llo colc-are tu-o e ne-llo leu-are tu-o

by DEF.SG.F way in-DEF.SG.M lie_down-INF POSS.2SG-SG.M and in-DEF.SG.M get.up-INF POSS.2SG-SG.M

Q3: אֵינֵּישֵׁירֵיטִי אֵיסִי אַלִי פִּילְיוֹלִי ווֹשְׁטְרִי אַפָּוֵילָאֵרִי אֵינֵּיסִי נֵילוֹסֵידֵירֵי טוּאוּ נֵילָקָסָה טוֹאָה אֵי נֵילוֹיִירֵי טוּאוּ
פֵּיר לָוִיאָה אֵינֵי לוֹ קוֹלְקָאֵרִי טוּאוּ אֵינֵי לוֹ לֵיבָאֵרִי טוּאוּ

Q3: *ennešereti essi alli filjoli uoštri a=fauellare enn=essi nello=sedere tuu nella=casa toa e nello=jire tuu per la=uia e=ne lo colcare tuu ene lo levare tuu*

S: אֶיט אִינְסֶינְיֵיאֵרֵיטֵי קְוֵוילִי אַלִי פִּילְיוֹלִי ווֹסְטְרִי אַ׳ פַּארְלַאר אִין קְוֵוילִי נֵיל סֵידֶיר טוּאוֹ נֵי לַה קַאסַה אֵי נֵיל קַאמִינַאר פֶּיר לַה וִויאָה אֶי נֵיל יַיאצֵיר טוּאוֹ אֶי נֵיל רִיצַאר טוּאוֹ

S: *et insenjerete queli ali filjoli uostri a' parlar in queli nel seder tuo ne la casa e nel caminar per la uia e nel jacer tuo e nel rizar tuo*

F, Q3, S: and you will teach them to your children to speak them while you sit in your home, and while you are walk on the way, and while you are lying down and while you come up

וכתבתם על מזוזות ביתך ובשעריך:

F: אֵי סְקְרִיווִי אֵיסִי סוֹפְּרֵי לִי בַּלֵיסְטְרַאטִי דִי לַה קַסַה טוֹאַה

F: *e scriu-i essi sopre li balestrat-i de la casa to-a*

and write-IMP.2SG DEM.PL above DEF.PL.M doorpost-PL of DEF.SG.F house POSS.2SG-SG.F

אֵי נֶילִי פּוֹרְטִי טוֹאִי:

e ne-lli port-i to-i:

and in-DEF.PL.F gate-PL POSS.2SG-PL

Q3: אֵי סְקְרֵיוֵירָאִי אֵיסִי סוֹפְּרֵי לִיבָלֵישְׁטְרָטִיקִי דֵי לַקָסָה טוֹאָה אֵינֵילִי פּוֹרְטִי טוֹאִי

Q3: *e screuerai essi sopre li=baleštratichi de la=casa toa e=nelli porti toi*

S: אֶי סְקְרִיוֵירָאִי קְוֶוילִי סוֹפְּרַה לִי סְטִיפִּידִי דֵי לַה קַאסַה טוּאַה אֶי נֶי לֵי פּוֹרְטֵי טוּאֵי

S: *e scriuerai queli sopra li stipidi de la casa tua e ne le porte tue*

F, Q3, S: and you will write [F: and write] them on the doorposts of your house and upon your gates

למען ירבו ימיכם וימי בניכם על האדמה אשר נשבע ה׳ לאבותיכם לתת להם כימי השמים על הארץ:

F: פֵּיר קִי סְמוֹלְטְפֵּיקַרָנוֹ לִי דִי ווֹסְטְרִי אֵי לִי דִי דֵי לִי

F: *per+chi se=moltepec-ar-anno li di uostr-i e li di de li*

for REFL.3=multiply-FUT-3PL DEF.PL.M day.PL POSS.2PL-M.PL and DEF.PL.M day.PL of DEF.PL.M

פִּילְיוֹלִי ווֹסְטְרִי סוֹפְּרֵי לַטֵירַה קִי אֶין פְּרוֹמִיסִי דוֹמְדֵית אַלִי פַּטְרִי

filjol-i uostr-i sopre la=terra che en+promise Domedet a-lli patr-i

son-PL POSS.2PL-M.PL above DEF.SG.F=earth REL promise.PRF.3SG Domedet to-DEF.PL.M father-PL

ווֹסְטְרִי אַדָרֵי אַאֵיסִי קוֹמִי דִי דֵילִי צֵילִי סוֹפְּרֵי לַטֵירַה:

uostr-i a=dare a=essi come di de-lli celi sopre la=terra:

POSS.2PL-M.PL to=give.INF to=DEM.PL as day.PL of-DEF.PL.M sky-PL above DEF.SG.F=earth

Q3: פֵּירְקִי סֵי מוֹלְטֵיפֵּיקָרָאנוֹ לִידִי וּוֹשְׁטְרִי אֵילִידִי דֵלִּי פִּילְיוֹלִי וּוֹשְׁטְרִי סוֹפְּרֵי לַטֵירָה קֵי אֶינְפְּרוֹמִיסֵי דוֹמֵדֵת אַלִּי פַּטְרִי וּוֹשְׁטְרִי אַדָּארֵי אַדֵיסִּי קוֹמֵי לִי דִי דֵילִּי צֵילִי סוֹפְּרֵי לַטֵירָה

Q3: *perchi se moltepecaranno li=di uoštri e=llidi delli filjoli uoštri sopre la=terra che enpromise Domedet alli patri uoštri a=dare ad=essi come li di delli celi sopre la=terra*

S: אַצִּייוֹ מוֹלְטִיפְּלִיקֵירַאנוֹ לִי ייוֹרְנִי ווֹסְטְרִי אֶי לִי ייוֹרְנִי דֵי לִי פִּילְיּיוֹלִי ווֹסְטְרִי סוֹפְּרַה לַה טֶירַה קֵי ייוּרוֹ אִיל סִינְיּיוֹר אָלִי פַּאדְרִי ווֹסְטְרִי אַ׳ דַאר אַ׳ קְוֵוילִי קוֹמֵי לִי ייוֹרְנִי דֵי לִי צֵיילִי סוֹפְּרַה לַה טֶירַה

S: *acio moltiplicherano li jorni uostri e li jorni de li filjoli uostri sopra la tera che juro il Sinjor ali padri uostri a' dar a' queli come li jorni de li cieli sopra la terra*

F, Q3, S: so that your days and days of your children will multiply on the land that God promised to your fathers to give to them as days of sky above the earth

ויאמר ה׳ אל משה לאמר:

F: אֵי דִיסֵי דוֹמְדֵית אַמֹּשֶׁה אַדִירֵי:

F: *e diss-e Domedet a=Mosce a=dire:*
and say.PRF-3SG Domedet to=Moshe to=say.INF

Q3: אֵי דִיסֵּי דוֹמֵדֵת אַמֹּשֶׁה אַדִּירֵי

Q3: *e disse Domedet a=Mmosce a=ddire*

S: אֶי דִיסֶי אִיל סִינְיּיוֹר אַ׳ מֹשֶׁה דִיצֶינְדוֹ

S: *e dise il Sinjor a' Mosce dicendo*

F, Q3, S: and God said to Moshe to say [S: speaking]

דבר אל בני ישראל ואמרת אליהם ועשו להם ציצת על כנפי בגדיהם לדרתם ונתנו על ציצת הכנף פתיל תכלת:

F: פַּוֵוילַה אַלִי פִּילְיוֹלִי דִי יִשְׂרָאֵל אֵי דִירַאִי אָאֵיסִי אֵי פַּרַנוֹ

F: *fauell-a a-lli filjol-i di Isra?el e dir-ai a=essi e far-anno*
talk.IMP-2SG to-DEF.PL.M son-PL of Israel and say.FUT-2SG to=DEM.PL and make.FUT-3PL

אַאֵיסִי פִּינַאלְיי סוֹפְּרֵי לִי לֵינְצוֹלֵי דֵי לִי פַּנֵי לוֹרוֹ אַלֵי

a=essi pinnalj-i sopre li lenzol-i de li pann-e loro a-lle
to=DEM.PL tassel-PL above DEF.PL.F flap-PL of DEF.PL.M garment-PL POSS.3PL to=DEF.PL.F

יינוֹרָאצִיאִי לוֹרוֹ אֵי דָרְנוֹ סוֹפְּרֵי לִי פֵּינַאלְיי לַה לַנְצוֹלַה אוּנוֹ פִּילוֹ

jenorazi-i loro e dar-anno sopre le pennalj-i la lanzola uno filo
generation-PL POSS.3PL and give.FUT-3PL above DEF.PL.F tassel-PL DEF.SG.F flap one thread

דִי וֵוינֵיטוֹ

de ueneto
of azure

Q3: פַּוֵילָּה אַלִּי פִּילְיוֹלִי דְיִשְׂרָאֵל אֵי דִירָאִי אַה אֵיסִי אֵי פַּאצָּנוֹ אַדֵיסִּי אַפֵּינַּלְיי סוֹפְּרֵי לִי לַנְצוֹלִי דֵילִּי פַּאנִּי לוֹרוֹ אַלְּיֵינוֹרַצִּיאִי לוֹרוֹ אֵי דָרָאנּוֹ סוֹפְּרֵי לִיפֵּינַּלְיי דֵילַּלַנְצוֹלָה פִּילוֹ דֵיוֵינִיטוֹ

Q3: *fauella alli filjoli de=Isra?el e dirai a essi e facciano ad=essi a=pennalji sopre li lanzoli delli panni loro alli=jenorazii loro e dar-anno sopre li=pennalji della=lanzola filo de=ueneto*

S: פַּארְלַה אַ׳ לִי פִּילְיּיוֹלִי דֵי יִשְׂרָאֵל אֶי דִירַאִי אַ׳ קְוֵוילִי אֶי פַּארַאנוֹ אַ׳ קְוֵוילִי פֶּינְדַאלְיי סוֹפְּרַה לִי קַאנְטוֹנִי דֶי לִי וֵוסְטִימֶינְטִי לוֹרוֹ אַלִי יֶינֶירַאצִיּוֹנִי לוֹרוֹ אֶי פּוֹנֵירַאנוֹ סוֹפְּרָה לִי פֶּינְדַאלְיי דֶיל קַאנְטוֹנֵי אוּן פִּילוֹ צֵילֶיסְטוֹ צִייוֹאֶי דֶי יַיאצִינְטוֹ

S: *parla a' li filjoli de Isra?el e dirai a' queli e farano a' queli pendalji sopra li cantoni de li uestimenti loro ali jenerazioni loro e ponerano sopra li pendalji del cantone un filo celesto cioe de jacinto*

F, Q3, S: talk to the sons of Israel and you will say to them and they will make tassels on the corners of their garment in their generations and they will add the azure thread to tassels on corners of flap [S: it means, of hyacinthine]
[…]

Šemona ʕEśre

ה׳ שפתי תפתח ופי יגיד תהלתך:

F: דוֹמְדֵית לִי לַבְּירִי מֵיאִי אַפְּרִי אֵי לַה בוֹקַה מֵיאַה

F: *Domedet*	*li*	*labber-i*	*me-i*	*apr-i*	*e*	*la*	*bocca*	*me-a*
Domedet	DEF.PL.F	lip-PL	POSS.1SG-PL	open.IMP-2SG	and	DEF.SG.F	mouth	POSS.1SG-SG.F

אַנוּנְצֵיאַרָה לָה לַאווֹדַה טוֹאַה:

annunce-ar-a	*la*	*lauoda*	*to-a:*
announce-FUT-3SG	DEF.SG.F	glory	POSS.2SG-SG.F

Q3: דוֹמֵדֶת לִי לַבְּרִי מֵיאִי אַפְּרִי אֵי לַבּוֹקָה מֵיאָה דֵינוּנְצִיאָרָה לַלַבְּדָה טוֹאָה
Q3: *Domedet li labbri mei ap-ie lla-vocca mea denunciara la=lavda toa*

S: סינייור לי לאברי מיאי אפרי אי לה בוקה [מיאה] אנונציארה לה לאבדה טואה
S: *Sinjor li labri mei apri e la boca [mea] anunciara la lavda toa*
F, Q3, S: God, open my lips and my mouth will announce your glory

ברוך אתה ה׳ אלהינו ואלהי אבותינו אלהי אברהם אלהי יצחק ואלהי יעקב

F: בְּינְיְדֵיטוֹ סִיאִי טוּ דוֹמְדֵית דֵית נוֹסְטְרוֹ אֵי דֵית דֵי לִי פַּטְרִי נוֹסְטְרִי

F: *bened-ett-o*	*si-i*	*tu*	*Domedet*	*Det*	*nostro*	*e*	*Det*	*de*	*li*	*patr-i*	*nostr-i*
bless-PTCP-SG.M	be.IMP-2SG	2SG	Domedet	Det	POSS.1PL	and	Det	of	DEF.PL.M	father-PL	POSS.1PL

דֵית דֵי אַבְּרָהָם דֵית דֵי יִצְחָק אֵי לוֹ דֵית דֵי יַעֲקוֹב:

Det	*de*	*Avraham*	*Det*	*de*	*Yiṣḥaq*	*e*	*lo*	*Det*	*de*	*Yaʕaqov:*
Det	of	Avraham	Det	of	Yiṣḥaq	and	DEF.PL.M	Det	of	Yaʕaqov

Q3: בֶּנֵידֵיטוֹ טוּ דוֹמֵדֶת דֵית נוֹשְׁטְרוֹ אֵי דֵית דֵילִּי פַּטְרִי נוֹשְׁטְרִי דֵית דֵי אַבְּרָהָם דֵית דֵיִצְחָק אֵי דֵית דְיַעֲקֹב
Q3: *benedetto tu Domedet Det noštro e Det delli patri noštri Det de Avraham Det de Yiṣḥaq e Det de=Yaʕaqov*

S: לוֹדַאטוֹ סֶיאִי טוּ סִינְיִיוֹר אִידִיאוֹ נוֹסְטְרוֹ אֵי דִיאוֹ דֵי לִי פַּאדְרִי נוֹסְטְרִי אִידִיאוֹ דֵי אַבְרָהָם אִידִיאוֹ דֵי יִצְחַק אֵי אִידִיאוֹ דֵי יַעֲקֹב
S: *lodato sei tu Sinjor Idio nostro e Dio de li padri nostri Idio de Avraham Idio de Yishaq e Idio de Yaʕaqov*
F, Q3, S: blessed [F: let be; Q3: -; S: is] you Lord our God and God of our fathers, God of Abraham, God of Isaac and God of Jacob

האל הגדול הגבור והנורא אל עליון גומל חסדים טובים וקונה את הכל וזוכר חסדי אבות ומביא גואל לבני בניהם למען שמו באהבה:

F: לוֹ דֵית גְּרַאנוֹ אֵי בָּרוֹנֵי אֵי טְימוּטוֹ דֵית אַלְטִיסִימוֹ קֵי

F: *lo Det grann-o e barone e tem-ut-o Det Alt-issim-o che*

DEF.SG.M Det great-SG.M and strong and awe-PTCP-SG.M Det High-SUPERL-SG.M REL

רֵימֵירְיטִי מִיסֵירִיקוֹרְדִיאִיי בּוֹנִי אֵי אַקְוֵויסְטִי אוֹנְי קָווֹסַה אַרֵינְקוֹרְדַה

remeret-i misericordi-i bon-i e aquest-i onne cauosa arrencord-a

recompense.PRS-2SG mercy-PL good-PL and acquire.PRS-2SG every thing remember.PRS-3SG

לִי מִיסֵירִיקוֹרְדִיאִי אַלִּי פַּטְרִי אֵי פַּאִי וֵוינִירֵי לוֹ סְקוֹנְפֵּירַטוֹרֵי

li misericordi-i alli patr-i e fa-i uen-ire lo sconper-atore

DEF.PL.F mercy-PL to-DEF.PL.M father-PL and do.PRS-2SG come-INF DEF.SG.M redeem-AGENT

אַלֵּי פִּילְיוֹלִי דֵּי לִי פִּילְיוֹלִי לוֹרוֹ פֵּיר לוֹ נוֹמֵי סוּאוֹ אֵין אָמוֹרֵי:

a-lle filjol-i de li filjol-i loro per lo nome su-o en amore:

to-DEF.PL.M son-PL of DEF.PL.M son-PL POSS.3PL for DEF.SG.M name POSS.3SG-SG.M in love

Q3: דֵית גְּרַאנֵּי אֵי בָּרוֹנֵי אֵי טֵימוּטוֹ דֵית אַלְטִיסִּימוֹ קֵי רֵימֵירִיטָה מִיסִירִיקוֹרְדִיאִי בוֹנֵי אֵי אַקְוִישְׁטָטוֹרֵי דֵי אוֹנֵי קָבוֹסָה אַרֵינְקוֹרְדָה לַמִיסִירִיקוֹרְדִיאָה דֵילִּי פַּטְרִי אֵי פָּאוֹ וֵינִירֵי סְקוֹנְפֵּירָטוֹרֵי אַלִּי פִּילְיוֹלִי דֵילִּי פִּילְיוֹלִי לוֹרוֹ פֵּיר לוֹ נוֹמֵי סוּאוּ קוֹן אָמוֹרֵי

Q3: *Det granne e barone e temuto Det Altissimo che remerita misiricordii bone e aquištatore de onne cavosa arrencorda la=misiricordia delli patri e fao uenire sconperatore alli filjoli delli filjoli loro per lo nome suu con amore*

S: אִידִיאוֹ גְרַאנְדֵי אֵי פּוֹטֵינְטֵי אֵי טֵימוּטוֹ אִידִיאוֹ אֵיצֵילְסוֹ קְוַואל רִימֵירִיטַה מִיסֵירִיקוֹרְדִיאֵי בוֹנֵי אֵיט אַקְוִויסְטַאטוֹר דֵיל טוּטוֹ אֵי סִי רִיקוֹרְדַה דֵי לִי מִיסֵירִיקוֹרְדִיאֵי דֵי לִי אַנְטִיקִי אֵי קוֹנְדוּצֵי סְקוֹמְפֵּירַאטוֹר אַ׳ לִי פִילְיוֹלִי דֵי לִי פִילְיוֹלִי לוֹרוֹ פֵּיר אִיל נוֹמֵי סוּאוֹ קוֹן אַמוֹרֵי

S: *Idio grande e potente e temuto Idio ecelso qual rimerita misericordie bone et aquistator del tuto e si ricorda de li misericordie de li antichi e conduce scomperator a' li filjoli de li filjoli loro per il nome suo con amore*

F, Q3, S: God great and strong and awful, Highest God that recompense [F: that You recompense] good merciful deeds and <is> owner [F: that You acquire] of everything and remember merciful deeds of our fathers and bring [F: You bring] redeemer to the children of their children with love

מלך גואל עוזר ומושיע ומגן. ברוך אתה ה׳ מגן אברהם:

F: רֵי סְקוֹנְפֵּירָטוֹרֵי אַיוּטַטוֹרֵי אֵי סַאלְוַודוֹרֵי אֵי סְקוּדִיאַטוֹרֵי בֵּינֵדֵיטוֹ סִיאִי טוּ דוֹמֵדִית קֵי סְקוּדִיאִי אַבְרָהָם:

F: *re sconper-atore aiut-atore e salu-adore e scudi-atore.*

king redeem-AGENT help-AGENT and save-AGENT and protect-AGENT

bened-ett-o si-i tu Domede che scudi-i Avraham:

bless-PTCP-SG.M be.IMP-2SG 2SG Domedet REL protect.PRS-2SG Avraham

F: King redeemer helper and savior and protector. Blessed will be you Lord that protect Abraham

Q3: רֵי סְקוֹנְפָּרָטוֹרֵי אֵי אַיוּטָטוֹרֵי אֵי סַלְבָּטוֹרֵי אֵיסְקוּדִיאָטוֹרֵי. בֵּנֵידֵטוֹ טוּ דוֹמֵדֵת סְקוּדִיאָטוֹרֵי דְאַבְרָהָם

Q3: *re sconparatore e aiutatore e salvatore e-scudiatore. benedetto tu Domedet scudiatore de=Avraham*

Q3: King redeemer and helper and savior and protector. Blessed You Lord protector of Abraham

S: רֵי אַיוּטַטוֹר אֶי סַאלְוַואטוֹרֵי אֶי סְקוּדוֹ. לַאוֹדַאטוֹ סִיאִי טוּ סִינְיוֹר סְקוּדוֹ דֵי אַבְרָהָם

S: *re aiutator e saluatore e scudo. laodato sii tu Sinjor scudo de Avraham*

S: King redeemer and savior and shield. Praised will be You Lord shield of Abraham

אתה גבור לעולם ה׳ מחיה מתים אתה רב להושיע

F: טוּ סִי בַּרוֹנֵי אַסֵינְפְּרֵי דוֹמְדֵית רַבֵּיפְּיקִי לִי מוֹרְטִי

F: *tu si barone a=senpre Domedet rabbefech-i li mort-i.*
2SG be.PRS.2SG strong to=forever Domedet revive.PRS-2SG DEF.PL dead-PL

טוּ סִי גְּרַאנוֹ אַסָאלְוַורֵי:

tu si grann-o a=salu-are:
2SG be.PRS.2SG great-SG.M to=save.INF

Q3: טוּסִי בָּרוֹנֵי אַסֵּינְפְּרֵי דוֹמֵדֵת קֵי אַרבֵּיפִּיקִי לִי מוֹרְטִי טוּסִּי גְרַאנֵּי אַסַלְבָּארֵי

Q3: *tu=si barone a=ssenpre Domedet che arrabbefichi li morti tu=ssi granne a-salvare*

S: טוּ סֶיאִי פּוֹטֵינְטֵי אִין אֵיטֶירְנוֹ סִינְיוֹר קְוַואל פַּה רֵיוִיוֶויר לִי מוֹרְטִי סִיאִי טוּ אֶי פַּאדְרוֹן אַ׳ סַאלְוַואֵרי

S: *tu sei potente in eterno Sinjor qual fa reuiuer li morti sii tu e padron a' saluare*

F, Q3, S: You are strong forever Lord, [Q3, S: that] revive the dead, You are great to save

משיב הרוח ומוריד הגשם

F: פַּאוֹ פְּיַיטָארֵי לוֹ וֵוינְטוֹ אֵי פַּאוֹ שֵׁינְיֵירֵי לַפְּיוֹיַיה:

F: *fao fiat-are lo uento e fao scennj-ere la=pjojja:*
do.PRS.3SG blow-INF DEF.SG.M wind and do.PRS.3SG descend-INF DEF.SG.F=rain

Q3: קֵי פָּה פְּלַטָארֵי לוֹבֵּינְטוֹ אֵיפָּה אַשֵׁינְיֵירֵי לַפְּלוֹיָיה

Q3: *che fa flatare lo=vento e=fa a=scennjere la=plojja*

S: לוּאִי פַּה סוֹפְיַיאר אִיל וֵוינְטוֹ אֶי פַּה דִישֶׁינְדֵיר לִי פִּיוֹיֵי

S: *lui fa sofiar il uento e fa discender li piojji*

F, Q3, S: [Q3: that; S: who] makes blow the wind and makes descend the rain

מכלכל חיים בחסד מחיה מתים ברחמים רבים סומך נופלים ורופא חולים מתיר אסורים

F: גּוֹוֵירְנַה לִי וִיוִוי אִין מִיסֵירִיקוֹרְדִיאֵי רָבֵּיפִּיקִי לִי מוֹרְטִי

F: *gouern-a li uiu-i en misericordi-e rabbefech-i li mort-i*
feed.PRS-3SG DEF.PL.M live-PL in mercy-PL revive.PRS-2SG(?) DEF.PL.M dead-PL

אִין רַפְּיִיטַמֵינְטִי מוֹלְטִי סְפּוֹנְצוֹלַה לִי קַדוּטִי אֵי גְוַורִישֵׁי

en rappjitament-i molt-i sponzol-a li cad-ut-i e guarisc-e
in compassion-PL many-PL sustain.PRS-3SG DEF.PL.M fall-PTCP-PL.M and heal.PRS-3SG

לִי אַמָלַאטִי אֵי שׁוֹלְיֵי לִי אֵינְפְּרֵיסוֹנַטֵי

li ammal-at-i e sciolj-i li enpreson-at-e
DEF.PL.M ill.PTCP-PL and dissolve.PRS-3SG DEF.PL.M imprison-PTCP-PL

Q3: גּוֹבֵּירְנָה לִיוִיבִּי קוֹן מִיסֵירִיקוֹרְדִיאָה אֵי אַרבֵּיפֵּיקָה לִי מוֹרְטִי קוֹן פְּיָיטַדִי מוֹלְטִי אֵי סְפּוֹנְצוֹלָה אַקְוֵילִי קֵי קַדֵינוֹ אֵי גְוַארִישֵׁי לַמָלָאטִי אֵישׁוֹלְיֵי לִינְפְּרֵיסוֹנָאטִי

Q3: *governa li-uivi con misericordia e arrabbefeca li morti con piatadi molti e sponzol-a a=quelli che cadeno e guarisce l=ammalati e-sciolje l=inpresonasti*

S: גּוֹבֵירְנָה לִי וִיוִוי פֶּיר סוּאַה מִיסֶירִיקוֹרְדִיאָה אֶי פַּה רִיסוּרֶייר לִי מוֹרְטִי פֶּיר לִי סוֹאִי גְרַאן קוֹמְפַּאסִיוֹנִי סוֹסְטִיֵינִי לִי קַאדוּטִי אֶי גְוַארִישֵׁי לִי אִינְפֶּירְמִי אֶי שׁוֹלְיֵי לִי אִינְקַאלְצֵירַאטִי

S: *governa li uiui per sua misericordia e fa risurjer li morti per li soi gran compasioni sostiene li caduti e guarisce li infermi e sciolje li incalcerati*

F, Q3, S: feeds the live in His mercy, revives the dead in his great compassions, sustains the fallings and heals the infirms and dissolves the imprisoned

ומקיים אמונתו לישיני עפר

F: אֵי אַפֵּירְמַה לַה וְוירֵיטַאדֵי סוֹאַה אַקְוֵוילִי קֵי דוֹרְמֵינוֹ

F: *e afferm-a la ueretade so-a a=quelli che dorm-eno*
and affirm.PRS-3SG DEF.SG.F truth POSS.3SG-SG.F to=DEM.DIST-PL REL sleep.PRS-3PL

אַה לַה פוֹלְוֵוירַה

a la poluera
to DEF.SG.F dust

Q3: אֵי אַפֵּירְמָה לַוֵירֵיטָאדֵי סוֹאָה אַקְוֵוילִי קֵי דוֹרְמֵינוֹ נֵילַּפוֹלְבֵּירֵי

Q3: *e afferm=a la=ueretade soa a=quelli che dormeno nella=polvere*

S: קוֹנְפֵירְמָה לַה וֶוירִיטָה סוּאַה אַ׳ קְוֶוילִי קֵי דוֹרְמוֹנוֹ נֵי לַה פוֹלְוֶוירֶי

S: *conferma la uerita sua a' queli che dormono ne la poluere*

F, Q3, S: [F, Q3: and] affirms His truth to those that sleep in the dust

מי כמוך בעל גבורות ומי דומה לך מלך ממית ומחיה ומצמיח לנו ישועה. ונאמן אתה להחיות מתים. ברוך אתה ה׳ מחיה המתים:

F: קֵי אֵי קוֹמֵי טִי פַּטְרוֹנֵי דֵי בַּרוֹנִיאִי אֵי קִי סְרַאסוֹמִילְיִי

F: *che e come ti patrone de baroni-i e chi se=rassomilj-i*
who be.PRS.3SG as 2SG.DAT lord of strength-F.PL and who REFL.3=be.like.PRS-3SG

אַטִי רֵי קֵי אוּצִידִי אֵי רַבֵּיפְּיקִי פַּאוֹ פְּיוֹרִירֵי אַנוֹאִי

a=ti re che uccid-i e rabbefech-i fao fior-ire a=noi
to=2SG.DAT king REL kill.PRS-2SG and revive.PRS-2SG make.PRS.3SG bloom-INF to=1PL.DAT

סַאלְוֵויצְיאוֹנֵי אֶין אַפְּרֵיסוֹ אֵי וְוירֵיטֵיוּולֵי סִי טוּ פֵּיר רַבֵּיפְּיקַרֵי לִי מוֹרְטִי

saluezione en appresso e uereteuole si tu per rabbefec-are li mort-i.
salvation in near and truthful be.PRS.2SG 2SG for revive-INF DEF.PL dead-PL

בְּינְדֵיטוֹ סִיאִי טוּ דוֹמְדֵית קֵי רַבִּיפְּיקִי לִי מוֹרְטִי:

bened-ett-o si-i tu Domedet che rabbifech-e li mort-i:
bless-PTCP-SG.M be.IMP-2SG 2SG Domedet REL revive.PRS-2SG DEF.PL dead-PL

Q3: קֵי אֵי קוֹמֵי טִי פַּטְרוֹנֵי דֵי בַּרוֹנִיאִי אֵיקִי סֵירֵיסֵימִילְיָה אַטִי רֵי קֵי אוֹצִידֵי אֵי אַבֵּיפִּיקִי אֵיפָּה פְּלוֹרִירֵי אַנוֹאִי סַלְבָצִיאוֹנֵי דַפְּרֵיסוֹ אֵיוֵירֵיטֵיוֵילֵי סִיטוּ אַרֵבֵּיפֵּיקָארֵי לִימוֹרְטִי. בֵּנֵידֵיטוֹ סִיטוּ דוֹמֵדֵת קֵיאַרֵבֵּיפֵּיקִי לִימוֹרְטִי

Q3: *chi e come ti patrone de baronii e=chi se=ressemilja a=tti re che occide e abbefichi e=fa florire a=nnoi salvazione d-appresso e=uereteuele si=tu arrabbefecare li=morti. benedetto si=tu Domedet che=arrabbefechi li=morti*

S: קֵי אֵי קוֹמֵי טוּ פַּאדְרוֹן דֵי לֵי פוֹטֵינְצֵי אֵי קִי סִי רַאסִמִילְיָיה אַ׳ טֵי רֵי קְוַואל פַּה מוֹרִיר אֵי רִיסוּרְיֵיר אֵי פַּה פִּייוֹרִיר סַאלוּטֵי אֵי סִיאִי רֵיאַלֵי פֵּיר פַּאר רִיסוּרְיֵיר לִי מוֹרְטִי. לוֹדַאטוֹ סִיאִי טוּ סִינְייוֹר קֵי פַּאִי רִיסוּשִׁיטַאר לִי מוֹרְטִי

S: *che e come tu padron de le potenze e chi si rassimilja a' te re qual fa morir e risurjer e fa fiorir salute e sii reale per far risurjer li morti. lodato sii tu Sinjor che fai risuscitar li morti*

F, Q3, S: who may be compared to You, Lord of forces and who is similar to You, King that kills and revives and makes salvation bloom to us and is truthful to revive the dead. Blessed [S: Praised] will be You, that revives the dead.

3.3 Initial fragment of the sermon by R. Samuel di Rafael da Modena (1535) Moscow Russian State Library, Ms. Guenzburg 1317, 184b-185a (the text is unvocalized, so the vowels are reconstructed)

The Hebrew title and its translation

זאת הדרשה נשאה האלוף כמ״ר שמואל ממודינה יצ״ו לתלמידו הנער כמ״ר בן ציון יצ״ו
ואמרה ביום שבת קדש וחנוכה רצ״ה ליצירה
אלקים יחנך בני [ברא׳ מג כט]
מדרש במדבר סיני רבה פרשת נשא [יא, ו] דרשו רז״ל. ויחנך [במ׳ ו כה] הרי הם מבורכים ושמורים
ושכינה ביניהם. ומניין אף חנוני בדעת ובינה. ת״ל ויחנך. כמה דמצלינן אתה חונן
לאדם דעת ומלמד לאנוש בינה. ד״א ויחנך. יחנה ה׳ אצלך. ד״א ויחנך יתן חנו עליך.

This sermon was delivered by the honorable Rabbi Samuel from Modena to his pupil the young Rabbi Ben Zion and he recited it on Holy Saturday and Ḥanukka of the year [5]295 (1535) from the Creation of World. "God will have compassion with you, my son" (Gen 43:29). Midrash Bemidbar Sinai Rabbah pericope Naśo [11:6] Rabbis explained "and will have compassion with you" [Num 6:25]: therefore they are blessed and guarded and Šeḵina is between them. And how do we know that they are granted knowledge and understanding? It is written "and will mercifully grant you" [another possibility to translate ויחנך]. As we pray "You mercifully grant to man knowledge and teach humankind understanding". Another explanation of ויחנך: God will make his camp near you. Another explanation ויחנך: will give His grace on you.

The sermon

ווינירא‍בילי אי אצילי[נ]טיסימי סינייורי. פיר פלו ראשוני אווידינטי אי
Venerabil-i e eccele[n]t-issim-i signor-i. Per plu rascion-i evident-i è
venerable-PL.M and eminent-SUPERL-PL.M lord-PL.M for more reason-PL evident-PL be.PRS.3SG
Venerable and eminent Sirs, for evident reasons it is

קוסה קייארה אי מניפיסטו. קי לריפריסינטיציאונה מיאה אין קוויסטו
cosa chiar-a e manifest-o. Che la=reppresenteziona mi-a in questo
thing clear-SG.F and evident-SG.M COMP DEF.SG.F=performance POSS.1FSG.F in DEM-M
a clear and manifest thing that my speech in this

מקום קדוש אי מולטו אינקוויטאינטי אי אוני לאלטירי אריקורדירימו
maqom qadoš è molto inquetante e onne altr-e arrecord-er-emo
place^{H} sacred^{H} be.PRS.3SG very disquieting and every other-PL recall-FUT-1PL
sacred place is very disquieting and from all other <reasons> let us recall

סולה קוויסטה אונה. קי איסינו איאו מינורי אין ספק קי נון אי
sol-a quest-a un-a. Che esse-nno io minore ʔen safeq che non è
sole-SG.F DEM-SG.F one-F COMP be.GER 1SG minor NEG.EXIST doubt^{H} COMP NEG be.PRS.3SG
only this one, that for me as a minor there is no doubt that it is not

ליציטו אמי אפרירי בוקה אדובה סיאנו לי מייורי.
lecito a=mme apr-ire bocca addova si-ano li magior-i.
legitimate to=1SG.DAT open-INF mouth where be.SBJV-3PL DEF.PL.M elder-M.PL
legitimate to open the mouth before elders.

קומו דיצינו חכמי׳ אין מס׳ ברכות קי אסור אאון תלמיד
Como dic-eno ḥakam-i<m> in mass<ek̲et> Berak̲ot che ʔasur a=un talmid
as say.PRS-3PL wise-PL^{H} in tractate^{H} Berakot^{H} COMP forbidden to=one.M pupil^{H}
As the Sages say in the tractate *Berak̲ot* it is forbidden to a pupil

אפי׳ לתת שלום לרבו. נון שטאנטי די אווירי אונה סימילה
ʔafi<llu> la-tet šalom le-rabb-o. Non.štante di av-ere una simil-a
even^{H} to-give^{H} salute^{H} to-teacher-POSS.3SG.M^{H} all.the.more.so of have-INF one.F similar-SG.F
even to say "Šalom" to his teacher, all the more to have such a

פרוסינציאונה איננצי אונה ריפלובקה. סימיל מינטו אין לו ירושלמי
prosunzion-a innanzi una replubbeca.Simil.mente in lo Yerušalmi
presumpion-SG.F before one.F assembly similarly in DEF.SG.M Yerušalmi^{H}
presumption before an assembly. Similarly, in the Jerusalem Talmud

דמס׳ ברכות פ׳ היה קורא דיצי [...] אדונקה וואי
de-mass<ek̲et> Berak̲ot p<ereq> haya qore dic-e […] Adunca voi
of-tractate^{H} Berakot^{H} chapter be.PST.3SG read.PTCP.SG.M say.PRS-3SG […] so 2PL
in the tractate Berak̲ot , in the chapter "He was reading", it is said […] So you

ווידינטי קי׳ אפי׳ ר׳ אלעזר. קי אירה גדול בתורה וגדול
ved-ent-i che ʔafi<llu> R. ʔElʕazar. Che era gadol be-Torah we-gadol
see-PTCP-PL COMP even^{H} R. Elazar COMP be.PST.3SG great^{H} in-Torah^{H} and-great^{H}
see that even R. Elazar that was (more) eminent in Torah and old(er)

בשנים. נון סי ארדיווה אפי׳ לשאול בשלו׳ ר׳ יוחנן
be-šan-im. Nonsi ard-iv-a ʔafi<llu> li-šʔol bi-šlo<m> R. Yoḥanan
in-year-PL^{H} NEG REFL.3 dare-PST-3SG even^{H} to-ask.INF^{H} in-salute^{H} R. Yohanan
in years. He did not dare even to greet R. Yohanan

לפי שהיה גדול ממנו בחכמה, טאנטו מייור מינטי קי
lef̲i še-haya gadol mi-mmennu be-ḥok̲ma, tanto maggior.mente che
according^{H} COMP-be.PST.3SG^{H} great^{H} of-him^{H} in-wisdom^{H} so much.more.ADV CONJ
because he was more eminent than him in wisdom, all the more so as

נון אי ליציטי אאון נער מנוער דיספוליאטו די טוטי לי חכמות
non è lecito a=un naʕar menoʕar dispogli-at-o di tutt-i li ḥok̲m-ot
NEG be.PRS.3SG legitimate to=one.M youth^{H} shaken.out^{H} strip-PTCP-SG.M of all-PL DEF.PL wisdom-PL
it is not legitimate to a youth stripped of all wisdoms

קומי מי אוסארי אונה סימילה פרוסינציאונה. פיר קויסטו איאו פרינציפיאאו
come me us-are una simil-a prosunziona. Per questo io princip-ao
as 1SG.ACC use-INF one similar-SG.F presumption. For DEM.M 1SG begin-PRF.1SG
like me to use such a presumption. For this reason I began

אי דיסי אלקים יחנך בנו. ר״ל
e diss-i ʔEloqim yo-ḥnə-k̲a ben-i. R<otse> l<-omar>
and say.PRF-1SG God^{H} FUT.3SG-have_misery-2SG.M^{H} son-POSS.1SG^{H} want.PTCP.SG.M^{H} to-say.INF^{H}
and said "God will have compassion with you, my son." It means,

לקאוויסה קי מי אה אינדוטו אקוויסטו אי סטאטו
la=cauesa che mi ha indo-tt-o a=questo è st-at-o
DEF.SG.F=reason REL 1SG.ACC have.PRS.3SG induce-PTCP-SG.M to=this be.PRS.3SG stay-PTCP-SG.M
the reason that has induced me to do this was

לו קומנאמינטו די לו מיאו סופרייורי אונורנדיסימו פאטרי קי
lo comannamento de lo mio superiore onorand-issim-o patre che
DEF.SG.M command of DEF.SG.M POSS.1SG.M superior honorable-SUPERL-SG.M father REL
a command of my superior honorable father that

מי הא דיטו אלקים יחנך בנו.
mi ha dett-o ʔEloqim yo-ḥnə-ḵa ben-i.
1SG.ACC have.PRS.3SG say.PTCP-SG.M God^H FUT.3SG-have_misery-2SG.M^H son-POSS.1SG^H
said to me: "God will have compassion with you, my son."

קומי און דירמי אנקי קי נון סיאה ליציטו אטי
Come un dir-mi anche che non si-a lecito a=tte
As one say.INF-1SG.DAT also CONJ NEG be.SBJV-3SG legitimate to=2SG.DAT
As if he had said, even if it is not legitimate for you

לריפריסינטיציאונה דקויסטו מקום קדוש פיר איסירי מינורי
la=representazion-a de=questo maqom qadoš per ess-ere minore
DEF.SG.F=performance-SG.F of=DEM.M place^H sacred^H for be-INF minor
to preach in this sacred place because you are minor,

נון טידוביטארי אלקים יחנך בנו יתן
non ti=dubit-are ʔEloqim yo-ḥnə-ḵa ben-i yitten
NEG 2SG.DAT=hesitate-INF God^H FUT.3SG-have_misery-2SG.M^H son-POSS.1SG^H FUT.3SG-give^H
do not hesitate. "God will have compassion with you, my son, he will grant you mercy."

חנו עליך קומי סי טו פוסי גדול בתורה וגדול
ḥinn-o ʕale-ḵa come se tu foss-i gadol be-Torah we-gadol
mercy-POSS.3SG.M^H upon-2SG.M^H as if 2SG be.PST.SBJV-2SG great^H in-Torah^H and-great^H
[…] as if you were learned in Torah and old(er)

בשנים. קי לו לשון די יחנך אנקי קי סי
be-šan-im. Che lo lašon di yo-ḥnə-ḵa anche che se
in-year-PL^H CONJ DEF.SG.M language^H of FUT.3SG-have_misery-2SG.M^H also CONJ if
in years. Because the expression יחנך even if

איטרַ[א]פיטה לשון די קורדולייו פורטה בין אנקי לשון די חן.
<?> etrapet-a lašon di cordoglio port-a ben anche lašon di ḥen.
REFL.3 interpret.PRS-3SG language^H of pity bear.PRS-3SG well also language^H of grace^H
explained as having a meaning of "compassion" has also the meaning of "grace".

קומי טרווימו קי חכמים דרשו לו לשון די
Come trov-imo che ḥakame-nu darš-u lo lašon di
As find.PRS-1PL COMP wise.PL-POSS.1PL^H interpret.PST-PL^H DEF.SG.M language^H of
As we find that our Sages have interpreted the expression

ויחנך אינקויסטו מידיסמו לשון די חן אינקוילו נוסטרו
w-i-ḥunne-ḵa in=questo medesimo lašon di ḥen in=quello nostro
and-FUT.3SG-have_misery-2SG.M^H in=DEM.M same language^H of grace^H in=DEM.DIST.M POSS.1PL
ויחנך in the same meaning of "grace" in the

מאמר פריציפיאטו די לו מדרש במדבר סינירבה פרשת נשא.
maʔamar princip-at-o de lo midraš Be-midbar SinayRabba parašat Neśo.
saying^H begin-PTCP-SG.M of DEF.SG.M midrash^H in-desert.CS^H SinayRabba^H section.CS^H Neśo^H
beginning chapter from the Midrash Bemidbar Sinai, pericope Neśo.

קומו ווידימו דיקלראטו. סימיל מינטו סימו דיקלירארי
Come ved-emo declar-at-o. Simil.mento simo declar-are
As see.PRS-1PL explain-PTCP-SG.M Similarly be.PRS.1PL explain-INF
As we see it was explained. Similarly we must explain

יחנך לשון חינוך [...] אי לנטינציאונה סיאי קי
yo-ḥnə-ḵa lešon ḥinnuḵ [...]. E l-intenziona si-i che
FUT.3SG-have_misery-2SG.M^{H} language.CS^{H} education^{H} [...] and DEF.SG.F-intention.SG.F be.IMP-3SG
יחנך as having a meaning of "education" [...] And I must explain

למעלה די לו מיאו אונוראנדיסימו פאטרי
che la-maʕala de lo mi-o onorand-issim-o patre
COMP DEF.SG.F-highness^{H} of DEF.SG.M POSS.1SG.M honorable-SUPERL-SG.M father
that his highness, my honorable father

מי אה דיטו אנקורה. אין פינה אמו קי אנקורה טו נון אירי
mi ha dett-o ancora. In.fina a=mo che ancora tu non er-i
1SG.DAT have.PRS.3SG say.PTCP-SG.M yet until to=now CONJ yet 2SG NEG be.PST-2SG
has said to me also: up to now when you have not yet

איסוטו די לו כלל די נער. לוטואו קאריגו די איסיריטי
ess-ut-o de lo kelal di naʕar. Lo=tuo carigo di ess-ere-ti
come_out-PTCP-SG.M of DEF.SG.M rule^{H} of youth^{H} DEF.SG.M=POSS.2SG.M burden of be-INF-2SG.DAT
come out from the stage of youth, the burden will be on you

מחנך בדברי חכמה ותוכחה אירה לו מיאו. כדאיתא
meḥanneḵ be-diḇre ḥoḵma we-toḵaḥa er-a lo mio. Ke-de-ʔiṯa
educator^{H} in-word.CS.PL^{H} wisdom^{H} and-admonition^{H} be.PST-3SG DEF.SG.M POSS.1SG.M as-REL-EXIST
educator in matters of wisdom and admonition was mine. As it is written (Aramaic)

בבראשית רבה צריך אדם ליטפל עם בנו עד י״ג שנה
be-Berešit Rabba ṣariḵ ʔadam li-ṭappel ʕim ben-o ʕad y"g šana
in-Bereshit^{H} Rabbah^{H} must^{H} man^{H} to-take.care.INF^{H} with^{H} son-POSS.3SG.M^{H} until^{H} 13^{H} year
in Bereshit Rabbah (63:10) man must take care of his son until he is 13 years old,

מכאן ואילך יאמר ברוך המקום שפטרני
mi-kan we-ʔelaḵ y-omar baruḵ ha-Maqom še-petara-ni
of-here^{H} and-later^{H} FUT.3SG-say^{H} blessed^{H} DEF-Place^{H} REL-free.PST.3SG-1SG^{H}
after that will say "Blessed be God that freed me

מענשו של זה. אדונקה מו קי טו סי אינטראטו
me-ʕonš-o šel ze. Adunqa mo che tu si entr-at-o
of-punishment-POSS.3SG.M^{H} of^{H} DEM.M^{H} So now CONJ 2SG be.PRS.2SG enter-PTCP-SG.M
from his punishment." So now when you have have began

אין לו חייוב די מן התורה טו סי א הב״ה קומו און פילייו
in lo ḥiyyuḇ di min ha-Tora tu sia a HB"H como un figlio
in DEF.SG.M duty^{H} of of DEF-Torah^{H} 2SG be.PRS.2SGto Saint_be_blessed_He^{H}as one son
your duty <to observe precepts> from the Torah you are for God as a son

אפריסו לופאטרי. אי פירצו אלקים יחנך בנו.
apresso lo=patre. E perciò ʔEloqim yo-ḥn-ḵa ben-i.
near DEF.SG.M=father and because.of.it God^{H} FUT.3SG-have_misery-2SG.M^{H} son-POSS.1SG^{H}
for a father. And this is the reason why God will be merciful to you, my son.

Abbreviations

Judeo-Italian translations of the Siddur:

F = *Editio princeps*, Fano 1506

Q1 = Ms. Parma de' Rossi ital. 7 (y. 1484)

Q2 = Ms. London 625 [Or. 2443] (y. 1483)

Q3 = Ms. JTS Mic. 4076 (15th century)

S = Ms. London Or. 10517 (17th century)

References

Aprile, Marcello. 2012. *Grammatica storica delle parlate giudeo-italiane*. Galatina, Lecce: Congedo Editore.

Bene Kedem 1932. "Gnora Luna – Scene di vita ebraica fiorentina." *Rassegna Mensile di Israel* 6: 546–579.

Bonfil, Robert. 1994. *In the Enchanted Mirror (Jewish life in the Renaissance Italy)*, Jerusalem 1994 (in Hebrew)

Bonfil, Robert. 2012. "La costruzione del tempo sociale in un calendario ebraico del secolo XVI." In: Danièle Iancu-Agou and Carol Iancu (eds.). *L'Écriture de l'Histoire Juive, Mélanges en l'honneur de Gérard Nahon*, Paris-Louvain-Walpole: Peeters, 515–521.

Calò, Mirella. 1990. *Chiacchere alla giudia*, Rome: Carucci.

Cassuto, Umberto. 1929. "Un'antichissima elegia in dialetto giudeo-italiano." In *Archivio Glottologico Italiano*, 28–29 (= *Silloge linguistica in onore di Graziadio Isaia Ascoli*), 349–408.

Cassuto, Umberto. 1930a. "La tradizione giudeo-italiana per la traduzione della Bibbia." *Atti del I Congresso per le tradizioni popolari*, Firenze 1930, 114–121.

Cassuto, Umberto. 1930b. "Les traductions judeo-italennes du ritual." *Revue d'Études Juives* 89: 260–281.

Cassuto, Umberto. 1930c. "Il Libro di Amos in traduzione giudeo-italiana." In: Elia S. Artom et al. (eds.). *Miscellania di studi ebraici in memoria di H.P. Chajes*. Firenze: Casa editrice Israel, 19–38

Cassuto, Umberto. 1934. "Saggi delle antiche traduzioni giudeo-italiane della Bibbia." *Annuario di studi ebraici* 1: 101–13.

Colorni, Vittore. 1970. "La parlata degli ebrei mantovani." *Rassegna Mensile di Israel* 36, N. 7–8–9: 109–164.

Contini, Gianfranco (ed.). 1960. *Poeti del Duecento*, vol. 1. Milano-Napoli: Ricciardi.

Croce, Benedetto. 1952. "La letteratura dialettale riflessa. La sua origine nel Seicento e il suo ufficio storico." In: Id. *Filosofia. Poesia. Storia, pagine tratte da tutte le opere a cura dell'autore*. Milano-Napoli: Ricciardi, 355–364.

Cuomo, Luisa. 1974. *Le glosse volgari dell'Arukh si r. Nathan ben Jechi'el da Roma*. Unpublished PhD dissertation, Jerusalem.

Cuomo, Luisa. 1976. "In margine al giudeo-italiano; note fonetiche, morfologiche e lessicali." *Italia* 1: 30–53.

Cuomo, Luisa. 1977 "Antichissime glosse salentine nel codice ebraico di Parma, De Rossi 138." *Medioevo romanzo* 4: 185–271.

Cuomo, Luisa. 1985. "Pesicheta Rabbati: un florilegio midrascico giudeo-italiano al confine tra Toscana e Umbria nel XVI sec." In: Isaac Benabu and Joseph Sermoneta (eds.). *Judeo-Romance Languages*. Jerusalem: Misgav Yerushalayim, 69–126.

Cuomo, Luisa. 1986. "Pesicheta Rabati: une traduction en judeo-italien." *Massorot* 2: 81–92.

Cuomo, Luisa. 1988a. *Una traduzione giudeo-romanesca del libro di Giona*, Tübingen: Niemeyer.

Cuomo, Luisa. 1988b. "Preliminari per una rivalutazione linguistica del Maqre Dardeqe." In: Dieter Kremer (ed.). A*ctes du XVIIIe Congrès International de Linguistique et de Philologie Romanes*. Tübingen: Niemeyer, 159–167.

Debenedetti Stow, Sandra (ed.). 1990. *Yehuda ben Moshe ben Daniel Romano, 14th cent. La chiarificazione in volgare delle 'espressioni difficili' ricorrenti nel Mishneh Torah di Mose Maimonide: glossario inedito del XIV secolo*. Rome: Carocci.

Del Monte, Crescenzo. 1927. *Sonetti giudaico-romaneschi con note esplicative e un discorso preliminare sul dialetto giudaico-romanesco e sulle sue origini*. Rome: Cremonese.

Del Monte, Crescenzo. 1932. *Nuovi sonetti giudaico-romaneschi con note esplicative ed alcune osservazioni sulle pecularitàe sulla presumibile derivazione del dialetto romano giudaico*. Rome: Cremonese.

Del Monte, Crescenzo. 1935. "Il dialetto di Roma al sec. XVI e le sue sopravvivenze. Alcune battute romano vernacole di una commedia del '500 con versione giudaico-romanesca." *Rassegna Mensile di Israel* 10: 290–296.

Del Monte, Crescenzo. 1955. *Sonetti postumi giudaico-romaneschi e romaneschi*. Rome: Cristoforo Castelletti.

Ernst, Gerhard. 1970. *Die Toskanisierung des römischen Dialekts im 15. und 16. Jahrhundert*. Tübingen: Niemeyer.

Fiorentino, Giuliana. 1937. "Note lessicali al Maqre Dardeqe." *Archivio Glottologico Italiano* 29: 138–159.

Fiorentino, Giuliana. 1951. "The general problems of the Judeo-Romance in the light ot the Maqre Dardeqe." *Jewish Quarterly Review* 42 (1951–1952): 57–77.

Mancini, Marco. 1992. "Sulla Formazione dell'Identita Linguistica Giudeo-Romanesca fra Tardo Medioevo e Rinascimento." In: *Roma nel Rinascimento*, 53–122.

Massariello Merzagora, Giovanna. 1980. "La parlata Giudeo-Piemontese." *L'Archivio Glottologico Italiano* 54, Fasc. 1–2: 105–136.

Mayer-Modena, Maria-Luisa. 1997. *"Le parlate giudeo-italiane."* In: Corrado Vivanti (ed.). *Storia d'Italia. Annali 11/2. Gli Ebrei in Italia*. Torino: Einaudi, 937–963.

Mayer-Modena, Maria-Luisa. 2001. "La Masseket Hamor di Gedalya ibn Yahia." *Italia* 13–15: 303–342.

Mayer-Modena, Maria-Luisa and Giovanna Massariello Merzagora. 1973. "Il giudeo-modenese nei testi raccolti da A. Giacomelli." In *Rendiconti dell'Istituto Lombardo. Accademia di scienze e lettere, classe I lettere* 107: 869–938.

Marazzini, Claudio. 1993. *"Le teorie."* In: Luca Serianni and Pietro Trifone (eds.). *Storia della lingua italiana*, vol. I: I luoghi della codificazione, Torino: Einaudi, 231–330.

Migliorini, Bruno. 1987. *Storia della lingua italiana*. Firenze: Bompiani.

Milano, Attilio. 1963. *Storia degli Ebrei in Italia*. Torino: Einaudi.

Natale, Sarah. 2018. *L'elegia gudeo-italiana. Editizione critica e commentata*. Pisa: Pacini.

Rohlfs, Gerhard. 1966–1969. *Grammatica storica della lingua italiana e dei suoi dialetti*, Torino: Einaudi.

Roth, Cecil. 1950. "Un'elegia giudeo-italiana sui martiri di Ancona (1556–57)." *Rassegna Mensile di Israel* 16: 147–156.

Ryzhik, Michael. 2007. "The linguistic traits of the Judeo-Italian prayer book translation according to the Fano edition, 1506." *Italia* 17: 7*–17* (in Hebrew)

Ryzhik, Michael. 2008. "I cambiamenti nel giudeo-italiano in corso del Cinquecento: le prediche." In: Francesco Aspesi, Vermondo Brugnatelli, Anna Linda Callow, and Claudia Rosenzweig (eds.). *Il mio cuore è a Oriente, לבי במזרח. Studi di linguistica storica, filologia e cultura ebraica dedicati a Maria-Luisa Mayer Modena*. Milano: Cialpino Istituto Editoriale Universitario, 527–545.

Ryzhik, Michael. 2009. "La proposizione nominale nelle traduzioni giudeo-italiane dei formulari di preghiera e della Bibbia." *Medioevo Romanzo* 33: 121–149.

Ryzhik, Michael. 2010. "The language and the prayer traditions in the Judeo-Italian prayer book translations." *Italia* 20: 7–28. (in Hebrew)

Ryzhik, Michael. 2012. "From the manuscripts to the printed editions: development of the tradition of the vocalization in the Italian Siddur editions at the end of the 15th and in the first half of the 16th centuries." *Leshonenu* 74: 333–357. (in Hebrew)

Ryzhik, Michael. 2013a. "Preliminaries to the critical edition of the Jewish-Italian translation of the Siddur." *Journal of Jewish Languages* 1 (2): 229–260.

Ryzhik, Michael. 2013b. "Le didascalie per la cena pasquale nella tradizione degli ebrei nell'Italia meridionale." In: Fabrizio Lelli (ed.). *Gli ebrei nel Salento (secoli IX-XVI)*, (= Università di Salento, Studi Storici 106). Galatina, Lecce: Congedo Editore, 379–406.

Ryzhik, Michael. 2014. "La traduzione delle poesie antiche per la festa delle Capanne (Hosh'anot) nei volgarizzamenti del libro di preghiere ebraico in giudeo-italiano." In: Ivano Pavoncello and Elisa Gregori (eds.). *Lingue, testi, culture. L'eredità di Folena, vent'anni dopo (Atti del XL Convegno Interuniversitario, Bressanone-Brixen, 12–15 luglio 2012)*. Padova: Esedra, 173–184.

Ryzhik, Michael. 2017. "La lingua dei calendari ebraici veneziani cinquecenteschi." *Rassegna Mensile di Israel* 83/2–3: 119–131.

Sermoneta, Joseph Baruch. 1967. "Il 'Libro delle forme verbali', compendio volgare del Mahalakh Sevile ha-daʕath di M.R.J. Qimchi." In: *Scritti in memoria di Leone Carpi*. Jerusalem: S. Mayer, 59–100.

Sermoneta, Joseph Baruch. 1969. *Un glossario filosofico ebraico-italiano del XIII secolo.* Rome: Edizioni dell'Ateneo.

Sermoneta, Joseph Baruch. 1976. "Considerazioni frammentarie sul giudeo-italiano." *Italia* 1: 1–29.

Sermoneta, Joseph Baruch. 1978. "La traduzione giudeo italiana dei Salmi e i suoi rapporti con le antiche versioni latine." In: *Scritti in memoria di Umberto Nahon*. Jerusalem: Fondazioni S. Mayer, 196–239.

Sermoneta, Joseph Baruch. 1990. "Testimonianze degli ebrei pugliesi a Corfù." *Medioevo Romanzo* 15/3: 408–437.

Terracini Benvenuto.1937. *"Due composizioni in versi giudeo-piemontesi del secolo XIX." Rassegna Mensile di Israel* 12: 164–183.

Terracini, Benvenuto. 1951. "Residui di parlate giudeo-italiane raccolti a Pitigliano, Roma, Ferrara." *Rassegna Mensile di Israel* 17: 3–11, 62–72, 111–121.

Terracini, Benvenuto. 1956. "Review of Max Berenblut and Menahem Banitt. 1949. *A comparative study of Judaeo-Italian translations of Isaiah*." *Romance Philology* 10 (1956–1957) (= E.P. Armstrong Memorial, Part I), 243–258.

Terracini, Benvenuto. 1962. "Le parlate giudaico-italiane negli appunti di Raffaelle Giacomelli." *Rassegna Mensile di Israel* 28: 260–295.

Tirosh-Becker, Ofra. 1990. "Arabic glosses in *Maqre Dardeqe*, Italian version – what is their nature?" *Italia* 9: 37–77. (in Hebrew)

Judeo-French

Alexandra B. Edzard, Bildungszentrum Nürnberg

1. Introduction

1.1 Historical overview

Judeo-French, also called Zarphatic or Western Loez[1], is the written language of the Northern French Jewry, which is documented in French texts composed in Hebrew characters dating from the second half of the 11th century until the first half of the 14th century in France. The term Judeo-French will be used in this contribution because of its convenience, regardless of the debate on its linguistic status.[2]

Before the 14th century, the texts mainly come from Northern and Eastern France, these parts of the country being the most important cultural centers for French Jewry, as far as one can deduce from the texts. The central Jewish communities in Northern France were situated in Champagne with Troyes as its main center, Normandy with its capital Rouen, and Lorraine. The Northern and Eastern French communities were culturally oriented towards that of Rhenish Jewry with the central Jewish communities of Speyer, Worms, and Mainz.[3] Judeo-French texts were also composed in Norman England, as the Jewish communities of England were closely linked with the communities in Normandy, until the expulsion of the English Jews in 1290.[4]

The use of French words written in Hebrew characters in France is first documented in texts composed by commentators of the Bible, notably Rabbi Solomon ben Isaac, better known as Rashi, in Troyes (1040–1105). At this period, single French words and expressions were integrated in otherwise Hebrew texts, in order to explain the precise meaning of the Hebrew words to French Jews.[5] This genre developed into Hebrew-Old French biblical glossaries, which shows that the process of writing in Old French – with the use of the Hebrew alphabet – got more and more important to French Jews.

The production of Judeo-French texts declined and finally disappeared with the two main waves of expulsion of the Jews from the Kingdom of France in 1306 and 1394.[6] By this time, a rich literature entirely composed in Old French in Hebrew letters had developed. From the beginning of the 14th century, the declining period of Jewish-French literary productivity, there exist only texts originating from the East of France.

1 Weinreich 2008, vol. 1: 101.

2 For further information about this question, cf. Banitt 1963, 1971/1972.

3 Cf. Battenberg 1990: 60; Preißler 2015: 1; Dahan 1997: 6.

4 Cf. Olszowy-Schlanger 2018: 70.

5 Cf. Banitt 1997: 192; Kiwitt 2013: 161.

6 Cf. Battenberg 1990: 90f., 95.

In this context, it has to be said, however, that between 95% and 98% of the texts produced in France by Jews has disappeared and been destroyed in the course of time.[7] Therefore, we only have a small impression of the literature created by French Jews in the Middle Ages.[8]

There exist different kinds of texts. Taking the two essential kinds of texts – religious and profane – together, the following classification can be established (cf. also Kiwitt 2013: 19f.):

1) Commentaries of the Bible and the Talmud written in Hebrew, which include some Old French glosses. This genre begins at the latest with Rashi in the 11th century in Champagne.

2) From the beginning of the 13th century on, we find biblical and onomasiological glossaries in Hebrew and Old French, which represent the prominent sources for Jewish use of French in Hebrew characters. The Biblical glosses were intended to explain the the Bible and the Talmud to French rabbis in order to ensure the correct understanding of the holy texts.[9]

3) This productivity allowed the development of literature starting in the middle of the 13th century, both religious and profane, either entirely written in Judeo-French or in two (Hebrew alternating with Old French) or even more languages. This category includes medical texts – as for instance the treatise on fever *Fevres*, alongside with recipes and adjurations, and astrological texts – as for instance the translation into (Latin-lettered) French of Abraham Ibn Ezra's astrological works made by Hagin le Juif.[10] Examples of writings connected to the historical and religious sphere are the *Elégie de Troyes* – which treats the auto-da-fé of 13 Jews on April 24, 1288, prayers in French, and two Wedding Songs.[11]

The development towards an own literature written in Hebrew-spelled Old French shows the self-concept which French Jews must have had. The self-concept indicated by the texts points towards a strong sense of being a part of the Latin-Christian environ-

7 Sirat 1994: 193; Battenberg 1990: 89.

8 For an overview over Judeo-French literature cf. Fudeman 2010: 155–158; Kiwitt 2013: 15–27; Sala 1998: 386f.

9 Cf. Dahan 1997: 7f.

10 This translation, *Comencement de sapience*, from 1273 is generally considered as Judeo-French, even though it uses Latin characters instead of Hebrew ones, due to some typical linguistic particularities. Cf. Kiwitt 2013: 21f. Fudeman (2010: 5) is more skeptical when it comes to marking this text as French Jewish or even Judeo-French.

11 David Simon Blondheim edited one bilingual Wedding Song (1927): "To the hill of frankincense" (English by Fudeman 2010: 124), from the 13th century, included as an addition in the compilation of prayers Maḥzor Vitry. The second Wedding Song known today, "Arise, come toward me, beautiful one, noble and worthy bride" (edition and English by Fudeman 2010: 124), has been found in ms. Heid. 51, Zentralbibliothek Zürich. The main parts of the manuscript Heid. 51 were written between 1402 and 1439, but the part (the end) in which the Wedding Song is located, is undated. Fudeman considers a time in the late 14th and early 15th century as likely for the composition of the song; cf. Fudeman 2010: 131f.

ment,[12] linked at the same time to an equally strong sense of forming an important particular entity, the Hebrew-Jewish one. The first aspect is illustrated by the use of Old French, the second by the use of Hebrew characters.[13] A particularly striking example which proves the double identity of French Jewry in the Middle Ages are poems, where Hebrew and Old French alternate.[14] Here, this fact appears both in the external aspect – the use of the two languages, as in the choice of topics and the resulting allusions to both cultures, which realize the topic.[15]

When the French Jews were expelled from the territory ruled by the French crown in 1306, they continued speaking French and copying French texts in their new homes in Germany, Hungary, and Italy, but their French changed from the one their ancestors spoke when living in France in a French society.[16] The productivity of French Jews in exile can be seen in the latest extant Hebraïco-French text, a recipe for a sweet paste made of fruits and nuts (*ḥaroset*), enclosed in a prayer book from 1470, including French words for various ingredients.[17]

For an overview of texts containing or consisting of Old French in medieval Jewish texts, one can refer to the works by Levy (1964), Banitt (1972; 1995), Fudeman (2010: 155–158), Kiwitt (2013: 15–27), and Olszowy-Schlanger (2018: 70–77), this last one in particular regarding Jewish texts containing Anglo-Norman dialectal elements.

1.2 State of the research

Research on Judeo-French started with the scholars Arsène Darmesteter (publications from 1872 to 1937), David Blondheim (publications from 1910 to 1937), and Raphael Levy (publications from 1927 to 1964), just to mention some of the most important names. This field of research on the intersection of French and Hebrew linguistics came to a broader attention again with Menahem Banitt (publications from 1961 to 2005), Cyril Aslanov (publications beginning with 1998), Kirsten Anne Fudeman (publications beginning witt 2003), and Marc Kiwitt (publications beginning with 2001). The bibliography on Judeo-Romance linguistics compiled by Paul Wexler (1989) and the publications by Menachem Banitt[18] provide the best overview over the state of the research concerning the first set of studies; for a survey also including more recent works see Zwink 2017: 17–22 and Kiwitt 2016: 161–167.

The question of the status of Hebrew-written Old French is a central one in many studies; an overview over the most important works concerning this question can be found in Kiwitt 2013: 173–184.

12 Cf. Marcus 2002: 450/451; Marcus 2002: 449: Jews and Christians mixed culturally, economically and socially: in early Christian Europe, there did not exist ghettos. Marcus calls this co-existence social-economic and social-religious cohabitation (cf. p. 250).

13 In this context it is important to note that Jews more often learned to write and read in Hebrew in their own schools; the majority was not able to read in Latin, except some scribes, cf. Banitt 1972 (vol. I: Introduction): 58; Kiwitt 2013: 50; Hagège 2006: 85; Fudeman 2010: 14f.

14 Cf. the two cited Wedding Songs.

15 For more information on this point cf. Rosenberg 1992, Fudeman 2010, Edzard 2014.

16 Fudeman 2010: 38.

17 The recipe can be found in the French prayer book Cod. Parm. 1902, cf. Fudeman 2010: 108.

18 Especially Banitt 1967: 188–191.

1.3 Sources on which this contribution is based

In order to provide as wide a variety of examples of Hebrew-written Old French as possible, on which this description is based, three Bible glossaries will be taken for illustration: first, the Glossary BN ms. hébreu 302 from the beginning of the 13th century, written by a single writer but probably vocalized by a different person,[19] edited by Mayer Lambert and Louis Brandin, second, the Glossaire de Bâle, composed in the first quarter of the 13th century by many different writers,[20] and finally, the Glossaire de Leipzig, composed at the end of the 13th century or in the beginning of the 14th century.[21] The last two mentioned glossaries have been edited by Menachem Banitt.

BN ms. hébreu 302 (in the following MS 302) is mostly written in the Francien dialect with some elements typical of the North East of France.[22] The Glossaire de Bâle uses the dialect of the South East of Champagne,[23] as it was created in Troyes.

The Glossaire de Leipzig, a trilingual glossary using Hebrew, Old French, and Middle High German, shows strong elements belonging to the Anglo-Norman dialect, which leads to the assumption that it has been composed in Rouen, at that time a flourishing center of Jewish cultural activity.[24]

Furthermore, the already mentioned manuscript of the treatise on fever *Fevres* (Ms. Or. Oct. 512, Berlin), produced at the end of the 13th century/beginning of the 14th century in the North of France by a single writer – the text using the Francien dialect with some linguistic hints to Northern Burgundy, South West of Champagne, or Lorraine[25] – will be taken into consideration, and finally the two Jewish Wedding Songs.

The earlier Wedding song is called by its incipit "To the hill of frankincense our bridegroom has come" and found in the manuscript *Maḥzor Vitry* owned by the Jewish Theological Seminary of America (MS 8092, fol. 160v), probably dating from the second half of the 13th century.[26] The later one, "Arise, come toward me, beautiful one, noble and worthy bride" is included at the end of manuscript Zentralbibliothek Zürich, ms. Heid. 51 and was written in the late 14th or the early 15th century.[27] Both songs are composed in the Lotharingian dialect.[28]

19 Lambert / Brandin 1905/1977: IV.

20 Banitt 1972 (vol. I: Introduction): 10–12.

21 Banitt 2005 (vol. I: Introduction): 42.

22 Lambert / Brandin 1905/1977: XII; Edzard 2011: 179.

23 Banitt 1972 (vol. I: Introduction): 23; 71.

24 Cf. Banitt 2005 (vol. I: Introduction): 19; 24.

25 Cf. Kiwitt 2001: 17/18; 57; Zwink 2017: 164.

26 Cf. Fudeman 2010: 125–128 for thoughts on the dating of the manuscript *Maḥzor Vitry*.

27 Cf. Fudeman 2010: 128–132; the Wedding Song has been edited by Fudeman in Fudeman 2010: 159–173.

28 Cf. Fudeman 2010: 160; Rosenberg 1992: 23.

2. Graphical, phonetical, and grammatical characteristics of Judeo-French

2.1 Writing system: orthography

Jewish-French writers used the Hebrew alphabet when writing Old French texts, adapting the Hebrew system of consonants and vowel marking – according to the Tiberian system – to the French language. This writing system, having developed since at least the 11th century onward, had become a distinct convention created by the Tossafists (< *tosafot* 'additions to Rashi's Talmud commentary'), who themselves oriented their tradition towards their teacher Rabbi Solomon ben Isaac, better known as Rashi. In addition to the Hebrew letters and their pointing, other elements of the Hebrew language were adopted in Hebrew-written Old French, though in each text to a different extent, as for example the norm of pointing all consonants except for the final one.

At the same time, Jewish Old French writing clearly reflects Latin writing traditions and is not a mere phonetic reproduction of the spoken language, a circumstance, which proves the writers' familiarity with Latin-written French. We know about individual Jewish scholars, for example Rashbam[29] (1085–1174) and the anonymous writer of the treatise on fever,[30] who cite from Latin works and therefore were obviously able to read in Latin.[31] For most of the Jewish writers, however, it must have been more natural to read and write in Hebrew characters, as they only learned Hebrew in school.[32] The translator from Hebrew into French of the astrological works of Abraham Ibn Ezra, Hagin (Ḥayyim) le Juif, seems to support the theory of Jews not being comfortable in writing in French at the time, as he dictated the text to a Christian writer instead of writing down the translation directly.[33]

A sort of convergence between the learned language – Hebrew – and the scientific tradition which involved the knowledge of Latin, and in addition the influence of the mother tongue French, must have led to the influences of Latin orthographic traditions on Hebrew-written Old French. The same influence is evident in Hebrew citations made by the writers, as one can find many orthographical and grammatical misrepresentations in the Hebrew parts of the Bible glossaries.[34]

The orthography in all texts gives evidence about the interaction between the different languages, even if in the French-written parts the phonetic way of writing plays an important role as well, especially as regards short words like the relative pronoun קִי *qī* (*Fevres*), or 2SG.PRES of "to be", אֶט *eṭ* (*Fevres*), showing up in the orthographical variation of אֵיט *ēṭ* in Wedding Song I, or אֵיטוֹפְּאמֵינט *ēṭōpəmēnṭ* 'constipation' (*Fevres*), without the <s>.[35]

29 An acronym of Rabbi Shlomo (Samuel) ben Meir.

30 Cf. Kiwitt 2001: 15f. on the question of how many writers were involved.

31 More information concerning the discussion about the status of Latin writing amongst Jews in French Middle Ages is found in Banitt 1972 (vol. I: Introduction): 58, extenuated by Kiwitt 2013: 49f.; Banitt 1997: 195; Fudeman 2010: 22–24.

32 Hagège 2006: 85.

33 Cf. Levy 1927: 19–23.

34 Cf. also Banitt 2005 (vol. I: Introduction): 92f.; 154.

35 This contribution follows for the transliteration of Hebrew written Old French words into Latin letters the way practiced by Kiwitt 2001, who himself follows the system used in Semiticist research;

The influence of Christian Old French appears especially in the morphological elements of Judeo-French, i.e. the terminations of verbs and nouns, as the following examples from MS 302 show, but also the words' stems: (1051) אַקֻוּבֵּיטוֹנְץ *aqāūḇēṭōnṣ* 'floating' (PTCP), (1) אַאַקְלַרְזִיר *a-aqlarzīr* 'to enlighten' (PREP+INF)[36], (14) רְגַרְדְּרָשׁ *rgardrāś* (*regarderas*) 'you will see' (FUT.2SG), (19) אֵיקֻוּטֵישְׁמוֹיי *ēqāūṭēś-mōyy* (*écoutez-moi)* 'listen to me' (IMP.2.PL-1SG). The fact that the last consonant of the ending usually gets no vowel point, except for words that are immediately connected with a function word, show the mere imitation of the Latin-written model of a grammatical ending that was not pronounced in (Old-)French.

Note also the use of geminate consonants, which sometimes can be observed:[37] (53) אַנְפּוֹרְרָלוא *anp̄ōrrā-lwʔ* (*anforra lu*) 'he will put it into the sheath' (FUT.3.SG + PRON), (817) דֵיגוֹטְטְא *dēgōṭṭə* (*degotte*) 'overflow', (Bâle 1803) פִּיֵּירְרשׁ פְּזַאנץ *piyērrś pzanṣ* (*pierres pesants*)[38] 'heavy stones'.

One graphic element of influence from Hebrew on French orthography is worth mentioning, the expression of feminine substantival and participle endings on *-ée* appearing in the Hebrew script as אֶה, e.g., נֶייאֶה *näyyəh* 'snow'.

Another example of the influence of the Latin model on Hebrew written Old French is [ɛ] written <ay> like in קָאַיְינא *q̄eayynʔ* 'chain' (Glossaire de Leipzig 8293) alongside with the phonetical orthography <ē> in MS 302 (425) מִיגְרֵינְא *mīgrēnə* 'pomegranate', in fact representing the expected writing with <e> after the monophthongization of <ai>, which never gained ground in Old French.[39]

Indecision in writing can often be observed, as in the writing of Christian authors, cf. the last syllable of *maladies* in the treatise on fever, which is written in three different ways,[40] and many other examples in all Judeo-French texts. The second Wedding Song cited below shows this un-fixedness of orthography in Hebrew-written French in an especially distinct way, as the first and the last stanzas are identical, but show many orthographical differences concerning both the consonants and the punctuation.

A comparison of different texts shows the varying role of the Latin-written model in Hebrew Old French: for the Bâle writer(s), it seems to have been more important than to the writer of MS 302, as the examples cited above and further examples in Banitt 1972 (vol. I: Introduction: 58) show.

Kiwitt 2001: 25ff. The numbers in front of the words cited here from MS 302 refer to the glossary of Judeo-French words examined from the Bible Glossary MS, Paris, BN 302 in Edzard 2011: 184–387. For the *Glossaire de Bâle* and *de Leipzig*, the respective numeration is taken from Banitt's editions (1972 and 2005).

36 In this example the use of *zayin* for Latin <ci> is astonishing as this letter ordinarily renders [z]; the use of the letters *tsade* or *sin* would have been more likely.

37 Cf. also Banitt 1972 (vol. I: Introduction): 58.

38 The writer does not use the feminine form of the adjective constantly, as one can see in this example. This fits with the fact that feminine adjectives derived from Latin two-termination adjectives generally got the *-e*-ending in analogy with feminine adjectives derived from Latin three-termination adjectives not earlier than at the beginning of the 14th century (Pope 1952: 306 § 779ff.). The manuscript shows the same adjective in its feminine form earlier: 1699 פְּזַאנְטשׁ *pzānṭś* (*pesantes*): PL.F.

39 Cf. Rheinfelder 1953: 31 (§79), 106 (§ 272, 273).

40 Kiwitt 2001: 23.

Wedding Songs I and II agree with common usage, too: The rhyme shows that final *-s*, *-t*, and *-r* were silent, even though they generally appear in the orthography. This matches the overall evolution of French, as the pronunciation of final *-s*, *-t*, and *-r*, preceded by the high vowels *e* and *i*, ceased from the beginning of the 13th century on.[41]

2.1.1 Graphemes: Consonants

The writers do not use all Hebrew letters when writing in Old French: *kaph* (כ), *samekh* (ס) and *tav* (ת) are the letters which are mostly reserved for writing in Hebrew and almost never appear in Old French words. *Ḥet* (ח) and *ʕayin* (ע) are not used at all.

In the context of Old French, *kaph* and *samekh* only appear in loanwords as for instance in *Fevres*[42] אֵיסְטוֹמַכְא *ēsṭōmakə* 'stomach'[43], סֻוֹכֵּר *sūker* 'sugar'[44], and דְרַכְּמְא *drak̲mə*[45] 'drachma', or in the Glossaire de Bâle (290) סוּקְרָא *sūqrə* 'sugar'. The letter *samekh* can in addition be found in Hebrew and Latin words in *Fevres*.

The letter *tav* is extremely rarely to be found in Old French words, Banitt gives one single example from the Glossaire de Leipzig: (844) אִיאִיתֵיאֵינְט רוֹלָנט *īītēēnṭ rōlānṭ*[46] 'and they were rolling' ("et ils roulaient") and explains the use of this letter by its position between two vowels.[47]

The letter *sin*/*šin*, whose pronunciation in Hebrew depends on the place of the dot on the letter, is used differently in Judeo-French. In Hebrew, the dot on the left part of the letter marks *ś* [s], whereas it marks *š* [ʃ] on the right part. The Judeo-French writing system only uses the letter with the dot on the right side, systematically referring to *ś* [s].

The Hebrew letters and their use in Judeo-French are the following:

– *ʔaleph* expresses the glottal stop and functions – then called a *mater lectionis* – as a means to introduce the vowels [a], [e], [i], [o], [u], and [y] in combination with vowel-pointing for the vowels [a], [e], and [i], or together with *yod* or *vav* in order to express <ī> and <ē> (*ʔaleph* in combination with *yod*)[48], and [o], [y] and [u] (*ʔaleph* and *vav*).

Inside a word, *ʔaleph* expresses either French [ə], which corresponds to Hebrew *schwa mobile*, or zero vowel, which corresponds to Hebrew *schwa quiescens*.

Furthermore, *ʔaleph* indicates the hiatus (glottal stop) and final [ə] and final [a]. It can also be combined with the letter *he* (ה) at the end of a word and in this case indicates the feminine ending. This is an element which follows the Hebrew grammar.

41 Cf. Pope 1952: 159 (§ 401 for final *r*).

42 Cf. Kiwitt 2001: 19f.

43 Kiwitt 2001: 60 (20r.–6).

44 Kiwitt 2001: 74 (181r.–22), the signification of *rafe* on top of the letter *kaph* is not clear.

45 Kiwitt 2001: 76 (215r.–8).

46 Banitt 2005 (vol. I: Introduction): 62/63.

47 Banitt 2005 (vol. I: Introduction): 193.

48 The macron on <i> and <e> does not necessarily signify a long vowel, but marks the difference between the writing *ʔaleph* + *ṣere* or *ḥiriq* + *yod* and the writing without *yod*.

Moreover, *ʔaleph* is used in order to strengthen an otherwise weak consonant (with high sonority), as for instance <r>. This phenomenon occurs at the end of words.[49]

– *Bet* corresponds to *b*. In Hebrew, it can bear a *dagesh*, i.e. a dot inside the letter (the same works for the letters ב, ג, ד, כ, פ, ת, the *bəgāḏkəp̄aṯ*-letters) and indicates the occlusive pronunciation of the letter.

Jewish writers in France use *dagesh* variably when writing Old French. In some manuscripts, it constantly appears, as in the Glossaire de Bâle, whereas in other manuscripts, it is found rarely or even not at all, as for instance in MS 302 and in the treatise on fever. Writers who work without *dagesh* rather do not mark the occlusive character of a letter at all, but instead mark the spirantized one by use of the diacritic sign *rafe*, a horizontal line on the above listed *bəgāḏkəp̄aṯ*-letters.

– *Gimel* corresponds to [g], and, with a *haček* or a *rafe* on the top, to [ʒ].[50] Sometimes, it is represented by single or double *yod*, cf. the Glossaire de Bâle, where [ʒ] appears as two *yod* with *rafe*. In *Fevres*, it appears without *rafe*.[51]

The consonant with *haček* or *rafe* renders both: older [dʒ] and more recent [ʒ], into which the phoneme [dʒ] developed from the beginning of the 13th century on.[52]

– *Dalet* corresponds to *d*. Sometimes and depending on the document, it can carry a *dagesh* which shows the letter's occlusive pronunciation, though most of the texts used here do not mark the occlusiveness of *dalet* at all, as its fricative version never is applied. In the Glossaire de Bâle, *dalet* always appears with *dagesh*,[53] MS 302 uses *dagesh* irregularly, *Fevres* does not display it at all.

– *He* renders *h aspiré* in the initials of French words. Furthermore, it sometimes works as a *mater lectionis* for [a] and [ə]; the former sometimes for the preposition *a* and PRS.3SG of *avoir*. The latter especially renders final *-ée*, <əh>, for feminine nouns and adjectives/participles.

– *Zayin* renders [z]. In some texts, *zayin* can bear a *haček*, which does not change the phonetic realization of the letter, though.[54]

Sometimes, *zayin* takes over the task to express [s], cf. all Bible glossaries, but also Wedding Song II. Cf. MS 302 below: אַאקְלַרְזִיר *a aqlarzīr* 'to enlighten', for Latin <ci>, Wedding Song II, 3.1: רֵייפּוּזֵייאָה *rəypūzēyəh* 'turned away' (F), where *zayin* stands for *sin*.[55]

Zayin often transcribes recent intervocalic [d], and [d] in contact with [r]; sometimes the scribes chose *dalet* with (or without) *rafe* for the same consonant.

– *Ṭet* expresses [t]; very rarely in the Bâle and Leipzig glossaries, *tav* is used for [t].

49 Cf. Banitt 1972 (vol. I: Introduction): 83.

50 Banitt states that *gimel* with *haček* or *rafe* mirrors the Latin model; cf. 2005 (vol. I: Introduction): 200. All the texts consulted here use *haček*, except for *Fevres*, whose writer uses *rafe* instead.

51 Cf. Zwink 2017: 133; Kiwitt 2001: 22.

52 Rheinfelder 1963: 164; Pope 1934: 93f.

53 Cf. Banitt 1972 (vol. I: Introduction): 60.

54 Cf. Darmesteter 1874: 459; Fudeman 2006: 561, fn. 59.

55 Cf. also Banitt 1972 (vol. I: Introduction): 63; Banitt 2005 (vol. I: Introduction): 199.

– *Lamed* corresponds to Latin *l*; it can be barred when palatalized, as it constantly is in the Glossaire de Bâle, cf. (3) אַבִֿללאנץ *abillanṣ* (in the Hebrew script, the first lamed carries a diagonal stroke) 'they committed crimes', (56) טַאללֵייאֶש *ṭallēyəś* 'cut', PTCP.PASS.PL.F, (57) אַשוּיילל *aśūyll* 'on the threshold' (preposition + noun). The palatalization of *l* can also be marked by two *yod* in front of or after *l*, which also is the case in the Glossaire de Bâle, from a different part of the glossary – the Book of Isaiah – onwards:[56] (6985) אַקוֹנְטַרְאַלֵייר *aqōnṭarialēyr* 'to irritate' (preposition *à* + infinitive), and which constantly is the case in the Glossaire de Leipzig, the Bible Glossary MS 302, as well as in the first Wedding Song analyzed in this paper. The treatise on fever *Fevres* only sporadically shows a single *yod* in order to indicate palatalization.

– *Mem* corresponds to *m*; at the end of a word it takes the form ם. In the Glossaire de Bâle, it sometimes gets a *dagesh* in order to indicate that there is no nasalization.

– *Nun* stands for Latin *n*. When closing a vowel, it marks a nasal, as it does in Latin-written French texts, but it often is omitted without further indication; cf. Bâle (892) דַאנְקוֹטְרָא *danqō<n>ṭrə*[57] 'opposite', where the second *nun*, marking the second nasal, is omitted; Wedding Song II 6.1: אֶטְנִדוּ *əṭnidū* 'heard' (PTCP.PASS.SG.CO.M) for 'entendu'. Most of the time, *nun* is used in the context of nasals instead of <m> in Latin writing: MS 302: (163) קוֹנְפְּלֵיינְדְרַ *qōnplēyndra* instead of *complaindra* 'he/she will complain' (FUT.3.SG), (822) אוֹנְבְּרָא *ōnbrə* instead of *ombre* 'shade'.

Two *yod* preceding or following *nun* often express the palatalization of the consonant (modern French <gn>), cf. MS 302 (259) אוֹנְצֵיינֵר *ōnṣēyner* 'enseigner' ("instruct" INF; there is supposed to be a *yod* before the final *resh* in order to express the infinitive-ending, but this is missing in this example). In the Glossaire de Bâle, this phenomenon is expressed by either a *nun* carrying a *haček* when palatalized, or by its being preceded or followed – sometimes in addition to the *haček* – by one or two *yod*.[58] At the end of a word, *nun* has a special form: ן.

– *Samekh* and *ʕayin*: see above.

– *Pe* corresponds to [p] or, with a *rafe*, to [f].

– *Ṣade* renders Old French [ts] or [s], to which [ts] evolved around the year 1200.[59] The differently developed sounds of [s] are often randomly expressed either by *ṣade* or by *śin*, which illustrates their concurrence. Some examples from MS 302 are (41) שְׁפּוֹייְאֵיץ *śpōyyēṣ* 'lean against' (PST.PTCP.M.PL) versus (50) אַמָשֵׁישׁ *amāśēś* 'assembled' (PST.PTCP.M.PL); (14) רְגַרְדֵיץ *rgardēṣ* 'look' (PRS.2PL) versus (51) אַמְנֵיש *amnēś* 'bring' (PRS.2PL). As the examples with *ṣade* show, the letter has a special form when at the end of a word.

– *Qof* stands for Old French [k]; when it carries a *haček* or a *rafe*,[60] it expresses [tʃ] or later [ʃ].

56 Banitt 1972 (vol. I: Introduction): 60.

57 Banitt (1972) marks absent nasal-*nun* in the Latin transcription by an *n* in pointed brackets.

58 Banitt 1972 (vol. I: Introduction): 60.

59 Rheinfelder 1953: 164 (§397/398).

60 The treatise on fever uses *qof* with *rafe*, the other here consulted texts all use *haček*.

– *Resh* represents [r]. In the Bâle and the Leipzig glossaries, it often carries a *dagesh*, which has the role of strengthening its pronunciation and preventing its becoming silent, especially in final, intervocalic and pre-consonantal inner position of a word.[61]

– *Śin*/*šin* are not used following the Hebrew pattern, as *šin*, with a dot on the right in the Hebrew system, appears as *śin* in the Hebrew-written French texts; *śin* renders simple [s]. The dot is often omitted.

Generally, the Bâle and Leipzig glossaries, and to a minor degree also MS 302, use many diacritic signs; besides the *haček* and the *rafe*, the *dagesh* plays an important role in the first two glossaries in assuring the pronunciation of the concerned letters in French, which were considered as uncertain and easily neglected by the scribes.[62] In order to assure their pronunciation, the scribes marked these consonants with a *dagesh*, or – in the case of *resh* – they add a second one, or an *ʔaleph*.[63] The use of *dagesh* in this sense applies to many other letters in intervocalic, pre-consonantal, or final position: *ʔaleph*, *gimel*, *dalet*, *zayin*, *ṭet*, *lamed*, *mem*, *nun*, *pe*, *ṣade*, *qof*, and *śin*.[64]

Sometimes, final letters are dropped because they were not pronounced at all. The more current way of indicating their silentness is the lack of pointing, though.

2.1.2 Graphemes: Semi-vowels

– *Yod* can serve as consonant, expressing [ʒ], which otherwise is often represented by *gimel* with *haček* or *rafe*, cf. the explanations above sub *gimel*.

Furthermore, *yod* serves as *mater lectionis* inside a syllable for *i* and *e*.

Double-*yod* functions in order to express the diphthong [ei] or long [e:], with a *ṣere* under the preceding consonant, or, when a diphthong is excluded for etymological reasons, it designates the word accent[65], present until the end of the 17th century.[66]

Furthermore, double-*yod* expresses the nasal and the palatalization of a consonant, as described above sub *lamed* and *nun*.

Wedding Song II differs from the otherwise observed use, as it features double-*yod* instead of *ʔaleph* after *schwa mobile*: cf. 3.1 רְייפֻּוזֵייאְה *ryypūzēyəh* (*repoussée*) 'turned away'; 4.2 שְׂיי *śyy* (*ce*) 'it'; 4.3 דְיילַיְימוֹנְט *dyylayymōnṭ* (*delaiement*) 'delay'; 6.2 קְייוַואַקְָא *q̄yywwaaq̄ə* (*chevache*) 'ride' (IMP).

– *Vav* as a consonant – single or double – renders *v* [v], just as does *bet* with *rafe*. There seems to be no rule as to when writers choose *bet* with *rafe* or *vav* instead, or when they do use both at all; it could though be that *vav* as [v] represents an imitation of the Latin-written model.[67] This is the case in the Bible glossaries Leipzig and MS 302 and also in

61 Pope 1952: 156 (§395); Banitt 1972 (vol. I: Introduction): 61, 82; Banitt 2005 (vol. I: Introduction): 202; 223.

62 Banitt 2005 (vol. I: Introduction): 201/202; 1972: 71.

63 Banitt 1972 (vol. I: Introduction): 82/83.

64 For a detailed summary cf. Banitt 2005 (vol. I: Introduction): 201/202 and Banitt 1972 (vol. I: Introduction): 71.

65 Zwink 2017: 134/135.

66 Pope 1952: 103 (§ 223).

67 Banitt 2005 (vol. I: Introduction): 194.

the treatise on fever, but not in the Glossaire de Bâle: here, [v] is rendered exclusively by *bet* with *rafe*.[68]

Vav can stand at the beginning of a word or it can introduce a new syllable. As *mater lectionis* it stands for *u* and *o*, and in the treatise on fever even for *i*, combined with certain vowel-points.

2.1.3 Graphemes: Vocalization

When one compares different manuscripts, it appears that even though Jewish writers generally resorted to the same writing system, the use and degree of punctuation differs from manuscript to manuscript. While five of the six texts examined here are almost fully punctuated, one text renounces punctuation nearly completely, cf. Wedding Song I ("To the hill of frankincense our bridegroom has come").

The points and dashes, marking the vowels in the Hebrew written Old French words, can either stand with *ʔaleph*, *vav*, or *yod* as *matres lectionis* (then called *plene*), or only under the consonant in question. Influenced by the tradition of Hebrew, final letters in Jewish Old French get no pointing.

The system, as a summary of all the texts studied, functions as follows:

1) French [a] is generally rendered by *pataḥ* (x̱; אַ) or *qamaṣ* (x̧; אָ), depending on its length.

In the treatise on fever, most of the time *pataḥ* is used, almost exclusively with *ʔaleph* as *mater lectionis*. *Fevres* resorts to *qamaṣ* for Hebrew words only and sometimes for final *-a* of Latin words.[69]

In the other texts, both *pataḥ* and *qamaṣ* appear; without *ʔaleph* as *mater lectionis*, the [a] is short, with *mater lectionis*, it is longer. The lengthening by use of *ʔaleph* generally appears when a consonant had been effaced and in verbal endings.[70]

Even if Wedding Song I is not punctuated, the consonants hint at a system that resembles the Bible glossaries: cf. stanza 2, verse 1: לבטיילא *l bṭyylʔ* (*la bataille* 'the battle'), with two short [a]s, but, in the next verse: האלטא *hʔlṭʔ* (*haute* 'high'), with a long one.

Wedding Song II differs as to its orthographic system compared to the other texts consulted here, cf. double-vowels:[71] a consonant gets a vowel sign followed by an *ʔaleph* with an own vowel sign as in 2.2 פַּאָטְ *paāṭ* < *faut* 'need'; 2.3, 7.3 פַּאָשׂ *paāś* < *pas* 'step'. Exceptionally, in 3.4 and 5.2, we find פַּאשׂ *paś* < *pas* 'step' with just one vowel.

2) French [e] and [ɛ] are expressed with *ṣere* (אֵ), sometimes with *segōl* (אֶ), generally followed by a *yod* as *mater lectionis*. In the treatise on fever however, *segōl* only appears in Hebrew words, in the Glossaire de Bâle it marks a distinction between other <e>s within a word or group of words.[72]

68 Banitt 1972 (vol. I: Introduction): 59: 7.1.11; 63: 7.1.37.

69 Kiwitt 2001: 22f.

70 Banitt 1972 (vol. I: Introduction): 65; Banitt 2005 (vol. I: Introduction): 202; Pope 1952: 96 (§ 199).

71 Cf. Fudeman 2010: 160.

72 Cf. Banitt 1972 (vol. I: Introduction): 66.

Long [e:] and [ɛ:] have double *yod* as *matres lectionis*. However, double *yod* is difficult to interpret unambiguously for all texts, as it not only can express [e:] and [ɛ:] as just mentioned, but also the diphthongs [ej] and [ɛj], as explained earlier.[73] This ambiguity, which is the same for Christian Old French written texts of the Middle Ages, as orthography does not always reflect the newest developments of sounds,[74] can thus not be definitely illuminated by the writing of French in Hebrew letters.

3) French [i] is represented with *ḥiriq* (אִ), most of the time followed by a single *yod*. As first element of a diphthong, double *yod* is preceded by a *ḥiriq*.

4) French [o] is transcribed with *ḥolam magnus*, which is a *ḥolam* in combination with *vav* as *mater lectionis* (וֹ); sometimes, the *vav* is omitted.

Long [o:] gets an *ʔaleph* in addition, preceding *ḥolam magnus*, in both the Bâle and the Leipzig glossaries: Leipzig (13774) פְּאוֹטֵייר *pʔōṭēyr* < Lt. *posse, *potere* ('to be able to'; in this context: 'to rule'); Leipzig (17980) פְּאוֹשְׂטֵיה *pʔōśṭēh* ('power').[75] The other texts examined here do not distinguish between [o] and [o:]

Ḥolam magnus furthermore expresses some diphthongs in connection with *yod*: the French diphthong <oi> [wɛ] appears either imitating its Latin-written model as *ḥolam magnus* followed by two *yod* and vocalized by *schwa*, cf. MS 302 (762) מַנוֹייְרְשׂ *manōyyrś* ('manor houses'), or vocalized by *ṣere*, then illustrating the phonetic realization.[76]

The diphthong [ou] is written with *ḥolam magnus* followed by *ʔaleph* and *vav*, cf. Wedding Song II, 2.4: טוֹאוּטְ *ṭōʔūṭ* ('all' SG.F) and MS 302 (164) פְּלוֹאוּט *plōʔūṭ* ('please!').

5) For the French phonemes [ø], [œ] and [u], [y], there are more varieties in the use of points and *matres lectionis* to be found, and the question as to how letters and sounds are to be attributed is more complicated here, a question equally important for Latin- and Hebrew-written French.

The fact that for the phonemes [y], [ø] and [œ], there do not exist special graphemes in the Hebrew script adds to the complexity of the situation concerning the differentiation between these phonemes in Hebrew Old French.

The following figure summarizes the overall situation:

	[y]	[u]
MS 302	*šuruq*/ *qubuṣ*	*ḥataf qamaṣ* (+ *šuruq*)/ *šuruq*
Bâle	*šuruq*/ *qubuṣ*	*šuruq*

73 Cf. Kiwitt 2001: 23; 2013: 63; 78f.; Banitt 1972 (vol. I: Introduction): 66.

74 Cf. Gossen 1967: 149; Pope 1958: § 689 ff.; esp. § 698.

75 Banitt 2005 (vol. I: Introduction): 205; 1972 (vol. I: Introduction): 68, the long [o:] resulting from muted *l*, *r*, and *s*.

76 Cf. also Kiwitt 2001: 23; Zwink 2017: 148; Banitt 1972 (vol. I: Introduction): 77.

	[y]	[u]
Leipzig	*šuruq*/	*šuruq*
	qubuṣ/	
	vav + *ḥolam*	
	šuruq + 2 *yod*	

	[y]	[u]
Fevres	*qubuṣ* + *vav*/	*qubuṣ*/
	vav + *ḥiriq*	*vav* + *ḥiriq*
	šuruq (sometimes)	
WS II	*šuruq*/	*qubuṣ* + *vav*
	qubuṣ + *vav*	

	[œ] and [ø]	[o]
MS 302	*šuruq* / *vav* + *ḥolam*	vav + *ḥolam*
Bâle	*qubuṣ*	"
Leipzig	*vav* + *ḥolam*	"
Fevres	*qubuṣ* + *vav*/	"
	vav + *ḥiriq*/	
	vav + *ḥolam*	
WS II	Ø	"

5.1) [ø] and [œ]

The resulting confusion is for instance distinct in the treatise on fever,[77] where *qubuṣ* (ֻx) followed by *vav* in Hebrew-written Old French can correspond to [œ] and [ø], as in בֻּובְּרַאגָֿא *būḇragā̄ə* 'potion' (f. 181v: 19; 182r: 1; 5) or קָֿאלֻור *q̄alūr* 'heat' (f. 180v: 7). Moreover, the writer of *Fevres* uses *vav* pointed either with *ḥolam* or with *ḥiriq*, where Latin writers would choose either <o> or <eu>: this leads to an orthography different of the example just presented above: קָֿאלוֹר *q̄alōr* 'heat' (fol. 180r: 7), alongside with קָֿאלוִר *q̄alwir* (fol. 182r: 5); פוֹ *pō* 'some' (fol. 180v: 1), דוֹלוִר *dōlwir* 'pain' (fol. 181v: 13).

Banitt[78] shows that in the Bible Glossaire de Leipzig, *ḥolam* stands for these phonemes as in the word (15471) אָבוֹבְּרוֹנְט *ābōḇrōnṭ* 'they will give water' alongside with (15474) אָבֵיבְּרַנְט *ābēḇranṭ* 'watering', or in (262) פּוֹיְילְא *p̄ōyylə* 'leaf'.

In the Glossaire de Bâle, *qubuṣ* stands for [œ] or [ø].[79]

In MS 302, *šuruq* and *ḥolam* can, alongside with [y] and [o], also express [œ] and [ø], respectively; cf. (654) נְווֹא *nvōʔ* 'nephew', (3) פְּלוּבוֹיְיר *plūḇōyyr* (*pleuvoir*) 'to rain' for [ø], and for [œ]: (380) קָלוֹרְא *q̄ālōrə* 'heat', (636) אוֹבְרְא *ōḇrə* 'œuvre'.

In Wedding Song II, there are no examples for the phonemes [œ] or [ø].

77 Kiwitt 2001: 75 f. 182r; Zwink 2017: 130, 159.

78 Cf. Banitt 2005 (vol. I: Introduction): 205: 7.1.9.6; 204: 7.1.9.4 and 220: 7.2.2.3 and 221.

79 Cf. Banitt 1972 (vol. I: Introduction): 69.

5.2) [y] and [u]

The ambiguity stated earlier for the way vowels appear in the documents holds for the French vowels [y] and [u] as well. Letters and pointing that the writers use, can often be interchanged. The tendency in the application of signs as they can be found in the different texts is as follows:

5.2.1) [y]

In the Glossaire de Bâle, [y] is mostly expressed by *šuruq* (וּ) and, some rare times, by *qubuṣ*, which Banitt analyzes as a more modern orthography, showing the graphical reaction to the development of this new sound.[80]

In MS 302, it is likewise *šuruq* that most of the time represents [y], cf. (28) אַוֹנְטוּרָא *awōnṭūrā* 'he strayed', but sometimes [u]: (46) אָגוּטֵיאָה *āgūṭēəh* 'adjoined' (SG.F). Similarly to the use observed in the Glossaire de Bâle, the vowel sign *qubuṣ* appears rarely in this glossary.

The Glossaire de Leipzig has some more ways of writing [y]. It resembles the two other glossaries as it uses *šuruq* and some rare times *qubuṣ*,[81] but Leipzig furthermore features *ḥolam* in order to express [y] as in (2697) אָלוֹמְרַש *ālōmraś* 'you will light' (FUT. 2SG) and in (18766) אָנְדוֹרְצִי *āndōrṣī* 'hardened' (PTCP.PASS). With ויי, the glossary uses yet another way of writing [y].[82]

Wedding Song II is similar to the glossaries in this respect. However, Wedding Song II uses several times *qubuṣ* followed by *vav* to designate [y] – but also [u] – as can be seen in the following examples: [y] in 1.4: טֻו *ṭū* 'you'; 2.1: נֻולְא *nūlə* 'no'; 2.4 אַקוֹטֻומֵייאָה *aqōṭūmēyəh* 'customary' (SG.F), but in 3.1: רֵייפֻוזֵייאָה *ryypūzēyəh* 'turned away' (< Lt. *pulsare*). Regarding the last example, the evolution of sounds prove that *qubuṣ* and *vav* must stand for [u], as this is the vowel, to which CLatin short *u* developed in closed syllables.[83]

In *Fevres*, *qubuṣ* can equally express [y], cf. אַקֻונְא *aqūnə* 'some', but the writer of the fever treatise in addition uses *vav* vocalized with *ḥiriq* for the sound [y] – as mentioned earlier, this sign also expresses [œ] – cf. f.180 r: 12: דְאשׁוִץ *dəświṣ* 'about'. This way of writing [y] seems to be idiosyncratic, as it differs from the use in all the other Jewish-French texts.[84]

In this context, the French diphthong <uï> [yi] has to be mentioned, which appears as *šuruq* (וּ) + two *yod* in the Glossary MS 302, cf. (32) פּוּיְירוֹנְט *pūyyrōnṭ* ('they will escape'), but as *vav* + *ḥiriq* in *Fevres*: קוֹנְדוִץ *qōndwiṣ* 'conducts' (f. 180r: 18).

The writer of the Glossaire de Leipzig shows a tendency of omitting the second part of the Francien diphthong [yi], as, e.g., (670) פּוּזְרֵישֵׁש *pūzrēśeś* 'drawer of water' (PL.F).

80 Cf. Banitt 1972 (vol. I: Introduction): 70.

81 Cf. Banitt 2005 (vol. I: Introduction): 205: 7.1.9.7.

82 Cf. Banitt 2005 (vol. I: Introduction): 205: 7.1.9.7.

83 Cf. Rheinfelder I 1976: 26 (§59).

84 Cf. Kiwitt 2001: 23; Zwink 2017: 130; Banitt 1971/72 (Judeo-French): 424; Banitt 1971–1972: 424.

5.2.2) [u]
The sound [u] – in Latin-written Old French represented by the digraph <ou> from the late 12th century onwards[85] – is realized by *šuruq* in the Bâle and the Leipzig glossaries,[86] which means that the writers use the same sign as for [y]. The treatise on fever uses again *qubuṣ* for [u], alongside with *vav* + *hiriq*.[87] This shows once more that the phonemes [y] and [u] – and furthermore [ø] and [œ] – are not easily to be separated.

In Wedding Song II, the vowel [u] is expressed by *qubuṣ* + *vav* as in 3.1, as mentioned under [y], but also with *vav* + *ḥolam* as in לַאבּוֹרֵייְאָה *labōrēyəh* 'worked'.

Concerning the French vowel [u], MS 302 differs from the system used by the other texts, with some few exceptions where the writer uses *šuruq*:[88] MS 302 transcribes [u] by the composition of two signs: either *ʔaleph* vocalized with *ḥataf qamaṣ* (אֳוּ), or only *ḥataf qamaṣ* without the *ʔaleph* as *mater lectionis*, followed by a *šuruq*, as for instance in (19) אֵיקֳוּטֵישְׁמוֹיי *ēqaūṭēś mōyy* 'hear me' (IMP), or (24) אִיאָטֳוּקָא *ī aṭaūqa* 'and touched' (conjunction + PRF). This double sign for the vowel [u] follows the Latin-spelled French model developing at that time.

Schwa plays two roles, similar to the Hebrew system: it can be quiet [Ø] (*schwa quiescens*) or realized as [ə] (*schwa mobile*), the difference between the Hebrew *schwa mobile* and the French one consisting in the fact that the Hebrew one depends on the surrounding consonants and phonotactics. The treatise on fever marks the differentiation of the two *schwa*s constantly by writing *ʔaleph* after *schwa mobile* also inside a word, which can be considered a new element in Hebrew written Old French.[89] The writers of the other texts only mark [ə] with an *ʔaleph* following *schwa* at the end of a word (cf. text samples below). This is also true for the Glossaire de Leipzig, even though the glossary dates from the same period as *Fevres*, end of 13th / beginning of 14th century. This shows that the writer of the medical treatise is proceeding in more systematic a way than his colleagues, and that this seems not to be a general evolution of Hebrew Old French spelling rules, but the proper initiative of the treatise's writer.

2.2 Phonetics and phonology – linguistic particularities of Judeo-French vowels
In the following, I will give a condensed overview over the most important phonetic and phonological features deviating from Francien, which can be deducted from the texts treated here. The editions of the texts all provide a detailed description, to which I refer for further information.

85 Pope 1952: 278 (§ 698); 457 (§ 1220); Rheinfelder I 1976: 43 (§113/114 and § 60).
86 Cf. Banitt 1972 (vol. I: Introduction): 68; Banitt 2005 (vol. I: Introduction): 194: 7.1.1.3.
87 Kiwitt 2001: 23/24.
88 E.g., שׁוּפְּלָא *śūp̄la* 'blew' (PRF.3SG).
89 Cf. Kiwitt 2001: 24.

2.2.1 Vowels

1) Pretonic [a] often appears as [ə] or [ɛ] in the treatise on fever and the Bible glossaries.[90] In the text-sample of *Fevres*, there appears twice the form אֵיפּוֹשְׁטוּמְא *ēpōšṭūmə* for *apostume* 'abscess', but the form with *a*- is likewise represented.

2) Both Wedding Songs and the Bible glossaries MS 302 and Bâle show a change of vowel from [e] to [a] in tonic and in pre-tonic syllables at the beginning of a word. In some cases, it is [e] preceding [s] that becomes [a], or preceding the nasal-consonant <n>; sometimes it is the Latin prefix *ex*- changing to *ad*-. Wedding Song I is unvocalized, but the writer makes explicit by writing *ʔaleph* following the initial consonant and preceding the nasal-consonant that he intends to express [a], cf. 2.9 באנרש *b̠ʔnrś* for *viendras* 'you will come' (FUT.2SG) and ראנדרא *rʔndrʔ* for *rendre* 'deliver' (INF), and in 6.4; 4.1 אַפּרינש *ʔ[m]pryns* for *empris* 'untertaken' (PTCP.PASS) etc. Wedding Song II has 2.4 אַטְרְא *aṭrə* for *estre* 'to be' (INF) and 6.2 טַרַאטְא *ṭ'araṭə* for *(t')arreste* 'you-stop' (PRN.SG.CO + IMP.SG); the Bible Glossary MS 302 (355) אַגָרָא *agārā* (PST.3SG) for *esgarer* 'stray'; furthermore, there are various examples of the verb אַנְקוֹנְטְרֵיר *anqōnṭrēr* for *encontrer/ancontrer* 'meet' (INF).

The sample of the Glossaire de Bâle shows the following example: אַנְקוֹטְרְא *anqōṭrə* for *encontre* 'encounter, battle'.

Leipzig demonstrates an evolution of free [e] towards [i] in almost all positions,[91] for which MS 302 only has some rare examples, as in (374) אַנְגְרִיגְא *angrīgə* 'became aggravated', cf. *engregier*. The other texts do not present this element.

3) In the Bâle as well as the Leipzig glossaries, *-er-* is often rendered as *-ar-*[92] as the text sample below from Bâle shows: דְפְּצַרָא *dpṣara* for *depeciera* 'break' (FUT.3SG). This is in line with the use in Latin-written Old and Middle French, as Pope describes, especially in eastern France.[93]

4) Vulgar Latin accentuated [ɛ] in open and closed syllable and accentuated [a] after a palatal ordinarily developed to the diphthongs [iɛ] and [ie][94], but in all texts consulted here, this vowel appears as long or short monophthong [ɛ] / [e] or diphthong [ɛi] / [ei] – depending on how this digraph has to be interpreted in the respective case.[95]

This holds for all analogue cases, i.e. verbal and substantival endings, where the diphthong [iɛ] and [ie] came along.[96]

90 Cf. Kiwitt 2001: 32; Banitt 1972 (vol. I: Introduction): 72, cf. (1832) טְרְאבֵירש *ṭrəb̠ērś* (*travers*) 'across'; Banitt 2005 (vol. I: Introduction): 218, Edzard 2011: 52, cf. (614) אֵטְרֵיט *eṭrēṭ* (*atrait*) 'attraction'.

91 Cf. Banitt 2005 (vol. I: Introduction): 219.

92 Cf. Banitt 1972 (vol. I: Introduction): 73; Banitt 2005 (vol. I: Introduction): 220.

93 Cf. Pope 1952: 187 (§ 496).

94 Cf. Rheinfelder I 1976: 27 (§ 64); 91 (§ 225); Pope 1952: 103 (§ 225), 163 (§ 414).

95 For all Jewish Old French texts the question arises if consonant with *ṣere* + double-*yod* corresponds to [ɛ:] or must be considered a diphthong [ei]; cf. Kiwitt 2013: 63; 78; Banitt 1972 (vol. I: Introduction): 66; but Fudeman 2010: 160; in Zwink 2017: 134, *ṣere* + double-*yod* is interpreted as either diphthong or monophthong carrying the word-accent.

96 Cf. examples in Kiwitt 2001: 28f.; Zwink 2017: 145f.

Examples: the Bible Glossary MS 302 (552) has מוֹנְגֵּייְר *mōnǧēyr*, for *mangier* 'food', in the Glossaire de Bâle the same noun (*mangēyr*) is documented, slightly differently vocalized, as the text sample below shows.[97]

In the Glossaire de Leipzig, an analogue development can be found, regarding the Latin suffix *-ariu*,[98] cf. פָּנֵייר *panēyr* 'basket' in the text sample below.

The text sample of *Fevres* presented below provides many examples as well, cf. [ie] + nasal, which appears as בֵּיינְט *ḇēynṭ* 'comes' (PRS.3SG); the "gallbladder" is represented in the Anglo-Norman form פֵּייל *p̄ēyl*, corresponding to *fel* in Latin-written Françien.[99]

Wedding Song I consistently uses the ending *-ēyr* (-ʔyyr) for *-ier* for nouns – if the supposed pointing here is right, it would be a consonant punctuated with *ṣere* followed by two *yod* and *resh* – as for example in 2.4 רִיבֵּיירא *riḇēyrə* for *riviere* 'river' or in 4.6 ארבלטייר *arbaleṭēyr* for *arbalestier* 'cross-bowman', and in all nouns finishing the French lines of stanza 5.

In Wedding Song II, the general use of double-*yod* after all consonants vocalized with *ṣere* or *segōl* is striking: cf. 4.3 מֵייטְרֵיי *mēyṭrēy* 'put' (FUT.1SG); all class I infinitive endings are written *-ēyr* with two *yod*, cf. 1.3 פַּשֵׂייר *paśēyr* 'pass'.[100]

5) Vulgar Latin accentuated [e] in open syllable, which developed into the diphthong [oi] by way of [ei][101] appears differently in the different documents: the treatise on fever mostly writes וֹיֵי, which Kiwitt transcribes as <ōyē> as in דרוֹיֵיט *drōyēṭ* 'droit' (f. 20v: 13), the vowel sign *ṣere* pointing at a phonetic realization by [wɛ].[102]

The Bible Glossary MS 302 tends more to the older form [ei], as visible in (767) פָּרַיְיץ *parayyṣ* 'paroi' [parai] ('wall') < Lt. *paries* or in (676) רֵייְאַמְשׂ / רֵייְאַמְא *rayyaməś* / *rēyamə* 'royaume(s)' ('kingdom(s)') < Lt. *regimen* + *regalis* and (911) וֵייאוֹנְץ *wēyyʔōnṣ* 'seeing' (PTCP.PRS.ACT). Alongside these forms, there appear several examples for [oi], as in (753) אַבְוִייְר *aḇwyyr* 'possessing' or (882) אַרְשׂוֹיְיר *ar-śōyyr* 'yesterday night' and analogically (819) פּוֹיְיץ *pōyyṣ* 'pitch'.

The Glossaire de Bâle uses the digraph <oy>, often written with two *yods* and unvocalized in order to make sure that *vav* and *yod* must be considered as consonants following the Latin-written model. Banitt states though that the pronunciation here must be [ɛ], as the punctuation with *ṣere* in other examples shows:[103] (310) פֵּוֹילְלא *peōyllə* 'hair'; (312) בֵּיאֵוִיט *ḇēewyṭ* 'he saw' (IPF.3SG).

For the Glossaire de Leipzig, one cannot determine a homogeneous tendency of how [oi] is rendered;[104] generally, forms on <ay>, <ei>, <e>, and <u> can be deduced from the text, as it is characteristic of the orthography in Anglo-Norman writing, which

97 Cf. Banitt 1972 (vol. I: Introduction): 74.

98 Cf Rheinfelder I 1976: 107 (§ 275); Banitt 2005 (vol. I: Introduction): 214, 221.

99 Cf. Zwink 2017: 173.

100 Cf. Fudeman 2010: 160.

101 Cf. Rheinfelder I 1976: 20 (§ 40); Pope 1952: 105 (§ 228ff.) and 194 (§ 518f.).

102 Cf. Kiwitt 2001: 30.

103 Cf. Banitt 1972 (vol. I: Introduction): 77.

104 Cf. Banitt 2005 (vol. I: Introduction): 214.

did not follow the development from [ei] to [oi].[105] Some examples from the edition of the glossary can illustrate these different writings, besides the mostly used digraph ויִי, which renders the Latin-written model, cf: (582) אָרְשׁוֹיְיר *ār-śōyyr* 'yesterday night', the text has (936) אָרְשֵׁייר *ār-śēyr*, (697) אָבַיְינְא *āḇayynə* 'oats', (379) אָדֵיטְרְרַיי *ādēṭrrayy* 'go to the right' (FUT.2SG), (7329) נוֹרְצִירֵינט *nōrṣīrēnṭ* 'darken' (FUT.3PL).

Wedding Song I (3.7) has דיפלאייר *dyplʔyyr* 'unfurl' (INF) < Lt. *des+plicare*, which represents the older form with diphthong [ei].

In general, Wedding Song II shows a preference for <*ēy*> in every possible phonetic context. As to the category presented here, the song prefers the older form with <*ēy*>, cf. 2.4: דֵייט *dēyṭ* 'must' (PRS.3SG).

Old French <e> often appears as <ei> in Jewish texts – similar to the before mentioned <ei> resulting from Latin *a* (cf. topic 4), but this is specially striking in Wedding Song II: cf. 7.4 טַאיירְא *ṭayyrə* 'land' (compare to WS I 3.6: טֵירא *ṭērʔ*); *ēy* for <e> in front of a consonant,which entails the omission of the consonant, cf. 3.2 דֵייטִינֶייאה *dēyṭīnäyyəh* 'destiny'; 3.4 מַיילֶייאְה *mayyläyyəh* for *malaise* 'difficulty'. Furthermore, Wedding Song II writes *ēy* for <e> (< Lt. short <i>), cf. 4.3 מֵייטְרֵיי *mēyṭrēy* for *mettrai* 'put' (FUT.1SG).

6) The diphthong [ai], from Lt. *a*, preceding a consonant, developed to open [ɛ] in western Old French and in Anglo-Norman, whereas it was maintained as a diphthong in eastern regions.[106] The diphthong [ai] developed to closed [e] when final.[107]

There are examples in the text samples showing by their vocalization or the use of one single *yod* instead of two that this sound is realized in many cases as a monophthong in the texts studied here: MS 302 פֵּייזוּנְט *pēyzwnṭ* (PTCP.PRS.ACT) 'doing'; Bâle מֵיטְרְא *mēṭrə* 'educator'; Leipzig פֵּיר *pēr* (INF) 'to do'; alongside with this representation of the Anglo-Norman pronunciation [ɛ], the glossary shows examples with the original diphthong, which can be explained by the graphical imitation of the Latin-written model;[108] *Fevres* פֵּייטֵייץ *pēyṭēyṣ* (IMP.PL) 'make';Wedding Song I פאיי *pʔyy* (IMP.SG) 'do'; Wedding Song II 1.2 פֵּיירְא *pēyrə* (INF) 'to do'; 2.2 מַיי *mayy* 'but', 3.4 מַיילֶייאְה *mayyläyyəh* 'difficulty', and 7.4 נֶייאְה *näyyəh* 'snow'.

7) Pretonic [i] has the tendency of becoming [e] in the Glossaire de Leipzig, as (15867)[109] דֵירוֹנְט *dērōnṭ* (FUT.3PL) for *diront* 'they will say'.

8) The texts reveal a confusion in the graphical representation of the vowels before a nasal consonant:

Latin-written vowel + *n*/*m* appear mostly as <on>, sometimes as <an> and very rarely as <in> in the Bible Glossary MS 302, e.g., (574) גִינְפְלְא *gīnplə* 'veil'. A special feature of this glossary is the sometimes appearing diacritic sign on the nasal-vowel indicating the nasal, instead of <n>, as for example in (410) גֵירמוֹנְמוֹט *germōnmōṭ* 'germination'.

105 Cf. Pope 1952: 458 (§ 1223).

106 Pope 1952: 199 (§ 533); 444 (§ 1157).

107 Pope 1952: 197 (§ 528 ff.).

108 Banitt 2005 (vol. I: Introduction): 219.

109 Cf. Banitt 2005 (vol. III): 1197.

Bâle uses mostly <an>, an orthography which includes older forms on <en>.[110] In this respect, *Fevres* shows the same development.[111] Furthermore, the glossary reveals graphic realizations of nasal vowels on <en> and <on>.

The Glossaire de Bâle regularly vocalizes the vowel next to the ending *-ment* with *pataḥ* as in אַפְּרֵינַמַּאנט *aprēnamanṭ* for *aprenement* 'teaching', the Glossaire de Leipzig writes *schwa* preceding the ending, and *pataḥ* within it, as in (8) אֵיטַנְדְמַנְט *ēṭandmanṭ* 'firmament'.

Apart from that, the Glossaire de Leipzig uses <in> with *hiriq* which mirrors the Latin writing, as well as <en> and <on>.

The Bible Glossary MS 302 and Wedding Song II follow the same rules concerning the orthography of the Latin-French ending of nouns *-(e)ment:* they appear as *-(e)mont* vocalized with *o* in Hebrew-written French, cf. Wedding Song II, stanza 4.3: דְיילַייְמוֹנְט *dəylayymōnṭ* 'delay'.

The treatise on fever however uses the vowel-signs and letters much more closely following the Latin-French model: *-(e)ment* is vocalized with *e*: cf. אֵיטוֹפְּאמֵינְט *ēṭōpəmēnṭ* 'constipation'.

In Wedding Song I, the nasal consonant <n> often appears alone, but sometimes, a *vav* shows that the nasal vowel is <o>, as can be seen in 2.6 קלונקלוזא *qlwnqlwzʔ* 'closed' (PTCP.PASS.SG.F). The consonants reveal furthermore that Latin-written <en> is realized as <an>, cf. 2.9; 6.4 and 4.1, already mentioned above. This is similar to the Glossaire de Bâle and *Fevres*. Wedding Song II uses in most of the cases <en> and <on>.

9) *Fevres* and the Glossaries of Leipzig and Bâle tend to reduce the Francien diphthong [yi] to [y], which points to dialects of eastern Gaule.[112] The text sample of *Fevres* presented below, however, only provides one example, where the writer does use the diphthong. In MS 302, the diphthong is attested. In the two Wedding Songs, there is no hint at this reduction either.

2.2.2 Consonants

1) MS 302, the Glossaire de Leipzig, *Fevres*, and both Wedding Songs do not use <d> as epenthetic consonant between *n* and *r*, or *l* and *r*, a widespread phenomenon in the northern and eastern Old French dialects, also of Lorraine.[113]

The Glossaire de Bâle differs on that point, the writers do use the epenthetic consonant with *l* and *r*, the only exception being derived forms of *prehendere*.[114]

2) Intervocalic secondary *d* (having developed from t) or *d* in contact with *r* opens sometimes into a fricative and is then rendered with *zayin*, as for example in MS 302,

110 Rheinfelder I 1953: 75 (§ 193).

111 Kiwitt 2001: 32.

112 Banitt 1972 (vol. I: Introduction): 77; Banitt 2005 (vol. I: Introduction): 206; Zwink 2017: 149; Rheinfelder I 1953: 99; Pope 1952: 194 (§ 517).

113 Cf. Banitt 2005 (vol. I: Introduction): 222; Edzard 2011: 57; Kiwitt 2001: 34. Wedding Song I uses the <d> once in 2.9: ראנדרא *rʔndrʔ* 'deliver'.

114 Cf. Banitt 1972 (vol. I: Introduction): 78/79.

where all forms of *tarder* ‘hesitate, be late’ appear with *zayin*, as it is likewise the case in the Glossaire de Bâle and in the treatise on fever.[115] Banitt states for the Glossaire de Leipzig, that there only are some relicts of fricative *d*.[116]

3) Pre-consonantal [n] and [m] after nasalized vowel are sometimes omitted, cf. Wedding Song II 1.3 קוֹוִיֵין *qōwīēn* for *convient*, 4.4 מֵייטְנִיר *mēyṭnīr* for *maintenir* ‘maintain’, 6.1 אְטְנְדוּ *əṭn(i)du* for *entendu* ‘heard’ and also 4.2 גְרֹאְט *groəṭ* for *gront* ‘big’; these examples show that at the time this song was written, the nasal consonant phonetically had merged with the preceding nasal vowel, a phenomenon, which Pope (1952: § 436) accordingly locates in the Middle French period. In the verbal and nominal endings, however, the *n* appears, again following the Latin-written model. The rhyme in Wedding Song I, stanza 4, where the participle passive words on *-prins* rhyme with the noun *pris* ‘renown’, shows that the nasal consonant [n] had merged with the nasal vowel *i* as well.[117]

The same observation is true for the Bâle and the Leipzig glossaries.[118] The example from the beneath cited text-sample from Bâle can illustrate this: אַנְקוֹטְרָא *anqōṭrə* ‘encounter; battle’. Also *Fevres* has examples of this writing.[119] This phenomenon can not be found in MS 302.

4) With the intention of making the two hemistichs in Wedding Song II 3.4 rhyme properly, the writer omits the intervocalic *-s-* in מַיילֶייאָה *mayyläyyəh* for *malaise* ‘difficulty’.

5) Pre-consonantal *l* is often omitted without the development of a diphthong, contrary to the consequence of the vocalization of pre-consonantal *l* to *u* in Francien.[120] This omission has to be reckoned among dialectal elements of the north-eastern regions of France (Picardy, Wallonie, Lorraine, Champagne).

This is true for the Bible Glossary MS 302, cf. (316) קָאפָּא *qāpā* ‘heated’ (PRF.3SG), (388) הָטוּרְשׁ *haṭūrś* ‘height’.

In the Glossaire de Leipzig, the non-pronunciation of pre-consonantal <l> is made explicit by the vocalization with *schwa*, cf. Leipzig (3225) with preceding <o> in פּוֹלְשְׁטֵיה *pōlśṭēh* ‘falseness’.[121] After <a>, <l> is omitted: cf. Leipzig (208) אַנְא *anə* for *aune* ‘cubit’.

The Glossaire de Bâle shows a similar development. Here, the elongated <a> preceding the original place of <l> is often supported by a supplementary <s>: (425) אַשְׁטְרָא *aśṭrə* for *autre* ‘other’.[122]

Wedding Song I: 1.7 שאבֿיר *śʔḇyr* ‘save’ < Lt. *salvare* for *sauver*; but: 2.4 האלטא *hʔlṭʔ* ‘high’ < Lt. *altus* for *haute*; and *s* for *u* or *l* can be found in: 4.4 מושט *mwśṭ* ‘much’ < Lt. *multus* for *molt*/*mout*; but: 6.7 מוט *mwṭ* ‘much’.

115 Cf Banitt 1972 (vol. I: Introduction): 70; Edzard 2011: 259 (354); Kiwitt 2001: 32.

116 Cf. Banitt 2005 (vol. I: Introduction): 222.

117 Pope 1952: 170, §§ 436 – 438; cf. as well Fudeman 2010: 162.

118 Cf. Banitt 1972 (vol. I: Introduction): 61; Banitt 2005 (vol. I: Introduction): 206.

119 Zwink 2017: 137.

120 Zwink: 150; Pope: 154 (§ 385ff.); Kiwitt 2001: 33; Banitt 1972 (vol. I: Introduction): 81.

121 Banitt 2005 (vol. I: Introduction): 222

122 Banitt 1972 (vol. I: Introduction): 81.

Wedding Song II: 1.4 and 1.8 וורָא *wwarā* < Lt. *valere* for *valdra/vaudra* 'will be worth'; 2.2 פַּאָט *paāṭ* 'need' < Lt. *fallere* for *falt/faut*;[123] 2.3 מָאה *māh* 'evil' < Lt. *malus* for *mal*; 6.4 and 7.3 דוש and דוֹשׂ *dwś/dōś* < Lt. *dulcis* for *dolce/douce* 'sweet'.

For *Fevres* cf. the text-sample beneath regarding <l> after <a>: אַקוּנְא *aqūnə* for *alcun/aucun* 'some, someone'; אַטְרְא *aṭrə* for *altre/autre* 'other' (f. 40r.-2),[124] alongside with אַאוֹטְרְא *aōṭrə* 'other', attested twice in the text sample beneath, a form which imitates the Latin-written model <au>.[125]

Furthermore, <l> following <o> is omitted as in פּוֹרְא *pō(d)rə* for *poldre/poudre* 'powder' (f. 220v.-1).

6) The exchange of the lateral consonants /l/ and /r/ following or preceding a labial plosive or fricative is current in the texts: cf. some examples from MS 302: (415) אַלְבְרְשׂ *albrś* 'trees'; (403) מַלְבְרְא *malbrə* 'marble'; (615) אַפְּרִיאַמוֹנְט *aprīamōnṭ* 'oppression' for OFr. *afliement* 'affliction', the latter is likewise documented in the Glossaire de Leipzig.[126] This form with <r> for <l> is attested in all texts in Romance languages composed in Hebrew letters, as *REW* article 263 documents.

In the Glossaire de Bâle, there are examples attested, cf. (181) אַפְּלֵיטְרַאשׂ *aplēṭraś* 'you will succeed', which can be found in MS 302 as well. Neither *Fevres* nor Wedding Song I or II do show this phenomenon. In the Glossaire de Bâle, <r> is sometimes dropped (cf. the text sample below): אַבְּרְשׂ *abrś* 'trees', a phenomenon also attested in Christian Old French.[127]

7) Pre-consonantal *s* of etymological origin is in almost all cases missing in most of the texts presented here.[128] In MS 302, this *s* turns up only very rarely, as in אֵישְׁטוֹרְדִיזוֹן *ēśṭōrdīzōn* 'bewilderment' (see text sample below).

This is the case for the Glossaire de Bâle as well, as the text sample below demonstrates: מֵיטְרְא *mēṭrə* 'educator' and דְפְּצַרַא *dpṣara* 'break' (FUT.3SG). Sometimes though, *s* appears, marked with a *schwa*, but its function is only to lengthen the vowel before.[129] This is reminiscent of Latin-written texts, where etymological *s* often is written as well, with the same vowel-lengthening function. The Glossaire de Leipzig does not feature pre-consonantal *s* as the text sample below shows: אֵיטְרְא *ēṭrə* 'to be' (INF); קְאֵנֵישׂ *q̄enēś* 'oak trees' (PL); דְטוֹרְבְא *dṭōrbə* 'trouble'. In *Fevres*, both forms like *apōśṭūmə/ēpōśṭūmə* 'abscess' and *ēṭōpəmēnṭ* 'constipation' are attested.

There is no instance of *s* before consonant in Wedding Song I, cf. two examples in the first stanza: קְטיאיי *q̄ṭyʔyy* for *chastel* and מיקְביר *myq̄byr* for *meschever* 'fail in'. Wedding Song II drops the <s> in all cases but one in stanza 5.4, where the *s* serves to avoid the hiatus, מִיישַׂאָיְישְׂא *mīyśaāyyśə* (*mesaise* 'trouble'), as in the Latin-written model.

123 Cf. Fudeman 2010: 160.

124 Kiwitt 2001: 33.

125 Cf. Zwink 2017: 127 for further examples.

126 Banitt 2005 (vol. I: Introduction): 223.

127 Cf. Pope 1952: 156f (§§ 396, 397).

128 Cf. Zwink 2017: 153f., Banitt 2005 (vol. I: Introduction): 223.

129 Cf. Banitt 1972 (vol. I: Introduction): 85.

8) Apart from the rhyme in the Wedding Songs, the writers of all texts make the silence or, in the opposite case, the pronunciation of final consonants clear by either refraining from vocalizing them, or by adding a strengthening *ʔaleph* or *he* after them, respectively.[130] The *r* of the infinitive ending *-ir* for instance is clearly silent in Wedding Song II 4.4, which can be classified among the dialectal elements of Lorraine.[131]

The weakness of the pronunciation of *r* also holds for its position inside a word, before a consonant. In this position, the writers resort to the means of duplicating the *resh*, or putting a *dagesh* into it, in order to strengthen it.[132]

9) The metathesis involving *r* is a phenomenon that appears often in the texts,[133] as for example in MS 302 (486) לֵישׁדַגְרוֹנְץ *lēś dagrōnṣ* 'the dragons' or in the Glossaire de Bâle (2267) דַגְרוֹנְמַאנט *dagrōnmanṭ* 'monstrosity'.

Fevres shows the metathesis of [-rə] to [-er] as in סֻוכֵר *sūker* 'sugar', which shows a closer resemblance of the form to its Arabic etymology.[134]

2.3 Morpho-syntax

In most ways, Hebrew-written Old French texts follow the Old French language used in the respective parts of France, including some expressions with characteristic traits from dialects of Eastern France and sometimes from dialects of Southern France. The latter can be explained by the exchange, copying, and integrating of manuscripts or parts of manuscripts originating from Jewish cultural centers in the South of France (Narbonne) in documents composed in Northern and Eastern France.[135] There are only few particularities which exclusively appear in Jewish written Old French texts, which are linked to the Hebrew alphabet and the cultural characteristics, to which the texts belong.

In this part, I will shortly relate Hebrew-written Old French to Latin-written Old French regarding the grammatical system as a whole, and then describe the most important differences between the two.

As in all Hebrew Old French texts, function words such as prepositions, articles, pronouns, possessive pronouns and relative pronouns are often merged into a single string with their word of reference, thus reflecting the tradition of the orthography in Semitic languages.

Concerning the two-case system, distinguishing between nominative case (CR) and oblique case (CO) in nouns, adjectives/participles, and articles, which more or less was installed in Old French[136] until it got progressively lost in all French dialects from the 12th century onwards, Judeo-French texts display it to a variable, but on the whole small degree. The two oldest texts examined here, the Bible glossaries MS 302 and Bâle, can be considered as rather differing from each other in this respect: MS 302 has

130 Cf. Banitt 1972 (vol. I: Introduction): 82ff.

131 Pope 1952: 158, § 401 and p. 495, § XXI.

132 Cf. Banitt 1972 (vol. I: Introduction): 83.

133 Cf. Banitt 1972: 83f.

134 For more examples cf. Zwink 2017: 139.

135 Cf. Banitt 1963: 267.

136 Cf. Buridant 2000: § 48: "N'ayant qu'une valeur fonctionnelle négligeable, la déclinaison est généralement flottante dans les textes, ..."

some rare remainders among nouns and adjectives,[137] more among the participle-present forms and participle-perfect forms,[138] whereas the Glossaire de Bâle almost completely renounces using the cases – apart from very rare visible traces.[139] The treatise on fever does not distinguish between the two cases either,[140] whereas the Glossaire de Leipzig observes the cases, as some examples of nouns in the subject case both for SG.M and PL.M show.[141]

In Wedding Song I, there appear many participle-past forms in CR, which leads to the assumption that at least for this scribe, the system was alive, at least related to these forms. Apart form that, there is only one noun in CR SG (6.4 ליקאטייש *ly-q̄ʔṭyyś* 'the castle') and one pronoun in the same case (1.7 נוש *nwś* 'no, none'), for the rest of the nouns the system is not applied. This stands in contrast to Wedding Song II, which does not show any signs of the two-case system.[142] One must point to the fact, though, that perfect participles constructed with *être* are much less in use here, and when they are, they appear in feminine gender, where the *-s* indicating CR SG generally rarely appears in analogy to the masculine forms:[143] קוֹזְא קִייאֵייט אַקוֹטֵומֵייאְה דֵייט אַטְרֵא טוֹאוּטְ אוֹטְרְייֵאְה *q̄ōzə qīyēyṭ aqōṭūmēyəh dēyṭ aṭre ṭōūṭ ōṭryēəh* (*Chose qui eit acotumeie, deit etre tout otreieie*) 'something that is customary must be granted freely' (2.4); נוֹן שְׁרַאַש רְייפֻּוזֵייאְה *nōn śraaś rəyypūzēyəh* [...] 'you will never be turned away' (3.1); טַאיירְא קִי אֵייט לַאבוֹרֵייאְה *ṭayyrə qī ēyṭ labōrēyə* (*Taire qui eit laboreie* [...]) 'land that is worked' (7.4).

2.3.1 The noun

Generally, the formation of nouns follows the usual mechanisms of Latin-written Old French. For an overview related to the different categories of the Old French noun's suffixes in general, see Nyrop (1908), Meyer-Lübke/Piel (1966), and specially aiming at Jewish Old French, Banitt (1963) and Edzard (2011).

Regarding the Bible glossaries, the mission of which is to transfer Hebrew expressions into French, it is particularly interesting to look at the formation of nouns, as due to the process of translation, a phenomenon can be noticed: the patterns of the Hebrew source words, the basis of which are verbal, find their way into the French target.[144]

Banitt emphasizes that while the Old French nouns written in Hebrew characters often seem to be formed on the Hebrew model (*calque*), they exist at the same time in non-Jewish texts as well.[145] The relatively free formation of nouns by help of suffixes implicates an hierarchy of these suffixes. In the glossaries of Bâle, Leipzig, and MS

137 Edzard 2011: 116; 126.
138 Edzard 2011: 131f.; 137f.
139 Cf. Banitt 1972 (vol. I: Introduction): 86: "La distinction des cas a pratiquement disparue: *s* est le signe du pluriel."
140 Cf. Kiwitt 2001: 35, Zwink 2017: 155.
141 Banitt 2005 (vol. I: Introduction): 225.
142 Cf. also Fudeman 2010: 162.
143 Buridant 2000: § 39–41.
144 Cf. Banitt 1972 (vol. I: Introduction): 102f.
145 Cf. Banitt 1972 (vol. I: Introduction): 96.

302, the following most often used suffixes can be detected: *-ement*, *-ure*, and *-ance*,[146] cf. the text sample from the Glossaire de Bâle: אַפְרֵינַמַאנט *aprēnamant* ‘teaching’, a noun usual in Latin-written texts as well.

Concerning the derivation of nouns from verbs, the Hebrew underlying word is often a participle or adjective, and the writers translate by a substantivated adjective,[147] like for example in MS 302 (668) לַפְרוּמְרוּייגָא *la-prūmrūyygə* ‘the-firstborn (F)’, derived from the adjective *premerain* ‘first, initial’. *La-prūmrūyygə* is the translation of Hebrew הַבְּכִירָה *hab-bəkīrā̊* (Gen 19:31), a feminine adjective form.

Bâle translates Hebrew מַכּוֹלֶת with OFr. *mangēyr*, a noun derived from an infinitive, unlike the original Hebrew noun pattern.

These particularities belong to the field of translation, of which the Bible glossaries are a part. The treatise on fever, accordingly, does not show these elements; at most, a tendency towards the formation of nouns with the suffixes *-eté* and *-at* can be detected.[148]

Wedding Song I has no unusual elements in the formation of nouns. The noun for “castle” shows the uncertainty of forms and orthography which is likewise distinct in Latin-written OFr. texts: stanza 1: object-form קְטיאיי, stanza 4: object-form קְטיל and stanza 6: subject-form קאטייש with the CR-article לי in front.

Wedding Song II has usual Francien forms of nouns as well, apart from *māh* for ‘mal’ (2.3). The feminine ending *-ée* is rendered by ייאה-.

2.3.2 The definite article

The sample of MS 302 beneath shows one definite article masculine attached to the determined noun: *l-ēṭōndmōnṭ*, one feminine: *lā-śäqṭēh* and one plural: *lyś-dgrwnṣ*.

The text corpus underlying Edzard 2011 shows moreover that the MS’s writer uses the definite article *lu* when determining masculine nouns beginning with a consonant, which constitutes an Anglo-Norman element (originally for casus obliquus.[149] *La* determines feminine nouns and *le* stands with both masculine (beginning with a vowel) and feminine nouns, this last case, *le* as feminine definite article, being an element from Picardie. The Francien CR-form *li* for masculines does not appear in this Bible glossary.

The article’s vowel is not necessarily omitted in front of a noun beginning with a vowel: sometimes, the <l> belonging to the article gets the punctuation which covers the noun’s vowel (and always forms an orthographical unity with the noun), sometimes the article’s consonant gets an own vowel sign, cf. below in the text sample (378) לְאֵיטוֹנְדְּמוֹנְט *l-ēṭōndmōnṭ* ‘the firmament’, with *lamed* vocalized with *schwa*, but: (843) אַלַאמַשְׂמוֹנט *a-l-amaśmōnṭ* ‘of the gathering’, with *lamed* vocalized with *pataḥ*.

146 Cf. Banitt 1972 (vol. I: Introduction): 102–109 for a detailed list of suffixes applied in the formation of nouns.

147 Cf. Banitt 2005 (vol. I: Introduction): 225, § 7.3.4.2; Banitt 1972 (vol. I: Introduction): 101, § 7.24.1.3f.

148 Kiwitt 2001: 55.

149 Cf. Buridant 2000: § 71; Pope 1961: § 1252; Edzard 2011: 139–141.

For nouns in plural, MS 302 displays several forms: *lēś*, *lēyś*, or *le*, cf. (480) לְווֹלִילְץ *le-wōlīlṣ* 'the poultry', or (742) לֵיְישׁ פּוֹיְיזְרֵישֶׁישׁ *lēyś pōyyzrēśəś* 'the water drawers (F)'.

The case-system plays no role regarding the definite articles of MS 302.

In the Glossaire de Bâle, the definite article masculine is *lo*, an element that points to the western regions of France.[150] Some rare examples of *le* and even less for *lu* can be located in the glossary. For feminine nouns, the writers use the form *la*, and *le* in front of a noun beginning on a vowel. Comparable to MS 302, Bâle uses *lēś* for the plural article (see sample below, here unconnected to the noun). The indefinite article does not appear in the glossary.

The sample of the Glossaire de Leipzig shows לָא *la* as feminine article, once connected with its antecedent (לָאפִּין *la-pīn* 'the-end'), once unconnected (לָא דְטוֹרְבָא *la dṭōrbə* 'the trouble'), and twice the plural article *lēś*, unconnected to its antecedent. Banitt explains[151] that the article SG masculine is written *lo* but pronounced as [lœ]. The most common form of the feminine SG is *la*, sometimes *le*. The forms of the definite article PL do not differ from the Francien forms, either. The glossary does not provide any examples of the indefinite article.

Fevres uses *lī* for feminine SG as in *lī-unə* and *lī aōṭrə*, which is a form from Picardie.[152] Zwink (2017) cites some instances of *li* as CR-form masculine SG and PL in her edition.[153] The form *lə* appears connected to masculine nouns (לְאקוֹרְץ *lə-qōrṣ* 'the body'). The sample below has two examples for the definite article PL, לֵישׁוֹרְצִילְשׁ *lē-śōrṣīlś* 'the eyebrows' and לֵיישׁאֶנְשֵׁינֵייץ *lēyś-enśēnēyṣ* 'the signs'. The picture provided by the text sample shows thus that *Fevres* follows the common Francien forms in general. The indefinite article does not differ from the Francien forms either.[154]

Wedding Song I has two times the definite article CR combined with a noun in CR: 6.4 ליקאטייש *li chateys* 'the castle', and *ly* unconnected to its Hebrew antecedent: 7.4 לי חתן *ḥatan*. The use of this form corresponds to common Francien use in Old French.[155]

Wedding Song II has one definite article SG in CO in stanza 4.4, connected to its antecedent: לְוזַאָגְא *l-ūzaāḡə* 'the custom'.

As to the enclitic forms, the text sample from MS 302 below shows the preposition *a* + *le* in front of a vowel: אֲלַאמַשְׁמוֹנט *a-l-amaśmōnṭ*. Edzard 2011 has an example for *de* + *lu*: (472) דוֹקָאמֵיי *dō-q̄amēy* 'of the camel' and preposition *də* + plural article *lēś*: (443) דֵישׁוָאלֵיאְשׁ *dēś-wālēə-ś* 'of the valleys'.

Fevres shows the same enclitic form *dō* in the excerpt below: דוֹפֵּייל *dō-p̄ēyl* 'from the gallbladder', and דוֹפּוֹייאָה *dō-p̄ōyyəh* 'from the liver'.

150 Cf. Banitt 1972 (vol. I: Introduction): 86/87, § 7.22.11 – 7.22.114; Buridant 2000: § 71.

151 Cf. Banitt 2005 (vol. I: Introduction): 224, § 7.3.1.

152 Cf. Buridant 2000: § 71.

153 Cf. Zwink 2017: 156.

154 Cf. Kiwitt 2001: 36/37.

155 Cf. Buridant 2000: § 71.

2.3.3 The pronoun

2.3.3.1 Possessive pronoun

In MS 302, only the unstressed forms are used – as in all the other Jewish Old French texts – and the case-system is not applied. The forms appearing in the glossary correspond to common use in Old French. The possessive pronouns are randomly attached or not to the corresponding noun, and their position follows the French and not the Hebrew model, i.e. in front of the antecedent.[156] The feminine forms SG – usually *ta* – becomes *te* in front of nouns starting with a vowel. There is one example of a possessive pronoun in the text sample of MS 302 below: *ā-śā-gīz* 'in-his/her-manner'. The same observations are true for the Glossaire de Bâle.[157]

The Glossaire de Leipzig has a similar system. Here too, the feminine SG form rarely appears as *te* instead of common *ta*, which apparently has nothing to do with the initial character of the word, and the writer choses the masculine SG form *son* in front of feminine nouns beginning with a vowel, like in modern French.[158]

Also the treatise on fever follows the common Francien system of the possessive pronouns, the only exception being – like in MS 302 – that the vowel in the feminine pronoun in front of a vowel changes towards <ə>, as can be seen in the text sample below: *śə-ōrīnə* 'his urine'.

In Wedding Song I, the unstressed second person SG טון *ton* is attested three times, the form of CO (stanzas 1, 4, and 5), even though it once designates a nominative (stanza 4). In all three instances, the possessive pronoun is unconnected to its antecedent. In stanza 3, the feminine for טַא *ta* appears, likewise unconnected to its antecedent.

Two forms of the plural can be found; נוטרא *notre* (1PL) in stanza 1 and שאייש *ses* (3PL) in the last stanza. There are no particularities concerning the possessive pronoun in this text.

In Wedding Song II, line 1.2 shows the unstressed form of the first person SG feminine מָא *ma* connected to its antecedent "pensée".

The second person SG masculine only occurs in CO (1.4; 2.2; 4.4; 8.4), although in one case, it is connected to the subject of the sentence (1.4/1; 8.4/1). In line 2.2, the whole Old French hemistich appears without any spaces between the words, for which reason the possessive pronoun (*ton*) is linked to the precedent and the following words and is no longer written imitating the Latin model as in the other cases. Twice, the feminine form *ma* is attested (6.1 and 7.2), both times orthographically connected to its antecedent. Line 3.4 contains the third person SG feminine *sa*, connected to its antecedent. All forms of the possessive pronouns are common forms.

2.3.3.2 Demonstrative pronoun

In Old-French, there exist two parallel sets of forms of the demonstrative pronoun, resulting from the Latin forms *iste* + *ecce* and *ille* + *ecce*, which developed to *cist*/*ceste*,

156 Cf. Edzard 2011: 151ff.

157 Cf. Banitt 1972 (vol. I: Introduction): 88 § 7.22.144.

158 Cf. Banitt 2005 (vol. I: Introduction): 224 § 7.3.3.

cil/*cele*, and the neuter form *ço*/*cel*, and combined with the adverb *ici*, the forms *icil*, *icist* and *icel*, *icest* were created.[159]

In Hebrew-written Old French, the demonstrative pronoun rarely appears; the text samples of the Bible glossaries do not provide any examples. In MS 302, שֵׁישׁ *śēś* 'this' (fol. 105 a, l. 14) is attested rendering Hebrew זאת *zō(ʔ)ṯ* (Amos 2:11: הַאַף אֵין־זֹאת).

According to Menahem Banitt,[160] the Glossaire de Bâle uses *icet* when the Hebrew pronoun is preceded by an article and otherwise *cet.* The forms *icel* or *icet* also appear for the Hebrew form הַלֵּזוּ *hallēzū*. *Ce* is the neutral pronoun.

In the Glossaire de Leipzig,[161] there exists a more differentiated system: the forms *cet*, *cete*, *ces* are in use for the Hebrew forms masculine SG, feminine SG, and PL, respectively; *icet*, *icest* for the more rare Hebrew forms הַלָּזֶה *hallåzɛ*, הַלֵּזוּ *hallēzū*, הָאֵלֶּה *håʔēllɛ*, and the case CR masculine SG is marked by *cis* and *ices*.

Fevres shows no particularities: *śēlə* SG.F is attested in the text sample; Kiwitt moreover lists the forms *celi*, *ceti*; *ceti-ci.*

In both Wedding Songs, the demonstrative pronoun is only used once and in both songs it is the same one: Wedding Song I: צא *ṣʔ* < *ce* 'this' (7.7); Wedding Song II: שְׁיי *śəy* < *ce* 'it' (4.2).

2.3.3.3 Personal pronoun

All Bible glossaries follow the Hebrew syntax as far as the Old French personal pronoun is concerned, which means that its position is after the verb and it most of the time is orthographically attached to it. The post-verbal position of the personal pronoun explains the exclusive use of stressed forms as can be seen in MS 302.[162] Both CR and CO-forms appear in the glossary:[163]

1SG	CR	*ḡē*	CO	*mōyy*
2SG		*ṭū*		*ṭūy* alongside common form *toi* (written *tōy*)
3SG.M		*ēl; īl; īlə* (f. 165b, l. 11)		*lūyy*, *lōyy*
3SG.F	CR	*ēlə* (f. 101a, l. 16)	CO	*lī*
1PL		*nōś* or elsewhere not documented *nōnś*		
2PL		*ḇūś* (f. 5b, l. 22)		
3PL.M	CR	–	CO	*aś* instead of *els* > *eus*
3PL.F		*äls* (אֶילְשׁ), *īls* (f. 164a, l.23)		

159 Buridant 2000: 122/123 § 90/91; Pope 1952: 325 § 844ff.

160 Cf. Banitt 1972 (vol. I: Introduction): 87, § 7.22.141.

161 Cf. Banitt 2005 (vol. I: Introduction): 224, § 7.3.2.

162 Edzard 2011: 144ff.

163 Cf. Rheinfelder 1963 II: 91/106; Pope 1952: 320 (§828); 322 (§ 833).

The Glossaire de Bâle has similar forms as MS 302, but does neither use 3SG.M *ēl*, 1PL *nōnś*, nor 3PL.M *aś*.[164]

The Glossaire de Leipzig does not display any particularities regarding the personal pronoun, apart from *ēl* for CR SG.M, which we find in MS 302, too. For 3PL.M and PL.F, Banitt lists some minor orthographical aberrations.[165]

In the treatise of fever, there are no peculiarities compared to a Latin-written Old French text; the text sample below shows the following examples: CR *īl* 3SG.M and *ēlə* 3SG.F often appear, CO 3SG.M (unstressed) *lī*, alongside with *lə*. CO 3PL (unstressed) *lēyś*.

Concerning CR, Wedding Song I has two times 1SG of the personal pronoun: *je* (stanzas 3 and 5, written ייא) and unconnected to the word before or after. 2SG, *tu*, appears two times (stanza 1 and 7), both connected with the word before or after the pronoun. 3SG, *il*, can be found four times (stanzas 6 and 7), once connected to the following word (stanza 6). Wedding Song I does not often exhibit the subject pronoun, which is common Old French use.[166]

For CO, only the 2SG and 3SG are represented. The direct and indirect forms of the 2SG, *te*, figures 3 times in the song, each time connected to the following word (stanza 3), once to the preceding as well as to the following word (stanza 1). In stanza 5, the writer uses the Picard form of the independent object pronoun (טי *ti*), after having opted for its Francien form in stanza 2 (preposition followed by טויי *toi*). The 3SG (לי *li*) is represented 4 times, three of which connected to another word (stanzas 1 and 6), once unconnected (stanza 6).

Wedding Song II uses the common forms of the personal pronoun. It has an orthographically special feature, though, as the forms *le*, *me*, and *te* often are written with two *yod* (5.3; 6.4: לייטייפרומיש *lyy-ṭyy-prwmy-ś* ‘[I] promise this to you’); instead of only a *schwa* as in all the other texts.

In a similar way, *je* is always written *ḡəy* (2.1; 4.1; 5.3, etc), with two *yods*, in Wedding Song II, as well as *śəy* < *ce* ‘it’ (4.2) and *mēy* < *me* (unaccented) ‘me’ (5.3).

2.3.4 The verb

The verbs show influences from both French and Hebrew in their morphological structure. On the one hand, the Hebrew-written Old French verbs show the Latin morphology concerning the verb endings.

On the other hand, as to the Bible glossaries, the writers try to transfer the Hebrew verb into the French one by simultaneously explaining its structure, which is the reason why we continuously find prefixes attached to the French verb that corresponds to the underlying Hebrew verbal patterns (*binyanim*). Example: Bible Glossary MS 302 (246) אֵידֵוִיווֹלָא *ē-dēvīvōla* instead of *viola* for Hebrew וַיָּחֶל *way-yā̊ḥεl* ‘and he profaned’ (Gen 9:20). In this example, the prefix *de-* imitates the Hebrew causative binyan *hifʕīl*. For a detailed analysis see Banitt *Introduction* 1972: 99–101, Banitt *Introduction* 1995–2005:

164 Banitt 1972 (vol. I: Introduction): 87, § 7.22.143.

165 Banitt 2005 (vol. I: Introduction): 226, § 7.3.5.

166 Cf. Buridant 2000: § 339.

380–382, and Kiwitt 2013: 108f. As Banitt states though (1972: 100), this is not always the case, as several *binyanim* often correspond to one single French prefix.

Concerning the endings of the verb forms, there do not exist important differences compared to the forms in Latin-written Old French. The most important elements will be listed here; for MS 302, additional details can be found in Edzard 2011.

MS 302: following a rather phonetical way of writing, the PRS.IND.3PL and PST.IND forms use the ending *-(e)t* instead for *-ent* and IPF.IND.3PL *-ēynṭ* instead for *-eient*.

Forms of *prendre*: the stem for PST as continuation forms of Vlt. *prensum*: 1SG *prīn* for common Ofr. *pris*; 3SG *prīnṭ* for *prist*, 3PL *(por)prīnrṭ* for *(por)prisdrent*.

In some instances, the verb stems in the glossary differ from its common Ofr. parallel. This is often due to a different process of the formation of the respective word, cf. (166) לָמוֹנִיאֵיר *lamōnīēr* instead of common *lamenter* (Hebrew לִסְפֹּד *li-spōḏ* (Gen 23:2)), which is a denominal derivation from *lamoniement*. Another example is (257) דֵיזַשְׁרוֹרְאגָֿאָרָא *dēzaśrōḡəra* 'he will marry the brother's wife, perform levirate marriage' derived from Lt. *sororius*. This word translates the Hebrew imperative form יַבֵּם *yabbēm* in Gen 38:8 and the second element אֹתָהּ *ʔōṯ-āh* 'her' (ACC).

The ending for 1PL.FUT is *-ōmś* instead of common *-ons*; the Hebrew written form is influenced by the Lt. form *sumus* > OFr. *somes*. The form found in Hebrew letters is similar to PRS.1PL *-omes* in the north-eastern regions Picardie and Wallonie.[167]

Concerning the conditional, the form for 1PL is (158) טְרוּבְרֵיימְשׁ *ṭrūbr-ēymś* for *trover-iiens*; possibly, the same influence underlies here from Lt. *sumus* as for the FUT. 1PL.

The *Introduction* by Banitt to the Glossaire de Bâle consecrates a detailed section to the verb.[168] The present tense is rarely used, because is rarely occurs in the Hebrew original passages. Instead, constructions with the participle present reflect the present tense forms.[169]

Imperfect forms have the common Francien endings, the 3SG appearing either as *-wyṭ* (without punctation), or as *-ēṭ*. An exception is found in the form for 3PL *-īanṭ*. The ending of 1PL.FUT is the same as in MS 302: *-ōmś*.

The perfect forms are common, except for uncertainties in the third conjugation.

As the text-sample shows, the writer uses an element from Picardie in the verbal inflections: 1.SG.FUT has the ending *-a* instead of *-ai* or *-e*, אֵידְפְּצַרָא *ē-dpṣar-a* 'and I will break'.[170]

Also for the Glossaire de Leipzig, Banitt provides a detailed analysis of the verb's morphology;[171] here, the most important elements will be presented.

As to the infinitives, the verbs in the Glossaire de Leipzig often differ from Francien forms as to the vowels *i* and *e*, which means a change of conjugation.

167 Cf. Pope 1952: 339 (§ 895); Buridant 2000: 270 (§ 217).

168 Banitt 1972 (vol. I: Introduction): 88ff.

169 Cf. Banitt 1972 (vol. I: Introduction): 89.

170 Cf. Buridant 2000: 270 (§217).

171 Banitt 2005 (vol. I: Introduction): 226ff.

The glossary follows the Latin-written model as to most verbal endings, for instance as regards the past participle.

The forms of the present tense, appearing rarely in the glossary out of the same reasons mentioned for the Glossaire de Bâle, are common.

The forms of the perfect show some peculiarities, as for example forms on *i* instead of common *a* for the first conjugation (*-er*). The second conjugation (*-ir*) is common. The third conjugation (*-ir*, *-eir*, and *-re*) shows many unexpected analogical forms to the first conjugation.

The imperfect forms do not show special elements, which holds for the endings for the future, too, except for 1PL *-ōmś*, like in MS 302 and the Glossaire de Bâle, which hints at a common usage of this form within Biblical education, transcending the initial dialectal realm.[172]

The forms of the imperative do not differ from the usual forms used in Latin-written Old French texts.

Fevres has some examples of northern- and northeastern-French variants for 1PL.PRS *-ōmēyṣ* alongside with the more often used Francien form *-ōnś*,[173] for which the text sample below is a reference.

Furthermore, infinitives on *-ier* (< Lt. *-are*) appear in the treatise, with the termination *-ir*, which points to north-eastern France.[174]

Wedding Song I displays the common Francien forms, only the additional <n> in all inflected forms connected to *prendre* represents an exception, as stanza 4 shows.

Wedding Song II 1.4 has לַייְרָאשׁ *layyrāś* (2PS.SG.FUT) < *lai*(*i*)*er* for *laisseras*; this form is typical of the eastern parts of France, and for Picardie and Wallonie.[175] The endings follow the Latin-written model.

2.4 *Elements of syntax*

The Bible glossaries do not show much evidence concerning the syntax, due to the fragmented nature of the sentences represented.

Nevertheless, some elements are striking even in the glossaries, and they can be explained by the writer's wish to enlighten the construction of the underlying Biblical expression in the process of translation:

– The indefinite article is not used in the glossaries because it does not exist in Hebrew.

– Hebrew prepositions are often transported to the Old French gloss and directly attached to the gloss, as are all sorts of function words (prepositions, articles, etc., see above), following the Hebrew model – this is an element valid not only for glossaries. Cf. the examples from the different Bible glossaries presented below:

MS 302: אַלַאמַשְׂמוֹנט *a-l-amaśmōnṭ* 'to the accumulation' < לַמִּקְוֵה *lam-miqwɛ*;

MS 302: אָשָׂאגִיז *ā-śā-gīz* 'in her manner' < לְמִינָהּ *lə-mīn-å̄h*.

172 Cf. also Kiwitt 2013: 99.

173 Kiwitt 2001: 38; Zwink 2017: 155.

174 Zwink 2017: 154/155.

175 Cf. Buridant 2000: 285, § 227.

Glossaire de Bâle: אֲבוֹקַ̄אגְ̄א *a-bōq̄agā̄* 'to woodland (Lebanon)' < לְבָנוֹנָה *ləḇāḇōn-ā̊*.
Glossaire de Leipzig: אַנְקוֹרְדְא *an-qōrdə* 'by way of cord' < בָּחֶבֶל *bā̊-ḥɛḇɛl*.

The personal pronoun in the accusative or dative is most of the time positioned after the verb and therefore the stressed one, hereby likewise reflecting the Hebrew original expression with suffix. An example from the Glossaire de Bâle is the following:
אֵידְפְּצַרָא אוֹשׂ *ē-dpṣara ōś* וּנְפַּצְתִּים *u-nəp̄aṣtī-m* 'and I will break them'. The object pronoun of the French gloss is exceptionally separated from the verb.

Regarding syntactical elements in the three running texts chosen here, the use of the subject pronoun is interesting. In Latin-written Old French, the subject pronoun was much less frequently expressed in main clauses than in subordinate clauses until the 13th century.[176] As Zwink shows for *Fevres*, the use of the subject pronoun, contrary to the use in Latin-written Old French texts, can be observed in main clauses, whereas only main clauses beginning with a conjunction (*si*, *por ce*, *o ... o*,) rather follow the general use of dropping the pronoun (*pro-drop*).[177] The text sample presented below provides many examples of the use of the 3SG.F pronoun *ele*, which replaces the noun *īqṭīrīṣīāh* 'icterus'. This pronoun is never dropped; the same holds for the 3SG.M pronoun *il*, designating the sick person and his body, or being the impersonal pronoun. In the sample's first two sentences, the author speaks of himself when he presents a sort of parenthesis on the subjects he already has written about and the subjects he wants to deal with in the following. In these two sentences, he drops the subject pronoun *nous*.

As the excerpt from the fever treatise otherwise gives recommendations on the care of the sick, only verb forms in imperative are used, were a pronoun is not required.

The syntax of the Wedding Songs is conform to the use otherwise attested in versified literature of the time.[178]

The most frequent examples in Wedding Song I for *pro-drop* is the reference to an already mentioned subject, cf. the Hebrew line 2.1, where the subject is the "beloved", with the French line 2.2, where the personal pronoun, referring to the same "beloved" is dropped. In a similar way, the references to the respective subject are settled in stanza 3: here, the groom addresses the bride and warns her about the events she shall experience, and the subject pronouns – 1.SG for the groom and 2.SG for the bride – are all dropped after the groom's initial metaphorical designation of his bride. According to common use again, the subject pronoun is expressed in subordinate clauses, cf. 1.6; 4.9.

In Wedding Song II, impersonal *il* is not expressed, cf. 1.3, 5.4. In stanzas 2 and 4, the respectively first French line starts on the subject pronoun *je*, designating the groom and forming a contrast to the following verses, where the groom tells the bride what she is supposed to do and to think; the same is true for 5.3 and 5.4, but here it is the bride, who reassures her groom; thus, the expression of the subject pronouns underlines the change of protagonist in the respective situation.

After *ja* 'indeed', the subject pronoun is always omitted in the song: Stanza 3 starts on an Old French assertive *ja*, which represents a link to the preceding verses on the

176 Buridant 2000: § 338ff. (424).
177 Zwink 2017: 163.
178 Buridant 2000: 425–432, especially §§ 341, 344, 346.

bride; in stanza 5, the bride starts responding by *ja*, thereby underlining her approval to the groom's plans.

Line 3.3 expresses the subject pronoun only in the subordinate clause – which is true for almost all subordinate clauses of the song and again conform to common Old French use, the only exception being 6.3: *se retien* 'if [I] hold back', where the subject pronoun is dropped.

2.5 Lexicon

This section summarizes the lexical tendencies, which each of the following text samples exhibit. Regarding a detailed study of the respective texts' lexicon, I refer to the studies by Banitt for the glossaries of Bâle and Leipzig, by Edzard for MS 302, and by Kiwitt and Zwink for *Fevres*.

Alongside the three French etymological dictionaries *FEW* by Walther von Wartburg, *REW* by Wilhelm Meyer-Lübke, and *DEAF* by Kurt Baldinger and Frankwalt Möhren, the two Old French dictionaries by Frédéric Godefroy and by Adolf Tobler and Erhard Lommatzsch, the dictionaries specifically targeting the vocabulary documented in texts written by French Jews in the Middle Ages by Raphael Levy, *Recherches lexicographiques sur d'anciens textes français d'origine juive*, the *Contributions à la lexicographie française selon d'anciens textes d'origine juive*, and the *Trésor de la langue des Juifs français au moyen âge* underlie this section.

The vocabulary of all the texts used here mostly represents the common Old French one of the respective period and region, in which the text was created. The specific element, though, is the existence of archaisms, i.e. words that have not found their way into Old French from their Latin or Greek origin,[179] especially in religious context, e.g., the verb אֵיאִיגֵּיר *ēīḡēr* 'build' (< Latin *aedificare*), *FEW* 24, 205a.

Another typical element concerning the Bible glossaries is the word formation of French words by *calque* of the Hebrew initial expression explained earlier, which leads to new variations of otherwise common words in Christian context. Differences occurring on the morphological level of the Old French words can therefore partly be explained by the process of translation already mentioned, which consists in the attempt of modeling the Old French word on the Hebrew original by reproducing the structure of the *binyanim* – but which not necessarily represents a rule, as Banitt states.[180] This is true for all Bible glossaries; cf. some examples from MS 302: (371) פּוֹרְבֵּיְיא *pōrḇēyə* 'travel through' (IMP), translating Hebrew הִתְהַלֵּךְ *hiṯhallēḵ* (Gen 13:17): this French verb with its prefix *por-* is modelled on the Hebrew reflexive *binyan hitpaʕʕēl*. Another example from MS 302 is (370) פּוֹרְאָלָא *pōrālā* 'journey through' PRF.3SG, rendering Hebrew מִתְהַלֵּךְ *miṯhallēḵ* (Gen 3:8).

Words in MS 302 which differ semantically and formally from otherwise documented Old French,[181] are for example (237) אוֹנְפְּלַיְיָאָה *ōnplayyāh* PST.3SG > *onplayer*/ *anployer* 'finish'; (422) פָּאוּוּי *pāōūy* 'pinewood' and (831) שׂוֹנְבְּלְטוֹנְץ *śōnblṭōnṣ* 'appear-

179 Banitt 1963: 264f. and 1972: 110f.; Edzard 2011: 244; Kiwitt 2013: 208f.

180 Banitt 1972 (vol. I: Introduction): 97; Banitt 2005 (vol. I: Introduction): 237f.

181 Cf. the list in Edzard 2011: 165–177.

ance, resemblance'. Apart from the form *śōnblṭōnṣ*, in many Hebrew-written French texts the form *śenblṭūnə* or *-ōnə* is found, which likewise is a form exclusively represented in texts composed by Jews, and the meaning of which varies from "appearance" to "looks of a patient" in the special medical context of *Fevres.*[182] A few words originate in Arabic, as in MS 302 (Edzard 2011): (448) כַּפְּרְא *kap̄rə* 'camphor' < Arabic *kāfūr*, without <n> or <m>, or כַּנְפּוֹר *kanp̄ōr*, as the form is documented in *Fevres*, with lacking final [ə], which makes it a form not represented in Latin-written Old French texts,[183] and (755) הַדִּיאְה *hadīəh* 'gift' < Arabic *hadīya*; they may have come into the writer's vocabulary from other glossaries originating from the south of France.[184]

In his work on the Glossaire de Bâle, Banitt presents a list of words[185] that "présentent quelque intérêt du point de vue sémantique, soit par le nombre des acceptions nuancées relevées, soit par le nombre des racines hébraïques qu'elles rendent, soit encore pour leur datation [...].[186]

In the study of the Glossaire de Leipzig, as well as in that of Bâle, Banitt introduces the subject of lexicon by way of a section on the formation of verbs and nouns, in which he explains the glossary writers' choice of the French translation of a Biblical term and the emergence of derivations from French words by use of prefixes, which Banitt calls *la nomenclature des dérivations*.[187]

Also for the Glossaire de Leipzig, Banitt presents a list of words representing an amplification of the Old French lexicon.[188]

In *Fevres*, there are three different categories of languages involved: Old French, Latin, and Hebrew.

The Latin vocabulary mostly consists of the designation of plants, pharmaceutic preparations, and medical terms, the very sporadic Hebrew vocabulary basically belongs to the common language.[189]

Regarding Old French, one must distinguish between two sorts of vocabulary: the special technical-medical one and the common every-day one. The main part of the last-mentioned vocabulary in *Fevres* belongs to common Old French vocabulary; beyond that, the treatise shows some instances of words well documented in later Latin-written Old French documents, thereby proving a much greater age than supposed and documented in *FEW*.[190] Furthermore, Kiwitt points out eight words within the corpus of texts examined in Kiwitt 2001, which are exclusively documented in *Fevres*, and one word –

182 Zwink 2017: 487.

183 Cf. Zwink 2017: 356.

184 Cf. Banitt 1963: 265ff.

185 Banitt 1972 (vol. I: Introduction): 112 – 165.

186 Cf. Banitt 1972 (vol. I: Introduction): 112.

187 Cf. Banitt 2005 (vol. I: Introduction): 232ff.

188 Banitt 2005 (vol. I: Introduction): 255–342.

189 Kiwitt 2001: 41f.; Zwink 2017: 174f.

190 Kiwitt 2001: 43f.; Zwink 2017: 169.

colonbe, usually meaning 'column, pillar', which has a signification not accounted for in other documents.[191]

Wedding Song I uses common Old French, the only exception being two Hebrew words in the first and the last stanza, more precisely in the first and the last line of the song: חָתָן *ḥā̊ṯā̊n* 'bridegroom' and כַּלָּה *kallā̊* 'bride'. The use of these two Hebrew words must have a symbolic signification, as they – indicating the two main persons of the song – provide a frame for the otherwise purely French text. These two Hebrew keywords place the text, which does not differ from Christian writing, neither linguistically – apart from the Hebrew characters – nor regarding the content, as the realization of the subject at least on the surface represents a typical Christian literary model, in the cultural context, to which this song belongs.[192]

For Wedding Song II, nearly the same observations and interpretations are true; the whole text uses common Old French vocabulary, with the exception of the word כַּלָּה *kallā̊* 'bride' in the identical first and last stanza.

3. Text samples

For the transliteration of all the text samples I adopt the system, which Marc Kiwitt uses in the edition of the fever treatise *Fevres* (2001).[193]

3.1 Bible Glossary Paris, Bibliothèque Nationale, fonds hébreu no. 302.

The time of composition is the beginning of the 13th century; the dialect is Francien with an admixture of elements from the North-East of France.

Fol. 1r, 1 – 11, the following glosses refer to Genesis 1:1–16.
Each gloss is followed by the abbreviation ב֗ל for בלעז *be-laʕaz* 'in [the French] foreign language' (not transliterated in the following). The numbers in parentheses after the Bible location refer to the word lists in Edzard (2011).

בראשית בתרג[ום] בקדמין אֵיינְשׂוֹיְיִשׂ בְּל֗

bə-rē(ʔ)šīṯ bat-targ[ūm] bə-qaḏmīn ēynśōyyś (Gen 1:1; 1066)
in-beginning^H in.DEF-Targum^H in-beginning^Aram first.ADV (Godefroy: *ainçois*)
in [the] beginning = in [the] beginning in the [Aramaic] Targum = at first

כמו הראשון אדם תולד

kəmō hā-rī(ʔ)šōn ʔāḏām tiwwālēḏ
as^H DEF-first^H human^H give_birth.PASS.IPFV.2SG.M^H
as are you the first human (ever) born (cf. Job 15:7)

תוהו אֵישְׂטוּרְדִיזוֹן ב֗ל

tōhū ēśṭwrdīzōn (Gen 1:2; 884)
chaos^H bewilderment (OFD: *estordison*)
chaos = bewilderment

191 Kiwitt 2001: 103.
192 Cf. Edzard 2014.
193 Cf. Kiwitt 2001: 25–27.

לשו[ן] שממון **ובוהו** אֵיבֿוּיְדְטֵי בֿל
ləšō[n] šimmāmōm wə-ḇōhū ē-ḇūyydṭē (Gen 1:2; 860)
term.CS[H] desolateness[H] and-emptiness[H] and emptiness (Godefroy: *et vuideté*)
a synonym of desolateness and emptiness = emptiness

לשון ריקנות **מרחפת** אַקֻוּבֵֿיטוֹנְץ בֿל
ləšōn rēqānūṯ mərahepeṯ aqāūḇēṭ-ōnṣ[194] (Gen 1:2; 1051)
term.CS[H] emptiness[H] float-PTCP.SG.F[H] float-PTCP (Godefroy: *acoveter*)
a synonym of emptiness floating = floating

יהי שׂוֹיְיט בֿל
yəhī śōyy-ṭ (Gen 1:3; 309)
be.3SG.PRS.JUSS[H] be.SBJV-3SG (*soi-t*)
it shall be = it shall be

ורשי׳ פי׳ יתחזק **הרקיע** לְאֵיטוֹנְדְּמוֹנְט בֿל
wə-rāšī pē[rūš-ō] yiṯḥazzēq hā-raqīʕ l-ēṭōndmōnṭ (Gen 1:7; 378)
and-Rashi explanation-3SG.M become_strong.IPV.3SG.M DEF-firmament[H] DEF-firmament (Godefroy: *e(s)tendement*)
and Rashi's explanation is confirmed; the firmament = the firmament

ויהי אֵיפּוּי בֿל
wa-yhī ē-pūy (Gen 1:3; 309)
and-be.3SG.M.PRET[H] and-be.3SG.PF (*et-fu-t*)
and it was = and it was

אור קְלַרְטֵי בֿל
ʔōr qlarṭē (Gen 1:3; 821)
light[H] brightness (*clarté*)
light = brightness

ויבדל אִיאֵשֵׂיבְרָא בֿל
way-yaḇdēl ī-ēśēbr-ā (Gen 1:4; 345)
and-part.3SG.M.PRET[H] and-part-3SG.PRF (*et-dessevr-a*)
and he parted = and parted

ויעש אִיאָפֵיטָה בל
way-yaʕaś ī-āpēṭ-āh (Gen 1:7; 226)
and-make.3SG.M.PRET[H] and-arrange-PRF.3SG (*et-afait-a*)
and he made = and he arranged

כמו ועשתה צפורניה
kəmō wə-ʕāśəṯā ṣipporne-hā
as[H] and-do.PF.3SG.F[H] fingernail.CS.PL-3SG.F[H]
as "and she clipped ("did") her fingernails" (cf. Dt 21:12)

יקוו המים שֵׂיְנְט אַמָשֵׂיאְשׂ בֿל
yiqqawu ham-mayim śēy-nṭ amāś-ēś (Gen 1:9; 50)
assemble.3PL.M.PASS.JUSS[H] DEF-water.PL[H] be-SBJV.3PL assemble-PTCP.PASS.PL.F (*soi-ent amass-ées*)
the water shall be assembled = they should be assembled

194 The vowel sign beneath the *qof* combined with a *vav*, sometimes a *vav* with a *šūruq*, is often used in order to express [u] in this glossary.

לש[ון] אסיפה **ותראה** אֵישְׁרָבֵיאוּ בל׳

ləš[on] *ʔăsīpā* *wə-ṯērāʔe* *ē-śr-ā-ḇē-ʔū* (Gen 1:9; 18)
term.CS^{H} assembly^{H} and.see.3SG.F.IPFV.PASS^{H} and-be-FUT.3SG-see.PTCP.PASS.SG.M (*et-ser-a-vu*)
a synonym of assembly and it will be seen = it will be seen

היבשה לָשֵׁיקְטֵיה בל׳

hay-yabbāšā *lā-śäqṭēh* (Gen 1:9; 820)
DEF-dryness^{H} DEF.F-dryness (*la-secheté*)
the dryness = the dryness

למקוה אַלְאמַשְׁמוֹנט בל׳

lə-miqwē *a-l-amaśmōnṭ* (Gen 1:10; 843)
to-gathering_of_water.CS^{H} to-DEF-gathering (*a-l'-amassement*)
to the gathering (of) = to the gathering

ימים מירש בל׳

yammīm *myr-ś* (Gen 1:10; 397)
sea.PL^{H} sea-PL (*mer-s*)
seas = seas

התנינים לישדגרונץ בל׳

hat-tannīnīm *lyś-dgrwn-ṣ* (Gen 1:21; 486)
DEF-dragon.PL^{H} DEF.PL-dragon-PL (*les-dragon-s*)
the dragons = the dragons

תדשא אֵירְבֵייְרָא בל׳

tadšē(ʔ) *ērbēyr-ā* (Gen 1:11; 4)
let_blossom.JUSS.3SG.F^{H} blossom-FUT.3SG (*erbeer-a*)
let it blossom = it will blossom

דֶשֶׁא אֵירְבִיץ בל׳

dešeʔ *ērbīṣ* (Gen 1:11; 438)
grass^{H} herb (Latin – OFr. *erbiz* 'field, meadow, pasture'; *erbe* 'grass, herb, plant, field')
grass = herb

עשב אֶרְבָא בל׳

ʕēśeḇ *ärbə* (Gen 1:11; 437)
grass^{H} grass, herb (*erbe*)
grass = grass, herb

מזריע זרע שְׁמוֹנְשׁוֹנְץ שְׁמוֹנְצָא בל׳

mazrīʕ *zeraʕ* *śmōnś-ōnṣ* *śmōnṣə* (Gen 1:11; 896; 412)
SOW.PTCP.SG.M^{H} seed^{H} sow-PTCP seed (*semenci-ant semence*)
sowing seed = sowing seed

עושה פֵייזוּנְט בל׳

ʕōśe *pēyz-wnṭ* (Gen 1:11; 976)
do.PTCP.SG.M^{H} do-PTCP (*fais-ant*)
doing = doing

למינה מפיק הי אָשָׁאגִיזְ

lə-mīn-āh *mappīq* *hē* *ā-śā-gīz* (Gen 1:24)
to-manner.3SG.F^{H} consonantal_dot^{H} *he*^{H} in-3SG.POSS.SG.F-manner (*a-sa-guise*)
(according) to her manner with a *mappiq* (in the letter) *he* = to her manner

מאורת קְלַרְטֵיץ בׄל

məʔōrōṯ *qlarṭē-ṣ* (Gen 1:14; 1012)
illuminated-body.PL^H brightness-PL (*clarté-s*)
illuminated bodies = brightnesses

להאיר אַאַקְלַרְזִיר בׄל

lə-hāʔīr *a-aqlarz-īr* (Gen 1:15; 1)
to-illuminate.INF^H to-enlighten-INF (Godefroy: a-aclairc-ir; TL: *aclar-ir*)
to illuminate = to enlighten

לממשלת אַפוֹטֵיר בׄל

lə-memšeleṯ *a-pōṭ-ēr* (Gen 1:16; 214)
to-governance.CS^H to-be_able-INF (*a-po-eir* / *po-oir*)
to the governance of = to be able

3.2 Glossaire de Bâle, MS A III 39 (23)

The time of composition is the first quarter of the13th century; the dialect reflects the region of South-East Champagne.

Fol. 27r, l. 1–11, the following glosses refer to 1 K 5:12–29.[195]

שירוֹ שִׁיר שֶׁלוֹ שׂוֹן קָאנט.

šīr-ō *šīr* *šell-ō* *śōn* *q̄anṭ* (1 K 5:12)
song-3SG.M^H song of-3SG.M^H 3SG.POSS.SG.M song
his song a song of his = his song

וַאֱלֶף אֵימֵיטְרָא

wa-ʔālep̄ *ʔy-{mē-}mēṭrə*[196] (1 K 5:12)
and-thousand^H and-educator
and thousand = and educator

י״א אִיאַפְּרֵינַמַאנט.

y[eš] ʔ[omrim][197] *ī-aprēnamanṭ*
exist^H say.PTCP.PL^H and-teaching
and some say and teaching

הֵנִיחַ אַשׂוֹאַגָאה

hēnīaḥ *aśōag̈-ah*[198] (1 K 5:18)
grant_peace.PF.3SG.M^H establish_peace-PF.3SG
he granted peace = he established peace

195 For a facsimile of the folium cf. Banitt 1972 (vol. 1: Introduction): 2; edition of the glosses quoted here: Banitt 1972 (Texte): 60, starting with nr. 1678.

196 Here, the glossarist has misunderstood the meaning of the root at this place. While the Masoretic voweling וָאֶלֶף indicates 'and thousand', the voweling of the glossarist וַאֱלֶף suggests the verb from 'and he taught'.

197 Cf. Banitt 1972 (vol. 1: Introduction): 15 (2.51.): abbreviation for יֵשׁ אוֹמְרִים 'there are some who say'; 'one can translate with'.

198 Possibly the same verb as in MS 302: 161 *aśōyygāəś* < *aśōygēr* 'to be pleasant' < Lt. *sedicare*, *FEW* XI, 409b?

פֶּגַע אוֹצִי

pegāʕ *ōṣī* (1 K 5:18); MS 302: (545) לֵיש אוּצִיש
obstacle^H murder.PTCP.PASS.SG.M
obstacle = murder

י״א אַנְקוֹטְרָא.

y[eš] ʔ[omrim] *anqōṭrə*
exist^H say.PTCP.PL^H encounter; battle
and some say encounter; battle

הָעֵצִים לֵיש אַבְּרְש לשׁ׳[199] אִילָנוֹת.

hā-ʕēṣīm *lēś abr-ś* *ləš[ōn]* *ʔīlānōt* (1 K 5:20)
DEF-tree.PL^H DEF.PL tree-PL gloss.CS^H tree.PL^H
the trees = the trees, a synonym of trees

בְּרוֹשִׁים ברושים בְּרוֹיש.

bərōšīm *brws-ym* *brōy-ś* (1 K 5:22)
cypress_wood.PL^H cypress_wood-PL^H bush, brushwood-pl (*broce* (sf.) cf. Hindley/Langley/Levy s.v.)
cypress woods = bushes

יַמָּה [200]כמ[ו] לַיָּם.

yāmm-ā(h) *kəm[ō]* *lay-yam*(1 K 5:23)
sea-DIR^H as^H to.DEF-sea^H
to the sea (just) as to the sea

דּוֹבְרוֹת רוֹיץ

dōḇərōt *rōy-ṣ*
raft.PL^H net-PL (OFr. *rois* F and M)
rafts = nets

י״א רְאזֵייאש קוֹרוֹת גְדוֹלוֹת טָעֲנוּ עֵצִים הוֹלְכוֹת בַּיָּם

y[eš] ʔ[omrim] *rəzēyə-ś*[201] *qōrōt* *gədōlōt* *ṭaʕănū* *ʕēṣīm* *hōləḵōt* *bay-yam*
exist^H say.PTCP.PL^H float-PL; raft-PL ^H bridge.PL big.PL.F load.3PL.PF tree.PL go.PTCP.PL.F in.DEF-sea^H
and some say floating rafts, large bridges they loaded with trees that went on the sea

בְלֹא סְפִינָה וְאָדָם עֲלֵיהֶם הַמַנְהִיגָם.

bəlō *səpīna* *wə-ʔāḏām* *ʕălē-hem* *ham-manhīg-am*
^H without boat and-human upon.3PL DEF-steer.PTCP-3PL.OBJ^H
without any boat or man upon them that would steer them

וּנְפַּצְתִּים אֵידְפְּצַרָא אוֹש

wə-nippaṣtī-m *ē-dpṣar-a* *ōś*
and-disassemble.CONSEC.PF.1SG-3PL.M^H and-break-FUT.1SG (*et-depecier-a*) 3PL.M.OBJ (*eus*/*aus*)
and I will disassemble them = I will break them (accentuated form)
(cf. Buridant 2000: 270)

כְּמוֹ וְנִפֵּץ [אֶת] עֹלָלַיִךְ.

kəmō *wə-nippeṣ* *[ʔeṯ]* *ʕōlālay-iḵ* (Ps 137:9)
^H like smash.CONSEC.PF.3SG.M ACC descendent.PL.CS-3SG.F^H
like and he will smash your descendants

199 Abbreviation for *ləšōn* 'term for', introduces a Hebrew synonym, cf. Banitt 1972 (Introduction): 15 (2.51).

200 Abbreviation for כְּמוֹ *kəmō* 'as', cf. Banitt 1972 (Introduction): 15 (2.51).

201 For the alveo-palatal version of [z] in this word, cf. Banitt 1972 (vol. 1:Introduction): 71 (7.1.63).

מַכּוֹלֶת מַנְגֵּייר כ[מו] מַאְכֹלֶת ויהוה נתן: הפטרה

makkōleṯ mangēyr (1 K 5:25) *kəmō ma(?)ḵōleṯ wə-YHWH nāṯan haṗṭārā*
food^{H} food (*mangier*) ^{H}as food and-God give.PF.3SG chapter_from_Prophets^{H}
food = food as food and God gave a chapter from the Book of Prophets

וְיִקְחוּ לִי תְּרוּמָה

we-yiqḥū l-ī tərūmā (Ex 25:2)
^{H}and-take.JUSS.3PL.M for-1SG task^{H}
and they shall take for me a task

לְבָנוֹנָה אַבוֹקָאגְא.

ləḇānōn-a(h) a-bōq̄agə (1 K 5:28)
Lebanon-DIR^{H} into-woodland, grove (*a-boschage*)
to Lebanon = into woodland

חֲלִיפוֹת חֹדֶשׁ קָאנְגַּמַאנט

ḥălīṗōt ḥōdeš q̄angamanṭ
alternation.PL.CS^{H} month^{H} alternation
(in) changes of a month = alternation

כלומ׳ כֹּל חֹדֶשׁ הוּא מְחַלְּפִים שְׁלֹשֶׁת אֲלָפִים.

kə-l-ōm[ar] kol ḥōdeš hū(?) məḥalləṗīm šəlōšeṯ ʔălāṗīm
^{H}as-to-say.INF every.CS month 3SG change.PTCP three.CS thousand.PL^{H}
so to speak every month he exchanged three thousand.

נוֹשֵׂא סַבָּל פּוֹרְטַאנט הוֹטְא

nōśē? sabbāl pōrṭ-anṭ hōṭə (1 K 5:29)
bear.PTCP.CS^{H} porter^{H} bear-PTCP.PRS basket
bearing porter = bearing basket

3.3 Glossaire de Leipzig, MS 1099 of Catalogue Vollers

The time of composition is the end of the 13th century/the beginning of the 14th century; the dialect is Anglo-Norman.

Fol. 119v, l. 1–7, the following glosses refer to Amos 7:12–8:4.[202]

זִי וְוִישְׁזַאגּוּנְדְּא **תנבא** שְׂרַשׂ פְּרוֹפְּצִיאַנְט

zī wwīśzagūndə tinnāḇē(?) śr-aś prōṗṣī-anṭ (Amos 7:12; Banitt 12574)
be.IMP.SG^{Y} prophecize.PTCP^{Y} be_prophet.2SG.M.JUSS^{H} be-FUT.2SG predict-PTCP.PRS
you shall prophesize

וכן **להנבא** אֶאֵיטְרְא פְּרוֹפְּצִיאַנְט

wə-ḵēn lə-hinnāḇē(?) ā-ēṭrə prōṗṣī-anṭ (Amos 7:13; Banitt 12575)
and-indeed^{H}to-prophesize.INF^{H} to-be.INF predict-PTCP.PRS
and indeed, to prophecize = to be predicting

רִינְדּוּר הֵירְטְא אִיךְ **בּוֹקֵר אנכי** בּוֹבְיֵיר רועה בקר:

rīndūr hērṭə īḵ bōqer ʔănōḵī bōbyēr rōʕē(h) bōqer (Amos 7:14; Banitt 12576)
reindeer^{Y} herd^{Y} 1SG^{Y} ox-driver^{H}1SG^{H} pasture herd ox/cattle
I am a reindeer herd

202 Facsimile cf. Banitt 1998 vol. 2: Planche II (p. 1024); edited text: p. 947.

ובוֹלֵס אֶצֵירְקָנְט כמו ויחפש

u-ḇōlēs *e-ṣērq̄-anṭ* *kəmō wa-yḥappēś* (Banitt 12577)

and-grow_figs.PTCP.SG.M^{H} and-search-PTCP.PRS as^{H} and-search.CONSEC.IPFV.3SG.M^{H}

and growing figs and searching like and he searched

דמתרג[מו] ובלש

di-mətargəm-ō *u-ḇəlaš*

of-translate.PTCP.SG.M-3SG.M^{Aram} and-search.PF.3SG.M^{Aram}

of his translator (to Aramaic) and he searched

ונ׳ אוּר זוֹכּוּר

wn' *ʔūr zōḵūr*

and^{Y} searcher^{Y} ("Ersucher")

and searcher

אֵיכְלוּן **שִׁקְמִים** קֶאֱנֵיש:

ʔēḵlūn *šiqmīm* *q̄enē-ś* (Banitt 12578)

eat.PF.3PL.M^{Aram} sycamore.PL^{H} oak_tree-PL

they ate sycamores = oak trees

תטיף פרופציארש כמו אל תטיפון לש[ון] נבואה

taṭṭīp̄ *prwpṣyʔr-ś* *kəmō ʔal* *taṭṭīp̄ūn* *ləš[ōn]* *nəḇūʔā*

prophecize.IPFV.2SG.M^{H} prophecize-FUT.2SG like^{H} PROH^{H} prophecize.IPFV.2PL.M^{H} term.CS^{H} prophecy^{H}

you shall prophecize like do not prophecize, a synonym of prophecy

זוֹלְטוֹ וִוישְׁזַגוּן

zōlṭō *wwīśzagūn* (Amos 7:16; Banitt 12579)

shall.PRS.2SG^{Y} prophecize.INF^{Y}

you shall prophecize

מִיט (מְ) זֵייְלְא זוֹל וֶוְרְדוּן גְטֶילוּט

mīṭ *(m)* *zēylə zōl* *wwärdūn* *gṭǣlūṭ* (Amos 7:17; Banitt 12580)

with^{Y} DEF.M.DAT^{Y} cord^{Y} shall.PRS.3SG^{Y} AUX.INF^{Y} divide.PPP^{Y}

with a measuring cord it shall be divided

בחבל תחלק אַנְקוֹרְדְא שְׁרָא פַּרְטִיאָה:

ba-ḥeḇel *təḥullaq* *an-qōrdə* *śr-ā* *parṭī-əh*

with.DEF-measuring_cord^{H} devide.IPFV.PASS.3SG.M^{H} by_way_of-cord be-FUT.3SG divide-PTCP.PASS.F

with a measuring cord it shall be divided

כְּלוּב קָיִץ פָּנֵייר דְפִיאָה סל מלא תאנים קוֹרְפְּ

kəlūḇ *qāyiṣ* *panēyr d-pīəh* *sal* *məlēʔ* *təʔēnīm* *qōrp* (Amos 8:1;

basket.CS^{H} sommer(-fruit)^{H} basket of-fig.SG.COLL basket^{H} full.CS^{H} fig.PL^{H} basket Banitt 12581)

a fruit basket = a fig basket = a basket full of figs = a basket

מְכָא אֶנְדְא **הקץ** לַאפִין

mkə *endə* *haq-qēṣ* *la-pīn* (Amos 8:2; Banitt 12582)

make.IMP.SG^{Y} end^{Y} the-end^{H} DEF.F-end

make an end = the end = the end

שירות לֵיש קַנְץ לש[ון] שיר בְזֶינְגְא

šīrōṯ *lēś* *q̄an-ṣ* *leš[on]* *šīr* *bzǣngə* (Amos 8:3; Banitt 12583)

song.PL DEF.PL song-PL gloss.CS song singing

songs = the songs, a synonym of song, singing

דוּר קוֹרפּוּל **הפגר** לָא דְטוֹרְבָא

dūr qōrpūl hap-peğer la dṭōrbə (Banitt 12584)

DEF.M body? DEF-corpse DEF.SG.F trouble, harm (OFr. *destorbe*)

the body = the corpse the harm

הס אוטא כלומר השלך וסלק והסר

hās ʔwṭʔ kə-l-ōmar hašlek̠ wə-slaq we-hāsēr

quiet.ADV^{H} remove.IMP as-to-say.INF^{H} send.IMP.SG.M^{H} and-go_up.IMP.SG.M^{H} and-drive_away.IMP.SG.M^{H}

quiet remove so to speak send and go up and drive away

טוֹאַבָא

ṭōab̠ə (Banitt 12585)

do.IMP.SG.down

put down

דֵי דָא שלִינְדוּנְט **השאפים** לֵיש גוֹלוֹיְיזָנְץ

dē dā šlīndūnṭ haš-šōʔăpīm lēś gōlōyyz-ānṣ (Amos 8:4; Banitt 12586)

3PL^{Y} REL^{Y} swallow.PRS.3PL^{Y} DEF-yearn/tread_on.PTCP.PL.M DEF.PL eat .PTCP-PL (gluttonously) (OFr. *goloser*)

those who swallow = the yearning ones = the gluttonous eaters

וְנ' צוֹ בוּר שְׁטוּרן **ולשבית** אֵיאָפֵּיר דְטוֹרְבֵיר

wn' ṣō b̠ūr šṭūrn wə-l-ašbīṯ ē-ā-pēr dṭōrbēr (Banitt 12587)

and^{Y} to^{Y} disturb^{Y} ("verstören") and-to.stop.INF^{H} and-to-do.INF disturb.INF (OFr. *destorber*)

and to disturb = and to stop = and to do disturb

כמו משבית מלחמות

kəmō mašbīṯ milḥāmōṯ (Ps 46:10)

like^{H} stop.PTCP.SG.M^{H} war.PL^{H}

like stopping wars

*3.4 The Old-French treatise on fever (*Fevres*), Ms. Or. Oct. 512, Berlin*

The time of composition is the end of the 13th century/the beginning of the 14th century (cf. Zwink 2017: 164); the dialect is Francien with an admixture of elements of Northern Burgundy, South-West of Champagne, and Lorraine (cf. Zwink 2017: 164).

Fol. 180r and 180v.

אֻנְקוֹרְא בוֹלוֹנְשׁ פַּרְלֵייר דְא אִיקְטִירִיצִיאַה

ūnqōrə b̠ōl-ōnś parl-ēyr də īqṭīrīṣīah

again want-PRS.1PL speak-INF about/of icterus

We want to speak again about icterus.

אַשֵׂייש אַבוֹנְץ פַּרְלֵי דְא דְאשוִץ דְא אוֹ אֵילְא בֵּיינְט

aśēyś ab̠-ōnṣ parl-ē də dəświṣ də ō ēlə b̠ēyn-ṭ.

enough have-PRS.1PL parler-PTCP.M of about of where 3SG.F come-PRS.3SG

We have talked enough about where it comes from.

אַקֻונְא פּוֹיֵיץ אֵילְא בֵּיינְט דוֹפֵּייל קִי אֵט טְרוֹף פְּלֵיין

aqūnə pōyēṣ ēlə b̠ēyn-ṭ dō-pēyl qī eṭ ṭrōp plēyn.

some time.PL 3SG.F come-PRS.3SG from.DEF.SG.M-gallbladder REL be.PRS.3SG too full

Sometimes it comes from the gallbladder which is too full.

אוֹ אִיל אַה דְאדֵיינְץ מַאלַאדִיאְה אוֹ אַפּוֹשְׁטֻומְא

ō īl ah dədēynṣ maladīəh ō apōśṭūmə.
or 3SG.M have.PRS.3SG inside disease or abscess
Either there is a disease or an abscess inside.

אוֹ אֵילְא בֵּיינְט דוֹפּוֹייאְה אוֹ דְאלֵיפְּלֵיין

ō ēlə b̲ēyn-ṭ dō-pōyyəh ō də-l-ē<ś>plēyn.
or 3SG.F come-PRS.3SG from.DEF.SG.M-liver or from-DEF.SG.M-spleen
Either it comes from the liver, or from the spleen.

קַאנְט אֵילְא בי בֵּיינְט דוֹ פּוֹייאְה אוֹ אֵילְא בֵּיינְט פַּר גְרַאנְט קַאלוֹר

qanṭ ēlə{by}[203] *b̲ēyn-ṭ dō pōyyəh ō ēlə b̲ēyn-ṭ par granṭ q̄alōr*
when 3SG.F come-PRS.3SG from.DEF.SG.M liver or 3SG.F come-PRS.3SG with great.SG.F heat
When it comes from the liver, it either comes with great heat

דוֹפּוֹייאְה אוֹ פַּר אֵיטוֹפְּאמֵינְט דְא שֵׁייץ קוֹנְדוִץ

dō-pōyyəh ō par ēṭōpəmēnṭ də śēyṣ qōndwi-ṣ
from.DEF.SG.M-liver or with constipation of POSS.3PL canals-PL
from the liver or with constipation of its canals.

רֵיאֵייץ אַרַאזְאוִיר לֵישׁוֹרְצִילְשׁ דוֹנֵיישׁ לִי אַבוֹייְבָּרְא

rē-ēyṣ a-razəwīr lē-śōrṣīl-ś, dōn-ēyś lī a-bōyyb̲-rə
shave-IMP.PL with-razor DEF.PL-eyebrow-PL give-IMP.PL 3SG.M.OBJ to-drink-INF
Shave the eyebrows with a razor, give him to drink

מֵרְדְא דְאאוֹאְה אוֹ מֵרְדְא דְאקָאבַל דֵיטְרֵינְפְּרֵי דְאבִין

merdə də-owəh ō merdə də-q̄əb̲al dēṭrēnpr-ē də-b̲īn.
excrement of-goose or excrement of-horse dissolve-PTCP.PASS.M of-wine
excrement of goose or excrement of horse dissolved in (some) wine.

אֻון אַאוֹטְרְא פְּרֵינֵייץ שְׁאמֵנְצְא דְאקֵנְבּוִץ שֵׁיק

ūn aōṭrə prēn-ēyṣ śəmenṣə də-q̄enb̲wiṣ śēq
INDEF.SG.M other take-IMP.PL seed of-hemp dry
Another one: take dry seed of hemp

שִׁי לְאבְרוֹייְאֵייץ מֵינוּ אֵיפּוִץ שִׁי לְאפֵּטְרִישֵׁייש

śī lə-brōyy-ēyṣ mēnū ē-pwiṣ śī lə-peṭrīś-ēyś
so 3SG.M.OBJ-pulverise-IMP.PL fine and-then so 3SG.M.OBJ-knead-IMP.PL
(so) you pulverise it finely and (so) you then knead it

Fol. 180v

אַבְּיקְא אֻון פּוֹ דְאמֵיל אֵיאִימֵיטֵייץ דְאלַאפּוֹייְץ נויי נוֹייְרְא מֵינוְאְה

ab̲ʿēʾqə ūn pō də-mēl ē-ī-mēṭ-ēyṣ də-la-pōyyṣ{nwyy} nōyyr-ə mēnwi-əh
with INDEF.SG.M little of-honey and-in-put-IMP.PL of-DEF.SG.F-pea black-SG.F small-SG.F
with a little of honey and put some small black pea in.

שִׁי לְאמֵיטֵייץ שׁוִר לְאאוֹנְבְּרִיל מוֹייְטְא

śī lə-mēṭ-ēyṣ świr lə-ōnbrīl mōyyṭə.
so it-put-IMP.PL on DEF.SG.M-navel moist
So put it on the moist navel.

203 In accordance with the tradition, the scribe uses this first part of the following word (without punctuation) in order to fill the rest of the line.

אֻונְקוֹרְא פְּרֵינֵייץ דְאפַּרִינְא שִׁי פֵּיטְרִישֵׁייש אַבֵּיקְא שׁוֹרִינְא

ūnqōrə prēn-ēyṣ də-pārīnə śī pēṭrīś-ēyś aḇēqə ś-ōrīnə

furthermore take-IMP.PL of-flour so knead-IMP.PL with 3SG.M.POSS-urine

Furthermore, take some flour, so knead (it) with his urine.

שִׁי אֵנְפֵּייטֵייץ טוֹרְטִיאַש פְּאטִיץ אֵי רוֹנְצְא

śī en-pēyṭ-ēyṣ ṭōrṭīa-ś pəṭī-ṣ ē ron-ṣə

so thereof-make-IMP.PL bread-PL.M small-PL.M and round-PL.M

Then make small and round breads from it.

שִׁי לֵייש דוֹנֵייץ אַמַאלַאדְא אַמַאנְגֵּייר טְרֵייץ קֵיקוֹן מַאטִין

śī lēyś dōn-ēyṣ a-maladə a-manḡ-ēyr ṭrēyṣ q̄ēqwin maṭīn

so 3PL.PRON.OBJ give-IMP.PL to-the sick to-eat-INF three each morning

So give them the sick to eat, three each morning

יוֹק אַטְרֵייץ יוֹרְץ

yōq a-ṭreyṣ yōr-ṣ

until in-three day-PL.M

for up to three days.

אִיקְטִירִיצִיאָה קִי בֵּיינְט דוֹקָאלוֹר דופו דוֹפּוֹייאָה

īqṭīrīṣīāh qī ḇēyn-ṭ dō-q̄ālūr[204] *{dwpw} dō-p̄ōyyəh*

icterus REL come-PRS.3SG from.DEF.SG.M-heat from.DEF.SG.M-liver

Icterus, which comes from the heat of the liver:

אֵילְא בֵּיינְט אֵן דוִץ מַאנֵיירְץ

ēlə ḇēyn-ṭ en dwiṣ manēyr-ṣ

3SG.F come-PRS.3SG in two way-PL.F

it comes in two ways;

לִיאוּנְא שִׁי בֵּיינְט פַּר אֵיפּוֹשְׁטֻומְ אֵי לִי אָאוֹטְרְא שַׁאנְט אֵיפּוֹשְׁטֻומְא

lī-ūnə śī ḇēyn-ṭ par ēpōśṭūm<ə> ē lī aōṭrə śanṭ ēpōśṭūmə

DEF.SG.M-one.F so come-PRS.3SG from abscess and DEF.SG.M other without abscess

The first one comes with an abscess, the other one without the abscess.

שֵׁילְא קִי אֵט אַבֵּיקְא אַפּוֹשְׁטֻומְא

śēlə qī eṭ aḇēqə apōśṭūmə

DEM.SG.F REL be.PRS.3SG with abscess

The one which is with abscess.

שְׁא שׁוֹנְט לֵיישאֵנְשֵׁינֵייץ אִיל שֵׁיטֵיינְא

śə śōnṭ lēyś-enśēnēy-ṣ īl ś-ēṭēyn-ə

DEM.SG.M be.PRS.3PL DEF.PL-sign-PL 3SG.M REFL-lose_consciousness-PRS.3SG

These are the signs: he loses consciousness

אֵיבַאלְא אֵירוֹטְא אֵילִידוִיֵּיט לְאדֵיטְרְא קוֹטֵי

ē-ʾḇʾal-ə ē-rōṭ-ə ē-lī-dwiyē-ṭ lə-dēṭrə qōṭē

and-be_healthy-PRS.3SG and-spew-PRS.3SG and-3SG.CO.M-hurt.PRS.SG DEF.SG.M-right flank

and is healthy (again) and spews and the right flank hurts him.

לְאקוֹרְץ שַׁאפֵּיבְלִיט אֵי שַׁאמֵיגְרִיט

lə-qōrṣ ś-āp̄ēblī-ṭ ē ś-amēgrī-ṭ

DEF.SG.M-body REFL-weaken-PRS.3SG and REFL-become_thinner-PRS.3SG

the body weakens and becomes thinner

204 In fact, *chalor* is feminine, but here the form דן constantly treated as masculine, e.g., *grant chalor.*

פֿוֹר קאָ אִיל נְאפּוִט קוֹנְפְּירָא שׂונמא שׂוֹנְמַאנְגֵייר

pōr qə īl nə-pwi-ṭ qōn p̄-īrə {śwnmʔ} śōn-mānḡēyr
because 3SG.M NEG-can-PRS.3SG prepare-INF 3SG.M.POSS-food
because he cannot prepare his food,

אֵי שְׂאוֹרִינָא אֵט קוֹם שַׂנְקָא

ē śə-ōrīnə eṭ qōm śanqə[205]
and 3SG.F.POSS-urine be.PRS.3SG as blood
and his urine is as blood.

3.5 Wedding Song I

ʔel gibʕat hal-ləbōnā notre ḥatan eit ariveiz – To the hill of frankincense our bridegroom has come, in: Maḥzor Vitry MS 8092, fol. 160vץ. The time of composition is the second half of the 13th century; the dialect is Lotharingian.

This song consists of seven stanzas, with nine Hebrew and French lines alternating, except lines 6 and 7, which both are always in French. The last stanza only has eight verses, the sixth and seventh are again both in French.

The song is almost unvocalized; the *qof* corresponding to *q̄* wears a sort of *haček* in the manuscript, in the following represented by a *rafe*. This writer sometimes uses a sign, which does not appear in the other texts here consulted, but in the elegy of Troyes: a *zayin* with a *haček* (corresponding to [z]) – in the following again represented as a *rafe*. According to Darmesteter, the *haček* does not have an influence on the phonetic realization of the letter.[206] The English translation is taken from Fudeman 2006.

(1

אל גבעת הלבונה

ʔel giḇʕaṯ hal-ləḇōnā
to height.CS DEF-frankincense
To the hill of frankincense (cf. Song 4:6)

נוטרא חתן אֵיט אריבֿיץ

nwṭrʔ ḥatan ēṭ ʔryḇy-ṣ
1PL.POSS bridegroom be.PRS.3SG arrive.PTCP.PASS-SG.CR.M
Our bridegroom has come

אור חמה ולבנה

ʔōr ḥāmā wə-ləḇānā
light.CS sun and-moon
Light of the sun, light of the moon! (cf. Is 30:26)

טון קֿטיאיי פֿאיי דליבֿריר

ṭwn q̄tyʔyy p̄ʔyy dlyḇr-yr
2SG.M.POSS castle do.IMP.SG surrender-INF
Surrender your castle!

205 An old-Vallonian form: cf. *FEW* 11, 170a; Zwink 2017: 173.
206 Cf. Darmesteter 1874: 459; Fudeman 2006: 561, fn. 59.

כי בידי חרב יונה

kī b-īḏē ḥereḇ yōnā

because in-hand.PL.CS sword oppress.PTCP.SG.F

For in his hand is a blood-red sword. (cf. Jer 46:16/50:16)

שטו נליבאייש ליבֿרֵיר

ś-ṭw n-ly-bʔ-yyś[207] *lyḇr-ēr*

if-2SG NEG-3SG.CO-go-PRS.1SG turn_over-INF

If you are not going to turn it over to him,

נוש נטנפורייט שאבֿיר

nwś n-ṭ-n-pwr-yyṭ śʔḇ-yr

none.SG.CR not-2SG.CO-of_it-be_able-COND.3SG save.INF

No one could save you from him;

לא ישוב אל נדנה

lō(ʔ) yāšūḇ ʔel nəḏān-āh

NEG return.IPFV.3SG.M to sheath.3SG.F

The sword won't return to its sheath. (cf. 1 Chron 21:27)

איינץ איפורייש טאוט מיקֿביר

ʔyynṣ ʔy-pwr-yyś ṭʔwṭ myq̄byr

rather there-be_able-COND.2SG everything.SG.CO fail

You stand to lose everything here.

(2

יבא דודי להלחמה

yāḇō(ʔ) dōḏ-ī lə-hal-loḥmā

come.JUSS.3SG.M beloved.1SG for-DEF-fight

Let my beloved come fight (cf. Song 4:16)

לבטיילא נרפֿוזֿא

l-bṭyylʔ n-rp̄wz̄-ʔ

DEF.SG.F-battle NEG-refuse-PRS.3SG

He does not refuse the battle

אל עיר דלתים וחומה

ʔel ʕīr dəlāṯīm wə-ḥōmā

to city.CS door.PL and-wall

To a city of [with] doors and a wall

האלטא ריבֿיירא בנא איקלוזא

hʔlṭ-ʔ ryḇyyrʔ bnʔ ʔyqlwzʔ

high-SG.F river sluice-gate lock

High river, sluice-gate, lock,

על אפיקה אייל יצמה (sic)

ʕal ʔăp̄īq-ah ʔayyāl yiṣmaʔ

on water_source-3SG.F stag be_thirsty.IPFV.3SG.M

The stag is thirsty for his brook (cf. Ps 42:2)

ייַא פר טויי נאיירט קלונקלוזא

yyʔ pr ṭwyy n-ʔyyr-ṭ qlwnqlwz-ʔ

indeed through 2SG.CO NEG-be-FUT.3SG close.PTCP.PASS-SG.F

By you the lattice door will never be closed.

207 The scribe writes 1SG, but certainly means 2SG (*vas*).

אנפוליאה שוייש אישוייש

ʔn-pwlyʔh śwyy-ś ʔy-śwyy-ś
in-folly[208] be-IMP.SG and-be-IMP.SG[209]
In folly be and be
(Or, after the emendation by Fudeman:) May you be faint-hearted in folly.

אל עיר משוח מלחמה

ʔel ʕīr məšūaḥ milḥāmā
to city anoint.PTCP.PASS.CS war
To the city anointed for war (cf. Mishna, *Soṭa*, viii, 1; *Mak.*, ii, 6)

בֿאנרש פור ראנדרא למוזא

ḇʔnr-ś pwr rʔnd-rʔ l-mwzʔ
come-FUT.2SG for deliver-INF DEF.SG.F-amusement
You will come, leaving dalliance behind.[210]

(3

עפרת חן במחולות

ʕop̄raṯ ḥēn bam-məḥōlōṯ
hind.CS grace in.DEF-dance.PL
Hind of grace in the dances

טשוי בֿנוץ פור פראייר

ṭ-śwy ḇnw-ṣ pwr pr-ʔyyr
2SG.CO-be.PRS.1SG come.PTCP.PASS-SG.CR.M for beseech-INF
I have come to beseech you,

או במלחמות גדולות

ʔō bə-milḥāmōṯ gəḏōlōṯ
or in-war.PL big.PL.F
Or in great wars (cf. 1 Chron 22:8)

טבֿירי ייא דפֿיאייר

ṭ-ḇy[n]r-y yyʔ dp̄y-ʔyyr
2SG.CO-come-FUT.1SG 1SG challenge-INF
I will come to challenge you,

מלחמה בתחבולות

milḥāmā bə-ṯaḥbūlōṯ
war with-trick.PL
a war with tricks (cf. Prov 24:6; 20:18)

208 Fudeman 2006: 561 sees a "*ja* that seems to be appended to the first word", which in fact does not seem to be there – rather the extended letter *he* that completes the line, as is usual in all Hebrew and Arabic written documents of the Middle Ages. The *he* belongs to the preceding ʔaleph and constitutes the usual feminine ending of a feminine noun having the accent on the last syllable (cf. also MS 302: גֵּילֵיאָה *gēlēəh* 'frost' (382); נוּאָה *nūəh* 'cloud' (383); וִיאָה *wīəh* 'life' (547); אוּאִיאָה *ūīəh* 'ear' (522).

209 Rosenberg (1992: 30) as well as Fudeman (2006: 561) suggest solutions in order to give sense to this line which reads *an folie sois et sois*. The second *sois* seems to be an error of the scribe, Rosenberg opts for *muse* 'waste one's time' instead, Fudeman for *oisus (oisos)* 'faint-hearted'.

210 This is Rosenberg's translation (1992: 26), which fits in better here, as Fudeman's translation goes far away from the literal sense: 'You will come to give up your independence.', cf. Fudeman 2006: 561.

שור טַא טֵירא פור פראייר

śwr ṭā ṭēr? pwr pr-?yyr
on 2SG.F.POSS land for plunder-INF
To plunder on your land.

בֿירש בנאיירא דיפלאייר

b̲yr-ś bn?yyr? dypl-?yyr
see-FUT.2SG banner unfurl-INF
You will see a banner unfurl

אל גבעת הערלות

?el gib̲ʕat̲ hā-ʕărālōt̲
to height.CS DEF-foreskin.PL
to the hill of foreskins.

בֿירש באייש קוש אנפלאייר

b̲yr-ś b?yy-ś qw-ś ?npl-?yyr
see-FUT.2SG fine-PL.CO.M blow-PL.CO employ-INF
You will see fine blows struck.

(4

אמיץ רב בגבורים

?āmīṣ rāb̲ bag-gibbōrīm
brave great in.DEF-hero.PL
(Oh) very brave among the heros (cf. Amos 2:16)

קי לֿבטיילא אַש אַפרינש

qy l-bṭyyl? aś a[n]pryn-ś
who DEF.SG.F-battle have.PRS.2SG undertake.PTCP.PASS-SG.CR.M
Who have undertaken the battle

אז לֿחם בשערים

?āz lāḥem baš-šəʕārīm
then battle in.DEF-gate.PL
There will be war at the gates (cf. Judges 5:8)

מושט אניירט קריאוץ טון פריש

mwśṭ ?n-yyrṭ qry?w-ṣ ṭwn pryś
much thereby-be.FUT.3SG increase.PTCP.PASS-SG.CR.M 2SG.M.POSS renown
Your renown will be greatly increased.

שמעו נא לי המורים

šimʕū-nā(?) ham-mōrīm
listen.IMP.PL-COH DEF-be_reluctant.PTCP.PL.M
Listen, you reluctant ones (cf. Num 20:10)

ארבלטייר באיין אפרינש

ʔrblṭyyr *bʔyyn* *ʔpryn-ś*
cross-bowman.PL.CR.M[211] well teach.PTCP.PASS-PL.CO.M[212]
Well-taught crossbowmen,

טוייץ אייטְש צי אנטרפרינש

ṭwyy-ṣ *ʔyyṭś* *ṣy* *ʔnṭrpryn-ś*
all-PL.CO.M be.PRS.2PL here in_difficulty-PL.CO.M
You are all under attack.

יעלו אבר כנשרים

yaʕălū *ʔēḇer* *kan-nəšārīm*
go_up.IPFV.3PL.M wing as.DEF-eagle.PL
They will ascend with [their] wings as the eagles. (cf. Is 40:31)

אַקְטיל איינץ קי שייט פרינש

a-q̄tyl *ʔyynṣ q-y* *śyyṭ* *pryn-ś*
in-castle.SG.CO before COMP-3SG.M be.SBJV.PRS.3SG take.PTCP.PASS-SG.CR.M
In the castle before it is taken.

(5

בחמת קרי וזעם

ba-ḥămaṯ qerī *wə-zaʕam*
in-heat.CS confrontation and-anger
In the heat of confrontation and anger (cf. Lev 26:28)

שרא בטוץ טון שנטייר

śrʔ *bṭw-ṣ* *ṭwn* *śnṭyyr*
be-FUT.3SG beat.PTCP.PASS-SG.CR.M 2SG.M.POSS path
Your path will be beaten.

אמותה אך הפעם

ʔāmūṯ-ā(h) *hap-paʕam*
die.IPFV.1SG-COH DEF-time (instance)
Let me then die this time (cf. Gen 46:30)

שור איקו בלנק דקרטייר

śwr ʔyqw *blnq* *d-qrṭyyr*
on shield white.SG.M of-quarter
On a white quarter(ed) shield[213]!

לחם סתרים ינעם

leḥem *sətārīm* *yinʕām*
bread hidden_place.PL be_pleasant.IPFV.3SG.M
Bread at a hidden place is sweet. (cf. Prov 9:17)

211 The plural word המורים in the Hebrew line before (שמעו נא לי המורים), and the continuation in the plural in the next line, leads us to the certainty that *arbaletier* 'cross-bowman' really stands in CR PL, without *-s*, which follows the so-called two-case-system and is a very rare example in Old-French Jewish texts, where the plural usually always gets an *-s* in the ending (after the rule only intended for CO PL) just as it later became established everywhere.

212 This participle shows the ending, which the system reserved for CR SG and CO PL; for CR PL, it should not have the *-s*, just like in *arbaletier*. It could be that the scribe simply forgot the *-s* in *arbaletier*, as he seems to follow the habit already common at that time to generalize the plural-*s*.

213 The Old French – English Dictionary has *escu de cartier* 'quartered shield'.

ברגינא ניאה מיטייר

brgynʔ n-y-ʔh mytyyr
bargain NEG-there-have.PRS.3SG need
Bargaining is useless!

קא ייא טי רמיינא אנטייר

qʔ yyʔ ṭy rmyyn-ʔ ʔnṭyyr
COMP 1SG 2SG.CO stay-SBJV.PRS.1SG whole.SG.CO.M
May I stay whole for you

יש בגיד נותן טעם

yeš bag-gid noten ṭaʕam
EXIST in.DEF-sinew give.PTCP.SG.M taste
There is something in the sinews that gives taste.

מאוט אַה צי קורטייש מיטייר

mʔwṭ ah ṣy qwrṭyy-ś myṭyyr
very have.PRS.3SG here courtly-SG.CR.M business
It has a very courtly role to play.

(6
חמתו דוד אל יעיר

ḥămāṯ-ō dōḏ ʔal yāʕīr
anger.3SG.M beloved PROH awake.JUSS.3SG.M
May [my] beloved not awake his anger. (cf. Ps 78:38)

אילנשווייט פרוש איפרדוץ

ʔyl-n-śwyy-ṭ prw-ś ʔyprdw-ṣ
he-NEG-be-SBJV.PRS.3SG valiant-SG.CR confused.PTCP.PASS-SG.CR.M
Let him not be a valiant man who is out of control.

כי לימים רך וצעיר

kī lə-yāmīm raḵ wə-ṣāʕīr
because to-day.PL tender and-young
because tender of age and young (cf. Job 32:6)

ליקאטייש לי איט ראנדוץ

ly-qʔṭyy ś ly ʔyṭ rʔndw-ṣ
DEF.SG.CR.M-castle-SG.CR 3SG.M.CO be.PRS.3SG hand_over.PTCP.PASS-SG.CR.M
The castle is handed over to him.

והיה כי תקרב אל עיר

wə-hāyā kī tiqraḇ ʔel ʕīr
and-be.IPFV.CONSEC.3SG.M as approach.IPFV.2SG.M to city
And it will happen as you approach a [the] city (cf. Deut 20:10)

אישי ליאירט דיפֿאנדוץ

ʔyśy ly-ʔyrṭ dyp̄ʔndw-ṣ
thus 3SG.M.CO-be.FUT.3SG defend.PTCP.PASS-SG.CR.M
That it will be defended against the aggressor.

איל ליאיירט מוט קֿיאייר בֿאנדוץ

ʔyl ly-ʔyyrṭ mwṭ q̄yʔyyr ḇʔndw-ṣ
3SG.M 3SG.M.CO-be.FUT.3SG very dearly sell.PTCP.PASS-SG.CR.M
It will be sold to him very dearly.

ישפוט אל הר שעיר

yišpōṭ	*ʔel*	*har*	*śēʕīr*
reign.IPFV.3SG.M	to	mount.CS	PN

He will reign on mount Seir. (Rosenberg: Gen 14:6; Deut 1:2; 33:2, etc.)

אפֿורקֿשֿ שאייט איל פאנדוץ

ʔ-p̄wrq̄-ś	*śʔyy-ṭ*	*ʔyl*	*pʔndw-ṣ*
on-gallows-PL.F	be-SBJV.PRS.3SG	3SG.M	hang-PTCP.PASS-SG.CR.M

Let him be hung on the gallows!

(7

את שן סלע האיתן

ʔeṯ	*šen*	*selaʕ*	*hā-ʔēṯān*
ACC	point.CS	rock	DEF-hard

The point of the hard rock (cf. Numbers 24:21; Job 39:28)

טובֿירש יַא איפרובֿיר

ṭw-ḇy[n]r-ś	*iā*	*ʔyprwḇ-yr*
2SG.CR-come-FUT.2SG	surely	experience-INF

You will soon experience (it)

אל תוך גנת הביתן

ʔel	*tōḵ*	*ginnaṯ*	*hab-bīṯān*
to	inner_part.CS	garden.CS	DEF-palace

To the inner part of the palace garden (cf. Esther 7:7)

או לי חתן פֿו ליבֿריץ

ʔw	*ly*	*ḥatan*	*p̄w*	*lyḇry-ṣ*
where	DEF.SG.CR.M	bridegroom[H]	be.PRF.3SG	hand_over.PTCP.PASS-SG.CR.M

Where the bridegroom was turned over,

החתן קולו נתן

hā-ḥāṯān	*qōl-ō*	*nāṯān*
DEF-bridegroom	voice-3SG.M	give.PF.3SG.M

The bridegroom produced his voice (cf. Jer 7:34)

איל אדיט אשאייש פריבֿיץ

ʔyl	*ʔ-dy-ṭ*	*ʔ-śʔyy-ś*	*pryḇy-ṣ*
he	have.PRS.3SG-say-PTCP.PASS-SG.CO.M	to-CO.3PL.M.POSS	attendant-PL.CO.M

He has said to his attendants:

ביא קֿאנטיר אינוייאה צא שבֿיץ

byʔ	*q̄ʔnṭ-yr*	*ʔynwyy-ʔh*	*ṣʔ*	*śḇ-yṣ*
fine	sing-INF	annoy-PRS/PRF[214].3SG	DEM.SG.M	know-PRS.2PL

"I'm bored by this fine singing, you know."

לחתן אֵי לכלה אן לקֿאיירא שוש לביץ

l-ḥatan	*ʔy*	*l-kalla*	*ʔn*	*l-q̄ʔyyrʔ*	*śwś*	*lby-ṣ*
DEF.SG.CO.M-bridegroom	and	DEF.SG.F-bride	in	DEF.SG.F-seat	on	raise-IMP.PL

Raise the bridegroom and the bride upon the throne!

214 The ending אה- corresponds to both *-a* (PRF) and *-e* (PRS), depending on the punctuation.

3.6 Wedding Song II

ʕUri liqraʔti yap̄a – Arise, come toward me, beautiful one, MS Heid. 51. The time of composition is the late 14th or early 15th century; the dialect is Lotharingian.

In this song, each of the eight stanzas is composed of four verses, the first three of which are in Hebrew in the first half, in the second half in French. The last verse of each stanza is in French only. The first and the last stanzas are identical. The French parts of the song are fully punctuated, except for stanza 6, verses 3 and 4, and stanza 7, verses 1 and 2.

Also the writer of this text used *haček* on *gimel* in order to express [dʒ] and [ʒ] and on *qof* in order to render [tʃ] and [ʃ]; the *haček* will here be replaced by *rafe*. For the Hebrew parts see also Fudeman 2010: 164ff. The translation into English also follows Fudeman.

(1

עורי לקראתי יפה ‏ ‏ ‏ ‏ גֿנְטִיש כַלָה אֶיינוֹרֵייאְה

ʕūrī liqra(ʔ)t-ī yāp̄ā ‏ ‏ *ḡnṭī-ś kallā äyynōrēy-əh*

arise.IMP.SG.F towards-1SG beautiful.SG.F ‏ ‏ noble-SG.CR bride[H] worthy-SG.F

Arise, come toward me, beautiful one ‏ ‏ noble and worthy bride

ארים ניסי במצפה ‏ ‏ ‏ ‏ פּוֹר אְנְפֵּייְרא מָאפְּנְשֵׂייאְ

ʔārīm niss-ī bam-miṣpe(h) ‏ ‏ *pōr ən-pēy-rə mā-pnśēyə*

raise.IPFV.1SG banner-1SG in.DEF-watchtower ‏ ‏ for of-do-INF 1SG.F.POSS-intention

I will raise my banner on the watchtower ‏ ‏ to accomplish what I intend

אל תראי אחותי ‏ ‏ ‏ ‏ פַּשֵׂייר טִיקוֹוִייֵן פַּרְשִׂי

ʔal tīrəʔī ʔăḥōṯ-ī paś-ēyr ṭī-qōwīēn par-śī

PROH be_afraid.JUSS.2SG.F sister-1SG pass-INF 2SG.CO-be_necessary.PRS.3SG through-here.

Do not be afraid, my sister, ‏ ‏ you must pass this way

נִיוּוֵרָא טוֹן בְּרְנַאגָֿא ‏ ‏ ‏ ‏ טֻוֹלַייְרָאשׂ אִישִׂיט טוֹן גַאגָֿא

nī-wwar-ā ṭōn brnaḡə ṭū-layyr-āś īśīṭ ṭōn gaḡə

NEG-be_of_value-FUT.3SG 2SG.M.POSS knighthood 2SG.CR-leave-FUT.2SG here 2SG.M.POSS pledge

your noble strength will be of no avail, you will leave your pledge here!

2

מכלל י[ו]פי שמעי לי ‏ ‏ ‏ ‏ גֿייטְדִי שְׂנֻוֹלְאפַּלְא

miḵlal yop̄ī šimʕī l-ī ḡəy-ṭ-dī ś-nūl-ə-palə

perfection.CS beauty listen.IMP.SG.F to-1SG 1SG-2SG.CO-say.PRS.1SG so-no-SG.F-error

Perfection of beauty, listen to me, ‏ ‏ I tell you, without a doubt

לא בכסף תגאלי ‏ ‏ ‏ ‏ מַייטוֹקוֹרְשְׂפַּאָטְקְטֻוּבַאלְישׂ

lō(ʔ) bə-ḵesep̄ tiggāʔēlī ‏ ‏ *mayy-ṭō-qōrś-paāṭ-q-ṭū-bal-əś*

NEG with-silver redeem.PASS.IPFV.2SG.F ‏ ‏ but-2SG.M.POSS-body-need.PRS.3SG-that-2SG.CR-surrender-SBJV.PRS.2SG

You will not be redeemed with silver, but you will have to surrender your body.

ערום מבלי שלמה ‏ ‏ ‏ ‏ נְטִיטֵיינָ[ר]אשְׂ פַּאָשׂ אַמָאה

ʕārōm mib-bəlī śalmā n-ṭī-ṭēyn̄[r]-aś paāś a-māh

naked from-without garment NEG-2SG.CO-hold-FUT.2SG step.NEG to-evil

Naked without a garment ‏ ‏ do not think you will be doing something wrong.

קֿוֹזְא קִייֵאיְט אַקוֹטֻומֵייאְה דֵייט אַטְרֵא טוֹאוּטְ אוֹטְרְייֵאְה
q̄ōzə qīy-ēyṭ aqōṭūmēy-əh dēy-ṭ aṭre ṭōūṭ ōṭryē-əh
thing REL-be.PRS.3SG customary-SG.F must-PRS.3SG be.INF all.SG.F grant.PTCP.PASS-SG.F
Something that is customary must be granted freely.

(3

שאלי מני ואתנה גַֿאָה נוֹן שְׂרַאַש רְייפֻוזֵייאְה
šăʔalī wə-ʔettən-ā(h) ḡaāh nōn śra-aś rəypūzēy-əh
ask.IMP.SG.F and-give.COH.1SG indeed NEG be-FUT.2SG turn_away-PTCP.PASS.SG.F
Ask and I shall give. You will never be turned away.

שאר כסות ועונה אַבְֿרַאש בוֹנְאה דֵייטִינֶייאה
šəʔēr kəsūṯ wə-ʕōnā aḇr-aś bōn-əh dēyṭīnäyy-əh
meat covering and-conjugal_right have-FUT.2SG good-SG.F destiny-SG.F
Meat, clothing, and conjugal rights. You will have a good destiny!

אל תאמרי נואש גַרְדְּאה בִּייֵן קְטֻופְֿרָאש
ʔal tō(ʔ)mərī nōʔāš gard-ə bīēn q-tū-p̄r-āś
PROH say.JUSS.2SG.F despair.PTCP.PASS.SG.M take_care-IMP.SG well REL-2SG.CR-do-FUT.2SG
Do not say "desperate", be careful what you do

נִינוֹן [פִ]יירא פַּאש מַיילֶייאְה פִּייָא נְפֻוטְא אוֹנְקְש שַׂלֵייאְה
nī-nōn pyy-rə paś mayyläyy-əh pīyā n-pūṭ-ə ōnqś śa-lēy-əh
nor-NEG do-INF step.NEG hardship-SG.F magpie NEG-plunder-PRS.3SG never 3SG.F.POSS-bed[215]-F
and do not fight: A magpie does not plunder its own nest [lit.: bed].

(4

הרחיבי מקום אהלך גְֿייטְפְּרִיא מַאדוֹשְ אַמִיאְה
harḥīḇī məqōm ʔōhŏl-ēḵ ḡəy-ṭ-prī-ʔ ma-dō-ś amīəh
make_wide.IMP-SG.F place.CS tent-2SG.F 1SG-2SG.CO-beg 1SG.F.POSS-sweet-SG.F friend.SG.F
Make wide the place of your tent, I beg you, my sweet beloved,

ואל תשמיעי קולך קָר שְׂיישְׂרֵייט גְרֹאְט פוֹלִיאְה
wə-ʔal tašmīʕī qōl-ēḵ qār śəy-śr-ēyṭ groə-ṭ p̄ōlīəh
and-PROH make_hear.JUSS.2SG.F voice.2SG.F because it-be.COND.PRS.3SG great-SG.F folly
And do not let your voice be heard for that would be a great folly.

יתד במקום נאמן מֵייטְרֵיישְׂאְן דְיילַיְימוֹנְט
yāṯēḏ bə-māqōm neʔĕmān mēyṭr-ēy-śən dəylayymōnṭ
peg in-place secure put.FUT-1SG-without delay
I'll put a peg in a sure place without further ado

פוֹר אַבוֹר טוֹן פֻּושְׂלַגְֿא שֶׂייטְ פּוֹר מֵייטְנִיר לֻוזַאָגְֿא
pōr abō[i]r ṭōn pūślaḡə ś-äyyṭ pōr mēy[n]ṭn-īr l-ūzaāḡə
for have.INF 2SG.M.POSS maidenhood indeed-be.PRS.3SG for maintain-INF DEF.SG-custom
to have your maidenhood – it is to uphold custom!

(5

ידיד צלח רכב גַֿאָה נַוְרַאש נֻולְא דֵייפּֿוֹנְשְׂא
yəḏīḏ-ī ṣəlaḥ rəḵaḇ ḡaāh n-awra-ś nūl-ə dēyp̄ōnśə
lover-1sg come_fourth.IMP.SG.M ride.IMP.SG.M indeed NEG-have.FUT-2SG none-SG.F resistance
Come fourth and ride, my lover! You will never meet any resistance.

215 Regarding the interpretation of this form, I agree with Fudeman 2010: 167.

על אשר תאמר אשכב נוֹאֶן שַׁאֵייְש פַּאש אֶנדוֹטְנְש

ʕal ʔăšer tō(ʔ)mar ʔeškab̲ nō-ən śaayy-ś paś ən-dōṭnś

upon REL say.IPFV.2SG.M lie_down.IPFV.1SG NEG-about it be-IMP.SG step.NEG in-doubt

According to what you say, I will lie down. Don't be afraid!

אחלי יכונו דודי גֵ̆ייטְפְּרִיא קָרְא מֵייקוֹזִ[י]

ʔaḥălē yikkōnū dōd̲-ī ğəy-ṭ-prī-ʔ qārə mēy-q̄ōzi

would_that be_steadfast.IPFV.PL.M beloved-1SG 1SG-2SG.CO-beg then (please) 1SG.CO-see.PRF.2SG

Oh that my beloved be steadfast. Please, look at me

דוֹשְׁמוּנְט אֵיידְבוֹנֵיירְא נִייה מִיישַׁאֵיְשא פַּאָש אַבֵייְרא

dōśmwnṭ äyy-dbōnēyrə n-ī-yh mīyśaāyyśə paāś a-b̲äyy-rə

tenderly and-gentle NEG-there-have.PRS.3SG trouble step.NEG to-observe-INF

gently and graciously, there is really nothing wrong in it!

(6

קולך דודי שמעתי גֵ̆ייאֶטְנִדוּ טַרְאקֵייטְא

qōl-k̲ā dōd̲-ī šāmaʕtī ğ-ēy-əṭnid-ū ṭa-rəqäyyṭə

voice-2SG.M beloved-1SG hear.PF.1SG 1SG-have.PRS.1SG-hear-PTCP.PASS.SG.CO.M 2SG.F.POSS-petition

Your voice, my beloved, I heard, I heard your petition.

כדודיך חשקתי קֵייוַאקְא אֵיינְטַראטְא

kə-d̲ōd̲ē-k̲ ḥāšaqtī q̄əwwaaq̄-ə ēy-n-ṭ-araṭ-ə

as-love.PL-2SG.M desire.PF.1SG ride-IMP.SG and-NEG-2SG.CO-stop-IMP.SG

As I have desired your love-making ride and don't stop!

גווי למכים אתן שייאשאן פור טוטא שרטייאן[216]

gēw-ī lə-makkīm ʔettēn śyy-ʔśʔn pwr ṭwṭ-ʔ ś-rṭyyʔn

si-assene por tote se-retien

back-1SG to-strike.PTCP.PL.M give.IPFV.1SG so-succeed.IMP for pillaging if-hold_back.PRS.1SG

I will give my back (body) to those who strike [me]

גֵ̆ייה לייטייפרומיש דוש שירא גֵ̆אה נימוראש מוט דירא

g̅yyh lyy-ṭyy[217]-prwmy-ś dwś śyrʔ g̅ʔh

1SG PRON.3SG.CO.M-2SG.CO-promise.PRS-1SG sweet.SG.M lord indeed

ny-m-wrʔ-ś mwṭ dy-rʔ

NEG-1SG.CO-hear.FUT-2SG word say-INF

I promise you, gentle lord, you will not hear me say a word.

216 This and the following verse are unpunctuated; the translation into Latin Old-French is an interpretation by Fudeman (2010: 168), reading for this line: 'stop and carry me off if I hold back.' The first OFr element of the verse is a point of discussion. Here comes Fudeman's interpretation: שייאשאן *ceisse-en* ... stop.IMP-of.it ... In contrast, I see a different interpretation of this first element of the French part of the verse: if one assumes that the scribe sometimes and as done in the following verse (6.4), uses two *yod* in order to express [i] instead of only one, the word(s) could be read as *si asēne* < OFr. *acener* 'to call' or OFr. *assener* 'to succeed'. The verse would than read: 'so call for/succeed to pillaging if I hold back'. This seems to be more convincing also in the context of the previous verse (6.2), where the bride tells the bridegroom not to stop: [...] *chevache et ne t'arete!* 'ride and don't stop!'

217 These two pronouns usually only get one single *yod*, cf. 1.3; 2.3; but in the last stanza, verse 3, it gets two *yod* again.

(7

חזק ב[ד]ק הבית פוראש פאמה שי מאריאה

ḥazzēq *beḏeq* *hab-bayiṯ* *pwrʔ-ś* *pʔmh* *śy* *mʔry-ʔh*

make_strong.IMP.SG.M crack.CS DEF-house take.FUT-2SG wife indeed[218] marry.PRS-1/3SG[219]

Repair the crack in the house. You will be taking a wife, indeed you marry,

ואז שמיר ושית נאווראש אנטפראייריאה

wə-ʔaz *šāmīr* *wa-šayiṯ* *nʔ-wwrʔ-ś* *ʔn-ṭ-prʔyyryʔh*

and-then thorn and-thorn(-bush) NEG-see.FUT-2SG in-2SG.F.POSS-meadow

And then you will see no more briars or thorns in your meadow,[220]

כרמך עולל לתמיד נׄאשַׁייְאש פַּאָש אֽוֹנְטוֹמִיש דוֹשְׁ שִׁירְא

karme-ḵā *ʕōlēl* *lə-ṯāmīḏ*

vineyard-2SG.M glean.PTCP-SG.M to-always

noʔ-śayə-ś *paāś* *əwnṭō*[221]*-mī-ś* *dō-ś* *śīrə*

NEG-be.IMP-SG step.NEG shy-1SG.CR.POSS-M sweet-SG.CR.M lord

As you always glean your vineyard. Don't be shy, my gentle lord.

טַאיירְא קִי אֵייט לַאבוֹרֵייאְה פוֹרְטְאה מֻואְש אְנְשֵׁייל׳וּנֶייאְה

ṭayyrə *qī* *ēyṭ* *labōrēy-əh* *pōrṭ-əh* *mūəś* *anś-ēyl-w-näyyəh*

land REL be.PRS.3SG work.PTCP.PASS-SG.F bear.PRS-3SG better before-frost-or-snow

Land that is worked bears best before frost or snow.

218 Fudeman (2010: 169) translates *si* with 'if', which would be the Modern French signification of the word. Yaalah Cohen called attention to this matter during the conference on Jewish Languages in Jerusalem (June 20–23 2016).

219 Fudeman (2010: 166) emends this verb to 2SG, as the loss of *-s* frequently appears before a pause (cf. Fudeman 2010: 162).

220 In this verse, Hebrew and French work together as one single entity.

221 Fudeman 2010: 168 discusses this word which can be transcribed in Latin letters as *onto*, in which case the first letter *ʔaleph* is omitted though, and probably corresponding to OFr. *hontos* meaning, *inter alia*, 'ashamed, shy'. Fudeman argues that, supposed that her reading is right, the letter *h* has been omitted because neither *ḥet* nor *he* would be considered adequate, as *ḥet* never has been used in Jewish Old French, and *he* only is used in order to represent vowels in this Wedding Song. The statement regarding *he* is not convincing, as the word in question is the only word requiring an initial *h* in this text, so that there is no material for comparison, and furthermore, *he* for Latin *h* does frequently appear in other Jewish Old French texts, apart from this letter's functions in context with vowels. Some examples from MS 302 (Edzard 2011) can illustrate this: (141) הוּמֵיר *humēr* 'imbibe'; the parts of the glossary examined has five times (178) הַייאִיר *hayyīr* 'hate' etc.

A different interpretation of אֽוֹנְטוֹמִיש, separated in two words אֽוֹנְטוֹ and מִיש by Fudeman, can be suggested when taken as one single word and would then be a participle past to *entomir* 'be drowsy, sleepy'. In this case, only the *schwa* under the first *ʔaleph* would be a misspelling of the scribe, and the meaning of the word would well fit into the line in context with the preceding parts of the stanza and the last line (7.4): 'Don't be sleepy, gentle lord. Land that is worked bears best before frost or snow.' The bride allegorically encourages her groom to have energy and to go on with the work on his fields. Furthermore, Latin-written French *en/em* almost always appears as *on* (or *an*) in Hebrew-written Old French, cf. 4.2 גְרֹאְט *gront* 'great'; 5.1 דֵייפּוֹנְשָׁא *defonse* 'resistance'; MS 302: (11) אוֹנְקַרְגִיאָה *ōnqarḡyāh* 'bear, carry', (20) אוֹנְטוֹנְדְרַש *ōnṭōndraś* 'you will hear'. The fact that the bride simply addresses her groom with דוש שירא *dos sire* 'gentle lord' in 6.4 instead of *mis dos sire*, suggested by Fudeman for 7.3, seems to support the reading as *ontomis* even more.

(8

עורי לקראתי יפה גְנְטִיש כַלָה אֶיינוֹרֶייאְה

ʕūrī liqra(ʔ)t-ī yāpā ḡnṭī-ś kallā äyynōrēy-əh

arise.IMP.SG.F towards-1SG beautiful.SG.F noble-SG.CR bride^H worthy-SG.F

Arise, come toward me, beautiful one noble and worthy bride

ארים ניסי במצפה פוֹר אְנפֵּייְרְאה מַאפְּנְשֵׁייאְה

ʔārīm niss-ī bam-miṣpe(h) pōr ən-pēy-rəh ma-pnśēyəh

raise.IPFV.1SG banner-1SG in.DEF-watchtower for of-do-INF 1SG.F.POSS-intention

I will raise my banner on the watchtower to accomplish what I intend

אל תראי אחותי פַשֵׁייר טִייקוֹבִיֶין פַרְשִׁי

ʔal tirʔī ʔăḥōṯ-ī paś-ēyr ṭīy-qōbīän par-śī

PROH be_afraid.JUSS.2SG.F sister-1SG pass-INF 2SG.CO-be_necessary.PRS.3SG through-here.

Do not be afraid, my sister, you must pass this way

נִי ווָרָא טוֹן בְרנַגְּא טוּלַייְרָש אִישִׁי טוֹן גָאגְּא

nī-wwār-ā ṭōn brnaḡə ṭū-layyr-āś īśī ṭōn gāḡə

NEG-be_of_value-FUT.3SG 2SG.M.POSS knighthood 2SG.CR-leave-FUT.2SG here 2SG.M.POSS pledge

your noble strength will be of no avail, you will leave your pledge here!

References

Aslanov, Cyril. 2003. "Le déchiffrement des gloses judéo-romanes: essai de rétrospective." *Helmántica* 163: 9–42.

Baldinger, Kurt and Frankwalt Möhren. 1974–. *Dictionnaire étymologique de l'ançien français* (= *DEAF*). 6– vols. Québec/Tübingen/Paris: Niemeyer.

Banitt, Menachem. 1963. "Une langue fantôme: le judéo-français." *Revue de Linguistique Romane* 27: 245–294.

Banitt, Menachem. 1966. "Les poterim." *Revue des Etudes Juives* 125: 21–33.

Banitt, Menachem. 1967. "L'étude des glossaires bibliques des Juifs de France au moyen âge. Méthode et application." In: The Israel Academy of Sciences and Humanities (ed.). *Proceedings. Vol. II. No. 10.* Jerusalem: Central Press: 188–210.

Banitt, Menachem. 1971–1972. "Judeo-French." *Encyclopaedia Judaica*, vol. 10: 423–425.

Banitt, Menahem. 1972. *Le Glossarie de Bâle, Introduction* and *Texte*, 2 vols. Jerusalem: The Israel Academy of Sciences and Humanities.

Banitt, Menahem. 1995–2005. *Le Glossarie de Leipzig, Introduction* and *Texte*, 4 vols. Jerusalem: The Israel Academy of Sciences and Humanities.

Banitt, Menahem. 1997. "Une vue d'ensemble sur les glossaires bibliques juifs de France au Moyen Age." In: Gilbert Dahan et al. (eds.). *Rashi et la culture juive en France du Nord au moyen âge.* Paris/Louvain: Peeters: 191–201.

Battenberg, Friedrich. ²2000. *Das europäische Zeitalter der Juden. Zur Entwicklung einer Minderheit in der nichtjüdischen Umwelt Europas*, 2 vols. Darmstadt: Wissenschaftliche Buchgesellschaft.

Bäuml, Franz. 1968. "Übergang mündlicher zur artes-bestimmten Literatur des Mittelalters." In: Gundolf Keil (ed.). *Fachliteratur des Mittelalters.* Stuttgart: Metzler: 1–10.

Blondheim, David Simon. 1927. *Poèmes judéo-français du moyen âge.* Paris: H. Champion.

Bunis, David. 1975. *Problems in Judezmo Linguistics* (Working Papers in Sephardic and Oriental Jewish Studies) vol. 1. New York: The American Sephardi Federation.

Buridant, Claude. 2000. *Grammaire nouvelle de l'ancien français.* Paris: Sedes.

Chambon, Jean-Pierre. 2006. "Lexicographie et Philologie: réflexions sur les glossaires d'éditions de textes (français médiéval et préclassique, ancien occitan)" *Revue de Linguistique Romane* 70: 123–142.

Chazan, Robert. 1973. *Medieval Jewry in Northern France. A Political and Social History*. Baltimore: Johns Hopkins University Press.

Dahan, Gilbert et al. (eds.). 1997. *Rashi et la culture juive en France du Nord au moyen âge*. Paris/Louvain: Peeters.

Darmesteter, Arsène. 1874. "Deux élégies du Vatican." *Romania* 3: 443–486.

Dieckhoff, Alain. 2007. "France." In: Michael Berenbaum and Fred Skolnik (eds.). *Encyclopaedia Judaica*, 2nd ed., vol. 7. Detroit: Macmillan: 146–170.

Edzard, Alexandra. 2011. *Varietätenlinguistische Untersuchungen zum Judenfranzösischen*. Frankfurt/Main: Peter Lang.

Edzard, Alexandra. 2014. "A Judeo-French wedding song from the mid-13th century: Literary contacts between Jews and Christians." *Journal of Jewish Languages* 2: 1–21.

Fudeman, Kirsten A. 2006. "'They have ears, but do not hear': Gendered Access to Hebrew and the Medieval Hebrew-French Wedding Song." *The Jewish Quarterly Review* 96/4: 542–567.

Fudeman, Kirsten A. 2010. *Vernacular Voices – Language and Identity in Medieval French Jewish Communities*. Philadelphia/Oxford: University of Pennsylvania Press.

Godefroy, Frédéric. 1880–1902. *Dictionnaire de l'ancienne langue française et de tous ses dialectes du IXe au XVe siècle*. 10 vols. Paris: Vieweg.

Golb, Noram. 1982. "Nature et destination du monument hebraïque découvert à Rouen." *Proceedings of the American Academy for Jewish Research* 48: 101–182.

Hagège, Claude. 2006. "Les gloses de Raschi, rabbin champenois du XIe siècle, document exceptionnel pour l'histoire du français parlé… et de l'hébreu." In: René-Samuel Sirat (ed.). *Héritages de Raschi. Actes du colloque scientifique réuni à l'occasion de la commémoration du 900ème anniversaire de la disparition de Raschi, Troyes – Paris, 27, 28 et 29 juin 2005*. Paris/Tel Aviv: Editions de l'éclat: 77–94.

Hindley, Alan, Frederick W. Langley, and Brian Levy. 2004. *Old French – English Dictionary*. Cambridge: University Press.

Kiwitt, Marc. 2001. *Der altfranzösische Fiebertraktat Fevres*. Würzburg: Königshausen und Neumann.

Kiwitt, Marc. 2013. *Les gloses françaises du glossaire biblique B.N. hébr. 301*. Heidelberg: Universitätsverlag Winter.

Kiwitt, Marc and Stephen Dörr. 2016. "Judeo-French." In: Lily Kahn and Aaron D. Rubin (eds.). *Handbook of Jewish Languages*. Leiden/Boston: Brill: 138–177.

Lambert, Mayer and Louis Brandin. 1905. *Glossaire hébreu-français du XIIIe siècle*. Paris: Ernest Leroux. Reprint: 1977. Genève: Slatkine Reprints.

Levy, Raphael. 1932. *Recherches lexicographiques sur d'anciens textes français d'origine juive*. Baltimore: Johns Hopkins University Press.

Levy, Raphael. 1960. *Contributions à la lexicographie française selon d'anciens textes d'origine juive*. Syracuse: Syracuse University Press.

Levy, Raphael. 1964. *Trésor de la langue des Juifs français au moyen âge*. Austin: University of Texas Press.

Marcus, Ivan. 1996. *Rituals of Childhood: Jewish acculturation in medieval Europe*. New Haven: Yale University Press.

Marcus, Ivan. 2002. "A Jewish-Christian symbiosis: The culture of early Ashkenaz." In: David Biale (ed.). *Cultures of the Jews: A new history*. New York: Schocken: 449–516.

Meyer-Lübke, Wilhelm. 1992. *Romanisches etymologisches Wörterbuch* (= *REW*). Heidelberg: Winter.

Meyer-Lübke, Wilhelm and Joseph Maria Piel. 1966. *Historische Grammatik der französischen Sprache*, vol. 2: Wortbildungslehre. Heidelberg: Winter.

Nyrop, Kristoffer. 1967. *Grammaire historique de la langue française*, vol. 2: Morphologie. Copenhague: Gyldendal.

Olszowy-Schlanger, Judith. 2018. "Manuscrits hébreux de Normandie et d'Angleterre au Moyen Âge." In: Nicolas Hatot and Judith Olszowy-Schlanger (eds.). *Savants et Croyants: Les Juifs d'Europe du Nord au Moyen Âge*. Rouen: Snoeck: 70–77.

Pfeffer, Wendy.1989. *Three Medieval Views of Women*. New Haven: Yale University Press.

Pfeffer, Wendy. 2001. *Songs of the Women Trouvères: An Anthology*. New Haven: Yale University Press.

Pope, Mildred K. 1952. *From Latin to Modern French with Especial Consideration of Anglo-Norman: Phonology and Morphology*. Rev. ed. Manchester: University of Manchester Press.

Rosenberg, Samuel. 1992. "The Medieval Hebrew-French Wedding Song." *Shofar* 11/1: 22–37.

Sala, Marius. 1998. "Die romanischen Judensprachen." In: Günter Holtus, Michael Metzeltin, and Christian Schmitt (eds.). *Lexikon der Romanistischen Linguistik*, vol. 7. Tübingen: Niemeyer: 372–395.

Sirat, Colette. 1994. *Du scribe au livre. Les manuscrits hébreux au Moyen Age*. Paris: CNRS Editions.

Sirat, Colette. 2002. *Hebrew Manuscripts of the Middle Ages*. Edited and translated by Nicholas de Lange. Cambridge: Cambridge University Press.

Steinschneider, Moritz. 1938. *Allgemeine Einleitung in die jüdische Literatur des Mittelalters*. Jerusalem: Bamberger und Wahrmann.

Tobler, Adolf, Erhard Lommatzsch, and Hans Helmut Christmann. 1925–2002. *Altfranzösisches Wörterbuch* (= *TL*). 11 vols. Berlin/Wiesbaden: Weidmann.

Wartburg, Walther von. 1950–. *Französisches etymologisches Wörterbuch* (= *FEW*). 25 vols. Tübingen: J.C.B. Mohr.

Weinreich, Max. 1973. *Geshikhte fun der Yidisher Shprakh*, 4 vols. New York: Yidisher Visnshaftlekher Institut = 2008. *History of the Yiddish Language*, 2 vols. YIVO Institute for Jewish Research/Yale University Press.

Zwink, Julia. 2017. *Altfranzösisch in hebräischer Graphie – Teiledition und Analyse des Medizintraktats "Fèvres"*. Berlin/Boston: Walter de Gruyter.

https://en.wikipedia.org/wiki/Goliard: "Goliardic culture"

Judeo-Provençal

Cyril Aslanov, Aix-Marseille Université / Institut Universitaire de France

1. Introduction

In this chapter[1] we will follow the development of Judeo-Provençal or rather of the various varieties of Occitan or Provençal used by Jews throughout the history of Jewish presence in what is today Southern France. Max Weinreich stated that Provençal Jews spoke the so-called *Chuadit* since the beginning of their existence as a distinct Jewry (Weinreich 1980: 101; 159). This assumption of Weinreich relies on Zośa Szajkowski's short study (Szajkowski 1948: 4–5) where the author considers the word *chuadit* (possibly a corruption of יהודית "Jewish") the usual name for the language of the Jews of Comtat Venaissin. However, it is absolutely not certain that modern time Provençal Jews ever used this word *chuadit* in order to refer to their language. In the parodic play *Harcanot et Barcanot* that was written by Israël Bédarride around 1820, the word used in order to refer to the specifically Jewish way of speaking Provençal is *lassan hakodes*, i.e. *ləšon ha-qodeš* 'Hebrew' (Pansier 1925: 136). Actually, it is not really Hebrew, but rather a variety of Provençal strongly relexified through a high contingent of Hebrew (often corrupted) words. A similar use of the word *ləšon ha-qodeš* (*ləschaun əkaudesch)* is found in Alsace and Baden in order to refer to an encrypted variety of Western Yiddish, and in Rome (*scionaccodesce)* in order to refer to a similarly encoded register of the Roman variety of Judeo-Italian (*giudaico-romanesco*). This term *lassan hakodes* that is paralleled in German- and Italian-speaking countries in order to refer to a cryptolalic way to resort to Hebrew in order to encode the language has nothing to do with the spontaneous use of the Provençal vernacular in Jewish context.

Thus it would be vain to assume a continuity from the first attestation of Occitan written in Hebrew letters (glosses inserted in David Qimḥi's *Sefer Ha-Šorašim*) to the last echoes of the Jewish variety of Modern Provençal in Armand Lunel's writing. Unlike Yiddish or Judeo-Spanish, Judeo-Provençal cannot be considered a single language that owes to be described as a system of its own. The very term "Judeo-Provençal" could give the wrong impression that there was a distinct language used by the various Jewish communities that developed in Occitania from the time of Charlemagne until the beginning of the twentieth century. Actually, each region where Jews are documented throughout the history of Occitania has its own variety of the local blend of Occitan used at the same time by the Gentile surroundings.

1 This research was conducted thanks to the funding of the Russian Science Foundation (project №15-18-00062), St. Petersburg State University.

2. Overview

2.1 Origin

The first traces of Jewish presence in Southern Gallia (Gallia Narbonensis) go back to the Roman time. However, there is no guarantee that the Jews attested in Occitania since the early Middle Ages are a direct continuation of the Jewish colonies on Gaulish soil. Actually, the first attestation of an important community is connected with Frankish-ruled Narbonne where Pepin the Short established the Babylonian Jew Makhir ben Yehudah Zakkai as the head of a Jewish feud. There is no clear evidence as to the language those Narbonese Jews spoke in that remote time, but one thing is sure: it could not have been Provençal since this language is not attested before the *Song of Saint Fides* (ca. 1060). Judging from the Babylonian origin of the Davidic aristocracy of this Jewish colony in Narbonne, it might be that they remained Arabic-speaking for quite a long time. However, when Joseph Qimḥi settled in Narbonne short after 1147, it seems that the local Jewry there was no longer connected with Arabophony, as shown by the fact that his son David found it necessary to write his *Sefer Ha-Šorašim*, which is roughly an adaptation of Ibn Janāḥ's *Kitāb al-ʔUṣūl* to an audience unable to understand Arabic.

During the twelfth-thirteenth century, the main bulk of Occitan Jewry was gathered in Languedoc, and more specifically in the area near Beziers, in a territory that corresponds to today's Hérault. However, after the annexation of Languedoc to the Kingdom of France in 1229 and the repeated expulsions of the Jews from the Kingdom between 1306 and 1394, many Jews had to leave Languedoc for Provence, east of the Rhône, a territory that was still out of the reach of France.

However, in 1482 the Kingdom of Provence became a personal possession of the King of France, which provoked a second exodus of Occitan-speaking Jews either outside Provence or to the parts of Provence that belonged to other powers: to Comtat Venaissin, a possession of the Holy See since 1274, and to Nice and the surroundings that belonged to the House of Savoy since the handing over of Nice to Amadeus VII in 1388.

The synagogue of Carpentras

In the Comtat Venaissin and in Nice the Jews were compelled to gather in ghettos starting from 1555 when Pope Paul IV issued the bull *Cum nimis absurdum*. In the Comtat Venaissin those ghettos were called *carriero* 'streets' because they were actually limited to one unique street in the four cities where the presence of Jews was still allowed (Avignon; Carpentras; Cavaillon; L'Isle-sur-la-Sorgue). In Nice, the Jewish quarter was known as *lou guet*, a Provençal adaptation of Italian *il ghetto/lo ghetto*. In Early modern times the Jews of the *carriero* produced interesting texts known as *obro* 'works', a Provençal term that could be considered an approximative equivalent of *piyyuṭ* 'liturgical poem'. The peculiarity of the *obro* is that they intertwine Hebrew and Provençal written in Hebrew letters.

After the abolition of the *carriero* in 1791, a consequence of the annexation of the Pontifical enclave of Comtat Venaissin to revolutionary France, the Jews of the four cities began to settle in other cities throughout Southern France. Many Jews of Provençal background assimilated to the Gentile population. Those who remained faithful to Judaism were overwhelmed by the arrival of non-Provençal Jews in Southern France throughout the nineteenth-twentieth centuries: Alsatians; East European Ashkenazim; Sephardites from Greece and Turkey and more recently North African Jews.

In spite of those demographic transformations that brought to the disappearance of a specific Provençal Jewish identity, some remnants of the ancestral language once spoken by Provençal Jews are still preserved by the descendents of the *Carriero* Jews. An association called *Association culturelle des Juifs du Pape* publishes a newsletter entitled *L'Écho des Carrières* where studies about the legacy of the Provençal Jewry help preserve the memory of a vanished world.

2.2 Script

Throughout the Middle Ages what makes the specificity of Judeo-Provençal is mostly the use of Hebrew letters in order to write the common language of Gentiles and Jews. By itself, the Provençal found in David Qimḥi's *Sefer Ha-Šorašim*, in Joseph Caspi's *Šaršot Ha-Kesef*, or in Crescas del Caylar's *Roman d'Esther* is not different from the language used in Narbonne or in Arles. The situation is reversed in early modern times. By then, the specificity of Judeo-Provençal in terms of graphematics is not any more connected with the fact that the Provençal words are written in Hebrew letters but conversely, it is related to the fact that some Hebrew words integrated within the remnants of modern Judeo-Provençal are written with Latin letters, which makes their identification sometimes extremely difficult.

Provençal was sometimes written by means of Hebrew letters. It is worth noting that not all of the 22 letters of the Hebrew alphabet were actually used in order to write Provençal. 6 of them (*zain*; *ḥet*; *kaf*; *samekh*; *ʕain*; *tav*) had no relevance for the writing of Provençal in Hebrew letters. The following table includes some letters with diacritics (*gereš* above the *gimel*; *rafeh*).

Hebrew letters (with their traditional phonetic value in the mainstream pronunciation of Hebrew)	Medieval Judeo-Provençal value
א ʔ	[a]: רומאן *roman* "Romance (language)"
	every initial vowel (followed by ו or י when representing a vowel other than [a]): אירא *era*, indicative imperfect 3rd person sg. of *esser* 'to be'
-א -ʔ	[-a] (word end): טיסטא *testa* 'head'
ב b	[b] at the beginning of word: בריגאדה *bregada* 'brawl'
	[v] in intervocalic position: אמנוביט *amanovit* 'prepared'
	[w] as a second element of diphthong: סיבטאט *ciutat* 'city'
ג g	[g] before [a], [o], [u], [y] or consonant: גרדיר *grazir* 'to please'
	[dʒ] before [e] and [i] with or without a diacritic use of י/יי *y/yy*: גיינולס *genols* 'knees'
	[tʃ] at the end of the word (with or without a preceding יי *yy*): לישקריג *l'escrig* 'the writing'; פאייג *fag* 'deed'
ג́ *gimel* with a diacritic above	[tʃ] (mostly at the end of the word): דריג́ *dreg* 'right'
ד d	[d]: דימאנדאר *demandar* 'to ask for'
ד̄ *daleth rafeh* = [ð] (diacritic not necessarily noted)	[z]: אבד̄יר *auzir* 'to hear'
-ה -*a(h)* (*mater lectionis* for final [a])	[-a] (end of the word): פירדוננצה *perdonansa* 'forgiveness'
ו w/v/u/o	[v] וינק *venc* 'came'
	[w] (first element of the diphthong [we]) פוייש *pueis* 'afterward'
	[o] אום *om* 'man'
	[y] נולייא *nulha* 'none'
ט ṭ	[t] טוט *tot* 'all'
י j/i	[i] אי *i* 'there'
	[e] אין *en* 'in'
ל l	[l] לאש *las* 'the' (definite article feminine plural)
לי ly	[ʎ] ליי *lhi* 'to him'
יל yl	[ʎ] קונשייל *conselh* 'counsel'
מ m	[m] מורט *mort* 'death'

נ n	[n] נוש *nos* 'us'
ני ny	[ɲ] שניור *senhor* 'sir'
פ p	[p] פיר *per* 'for'
פֿ f *pe rafeh* (diacritic not necessarily noted)	[f] פין *fin* 'fine'
צ ṣ	[s] אצירטא *acerta* 'it asserts'
-טץ -ṭṣ (word end)	[-ts] שירוויטץ *servitz* 'served'
ק q	[k] קוד̄ינא *cozina* 'kitchen'
ר r	[r] ריי *rei* 'king'
ש š	[s] שיגון *segon* 'according to'

2.3 Phonology

From the twelfth to the fifteenth century the Provençal written in Hebrew letter do not seem to diverge phonetically from the language used by the Gentile surroundings. This makes the decipherment of the glosses or of the continuous texts (*Roman d'Esther*; translation of prayer books) quite easy.

The situation may be slightly different in early modern times when the Jewish population of Provence was ghettoized in the Jewish *carriero* (streets) of Avignon, Carpentras, Cavaillon, L'Isle-sur-la-Sorgue and quite isolated from the Christians. Although there was an improvement of the Jewish condition toward the end of the *carriero* period and the barriers of the ghetto were partly lifted at least informally, it seems that the isolation of the Jews brought about a slightly different pronunciation of the Provençal dialect in use in the Comtat Venaissin (Provençal rhodanien).

One of the proofs that may be adduced in order to corroborate this assumption is the existence of a satiric play in Provençal where the Jews of the *carriero* are ridiculized through their speech and more specially through their way of pronouncing the local dialect. And in *Harcanot et Barcanot* (Bibliothèque Inguimbertine, ms. 1005–7; Pansier 1925), another satiric play written by the Provençal Jew Israël Bédarride (1798–1869), the accent of Carpentras Jews is mocked in a way that betrays that in the *carriero* the [dʒ] was pronounced as a [tʃ] or as a [ʃ], as in the word *jamai* 'never' that becomes *chamai* (Szajkowski 1948: 54).

This difference in the pronunciation of [dʒ] may be due to the fact that in modern Provençal, the etymological [dʒ] becomes [dz]. Apparently, the shift [dʒ] > [dz] was not shared by the Jews of the Comtat, maybe because of the Languedocian origin of many Comtadine Jews who left Languedoc for Provence after the reiterated expulsions of the Jews from the Kingdom of France in the fourteenth century. The Languedocian accent of the *carriero* Jews may have prevented them from pronouncing the postpalatal voiced affricate [dʒ] as a dental affricate [dz]. However, the preservation of the postpalatal nature of the affricate was followed by a devoicing of [dʒ] into [tʃ]. This seems to be a way of adapting the Languedocian phonology to the phonology of the local (Rhodanian) Provençal dialect. Another explanation has been proposed by Marie-Claire Viguier for this strange devoicing of the affricate [dʒ]. Viguier prefers to ascribe this evolution to a Spanish influence connected with the evolution of [dʒ]/[ʒ] to [ʃ], the last stage before the shift from [ʃ] to [x] (as in *hijo* or *mujer*) (Viguier 1988). Whatever the explanation might be, it remains beyond doubt that in early modern times, the Comtadine Jews had a slight different way of pronouncing the affricate [dʒ].

Another interesting point relates to a specific realization of some occurrences of [s] in the Hebrew component of modern Judeo-Provençal. As a matter of fact, most of those occurrences are actually connected with the pronunciation of *tav rafeh*, *śin* and *samekh* in a way that seems to oscillate between [s] and [f], perhaps as an interdental [θ] (Jochnowitz 1978: 70; Aslanov 2014): e.g., *guenevuf* < גנבות 'stealing'; *afani* < עָשַׂנִי 'made me'.

2.4 *Morphology and morphosyntax*

There is not very much to say about the morphology of the various strata of Provençal in Jewish context. The first continuous text written in Judeo-Provençal, the *Roman d'Esther*, does not display any difference from the literary *koiné* that was still in use in the first half of the fourteenth century. The only feature of the language that could be ascribed to an influence of the Hebrew language is a kind of *smikhut kfulah,* i.e. a redundant marking of the relation of possession between the possessor and the possessed: *sapiam de Vasti sa sentencia*, literally "let us know of Vasti her judgment", i.e. 'let us know the judgment regarding Vasti'. We find a similar construction in Ladino where the Aramaic formula בריך שמה דמרא עלמא 'blessed be the name of the lord of the world' is translated as *bendicho su nombre de el sinior del mundo*. In the *Roman d'Esther,* this redundant way of expressing possession is combined with a reverted construction whereby the possessor precedes the possessed.

2.5 *Lexicon*

As mentioned above, the Hebrew component appears mainly in the cryptolalic register known as *lassan hakodes*. However, the indiosyncratic way of pronouncing Hebrew in the communities of Comtat Venaissin and the total integration of the Hebrew words to the morphophonemic scheme of the local Provençal dialect made the Hebrew merged in the vernacular sometimes extremely difficult to recognize. As a matter of fact, Max Weinreich's distinction between merged and whole Hebrew is hardly relevant here since even the whole Hebrew was pronounced in a very awkward way (Szajkowski 1948: iii).

Since the *lassan hakodes*, which Armand Lunel used to name *argot hébraïco-provençal* "Hebrew-Provençal slang", was nothing but a cryptolalic register used only in very specific circumstances by a few people initiated to this way of speaking, it is difficult to consider it a genuine example of the way the Provençal of the Jews integrated the Hebrew component. In order to have a more authentic picture of the Hebrew component in the Jewish variety of Provençal, it is perhaps sounder to resort to more neutral varieties of the language. Thus in a text written around 1557 in Latin letters in order to make the by-laws of the community of Carpentras available to the pontificial administration, we find the form *hermatz* 'confiscated as a result of an anatheme', where we can recognize the past passive participle masculine plural of a verb *hermar*, a denominative verb derived from the Hebrew word *ḥerem* 'anathema' (Aslanov 2006: 26). Even when the anonymous scribe wanted to make the text understandable for the Gentiles, he was unable to find a proper term able to transpose the notion conveyed by *hermar*, probably a translation of הֶחֱרִים 'to confiscate; to anathemize', if we take into account that the original of those by-laws *(haskamot/escamot)* was probably in Hebrew.

Conversely, it seems that many Hebrew culture words that are usually expressed in Hebrew in most of the Jewish languages or ethnolects have been translated into Provençal by the local Jews. Thus such words as *miqweh* ritual bath', *maṣah* 'azyme', or *šofar* 'ram's horn' are transposed into Provençal as *cabussadou* (from the verb *cabussar* 'to plunge'), *coudolo*, and *cornet*, respectively (Szajkowski 1948: 18).

3. Text samples

3.1 Extract from Crescas del Caylar's (ישראל קשלרי) Roman d'Esther *(ca. 1322)* (Neubauer-Meyer 1892)

Although the text of the ms. (London, Adler 28) is written in Hebrew letters (see above the norms of transliteration of Provençal into Hebrew letters), I have chosen to quote it in transliteration. I have slightly changed the transliteration already used by Paul Meyer in order to make more conform to the spelling rules of the Provençal literary koiné in the Middle Ages.

ציל קאוואלייר אויאה דוש נומש

Cel cavalier av-ia dos nom-s
DEM.M.SG knight:SG have-3SG.PST.IPF two name-PL
This knight had two names

המן אירא שון נום אינלאייק

Haman era son nom en laic
Haman be:3SG.PST.IPF POSS.3M.SG name:SG in laic:M.SG
Haman was his name in lay

מיש און לאפילאווא אינאבראייק

Mes on l'-apela-va en ebraic
However PRON.INDF.3SG PRON.OBJ.3M.SG-call-3SG.PST.IPF in Hebrew:M.SG
However people used to call him in Hebrew

ממוכן אין אקישט אינויט

Memucan, en aqu-est envit,
Memucan in DEM-M.SG invitation:M.SG
Memukan in that invitation

קי וול דיר אין רומאן אמנוביט

Que vol dir en roman a-manov-it
REL will:PRS.3SG say:INF in Romance:M.SG be-at-hand:PST.PTCP.M.SG
Which means 'prepared' in Romance

דמאל אפאר אירא בין אפארילייאט

De mal a far era ben aparelha-t,
of evil to do:INF be.PST.IPF good.ADV equip:PST.PTCP.M.SG
He was well prepared for doing evil

אי אקו אירא בין טאלייאט

E aco era ben talha-t.
and DEM.N.SG be:PST.IPF good.ADV cut-PST.PTCP.M.SG
And this was well shaped

שונום מיטיבש אירא גארינט

So nom meteus era garent
POSS.3M.SG name:M.SG itself:M.SG be:PST.IPFV garant:SG
Even his name was a guarantee

קי איל אנאבא מאל קירינט

Que el ana-va mal quer-ent;
COMP 3SG go-PST.IPF.3.SG evil.SG look_for-PR.PTCP
Because he was continuously searching for evil

פיר אקו אק נום ממוכן

Per aco ac nom Memucan;
For 3N.SG have.PRF.3SG name:SG Memucan
Therefore he was called Memukan

נון ליי שאיי פאר שינון עכן

Non lhi sai par se non ʕAkhan
NEG DAT.SG.3 know:PRS.1SG equal:SG if NEG ʕAkhan
I do not know anybody equal to him if not Achan (v. 286–296)

The Jewish character of this rewriting of the Book of Esther according to the formal pattern (octosyllabic rhymed couplet) of Provençal narrative or didactic poems like *Jaufré* (end of the twelfth century-beginning of the thirteenth), the *Romance of Flamenca* (ca. 1234–5) or Matfre d'Ermengau's *Breviari d'amor* (after 1288) is mainly connected with the use of Hebrew letters in order to transcribe or rather transliterate Provençal. However, the content and more precisely the ability to make cross-linguistic puns between Hebrew and Provençal could be considered an additional mark of the Jewishness of this text. Crescas del Caylar tries to find the etymology of the name Haman, which he connects by way of a cross-linguistic paronomasia to the past participle of the verb *amanovir* 'to put at hand'.

3.2 Translation of a prayer book for women (Leeds, Roth 32, 14th century)

I adopted a slightly different transliteration from the one used by George Jochnowitz in his study on this prayer book and I corrected his reading of בֶּנְדִיג from *benedich* to *bendich* (Jochnowitz 1981).

בנדִיג טוּ שנט בינידִ̄יט נושטרי דייב

Bendich tu sant benezet nostre Dieu
bless:PST.PTCP.M.SG 2SG holy:M.SG the_blessed_one:M.SG POSS.1PL.M.SG God:M.SG
Blessed art thou, holy blessed, our God,

רֶי דיל שיגלי קי נוֹן פיש מִי שירבנטה

rei de-l segle que non fis mi servant-a
king:M.SG of-DEF.M.SG world:SG REL NEG make:PRF.3SG OBJ.1SG servant-F.SG
king of the universe, who did not make me a servant

בנדִיג טוּ שנט בינידֿיט נושטרי דייב
Bendich tu sant benezet nostre Dieu
bless:PST.PTCP.M.SG 2SG holy:M.SG the_blessed_one:M.SG POSS.1PL.M.SG God:M.SG
Blessed art thou, holy blessed, our God,

רֶי דיל שיגלי קי נוֹן פיש מִי גויה
rei de-l segle que non fis mi goy-a
king:M.SG of-DEF.M.SG world:SG REL NEG make:PRF.3SG OBJ.1SG gentile-F.SG
king of the universe, who did not make me a Gentile

בנדִיג טוּ שנט בינידֿיט נושטרי דייב
Bendich tu sant benezet nostre Dieu
bless:PST.PTCP.M.SG 2SG holy:M.SG the_blessed_one:M.SG POSS.1PL.M.SG God:M.SG
Blessed art thou, holy blessed, our God,

רֶי דיל שיגלי קי פיש מִי פֵינה
rei de-l segle que fis mi fena
king:M.SG of-DEF.M.SG world:SG REL make:PRF.3SG OBJ.1SG woman:SG
king of the universe, who made me a woman

This excerpt is a calque-translation of three Hebrew blessings recited in the frame of the blessing of the dawn. The omission of the copula in Hebrew (ברוך אתה lit. "blessed thou") is reproduced as such in the target language although a verb in the subjunctive would have been expected in this syntactic context. The original formulation of the blessing in Hebrew contains the substitute of the Tetragrammaton (ה'), pronounced *Adonai*. The Provençal translation replaced it by the formula *sant benezet*, lit. "holy blessed", which is a calque-translation of Aramaic/Hebrew קודשא בריך הוא/ הקדוש ברוך הוא 'the Holy one, blessed be He'. The Hebrew passive participle ברוך is translated in two different ways: first as *bendich*, the past passive participle of *bendir* 'to bless'; second as *benezet*, a form that is not part of the conjugation of *bendir* since it is the direct continuation of the Latin past passive participle *benedictus* from *benedicere*.

3.3 Ḥad Gadya *'one kid' in Provençal*

A Passover cumulative song written originally in Aramaic and first attested in an Ashkenazi Haggada from 1406. It has been translated into many languages, including Provençal. The present version was sung by Armand Lunel, the last depositary of the Jewish-Provençal tradition.

Un cabri, un cabri
INDEF.M.SG kid:SG INDEF.M.SG kid:SG
A kid, a kid

Que av-ié achat-a m-oun paire
REL have-PST.IPF.3SG buy:PST.PTCP.M.SG POSS.1M.SG father:SG
Whom my father had bought

Un escu, dous escu
one:M.SG crown:SG two crown:PL
One crown, two crowns

Ḥad Gadya (Aramaic)
one.M kid
One kid

Es ven-g-u lou cat
be:PRS.3.SG come-PST.PTCP.M.SG DEF.M.SG cat:M.SG
The cat has come

A mangi-a lou cabri
have:PRS.3.SG eat-PST.PTCP.M.SG ART.M.SG kid:M.SG
Has eaten the kid

Que av-ié achat-a m-oun paire ...
REL have-PST.IPF.3SG buy:PST.PTCP.M.SG POSS-1M.SG father:SG
That my father had bought ...

3.4 Bilingual obro (piyyuṭ) *from the first half of the eighteenth century*

אֶפְתַּח נָא שְׂפָתַי בְּרִנָּה

ʔEftaḥ na śefat-ay be-rinah
open.JUSS.1SG COH lip.DU.CS-POSS.1SG in-joy
Let me open my lips in joy

קַנטארֵים דֵימָה אַ אַדִינָה

Cantar-em dema a adina
sing-FUT.1PL tomorrow:ADV for have_dinner:INF
Tomorrow we will sing during the meal

יִרְאַת ה׳ לְמַעֲנָהּ

Irʔat Adonai le-maʕan-ah
fear.CS God ("my lords") for-sake-POSS.3F.SG
The fear of God stays for its own sake

קַאקוֹ אֵיש לוּ גְראַן מֵישְׁטְרֵ

Qu'aco es lou gran mestre
because:CONJ'DEM.NEUTR.SG be:IND.PRS.3SG DEF.M.SG great:M.SG master:SG
Because He is the great lord

וְאוֹדֶה נָא לָאֵל עֶלְיוֹן

ve-ʔodeh na le-ʔel ʕeliyon
and-praise.JUSS.1SG COH for-God high
And let me praise God the Most High

דֵישוש טמבוּרִין אַי אי ביוּלוֹן

dessus tambourin e i vioulon
on tambourin:PL (unmarked) and in.DEF.PL violin:PL (unmarked)
on tamboourines and violins

אַבְרָם אֵיש אֵישְׁטָה קוֹמַנְדָה

Abram es est-a comand-a
Abram be IND.PRS.3SG be.PST.PTCP.M.SG summon PST.PTCP.M.SG
Abram has been summoned

לִכְרוֹת בְּשַׂר עוֹרְלָתוֹ

li-khrot beśar ʕorlat-o
for-cut:INF flesh.CS foreskin.CS-POSS.3M.SG
to cut the flesh of his foreskin

א דייב נאבטגֵי פאש רֵיפוּדָה

A Diou n'autg-é pas refus-a
to God:SG NEG(first part) 'dare-PF.3SG NEG(second part) refuse INF
He did not dare to refuse to God

לָמוּל בְּשַׂר עוֹרְלָתוֹ

li-mol beśar ḥerpat-o
for-circumcise:INF flesh.CS pudendum.CS-POSS.3M.SG
to circumcise the flesh of his pudendum

טרֵיש גור אפרֵיש פוּגֵי מלאב

Tres jour après fugu-é malau
three day:PL (unmarked) afterwards be-PF.3SG sick:M.SG
Three days afterwards he was sick

וַיִּשְׁלַח מַלְאָכָיו אֵלָיו

va-yišlaḥ malakh-av ʔel-av
and-send.PRET.3M.SG messenger.PL.CS-POSS.3M.SG to-3.M.SG
He sent his messengers to him.

לִי רֵיצֵיבֵי פוֹרט בוֹלוּנטיאֵרש

Li recev-é fort voluntiers
ACC.3PL receive-PF.3SG strong:ADV willing:ADV
He received them very willingly

רָץ אֶל הַמֵּמִית בַּעֲלֵי חַיִים

raṣ ʔel ha-memit baʕalei ḥayim
run:PF.3.M.SG to DEF-kill.PTCP.M.SG owner.PL.CS life
He ran to the slaughterer

אמֵי אוּנוֹ גרנדוֹ אמִיטִיאֵי

Amé un-o grand-o amitié
with INDEF.F.SG great-F.SG friendship:SG (French loanword)
With a great friendship

אָמַר: יוֹחַז נָא מַיִם

ʔamar: yoḥaz na mayim
say:PF.3M.SG take:PF.3M.SG COH water
He said: let him take water

אֵי אפרֵיש קֵי טוּט פוּגֵה פרֵיש

E après que tout fugu-é près
and after CONJ all:M.SG be-PF.3SG ready:M.SG
And after everything was ready

מנגֵירוּן דֵישוש לארבַרֵי פרֵיש

mang-eroun desous l'arbre frès
eat-PF.3PL under DEF.M.SG'tree:SG (French loanword) fresh:M.SG
they ate under the fresh tree

3.5 Harcanot e Barcanot, *a parodic play written by Israël Bédarride around 1820* (Pansier 1925: 134–135)

Barcanot:

Nous plaignissen de rèn moussu lou haoumoun,
1PL.REFL complain:IND.PRS.1PL of nothing sir:SG^{F} (< *monsieur*) DEF.M.SG archbishop:SG^{H} (< הֶגְמוֹן)
We are not complaining about anything, Sir Archbishop,

s-ian dóu matin chusqu' au soir
be-IND.PRS.1PL from.DEF.M.SG morning:SG until^{F} (< *jusqu'*) to.DEF.M.SG evening:M.SG^{F}
we are from morning to evening

au bardat de Cancan; la velho de chontou aqui
in.DEF.M.SG square:SG of gossip:M.SG DEF.F.SG eve:F.SG of holiday:SG^{H} (< יום טוב) here
on the Esplanade of Gossip. On festival eve here

tout kahal pass-e; qui dabèr-on tout
all:M.SG congregation^{H} pass_by-IND.PRS.3SG here speak^{H}-IND.PR.3PL (< דִּבֵּר) all:M.PL (plural unmarked)
all the congregation passes by. Here everybody comment whatever

de que i a dins la plaço S'a-n sahat-a
of REL there have:IND.PRS.3SG in DEF.F.SG square:SG if'have:IND.PRS.3PL slaughter^{H}-PST.PTCP.M.SG (< שָׁחַת)
there is on the square. If they have slaughtered

un bióu, se se fai un berif,
INDEF.M.SG ox:SG if 3SG.REFL do:IND.PRS.3.SG INDEF.M.SG circumcision:M.SG^{H} (< בְּרִית)
an ox, if a circumcision is performed

S'un tau a pas manc-a ni minrha
if'INDEF.M.SG such:M.SG have:IND.PRS.3SG NEG fail-PST.PTCP.M.SG neither afternoon.prayer:SG^{H} (< מִנְחָה)
If someone by any chance failed to go to the afternoon prayer

ni arvif; En un mot se dis tout,
nor evening.prayer:SG^{H} (< עַרְבִית) in one.M word:SG 3SG.REFL say:IND.PRS.3SG all:M.SG
or to the evening prayer. In one word, everything is said,

e pèr fini l'afaire Vous daberer-ai dounc ...
and for end:IND DEF.F.SG 2PL.DAT speak-IND.FUT.1SG thus ...
and in order to end the account I shall thus speak to you ...

Moun fils, ves-qui t-oun paire.
POSS.1M.SG son, see:IND.PRS.2SG-here POSS-2M.SG father.
My son, behold your father.

References

Aslanov, Cyril. 2006. "The Translation of the 1557 *Escamot* into Provençal: Preservation or Blurring of the Jewish Linguistic Identity?" *Massorot: Studies in Language Traditions and Jewish Languages* 13–14: 25–39. (in Hebrew)

Aslanov, Cyril. 2014. "On the Realization of Some Consonants in the Tradition of Hebrew of Provençal Jews in Modern Times and on Its Signification Regarding the Issue of Judeo-Provençal." In: Moshe Bar-Asher and Irit Meir (eds.). *Niṭʕe Ilan: Meḥqarim ba-lašon ha-ʕivrit u-ve-ʔaḥayote-ha mugašim le-Ilan Eldar*. Jerusalem: Carmel, 357–368. (in Hebrew)

Guggenheim-Grinberg, Florence. 1954. "The Horse Dealers' Language of the Swiss Jews in Endingen and Lengnau." In: Uriel Weinreich (ed.) *The Field of Yiddish: Studies in Language, Folklore, and Literature*. New York: Linguistic Circle of New York, 48–62.

Jochnowitz, George. 1978. "Judeo-Romance Languages." In: Herbert H. Paper (ed.) *Jewish Languages: Themes and Variations* (Proceedings of Regional Conferences of the Association for Jewish Studies Held at the University of Michigan and New York University in March-April 1975). Cambridge, MA: Association for Jewish Studies, 65–73.

Jochnowitz, George. 1981. "… Who Made Me a Woman." *Commentary* 71/4: 63–64.

Neubauer, Adolf Zvi and Paul Meyer. 1892. "Le roman provençal d'Esther par Crescas du Caylar, médecin juif du XIVe siècle." *Romania* 21: 194–227.

Pansier, Pierre. 1925. "Une comédie en argot judéo-provençal de la fin du XVIIIe siècle." *Revue des Études Juives* 81: 113–145.

Szajkowski, Zośa. 1948. *The Language of the Jews in the Four Communities of Comtat Venaissin*. New York: Yivo. (in Yiddish)

Viguier, Marie-Claire. 1988. "Le judéo-occitan existe… Essai sur la 'lenga juzieva'." In: Marie-Claire Viguier and Dominique Alibert (eds.). *Juifs et source juive en Occitanie*, Valderiès: Vent Terral, 193–209.

Weinreich, Max. 1980. *History of the Yiddish Language*, trans. Shlomo Noble. Chicago-London: The University of Chicago Press.

Judeo-Greek

Julia G. Krivoruchko, University of Cambridge

1. Introduction

1.1 Glottonyms

During the Hellenistic period and Middle Ages, authors writing in Hebrew and Aramaic referred to the Greek language, including the Greek used by Jews, using derivatives from the root יוון *yavan*, e.g., לשון יוון *lešon yavan* / לעז יווני *laʕaz yavan*, יוונית *yavanit*. The printers of the early modern period continued this practice.

Greek Jewish language varieties of the modern period usually received their names from the locations and social settings. For example, in Ioannina, where the community historically resided in the Castle and by the marketplace, the terms *kastriná*, lit. '[the language variety] of the Castle', or *kourmaniótika*, lit. '[the language variety] of the market' were used. Such terms were exo-glottonyms of limited local usage. The general endo-glottonym was the name of the principal surrounding language: ἑλληνικά 'Hellenic, Greek' (see Sample 3 below). There is no evidence that late-medieval or early-modern Greek Jews were eager to emphasize linguistic differences between themselves and their non-Jewish neighbours through a specific term, much more so one covering all the language varieties used by Greek-speaking communities.

In J[udeo-]G[reek] speech Greeks and occasionally other Christians were commonly called יוונים *yavanim/yevanim*, and their vernacular *yavanitika/yevanitika*. This latter term could be applied to JG by way of synecdoche, *qua* a variety of Greek. However, Greek Jews characterized themselves as *Εβραίοι*, *Ισραηλίτες* or *yehudim*, with *yevanim* appearing only as exo-ethnonym for differentiation purposes in intercommunal contexts. Thus, the names for JG are typologically similar to those found in other Jewish communities.[1]

In the scholarly milieu, researchers of pre-modern Judeo-Greek (including deniers thereof) called and continue to call the object of their enquiry 'Jewish Greek' or 'Jud(a)eo-Greek'.[2] However, some linguists of Yiddish found these terms unacceptable for ideological reasons, as presumably invalidating Jewish subjectness, and promoted instead 'Yevanic' for post-Hellenistic JG.[3] The term was adopted in the *Ethnologue*, a handwritten checklist of languages drafted in the SIL for practical convenience.[4] In 1958 *Ethnologue* became a printed reference book and gained popularity in the English-speaking world. Later, USA standard authorities incorporated the SIL-created list into the international standard for naming languages, and as a result towards the end of the

1 On the typology of Jewish glottonyms see Bunis 2008.

2 E.g., Horsley 1989; George 2010; van der Horst 2015; Wexler 1985; Bubenik 1997; Hollender and Niehoff-Panagiotidis 2011; Aslanov 2012.

3 Timm 2011; Weinreich 1954: 34; Gold 1987; for background see Sunshine 1995.

4 The current edition is Simons and Fennig 2020.

twentieth century the designation started appearing in other languages, e.g., French *yévanique*, Greek *γεβανικά*. However, it remained rare as far as scholarly use is concerned, ceding to chronologically wider *Judeo-Greek* (JG).

1.2 Historical outline

Contacts between Jews and Greek-speakers started as early as the first millennium BCE and intensified during the Hellenistic and Roman period. The increasing influence of Greek in Palestine resulted in some Jews becoming Greek-L2 and Greek-L3 learners and later Hebrew-/Aramaic-Greek bilinguals. In diaspora, Hebrew-L1 or Aramaic-L1 attriters also became Hebrew-/Aramaic-Greek bilinguals, with later generations developing Greek monolingualism and eventually preserving Hebrew as their heritage language.

The need for a lingua franca and the prestige of Greek resulted in the spread of Greek education across the Mediterranean. Having received Greek education, the acculturated Hellenistic/Roman Jews would normally use Greek script for writing down their varieties of Greek, which could be as different as those of Ezekiel the Tragedian (2nd century BCE), Philo (10/15 BCE – after 40 CE) and Josephus Flavius (37/38 – after 100 CE). The Septuagint (250 BCE – 100 CE), the most important Jewish linguistic product of the Hellenistic period, exhibits rich evidence of language contact: neologisms of Semitic origin, semantic shifts in Jewish-specific vocabulary, and impact of the Semitic syntax. However, being a translation, the LXX cannot provide information about the non-translational JG language varieties, and documentary evidence that could shed light on such varieties is scarce.

During the Hellenistic and Roman period Greek was used by Jews in the remote corners of the Mediterranean including modern Spain and France.[5] JG in these territories became a non-co-territorial Jewish language, but its existence in this capacity was short-lived: with the division of the Roman Empire Western JG was gradually abandoned in favour of local Romance varieties.

The decline of Greek after the Islamic conquests in the seventh century halted Greek education among the local Jews and lead to their switching to Arabic across the Middle East and North Africa. In Asia Minor, northern Syria, the Balkans, South Italy and Sicily, Greek continued to be widely spoken, yet the encroaching Rabbinic Judaism introduced Hebrew Bible instruction and triggered the shift from Greek to Hebrew script. From that period on, writing Greek in Hebrew letters became a common practice among Greek-speaking Jews. The absolute majority of JG materials preserved in the Cairo Genizah are written in Hebrew script.[6]

By the early Middle Ages most Greek-speaking Jews were surrounded by speakers of the same language, and the development of JG reflected the processes characteristic to the majority Greek. The differences between the local varieties of spoken language started to deepen, splitting the relatively uniform koine into a range of dialects.[7] Jewish forms of speech must have shared the features of local dialects. However, internal

5 On the epigraphical evidence see Kant 1987.

6 A representative sample of Genizah texts is de Lange 1996.

7 The difficulties of assessing this process are highlighted in Horrocks 2010: 281.

migrations of Jews in Greek-speaking territories due to natural catastrophes, economic vicissitudes, and persecutions. led to their carrying with them the linguistic features of their previous surroundings. Unfortunately, not enough material has survived to judge whether Jewish groups were indeed perceived as linguistically distinct, to what extent and in which places. Whether some koineization of the JG dialects took place at this stage is currently impossible to say.

The sociolinguistic repertoire of the language varieties available for JG speakers was significantly different from that of the Orthodox Christian Greek majority. Ordinary Greek Jews had little or no exposure to socio-pragmatic contexts where Ancient Greek classics were taught, admired, and imitated. Thus, high registers of Christian Greek were largely unknown to them. Instead, the established translations of the Hebrew Bible (LXX, Aquila) commanded respect and were followed as prestigious examples in genres such as paraliturgical poetry. It is probable that women, normally less educated, had little competence even in these registers, using colloquial JG throughout.

As parts of Byzantium succumbed to the Seljuk and Ottoman Empires, multilingualism with Turkish, the new prestigious language of administration, spread across the Jewish communities. The lexical and morphological impact of Turkish is easily traceable in JG texts.[8] In the parts of the Greek-speaking world that did not fall to the conquerors and maintained stronger connections with the West, JG was enriched by loans from Italian and Judaeo-Italian, while the coexistence with Sephardi Jews exposed Romaniotes to Judeo-Spanish vocabulary.

Hardly any evidence of lower registers of JG has reached us from the pre-modern period. The economic and numerical weakness of JG communities made publishing in JG relatively unprofitable. Thus, texts with literary ambitions and/or secular content had to be either written in other languages or were doomed to manuscript transmission. The few copies produced vanished in the turbulent centuries to come, and even texts on religious topics survived in tiny numbers.

Towards the end of the eighteenth century several major Greek dialect zones, such as Northern, Cretan, Ionian and hypothesized Southern, had a resident Romaniote population.[9] Wandering teachers of Hebrew scripture continued the ages-old tradition of JG Biblical translations. Catering for minor communities, they must have acted as agents of koineization inside these zones.

Due to military activity during the nineteenth century the area of Romaniote settlement in the Peloponnese dwindled, and urbanization levels increased. Greek-speaking Jews founded their synagogue in Athens, the first synagogue of the capital. The Enlightenment entailed education in non-Hebrew scripts, Latin and/or Greek. As the majority Greek language variety became accessible to wider Jewish masses and individual creative JG writing was no longer limited to the Hebrew script, the decline of the JG dialect environment became a visible prospect. The depopulation of Romaniote communities by the Nazis resulted in the even quicker disintegration of their language environment. Following WWII and the civil war, many Jews moved from the provincial towns

8 E.g., Matsa 1971–1981.

9 For an attempt of general classification of the dialects see Trudgill 2009; on the Southern zone see Pantelidis 2016.

of the north to major urban centres (Athens, Thessaloniki), where the language was already significantly standardized. Local JG phonetic and grammatical features were lost. Isolated enclaves of Romaniotes abroad, untouched by the war, preserved more elements of early-twentieth century JG.

JG of the twenty-first century does not diverge from its non-Jewish counterpart,[10] but includes a constantly developing Jewish-specific vocabulary based on borrowing from (Ashkenazic and Israeli) Hebrew and (Jewish) English.

2. Grammatical sketch

2.1 Writing system and phonology

Since most surviving texts contain traditional religious material, few manuscripts can claim to represent a synchronic picture of orthography. Vocalization is often not contemporaneous with the initial consonantal text. The amount and nature of evidence make telling apart distinct orthographic traditions extremely difficult. This situation is typical for language varieties without a developed printing culture: a relatively high level of spelling regularization normally follows printing, while handwritten production may remain immune to normalization for centuries.[11] Most orthographic practices used in manuscripts and early prints are based on the common principles summarized below.

The JG writing system is primarily a phonetic transcription.[12] Major exceptions to this rule are Hebrew proper names, which predominantly appear in their original spelling. The evidence for knowledge of Greek spelling is rare and uncertain. Scribes do not distinguish between vowels recorded as digraphs vs. those represented by singular graphemes in historical SMG spelling: ε [e] and αι [e] are written down similarly, and so are ι [i], ει [i], υ [i], etc. No historical spelling is reproduced in consonant clusters: γγ [ⁿg] is recorded as נג, not גג, etc. On the other hand, while historical Greek spelling conventions are not enforced, JG writers may refrain from writing down the sounds that are not recorded in Greek spelling.

JG consonant phonemes are represented by the following Hebrew graphemes:

		Labial	Dental	Alveolar	Velar
Nasal		m מ		n נ ן	
Plosive	**voiceless**	p פ פּ		t ט תּ ת	k ק כּ כ
	voiced	b ב בּ		d ד דּ	g ג גּ
Fricative	**voiceless**	f פ פֿ	θ ת	s ס שׁ שׂ שׁ	x כֿ כ ח
	voiced	v בֿ ב ו וו	ð ד	z ז	ɣ ג
Rhotic				r ר	
Lateral				l ל	

Rafe and *dagesh lene* are used to mark fricatives and stops, respectively, at times redundantly. It is unclear, whether *dagesh* was ever used as *forte*, since no data can be

10 This has been pointed out already by Drettas 1999.

11 Voeste and Baddeley 2012.

12 The orthographic systems used in some texts are closer to phonemic transcription.

reliably attributed to the areas where geminates were pronounced.[13] The extent of the diacritics' usage depends on the intended use of the text: private notes and marginalia exhibit fewer diacritiscs than the texts deemed important.

The cluster [t͡s], believed by some researchers to be a phoneme, is notated as צ (ṣ).[14] Its voiced counterpart [d͡z] is written as ז following the traditional Romaniote pronunciation of this letter.[15] Some scribes distinguish [z] from [d͡z] through *geresh*, others make no distinction, which does not present a problem due to the relative rarity of [d͡z] and lack of phonemic load on the opposition.

Since Greek /s/ can be realized as an advanced postalveolar or a retracted alveolar,[16] both ס and ש can be used to notate it.

Word-initial [v] is notated with *vav(s)* due to the impact of Hebrew spelling and the limitations of Hebrew morphophonetics.

The rhotic, normally written as ר, can appear on the odd occasion as ג, which suggests that it can be realized as an uvular fricative [ʁ] or velar [ɣ], cf. Standard Greek (SG) realization as an alveolar tap or trill.[17]

Palatals [c, ɟ, ç], being allophones of velars /k, g, x/ before the front vowels, are notated as the corresponding velars. Their counterpart palatal fricative [ʝ], an allophone of /ɣ/, is not distinguished in writing from the palatal approximant [j], believed to be an allophone of unstressed /i/ before vowels. Both can be written as double or single *yod*.[18] JG writing does not normally record devoicing of [ʝ] > [ç] after voiceless consonants wherever j originates from [i] followed by a back vowel in the same syllable. This might be due to: (a) low degree of such devoicing; (b) the fact that in some regions [i] did not lose its vowel quality, or perhaps was (still) pronounced as a separate syllable, and the resulting spelling was preserved/spread into other regions; (c) imitation of Greek spelling, which does not reflect this phenomenon. Palatal allophones of /l/ and /n/ are notated as clusters [nj], [lj].[19]

The grapheme *ʕayin* has zero phonetic value, being used only in Hebrew borrowings. *Hei* has no consonant value; it is mostly used for word final [a], see below, and in Hebrew borrowings.

13 For the geographic spread of the phenomenon see Manolessou and Bassea 2012.

14 For a summary of the argumentation see Arvaniti 2007: 114–117.

15 Drettas 1999: 281.

16 Arvaniti 2007: 106–107.

17 Here and below SG refers to modern SG.

18 For the sake of simplicity [j] is used in transcriptions for all such cases below.

19 See Krivoruchko 2021 for examples.

JG vowel phonemes to graphemes:[20]

IPA	word-initially	word-medially	word-finally
a	א- אַ- אָ-	-א- -∅- -ַ- -ָ-	-א -ה -אַ -אָ -הַ -הָ
e	אֶי- א- אֵ- אֶ- אֵי-	-י- -∅- -ֵ- -ֶ-	-ה -הֵ -הֶ
i	אי- אִי-	-י- -אִי- -ִ-	-י -אי
o	אוֹ- או-	-ו- -וֹ-	-אוֹ -או
u	אוּ- או-	-וּ- -ו-	-אוּ -או

The distribution of *pataḥ* vs. *qameṣ* and *seghol* vs. *ṣere* is mostly random; the allophonic difference between the stressed and unstressed (accented vs. non-accented) JG vowels is not reflected in spelling. *Shwa* has zero phonetic value, a second consecutive *shwa* occasionally may reflect [e].

2.2 Word division

Since JG writing is based on phonetic criteria, its written word often coincides with a host-and-clitic group. A typical nominal group consists of preposition, definite article, host (mostly a noun) and a weak possessive pronoun, or a subset of this set. While this type of word division could be deemed to imitate Hebrew, the verbal clitic groups show that it is not the case, as their morpho-syntactic structure is typically Greek. Such groups may comprise a complementizer (conjunction or relativizer), negation, particle, pronominal object and verb. Other (types of) groups involving adverbs and pronouns are also possible.[21] Biblical JG tends to isolate Hebrew proper names from their clitics, possibly to facilitate the comparison with the Hebrew original. *Meteg* may be used to mark stress(es) in phonological words.

2.3 Nonstandard dialect phonology

Phonological systems of Greek dialects include numerous sounds and phonemes not mentioned in the above description, such as near-open vowels in place of rising diphthongs, labialized vowels, palato-alveolar, alveo-palatal and aspirated consonants resulting from fronting velars, etc. In absence of contrary evidence it is safer to hypothesize that JG varieties shared the phonological profile of the coterritorial populations, although the orthographies do not always shed light on these phenomena. Some traceable features are discussed below in Samples A and B.

2.4 Vocabulary and related morphological and syntactic phenomena

The phonetics and morphology of early modern and modern JG varieties, in as far as they appear in the texts, exhibit no marked difference from their non-Jewish correlates. The major aspect of the JG distinctiveness is its vocabulary, primarily the specifically Jewish vocabulary. Distinctions existed also in not characteristically Jewish lexical stock, such as in names of household objects, but little data is available in this regard.

20 This approximate representation of vowels is traditional in Greek linguistic literature, and it is followed in the sample transcriptions below. "Word" here refers to the phonological word, see below.

21 See Krivoruchko 2002.

Most Jewish-specific vocabulary in JG derives ultimately from Hebrew and Aramaic, either directly or via other Jewish languages, such as Judezmo, Judeo-Italian, or Yiddish. The accommodation of Hebrew-Aramaic (HA) loans in JG continued for centuries, from the pre-Masoretic period to Israeli Hebrew. A chronological span that large inevitably results in a complex picture: varying processes of morphological adaptation and de-adaptation took place with varying results, and many HA lexemes were reimported into JG time and again. In recent years due to the activity of international Jewish organizations the stream of new borrowings, mostly non-adapted, has substituted the old Romaniot lexical stock. The description below concentrates mainly on the traditional vocabulary, recorded in Greek script up to the end of the twentieth century.

Educated Jews writing in the Greek alphabet used a historical spelling based on the Septuagint up to the last quarter of the twentieth century; some publications follow this practice nowadays. The influence of Israeli Hebrew and (Jewish) English in recent years led to the increased adoption of phonetic spellings. Below the examples taken from writen sources are spelled as in the original, hence mostly with endings *-ημ*, *-ωθ*, *-ηλ*, etc., while the examples recorded during fieldwork are spelled phonetically. The accent is not marked wherever its position is uncertain or variants occur.

The majority of HA loans are morphologically unadapted. The more learned the word, the likelier it is to keep the gender of its HA precursor and less likely to decline, and vice versa: if the word is related to everyday life and used by women, it usually adapts to standard Greek paradigms.[22]

Direct HA loans into JG sprung from phonetic words, mostly nominal forms, or, less frequently, small syntactic units, in particular annexations (status constructus), e.g., ראש חודש [roˈsxodes] < *το ρισχόδες / ρεσχόδες / ροσχόδες* 'the beginning of the month', בְּרִית מִילָה [beriθmiˈla] > *το μπερίθ μιλά* 'circumcision'. Eventually, entire biblical phrases could be lexicalised, as in *βεραχουμ* 'physical punishment of a child' [verahum] < [ve^{h}uraxum] וְהוּא רַחוּם 'He, being full of compassion' (Ps 78:38). Hebrew nouns are borrowed without the definite article, with the exception of הקדוש [akados] > *ο Ακαδως* 'the Holy One'. Aramaic nouns are borrowed together with their suffuxed article, perceived as part of the noun אדרא [idaˈra] '*Idra* (part of *Zohar*)' > *το ινταρά* 'a memorial'. Nouns that are plural in the source language may be adopted as singular, e.g., heortonyms (terms denoting holidays) סוכות > *το Σουκώθ* 'Sukkot' and פורים > *το Πουρίμ* 'Purim', and vice versa, original singulars may be constructed as plurals *ad sensum*, e.g., סנהדרין [saneˈdrin] > [saniˈdrin] > *οι Σανιδρήν* 'the [wise men of the] Synedrion'.

It has been shown that the main factors that determine the morphological adaptation of loanwords in Modern Greek are the auslaut and the accent pattern of the source, while gender ascription depends upon the semantics of the noun, its gender in the source language and the gender of its equivalent in Greek.[23] The HA loans comply with the general rules. Oxytone nouns with stress on the ultima and with consonant auslaut constitute the largest category of the Hebrew vocabulary, and their borrowing proceeds as follows: if the noun denotes a non-human entity, it becomes neuter and receives the ending /- i/, e.g., שבת [saˈbaθ] > *το *Σαμπάθι*, gen. *του Σαμπαθιού* 'Shabbat', cf. un-

22 More on this in Krivoruchko forthcoming a.

23 Anastasiadi-Symeonidi 1994, Ralli 2002, Kyranoudis 2009.

adapted *του Σαμπάθ*. If the noun characterizes a person, further adaptation will depend on the pragmatic context: negative value load will lead to the acquisition of neuter; otherwise, a masculine will receive -ης and a feminine -ω in accordance with natural gender,[24] e.g.: קמצן [kam'tsan] > **το καμτσάνι* > *το καμτσάμ'* (Ioannina) 'a stingy person', אברהם [avra'am] > [a'vram] > *ο Αβράμης*, gen. *του Αβράμη* 'Abraham', מזל [ma'zal] > *η Ματζάλω*, gen. *της Ματζάλως* 'Mazal'.

In the case of nouns ending in fricative sibilants, the latter are re-analysed as Gr. nom. masc. endings. Such nouns bild an asigmatic genitive after the paradigm of *ψωμάς*: שמש [sa'mas] > *ο σαμάς*, gen. *του σαμά* 'beadle', פרנס [par'nas] > *ο παρνάς*, gen. *του παρνά* 'community leader'.

JG employs a pluralizer [-im] < Heb. ים- to form indeclinable plurals, mostly masculine, e.g., אשכנזי > JG [askena'dzi] > *οι ασκενατζήμ* 'Ashkenazic Jews', ערל JG [a'rel] > *οι αρελήμ* 'uncircumcized', 'non-Jews', תלמיד > JG [tal'mið] *καλοί ταλμιδήμ* 'good students'. This plural marker was nativized, e.g., *μη μας ακούσουν τα κατανίμ* 'lest children hear us', with [kata'nim] 'small (pl.)' < [ka'tan] + [-im] rather than [*ketanim] or [*ktanim], which would be expected if imported directly. The allocation of the neuter gender here results from the analogy with Gr. *παιδιά* 'children'. Properly formed plural segolates also occur, e.g., *τα κελαβίμ* (< כלבים) *οι Γερμανοί* 'these German dogs', with gender change due to derogatory contexts and/or influence of the Greek synonym *τα σκυλιά*.

An extra Greek plural neuter ending can be appended to Hebrew plurals in [-im], e.g., רימונים [rimo'nim] 'pomegranates' > *τα ριμονίμια* 'womens' breasts', שדים [se'dim] > *τα σεντίμια* 'evil spirits, demons'.

The Hebrew precursors with vocal auslaut [-i] or [-e] typically acquire [-s] for masculine, e.g., משה [mo'se] > [mu'se] > *ο Μουσές* 'Moisis', טָמֵא [ta'me] 'unclean' > *ταμές* 'Christ', 'cross', 'icon', לוי [le'vi] > Λεβής 'Levi', אֵלִיָּהוּ הַנָּבִיא [eli'jahu ana'vi] > *Λιαχανεβής* 'prophet Elijah'. Plurals, if built, are anisosyllabic (i.e. have a different amount of syllables in the nominative and other cases, a post-koine phenomenon for this type of the nouns): *ταμέδες*.

Another large group of JG nouns are those derived from Hebrew nouns in [-a]. They may be accommodated as feminine or neuter, with the former group at times building the genitive singular in [-s], e.g., מנורה [meno'ra] > *η μενορά* 'menora', כתובה [ketu'ba] > *η κετουμπά* 'dowry agreement', סוכה [su'ka] > *η σουκά* 'booth, tabernacle', genitive *της σουκάς*, but שכינה [sexi'na] > *το Σχινά* 'Divine presence', צדקה [t͡seda'ka] > *το τσεδακά* 'alms'. Some Hebrew etyma are reflected as both feminine and neuter: תיבה [teva] > *το τεβά* or *η τεβά* 'pulpit', חובה [xo'va] > [xu'va] 'obligation' > *το χουβά* or *η χουβά* 'Passover seder', חנוכה [xanu'ka] > *το Χανουκά* or *η Χανουκά* 'Hanukkah'. The plural forms are formed in [-oθ] < Hebrew ות-, or, under the influence of Judeo-Spanish, in [-ot] and can be neuter: סליחות [seli'xoθ] > *τα σελιχόθ* 'penitential prayers', צרות [t͡sa 'roθ] > *τα τσαρόθ* 'misfortunes', but also feminine: *οι μιγκλότ 'scrolls'* < מגילות [megi 'loθ] > [me'gloθ] > [mi'gloθ]. Like masculine plurals, feminine in [-ot] can be re-pluralized through adding [-ia].

24 Cf. Mladenova 2001.

HA loanwords serve as the basis for nominal and verbal derivation in accordance with standard Greek patterns. So, diminutives can be built with the suffix [-aki-]: *το κατανάκι* 'very young child, baby', ultimately from [ka'tan] 'small'; with [-pulo]: *Πουριμόπουλο or Προμόπλο* [pro'moplo] < [pri'moplo] < [puri'moplo] < [puri'mopulo] 'Purim of Sicilians, local Purim, Purim Katan' < פורים [pu'rim]. Agentive nouns can be derived through masculine [-otis], feminine [-tra], etc., e.g., *η τεβιλίστρα* 'woman attendant in mikveh', via [*tevi'lizo] or [*tevi'lo] 'to immerse', ultimately from טבילה [tevi'la] 'ritual immersion', *χεβριώτης* [xe'vr^j^otis] 'member of the burial society' < חברה [xe'vra] (sc. Chevra Kadisha, burial society, lit. 'Holy Society').

3. Text samples

Samples A and B represent the period between the 17th and 19th centuries. Both were originally written in Hebrew script. Extensive comparable material from other Greek religiolects facilitates the assessment of the JG material. Sample C illustrates the recent state of the JG language variety in the New York Romaniot community.

3.1 Sample A

Two mantinadas have been preserved on a flyleaf of the seventeenth-century manuscript of Pirqe Avot from Chania, Crete.[25] Mantinada is a strophe of two rhyming decapentasyllabic verses, normally iambic heptameters, with a caesura after the eighth syllable. Mantinada has been a popular genre of folk poetry since Byzantine times. Fixed texts circulate, but can also be improvised on various topics and occasions.[26]

No date or authorship appear in the manuscript, yet the linguistic profile of the poem concurs with the data on Cretan Greek, well researched, as it served as a vehicle for the large corpus of Renaissance literature. The crossed-out verse with confused wording (in the ms after l. 2, not reproduced here) increases the probability that the text is a copy rather than a protograph.

The interest in journeys to the underworld is characteristic of the earlier period of Cretan literature spanning 1350–1580; the rhymed couplet is also unlikely to predate the fourteenth century. More precise geographic localization of the text is hardly possible: while present forms in -ουν in the third person plural are believed to have spread from the eastern parts of the island, the data about the process is inconclusive and the size of the text too small.

3.1.1 Writing system and phonetics

The text is characterized by unsystematic use of *matres lectionis yod* and *ʔaleph*. Final [-a] is consistently spelt with א. *Schwa* alternates with *ṣere* for [e], cf. the spelling of the same verb in a similar phonetic environment as אַנִינֵי and קֵיאַנִינְי. No accents were marked by the scribe.

25 For more information about the manuscript see the first publication of the text by de Lange 2008, where it is wrongly located in the Jewish National and University Library. In fact it is in the Israel Museum, Jerusalem.

26 For the performative context of mantinadas see Sykäri 2009, for structural analysis see Topintzi and Versace 2015.

The clusters [tr], [dr], [ðj] are vocalized with *ṣere*. Were they pronounced with [e], this epenthetic vowel would better be short, i.e. [ðed^{e}ri'ka], [ð^{e}ja'vazu], [jat^e'revγun], [jat^e'ri] in order to preserve the meter. It is therefore more likely that *ṣere* could be realized as [∅] as a result of its confusion with *schwa*. In [s^{e}ta=sko'lja] *yod* is used in the initial cluster, increasing the possibility of the vowel being pronounced.

The transcription below is given on the presumption that צ reflects alveopalatal [t͡ɕ], as in modern Cretan. No use of ס is made, which may – but need not – reflect the shift toward a more palatal articulation of [s] in Cretan Greek.[27] Double *vav* is consistently used for [v] inside the word, possibly pointing to the fixed interpretation of ב as [b] in the orthographic system of the scribe or his prototype.

Typically for Crete, a nasal+dental cluster loses its nasal: [ðedri'ka], cf. SG ['ðe$^{(n)}$dra].[28]

The preference for a syllabic structure of CV type is evident: the particle [an] 'whether' appears as [ane] before consonants and [an] before vowels, while the distinctive Cretan acc. pl. article *τσι* < SG *τους* appears apocopated before the vowel: t͡ɕ=arosti 'menus. The final [n] of the present verb 3PL is elided before a consonant but preserved before a vowel: [ðja'vazu sta …], but [jat^e'revγun I …].[29]

The [o] in the final syllable of the verb ['psalo] for expected [u] may be explained as either a) a copyist's mistake, if a compound with [psilo-] was anticipated; b) a mechanical mistake in pointing; c) a local phonetic feature; d) impact of another linguistic variety or even another language: Jews of different origins are known to have inhabited Crete at this period.[30]

Infixing [γ], as in [ja'trevγu], cf. SG *γιατρεύουν*, is a widespread phenomenon known already since the Hellenistic koine.[31]

As opposed to modern Cretan, no simplification of the cluster [zm] > [m] in participles takes place.[32]

3.1.2 Syntax and Lexicon

[ce='psalo sina'γoja] is not a predicate + subject construction: in JG *συναγώγι* is not a congregation, but a building, and medieval-early modern Greek poetics would not allow a metonymic subject for 'they chant'. Phonetic disappearance of στα through assimilation *στα συναγώγια* > *σα συναγώγια* > *σσυναγώγια* > *συναγώγια* is possible in some dialects, but unlikely for Cretan. [sina'γoja] is therefore a prepositional phrase without the preposition, tolerated because its closeness to *στα σκολιά* in the same line.

The forms of *είναι* 'to be' are commonly used in Cretan for *υπάρχω* 'to exist'.[33] Neuter plural of the adjective *δενδρικός* is used as a plurale tantum for 'trees' (SG

27 Kontosopoulos 2008: 30.

28 Cf. Henrich 1998: 90, Kontosopoulos 2008: 30–31.

29 The manuscript reading of *nun* is uncertain.

30 See Schoenfeld 2007.

31 Horrocks 2010: 367–368; Kontosopoulos 2008: 31.

32 Kontosopoulos 2008: 31.

33 Kontosopoulos 2008: 32, n. 1.

δένδρα) in the contemporaneous Cretan poetry, e.g., Erotocr. 1.1883, Thes. 7.[573]. *ογιά* for *για* survives in Crete until nowadays.

Neuter *συναγώ(γ)ι* is a common vernacular form for SG *συναγωγή*, as is already Byzantine *σκολιό* for SG *σχολείο*.[34]

3.1.3 Text

The manuscript text is followed by the reconstructed IPA, glossing, standardized Greek version and English translation.

אַנִינֵי שְׁטוֹנַדִי דֵידֵרִיקַא   קֵיאַנִינְי פֵּרִיווֹלְיָיא

aˈn=ine s=toˈn=aði ðedriˈka ce=aˈn=ine periˈvolja

if=be.PRS.3SG in=DEF=Hades.ACC tree.PL and=if=be.PRS.3SG garden.PL

Αν είναι στον Άδη δενδρικά και αν είναι περιβόλια;

Are there trees in Hades and are there gardens?

קֵיאַנֵידֵיָיוַזוּ שְׁיטַשְׁקוֹלְיָיא   קֵיפְשַׁלוֹ שִׁינַגוֹיָיא

c^e=ane=ðjaˈvazu s^e=ta=skoˈlja ce=ˈpsalo sinaˈγoja

and=if=read.PRS.3PL in=DEF=school.PL.ACC and=chant.PRS.3PL synagogue.PL

Κι άνε διαβάζουν στα σκολιά και ψάλο[υν] συναγώγια;

And do they study in the schools and chant [in the] synagogues?

אֵכִי אוֹאַדִיש קְרֵיָיאנֵירָא   אוֹיַיא צִידִיפְשָׁזְמֵינוּש

ˈeçi o=ˈaðis ˈkrija neˈra oja t͡ɕi=ðipsaˈzmenus

has DEF=Hades cold.PL.N water.PL for DEF=thirsty.ACC.PL.M

Έχει ο Άδης κρύα νερά ογιά τσ' διψασμένους;

Does Hades have cold water for the thirsty?

קֵי אַנֵי יָיאטֵרְיוְוגוּן אִייָטֵרִי   אִיקִי צָרוֹשְׁטִימֵינוּש

ˈc^e=ane jaˈtrevγun i-jaˈtri eˈci t͡ɕ-arostiˈmenus

and=if heal.PRS.3PL DEF=doctor.PL there DEF=sick.ACC.PL.M

Κι άνε γιατρεύουν οι γατροί εκεί τσ' αρρωστιμένους;

And do the doctors heal the sick there?

3.2 Sample B

The text offered below is a passage from the JG translation of the prophetic reading (Is 40:1–26) following the weekly Torah reading (*parasha) Va'etchanan*, to be read on Shabbat *Nahamu*. Chanting Greek prophetic readings (*haftaroth)* during the service was practiced in some Romaniote communities until the early twentieth century.[35]

The manuscript has no colophon and there is no data about its previous owners or acquisition.[36] Sznol suggested that its text 'illustrates special features of the medieval language of the region of Ioannina'.[37] Yet the sample contains features that cannot be at-

34 See Dimitrakos 1953–64: 6857, s.v. *συναγώγιον* 2; Horrocks 2010: 283, cf. sample C below.

35 Belléli 1897: 137–138, Matsas 1953: 11, n. 1.

36 It is currently preserved in Yad Ben-Zvi Institute, Jerusalem, MS 3519; for the images see Sznol 2000. The sample is taken from fol. 1r-2v. Parts of the manuscript have been previously published in Krivoruchko 1999: 654–660; Sznol 2000: 15–17.

37 Sznol 2000: 10.

tributed to this area, and its Epirus Greek (EG) characteristics are relatively few. It also lacks the phenomena characteristic to the nineteenth-century Jewish Ioanniote language variety. Thus, while the *haftara* could have been copied in nineteenth-century Epirus, it is a reworking of an older translation of non-Epeirote provenance.[38]

3.2.1 Writing system[39]

Consonants

		Labial	Dental	Alveolar	Palato-alveolar	Velar
Nasal		m מ		n נ		
Plosive	**voiceless**	p פּ		t תּ ט		k כּ ק
	voiced	b בּ		d ד דּ		g גּ
Fricative	**voiceless**	f פ	θ ת	s ס	ʃ ש	x ח כ
	voiced	v ו ב	ð ד	z ז	ʒ ז'	ɣ ג
Affricate	**voiceless**			t͡s צ		
	voiced			d͡z ז		
Rhotic				r ר		
Lateral				l ל		

The writing system employs Tiberian principles: *dagesh* serves to distinguish plosive vs. fricative articulation in homorganic pairs of voiced and voiceless labials and velars. Affricates occur in loanwords.

Apart from *dagesh*, the scribe uses another diacritic, a point above the middle part of the letter, further called an 'overdot'.[40] The state of the manuscript does not allow defining the exact inventory of letters that can bear such a diacritic. The mark is found with some consistency only above *qof* and *kaf*.[41]

In one of his later publications Ioannina philologist J. Matsas observed: "to mark the most popular phonetic sound *ke*, *ki*, they wrote ק' (q).[42] As a native speaker knowledgeable of the JG tradition Matsas failed to mention the exact shape of the diacritic, neither did he care to reproduce it in his edition.[43] However, it can be little doubt that the diacritic in question was not *geresh*, but an overdot. Since in Matsas's native Epirus dialect voiced velars did not shift to affricates or fricatives, one may presume that he envisioned a palatalized [c], noted by Epirus dialectologists on many occasions. Indeed, in the text of the *haftara* ק' appears either before the front vowel or in the position were

38 For the discussion of the prehistory of the text see its edition in Krivoruchko forthcoming b.

39 The manuscript employs two different orthographic systems; the present description refers only to the sample below.

40 It is represented here as (') *after* the letter for technical reasons.

41 More on the use of overdot in Krivoruchko forthcoming b.

42 "לציון הצליל הפונטי השכיח ביותר ke, ki רשמו ק' " Matsa 1971–1981: 242.

43 ק'סמ'ס on p. 243 ibid. is a misprint of קֹסמֹס.

such vowel may be reconstructed: *και* (throughout the text), *πιλέκιτο* (40:19), *λακκια* (40:4). No counter-examples occur: 'ק is not found before the back vowels without an underlying /e/ or /i/ in between.

More supporting evidence can be gleaned from Matsas' earlier book in Greek script, where a diacritic (inverted breve) was used not only with *κ*, e.g., *Γιτσχαȋκή*, but also above *χ*: *Χ̂έφετς*.[44] In the text of the haftara adduced below, the overdot appears above כ in the following words: *χερι* (50:11), *χέρα* (40:10), *ράχη* (40:4), *ραχες* (40:12), *χύνει* (40:19), *χρυσκός* (ibid.), *χρυσκος* (ibid.), *χρυσαφι* (ibid.), *αρχη* (40:21), *αχερον* (40:24). It can be seen that the front vowel directly follows the consonant in all cases but the derivatives of the root *χρυσ-*. In these latter the palatalization of [x] looks likely, if we consider that the clusters /velar + r/ elsewhere in the manuscript receive an epenthetic [i] that should provoke palatalization: [kir'jas] (49:26) 'meat', [aγirjo'vojiðo] (51:20) 'wild ox'.[45] No contradicting evidence is found: the words ['xnumi] (40:13, 15) SG *χνούμι*, [efto'xos] (40:20) SG *εφτωχός* bear no palatalization mark. Thus, it can be hypothesized that overdot was used to mark palatalization.

The hypothesis can be further supported by the fact that *zayin* with overdot is likely to have reproduced [ʒ], e.g.ת [ʒi'ɣosun] (40:16); this use of the diacritic is, however, inconsistent, cf. ['zi[jise]] (40:12).

Vowels

Vocalization is thorough: most consonants have niqud. Mid-word [a] is *pataḥ* or *qamaṣ;* final [a] is a combination of *qamaṣ* and *ʔaleph*; [e] is represented by *ṣere* followed by *yod* or without it, occasionally *seḡol* with or without *yod*; [i] in the majority of cases is represented by *ḥiriq male*, at times only by *ḥiriq*. [o] is *ḥolem* with *vav* or without it, [u] is *šuruq*, *schwa* is [∅].

Word division

The scribe tends to keep clitics separate from their hosts, and at times even breaks autosemantic parts of speech into pieces. As a result of this piecemeal approach, which may – but must not – be due to copying practices, the text represents fewer sandhi phenomena than could be expected.

3.2.2 Phonetics

The text contains instances of mid-vowel raising: unstressed [o] > [u], e.g., [a'pano] > [a'panu] (40:9) SG *απάνω*, ['tipotes] > ['tiputes] (40:17) SG *τίποτε*. Shift of unstressed [e] to [i] typically occurs in augment, e.g. [e'sostepse] > [i'sostipse] (40:2) EG *εσώστεψε*, [e'pire] > [i'pire] (ibid.) SG *πήρε*; in the 3SG ending, e.g., [for'tonete] > [for 'tonite] (40:11), [ðe'niniti] (40:23) SG *δεν γίνεται*, ['rixnete] > ['rixnite] (40:15), as well as in [pilecito] (40:18, 20) SG *πελεκιτό*, [ka'totira] (40:17) SG *κατώτερα*, ma'θitipse (40:13) SG *μαθήτευσε/μαθήτεψε*.

44 Matsas 1956: 101, 102.

45 This conclusion relies on the presumption that a unified linguistic/phonological profile can be reconstructed behind all parts of MS 3519. Arguments in favor of this hypothesis are discussed in Krivoruchko forthcoming b.

Some forms appear with their unstressed vowel deleted: [opu] > [op] (40:15, 18, 19), [sxariˈceftra] (40:9) < [siᵑxariˈceftra] EG **συγχαρικεύτρα*; [ˈʃaste] (40:3) < [iˈʃaste] SG *ισιάστε*, [ˈʃaði] (40:4) < [iˈʃaði] Early MG *ισιάδι*.

[s] appears palatalized before [i] or underlying [i], as in two latter examples, various forms of *σηκώνω*, e.g., [ʃiˈkoni] (40:24), [ˈʃiklo] (40:14), [niˈʃotes] (40:15) SG *νησιώτες*, [xriʃkos] (40:18) SG obs. *χρυσικός*, as well as before [k], e.g., [voˈʃkaj] (40: 11) SG *βοσκάει*. [z] is palatalized before [i] in root morphemes, e.g. [ʒiˈɣosun] (40:16), [ʒiˈti] (40:20), but not in verbal suffixes *-ίζω*, *-άζω*.

Clusters with second [θ] are subject to defricativisation: [sθ] > [st], e.g., [miˈstos] (40:10), [rθ] > [rt], e.g. [ˈerti].

A prothetic vowel appears before the initial cluster in [evraˈxona] (40:11). Development of [j] is observed in intervocal position in [iˈanθi] > [iˈjanθi] (40:6); [ievraˈxona] > [ijevraˈxona] (40:10).

3.2.3 Morphology

The third-person pronoun builds its forms from a suffixed stem: genitive *αυτουνού*, etc. An unstressed augment is preserved in past forms, e.g., [iˈpire] (40:2) SG *πήρε*. The future is built with the particle [θa], but a form with [θana] also occurs (40:3).

3.2.4 Syntax

Biblical JG (BJG) is capable of calquing the structure of the Hebrew original with great precision, often providing a morpheme-to-morpheme mirror of the Hebrew text.[46] The translator never omits any part of the original deemed holy. Hebrew word order is disregarded only on rare occasions. The division into syntactic units follows that defined by Hebrew cantillation. However, calquing is never perfect, since other considerations - practical and ideological – may intervene. The translator of the sample text inserts, with some consistency:

- articles in accordance with Greek rules of article placement;
- comparative particles, in particular when the anthropomorphic perception of God is to be avoided or when prophetic language should not be taken too literally;
- copulas, such as forms of *είναι* ‘to be’ and *γίνομαι* ‘to become’, but also pseudo-copulas with some semantic content of their own, to compensate for the perceived lack of coherence of Hebrew nominal sentences;
- subordinating conjunctions;
- prepositions in accordance with the government requirements of Greek verbs;
- weak pronouns as verbal objects, to increase coherence between sentences.

On an *ad hoc* basis, the translator also inserts autosemantic parts of speech, mostly nouns and adverbs, sourced from traditional translations and commentators in order to facilitate the understanding of the chanted passage. Generally these accommodations are sufficient to create a text comprehensible to those unfamiliar with the original.

46 More on the BJG translations in Krivoruchko 2014.

The preposition [san] may be used with the nominative (40:8, 11) and the accusative (40:23), cf. the SG accusative.

3.2.5 Text

Some parts of the manuscript are damaged; only complete sentences not requiring major textual reconstruction were sampled. The reconstructed text is indicated by [ ].

The JG manuscript text (1) is followed by:

2) Hebrew Biblical text, of which (1) is a translation;[47]
3) version of (1) in IPA. Original accents of the manuscript are marked ″, accents reconstructed per SG rules as ˈ; in case of incongruity priority is given to the manuscript evidence. Clitic groups are split as per SG rules and adjoined through = ; the coincidences with the word division of the manuscript are marked ≡. The reading of the Divine name is presumed identical throughout the text and spelled as in the manuscript in 40:10 with accent assigned;
4) glossing;[48]
5) SG translation of the original Hebrew (2), reproduced from Today's Greek Version (TGV) for the purpose of comparison;[49]
6) English translation of the JG text (1), based on that of Jewish Publication Society.[50]

פַּרִיגוֹרֶטֵי פּריגורטי טוֹ לָאוֹמוּ .לֵי או תֵיאוֹסָס:

נַחֲמוּ נַחֲמוּ עַמִּי יֹאמַר אֱלֹהֵיכֶם

pariɣo″rate[51] *pariɣoˈrate* *to=″lao≡mu*

console:IPFV.IMP.PL console: IPFV.IMP.PL DEF=people:ACC.M=POSS.1SG

le[52] *o=θeˈo≡sas||*

say:PRS.3SG DEF=god:NOM.SG=POSS.2PL

«Παρηγορείτε, παρηγορείτε το λαό μου», λέει ο Θεός σας.

Is 40:1 ‘Comfort ye, comfort ye My people’, saith your God.

47 BHS 1977.

48 Suffixed weak pronouns functioning as possessive are tagged POSS; perfective past as AOR, perfective future as AOR.FUT. The same tags are also used in Sample 3. Minor pauses are marked |, major pauses, mostly coinciding with verse ends, as ||.

49 Hellenic Bible Society 1997.

50 Young and Margolis 1917.

51 The imperfective imperative in [-a], [-ate] is common for this verb in SG, although the fact is not properly reflected in standard descriptions. The *Dictionary of Modern Greek* 1998 (further LKN), for example, classifies the verb as adopting the paradigm P10.9 (= 2nd conjugation, type A of Holton 2004), which it indeed follows in most, but not all forms.

52 A colloquial form resulting from the loss of intervocalic voiced fricative (< *λέγει*), cf. also *διαλέ* (Is 40:20) below.

אוֹמִילְטֵי אַפַּנוֹ טִין קַרְדְיָא טִיס יְרוּשָׁלַיִם קֵ׳יקְרַסְטֵי
דַּבְּרוּ עַל-לֵב יְרוּשָׁלַםִ וְקִרְאוּ

omi″late *a'pano*[53] *tin=kar'ðja* *tis* *jeruʃa'lajim*[54] *ce≡'kraste*
talk: IPFV.IMP.2PL on DEF =heart:ACC DEF.GEN.F Jerusalem and=call: AOR.IMP.PL
«Βεβαιώστε την Ιερουσαλήμ και φωνάξτε
40:2 Talk to the heart of Jerusalem, and call

אִסְאַפְּתִין. אֵיפִּידִי אִיסוֹסְטִיפְּסֵי אוֹקֵ׳ירוֹסְטִיס. אֵיפִּידִי
אֵלֶיהָ כִּי מָלְאָה צְבָאָהּ כִּי

is≡a'ftin | *epi″ði*[55] *i'sostipse*[56] *o≡ce'ros≡tis*| *epi'ði*
to=she:ACC because end:AOR.3SG DEF=time=POSS.3SG.F because
της ότι τέλειωσε της δουλείας της ο καιρός, ότι
unto her, as her time hath ended, as

אֵימִורוֹתִיקֵי טוֹקְרִימָטִים. אֵיפִּידִי אִיפְּיְרֵי אַפוֹטוֹ
נִרְצָה עֲוֹנָהּ כִּי לָקְחָה מִיַּד

em^j^u'roθice[57] *to≡'krima≡tis*| *epi'ði* *i″pire* *a'po≡to*
cover=AOR. PASS.3SG DEF=sin=POSS.3SG.F because take:AOR.3SG from=DEF.N
η ανομία της συγχωρήθηκε, ότι τιμωρήθηκε
her guilt is covered, that she hath received

כֵירִי טוּ ה׳. דִפְּלוֹן טוֹסוֹ
יְהוָה כִּפְלַיִם

″çeri *tu* *aðo'naj* | *ði'plon* *'toso*
hand:ACC DEF.GEN.M Lord double:ADJ.N.SG that.much:N.SG
από τον Κύριο με το παραπάνω,
of the hand of Lord double

דְיָאוֹלָא טַפְטֵיקְסִימַטָטִיס: סַמַנְדַא פוֹנִי קְרָזִי.
בְּכָל-חַטֹּאתֶיהָ. קוֹל קוֹרֵא

ðia≡″ola *ta≡fteksima″ta≡tis* || *″sa≡manda*[58] *fo″ni* *″kraz-i* |
for=all.ACC.N.PL DEF=fault.ACC.N.PL=POSS.3SG.F as.if voice.NOM.SG call:PRS.3SG
για όλες τις αμαρτίες της». Ακούστε! Κάποιος φωνάζει:
for all her sins. 40:3 Hark! one calleth:

53 BJG calque of the Hebrew preposition על *ʕal*, where SG would require an indirect object.

54 BJG tends to use the Hebrew proper nouns in their original form, only occasionally adapting them to Greek morphology. Cf. SG declinable *τα Ιεροσόλυμα* vs. more formal *η Ιερουσαλήμ*.

55 A translational Hebraism, aimed to reflect the causative meaning of Hebrew כי *kī*.

56 From *εσώστευσε* < *σωστεύω* 'to come to an end, become full, complete', with mid-vowel raising. Derivatives of the root are common in the EG contemporaneous with the manuscript, e.g., *ἄσωστος* (Vilaras), and modern EG, e.g., ό σώστης (Bonkas 1964: 379).

57 From the verb *μουρώνω*, explained by Somavera as 'camuffare'. The *ḥiriq* may reflect the palatalization of the initial [m], cf. EG μιανούλα for *μανούλα*, Bonkas 1964: 336.

58 'As if' here and below is inserted to avoid anthropomorphism.

אַדְיָסְטֵי אִיסטוֹן אֱירִימוֹ טוֹדְרוֹמוֹ טוּ ה.
בַּמִּדְבָּר פַּנּוּ דֶּרֶךְ יְהוָה

a'ðjas-te is≡ton 'erimo[59] *to≡'ðromo tu aðo'naj* |
empty:AOR.IMP.2PL in=DEF= desert.ACC.SG.M DEF=way.ACC.SG.M DEF Lord
«Ετοιμάστε στην έρημο ένα δρόμο για τον Κύριο,
'Clear ye in the wilderness the way of the Lord,

שַׁסְטֵי אִסְטוֹ פְּלָיֵי מוֹנוֹפָּטִי טוּ תֵיאוּמָס
יַשְּׁרוּ בָּעֲרָבָה מְסִלָּה לֵאלֹהֵינוּ.

"ʃaste "is=to "plaji "mono"pati tu= θe"u≡mas ||
straighten:AOR.IMP.2PL in=DEF slope path DEF=god=POSS.1PL
ισιώστε εκεί το δρόμο να περάσει ο Θεός μας.
straighten on the slope a path for our God.

קָתֵי פְּלָיֵי תַנַשִׁיקוֹתִי קֵיקָתֵי בוֹנוֹ
כָּל-גֶּיא יִנָּשֵׂא וְכָל-הַר

"kaθe "plaji θana≡ʃiko'θi ce≡'kaθe vo'no[60]
every slope FUT.PART=rise: AOR.SBJ.PASS.3SG and=every mountain
Κάθε φαράγγι ας υψωθεί, κάθε βουνό
40:4 Every slope shall rise up, and every mountain

קֵ'י רָכִ'י תַחַמְבִּילוֹסוּן. קֵ'יתָאִינֵי אוֹ סְטְרָבוֹדְרוֹמוֹס
וְגִבְעָה יִשְׁפָּלוּ וְהָיָה הֶעָקֹב

ce="raçi[61] *θa≡xambi'losun*[62]| *ce≡θa≡"ine o stra"voðromos*[63]
and=hill FUT=lower:3pl and=FUT=be:3SG DEF tortuous.way
και κάθε λόφος ας χαμηλώσει· το έδαφος το ανώμαλο
and hill shall lower; and the tortuous way

59 BJG calques the gender; in SG the noun is feminine.

60 SG *βουνό*, cf. EG το βονί (Kotzageorgis 1997: 100) with the same vocalism.

61 In SG *ράχη* is predominantly used for mountain peaks, but in Epirus toponimics it is applied to hills and smaller heights, see Bonkas 1964: 324. Similar usage is witnessed for Macedonia, Thessaly, Sterea Ellada, and Corfu, cf. also Papaioannou 1976: 109.

62 SG *χαμηλώνω*. For the infix [b] see *χαμbλώνου* and other derivatives from the root in Bonkas 1964: 426; Kosmas 1997: 26; cf. *χαμπηλά* in Matsas 1953: 37; Altbauer and Shiby 1971–1981: 413.

63 The word *στραβόδρομος* is not found in the dictionaries, but its derivational pattern is common, cf. SG *πεζόδρομος* 'pedestrianized street', *χωματόδρομος* 'dirt road', *σιδηρόδρομος* 'railway', etc. The derivative verb *στραβοδρομώ* occurs as a hapax in 'Great Chimera' (1936) by M. Karagatsis.

יַשָּׁדִי. קֵ׳י אִפְּסִילוֹטוֹפִּי יַלַקַ׳א. טוֹטֵס תַפַנֵירוֹתִי
לְמִישׁוֹר. וְהָרְכָסִים לְבִקְעָה וְנִגְלָה

ja≡ˈʃaði|	*ce=i≡psiˈlotopi*[64]	*ja≡laˈca*[65]|	*ˈtotes*	*θa≡faneroˈθi*
for=straight.place	and=DEF=high.place.PL	for=pit.SG	then	FUT=reveal:3SG

ας γίνει πεδιάδα και τα μέρη τ' απόκρημνα, κοιλάδα. Τότε

shall become straight, and the high places [shall become] a pit. 40:5 Then shall be revealed

אִיטִימִי טוּ ה׳. <...>[66] דְיָאוֹטִי אוֹלוֹגוֹס טוּ ה׳
כְּבוֹד יְהוָה <...> כִּי פִּי יְהוָה

i≡tiˈmi	*tu=aðoˈnaj|*	<...>	*ðja≡ˈoti*	*o≡ˈlogos*	*tu=aðoˈnaj*
the=honor	DEF.GEN=Lord		for=that	DEF=word	DEF.GEN=Lord

η δόξα του Κυρίου θα φανερωθεί <…>, γιατί ο Κύριος ο ίδιος

the honor of the Lord <…>, for the word of the Lord

אוֹמִילִיסֵי: פוֹנִי לֵי קְרַקְסֵי. קֵ׳ילֵי
דִּבֵּר. קוֹל אֹמֵר קְרָא וְאָמַר

oˈmilise ||	*foˈni*	*le*	*ˈkrakse|*	*ce≡ˈle*
speak:AOR.3SG	voice	say:PRS.3SG	call:IMP.SG	and=say:PRS.3SG

μίλησε». Μια φωνή λέει: «Φώναξε!» Κι εγώ ρωτάω:

hath spoken.' 40:6 A voice saith: 'Proclaim!' And he saith:

טִי נַקְרַקְסוֹ. אוֹלִי אִיסַרְקָא תַמַרַתִי
מָה אֶקְרָא כָּל-הַבָּשָׂר

ti	*na≡ˈkrakso |*	*ˈoli*	*i≡ˈsarka*	*θa≡maraˈθi*
what	SBJ=call: AOR.SBJ.1SG	all:F.NOM	DEF=flesh	FUT=wither: AOR.SBJ.PASS-3SG

«Τι να φωνάξω;» «Ότι ο κάθε άνθρωπος είναι

'What shall I proclaim?' 'All flesh will wither

סַחוֹרְטָרִי. קֵי אוֹלִי אִיקָלוֹסִינִיטוּ סַן אִיַנְתִי
חָצִיר וְכָל-חַסְדּוֹ כְּצִיץ

sa≡xorˈtari |	*ce=ˈoli*	*i≡kaloˈsini≡tu*	*san*[67]	*i≡ˈjanθi*[68]
like.PART=grass	and=all.F	DEF =goodliness=POSS.3SG.M	like.PART	DEF=flower.F

σαν το χορτάρι [», μού απαντά η φωνή, «]κι η δόξα του όλη φευγαλέα σαν το αγρολούλουδο.

like grass, and all the goodliness thereof [will wither] as the flowers

64 Assuming that the article of the prototype was given a representation, the reading *οι-ψηλότοποι* is preferable to **υψηλότοποι*. Although the lemma *ψηλότοπος* does not appear in the Epirus lexicography, its derivational pattern is common, cf. EG *βραχότοπος* 'rocky place', *λιβαδότοπος* 'meadowland' (Vilaras), SG *ερημότοπος* 'wilderness, desert', etc.

65 The form is defined as singular on presumption of parallelism with the original, cf. EG *λακκιά* 'gorge' (Bonkas 1964: 208).

66 The translation of the clause וְרָאוּ כָל-בָּשָׂר יַחְדָּו was accidentally omitted by the copyist; it is supplied after the end-mark of the *haftara*.

67 In SG the preposition requires accusative.

68 The feminine form *η άνθη* did not survive in SG, which has only *το άνθος* 'flower' and *ο ανθός* 'blossom, bloom','blooming season'.

טוּ קַמְפּוּ: אַפַּנוּ בוֹנוֹ פְּסִילוֹ אַנֵיבָא
הַשָּׂדֶה. עַל הַר-גָּבֹהַ עֲלִי-

tu='kampu || a'panu vo'no psi'lo a″neva
DEF=field.GEN on.top mountain high.N climb:IMP.SG
<…> Ανέβα πάνω σε ψηλό βουνό,
of the field.' <…> 40:9 Get thee up into the high mountain,

אֵיסֵינָא סְחַרִיקֵ׳פְּטְרָא טִיס צִיוֹן. פְּסִילִינֵי מֵידִינָמִי
לָךְ מְבַשֶּׂרֶת צִיּוֹן הָרִימִי בַכֹּחַ

e″sena[69] sxari'ceftra[70], tis=t͡si'on| 'psiline[71] me≡'ðinami
you:ACC bearer.of.good.news.F DEF.GEN.F=Zion lift:IMP.AOR.SG with=strength
Σιών, και διακήρυξε τη χαρμόσυνη αγγελία. Βάλε φωνή με δύναμη,
o thou that tellest good tidings to Zion, lift up thy voice with strength;

טִיפוֹנִיסוּ. סְחַרִיקֵפְּטְרָא טִיסְיְרוּשָׁלַיִם. פְּסִילִינֵי מִי פוֹבָסֵי.
קוֹלֵךְ מְבַשֶּׂרֶת יְרוּשָׁלִָם הָרִימִי אַל-תִּירָאִי

ti≡fo'ni≡su| sxari'ceftra tis≡jeruʃa'lajim| 'psiline 'mi=fo'vase|
DEF=voice=POSS.2SG bearer.of.good.news.F DEF:GEN.F=Jerusalem lift:IMP.AOR.SG NEG=fear.IMP.SG
Ιερουσαλήμ, και διακήρυξε τα νέα τα ευχάριστα. Φώναξε, μη φοβάσαι!
o thou that tellest good tidings to Jerusalem, lift it up, be not afraid;

פֵּס אִיסְטִסְחוֹרֶ[ס] טוּ יְאוּדָה. אִידוֹ אוֹתֵאוֹסָס:
אִמְרִי לְעָרֵי יְהוּדָה הִנֵּה אֱלֹהֵיכֶם.

pes is≡ti's≡xore[s][72] | tu jeu'ða[73] 'iðo[74] o≡θe'o≡sas||
say:IMP.AOR.SG to=DEF=city:ACC.PL DEF.GEN Judah behold DEF=god=POSS.2PL
Στις πόλεις του Ιούδα πες: «Να ο Θεός σας!
say unto the cities of Judah: 'Behold your God!

69 In SG this type of construction would require a weak pronominal form rather than emphatic, see Holton 2014: 115.

70 A derivative of *σχαρικεύω* < **συγχαρικεύω* 'to bring good news' (Macedonia), cf. *συγχαρεύω* 'the same' (East Macedonia), *συγχαριάζω* 'to greet' (Sterea Ellada, Peloponnese), *σχάρω* < *ἐσυχάρην* (Cappadocia, Chatzidakis 1905: vol.2, 541), and widespread *συγχαίρομαι*. A masculine agent noun *συγχαριστής* is recorded in Vlaxos (1659). EG preserves only *τά š'χαρίκια* 'tip given to the bearer of pleasant news' (Bonkas 1964: 375, cf. Kosmas 1997: 114, 31). In JG the root provides conventional translations for בשר 'to announce (sc. good news), reveal', cf. *σχαρικέψεις* in Matsas 1953: 50 with reference to prophet Elijah.

71 The de-adjectival verb is built from *ψηλός* 'high' after the model *λαμπρός* 'brilliant' > *λαμπρύνω* 'to brighten', *εύκολος* 'easy' > *ευκολύνω* 'to facilitate'. It is recorded in Pontic area and in Erikousa.

72 In modern SG the word means 'countries.' In late Medieval and Early Modern period, as well as in more recent EG *χώρα* meant 'town' or 'major/central village', see Bongas 1964: 438. In JG it served as a translational equivalent for עיר 'town', cf. *αγια χωρα* 'holy city' (= Jerusalem) (Is 52:1, fol. 6v of this manuscript).

73 Unlike the majority of cases, Hebrew spelling of the proper noun is not followed here.

74 The particle could have resulted from the contamination of *ἰδού*, the traditional translational equivalent of הִנֵּה in LXX, with the adv. *εδώ*. In the following verse it is accented paroxytonally, which possibly can be generalized to all cases.

אִידוֹ ה׳ אוֹתֵי אוֹס מֵיכֵ׳יךָא דִינָטִי
הִנֵּה אֲדֹנָי יְהוִה בְּחָזָק

ˈiðo aðoˈnai o=θeˈos me=ˈˈçera[75] *ðinaˈti*
behold Lord DEF=god with =hand strong:F
Ο Κύριος, ο Θεός, έρχεται να εξουσιάσει με δύναμη.
40:10 Behold, the Lord God will come with mighty hand,

תָאֵרְטִי קֵיאִי יֵבְרַחוֹנָאטוּ תָאוֹרִיסִי אַפְטוּנוּ. אִידוֹ
יָבוֹא וּזְרֹעוֹ מֹשְׁלָה לוֹ הִנֵּה

θa≡ˈerti ce≡i=jevraˈxona≡tu θa≡oˈˈrisi aftuˈnu | ˈˈiðo
FUT=come:3SG and=DEF=arm=POSS.3SG.M FUT=rule: AOR.SBJ.3SG 3SG.GEN behold
Φέρνει μαζί του
and His arm will rule for Him; behold,

אִפְּלֵירוֹמִיטוּ מֵטַפְטוֹן. קֵי אוֹמִסְטוֹס טִסְקַטַנְדְיַסְטוּ אֹמְבְּרוֹסְטָטוּ:
שְׂכָרוֹ אִתּוֹ וּפְעֻלָּתוֹ לְפָנָיו.

i≡pleroˈˈmi≡tu me≡ˈˈtafton| ce o≡miˈstos tis≡katanˈdjas≡tu[76]
DEF=payment=POSS.3SG.M with=him and=DEF=salary DEF=success.GEN=POSS.3SG.M
ombroˈˈsta≡tu||
in.front=him.PRON.3SG.M
αυτό που κέρδισε.
His reward is with Him, and His recompense before Him.

סַן אוֹפִּסְטִקוֹס
כְּרֹעֶה

san o≡pistiˈkos
like DEF=shepherd
Καθώς βοσκός
40:11 As a shepherd

פּוּטוֹ מַנְדְרִיט'וּ בוֹשְׁקַי. מֵיטִין אֵבְרַחוֹנָטוּ סִימָזוֹנִי אַרְנְיָא
עֶדְרוֹ יִרְעֶה בִּזְרֹעוֹ יְקַבֵּץ טְלָאִים

pu≡to manˈdri[77]*≡tu voˈʃkaj*[78]*| me≡tin=evraˈxona=tu ˈˈsimaˈzoni arˈnja*
REL=DEF flock=POSS.3SG.M graze.PRS.3SG with=DEF=arm=POSS.3SG.M gather:PRS.3SG lamb:ACC.PL
βοσκάει το κοπάδι του· το συναθροίζει με το χέρι του·
that feedeth his flock, that gathereth the lambs in his arm,

75 Both archaic feminine *χέρα* and commoner neuter *χέρι* can be used for the Divine hand, cf. 40:2 of this sample for the neuter version, and Matsas 1953: 52 for feminine.

76 The transcription and translation are tentative, as the noun can be both paroxytone and oxytone. Earlier witnesses record paroxytone, e.g. Somavera, who interprets it as 'il farsi de qualche cosa', while more recent lexicographers register oxytone. The oxytone version from Epirus and Sterea Ellada combines abstract meanings 'success, economic progress' with concrete 'estate, belongings'. In SG *kaˈtandja* evolved to mean 'miserable physical, moral or mental state, a predicament'.

77 Μαντρί in sense of 'flock' is atypical for the Epirus area, where the word means 'corral', as in SG. The meaning 'flock' is widely represented in the Aegean (Dodecanese, Cyclades, Kythera), e.g., *ήθελα να μουβ βόσκισσα να 'οσκα το μαντρίσ σου* (Carpathos, Michaēlidēs Nouaros 1932: vol. 1, 41). According to Chatzidakis (1905: vol. 2, 257), this was also the usage in Pontos.

78 Or *voˈʃkai.*

קֶסְטוֹן קוֹרְפוֹטוּ טַפוֹרְטוֹנִיטֵי. טַמִקְרָא טוֹן בִיזַסְטְרוֹן קוֹלַנְדְּרִיזִי:

וּבְחֵיקוֹ יִשָּׂא עָלוֹת יְנַהֵל.

ce≡s≡ton 'korfo≡tu| *ta≡for'tonite* *ta≡mik'ra* *ton=viza'stron*

and=in=DEF=bosom=POSS.3SG.M them=load:PRS.3SG DEF=small:ACC.PL DEF= suckling:GEN.PL

kolan"drizi[79]*||*

lead:PRS.3SG

βαστάει στο στήθος του τ' αρνάκια, και τις μανάδες τους προσεκτικά τις οδηγεί».

and carrieth them in his bosom, [and] small of kids of sucklers he gently leadeth.

פְּיוֹס אִימֵטְרִיסֵי מֵטִיחוּפְטַטוּ טָנֵרָא. קֵיטוּס אוֹרָנוּס

מִי-מָדַד בְּשָׁעֳלוֹ מַיִם וְשָׁמַיִם

pços i"metrise *me≡ti≡ 'xufta≡tu* *ta≡ne'ra |* *ce≡tus ora'nus*[80]

who measure:AOR.3SG with=DEF=handful=POSS.3SG.M DEF=water:ACC.PL and=DEF=sky:ACC.PL

Ποιος τα νερά της θάλασσας μπόρεσε ποτέ με τη χούφτα να μετρήσει, τα ουράνια

40:12 Who hath measured the waters in the hollow of his hand, and meted out heaven

מֵיטִין פִּיתָמִי אֵילוֹגַרְיָסֵי. קֵיאִי מֵטְרִיסֵי מֵיטוֹמֵיטְרוֹ טוֹ חוֹמָא

בַּזֶּרֶת תִּכֵּן וְכָל בַּשָּׁלִשׁ עֲפַר

me≡tin pi'θami *elo'γariase|* *ce=i'metrise* *me≡to≡ 'metro* *to "xoma*

with=DEF=span calculate:AOR.3SG and= measure:AOR.3SG with=DEF=measure:ACC DEF=earth

να υπολογίσει με τη σπιθαμή, να βάλει σε σακί της γης το χώμα,

with the span, and measured in a measure the dust

טִיסְאִיִס. קֵיאִיזִי[יסֵי מֵי]טוֹ סַטֵרִי טַיְבוּנָא. קֵיטִסְרַכֵ׳ס

הָאָרֶץ וְשָׁקַל בַּפֶּלֶס הָרִים וּגְבָעוֹת

tis≡i'jis| *ce≡i'zi[jise* *me] to sa"teri*[81] *ta≡jvu'na*[82]*||* *ce≡tis≡"raçes*

DEF=earth:GEN and=weight=AOR.3SG with DEF=scales DEF=mountains:ACC.PL and=DEF=hills:ACC.PL

με την πλάστιγγα να ζυγίσει τα βουνά ή με τη ζυγαριά τους λόφους;

of the earth, and weighed in scales the mountains, and the hills

מֵיבִילַנְזֶיס: פְּיוֹס אֹרְדִנְיַסֵי טוֹתֵלִימָא טוּ ה׳.

בְּמֹאזְנָיִם. מִי-תִכֵּן אֶת-רוּחַ יְהוָה

me≡vi'landzes[83]*||* *pços or'ðiniase*[84] *to≡"θelima* *tu aðo'naj|*

with= balance:ACC.PL who advise:AOR.3SG DEF=will DEF.GEN.SG=Lord

Ποιος μπορεί να κατανοήσει το Πνεύμα του Κυρίου,

in a balance? 40:13 Who hath commanded the will of the Lord?

79 The meaning of the verb continues its Turkish etymon *kullandirmek* 'to drive, to use', cf. 'maneggiare' (Somavera 1709), Altbauer and Shiby 1971–1981: 407 translating נוהג (Eccl. 2:3), without semantic lowering found in SG *κουλαντρίζω* 'to tease, to provoke'. In EG the verb develops the meanings 'to treat, nurture, care systematically (as about child or sick person)'.

80 The plural is a translational Hebraism.

81 The form is attested in EG, cf. SG *στατήρας*.

82 From [ta=ivu'na] with shortening of [i], [ivu'no] being a common EG form for SG *βουνό*.

83 The loan reflects Calabro-Sicilian *vilanza*, cf. SG *παλάντζα* and *μπαλάντζα*, which goes back to *balanza,* a form of Venetian, Tuscan, and some other Central and Northern Italian dialects.

84 The semantics of the verb extends from 'to order, command, dictate, manage, correct, arrange' documented in texts and early lexicographers (Somavera) to 'advise' in the dialects of Dodecanese and Thrace.

קִיטְִי[נוּס אנְ]תְרוֹפּוּ טִין אוֹרְמִנְיַאטוּ טוּמַתִיטִפְּסֵי.
וְאִישׁ עֲצָתוֹ יוֹדִיעֶנּוּ.

ci≡″ti[nus an]ˈθropu tin=ormiˈnja≡tu tu≡maˈθitipse||
and=who:GEN man:GEN.SG DEF=order=his he:GEN=instruct:AOR.3SG
και ποιος μπορεί να τον διδάξει ή να του δώσει συμβουλές;
And from which man hath He learnt His commandment? <…>

אִֽידוֹ טָאֵתְנָא סָא סְטַלַמַטְיָא אַפּוֹ שְׁקְלוֹ. קֵ'יסַכְנוּמִי
הֵן גּוֹיִם כְּמַר מִדְּלִי וּכְשַׁחַק

″iðo ta≡eθna sa stalamaˈtja apo ″ʃiklo| ce≡sa≡″xnumi[85]
here[86] DEF=people:PL as=drop:ACC from=bucket:ACC and=as=lightweight.remnants
Τι ’ναι τα έθνη; Σαν μια σταγόνα σ’ έναν κάδο με νερό, σαν κόκκος σκόνης
40:15 Behold, the nations are as a drop of a bucket, and are counted as the small dust

אַפּוֹ וִילַנְזֶיס לוֹגַרְיַזוֹנְדֵי. אִֽידוֹ אִינִישׁוֹטֶיס סָא
מֹאזְנַיִם נֶחְשָׁבוּ הֵן אִיִּים כַּדַּק

aˈpo viˈlandzes loɣarˈjazonde| ″iðo i-niˈʃotes[87] *sa*
from= balance:ACC.PL PRS:3PL here DEF=islanders:PL as
πάνω στην πλάστιγγα. Πόσο ζυγίζουν τα νησιά;
of the balance; behold the islanders are as

פְּסִילוֹ כְנוּמִי אוֹפְּרִיכְנִיטֵי: קֵ'י מֵטַדֶנְדְרָא טוּ לְבָנוֹן. דֵי פְּטַנִי
יִטוֹל. לְבָנוֹן אֵין דֵּי

″psilo ″xnumi[88] *op≡ˈrixnite|| ce me≡ta≡ˈðendra tu levaˈnon*[89]*| ðe ″ftani*
fine.coal.dust that=throw.3SG.PASS and with=DEF=tree.PL DEF=Lebanon NEG=suffice.3SG
Όσο της άμμου ο κόκκος. Όλα τα δέντρα του Λιβάνου δεν αρκούν
a mote in weight. 40:16 And with the trees of Lebanon there is not sufficient

יַנַקְסַנַפְּסוּן. קֵ'ימֵטָתֵרִיאָטוּ. דֶיפְּטָנִי יַנַזְ'יגוֹסוּן אוֹלוֹכַּפְטוֹ:
בָּעֵר וְחַיָּתוֹ אֵין דֵּי עוֹלָה.

ja≡na≡ksaˈnapsun| ce≡me-ta≡θeˈria=tu| ðe≡ˈftani
for=PART=rekindle= AOR.SBJ.3PLand=with=art=beast:PL=POSS.3SG.M NEG=suffice:PRS.3SG
ja≡na≡ʒiˈɣosun oˈlokafto||
for= PART=approach=AOR.SBJ.3PL burnt.offering
για τη φωτιά ούτε όλα του τα ζωντανά για τ’ ολοκαύτωμα.
fuel, nor the beasts thereof sufficient for burnt-offerings.

85 The lexeme *χνούμ’, ή* has several possible interpretations: in EG it may mean ‘bits of ears of cereals separated during threshing and winnowing’, which in some areas of Epirus evolved into ‘any lightweight object’. In the urban dialect of Ioannina, it used to mean ‘fine dust that remains in the bucket after the coal has been removed’, see Bonkas 1964: 433.

86 The translation of the lexeme here and in the following verse is tentative.

87 The translation reflects the traditional understanding of the verse going back to Targum Jonathan ad loc. The corresponding modern Ianniote form *ν’σιώτ’ς* in Kosmas 1997: 98 is not transcribed as containing ʃ.

88 SG would require an article in this position.The noun is a compound **το ψιλοχνούμι*, which seems unwitnessed, but is built with popular first compound *ψιλο-*, see LKN s.v. *ψιλο-* 4a. It cannot be read as noun phrase, because this would require an accent on the final syllable *ψιλό*, and would violate the rule of one-to-one equivalence between the source and translation.

89 The Hebrew toponym is preserved indeclinable, cf. SG *ο Λίβανος*.

אוֹלָא טָאֶתְנָא סַמַנְדָּא דֶנִיטָא קַטַגְנַדִּנְטוּ.
כָּל- הַגּוֹיִם כְּאַיִן נֶגְדּוֹ

'Ola ta='eθna samanda ðen-ita[90] *kataɣna'din-tu|*
all:N.PL DEF=nations:N.PL as.if NEG=was opposite=him
Όλα τα έθνη είν' ένα τίποτα μπροστά του·
40:17 All the nations are as nothing before Him;

קַטוֹטִירָא אַפּוֹ טוֹדִיחוֹס קֶ׳יקַנְטִפּוּטֶס לוֹגַרְיַזוֹנְדֵי אַפְטוּנוּ:
מֵאֶפֶס וָתֹהוּ נֶחְשְׁבוּ-לוֹ.

ka"totira a'po to≡'ðixos ce≡kan≡'tiputes loɣa'rjazonde aftu'nu||
low:COMP.N.PL from=DEF=without and=NEG=nothing consider:3PL.PASS he:GEN
τα λογαριάζει σαν μηδέν, ωσάν μηδαμινότητα.
they are accounted by Him as things of nought, and vanity.

קֶ'ימֵי טוֹמְפְּיוֹן סִנְדּוֹמְנְיַזִיטֵי טוֹן תֵאוֹ. קֵיטִי
וְאֶל-מִי תְּדַמְּיוּן אֵל וּמַה-

ce≡me to^{m}*≡'pçon*[91] *si*^{n}*do'mnjazite*[92] *ton θe'o| ce≡'ti*
and with DEF=who:ACC.SG.M compare:PRS.2PL DEF god:ACC and=what
Με ποιον θέλετε να παρομοιάστε το Θεό; Και ποιο
40:18 To whom then will ye liken God? Or what

סִנדּוֹמְנְיַסִי אֹרְדִינְיַזִיטֵי אַפְטוּנוּ: טוֹפִּילֵיקִ׳יטוֹ אוֹפּ
דְּמוּת תַּעַרְכוּ לוֹ. הַפֶּסֶל

si'^{n}*domnjasi| orði'njazite aftu'nu || to≡pi"lecito op*
comparison arrange.PRS.2PL he.GEN DEF=carving that
ομοίωμα να πείτε πως του μοιάζει; Το είδωλο το
likeness will ye compare unto Him? 40:19 The image, which

כִּ׳ינִי אוֹמַסְטוֹרָס. קֶ׳יאֹכְ׳רִישְׁקוֹס מֵיטוֹ כִּ׳רִיסָפִּי
נָסַךְ חָרָשׁ וְצֹרֵף בַּזָּהָב

="çini o≡'mastoras | ce≡o≡çri'ʃkos[93] *me≡to çri'safi*
pour.PRS.3SG DEF=master and=DEF=goldsmith with=DEF gold
χύνει ο τεχνίτης κι ο χρυσοχόος το επιχρυσώνει
the craftsman melteth, and the goldsmith

90 The use of past tense could have been provoked by the following verb.

91 In SG no article is required before the interrogative pronouns, see also below in 40:24.

92 JG regularly records a glide in this root, cf. *ὀμνιότη* (Const. Pent. Deut. 33:28); *ομνιάζω* Altbauer and Shiby 1971–1981. The verb *συντουμιάζου* 'to liken', 'to confuse a person with someone else' and its medial form *συντουμιάζουμι* 'to be alike' were recorded in Ereikousa and Kavakli (Eastern Rumelia, now Topolovgrad, Bulgaria).

93 According to Bonkas 1964: 437, the noun *χ'σ'κός* in EG referred to one who is 'both goldsmith and silversmith'.

טוֹ אַפְּלוֹנִי. קֵימֵיאַלִיסוּס אַסִימֵנְיוּס אוֹ כְ'רִשְׁקוֹס:

יְרַקְּעֶנּוּ וּרְתֻקוֹת כֶּסֶף צוֹרֵף.

to a″ploni | ce≡me≡ 'alisus[94] *asi 'menjus o=çri 'ʃkos||*

it:ACC.SG spread:PRS.3SG and=with=chain:ACC.PL silver:ADJ.ACC.PL.M DEF=goldsmith

και το στολίζει με αλυσίδες αργυρές.

coverth it with gold and with silver chains, the goldsmith?

אוֹאֵפְּטוֹכוֹס יַחוֹרִיזְמָא. קְסִילוֹ אוֹפְּדֵי סַרַקְוֹנִיטֵי דְיָלֵי.

הַמְסֻכָּן תְּרוּמָה עֵץ לֹא-יִרְקַב יִבְחָר

o=efto 'xos ja= 'xorizma| 'ksilo op≡ðe| sara″konite[95] *ðja 'lei*[96]*|*

DEF=poor for=partition:ACC.SG wood that=NEG=be.worm-eaten:PASS.3SG choose:PRS.3SG

Όποιος είναι φτωχός διαλέγει για την προσφορά του ξύλο που δεν το τρώει το σαράκι,

40:20 A poor man for division, chooseth a tree that will not be worm-eaten;

מַסְטוֹרַן סוֹפוֹן זְ'יטִי דְיַטַ[פְטוֹן] יַנַאוֹרְדִינְיַסִי

חָרָשׁ חָכָם יְבַקֶּשׁ-לוֹ לְהָכִין

'mastoran so 'fon ʒi 'ti ðja 'ta[fton] ja≡na≡orð i 'njasi

master:ACC wise:ACC search:PRS.3SG for=this.ACC.SG PRP= SBJPART =order:AORSBJ.3SG

κι αναζητάει έναν τεχνίτη ικανόν να του φτιάξει

he seeketh unto him a cunning craftsman to order

פִּילֵיקִ'יטוֹ פּוּנַמְדֵן אַגְלִסְטְרֵי [:]אוֹפִּיאוֹס דְינִי

פֶּסֶל לֹא יִמּוֹט. <…> הַנּוֹתֵן

pi″lecito pu≡na≡m 'ðen aɣli″stri[97]*[||] 'opços ″ðini*[98]

carving:ACC.N that= SBJPART=NEG slide.PRS.3SG whoever give:PRS.3SG

είδωλο που να ’ναι στέρεο. <…> Αυτός

a carved image, that shall not subside.<…> 40:23 [He] that taketh

טוּס אַפֶּנְדָּדֶס סַמַנְדָּא דֶנְאִינִיטִי. טוּס קְרִיטָדֶיס טִסְאִיִּיס

רוֹזְנִים לְאָיִן שֹׁפְטֵי אֶרֶץ

tus afe 'ndaðes 'samanda ðen≡″initi | tus=kri″taðes tis=i 'jis

DEF=lord.ACC.PL as.if NEG=become:PRES.3SG DEF=judges:ACC.PL DEF=earth:GEN.SG

τους ηγεμόνες τούς εκμηδενίζει κι

lords for nothing; He maketh the judges of the earth

סַן טוּס קַטִיפּוֹטֶרְנְיוּס קָנִי: אַפַּטָא סַמַנְדָּא

כַּתֹּהוּ עָשָׂה. אַף בַּל-

san tus=katipoter 'njus[99] *″kani|| apa 'ta 'samanda*

PART DEF=negligible.ACC.PL.M do:PRS.3SG PART as.if

εξαφανίζει τους κριτές της γης. Μοιάζουν

as a thing of nought. 40:24 As if they

94 For the gender ascription (masculine rather than SG feminine) see Chatzidakis 1905: vol. 2, 140; Bonkas 1964: 41.

95 Cf. SG σαρακιάζεται.

96 Or *ðja 'lej.*

97 Here conjugated after P10.9 (LKN), cf. SG *γλιστράει* following P10.1. For the prothetic vowel cf. EG *ἀγλιστράου* Kosmas 1997: 16, Bonkas 1964: 9.

98 Literal translation of the Hebrew phraseologism ‘to give X to Y’ = ‘to compare X with Y’, which has no parallel in SG.

99 *κα* < *κἄν* is added to reinforce the negative meaning, cf. *καένας, κατ'νους* Kosmas 1997: 43. On the development of [r] see Bonkas 1964: 10, Kosmas 1997: 28.

דֵן אֵפִיטֶפְטֵי קָן אַפַּטָא סַמַנְדָא דֵן אִסְפִּרְטִיקָן. אַפַּטָא

נִטָּעוּ אַף בַּל-זֹרָעוּ אַף

ðen efi'tefte kan apa'ta 'samanda ðen i'spirtikan| apa'ta

NEG plant:AOR.PASS.3PL PART as.if NEG sow:AOR.PASS.3PL PART

με νεαρά φυτά που τώρα μόλις σπάρθηκαν,

were not planted, as if they were not sown, as if

סַמַנְדָא דֵן אֵרִיזְוֹתִיקֵי אִסְטִין אִיִין טוֹ קוּצִירוֹ טוּס. קֵ׳יאַפַּטָא

בַּל-שֹׁרֵשׁ בָּאָרֶץ גִּזְעָם וְגַם-

'samanda ðen eri"zoθike is≡tin=i'jin to='kuts͡i'ro tus, ce apa'ta

as.if NEG=take.root:AOR.PASS.3SG in=DEF=earth:ACC.SG DEF= = POSS.3PL.M and PART

που μόλις ρίζωσαν στη γη. Όταν

their stock hath not taken root in the earth; and

פִּיסַי סֵטַפְטוּנוּס קֵיסְטֵגְנוֹנוּן. קֵ׳י אַנִימוֹסְטְרוֹפִילָס סַנְטוֹן

נָשַׁף בָּהֶם וַיִּבָשׁוּ וּסְעָרָה

fi'saj se≡taftu'nus ce≡ste'γnonun| ce animo'strofilas[100] *san≡ton*

blow:PRS.3SG in=this:ACC.PL and=dry:PRS.3PL and= whirlwind like=ART:ACC

ο Κύριος πάνω τους φυσήξει θα ξεραθούν, κι ο ανεμοστρόβιλος σαν

when He bloweth upon them, they wither, and the whirlwind

אַכֵ׳ירוֹן טוּס שִׁיקוֹנִי: קֵי מֵי טוֹנְפְּיוֹן מֵיסִין דוֹמְנְיַזִיטֵי

כַּקַּשׁ תִּשָּׂאֵם וְאֶל-מִי תְדַמְּיוּנִי

'açeron[101] *tus=ʃi'koni|| ce=me ton='pçon me=sin do'mnjazite*

straw:ACC.M they:ACC=lift:PRS.3SG and with DEF=who:ACC.SG.M I:ACC=compare:PRS.2PL

άχυρο θα τους αρπάξει. «Με ποιον θα με παρομοιάσετε, λοιπόν;»

taketh them away as straw. 40:25 And to whom will ye liken Me,

פוּנָאוֹמְנְיָסוֹ. לֵי אוֹ אָיוֹס:

וְאֶשְׁוֶה יֹאמַר קָדוֹשׁ.

pu≡na≡o'mnjaso| le o="ajos||

that=SBJ.PART=be.alike:AOR.SUBJ.1SG say:PRS.3SG DEF=holy:NOM.M

λέει ο Άγιος Θεός, «με ποιον θα ταυτιστώ;»

that I should be equal? saith the Holy One.

3.3 Sample C

The following sample is a transcription of oral interview with a congregant of Kehila Kedosha Janina in New York, male, born in 1929 in the family of Romaniote immigrants from Ioannina. It was conducted by D. Kaufman in 2014 as a part of a project to record the endangered languages of New York City. [102] In terms of typology of speakers

100 The EG form *ἀνιμουστρόφ'λας* Kosmas 1997: 26, *μ'στρόφλας* Bonkas 1964: 243, cf. SG *ἀνεμοστρόβιλος*, results from the folk-etymological association of the second part of the compound with *στρέφω* 'to turn'.

101 In SG *άχυρο* is neuter.

102 The recording is accessible on http://www.youtube.com/watch?v=9NRqqjflY7Y&t=143s (5:59 min in total; fragments 2:50–55 and 4:19–27 were omitted from the transcript below as repetitive and not adding new data).

the interviewee can be characterized as a terminal speaker.[103] His dysfluency is obvious in frequent aborting of the projected words and numerous switches to the languages, in which he feels more at ease: English, Hebrew, and Spanish. The transcript allows an assessment of the advanced level of attrition of morphology, syntax and vocabulary.[104]

3.3.1 Phonetics

The phonetic influence of English is evident throughout: many vowels, in particular [a] and [e], differ from their Epirus and SG counterparts; initial stops [t, p] are aspirated; interdentals can also be realized as stops with secondary aspiration.

Northern Greek vocalic phenomena of an extreme type are widely represented: unstressed high vowels in word-final and word-internal positions are deleted, unstressed mid vowels raised and eventually also deleted. The extent of reduction and final deletion in the sample is remarkable: even unstressed [a] can be reduced and, if final, deleted. Vowels in unstressed positions appear strongly centralized. [i] and [u] in clitics tend to merge into [ɯ]. The negation [ðen] has its vowel backed into [ɤ].

As it is usual for northern language varieties, a vowel develops between the final [-s] of the noun, voiced into [z], and the initial [m-] of the weak possessive pronoun: [opaˈterazim].[105] [s] before [i] is realized as voiceless palato-alveolar sibilant [ʃ], cf. Sample B.

3.3.2 Morphology

The sample shows a lack of article in the positions where it is expected, e.g., [xaˈxam] for [o=xaˈxam]. A neutral article appears to be generalized for masculine and feminine nouns ([t=jaˈɲotᵊs], cf. SG *οι Γιαννιώτες*; [tu=oˈxam] for *[o=oˈxam] > [oˈxam], [tu=cei ˈla] for *[i=ceiˈla]).

The lack of distinction between the article forms *τους* and *τις* is due to their similar pronunciation (see Phonetics above) which must have contributed to the loss of gender distinctions.

The genitive plural is used in the fixed phrase [X xruˈnon] 'x years old', but does not occur anywhere else. The genitive of both singular and plural is replaced through the periphrastic constructions *από* 'from'+ acc. and *οπ'είναι σε* 'which is in' + acc.

The accusative of direct object is suppressed in favor of the nominative on one occasion: in '[they sent] my father' the object is expressed through [opaˈterazim].

Pluralization is still preserved in all three genders, however, on one occasion a neutral plural is used for singular: [t=uˈnomata]. More research is needed to establish whether it is more than an accidental slip of tongue.

The loss of genitive and weakening of accusative resulted in significant simplification of the nominal paradigm. Even more advanced are the changes in the verbal system: the category of verbal aspect appears to have been lost: perfective aspect is genera-

103 For the classification of speakers see Grinevald and Bert (2011). For the background of the interviewee, including his language repertoire, see http://www.youtube.com/watch?v=EdWIHdN675k.

104 For more data on the New-York JG see Vlachou et al. 2014.

105 Kontosopoulos 2008: 98–99.

lized for all forms of the past ([ˈpiγa] for [ˈpijena]) and subjunctive ([na=ðjaˈvasumi] for [na=ðjaˈvazumi]).

3.3.3 Syntax

Directional construction may appear with or without the preposition σε, occasionally producing an output [ci=ˈpiγa ˈena talˈmud toˈra], whose SG equivalent **πήγα ένα σχολείο* is ungrammatical.[106]

The interviewee inserts *σε* 'in' into the time expression 'in 1929', where SG requires the accusative, under the influence of the languages requiring a preposition (English *in*, Hebrew *be-*, Spanish *en*).

3.3.4 Lexicon

Even the basic Greek vocabulary ('school', 'young', etc.) appears to have been lost. The semantic range of some lexemes does not fully correspond to that of SG or EG: e.g., [ˈama] appears overgeneralized, replacing every type of temporal conjunction; the speaker is unsure of the polysemy of *μαθαίνω* 'to learn/teach'.

Obsolete vocabulary, currently out of use with Ioannina Romaniotes, is preserved due to the isolation of the New York community: *κρίνω* 'to speak' (SG *μιλώ*), *λίμπρο* 'book, genealogical record' (possibly reinforced in the speaker's idiolect by Spanish *libro*; SG *βιβλίο*, *κατάλογος*, *μητρώο*). The glottonym *Ελληνικά* is pronounced with [e] in the second syllable, either influenced by English *Hellenic* and Spanish *helénico*, or continuing a dialect form.[107]

The phonetic form of the HA loanwords is influenced by the Sephardic tradition of reading Hebrew: [briθmiˈla] < ברית מילה 'circumcision' occasionally preserves its [θ] in the root, but not in the plural ending [briθmilot]; cf. [talˈmud] rather than [talˈmuð]. Polymorphism of the place name [saloˈnik] and [saˈlonika] 'Thessaloniki' (SG *Θεσσαλονίκη*) is also due to the impact of Judeo-Spanish.

3.3.5 Text

The transcription is followed by the SG version, glossing and an English translation. The conventions of the transcription follow the practice of the Linguistic Data Consortium: single dash (-) is used to indicate the point at which a word was broken off. An asterisk (*) precedes obviously mispronounced words. Double brackets (()) mark unclear passages of the recording. A plus sign (+) disambiguates the word intended by the speaker, which was uttered in a truncated form. Due to space limitations filled pauses, hesitation sounds and verbatim repetitions were ignored. Numerous speaker's restarts, indicated with double dash (--), are not transcribed, unless the rephrased utterance resulted differently from the initially intended one. Switches to other languages are not transcribed and glossed, being marked {–}. Semantically identical repetitive utterances

106 While '*πήγα σχολείο*' 'I went to school' (in generalized meaning 'I studied/received my education') is acceptable in SG, the use of an articulated form would require a preposition, i.e. either '*πήγα σ'ενα σχολείο*' or '*πήγα στο σχολείο*' 'I went to a/the school'.

107 The form has been recently reported in the neighboring Northern Epirus dialect: Brown and Joseph (2015). In the nineteenth century it was widespread in the Greek-speaking realm as far as Pontic.

in other languages are omitted from the English translation and the SG version. The SG version provides SG equivalents for HA loanwords and translates the Hebrew and English switches.

'ama i^{j}i'niθka -- 'monaxa[108] *a^{ŋ}gli'ka 'emaθa|*
after bear.AOR.PASS.1SG only English.NEUT.PL learn.AOR.1SG
Αφότου γεννήθηκα μόνο αγγλικά μάθαινα.
Since I was born I have been studying only English,

al- -- 'ama 'imun eks^{i} xru'non|
but when be.AOR.1SG 6.NUM year.GEN.PL
Αλλά όταν ήμουν έξι χρονών
but when I was six years old

^{e}'piγa s=tu Hebrew school| Talmud Torah|
go.AOR.1SG to=DEF {-} {-} {-} {-}
πήγα στο εβραϊκό σχολείο, [που ήταν] θρησκευτικό σχολείο.
I went to a Hebrew school, Talmud Torah.

ci='piγa 'ena tal'mud to'ra 'p=itan Syrian|
and=go.AOR.1SG ART.N Talmud Torah REL=be.AOR.3SG {-}
Πήγα σ' ένα εβραϊκό θρησκευτικό σχολείο που ήταν συριακό.
I went to a Talmud Torah, which was Syrian,

and ci=^{e}'piγa s=tus -- s=tu Hebrew school 'kaθi
{-} and=went.AOR.1SG to=DEF.M.PL -- to=DEF.N.SG {-} every
Πήγαινα στο εβραϊκό σχολείο κάθε
and I have been going to Hebrew school every

'mera ja='t^{h}eseris 'ores| 'ðjo 'ores
day for=4.NUM.FEM hour.ACC.PL 2.num hour.ACC.PL
μέρα για τέσσερις ώρες. Δύο ώρες
*day for four hours. For two hours

em-- 'emaθan na=ðja'vasumi| ce='ðjo 'ores na='krinumi[109]
teach.IMPF.3PL PART=read.AOR.SUBJ.1PL and=2.num hour.ACC.PL PART=speak.AOR.SUBJ.1PL
[μας] μάθαιναν να διαβάζουμε, και δύο ώρες να μιλάμε,
[they] taught us to read, for two hours to talk,

108 The accent *μόναχα* 'only' (SG *μονάχα* or *μοναχά*) was common in the 19th century in many regions, including Epirus, e.g., Politis (1904: 949).

109 The verb has homonymic forms of the present and aorist subjunctive. It is identified as an aorist by analogy with the surrounding forms.

na='maθumi *ivrit| Hebrew| -- 'ets͡i* *'emaθa* *-- hebreo| Hebrew|*

PART=learn.AOR.SUBJ.1PL {-} so learn.AOR.1SG {-} {-}

για να μάθουμε εβραϊκά. Έτσι έμαθα εβραϊκά.

[so that] we would learn Hebrew. That's how I learnt Hebrew.

O=pa'teraz^{i}=m *'itan* *-- a traveling--* *I get to know how to say it in Greek*

DEF=father=POSS.1SG be-AOR.3SG {-} {-}

Ο πατέρας μου ήταν

My father was – I get to know how to say it in Greek –

-- a traveling merchant and used to sell goods| ce='otu *xa'xam|* *rabbi*

{-} and=when rabbi=NOM.SG {-}

πραματευτής, πουλούσε εμπόρευμα. Και όταν ο ραβίνος {-}

a traveling merchant and used to sell goods. And when the Rabbi

a'p=itan *s=ta='janina* *'p^{h}eθane|* *ci=t=ja'ɲot's*

REL[110]=be.AOR.3SG in=DEF=Ioannina.ACC.PL die.AOR.3SG and=DEF.PL.N=Ioannina.inhabitants.PL.M

των Ιωαννίνων πέθανε, οι Γιαννιώτες

of Ioannina died, the Ioanniotes,

sent *o=pateraz$^{i=}$m* *-- s=tu salo'nik* *ci -- he became ordained*

{-} DEF=father.POSS.1SG in=DEF=Thessaloniki and= {-}

[έστειλαν] τον πατέρα μου στη Θεσσαλονίκη και χειροτονήθηκε

[sent] my father to Thessaloniki, and [later] he became ordained

stɘ --| *ci='ama* *'itane* *s=tu=sa'lonika* *'emaθi*

in=DEF and=when be.AOR.3SG in=DEF=Thessaloniki learn.AOR.3SG

στ … . Και όταν ήταν στη Θεσσαλονίκη έμαθε

in … . And when he was in Thessaloniki, he learnt

beriθmi'lot *a -- and and le- le -- +learnt to be a shochet[111]|*

circumcision.PL^{H} {-}

[να κάνει] περιτομές και να είναι θρησκευτικός σφαγέας.

[to perform] circumcisions and to be a *shochet.*

ka'topi *'jirise* *s-- apo= ta='janina*

after turn.AOR.3SG from= DEF=Ioannina

Κατόπιν γύρισε στα Γιάννενα

Later he returned to Ioannina

110 The vowel [a] must be due to the contamination of [a'po] and ['opu], both of which are used by the interviewee for paraphrasing the genitive.

111 Hebrew שׁוֹחֵט *šoḥeṭ* 'butcher'.

ci='itan tu=o'xam a'po ta='janina ci=s=tun=zu'it
and=be.AOR.3SG DEF=rabbi^{H} of=DEF=Ioannina and=in=DEF=life.POSS.3SG
και έγινε ραβίνος Ιωαννίνων, και στην ζωή του
and became the Rabbi of Ioannina, and in his life

'ekame eksa'kofa briθmi'lot| he performed six hundred briθmi'lot|
do.AOR.3SG 600.NUM.N circumcision.ACC.PL^{H} {-}
έκανε εξακόσιες περιτομές.
he performed six hundred circumcisions.

ci='ola ja='tiputa| pro bono as they say today| ((ðe='don))[112]
and all.PL.N for=nothing {-} {-} NEG=he.ACC.SG
και όλα δωρεάν, pro bono, όπως το λένε τώρα, [τίποτα] δεν
And all for free, *pro bono* as they say today, he

*e'biri| ci=e'go 'imi o=*jaɲot the youngest*
take.AOR.3SG and=I am DEF=* {-}
πήρε. κι εγώ είμαι ο νεώτερος
received nothing. And I am the youngest

apu='ðeka pi'ðja| ci=o=pa'teraz^{j}=m 'ekame tu=briθmi'la
of=10.NUM child.ACC.PL and=DEF= father .POSS.1SG make.AOR.3SG DEF=circumcision^{H}
από δέκα πεδιά, κι' ο πατέρας μου έκανε την περιτομή
of ten children, and my father circumcised

ja-- si='pendi ap=t^{j}=pi'ðja=t|
to=5.NUM of=DEF=child.PL=POSS.3SG
στα πέντε (από τα) παιδιά του,
five of his children,

ci=tu='ekt pi'ði 'ðon 'to=kme
and=DEF=sixth.NUM.N child NEG=it.CL.ACC.SG.N=make.AOR.3SG
δεν το έκανε
and he didn't circumcise the sixth,

((jat='ðon t='içe)) 'itan licensed –
because=NEG PRON.ACC.SG.N[113]=have.AOR.3SG be.AOR.3sg {-}
γιατί δεν είχε {άδεια}, [δεν] ήταν εξουσιοδοτημένος,
because he didn't have it, he wasn't licensed,

112 The interpretation is tentative because of an unclear recording.

113 On the presumption that neuter *το* is meant.

**op 'ðon 'kser na=t='po license*
NEG=know.PRES.1SG PART=PRON.ACC.SG.N=say.AOR.1SG
δεν ξέρω να πω 'άδεια'
I don't know how to say 'license'

sta=eleni'ka| ce='itan xa'xam is=tu=sina'γoi ap=ta='janina [...]
in=DEF=Greek.PL.N and=be.AOR.3SG rabbi in=DEF=synagogue of=DEF=Ioannina
στα ελληνικά. Και ήταν ραβίνος στη συναγωγή των Ιωαννίνων [...]
in Greek. He was a Rabbi in the synagogue of Ioannina [...].

Tu='libru ap -- apu-t- ta= o'nomata ap=ta=pe'ðja pu='ekame briθmi'la --
DEF=book from=DEF=name.PL from=DEF=child.PL REL=do.AOR.3SG circumcision[H]
Το βιβλίο με τα ονόματα των παιδιών που [τους] έκανε περιτομή ...,
The book with the names of children that he circumcised ...,

'eçi 'ena 'libru ce=tu='libru 'ine e'ðo sto museum upst- +upstairs e'pan|
have.PRS.3SG ART.N=book and=DEF=book be.PRS.3SG here in=DEF {-} up
έχει ένα βιβλίο, και το βιβλίο είναι εδώ στο μουσείο επάνω.
there is a book, and the book is here in the museum upstairs.

'itan xa'xam ci='itan depression years|
be.AOR.3SG rabbi and=be.AOR.3SG {-}
Ήταν ραβίνος και ήταν τα χρόνια της οικονομικής ύφεσης
He was a Rabbi, and [those] were depression years,

'ama eγo -- eγo je'niθka
when=I=bear.AOR.PASS.1SG
όταν γεννήθηκα εγώ
when I was born,

se='çiʎa eɲa'koʃa 'ikoʃi e'ɲa| 'tora 'imi o'γðonda 'pendi xro'non|
in=1929.NUM.N now am 85.NUM year.GEN.PL
το χίλια εννιακόσια είκοσι εννιά. Τώρα είμαι ογδόντα πέντε χρονών.
in 1929. Now I am eighty five years old.

ci= o=pa'teraz=im eci-p-- 'içi ipomo'ni
and=DEF=father.POSS.1SG have.AOR.3SG patience.ACC
και ο πατέρας μου είχε υπομονή
My father had patience

na='maθi 'mena na m-- how do you say teach me--na= 'krinu
PART=teach.AOR.SUBJ.3SG me.EMPH.ACC {-} PART=speak.PRES.SUBJ.1SG
να με μάθει να μιλώ
to teach me to speak

ivrit| ci=eleni'ka 'vevja stu='spit we only spoke eleni'ka|
{-}^{H} and=Greek.PL.N certainly in=DEF=home.ACC.SG {-} Greek.PL.N
εβραϊκά, και ελληνικά βέβαια. Στο σπίτι μιλούσαμε μόνο ελληνικά.
Hebrew, and of course Greek. At home we only spoke Greek.

and o=pa'terazi=m 'itan po'li charitable| ol ta=briθmi'lot
{-} DEF=father.POSS.1SG be.AOR.3SG very {charitable}. all.PL.N DEF=circumcision.PL^{H}
Ο πατέρας μου ήταν πολύ φιλάνθρωπος. Όλες τις περιτομές
My father was very charitable. All the circumcisions

jat=fa^{m}'ʎa=t ci=ja=ta friends and relatives ja='tipota
for=DEF=family.ACC.SG=POSS.3SG and=for=DEF.PL.N {-} for=nothing
για την οικογένειά του και τους φίλους και συγγενείς [τις έκανε] δωρεάν,
for the family, friends and relatives [he did] for free,

(('ðon)) 'epiri ut='ena sent|[...]
NEG=take.AOR.3SG NEG.CONJ=1.NUM=cent
δεν πήρε ούτε ένα σεντ. [...]
he didn't take a single cent. [...]

a'la 'ama 'ekmi| s=tu='libru 'lei| 'ama 'itan
but when do.AOR.3SG in=DEF=book.ACC say.PRS.3SG when be.AOR.3SG
αλλά όταν έκανε [τις περιτομές], στο βιβλίο έλεγε ... όταν έκανε
But when he did, in the book it says … when he did

milat tu o=pateras |the name | I forgot it | *ap=tu=pa'tera=t* of the father|
circumcision.POSS.3SG^{H} DEF=father {-} of=DEF=father.ACC=POSS.3SG {-}
την περιτομή ο πατέρας ...{έγραφε το όνομα} του πατέρα
a circumcision, [my] father .. [wrote] the name, I forgot it, of the father

ci=dt-- ci=t=u'nomata ap=tu=pi'ði op='ekame britmi'la
and=DEF=name.PL of=DEF=child.ACC REL=do.AOR.3SG circumcision.ACC^{H}
και το όνομα του παιδιού στο οποίο έκανε την περιτομή.
and the name of the child whom he circumcised.

a'la am='ekame britmi'la ja=tu=pi'ði=t i ja=ta=pi'ðja=t
but when= do.AOR.3SG circumcision.ACC^{H} for=DEF=child=POSS.3SG or for=DEF=child.PL= POSS.3SG
Αλλά όταν έκανε για το παιδί του ή για τα παιδιά τους
But when he circumcised his child or their children

'eγrapse s=tu='vreika
write.AOR.3SG in=DEF=Hebrew.ACC.PL
έγραφε στα εβραϊκά:
he wrote in Hebrew:

ביום שלישי בשבת חנני השם בן ונולד[114] ונשמע שמו בישראל שלמה | כן -- ונמועל ע"י ב- |
"Την τρίτη ημέρα [μετά] το Σάββατο κατηξίωσε ο Θεός και γεννήθηκε ο γιός μου και εκλήθη το όνομά του στο Ισραήλ Σελομό. Και περιετμήθη υπ' εμού..."
'On the third day of Shabbat by Divine mercy the son was born [to me], and his name in Israel [will] be called Shlomo. He was circumcised by me on ... ,'

he will give the month and the day and the year כן שזכה ל- | -- *ci='egrapse*
{-} {-} {-} and= write.AOR.3SG
[Εδώ] θα έγραφε το μήνα, την ημέρα και το έτος, και θα έγραφε
[here] he will give the month and the day and the year. 'As he merited ...,' he wrote ... .

כן שזכה ל- | *he wrote only for his children*
{-} {-} {-}
"όπως αξιώθηκε ...". Το έγραφε μόνο για τα παιδιά του:
'As he merited ...,' he wrote only for his children.

כן שזכה לברית מילה כן יזכה לתורה למצוות ומעשים טובים ולחופה אמן כן יהי רצון |
"Όπως αξιώθηκε την περιτομή, ας αξιωθεί και την Γραφή, τις εντολές, τις αγαθουργίες και την γαμήλια τελετή. Αμήν, γένοιτο."
'As he merited the circumcision, let him merit [the study of] Torah, mitzvoth, good deeds and marriage. Amen, may it be.'

i'fto *'egrapse*
PRON.ACC.SG.N write.AOR.3SG
Αυτό έγραφε
This he wrote

'monaxa *ja=t=pi'ðiat* *i=ja=t=$e^{ŋ}$goɲa=t^{e}s*
only for=DEF=child.ACC.PL=POSS.3SG or=for=DEF=grandchild.ACC.PL=POSS.3SG.M
μόνο για τα παιδιά του και για τα εγγόνια του.
his grandchildren
{-}
only for his children and grandchildren.

ce=tu='libru *op='eçi* *olu* *tu=mi'lot* *'eni* *e'ðo*
and=DEF=book.NOM REL=have.PRS.3SG all.SG.N DEF=circumcision.PL^{H} be.PRS.3SG here
Και το μητρώο που καταγράφει όλες τις περιτομές είναι εδώ
And the register that has all the circumcisions is here

s=to museum *ap=tu=cei'la* *'janina* *{{in}} New York*
in=DEF {-} from=DEF=community.ACC Ioannina.NOM {-}
στο μουσείο της κοινώτητας Ιωαννίνων στην Νέα Υόρκη.
in the museum of the Ioannina congregation in New York.

114 Pronounced [ni'.lad].

References

Altbauer, Moshe, and Yakov Shiby. 1971–1981. "A Judeo-Greek Glossary of the Hamesh Megillot." *Sefunot* 15: 367–421.

Anastasiadi-Symeonidi, Anna. 1994. *Νεολογικός δανεισμός της Νεοελληνικής. Άμεσα δάνεια από τη γαλλική και την αγγλοαμερικανική. Μορφοφωνολογική Ανάλυση [Neological borrowing in Modern Greek: direct loanwords from French and English. Morphophonological analysis]*. Thessaloniki: Aristotelean University of Thessaloniki Press.

Arvaniti, Amalia. 2007. "Greek Phonetics: The State of the Art." *Journal of Greek Linguistics* 8: 97–208.

Aslanov, Cyril 2012. "Homer within the Bible: Homerisms in the Graecus Venetus." In *Homer and the Bible in the Eyes of Ancient Interpreters*, edited by Maren R. Niehoff, 199–218. Leiden: Brill.

Belléli, Lazare. 1897. "Review of: D. C. Hessling. Les cinq livres de la loi (le Pentateuque)." *Revue des Études Juives* 35: 132–155.

BHS = Alt, Albrecht, Otto Eissfeldt, Paul Kahle, Rudolf Kittel, Hans Bardtke, and Adrian Schenker, eds. 1977. *[Torah, Nevi'im U-Khetuvim]: Biblia Hebraica Stuttgartensia quae antea cooperantibus A. Alt, O. Eissfeldt, P. Kahle ediderat R. Kittel adjuvantibus H. Bardtke ... [et al.] cooperantibus H. P. Rüger et J. Ziegler ediderunt K. Elliger et W. Rudolph, textum masoreticum curavit H. P. Rüger masoram elaboravit G. E. Weil. Editio quinta emendata opera A. Schenker.* Stuttgart: Deutsche Bibelgesellschaft.

Bonkas, Evangelos A. 1964. *Τα γλωσσικά ιδιώματα της Ηπείρου (βορείου, κεντρικής και νοτίου): Γιαννιώτικο και άλλα λεξιλόγια [The dialects of Epirus (Northern, Central and Southern): Gianniote and other lexicons]* 2 vols. Vol. 1. Ioannina: Etaireia Ipeirotikon Meleton.

Brown, Christopher G., and Brian D. Joseph. 2015. "On Hybrid Forms in Language Contact: Some Evidence from the Greek of Southern Albania." *Albanohellenica* 6: 1–8.

Bubenik, Vit. 1997. "Judeo-Greek or Hellenistic Koine with Structural Semitisms?" *Μελέτες για την Ελληνική Γλώσσα [Studies in Greek Linguistics]* 17: 42–56.

Bunis, David M. 2008. "The Names of Jewish Languages: A Taxonomy." In *Il mio cuore è a Oriente: Studi di linguistica storica, filologia e cultura ebraica dedicati a Maria Luisa Mayer Modena*, edited by Francesco Aspesi, 415–433. Milano: Cisalpino.

Chatzidakis, Geōrgios N. 1905. *Μεσαιωνικά και νέα Ελληνικά [Medieval and Modern Greek]*. Athens: Sakellariou.

de Lange, Nicholas R. M. 1996. *Greek Jewish Texts from the Cairo Genizah*. Texte und Studien zum antiken Judentum. Tübingen: J.C.B. Mohr (Paul Siebeck).

de Lange, Nicholas R. M. 2008. "Some Lines of Greek Verse in a Hebrew Manuscript from Seventeenth-Century Crete." *Bulletin of Judaeo-Greek Studies* 42: 29–30.

Dimitrakos, Dimitrios V. 1953–1964. *Μέγα λεξικόν όλης της ελληνικής γλώσσης (δημοτική, καθαρεύουσα, μεσαιωνική, αρχαία) [Great dictionary of the whole Greek language (demotic, katharevousa, medieval, ancient)]*. 15 vols. Athens: Domi. First published 1936–1950.

Drettas, Georges. 1999. "Propos sur la judéïté grécophone." In *Vena Hebraica in Judaeorum Linguis: Proceedings of the 2nd International Conference on the Hebrew and Aramaic Elements in Jewish Languages (Milan, October 23–26, 1995)*, edited by Shelomo Morag, Mosheh Bar-Asher, and Maria Mayer-Modena, 271–288. Milan: Centro Studi Camito-Semitici.

George, Coulter H. 2010. "Jewish and Christian Greek." In *A Companion to the Ancient Greek language*, edited by Egbert J. Bakker, 267–280. Chichester: Wiley-Blackwell.

Gold, David L. 1987. "A Few Notes on Yevanic." *Jewish Language Review* 7: 132–138.

Grinevald, Colette, and Michel Bert. 2011. "Speakers and Communities." In *The Cambridge Handbook of Endangered Languages*, edited by Peter K. Austin and Julia Sallabank, 45–65. Cambridge: Cambridge University Press.

Hellenic Bible Society. 1997. *Η Αγία Γραφή σε μετάφραση στη δημοτική [The Holy Scripture translated into Demotic]*. Athens: Hellenic Bible Society.

Henrich, Günther Steffen. 1998. "Στοιχεία σημερινών κρητικών ιδιωμάτων τεκμηριωμένα ήδη στην Κρητική Λογοτεχία [Elements of contemporary Cretan dialects documented already in Cretan literature]." *Cretan Studies* 6: 89–108.

Hollender, Elisabeth, and Johannes Niehoff-Panagiotidis. 2011. "*Mahzor Romania* and the Judeo-Greek Hymn ΕΝΑΣ Ο ΚΥΡΙΟΣ: Introduction, Critical Edition, and Commentary." *Revue des Études Juives* 170 (1–2): 117–171. doi: 10.2143/rej.170.1.2126642.

Holton, David, Peter Mackridge, and Irene Philippaki-Warburton. 2004. *Greek: An Essential Grammar of the Modern Language*. London, New York: Routledge.

Horrocks, Geoffrey. 2010. *Greek: A History of Language and its Speakers*. 2 ed. Chichester: Wiley-Blackwell.

Horsley, Gregory H. R. 1989. "The Fiction of 'Jewish Greek'." *New Documents Illustrating Early Christianity* 5: 5–40.

Institute for Modern Greek Studies [Manolis Triandafyllidis Foundation]. 1998. LKN = *Λεξικό της Κοινής Νεο-ελληνικής [Dictionary of Modern Greek]*. Thessaloniki: Institute for Modern Greek Studies [Manolis Triandafyllidis Foundation].

Kant, Laurence H. 1987. "Jewish Inscriptions in Greek and Latin." In *Aufstieg und Niedergang der Römischen Welt*, edited by Wolfgang Haase and Hildegard Temporini, 672–713. Berlin, New York: de Gruyter.

Kontosopoulos, Nikolaos G. 2008. *Διάλεκτοι και ιδώματα της Νέας Ελληνικής [Major and minor dialects of Modern Greek]*. 5 ed. Athens: Grigoris.

Kosmas, Nikos B. 1997. *Το γλωσσικό ιδίωμα των Ιωαννίνων [The dialect of Ioannina]*. Athens, Ioannina: Dodoni.

Kotzageorgis, Fokion. 1997. *Το ισλάμ στα Βαλκάνια. Ένα ελληνόφωνο μουσουλμανικό χειρόγραφο από την Ήπειρο του 18ου αιωνα [Islam in the Balkans: An eighteenth-century Muslim manuscript from Epirus in Greek language]*. I kath' imas Anatoli. Athens: Sindesmos ton en Athinais Megalosxoliton.

Krivoruchko, Julia G. 1999. "Τα ελληνικά χειρόγραφα σε Εβραϊκή γραφή, η προέλευση και τα κύρια χαρακτηριστικά της γλώσσας τους [The Greek manuscripts in Hebrew script: the principal linguistic features and provenance]." In *Ο Ελληνικός κόσμος ανάμεσα στην Ανατολή και τη Δύση 1453–1981. Πρακτικά του Α' Ευρωπαϊκού Συνεδρίου Νεοελληνικών Σπουδών, Βερολίνο 2–4 Οκτωβρίου 1998 [The Greek World between East and West. Proceedings of the First European Congress of Modern Greek Studies, Berlin, 2.–4.10.1998]*, edited by Asterios Argyriou, Konstantinos Dimadis and Anastasia .D. Lazaridou, 647–660. Athens: Ellinika Grammata.

Krivoruchko, Julia G. 2002. "Prosodic Nature of Word Segmentation in Modern Biblical Judeo-Greek (MBJG)." In *Recherches en linguistique grecque: Actes du 5-e Colloque international de linguistique grecque, Sorbonne, 13–15.09.2001*, edited by Christos Clairis, 47–50. Paris: L'Harmattan.

Krivoruchko, Julia G. 2014. "Medieval and Early Modern Judaeo-Greek Biblical Translations: A Linguistic Perspective." In *The Jewish-Greek Tradition in Antiquity and the Byzantine Empire*, edited by James K. Aitken and James Carleton Paget, 152–170. Cambridge: Cambridge University Press.

Krivoruchko, Julia G. 2021. "A Sixteenth-Century Trilingual Dictionary of Hebrew." Taylor-Schechter Genizah Research Unit: Fragment of the Month, January 2021, https://www.lib.cam.ac.uk/collections/departments/taylor-schechter-genizah-research-unit/fragment-month/fotm-2021/fragment.

Krivoruchko, Julia G. Forthcoming a. *Lexicon of the Hebrew/Aramaic component in Modern Judeo-Greek*. Jerusalem: The Hebrew University of Jerusalem.

Krivoruchko, Julia G. Forthcoming b. "Haftaroth from Isaiah."

Kyranoudis, Panagiotis. 2009. *Μορφολογία των τουρκικών δανείων της ελληνικής γλώσσας [Morphology of Turkish loans in the Greek language]*. Thessaloniki: Institute for Modern Greek Studies.

Manolessou, Io, and Christina Bassea-Bezantakou. 2012. "Τα διπλά σύμφωνα στις νεοελληνικές διαλέκτους: Συγχρονική και διαχρονική προσέγγιση [Double consonants in Modern Greek dialects: Synchronic and diachronic approach]." In *Selected Papers of the 10th International Conference of Greek Linguistics*, edited by Zoe Gavriilidou, Angeliki Efthymiou, Evangelia Thomadaki, and Penelope Kambakis-Vougiouklis, 950–959. Komotini: Democritus University of Thrace.

Matsa, Joseph. 1971–1981. "Jewish Poetry in Greek (in Hebrew)." *Sefunot* 15: 235–365.

Matsas, Joseph. 1953. *Γιαννιώτικα εβραϊκά τραγούδια [Ianniote Jewish songs]*. Ioannina: Epeirotiki Estia.

Matsas, Joseph. 1956. "Τα ονόματα των Εβραίων στα Γιάννινα [The names of Jews in Ioannina]." In *Αφιέρωμα εις την Ήπειρον. Εις μνήμην Χρίστου Σούλη (1892–1951) [Dedicated to Epirus: In memory of Christos Soulis (1892–1951)]*, edited by Leandros Vranousis, 95–102. Athens: Mirtidi.

Michaēlidis Nouaros, Michaēl G. 1932. *Λαογραφικά σύμμεικτα Καρπάθου [Studies on Karpathos folklore]*. 2 vols. Athens: Ta Chronika.

Mladenova, Olga M. 2001. "Neuter Designations of Humans and Norms of Social Interaction in the Balkans." *Anthropological Linguistics* 43 (1): 18–53.

Pantelidis, Nikolaos G. 2016. "Μία νοτιοελλαδική διαλεκτική ζώνη." *Μελέτες για την Ελληνική Γλώσσα [Studies in Greek Linguistics]* 36: 303–313

Papaioannou, Miltiadis I. 1976. *Το γλωσσάριο των Γρεβενών [The glossary of Grevena]*. Thessaloniki: Μακεδονική Βιβλιοθήκη [Macedonian Library].

Politis, Nikolaos G. 1904. *Μελέται περί του βίου και της γλώσσης του ελληνικού λαού: Παραδόσεις – Μέρος Β΄ [Studies on the life and language of the Greek people: Traditions – Part B]*. Athens: Sakellariou.

Ralli, Angela. 2002. "The Role of Morphology in Gender Determination: Evidence from Modern Greek." *Linguistics* 40, 3 (379): 519–551.

Schoenfeld, Andrew J. 2007. "Immigration and Assimilation in the Jewish Community of Late Venetian Crete." *Journal of Modern Greek Studies* 25: 1–16.

Simons, Gary F., and Charles D. Fennig, eds. 2020. *Ethnologue: Languages of the World*. 23rd ed. Dallas, Texas: SIL International.

Somavera, Alessio de. 1709. *Θησαυρός της Ρωμαϊκής και της Φραγκικής γλώσσας. Tesoro della lingua italiana e greca-volgare*. Paris: Michele Guignard.

Sunshine, Andrew. 1995. "History of Jewish Interlinguistics: A Preliminary Outline." In *History of Linguistics. 1993: Papers from the Sixth International Conference on the History of the Language Sciences (ICHoLS VI), Washington DC, 9–14 August 1993*, edited by Kurt R. Jankowsky, 75–82. Amsterdam: Benjamins.

Sykäri, Venla. 2009. "Dialogues in Rhyme: The Performative Contexts of Cretan Mantinádes." *Oral Tradition* 24 (1). doi:10.1353/ort.0.0058.

Sznol, Shifra. 2000. "A Judaeo-Greek Translation of the Haftara of Vaethanan for the Sabbath of Consolation (Isaiah 40, 1–26) (in Hebrew)." *Textus* 20: 9–32.

Timm, Erika, ed. 2011. *Salomo / Solomon A. Birnbaum: Ein Leben für die Wissenschaft. A Lifetime of Achievement*. Vol. 1, Linguistics. Berlin: De Gruyter.

Topintzi, Nina, and Stefano Versace. 2015. "A Linguistic Analysis of the Modern Greek Dekapentasyllavo Meter." *Journal of Greek Linguistics* 15: 235–269.

Trudgill, Peter. 2009. "Greek Dialect Vowel Systems, Vowel Dispersion Theory, and Sociolinguistic Typology." *Journal of Greek Linguistics* 9: 165–182.

van der Horst, Pieter Willem 2015. *Saxa Judaica loquuntur: Lessons from Early Jewish Inscriptions:* Radboud Prestige Lectures 2014. Leiden: Brill.

Vlachos, Gerasimos. 1659. *Θησαυρός της εγκυκλοπαιδικής βάσεως τετράγλωσσος μετά της των επιθέτων εκλογής, και διττού των λατινικών τε και ιταλικών λέξεων πίνακος' εκ διαφόρων παλαιών τε και νεωτέρων λεξικών συλλεχθείς παρά Γερασίμου Βλάχου του Κρητός [...]. = Thesaurus encyclopaedicae basis quadrilinguis cum epithetorum delectu ac duplici latinarum, ac italicarum dictionum indice de pluribus antiquis ac recentioribus dictionariis collectus a P. Gerasimo Vlacho Cretensi [...]*. Venice: Ex typographia ducali Pinelliana.

Vlachou, Evangelia, Giorgos Kotzoglou, and Chrysoula Papadopoulou. 2014. *"Πριν σβήσει η φλόγα: Καταγραφή της γεβανικής διαλέκτου [Before the flame goes out: Recording the Yevanic dialect]."* In Κοινωφελές Ίδρυμα Ιωάννη Σ. Λάτση [John S. Latsis Public Benefit Foundation].

Voeste, Anja, and Susan Baddeley, eds. 2012. *Orthographies in Early Modern Europe*. Berlin: de Gruyter.

Weinreich, Max. 1954. "Prehistory and Early History of Yiddish: Facts and Conceptual Framework." In *The Field of Yiddish: Studies in Yiddish Language, Folklore, and Literature*, edited by Uriel Weinreich, 73–101. New York: Linguistic Circle of New York.

Wexler, Paul 1985. "Recovering the Dialects and Sociology of Judeo-Greek in Non-Hellenic Europe." In *Readings in the Sociology of Jewish languages*, edited by Joshua A. Fishman, 227–240. Leiden: Brill.

Young, Arthur William, and Max Leopold Margolis. 5677 [1917]. *Tōrah nevi'īm ū-k͡hetūvīm. The Holy Scriptures according to the Masoretic Text: A New Translation with the Aid of Previous Versions and with Constant Consultation of Jewish Authorities*. 2nd impression ed. Philadelphia: The Jewish Publication Society of America.

Early Judeo-Persian

Ludwig Paul, University of Hamburg

1. Introduction

Judeo-Persian literature is conventionally divided into works that were composed before, and those that were composed after the Mongol invasion of Iran (1220–1260). The language of the pre-Mongol phase of Judeo-Persian literature is called "Early Judeo-Persian" (EJP). It shows dialectal and archaic features that distinguish it from the form of Persian that was written during the same time by Muslim Iranian authors, in Arabic script. After the Mongol invasion, Judeo-Persian gradually lost its dialectal features and became more or less identical grammatically to the language of contemporary classical Persian authors, its only remaining distinctive feature being the Hebrew script in which it was written.

The extant literature of Early Judeo-Persian (which is the main focus of the present contribution) spans a period from the 8th to the 12th century C.E.; EJP manuscripts were composed in such diverse areas as southwest Iran (Khuzestan), central Iran (Zefre), Afghanistan (Bāmiyān), Central Asia (Bukhara), and west China (Dandān Uiliq). A large part of the EJP manuscripts were found in the form of detached sheets of writing in one of two Genizahs. This means that they are fragmentary, and seldom contain colophones or other indications as to authorship or date, and it is not easy to determine their provenance. Texts attributed to Bukhara may have travelled to other parts of Iran. This is no doubt the case with the large (226-page) codex containing a tafsīr of the Book of Ezekiel, written in two different hands and in two dialects of Persian, in a manuscript held at the National Library of Russia in St. Petersburg. The texts found so far undoubtedly represent only a fraction of a much more extensive literary output.

The compositions in EJP from the Cairo Genizah amount to ca. 900 manuscript pages and are predominantly of religious nature. Most of them can be classified as *tafsīrs*, i.e. translations and exegesis on portions of the Hebrew Bible. The texts dealing with non-religious topics, which make up less than 10% of the corpus, consist of ca. 25 documents (private and commercial letters, two legal deeds), and of a small number of literary pieces, consisting of *piyyuṭ* (= liturgical poetry), medical and grammatical treatises, and a few other texts. The documentary fragments from the Cairo Genizah derive partly from a family archive of the Tustari family, who had come to Fusṭāṭ from Ahwāz in south-western Persia. Members of this family are known to have held positions of high influence in the administration of the Fatimid Empire (909–1171). They belonged to the Karaite sect and were counted among the leaders of the Jewish community in Egypt.

The second largest group of EJP manuscripts is the so-called "Afghan Genizah". It was found towards the end of the last century in Afghanistan at an undisclosed location by local people and was held by several antique dealers in Europe. A small portion of it was eventually acquired by the National Library of Israel. The whole hoard of "Afghan Genizah" manuscripts probably exceeds 300 sheets of written paper. Most of these fragments are still in the hands of dealers, but two scholars have managed to get access to them (Shaul Shaked and Ofir Haim). The Afghan Genizah material consists of fragments of writing in a variety of languages: Hebrew, Aramaic, Standard Persian, Standard Arabic, (Early) Judeo-Persian and Judeo-Arabic. The EJP language of these texts is different dialectally from that of the Cairo Genizah texts. The Afghan Genizah material is of great importance, but work on it has been hampered so far by the fact that they are not in the public domain, that the photos available are not professional, and that the originals have not been fully treated for restoration.

The Afghan Genizah contains EJP tafsīrs, fragments of literary texts, among them chiefly portions of early Karaite treaties, a number of interesting poetical compositions in EJP, several private and commercial letters, legal acknowledgement of debts (*iqrār*), and fragments of commercial account-books (*daftar*). All the documentary texts of the Afghan Genizah probably belong to the archive of a Jewish trader (ʔAbū Naṣr ben Dāniēl) from Bāmiyān.

There are only few EJP manuscripts that do not derive from the Cairo Genizah or from the hoard of manuscripts found in Afghanistan. They comprise one tafsīr fragment of the Psalms of four pages that was acquired from private people in Zefre (northeast of Isfahan) in the 1970s, or two private letters from the 8th century that were found in archaeological excavations in Dandān-Uiliq (west China); together with a short tombstone inscription from Tang-i Azao (Afghanistan), these two letters are the oldest known EJP texts.

In the post-Mongol period, tafsīrs remained a popular genre of Judeo-Persian literary production; unlike in pre-Mongol times, some post-Mongol JP tafsīrs have preserved (almost) complete books of the Hebrew Bible. Besides tafsīrs, liturgical and narrative poetry were very popular. The acme of Judeo-Persian literature was reached in the 14th century, when the most admired author Šāhīn (from Šīrāz) composed a large-scale poetic work covering much of the narrative parts of the Hebrew Bible. His works include poetic narratives of the Pentateuch, namely the *Berešīt-nāma* (Book of Genesis) and the *Mūsā-nāma*, as well as a versified version of the Book of Esther, known as *Ardašīr-nāma*. Another well-known Judeo-Persian poet is ʕImrānī, who lived in the 16th century and continued the big project of Šāhīn by composing poetry inspired by the narrative parts of some of the biblical books not covered by his predecessor. Thus there arose a full-fledged Judeo-Persian literature, that was aware of the trends in the Classical Muslim Persian literature and sought to emulate them. A historiographic epic by Bābāʔī ben Luṭf (17th century), called *Ketāb-e anusi*, recounts a sad episode of persecution of the Jews of Kāšān.

2. Grammatical sketch

2.1 Phonology

2.1.1 The phonemic system

The phonemic system of Early Judeo-Persian (EJP) includes the following system of 29 consonants (including two semi-vowels) and 11 vowels:

		labial	(-dental)	dental	palatal	velar	uvular	laryngeal
plosive	voiceless	p		t		k	q	(ʔ)
	voiced	b		d		g		
affricate	voiceless				č			
	voiced				j			
fricative	voiceless		f	s	š	x	(xw)	h
	voiced	(β)	(v)	z (δ)	(ž)		γ	
liquid	nasal	m		n		(ŋ)		
	lateral			l				
	rolled			r				
semi-vowels	(glides)	w			y			

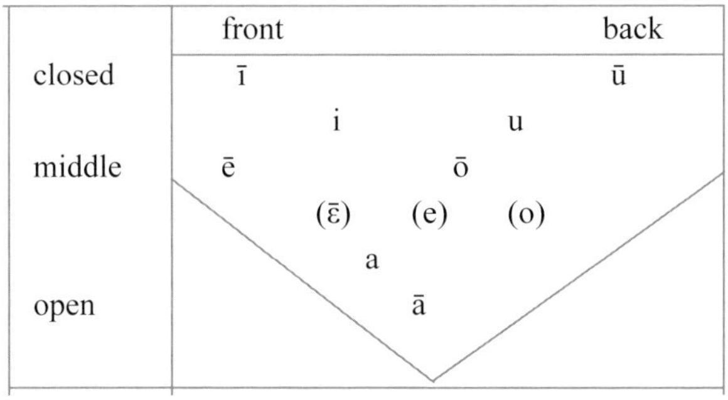

The sounds in brackets are controversial, or allophones (see below).

2.1.2 Writing system and orthography

The Hebrew alphabet was used to represent these sounds as follows:

א ʔ (*ʔāleph*)	ʔ, a, ā	ל l (*lāmed*)	l
ב b (*bēt*)	b, (β), (v)	מ m (*mēm*)	m
ג g (*gimel*)	g, γ, j, (ž)	נ n (*nūn*)	n
ד d (*dālet*)	d, (δ), {ḍ}	ס s (*sāmekh*)	s
ה h (*hē*)	h; -a, -ā	ע ʕ (*ʕayin*)	{ʕ ayin}
ו w (*wāw*)	w, (β), (v); ū, u, ō, o	פ p (*pē*)	p, f
ז z (*zayin*)	z, j, (ž)	צ ṣ (*ṣādē*)	č, j, {ḍ, ẓ, ṣ}
ח ḥ (*ḥēt*)	{ḥ}	ק q (*qōph*)	k, q
ט ṭ (*ṭēt*)	{ṭ, ḍ, ẓ}	ר r (*rēš*)	r
י y (*yōd*)	y; ī, i, ē, e, (ɛ̄)	ש š/ś (*šīn/śīn*)	š, (ž), {ś}
כ k (*kaph*)	k, x	ת t (*tāw*)	t, {ϑ}

The sounds in {braces}, which are not part of the EJP phonemic system, belong to the Arabic or Hebrew phonemic systems and occur in loanwords from these languages only; their actual pronunciation in EJP is doubtful.

It is obvious from the table above that the Hebrew alphabet does not exactly match the phonemic system of EJP; a one-to-one correspondence of character and phoneme/sound holds only for a small number of sounds (*l*, *m*, *n*, *s*, *r*). The Hebrew *begadkefat* rule is applied wherever possible, most regularly for *gimel* [g, γ], *kaph* [k, x], and *pē* [p, f], but it remains "alien" to the EJP phonemic system in the sense that it does not show stop/fricative-alternations within a given inflectional paradigm.

There are Hebrew characters, to which no EJP phoneme or sound corresponds (e.g., *ḥēt*, *ʕayin*), and EJP sounds, which are not represented in the Hebrew alphabet (*č*, *j*). A variety of conventions to write these sounds is found in the EJP documents. These may have evolved out of *ad hoc*-solutions of individual writers, or in contexts of writing "schools", in various regions at various times.

Hebrew diacritics could be used and occur in EJP, in a way different from manuscript to manuscript, and often inconsistently within one and the same manuscript. The most important consonantal diacritics are:

– *rāphē*, a horizontal stroke on top of the letter, to mark a fricative, e.g., גֿם *ḡm* [γam] 'sorrow'

– *dāgēš lene*, a dot inside a letter, to mark the pronunciation as a stop, e.g., אבּר *ʔbr* [abr] 'cloud'

– a dot on top of the letter *gimel*, indicating [j], e.g., גׄא *ġʔ* [jā] 'place'; on top of *ṣādē*, indicating [č] or [ḍ], e.g., צׄון *ċwn* [čōn] 'how', פצׄל *pċl* [faḍl] 'virtue'; on top of *ṭēt*, indicating [ḍ] or [ẓ], e.g., חטׄרת *ḥṭ̇rt* [ḥaḍrat] 'presence', נטׄר *nṭ̇r* [naẓar] 'view'.

The vocalic diacritics of the Tiberian and Babylonian systems were applied in EJP less often than the consonant diacritics, and their inconsistent use in some manuscripts leaves a lot of questions open, especially for the Babylonian system. For an overview, see Paul 2013, §§ 8f.

Each EJP consonant phoneme may be spelled with the following character(s), also taking into account some of the more important diacritics:

p	is written	p (i.e. pē)	x	is written	k, ḵ
t		t	(xw)		kw, ḵw
k		k, q	h		h
q		q	z		z
(ʔ)		ʔ	(ž)		š, ġ, z
b		b	γ		g, ġ
(β)		b, ḇ, w	m		m
d		d	n		n
(δ)		d, ḏ	(ŋ)		ng
g		g	l		l
č		ṣ, ṩ	r		r
j		ṣ, g, ġ, z	w		w, ww, (b?)
f		p, p̄	(v)		b, ḇ, w
s		s	y		y, yy
š		š			

Certain EJP writing conventions changed over time, mainly as an effect of the large number of Arabic loanwords that entered Persian during the first centuries of Islam. In the earliest EJP documents (Dandān Uiliq letters, 8th century C. E.), for instance, *kaph* was still used for [x] and *qōph* for [k]; there were very few Arabic loanwords with [q]. When many Arabic loanwords entered Persian in the following centuries, bringing the sound [q] with them, *qōph* came to be used for [q], and *kaph* remained for both [k] and [x].

Similarly [j], a sound not occurring in Hebrew, was written with *ṣādē* in the earliest documents, like its voiceless counterpart [č]. When Arabic loanwords entered Persian, whose *jīm* was pronounced like a palatalized *gimel* in Egyptian Arabic, the [j]'s in Arabic loanwords were written *gimel*, and later on, also the [j] in Persian words. Other spelling variations like that of *zayin* for [j] (in 3 EJP manuscripts) can only be described as a divergent individual, or regional, "solution" of the basic problem posed to the scribe of how to write [j] with the Hebrew alphabet. Word-final *-a* was mostly written with *ʔāleph* but in Du1/2 and (partly) in Ez, with *hē*. The Hebrew alphabet allows both writings, the writings in Du and Ez may represent individual or regional variations.

The writing of the [ḍ] of Arabic loanwords as *ṣādē*, dotted *ṣādē*, *dālet*, *ṭēt*, or dotted *ṭēt*, represents various conventions, but has little bearing on the EJP phonemic system. It is mentioned here because besides [k] and [j], [ḍ] is the most "diversely written" and interesting sound with respect to the EJP writing conventions. The following overview should give an impression of the writing conventions concerning [k], [j], and [ḍ] in various texts:

	[k]	[j]	[ḍ]
Ta	q	(?)	(?)
Du1/2, Is	q	c	
Kd	k	z / g	c
Lr, L3	k	c g	c
L4, L6	q k	c	c
L5	k	c (P./Ar.) g	c / d
L7, L15	k	c	
L11, L17/21	k	c	c
L12	k	c (P./Ar.) g	d
L18	k	c	c, ċ
L19		z	
Gr	k	c g	c, ċ
Db	q k	c	d
Ar	k	c / z	
Ez1	k	ġ	ċ ṭ, ṭ̇
Ez2	k	c	ċ ṭ
Gen, Jer	k	g, ġ	ṭ
Zefre		c ġ	d

2.1.3 Specific phonological phenomena / processes

(a) Historical long *ā* often remained unwritten in EJP before *h*, e.g., אגה *ʔgh* 'aware', רה *rh* 'way' (historically pronounced: [āgāh, rāh]), but also in other phonetic contexts (בש *bš* 'be!', חהר *chr* '4', etc.). A similar phenomenon is known from Classical Persian poetry, where an (etymologically) long [ā] can be left unwritten, and is assumed to have been realized, by "poetic license", as a short [a]. On account of the EJP data, it seems preferable to interpret this not as a (casual or poetic) shortening of [ā], but as a (partial) neutralization of the opposition *a*/*ā* in EJP and ENP.

(b) *Imāla*. Arabic [ā] is occasionally written with *yōdh* in various EJP text (instead of *ʔāleph*), which shows its intermediate articulation between [ā] and [ē], probably as a long, open [ā] inclining towards [ē], e.g., אנציף *ʔ*$_i$*nc*$_ē$*yp* [inṣā/ēf] 'justice' (L7.14). Sometimes the [ā/ē] is vocalized, e.g., כילִיף *k*$_i$*yl*$_ē$*yp* [xilā/ēf] 'opposition' (Ez5.7).

(c) The MP initial groups *fr-*, *dr-*, and *xr-* may take an epenthetic palatal vowel in EJP, probably *-i-* that corresponds to an *-a-* in later NP, e.g., *pyrzʔm* [firzām] 'end' (NP *farzām*).

(d) Word-internal clusters like *-fr-*, *-xr-*, or *-xl-*, underwent a metathesis from Middle to New Persian, e.g., ZMP *taxl* 'bitter' > NP *talx*, MP *wafr* 'snow' > NP *barf*. In EJP, this metathesis had not yet taken place in *thl* [tahl] 'bitter' and *bpr* [bafr] 'snow', but it had already occurred in *crk* [čarx] 'wheel'.

(e) Many EJP (and ENP) words preserve an MP initial *a-* that was lost in later NP, e.g., EJP *ʔbʔ* [abā] 'with', *ʔnyz* [anīz] 'also' (NP *bā*, *nīz*). In the 8th century document Du.2, however, the word *yʔr* [yār] 'friend' (MP *ayār*, NP *yār*) shows that the dropping of *a-* must have started in some areas quite early.

(f) Old Iranian initial groups like *st-*, *sp-*, *šn-* are preserved as such in ZMP but may take a prothetic *i-* in MMP, e.g., ZMP *stadan* / MMP *istadan* 'take'. In EJP, variations with and without a prothetic vowel occur (e.g., PP *ʔstd* [istad] or *std*, present stem *ʔystʔn-* [istān-]); the form *std* was probably pronounced with an epenthetic *-i-*, as it was in later NP *sitad*.

(g) An additional *ʔāleph* at the end of certain Arabic loanwords (e.g., *ḥcrʔ* 'present', *lzmʔ* 'necessary', *ʔstʕmlʔ* 'usage'), of unknown function and origin, is here interpreted as a merely graphic feature, and the words are read as: *ḥāḍir*, *lāzim*, *istiʕmāl*.

2.2 Morphology

2.2.1 The noun

2.2.1.1 Morphological categories

EJP nouns distinguish number (Sg./Pl.) and have a suffix of indefiniteness (*-ē*); there is no morphological distinction of case, gender, or animacy.

2.2.1.2 Form

(a) The EJP nominal suffixes *-ī(h)* and *-išn*/*-išt*, building abstract nouns and action nouns, respectively, are typical of EJP: unlike (E)NP, they partially preserve the MP form (*-īh*; *-išn*), e.g., EJP *durustī(h)* 'rightness', *āfarīnišn* 'creation' (corresponding to NP *-ī*, *-iš*, as in *durustī*, *āfarīniš*).

(b) EJP *barādar* 'brother' occurs seldom without *-ar* (i.e. as *barād*), reflecting the remnant of a MP casus rectus form. Unlike MP *brād*, however, EJP *barād* is used indiscriminately from *barādar*, i.e. *barād*/*barādar* does not show a case distinction. For other kinship terms like *pidar* 'father', no forms without the *-ar* are attested in the EJP corpus.

2.2.1.3 Definiteness

The simple noun may be definite, indefinite, or generic, in various syntactic functions, e.g.:

ks (indefinite subject) *nʔ dʔnyst* [kas na dānist] – 'no one knew (it)' (T11-1.7)

rh (definite direct object) ... *dʔnd* [rah ... dānad] – 'he knows the way' (Arg.c6)

dynʔr (generic direct object) *prwktwm* [dēnār furōxtom] – 'I bought dinars' (Lr.12)

The *-ē* of indefiniteness and unit

(a) When a noun is indefinite, it often takes the suffix *-ē*, e.g. (in various functions):

nʔmy (subject) *by ʔmd* [nāma'ē be āmad] – 'a letter came' (L5.10)

kwhyd tysy (direct object) *dyhydʔt* [xwāhed tis-ē dihed-a-t] – 'he wants to give you something' (L11.5)

bʕd ʔz mwdty (prepositional complement) [baʕd az muddat-ē] – 'after a while' (L5.10)

(b) The notion of indefiniteness often goes along with that of unit. Sometimes, the unit notion is more prominent, e.g.:

sʔly wnym [sāl-ē u-nēm] – 'one year and half / one and a half years' (Ez183.1)

(c) An *-ē* may also be attached to an indefinite noun to show that it is specific, especially if the noun governs a relative clause, e.g.:

sʔlyʔn bsyʔr mrdy [mard-ē] *by ʔyyd* – 'for many years, a (certain) man comes' (Arg.p2)

kwdʔhy [xwadāh-ē] *hyst ypʔ pyšwbʔ ʔgh bwd* –
'he is a god who is aware beforehand' (Arg.a10)

2.2.1.4 Plural

To mark an EJP noun as pluralic, the two morphemes *-(y)hʔ* [-ihā] and *-(g)ʔn* [-(g)ān] are used. In principle, *-(g)ān* is used for animate, *-ihā* for inanimate nouns, but there are exceptions to this rule. *-gān* (with *-g-*) is a historical form that occurs after nouns whose MP precursor ended in *-g* (e.g., EJP *firešta* 'angel', PL *fireštagān*, from MP *frēštag* 'angel'. *-ān* is sometimes written without *ʔāleph* (e.g., *prznd*n [frazandān] (Arg.s11), see also section 2.1.3 (a)). *-ihā* is written *-yhʔ* or *-hʔ* (in certain texts like Ez1 almost exclusively *-yhʔ*); the adverbial origin of *-ihā* (< MP *-īhā*) is still recognizable from *ʔzdyhh* [āzādihā] 'nobly' (Du2.9) (*-ihā* is exceptionally written *-yhh* here). In ENP, *-ihā* occurs rarely, besides regular *-hā* (Lazard 1963, § 152).

Arabic and Hebrew loanwords in EJP may form a plural either by indigenous morphological means, notably Arabic "broken" plurals in words like *fiʕl* 'deed', PL *afʕāl*, or the Hebrew PL *yhwdym* 'Jews'; or with the Persian plural endings, e.g., *lwgthʔ* [luɣat-hā] 'words' (< Ar. *luɣa(t)*), *ʕwrlʔhʔ* [ʕorlahā] 'foreskins' (< Heb. *ʕorlā*); or with a combination of both, e.g., *ʔkbʔryhʔ* [axbārihā] 'notices' (cf. the Arabic broken plural *ʔaxbār*), *gwymʔn* [goyīmān] 'gentiles' (Hebrew plural *goyim*).

2.2.2 Adjectives, Adverbs

2.2.2.1 Form and function

(a) It is not always possible to distinguish EJP adjectives from nouns, e.g., adjectives like *pyr* [pīr] 'old' or *pʔdywnd* [pādyāwand] 'strong' that may be used as nouns *ad hoc* (e.g., as head of a nominal phrase), or ethnonyms like *tʔzy* [tāzī] 'Arab'.

(b) Certain adjectives can modify verbs and thus be used as adverbs, e.g., *nykw* [nēkō] 'good', *skt* [saxt] 'strong', used as adverbs in the sense of 'well' and 'very', respectively.

(c) Adjectives usually follow the noun they qualify with an *ezafe* (but see below). The following adjectivizing suffixes occur in EJP:

-yn [-ēn], denoting materials or temporal/local relations, e.g., *gwštyn* [gōštēn] 'fleshy', *pyšyn* [pēšēn] 'former', *zyryn* [zērēn] 'lower'

-gyn [-gēn], emotional states, e.g., *gmgyn* [γamgēn] 'sad'

-y [-ī], places of origin (*nisba*) and various other adjectives, e.g., *bgdʔdy* [Baγdādī] 'from Baghdad', *cyny* [čīnī] 'Chinese'; *grʔmy* [girāmī] 'dear'

-wmnd [-ōmand], e.g. *zyʔnwmnd* [ziyānōmand] 'harmful'

-ʔsʔ [-āsā], e.g., *ʔb ʔsʔ* [āb-āsā] 'like water'

The last two suffixes are often written separately from the word, to which they are suffixed.

The EJP adverbs may be divided into the following groups:

– local, e.g., *ʔyngʔ* [ēnjā] 'here', *ʔydr* [ēdar] 'here'

– temporal, e.g., *ʔbʔ(z)* [abā(z)] 'again', *(ʔ)nwn* [(a)nūn] 'now'

– manner, e.g., *ʔydwn* [ēdōn] 'thus', *tn(y)hʔ(n)* [tan(i)hā(n)] 'only'

2.2.2.2 Comparative

(a) EJP comparative adjectives are derived from the plain adjective with the suffix *-tar*, e.g., *bwzwrgtr* [buzurgtar] 'bigger', *pʔdywntr* [pādyāwantar < *pādyāwand-tar (with assimilation)] 'stronger'.

(b) Besides, there still exists a small number of historical (MP) comparatives without *-tar* in EJP, e.g. *byh* [beh] 'better', *myh* [meh] 'greater', sometimes besides the *-tar*-form (e.g., *byhtr* [behtar] 'better').

2.2.2.3 Comparative constructions

(a) The standard of comparison, governed by the preposition *az* 'from', usually follows the comparative adjective:

byh ʔz ʔn [beh az ān] – 'better than that' (Du1.28)

ġlyl tr ʔz ʔyn [jalīltar az ēn] – 'more glorious than this' (Ez177.25),

but may also precede it:

ʔzyšʔn ǧlyl tr [az-ēšān jalīltar] – 'more glorious than they (are)' (Ez174.15)

(b) Superlatives are paraphrased with comparative constructions using words like *hama* 'all', e.g.:

nbyltr ... hyst ʔz hmʔ šyrh hʔ – 'it is the noblest of ('nobler than') all songs' (Gr3r.18)

2.2.2.4 Certain adjectives (pronouns)

(a) Quantitative, indefinite, and interrogative adjectives normally precede the noun they qualify:

wbs tys [u-bas tis] ... *ʔwryd* – 'and He created many things' (Arg.b4)

pʔ ʔndq zmʔn [pa andak zamān] – 'for a short time' (Is1.8)

cy tgyyr nʔ bwd [čē taγyīr na būd] – 'there was not any change' (Gen11.35)

cyz ʔndwh mʔ kwr [čē-z andōh ma xwar] – 'do not suffer any anxiety' (Du1.30)

pwlʔn ks [fulān kas] – 'the so-and-so' (Ez10.23)

Note the adjective *čē(z)* 'any' (in negative sentences) that had developed from *čē* 'what?', with a generalizing *-iz* '-ever'; as a pronoun, *čē(z)* 'anything' is the basis for (later) NP *čīz* 'thing'.

Some adjectives from this group may follow the noun with the *ezafe*, e.g.:

bʔyndʔ ydygr – 'another bird' (Arg.c4)

(b) The demonstrative adjectives *ʔyn* [ēn] 'this', PL *ʔynʔn* [ēnān] 'these', and *ʔn* [ān] 'that' (no plural attested), as well as the cardinal numbers, also precede the noun without the *ezafe*.

Cardinal numbers could be written phonetically, or with the appropriate letter of the Hebrew alphabet, marked by a dot or stroke, e.g., בּ̇ *ḃ* [dō] '2', ז̇ *ż* [haft] '7'. A noun that is qualified by a cardinal number remains in the singular, e.g.:

byst nʔmh [bīst nāma] – '20 letters' (Du1.2)

The following examples show how dates are expressed in EJP:

k̇ż pʔ mhyʔn nysʔn [bīst-u-haft mahyān i Nīsān] – '(on) the 27th ('in the month') of Nisan' (L18.6)

pʔ byst wpnc sgd [pa bīst-u-panj saγd] – 'on the 25th (day) (lit., "on 25 passed")' (Du2.28)

... *(ṭ)z ʔb sʔl hzr wd(wys)t wšst wdw šmʔr yšṭrwt* – '(on?) the 16th of Ab (of the) year 1262, according to the Seleucid era' (Kd.2)

Note that *sgd* [saγd], lit. "passed", occurring only in Du, may be a loan from Sogdian.

2.2.3 Noun phrases

When an EJP noun is modified by another noun or adjective in possessive or descriptive function, the latter normally follows the former with an enclitic particle, pronounced [i], that is traditionally called *ezafe* (< Arabic *ʔiḍāfa* 'addition'). The noun that is modified is called the "head noun" (H), the noun or adjective that is following it is called the "modifier" (M). The H and M, together with the *ezafe* (H i M), form a noun phrase.

2.2.3.1 Writing/spelling of the *ezafe*

Being a short vowel, the *ezafe* may be written, or left unwritten, in any EJP text. In the earliest texts Du1/2, and in Ar (twice out of 189x), it may be written as an independent word *ʔy* [i] between H and M. In all other texts the *ezafe* is written (if it is written at all) with a plain *yōd*, either affixed to the head, or prefixed to its modifier (i.e. "Hy M" or "H yM"). Here are examples:

M = possessive complement:

– *ezafe* written independently as *ʔy*:

mrdwmʔn ʔy šhr [mardumān i šahr] – 'the people of the city' (Du1.11)

nʔm ʔy zkrwt [H.] – 'the name of masculinity' (Arg.t13)

– *ezafe* unwritten:

by dst mʔ [be dast i mā] – 'to our hand' (Du2.21)

dwktr rʔwbn [duxtar i R.] *ybzʔz* – 'the daughter of Reuben, the clothes-dealer' (L11.11)

The *ezafe* may be unwritten even after a H ending in long vowel, e.g.:

zyʔnhʔ kwdtʔn [ziyānhā i xwad-itān] – 'your own losses' (L3.34)

– *ezafe* written *y-*, prefixed to the modifier:

nʔmh yšmʔ [nāma i šumā] – 'your letter'Du2.6

mylk ybrʔdrʔnwm [milk i barādarānum] – 'the property of my brothers' (Lr.6)

– *ezafe* written *-y*, affixed to the head:

ʔbr sry ʔyšʔn [sar-i ēšān] – 'over their heads' (Ez2.21)

kʔry ʔw [kār-i ō] – 'his work' (Gen5.16)

M = descriptive complement

– *ezafe* written independently as ʔy:

ʔz šmr ʔy kwš [šumār i xwaš] – 'from the good account' (Du1.21)

– *ezafe* unwritten:

mrw'khwn [murwārīd i kahwan] – 'old pearl(s)' (L3.25)

ʔktyʔr bd [ixtiyār i bad] – 'a bad choice' (Ez191.22)

– *ezafe* written *y-*, prefixed to the modifier:

swd (y)nyyk – 'a good profit' (L3.24)

p(ws)r yhšt rwzʔ – 'the son of eight days (old)' (Arg.s8)

– *ezafe* written *-y*, affixed to the head:

mġlysy nykw – 'a nice gathering' (Ez30.30)

rwzy sywm – 'the 3rd day' (Gen5.29)

2.2.3.2 Further rules

(a) Concord of number is not obligatory for descriptive noun phrases, cf.:

myhtrʔn grʔmyʔn [mehtarān i girāmīyān, plural] – '(oh) dear elders' (L7.2)

brʔdrʔn grʔmy [barādarān i girāmī, singular] – '(oh) dear brothers' (L15.8)

(b) Most quantifying, indefinite (etc.) adjectives precede the noun they qualify without *ezafe* (see above); rarely, also certain other (descriptive) adjectives may precede the head, e.g.:

skwn ʔy bd mrdwm [bad mardum] – 'the words of the bad people' (Du2.12)

kwr dwd [kūr Dawid] – 'David the blind' (L18.22)

(c) When the head of a noun phrase is marked as indefinite by the suffix *-ē*, it can be modified by an adjective without *ezafe*, e.g.:

*ʔyn tysy*ᵉ *kwʔr* [tis-ē xwār] *ʔysty*ᵉ*d* – 'this is a light thing' (L6.4)

šrḥy dygr [šarḥ-ē dīgar] – 'another explanation' (L12.12)

ʔyynʔy symyn [āyēna-ē sēmēn] – 'a silver mirror' (L15.16)

(d) When a M is modified by another M, a chain of two (or more) *ezafe* constructions can occur:

cypt yzʔnwrhʔ yʔbʔry [ṣifat i-jānwarhā i-abārī, N N A] – 'the quality of other animals' (Arg.b6)

byʔnhʔ yʔrʔyšn yʔn rwmy [biyānhā i-ārāyišn i-ān Rōmī, N N N] – 'the tents of the adornment of that Byzantine' (Db3.4)

Here also, one or all *ezafe*s can be left unwritten:

prznd ʔn rmy tw [farzandān i ram-i tō] [N N N] – 'the children of your people' (Ez211.22)

2.2.4 Pronouns

2.2.4.1 Personal pronouns

(a) There are two series of EJP personal pronouns, a full and an enclitic one. The pronominal system of the earliest texts (Du) differs substantially from that of all other EJP texts. The full forms, with the Du1/2-forms (where they are different) given separately, are:

	SG	(Du1/2)	PL	(Du1/2)
1	*mn* [man] 'I'	(id.)	*ʔymʔ(n)* [ēmā(n)]	*mʔ* [mā] 'we'
2	*tw* [tō] 'you'	(id.)	*š(w)mʔ(n)* [šumā(n)]	*(y)šmʔ* [(i)šmā/š(i)mā] 'you'
3	*ʔw(y)* [ō(y)]	*w(y)* [wa(y)] 'he, she, it'	*ʔyšʔn* [ēšān] 'they'	(id.)

(b) The EJP enclitic personal pronouns may be attached to most parts of speech (noun, adjective, preposition, verb, conjunction), and serve the same syntactic functions as do the full pronouns, except that of the subject. The forms occurring in the EJP texts are:

	SG	PL
1	*-(w)m* [-um]	*-mʔn* [-mān]
2	*-(y)t* [-it]	*-tʔn* [-tān]
3	*-(y)š* [-iš]	*-(y)šʔn* [-(i)šān]

2.2.4.2 Reflexivity

EJP Reflexivity is expressed in a way similar to ENP, with *xwēštan* (for direct and indirect objects, prepositional complements) and *xwēš* (possessive complements), e.g.:

šwyʔʔn hynd kwyštn rʔ (direct object) [šōyān hend xwēštan rā] – 'they are washing them-selves' (Gr8v.5)

pʔ kwyštn (prepositional complement) *ʔndyšydwm* [pa xwēštan andēšīdom] – 'I thought by myself' (Arg.g4)

ʔ kʔr y kwyš [u/a kār i xwēš] (possessive complement) *dʔnd šwdn* – 'he knows to go to his business' (Arg.b9)

The element *xwad* had not yet turned into a reflexivity marker (as it would do in later NP), but was still used as an emphatic:

qw kwd krydy wkwd prwkty – 'which you bought *yourself*, and sold *yourself*' (Du1.19)

wʔqpʔ kwd hm hyst kw [wāqif xwad ham hest ku] – 'he is *even* informed that …' (L4.5)

2.2.5 Verbs and verbal syntax

2.2.5.1 Stem formation

EJP simple verbs derive their forms from two verbal stems, present and past. The past stem of each EJP verb ends in *-d* or *-t*, depending on whether the preceding sound is voiced or not (e.g., *kerd* 'done', *guft* 'said'). The infinitive, in which the EJP verbs are normally quoted, is formed from the past stem with *-an* (*kerdan* 'do').

There is no clear-cut distinction between regular and irregular verbs, but rather a scale of (decreasing) regularity of stem formation, and the classification of the verbs into stem groups is a matter of convention.

(a) Those EJP verbs are categorized here as regular with respect to stem formation that derive their present stem through the deletion of one out of four past formants, e.g.:

-īd: past *andēšīd* 'think' > present *andēš-*; *kašīd* 'draw' > *kaš-*

-ist: *dānist* 'know' > *dān-*; *šāyist* 'be possible' > *šāy-*

-ād: *ōftād* 'fall' > *ōft-*; *nehād* 'take' > *neh-*

-d (after *n* or *r*): *bizārd* 'explain' > *bizār-*, *kand* 'dig' > *kan-*

or through the regular replacement of a past through a present formant:

-ūd > *-āy*: *firmūd* 'order' > *firmāy-*

-ft > *-b*: *(a)yāft* 'find' > *(a)yāb-*

(b) The irregular verbs derive their present stem by replacing it through another, less predictable formant:

-xt > *-j*/*-s*/*-š*/*-z*: *šināxt* 'know' > *šinās-*; *āmōxt* 'teach' > *āmōz-*

-št/*-st* > *-s*/*-š*/*-z*: *nibišt* 'write' > *nibēs-*; *xāst* 'rise' > *xēz-*

-št/*-st* > *-r*/*-h*/*-n*/*-l*: *dāšt* 'had' > *dār-*; *šikast* 'break > *šikan-*

Besides, there are "more strictly irregular" verbs that do not fit into any of the above categories, e.g. *dād* 'give' > *deh-*; *burd* 'carry' > *bar-*; and a small number of suppletive stems that do not show a phonetic or etymological relation with each other, like *āmad* 'come' > *āy-*, or *dīd* 'see' > *wēn-*.

The following prepositions/adverbs occur as preverbs in EJP:

– *(a)bāz* 'back (to)', e.g., in *(a)bāz āmadan* 'return'

– *abar* 'upon' *abar dāštan* 'raise'

– *andar* 'in' *andar āmadan* 'enter'

(a) There are various verbal particles and affixes in EJP: durative *(ha)mē*, emphasizing *be*, and hortative *(h)ē*. Especially the first two are not yet fully grammaticalized in EJP.

(b) Verbs are negated through the particle *nē* in most texts, in some through *na*. Since *nē* was the MP particle of negation, and *na* occurs mainly in northern EJP texts, it is likely to be of later, northeastern dialectal origin. The prohibitive particle is *ma* in all EJP texts.

There are various EJP participles whose use, especially in verbal constructions, differs considerably from text to text, and which therefore can only be mentioned here:

– based on the present stem: in *-ā* (e.g., *gōyā* 'saying'), *-anda* (*šawanda* 'going')

– based on the past stem: plain past stem (*kušt* 'slain'), with *-a* (*kušta* 'slain'); *-dār*/*-tār* (*pursīdār* 'asking'), *-agī* (*nimūdagī* '(the act of) showing')

2.2.5.2 Present tense

The EJP present indicative is built from the present stem and the following endings:

	SG	PL
1	*-wm* [-om]	*-ym* [-ēm]
2	*-y* [-ī]	*-yd* [-ēd]
3	*-yd* [-ed] (*-d* [-ad])	*-ynd* [-end] (*-nd* [-and])

The varieties 3SG/PL *-ad*/*-and* often occur in northern texts like Ez1 or Gen.

(a) Present forms with *(h)my* [(ha)mē] may yield a durative or iterative sense, or point to the fact that an action is going on at the moment of the speech act ("progressive"), e.g.:

hr wqty my ʔrynd [mē ārend] ... *swd ynyyk pdyš my kwnynd* [mē kunend] – 'whenever they bring (it), they make a good profit with it' (L3.23)

ʔyn nʔmʔ hmy nbyswm [hamē nibēsom] ... – 'I am writing this letter' (L15.8)

(b) The particle *by* [be] which would become a subjunctive marker in later NP, is even less grammaticalized in EJP (and ENP) than *(ha)mē*. Its exact functions are difficult to describe, its occurrence seems to depend mainly on the verb's "degree of semantic autonomy" (Lazard 1963, §§ 395, 403).

EJP has preserved a MP subjunctive form in 3SG *-ād* that usually expresses a wish, often as an invocation of God, e.g.:

drwd wʔpryn pʔ šwmʔ bʔd [bād] – 'may greeting(s) and blessing(s) be upon you' (L18.4)

In all EJP, only one non-3SG subjunctive form is possibly attested in:

krʔm [xirām] – 'we may buy' (uncertain meaning) (Du1.12)

(a) The imperative SG is formed with the plain present stem, e.g., *kwn* [kun] 'do!', and the PL with the ending *-yd* [-ēd]: *kwnyd* [kunēd] 'do (ye)!' The particle *by* may precede imperative verbs (*by kwn* 'do!'), but its occurrence is unpredictable, since *by* (cf. last paragraph) had not yet been grammaticalized in EJP.

(b) The prohibitive is formed with the prefix *ma*, e.g., *mʔ kwn* [ma kun] 'do not!'

Other noteworthy present tense constructions, occurring seldom in the EJP corpus, include:

– the present indicative, together with a hortative particle *ʔy* or *hy* [(h)ē], e.g.:

ʔy yʔr bʔšd [ē yār bāšad] – 'may (God) be a helper' (Du1.1)

– a present verbal form, with an irrealis suffix *-y* [-ē]:

tʔ … ʔyspnc gyrwmy [ispanj gīrom-ē] – 'so that I would take a dwelling' (Zef3.11)

2.2.5.3 Past tenses

The Simple Past (Preterite)

The EJP Simple Past is the unmarked past tense, used as a general narrative past. It is built from the past stem and the following personal endings:

	SG	PL
1	*-(w)m* [-om]	*-ym* [-ēm]
2	*-y* [-ī]	*-yd* [-ēd]
3	-Ø	*-ynd* [-end] (*-nd* [-and])

Although EJP is clearly an accusative language, reflexes of MP ergativity may be seen in the agentless/passive use of 3SG past forms like in:

nbyšt ʔyn nʔmʔ [nibišt ēn nāma] … *rwz b* – 'this letter was written … on Monday' (L3.45)

cyst wʔz cy grypt [az čē girift] – 'what is it and from what has it (the word) been derived?' (Gr7r.16)

(a) The particle *(ha)mē* has, with a past verb, the same durative/habitual meaning as with a present verb, see above and:

kʔr (pdyš) hmy krdnd [hamē kerdand] – 'they continued to act according to it' (Arg.r2)

(b) The use of *be* with past verbal forms follows the same vague, partly stylistic rules as for the present. Besides, traces of an older MP lexical meaning of *be* as 'out, away' (as in ENP) may be seen in:

ʔn tys by bwrd [be burd] ʔwy rʔ ʔz dyl ymn – 'that thing carried it (away) from my heart' (Arg.h1)

An invariable past tense in *-agē*, derived from the PP, is occasionally used as a full verbal form in the texts Ez and Gen, and may be compared to modern Tajik forms like *omadagi* '(he) has come', often with a resultative meaning, e.g.:

rwʔ hst ky mwktcr krdgy [muxtaṣar kerdagē] – 'it is possible that he has made it short' (Ez15.32)

An EJP irrealis is formed with the simple past and the suffix *-y(h)* [-ē(h)] that is attached to the personal ending. It can be used independently or in conditional clauses, e.g.:

wʔylʔ mn by nybštwmyh [be nibištomēh] *pyš šyyk ... tʔ prysty(d)yh* [firistīdēh] – 'otherwise I should write to Sheikh … so that he may send (it)' (L15.32)

bʔysty ky ... mwḥtrz bwdndy [būdandē] – 'they … should have been cautious' (Ez179.4)

ʔgr mwkʔlpyh ... ny bwdy [nē būdē] … *hmgʔn i bwdndy* [hamagān yak būdandē] – 'if there were no disagreement … they would all be one' (Arg.f8)

2.2.5.4 Compound past tenses

There are two compound past tenses in EJP, present and past perfect, each of which may be formed with either the plain past stem or the past participle in *-a* together with the present or past form of the verb "to be". The variants with the past stem form the more regular past tenses, while the forms with the participle in *-a* often have an adjectival-static meaning, owing to the adjectival origin of the participle; i.e. *nibišt hest* 'he has written' vs. *nibišta hest* 'it is written'.

The present perfect

(a) The Present perfect with the plain past stem describes an action or state that is conceived to be effective until the present, see:

tysy krd (h)yst [kerd hest] *ʔzmr ymn šmwʔl rʔ* – 'he has done something towards me, Samuel' (Kd.4)

A plain past tense form, followed by a present perfect form of the same verb in more lively direct speech, serves to show a typical function of this tense:

nʔmy by ʔmd [be āmad] ... *kw nʔmʔ ʔlš[yx] ... ʔmd hyst* [āmad hest] – 'a letter came … (saying) that: "the letter of Sheikh … has arrived"' (L5.10)

In non-3SG forms, a peculiar construction occurs where the personal ending is attached not to the auxiliary but to the verbal past stem:

ʔb prystʔdnd hyst [āb firistād-end hest] – 'they have sent water' (Ez171.31)

(b) The present perfect with the past participle in *-a* has not yet been fully grammaticalized as a tense; the original adjectival/stative character of the past participles in *-a* continues to prevail, e.g.:

ʔgr tysy ʔz cʔmʔ mndʔ hyst [mānda hest] – 'if anything of the clothes has remained' (L7.8)

ḥq ʔn hynd ymn pdyš ʔystydʔ hwm [ēstāda hom] – 'the truth is those (things) on which I stand' (Arg.g1)

cwn nbyštʔ hyst [nibišta hest] – 'as it is written' (Arg.x6)

In the whole EJP corpus, only two present perfect forms of the *kardastam*-type occur, e.g.:

ktʔbʔ ḥtmy krdystym [kardistēm] – 'we have sealed the book' (L19.1)

Pluperfect

(a) The following are examples of pluperfect with the plain past stem:

ʔyn q̇ q̇ s ynbyšt bwd – 'these 200 s.(?) which he had written' (L4.18)

bʔry dygr šnyd bwd – '(because) he had heard (it) another time (Ez5.25)

For non-3SG persons, the same peculiar construction as for the present perfect (see above) obtains:

pʔ pyš ... gwptwm bwd [guft-om būd] – 'I had said before' (Ez3.16)

ʔbʔz ʔmdnd bwd [āmad-and būd] – 'they had returned' (Ez187.23)

(b) Like the present perfect, transitive forms of the pluperfect with *-a* usually have an adjectival-passive meaning:

[p]rwkth bwd – '(it) was sold (unclear context, maybe *buwad* 'it is (being) sold'?) (Du1.11)

rwʔ hst ky ... ġ klymʔ nybyštʔ bwd – 'it is possible that the three words were written' (Ez5.21)

nʔmhʔ ... yʔbr cwb nbyštʔ bwd – 'names that were written on the stick' (Ez212.4)

Less often, transitive verbs are used accusatively with a past meaning, e.g.:

ʔyn nbyʔ ykwdʔ by mrdwmn prstydʔ bwd – 'this prophet whom God *had sent* to mankind' (Arg.h12)

2.2.5.5 Overview of the EJP tense and mood system

The EJP tenses cannot be presented as a fixed and cohesive system, because the language itself is not unified in time or space. The following schedule of 3SG forms aims to summarize the most important tenses of EJP; the forms in (brackets) are marginal and occur very rarely.

Present	
Indicative	*rased* 'he arrives' (etc.)
– progressive	*(ha)mē rased*
– "independent"	*be rased*
Subjunctive	*rasād*
Hortative	*(h)ē rased*
Imperative	*(be) ras*
Present Irrealis	*rasom-ē*
Past	
Simple	*rasīd*
– durative	*(ha)mē rasīd*
– stylistic	*(be) rasīd*
Resultative	*(rasīdagī)*
Past Irrealis	*rasīdē(h)*
Present Perfect: – plain past stem	*rasīd(-end) hest*
– with PP in *-a* (passive-adjectival)	*rasīda hest*
– kardastam-type	*(rasīda'st)*
Pluperfect: – plain past stem (active)	*rasīd(-end) būd*
– with PP in *-a* (passive-adjectival)	*rasīda būd*

2.2.5.6 Passive, Causative

(a) An EJP morphological passive is derived from the present stem with the suffix *-(y)h* [-ih] (< MP *-īh*), the past stem with *-(y)h(y)st* [-ihist], e.g., in the examples:

ʔprynhyd [āfarīnihed] 'he will be blessed' (Is2.11)

tbhhysty [tabāhihistē] 'it would have been ruined' (Arg.e9)

(b) A passive may alternatively be paraphrased with *āmadan* 'come', e.g.:

kwštʔ ʔmdnd [kušta āmadand] – 'they were slain' (Ez132.22)

ʔprydʔ ʔyyd [āfarīda āyad] – '(that) it would be created' (Gen2.8)

EJP causatives are derived from the present stem with the morpheme *-n* [-en] or *-ʔn* [-ān], e.g.:

ʔghn- [āgahen-] 'inform' (Du2.6/L7.9)

hmy ʔmwzʔnnd [hamē āmōzānand] 'they are teaching' (Ez9.18)

2.2.5.7 Special verbs

(a) The EJP substantive verb "to be" has the following present tense forms:

	SG	PL
1	*hwm* [hom]	*hym* [hēm]
2	*hy* [hī]	*hyd* [hēd]
3	*h(y)st* [hest, hast]	*h(y)nd* [hend, hand]

The 3SG form is *hest* in most southern texts, *hast* in most northern texts, but there are exceptions to this rule. The negative form of the substantive verb ist *nyst* [nēst] (only 3SG forms are attested).

(b) An enclitic substantive verb (copula) without *h-* occurs only in two verbal forms in the EJP corpus, e.g.:

gwhwm [guwāh-om] – 'I am witness' (Koll.2)

Further forms of the substantive verb include the verb *būdan* 'be' in the full present stem *baw-* and the shortened present stem *b-*; *bāš-* (mostly used for imperative); and *ʔyst-* [ēst-], possibly from *ēstādan* 'stand', e.g.:

šʔd hmy bwm [hamē buwom] – 'I am glad' (L5.4)

spyd bynd [s(i)pēd bend] – 'they will be white' (Db3.10)

ʔgh bʔš [āgah bāš] *kw* – 'be informed that …' (L15.9)

ʔyn tysy^ē kwʔr ʔystyⁱd [ēsted] – 'this is(?) a light thing' (L6.4)

(a) The following modal verbs occur in the EJP texts:

(ʔ)bʔyd, (ʔ)bʔyst [(a)bāyed, (a)bāyist] – 'it is necessary, one must'

dʔnystn, dʔn- [dānistan, dān-] – 'know, be able'

kwʔstn, kwʔh- [xwāstan, xwāh-] – 'want'

s(ʔ)zd/syzd (Ar/Lr) [sāzad/sezad] – 'it is proper, fitting, right'

šʔh(y)d/šʔyd, šʔhyst – 'it is possible, one can' (L6.10 *šʔyhyd* [šāyihed]) [šāhed/šāyed, šāhist]

twʔnystn, twʔn- [tawānistan, tawān-] – 'can, be able'

(b) Both personal and impersonal EJP modal verbs govern an infinitive, cf. personal:
ʔkʔr ykwyš dʔnd šwdn [dānad šudan] – ‘it knows to go to its (own) business’ (Arg.b8)
ny$^{\bar{e}}$ *my*$^{\bar{e}}$ *twʔnm šwdn* [nē mē tawānom šudan] *ʔcʔyy*$^{\bar{e}}$ – ‘I cannot go to any place’ (L6.8)
and impersonal:
cy ʔbʔyd krdn [abāyed kardan] – ‘(it knows) what it is necessary to do’ (Arg.c7)
cy šʔhyd k(y)rdn [šāhed kerdan] *ʔylʔ šwkr y'y' bwrdn* – ‘what can one do except thanking God?’ (L3.30)
(c) Impersonal modal verbs may alternatively govern a dependent clause with a finite verb, e.g.:
šʔhd ky [šāhed ki] *gwyy ky* – ‘you may (“it is possible that you”) say that …’ (Ez6.15)
bʔyd ky [bāyad ki] *šwkr ʔrwm* – ‘I must thank (him) (“bear thank(s)”)’ (Ez177.26)

EJP nouns and adjectives can be combined with basic verbs like “do”, “have”, etc., to form “compound verbs”, i.e. more or less firm lexical/syntactic units that often correspond to English simple verbs, e.g.:
mšh drwst krdy [durust kerdī] – ‘you have confirmed (the prophethood of) Moses’ (Arg.j9)
(ʔ)w(m)yd dʔrwm [umēd dārom] *kw p(ʔ š)lwm rsydy* – ‘I hope that you arrived in peace’ (L3.8)
nbyʔ ʔndrz krd [andarz kard] *ʔwrʔ* – ‘the prophet admonished him (“made (to) him advice”)’ (Ez10.2)

2.2.6 Particles

2.2.6.1 Prepositions

(a) The following simple prepositions occur in Early Judeo-Persian:

ʔbʔ(z) [abā(z)]	1. ‘with’; 2. ‘back (to, from)’; ‘to’
ʔbr [abar] (Lr.2 *ʔwr* [aβar])	‘upon’
ʔby [abē]	‘without’
ʔndr [andar]	‘in(to)’
ʔ(w), w- [u, a?]	1. ‘to, towards’; 2. (direct object marker)
ʔz [az]	‘from’
by/b(ʔ) [be/ba]	‘to, towards’
cwd/gwd/zwd [jud]	‘except’
cwn [čūn]	‘like’
p(d), pʔ [pa(d)]	1. ‘with, by’; 2. ‘in, on, at’; 3. ‘to(wards)’
tʔ [tā]	‘until’

The preposition *u* ‘to’, later *a*, may be infixed (written with *ʔāleph*) between finite verbal forms and a personal suffix, e.g.:
gwptyndʔš [guftend-a-š] – ‘they said to him’ (Lr.6)
kwhyd tysy dyhydʔt [dehed-a-t] – ‘he wants to give you something’ (L11.5)
(w)by prystydyʔm [firistīdī-a-m] – ‘(and) you sent (it) to me’ (L15.24)

The “normal” suffixes in these cases, without infixed *a* and without directional meaning, would be *-yš*, *-wm*, etc.

2.2.6.2 Prepositions with the *ezafe*

Certain EJP prepositions (some of which are actually nouns, adjectives or adverbs) govern a noun with the *ezafe*, e.g.: *ʔzyr* [azēr i] 'below', *cʔdʔ/gʔdʔ* [jāda i] 'concerning, because of', *myʔn* [miyān i] 'between', *nz(d)yk* [naz(d)īk i] 'near', *ps* [pas i] 'after'.

Another group of prepositions combine a simple preposition with the nouns, adjectives or adverbs just mentioned, and govern the noun also with an *ezafe*, e.g.: *ʔnzdyk* [a-nazdīk i] 'among', *ʔpyš* [a-pēš i] 'to, before (sb.)', *ʔz myʔn* [az miyān i] 'from among', *pʔ nzdyk* [pa nazdīk i] 'near to'.

(a) The postposition *rʔ* [rā] has the following meanings in EJP, some of which overlap with meanings of certain prepositions (e.g., *u/a* as a direct and indirect object marker):

– direct object: *kwdʔ mn rʔ* [man rā] *prstyd* – 'God has sent me' (Arg.n2)

– indirect object: *gwptwm twrʔ* [to rā] *ky* – 'I told you that …' (Ez4.17)

– possessive: *tysy mn rʔ* [man rā] *ʔpyš ʔyn shl ... hyst* –
'I have ("to me is") something before this Sahl' (Lr.9)

– benefactive: *šbʔnʔn rʔ* [šubān-ān rā] *bgdw ... hdyh* –
'for the shepherds, one *bgdw* (=?) as a present' (Du2.20)

– "as for …": *wmrdwmyh rʔ* [u-mardomīh rā] *cypt ... ny ʔydwn ʔwrydʔ hyst* –
'and as for mankind, their quality … has not been created so' (Arg.d2)

– causal: *wbs ʔndyšʔyh rʔ* [bas-andēša'īh rā] *i ʔbʔ dygr kwhnd* – 'and because of (this) great occupation, they trample on one another' (Arg.d5)

(b) *rā* occurs together with the preposition *u/a*, to form the circumposition *u/a ... rā*, as which it is used in all functions of *rā*, e.g.:

mwkʔlp hynd i ʔdygr rʔ [yak u-dīgar rā, Oi] – 'they are opposed to one another' (Arg.h4)

yʔymʔ ʔʔwy rʔ [u-ōy rā, Od] ... *pdyrptym* – '(that deputy) whom we accepted' (Arg.p12)

nbyʔ bwd ʔʕlmʔ rʔ [u-ʕālam rā, poss.] – 'the world had a prophet' (Arg.a3)

2.2.6.3 Conjunctions

The following main simple sentence conjunctions occur in Early Judeo-Persian:

ʔgr [agar]	'if'
ʔylʔ [illā]	'except'
ʔyyb/yʔw/yw [ayāb/yāw/yaw Ar/L4,Is/Gr,Ez2]	'or'
by [be/ē] (only Arg)	'but'
cwn [čūn]	'as, how'
cy [čē]	'for, because'
kʔ [ka] (only Arg)	'if, when'
kw/qw [ku]	'that' (subordinating)
ky [ki]	'that' (subord.); 'that, which' (rel.)
tʔ [tā]	'so that, until'
w [u, wa]	'and'
wʔmʔ [wa-ammā]	'but'
wlykyn [walēkin]	'but'

3. Texts

3.1 Text 1: The Ahwaz Law Report (ed. Asmussen 1965, transl. MacKenzie 1966)

אידון בוד אפיש יאימאן סהדאן יכט מאן

(1)*ēdōn būd a-pēš i-ēmān sahad-ān i-xaṭṭ-mān*

thus be.PST.3SG to-before EZ-we witness-PL EZ-script-our

It was thus before us witnesses, whose signature

אזיר אין מחצר נבישתא היסת פא הורמשיר

azēr (i-)ēn maḥḍar nibišt-a hest pa Hurmšīr

under EZ-this record write.PST-PPP COP.3SG by (PN)

is written below this record, in Hurmšīr (= Ahwāz),

שהרי אז צומלא כוזיסתאן כו איסתאדא היסת

šahr-ē (2)*az jumla (i-)Xūzistān ku ēstād-a hest*

town-INDEF from whole (EZ-)(PN) which stand.PST-PPP COP.3SG

a town of the whole of (the towns of) Khuzistān, which is situated

אור רוד יאולי פא מהיאן ישבט

awar rōd i-Ulai pa mahyān i-šebaṭ

on river EZ-(RN) by month EZ-Shebat

on the river Ulai (Eulaios), in the month of Shebaṭ,

סאל אלשלב למנין שטרות

sāl ʔlšlb lə-minyå̄n šəṭå̄r-ōṯ

year 1000+300+30+2^{H} for-reckoning.CS^{H} document-PL^{H}

(in) the year 1332 in the reckoning of the documents (i.e. of the Seleucid era) (= 1020/21 C.E.)

חצרא בודינד אפיש מאן חנה בת ישראל

(3)*ḥāḍir būd-end a-pēš mān Ḥannå̄h baṯ Yiśrå̄ʔēl*

present be.PST-3PL to-before our (FN)^{H} daughter.CS^{H} (MN)^{H}

There were present before us Ḥannah, daughter of Israel

בן יעקוב נוחו עדן

ben Yaʕăqōḇ nūḥ-ō ʕēḏen

son.CS^{H} (MN)^{H} rest-3M.SG^{H} paradise^{H}

b. Jacob, *his rest (be in) Paradise*,

ואחצרא כירד אדניאל בן ראובין יעזריה ימערופ פא בצא

u-iḥḍār kerd a-Dāniyēl ben Rəʔūḇēn i-ʕĂzaryāh i-maʕrūf(4)*pa bačča*

and-summons make.PST.3SG to-(MN) son.CS^{H} (MN)^{H} EZ-(MN)^{H} EZ-known by child

and he summoned Daniel b. Reuben, (son of?) ʕAzariah, who (is) known by (the name) "Baby"

ואידון גופת אין חנה בת ישראל כו

u-ēdōn guft ēn Ḥannå̄h baṯ Yiśrå̄ʔēl ku

and-thus say.PST.3SG this (FN)^{H} daughter.CS^{H} (MN)^{H} that

and thus said the above-mentioned Hannah, daughter of Israel:

שוד היסת אין דניאל בן ראובין ידאמאדום

šud hest ēn Dāniyēl ben Rəʔūḇēn i-dāmād-om

go.PST.3SG COP.3SG this (MN) son.CS^{H} (MN^{H}) EZ-son_in_law-my

"This Daniel b. Reuben, (who is) my son-in-law, has gone,

אבי פירמאנום ואבי שהותום וכנד
abē firmān-um u-abē (5)šahwat-um u-kand
without order-my and-without wish-my and-pull.PST.3SG
without my order and without my wish, and taken

אז סרא יבראדראנום יפא מיצר הינד שש צופת דר
az sarā i-barādar-ān-um i-pa Miṣr hend šaš juft durr
from house EZ-brother-PL-my EZ-in (PN) COP.3PL 6 pair pearl
from the house of my brothersת who are in Egypt, six pairs (of) pearls,

ופרוכת פא ביסת ופנץ דינאר ואין סרא
u-furōxt pa bīst u-panj dēnār u-ēn sarā
and-sell.PST.3SG by twenty and-five dinar and-this house
and sold (them) for twenty-five dinars. And this house

מילך יבראדראנום בוד סהל ויוסף וסעיד
(6)milk i-barādar-ān-um būd Sahl u-Yōsep̄ u-Saʕīd
property EZ-brother-PL-my be.PST.3SG (MN) and-(MN)^{H} and-(MN)
was the property of my brothers Sahl, Joseph and Saʕīd,

בני ישראל בן יעקוב נוחו עדן
bən-ē Yiśrā̊ʔēl ben Yaʕăqōḇ nūḥ-ō ʕēḏen
son.PL.CS^{H} (MN)^{H} son.CS^{H} (MN)^{H} rest-3.M.SG paradise^{H}
sons of Israel b. Jacob, his rest (be in) Paradise”

וגופתינדאש פיראן כו בד כירדי אין כירדי כו
u-guft-end-a-š pīr-ān ku bad kerd-ī ēn (7)kerd-ī ku
and-say.PST.3SG-to-him old-PL that bad do.PST-2SG this do.PST-2SG that
And the elders said to him, “You did wrong (that) you did this, that

דסת אנדר בורדי פא מילך יצוד אז כודית
dast andar burd-ī pa milk i-jud az xwad-ɪt
hand inside carry.PST-2SG by property EZ-separate from self-your
you laid hand(s) on property other than your own,

ונא חלאלית היסת פאין יכירדי
wa na-ḥalālī-yat hest pa-ēn i-kerd-ī
and not-lawful-your COP.3SG by-this EZ-do.PST-2SG
and yours is a (state of) lawlessness for what you have done.”

וצואב דאד כו פא צרורא כירדום
u-jawāb dād ku pa (8)ḍarūra kerd-om
and-answer give.PST.3SG that by necessity do.PST-1SG
And he answered, “I did (it) out of necessity,

אז דסת ידילומ כו מופתלא בודום
az dast i-dil-um ku mubtalā būd-om
from hand EZ-heart-my that suffering be.PST-1SG
out of my’ heart(’s desire) (i.e. out of greed), because I was suffering”.

וגופתינדאש פיראן כו ואגיב היסת אור תו
u-guft-end-a-š pīr-ān ku wājib hest awar tō
and-say.PST-3PL-to-him old-PL that necessary COP.3SG upon you
And the elders said to him, “It is incumbent upon you,

דניאל בן ראובין עוציש דאדן

Dāniyēl ben Rəʔūḇēn (9) *ʕawaḍ-iš dādan*

(MN) son.CS^{H} (MN)^{H} exchange-his give.INF

Daniel b. Reuben, to give recompense for it

ואחולא כואסתן אז כודאונדאן ימילך

u-(a-?)ḥawāla xwāstan az xwadāwand-ān i-milk

and-assignment ask.INF from owner-PL EZ-property

and to ask for a (note of) assignment from the owners of the property".

וגופת אין דניאל בן ראובין כו

u-guft ēn Dāniyēl ben Rəʔūḇēn ku

and-say.PST.3SG this (MN) son.CS^{H} (MN)^{H} that

And the above-mentioned Daniel b. Reuben said,

תיסי מן רא אפיש אין סהל ויוסף

tis-ē man rā a-pēš (i-?)ēn Sahl (10) *u-Yōsep̄*

thing-INDEF I for to-before (EZ-?)this (MN) and-(MN)^{H}

"There is something of mine with ("before") these (men) Sahl, Joseph,

וסעיד בני ישראל בן יעקוב נוחו עדן היסת

u-Saʕīd bənē Yiśrā̄ʔēl ben Yaʕăqōḇ nūḥ-ō ʕēḏen hest

and-(MN) son.PL.CS^{H}(MN)^{H} son.CS^{H} (MN)^{H} rest-3M.SG^{H} paradise^{H} COP.3SG

Joseph and Saʕīd, *sons of Israel b. Jacob, his rest (be in) Paradise*,

וראצי הום אפיש ישומאן פיראן כו נביסיד

u-rāḍī hom a-pēš i-šumān pīr-ān ku nibēs-ēd

and-content COP.1SG to-before EZ-you old-PL that write.PRS-2PL

I am content before you elders that you write

ודריסת כוניד אברם פאן ידריסת בוד כו ראצי בודום

u-d(i)rist kun-ēd (11) *abar-um pa-ān i-d(i)rist buw-ad ku rāḍī būd-om*

and-right do.PRS-2PL upon-me by-that EZ-right be.PRS-3SG that content be.PST-1SG

and adjust (it) upon (i.e. against) me, in that which it is correct that I (should?) have been content.

היסת כו עוץ יאין דרהא איסתאנינד

hest ku ʕawaḍ i-ēn durr-hā estān-end

COP.3SG that exchange EZ-this pearl-PL take.write.PRS-3PL

There is (something) that they (will) take as a recompense for these pearls.

אזיר ידסתשאן עוצ אין דינאר פרוכתום

azēr i-dast-išān ʕawaḍ (i-)ēn (12) *dēnār f(u)rūxt-om*

under EZ-hand-their exchange (EZ-)this dinar sell.PST-1SG

I have secretly ("under their hands") sold dinars as a recompense for this,

וסתדום כה דינאר יקואמי יסלטאני

u-stad-om kḣ dēnār i-qawāmī i-sulṭānī

and-take.PST-1SG 20+5 dinar EZ-regular EZ-sulṭānī

and taken (for it) 25 regular(?) sulṭānī dinars".

וראצי בוד וקנין סתדים אז דסת

u-rāḍī būd u-qinyān stad-ēm az dast

and-content be.PST.3SG and-possession^{H} take.PST-1PL from hand

And he was content, and we took possession from the hand

אין דניאל בן ראובין יעזריה ימערופ פא בצא

i-ēn Dāniyēl ben Rəʔūḇēn (13) *i-ʕĂzaryāh i-maʕrūf pa bačča*

EZ-this (MN) son.CS^H (MN)^H EZ-(MN)^H EZ-known by child

of the above-mentioned Daniel b. Reuben (son of?) ʕAzariyah, who (is) known as "Baby",

פא צאמא סיזיד קנין סתדן

pa jāma (i-?)sez-ed qinyān stadan

in garment (EZ-?)fit.PRS-3SG possession^H take.INF

in the garment (in which) it is fitting to take possession,

פא חקי סיני ואמרי חורב לרצונו ותאותו

pa ḥuqqē Sīnay wa-ʔimrē Ḥōreb li-rṣōn-ō wə-taʔăwat-ō

by law.PL.CS^H (PN)^H and-word.PL.CS^H (MN)^H to-wish-3M.SG^H and-desire-3M.SG^H

by *the laws of Sinai and the sayings of Ḥoreb, at his wish and desire.*

ובטלא כירד אין דניאל בן ראובין יעזריה

u-bāṭil kerd (14) *ēn Dāniyēl ben Rəʔūḇēn i-ʕĂzaryāh*

and-void make.PST.3SG this (MN) son.CS^H (MN)^H EZ-(MN)

And the above-mentioned Daniel b. Reuben (son of?) ʕAzariyah abandoned

הר מודעי עד סוף כל מודעין

har muddaʕ-ē ʕad sōp̄ kol muddaʕīn

every claim^H-INDEF until^H end^H all^H claim.PL^H

all (further) claim (on it), *until the end of all claim(s).*

ונבישתים ודאדים פא דסת יחנה

u-nibišt-ēm u-dād-ēm pa dast i-Ḥannā̊h

and-write.PST-1PL and-give.PST-1PL to hand EZ-(FN)^H

And we wrote and gave (it) into the hand(s) of Ḥannah,

בת ישראל בן יעקוב נוחו עדן

bat Yiśrā̊ʔēl ben (15) *Yaʕăqōḇ nūḥ-ō ʕēḏen*

daughter.CS^H (MN)^H son.CS^H (MN)^H rest-3M.SG^H paradise^H

daughter of Israel b. Jacob, *his rest (be) in Paradise*,

תא בוד אזמרש בוזישת וחוצת

tā buw-ad azmar-iš bōzišt u-ḥujjat

so_that be.PRS-3SG for-her relief and-proof

that there may be a relief and proof for her.

עזריה בן אברהם בן עמאר סעדאן בן דניאל בן סעדאן

ʕĂzaryāh ben Abraham ben ʕAmmār (16) *Saʕdān ben Dāniyēl ben Saʕdān*

(MN)^H son.CS^H (MN)^H son.CS^H (MN) (MN) son.CS^H (MN) son.CS^H (MN)

(Signed:) ʕAzariah b. Abraham b. ʕAmmār, Saʕdān b. Daniel b. Saʕdān.

3.2 Text 2: The Cairo Genizah "Letter nr 3" (ed. Paul, forthcoming)

פניי דירזאישן ביה פירזאם מאדר

Recto(1)*p(ad) n(ām i) *xudā* (2)*dēr-zihišn beh firzām mādar*

by name (of) God long-life good end mother

In the name of God. (Oh) mother, (may you have) a long life and a good end,

ובראדראן יגראמי יפא אפר <<? ʔAbū Mūsā, Ḥayyim>>
u-barādar-ān i-girāmī i-pa afr(āz?) ... (3)*(u-)ʔAbū Mūsā, Ḥayyim*
and-brother-PL EZ-dear EZ(REL)-by acclivity(?) (and-)ʔAbū Mūsā, Ḥayyim
and dear exalted brothers ... (to) ʔAbū Mūsā, Ḥayyim

ואהרן יסולימאן (א)[ז] תנחום סולימאן צאידא(ן) ... (א)פ(רי)ן יי
u-ʔAharon i-Suleymān (a)[z?] Tanḥum Suleymān jāyedān ...(4) *(ā)f(rī)n (i-)*xudā*
and-Aron^{H} EZ-Suleyman from? Tanhum Suleyman eternal blessing (EZ-)God
and Aaron, sons of Sulaymān, (from?) Tanḥūm, son of Sulaymān, eternal ... may God's blessing

פ(א) תן וצאן י(שמא בא)[ד] פאן הפתא נאמא תאן
p(a) tan u-jān i-(šumā b-ā)[d] pa-ān hafta nāma tān ...
by body and-soul EZ-you be.PRS-SBJV.3SG by-that week letter your
be upon your body and soul. In that week, your letter ...

בגדאד פא דיליש ואמא יי א(ב)ר מאדר יגראמי
(5)*Bagdād pa dil-iš u-ammā *xudā a(ba)r mādar i-girāmī*
(PN) by heart-his and-but God upon mother EZ-dear
Baghdad in his heart. But the Lord [may ...?] upon the dear mother

ו(ב)[ראדראן] ... אגה בודום
u-(ba)[rādar-ān] ... (6)*āgah būd-om*
and-brother-PL aware be.PST-1SG
(and) [brothers?] ... I was aware.

בג נאמא צואב פא שרח נבישתום תאן ...
dō-sih nāma jawāb pa šarḥ nibišt-om tān ...
2-3 letter answer by explanation write.PST-1SG you ...
I wrote you two (or) three letters (in) response, for explanation ...

דירזהישן ابو الحسن اعزه الله وارجو
(7)*dēr-zihišn ʔAbū 'l-Ḥasan ʔaʕazza-hu allāh wa-ʔarǧ-ū*
long-life (MN) make_strong.PRF-him God and-wish.IPFV-1SG
ʔAbū l-Ḥasan, may he have a long life, *(and) may God give him strength. And I wish*

כו (דס)תאן (ר)סיד נבישתי כ(ו) ... כוהום ש(ו)דן ...
ku (das)t-ān (ra)s-ed nibišt-ī k(u) ... (8)*xwāh-om šudan*
that hand-PL arrive.PRS-3SG write.PST-2SG that want.PRS-1SG go.INF
that it arrives at (your?) hands. You wrote th(at) ... I want to go.

אומיד דארום כו פ(א ש)לום רסידי ונאמאת פר(ס)[תאדי]
ummēd dār-om ku p(a ša)lom rasīd-ī u-nāma-t firi(s)[tād-ī]
hope have.PRS-1SG that by peace^{H} arrive.PST-2SG and-letter-your send.PST-2SG
I hope that you arrived in peace, and (that you) sent your letter

(ס)למתי אז בצרה פא זודיה אן שאללה ומן שב ורוזום
(9)*(sa)lāmatī az Baṣrah pa zūdīh ʔin šāʔa llāh u-man šab u-rōz-om* ...
health from (PN) by speed if^{Ar} want.PRF.3SG^{Ar} God^{Ar} and-I night and-day-my ...
(in?) health from Basrah quickly, *God willing*. And (by) my day and night, I ...

תא דידן תאן ואיד(ו)ן עזמום ה(יס)ת כו
(10)*tā dīdan tān u-ēd(ō)n ʕazm-um h(es)t ku*
so_as see.INF your and-thus wish-my COP.3SG that
so as to see you, and so it is my resolution that

בעד אז פסח בי (א)[ים] ונא דאנם כו

baʕd az Pesaḥ be (ā)[y-om] ... (11) *u-na dān-om ku*

after from Pessach[H] VPT come.PRS-1SG and-not know.PRS-1SG that

(I come?) after Passover ... And I do not know

צי רסידאם וליכין אזאן יפא דילום מי בו[ד] ...

če rasīd-a-m wa-lēkin az-ān i-pa dil-om mē buw-ad ...

what arrive.PST.3SG-to-me and-but from-that EZ-by heart-my VPT be.PRS-3SG ...

what has befallen me, but of that which is in my heart ...

גונא גונא פא סבב תאן ופא סבב דיר(ז)ה(י)שן מאדר

(12) *gōna-gōna pa sabab tān u-pa sabab (i-)dēr-zihišn mādar*

sort-sort by reason your(PL) and-by reason (EZ-)long-life mother

all kinds of things, on account of you and on account of mother, may she have a long life,

וכהר[אן יגראמי] ... וצפ(י)ש נא דאנם נבישתן

u-xwāhar-[ān i-girāmī?] ... (13) *waṣf-(i)š na dān-om nibištan*

and-sisters-PL EZ-dear description-his not know.PRS-1SG write.INF

and the [dear?] sister[s] ... I cannot describe it in writing.

תא ״י״ רושן כונאד אבר אנדא(ם) [ישמא]

tā xudā rōšn kun-ād abar andā(m) [i-šumā?] ... (14)

so_that God bright do.PRS-SBJV.3SG upon body EZ-you.PL ...

May God illuminate upon [your] body ...

והמא ישראל ופרציש בי פרי(ס)תאד פא פצליש ורח[מתיש]

u-hama Yiśrå̄ʔēl u-faraj-iš be firist-ād pa faḍl-iš u-raḥmat-iš ...

and-all Israel[H] and-relief-his VPT send.PRS-SBJV.3SG by grace-his and-mercy-his ...

and the whole of Israel, and may He send His relief by His grace and me[rcy] ...

כ ס נ(ב)ישתי כו דאדום אגה ב(וד)ם

(15) **panj-sad s. ni(b)išt-ī ku dād-om āgah būd-om*

five-hundred s. (=?) write.PST-2SG that give.PST-1SG aware be.PST-1SG

You wrote, "I have given 500 s". I was aware (of it)

ואנ(יז) פיש אזין ס(ו)[פתא] ... פא ש׳ ס פ(ר)יס(תא)דם

u-anēz pēš az-ēn s(u)[fta] ... (16) *pa *sē-sad s fi(r)is(tā)d-om*

and-also before of-this bill by three-hundred s. (=?) send.PST-1SG

and I also sent, before this, a bi[ll of exchange] over 300 s

תא פא [הו](ל)ת דה(י)ד .. (?) .. כש(א) .... סיניזי פס

tā pa (?)hawālat dah-(e)d..(?).. (?)kaša .... (17) *Sīnīz-ī pas*

so_that by cheque give.PRS-3SG (?) (PN)-ADJ then

so that you (pl.) may give it through a (?)cheque .... Sīnīzī fabric. Then,

פס אוי אז הולת סופ[ת]אי פא ק׳ ס בי נביסת

*ōy az hawālat suf[t]a-ē pa *sad s. be nibišt*

he from cheque bill_of_exchange-INDEF by 100 s. VPT write.PST.3SG

from the (?)cheque, he wrote a bill of exchange over 100 s.

(ק) [ס] באז דאדום פס פא רוז ק׳ ק׳ בי דה(י)ד

*(*sad) [s.]* (18) *bāz dād-om. pas pa rōz *dō-sad be dih-(ē)d*

100 s. back give.PST-1SG then by day two-hundred PTV give.PRS-2PL

I have given back (the) 100 [s]. Then, (if?) you give 200 on the day,

אין עלי אבא(ז) א(י)[ד] (ו)אבזון קבצי
ēn ʕAlī abā(z) ā(y)[-ed] (19) (u-)abzōn qabḍ-ē
this (PN) back come.PRS-3SG and-interest invoice-INDEF
this ʕAlī comes back and takes an interest invoice

אזיש סתאנד אב(ר) יהושו(ע) דריא מוסי הר(ו)ן
az-iš stān-ad ab(ar) Yəhōšū^{a}ʕ Daryā Mūsā (20) Hārūn.
from-him take.PRS-3SG upon (MN)^{H} (MN) (MN) (MN)
from him, upon (the account of) Joshua, Daryā, Mūsā (and) Hārūn.

צותר מא כוהי(ד) (ו)כאר תאן בי בזאריד
juttar ma kun-ēd u-kār-tān be bizār-ēd.
separate not do.PRS-2PL and-work-your VPT fulfill.PRS-IMP.2PL
Do not act otherwise and fulfill your work.

נבישתי כו יכי אז שאם אמד
nibišt-ī ku yak-ē (21) az Šām āmad
write.PST-2SG that one-INDEF from (PN) come.PST.3SG
You wrote that someone came from Damascus

ויאקות וזמרוד ומרו׳ אוורד
*u-yāqūt u-zumurrud u-*murw(ārīd) āwurd*
and-ruby and-emerald and-pearl bring.PST.3SG
and brought rubies, emeralds and pearls

פא אל׳ דינר ופא בגדאד פרוכת
*pa *hazār dēnār u-pa (22) Baɣdād f(i)rōxt.*
by 1.000 dinar and-by (PN) sell.PST.3SG
for 1000 dinar and sold (them) in Baghdad.

אגה באש כו אין אז חלב וחימס ואן סאמאן אוורד
āgah bāš ku ēn az Ḥalab u-Ḥims u-ān sāmān (23) āwurd.
aware be.IMP that this from (PN) and-(PN) and-that region bring.PST.3SG
Know (sg.) that he brought this from Aleppo and Hims and that region.

והר וקתי מי ארינד אז אן סאמאן אידר פא בסיארי
u-har waqt-ē mē ār-end az ān sāmān ēdar pa bisyārīh
and-every time-INDEF VPT bring.PRS-3SG from that region here by abundance
Whenever they bring (it) from that region, (it is) in abundance here

וסוד(י)נייך פדיש מי כונינד צי פאן סא(מ)א(ן)
(24) *u-sūd (i-)nēk pad-iš mē kun-end čē p(a)-ān sā(m)ā(n)*
and-profit (EZ-)good by-it VPT do.PRS-3PL for by-that region
and they make a nice profit with it, because in that region

ארזאן מי אופתיד פס הרצ יאזין גונא אופתיד
arzān mē (25) uft-ed. pas harč i-az-ēn gōna uft-ed
cheap VPT fall.PRS-3SG then all_that EZ-from-this kind fall.PRS-3SG
it comes (lit., "falls") cheap. Then, anything of this kind that comes (along),

ארזאן כריד ומרו׳ כהון כריד צי אידר פא בהא היסת
*arzān xir-ēd. u-*murw(ārīd) (26) kahwan xir-ēd čē ēdar pa bahā hest.*
cheap buy.PRS-IMP.2PL and-pearl old buy.PRS-IMP.2PL for here by value COP.3SG
buy (pl.) (it) cheap. And buy old pearls, because they are valuable here.

פאים סאל מגרביאן ב(ס)יאר אמדינד וכרידינד

pa-im sāl maγribī-yān (27) bisyār āmad-end u-xarīd-end.

by-this year Maghrebinian-PL many come.PST-3PL and-buy.PST-3PL

This year, many Maghrebinians came and made (their) purchases.

וצנד נוסכא יבסיאר נבישתום ת(א)ן והרצ ניבשתום

u-čand nusxa i-bisyār nibišt-om tān (28) u-harč nibišt-om

and-some copy EZ-many write.PST-1SG you and-whatever write.PST-1SG

And I wrote you (pl.) quite some copies (i.e. letters), and whatever I wrote,

כאר אזיש כוניד תו דירזהישן מאדר יגראמי

kār az-iš kun-ēd. tō dēr-zihišn mādar i-girāmī

work from-it do.PRS-IMP.2PL you long-life mother EZ-dear

act according to it. You, dear mother – (may you have a) long life –,

אגה באש כו הרצ נבישתי אגה בודום

(29) āgah bāš ku harč nibišt-ī āgah būd-om

aware be.IMP.2SG that whatever write.PST-2SG aware be.PST-1SG

know that anything you wrote, I was aware

אז תהלההא ירסידאת וליכין צי שאהיד כ(י)רדן

az tahlīh-hā i-rasīd-a-t (30) wa-lēkin čē šāh-ed kerdan

of bitterness-PL EZ-arrive.PST.3SG-to-you and-but what may.PRS-3SG do.INF

of the bitternesses that have befallen you, but what can one do

אילא שוכר יי כירדן הרצ אוי כונאד

*illā šukr (i-)*xudā kerdan? harč ōy kun-ād*

except thanks (EZ-)God do.INF whatever he do.PRS-3SG

except thanking the Lord? Whatever He does,

המא דאוריה ראסת היסת ביש אזין מאנדא

(31) hama dāwarīh (i-)rāst hest. bēš az-ēn mānda

all judgement (EZ-)right COP.3SG more of-this remain.PPP

all (of it) is just judgement. (?Even if) more of this has remained,

זנאד מאן סכתיה ובס בי כונאד

zan-ād mān (32) saxtīh u-bas be kun-ād

strike.PRS-SBJV.3SG us hardship and-much VPT do.PRS-3SG

let Him strike us (with) hardship, and may He end (it),

פא פצליש ורחמתי(ש) אנ(ו)ן נאדאנם נבישתנית אז גם

pa faḍl-iš u-raḥmat-iš. anūn na-dān-om (33) nibištan-it az γam

by grace-his and-mercy-his now not-know.PRS-1SG write.INF-you of grief

with His grace and mercy. I cannot write you now of (my) grief

פא סבב תאן (ו)פא סבב כוהראן יגראמי

pa sabab tān u-pa sabab (i-)xwāhar-ān i-girāmī.

by reason your and-by reason (EZ-)sister-PL EZ-dear

because of you and because of the dear sisters.

וגילא בראד אבו עמר נבישתי

(34) u-gila (i-)barād ʔAbū ʕUmar nibišt-ī

and-complaint (EZ-)brother (MN) (MN) write.PST-2SG

And (as for) the complaint(s) of brother ʔAbū ʕUmar, (of which) you wrote,

וזיאנהא בוד תאן ציז נא שאהיד כ(י)רדן

u-ziyān-hā (i-)būd tān (35)čē-z na šāh-ed kerdan.

and-loss-PL (EZ-)be.PST.3SG your thing-too not may.PRS-3SG do.INF

and the losses (which) they were for you, one cannot do anything.

פס פאין סבבהא חילי מי כונום כו

Verso(1)*pas pa-ēn sabab-hā ḥīl(a)-ē mē kun-om ku*

then by-this reason-PL stratagem-INDEF VPT do.PRS-1SG that

Then, for these reasons, I (will) arrange (it)

בעד א(ז) פסח׳ בי אים צי דילום א(ר)אם ניסת

baʕd a(z) Pesaḥ be āy-om (2)čē dil-um ā(r)ām nēst.

after of Pessach^{H} VPT come.PRS-1SG for heart-my calm is_not

to come after Passover, because my heart is not calm.

תא יי רושן כונאד אבר א[...] ישמא

*tā *xudā ʕazza wa-jalla rōšan kun-ād abar*

may_that God be_mighty.PRF.3M.SG^{Ar} and-be_lofty.PRF.3M.SG^{Ar} bright do.PRS-SBJV.3SG upon

May the Lord, *the Exalted and Mighty*, illuminate your body

המא ישר׳ פא פצל(יש) ורחמת(י)ש וכאר תאן בי בזאריד

a[ndām?] (3)i-šumā hama Yiśrāʔēl pa faḍl(-iš) u-raḥmat-(i)š. u-kār tān be

body EZ-your all Israel^{H} by grace-his and-mercy-his and-task your VPT

your body (and) the whole of Israel, by His grace and mercy. And fulfill your task

ומודארא בראד אבו עמר כוניד כו שאהיד כו

(4)*bizār-ēd u-mudārā (i-)barād ʔAbū ʕUmar kun-ēd ku šāh-ed ku*

fulfill-IMP.2SG and-kindness (EZ-)brother (MN) (MN) do.PRS-IMP.2PL for may.PRS-3SG that

and treat brother ʔAbū ʕUmar well, for it is possible that

אין ה אל׳ ס בעד אז המא אין סאלהא באז דהיד תאן

ēn (5)panj hazār s baʕd az hama ēn sāl-hā bāz dah-ed tān.

this five 1.000 s after of all this year-PL back give.PRS-3SG you

he may return to you these 5.000 s after all these years,

צי דאנם כו יכ יכי סוד ביש פדיש כירד

(6)*čē dān-om ku yak-yakē sūd beš pad-iš kerd.*

for know.PRS-1SG that one-one profit more by-it make.PST.3SG

because I know that he has made some profit with it.

ואין נא דהיד אז יי אין מי כוניד

*u-ēn na (7)dah-ed az *xudā ēn mē kun-ed*

and-this not give.PRS-3SG from God this VPT do.PRS-3SG

And (if?) he does not give this, from the Lord (I beg) he (will?) do this,

יי רחמתאן פא דיליש אבגנאד אמן

**xudā raḥmat-(t)ān pa dil-iš (8)abgan-ād ʔāmēn.*

God mercy-your by heart-his throw.PRS-SBJV.3SG amen^{H}

may the Lord put ("throw") mercy for you (lit., "your mercy") in his heart, amen.

אנון פא חילי כאר בזארדן (ב)[ש] פא הר גונא היסת

anūn pa ḥīl(a?)-i kār bizārdan (bā)[š] pa har (9)gōna [i-]hest

now by stratagem-EZ work fulfill be.IMP by every sort COP.3SG

Now, arrange to fulfil (your) task (and), in any way there is,

נאמא תאן מא בוריד דרוד ואפרין יי

*nāma tān ma burr-ēd. durōd u-āfrīn (i-)*xudā*
letter your PROH cut.PRS-IMP.2PL health and-blessing (EZ-)God
do not stop (writing) ("do not cut off") your letter(s). May the Lord's blessings

פא תן וצאן ישמא באד נבישת אין נאמא

pa (10) *tan u-jān i-šumā b-ād. nibišt ēn nāma*
by body and-soul EZ-you be.PRS-SBJV.3SG write.PPP this letter
be upon your body and soul. This letter (was) written

אז בית אלמקד(ס) (ר)וז ב ש כ פא טיבת

az Bayt al-maqdis (11) *(r)ōz 2-š(amba)20 pa Ṭevet*
from house[Ar] DEF-holy[Ar] day Monday 20 by Ṭevet[H]
from Jerusalem, (on) Monday, the 20th of Ṭevet.

ד(ר)וד פ(די)ר(י)ד אז כאנא מאן אבר כוציכ בזורג תאן

(dur)ōd pa(dī)r-(ē)d(?) az xāna mān abar (12) *kūčik- buzurg tān*
greeting accept.PRS-IMP.2PL from house our upon small big your
Accept greeting(s) from our house, upon young and old of you.

דרוד צהד פא כונדן אבר כודכ די(ר)זהשן כוהר יגראמי

durōd. jahd pa xwāndan abar kōdak dē(r)-zihišn (13) *xwāhar i-gerāmī*
health effort by read.INF upon young long-life sister EZ-dear
Greetings. And make an effort to read (it) to my dear young sister, may she have a long life,

בי כוניד תא (פ)א זדיה (ני) כואנד

be kun-ēd tā (p)a zudīh (be?) xwān-ed
VPT do.PRS-IMP.2PL so_that by speed VPT read.PRS-3SG
so that she reads (it) quickly.

ונא(מ)א[תאן] נביס(י)דאם ת(א) יי

u-nā(m)a[-tān] (14) *nibēs-(ē)d-a-m t(ā) *xudā*
and-letter-your write.PRS-IMP.PL-to-me so_that God
And write me your letters, May that the Lord

(א)ין עלמא מא בראדאם תא באז בינם תאן

[i-]ēn ʕālam ma burr-ād-a-m tā bāz bēn-om (15) *tān*
[of-]this world PROH cut.PRS-SBJV.3SG-to-me so_that again see.PRS-1SG you
of this world not cut me off, so that I may see you again,

פא פצליש דרוד מצחפהא י(ת)רא ידרוסת הר[צ]

pa faḍl-iš. durōd. muṣḥaf-hā i-(to)rā i-durust ha[r]č
by grace-his greeting book-PL EZ-(To)rah EZ-right all_that
by His grace. Greetings. Fine Torah codices, anything that

איא[ד] אז בצרה ובגדאד בי כריד

āy-ā[d] (16) *az Baṣrah u-Baγdād be xir-ēd*
come.PRS-SBJV.3SG from (PN) and-(PN) VPT buy.PRS-IMP.2PL
may come from Basrah and Baghdad, buy (it),

צי סוד נייך פדיש היסת

čē sūd (i-)nēk pad-iš hest.
for profit (EZ-)good by-it COP.3SG
for there is a good profit in it.

3.3 Text 3: Tafsir Ezekiel 3.13-14 (ms. p. 8.6-21) (ed. Gindin 2007)

וקול כנפי החיות משקות אשה

[3.13] (6) *wə-qōl kanpē ha-ḥayyōṯ maššīqōṯ ʔiššā̊(h)*

and-voice.CS^{H} wing.DU.CS^{H} DEF-creature.PL^{H} touch.PTCP.PL.F^{H} woman^{H}

And the noise of the wings of those living creatures that touched one another, (rest of verse: *and the noise of the wheels over against them, and a noise of a great rushing*)

אל אחותה ובאנג פריהא אן ג׳אן דאראן

(7)*ʔɛl ʔăḥōṯ-ā̊h u-bāng (i-)par-ihā (i-)ān jān dār-ān*

to^{H} sister.CS-3SG.F^{H} and-noise (EZ-)wing-PL (EZ-)that life having-PL

And the noise of the wings of those living creatures

שקשק זנאן בודנד הר יכי אבא המבאז או

(?)šaqšaq zan-ān būd-and har yakē abā hambāz (i-)ō

(?) striking-PL be.PST-3PL every one with companion (EZ-)it

(that?) were (?)fluttering each one with its companion,

ובאנג אן בכראיהא פא בראבר אישאן בודנד

(8)*u-bāng (i-)ān (?)baxirā-ihā pa barābar (i-)ēšān būd-and*

and-noise (EZ-)that (?)-PL by against (EZ-)them be.PST-3PL

and the noise of the (?)wheels that were over against them,

ובאנג לרז זלזלא בוזורג

u-bāng (i-)larz (i-)zilzila (i-)buzurg

and-noise (EZ-)trembling (EZ-)earthquake (EZ-)great

and the noise of the trembling of a great earthquake.

בי נמוד כי אין באנג כי אן וקת שנידום

be namūd ki ēn bāng (9)*kē ān waqt šanīd-om*

VPT show.PST.3SG that this noise which that time hear.PST-1SG

(Commentary:) He intimated that: The sound which I heard at that time

כי אין כנפים יכ פא יכ המי זדה אמדנד

kē ēn kənā̊payim yak pa yak hamē zada āmad-and

which this wing.DU^{H} one by one VPT beaten come.PST-3PL

(was that?) which these *wings* were beating against one another,

פא קיבל אן כי משיקות אבר כנפים פיוסתה הסת

pa qibal (i-)ān ki (?)maššīqōṯ(10) *abar kənā̊payim paywasta hast*

by side (EZ-)that that (?)touch.PTCP.SG.F^{H} upon wing.DU^{H} bound is

because *maššīqōṯ* refers to *wings*.

וגופתן וקול האופנים לעומתם גופת כי

u-guftan wə-qōl hā̊-ʔōpannīm lə-ʕummā̊ṯ-ā̊m guft ki

and-say.INF and-voice.CS^{H} DEF-wheel.PL^{H} to-opposite-3PL.M^{H} say.PST-3SG that

and saying: *and the noise of the wheels were over against them* said (i.e. means) that

באנג אן אופנים כי ברמבר אן חיות בודנד בי שנידום

bāng (i-)ān ʔōpannīm(11) *kē barambar (i-)ān ḥayyōṯ būd-and*

noise (EZ-)that wheel.PL^{H} that against (EZ-)that creature.PL^{H} be.PST-3PL

The sound of those *wheels* which were facing those *creatures*,

בי שנידום פא פסוק פיש גופת

be šanīd-om pa pasuq (i-)pēš guft
VPT hear.PST-1SG by verse (EZ-)before say.PST.3SG
I have heard (it). In the preceding verse, he said:

קול רעש גדול ברוך כבוד יי ממקומו

qōl raʕaš gā̊ḏōl bā̊rūḵ kəḇōḏ (12)*y'y mim-məqōm-ō*
voice.CS^H trembling^H big^H blessed^H glory.CS^H God^H from.place.CS-his^H
a noise of a great trembling (and I also heard that) the glory of the Lord was praised from its place

ואבאז אידר גופת וקול רעש גדול

u-abāz ēdar guft wə-qōl raʕaš gā̊ḏōl
and-again here say.PST.3SG and-voice.CS^H trembling^H big^H
and here again he says: *and a noise of great trembling*

ומאניד כי ג באנג שניד הסת

u-mān-ed ki se bāng šanīd hast
and-seem.PRS-3SG that 3 noise hear.PST.3SG COP.3SG
it seems that he has heard three sounds:

אולא קול רעש בי שניד ואניז

awwala(n) (13)*qōl raʕaš be šanīd u-anīz*
first voice.CS^H trembling^H VPT hear.PST.3SG and-also
first, he heard a *noise of trembling*, and also

הם פא אן רסם בי שניד תא המי גופת

ham pa ān rasm be šanīd tā hamē guft
even by that manner VPT hear.PST.3SG so_that VPT say.PST.3SG
in the same manner, he heard so that he said:

ברוך כבוד יי ממקומו

bā̊rūḵ kəḇōḏ y'y mim-məqōm-ō
blessed^H glory.C^HS God^H from-place.CS-3SG.M^H
blessed be the Lord of the glory from his place

ואבאז קול רעש גדול בעד אז אן בי שניד

(14)*u-abāz qōl raʕaš gā̊ḏōl baʕd az ēn be šanīd*
and-again voice.CS^H trembling^H big^H after of this VPT hear.PST.3SG
and again he heard afterwards a *noise of great trembling*

צונין פא אין פסוק גופת וקול רעש גדול

čunēn pa ēn pasuq guft wə-qōl raʕaš (15)*gā̊ḏōl*
so by this verse say.PST.3SG and-voice.CS^H trembling^H big^H
so he says in the present verse: *and a noise of great trembling.*

ורוח נשאתני ותקחני

[3.14] *wə-rūᵃḥ nəśā̊ʔaṯ-nī wat-tiqqā̊ḥē-nī …*
and-spirit^H lift.PF.3SG.F-me^H and.CONS-PRET.3SG.F-me^H
And the spirit lifted me up, and took me away, (rest of verse: *and I west in bitterness, in the heat of my spirit; but the hand of the Lord was strong upon me*)

ובאד אבר דאשת מרא ובי סתאד מרא

u-bād abar dāšt ma-rā u-be stād (16) *ma-rā*
and-wind up hold.PST.3SG I-DO and-VPT take.PST.3SG I-DO
And a wind lifted me up and took me,

ובי רפתום ... תהליגאן פא גרמי ג׳אן מן

u-be raft-om ... tahlgēn pa garmī (i-)jān (i-)man
and-VPT go.PST-1SG bitter by heat (EZ-)spirit (EZ-)I
and I went [....] bitter in the heat of my spirit,

ופיאמברי יי אבר מן סכת קוי בי בוד

u-payāmbarī (i-)y'y abar man saxt qawī be būd
and-prophecy (EZ-)God upon I very strong VPT be.PST.3SG
and the prophecy of God was very hard upon me.

בי נמוד כי גמגין ואנדוהגין ותהלגין בוד

be nimūd (17) *ki ɣamgēn u-andōhgēn u-tahlgēn būd*
VPT show.PST.3SG that sorrowful and-worryfull and-bitterfull be.PST.3SG
(Commentary:) He intimated that he was full of sorrow, worry and bitterness

פא קיבל אין כי גונאיהא כי יי גופת אורא כי

pa qibal (i-)ēn ki gōnā(y)-ihā ki y'y guft ō-rā ki
by side (EZ-)this that sin-PL which God say.PST.3SG he-to that
because of the sins concerning which the Lord said to him that

ישראלן לא יאבו לשמוע אליך

yiśrå̄ʔēl-ān (18) *lō(ʔ) yō(ʔ)ḇū li-šmōᵃʕ ʔēlɛ-ḵå̄*
Israelite[H]-PL not[H] want.IPF.3PL.M[H] for-hear.INF[H] to-you.SG.M[H]
the Israelites *will not hearken unto thee*

וגופת כי בית מרי הנד

u-guft ki bēṯ mərī hand
and-say.PST.3SG that house.CS[H] rebellion[H] COP.3PL
and he says that they are *a rebellious house*.

וגופתן ויד יי עלי חזקה

u-guftan wə-yad y'y ʕala-y ḥăzå̄qå̄(h)
and-say.INF and-hand.CS[H] God[H] upon-1SG[H] strong.F[H]
And (as) to the words *the hand of the Lord was strong upon me*

מאניד כי גופת כי אין נבואתיהא סכת הסת

mān-ed ki guft ki ēn (19) *nabawāt-ihā (i-)saxt hast*
seem.PRS-3SG that say.PST.3SG that this prophecy-PL (EZ-)hard COP.3SG
it seems that he said that these are the severe prophecies

כי יי יחזקאל רא אגה בי כרד

ki y'y yiḥɛzqēl rā āgah be kerd
that God[H] Ezekiel[H] for known VPT make.PST.3SG
that the Lord informed Ezekiel

כי פא ישראלן כואהד כרדן

ki pa yiśrå̄ʔēl-ān xwāh-ad kardan
that by Israelite[H]-PL want.PRS-3SG do.INF
that he would inflict on the Israelites.

ואין מאניד צ׳ון כחזקת היד וסרני מלכת

u-ēn mān-ed (20) *čon kə-ḥɛzqaṯ hay-yā̊ḏ wə-yissərē-nī mil-lɛḵɛṯ*

and-this seems.PRS-3SG like as-strength.CS^{H} DEF-hand^{H} and-admonish.PF.3SG.M-1SG^{H} from-go.INF^{H}

And this seems like *while his hand was strong upon me and warned me not to walk* [Is 8.11].

ומעני חזוק יד פא אין ג׳אגה

u-maʕnī(-ye) ḥăzōq yaḏ pa ēn jāgah

and-meaning(-EZ) strengthen.INF.CS^{H} hand^{H} by this place

And the meaning of *ḥăzōq yaḏ* (= the strengthening of the hand) in this place (is):

אכבאר סכתיהא כי כואסת כי אברד אבר ישראלן

axbār (i-)saxtī-hā ki xwāst(21) *ki āβar-ad abar yiśrā̊ʔēl-ān*

news (EZ-)severity-PL which want.PST.3SG that bring.PRS-3SG upon Israelite^{H}-PL

make known the severities that he wanted to bring upon he Israelites.

Abbreviations

Arg. An Early Jewish-Persian Argument (ed. MacKenzie 1968)
Db. EJP commentary on Daniel, text b (ed. Shaked 1982)
Du1. 1st EJP. letter from Dandān-Uiliq (ed. Utas 1969)
Du2. 2nd EJP. letter from Dandān-Uiliq (ed. Zhan/Guang 2008)
Ez. EJP. tafsir of Ezekiel (ed. Gindin 2007)
Gen. EJP. tafsir of Genesis (unpublished)
Gr. EJP Grammatical texts (ed. Khan 2000)
Is. EJP. tafsir of Isaiah (unpublished)
Kd. Karaite document (ed. Shaked 1972)
Koll. Kollam plates (ed. Cereti 2009)
L1–L23 EJP. letters 1–23 from the Cairo Genizah (mostly unpublished, except L2, L6, ed. Shaked 2011, and L3, ed. Paul 2021
Lr. EJP. Law report (ed. Asmussen 1965, transl. MacKenzie 1966)
T1–T11 Tafsirs 1–11 (unpublished)
Zef. EJP. psalms from Zefre (ed. Netzer 2002)

References

Asmussen, Jes P. 1965. “Judaeo-Persica II. The Jewish-Persian Law Report from Ahwaz, A. D. 1020.” *Acta Orientalia* 29: 49–60.

Cereti, Carlo G.. “The Pahlavi Signatures on the Quilon Copper Plates (Tabula Quilonensis).” *Exegisti monumenta. Festschrift in Honour of Nicholas Sims-Williams*, eds. Werner Sundermann, Almut Hintze, and François de Blois. Wiesbaden: Harrassowitz, 31–50.

Gindin, Thamar E. 2007. *The Early Judaeo-Persian Tafsīrs of Ezekiel: Text, Translation, Commentary. Vol. I: Text. Vol. II: Translation*. Vienna: Verlag der Österreichischen Akademie der Wissenschaften.

Khan, Geoffrey (ed.). 2000. *Early Karaite Grammatical Texts* (Masoretic Studies 9). Atlanta: Society of Biblical Literature.

Lazard, Gilbert. 1963. *La langue des plus anciens monuments de la prose persane*. Paris: C. Klincksieck.

MacKenzie, David N. 1966. “Ad Judaeo-Persica II Hafniensa.” *Journal of the Royal Asiatic Society* 1966: 69.

—. (ed.). 1968. “An Early Jewish-Persian Argument.” *Bulletin of the Society of Oriental and African Studies* 31: 249–269.

Netzer, Amnon 2002. "An Early Judaeo-Persian Fragment from Zefreh. Psalms 44:24–27, 45:1–9 and 55:2–16." *Jerusalem Studies in Arabic and Islam* 27: 419–438.

Paul, Ludwig. 2013. *A Grammar of Early Judaeo-Persian*. Wiesbaden: Harrassowitz.

—. (ed.). 2021. "The Early Judaeo-Persian Letter L3 (T-S 18 J 3.16)." *Journal of Jewish Languages* 9: 77–99.

Shaked, Shaul. 1972. "Teʕuda qaraʔit qeduma be-parsit yehudit." *Tarbiz* 4: 49–58. [An early Karaite document in Judaeo-Persian]

—. (ed.). 1982. "Fragments of two Karaite Commentaries on Daniel in Judaeo-Persian". *Irano-Judaica* [I]: 304–322.

—. (ed.). 2011. "Persian-Arabic bilingualism in the Cairo Genizah documents." *From a sacred source: Genizah Studies in Honour of Professor Stefan C. Reif*, eds. Ben Outhwaite and Siam Bhayro. Brill: Leiden, 319–330; 416–417.

Utas, Bo. 1968 (1969). "The Jewish-Persian fragment from Dandān-Uiliq." *Orientalia Suecana* 17: 123–136.

Zhang Zhan, Shi Guang. 2008. "A Newly-discovered Judaeo-Persian Letter." *Journal of the Dunhuang and Turfan Studies* XI: 71–99.

Juhuri / Judeo-Tat(i) / the Language of the Mountain Jews

Dan Shapira, Bar-Ilan University

1. Introduction

Juhuri / Judeo-Tat(i) / the Language of the Mountain Jews (*zuhun tati*; *zuhun juhuri*) is an Iranian language derived from a spoken form of a sister-language of Early New Persian [NP] and heavily influenced by Azeri Turkic and Russian. It was traditionally spoken in Jewish communities of the Eastern and Northern Caucasus (Northern Azerbaijan, Southern-Central Dagestan, Nalchik, Grozny, and more), known as the Mountain Jews (*dağ-çifut*; *gorskie jevrei*; *yehudim harariyim / qavqaziyim*). All speakers, especially males, were and are multilingual (Azeri and other languages in Azerbaijan, Azeri, and/or Qumıq and other languages in Dagestan, Balqar/Malqar in Nal'chik, in addition to Russian, and to some extent, Hebrew. By now, the heritage-speakers of Juhuri speak Russian, Hebrew, English, and Azeri, sometimes, even all of these.

There are two very similar dialects, the Northern, Derbendi, in Dagestan and Nal'chik, and the Southern, Qubai, in Azerbaijan; the first one is sometimes more archaic than New Persian and is more remote from NP than the second one (Griunberg 1982: 232). Judeo-Tat does not reflect dialectal unity with neighboring Tati dialects, spoken, mostly in the past, by Muslim populations (both Sunni and Shiʕi dialects[1]); these Tati Muslim dialects of Azerbaijan and Dagestan, in turn, are to be distinguished from the so-called Southern Tati dialects of northern Iran.[2] On the other hand, Judeo-Tat is close to a dialect of the New Persian type spoken, in the past, by a small Armenian-Grigorian community in north-western Azerbaijan. During the 19th and 20th centuries, Judeo-Tat was adopted by smaller Jewish linguistic minorities of Transcaucasia and northern Caucasus (speakers of Neo-Aramaic, Kurdish, Azeri, and probably Adyge-Circassian[3]). Though Jewish populations had been recorded in northern and central Dagestan more than a millennium ago, we cannot be certain that there is a continuous link between these Jewish populations and the Mountain Jews of southern Dagestan and northern Azerbaijan.

There is no linguistic evidence to support the claim that the Mountain Jews descend from Iranian military colonies established during the Sassanid period (226–641 CE) on

1 See Griunberg 1963a, 1963b; these two works do not treat Judeo-Tat, rather the Muslim-Tati dialects. On varieties of the Tati dialects cf. also Vsevolod Miller 1892, 1901, 1905, 1907, as well as Boris Miller 1945.

2 Yar-Shater 1969. The word "Tat" means "a settled Iranian population subjugated to Nomadic Turks and living in a symbiosis between land-toilers and Nomads". The term is widely used across Eurasia, compare the (obsolete and now offensive) Hungarian word for Slovaks and (rarer) Slovenes, *Tót* (pl. *Tótok*).

3 On the last one, cf. Shapira 2010.

the northern frontier of the empire. The ancient / early-medieval Caucasian-Albanian/ Aghvanian Christian texts referred to the Jews as "merchants" (*vačar*)[4].

In 1459, in Shirvān (now northern Azerbaijan), Moshe ben ʔAharon ben Sheʔrith composed a dictionary of the Hebrew language, titled *Egron*, with translations into standard Jewish New Persian of the post-Mongol period[5]. It seems that the ancestors of the Mountain Jews migrated from Iran to Transcaucasia and the eastern and northern Caucasus during the post-Mongol, and, especially, Safavid period, where they adopted the already existing Tati dialects spoken by local Muslims. In 1612, Shāh Abbās I, the Great (reigned 1588–1629), had established a new capital at Faraḥābād (Sārī in Māzandarān), where he settled, *inter alia*, thousands of Jewish families from the Caucasus. After his death, many inhabitants abandoned the city with some returning to their native places. Jews suffered badly during the 1741–1745 Nādir-Shāh's campaign in Dagestan. In the 18th and the early 19th centuries, more Jews from the neighboring Gīlān came to the Caucasus, where their descendants are still known as a semi-separate group among the Mountain Jews. Between 1804 and 1828, the Russian Empire conquered from Iran, *inter alia*, what is now Dagestan and Azerbaijan. These were times of tribulation for the ancestors of the Mountain Jews, who began to leave the mountain villages, where they had been dispersed, and moved to the safety of Russian fortresses, especially Derbend/ Darband, later Petrovsk (now Makhachkala/Mahaç-Qalʕah, Dagestan), and Quba (northern Azerbaijan). Nowadays, the Mountain Jews are found mainly in Israel, as well as in well-organized communities in Quba, Moscow, New York, Derbend, and Nal'chik.

In the 19th century, the Mountain Jews used a variant of the Hebrew script, called by them *bağdadi*, to write letters and notes. No Judeo-Tati texts from the 19th century are known. The only text written in Hebrew characters from the 19th century, known as being composed by a Mountain Jew, was in a Turkic language, Azeri or Qumıq (published in Shapira 2001–2002: 495f.). Before 1917 only two printed books existed in Judeo-Tat, both translated from Hebrew, *Metleb Sioniho* 'Zionists' Aim', and a Sephardi prayer book, both printed at Vilna. In the days of the First World War, a Hebrew newspaper appeared, *Hed Harım* 'Mountains' echo'. In the Soviet period, the Mountain Jews were recognized as one of the nationalities of the Republic of Dagestan, and their language ("Tati", actually, the Derbend dialect) became one of the five official languages of the Dagestan Republic. In 1928/1929, as a measure of secularization, the Latin alphabet was imposed on this language, replacing the Hebrew alphabet used in Dagestan (in Nal'chik in 1930). This happened in the context of the general Latinization politics in the USSR, which would include also Russian. However, by 1939 the language politics changed and all the Latin scripts were replaced by the Cyrillic alphabet. In the Soviet period, especially ifrom the 1920s to the 1940s, there existed many Judeo-Tat schools, newspapers, and other publications.[6] In the 1960s, some community leaders in Soviet Dagestan (but not in Azerbaijan) promoted the politics of "Tatization", claiming a non-Jewish origin of the Mountain Jews and encouraging them to register as "Tats". How-

4 Shapira 2015: 16.

5 Netzer 1999: 29–30.

6 See Zand 1985 and 1986.

ever, there were no registered "Tats" other than the Mountain Jews". Though withering, this language (the Derbendi dialect) is now one of the 14 official languages of Dagestan.

Since 1956, a literary almanac in Tati (*tatskij*, actually, Judeo-Tati/Juhuri), *Sovet Vatanimu* (Совет Ватаниму, 'Our Soviet Homeland') has been published yearly. In the 1959 Soviet census, about 30,000 Jews declared Tati (*tatskij*) as their mother tongue. By now, Judeo-Tat is an endangered language, and almost all Mountain Jews of Dagestani origin now speak Russian and/or Hebrew. The dialect of Quba in Azerbaijan seems to be more of a living language,[7] but it is barely known to scholars. There are limited publishing activities in Israel and Russia, restricted, however, to Hebrew and Russian.

2. Grammatical notes

2.1 Phonology

The language is derived from a sister-dialect of Late Middle / Early New Persian, and its grammar is very similar to that of the spoken variety of New Persian of Iran. As in spoken NP, *ā* shifts to *ō*, and sometimes to *ū*. Unlike in NP, the older intervocalic *-t-* shifts to *-r-* (rhotacism;[8] in NP, *-t-* shifts to *-d-*).

The sound *v-* did not shift to *b-* (**vāta-* 'wind' > **vār* > *vor*, cf. NP *bād*/*bōd*; **varka-* 'leaf' > *valg*/*vəlg*, cf. NP *barg*); Qubai *ov* 'water' vs. Derbendi *ʕav* represents another development.

Due to the impact of Azeri/Qumıq, there are two vowels *ü* and *ö*. Also, there are elements of Turkic-derived vowel harmony.

In the 1950s to 1960s, the sounds *ʕ* and *ḥ* still existed in the speech of older speakers, not only in Hebraisms, but also in words of Iranian origin, e.g., *ʕasb* 'horse' (– [equally in this word in post-Mongol Judeo-Persian written with *ʕayin*], *ḥozor* 'thousand', *ḥofd* 'seven', *ḥoftə* 'week').

The quality of the reduced / open sound written as *ə* in Latinized and Cyrillic Azeri and pronounced as *æ* in Azeri is uncertain. Here, it is transcribed as *e*, *a*, *ə*, and *æ*. It seems that in the older forms of Derebendi and Quba'i, there were different realizations of this vowel.

2.2 Morphology and syntax

Basically, Juhuri grammar is very similar to that of NP, with a number of differences:

Unlike in NP, the adjective precedes the noun, with unstressed *-æ*/*-ə*/*-a* added to the adjective: *xúb-æ xunæ* '[a] good house (NP: *xāne-yi xub* / *xune-ye xub*).

The *Izāfet* (NP: *xāne-yi xub* / *xune-ye xub*; *Īrān-e mā* 'Iran of us / our Iran') is almost lost, appearing after vocalic end only: *sula-i sičan* 'hole of [a] mouse', but *duvar xunæ* '[the] wall of [the] house'. Another construction mimics the Turkish *Izāfet* (actually, the Azeri one: *peder-i-n ev-i* 'of [the] father his house'): *piyær-æ xune-y-i*.

7 Cf. Borjian and Kaufman 2016.

8 Other forms of rhotacism can be noted in Iranian loanwords in Classical Armenian, in Talyshi, in Gilaki/Giliki, and in Mazruni.

Unlike NP that has one postposition *-rā* only, Juhuri has several ones, e.g., the instrumental-comitative combination of a preposition and two postpositions [**ba- >*] *e/ə … rə+voz* [< **rāδ/rā+*apāč/bāz*] 'with'.

As in NP and in most Iranian languages and dialects, the verb has two bases, that of the past and that of the present/future. However, in Juhuri, the *mi*-present (*mī kon-am* 'I do / I will do') shifted to the eventualis, with a new form arising, probably, under the impact of a similarly-formed Lezgian form, built on the infinitive, whose base-form in Iranian is normally in the sphere of the past. As the final *-n* of the Infinitive *[-d]en* has dropped, after having been nasalized but having been retained in the new present form, the derivation became less transparent. Here is the paradigm for 'I, etc., do / am doing (base s*ox*- 'do'):

	SG	PL
1	*sox-d-e-n-um*	*sox-d-e-n-im*
2	*sox-d-e-n-i*	*sox-d-e-n-it*
3	*sox-d-e-n-i*	*sox-d-e-n-ut*

Only in the Northern (Derbendi) dialect an optative is found (from an older conjunctive):

	SG	PL
1	*-om*	*-oym*
2	*-oš*	*-ošit*
3	*-o*	*-ošut*

2.3 Lexicon

There are a number of Hebrew and Aramaic loanwords, *e.g., e.g., malaxomovit* (מלאך המות), *memiriz/məmzir* (ממזר), *gid* (גט), *miʕit* (מועד), *gennadim* (גן עדן), *boruxo* [ברוכה, from Aramaic], etc. It seems that the older stratum of Hebrew/Aramaic loanwords reflects a different pronunciation of the Hebrew language than the younger loanwords.

3. Texts

3.1 Sample Text 1

The following is taken from the oldest extant Judeo-Tati text. It certainly dates more than a couple of centuries back, but was linguistically updated several times, as was the case with all Jewish Bible translations. It is taken from the prayer book (סדור קול תפלה אה עדת ג׳מעת האי ספרדי, אסף בה״ר יותם פינחסאוו, ווילנא תרס״ט בדפוס י׳ פיראזשניקאוו) and the Biblical verses in it are translated, thus being part of the traditional *Targum*. The late Professor Michael Zand was of the opinion that the language was heavily Persianized.

Neh 9:5–6 (*Siddur*, pp. 70–71):

ויברכו שם כבודך ומרומם
וַא ברוכה בִּירַת נומי עוזַתְתו וא בּוּלונדָורי תּו

və boroxo birat num-i ʕüzzet-ə-tü və bülündür-i-tü
and blessing be.OPT[9].3SG name-IZAF[10] glory-of-2SG and exalted-of-2SG
Blessed be Your exalted name of glory

על כל ברכה ותהלה אתה הוא ה׳ לבדך
אַסר המי בּרוכה הא ותחריפ-יַתִיהָא תוני או ה׳ אַה תחנַיִתו

a-sar hami boroxo-ho və təḥərifiyat-i-ho tü-n-i u H a taḥna-yi-tü
to[11]-head all blessing-PL and praise[12].PL[13]-IZAF-PL 2SG-COP-2SG he God to[14] only[15]-IZAF-2SG
above all blessings and praises. You are He, God, (to) You alone,

אתה עשית את השמים שמי השמים וכל צבאם
תו סכדָי אָסמורה אסמוי אסמו הָרא והמי לשגַר השורַא

tü saxdi asmu-ra asmu-yi asmu-ho-ro və hami lašgar-ho-šu-ro
2SG do.PAST.2SG sky-ACC.POSTP sky-IZAF sky-PL-ACC.POSTP and all army-PL-POSS.3PL-ACC.POSTP
You made the heaven, the heaven of heavens and all their army/host,

הארץ וכל אשר עליה הימים
כרירה וַא המי אסר יו וריהרא דריהּהָרא

xori-ro və hami a-sari-y-u vari-ho-ro dariyo-ho-ro
earth/land-POSTP and all to[16]-head-IZAF-POSS.3SG on[17]-PL-POSTP sea-PL-POSTP
the earth[18], and all things that are therein

וכל אשר בהם ואתה מחיה את כלם
והמי אַיִשוְ דרִי הרא תו זוהונדַני הממשורא

və hami a-yi-šü dar-i-ho-ro tü zühünda-n-i hammi-šu-ro
and all in-IZAF-3.POSS.PL in[19]-IZAF-3PL-POSTP 2SG making.alive-PRES-2SG all-3POSS.PL-POSTP
the seas, and all that is therein, You preserve them all,

9 This is an archaic form not in use anymore.

10 The *izāfet* here is archaic or mimics NP usage.

11 **p/bad* > *e/a/æ/ə* (deletion of the consonants).

12 Possibly, **taʕrīf*.

13 Classical NP/ Arabic plural.

14 A calque of Hebrew *lə-* in *lə-ḇad-əḵā*.

15 NP *tanhā*, here with metathesis and *h* > *ḥ*.

16 **p/bad* > *e/a/æ/ə*.

17 The use of this preposition is one of the pieces of evidence testifying to the fact that the translation is old/archaic, or that it had a NP *Vorlage*, or that it represents a dialect now dead. *bar-i* is 'Tati' form of the Classical Persian *ba-rā-y-i* / Dari (Afghanistani Persian) *bar-i* 'for', contaminated with *bar*, 'on, above'. The Southern Tati (Muslim dialects of Azerbaijan) form is *bei* / *bäri*, the Derbendi form is *er-i* (both from **pat* + **rā-i*, see Griunberg and Davydova 1982: 279). The form as in this Bible translation is unattested outside this *siddur*.

18 A word of unknown etymology.

19 NP *dar* (Middle Persian *andar*) has no correspondence in Tati (see Griunberg and Davydova 1982: 279). Thus, here it is an archaism or reflects a NP *Vorlage*.

וצבא השמים לך משתחוים
וא לשַׁגַרהָיֵי אסמו אַתו סַר זַרנות

və lašgar-ho-yi asmu a-tü sar zar-n-ut
and army-PL-IZAF sky to-2SG head hit[20]-PRES-3PL
and the hosts of heaven worship You.

3.2 Sample Text 2[21]

The excerpt is taken from the following source: *Sifir en Yuno. Sifir ez Tanax. Novi Yuno, kuk Amitay Terjüme ə zuhun juhuri doği / Sifir ən Yuno. Sifir əz Tanax. Novi Yuno, kuk Amitay Targum ə zuhun cuhuri doği*, published in Israel in 2011.

Jonah 1:1–9

וַיְהִי דְּבַר ה׳ אֶל יוֹנָה בֶן אֲמִתַּי לֵאמֹר:

bisdo gof Adonoy ə-kin Yuno kuk Amitay və gufdi:
become.PST.3SG speech[22].of God to[23]-wards[24] Jonah son Amittai and say.PST.3SG
It became speech of God to Jonah son of Amittai and He said:

קוּם לֵךְ אֶל נִינְוֵה הָעִיר הַגְּדוֹלָה

vəxiz bura ə Ninvi ə kələ šəhər
arise[25].IMP.2SG go[26].IMP.2SG to[27] Nineveh to big city
Arise, go to Nineveh, to the big city

וּקְרָא עָלֶיהָ

və noviyəti sox ə tovun ənu-ho
and prophecy[28] make.IMP.2SG to about of-3PL
and [make] prophecy about them

כִּי עָלְתָה רָעָתָם לְפָנָי:

čün-ki bəd-i-ho-y ənu-ho vəromorət ə pušo-y mə
because[29] bad-ABSTR.SUBST.SUFF-PL-IZAF of-3PL arise.PST.3SG[30] to before[31]-IZAF 1SG
for their badness arose before Me.

20 "to hit with one's head", a calque from Azeri *baš urmaq*, means "to ask humbly". NP *zadan* (from **zata-*), where *-d-* is part of the base and not the infinitive ending *–den*, corresponds to Old Tati **zaran*; probably, an uncertain vowel was pronounced between *-r+n-*.

21 Der Imidi Publishing, Inc P.O. Box 51 Belfast, ME 04915, USA. www.derimidi.com.

22 New Persian *gap*, from the same root as *guftan*.

23 From Middle-Persian *pat* > *pad* / New Persian *be*.

24 Probably, *kin* in *ə kin* is an archaism or a dialectal form. Agarunov 2005: 84: *əki*. Cf. Authier 2012: 69: "les prépositions *eki* et *ezki* sont sans doute issues de la grammaticalisation du nom *kin* qui existe encore sous la forme diminutive *kinle* 'foyer', avec chute du /n/ final".

25 Corresponds regularly to NP *bar-xīz*.

26 Corresponds regularly to NP *bo-ro*.

27 Corresponds regularly to NP *b-e*.

28 A Persian-like abstract noun formed from a Hebrew word in the pronunciation of the Mountain Jews / Iranian Jews.

29 A Persian word borrowed through Azeri.

30 Corresponds regularly to NP *bar-āmad*-3SG-*ət*.

31 Corresponds regularly to NP *pīš*.

וַיָּקָם יוֹנָה לִבְרֹחַ תַּרְשִׁישָׁה מִלִּפְנֵי ה'

ommo vəxüšd Yuno əri virixdə ə Taršiš əz pušo-y Adonoy
but arise[32].PST.3SG Jonah in.order.to escape.INF[33] to Tarshish from before-IZAF God
But he arose, Jonah, and escaped to Tarshish from before God,

וַיֵּרֶד יָפוֹ וַיִּמְצָא אֳנִיָּה

fur-omo ə Yəfo ofd gəmi-rə
descend[34]-PST.3SG to Jaffa find.PST.3SG[35] ship-*ra*.POSTP
he went down to Jaffa, he found the ship,

בָּאָה תַרְשִׁישׁ

ə Taršiš raf-də-n-bu-ho-rə
to Tarshish go.*ede*-*n*-be.PST-3PL-*ra*.POSTP[36]
exactly the one which went to Tarshish,

וַיִּתֵּן שְׂכָרָהּ וַיֵּרֶד בָּהּ

do müzd rəħ-rə və fur-omo ə gəmi
give.PST.3SG[37] reward road-*ra*.POSTP[38] and go.down-PST.3SG to ship
he paid the payment of the route and he went down to the ship

לָבוֹא עִמָּהֶם תַּרְשִׁישָׁה מִלִּפְנֵי ה':

əri rafdə ə u-ho-rə-voz ə Taršiš əz pušo-y Adonoy
in-order-that go.INF[39] with them[40] to Tarshish from before-IZAF God
in order to go with them to Tarshish from before God.

וַה' הֵטִיל רוּחַ גְּדוֹלָה אֶל הַיָּם

umohoy Adonoy ə dəryoh vəxüzünd kələ kulok
then God to sea arise[41].PST.3SG big wind
Then God arouse a big wind to the sea,

וַיְהִי סַעַר גָּדוֹל בַּיָּם

və Adonay ə dəryoh zurbo-yə šar
and God to sea blow.PL-IZAF ?[42]
and God made blows to the sea[43]

32 NP *bar-xāstan*.

33 NP *gerīxtan*. Here, a quasi-infinitive form.

34 NP *foru-āmadan*.

35 NP *yāftan*. The loss of the initial *y-* is unexplained by scholars.

36 The past of a rare form, what Authier 2012:177–180 calls this 'le focalisateur progressif-constatif *ede-*'. Note the double use of the postposition *rə* (used in the sense of accusative): 'that ship [ACC] that-was-bound-to-go-to… [ACC]. This mimics slightly a Turkic construction.

37 NP *dād*.

38 *ra* > *ə*.

39 NP *raftan*. Here, a quasi-infinitive form.

40 See above, a preposition and two postpositions [**ba-* >] *e/ə* … *rə-voz* [< **rāδ/rā+*apāč/bāz*], 'with'.

41 Causative (*və-xüzündə*) of *və-xüšdə* (NP *bar-xāstan*).

42 Possibly, misprinted NP **šod* 'it became' or Arabic *šarr* 'evil'?

43 This line seems to be another targum, possibly with a misprint in the last word. *zurbo*, from Arabic *ḍarba*, obviously means 'a blow / blows' (*zurba-ho* > *zurbo*).

וְהָאֳנִיָּה חִשְּׁבָה לְהִשָּׁבֵר׃

yəkəm mundən-bu əri gəmi xürd birə

a_bit leave[44]-be.PST.3SG so_that[45] ship break[46].PPP.3SG be.PF.3SG

little was left so that the ship would be broken.

וַיִּירְאוּ הַמַּלָּחִים וַיִּזְעֲקוּ אִישׁ אֶל אֱלֹהָיו

tərsir-üt gəmi-či-ho və dəšənd hər mərd ə xudo-y xüšdə

fear[47]-PST.3PL ship-či[48]-PL and cry[49].PST.3SG every man to god-IZAF his[50].own

They feared, (the) shipmen, and he cried, every man to his own god,

וַיָּטִלוּ אֶת הַכֵּלִים אֲשֶׁר בָּאֳנִיָּה אֶל הַיָּם

və dəšənd-üt ə[51] gəmi və-bir-üt-ho či-ho-rə ə dəryoh

and throw[52]-PST.3PL from ship on-be-PPP.3PL[53]-PL thing[54]-PL-*ra*.POSTP to sea

and they threw from the ship the things that were found on it into the sea

לְהָקֵל מֵעֲלֵיהֶם

əri gəmi suk birə

so_that ship light[55] be.PF.3SG

so that the ship would be lighter.

וְיוֹנָה יָרַד אֶל יַרְכְּתֵי הַסְּפִינָה וַיִּשְׁכַּב וַיֵּרָדַם׃

ommo Yuno fur-omo ə dorun gəmi dəgəšd xisi

but Jonah come_down-PST.3SG to inner ship lay[56].PST.3SG sleep.INF

But Jonah had descended to the inner part of the ship, he had laid himself to sleep.

וַיִּקְרַב אֵלָיו רַב הַחֹבֵל וַיֹּאמֶר לוֹ

sərvor gəmi künd bisdo ə kin ən-u və gufdi

commander ship close become.PST.3SG towards to-3SG and say.PST.3SG

The commander of the ship got close to him and said:

מַה לְּךָ נִרְדָּם קוּם קְרָא אֶל אֱלֹהֶיךָ

tü əri čü xisirəy? vəxiz minət sox ə Xudo-y-tü

2SG for what sleep.PRS.2SG arise.IMP.SG supplication make.IMP.SG to God-IZAF-2SG

Why do you sleep? Arise, make a supplication to your god

44 NP *māndan*.

45 Authier 2012: 155: 'particule d'exhortation. Le mot *heri* qui signifie 'oui' en réponse, s'emploie aussi avec les modes injonctifs'.

46 NP *xordan*, frequently used in composite verbs with the meaning 'to be exposed to something unpleasant'.

47 NP *tarsīdan*.

48 The Turkic suffix of professional duties.

49 *dəšəndə*(*n*).

50 her, its, *etc*.

51 A mistake, or an assimilation for **az*.

52 *dəšəndə*(*n*), an homonym of 'to cry'.

53 *və* (NP *bar*, 'on / above') *bir*, past base of 'to be', *üt*, 3PL.

54 NP *čīz*.

55 NP *sobok*.

56 NP *dar-gaštan*.

אוּלַי יִתְעַשֵּׁת הָאֱלֹהִים לָנוּ וְלֹא נֹאבֵד׃

bəlkəm yəzuğ omo Xudo-rə ə imu və puč ni-bošim

perhaps[57] regret come.PST.3SG God+*ra*.POSTP to 1PL and destroy.PPP NEG-be.OPT.1PL

perhaps (your) god would express regret to us and we would not be destroyed.

וַיֹּאמְרוּ אִישׁ אֶל רֵעֵהוּ

gufdir-ü gəmi-či-ho dü ə-yəki

say-PST.3PL ship-man-PL two to-one.one

They said, the sailors, one to another:

לְכוּ וְנַפִּילָה גוֹרָלוֹת וְנֵדְעָה

biyoyt čüp dəšən-im və dan-im

come.2PL wood throw-1PL and know-1PL

Come on, let us throw woods (lots) and we will know

בְּשֶׁלְּמִי הָרָעָה הַזֹּאת לָנוּ

ə sərəbot-i kom-inimun-i-gə omori-ho i bəd-i ə səri-mu

on-account-of[58] whose-of-one.1PL come-PST.3PL this bad-ABSTR.SUFF to head-1PL

on account of whom of us the badness has come on us (lit. “to our head”),

וַיַּפִּלוּ גּוֹרָלוֹת וַיִּפֹּל הַגּוֹרָל עַל יוֹנָה׃

čüp dəšəndit čüp ofdo ə sər Yuno

wood throw.PST.3PL wood fall.OLD.SUBJ.3SG to head (of) Jonah

they threw woods (lots), the lot fell on Jonah (lit. “to Jonah’s head”).

וַיֹּאמְרוּ אֵלָיו הַגִּידָה נָּא לָנוּ

pəsdə unə-gür gufdir-üt ə u xosdən-im məhlüm di ə imu

then[59] that-because_of[60] say-PST.3PL to[61] 3SG want.PRS-1PL known[62] give.IMP.SG to 1PL

So they said to him: We want that you make known to us

בַּאֲשֶׁר לְמִי הָרָעָה הַזֹּאת לָנוּ

ə sərəboti ən čü kor-tü omor-i ə sər-imu i bəd-i

to reason[63] of what work-(IZAF.)2SG come-PST.2SG to head-1PL this bad-ABSTR.SUFF

because of what work of yours did you come on us (lit. “our head”) with this badness,

מַה מְּלַאכְתְּךָ וּמֵאַיִן תָּבוֹא

čü-n-i pišə-y-tü əz komi-n-co omor-əy

what-COP.2SG-COP craft[64]-IZAF-2SG from which[65]-place[66] come-PF.2SG

what is your craft, from which place did you come,

57 A borrowing from Azeri.

58 Agarunov 2005:2 29b: *ə səribəti*.

59 Agarunov and Agarunov 1997: 135b: “the Derbendi form of *bəqdə*”.

60 Agarunov and Agarunov 1997: 171b: *unə-gyrə*.

61 *be.

62 From Arabic *maʕlūm*.

63 Seems to be a misprint for *səḇəboti.

64 NP *pīšeh*.

65 *komi* (NP *kodām*), ‘which’; *komini*, ‘which one exactly, that which’.

66 NP *jāh*.

מָה אַרְצֶךָ וְאֵי מִזֶּה עַם אָתָּה:

əz komi xori-n-i tü və əz komi ğəym-i tü?
from which land.COP.2SG 2SG and from which nation[67].COP.2SG 2SG
from which land are you, and from which nation are you?

וַיֹּאמֶר אֲלֵיהֶם עִבְרִי אָנֹכִי

Ħivri-n-üm mə cohob do u u-ho-ra
Hebrew-COP.1SG.1SG 1SG answer[68] give.PST.3SG[69] 3SG 3SG-3PL-*ra*.POSTP
He answered: I am a Hebrew,

וְאֶת ה׳ אֱלֹהֵי הַשָּׁמַיִם אֲנִי יָרֵא

əz Adonoy-Xudoy asmu tərs-irən-üm
from God-God.IZAF sky fear-PRS-1SG
I fear God of Heaven,

אֲשֶׁר עָשָׂה אֶת הַיָּם וְאֶת הַיַּבָּשָׁה:

komi-ki dəryoh nə-xüšgi-rə ofirri-ho
he-who sea and[70]-dry_land-*ra*.POSTP create.PST.3SG-3PL
he who created the sea and the dry land.

3.3 Sample Text 3

The following excerpt is taken from Borjian 2017: 273. It constitutes an excerpt from a text in the Quba dialect, recorded by Yakov Abramov in 2014 in New York (note that the loanwords *gorskiy* and *raznitsa* are taken from Russian and the loanword *hibru* from English):

e qed en zuvun gorskiy juvur-ho ambar-a gof-ho-y en hibru der-i
in interior of language mountain Jew-PL many-ATTRIB word-PL-GEN[71] of Hebrew be.in-3SG
In the language of the Mountain Jews are many Hebrew words.

i raznitsa en gorskiy juvur-ho ne tat-ho uni-ki.
this difference of mountain Jew-PL and Tat-PL thereof
This is the difference between the Mountain Jews and [the Muslim] Tat.

3.4 Sample Text 4

The text below is taken from Authier 2012: 13–14. From the outset, this text looks like belonging to the folkloric genre, but it is, in fact, a learned version of folk-history based on R. Sherbet. The following changes were made in the transcription: *ç* to *č* and *ş* to *š*.

67 From Arabic *qawm*.

68 From Arabic *jawāb*.

69 NP *dād* / *dod*.

70 The 'real' Tati for 'and', not the NP-derived *ve* as in previous examples.

71 I.e., *Izafet*.

imu ez Iron[72] *vedir-omori ho.*
we from Iran PREF-come.PPP 3PL
We (are those who) came from Iran.

az Iron vedir-omoreym imu e vileyet Modey[73] (araluq[74] Iron ne Azerbijan).
from Iran PREF-come.PF.1PL 1PL to country.of Media in.between[75] Iran and Azerbaijan
From Iran we came to the country of Media (between Iran and Azerbaijan).

zihisd-im imu e unjo ye čend sal e des en parčo y Peres ne Modey
live.PST-1PL 1PL to/in there[76] one several year in/to hand[77] of part IZAF Persia and Media
We lived there for several years in the area of part(s) of Persia and Media.

ez Modey nime y en juhur-(h)o raf-di e Samarkand[78] *ne Buxore,*[79]
from Media half IZAF of Jew-PL go.PST-3SG to Samarqand and Bukhara.
from Media (one) half of Jews went to Samarqand and Bukhara.

ommon imu omo-reym ä xori-ho y en Yevloq[80]
but[81] 1PL come-PF.1PL to land-PL IZAF of Yevlaq.
But we came to the lands of Yevlaq,

en Gyokčoy,[82] *Barda,*[83] *Mir-Bašir,*[84] *en Agdam.*[85]
of Gökçay Barda'ah Emir-Bashir of Aqdam
of Gökçay (Blue River), Barda'ah, Emir-Bashir, and Aqdam.

72 The authentic Juhuri form for "Iran", with the shift *ā* > *o*.
73 Hebrew *Māday*.
74 An assimilated Azerbaijani form of "what is between".
75 From Azeri.
76 **ān jāh* 'this place'.
77 **dast*.
78 The Russian form of Samarqand.
79 An authentic Juhuri pronunciation for Bukhara, obviously an old form.
80 Yevlax/Yevlakh, 265 km west of Baku.
81 Arabic *ʔammā*; Judeo-Tat used to have nasalization, a point that remains understudied.
82 The older Russian pronunciation of Göyçay, a region in the middle of Azerbaijan.
83 Barda'ah/Partev – an important historical city in the Wet of Azerbaijan.
84 Tərtər/Tartar, 330 km west of Baku. The name is used here in the Russian form of the Soviet-Azerbaijani name Mirbəşir (called after a Communist leader during the Soviet period).
85 The form of the name of the city of Ağdam (365 km west of Baku) is Russian.

ez Agdam juhuro-ho-y-mu ve-raf-dut e Zakatali,[86]
from Agdam Jew[87].PL-PL[88]-IZAF-POSS-1PL PREF[89]-go.PST-3PL to Zaqataly,
From Agdam, our Jews went to Zaqataly,

ez Zakatali raf-dut e Rutul,[90] *pesde ez Rutul furamor-ut e-Axti.*[91]
from Zaqataly go-PST.3PL to Rutul then[92] from Rutul come_down.PST-3PL to-Akhti
from Zaqataly they went to Rutul, from Rutul they descended to Akhti.

ez Axti yek-i-ho raf-dut e Kusari u-ho häy-säʕät zihisden-üt ä-Qube[93]
from Akhti one.IZAF-PL go.PST-3PL to Kusari 3SG-PL this-hour live.PRS-3PL in-Quba
From Akhti some of them went to Kusari, now they live in Quba,

yek-i ho raf-dut e Derrey-Qatta e lo y Mejelis[94]
one-IZAF PL go.PST.3PL to Derrey-Qatta to layer IZAF Mejelis
some of them went to Qatta Valley, to (where is) near Mejelis.

yek-i ige y ho š e Aksay ez unj ige e Xasavyurt.[95]
one-IZAF other[96] IZAF PL POSS.3SG to Aqsay from there other to Xasavyurt
Some others of them[97] (went) to Aqsay, from there to Khasavyurt.

References

Agarunov [Aharonov], Jakov Mikhailovich 1997. *Татско(еврейско)-русский словарь*. Moscow (1997. *Tati(Jewish)-Russian Dictionary*. Moscow).

Agarunov, Mikhail. 2005. *Jazyk gorskix jevrejev*, Vol. 1. Abilov. Zejnalov i synovja. Baku.

Anisimov, Nikolai [Naftali Tsevi].A. 1932. *Grammatik zuhun tati*. Moscow [in Judeo-Tat].

Authier, Gilles. 2012. *Grammaire juhuri, ou judéo-tat, langue iranienne des Juifs du Caucase de l'est.* Wiesbaden: Ludwig Reichert.

86 The Russian form of Zaqatala, a multi-ethnic mountainous town in Azerbaijan near the borders of Georgia and Dagestan.

87 **yəhūδ > juhur*, with Rhoticism, > *čuhur*; *čuhuri* = Jewish.

88 Double PL; the first form was **čuhur(h)o*, then *o* lost its PL sense and a new full form was added.

89 Corresponds vaguely to NP *bar-(raftan)*.

90 The Russian name of the village, the area, and a tiny Lezgian language on the Dagestani-Azerbaijani border.

91 A Lezgian village in Southern Dagestan.

92 Acts as filler; Derbendi.

93 A big Jewish town in Northern Azerbaijan, sometimes called 'the last Jewish *shtetl*' in the press.

94 One of the oldest Jewish settlements in Dagestan, in the mountains above Derbend. Founded in 1581 as the capital of the Qaytaq Utsmidom, whence the name ('seat of the ruler'). Avraham Firkowicz "found" there a pseudo-historical document, see Shapira 2006.

95 The Russian (from Qumıq) form of the Avar-Chechen-Qumıq-populated city in West-Northern Dagestan, close to the border with Chechnya.

96 *ige*, from **digar / dige*.

97 *-š*, being SG, refers to PL.

Borjian, Habib. 2017. "Judeo-Iranian Languages", *Handbook of Jewish Languages. Revised and Updated Edition*, ed. by Lily Kahn and Aaron D. Rubin. Leiden and Boston: Brill, 234–297.

Borjian, Habib, and Daniel Kaufman. 2016. "Juhuri: From the Caucasus to New York City", *International Journal of the Sociology of Language* 237: 59–74.

Griunberg ,Aleksandr Leonovich. 1963a. *Язык северо-азербайджанских татов*. Moscow (*Yazyk severo-azerbay-dzhanskikh Tatov*. Moscow).

Griunberg, Aleksandr Leonovich. 1963b. "Система глагола в татском языке." *Иранский сборник*. Moscow, 121–149.

Griunberg Aleksandr Leonovich, and Lidia Xanonova Davydova. 1982. "Tati Language." *Foundations of the Iranian Linguistics. New Iranian Languages: the Western Group, the Caspian Languages*. Moscow: Nauka, 231–228.

Miller, Vsevolod F. 1892. *Материалы для изучения еврейско-татского языка. Введение, тексты, словарь*, СПб. (*Materialy dlya izucheniya yevreyskotatskogo yazyka; Vvedenie, teksty, slovar'* (St. Petersburg 1892) / *Materials for Study of the Judeo-Tat Language. Introduction, Texts, Glossary*).

Miller, Vsevolod F. 1901. *Очерк морфологии еврейско-татского наречия*. Moscow (*Ocherk morfologii ievrejsko-tatskago narechia*. Moscow / *An Essay on morphology of the Judeo-Tati dialect*. Moscow).

Miller, Vsevolod F. 1905. *Татские этюды, Ч.1. Тексты и татско-русский словарь*. Moscow (*Tati Studies. Part I. Texts and Tat-Russian Dictionary*. Moscow).

Miller, Vsevolod F. 1907. *Татские этюды. Ч. II. Опыт грамматики татского языка*. Тр. Лазаревского ин-та вост. языков. Вып. 26. Moscow (*Tati Studies, Part II. An Attempt at a Grammar of the Tati Language*,. Trudy Lazarevskago Instituta Vostochnykh iazykov, 26.Moscow).

Miller, Vsevolod F. 1945. "Татские тексты", *Иранские языки*, I. М.-Л., 1945 ("Tati texts", *The Iranian Languages*, Vol.1. Moscow-Leningrad).

Nazarova, Evgenia. 2021 (in print). Терминологическая ситуация с названием языка горских евреев ("Terminological Situation of Juhuri"). *Judeo-Slavic Journal.*

Shapira, Dan. 2001–2002. "Miscellanea Judaeo-Turkica: Four Judeo-Turkic Notes (Judaeo-Turcica IV)." *Jerusalem Studies in Arabic and Islam* 27 [Shaul Shaked Festschrift]: 475–496.

Shapira, Dan. 2006. "Remarks on Avraham Firkowicz and the Hebrew *Mejelis 'Document'*." *Acta Orientalia Academiae Scientiarum Hungaricae* 59/2: 131–180.

Shapira, Dan. 2007. "Judeo-Tat (Zuhun Tati; Zuhun Juhuri)." *Encyclopaedia Judaica, Second Edition*, vol. 11: 560b–561b.

Shapira, Dan. 2010. "The Mamshukh Circassian Jews: A Jewish Community that never existed." *Studia Anthropologica. Festschrift in Honour of Michael Chlenov*, ed. by A. Fedorchuk and S. Chlenova. Gesharim: Moscow and Jerusalem, 139–144.

Shapira, Dan. 2014. "*'We Are a Very Ancient People.'* The Antiquity Discourse among the Jews of North-eastern Caucasus, Georgia, and Central Asia." *Studies in Caucasian, Georgian, and Bukharan Jewry. Historical, Sociological and Cultural Aspects,* ed. by Golda Akhiezer, Reuven Enoch, Sergei Weinstein. Ariel University, Institute for Research of Jewish Communities of the Caucasus and Central Asia, 20–34.

Shapira, Dan. 2015. "Studies on the Questions Regarding the Ancient Jewish Settlements in the Northern Iranshahr (Azerbaijan and Daghestan) According to the Caucasian Albanian, Islamic and Jewish (The Answer of the Khazar King Joseph) Sources." *ABBA* 8: 9–48 [in Hebrew].[98]

Sifir en Yuno. Sifir ez Tanax. Novi Yuno, kuk Amitay Terjüme ə zuhun juhuri doği / Sifir ən Yuno. Sifir əz Tanax. Novi Yuno, kuk Amitay Targum ə zuhun cuhuri doği. Belfast, ME: Der Imidi Publishing, 2011.

Yar-Shater, Ehsan. 1969. *A Grammar of Southern Tati Dialects*. The Hague: Mouton.

Zand, Michael. 1985–1986. "The literature of the Mountain Jews of the Caucasus." *Soviet Jewish Affairs* 15/2: 3–22; 16/1 (1986): 35–51.

98 אב"א, acronym of איראן, בוכרה, אפגניסטן.

Judeo-Turkic languages and dialects: Judeo-Crimean-Turkic, Krymchak, Karaim, and other varieties

Dan Shapira, Bar-Ilan University

1. Introduction

1.1 Some introductory remarks on terminology

Turkic and Turkish: in English and some other languages, there is a difference between "Turkic", meaning "any one of some forty languages belonging to the Turkic language group/family, including Turkish of Turkey", and "Turkish", reserved to the "Turkish of Turkey". In the last-mentioned language, there is no difference, purportedly, between these two meanings, with both expressed just by "Türk" (with "Turkish of Turkey" being called *Türkiye Türkçesi*).

"Tatar": this is another highly ambiguous term; originating in Mongolia, the term spread during the Mongol conquests of the 13th century westwards, becoming sometimes a sobriquet name of almost all Turkic-speaking Muslims in contact with Christians, especially, with the Poles, Lithuanians, and Russians.[1] Once ago, the name was used to claim heritage to Chingis-Khan. By the early twentieth century, Russians called the people we now call Azeris/Azerbaijanis by the name of "Caucasian Tatars", and spoke of "Lithuanian, Crimean, Volgan, Sibirian, Minussinsk, etc. Tatars". The Turkic languages used to be known in Russian and other languages as "Turkish-Tatar languages". As Chingis-Khan's heritage in Northern Eurasia happened to fall into the hands of the Muscovy Czardom/the Russian Empire/USSR and its vassal states, and as the vast majority of the speakers of Turkic languages used to live in these areas, these Russian conventions were frequently adopted by non-Russian scholars alike.[2] Nowadays, there are several hardly-connected Turkic ethnicities using the ethnonym "Tatar", generally, together with an adjective, e.g., the Crimean Tatars.[3] When the Russians and the early Soviets spoke of Crimean Tatars and their language[s], they meant the Turkic-speaking Muslims living in the Crimea, while some of these people would preferred to be called "Crimean Turks/Türks" or "Qırımčaqs/ Qırımçaqs" (another ambiguous term, see below), or simply "Crimeans". However, the Crimean Peninsula was not a homogenous entity, neither politically nor linguistically.

1 With an important exception of the Bashkirs, who were one of the estates (social classes) of the realm of their own.

2 For instance, the earliest scholarly article dealing with the Karaim language, written by an Austrian Pole, bore the title "Ein türk-tatarischer Dialect … in Halicz" (Grzegorzewski 1903).

3 The term "Tatar" is sometimes perceived as slightly pejorative, and among some Volgan-Tatar nationalists, there is movement, whose aim is changing their ethnonym to "Bulgar", after the Medieval Islamic Volgan Bulgaria. It is quite possible that in the future the Crimean Tatars will adopt "Q[ı]rımčaq" as their ethnonym.

1.2 The names of the languages and dialects

The Turkic-speaking Karaites were aware that they used three different Turkic languages, labeled by them *Lešon Qedar* (Karaim), *Leshon Yišmaʕel* (Turkish), and *Lešon Tatar* (Crimean-Tatar), sometimes mixing up these names. When the Karaites of the Russian Empire were discussing their linguistic future in the early twentieth century, they were divided as to the choice between Russian or "Tatar" (see the name of the article by Kokizov 1911), with some even optioning for Hebrew. The Rabbanite Jews (Q[ı]rımčaqs, Krymchaks, Krimchaks, etc.) of the Crimea called their Turkic language *Tatar Tili*. It is quite possible that the use of the glossonym "Tatar" by the Jews began in the Russian Imperial period only.

1.3 Turkic languages

The Turkic languages, together with the Mongolic and Tungusic language groups (and probably Korean and Japonic languages)[4], are generally seen to belong to the Altaic family of languages.

It is impossible to provide here even a short sketch of the basic Turkic grammar features, let alone all the dialects. Generally speaking, the Turkic languages belong to the SOV type, are pro-drop languages, are characterized by vowel harmony, agglutination of suffixes and post-positions (there are no prepositions), lack of grammatical gender, and lack of articles.

However, all the major Turkic languages have been part of the Islamic world, and their original speakers had been islamized through the vehicle of Classical/Early New Persian. Persian, with its Arabic component, had a profound impact on all Islamic Turkic languages and influenced, to different degrees, their inner structures (Ottoman and Modern Turkish, Azeri/Torkī of Iran, Chağatay, and Modern Uzbek are good examples; but this hardly applies to the Judeo-Turkic varieties, for Persian never was on the Judeo-Turkic curricula). It should be remembered that all the Turkic Muslim authors (those educated prior to the 1930s in the cases of the Russian Empire/USSR and the Ottoman Empire, or prior to the 1950s in the case of the People's Republic of China) and their readership was educated in Persian and Arabic.[5] Hence, the Muslim Turkic languages had developed grammatical and lexical means to render non-Turkic (Persian and Arabic) grammatical features, such as the definite article of Arabic (by *ol*, from an archaic form of pronoun of the 3SG[6]), or the use of the Persian conjunction *kī*.[7] In literary Mus-

4 According to the so-called "Macro-Altaic" theory. In the past, the Uralic languages (Finno-Ugric [like Finnish, Estonian, Saami, and the Fennic languages of the Middle Volga, as well as Hungarian and Hanty-Mansi [Ostyak-Vogul]; and more) were sometimes grouped together with the Altaic languages. Indeed, the two families have a great deal of structural similarity (agglutination, a large number of grammatical cases, lack of grammatical gender, use of postpositions, vowel harmony, and more).

5 Arabic, Persian, and Turkish, in this order, constitute the so-called "three-languages" (*elsine-i seláse*) in education, with the emphasis on Persian.

6 The same happened in Judeo-Turkic in order to render the Hebrew definite article. The direct object marker *ʔet* is generally rendered by *šol* + ACC in Karaite Crimean texts and *osol* < *ošol* + ACC in Halicz Karaim, by *ošol ol* + ACC in Krymchak Bible translations, by *ol* + ACC in Troki Karaim, and by *ʔošol* + ACC in Firk I Bib 143 (Num 19.10: *ʔošol ṭonlārini* = אֶת בְּגָדָיו; Num 19.13: *ʔošol miškan*

lim Turkic languages, there existed code-switching, applying to phrases or complete sentences in Persian and Arabic, similarly to what existed in Jewish languages with regard to Hebrew and Aramaic.

In addition, in the case of Ottoman-Turkish authors, their mother tongues were of such different provenance as Southern Slavic, Greek, Circassian, Hungarian, Georgian, Albanian, and more. By the mid-19th century, almost all authors in Ottoman-Turkish were fluent in French, while those writing in Muslim Turkic languages in the Russian Empire were educated in Russian, frequently with some knowledge of French, too. This contact with languages of genealogically unrelated language families account for similar characteristics of the Muslim Turkic languages and the Jewish languages.

In addition, new grammatical categorizations were made in Karaim of the Eastern Europe in the 20th century, such as adding the instrumental case into the paradigm, or the re-categorization of tenses (or even acquiring the ability to render Slavic modes in the verbal system), all this because of the speakers' Russian and Polish education and multilingualism.

1.4 Classification of the Turkic Languages

All the Turkic languages are divided into two uneven groups – one living language belongs to the Oğur, or "Lir-Turkic", and the rest are called the Common Turkic, or "Shaz-Turkic".

The common Turkic languages and dialects are classified using various parameters and there are many different classifications. For our purposes, only two subgroups of the Common Turkic languages are relevant, the Oğuz (or Southwestern) and the Qıpčaq/ Qıpçaq (or Northwestern) subgroups. The majority of Judeo-Turkic idioms are Qıpčaq, a small minority are Oğuz, but many Qıpčaq varieties have Oğuz features, too.

1.4.1 Oğuz

This group includes Turkish, including Osmanlı (Ottoman) Turkish, various Turkish dialects (Rumelian, Anatolian, Karamanlı, Southern-Crimean, etc.), Azeri, Türkmen, Gagauz, and some other dialects/langauges in Iran, Syria, Iraq, the Balkan states, and China.

The Ottoman *eyâlet* (greater province) of Qırım included the Southern Coast and the Montaneous Crimea (Keffe/Caphá/Feodosija, the *Yayla*, Mangup), where a local Turkish dialect was spoken.[8]

In the Crimean Khanate (Bâhçe-Sarây, Gözleve/Jevpatorija, Qarasub/Qarasubazar/ Belogorsk), the Central Crimean-Tatar dialect was spoken containing both Qıpčaq and

ywy niŋ murdar-lādi = אֶת מִשְׁכַּן ה' טִמֵּא; Num 24.21: *d-kwrdy ʔwšwl qyny ny* = וַיַּרְא אֶת הַקֵּינִי). Note that the Troki Karaim and Karaite Crimean had traditions different from those of the three other ones. Cf. Olach 2013: 226.

7 Which happened to sound as the Hebrew *kī*, with roughly the same meanings. An example from Turkish: *bir adam ki öğüt din-le-mez*, lit. "a man that/who doesn't listen [to] advice", is now regarded "un-Turkish"; the standard form should be *öğüt din-le-me-y-en bir adam*, lit. "advice listen nothing one man".

8 For texts from the late 17th to the late 19th century, cf. Shapira 2001; 2002a; 2014a; 2015.

Oğuz traits.[9] In the northern Steppes, the Qıpčaq dialect/language of the nomadic Noğays was spoken; no Jewish varieties existed.[10]

1.4.2 Qıpčaq

This group includes, e.g., the language of a Christian collection of different compositions known as *Codex Cumanicus*;[11] Mamluk-Qıpçaq of Egypt and Syria;[12] Armeno-Qıpçaq of Galicia and Podolia;[13] Qumıq/Qumuq and Qaračay-Balqar/Malqar of the Northern Caucasus; the languages called "Tatar" of Qazan, Siberia, Astrakhan, the Central Crimea, etc.; Qazaq/Qazak and Qırğız; Noğay of the Northern Caucasus, Dobruca in Rumania and the Steppe-Crimea; and also the Karaim of Lithuania and Wolhynia-Galicia.[14]

The newly identified Jewish written language of the Golden Horde (dated by *circa* 1470–1500), even though possessing some Oğuz traits, belongs here, too.

1.4.3 "Crimean-Tatar"

The "modern" Crimean-Tatar language did not appear before 1928, when it was "engineered" by a Soviet commission. Prior to that, since the late 15th century, a local version of Ottoman Turkish, with many Qıpčaq traits, was used for writing. In the second part of the 19th century, the Crimea became the center of an interesting attempt to create an all-Turkic literary language. Ismail Gasprinski (1851–1814) was editing his journal, *Tercümân*, in a kind of a Turkic Esperanto devised by him ("the language of *Tercümân*");[15] then came the Nativist-oriented angry young men, who opposed Gasprinski's

9 Samojlovich 1916; 1929.

10 A unique text from 1860s in a Turkic language used in some contexts by the Montain Jews of the Eastern Caucasus, encouraging to *ʕaliyah* to Jerusalem, was published as Part IV in Shapira 2001–2002.

11 A Latin-Persian-Coman dictionary composed by the Italian monks at Sulkhat in 1294/1295; the MS was copied in 1303 on the Volga, at the Catholic St. John Monastery, and in the 1340s, the German monks added to it local Coman translations of the New Testament, the Catholic Prayerbook, a dictionary, and various texts. The *Codex Cumanicus* [Grønebech, K. 1942. *Komanisches Wörterbuch.* Einar Munskgaard: København; Golden, Peter B. 1992. "The Codex Cumanicus". In: *Central Asian Monuments*, edited by H.B. Paksoy, ISIS Press. https://web.archive.org/web/20050307164248/http://eurasia-research.com/erc/002cam.htm] is the only known document of purely Qıpčaq provenance.

12 In Mamluk-Qıpčaq works from Egypt and adjacent countries, the Qıpčaq elements are frequently mixed up with those Oğuz (identified as Turkmen). Cf. Pritsak 1959b.

13 Armeno-Qıpčaq (*xïpčax tili, tatarča*) documents from the 16th-17th century from Kamieniec-Podol'ski[ij] or books printed in L'vov/Lwów/Lemberg/Lemberik (Armeno-Qıpčaq: *Ilov*). See Grunin 1967.

14 Grammars and grammatical studies on the Karaim Language: Musaeev 1964 and Németh 2011 (both Halicz and Troki dialects); Kowalski 1929 (cf. Kowalski 1927); Pritsak 1959a; Németh 2010; 2012; 2014ab2015ab. Views on the body of the "Karaim Language": Kowalski 1926; Szapszał 1928; Shapira 2003; 2005; Jankowski 1997; 2003; 2015a; 2015b; Jankowski et alii 2019 (Introduction, the concept, and the title). Some editions of texts: Kowalski 1929; Sulimowicz 1972–73; Jankowski 2011; 2014; Németh 2014c 2015cd; 2016; Olach 2013; 2016; Shapira 2013.

15 It seems that Gasprinski followed the clue of A. Firkowicz, see Shapira 2003.

All-Turkic tendencies, and began to write in the local language;[16] only then the Soviet-designed Literary Crimean-Tatar emerged.

By the late 1930s, all the Crimean-Tatar intellectuals using the Soviet-designed "Crimean-Tatar" language were annihilated; in 1944, all the Muslim speakers of it were deported, and their language was banned. So while speaking of "Krymchak", "Crimean-Karaim", or "Crimean-Tatar", one should keep in mind that these languages existed only in a short period as "modern" languages, and when one uses terms like "Tatar", "Tatarization", regarding the earlier periods, one refers to some hardly known varieties. The only texts in any variety of "Crimean-Tatar" written in the 19th century one is aware of were written, in fact, in Hebrew characters (and rarely, in Cyrillic) by Karaites and Krymchaks. One lacks comparable material written by Muslims, except for some late recordings of folklore.

1.4.4 Judeo-Turkic

There used to be the following forms of Judeo-Turkic languages in Eastern Europe (including the Crimea):

– the Qıpčaq Karaim dialect of the Karaite Jews of ethnic Lithuania (the "Troki/Troch/Trakai dialect");

– the Qıpčaq Karaim dialect of the Karaite Jews of Galicia and Wolhynia (two subdialects: the "Halicz/Halič/Galič dialect and the Łuck/Lutsk/Luck dialect");[17]

– the mixed Qıpčaq-Oğuz dialect of the Karaite and Rabbanite Jews in the Crimean Khanate (apparently, with many sub-variants prior to the mid-19th century and with differences in the speech of the Karaites and Rabbanites);

– the Oğuz Turkish with some occasional Qıpčaq elements of the Southern Coast of the Crimean Peninsula spoken by the Karaite and Rabbanite Jews (of this variety, we have very little information as about these Ottoman and post-Ottoman communities of the Southern Crimea in general).

The Karaim language will be discussed later in section 3.3 of this chapter.

2. Orthography of the Judeo-Turkic dialects written in Hebrew script

The Hebrew script used by Turkic-speaking Jews was of Byzantine provenance, with Eastern and sometimes Ashkenazi admixtures. Sometimes, *ʕayin* is used non-etymologically or as a vowel sign, and *ḥē̱t* for *he* (in Karaim texts from the late 19th century, *ḥē̱t* was used for *x*[18]). *Taw* was rarely used, mostly in Hebrew and Arabo-Persian words where it was etymological, but generally, the etymological *taw* was spelled with *ṭē̱t*, even in Hebrew words (like טרפים for Hebrew תְּרָפִים 'kind of house gods' in a Krymchak *Genizah* fragment of Hosea 3:4). *Ṣade* stood for *č*, and in the Judeo-Turkic pronunciation of Hebrew, every *ṣade* in Hebrew words was pronounced [č] (the Southern dia-

16 Cf. Samojlovich 1916; 1927.

17 Grammar: Dictionary of the Karaim and of the written Crimean-Turkic of the Karaites (cited there as the third, the Crimean Karaim dialect): the *KRPS* (an important review to which much can be added: Altbauer 1979–1980); Dictionary of the Crimean Karaite-Turkic (mostly, based on the material of the *KRPS*): Aqtay and Jankowski 2015.

18 Nemeth 2015: 175.

lect of Karaim later developed the shift *č* > *c* [= *ts*]). *Bē<u>t</u>* stood for *b* and *v*; the latter was spelled either ו ,בֿ, or וו. The phoneme *f* is not germane in Turkic languages, appearing in borrowings only, and was mostly left undistinguished from *p*. We cannot always be sure what *qof* stood for, as, in many Qıpčaq (and Oğuz) dialects, it underwent the shift *q* > *x* in certain positions. In Firk I Bibl 143, for instance, the same words are sometimes written with the etymological *q*, and sometimes with כ, indicating the *q* > *x* shift (כלאיך 'people'). In later Karaim texts, when the sound *q* was lost, ק stood for *k*, and קֿ for *x* in the Northern Karaim. By the 19th century, if not earlier, the dialects of Karaim lost the Turkic sound *ğ*, pronounced similar to *ġayn*; prior to that and in the non-Karaim texts, it was left undistinguished from *g*, or distinguished by a dot or stroke over the letter *gimel* (גֿ), sometimes, on the left corner.

Examples from Firk I Bibl 143:

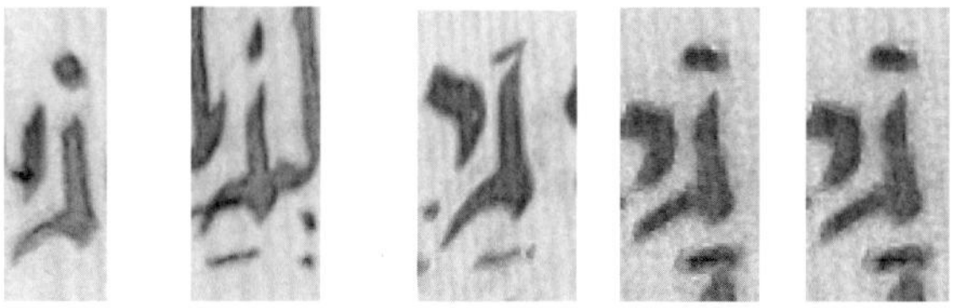

oğurliki olğalangay ğariplar ğaripniyg buğa

As such, it was sometimes undistinguished from *j* (*dž/ǯ*), which was sometimes spelled with just a *gimel* and sometimes by a *gimel* with a dot or a stroke.

Examples from Firk I Bibl 143:

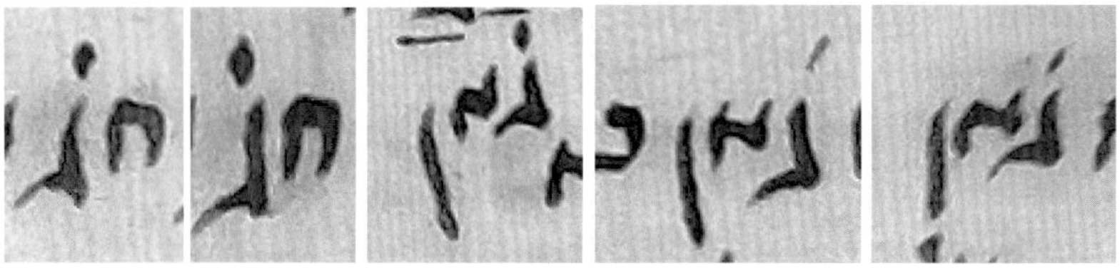

However, Firk I Bibl 143 was, apparently, written in a *ǯ*-dialect (the well-known non-prestigious[19] Qıpčaq shift of the initial *y* to *j* attested in different Turkic dialects and languages), what is called by Russian Turkologists джеканье *dzhekanie*. This feature is characteristic of the Steppe Crimean-Tatar dialect (basically, it is a Noğay dialect), of some sub-dialects of the so-called "Middle" Crimean-Tatar, of Modern Qazakh/Kazakh, Qarachay-Malqar, Qara-Qalpaq, the J-dialect of Modern Uzbek, etc. When using consonantal script, *j* was generally not recorded in writing and was probably seen as an accent feature not hampering comprehension. In one passage we find the same word written once with a *y* and then with *j*.

19 This probably means that the dialect of this manuscript was spoken in an area where no prestigious Turkic literary language was in use, as in some Slavic territory.

Lev 13:40–41

וְאִישׁ כִּי יִמָּרֵט רֹאשׁוֹ קֵרֵחַ הוּא
דאיר כישי איגר יולקונסא באשי קַשְׁקַא דִיר ~~טִיר~~ אול

d-ʔyr kyšy ʔygr ywlqwnsʔ bʔšy qašqaʔ diyr ~~ṭyr~~ ʔwl
and-male person if tear_out-COND.3SG head-POSS.3SG bald COP.3SG ~~COP.3SG~~ 3SG
And if a male person would have his head torn out, he is bald

טָהוֹר הוּא
ארוב דיר אול

ʔrwb dyr ʔwl
pure COP.3SG 3SG
he is pure.

וְאִם מִפְּאַת פָּנָיו יִמָּרֵט רֹאשׁוֹ גִּבֵּחַ הוּא טָהוֹר הוּא
דאיגר בוצקקינדן יוזיני ג׳ולקונסא באשי

d-ʔygr bwṣqq-yn-d ywz-y<n>y jwlqwnsʔ bšy[20]
and-if corner-POSS.3SG-ABL face-POSS.3SG-GEN tear_out-COND.3SG head-POSS.3SG
If from the corner of his face his head would be torn out

טיר אול ארוב דיר אול

ṭyr ʔwl ʔrwb dyr ʔwl
COP.3SG 3SG pure COP.3SG 3SG
…[21] is, he is pure.

This probably means that every word with an initial *y* was pronounced with a *j*, which was just not recorded in writing.

In Early Modern / Late Karaim, new combinations of letters and diacritics were used for newly developed sounds: זד and צ̌ for *ʒ*, ז̄ד, ז́ד́, and צ̌ for *ǯ*. As to the etymological Turkic *ŋ* (appearing, inter alia, in some formants, and thus of high frequency), it was written by נ or ג, or ג̄ in texts from Istanbul, Southern Crimea, and Central Crimea, and it is sometimes difficult to discern between both; in both Northern and Southern Karaim, however, it was always written as נ and ן-. In Firk I Bibl 143 it was written נג, as in the Türki of the Golden Horde or in Mamluk-Qıpčaq, and sometimes ג. So the scribal tradition of this latter manuscript had no continuation. Later on, by the late 17th century,[22] the etymological *ŋ* (if it ever existed in the developed varieties) became develarized into *n* in the Southern dialect of the Karaim language, and was shifted to *y* and *n*/*ń* in the Northern dialect. By the late 18th century, the Southern dialect of the Karaim language began to shift *š* to s; this can be easily seen, for instance, in letters and copies by Avraham Firkowicz, where sometimes the original *s* was rendered hyper-correctly as *š*.

By the 18th/19th centuries, the opposition between the front vowels and the back vowels disappeared in the Karaim language (*ö* > *e*, *ü* > *i* in the Southern dialect, and *ö* > *'o*, *ü* > *'u* in the Northern dialect). Most probably, this happened because the numbers of the speakers shrank dramatically as a consequence of the Second Northern War, and the few survivors became exposed more and more to the speech of their Slavic neighbors,

20 Blank space left.

21 The word (possibly) synonymous with the word for "bald" used in the previous verb is omitted, for the lack of a Turkic equivalent.

22 Jankowski 2014: 35–37; Németh 2015b: 169–170.

with its systematic palatatalization. The result was that the vowel harmony of the Turkic languages (the first vowel determines the quality of the vowel in the next syllable) became transformed into a consonant harmony, where the consonants must agree according to palatality/non-palatality.[23] As a consequence, there arose a need for recording this palatality in writing, and the Karaim developed a Polish-influenced orthography: כּיוֹכּ, *k'ok* 'sky' (in the latinized orthography of the Inter-War period and further: *kiok*); כּיוֹמיוּר, *k'om'ur* 'coal' *kiomiur*.

The vowel *a* is written with a *pataḥ*, rarely with a *qamaṣ*. In texts from the Crimea, *pataḥ* renders not only *a*, but also *æ* and an open *e* / *ɛ*; *ṣere* is used for the closed *e* and rarely for *e* / *ɛ*; *segol* is rarely used in either the texts from the Crimea or in those in the Karaim language. The Turkic vowel *ı/ĭ* (*y*, in latinized Karaim) has no special sign and was written in the same way as *i*, by a *ḥiriq*, or *ḥiriq* + *yod*. For *u/ü*, a *ḥolam* + *waw*, and for *o/ö*, a *shuruq* + *waw* were used.

It was only in Firk I Bibl 143 that the Babylonian vocalization was used in a dozen cases; in this manuscript, sometimes a *qubbuṣ* precedes a *waw* to indicate the front pronunciation *ü*, not *u*:

kün  *ʔüzün* 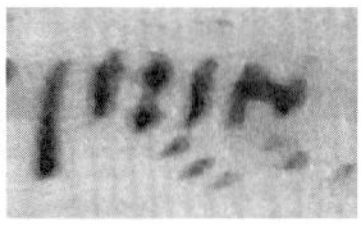

kündüz 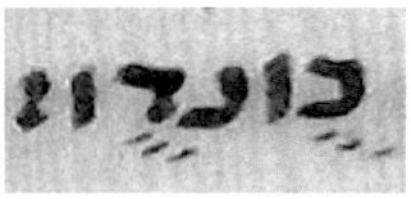 *ṭüz* 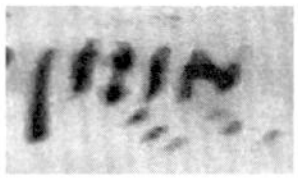

ʔwlṭüyrgyn … ʔwlṭüyr 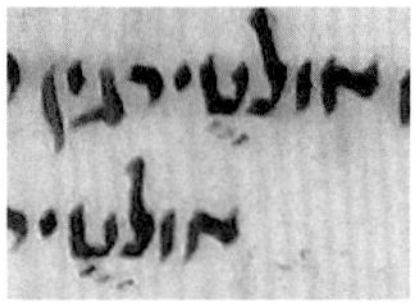

3. Texts and varieties

3.1 The oldest Judeo-Turkic text (title/author and provenance unknown)

The oldest Judeo-Turkic text known so far was written by the late 15th century, in the last days of the Golden Horde.[24] This is what is left of a translation of the Pentateuch, beginning in the middle of Ex 21.10 and ending in the middle of Num 28.15. The translation reflects a very archaic Qıpčaq dialect with some Oğuz influences; it cannot be stated at this stage where exactly in (or outside) the Golden Horde the translation (or its copy, see below) was made. The translation is Rabbanite, not Karaite (we have so far no Rabbanite Judeo-Turkic translation of the Pentateuch, except this MS). The language and the modes of translation had no continuity (though Karaite Pentateuch translations go back to a prototype to which this MS can be related as well).

23 Németh 2014b: 353–369.

24 The paper used in the MS was dated by Dr. Alexander Grishchenko (Moscow State University of Education; Institute for Slavic Studies of the Russian Academy of Sciences, Moscow) and Dr. Alexandra Soboleva (Vinogradov Russian Language Institute, Moscow) in April 2017.

The MS was found by Avraham Firkowicz in 1844, either in Qarasubazar or in Keffeh in the Crimea, apparently, in a Rabbanite *Genizah*;[25] this MS, Evr 1 Bibl 143, is not an original translation, but rather a copy that contains omissions and corrections, and is partially vocalized in at least two different systems:

da-bar-gay 'let him give', revocalized to *da-bēr-gay*; the dialect of the earlier vocalizer had the backward open *æ* rendered by a *pataḥ*, the dialect of the later vocalizer had it the forward closed *é*.

The MS escort of Evr 1 Bibl 143 is Rabbanite (or, rather, non-Karaite), possibly with the exemption of Evr 1 Bibl 146 (Harkavy and Strack 1875: 170), which is ten folios of a Judeo-Turkic translation of the Book of Psalms,[26] whose language, but not its writing/spelling, is rather close to Evr 1 Bibl 143. Evr 1 Bibl 144, however, is a 18th century Karaite translation of the Pentateuch.

The provenance of Evr 1 Bibl 143 can be one of the following: Kyiv,[27] the Golden Horde's capitals of the New Sarây and the Old Sarây on the Volga, the Crimean Peninsula, the steppes of the Northern Caucasus and its shores of the Black Sea, and Qazan. All these places are possible, based on different linguistic and historical observations. Another possibility is that the translation was made in the entity called *Yagalday* or *Yagalday*'s *tümen* (in Medieval Russian: Ягалдасва тьма), a Lithuanian-Tatar principality established ca.1438 in the vicinity of present day Belgorod in the South-Western federal subject of Russia (this little-known entity is sometimes seen as a precursor of the Ukrainian Cossack state).[28]

25 In Avraham Firkowicz' MS collection catalogue, written around 1845 (OR RNL f. 946 op. 1 N 128), he wrote that on Sunday 26 Nisan B / April 2, 1844 and on Wednesday 29 of Nisan (sic), he found the following manuscripts in the *Genizah* of the Qarasubazar Rabbanites and in the city of Qafa? (sic)/Keffe/Capha/Feodosija: a Pentateuch with a Persian translation, 44 fol.; a Persian translation of Job, 9 fol.; some (קצת) of a translation of the Pentateuch בלשון צגאטאי *be-lašon ṣagaṭay*, 130 fol.; a translation of Ezekiel and the Minor Prophets belonging to/made by the Rabbanites in the same language (בלשון ההיא *bal-lašon ha-hi*): another Pentateuch translation בלשון צגאטאי. In two other documents kept in Kyiv, Firkowicz provided two other versions of the circumstances of his finding these MSS. Firkowicz used *ṣagaṭay* for the language of old MSS coming from the Krymchaks; a rather similar (*čaltay*) term for the dead Turkic language of the Bible translation was used in Gordelvskij 1928: 87; he was followed by Pritsak 1959a, and, more importantly, Filonenko 1972 claimed that the Krymchak Rabbanite Jews called their older language *čagaday*, referring, apparently, not to their spoken language, but rather to the language of the old Bible translations. There can be no doubt that the Karaite and Krymchak terms *čaltay* / *čagaday* are connected.

26 This was written by the end of the 18th century, after 1789.

27 The MS is in some way connected to R. Moshe ha-Goleh of Kyiv and/or to Zekharia, the copyist of scientific texts for R. Moshe (cf. Shapira 2018b).

28 This assumption is based on the etymology of the word *čaltay* (this was how the Rabbanite Jews of the Crimea designated the language of their older texts; later the word was corrupted into *čağatay*). According to Tenišev 1995, *čaltay* was derived from the Mongol word *zagaltay* and its relatives (the word means a horse's color), used for the mid-15th Lithuanian-Tatar entity; on this entity, see Rusyna 2005; the Jews, who called their language *čaltay* (attested as early as 1799 in Ginzburg 1159, Moscow), have most probably come from there.

The dialect of Evr 1 Bibl 143 is the only *j/dzh/ǯ*-Judeo-Turkic dialect known where the (mostly intial) *y*- becomes *j/dzh/ǯ*- (the Kriáshen dialect of the Volga-Tatars spoken by Christian converts, the Noğay language/dialect, and many other Qıpčaq dialects share this feature).

Num 13:2

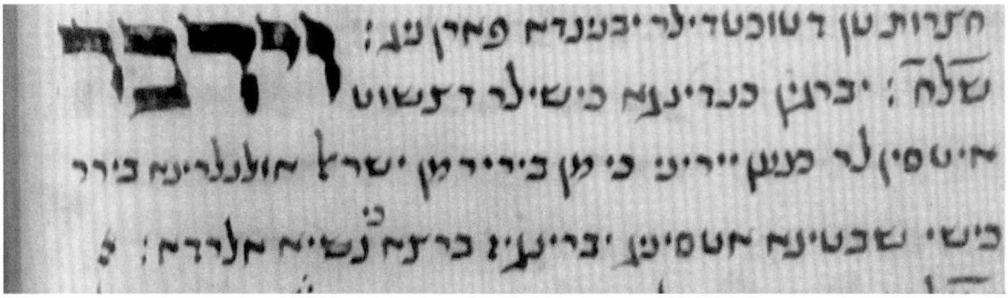

שְׁלַח לְךָ אֲנָשִׁים וְיָתֻרוּ

יברגין כנדינגא כישילר דצשוט איטסין לר

yibir-gin *kendi*[29]*-ŋ-ge* *kiši-ler* *da* *češüt* *eṭ-sin* *ler*[30]

send-IMP2[31].2SG self-PRON.2SG-DAT man-PL[32] and[33] spy do-IMP.3SG PL[34]

Send to yourself men and let them spy

אֶת אֶרֶץ כְּנַעַן אֲשֶׁר אֲנִי נֹתֵן

כנען ייריני כי מן ביריר מן

*k*æ*?naʕan* *yer-i-ni* *ki* *mæn* *ber-ir-men*

Kenaan:NOM place/country-POSS.PRON.3SG-ACC[35] that/what[36] I give:AOR.1SG

the land of Canaan that I give

29 The Oğuz form, relatively rare in this text, but seemingly on the verge of replacing the Qıpčaq *kensi*. KRPS, p. 305b: *kensi* th (two forms), quoting *ken'sisin'dia ušpu koun'niun'*, "on the same day", and p. 391b, *kense* k, quoting *kenseinde ušbu künnün*; Aqtay and Jankowski 2015: 206a: *kendi*, quoting *kendisinde ol uşbu kunniñ*, "on the same day" (Aqtay and Jankowsky, actually, cited the KRPS); cf. p. 165a, *gendi*; and cf. p. 206b, *kense*, "the same exactly" . It is obvious that this is an old frozen expression, and *kensi* was not part of the vocabulary of the Karaim-speakers in the last couple of centuries. No *kensi* or a similar form appear in Kowalski 1929 (which treats the Troki dialect) or in Németh 2011 (which treats both). Qazzaz's dictionary, p. 102b, Hebrew עצם: … *kēmik*, *swywk* ["bone"], *wyjwd* ["essence"]; בעצם היום הזה *bw gwnyŋ wyjwdynd?*, *bw gwnyŋ gndysynd?*.

30 A compound verb, typical of the Persian-influenced Muslim Turkic languages.

31 IMP2 (verbal root + *gin*) exists in 2SG only; IMP1.2SG = verbal root.

32 ACC=NOM to express the Hebrew indefinite "men".

33 Translates the Hebrew *waw* consecutive.

34 IMP.3SG is *-sVn*; IMP.3PL is *-sVn-lVr*; actually, the form used here is IMP.3PL, but from the point of view of the author/copyist, who wrote the pl suffix separately, these were two morphemes, not one.

35 The proper Turkic *izafet* is used, not copying of the Hebrew word order.

36 Persian; the "*ki*-construction" is regarded "un-Turkic".

לִבְנֵי יִשְׂרָאֵל
ישראל אולנלרינא

yisraʔel	*u/olan-lar-in-a*
Israel:NOM	lad/son-PL-POSS.PRON.3SG-DAT2[37]

to the sons of Israel

אִישׁ אֶחָד אִישׁ אֶחָד לְמַטֵּה אֲבֹתָיו
בירר כישי שבטינא אטסיניג

bir-er	*kiši*	*šebeṭ-in-e*[38]	*ata-sı-nıŋ*
one:DISTR.NUM	man.NOM	tribe[H]-POSS.PRON.3SG-DAT	father-POSS.PRON.3SG-GEN

one by one man to the tribe of his father

תִּשְׁלָחוּ כֹּל נָשִׂיא בָהֶם.
יברינגיז ברצא כי נשיא אלרדא

yib-ir-iŋiz	*barča-ni*	*nasiʔ*	*alar-da*
send-AOR-2PL	all/every-ACC	chief[H].NOM	they-LOC

you send every chief in them.

Ex 21:18

וְכִי יְרִיבֻן אֲנָשִׁים וְהִכָּה אִישׁ
וכי : דַאֵיגַר טַלַשְׁסַלַר כִּישִׁילַר דַאוּרְגַי כִּישִׁי

da	*egær*	*ṭalaš-sa-lar*	*kiši-lær*	*da*	*ur-g/ğay*	*kiši*
and[39]	if[40]	quarrel-OPT/COND-3PL	man-PL.NOM	and[41]	hit-SUBJ.3SG[42]	man:NOM

and if they would quarrel, and a man would hit

אֶת רֵעֵהוּ בְּאֶבֶן אוֹ
דוֹסְטוּנִי טַש בִּלַא יַא סַא

dosṭ-u-ni	*ṭaš*	*bila*	*yasa*
friend-POSS.PRON.3SG-ACC	stone:NOM	with:POSTP	or

his friend with a stone or

אוֹ בְאֶגְרֹף וְלֹא יָמוּת וְנָפַל לְמִשְׁכָּב
יוּמוּרוּק בִּלַא דַאוֹלְמַגִי אִלָא טוֹשְׁכַי טוֹשַׁכקָא :

yumruq	*bila*	*da*	*öl-mæ-g/ğæy*	*illæ*[43]	*töš-xay-sa*	*töšæ*x-xæ*[44]
fist:NOM	with:POSTP	and[45]	die-NEG-SUBJ.3SG	but[46]	fall-SUBJ-CONJ.3SG	bed-DAT

with a fist and he would not die, but would fall to bed.

37 The "Oğuz Dative". The proper Turkic *izafet* is used, no copying of the Hebrew word order.
38 Or: *šebeṭ-iŋ-ge*; the graphic forms is not enough decisive.
39 Mimics the Hebrew *waw* consecutive.
40 Persian.
41 Mimics the Hebrew *waw* consecutive.
42 It seems that SUBJ and OPT began to merge in this dialect.
43 **ʔllāʔ.*
44 Merger of *k* / *q* or an orthography convention?
45 Mimics the Hebrew *waw* consecutive.
46 *Arabic. Added by the translator.

Num 20:2–5

וְלֹא הָיָה מַיִם לָעֵדָה
דָא יוֹךְ אֵידִי סוּב אוֹל גָמַעַת קָא

dā yox[47] *ʔē-di suḇ ʔol gāmaʕat*[48] *qāʔ*
and there_is_not be-PST.3SG water.NOM this[49] assembly DAT
and (there) was not water to the/this assembly

וַיִּקָּהֲלוּ עַל מֹשֶׁה וְעַל אַהֲרֹן
דָאִיְיִלְדִילָר מֹשֶׁה אוּסְטִינָא דָאַהֲרֹן אוּסְטִינָא

dā il-di-lār mošeh üsṭināʔ[50] *dā ʔaharon üsṭināʔ.*
and people[51]-PST[52]-3PL Moses on.POSTP and Aharon on.POSTP
and they became people/assembled over/on Moses and over/on Aharon.

וַיָּרֶב הָעָם עִם מֹשֶׁה
דָא טָלַשְׁטִי אוֹל אוּלוּס מֹשֶׁה בִלָא

dā ṭālaš-ṭi ʔol ʔulus mošeh bilāʔ
and quarrel-PST.3SG[53] this.PRON.3SG[54] people/nation-NOM Moses with.POSTP[55]
and (it/he) quarreled, the/this nation, with Moses

וַיֹּאמְרוּ לֵאמֹר
דָאַיִיטְטִילָר דֵימָא

dā ayyiṭ-ṭi-lār dēymāʔ
and say-PST-3PL saying[56]
and they said saying

וְלוּ גָוַעְנוּ בִּגְוַע אַחֵינוּ לִפְנֵי ה׳
דָכַשְׁכָּא אוֹלְגַיְ-אֵדִיכְ אוֹלגַנְדָא

dā kaškāʔ öl-gæy[57] *ʔē-dik ʔol-gan-dāʔ*[58]
and would_that.ADV[59] die-OPT/SUBJ be-PST.1PL die-PRES/PST.PTCP-LOC[60]
and, Oh that we would die by dying

47 The final *-q*, as in many other Turkic dialects, >*-x*.

48 *j*/*dzh*/*ǯ* in this word is undotted, meaning that all undotted *gimel*s are *ǯ*.

49 Used to mimic the Hebrew definite article.

50 Possibly pronounced *üsti*/*ünæ*. This form with the middle *-i-* like vowel is unique among other Judeo-Turkic dialects.

51 The Old Turkic *il* translates Hebrew *qāhāl*; a denominative verb is formed, **ilmæk*/*x*, unattested in the infinitive. In later Karaite translations, Jankowski et al. 20129: 260 and Nemeth 2012: 725, two different verbs were used, with the meaning "they gathered".

52 In the sense of reflexive.

53 Note that here the Hebrew *waw* cum imperfect is rendered by the simple past.

54 Used to mimic the Hebrew definite article.

55 Modern Turkish: *ilen* / *-len*; Crimean Tatar: *bile* / *bilen* / *bilan* / *ilen*; Karaim: *bela* / *bıla* / *-ba* / *-be*.

56 Translates לאמור, grammatically a *maṣdar* / verbal noun.

57 Pronounced *ölgey* or *ölǧey*.

58 Pronounced *ölgændæ* or *ölǧændæ*.

59 From Persian. Attested also in Halicz Karaim, see KRPS, pp. 308b, 312a.

60 This form routinely translates the Hebrew construction *b-* + infinitive construct.

אַחֵינוּ לִפְנֵי ה׳
קַרְדַשְׁלָרִימִיז נִינְ יוֹי נִיג אַלְנִינָא

qardaš[61]*-lār-imiz niŋ ywy nig ʔalni-nāʔ*[62]
brother-PL-PRON.POSS.1PL GEN God GEN face-POSTP.3SG.DAT
of our brothers before God's face.

וְלָמָה הֲבֵאתֶם אֶת קְהַל יה׳
דָנֵיכְּ כֵלְטִירְדִי-נְגִיז גָמַעתִין יוֹי נִיג

dā nēk[63] *kēl-ṭir-di nŋiz jāmaʕat*[64]*-in ywy nig*
and what_for come-CAUS-PST PRON.2PL assembly/congregation-GEN[65] God GEN
and why did you (PL) cause to come God's assembly

אֶל הַמִּדְבָּר הַזֶּה לָמוּת
אוֹשְ בוּ יַבָן גָא אוֹלְמָא

ʔuš bu[66] *yābān gāʔ ʔol-māʔ*[67]
to this desert DAT die-GER/VN/INF
to this (very) desert (in order) to die

שָׁם אֲנַחְנוּ וּבְעִירֵנוּ
אַנְדָא בִיז דָא טוּבָרִימִיז

ʔandāʔ biz dāʔ ṭuḇār-<i>-miz
there we.PRON.1PL and cattle/goods[68]-i-PRON.POSS.1PL
in here we and our cattle / goods.

וְלָמָּה הֶעֱלִיתֻנוּ מִמִּצְרַיִם
דָנֵי אוּצוּן כוֹצִירְדִינְגִיז בִיזְנִי מִסִיר דַן
dā nēy ʔuṣun[69] *koč-ir-di-ngiz biz-n misir dan*
and what for-POSTP travel-CAUS-PST-PRON.2PL we-ACC Egypt ABL
and why did you (PL) cause us to migrate/nomadize from Egypt

לְהָבִיא אֹתָנוּ אֶל הַמָּקוֹם הָרָע הַזֶּה
כֵלְטִירְמָא בִיזְנִי בוּ יַמָן יֵירְגָא

kēl-ṭir-māʔ biz-ni bu yamān yyēr-gāʔ
come-CAUS-VN/INF we-ACC this bad.NO place/country-DAT
(in order) to cause us to come to this bad place/country

61 Possibly pronounced *qardæš*.
62 The form is identical to that of the Halicz Karaim.
63 Attested in both Karaim dialects and in Crimean-Tatar.
64 *j* / *dzh* / *ǯ* marked.
65 In the sense of ACC, as GEN forms were frequently used for ACC in some Qıpčaq dialects.
66 Sometimes written in one word, it was one of the ways to render the Hebrew definite article.
67 Pronounced *ölmæ*.
68 Possibly, an old Semitic borrowing (*דבר); used here in the sense of *māl* 'property'.
69 Pronounced *üčün*.

לֹא מְקוֹם זֶרַע וּתְאֵנָה וְגֶפֶן

טוּאוּל דִיר אוֹרְנִי אוּרְלוּךְ נִיג נֵי כִי אִינְגִ'יר נִיג יָא בוֹרְלָא נִיג

ṭuʔul[70] *dir* *ʔor<>n-i* *ʔurlux* *nig* *nēy* *ki* *ʔinjir* *nig* *yāʔ* *borlāʔ* *nig*

there-is-not COP.3SG place[71]-POSS.3SG seed GEN what for[72] fig GEN or vine/vineyard GEN

there is no seed's place, what for of fig or vine,

וְרִמּוֹן וּמַיִם אַיִן לִשְׁתּוֹת

יָא נַר נִיג סוּב דָגִה יוֹךְ טִר אִצְמָגָא

yāʔ *nar* *nig* *sub̲* *dāgi* *yox* *ṭir* *ʔič-mā-gāʔ*

or pomegranate GEN water.NOM and/also there_is_not COP.3SG drink-VN/INF-DAT

or of pomegranate, even water (there) is not (in order) to drink.

Num 21:28–30

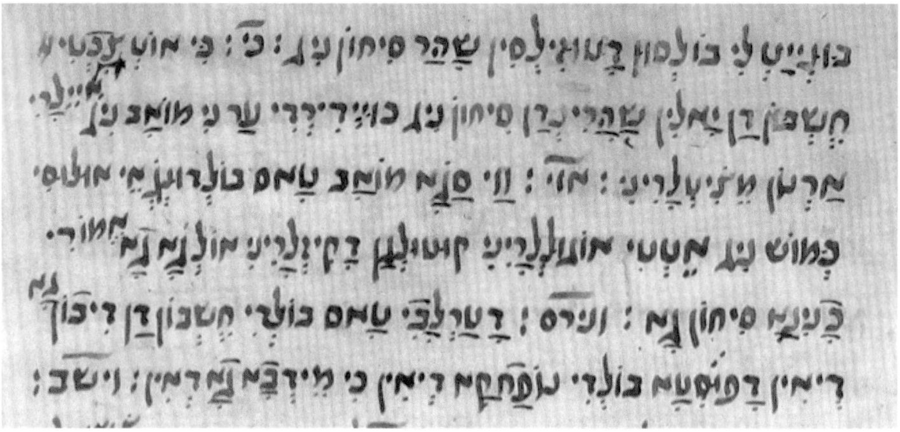

כִּי-אֵשׁ יָצְאָה מֵחֶשְׁבּוֹן

כִּי אוֹט צִכְּטִי חֶשְׁבוֹן דַן

ki *ʔoṭ* *ṣix-ṭi* *ḥɛšbon dan*

as/because.ADV fire.NOM go_out-PST.3SG Heshbon-ABL

for fire went (out) from Heshbon

לֶהָבָה מִקִּרְיַת סִיחֹן אָכְלָה עָר מוֹאָב

יָאלִין שָׁהַרדַן סִיחוֹן נִיג כוּיְידִירְדִי עַר נִי מוֹאָב נִיג

yāʔlin *šāhar-i<n>-dan* *siḥon* *nyg* *kuyy-dir-di* *ʕar* *ni* *moʔāb̲* *nig*

flame.NOM city^{P}-PRON.3SG-ABL Sihon GEN[73] burn-CAUS-PST.3SG Ar ACC Moab GEN[74]

flame from Sihon's city (it/he) caused to burn Moab's Ar

70 Modern Turkish *değil*, Crimean-Tatar *dugul* / *dügül*, Halicz Karaim *divil* / *tivil*, Troki Karaim *tiuviul*.

71 *orun*, > *orn-V* in declination or with possessive suffixes.

72 A similar form, *nege*, in Halicz Karaim.

73 This construction (found in the texts in the Karaim language) mimics Hebrew word order and is alien to any "normal" Turkic language (*Sihon-un şehr-i(n)-den*, in Modern Turkish: Sihon-GEN city-PRON.3SG-(n)-ABL).

74 See the previous note; Modern Turkish: *Moab-ı-(n) Ar şehr-i-(n)-i*, Moab-GEN-(n) Ar-NOM city-PRON.3SG-(n)-ACC.

בַּעֲלֵי בָּמוֹת אַרְנֹן
אִיֵילָרִי אַרְנוֹן מֵצִּיטְלָרִינִי

ʔiyyē-lār-i	*ʔarnon*	*mēčiṭ-lār-i-ni.*
master-PL-PRON.3SG	Arnon.NOM	mosque[75]-PL-POSS.3SG-ACC

Arnon's mosques' owners.

אוֹי לְךָ מוֹאָב אָבַדְתָּ
וַיֵ סַג׳א מוֹאָב טָאס בוֹלְדוּנְג׳

way	*saŋʔ*	*moʔāḇ*	*ṭāʔs*	*bol-d-unŋ*
vay!	you.PRON.2SG.DAT	Moab.NOM=VOC	lost/waste	become-PST-PRON.2SG

Woe to you, Moab, you became lost/waste

עַם כְּמוֹשׁ נָתַן בָּנָיו פְּלֵיטִם
אֵי אוּלוּסִי כְּמוֹשׁ נִיג אֵטְטִי אוֹגוּלְלָרִינִי קוּטוּלְגַן

ʔēy	*ʔulus-i*	*kəmoš nig*	*ʔēṭ-ṭi*	*ʔogul-lār-i-ni*	*quṭ-ul-gan*
oh!	people-PRON.3SG	Kemosh-GEN[76]	make-PST.3SG	son-PL.3SG-ACC	save-PASS-PRES/PST.PART[77]

Oh Kemosh's nation, (it/he) made his/their sons saved /having been saved/ ones

וּבְנֹתָיו בַּשְּׁבִית לְמֶלֶךְ אֱמֹרִי סִיחוֹן
דָא קִיזְלָרִינִי אוֹלְגָ׳אגַּא אֱמוֹרִי כָּנִינָא סִיחוֹן גָא

dā	*qiz-lār-i-ni*	*ʔoljā-ğā*	*ʔɛmori*	*xān-i-<n>-āʔ*	*siḥon*	*gāʔ*
and	daughter-PL.POSS.3SG-ACC	booty-DAT	Amorite.NOM	Khan-POSS.3SG-(n)-DAT	Sihon	DAT

and his/their daughters into booty to Amorite Khan, to Sihon.

וַנִּירָם אָבַד חֶשְׁבּוֹן
דָא טַרְלָבִי טָאס בוֹלְדוּ חֶשְׁבּוֹן דַן

dā	*ṭarlāḇ-i*[78]	*ṭāʔs*	*bol-du*	*ḥɛšbon*	*dan*
and	field/countryside-POSS.3SG	lost/waste	become-PST.3SG	Heshbon	ABL

and its/his field became lost/waste from Heshbon

75 This seems to be an indication that the original translation was made in the mid-14th century, some time after or during the Islamization of the Golden Horde, for there is equation of mosques (apparently, newly built) with the high places of the Baals.

76 Mimics Hebrew word order; Modern Turkish: *Kemoşun kavmı*, Kemosh-GEN people(*Arabic)-PRON.3SG.

77 The case is "inner ACC" = NOM.

78 KJV: We have shot at them Heshbon is perished even unto Dibon and we have laid them waste even unto Nophah, which reacheth unto Medeba. Gözleve 1841: *da-biz (gēl-ip)ʔowq ʔaṭ-ip ol-dur-di-k ʔalar-ni ṭas bol-di ḥešbon diḇon gah dēgin da-wēran ʔēṭ-ṭi-k šaḥar-lar-ni ṭaʔ nopaḥ-qah dēk*, "and we (having come) having shot arrow(s), we caused them to die / we killed them, lost/waste became Heshbon, until to Dibon, and desolate [a Persianism] we made towns, till to Nophah, until". Here נירם was analyzed, like in the KJV, as "we have shot".

עַד דִּיבֹ֑ן וַנַּשִּׁ֖ים עַד נֹ֔פַח
דִיבֺון גָא דְאִין דָא פוּסְטָא בוֹלְדִי נוֹפַּח קָא דְיאִין

dibon gāʔ dəʔin dā pusṭāʔ[79] *bol-di nopāḥ-qāʔ dəiʔin*
Dibon DAT up_to.POSTP[80] and wilderness/steppe[81] become-PST.3SG[82] Nophah-DAT up_to.POSTP
until Dibon and (it/he) became *Pusta* up to Nophah

אֲשֶׁ֖ר עַד מֵידְבָֽא
כִ מֵידְבָא גַא דְאִין

ki mēdbāʔ ğāʔ dəʔin
that Medeba DAT up_to.POSTP
that (is) up to Medeba.

3.2 Krymchak

The unified community of the Crimean Rabbanites was organized in Caphá/Keffeh/Feodosiya in 1506 by R. Moses ha-Ashkenazi of Kyiv.[83] The community had included Jews from Ashkenaz, Byzantium, Georgia, Italy, Iberian Peninsula, the Golden Horde, and other places. Their prayer book was basically Romaniot, the ritual Ashkenazi. We can assume that in the mid-15th century, if not earlier, *some* of the Crimean Rabbanites had been Turkic-speaking, though the evidence is not direct. By the late 17th century, the community was thoroughly turkified, deeply influenced by the Lurian Kabbalah and by popular Ottoman Sufism (see below).

It should be stressed that, despite the efforts of the afore-mentioned R. Moses in the beginning of the Ottoman rule in the Crimea to draw a line between the Rabbanites and the Karaites, the Rabbanites of the Crimea later fell under the authority of the Karaite leaders. Unlike in Constantinople, Jerusalem, Damascus, or Egypt, it was the Karaites, who headed the Jewish community in the Crimea until the early 19th century. This fact had linguistic implications, for the Bible translations made by the Crimean Karaites were, as it seems so far, modeled on the language used by the Crimean Karaites in their Bible translations (however, this assumption needs further elaboration and so far, this is just a working hypothesis). Cf. Ps 58:12 in the Rabbanite version of Firk I Bibl 146:

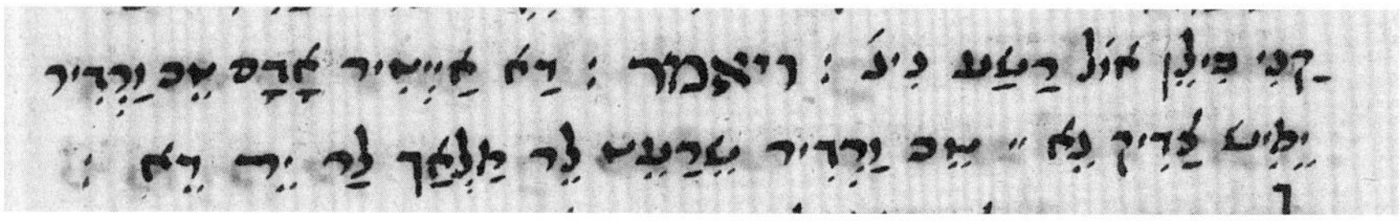

79 *pwsṭ?*, used in the MS for מדבר, שממה, שומם, לשומם, להישום, "desert, wilderness, to devastate, to be devastated", etc. (plus once for השמד 'to destroy, annihilate'), is a Slavic loan word meaning "a void place", "void". In Yiddish, *puste* / *pusto* / *pusta* means "desert", apparently borrowed from the same kind of Slavic and about the same time as our Judeo-Turkic word here and the Halicz and Troki Karaim *pusta* / *pustalyk* / *pustalyx* (Israeli Hebrew *pistin* 'waste terrain' comes directly from the 19th century Russian).

80 Crimean-Tatar *degin* (and *dek*), Modern Turkish *dehin*, Karim *deyin*.

81 A Slavic loan word, attested in Karaim, where it would be a later and independent borrowing.

82 Note the variation of the PST.3SG ending *-dw*/*-dy*; the actually pronunciation was most probably **dı*.

83 Shapira 2018b; 2019.

וְיֹּאמַר אָדָם, אַךְ-פְּרִי לַצַּדִּיק;
דַא אַיְטִיר אָדָם טֵכּ וַרְדִיר יֶמִיש צַדִיק גֵא

daʔ	*ʔayyṭ-iyr*	*ʔādām*	*ṭēk*	*war*	*diyr*	*yēmiyš*	*ṣadiyq*	*gēʔ*
and	say-AOR.3SG	man[H]	only	there_is	COP.3SG	fruit	righteous-one[H]	DAT

And says a man: “there is only a fruit to a righteous

אַךְ יֵשׁ-אֱלֹהִים, שֹׁפְטִים בָּאָרֶץ.
טֵכ וַרְדִיר שֵׁרַעֵט לֵר מַלְאַךְ לַר יֵר דֵא

ṭēk	*war*	*diyr*	*šēraʕēṭ*	*lēr*	*malʔax*	*lar*	*yēr*	*dēʔ*
only	there_is	COP.3SG	judgment/Shariat/judge	PL	angel[H84]	PL	place/soil	LOC

there is only judges, angels, in (the) land”.

After the Russian Empire had occupied the Crimean Khanate in 1771 and then annexed it in 1783 and took part in the partitions of Poland-Lithuania in 1772–1795, an influx of Polish Jews to the Crimea began. In order to distinguish between the Rabbanite Polish Jews and the Rabbanite Crimean Jews, the term “Krymchak” became current in the first third of the 19th century. By this name, the “Crimean-Tatar”-speaking Rabbanite Jews of Qarasubazar and Capha became known more and more, until the term became their self-appellation by the turn of the 19th and 20th centuries. Different forms of their Turkic language are sometimes described as an ethnolect of “Crimean-Tatar” and sometimes as an independent Turkic language.[85]

A “modern” version of Krymchak used to exist a couple of decades at most – the Crimea was Sovietized in late 1920, and schools teaching in Krymchak were opened in the mid-1920s, only to be shut down a decade later;[86] during WWII, almost all the Krymchaks were murdered by the Nazis and their helpers.[87] There was a twinkle of publications in the Perestroika and post-USSR years that have been produced mostly by very aged people. It should be added that, as a consequence of the Nazi genocide, many surviving members of the Krymchak community have undergone the process of ethnic de-Judaization (again, following in the steps of their Karaite neighbors), and many of them pretended to be a Turkic ethnic group endemic to the Crimean Peninsula and having had professed the Religion of Moses in the past.

To judge from the texts and studies published, the spoken Krymchak of the 20th century was basically a variety of the “Middle dialect of the Crimean-Tatar” (on which the Soviet “Crimean-Tatar” was based), having both Qıpčaq and Oğuz features in varying proportions. This means that this language/dialect[s]/ethnolect shared a great deal of

84 Hebrew; in Karaite versions (as in Tırıshqan, Gözleve 1841, see further): *da-ʔayṭir ʔādām ṭēk yēmiš ṣadiq qaʔ ṭēk bardir ṭagri šara'aṭ ʔēṭiwṣi ʔol yērdaʔ* ‘God (the) judgment-maker’.

85 Editions of texts from the 19th and early 20th centuries, and studies are: Ianbay and Erdal 1998; Erdal and Ianbay 2000; Ianbay 2017; Shapira 2016a; texts from the Soviet period: Ianbay 2002; Folklore texts: Filonenko 1930a; Filonenko 1930b; Filonenko 1972; studies: Ianbay 2001; Ianbay 2010; dictionaries: Ianbay 2016 (review: Shapira 2016c); Rebi 2016 (review: Shapira 2019); language and history: Polinsky 1991; Polinsky 1992; Shapira 2007; Shapira 2014b; Shapira 2016a; Shapira 2018b.

86 In Soviet terms, by 1936, the Krymchak became a *bespis'mennyj jazyk*, a language lacking script and literature.

87 See Feferman 2016.

grammar and vocabulary with Turkish, while sharing many phonological and morphological features with "Crimean-Tatar".

The situation was quite different in the written texts from the earlier period: there are two texts in a language we can define as being close to spoken Turkish and Ottoman Turkish in MSS from Keffeh/Caphá/Feodosija; the first text was recorded by a Karaite.

Sample text

A fragment of a poem in Turkish from mid-17th century Keffeh ; the author/copyist seems to be Moshe b. Eliyahu Halevi, a copyist and Ḥazzān in Kaffa, who traveled to Jerusalem in 1654/55 (*Ginzey Yisrael* I 31–43), and died in Çufut-Qalʕeh in 1667 (AZ 349); he penned *piyyuṭim* (one was printed in Siddur 1806, I.92ff., 96ff.; II.14ff.; *Meqabbeṣ* I; *Tehillot Yisrael* 48).

There is nothing "Jewish" about this text which was possibly part of the local folklore common to Muslims and others. Its Oğuz features are unmistaken: the use of the Oğuz form of DAT (no *-g/ğ/q/kV*), the Oğuz form of PRS.PTCP (no *–g/ğ/q/kV-n*), the use of the verb variants with *g-*, *d-* (*dut-* 'to hold'; *dil* 'tongue'; *gel-* 'to come'; *gün* 'day'), and *ol-* instead of *bol-* 'to become'.

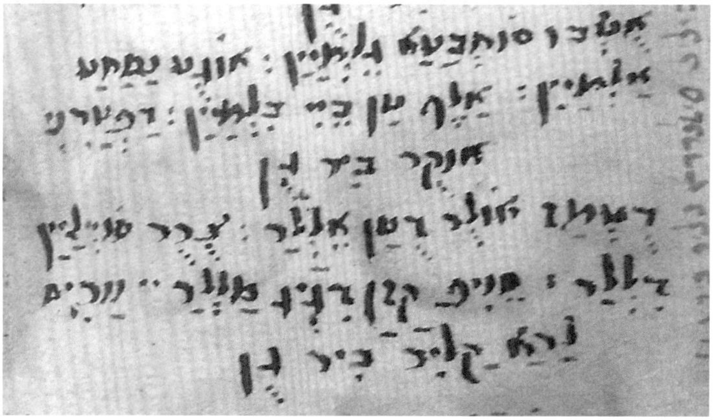

The reading and translation by Marcel Erdal:[88]

ušbu soxbätä gelmäyän	Whoever does not come to this chat,
ögüt nasahat bilmäyän	Whoever does not accept advice and counsel,
alef tän be'i bilmäyän	Whoever cannot distinguish alef from be,
däftärini oqur bir gün	Will read this inventory one day.

88 Marcel Erdal and Menashe Goldelman, "A mid-17th Century Pinkas of the Karaite Community in Caffa: Historical, Philological and Linguistic Considerations", from the Handout of a lecture held at *The Sixth International Congress of Misgav Yerushalayim: Languages and Literatures of Sephardi and Oriental Jews, June 11–15, 2000*, Mount Scopus, The Hebrew University of Jerusalem. The photo was taken by me. Cf. now Shapira 2018a.

dutmaz olur dutan ellär	Holding hands become unable to hold
çürür söyläyän diller	And singing tongues will rot.
sevip qazandığıŋ mallar	The belongings which you liked and amassed,
varislärä kalır bir gün	Will be left to the heirs one day.

אֱשְׁבו סוֹחְבַטַא גֶלְמַייַן :

uš-bu *soxbät-ä* *gel-mä-<y>-än*
to-this chat^{Ar}.DAT[89] come-NEG-PRS.PTCP
one is not coming to this chat

אוֹגֶט נַסַחַט אַלְמַייַן :

ögüt *nasahat* *al-mä-<y>än*
advice.NOM counsel^{Ar}.NOM take-NEG-PRS.PTCP
one is not taking advice (and) counsel

אלף טַן בֵיי בְלְמַייַן :

alef-tän *be-i* *bil-mä-<y>-än*
ʔalif^{Ar}-ABL bāʔ^{Ar}-ACC know-NEG-PRS.PTCP
from Alif (the) Bā (is) not knowing

דַפְטַרְנִי אוקֶר בִיר גֶן

däftär-i-ni *oq-ur* *bir* *gün*
register-POSS.PRON.3SG-ACC read/learn-AOR.3SG one.NOM day.NOM
his register he learns one day

דֶטַמַז אוֹלֶר דֶטַן אֶלְלַר :

dut-maz *ol-ur* *dut-an* *el-lär*
hold-AOR.NEG.3SG become-AOR.3SG hold-PRS.PTCP hand-PL.NOM
becoming not able to hold, (they), holding hands

צֶרֶר סוֹיְילַיַין דִלְלַר :

çür-ü *söylä-<y>-än* *dil-ler*
rot-AOR.3SG say-PRS.PTCP tongue-PL.NOM
(they) rot, saying tongues

סֶוִיפּ קַזַן דְגָיג מַלְלַר :

sev-ip *qazan-dığ-ıŋ* *mal-lar*
love-CVB earn-OBJ-PTCP.GEN possession^{Ar}-PL.NOM
with love earned possessions / possessions earned with love

וַורִיס לַרַא קַלִיר בִיר גֶן

varis-lär-ä *qal-ır* *bir* *gün*
heir^{Ar}-PL.DAT remain-AOR.3SG one.NOM day.NOM
to heirs remain one day

There are only seven Arabic words and one Persian-Arabic word (*daftar*) in this text. Compare the following text in Ottoman Turkish, recorded in Hebrew characters (many mistakes made in the text testify to the fact that the copyist[s] did not understand the text well); I counted 26 Turkic words or grammatical elements in the following text, the rest is Persian with Arabic words. This is very similar to how the official Ottoman-Turkic looked like.

89 The Oğuz DAT.

A text from the Rabbanite prayer books

There are three versions of the garbled Ottoman prayer for the well-being of the Ottoman Sultan Ahmed (III, r. 1703–1730), the Crimean Khan Mengli Giray Khan (II, r. 1724–1730 and 1737–1740), and his brother Selamet Giray Qalga Sultan (1691–1751, r. 1740–1743). The one quoted below is found in the Ukrainian National Library in Kyiv, F 321 op[is'] 5 N ORI [OPI] 834, new number 248, from the collection of Avraham Kaufmann, a Rabbanite prayer book for the "Ten Days of Repentance" (סדר התפלות לימים נוראים) according to *Minhag Kafaʔ* from the 18th century, containing 578+2+1 pages.[90]

כליקי ג׳יחניג׳ כי כלק אידופטיר ג׳יחני

haliq-i jihan-iŋ ki halq id-üp-tir[91] *jihan-i*

creator^{Ar}-IZAF world^{P}-GEN that creation/creature^{Ar} do-CVB-COP.3SG world-ACC

(The) Creator of (the) world, who had created His world,

עלמי לֵווחי וקלמי אול מולכו קדיר

ʕalem-i levḥ-i ve-qalem-i ol mülk-ü[92] *qadir*

world^{Ar}-POSS.3SG tablet^{Ar}-POSS.3SG and-pen^{Ar}-POSS.3SG this kingdom^{Ar}-IZAF mighty^{Ar}

His world is His Tablet and His Pen is this mighty kingdom[93]

קיום דיר כי וירופטיר ווסעת וסעדת פדישה לרא

qayyum dir ki ver-üp-tir vasʕat ve saʕadet padišah-lar-a

everlasting^{Ar} COP.3SG that give-CVB-COP.3SG abundance^{Ar}[94] and felicity^{P} king-PL-DAT[95]

The Eternal (God) who gives abundance and felicity to kings

וחוכמי סלטנת אג׳א לרא וא ביג׳ לרא

ve ḥükm-i saltanet ağa lar-a ve beğ ler-e

and rule^{AR}-IZAF sultanate^{AR} Agha PL-DAT[96] and Bek PL-DAT[97]

and the legal power of rulership to lords and princes

ועיזתיהו וא מולכו סלטנתיהו חי וקיים חי וקיים

ve ʕizzet-ihu[98] *ve mülk-ü*[99] *saltaneti-hu*[100] *ḥay-ve-qayyam*

and honour^{Ar}-POSS.3SG.M and kingdom^{Ar}-CS.NOM sultanate-POSS.3SG.M.GEN alive^{H}-and-existing^{H}

and His might and kingdom of His sultanate (are) living and everlasting

מודמא אול בארי כודא כי כלס איטופטיר

müdema ol bari xuda ki xilas id-üp-tir

as_long_as^{Ar} this creator^{Ar} god^{P} that salvation^{AR} do-CVB-COP.3SG

all time that the Creator (the) God who rescues

90 Published in Shapira 2017 and Shapira 2018b.

91 Compound verb, "to create".

92 The Persian *izafet* with Turkic vowel harmony.

93 The Ottoman Empire.

94 Serving as the equivalent of the related Hebrew תשועה *təšūʕā* 'deliverance'.

95 The Oğuz, *i.e.*, Turkish form of the Dative (not the Qıpčaq *–g/ğ/q/kA/E*).

96 The Oğuz, *i.e.*, Turkish form of the Dative (not the Qıpčaq *–g/ğ/q/kA/E*).

97 The Oğuz, *i.e.*, Turkish form of the Dative (not the Qıpčaq *–g/ğ/q/kA/E*).

98 Note *-i-* in Arabic GEN, maybe a scribal error or Turkic vowel harmony.

99 Here *-ü* in *mülk-ü* is the Ottoman Turkish pronunciation of Arabic NOM.

100 Note *-i-* in Arabic GEN, maybe a scribal error or Turkic vowel harmony.

הזרטֵי דוד קולוני חרבי עַאדוּ לרינדן אול

ḥazret-i davud/david qul-u-nı ḥarb-i ʕadu lar-ın-dan

Hazret-IZAF David.NOM=ACC slave-POSS.3SG.ACC sword^{H}-IZAF enemy^{Ar} PL-POSS.3SG-ABL

Hazret-i Davud/David, His slave, from sword of his enemies,

בארי כ׳ודא כי וירופטיר דרייא לר דא וא עזים סוב לרדא

ol bari xuda ki ver-üp-tir darya lar da ve ʕazim suv-lar-da

this creator^{Ar}god^{P} that give-CVB-COP.3SG sea^{P} PL LOC and mighty^{Ar} water-PL-LOC

The Creator (the) God who had made in seas and mighty waters

יול ודאריך. אול נורי שריפ׳ינדן

yol ve-darix ol nur-i šerif-in-den

way and-path(?)[101] this light^{AR}-IZAF noble^{Ar}-POSS.3SG-ABL

(a) way and guiding path from His noble light…s

... כי אול דור כ׳אלִיפֵאיִי זמ עלי

*... ki ol dur xalife-yi *zemin*[102]*/*zeman*[103] *ʕala[y]*

that/what this COP.3SG[104] Khalifa^{Ar}-IZAF land/time^{Ar} over^{Ar}

For he is the Khalifah of (the) *land/time over

ארצי מוקדשא וא מדינה מונאוורא

arz-i muqaddeše[105] *ve medine-*yi münevvere*

land^{Ar}-IZAF holy.FEM^{Ar} and Madinah^{Ar}-IZAF enlightened.FEM^{Ar}

(the) Holy Land and the Enlightened Madinah

וא כעבא שריפא וא ברריא וא בחרייא

*ve kaʕbe-*yi šerife ve barriye ve baḥriye*

and Kaʕbah^{Ar}-IZAF noble.FEM^{Ar} and of_dryland.FEM^{Ar} and of_seas.FEM^{Ar}

and the Noble Kaabah, and the dryland and the seas / the ground army and fleet

וא אתרפ׳י עַלֵמא חוכמו קאוו

ve etraf[106]*-i ʕalem-a ḥükm-ü*[107] *qavu*[108]

and sides^{Ar}-IZAF world^{Ar}-DAT rule^{Ar}-IZAF strong^{Ar}

and to (the) sides of (the) world (a) strong rule

וַסלטנתי אסתון אילא פדישחימיז ...

ve saltanet-i üstevan[109] *ile padišah-ımız ...*

and sultanate^{Ar}-IZAF solid with-POSTP Padishah-POSS.1PL …

with sultanate solid, our king …

101 Possibly, a Hebrew-Arabic contaminated word (דֶּרֶךְ *dere<u>k</u>* + طَرِيق *ṭarīq*).

102 If read *zem*in*.

103 If read (Persian) *zem*in*.

104 With vowel harmony depending on the open vowel of the preceding *ol*, **dir>dur*.

105 Arabic in Hebraized spelling. Note that "the Holy Land", apparently Palestine, appears on the first place, before the Muslim holy places.

106 Arabic, broken plural.

107 The Persian *izafet* with Turkic vowel harmony.

108 Arabic *qawi*, with Turkic vowel harmony *i* > *u*.

109 Persian *ustuwān*.

Haggada šel Pesaḥ

Another relevant text is the *Haggada šel Pesaḥ* with a Judeo-Turkic translation, printed in Petrokov (Trybunalski, Russian/Congress Poland) in 1904 by the printing house of Mordechai Zederbaum. The language of the translation is called "Tatar" (נערך ונעתק לשפת טאטר המֻדברת בינינו פה במדינת קרים) (available on Hebrewbooks.org.10967). Even though claimed to be a new translation, it was possibly based on much older translations.

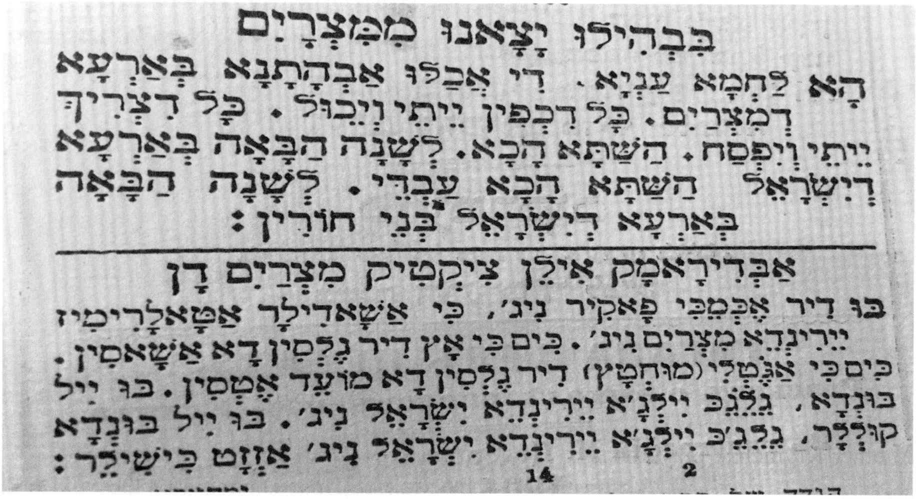
בבהילו יצאנו ממצרים

הא לחמא עניא. די אכלו אבהתנא בארעא
דמצרים. כל דכפין ייתי ויכול. כל דצריך
ייתי ויפסח. השתא הכא. לשנה הבאה בארעא
דישראל השתא הכא עבדי. לשנה הבאה
בארעא דישראל בני חורין:

אבדיראמק אילן ציקטיק מצרים דן

בו דיר אכמכי פאקיר ניג׳, כי אשאדילר אטאלרימיז
יירינדא מצרים ניג׳. כים כי אץ דיר גלסין דא אשאסין.
כים כי אגטלי (מוחטץ) דיר גלסין דא מועד אטסין. בו ייל
בונדא, גלג׳כ יילג׳א יירינדא ישראל ניג׳. בו ייל בונדא
קוללר, גלג׳כ יילג׳א יירינדא ישראל ניג׳ אזזט כישילר:

14 2

הָא לַחְמָא עַנְיָא
בוּ דִיר אֶכְמֶכִּי פָּאקִיר נִיג׳

bu dir ʔækmek-i faq/xi/ır-niŋ
this COP.3SG bread-POSS.3SG poor-GEN
this is (the) bread of (a) poor (one)

דִּי אֲכָלוּ אַבְהָתָנָא בְּאַרְעָא דְמִצְרָיִם
כִּי אַשָׁאדִילָר אַטָאלָרִמִיז יֵירִינְדֶא מִצְרַיִם נִיג׳

ki aša-dı-lar ata-lar-ımız yer-in-de Mičrayim-niŋ
that eat-PST-3PL father-PL-POSS.1PL place/country-POSS.3SG-LOC Egypt-GEN
that they ate, our fathers. In the land of (of) Egypt,

כָּל דִּכְפִין יֵיתֵי וְיֵיכוֹל
כִּים כִּי אָץ דִיר גֶלְסִין דָא אַשָׁאסִין

kim ki ač dir gel-sin da aša-sın
who/whoever that hungry.NOM COP.3SG come-IMP.3SG and eat-IMP.3SG
whoever that is hungry, let him come and let him eat,

כָּל דִּצְרִיךְ יֵיתֵי וְיִפְסַח
כִּים כִּי אַגֶ׳טְלִי (מוּחְטָץ) דִיר גֶלְסִין דָא מוֹעֵד אֵטְסִין

kim	*ki*	*ʔajjeṭ*[110]-li	(*muxtač*[111])	*dir*	*gel-sin*	*da*	*moʕed*	*et-sin*[112]
who(ever)	that	need-y.ADJ.NOM	(needy)	COP.3SG	come-IMP.3SG	and	annual_festival	do-IMP.3SG

whoever needy (needy)is, let him come and perform (the) annual festival.

הָשַׁתָּא הָכָא – לְשָׁנָה הַבָּאָה בְּאַרְעָא דְיִשְׂרָאֵל
בוּ יִיל בוּנְדָא גֶלֶגֶ׳כּ יִילְגָא יֵירִינְדֵא יִשְׂרָאֵל נִיגְ׳

bu	*yıl*	*bunda*	*gel-ejek*	*yıl-ğa*	*yer-in-de*	*yisrael-niŋ*
this	year.NOM	here	come-FUT[113].3SG	year-DAT[114]	place/country-POSS.3SG-LOC	Israel-GEN

this year here, to (the) coming year in (the) country of (of) Israel

הָשַׁתָּא עַבְדֵי – לְשָׁנָה הַבָּאָה
בוּ יִיל בוּנְדָא קוּלְלָר גֶלֶגֶ׳כּ יִילְגָא

bu	*yıl*	*bunda*	*qul-lar*	*gel-ejek*	*yıl-ğa*
this	year.NOM	here	slave-PL.NOM	come-FUT.3SG	year.DAT

This year – slaves, to (the) coming year

בְּנֵי חוֹרִין.
יֵירִינְדֵא יִשְׂרָאֵל נִיגְ׳ אַזָט כִּישִׁילֵר

yer-in-de	*yisrael*	*niŋ*	*azat*[115]	*kiši-ler*
place/country-POSS.SG-LOC	Israel	GEN	free[P]	man-PL.NOM

in (the) country of (of) Israel – free men.

Krymchak prayerbook, Kyiv MS 835

Another Krymchak prayerbook is F 321 op[is'] 5 N ORI [OPI] 835, new number 249, *Minhag Kafaʔ* for the days of fasting (מנהג כפא לימי צום), also coming from the collection of Avraham Kaufmann; the MS is also from the eighteenth century (the date corresponding to 1775/6 appears in the manuscript).[116] It contains, *inter alia*, partial translations to Turkic, Song of Songs and Ruth with a traditional commentary (called *targum*), both in Hebrew and in Turkic, and *Pirqe Avot* with a Turkic translation, and other texts. In this MS, the Turkic translation is called either *tefsir* or *twrqy* (fol. 55b), "Turkish".

110 *Arabo-Persian *ḥajjet* (pronounced *hajjet* [*haccet*] in Turkish), "need". *ḥ* fell out in all the Crimean-Turkic varieties.

111 *Arabo-Persian *muḥtāj* 'needy'. Note the change *ḥ* > *x* (also occurring in Karaite texts from the Crimea). A gloss to the older * *ḥajjet-li*, which probably was note understood well anymore; indeed, this word is not found in Krymchak dictionaries.

112 A composite verb translating Aramaic ויפסח.

113 Typically Oğuz.

114 Rendering Hebrew -ל *lə*-.

115 Persian *āzād*.

116 Yet Another Krymchak prayerbook is F 321 op[is'] 5 N ORI [OPI] 836, new number 250, Prayer according to *Minhag Kafaʔ* from 1776; it begins with rules for the morning prayer (דיני שחרית) and ends with the *Ḥad Gadya* (חד גדיא), the closing song of the Rabbanite Passover meal, and has no Turkic texts. Another Krymchak prayerbook previously kept in the Vernadsky Library was F 321 op[is'] 5 N ORI [OPI] 870, the introduction to the *Maḥzor* according to the rite of Qarsubazar (הקדמה למחזור נוסח קראסוב) in a 19th century copy, but I was not able to find this manuscript, and it was presumably lost. In addition, there is item F 321 op[is'] 5 N ORI [OPI] 837, new number 251, that contains different Turkic *piyyuṭim* in the Karaim language.

In the following, I provide fragments of the Krymchak translation of Songs of Songs according to my readings from the Kyiv MS 835 of , the equivalent fragments from the 1905 print, and an English translation. The differences – very minor – are underlined. One can see that both Krymchak text go back to the same Urtext, which was updated linguistically in the 1905 print.

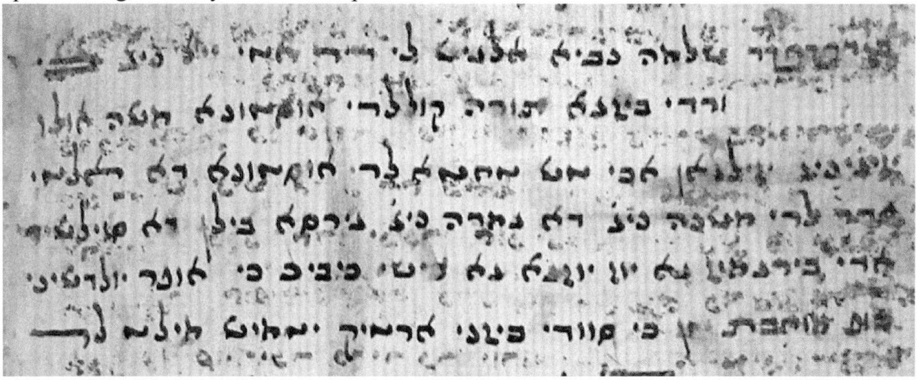

איטְטי שלמה נביא אלגיש לי דיר אטי ייו' ניג

ʔayṭ-ṭi	*šəlomoh*	*nābiʔ*	*ʔalgiš li*	*dir*	*ʔaṭ-i*	*YYW*	*niŋ*
ʔayṭ-ṭi	*šəlomoh*	*nābiʔ*	*ʔalgiš-li*	*dir*	*ʔād-i*	*ʔadonāy*	*niŋ*
say-PST_3SG	Salomon	prophet	blessing-ADJ.SUF	COP.3SG	name_POSS.3SG	God	GEN

Solomon the prophet said: the name of God is blessed

כי ורדי ביזגא תורה קוללרי אוסטונא משה

ki	*wer-di*	*biz-geʔ*	*torāh*	*qul-lar-i*	*ʔusṭuneʔ*	*mošeh*
ki	*wer-di*	*biz-geʔ*	*torāh ni*	*qul-lāʔr-i*	*ʔilen*	*mošeh*
because	give-PST.3SG	we-DAT	Torah-ABS/ACC	hand-PL-POSS.3SG	on/with	Moses

because He gave us the Torah on[117]/by hands [of] Moses

אולו יזיג'יניג יזילגאן אכי טש טחטאלר אוסטונא

	ʔulu	*yaz-iji-niŋ*	*yaz-il-gaʔn*	*ʔeki*	*ṭaš*	*ṭaḥṭaʔ-lar*	*ʔusṭuneʔ*
ʔol	*buyuk*	*yāʔz-iji niŋ*	*yāʔz-il-gān*	*ʔeki*	*ṭāš*	*ṭaḥṭāʔ-lar*	*ʔusṭuneʔ*
PRON.3SG[118]	big	write-SUF[119]-GEN[120]	write-PASS-PTCP	two	stone	tablet-PL-ABS	on

of the great Scribe written on two stone tablets

דא אלטי סדר לרי משנה ניג̇ דא גמרה ניג̇ גירסא בילן

daʔ	*ʔalṭi*	*seder*	*lar-i*	*mišnah*	*niŋ*	*daʔ*	*gəmarāh*	*niŋ*	*girsaʔ*	*bilen*
dāʔ	*ʔalṭi*	*seder*	*ler-i*	*mišnāh*	*niŋ*	*dāʔ*	*gəmārāh*	*niŋ*	*girsāʔ*	*ʔilen*
and	six	*seder*	PL-POSS.3SG	Mishnah	GEN	and	Gemara	GEN	*girsa*	with

and six Orders of Mishnah with the *girsa* of the Gemara,

117 Mimics Hebrew על ידי.

118 Mimics the Hebrew definite article

119 Suffix of professions or occupations, taken into other languages, like Arabic, Persian, Hebrew, etc.

120 This genitive refers to the whole chain "of Moses, the great scribe".

דא סוילשיר אדי בירגמיז גא יוז יוזגא

daʔ soyl-eš-ir ʔe-di bir-ge-miz geʔ yuz yuz-geʔ

dāʔ soyl-eš-ir ʔe-di bār-āʔ-bāʔr-i-miz-ğāʔ yuz yuz-geʔ

and speak-SUF-AOR.3SG he-be.PST.3SG together[121]-PRON.1PL-DAT face face-DAT

and He was speaking with us face to face,

גא כישי כיביכ כי אופר יולדשיני כופ מוחבת תן

kiši kibik ki ʔop-er yoldaš-i-ni kop muḥabbat ṭan

kiši kibik ki ʔop-er yoldāʔš-i-ni čoq-un-dān mahabbeṭ niŋ

man like that kiss-AOR.3SG comrade-POSS.3SG-ACC much/very-POSS.3SG love ABL/GEN

as a man kissing his friend (because of) much (of) / greatness of love

כי סוודי ביזני ארטיק יטמיש מילט לר דן

ki seḇ-di biz-ni ʔarṭiq yeṭmiš milleṭ ler den

ki seww-er biz-ni ʔarṭiq yeṭmiš milleṭ ler den

for love-PST.3SG/AOR.3SG we_ACC more seventy nation PL ABL

for He loved/loves us more that the Seventy Nations.

A Bilingual *Piyyuṭ* accompanying the *Teachings of the Fathers*

On Fol. 117 and further (the page cannot be turned without damaging the text) of the same Kyiv MS 835 there is the end of the *Teachings of the Fathers* (6:12 (פרקי אבות (with a slightly different text, ending at Isaiah 43:7); then follows the title with the name of the author and a Hebrew *piyyuṭ* translated into Turkic. The *piyyuṭ* found in other MSS of the Rabbanite prayer books according to the ritual of Romania (meaning the Byzantine realm), announcing Passover on the Great Shabbath (*šabbat ha-gadol,* the Shabbath preceding Passover), was discussed in Goldschmidt 1963/4: 226 (where the text is slightly different; Goldschmidt (p. 236 [רלו]) stressed the importance of future study of the prayer books from Corfu, Caphá, and Qarasubazar for establishing a better text of *Nusaḥ Romania*).

121 The MS version uses the older Qıpčaq *birge*; the printed version uses the Tatar word.

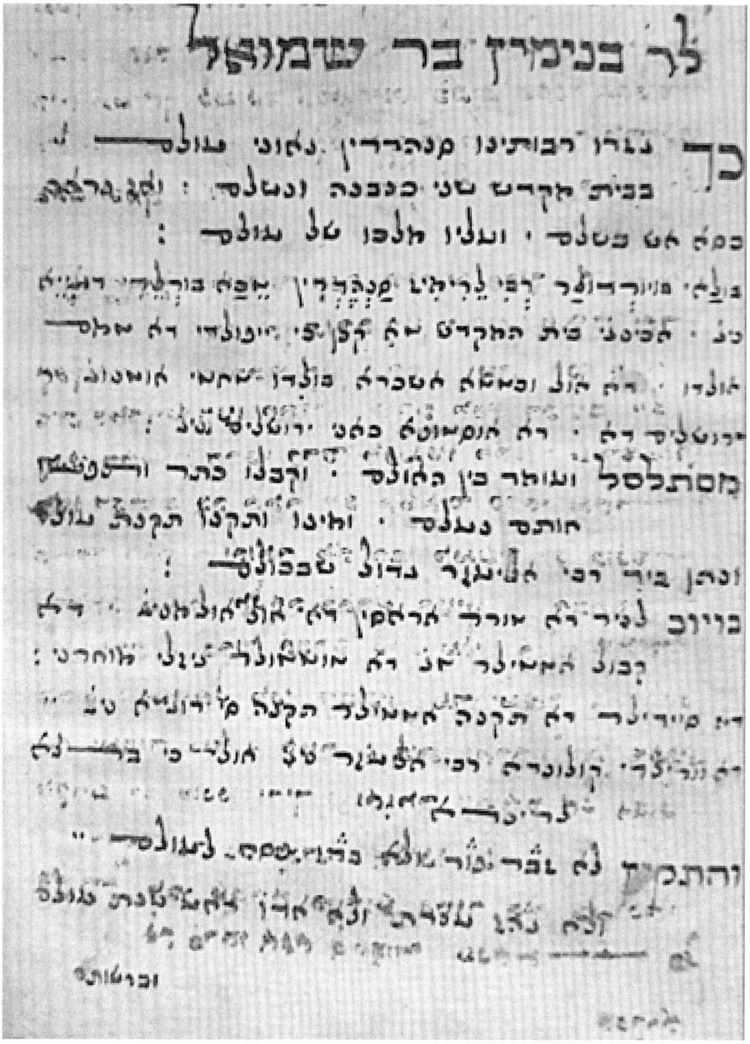

לר' בנימין בר שמואל

lə-binyamin bar šəmuʔel

to^H^-Binyamin son.CS^Aram^ Shemuʔel

By R. Binyamin Bar Shemuʔel

כך גזרו רבותינו סנהדרין גאוני עולם

בולַאי בויורְדולַר רְבִּי לֵרִימִיז סַנְהֶדְּרִין טֵכַּא בורְלֵרִי דוּנְיֵיא ניגֿ

bulay buyur-du-lar rbi ler-imiz sanhedrin ṭekaʔbur-ler-i[122] *duńyyaʔ-niŋ*

thus order-PST-3PL rabbi PL-1PL sanhedrin.NUM pride-PL.POSS.3SG world-GEN

Thus (they) ordered, our rabbis,[123] (the) Sanhedrin, prides of (the) world

122 *takabbur / tekabbür*.

123 In the Krymchak Turkic version from the 18th century, the pronunciation of the word רבי is dotted as in the 20th century pronunciation, *rbi / rəbi*.

בבית מקדש שני כנבנה ונשלם :

אכינגׄי בית המקדש טא קצן כי ייפולדי דא טמם אולדו

ekinji	*beyt hamiqdaš-ta*	*qačan*	*ki*	*yıp-ul-dı*	*da*	*tamam*	*ʔol-du*
second	Temple LOC	when	that/what	build-PASS-PST.3SG	and	complete	become-PST.3SG

in the Second Temple, when it was built and got finished

ואז נראה כסא אש

דא אול וכטטא אשכרא בולדו טכטי אוטנוגׄ

da	*ol*	*waxt-ta*	*aškara*	*bol-du*	*taxt-i*	*ʔot-nuŋ*
and	this	time-LOC	visible	become-PST.3sg	throne-POSS.3SG	fire-GEN

and that time (there) became visible a throne of fire

בשלם : ועליו מלכו של עולם :

ירושלים דא דא אוסטונא כאני ירושלים ניגׄ

yerušalayim-da	*da*	*üstünæ*	*xan-i*	*yerušalayim niŋ*
Jerusalem-LOC	and	on-POSTP[124]	Khan-POSS.3SG	Jerusalem-GEN

in Jerusalem and on it, Jerusalem's Khan.

מסתלסל ועומד בין האולם :

בויוכ לניר דא אוטר אראסין דא אול אולמניגׄ דא

büyük-len-ir	*da*	*tur-ar*	*ara-si-<n>-da*	*ol*	*ʔulam-niŋ*	*da*
become_big-REFL-AOR.3SG	and	stand-AOR.3SG	between-POSS.PRON.3SG-LOC	it/DEF	hall[H]-GEN	and

it grows bigger and stands between the Hall[125] and

וקבלו כתר ותפשו חותם נעלם :

קבול אטטילר טגׄ דא טוטטולר גיזלי מוחרני

qabul	*et-ti-ler*	*ṭaj*	*da*	*tut-tu-lar*	*giz-li*	*muḥ<u>r-ni*
reception[Ar]	do-PST-3PL	crown[P/Ar]	and	seize-PST.3PL	secret-ADJ.SUF	signet-ACC

they received (a) crown and they seized (the) secret signet

ומינו וקבלו ותקנו תקנת עולם

דא סיידילר דא תקנה אטטילר תקנה דונייא ניגׄ

da	*say-dı-lar*	*da*	*taqqanah*	*et-ti-ler*	*taqqanah-sı*	*düńya*	*niŋ*
and	count-PST-3PL	and	*taqqanah*/ruling	do-PST-3PL	*taqqanah*/ruling-POSS.3PL	world	GEN

and they appointed[126] and made (a) ruling, (an) eternal[127] ruling

ונתן ביד רבי אליעזר גדול שבכולם

דא וורילדי קולונדא רבי אליעזר ניגׄ אולי כי ברצא לרינדא

da	*ver-il-di*	*qul-u<n>-da*	*rbi*	*ʔeliʕezerniŋ*	*ulı*	*ki*	*barča-larin-da*
and	give-PASS-PST.3SG	hand-POSS.3SG-LOC	R.	Eliezer-GEN	great	that/what	all-POSS.3PL-LOC

and it was given in the hand[128] of R. Eliezer, the great(est) of them all.

124 The postposition does not rule anything, there is no pronoun or noun. This means it simply mimics the Hebrew *ʕal*.

125 The structure that stood at the entrance to the *Heykhal*, the inner sanctuary, in the Temple of Jerusalem.

126 The Turkic translator used here the calque-verb "to count, to charge" to render different and homonym Hebrew verbs that mean "to count" and "to put in charge".

127 Hebrew *ʕolām* means "eternity, place, time, world"; the Turkic translator just calqued Hebrew "eternal" by his "of the world", *dwńyyʔ nyŋ*.

128 References to the mystical Heykhaloth / Shiʕur Qomah literature.

והתקין לא ז'ב'ד' פור ולא ב'ד'ו' פסח לעולם

wə-hiṯqīn	*lo(?)*	*7'2'4*	*pur*	*wə-lo(?)*	*2'4'6*	*pesaḥ*	*lə-ʕolam*
and-decree.PF.3SG.M	NEG	7'2'4	Purim	and-NEG	2'4'6	Pesaḥ	for-eternity

And he ordered: Purim can never fall on Shabbath, Monday, and Wednesday; and not Pass-over on Monday, Wednesday, Friday;

ולא ג'ה'ז' עצרת ולא א'ד'ו' ראש שנות עולם

wə-lo(?)	*3'5'7*	*ʕăṣereṯ*	*wə-lo(?)*	*1'4'6*	*rō(?)š*	*šənoṯ*	*ʕolam*
and-NEG	3'5'7	feast_of_weeks	and-NEG	1'4'6	beginning.CS	year.PL.CS	world

and no Feast of Weeks on Tuesday, Thursday, Shabbath; and the Beginning of the worldly Years not on Sunday, Wednesday, Friday.[129]

The Turkic language here cannot be modeled on Karaite versions, for the text translated is strictly Rabbanite, and even the choice of the text to be translated can be seen as reflecting anti-Karaite tendencies. Nevertheless, we can see similarities with the language of Karaite Biblical translations copied in the Crimea. They included *barča* 'all/every' instead of the later *jümle*; the use of the pseudo-article *ol* and the specific "Karaim" genitive construction that renders the post-Biblical Hebrew one: *sanhedrin ṭekaʔburleri duńyyaʔniŋ* 'the pride[s] of the world (its prides, of world), [the members of the] Synedrion'; *xʔny yrwšlym nyŋ* 'Khan of Jerusalem, its Khan, of Jerusalem'; *ʔrʔsyn dʔ ʔwl ʔwlmnyŋ* 'in the middle of the *ʔUlam*'. Especially instructive is *ṭḥṭy ʔwṭnwŋ* 'a throne of fire' (its throne, of fire), translating *kisseʔ ʔēš* – not **ot taxtı* or **otnuŋ taxtı*. Noteworthy is the use of the Oğuz verb of being and becoming *olmaq* besides the Qıpčaq *bolmaq*.

3.3 Crimean Karaite-Turkic / Crimean-Tatar and Karaim

The Karaites in the Crimea spoke the same language as their neighbors – Muslims, Orthdox-Greek (*Urum*), or Armenians – i.e., in the areas of the predominance of the Oğuz Crimean-Turkish, or the Crimean dialect of the Ottoman Turkish, like Keffeh/Feodosia, Mangup, which were included in the Ottoman *eyālet* of Qirim/Keffeh. Their speech was basically Turkish, while in the areas of the Crimean Khanate proper, with its Qıpčaq-Tatar, they spoke Tatar. The first known Karaite immigrants to the Peninsula, those who moved to the new Mongol-ruled cities from Byzantine Constantinople in the second half of the 13th century, were speakers of Greek. This influx of the Greek-speaking Karaites from the former Byzantine provinces, both in Rumelia and in Anatolia, never stopped, but had two peaks. The first peak was in the late 15th / early 16th centuries, after Constantinople became the Ottoman Istanbul and the capital of the sultans was transferred there, on the one hand, and the new opportunities were opened in the Crimea, on the other. The second peak was in the mid-17th century, after a series of calamities befell the Karaites of Istanbul. However, this stream of Istanbul Karaites to the Crimea was continuing even in the early 20th century.

129 For the Crimean Rabbanites, who lived surrounded by the Karaite majority, these rules were to be emphasized.

Other early Karaite immigrants came to the Crimea, according to the early 19th century Karaite traditions (real or not), from Bukhara, Circassia, and Iran. This seems plausible, and indeed, Judeo-Persian MSS were found in the Crimean *Genizah*s.[130]

Beginning from the late 15th/early 16th century, we encounter religious teachers in the Crimean Karaite communities of Çufut-Qal'eh, Mangup, Keffeh/Feodosija, who were emigrants from Łuck/Luck/Lutsk, Kyiv, Halicz, Troki (and from Deražne in Keffeh in the late 17th century,[131] and from Kokizow in the early 18th century). For a century, from the mid-18th century up to mid-19th century, positions in religious education in the Karaite Crimea were filled, almost exclusively, by immigrants from Łuck (e.g., Simhah Yitshaq Łucki, Yitshaq Shlomo Łucki, David Kokizow, Mordechai Sultanski, Avraham Firkowicz, to mention the most prominent among them). In the Crimea, they had to learn the local Turkic idiom, but on the other hand, they diffused the passive knowledge of their mother tongue that did develop in the Crimea into a sort of the "language of the educated", which gained significant prestige, a situation not unknown to other Jewish immigrant sub-languages (Ivry-Taitsh [religious tranlation languages] vs. *Jargon*/Yiddish and Ladino [religious translation language] vs. Judeo-Spanish/Judezmo being good examples).

The language of the Bible translations written or copied in the Crimea thus does not tell us much about the languages spoken by the Crimea Karaites.[132]

A sample of Crimean Karaite-Turkic of Çufut-Qalՙeh from the 1820s

Here follows a specimen of a translation from Hebrew of a non-Biblical text, *Ṣel ha-ʕolam* (most probably, the 1733 Amsterdam print was used), which is, itself, a translation of a 1246 Old French encyclopedia, *L'Image du monde*, written by Gautier de Metz. The Crimean Judeo-Turkic version of *Ṣel ha-ʕolam* is now kept in New York, at the Jewish Theological Seminary in the Elkan Nathan Adler collection, NY JTS Ms. 3482 (ENA 117, F 32167).[133]

The translator or the owner of the MS was Abraham Shammash Bota, or Abraham ben Yaʕaqob ben Berakhah Botowicz,[134] a native of Çufut-Qalʕeh, who served in 1846/7 as a *shammash* in Sevastopol (it seems that a small Karaite community was established there after 1844). Apparently, Abraham Bota / Botowicz made his translation from Hebrew into his own dialect of Crimean Judeo-Turkic in order to be printed by the newly-established Karaite printing house at Gözleve, the city of Simḥah ben Shelomo ben Nahamu Babowicz (1790–1855), the richest man in the Crimean Peninsula, a philanthropist, and a contractor for the Russian Army (there is a dedication of the work to

130 Cf. Shapira 2008a.

131 Shapira 2018a.

132 For other opinions: Németh 2014c; 2015d; 2016; Jankowski 1997; 2003; 2015a; 2015b; see now Jankowski et al. 2019.

133 I would like to express my gratitude to Prof. Gad Freudenthal who drew my attention to this text and discussed various accepts of this work with me.

134 Samuel Poznanski in his unpublished *Encyclopedia of Karaites* made two different persons of him. In 1833/34, Abraham ben Yaʕaqob ben Berakhah Botowicz participated in financing the Karaite printing house in Gözleve and donated 300 Rubles, a considerable sum. He died prior to 1856/57, probably as a consequence of the Crimean War.

Babowitz in the MS); the idea of printing the originally 1246 French work in a "Tatar" translation fits into the atmosphere of the 1830s at Gözleve.[135]

The beginning of Chapter III.6/7: What is important about this translation linguistically are two facts. First, if the author was indeed Abraham Bota/Botowicz, a native of Çufut-Qalʕeh, so his maternal language was supposed to be the local dialect; second, he was living in relative isolation in Sevastopol.

His idiolect was less likely affected by the linguistic shift occurring at the 1820s "Tower of Babel" of Gözleve, where idiolects of newcomers from Mangup, Keffeh (like Yiṣḥaq Tirishqan, see below), Çufut-Qalʕeh, the former Ottoman villages near Kerch (like Babowicz himself), and Łuck and Kokizow (like Avraham Firkowicz, David Kokizov, YaSHaR Łucki, Mordekhay Sultanski) were merging into a new dialect. The idiolect of the translator of *Ṣel ha-ʕolam* seems to have been typical for the Central Crimea.

The beginning of Chapter III.6/7:

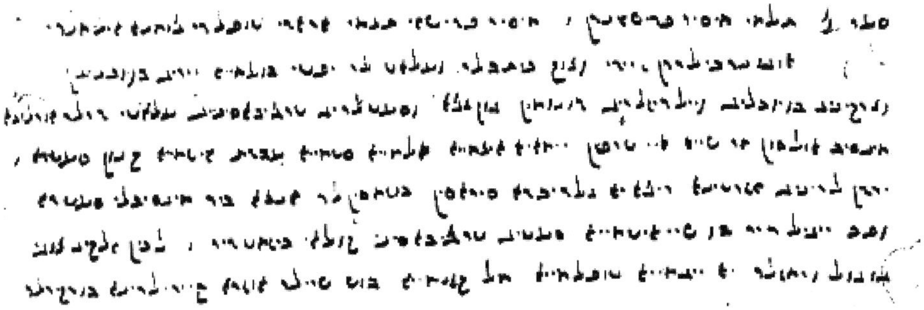

מן תלמי מלך מצרים
תלמי מיסיר פדישהנדן

talmay misir padišaḥ-in-dan
Ptolemy Egypt king-POSS.3SG-ABL
About Ptolemy, king of Egypt

תלמי מלך מצריי׳ אשר דרש ואסף
מיסיר פדישחי תלמי או אדי טופלדי

misir padišaḥ-i talmay o e-di ṭop-la-di
Egypt king-POSS.3SG Ptolemy PRON.3SG be-PST.3SG collect-SUF-PST.3SG
Ptolemy king of Egypt, he was (one who) collected

135 We know that the Karaites' choices of Hebrew books to be translated quite lately into their Turkic vernaculars were sometimes rather surprising: by the end of the 19th century, a Karaite copied an obscure Rabbinic work, *Yeriʕot Shelomo*, of an obscure late 19th century German Rabbi, Salomon Thien; I thank Professor Haggai Ben-Shammai, who called my attention to this author and his work. See Shapira 2014: 143.

החכמה מכל קדומיו

ג׳ומלא אילימלרי אונונדכילרדן זיידי

jumle il[i]m-ler-i oŋ-uŋ-da-ki-lar-in dan ziyadi

all science-PL-ACC before-GEN-LOC-KI[136]-PL-GEN ABL (too-)much

all (the) sciences more that those who were before him

וחיבר ספרי׳ רבי׳ וכלי׳ למצא גודל הארץ

וצוק כיתבלר ועלאט לר יפטי בולמיא יייריג בויוכליג

ve-čoq kitab-lar-i ve-ʕalaʔṭ-lar yap-ṭ bul-ma-ya yyer-iŋ buyuk-lig

and-much book-PL-ACC and-instrument-PL do_PST.3SG find-INF-DAT earth-GEN big-*lik*_SUF.ABS

and he made many books and instruments to find the greatness of the Earth

וגבה הגלגל ותנועת הככבי׳ יום ולילה

וצרקיניג בויוכליג ויילדיזלריג דונומין גון גג׳א

ve-čarq-i-n-iŋ buyuklig ve-yyildiz-lar-iŋ don-um-in gun-geje

and-wheel-POSS.3SG_N_GEN big-*lik*_SUF.ABS and.star-PL-GEN turn-SUF-ACC day-night

and the greatness of the Wheel and the tournament of the stars day and night,

וכלי מבחן השעות הנקרא אורלוג׳א

וסעטלריג טוג׳ריבאסיניג עלאטי דרלר אורלוג׳א

ve-saʕaṭ-lar-iŋ ṭojribeʔ-si-niŋ ʕalaʔṭ-i de-r-ler ʕorlojaʔ

and hour-PL.GEN trial-POSS.3SG-GEN instrument-POSS.3SG say-AOR-3PL *horloge*

and the instrument for judgment of the hours [that] they call *horloge*

יתכנו לכל דבר היות מבאר לאכול לשתות ליקח

מינסיב אולסון חר שייא איי זימן יימאיא איצמייא אלמייא

minsib ol-sun ḥer šeyy-eʔ iyyi ziman yye-me-yyeʔ ʔič-me-yyeʔ ʔal-ma-yyaʔ

suitable be-SUB-3SG every thing-DAT good time eat-INF-DAT drink-INF-DAT take[137]-INF-DAT

so it would suit for every thing in proper/good time, for eating, drinking, buying, and

למכור להתפלל בשעה קבועה

סטמייא עבדת איטמייא קנון סעטדא

saṭ-ma-yyaʔ ʕebadet ʔeṭ-me-yyeʔ qanun saʕaṭ-daʔ

sell-INF-DAT worship do-INF-DAT law hour/watch-LOC

selling, for worshiping in the lawful hour

ואל יהרסו בגשתם לבקש כבוד יוצרי׳ שלא הסדר כי אם אל נכון בשעה

ירדן לרניג חזרטיגא ריג׳א יא גלדיכדא סיראסין בוזמסין לר אנג׳א ביר מינסיבלי סעטדא

yarad-gan ler-iŋ ḥazreṭ-i-ğeʔ rijaʔ yaʔ gel-dik-deʔ sira-ʔsin

create-PTCP PL-GEN *hazret*-POSS.3SG-DAT request DAT come-GER-DAT row-OLD.INSTR

boz-ma-sin lar anja bir minsib-li saʕaṭ-daʔ

break-NEG-COND 3PL so_far one suitable_*li*-ADJ.SUF hour/watch-LOC

so much that they would not be made broken in time when they come to ask from His Honor their Creator at one suitable hour

ומאד קל הדבר לעשותו

ופכ ייגיל דיר בו שיי איטמייא

ve-pek yyiğ-il dir bu šey ʔeṭ-me-yyeʔ

and-very normal-ADJ.SUF COP.3SG this thing make-INF-DAT

and very correct/normal is for doing this thing;

136 The pronominal or "mixed" suffix *-ki*, cf. Lewis 2013: 66.

137 Used in the sense of "to buy".

מבחן השעות היא מלאכה קלה אמנ׳ רוב ההמון
סעטיג טרג׳יבאסיני קולאי כיזמט דיר לכין חלקיג צוגי
*saʕaṭ-iŋ *ṭojribeʔ-si-ni qolaʔy xizmeṭ dir lekin ḥalq-iŋ čoğ-i*
hour/watch-GEN trial-POSS.3SG-ACC easy service COP.3SG but people-GEN very-POSS.3SG
the judgment of the timepiece is an easy service. But the majority of people

לא ישיתו לבבם כי אם לכנוס ולאסוף לצרור הון
גוגול ורמזלר יא ייגמייא טופלמייא מל קזנמייא
goŋul ver-mez-ler ya yyiğ-me-yyeʔ ṭopla-ma-yyaʔ mal qazan-ma-yyaʔ
heart/soul give-NEG-3PL or collect-INF-DAT collect-INF-DAT property earn-INF-DAT
they do not give heart but for assembling, collecting [and] earning property

לבעלי נשואי נשיהן
בוש שיילר אוזרא קיידלריגא
boš šeyy-ler ʔuzereʔ qayydi<n>-lar-i-ğaʔ
empty thing-PL on woman-PL-POSS.3-DAT
[in order to spend it] on empty things for women.

The Qipčaq *-ğ/g/qV* dative form is rare[138] with mostly the Oğuz *-(y)V* being used (*dunyay̱a kolgu*); Qıpčaq forms (*kolgu*) appear alongside with the Oğuz *g̦orduğim g̦orume*. The verb *qomaq* ‘to put’ was analyzed or/and pronounced *qom-maq* (*ve-ʔadin qom-ṭu yisraʔel-de* ‘and He has his name put in Israel’).

While citing the Bible, the translator was mostly code-switching from his Crimean variety of Turkish (or, from the “Oğuz dialect of Crimean Tatar”) to the above-mentioned prestigious Karaim language of the teachers from the North (I:3, *ve-oṭurdu* [*šelomo xizireṭ*] *ṭaxṭ-i ʔüsṭüne H’ niŋ*, seat-POSS.3SG on.POSTP God GEN, וישב שלמה על כסא ה׳, Chr 1 29:23; a Modern Turkish translation: *RABBIN tahtı üzerine oturdu*).

He also used specifically Karaim religious terms such as *maxtuvlu* ‘the blessed one’ (an old borrowing from Mongolian), as in the phrase *maxṭuvli olsun qadir ṭeŋri* ‘let the Mighty God be blessed’.

3.4 Bible translations of Avraham Firkowicz and Yiṣḥaq Tirishqan

In 1831–33, Firkowicz, then living and teaching in Constantinople, printed his translation of the Pentateuch in an experimental Turkic language – the vernacular Turkish of the capital as spoken by minorities and the less educated, with a blend of grammatical constructions and vocabulary of his Karaim mother tongue.[139] The language of the translation was considered an outrage by the leaders of the Karaite community of Constantinople – who knew and spoke Turkish, but were native speakers of Greek.[140] It had no linguistic continuation, and in 1841 in Gözleve the biggest Judeo-Turkic project ever was launched, a printed translation of the whole of the Bible (except Chronicles), in

138 But see I:3, *qadir ṭeŋri ki yaraṭṭi ʔinsan-ni qiyafeṭi-len* ‘The Almighty God created the man by his/His own likeness’.

139 In Firkowicz’s private archive, kept in St. Petersburg, there are many drafts and lists of vocabulary prepared for this translation.

140 Shapira 2003a.

three volumes; it was formally dedicated to the future Russian Czar Alexander II on the occasion of his hasty wedding.

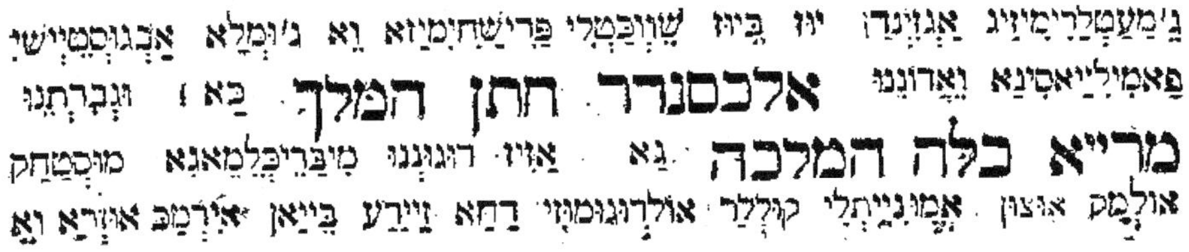
אלכסנדר חתן המלך
מריא כלה המלכה

In fact, the publication celebrated the newly gained administrative and religious independence of the Crimean Karaites, under the successful leadership of the above-mentioned Simḥah Babowicz, who was born into the only Jewish/Karaite family in a Muslim village in the formerly Ottoman Turkish-speaking area near Kerch and resided in the hub of Gözleve, where many Turkic dialects were intermingling, or at his estate near Qarasubazar (where a mixed Oğuzo-Qıpçaq dialect was spoken).

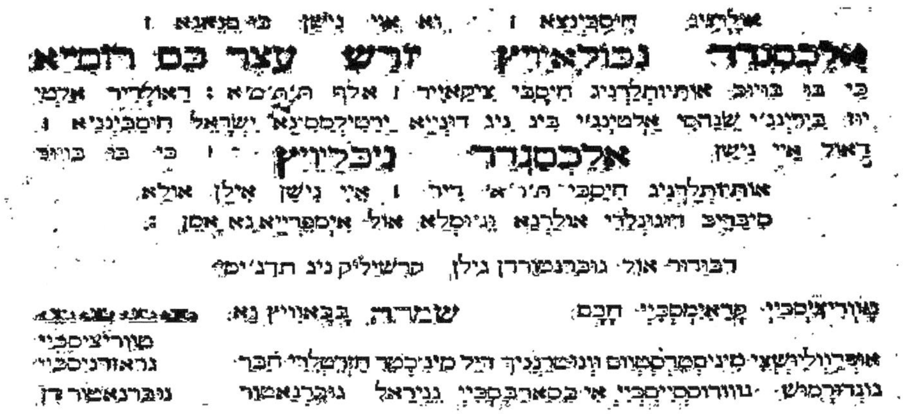

The translation was sponsored by the rich and educated merchant Mordechai Trıshqan/Tırıshqan, a native of Turkish-speaking Keffeh/Feodosija, who had moved to Gözleve. Trıshqan had a history of being involved in publishing projects and he participated somehow in Firkowicz's Constantinople edition. There was a team of scholars working with Trıshqan on the MSS taken as the basis of the printed edition. Avraham Firkowicz was not invited to this team; nevertheless, Tırıshqan's team adopted the same principles of editing a translation into a non-spoken and artificial Turkic language that Firkowicz had led a decade ago. Because of reservations about Firkowicz's radical linguistic engineering, because of lack of time, and because of lack of Turkic-speaking type-setters, Tırıshqan's team adopted the inner structure of the Bible translation as coagulated in the older MS translations, including the non-Turkic genitive construction rendering the post-Biblical Hebrew one. At the same time, they changed, rather consistently, several of the lexical and phonetic features, adopting them, to a certain degree, to the current speech (e.g., changing the Qıpčaq *k* and *t* to the Oğuz *g* and *d*, etc.). One important trait that distinguished the "Trıshqan edition"/"Gözleve edition" from the "Firkowicz edition"/"Constantinople edition" was that Tırıshqan's team kept the Qıpčaq dative form (changed by Firkowicz into the Oğuz one), a trait that provides the "Tırıshqan edition" its "Tatar" flavor. It should be remembered that practically nobody in Tırıshqan's team was a native speaker of "Crimean-Tatar" – they were mostly speakers of Łuck-Karaim or of Turkish (like Tırıshqan himself). The fact that many of the members of the team were themselves speakers of Łuck-Karaim, who had years of experience of teaching the Crimean-born Karaite children in the older Karaim-colored "language of the educated" only, strengthened their desire to adopt the language of the land and to settle down in the country. It would be interesting to follow up how the editing techniques of the team were changing over time: they had begun with the sincere desire to provide a new and better read-off translation than Firkowicz's PR disaster of 1831–33, but as they proceeded with their work, they felt that they were running out of time (as said, the future Czar's scandalous wedding came as a surprise for everyone), and they began to reproduce the "Firkowicz edition" first (while keeping their principles of adapting the text to a certain "ideal" reality of a Qıpçaq/"Tatar"-looking text), and then they just reproduced the MSS without change.

A problem with this "Tırıshqan edition" was their use of a system of vocalization that discerned a frontal *e* (*ṣere*), used a *qamaṣ* in Hebrew words, like in nouns, where it is found, but used the same sign, *pataḥ,* for both *a* and the backward closed *a/æ* (examples of such a vocalization are found, indeed, in the MSS). Another problem was the inexperience of the type-setters, who not infrequently did not understand the text. The result was a text full of printing errors. In an introduction to the Bible translation, the editors printed the following example of the real language the Karaites of Gözleve were speaking:

The Printers' Excuses

מצדיקי הרבים קונים חברים מקשיבים ניג אגזינדן

maṣ/čdiqey[141]	*ha-rabbim*	*qonim*	*ḥaḇerim*	*maqšiḇim-niŋ*	*ağz-ın-dan*
judge_honestly.PTCP.CS.PL	DEF-much.PL	buy.PTCP.PL	friend.PL	listen.PTCP.PL-GEN	mouth-POSS.3SG-ABL

From the mouth of *those who are charitable to the public, the buyers, the subscribers,*[142] *those who are ready to listen*

אווללא אללה ג׳א דועה

evvele[143]	*Allah*	*ğa*	*duʕah*
at_first^{Ar}	God	DAT^{Ar}	prayer^{Ar}

Firstly, a prayer to God

אכינג׳י התנצלות נאמי

ekinji	*hitnaṣ/čelut*[144]	*nam-i*
second	apology^{H}	book/missive[145]-POSS.3SG

Secondly, a letter of apology.

141 The first sign is graphic, the second one is phonetic.

142 People who prepaid the edition and thus made it possible.

143 Assimilated Arabic.

144 The *shwa mobile* is pronounced as a regular *e*-sound in the Karaite tradition.

145 Turkish from Persian.

עזרנו בשם יוי עושה שמים וארץ

ʕezre-nu be-šem YWY ʕośe šamayim wa-ʔareṣ/č[146]

help-1PL^{H} in-name.CS^{H} God^{HH} make.PTCP.CS^{H} heaven^{H} and-earth^{H}

Our support is in the name of the Lord, creator of Heaven and Earth.

דגין בו ואקיט צוק שוכורלר אללה תעלה גא כי

dağın bu waqıt čoq šükür-ler ʔAllah Taʕalah-ğa ki

again this time^{Ar} much thank^{AR}-PL God be_exalted^{AR}-DAT that.CONJ

Again, much thank be to God Almighty for that

שׁווכטלי מרחמטלי פּדישחימיזגיג גונונדא

ševketli merhametli padišax-ımız-gig[147] *gün-ün-de*

magnificent merciful padishah-POSS.1PL.GEN day-POSS.3SG-LOC

in the days of our mighty merciful King

ירילקאמאגי אילן המון העם אוצין

yarılqa-mağ-ı ʔilen hamon ha-ʕam ʔüčün

grant-INF.POSS.3SG with.POSTP mass.CS^{H} DEF-people^{H} for.POSTP

by/with his granting the common people

תּ׳נ׳ךְ ניג תרגומוני דפוס אידטירמייא ביזלרי

TaNaX-nıŋ targum-u-nı defus id-tir-me-ye bizler-i

Hebrew_Bible^{H}-GEN translation^{H}-POSS.3SG-ACC print^{H} do-CAUS-INF-DAT we-ACC

making us to print a translation of the Hebrew Bible

מוסטחק אידטירמיש גרצכ כי

mustaxaq id-tir-miš gerček ki

worthy^{Ar} do-CAUS-PST.PTCP true that.CONJ

having made (us) worthy. Though it is true that

דורלו סבבלר דן תרגום דפוסי ספצא אולממיש

dürlü sebeb-ler den targum defus-i sefa-ča ol-ma-mıš

of_all_kinds.ADJ reason^{Ar}-PL ABL translation^{H} print^{H}-POSS.3SG enjoyment^{Ar}-ADV be-NEG-PST.PTCP

the printing of the translation, for different reasons, had not become enjoyable,

ביר כי אשכנז מסדר לרי טאטר דילינִי

bir ki aškenaz mesadder-ler-i tatar dil-i-<n>-i

one that.CONJ Ashkenazi^{H} setter^{H}-PL-POSS.3SG Tatar language-POSS.3SG-ACC

one [reason being] that (the) Ashkenazi setters [not knowing the] Tatar language

בילמדיכלרינדן אוטרו אותיות לרני וא סוזלרני דאכי

bil-me-diklerin-den uturu otiyot lar-nı ve söz-ler-ni daxi

know-NEG-GER.PTCP.3PL-ABL against letter.PL^{H} PL-ACC and word-PL-ACC even

having not known, letters and even words

בירי ביריניג ירינא

bir-i bir-i-niŋ yer-i-<n>e

one-POSS.3SG one-POSS.3SG-GEN place-POSS.3SG-DAT

one instead of the other

146 The first sign is graphic, the second one is phonetic.

147 A misprint for **nyg* that stands for *-nıŋ*, GEN.

דגישיפ שאשיריפ קארישטיריפ דוזר איד לא
degiš-ip šaš-ır-ıp qarıš-tır-ıp düze-r idi-ler
change-GER wander-CAUS-GER mix-CAUS-GER order-AOR.3SG do_be-3PL
while they change, misplace and mix up (them)

וא צוק זַחְמֶטְלַר אִילַן הגהה אולונדוקטן סוגרא
ve čoq zaḥmetlar ilen haggaha ol-un-duq-tan soŋra
and much trouble^{Ar}PL with.POSTP proof_reading^{H} be-PASS-GER-ABL after.POSTP
And after much toiling, having had proofread,

גנא יגלישלר בולונויור זירא הגהה דן סוגרא דאכי
gene yaŋlıš-lar bul-un-uyor zira[148] *haggaha da soŋra daxi*
new mistake-PL find-PASS.PRS.3SG because^{P} proof_reading^{H} ABL after.POSTP even
new mistakes were found, for, after the proof-reading,

כסטיקלרי ואקיט מורכפ סולדיגי ואקיט
xastı-q-lar-ı vaqıt ta mürekkep sol-dıg-ı vaqıt
ill^{P}-ness-3PL-GEN time LOC ink^{AR} wane-GER-GEN time
during the illness, when the ink waned

יפּוּשופּ אותיות לר ירלרינדן ציקטיגי ואקיט איככנג׳אג׳י
yap-uš-up otiyot lar yer-ler-in-den čıq-tığ-ı vaqıt ikkenjaji
make-RECIP-GER letter.PL^{H} PL place-3PL-GEN-ABL go_out-GER-POSS.3SG time *Ashkenazi[149]
and when the prepared letters moved from their proper places, the *Ashkenazi,

דיל בילמייפ אותיות לרי ירלי ירינג׳א קויימז אדי
dil bil-me-yip otiyot lar-ni yerli yer-in-j[150]*e qoy-maz e-di*
tongue know-NEG-GER letter.PL^{H} PL-ACC proper place-POSS.3SG-DAT put-NEG be-PST.3SG
not knowing the language, did not put the letters to their proper places.

A sample of a Tirishqan edition compared with three other versions

Here I provide Jeremiah 1:5–12 in four Judeo-Turkic versions. The basic version presented here is the Tırıshqan version printed in 1841 at Gözleve. It was based on MSS copied in the Crimea for generations, and the first version in my notes is that of a late 18th century MS of the Pentateuch belonging to Mr. Alfred Eidlisz (one former owner of this MS was the renowned Karaite collector Koknay). It can be easily seen that these versions are almost identical, except such features are *barča* for "all" replaced by *jümle*, etc. The second version in the notes one is from a 19th century Krymchak MS kept at the Institute for Oriental Studies, St. Petersburg (B98, fols 68b–69a); I have published the Book of Obadiah from this MS (Shapira 2016a).

148 Persian. Possibly a misprint for **xastılıq*.

149 A misprint!

150 A misprint, *j* should be **g*.

From comparison, there can be seen both similarities (for both Karaite and Krymchak Turkic texts of Biblical translations go back to the same Middle-Qıpčaq tradition) and dissimilarities (being the result of bifurcation of the common inherited tradition).

The third version in the notes is from the Karaite hectograph / schapirograph edition of the Book of Jeremiah published in Halicz in 1927 in just 28 copies;[151] it was prepared by Josef Mardkowicz and edited by Zerach (Zarach) Zarachowicz and Noah (Nowach) Szulimowicz in anticipation of the sweeping religious reforms, by Seraja Szapszał, of Karaite religious life and Karaites' Turkic language in the inter-war Poland, just in the two years after this publication. What is important, this translation does not demonstrate the typically late Halicz (and Troki) shifts *ö* > *io* and *ü* > *iu*, meaning that a genuinely old MS was used, as stated in the authors' *Introduction* to this publication. It can be seen that this translation is both conservative, preserving the skeleton of Middle-Qıpčaq translations, and innovative.

Jer 1:5

בְּטֶרֶם אצורך (אֶצָּרְךָ) בַבֶּטֶן יְדַעְתִּיךָ

Tırıshqan יַרַטְמַסִימֶדַן בּוּרוּן סֵנִי קוּרְסַקְדַא בִּילְדִים סֵנִי

yar-aṭ-ma-si-m-dan	*burun*	*sēny*	*qursaq-daʔ*	*bil-dim*	*sēni*
split-CAUS-INF-POSS.3SG-POSS.1SG-ABL	before-POSTP	2SG-ACC	belly-LOC	know-PST.2SG	2SG.ACC

before my splitting you out / my creating you / of (the) belly I had known you

Eidlisz-Koknay ירטמסמדן בורין קורסקטא בילדים סני

yrṭmsmdn bwryn qwrs-qṭʔ[152] *byldym sny*

Krymchak יַרַטְמַסמְטַן בורון סני קורסק טא/ טן בילדים סני

yar-aṭ-ma-s-ṭan bwrwn sny qwrsq ṭʔ/n[153] *byldym sny*

Halicz יָארַטְמַסְמְדָן בוּרוּן סֵנִי קוּרְסַקְטָא בִּילְדִים סֵנִי

yāʔr-aṭ-ma-si-m-dān burun seni qursaq-ṭāʔ bil-dim seni

וּבְטֶרֶם תֵּצֵא מֵרֶחֶם הִקְדַּשְׁתִּיךָ

Tırıshqan דַצִיקְמַסִינְדַן בּוּרוּן קוּרְסַקְדַן אַיְרוּכְסִי אֵטְטִים סֵנִי

da-ṣiq-ma-si-ŋ-dan	*burun*	*qursaq-dan*	*ʔayruxsi*	*ʔeṭ-ṭim*	*seni*
and-exit-INF-GEN-POSS.2SG-ABL	before-POSTP	belly-ABL	holy	make-PST.1SG	2SG.ACC

and before your going out off the belly, I had made you holy

Eidlisz-Kokenay דציגרמסימדן בורין קורסקטן איירוקסי אטטים סני

d-ṣygrmsymdn bwryn qwrsq-ṭn ʔyyrwqsy ʔṭṭym sny

Krymchak דציקמסטן בורון אומיי דן חדיר לדים סני

d-ṣyqmsṭn bwrwn ʔwmyy dn ḥdyr ldym[154] *sny*

151 The number which demonstrates the demand existing in the dwindling community (thanks to generosity of Dr. Mikhail Kizilov, I possess one copy). In the 1920s–1930s, a small circle of Halicz Karaites was engaged in Sisyphus attempts to preserve the cultural heritage of the tiny community. Especially worth notice is the work of Zerah (Zara, Zarach) Zarachowicz, who copied MSs and translated Rabbanite and Karaite works into the Karaim language even in the days of WWII (see Shapira 2002b).

152 belly-LOC.

153 LOC/ABL.

154 "I prepared / I made special and ready".

Halicz דָא צִקְמַסִינְדָן בוּרוּן קוּרְסַקְטַן אַיְירִיקְסִי אֶטְטִים סֶנִי
dāʔ ṣiqmasindān burun qursaqṭan ʔayyriqsi ʔeṭṭim seni

נָבִיא לַגּוֹיִם נְתַתִּיךָ
נָבִיא אולוסֶלַרְגַא בֵּרְדִים סֵנִי

nābiʔ ʔulus[155]*-lar-gaʔ bēr-dim sēni*
prophet nation-PL-DAT give-PST.1SG 2SG-ACC
I made you as a prophet to nations.

Eidlisz-Kokenay נביא אולוס לרגא ברדים סני
nbyʔ ʔwlws lr-gʔ br-dym sny

Krymchak נביא אולוס לר גא קויידום סני
nbyʔ ʔwlws lr gʔ qwyy-dwm[156] *sny*

Halicz אַזִימֵי נָבִיאגֵי חַנְלִקְלַרְגַא בֵּרְדִים סֵנִי
ʔazimey nābiʔ-gay ḥanliqlargaʔ berdim seni

Jer 1:6

וָאֹמַר אֲהָהּ אֲדֹנָי ה׳ הִנֵּה לֹא יָדַעְתִּי דַּבֵּר כִּי-נַעַר אָנֹכִי
Tırıshqan דַאיְטְטִים וַה אֲדנַי טַגְרִי מוּנַא בִּילְמַדִים סוֹזְלַמָא כִּי אוֹגְלַנְדִיר מֵן
da-ʔayṭ-ṭim wah ʔadonai ṭaŋri munaʔ bil-ma-dim soz-la-māʔ ki ʔoglan-dir mēn
and-say-PST.1SG wah! Adonai God behold know-NEG-PST.1SG word-VERB.SUF-INF for lad-COP.3SG 1SG
and I said: "Oh Adonai God! Behold, I do not know to speak for I am a lad /young".

Eidlisz-Koknay דא איטים וַי אדני טגרי מונא בילמדים סויילמגא כי אוגלן מן
dʔ ʔyṭ-ṭym way ʔdny ṭgry mwnʔ byl-m-dym swyy-l-m-gʔ ky ʔwgln mn
—— Krymchak
Halicz דָא אַיְטְטִים אֲהָהא אֵי אֲדֹנַי טֶגְרִי מוּנָא בִלְמֵיְיְמֶן סַזְלֵיְימֵאָ כִי יְיָס מֵנְמֵן
dāʔ ʔayṭ-ṭim ʔahhāʔ ʔey ʔadonay ṭɛnri munāʔ bil-meyy-men sez-le-meʔ ki yyās men-men

Jer 1:7

וַיֹּאמֶר ה׳ אֵלַי אַל תֹּאמַר נַעַר אָנֹכִי כִּי עַל כָּל
Tırıshqan דַאיְטְטִי יוי מַגַא אַיְטְמַגִין אוֹגְלַנְדִיר מֵן כִּי ג׳וּמלֵא גַא
da-ʔayṭ-ṭi YWY magaʔ ʔayṭ-ma-gin ʔoglan-dir mēn ki jumlaʔ gaʔ
and say-PST.3SG God 1SG-DAT say-NEG-IMP.2SG lad-COP.3SG 1SG for all DAT
and God said to me 'Do not say "I am a lad"'. For all

Eidlisz-Kokenay דא אייטטי ה׳ מנה אייטמגין אוגלן דירמן כי ברצא גא
dʔ ʔyyṭ-ṭy Hʔ mnh ʔyyṭ-m-gyn ʔwgln dyr-mn ky brṣʔ[157] *gʔ*
Krymchak דא איטטי ה׳ מגה אטמגיסין אוגלן מן כי ברצא גא
dʔ ʔyṭ-ṭy YYY mgʔ ʔṭ-m-gy-syn[158] *ʔwgln mn ky brṣʔ nʔ gʔ*

155 This old Turkic word surviving from the Middle-Qıpčaq period; in Modern Turkish revitalized for "nation" in the modern sense. Note below how *goyim* was translated in other versions.

156 put-PST.1SG.

157 *barče* all', the older Qıpčaq word, retained as *bar* in Halicz and translated by Turkish-from-Arabic *jümlæ* in the Tırıshqan edition.

158 Note the form *ʔṭ-m-gy-syn*, say-NEG-IMP-2SG, is pseudo-learned, and possibly the result of a long copying tradition.

דָא אֵיְטְטִי הָ מָנָא אַיְטְמָגִין יַאס מֶנְמֶן.כִי בַר קַיְירִי Halicz
dāʔ ʔayyṭ-ṭi Hā mānāʔ ʔayyṭ-mā-gin yyāʔs men-men ki bar qayyri

אֲשֶׁר אֶשְׁלָחֲךָ תֵּלֵךְ וְאֵת כָּל אֲשֶׁר אֲצַוְּךָ תְּדַבֵּר
כִּי יִבִּירְסֶם סֵנִי וַרְגִין דָג׳וּמלַנִי כִּי סִימַרְלַסַם סַגַא סוֹזְלַגִין Tırıshqan
ki yibir-sēm sēni war-gin da-jumla-ni ki simarla-sam sāŋāʔ sozla-gin
what send-SUBJ.1SG 2SG-ACC go-IMP and-all-ACC what command-SUBJ.1SG 2SG-DAT say-IMP
wherever I would send you, you must go and all whatever I would command you, you must say.

כי ייברסם סני ברגין דאשול ברצה כי סוזלסם דנא סוזלגין Eidlisz-Kokenay
ky yybyr-sm sny br-gyn dʔ-ʔšwl brṣʔ ky swzl-sm snʔ swz-l-gyn
כי ייוורסם סני וורג׳ סין דא ברצא נא גא כי סימרלסם סגא סוֹיילֵגֵיסִין Krymchak
ky yywwr-sm sny wwr-ǧy syn dʔ brṣʔ nʔ gʔ ky symrl-sm sgʔ soyylē-gēy-sin
כִּי אִיְיסֶם סֶנִי בַרְגִין דָא אוֹסוֹל בַר נֶנִי כִי בוּיוּרְסָם סָנָא סֵזְלֵגִין Halicz
ki ʔiyy-sem sɛni bar-gin dāʔ ʔosol bar neni ki buyur-sām sānāʔ sezle-gin

Jer 1:8

אַל תִּירָא מִפְּנֵיהֶם כִּי אִתְּךָ אֲנִי לְהַצִּלֶךָ נְאֻם ה׳
קוֹרְקְמַגִין אַלְדְלַרִינְדַן אָלַרְנִין כִּי בִּירְגֵדִיר מֵן קוּתְקַרְמָא סֵנִי סוֹזִי יוי נִיג Tırıshqan
qorq-ma-gin ʔald-lar-in-dan ki birgē-ŋa-dir mēn qutqar-māʔsēni
fear-NEG-IMP face-PL-POSS.3PL-ABL for together-2SG-COP.3SG 1SG save-INF 2SG ACC
"Do not be afraid of their faces, for I am with you to deliver you,"
soz-i YWY niŋ
word-POSS.3SG God GEN
the word of God.

קורקמגין אלדילרדן כי בירגגא דיר מן קוטקרמא סני סוזי ה׳ ניג Eidlisz-Kokenay
qwrqmgyn ʔldy[159]lryndn ky byrŋgʔ dyr mn qwtqrmʔ sny swzy Hʔ nyŋ
קורקמגיי סין אללרין דן כי בירגג׳א מו /וט/רמא סני סוזו ייי ניג Krymchak
qwrq-m-gyy syn ʔl-lryn dn ky byrŋǧʔ mn qwtqr-mʔ sny swz-w YYY nyŋ
קוֹרְקְמֶגִין אַלִינְלָרִינְדָן אָלַרְנִין כִּי בִּרְגִינְיֵא סֶנִין בוֹלוּסְלוּגוּם מֶנִים קוּטְקַרְמא סֶנִי אָלַיְ אַיְטַדִי הָ Halicz
qorq-mā-gin ʔalin-lārin-dān ʔālar-nin ki birgie-nie senin boluslug[160]um menim quṭqar-māʔ seni ʔālayy ʔayyṭa-di Hā.

Jer 1:9

וַיִּשְׁלַח ה׳ אֶת יָדוֹ וַיַּגַּע עַל פִּי
דַסוּנְדוּ כָּבוֹדִי יוי נִיג קוּדְרַטִין דַתִייְדִרְדִי אַגְזִים אוּסְטוּנַא
da-sun-du kabod-i YWY niŋ qudraṭ-in da-tiy-dir-di ʔağz-im ʔusṭunah
and-stretch-PST.3SG honor-POSS.3SG God GEN power-ACC and-touch-CAUS-PST.3SG mouth-POSS.3SG on.POSTP
And God's Honor sent His Divine Power and made it touch my mouth

דאייטטי ה׳ מגא מינא ברדים סוזלרים ני אגזיגדא Eidlisz-Kokenay
d-ʔyyṭ-ṭy Hʔ mgh mynh br-dym swz-lr-ym ny ʔgz-yŋ-dʔ

159 Note the same mistake in the word for "face": *alın* > *adlı*.

160 *bolusluk* (help, N) + POSS.1SG < *עֶזְרִי.

Krymchak דאטטי ה׳ מגא מונא ורדים סוזלרים ני אגזיגדא
d? ?ṭ-ṭy YYY mg? mwn? wr-dym swz-lr-ym ny ?gz-yŋ-d?
Halicz דָא אַיְטְטִי הָ֣ מָנָא מוּנָא בֵּרְדִים סֶזְלֵרִי מְנִי אַוְזוּנְדָא סֶנִין
dā? ?ayyṭ-ṭi Hā mānā? munā? ber-dim sez-ler-im-ni ?awwz-un-dā? senin.

וַיֹּאמֶר ה׳ אֵלַי הִנֵּה נָתַתִּי דְבָרַי בְּפִיךָ
Tırıshqan דַאיְטְטִי יוי מַגַא מוּנָא בֵּרְדִים סוֹזְלֵר מְנִי אַגְזִיגְדַא
da-?ayṭ-ṭi YWY maŋa? munā? bēr-dim soz-lar-im-ni ?ağz-iŋ-da?
and-say-PST.3SG God 1SG-DAT behold give-PST.1SG word-PL-POSS.1SG-ACC mouth-POSS.2SG-LOC
And God said to me “behold, I have put my words into your mouth.
Eidlisz-Kokenay דאייטטי ה׳ מגא מינא ברדים סוזלרים ני אגזיגדא
d-?yyṭ-ṭy H? mgh mynh br-dym swz-lr-ym ny ?gz-yŋ-d?
Krymchak דאטטי ה׳ מגא מונא ורדים סוזלרים ני אגזיגדא
d? ?ṭ-ṭy YYY mg? mwn? wr-dym swz-lr-ym ny ?gz-yŋ-d?
Halicz דָא אַיְטְטִי הָ֣ מָנָא מוּנָא בֵּרְדִים סֶזְלֵרִי מְנִי אַוְזוּנְדָא סֶנִין
dā? ?ayyṭ-ṭi Hā mānā? munā? ber-dim sez-ler-im-ni ?awwz-un-dā? senin

Jer 1:10

רְאֵה הִפְקַדְתִּיךָ הַיּוֹם הַזֶּה
Tırıshqan כורגִין וַכִּיל אֵטַטִים סֵנִי בוּגוּן אוּשְׁבוּ כּוּן
kor-gin wakil ?ēṭ-ṭim sēn-i bu-gun? uš-bu kun
see-IMP appointee make-PST.1SG 2SG-ACC this-day/today this-that day
see, I appointed you today, this very day
Eidlisz-Kokenay כורגין וכיל אטטים סני אושבו כון
kwr-gyn wkyl ?ṭ-ṭym sny ?wš-bw kwn
Krymchak כורגין וכיל אטטים סני בו גון
kwr-gwn wkyl ?ṭ-ṭym sny bw gwn
Halicz כֵּרְגִין וַוַקִילְלֵדִים סֶנִי בִיגִין אוּסְפּוּ כִּינְדֶן
ker-gin wwaqil-le-dim sen-i bi-gin ?us-pu kin-den

עַל הַגּוֹיִם וְעַל הַמַּמְלָכוֹת לִנְתוֹשׁ
אוּל אוּלוּסְלַר אוּסְטוּנַא דַאוּל מַמְלַכַת לַר אוּסְטוּנַא טַשְׁלַמַא
?ol ?ulus-lar ?usṭunah da-?ol mamlakat lar ?usṭunah ṭaš-la-ma?
DEF nation-PL over-POSTP and-DEF kingdom PL over-POSTP move-VERB.SUF-INF
over the nations and over the kingdoms, to remove
Eidlisz-Kokenay אול אולוסלר אוסטינא דאול ממלכט לר אוסטונא טשלמה
?wl ?wlwslr ?wsṭyn? d-?wl mmlkt lr ?wsṭwn? ṭšlmh
Krymchak אול אולוס לר אוסטונא דא אול ממלכט לר אוסטונא קופרמגא
?wl ?wlws lr ?wsṭwn? d? ?wl mmlkt lr ?wsṭwn? qwp-r-m-g?
Halicz אוֹל חַנְלִיקְלַר אִיסְטִינֵיא דָא אוֹל בִייְלִיקְלֵר אִיסְטִינֵיא טַסְלָמָא
?ol ḥan-liq-lar ?isṭinie? dā? ?ol biy-liq-ler ?isṭinie? ṭas-la-mā?

וְלִנְתוֹץ וּלְהַאֲבִיד וְלַהֲרוֹס לִבְנוֹת וְלִנְטוֹעַ
דַבּוּזְמַא אֵטַס אֵטְמַא דַבּוּזְמַא קוֹנְדַרְמַא דַטוֹכְּמַא

da-boz-maʔ	*ʔēṭas*[161]	*ʔēṭ-maʔ*	*da-buz-maʔ*	*qon-dar-maʔ*	*da-ṭok-maʔ*
and-destroy-INF	lost	make-INF	and-destroy-INF	camp-CAUS-INF	and-plant-INF

and to destroy, to eliminate and destroy, to build and to plant

Eidlisz-Kokenay דבוזמה דטס אטמא דבוזמא קונדרמא דטיכמא
d-bwzmh d-ṭs ʔṭ-mʔ d-bwz-mʔ qwn-dr-mʔ d-ṭyk-mʔ

Krymchak דא בוזמגא דאטס אטמגא דבוזמגא יפמגא דא טיכמא
dʔ bwz-m-gʔ dʔ ṭs ʔṭ-m-gʔ dʔ bwz-m-gʔ yp-m-gʔ dʔ ṭyk-mʔ

Halicz דָא יַיִנְצְמָא דָא טַס אֵטְמֵי דָא בוּזְמָאֶ קוֹנְדַרְמָא דָא אוֹרְנַטְמַא
dāʔ yyanṣ-māʔ dāʔ ṭas ʔeṭm-ey dāʔ buz-māʔ qon-dar-māʔ dāʔ ʔornaṭ-maʔ

Jer 1:11

וַיְהִי דְבַר ה׳ אֵלַי
Tırıshqan דַבּוֹלְדִי סוֹזִי יוי נִיג מַנַא

da-bol-di	*soz-i*	*YWY*	*niŋ*	*maŋaʔ*
and-become-PST.3SG	word-POSS.3SG	God	GEN	1SG-DAT

and there was (a) word of God to me

Eidlisz-Kokenay דבולדו סוזי ה׳ ניג מגא
d-bwl-dy swz-y Hʔ nyg mgʔ

Krymchak דא בולדו סוזי ייי ניג׳ מגא
dʔ bwl-dy swz-w YYY nyŋ mgʔ

Halicz דָא בוֹלְדוּ נָבִיאלִיק סֶזִי הָ-נִין מַנַא
dāʔ bol-du nāḇiʔ-liq sez-i Hā-nin mānā

לֵאמֹר מָה אַתָּה רֹאֶה יִרְמְיָהוּ
Tırıshqan דֵמַא נֵא סֵן כּוּרַיְרֵרסַן יִרְמִיָהוּ

dēmaʔ	*nēʔ*	*sēn*	*koraydirsin*	*yirmiyāhu*
saying	what	2SG	see.2SG	Jeremiah

saying, “what do you see, Jeremiah?”

Eidlisz-Kokenay דמא נא סן כורײדיר סן ירמיהו
dmʔ nʔ sn kwr-yy-dyr sn yrmyhw

Krymchak דמא נא סן כורײדיר סן ירמיהו
dm-gʔ nʔ sn kwr-yyr-syn yrmyhw

Halicz אַיְיטַדוֹגַד נֵי סֶן כֵּירֶסֶן יִרְמְיָהוּ
ʔayyṭadogox ney sen keyr-e-sen yirmiyāhu

וָאֹמַר מַקֵּל שָׁקֵד אֲנִי רֹאֶה
Tırıshqan דַאֶיְטְטִים בַּדַם טַיַגִי מֵן כּוּרַיְדִירְמֵן

da-ʔayṭ-ṭim	*badam*	*ṭayağ-i*	*mēn*	*kor-ay-dir-mēn*
and-say-PST.1SG	almond	stick-POSS.3SG	1SG	see-PRS-COP-1SG

and I said, “A stick of an almond tree I see.”

Eidlisz-Kokenay דאייטטים בדם טטיג׳י מן כורײדיר מן
d-ʔyyṭ-ṭym bdm ṭyyğ-y mn kwr-yy-dyr mn

161 A misprint for *ṭas.

דא אטטים טייכ׳י בדם מן כוריירמן Krymchak

dʔ ʔṭ-ṭym ṭyyx-y bdm[162] *mn kwr-yyr-mn*

דָא אֶיְטְטִים בָדָם טָיָגִין מֵן כֵירֶמֵן Halicz

dāʔ ʔayyṭ-ṭim bādām ṭāyyāg-i-n mēn kēyr-ɛ-mēn

Jer 1:12

וַיֹּאמֶר ה׳ אֵלַי הֵיטַבְתָּ לִרְאוֹת

דַאְיְטְטִי הָ מַגַא יַכְשִׁי אֶטְטִיג כּוֹרְמָא Tırıshqan

da-ʔayṭ-ṭi	*Hā*	*maŋaʔ*	*yaxši*	*ʔeṭ-ṭiŋ*	*kor-māʔ*
and-say-PST.3SG	God	1SG-DAT	good	make-PST.2SG	sea-INF

and God said to me, "You have seen well,

דאייטטי ה׳ מגא יכשי אטטיג׳ כורמא Eidlisz-Kokenay

d-ʔyyṭ-ṭy Hʔ mgʔ yxšy ʔṭ-ṭyŋ kwr-mʔ

דא אטטי יי מגא יעשי אטטיג׳ כורמגא Krymchak

dʔ ʔṭ-ṭy YYY mgʔ yxšy ʔṭ-ṭyŋ kwr-mē-gēʔ

דָא אַיְטְטִי הָ מָנָא יַיכְסִי אֶטְטִין כֵּירְמִיֵא Halicz

dāʔ ʔayyṭ-ṭi Hā mānāʔ yyaxsi ʔeṭ-ṭin keyr-mieʔ

כִּי שֹׁקֵד אֲנִי עַל דְּבָרִי לַעֲשֹׂתוֹ

כִּי גַ׳חְט אֵטַיְדִירְמֵן מֵן סוֹזִים אוּצוּן קִילְמַא אַנִי Tırıshqan

ki	*jaḥṭ*	*ʔeṭ-ay-dir-men*	*soz-im*	*ʔuṣun*	*qil-maʔ*	*ʔani*
that	quick[163]	make-AOR-1SG	word-POSS.1SG	for-POSTP	do-INF	it.ACC

for I make quickly my word in order to do it.

כי ג׳חְט איטיידיר מן סוזים אוצין קילמא אני Eidlisz-Kokenay

ky jaḥṭ[164] *ʔṭ-yy-dyr mn swz-ym ʔwṣyn qyl-mʔ ʔn-y*

כי אטיכיידר מן סוזום אטמגא אני Krymchak

ky ʔṭyx-yy-dr mn swz-wm ʔṭ-m-gʔ ʔn-y

כִי פִילְנוֹבַט אֵטֵרְמֵן מֵן סֶזִים אִסְטִינִיֵא קִלְמָא אָנִיא Halicz

ki pilnoḇaṭ ʔeṭ-er-mēn mēn sɛz-im ʔisṭinieʔ qil-māʔ ʔān-iʔ

It can be seen that the text, which is very close to the one printed in Halicz in 1927, was used while editing the Gözleve Jeremiah.[165]

Karaim among other Judeo-Turkic varieties: Proverbs 1:1–9 in five versions

In order to demonstrate the closeness and differences between different Karaite versions and the Krymchak version, there follows below the text of Proverbs 1:1–9 in five versions. The first version is MS Ginzburg 1159, now kept in Moscow, written in 1799, the MS, in which the denomination of the language occurs. This is a Krymchak Rabbanite text having many similarities (and some distinct differences from) to the Karaite text as

162 Note the different type of genitive construction.

163 KRPS, pp. 172a and 176a, quotes this word as attested in Troki and Halicz dialects only. This might be one of the markers of a Northern proto-text.

164 Note the use of *jaxt*.

165 Jankowski et al. 2019.

given in Tırıshqan's edition (in notes). The second translation is in Troki Karaim, made by Shelemiel b. Shemuel in Poswoł (near Wilna-Troki) in the late 18th century.

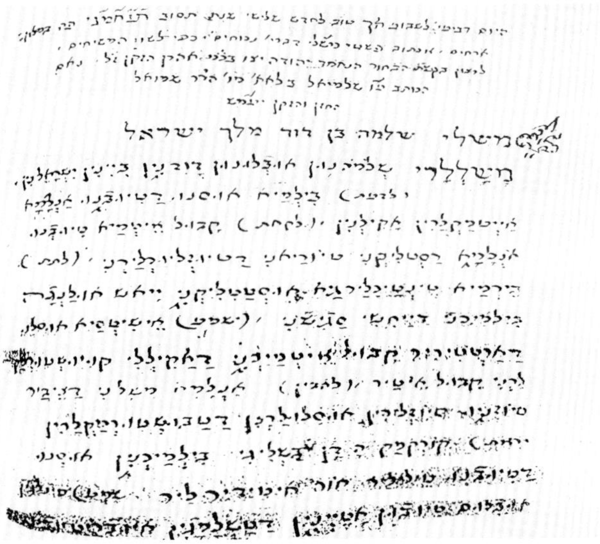

To this version is added (in notes) the Łuck translation made in 1750s by the illustrious Karaite sage, known as "the Karaite Raš"i" and *ʕOlām ṣāʕīr* 'the Microcosm', Śimḥāh Yiṣḥāq b. Mōše Łucki. This scholar moved from Łuck to Çufut-Qalʕeh in the Crimea in the mid-50s of the eighteenth century, in order to teach there, and where he died in 1762 (see on him Lasker 2015). This translation found in Firk I B 113, microfilm No 53791 in the Institute of Microfilmed Manuscripts at the Jewish National and University Library, Jerusalem, was written possibly in Çufut-Qalʕeh and copied in 1831 by *Samuil Abramovič Firkovič Luckij* (a son of the notorious Avraham Firkowicz). This translation is an example of the mid-18th century Łuck Karaim as copied in the early 19th century by a native speaker.

Prov 1:1

מִשְׁלֵי שְׁלֹמֹה בֶן דָּוִד מֶלֶךְ יִשְׂרָאֵל

Krymchak משל לרי שלמה ניג׳ אוגלו דוד ניג׳ כאני ישראל ניג׳

mšl lr-y šlmh nyŋ ʔwgl-w dwd nyŋ xʔn-y ysrʔl nyŋ

proverb PL-POSS.3SG Shlomo GEN son-POSS.3SG David GEN Khan-POSS.3SG Israel GEN

proverbs of Solomon the son of David, the Khan of Israel

Tırıshqan מָשָׁל לַרִי שְׁלֹמֹה נִיג אוֹגְלִי דָּוִד נִיג כַּנִי יִשְׂרָאֵל נִיג

māšāl lar-ı šəlomoh niŋ ʔoğl-ı dāwid niŋ xan-ı yisrāʔēl niŋ

Poswol מָשָׁלְלַרִי שְׁלֹמֹה נוּן אוּבְלוּ דָּוִד נִין בִּיינִין יִשְׂרָאֵלְנִין

māšāl-lār-i šəlomoh nun ʔublu dāwid nin biyy-i-nin yisrāʔēl-nin

proverb-PL-POSS.3SG Shlomo GEN son-GEN David GEN *biy*-POSS.3SG-GEN Israel-GEN

proverbs of Solomon the son of David, bey/*biy* (king) of Israel

S-Y Lucki, 1750s מָשָׁלְלָרִי שְׁלֹמֹה נוּן אוּבְלוּנוּן דָּוִד נִין בִּיִּינִין יִשְׂרָאֵל נִין

māšāl-lār-i šəlomoh nun ʔuvl-u-nun dāwid nin biyyinin yisrāʔēl nin

B556 Halicz מָשָׁלְלָרִי שְׁלֹמֹה נוּן אוּבְלוּנוּן דָוִדְנִין בִּיִנִין יִשְׂרָאֵלְנִין

māšāl-lār-i šəlomoh nun ʔuvl-u-nun dāwid-nin biyiynin yisrāʔēl-nin

Prov 1:2

לָדַעַת חָכְמָה וּמוּסָר לְהָבִין אִמְרֵי בִינָה

Krymchak בילמגא אוסול ליכ דא אוגוט אנלמגא אייטובלרי אקיל ניג

byl-mg-ʔ	*ʔwswl*	*lyk*	*dʔ*	*ʔwgwṭ*	*ʔnl-mg-ʔ*	*ʔyyṭ-wb-lr-y*	*ʔqyl nyŋ*
know-INF-DAT	rules[166]	ABST.SUF	and	counsel	understand-INF-DAT	say-NOM.SUF-PL-ACC	mind-GEN

to know rules and counsel, to perceive the words of understanding

Tırıshqan בִּילְמַא אוּסְנִי דַאוּגוּטְנִי אַנְלַמַא אַיְטוּבְלַרִין אַקִילְנִיג

bil-maʔ ʔus-nı da-ʔüğüṭ-ni ʔaŋla-maʔ ʔayṭub̲-lar-ın ʔaqıl-nıŋ

Poswol בִּילְמֵיא אוּסְנוּ דַטִיוּבְנוּ אַנְלָמָא אַיְטְמַקְלַרִין אָקִילְנִין

bil-mayʔ	*ʔus-nu*	*da-ṭiub-nu*	*ʔanlā-māʔ*	*ʔayyṭ-maq-lar-in*	*ʔāqil-nin*
know-INF	wisdom-ACC	and-knowledge-ACC	understand-INF	say-INF-PL-ACC	mind-GEN

to know wisdom and instruction, to perceive the words of understanding

S-Y Lucki, 1750s בִּילְמִיֵא אוּסְנוּ דָא טִיוּבְנוּ אַנְלָמָא אָקִילֵי אַיְיְטְמַקְלַרְנִי

bilmiēʔ ʔus-nu dāʔ ṭiuv-nu ʔanlā-māʔ ʔāqil-lēy ʔayyṭ-maq-lar-ni

B556 Halicz בִּילְמֵיא אָלַרְדָן אוּסְנוּ דָא טִיוּבְנוּ אַנְלָמָא אַיְ טְמַקְלָרִין אָקִילְנִין

bil-mēyʔ ālar-dān ʔus-nu dā ṭiuv-nu ʔanlā-māʔ ʔayyṭ-maq-lār-in ʔāqil-nin

Prov 1:3

לָקַחַת מוּסַר הַשְׂכֵּל

Krymchak אגלמגא אוגוט עקיל לנמגא

ʔgl-mg-ʔ	*ʔwgwṭ*	*ʕqil*	*ln-mg-ʔ*
understand-INF-DAT	counsel	mind	VERB.SUF-INF-DAT

to understand the counsel to learn

Tırıshqan קַבוּל אֵטְמַא אוּגוּטְנִי דַאַגְלַמַא

qabul ʔēṭ-maʔ ʔüğüṭ-ni da-ʔagla-maʔ

Poswol קָבוּל אֵיטְמַיא טיובנו אַנְלָמֵיא

qābul	*ʔēyṭ-mayʔ*	*ṭiub-nu*	*ʔanlā-māyʔ*
acceptance	make-INF	knowledge-ACC	understand-INF

to receive the instruction of wisdom

S-Y Lucki, 1750s קָבוּל אֵיטְמִיֵא טִיוּבּוּן אַנְלַמַקְנִין

qābul ʔēyṭmiēʔ ṭiuv-un ʔanla-maq-nin

B556 Halicz קָבוּל אֵיטְמֵיא טִיוּבּוּן אָנְלָמַקְנִין

qābul ʔēyṭ-mēyʔ ṭiuv-un ʔānlā-maq-nin

צֶדֶק וּמִשְׁפָּט וּמֵשָׁרִים

Krymchak דורוסט ליק דא שרעט דא דוגרו ליקלר

dwrwsṭ	*lyk*	*dʔ*	*šrʕṭ*	*dʔ*	*dwgrw*	*lyq-lr*
right	ABST.SUF	and	*shariʕah*	and	straight	ABST.SUF-PL

justice, and religious law, and straightfulness

166 If theArabic PL of *ʔaṣl*; it can also be a back formation of Turkic *us* 'wisdom' +ADJ.SUF *-lu* > *ul*.

רַסְטְלִיקְנִי דַשַׁרַעַטְנִי דַרוֹגְרִילִיקְלַרְנִי Tırıshqan

rasṭ-lıq-nı da-šara'aṭ-nı darogri[167]*-liq lar-nı*

רסטליקני טיוֹרַיאַנִי דַטיוּזְלִיוּקְלַיְרנִי Poswol

rasṭ-liq-ni ṭioray?-ni da-ṭiuz-liuq-layr-ni

right-ABST.SUF-ACC judgment-ACC and-straight-ABST.SUF-PL-ACC

justice, and judgment, and equity

רַסְטְלִיקְנִי דָא טיֵרֵיֵנִי דָא טִיזְלִיקְלִיֵרְנִי S-Y Lucki, 1750s

rasṭ-liq-ni dā? ṭiērie-ni dā? ṭiz-liq-liēr-ni

רַסְטְלִיקְנִי דָא טיוֹרֵיא נִי דָא טִיזְלִיקְלֵיְרנִי B556 Halicz

rasṭ-liq-ni dā? ṭioriē ni dā? ṭiz-liq-lēyr-ni

Prov 1:4

לָתֵת לִפְתָאיִם עָרְמָה לְנַעַר דַּעַת וּמְזִמָּה

ורמגא בוג׳לגא איירליק אוגלו גא בילמכ Krymchak

wr-mg-? bwŋ-l[r]-g? ?yyr-lyq ?wglw g? byl-mk

give-INF-DAT stupid-PL-DAT discern-ABST.SUF lad DAT know-INF

to give the stupid ones discerning, to (the) lad to know

בֵּרְמַא אַחְמַקְלַרְגַא פֵירַסְטַלִיק אוֹגְלַנְגָא בִּילוּב Tırıshqan

bēr-ma? ?aḥmaq-lar-ga? fērasṭa-lıq ?oğlan-ğa? bilüb̲

בִּיֶרְמַיא טיֶנְטַיכְלַיְרְגַיא אוּסְטַטְלִיקְנִי יַיאש אוּלַנְגָ׳א בִילְמַיכְנִי Poswol

bier-may? ṭienṭayk-layr-gay? ?usṭaṭ-liq-ni yya?š ?ulan-ğā? bil-mayk-ni

give-INF stupid-PL-DAT master-ABST.SUF-ACC young lad-DAT know-INF-ACC

to give subtlety to the simple, to the young man knowledge and discretion;

בִּיֶרְמִיֶא טִיֶטְטִיֶכְלִיֶרְגִיֶא אוּסְטַטְלִיק אוּלַן גָא בִילִיבְנִי S-Y Lucki, 1750s

biɛr-mie? ṭieṭṭiek-liēr-gie? ?usṭaṭ-liq-ni ?ulan-gā? biliv-ni

בֵּירְמֵיא טֵינְטֵיכְלֵירְגֵיא אוּסְטַטְלִיק אוּלַן גָא בִילִיב B556 Halicz

bēyr-mēy? ṭēynṭēyk-lēyr-gēy? ?usṭaṭ-liq ?ulan-gā? biliv

Prov 1:5

יִשְׁמַע חָכָם וְיוֹסֶף לֶקַח

דא פיכיר אישיטיר אוסלו דא ארטטירר עקיל Krymchak

d? fykyr ?yšyṭ-yr ?ws-lw d? ?rṭ-ṭyr-yr ʕqyl

and thought hear-AOR.3SG wisdom-ADJ.SUF and add-CAUS-AOR.3SG mind

and (the) wise would listen and will increase reason,

דַפִיכִּיר אֵשִׁיטִיר אוּסְלִי דַאַרְטְטִידִיר עַקִיל דַאַרְטְטִידִיר עַקִיל Tırıshqan

da-fikir ?ēšiṭ-ir ?us-lı da-?arṭ-ṭıd[168]*ır ʕaqıl ?al-maq-nı*

דַיַיחְשִׁי סַגִ׳ישְׁנִי אישיטסיא אוּסְלוּ דַאָרְטְטִירִיר קָבוּל אֵיטְמַיכְנִי Poswol

da-yyaḥši sağiš-ni ?iēšiṭ-say? ?us-lu da-?ārṭ-ṭir-ir qābul ?ēṭ-mayk-ni

and-good thought-ACC hear-SUB.3SG wisdom-ADJ.SUF and-add-CAUS-AOR.3SG acceptance make-INF-ACC

a wise man will hear and will increase learning,

167 With two misprints.

168 ד misprinted for *ר.

S-Y Lucki, 1750s דָא יַיַחְשִׁי סָגִישְׁנִי אֵיֵשִׁיטְטִין אוּסְלוּ דָא אַרְטְטִיֵרְסִין אָקִיל

dāʔ yyaḥši sāgiš-ni ʔiēšiṭ-ṭin ʔus-lu dāʔ ʔarṭ-ṭiēr-sin ʔāqil

B556 Halicz דָא יַחְשִׁי סָגִישׁ אֵשִׁיטְסֵיא אוּסְלוּ דָא אַרְטְטִירִיר אַקִיל

dāʔ yaḥši sāgiš ʔēšiṭ-sēyʔ ʔus-lu dāʔ ʔarṭ-ṭir-ir ʔaqil

וְנָבוֹן תַּחְבֻּלוֹת יִקְנֶה

Krymchak דא עקיל לי פיכיר לר סטין אליר

dʔ ʕqyl ly fykyr lr sṭyn ʔl-yr

and mind ADJ.SUF thought PL buying take-AOR.3SG

and a man of understanding would buy thoughts

Tırıshqan אַלְמַקְנִי דַאקִילְלִי אוּסְטַטְלִיקְלַרְנִי קַזַאנִיר

da-ʔaqıl-lı ʔusṭaṭ-liq-lar-nı qazaʔn-ir

Poswol דַאָקִילְלִי קוּיוּשְׁטוּרְמַקְלַרְנִי קָבוּל אִיֵטַיר

da-ʔāqil-li uyuš[169]-ṭur-maq-lar-ni qābul ʔiēṭayr

and-mindful-ADJ.SUF coagulate-CAUS-INF-PL-ACC acceptance make-AOR.3SG

and a man of understanding shall attain unto wise counsels,

S-Y Lucki, 1750s דָא אָקִילְלִי אוּסְטַטְלִיקְלַרְנִי קָבוּל אִיֵטְסִין

dāʔ ʔāqil-li ʔusṭaṭ-liq-lar-ni qābul ʔiēṭ-sin

B556 Halicz דָא אַקִילְלִי אוּסְטַטְלִיקְלָר קַבוּל אֵיטֵיר

dāʔ ʔaqil-li ʔusṭaṭ-liq-lār qabul ʔēyṭ-ēyr

Prov 1:6

לְהָבִין מָשָׁל וּמְלִיצָה דִּבְרֵי חֲכָמִים וְחִידֹתָם

Krymchak אגלמגא משל דא גלג׳י סוזלרי חכם לרניג׳ דא טפמג׳א לריני

ʔgl-mg-ʔ mšl dʔ gljy[170]swz-lr-y ḥkm[171] lr-nyŋ dʔ ṭpmjʔ lr-y-ny[172]

understand-INF-DAT proverb and ??? word-PL-POSS.3SG *ḥakam*ᴴ PL-GEN and riddle PL.POSS.3SG-ACC

in order to understand proverb(s), and ??? the words of the sages, and their riddles

Tırıshqan אַגְלַמַא מָשָׁל דַגַלְגֵ׳ינִי סוֹזְלַרִין אוּסְלוּלַרְנִיג דַחוּגֵ׳ט לַרִין

ʔaŋla-maʔ māšāl da-galjēy-ni söz-lar-in ʔuslu-lar-nıŋ da-ḥujēṭ[173]-lar-in

Poswol אַנְלַמָא משלני דַסִיֵבִיר סיוֹזְנִיוּ סיוֹזְלִירִין אוּסְלוּלַרְנִין דַטַבוּשְׁטוּרְמַקְלַרִין

ʔanla-maʔ mšl-ni d-ṣiēbayr[174] sioz-niu sioz-lyr-in ʔus-lu-lar-nin

understand-INF proverb-ACC and-pleasant? word-ACC word-PL-ACC wisdom-ADJ.SUF-PL-GEN

to understand a proverb, and the interpretation; the words of the wise,

169 Stands for תחבולות ונבון תחבלות יקנה ‘and a man of understanding will attain wise counsel’; here in the Troki version translated as if formed from another Biblical root, ḤBL IV ‘to coagulate, conceive (a foetus)’; KRPS, p. 345a: *kuyuštur- t vyzyvat’ sviortyvanije (moloka); zastavljat’ zastyt’ ... / powodować zsiadanie się (mleka); powodować krzepnięcie, gęstnienie* (coagulation (of milk); to coagulate).

170 The second occurrence of מליצה in the Bible, Habakkuk 2.6 (...הלא אלה כלם עליו משל ישאו ומליצה חידות), Tırıshqan’s edition: *munaʔ bular jumla-lār-ī ʔusṭunaʔ māšāl koṭarīr-lār dā-gālājī hujaṭ-lar*.

171 The Rabbanite version is the only one to render חכם as חכם, meaning here clearly חכמי המשנה.

172 Tırıshqan: *da-ḥujēṭlarin.*

173 Note that the word used is the same as in Łuck and Halicz versions; KRPS: *xidzet / chidzet h*, “enigma”, thus חידה. Note also that this is the word used in Judeo-Turkish version, see below in notes.

174 KRPS: *ceber h / čebiar t*, “milyj / *mily*”, something like דברי חמד.

da-ṭabu-š-ṭur-maq-lar-in[175]
and-find-VERB.SUF-CAUS-INF-PL-ACC
and their dark/enigmatic sayings

אַנְלָמָא מָשַׁלְנִי דָא צִיֵבִיֵר סִיֵזְנִי סִיֵזְלִיֵרִין אוּסְלוּלַרְנִין דָא חִיצ׳יֵטְלִיֵרִין אָלַרְנִין S-Y Lucki, 1750s
ʔanlāmāʔ māšal-ni dāʔ ṣiēbiēr siēz-ni siēz-liēr-in ʔus-lu-lar-nin dāʔ ḥiṣ'iēṭ-liēr-in ʔālar-nin

אַנְלַמָא מָשָׁלְנִי דָא צֵיבֵיר סיוֹזְנִי סיוֹזְלֵירִין חָכָמְלָרְנִין דָא חִיזְצֵיטְלֵירִין אָלַרְנִין B556 Halicz
ʔanla-māʔ māšāl-ni dāʔ ṣēybēyr sioz-ni sioz-lēyr-in ḥāḵām-lār-nin dāʔ ḥizṣēyṭ-lēyr-in ʔālar-nin

Prov 1:7

יִרְאַת ה׳ רֵאשִׁית דָּעַת
קורקובו יי׳ ניג אילכי עקיל ניג Krymchak

qwrq-wb-w	*YY'*	*nyŋ*	*ʔylky*	*ʕqyl nyŋ*
fear-NOM.SUF-POSS.3SG	God	GEN	first	reason GEN

the fear of God (is) the first reason

קוֹרקוּבִי יוי נִיג אִילְכִּי בִּילוּבְנִיג Tırıshqan
qorquḇ-ı YWY niŋ ʔilki bilüḇ-niŋ

קוֹרְקְמַק הָ דַן בַשְׁלִיגִי בִילְמַיכְנִין Poswol

qorq-maq	*Hā*	*dan*	*baš-lig-i*	*bil-mayk-nin*
fear-INF	God	ABL	head-ABST.SUF.-POSS.3SG	know-INF-GEN

the fear of the Lord is the beginning of knowledge

קוֹרְקוּבוּ הַ-נִין בַשְׁלִיגִידִיֵ אוּסְנוּן S-Y Lucki, 1750s
qorquv-u Hā-nin baš-lig-i-diē ʔus-nun

קוֹרְקְמָק הָדָן בַשְׁלִיגִידִי בִילִיבְנִין B556 Halicz
qorq-māq Hā-dān baš-lig-i-di biliv-nin

חָכְמָה וּמוּסָר אֱוִילִים בָּזוּ
רוסול ליק ני דא אוגוט ני דלי לר כ׳ורלדילר Krymchak

ʔwswl	*lyq*	*ny*	*dʔ*	*ʔwgwṭ*	*ny*	*dly*	*lr*	*xwr-l-dy-lr*
rules[176]	ABST.SUF	ACC	and	counsel	ACC	crazy	PL	despise-VERB.SUF-PST-3PL

crazy people despise rules/wisdom and counsel

אוּסְנִי דַאוּגוּטְנִי דֶלִילַר כוֹר אֵטְרְלַר Tırıshqan
ʔus-nı da-ʔüğüṭ-ni deli-lar xor ʔēṭ-er-lar

אוּסְנוּ דַטיוּבְנוּ טיֵלִילַיר חוֹר איטידירלַיר Poswol

ʔus-nu	*da-ṭiub-nu*	*ṭiēly-layr*	*ḥor*	*ʔyṭy-dyr-layr*
wisdom-ACC	and-knowledge-ACC	crazy-PL	despised	make-CAUS-3PL

but fools despise wisdom and instruction.

טיֵךְ אוּסְנוּ דַא טיוּבְוּן טיֵלִילִיֵר חוֹרְלַיְדִילַר S-Y Lucki, 1750s
ṭiēk[177] *ʔus-nu dāʔ ṭiuv-un ṭiēli-liēr ḥor-layy-di-lār*

175 KRPS: *xidzet* / *chidzet h* 'enigma', thus חידה. Note that this is the word used in the Judeo-Turkish version, see above.

176 If Arabic PL of *ʔaṣl*; can also be back formation of Turkic *us* 'wisdom' +ADJ.SUF *-lu* > *ul*.

177 *ṭiēk* 'only'.

B556 Halicz ווָלֵי טֵיילִילֵיר אוּסְנוּ דָא טִיוּבָֿנוּ חוֹרְלָיְיִדִילָר
wwālēy[178] *ṭēyyli-lēyrʔus-nu dāʔ ṭiuv-nu ḥor-layy-di-lār*

Prov 1:8

שְׁמַע בְּנִי מוּסַר אָבִיךָ
Krymchak אישיטכין אוגלום אוגוט אטג׳ ניג׳
ʔyšyṭ-kyn ʔwgl-wm ʔwgwṭ ʔṭ-ŋ nyŋ
hear-IMP son-POSS.1SG counsel father-POSS.2SG GEN
My son, hear the instruction of your father

Tırıshqan אֶשִׁיטְכִּין אוּגְלִים אוּגוּטִין אַטַגְנִיג
ʔēšiṭ-kyn ʔoğl-ım ʔöğüṭ-in ʔaṭa-ŋ-nıŋ

Poswol טִנְלָגִין אוּבלוּם טיוּבוּן אָטֵייְנִין
ṭinlā-gin ʔubl-um ṭiub-un ʔāṭ-[179]*eyy-nin*
listen-IMP son-POSS.1SG knowledge-ACC father-POSS.2SG-GEN
My son, hear the instruction of your father,

S-Y Lucki, 1750s טִינְלָגִין אוּבלוּם טִיוּבֿוּן אָטַנְנִין
ṭinlā-gin ʔuvl-um ṭiuv-un ʔāṭa-n-nin

B556 Halicz טִינְילַגִין אוּבלוּם טִיוּבֿוּן אָטָאנְנִין
ṭińlā-gin ʔuvl-um ṭiuv-un ʔāṭā-n-nin

וְאַל-תִּטֹּשׁ תּוֹרַת אִמֶּךָ
Krymchak דא טשלמגייסין תורה סי אנג׳ ניג׳
dʔ ṭš-l-m-gyy-syn twrh sy ʔn-ŋ nyŋ
and remove-VERB.SUF-NEG-IMP-SG Torah POSS.3SG mother-POSS.2SG GEN
and remove not the Torah of your mother

Tırıshqan דַכֶּמִישְׁמַגִין אוֹגְרַטְמַגִין אַנַגְנֵיג
da-kēmiš-ma-ğin ʔöğraṭ-mağ-in ʔana-ŋ-nıŋ

Poswol דַטַשְׁלָמַגִין איוּבְרַיטיוּביוּן אָנַייְנִין
da-ṭaš-lā-mā-gin ʔiubrayṭ-iub-iun ʔāna-yy-nin
and-remove-VERB.SUF-NEG-IMP teach-NOM.SUF-ACC mother-POSS.2SG-GEN
and forsake not the law of your mother:

S-Y Lucki, 1750s דָא טַשְׁלָמָגִין אִיבְֿרֵיטִיבִֿין אַנַנְנִין
dān ṭašlā-mā-gin ʔibriēṭib̠-in ʔana-n-nin

B556 Halicz דָא טָשְׁלַמָגִין איוּבְֿרֵיטִיוִין אָנָנְנִין
dā ṭāšla-mā-gin ʔiubrēṭiuw-in ʔānā-n-nin

Prov 1:9

כִּי לִוְיַת חֵן הֵם לְרֹאשֶׁךָ
Krymchak כי קושול מכי שירין ליך ניג׳ אלר בשג׳א
ky qwšwl mk-y šyryn lyx nyŋ ʔlr bš-ŋ-ʔ
for bind INF-POSS.3SG sweet ABST.SUF GEN they head-POSS.2SG-DAT
for they are bonds of grace for your head

Tırıshqan כִּי קוֹשוּלְמַגִי גֵיבֵּי שִׁירִינְלִיכּ נִיג דִיר אַלַר בַּשִׁיגַא
ki qošul-mag-ı gibi širin-lik niŋ dir ʔalar baš-ıŋ-aʔ

178 "but", from Western Slavic.

179 The border between the morphemes here is blurred by phonetical shifts.

Poswol כִּי שִׁירִין וְוִיֵנִיֵס כִּיבִיכ אָלַר בַשִׁיָא

ki širin wwiēniēs[180] *kibik ʔālar baš-iyy-āʔ*
for sweet crown like PRON.3PL head-POSS.2SG-DAT

for they shall be an ornament of grace unto thy head,

S-Y Lucki, 1750s כִּי שִׁירִין וְוִיֵנִיֵץ כִּיבִיקְטִי אָלַר בָשִׁינָא סִיֵנִין

ki širin wwiēniēs kibiq-ṭi ʔālar bāš-in-āʔ siēnin

B556 Halicz כִּי שִׁירִין וְוִיֵנִיֵץ כִּיבִיכְטִי אָלֶר בַסִינָא סֵנִין

ki širin wwēnēs kibix-ṭi ʔālɛr bas[181]*-in-āʔ sēnin*

וַעֲנָקִים לְגַרְגְּרֹתֶךָ

Krymchak דא בויון קיסטילר גרדן לריגא

dʔ bwywn qysṭy-lr[182] *grdn lr-yg-ʔ*
and neck necklace-PL neck[P] PL-POSS.2SG-DAT

and necklaces for your neck

Tırıshqan דַבּוֹי מִינְצַקְלַר גִיבִּי בּוֹגוּרְרַק לַרִיגַא

da-boy minṣaq-lar gibi bogurraq[183] *lar-iŋ-aʔ*

Poswol דַמוּנְד׳זַקְלַר בוֹיְנְלַרִיָא

da-mund'zaq[184]*-lar boyyn-lār-iyy-āʔ*
and-???-PL neck-PL-POSS.2SG-DAT

and chains about thy neck.

S-Y Lucki, 1750s דָא בוֹייְמוּנְזַצְקְלָר כִּיבִיקְטִי בוֹייְנוּנָא סִיֵנִין

dāʔ boyy-munṣ'aq-lār kibiq-ṭi boyynunāʔ siēnin

B556 Halicz דָא בוֹייְמוּנְזַצְקְלָר כִּיבִיכְטִי בוֹייְנוּנָא סֵנִין

dāʔ boyy-munzṣaq-lār kibix-ṭi boyynunāʔ sēnin

References

Altbauer, Moshe. 1979–1980. "O tendencjach dehebraizacji leksyki karaimskiej i ich wynikach w 'Słowniku karaimsko-rosyjsko-polskim'." In *Eucharisterion: Essays presented to Omeljan Pritsak on his Sixtieth Birthday by his Colleagues and Students* [*Harvard Ukranian Studies* III/IV, 1979–1980, Part I,], edited by Ihor Ševčenko and Frank E. Sysyn with the assistance of Uliana M. Pasicsnyk. Cambridge, MA, 51–60.

Aqtay, Gulayhan, and Henryk Jankowski. 2015. *A Crimean Karaim-English Dictionary. 10,000 Entries*, Prace Karaimoznawcze 2. Pod redakcją Henryka Jankowskiego i Piotra Muchowskiego. Department of Asian Studies. Faculty of Modern Languages and Literatures, Adam Mickiewicz University in Poznań, Poznań.

Erdal, Marcel, and Iala Ianbay. 2000. "The Krimchak Book of Miracles and Wonders". *Mediterranean Language Review* 12: 39–141.

Filonenko, V.I. 1930a. "Atalar sozy – karaimskie poslovicy i pogovorki." *Izvestija tavričeskogo obščestva istorii, arxeologii i étnografii* 3 (Simferopol 1929): 1–16.

—. 1930b. "Materialy po izučeniju karaimskoj narodnoj poezii – poslovicy i pogovorki". *Izvestija Krymskogo Pedagogičeskogo Instituta* 3 (Simferopol): 1–14.

—. 1972. "Krymčakskie Étjudy." *Rocznik Orientalistyczny* 25.1: 5–35.

180 Note that the T version uses the same Slavic word, unattested as belonging to this dialect in KRPS.

181 Note that in this word, **š* has already shifted to *s*.

182 Ianbay 2016, p. 164a, "necklace", where Song of Songs 4:9 is quoted.

183 This word is misprinted; **boğaz*?

184 KRPS, p. 411a: *mundzek h …*, cf. Ianbay 2016: 127b.

Grunin, T.I. 1967. *Dokumenty na poloveckom jazyke XVI v. (Sudebnyje akty kamenec-podol'skoj armjanskoj obščiny). Transcripcija, perevod, predislovije, vvedenije, grammatičeskij kommentarij i glossarij T.I. Grunina. Pod redakcijej Ė.V. Sevortjana. Statja. Ja.R. Daškeviča.* Pamjatniki Pis'mennosti Vostoka III. Moscow: Nauka.

Grzegorzewski, Jan v. 1903. "Ein türk-tatarischer Dialekt in Galizien – Vokalharmonie in den entlehnten Wörter der Karaimischen Sprache in Halicz." *Sitzungsberichte der Kaiserlichen Akademie der Wissenschaften, Phil-hist. Classe*, Vol. CXLVI. Wien, 1–80.

Ianbay, Iala. 2016. *Krimchak Dictionary*, Ben-Zvi Institute for the Study of Jewish Communities in the East / Wiesbaden: Harrassowitz.

—. 2017. *Pesn' Pesnej carja Solomona i targum na jazyke krymčakov*. Jerusalem.

Ianbay, Iala, and Marcel Erdal. 1998. "The Krimchak Translation of a Targum Šeni of the Book of Ruth." *Mediterranean Language Review* 10: 1–53.

Jankowski, Henryk. 1997. "A Bible translation into the northern Crimean dialect of Karaim." *Studia Orientalia Societas Orientalis Fennica* 82 (Helsinki): 1–84.

—. 2003. "On the Language Varieties of Karaims in the Crimea." *Studia Orientalia* 95: 109–130.

—. 2011. "Two Prayers for the Day of Atonement in Translation into the Luck-Halicz Dialect of Karaim." *Eastern European Karaites in the Last Generations*, edited by Dan D.Y. Shapira and Daniel Lasker. Jerusalem: Ben-Zvi Institute, 156–170.

—. 2014. "Two Karaim religious poems by Isaac ben Abraham Troki." *Karaite Archives* 2: 35–57.

—. 2015a. "Crimean Turkish Karaim and the old North-Western Turkic tradition of the Karaites." *Acta Orientalia Academiae Scientiarum Hungaricae* 68.2: 199–214.

—. 2015b. "Karaim and Krymchak." *Handbook of Jewish Languages*, edited by Lily Kahn and Aaron D. Rubin, Brill: Leiden, 451–488.

Jankowski, Henryk, with Gulayhan Aqtay, Dorota Cegiolka, Tülay Çulha, and Michal Németh [eds]. 2019. *The Crimean Karaim Bible. Vol. 1: Critical Edition of the Pentateuch, Five Scrolls, Psalms, Proverbs, Job, Daniel, Ezra and Nehemiah. Vol. 2: Translation*, Turcologica 119. Wiesbaden: Harrassowitz.

Khazanov, Anatoly. 1989. *The Krymchaks: A Vanishing Group in the Soviet Union*. The Marjorie Mayrock Center for Soviet and East European Research, The Hebrew University of Jerusalem, Research Paper No. 71, Jerusalem, November 1989.

Kokizov, D.M. 1911. "Russkij jazyk' ili tatarskij?" *Karaimskaja žizń* 2: 34–36.

Kowalski, Tadeusz. 1926. "Język karaimski." *Myśl Karaimska* I.3: 3–7.

—. 1927. "Pieśni obrzędowe e narzeczu Karaimów z Trok." *Rocznik Orientalistyczny* (1927): 216–254, 343–344.

—. 1929. *Karaimische Texte im Dialekt von Troki*. Kraków.

KRPS = *Karaimsko-russko-pol'skij slovar' / Słownik karaimsko-rosyjsko-polski*, edited by N.A. Baskakov, A. Zajączkowski, S.M. Szapszał/Shapshal/Šapšal. Moscow 1974.

Lasker, Daniel. 2015. *The Sage Simhah Isaac Lutski. An Eighteenth-Century Karaite Rabbi. Selected Writings*. Jerusalem: Ben-Zvi Institute [in Hebrew].

Monshi-Zadeh, Davud. 1969. *Das Persische im Codex Cumanicus*. Uppsala.

Musaev, Kenesbaj M. 1964. *Grammatika karaimskogo jazyka. Fonetika i morfologija*. Moscow.

Németh, Michał. 2011. *Unknown Lutsk Karaim Letters in Hebrew script (19th–20th Centuries). A Critical Edition* (= Studia Turcologica Cracoviensia 12). Kraków.

—. 2010. "North-Western and Eastern Karaim features in a manuscript found in Łuck." In *Studies on the Turkic Word*, edited by E. Mańczak-Wohlfeld and B. Podolak. Kraków, 75–94.

—. 2011. *Zwięzła gramatyka języka zachodniokraimskiego z ćwiczeniami*, Prace Karaimoznawcze 1, Pod redakcją Piotra Muchowskiego. Poznań.

—. 2012. "A North-Western Karaim manuscript found in Lutsk. A Case of Dialect Mingling?." *Studia Linguistica Universitatis Iagellonicae Cracoviensis* 129: 139–161.

—. 2014a. "A historical phonology of Western Karaim. Alveolars and front labials in the southwestern dialect." *Studia Linguistica Universitatis Iagellonicae Cracoviensis* 131/3: 247–267.

—. 2014b. "A historical phonology of Western Karaim. The evolution of consonant harmony in the north-western dialect." *Studia Linguistica Universitatis Iagellonicae Cracoviensis* 131/4: 353–369.

—. 2014c. "An early north-western Karaim Bible translation from 1720. Part 1. The Torah." *Karaite Archives* 2: 109–141.

—. 2015a. "A historical morphology of Western Karaim. The *-p + edi-* past tense in the south-western dialect." *Acta Orientalia Academiae Scientiarum Hungaricae* 68/2: 215–228.

—. 2015b. "A historical phonology of Western Karaim. The process of diversification into Dialects." *Studia Linguistica Universitatis Iagellonicae Cracoviensis* 132: 167–185.

—. 2015c. "An early North-Western Karaim Bible translation from 1720. Part 2: The Book of Ruth." *Karaite Archives* 3: 49–102.

—. 2015d. "An early North-Western Karaim Bible translation from 1720. Part 3: A contribution to the question of the stemma codicum of the Eupatorian print from 1841." *Karaite Archives* 3: 103–118.

—. 2016. "A Crimean Karaim handwritten translation of the Book of Ruth dating from before 1687. Another contribution to the history of Crimean Karaim and to the question of the stemma codicum of the Eupatorian printed edition of the Tanakh from 1841." *Türk Dilleri Araştırmaları* 26/2 [FS H. Jankowski]: 161–226.

Németh, Michał. 2021. *The Western Karaim Torah: A Critical Edition of a Manuscript from 1720.* The Languages of Asia Series. Leiden: Brill.

Olach, Zsuzsanna. 2013. *A Halich Karaim Translation of Hebrew Biblical Texts.* Turcologica. Herausgegeben von Lars Johanson. Band 98. Wiesbaden: Harrassowitz Verlag.

—. 2016. "A 'Lovely morning prayer': a new edition of a Karaite version." *Karaite Archives* 4: 77–116.

Polinsky, Maria S. 1991. "The Krymchaks: History and Texts." *Ural-Altaisches Jahrbuch* 63: 123–154.

—. 1992. "Crimean Tatar and Krymchak, classification and description." In : *The Non-Slavic Languages of the USSR*, edited by Howard I Aronson. Chicago: Chicago Linguistic Society, 157–188.

Pritsak, Omelian. "Das Karaimische." *Philologiae Turcicae Fundamentae*, ediderunt Jean Deny et al., vol. I, Aquis Mattiacis apud Francisum. Wiesbaden: Steiner, 318–340.

—. 1959b. "Das Kiptschakische." *Philologiae Turcicae Fundamentae*, ediderunt Jean Deny et al., Vol. I, Aquis Mattiacis apud Francisum.Wiesbaden: Steiner, 74–86.

Rebi, David I. 2016. *Krymčaksko-russkij i Russko-Krimčakskij slovari.* Simferopol' Diajpi 2016.

Rusina, Olena. 2005. *Studyji z ystoryji Kijeva ta Kijiv'skoj Zemli.* Kyjev.

Samojlovich, A. 1916. *Opyt kratkoj krymsko-tatarskoj grammatiki.* Petrograd 1916.

—. 1927. "Kistorii krymsko-tatarskogo jazyka." *Vestnik Naučnogo Obščestva Tatarovedenija* II Simferopol', 27–32.

Shapira, Dan. 2001–2002. "Miscellanea Judaeo-Turkica: Four Judeo-Turkic Notes (Judaeo-Turcica IV)." *Jerusalem Studies in Arabic and Islam* 27: 475–496.

—. 2001. "A Karaim Poem in Crimean-Tatar from Mangup: a Source for Jewish-Turkish History (Judaeo-Turcica III)." *Jewish-Turkish Encounters. Studies in Jewish-Turkish Relations Throughout the Ages*, ed. M. Tütütncü, SOTA. Haarlem, 81–100.

—. 2002a. "New Versions of the Karaim Poem in Crimean-Tatar from Mangup." *Vestnik Jevrejskogo Universiteta v Moskve*, 7 (Moscow-Jerusalem 2002 [in Russian]).

—. 2002b. "A New Collection of Documents on Karaites in Eastern Europe at the Ben-Zvi Institute." *Peʕamim* 90: 155–172 [in Hebrew].

—. 2003. *Avraham Firkowicz in Istanbul (1830–1832): Paving the Way for Turkic Nationalism.* KaraM Publishing Co, Ankara.

—. 2003b. "Beginnings of the Karaites of the Crimea Prior to the Early Sixteenth century", *A Guide to Karaite Studies: An Introduction to the Literary Sources of Medieval and Modern Karaite Judaism*, ed. Meira Polliack. Leiden Brill, 709–728.

—. 2005. "A Jewish Pan-Turkist: Serayah Szapszał's Work *Qırım Qaray Türkleri.*" *Acta Orientalia Academiae Scientiarum Hungaricae* (58:4): 349–380.

—. 2007. "Some Notes on the History of the Crimean Jewry from the Ancient Times Until the End of the 19th Century, With Emphasis on the Qrımçaq Jews in the First Half of the 19th Century." *Jews and Slavs* 19 (2007), ed. by Wolf Moskovich and Leonid Finberg, Jerusalem/Kyiv: Hebrew University; [Ukrainian] Institute of Jewish Studies, 65–92.

—. 2008. *The Tombstones of the Cemetery of the Karaite Jews in Çufut-Qalʕeh (the Crimea). Report of the Ben-Zvi Institute Expedition. A Collection of Studies*, edited by Dan D.Y. Shapira. Ben-Zvi Institute, Jerusalem [in Hebrew].

—. 2008a. "Persian, and especially Judeo-Persian, in the Medieval Crimea." *Irano-Judaica* VI, ed. Shaul Shaked and Amnon Netzer. Jerusalem, 253–289.

—. 2013. "The Karaim Translation of the Book of Nehemia Copied in the 17th century's Crimea and Printed in 1840/41 at Gözleve, on the Copyist of the Manuscript, and some Related Issues." *Karaite Archives* 1: 133–198.

—. 2014a. "A New Karaite-Turkish Manuscript from Germany: New Light on Genre and Language in Karaite and Rabbanite Turkic Bible Translations in the Crimea, Constantinople and Elsewhere." *Karaite Archives* 2 (2014): 143–176.

—. 2014b. "Review of Nesrin Güllüdağ, *Kırımçak Türkesi Grameri*". *Karaite Archives* 2 (2014): 235–240.

—. 2015. "A Hebrew Word-list Translated into a Jewish Variety of Crimean-Tatar from the Late 19th Century." *Karaite Archives* 3: 133–140.

—. 2016a. "A Krymchak Obadiah." *Karaite Archives* 4: 117–128.

—. 2016b. "A prayer in Turkish in Hebrew characters from 1727–1730 for the well-being of the Sultan Ahmet III, the Crimean Khan Mengli-Giray II, the Enlightened Medina and the Noble Kaʕba from a Crimean-Rabbanite prayerbook." *Moreshet Israel* 13 (March 2016), Ariel University, 33–43 [in Hebrew].

—. 2016c. "Review of Ianbay, Iala 2016. *Krimchak Dictionary*. Ben-Zvi Institute for the Study of Jewish Communities in the East / Wiesbaden: Harrassowitz, *Karaite Archives* 4: 191–204.

—. 2018a. "A 17th Century Pinkas of Capha / Keffe", *Moreshet Israel* 16 (March 2017), Ariel University, 39–66 [in Hebrew].

—. 2018b "Essay Review: Late Fifteenth-Century Hebrew-into-Ruthenian Translations of Philosophical Treatises and Their Significance. Apropos of: Moshe Taube, introd., ed. and trans. *The Logika of the Judaizers. A Fifteenth-Century Ruthenian Translation from Hebrew. Critical Edition of the Slavic Texts Presented alongside Their Hebrew Sources with Introduction, English Translation, and Commentary.* Jerusalem: The Israel Academy of Sciences and Humanities, 2016. 720 pages, glossaries, index, bibliography." *Aleph* 18.2: 295–312.

—. 2019. Review on Rebi, David I. 2016. *Krymčaksko-russkij i Russko-Krimčakskij slovari*, Simferopol' Diajpi 2016, *Kwartalnik Historii Żydów / Jewish History Quarterly* 3 [271]: 731–732.

—. 2021. "Preliminary Notes on Some Krymchak Texts from the Ukrainian National Library, Kyiv." *Kwartalnik Historii Żydów / Jewish History Quarterly* 3.

Sulimowicz, Józef. 1972–1973. "Materiał leksykalny krymskokaraimskiego zabytku językowego (druk z 1734 r.)." I–II, *Rocznik Orientalistyczny* 35.1 (1972): 37–76; *Rocznik Orientalistyczny* 36.1 (1973): 47–107.

Szapszał, Seraja. 1928 = Şapşaloğlu, Seraya. 1928. "Qırım Qarai Türkleri." *Türk Yılı*, Istanbul, 575–615.

Tenišev, É.R. 1995. "Kizučeniju tjurkskix jazykov Kryma." *Izvestija AN SSSR. Serija literatury i jazyka*, 54.1: 41–48.

Indices

Index of Hebrew Bible, Mishna, and Talmud passages

Hebrew Bible

Index of language groups, languages, dialects, and varieties

General terms such as "Arabic" or "Spanish" are only referenced *outside* the chapters dealing with the Jewish varieties of the respective language. In contrast, the specific Jewish and other varieties are referenced throughout.

Index of countries, regions, and cities

Index of groups and persons

Index of linguistic subjects

The listed entries comprise all relevant occurrences in the grammatical sketches and texts, but not grammatical marking in the interlinear glosses.

Index of cultural/religious and historical subjects